D0222291

A History of Economic Theory & Method

Sixth Edition

A History of Economic Theory & Method

Sixth Edition

Robert B. Ekelund, Jr.
Auburn University

Robert F. Hébert
Auburn University

Long Grove, Illinois

For information about this book, contact:
Waveland Press, Inc.
4180 IL Route 83, Suite 101
Long Grove, IL 60047-9580
(847) 634-0081
info@waveland.com
www.waveland.com

Cover illustrations by Robert B. Ekelund, Jr.

10-digit ISBN 1-4786-0638-X
13-digit ISBN 978-1-4786-0638-3

Printed in the United States of America

7 6 5 4 3 2 1

Our mentors have shed their mortal coils . . .
but their legacy lives in us, and those we touch.
This book is dedicated to the memory of
William Breit, James P. Payne, Jr.,
Alfred Chalk, and Ludwig H. Mai.

About the Authors

Robert B. Ekelund, Jr., earned baccalaureate and masters degrees in economics, with minors in ancient, medieval, and art history, at St. Mary's University. He earned his doctorate degree in economics and political science from Louisiana State University in 1967. He was professor of economics at Texas A&M University until 1979 when he joined the faculty at Auburn University. At Auburn Ekelund was Professor and Eminent Scholar in Economics, retiring at the rank of Eminent Scholar Emeritus in 2003. He was a Visiting Scholar at the Hoover Institute at Stanford University and was the Vernon F. Taylor Distinguished Visiting Professor at Trinity University in 2003. In 2006–2007 he served as Acting Director of the Jule Collins Smith Museum of Fine Arts at Auburn University. He is the author or coauthor of 30 books including (with Robert D. Tollison and Rand Ressler) *Economics: Private Markets and Public Choice* (7th ed. 2006); (with Tollison) *Mercantilism as a Rent-Seeking Society* (1981), *Politicized Economies* (1997), and *Economic Origins of Roman Christianity* (2011); (with David Saurman) *Advertising and the Market Process* (1988); (with Richard W. Ault) *Intermediate Microeconomics: Theory and Applications* (1995); (with Mark Thornton) *Tariffs, Blockades and Inflation: The Economics of the Civil War* (2004); (with Catherine Walsh) *The Persistence of Myth and Tragedy in Twentieth-Century Mexican Art* (2004); and (with E. O. Price III) *The Economics of Edwin Chadwick* (2012). He is a contributor to *Art Interrupted: Advancing American Art and the Politics of Cultural Diplomacy* (2012). He has published more than 200 articles, papers, and monographs on aspects of applied microeconomic theory, history of economic theory, economic history, the economics of regulation, cultural economics, and the economics of religion in such journals as the *American Economic Review*, the *Journal of Political Economy*, the *Quarterly Journal of Economics*, *History of Political Economy*, and *Politics and Religion*. Dr. Ekelund is an artist featured in a number of one-person exhibits over the past several decades and an amateur classical pianist who regularly enters the Van Cliburn Amateur Video contests.

Robert F. Hébert earned his PhD from Louisiana State University in 1970. He taught at Clemson University for four years (1970–74) and at Auburn University for over 25 years (1974–2000). At Auburn he served two terms as head of the economics department (1980–87; 1991–93) and was the Benjamin and Roberta Russell Foundation Professor of Entrepreneurial Studies for 13 years. In 1995 he was a Senior Fulbright Research Scholar and Visiting Professor of Economics at the Université de Paris I (Sorbonne). He also has been visiting professor at the Institut d'Administration des Entreprises de Caen (I.A.E.), Basse Normandie, France, and at the University of Louisiana at Lafayette. He is currently Russell Foundation Professor Emeritus, Auburn University. Dr. Hébert is past president of the History of Economics Society and former trustee of the Southern Economic Association. He served on the Board of Editors of the *History of Political Economy* for many years. He has published widely in major journals, including *Economica*, *Economic Inquiry*, *European Journal of the History of Economic Thought*, *History of Political Economy*, *Journal of Economic Behavior and Organization*, *Journal of Economic Perspectives*, *Journal of Political Economy*, *Southern Economic Journal*, and *Quarterly Journal of Economics*, on topics involving the history of economic thought, historical aspects of entrepreneurship, and the economics of religion. His books include *A History of Entrepreneurship* (with A. N. Link, 2009); *The Marketplace of Christianity* (with R. B. Ekelund, Jr., and R. D. Tollison, 2006); *Secret Origins of Modern Microeconomics: Dupuit and the Engineers* (with R. B. Ekelund, Jr., 1999); and *Sacred Trust: The Medieval Church as an Economic Firm* (with Ekelund, Tollison, G. M. Anderson, and A. B. Davidson, 1996).

Contents

Part VI
Back to the Future: The Twenty-First Century 619

Preface

With this edition, *A History of Economic Theory and Method* enters its fifth decade. It therefore seems safe to conclude that it has found a solid level of acceptance in the marketplace. It could not have done so unless it satisfied a demand that was fueled by many people, faculty and students, who have used this book. We are gratified that students and professors have found our work useful for over four decades, and grateful to all those who have provided us with their evaluations of past editions and suggestions for improvement. As authors, we are somewhat surprised, but clearly delighted, at the longevity of this work. A new edition offers an opportunity once again to reflect on the nature and scope of the history of economic theory and method.

Distinctive Features of This Book

This book offers an extensive survey of the wide range of economic ideas from ancient times to the present. We cannot be encyclopedic in scope, but we do attempt to substantially illustrate the broad panorama and remarkable continuity of economic analysis through the ages. As in previous editions, we have attempted to show the interaction between ideas and the course of historical institutions at key points throughout the book.

The student who has mastered the substance of this book will understand how past analytic contributions, both those that were successful and those that were not, shaped contemporary economic theory. He or she will also gain insights into different methods of problem solving that distinguished one pioneer or group of pioneers from another. By these smaller payoffs the ultimate gain to the student who masters this subject is a sense of perspective regarding economic analysis—an appreciation for the strengths and weaknesses of the discipline, its successes and failures.

As in all previous editions, we strived for clarity and probity in our survey of intellectual history. We believe that it is not enough merely to *catalog* history; we must also try to extract its valuable lessons. Hence, we connect our survey of pioneer performances with a running assessment (ours, to be sure) of the importance and subsequent impact of key ideas. We have also tried to impart the *international* character and scope of major contributions to economic analysis. Other books in this field all too often focus exclusively on the Anglo-Saxon tradition in economic thought to the exclusion of many critical contributions from other countries and cultures. Like most scholars, we are impaired by our limited understanding of different languages, yet we hope that we have made tentative amends in regard to earlier neglect of the multinational roots of economics, and encourage others to join the fray. These themes of clarity, probity, and cosmopolitanism that marked our earlier editions continue throughout the present one.

■ The Sixth Edition

This edition retains the structure and content of its immediate predecessor while expanding coverage of economic policy and its theoretical underpinnings in nineteenth-century Britain. The "evils" wrought by the Industrial Revolution—poor sanitation, disease, plague, low wages, and a highly skewed income distribution to name a few—provided the grist for socialist and "heterodox" reformers. Often ignored is the fact that "radical" reform ideas provoked a response from "orthodox" thinkers. This edition focuses on orthodox responses to hostile attacks by myriad "reformers" who gained currency during the era. Chapters 9 and 10 provide a detailed analysis of possible administrative solutions advanced by John Stuart Mill and Edwin Chadwick, defenders of orthodox economic theory who advanced sound and meaningful discussions of issues relating to social problems wrought (or exaggerated) by the Industrial Revolution. Their views on policies involving taxes, externalities, social cost, moral hazard, and human capital were important elements of an expanding orthodoxy that repay consideration, even today.

In this edition we have streamlined coverage in some respects and expanded coverage in others. The last three chapters, which bring us closest to the present, reflect the most significant changes. Chapter 26 expands on the role of psychology and "experiments" in broadening our understanding of demand and consumer behavior. In particular, psychologists have suggested relaxing the rationality assumption of standard economic theory in a way that must be considered for its impact on economics. Chapter 27, a new chapter, shows how modern economic theory is being drawn into closer alliance with other social sciences such as sociology, history, religion, and anthropology, which includes culture and archeology. These extensions are treated as complements rather than substitutes to standard economic analysis. Chapter 28, the final chapter, discusses the sociology of economics, including the achievements of Nobel laureates, the changing technology of dissemination of ideas, and the possible future directions of the science.

Another new feature of this edition is its attempt to trace the episodic development of the critical role of entrepreneurism as represented by the major economic thinkers of the past. We are compelled to mention several caveats about this effort. The first is that a historical survey of entrepreneurship, as established by the "builders" of economics, shows that the concept means different things to different people. As of this writing, there is no one, universal conception of entrepreneurship that dominates economics. Another caveat is that although entrepreneurship is a value-free concept in a strict, theoretical sense, in practice it is inevitably shaped by a society's reigning institutional framework. Culture and institutions determine whether entrepreneurial efforts result in the *creation* of wealth or its mere *distribution* (what economists today call rent seeking). Normatively speaking, there is "good" entrepreneurship and "bad" entrepreneurship, i.e., productive and unproductive enterprising behavior. Historically, its close connection to economic development means that entrepreneurism is almost always identified as salutary behavior. But rent-seeking societies do not necessarily have fewer entrepreneurs than market-oriented societies. We strive throughout this Sixth Edition to make these distinctions, identifying the key factor at play in whether entrepreneurship is productive or unproductive.

In addition to these substantive changes, the end-of-chapter notes for further reading have been revised and updated. As in the Fifth Edition, "Force of Ideas" segments seek to connect key ideas—which are sometimes addressed briefly in the text—to current economic thought or practice. These segments are intended to illustrate the remarkable continuity of ideas throughout the history of economics. The "Method Squabbles" segments attempt to convey the competing techniques, or analytical procedures, of different writers who made a lasting imprint on economics. These segments are intended to illustrate the pluralistic nature of economic method. How economists "do" economics is not a matter that has been conclusively settled, despite more than two centuries of economic inquiry.

A revised and updated instructor's manual is available to faculty. We hope that this manual proves highly useful, especially for instructors teaching the course for the first time. Prepared by the authors, each chapter of the manual contains five key elements:

- A summary of the text chapter, highlighting key issues or ideas
- A set of multiple-choice examination questions (and answers)
- A set of discussion questions (and answers)
- Suggestions for term paper topics
- Hints about how one's lectures might be extended on more detailed subject matter

■ Acknowledgements

Having survived four decades, it is not surprising that this book has generated an abundance of encouragement, advice, and criticism. It would be impossible to thank all of those users, reviewers, and colleagues who contributed to its success. Indeed, we hesitate to try for fear of offending someone by omission. But on this issue, silence is not an option. On a particular level we must acknowledge, first and foremost, our mentors (now all deceased): William Breit ignited our interest in the history of economic thought, and his persistent encouragement and pride in our accomplishments have sustained us throughout our professional careers. James P. Payne, Jr., taught us the nature and responsibilities of an academic economist (and more than a fair amount of price theory). Ludwig H. Mai and Alfred F. Chalk were seminal inspirations, perhaps more than they ever knew. These four individuals defined scholarship for us and taught by example. Our joint overall debt to them is incalculable and we hold their memories and their teaching forever close to our hearts.

A number of other people provided help and encouragement in bringing past and present editions to realization. We are grateful to all of them: Richard Ault (Auburn University), Randy Beard (Auburn University), Don Boudreaux (George Mason University), Elynor Davis (Georgia Southern University), George Ford (Phoenix Center), David E. R. Gay (University of Arkansas), John Jackson (Auburn University), Yvan Kelly (Flagler College), Roger Koppl (Fairleigh Dickinson University), John Merrill (Kansas State University), Frank Mixon (University of Southern Mississippi), the late Margaret O'Donnell (University of Louisiana at Lafayette), E. O. Price (Oklahoma State University), Rand Ressler (University of Louisiana at Lafayette), the late Larry Sechrest (Sul Ross State University), Parth Shaw (University of Michigan, Dearborn), John Sophocleus (Auburn University), Sven Thommesen (Auburn University), and Mark Thornton (Mises Institute). We owe a special debt of gratitude to Bob Tollison (Clemson University) and David Laband (Georgia State) for help on the Sixth Edition and to Audrey Davidson (University of Louisville) for excellent advice that spanned a number of editions.

Our graduate students, many of whom are now professors and mentors themselves, provided able assistance throughout five editions of this book. They include Frank Adams, Paula Gant, Thomas McQuade, Keith Reutter, Shawn Ritenour, John Thompson, Marc Ulrich, and Mark Yanochik. A special thanks to Matthew McCaffrey and Briggs Armstrong for research, editing, and design assistance with the Sixth Edition. Last, but far from least, we acknowledge the help of Waveland Press. We owe a special debt to our editor at Waveland Press, Jeni Ogilvie, whose interest, enthusiasm, and painstakingly careful attention to detail made this book far better than it otherwise would have been. Graphic artist, Tom Curtin, who transformed the sketches rendered by Robert B. Ekelund, Jr., into the cover of this Sixth Edition, exceeded our expectations.

As we have constantly reminded our students, there is no substitute for reading the "classics" in the original. We hope that our text, which for us has been a labor of love, energizes students to go to those wonderful and rewarding original sources. There are gems to be found in the past that, if polished now, will shine on the future.

Robert B. Ekelund, Jr.
Robert F. Hébert

1 Economics and Its History

Every aspiring economist, whether amateur or professional, must sooner or later confront the fact that economics is a heterogeneous discipline with numerous traditions, each based on a cluster of theories. Each theory uses observations, ideas, and assumptions about how the world works. Most theories produce models of human behavior of varying degrees of complexity. Different theories often give rise to opposing views on the nature of a problem, its significance, how best to formulate the problem, what method(s) to apply, and what policy judgments to make. Ignorance of this fact, or failure to appreciate its consequences, constitutes a serious deficiency in the training of any economist. This book is designed to provide awareness and appreciation of the variety and complexity of the field of economics, from its early and loose origins as household management in antiquity to its intricate and complex analysis of human action in contemporary economics.

The ancient Greeks gave us the word *economics*, but restricted its meaning to household management. Roman civilization infused economics with legalistic elements. Medieval society imbued it with ethical discourse. In the seventeenth century economics was overtly treated as a subset of moral philosophy, although a mutant strain developed called *political arithmetic*. In the eighteenth century a subtle bifurcation occurred, which on the one hand focused on the nature of enterprise economics, shorn mostly of it political integuments, and on the other hand focused on the essential interplay of politics and economics. From this latter focus emerged the "classical" form of economics known as *political economy*. As political economy evolved toward a mature statement in the nineteenth century, various strains (some virulent) of heterodoxy appeared. But owing to the further refinement and professionalization of economics in the twentieth century, political economy gave way to the preferred, simple term, *economics*, a consensus label for a body of principles and a method of analysis that can now be called "mainstream." This book is about the evolution of economics as it developed and consolidated into mainstream science. As such, it is *a* history of economic analysis, not *the* history of economic analysis.

Economics, like physics or meteorology, is a science inasmuch as it comprises a set of analytical principles that work with consistent regularity. Unlike the so-called natural sciences, however, economics is a *social* science because it studies human behavior rather than the disembodied workings of nature. Thus, it is appropriate to describe the subject, by analogy, as a set of tools. Just as a carpenter uses tools to build a house; or a printer uses tools to make a book; so an economist uses tools to build models designed to enhance understanding of human behavior and its consequences. Every social science makes the same claim, however. What distinguishes economics from, yet is sometimes applicable to, its "sister" social sciences, such as sociology or psychology, is that it studies human behavior within the context of markets. A *market* is an institutional arrangement that fosters trade or exchange. A market can be *explicit* as with the market for shoes or *implicit*, such as the market for marriage or religion. Modern economics, therefore, is primarily the study of how markets of both kinds work, in terms both of their internal logical mechanism, and how external forces bring about behavioral adjustments. From economics we gain insights into how value and prices are determined and how inputs relate to each other in production, for example, as well as how market participants adjust to changes in important parameters, such as tastes or income.

Exchange, or trade, is probably as old as mankind. So the *existence* of markets preceded the study of how markets work by a long period of time. For eons people exchanged goods and services as a matter of social necessity, or survival, without much thought given to the abstract nature of individual decisions made or the consequences for society at large. Only after markets had reached a mature stage of development and became a general feature of many (mostly Western) societies did attention become focused on abstractions regarding how they work and what consequences they have. Thus, it becomes possible to pinpoint, at least approximately, the birth of a science that treats these issues. But it is clear that there is a larger set of questions involved, namely: Where did the market come from? Is it the only way to organize economic activity? What are the viable alternatives and how might they work?

The history of economics is replete with writers who sometimes addressed how markets work, and sometimes explored what the alternatives are. Occasionally, but rarely, did a writer address both. Karl Marx was such a writer, which is perhaps why he is regarded as more than an economist. Most of the writers who achieved lasting fame as architects of the field of economics concentrated on how markets work, however. So dominant was this focus that the resulting analysis has come to be recognized as *mainstream*, or *orthodox*. By contrast, attempts to explore the second set of questions are typically regarded as *heterodox*, or outside the mainstream. Although this book focuses primarily on mainstream economic analysis, it does not ignore heterodox points of view (e.g., socialist, Marxist, radical, historical, institutionalist, or psychological)—mainly because criticism almost always has an impact on received ideas. Other writers may be disposed to treat the subject differently. Surely the marketplace of ideas encourages and accommodates variety. Our justification for the approach adopted in this book is twofold: (1) mainstream economics represents a consensus of what contemporary economics is all about; (2) a historical perspective on mainstream economics is apt to be more serviceable to you, the reader. In our historical survey of economics, therefore, economic heterodoxy enters the picture as a direct challenge to the reigning orthodoxy or as a variation on the basic theme of mainstream economics. Although this emphasis is a matter of choice, it does not obviate the fact that economics—in its past as well as its present (and more than likely its future)—is a vibrant form of intellectual discourse, not a settled body of principles.

Economics continues to ferment with the continual march of time. Even among mainstream economists, gnawing questions persist about the nature, scope, and method of economic inquiry and the value and place of economics among competing social sciences and its applicability to some of the subjects ordinarily dealt with by history, sociology, and politics. Disagreement persists about the proper boundaries of the subject, the role of the individual versus the group, the method of analysis to be employed, the desired level of abstraction, and the very usefulness of the subject. Hence, even though we emphasize continuity and consensus in the evolution of economic theory, we urge students of the history of economics to keep an open mind to alternative points of view and to seek gainful lessons, not only in the successes of past, but in its errors as well.

What Is the Value of Studying the History of Economics?

Historians are necessarily stationed at the border between the past and the present. By its nature history is backward looking, whereas economics—conceived as the study of human decision making—is forward looking. Is it reasonable, therefore, for historians of economics to concentrate on past triumphs and failures? Is this concern a waste of time, an obsession with irrelevant minutiae, an exercise in mere ancestor worship, or does it produce constructive results? To no one's surprise, the answer is: "It depends." Merely looking backward for nostalgia's sake is of no particular benefit. However, studying the past for lessons that might be learned, or fresh insights gained, can be of enormous benefit. Humans can judge where they are only in terms of where they have been, and since history is the study of humanity, we ignore history at the risk of not understanding ourselves. Because this book is about *intellectual* history, if properly used, it can provide insights into the ways of the mind: how our intellectual ancestors perceived economic problems, grappled with solutions, advanced their ideas and how shortcomings were modified.

One of the things that can be gained from a study of the past is a better understanding of the creative process. All the great intellectual pioneers held a skeptical, almost iconoclastic, attitude toward traditional ideas and maintained an open, almost naive, credulity toward new concepts. Out of this combination came the crucial capacity to see a familiar situation or problem in a new light. The creative process is always a wrenching away of a concept from its traditional context or meaning.

Another benefit from a study of the past is an appreciation for the kind of ideas that have staying power. What separates good ideas from bad ideas? Why do certain ideas survive in economic theory long after their emergence on the intellectual scene? Why do other ideas fizzle quickly? Traditional economics courses have little time for such issues, yet they are entirely appropriate within the context of intellectual history, and, it turns out, the answers have an enormous impact on the content of economics at any particular point of time.

Yet another benefit is a keener understanding of contemporary economic theory by exposure to the shortcomings of past theories and the obstacles overcome by the principles that survive. Some students will find the abstract theory of economics more palatable—indeed, more understandable—when it is presented in a historical context. But in the final analysis the only justification needed for studying the history of economic thought may be that the subject is interesting. Herpetology is the narrow study of reptiles, especially snakes. When asked by a brash young student what good snakes are, a noted herpetologist deftly replied, "Snakes are damned interesting, that's what good snakes are." This defense is equally apt to a study of the history of economics.

Aim, Scope, and Method

The title of this book is intended to convey a desire to impart, alongside the march of ideas, something of the intellectual framework that incubates and illustrates each writer's economics. Understanding the thought process of the great minds in economics provides valuable insights and lessons for today's economists. Thus, we employ the term "method" in an unpretentious way to convey a concern for the overall structure of thought within which theoretical contributions emerge, much as bricks and mortar, to hold the structure together. We do not identify "method" with *methodology*, which is the *study* of method. Some method, or *modus operandi*, is essential to any systematic form of reasoning, but we don't address how and why economists came to use the methods they did, or how analytical methods differ from one another. Methodology is closely related to the *sociology of knowledge*, which seeks to trace the origin of patterns of thought. Our historical treatment of economics leaves methodology and/or the sociology of knowledge to the specialists who work this field. Existing studies that confront these issues, such as the late Mark Blaug's *The Methodology of Economics, or How Economists Explain*, may be used profitably with *A History of Economic Theory and Method*, but unlike Blaug, we do not attempt to present a history of methodology. In practice, this separation of the history of economics from the methodology of economics is difficult to maintain because, according to the standard classification of economic literature established by the American Economic Association, periodical literature dealing with the former is lumped with periodical literature dealing with the latter. But we accept the personal mantra that writers of textbooks must be wary of trying to do too much, as well as actually accomplishing too little.

Principally, this is a textbook in the history of economic analysis, and its content is dictated, more or less, by the subjects that have been treated by past and present historians of economics, among whom we count ourselves. Some contributors to the field of economics have simply been successful, and must be included on this criterion alone. The names of Adam Smith, David Ricardo, Alfred Marshall, and John Maynard Keynes readily come to mind. In other cases, selective judgment must be exercised about whom to include and exclude. Although our selection of individuals and topics may seem idiosyncratic to some, we stand ready to abide by the wisdom of the marketplace, which is the ultimate arbiter of the usefulness of this book.

Standard history is the story of events. Intellectual history is the story of ideas. This book is an exercise in intellectual history. Its primary emphasis is the evolution of economic abstractions per se, although social and methodological issues are frequently discussed as integral parts of the intellectual landscape. We believe that economic theories do indeed have a life of their own, and that a study of their development is interesting and beneficial to an educated mind. Any book of limited scope will necessarily leave many questions unanswered, and this book is no exception. What role, if any, does the environment play in the development of economic theory? Do great empirical concerns (e.g., food shortages, income distribution, population demographics, or the magnitude of unemployment and inflation) temper the nature and direction of analytical inquiry? If economic abstractions really do have a life of their own, has insularity led theorists to shut out potential areas of interest and benefit to economics? How do ideas join forces and spread within countries and between countries? How are ideas related to the times in which they emerge? How does philosophy (or other disciplines) relate to economic theory? These and many other questions impinge on intellectual history. We do not have conclusive answers to these questions, but we offer this book as a device to deepen appreciation and understanding of the issues.

We have tried to free our historical survey from particular and/or idiosyncratic points of view, even while admitting the probability that this is impossible in a field as vast and varied as economics. We merely seek to expose the historical record for what it is, leaving others to take the measure of the advantages and disadvantages of any single view.

Suggestions on How to Use This Book

The history of economic thought is a vast field having many resources at its disposal. Insofar as historians of thought are inevitably involved in interpreting (and often reinterpreting) past ideas, it is a field that allows wide sway for different points of view. It is easy for the neophyte to be overwhelmed with historical material. Therefore we tentatively offer some guidance. The chapters in this book follow a chronological progression, more or less, beginning with the ancient Greeks and concluding with the first decade of the twenty-first century. We have tried to make each chapter reasonably self-contained, while emphasizing key issues (often debatable) along the way. Certain boxes have been placed in each chapter: One set of boxes is called "The Force of Ideas"; the other is labeled "Method Squabbles." The former underscores certain key ideas from the past that have had a particular impact on contemporary thought and practice. The latter marks certain procedural disagreements or alternative approaches to economics that have rubbed against each other through the march of time. Each box is freestanding, but it treats a topic that is intimately related to the subject of the chapter within which it appears. At the end of each chapter the reader will find a "References" section that contains bibliographic information for all citations made in the chapter. Finally, there is a "Notes for Further Reading" section, a bibliographic assemblage that offers more detail, depth, or sophistication on the key individuals, concepts, and issues treated in each chapter.

Because the river of economic thought runs deep and wide, instructors may find it necessary to impose narrower limits on the scope of their course than this book presents. Our book is composed in such a way as to allow individual instructors to select some chapters and omit others. In such instances, care must be taken by the instructor to supply necessary transitions, but we have tried to present the material in such a way as to minimize this effort.

Other Useful Resources and Information

In addition to the storehouse of secondary literature contained in the "Notes for Further Reading," there are many other useful resources for the novice and the advanced student alike. For the past several decades, Edward Elgar Publishing has been rendering a singular service to the field by turning out books on the history of economics, including multi-volume collections of reprints of primary and secondary literature in the history of economics. Perusal of a recent Elgar catalog will reward the interested scholar no less than the casually interested beginner with a number of desirable additions to one's library.

There are at least four English-language journals now devoted exclusively to the history of economic thought. They are, in order of longevity, *The History of Political Economy* (published at Duke University), the *Journal of the History of Economic Thought* (published under the auspices of the History of Economics Society), the *History of Economic Ideas* (published in Rome by an international group of editors), and the *European Journal of the History of Economic Thought* (published and distributed by Routledge). Global interest in the history of economic thought is also evident in the formation of societies to promote the subject in different countries. Some of these societies are informal (e.g., in the UK and Europe), without an official body of officers or constitution, whereas others are formal organizations with all the official trappings (e.g., in the U.S.). Australia and Japan as well as North America and Europe have established societies to promote the history of economics. If you are interested in the activities of these societies, or membership in any of them, ask your instructor for appropriate information, or search the Internet for details.

In a short span of time the Internet has become a superb tool for identifying, locating, and disseminating information. A Web search using the phrase "history of economics" will repay the effort multifold. But be forewarned—selection is called for. At this writing, the most popular Internet search engine, Google, boasted 538,000,000 entries under this rubric.

Part I

Preclassical Economics

Economic theory developed as a consequence of the attempt to construct a scientific explanation of society and the economy. This attempt reached a watershed in 1776 when Adam Smith published *An Inquiry into the Nature and Causes of the Wealth of Nations*. As monumental as Smith's work was in economics, he nevertheless built on an intellectual tradition of Western thought that reached back as far as ancient Greece. Among other things, Smith derived from his intellectual ancestors a belief in *natural law*. Natural law held that society was governed by an (unseen) order, or set of rules, and that the job of the philosopher/scholar/scientist was to discover those rules through reason. The ancient Greeks—in particular, Plato and Aristotle—formed the first wave of natural law philosophers. The second wave was represented by the medieval fathers of the Church, who are usually referred to as the Scholastics. The Enlightenment shaped the third wave, and it is at this juncture that we find Smith and many of his contemporaries.

Writers like Plato, Aristotle, and St. Thomas Aquinas lived in economic circumstances different from modernity. In the ancient and medieval societies basic economic decisions were taken by tradition and command rather than by individual economic agents acting within a system of open markets. Consequently, the lasting influence on Western social thought of the earliest writers lies not so much in their insights into the operation of market forces, but rather in their preconceptions regarding the nature of social laws. They had a "prescientific" vision that established a foundation on which "scientific" economics was slowly but surely erected through time.

Chapter 2 takes a brief foray into Asian and Arabic thought, but concentrates mostly on tracing the highlights of the Western natural law tradition as it developed from antiquity to the emergence of merchant capitalism, or mercantilism. Chapter 3 surveys the mercantile period, emphasizing economic history alongside the history of economic thought. Chapter 4 brings us closer to Adam Smith's pivotal influence by examining the ideas of his immediate predecessors who were inching ever closer to a systematization of economic thought. Throughout this section you should be alert to the progression of ideas over time, and the connection—sometimes immediate, sometimes remote—of thinkers with their predecessors. You should also be aware that as Western Europe moved from feudalism to capitalism the consequent changes in economic organization helped to shape intellectual activity.

2

Ancient and Medieval Economic Thought and Institutions

For most of human history, economics did not have a separate identity apart from social thought in general. As late as the eighteenth century Adam Smith viewed economics as a subset of jurisprudence. This makes the search for first principles of economic reasoning more difficult, not because the intellectual cupboard of antiquity was bare, but because the subject boundaries between the social sciences were blurred beyond recognition. Economics attained its distinctive identity when it came to be identified with a self-regulating market process, and the discovery of the market as a self-regulating process was an eighteenth-century phenomenon. However, the seeds of economic analysis were sown long before, in ancient Greece, the cradle of Western civilization.

Contributions of the Ancient Greeks

We start with the ancient Greeks because they gave us the best recorded history on which to base our intellectual safari. Although enterprise flourished in ancient Babylonia, Assyria, and neighboring lands, only scant surviving sources exist that would allow us to identify a *theory* of economic activity. This is no less true for Egypt, which, except for its military excursions, was more commercially self-contained than other parts of the Near East. At any rate, Edward Bleiberg ("The Economy of Ancient Egypt," pp. 1382–1383) maintains that the normal Egyptian state of affairs was a redistributive economy.

The Greeks also give us a convenient starting point because in the Western world our patterns of thought, the framework within which our ideas emerge and circulate, the forms of language in which we express ideas, and the rules that govern them, are all products of antiquity. Thus, as Theodor Gomperz wrote, "Even those who have no acquaintance with the doctrines and writings of the great masters of antiquity, and who have not even heard the names of Plato and Aristotle, are, nevertheless, under the spell of their authority" (*Greek Thinkers*, p. 528). The very word "economics" takes its name from Xenophon's instructional treatise on efficient management and leadership, the *Oeconomicus*.

What the ancient Greeks contributed to economics was a rational approach to social science in general. Their economy may be described as "premarket," not in the sense that trade was absent, but rather in the sense that products were neither uniform, nor traded on organized exchanges, nor analyzed for their own sake. Greek thinkers were interested primarily in economic and organizational efficiency. Their view of the world was anthropocentric, not mechanistic. In other words, man was the center of all things. The ancient Greeks placed great stock in the self-regulating capacities of individuals who sought to maximize human happiness by making rational decisions, but they did not discover the key principle of modern economics: the self-regulating marketplace.

Ancient Greek culture admitted two contrasting ideas of individualism. On the one hand, an authoritarian ruler was empowered to make administrative decisions on behalf of the interests of society. This led to the development of rational calculation based on the abstract definition of an individual as the basic social unit. On the other hand, each family was patriarchal and success-driven, which led to the development of the individual male citizen as a fundamental decision maker. These two contrasting forms of individualism, "macro" and "micro" as it were, contributed to the formal emphasis in Greek society on private household management (*oikonomics*) and to the development of a hedonic calculus of rational self-interest.

Because the Greeks concentrated on elements of *human* control, they developed the *art* of administration rather than the *science* of economics. Their economy, after all, was basic and simple. It consisted of primary agriculture and limited palace trade. The production of goods was supervised on large, landed estates and in the halls of military chieftains. Warfare dominated political and economic life from 500 BC to 300 BC. As the focal point of religious and military activities, the state had few nonmilitary expenditures. Nevertheless, in the course of elaborating the nature of administration, the ancient Greeks developed analytic structures that have significance for economic theory. In particular, the following components of modern economics originated in Greek thought: efficiency, resource allocation, the notion of subjective value, the hedonic calculus, and the concept of diminishing marginal utility. The major writers of this period who contributed to economic analysis were Xenophon, Plato, Protagoras, and Aristotle.

Xenophon on Organization, Value, and the Division of Labor

Philip Wicksteed, a noted British economist of the nineteenth century, wrote that economics "may be taken to include the study of the general principles of administration of resources, whether of an individual, a household, a business, or a State; including the examination of the ways in which waste arises in all such administration" (*Common Sense*, p. 17). He might have had in mind the Greek philosopher, Xenophon (c. 427–355 BC), whose writings are paeans to the science of administration. A decorated soldier and a student of Socrates, Xenophon couched his ideas in terms of the individual decision maker, whether he was a military commander, public administrator, or head of a household. He emphasized efficient, as opposed to inefficient, courses of action. In *Oeconomicus* he explored the proper organization and administration of private and public affairs, and in *Ways and Means* he prescribed the course of Athens' economic revitalization in the middle of the fourth century BC. For this Greek philosopher who regarded the material environment as fixed, the chief element of good administration was human capacity, honed into good leadership.

A good manager strives to increase the size of the economic surplus of whatever unit he supervises, whether it is family, city, or state. Xenophon maintained that this is accomplished through organization, skill, and division of labor. The division of labor became the linchpin of economic growth in the writings of Adam Smith, as we shall see in chapter 5, but its important economic implications were recognized in antiquity. Xenophon attributed an increase in both the quantity and the quality of goods to this organizing principle. Moreover, by exploring the relationship between population concentration and the development of specialized skills and products he supplied the basis of Adam Smith's famous dictum that specialization and division of labor are limited by the extent of the market.

Xenophon's emphasis on the nature and importance of leadership, though not formulated in the strict context of competitive markets, nevertheless provided a prototype for an important element of economics that gained traction in the eighteenth-century: the function and pivotal importance of the entrepreneur in a market economy (see chapter 4). Entrepreneurship and its role in economic theory, as we shall see throughout this volume, is a theme that has faded in and out of economic theory through time.

Modern economists would say that the deficiency in Xenophon's leader—that exceptional individual who organizes human activity—is that he confronts the powers of nature seemingly unaware of the forces of a competitive economy. Although the leader is motivated by self-interest, Xenophon decries acquisitive behavior as "unnatural." The "natural" economic process, he claims, consists of intelligent man using perception and reason to extract from nature what is necessary to avoid discomfort and fulfill human wants. The Greeks formalized the active and rational pursuit of pleasure and avoidance of pain in their doctrine of *hedonism*, an idea that resurfaced many centuries later in the subjective theory of value that separated neoclassical economics from classical economics (see chapters 12–17).

Even though his thinking is not set in an explicit market context, it is easy to see how Xenophon's concept of subjective value presages modern economic thought. In one of his works, *Hiero*, Xenophon remarks that "the greater the number of superfluous dishes set before a man, the sooner a feeling of repletion comes over him; and so, as regards the duration of his pleasure, too, the man who has many courses put before him is worse off than the moderate liver" (*Scripta Minora*, p. 9). The clear implication here is that *extra* satisfaction derived from consumption falls as the quantity consumed increases, an idea that eventually entered formal economic analysis as the principle of diminishing marginal utility. Xenophon also grappled with the distinction between a purely *individual* subjective concept of value and a more objective *general* concept of wealth, or property. His conclusion was that wealth is a relative concept. Thus, in his discussion of estate management he observed that "the same things are wealth and not wealth, according as one understands or does not understand how to use them. A flute for example, is wealth to one who is competent to play it, but to an incompetent person it is no better than useless stones . . . unless he sells it . . ." in which case, "it becomes wealth" (*Oeconomicus*, 1.10–13). Thus, in the end, "wealth is that from which a man can derive profit," but if it causes him harm, it is not wealth. "Even land is not wealth if it makes us starve instead of supporting us" (*Oeconomicus*, 1.8).

The idea that value comes not from a good itself but from the pleasure it produces lies at the center of utility/value theory in contemporary economics. Xenophon embellished the idea of subjective utility in the dialogue between Aristippus and Socrates, where Aristippus asks, "Do you mean that the same things are both beautiful and ugly?" Socrates replies, "Of course—and both good and bad. For what is good for hunger is often bad for fever, and what is good for fever is bad for hunger; what is beautiful for running is often ugly for wrestling, and what is beautiful for wrestling ugly for running. For all things are good and beautiful in relation to those purposes for which they are well adapted, bad and ugly in relation to those for which they are ill adapted" (Xenophon, *Memorabilia*, III.8.6–7). This resort to subjective evaluation in the measurement of good versus bad was an important premise of Greek thought from the time of the early Sophists through Aristotle.

Plato and the Administrative Tradition

Whereas Xenophon focused on the practical nature of leadership and policy, Plato (c. 427–347 BC) analyzed the entire political and economic structure of the state. Both writers shared the view that human activity is the primary variable of political economy and statecraft, but Plato searched for the optimum polity/economy by investigating and refining the moral imperative of justice. For Plato the optimum state is a rigid, static, ideal construct from which any deviation whatsoever is considered to be regressive.

Extending the concept of division of labor raised by Xenophon, Plato molds the argument into an explanation of the origin of cities, which is an outgrowth of exchange.

> The origin of the city . . . is to be found in the fact that we do not severally suffice for our own needs, but each of us lacks many things. We, being in need of many things, gather many into one place of abode as associates and helpers, and to this dwelling we give the name city or state. . . . And between one man and another there is an interchange of giving . . . and taking, because each supposes this to be better for himself. (*Republic*, vol. 1, p. 149)

A city can be viewed from many different angles, of course, but in his explanation, Plato starts us on the road to a theory of exchange. Specialization creates mutual interdependence, and mutual interdependence establishes reciprocal exchange. Although Plato did not go so far as to establish an actual *theory* of exchange, he did confront the nature of economic distribution—which is inevitable in any inquiry about justice.

Plato's first principle in his discourse on justice is that specialization and division of labor establish efficiency and productivity. How then, are the fruits of efficiency and productivity to be distributed? Plato answered that goods and services are distributed through a marketplace, with money as a token of exchange. But in typically Greek fashion, he did not consider the marketplace capable of self-regulation. He maintained that the marketplace, like the state, requires administrative control. The elements of control that Plato sponsored were fiat money, which must be managed to eliminate profit and usury, and certain "rules" of justice (i.e., custom and tradition), which would have the effect of establishing distributive shares according to strict mathematical principles.

In keeping with the ancient Greek administrative tradition, Plato based his ideal state on wise and efficient leadership. Xenophon had recognized that profit seekers make good managers as long as their excesses are curbed by appropriate administrative controls. Plato advanced this thinking further by devising the necessary controls. Convinced that all forms of profit (including interest—the profit on money) were threats to the status quo, he went to great lengths to insulate his leaders from corruption. He proposed that communism be imposed on the rulers so that they not be tempted by possessions or diverted from the task of wise governance. He sought to make philosophers out of soldiers, in order to shape a ruling class of "guardians," who would combine the strength and discipline of the warrior with the wisdom and understanding of the scholar. Aware of the benefits of specialization and division of labor, Plato championed a kind of "class specialization" whereby an elite group of capable and high-minded rulers would be trained to direct the political economy.

Plato on Democracy and "Public Choice"

The establishment of Plato's ideal polity depends on elitism rather than on any participative social process. Plato could only envision the ideal state as a consequence of authority. To safeguard stratified social interests, the governing elite were to be conditioned by censorship and communism of the family and property. In the final analysis, justice was the product of superior intellectual authority, tempered by administrative constraints. This view stands in stark contrast to those of Adam Smith and the classical economists we will meet in part II, who believed that a central value of liberty could only be achieved through individual participation and freedom of action constrained by competitive forces.

Despite his advocacy of this ideal, however, Plato may have sensed the implausibility of long-term equilibrium in a utopian society. He analyzed how states "declined" from the ideal, offering implicit and explicit criticisms of various foundations of the state known in his time. The following chart summarizes the regressive decline from the just society envisioned by Plato.

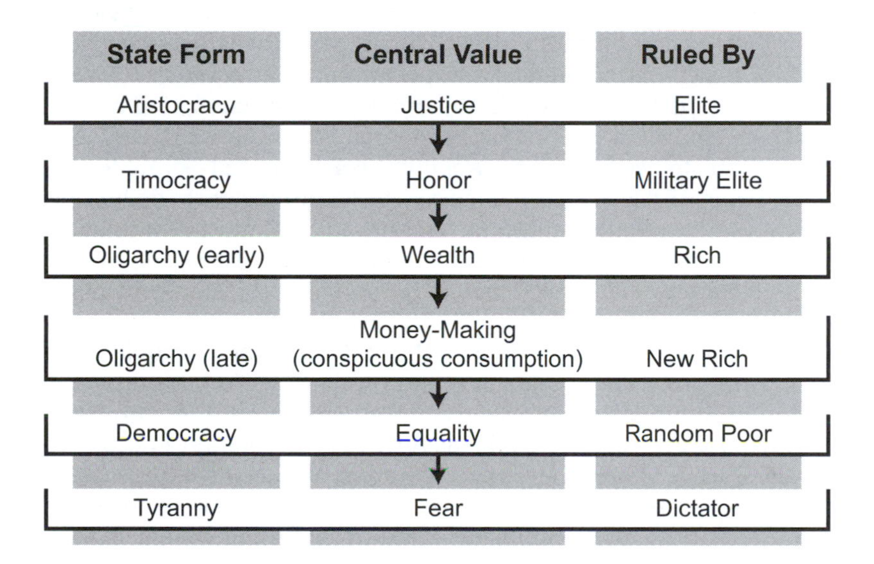

Plato maintained that states decline due to an excess of their central value. In his mind, lust, greed, and wanton acquisitiveness were major culprits that could undermine an established polity. From a contemporary perspective it is noteworthy that while Plato listed tyranny as the worst of all states, he cited democracy as a close second. Across the ages, Plato speaks to us derisively about a treasured form of Western government and its potential dangers. But remember that Plato's ideas were limited to his own experience. The ancient world witnessed many varieties of democracy, but none that mirrored the parliamentary or congressional forms of representative democracy that we know today.

In his analysis of comparative forms of government Plato addressed two important issues concerning democracy: (1) Why was it such an attractive state? and (2) Why was it basically unstable, leading in the extreme to dictatorship? In the first instance he maintained that democracy's appeal comes on the one hand from the individual liberty that permits each citizen to speak and act as she likes, and on the other from the diversity of individual characters that it permits. According to Plato democracy comprises a "bazaar of constitutions and characters," which allows individuals to choose their form of government "cafeteria-style," as it were. In the second instance, despite the political and economic charms of democracy as it was known, Plato considered it unstable. The logical outgrowth of democracy, he argued, is anarchy, because it treats people as equal, whether they are equal or not. Plato believed the excessive desire for liberty and equality that democracy promotes eventually leads to its destruction. Offices are obtained by lot (or worse, by "sale"). Furthermore, democracy tends to abuse those who obey authorities—as servile and contemptible—and reserves its approval, in private and public life, for rulers who behave like subjects and subjects who behave like rulers. In such a society the principle of liberty is bound to go to extremes. Tyranny, for Plato, was the logical consequence of democracy (*Republic*, vol. 2, pp. 305–307).

A democratic society is ripe for tyranny when a leader discovers that not everyone can be satisfied all of the time. Because the majority rules in a democracy, leaders rely on polls of public opinion and so base their judgments on sentiment, prejudice, and self-interest, rather than justice. Elected rulers gain political advantage by taking from the rich and giving to the poor. Thus, democracy encourages redistributive battles that intensify when a tyrant (in Plato's symbolic language, "the wolf") is raised up to "protect" the poor from their enemies. Once the tyrant has "disposed of his foreign enemies by treaty or destruction, and has no more to fear from them, he will in the first place continue to stir up war in order that the people may continue to need a leader" (*Republic*, vol. 2, pp. 323–325). Moreover, high taxation in times of war keeps the masses busy earning their daily bread—and away from ideas of freedom or rebellion—so that a tyrant must always be provoking war.

It follows that in Plato's political landscape the descent to tyranny from democracy is a natural evolution. Thus, it is no surprise that Plato placed his bet on authority rather than democracy to establish the ideal state. Ironically, however, the experience of Western civilization in the millennia since antiquity shows that where absolute authority exists it is more likely to impose despotism than harmony. As a result, democracy is upheld today as a Western ideal. To be sure, modern democracies have tried to erect bulwarks against their devolution into tyranny, with practices such as federalism and the separation of executive, judicial, and legislative powers. Nevertheless, representative democracies in the world today continue to grapple with many of the problems Plato warned against—which makes his important lessons worth remembering.

Protagoras and the Hedonic Calculus

Whereas Plato was an absolutist, Protagoras (c. 480–411 BC) was a relativist. He held that there was no objective truth, only subjective opinion. This subjectivism is exemplified in his famous maxim: "Man is the measure of all things." In other words, although truth cannot be discovered, utility can. According to Protagoras it is up to the citizens of a state to decide what constitutes social welfare and how to achieve it. As against the absolute authority of Plato, Protagoras extolled the democratic process. He put his faith in common sense rather than science, and trusted the practical social experience of mankind as opposed to the doctrines of moral and political theorists. Not surprisingly, Plato was one of his main critics.

Protagoras's subjectivism is based on the interaction between human perception and physical phenomena. Formulated at a time when vision was believed to be produced by light emanating from the eye (rather than entering it), it suggests an active rather than a passive view of individualism. Plato challenged Protagoras's philosophy in his dialogue with Theaetetus. Recalling Protagoras's dictum that "each one of us is the measure of the things that are and those that are not," Plato responded, "but each person differs immeasurably from every other in just this, that to one person some things appear and are, and to another person other things" (*Theaetetus*, p. 95). Hence, Plato did not see how relativism could be accepted as the basis for a proper polity. He rejected Protagoras's belief that means are more important than *ends*, stating that social stability is achieved by individual participation in the wise choice of ends. (By analogy, economics maintains that market stability is established by the active involvement of market participants.) Like the rest of the ancient Greek philosophers, Protagoras was interested in the effects of leadership and administration, but he insisted that the proper role of the administrator/leader was to offer advice, not to rule absolutely. Administration, in other words, would make its contribution through the informed choice of means to achieve given ends.

S. Todd Lowry makes certain claims on behalf of Protagoras. He asserts, simply: "What Protagoras claimed to teach sounds very much like political economy" ("Greek Heritage," p. 11). More specifically, Lowry claims that Protagoras's man-measure doctrine is the parent idea of both the labor theory of value and the idea of subjective individualism. He also asserts that Protagoras anticipated two of the most basic elements of modern economic theory: (1) the way the market maximizes utility through its function of allocating resources, and (2) the use of hedonic measurement in the evaluation of choice (*Archaeology*, p. 159). These claims are difficult to substantiate fully in view of the fact that Protagorean thought survives only in secondary sources. Nevertheless, the Sophists, of whom Protagoras was one of the earliest and greatest, definitely planted the seeds of certain ideas that were to flower in the nineteenth century.

Aristotle and Two-Party Exchange

Aristotle (c. 384–322 BC) was interested in the analytic potential of comparing utility measurements. In his *Topics* and *Rhetoric* he presented a systematic examination of the elements of choice appropriate to public decision making. Most important for modern economic theory, Aristotle discussed value in terms of incremental comparisons. However, his systematic comparisons of value based on subjective marginal utility developed in a way completely unrelated to contemporary price theory. It is most likely that Aristotle's analysis of exchange was an attempt to determine the criteria for fairness on which the Athenian legal system was founded. In any event, equity considerations dominated economic considerations in his analysis of exchange.

It is important to note that Aristotle set out to analyze *isolated* exchange as opposed to *market* exchange. The difference is vital to understanding both the procedure and conclusions of the Aristotelian model. Economists define isolated exchange as two parties exchanging goods in conjunction with their own subjective preferences, without reference to any alternative market opportunities. Market exchange, on the other hand, takes place when individual traders arrive at their decisions from their awareness of continuous, pervasive trading among large numbers of participants in an organized and informed market. In market exchange, the publicly known price is the end result of an impartial working out of the interests of many buyers and sellers. In isolated exchange, by contrast, there is no going market price established by large-numbers feedback. Absent the interplay of large numbers of market participants, the fairness of each transaction can only be determined by a disinterested third party, such as judge or arbitrator. Moreover, the judgment must be rendered on a case-by-case basis. Isolated exchange was a commonplace of Aristotle's experience, and it remains fairly common today in preindustrial economies, where primitive or idiosyncratic production techniques lead to highly differentiated products.

The Nature of the Polity. Although he was Plato's prize pupil, Aristotle rejected his master's notion of the ideal state. Instead he favored a mixed economy that allowed greater play for economic incentives. Unlike Plato, who defended private property only for the nonrulers, Aristotle defended private property for all classes—on the grounds that it promotes economic efficiency, engenders social peace, and encourages the development of moral character.

In Aristotle's day the Athenian polity functioned mainly as a distributive economy. Wealth and privilege were distributed by custom, tradition, and government directives. Among the things distributed were: honors of all sorts, free public meals, public entertainment, rations of grain, profits from the silver mines at Laurium, and payments to many citizens for jury duty and for attendance at public assemblies. These "entitlements" became the prerogative of every Greek citizen, and Aristotle viewed them as protection against an unfettered democracy. His central civic concern, therefore, was distributive justice.

The Nature of Trade. Aristotle's analysis of two-party exchange arose from his focus on distributive justice. He viewed exchange as a bilateral process that made both parties better off. Exchange is induced when two parties to a potential trade each have a surplus that they are willing to give up in return for one another's goods. Thus, exchange is built on the notion of reciprocity. His analysis proceeds on a judicial rather than a commercial footing. Consider the following passage in which Aristotle analyzes exchange by barter:

> Now proportionate return is secured by cross-conjunction. Let A be a builder, B a shoemaker, C a house, D a shoe. The builder, then, must get from the shoemaker the latter's work, and must himself give him in return his own. If, then, first there is proportionate equality of goods, and then reciprocal action takes place, the result we mention will be effected. If not, the bargain is not equal, and does not hold; for there is nothing to prevent the work of the one being better than that of the other; they must therefore be equated. . . . This is why all things that are exchanged must be somehow comparable. It is for this end that money has been introduced, and it becomes in a sense an intermediate; for it measures all things, and therefore, the excess and the defect—how many shoes are equal to a house or to a given amount of food. The number of shoes exchanged for a house must therefore correspond to the ratio of builder to shoemaker. For if this be not so, there will be no exchange and no intercourse. And this proportion will not be effected unless the goods are somehow equal. All goods must therefore be measured by some one thing, as we said before. Now this unit is in truth demand, which holds all things together . . . ; but money has become by convention a sort of representative of demand; and this is why it has the name "money"—because it exists not by nature but by law and it is in our power to change it and make it useless. There will, then, be reciprocity when the terms have been equated so that as farmer is to shoemaker, the amount of the shoemaker's work is to that of the farmer's work for which it exchanges. (*Nichomachean Ethics*, $1133^{a}5$–30)

This passage plus other elaborations by Aristotle became the subject of intense and repeated examination by the Scholastic writers of the Middle Ages (see this chapter, below), who were also concerned primarily with distributive justice. Notice that Aristotle's notion of demand is basically empirical; it is something "which holds all things together" and its popular measure is "money." It is not clear what meaning we should attribute to the phrase, "holds all things together," but one clear implication is that demand constitutes an essential element of trade. Obviously, supply is the other, and the interaction of the two, in Aristotle's mind, constitutes reciprocity.

Aristotle's analysis of two-party exchange does not move us very close to an analysis of market price because its rudimentary notions of demand and supply are limited to single market participants, and the "comparability" standard on which "equilibrium" rests, remains obscure. In the final sentence from the passage above it would appear that "equilibrium" trade depends on a rough equality between the work (effort) of the buyer and seller. Here, in embryonic form, we find the root of the idea that later came to be known as the labor theory of value in classical economics (see part II).

Later writers tried to give Aristotle's analysis geometric form. In his fourteenth-century commentary on Aristotle's works Nicole Oresme presented the diagram reproduced here as figure 2-1. Unfortunately, this geometric "model" does not clarify the fundamental economic issues. Despite its apparent resemblance to modern supply and demand curves, the cross-diagonals of figure 2-1 are not functional relationships in a mathematical sense. Furthermore, there is no recognition of price, although there is the suggestion of a kind of equilibrium that equates subjective utilities.[1] Moreover, the figure reveals nothing about the distribution of benefit between the two traders or of the justice of the exchange within the limits of voluntary choice.

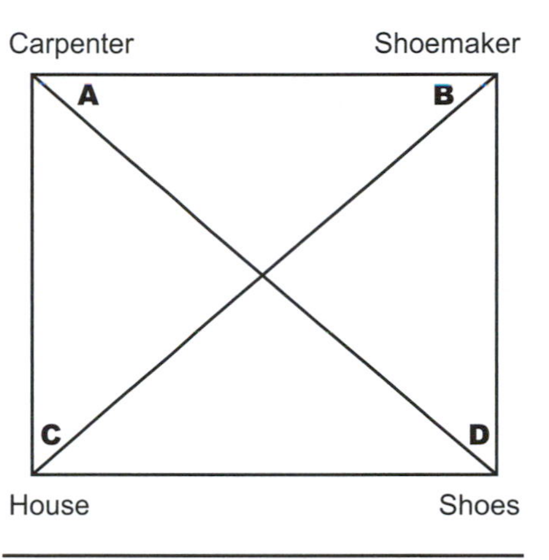

Figure 2-1 If the carpenter and the shoemaker trade at the intersection of the diagonals, then proportional compensation is achieved.

Persistent confusions about the Aristotelian exchange model should not be allowed to obscure the fact that it became an important foundation for the prolonged discussions of value that subsequently emerged in the Middle Ages (discussed below). If nothing else, Aristotle's exchange model established important preconditions for trade, and these premises became part and parcel of early economic analysis. For example, Aristotle clearly established the following propositions:

1. Trade arises only when surpluses exist.
2. There must be differing subjective estimates among traders of the worth of each surplus.
3. Traders must establish a rapport that recognizes the potential mutual advantage from exchange.
4. If a dispute arises in isolated exchange regarding the specific allocation of benefits, the proper shares will have to be determined by an administrative authority, taking into account the rules of common justice and the welfare of the state.

[1] In fact, the diagram is reminiscent of one used by W. S. Jevons, one of the founders of marginal-utility analysis, in 1871 (see chap. 14). Jevons acknowledged Aristotle's influence on his own thought.

Aristotle also left an imprint on the theory of value in other ways. For example, he approached the subject in terms of incremental comparisons. Thus, he observed that "a thing is more desirable if, when added to a lesser good, it makes the whole a greater good. Likewise, you should judge by means of subtraction: for the thing upon whose subtraction the remainder is a lesser good may be taken to be a greater good, whichever it be whose subtraction makes the remainder a lesser good" (*Topics*, 118^{b} 15). He also took account of scarcity and use value, alluding to the famous water–diamonds paradox elaborated by Adam Smith (see chapter 5). "What is rare is a greater good than what is plentiful," he maintained, "thus, gold is a better thing than iron, though less useful: it is harder to get, and therefore better worth getting" (*Topics*, 1364 20–25). "What is often useful surpasses what is seldom useful," Aristotle said, and quoted Pindar to the effect that "the best of things is water." His ordinal ranking of human wants in the *Politics* also presaged the theory of the great Austrian economist, Carl Menger (see chapter 14).

Aristotle on Money and Interest

Aristotle's theory of money rationalized both the origin of money and its functions. The passage about reciprocity quoted above from the *Ethics* underscores his perception of money as a standard of value and a medium of exchange. He also recognized money as a store of value by observing that "if we do not need a thing now we shall have it if ever we do need it—money is as it were our surety; for it must be possible for us to get what we want by bringing the money" (*Nichomachean Ethics*, 1133^{b} 10). Some scholars even argue that the modern idea of money as a contractual standard of deferred payment is implicit in Aristotle's analysis of usury.

Of course Aristotle wrote before the creation of paper money and banking, but he nevertheless spelled out the properties required of money in the fourth century, BC, when gold was the common currency. Although gold has been replaced by fiat currency in modern times, the properties of money designated by Aristotle are nevertheless just as meaningful now as they were then. The five properties specified by Aristotle are:

1. *Durability.* Gold makes good money because it won't evaporate, mildew, rust, crumble, break or rot. Gold is chemically inert, which makes for a lasting medium of exchange.
2. *Divisibility.* Whether bullion, dust, or coin, one ounce of gold is exactly 1/100 of one hundred ounces. Hence it is divisible without depreciation of its value. By contrast, when a diamond is split, its full value may be destroyed.
3. *Convenience.* Gold allows the owner to carry his money with him. Real estate stays where it is and equivalent value of many other metals may be too heavy to carry.
4. *Uniformity.* Only one grade exists for 24-carat gold, so there is no danger of owning 24-carat gold varying in quality. Pure gold is the same in every time and place because it is a natural element, unlike gemstones, artwork, land, corn, or other commodities.
5. *Intrinsic value.* Gold finds many uses other than money. Of all the metals, it is the most malleable, most ductile, and the least reactive. Next to silver (another popular form of money in ancient times), it is the most conductive of heat and electricity.[2]

[2] While these five characteristics, taken together, make gold uniquely suited as a medium of exchange and a store of value, it is important to note that arguments that gold's value is "mystical" are silly—it is simply one of the 92 natural elements.

Aristotle's concern with justice and the administrative nature of the economy led him to a discussion of money as an object of acquisitive behavior, and particularly to an examination of interest as an "unnatural" return. Modern economic thought regards acquisitive behavior as a healthy manifestation of self-interest, which can be demonstrated to have beneficial effects through the restraints placed on it by competition. To the Greek mind, however, which did not grasp the self-regulating character of the marketplace, unrestrained acquisitive behavior was a threat to social and economic stability. Aristotle believed that coined money permitted the development of "unnecessary" exchange, which was to be discouraged in the "good" state. In the context of ancient Greece, unnecessary exchange is exchange without a natural limit. Unlike the *necessary* exchange of households, which was restrained by the limited wants of the family and by diminishing marginal utility, unnecessary exchange (i.e., retail trade) occurs merely for the purpose of accumulating wealth for its own sake. In other words, although Aristotle recognized the use of exchange to satisfy (natural) individual and collective wants, he did not approve of the use of exchange as a mere device for accumulating wealth. Since such accumulation was without natural limit, its relentless pursuit runs the risk of impoverishing the many in order to profit the few—a violation of distributive justice.

To Aristotle, the natural use of money was to spend it. He regarded hoarding, or accumulation for its own sake, as unnatural and, therefore, condemned it. Insofar as there can be no lending without previous accumulation, lending, too, was suspect. It is this kind of thinking that underlies Aristotle's condemnation of interest as "unnatural." He equated interest with usury and condemned both because in his view it is not "natural" that money (considered as a medium of exchange) should reproduce itself solely by passing from hand to hand. Unfortunately, he never grappled with the question of why interest is paid in the first place. In other words, Aristotle did not develop a *theory of interest*, even though he had a primitive theory of money to which he linked interest.

Looking backward through the millennia, it is clear that what the Greeks contributed to Western thought was a rational approach to social science. Their ideas established a continuum that stretched from the microeconomic values of the basic production/consumption unit of the household to the macroeconomic values of happiness and self-sufficiency of the collective citizenry. What they did not grasp is the concept of the marketplace as a self-regulating mechanism. Thus, their framework of analysis was anthropocentric and administrative. (For more on the Greek legacy to economic thought, see the box, Method Squabbles 1: What Can Economists [or Anyone] Know?)

Method Squabbles 1: What Can Economists (or Anyone) Know?

In economics, as in any field of knowledge, one of the most fundamental questions that anyone can ask is whether and under what circumstances we can know anything. Alternative views about knowledge and change have shaped the way economists have analyzed the world.

This issue bedeviled the early Greek philosophers, who originated the mother of all method controversies. The critical issue is the basis of knowledge itself. Method controversies about the nature of change began to gather steam in the earliest days of Greek philosophy.* One group of pre-Socratics, led by the philosopher Heraclitus, based their arguments about change on a *perpetual* and *ever-fluctuating* view of the world. We might call this the *dynamic*

(continued)

method of analyzing change. The opposing view was that of another Greek philosopher, Zeno the Eleatic. He adopted a *static* view, which held that all change is mere surface appearance generated by unreal and unreliable sense experience. In this static view the world is unchanging and predictable.

Although daily events appeared to contradict Zeno's conception, philosophers such as Plato and Aristotle adopted the static view, and it became the dominant philosophical preconception for more than two thousand years. Zeno and his followers searched for the "permanent attributes" of nature that lay behind the surface world of sense experience. This world permitted change, but that change was "predictable" as in, say, regular cycles of business activity. This kind of world (in which A *causes* B; B causes C; therefore A *causes* C) was ultimately dubbed "static" and was said to be "deterministic." Perhaps more than anyone else, the French astronomer and mathematician, Pierre Laplace, captured the essence of determinism with his famous remark that if he knew the state of every particle in the universe at any given moment, he would be able to predict the future course of events throughout eternity. This static view of the world dominated Western thought and became an integral part of some sciences, including economics.

The opposing view—one of perpetual change—resurfaced in the nineteenth century in the work of Charles Darwin, whose *Origin of the Species* (1859) emphasized the dynamism of biological evolution. As a result, biology and other life sciences have come to be dominated by a more dynamic view of "how the world works," thereby providing a counterpoint to the more orthodox and accepted static view of other sciences.

Economics, as will become evident throughout this book, has not escaped this fundamental philosophical controversy about knowledge and what we can know. Formal or empirical economic *models* or *theories*, especially those within the main tradition of "neoclassical" economics that prevails today, are highly deterministic. In the standard economic "model" conditions surrounding some "event" are specified and the model then predicts the outcome. For example, if the demand for computer chips rises, given theorized or empirically specified supply conditions, the price and quantity of computer chips will rise. This kind of predictive theorizing is simply an extension of determinism and a belief in "natural laws" subscribed to by a wide variety of eighteenth century "Enlightenment" philosophers. As we will see in chapter 5, Adam Smith—the founder of economics—was one of these philosophers. His emphasis on the "invisible hand" as an immutable universal law of nature is a latter-day reflection of Zeno's view.

The static view had and continues to have an enormous impact on the method by which economists study their field. But Heraclitan dynamics has had an important influence, too. Shortly after the promulgation of Darwinian principles, the American economist Thorstein Veblen criticized orthodox economics as "old-fashioned" because it did not utilize dynamic and evolutionary methods (manifest by Darwinian biology). About this time another famous economist, Joseph Schumpeter, introduced a new evolutionary theory of economic development that relied heavily on dynamic theories of change. Veblen and Schumpeter did not convince their contemporaries to replace the static method with the dynamic one, but the study of economics periodically undergoes new "revolutions" aiming to analyze institutional change from a dynamic perspective.

Which view of change will ultimately dominate: Zeno's static view or Heraclitus's dynamics? One hindrance to dynamic discussions or theories of change is that if all factors relating to the economy or particular events are in constant flux, the future is not predictable. And economists, perhaps along with all scientists, want to be able to predict, at least within limits. Both of these views, as will be shown throughout this book, have support in the discipline of economics. The opposing views of two ancient Greek philosophers will continue to fuel debates over method in economics. Look for them as you read through this book.

*Some of this discussion follows Alfred Chalk, "Schumpeter's Views on Philosophy and Economics."

■ Roman and Early Christian Contributions

Economic details are available for only about two centuries of Roman history, circa 150 BC to AD 50. Little genuine analytical work emerged during this period, however, because the focus was mainly military and political. By the time Rome reached the pinnacle of its power, important commercial interests had developed and spread throughout the empire. And by the end of the Roman Republic there were enough economic problems—problems of trade, finance, war, colonization, and slavery, to name a few—to employ a legion of economists and government advisers. But for all its power and ensuing troubles, Rome shared the oligarchic ethic of ancient Greece. The major ways to accumulate wealth were by conquest, piracy, slave capture and trade, money lending, tax farming, and kindred predatory activities.

In other words, the social structure of ancient Rome was not congenial to purely entrepreneurial activities or to extensive reflection on the behavior of markets. From the bottom up, Roman society consisted of slaves, peasants, artisans, and traders, capped by a civil and military aristocracy. Although the aristocracy nurtured a considerable interest in Greek philosophy and art, it did so more as an avocation than a vocation, with the predictable result that little serious analytical advance in economics occurred.

The one great achievement of Roman society was the law. From a social standpoint, it was the crowning glory of one of the greatest empires in the history of the world. Roman law was divided into a civil law that applied only to relations between citizens *(jus civile)* and a kind of common law—though not in the English sense—that ruled commercial and other relations between noncitizens or between citizens and noncitizens *(jus gentium)*. This last body of law became a repository of economic principles that later provided a starting point for economic analysis, especially in the Middle Ages. The Roman law of property and contract, for example, subsequently became the mainstay of legal systems in the Western world. The concept of natural law, which can be traced back to Aristotle, found its way into Roman law, where it was used as a touchstone for determining the validity of human legislation. Finally, the modern doctrine of the corporation can be traced back to Roman law.[3] In general, Roman law provided a frame on which the economics of a later day was slowly but surely mounted. The focal point of later discussions of market price, for example, is found in the Justinian Code:

> The prices of things function not according to the whim or utility of individuals, but according to the common estimate. A man who has a son whom he would ransom for a very large sum is not richer by that amount. Nor does he who possesses another man's son possess the sum for which he could sell him to his father; nor is that amount to be expected when he sells him. In the present circumstances he is evaluated as a man and not as somebody's son. . . . Time and place, however, bring about some variations in price. [Olive] oil will not be evaluated the same in Rome as in Spain, nor, since here as well prices are not constituted by momentary influences, nor by occasional scarcity, will it be evaluated the same in times of prolonged sterility as in times of abundant harvest. (*Corpus Iuris Civilis*, in Dempsey, p. 473)

It is worth noting that from the time of the fall of Rome to the end of the eighteenth century, most of the writers on economics were by profession either businessmen or

[3] An excellent, brief historical treatment of the modern corporation is contained in Robert Hessen's *In Defense of the Corporation*. Curiously, Hessen does not trace the concept back as far as Roman law, stopping instead at the Middle Ages.

lawyers. If they were lawyers, moreover, they were either clergymen trained in canon law or jurists trained in civil law.

The rise of Christianity overlapped the decline of the Roman Empire and offered a different kind of civilizing influence. Rome's efforts at civilizing its annexations pretty much began and ended with the establishment of law and order. The only message it offered to those outside its jurisdictional limits was military surrender. Perhaps for this reason its social and political order was inherently unstable. Christianity offered a different message, one that proved to be an inspiration and a rallying point for millions of people, but one not especially fruitful for the advance of economic analysis until after a period of consolidation.

Early Christian thought treated the kingdom of God as being near at hand, and so it emphasized "other worldly" treasures. Production and material welfare would be superfluous in the kingdom of God. Indeed, earthly treasures were regarded as an impediment to the attainment of this heavenly kingdom. As the passage of time made the comings of this kingdom seem more distant, wealth came to be looked on as a gift of God, furnished to promote human welfare. Christian thought therefore came to center on the "right" use of material gifts, an idea that persisted in medieval economic thought. Thus, St. Basil (c. 330–379) wrote:

> The good man . . . neither turns his heart to wealth when he has it, nor seeks after it if he has it not. He treats what is given him not for his selfish enjoyment, but for wise administration. (*Works of St. Basil*, in Gray, p. 52)

This kind of writing is more prescriptive than analytical. The same could be said of the early writings of Saints John Chrysostom (c. 347–407), Jerome (c. 347–419), Ambrose (c. 339–397), and, to a lesser extent, Augustine (c. 354–430). Augustine went further than the others in that he pointed the way to a subjective theory of value, where wants are individually determined. See if you can detect the subtle influence of Aristotle and/or Protagoras in this passage from *The City of God*:

> There is . . . a different value set upon each thing proportionate to its use . . . very frequently a horse is held more dear than a slave, or a jewel more precious than a maid servant. Since every man has the power of forming his own mind as he wishes, there is very little agreement between the choice of a man who through necessity stands in real need of an object and of one who hankers after a thing merely for pleasure. (in Dempsey, p. 475)

By and large, however, the early Christian writers treated economic topics with indifference, if not hostility. They were primarily interested in the morality of individual behavior. The how and why of economic mechanisms seemed to be of no interest to the Church's leaders or its writers.

■ Chinese Economics in the First Millennium

China is one of the world's oldest civilizations, but its intellectual history remains inaccessible to many Westerners because of its long-time geographic, cultural, and linguistic isolation. Chang ("History of Chinese Economic Thought") maintains that Chinese economic thinking originated mainly during the Eastern Chou Dynasty (771–249 BC), a period that partially overlaps with the age of Greek antiquity. The Chou Dynasty was marked by steady decline in the authority of the monarchy and the aristocracy on the one hand and the emergence of the kingdom's fiefs as independent states on the other. Economically the productivity of land increased; monetization and specialization grew; merchants, cities, and marketplaces emerged; and the contrast between rich and poor became sharper. Three groups of writers, the Confucianists, the Legalists, and the Moists, dealt with economic issues during this golden age of Chinese philosophy.

Confucius and His Followers

Like his contemporaries in ancient Greece, Confucius (551–479 BC), was preoccupied with moral issues. He promulgated an ethical system of order that regulates all natural and social phenomena, including the movement of heavenly bodies, the variation of seasons, the rise and fall of governments, and all interpersonal relations. Aside from the sweeping nature of this system, one finds certain parallels with Greek antiquity. In the Confucian society, interpersonal obligations are reciprocal. The ascendancy of rulers is not based on heredity but on virtue and ability. The state is legitimized by a set of ethical norms and rules that are codified by legendary sages and is governed by men who derive authority through moral influence rather than law, coercion, or divine spirits. In Confucius's hierarchical society, each person has a unique role, and social harmony results only if every person understands and carries out his role. The ideal Confucian society is not driven by personal gain but is propelled by people's desire to serve the common good. These ideas, as simple and direct as they are, set the scope of Chinese economic thinking for centuries to follow. Chief among Confucius's precepts were:

1. Taxes should derive from people's productive abilities and should be limited to one-tenth of the produce of the land.
2. Government spending, which includes palace expenditures, should be adjusted to government revenues, not the other way around.
3. Living standards should conform to each person's social status, without extremes of lavishness or parsimony.
4. The foremost obligation of the ruler is the well-being of the people.
5. Government should maintain a general posture of noninterference, yet provide assistance to production and sustain equitable distribution of income when necessary.

Ambiguities in this program (for example, item 5) became increasingly troublesome after Confucius's death and led to squabbles among his followers about the essence of human nature and about the proper role of government in the economy. One of Confucius's disciples, Mencius (c. 372–287 BC), believed that individuals are inherently good and that government should promote the public welfare by a policy of noninterference; another, Hsun-tzu (c. 300–237 BC), held that people are dominated by evil impulses, and he advocated a more authoritarian government.

The Legalists

Han-fei-tzu (280–233 BC), one of Hsun-tzu's disciples, believed—following his teacher—that people are motivated primarily by self-interest. Han-fei-tzu believed that social order and economic progress would only result from the strict, centralized control of rewards and punishments. Aware that a Confucian society would function well only if individuals were guided by moral principles and kings were wise rulers, Han-fei-tzu argued that in reality societies are headed only by average rulers and that avarice is the rule rather than the exception. Another legalist, the innovative administrator Kuan Chung (c. 730–645 BC), rejected Confucian methods of decentralization, moral suasion, and personal virtue in favor of centralized state power and legal mechanisms of control. His followers, working vigorously to stamp out the remnants of the old aristocracy from Chinese society, wrote on such topics as monetary and fiscal policies, government monopoly, price stabilization, population, agriculture, and commerce.

The Moists

A third school of economic thinkers was led by Mo Ti (c. 479–438 BC), who studied under disciples of Confucius but later rejected their teachings. Disillusioned by Confucianists who rejected their learned principles in favor of personal gain, Mo Ti saw the Confucianists' failure to deal with existing chaos and misery as flaws in their thinking. Like Confucianists, Moists sought to promote economic harmony and welfare under existing monarchical regimes, but they differed on matters of implementation. Mo Ti believed in a kind of universal brotherly love as an antidote to mankind's natural inclinations toward selfishness and injustice. He was opposed to class distinctions, luxury, and ostentation. He favored social mobility, peace, order, national wealth, and a large population. His concept of division of labor, focusing on the advantages of specialization, was quite advanced for his time. Mo Ti was also strongly confident of government effectiveness if directed by a disciplined hierarchy and a strong sovereign. He organized his disciples according to strict military and authoritarian principles, which encouraged a religious zeal and authoritarian spirit unmatched in ancient China.

This kind of diversity of thought did more to highlight contentious issues than to produce a unified field of economic analysis. Like their Greek counterparts in the ancient Western world, Chinese philosophers cast economic inquiry in the frame of morality and ethics. Their analyses were influenced by the institutional makeup of the societies of their time, in which the marketplace was never conceived as a mechanism that was capable of regulating itself by allowing the free play of individual self-interest. Quite naturally, therefore, economics was regarded as a branch of moral philosophy—a tendency that continued in the East as well as the West well into the eighteenth century.

■ Medieval Arab-Islamic Economics

Whereas the contribution of ancient Greek philosophers to economic analysis is sometimes debated, the influence of Arab-Islamic thought has been persistently neglected. Historians acknowledge, however, that the death of the last Roman emperor in 476 ushered in a long period of secular decline in the West and a concomitant rise in the power and influence of the East. For five centuries, from AD 700 to 1200, Islam led the world in power, organization, and extent of government; in social refinements and standards of living; and in literature, scholarship, science, medicine, and philosophy. Moreover, it was Muslim science that preserved and developed Greek mathematics, physics, chemistry, astronomy, and medicine during this half millennium, while the West was sinking into what historians commonly call the Dark Ages. By 730 the Muslim empire reached from Spain and southern France to the borders of China and India; it was an empire of spectacular strength and grace. In this expanded capacity, the Arab world provided a bridge across which Greek and Hindu wisdom and culture traveled to the West. Perhaps the most significant, single innovation that the medieval Arab scholars contributed to the West was their system of writing numbers. Arabic numerals displaced the clumsy Roman numerals of the previous empire. In addition, one of the more eccentric Arab mathematicians, Alhazen, founded the modern theory of optics around the year 1000. But for our purposes, the most important contribution of Arab culture was its reintroduction of Aristotle to the West.

A substantial body of economic knowledge is attributable to no less than thirty Arabic scholars of the medieval period, who, like the clerics of medieval Christendom discussed in the next section, focused on the possibility of reconciling reason with faith. They viewed economics not as an end in itself but as a means to an end. The end was salvation; hence economic activities were seen as part of the earthly struggle to earn heaven. It can be said that Muslim society believed in *homo Islamicus*, not *homo oeconomicus*. Thus, Muslim philosophy showed little concern for the validity of certain economic formulations. Instead, it emphasized how economic ideas were treated in relation to ethical and political principles. In Islam there is no tradition of positive law derived from human reason. The law is derived from Shari'a, an expression of divine will, from which jurists and theologians develop ethical, social, and economic principles. This makes comparison between Muslim economics and Western economics highly problematic. Nevertheless, a brief review of Muslim medieval economic thought serves to underscore a strain of continuity between the philosophical inquiry of the ancient Greeks and that of medieval European scholars. Space constraints do not permit a comprehensive survey of the entire medieval Arabic intellectual tradition. Instead, we shall concentrate on the main link in a chain of Islamic thought that stretched from the eleventh to the fourteenth centuries.

Abu Hamid al-Ghazali (1058–1111) is a mirror of this tradition. He developed what might be called a social welfare function based on consideration of utilities *(masalih)* and disutilities *(mafasid)*. Although salvation is the ultimate goal of human action, the pursuit of economic activities is a necessary part of achieving that goal because human beings would perish without them (*Ihya*, 2:32, in Ghazanfar and Islahi, p. 384). Economic efficiency is therefore seen merely as an aspect of fulfilling one's religious imperatives (*Ihya*, 2:249, 3:236; *Mizan*, 377—in Ghazanfar and Islahi, p. 384). Following Aristotle, Ghazali stressed a "middle path," or "golden mean," and the "correctness" of intentions in all actions. When intentions are consistent with divine will, he asserted, then economic activities become a kind of worship—part of one's calling (*Ihya*, 2:83—in Ghazanfar and Islahi, p. 384).[4] He recognized three sources of wealth: individual earnings, profit from exchange, and acquisition by bequest or discovery. The European Scholastics (see next section) accepted many of his views and made them part of their medieval philosophy because he made science, philosophy, and reason subservient to religion and theology.

Ghazali made specific contributions to four major areas of economic thought: (1) voluntary exchange and markets; (2) the nature of production; (3) money and interest; and (4) public finance. For Ghazali, markets—the mechanism within which voluntary exchange takes place—evolve as part of the natural order of things. Trade adds value to goods by making them available at a convenient time and place. People are acquisitive by nature, and they will seek to maximize their individual situations. Although he did not regard wealth accumulation as the noblest of activities, he recognized it as essential to the proper functioning of a progressive economy.

[4] S. M. Ghazanfar and A. A. Islahi ("Economic Thought of an Arab Scholastic," p. 386) suggest that Ghazali laid the foundation for what later became known as the "spirit of capitalism." See, for example, Max Weber, *Protestant Ethic*.

The mutuality of exchange necessitates specialization and division of labor with respect to resources and regions, which leads, among other things, to the creation of profit-motivated middlemen. Although Ghazali did not grasp the modern technique of demand and supply analysis, his discussion of prices and profits fits easily into the modern framework. He had an intuitive understanding of the concept of price elasticity, and a primitive notion of equilibrium price.[5] Like all medieval writers, Ghazali based his discussion of markets on an ethical-moral code of conduct that roundly condemned secrecy, deception, manipulation, and profiteering.

Ghazali classified production activities in terms of their social importance, emphasizing fundamental Islamic principles of duty and responsibility. Apart from its moral roots, his hierarchy of production is reminiscent of Adam Smith's ranking many centuries later. For Ghazali, output resolves itself into primary production (agriculture), secondary production (manufacturing), and tertiary production (services). He regarded the first category as the most important—even to the extent of requiring the state to be a mediating force in order to prevent agriculture's decline. But he made it clear that proper social harmony requires the active pursuit and promotion of all three levels of production. Within any given level of production, Ghazali was conscious of the linkages that exist in the production chain. Thus, he speaks of how the farmer produces grain, the miller turns it into flour, and the baker converts the flour into bread. These linkages require specialization and division of labor as well as cooperation and coordination. In driving home his point, Ghazali described how needles are made by passing through multiple transformative stages—thus anticipating the famous pin factory example espoused by Adam Smith more than half a millennium later (see chapter 5).

Ghazali recognized that money evolved in order to overcome the deficiencies of barter: in particular, the lack of mutual coincidence of wants between traders. He seemed to be aware of the distinction between use value and exchange value, but he took the curious position that gold and silver money have no intrinsic value. In other words, he argued that gold and silver have no value other than exchange value. Although this is not a defensible argument today, it may have served to buttress Ghazali's arguments against hoarding for its own sake. Like Aristotle, Ghazali argued that usury is wrong because charging interest on the borrowing and lending of money deflects money from its key function, which is to facilitate exchange. We shall see in the next section that this fiction was perpetuated by the European Scholastics as well.

Ghazali was not shy about giving advice on the proper role and function of the state, which he considered a necessary institution to ensure the proper operation of the economy and the fulfillment of divinely ordained social obligations. His position in this respect echoes down through the ages of Islam: "The state and religion are inseparable pillars of an orderly society. Religion is the foundation, and the ruler, representing the state, is its promulgator and protector; if either pillar is weak, society will crumble" (*Ihya*, 1:17; *Mizan*, 297; *Counsel*, 59—in Ghazanfar and Islahi, p. 395). Although the inseparability of religion and state was later rejected in some Western traditions, other aspects of Ghazali's system were readily embraced: for example, his belief that the state must establish peace, justice, security, and stability in order to promote economic prosperity. His discussion of public finance, though insightful in some respects, was constrained by the religious, ethical, and cultural

[5] Throughout his economic writings, Ghazali talks of a "prevailing price, as determined by market practices." This concept was referred to as "just price" by some of his Arab contemporaries and was later adopted by European medieval philosophers. Still later it culminated in the notion of "equilibrium price," as discussed in the next section.

precepts of Islam. He seemed aware of the benefits-received and ability-to-pay principles of taxation (he advocated the latter as a matter of equity). He approved of government borrowing only if it is possible to secure repayment from future revenues. And he considered public goods to be a legitimate use of public funds, citing specifically the need to provide for a country's defense, education of its people, health care, law enforcement, and the construction of roads and bridges.

Ghazali had a number of students, who in turn influenced other students, so that a continuous line of economic inquiry (always as a subsidiary branch of morals) was established in the eleventh, twelfth, and thirteenth centuries. This intellectual tradition culminated in the fourteenth century with the work of Ibn Khaldun (1332–1404). It was Khaldun who first formulated the labor theory of value that subsequently preoccupied the classical economists of the eighteenth and nineteenth centuries. Writing against the backdrop of the dramatic rise of the Ottoman Empire, which served to spread medieval Muslim thought ever wider, Khaldun anticipated Adam Smith on a number of important facets of what was to become political economy.[6] But he was preceded in this endeavor by the medieval scholars of Christian Europe.

■ Medieval European Economic Thought

After the Spanish city of Toledo was recaptured from the Moors in 1085, European scholars flocked to that site in order to translate the ancient classics. The ancient texts were turned from Greek (which Europe had forgotten) through Arabic and Hebrew into Latin. In this last mode their philosophical gems were mined for the next four hundred years by the scholars of the medieval Church—that group of priests and philosophers who are known as the Scholastics. Like their Muslim counterparts, this group of writers wrote within the context of a dominant religious creed, which in this case was Christianity.

Economics in a Feudal Society

The dominant form of economic organization in the Middle Ages was feudalism. In a feudal system of production and distribution the ownership of land is neither absolute nor divorced of duties, as it had been in ancient Rome and was to become again in modern times. Instead, the king was the repository of all legal property rights. He assigned land in large parcels to his favored chiefs and noblemen, who could, in turn, assign the land to various subtenants. "Ownership" at the production level meant the mere *right to use* (usufruct), although this right tended to become hereditary. Usufruct remained, however, subject to the performance of certain military, personal, and economic duties.

Feudal property established the seat of political power in the medieval era. A strong, central authority requires social, economic, and political integration to an extent found lacking in the Middle Ages. Consequently each feudal lord was vested with numerous governmental functions, which he exercised in his particular fiefdom. Economic production took place on the manor, or agricultural estate. Output was produced on a small scale, using relatively primitive agricultural techniques. Labor services were provided by serfs who were attached to the land rather than to

[6] Besides the labor theory of value, among the key pillars of classical economics anticipated by Khaldun are: capital accumulation and its relationship to economic progress; the dynamics of demand, supply, prices and profits; the disentanglement of money and wealth; economic freedom and the (limited) role of government.

the person who "owned" it. There was no wage system on the manor. The goal of the manor was self-sufficiency; trading activities between regions and/or countries were severely limited. In sum, the economic and social framework of the manor was analogous in many respects to that of the *polis*, or Greek city-state. The principle of organization in both was status, not contract.

Two major factors that set the Middle Ages apart from Greek antiquity were its doctrinal unity, which was provided by the Roman Catholic Church, and the pervasiveness of the market mechanism, which was manifest mostly in the cities. Medieval society somewhat grudgingly nurtured a nascent form of capitalism, as economic markets (both in products and in factors of production) became more and more entrenched in the fabric of daily life. It was against this backdrop that Scholastic economics developed.

Scholastic Economic Analysis

The social hierarchy of medieval civilization was almost Platonic in its structure. One belonged to either the peasantry (who worked), the military (who fought), or the clergy (who prayed). The last group alone emphasized the importance of knowledge, and so it was, almost by default, that the clergy became the repository and the guardians of that knowledge, exercising a virtual monopoly of learning. Consequently, medieval economics was almost the exclusive product of the clergy, particularly a group of learned writers that we now refer to as Scholastics.[7] It was they who joined together the several strands of thought that constitute medieval economics: ideas gleaned from Aristotle and the Bible, from Roman law and Church law, and from Chinese and Muslim influences.

Scholastic economics is not held in high regard today. It is commonly perceived as a tissue of misplaced fallacies about market price, interest, and property. Although most Scholastic ideas have been expunged from the corpus of economic knowledge, they have some significance in the painfully drawn-out evolution of modern value theory. This last phenomenon deserves a close examination.[8]

The Scholastic Method. The method of Scholasticism was as follows: The writer posed a question, then followed it with a lengthy and detailed exposition of the view that was to be either refuted or reinterpreted. Attention was always paid to the weight of authority. Eventually, an answer was given, contrary views scrutinized, and documentation brought forth. The whole process was deductive in nature, depending not so much on the rules of logic or of human experience as on faith and the weight of authority. While this method may seem decidedly unscientific to a modern mind, it was the accepted procedure of the medieval period. There were many masters of this method, but five in particular stand out in the tradition of Aristotelian value theory. The five are Albertus Magnus (c. 1206–1280), Thomas Aquinas (c. 1225–1274), Henry of Friemar (c. 1245–1340), Jean Buridan (c. 1295–1358), and Gerald Odonis (c. 1290–1349).

As keepers of the moral code of medieval society, the main interest of the clergy was justice, not exchange. One form of justice is exchange justice (or commutative justice), which is exactly the issue broached by Aristotle in Book V, Chap. 5, of the *Nichomachean Ethics*. It was there that Aristotle developed his reciprocity model (see above), and it was from this point that Scholastic economics took its departure. The text of Aristotle's exchange analysis may have been garbled from the outset,

[7] As used in this context, the term simply means "professors" or "teachers."

[8] The following section follows very closely the excellent study of Odd Langholm, *Price and Value*.

but it seems certain that subsequent translations into Arabic, Hebrew, and Latin did little to remove any ambiguities. Perhaps it is not surprising, therefore, that the Scholastics spent four centuries trying to disentangle and clarify its meaning. In the process Scholastic analysis infused Aristotle's primitive notion of value with the idea of *equilibrium*. It also set the train of economic reasoning down two divergent tracks that were not to come together again for over half a millennium, namely cost-determined value on the one hand, and demand-determined value on the other.

Labor and Expenses: The Analysis of Albertus Magnus. Albertus Magnus, Dominican provincial, Bishop of Regensburg, and doctor of the Church, was the first great Latin Aristotelian. His place in the history of economics is assured by two things: his tutelage of Thomas Aquinas, who subsequently had an enormous impact on Western thought, and his commentaries on the Nichomachean Ethics, where he traduced ancient Greek ideas through the prism of medieval society, providing the point of departure for all subsequent thought on exchange and value. What Albert did was to plant in Western thought the persistent notion that value-in-exchange must comply with cost-of-production. In so doing, he set in motion a long train of thought that did not reach its fruition until the nineteenth century, notably in the work of Karl Marx (see chapter 12).

Earlier commentators on Aristotle's exchange model did not advance much beyond the question of the *measurement* of value. Recall that Aristotle said that money was the measure of demand. The Scholastics most commonly referred to the measure of value in terms of money *(nummisma)* and wants *(indigentia)*. But Albert, arguing that there is a natural order and an economic order in which things are valued differently, maintained that in the economic order goods are measured in relation to labor *(opus)*. He asserted that "labor and expenses," were elements of cost and that cost was a proper measure of value. Mere recognition of the role of cost in the measurement of value is not as important as Albert's use of the insight, however. He related costs of production to the "cross-conjunction" in Aristotle's model (see figure 2-1), noting that if the market price does not cover costs of production, production will eventually cease. This was an important analytical leap for two reasons: It suggested that price could be treated as an *equilibrium* value, and it established an economic variable (i.e., costs) as the *regulator* of value. Certainly Albert was a long way from presenting an integrated and systematic explanation for the determination of market price, but his analysis was nevertheless an important advance for the thirteenth century. The fact that he brought labor into the Aristotelian framework was a lasting contribution. In subsequent chapters of this book we shall see how much mileage later economic writers got from the same notion.

Human Wants, Thomas Aquinas, and "Just Price." Albert's brilliant pupil, Thomas Aquinas, did not really have any conflict with his teacher, but he tried to improve on Albert's labor theory, which he attempted by stressing human wants. Thomas reached back to St. Augustine for this point, noting that men will not always rank things according to the natural order. Stressing the natural order, Augustine had toyed with subjectivism by noting that men will often value a jewel more than a servant girl (see above). But he did not really distinguish between wants and pleasure. If Aquinas had followed Augustine's lead it might have accelerated the early development of demand theory. Instead, Aquinas chose to inject moral instruction into his economics, a practice that tends to discount pleasure. Consequently, Aquinas's demand theory never got beyond the simple notion of the human usefulness of goods as compared with their place in the natural order of creation.

Aquinas's formal contribution to Aristotelian value theory was two-pronged: one element conditioned the other. First, he reaffirmed the *double measure* of goods (value in use versus value in exchange) that Aristotle had established; second, he introduced wants into the price formula. This last contribution is especially important because it marked the earliest root of an analytical demand theory of value. Aquinas argued that *price varies with wants*. Thus, *indigentia* became a regulator of value. This contribution, however, was strictly formal. Aquinas did not explain his terms; he simply made the connection between wants and price. Nevertheless, that connection stood as an invitation to subsequent Aristotelians to work out a more complete theory of value, which they eventually did. In the Scholastic analysis that followed Aquinas, the concept of *indigentia* was gradually enlarged to include utility, effective demand, and even unmitigated desire.

It should be noted that Aquinas's mentor, Albert, did not overlook wants in his discussion of value, nor did Aquinas neglect costs. Rather it is the case that each in turn helped to develop more fully one particular side of the argument. Taken together, the discussion is fairly balanced, although there was still a long way to go toward an integrated, analytical understanding of the market mechanism.

Indeed, an opinion shared by many modern historians of economics is that Aquinas viewed market forces as antagonistic to justice. It is difficult to reconcile the medieval notion of "just price" with the modern notion of "market price," since the former is generally defended on normative grounds whereas the latter is held to be an objective result of impersonal forces. Certainly Aquinas's language was open-ended on many points, furthering the popular notion that his analysis was wrong-headed. For example, bowing to Aristotle, Aquinas wrote:

> If the price exceeds the quantity of the value of the article, or the article exceeds the price, the equality of justice will be destroyed. And therefore, to sell a thing dearer or to buy it cheaper than it is worth is, in itself, unjust and illicit. . . . The just price of things, however, is not determined to a precise point but consists of a certain estimate. . . . The price of an article is changed according to difference in location, time, or risk to which one is exposed in carrying it from one place to another or in causing it to be carried. Neither purchase nor sale according to this principle is unjust. (in Dempsey, p. 481)

David Friedman ("In Defense") has advanced a tolerant view of Aquinas by arguing that the concept of just price was a substitute for the unregulated, competitive, market price at a time in history when markets had not yet reached the stage of development that would guarantee socially efficient results. Modern competitive markets produce socially "efficient" prices only when large numbers of buyers and sellers, each possessing reliable information, interact. These conditions were not widespread in the Middle Ages. Medieval trade involved *few* buyers and sellers, in some cases approaching the technical condition of bilateral monopoly (one seller, one buyer). In these conditions, the relationship between "market" price and average costs of production was tenuous, at best, and it was relatively easy for one party to "exploit" another. Friedman argues, therefore, that the "just price" was, in essence, a kind of *arbitrated price*, involving the establishment of equity-based guidelines designed to preserve distributive justice in exchange and to resolve the kind of conflict endemic to limited-participation markets that could not "protect" consumers by the law of large numbers (i.e., vigorous competition).

From an analytical standpoint, "just price" is a vague and imprecise idea, unsuited to an operational theory that befits a science. But to paraphrase Alfred

Marshall (see chapter 15) economics, like nature, does not make sudden, gigantic leaps forward. During the Middle Ages, if anything, economics seems to have crawled rather than leaped forward, but it nevertheless headed in the right direction.

Aggregation and Scarcity: The Influence of Henry of Friemar. Aquinas had developed the concept of indigentia in a way that related primarily to the individual. But the modern notion of market demand is an aggregate notion that comprises the wants of all those buyers who participate in the market. The next step toward establishing indigentia as an aggregate measure was taken by the Augustinian friar, Henry of Friemar.

The Scholastics' concept of *indigentia* differs from the technical, contemporary notion of market demand. It is not quantity demanded as a function of price; its meaning is much less precise, including elements of supply as well as of demand. The meaning most commonly attached to the concept in Scholastic literature is "amount desired in relation to what is available" (i.e., demand in the face of scarcity). As we now recognize, genuine analytical progress in value theory required the separation (even if artificial) of the two notions "demand" and "supply." Failure to separate demand and supply as elements in the value formula was the fundamental defect in the Aristotelian market model. Unfortunately, the Scholastics, despite their long, inquisitive tradition, never quite remedied the defect. In fact, the remedy was not forthcoming until the full flowering of marginalism in the nineteenth century.

Progress, however slow, was nevertheless made by the Scholastics. Just as Aquinas had directed Albertus's analysis toward demand factors instead of costs, so Henry tipped Aquinas's formula in favor of aggregate (i.e., market) demand. Henry advanced the somewhat mixed notion that value is determined by "the common need of something scarce." This concept acknowledged that as long as there is abundance in the face of strong demand, *indigentia* will not raise price.

Odd Langholm has aptly pointed out that a theory of exchange value can start at any one of three stages of deduction. It can start with the conditions of the market, that is, with the abundance or scarcity of goods. Or it can start with the properties of goods that make the market conditions relevant. Or it can start with the wants of the people that make these properties in goods relevant, proceeding to market conditions from there. The medieval theory, which was rooted in Aristotelian soil and nurtured all the way into modern economics, started at the third level. Although the Scholastics were not alone in discussing economic matters in relation to human wants, they deserve credit "for taking this concept through aggregation and scarcity into a workable argument in the price formula" (Langholm, *Price and Value*, p. 115).

Effective Demand: The Contribution of Jean Buridan. The next major step in the evolution of value theory was taken by the rector of the University of Paris, Jean Buridan. Buridan was a master logician and thoroughgoing Aristotelian whose contributions to social science and philosophy are contained in some three dozen commentaries on Aristotle's works. He maneuvered the Scholastic notion of indigentia much closer to the modern concept of effective demand. Buridan described poverty as a state in which someone does not have that which he desires, which meant that indigentia could be applied to "luxuries" as well as "necessities" (the narrower sense given to it by Aquinas). In addition, Buridan made indigentia into desire backed by ability to pay.

This modification, as insignificant as it may seem, provided a way out of a nettlesome problem in medieval value theory. Both Aquinas and his fellow prelate, John Duns Scotus, were spokesmen for a "double rule" in medieval price theory. A seller who parted with a commodity at unusually high sacrifice to himself could, with the blessing of the Church fathers, compensate for his loss by charging a higher than normal price. But if the sacrifice was "ordinary," he could not charge a higher price merely to increase his profit. In the latter case, Aquinas argued that by profiting exorbitantly, the seller in effect sold something that was not his own (the same rationale applied to Scholastic condemnations of usury). Duns Scotus maintained that something is not precious in itself merely because of the buyer's strong preference. Both writers were basically arguing that it is wrong to take advantage of a buyer's intense wants.

There are several problems with this double rule. The most obvious is its basic analytical asymmetry: It is all right for a seller to do one thing if his want is high but not to do the same thing if the buyer's want is high. The other problem is how to define "unusually high want." Borrowing from both Aquinas and Henry of Friemar, Buridan advanced a line of thought that distinguished between individual "wants" and aggregate "wants." He tied value to aggregate wants, by which he meant effective demand, and argued that the conjunction of numbers of consumers and their purchasing power works to establish a just and normal state of affairs in the marketplace. A buyer, therefore, however desirous, must comply with the valuation of the market. This is the identical line of thought that led centuries later to the laissez-faire morality of Nicholas Barbon and Thomas Hobbes, the latter declaring that "the market is the best judge of value."

What is interesting about Buridan's achievement is that it was developed within an Aristotelian framework that permitted the metamorphosis of a narrow medieval concept, *indigentia*—which originally took the vague connotation of *need* into the indiscriminate generalization, "every desire which moves us to set store by things." It is to this notion that European price theory—as opposed to British classical value theory—owes its later success. Buridan spawned a tradition of economic inquiry that permeated not only his native France but eventually also Italy and, most especially, Austria. This tradition, with tentacles reaching all the way back to Aristotle, culminated in the nineteenth-century formulation of utility, and finally in the fusion of this last concept to the notion of the margin. This success was in no small part explained by an "emphasis on utility as a psychological experience, playing down considerations of the properties in goods which cause men to desire them, a preoccupation which is sure to take theorists away from the main point" (Langholm, *Price and Value*, p. 144).

Toward a Synthesis: Odonis and Crell. All through the Middle Ages, discussions of value theory constantly pitted a generalized concept of supply (based on labor costs) against a demand theory, so that the two were continually rubbing against each other. In these circumstances one would have expected a synthesis to be forthcoming, yet the Scholastic tradition stopped short of what we today call the "neoclassical synthesis." One man more than any other brought value theory close to this now familiar synthesis. He was a resourceful German sectarian theologian named John Crell (1590—c. 1633), whose powerful insight came from joining Buridan and another Scholastic, Gerald Odonis. Odonis was a French monk of the Franciscan order, which developed its own tradition in exchange theory. He had inherited a market model that exceeded that of Aquinas and bore the imprint of Henry of Friemar. The Franciscan tradition focused on raritas, by which it meant scarcity in the face of wants (the reverse of Henry's indigentia, which was wants in the face of scarcity).

Odonis rejected a simple labor-quantity theory of value and focused on the scarcity and quality of human productive skills. This led him to a theory of wage differentials that recognized the relative efficiencies of different skills and the relative cost of acquiring those skills. It was an important step on the path to ultimate recognition of the synthetic nature of labor and demand theories of value. Odonis's theory could explain, for example, why an architect earned more than a stonecutter, and it led to the inference that scarce labor commands a higher product price because of product scarcity. A complete synthesis requires an additional step: the recognition that every kind of labor is always to some extent scarce, and so brings forth a scarce product. Indeed, it is in this way that labor serves as a *regulator* of value. The inference was a long time coming; it was not made by Buridan because it required joining his own insight to that of Odonis, who had not yet written when Buridan wrote his commentaries. Born in the following century, a resourceful thinker like Crell was able to put the two together.

History tells us that the problem of value was not solved completely until economists came to understand that the cost theory and the demand theory were merely components of a single principle. Like a two-legged stool, the single principle rested on two legs. The first leg is that labor is a regulator of value only if it is spent on something useful. The second leg is that all labor is always (to some extent) scarce. Wants and costs are, to use Alfred Marshall's felicitous analogy, but two blades of the same scissors. Yet, it took a very long time to get that far in economic analysis. Ironically, in the seventeenth and eighteenth centuries a very able line of Italian and French economists had the two theories marching separately, with scarcity and utility carrying the burden of explanation. The British classical tradition somehow got off on the monotonous track of costs and failed to unite the two concepts, even though the idea that labor regulates product value through scarcity is very much in evidence in Nassau Senior's work (see chapter 7). In nineteenth-century France there was a sudden flash of genius, but this was not fully reflected in economic theory until after a hiatus of nearly three decades (see chapters 12–17).

The most interesting thing to surface from recent research into Scholastic economics is the remarkable continuity of the Aristotelian tradition through the years. The Scholastic economists advanced the Greek tradition, a fact that unfortunately serves to detract from the originality of their contributions. But one by one, they laid the bricks and mortar on which the edifice of value theory was slowly built. The chief architects of this edifice and the nature of their contributions are summarized in figure 2-2 on the following page.

The Doctrine of Usury

Insofar as interest is generally regarded as the price of money, a modern theory of interest is treated merely as a subset of the general theory of value. But medieval writers were concerned primarily with commutative justice, so they regarded the theory of interest primarily as an ethical issue. Few topics evoked as much controversy as the conditions under which interest was to be allowed. The Church, moreover, had an official position on the subject.

Although the idea that interest, or "profit," from loans is wrong can be traced back to the Old Testament (*Exodus* 22:25), the Roman Catholic Church did not make the injunction against usury (defined as a transaction "where more is asked than is given") part of its official doctrine until the fourth century AD when the Council of Nicaea banned the practice among clerics. During the reign of Charlemagne, the prohibition was extended to all Christians. Subsequent practice made

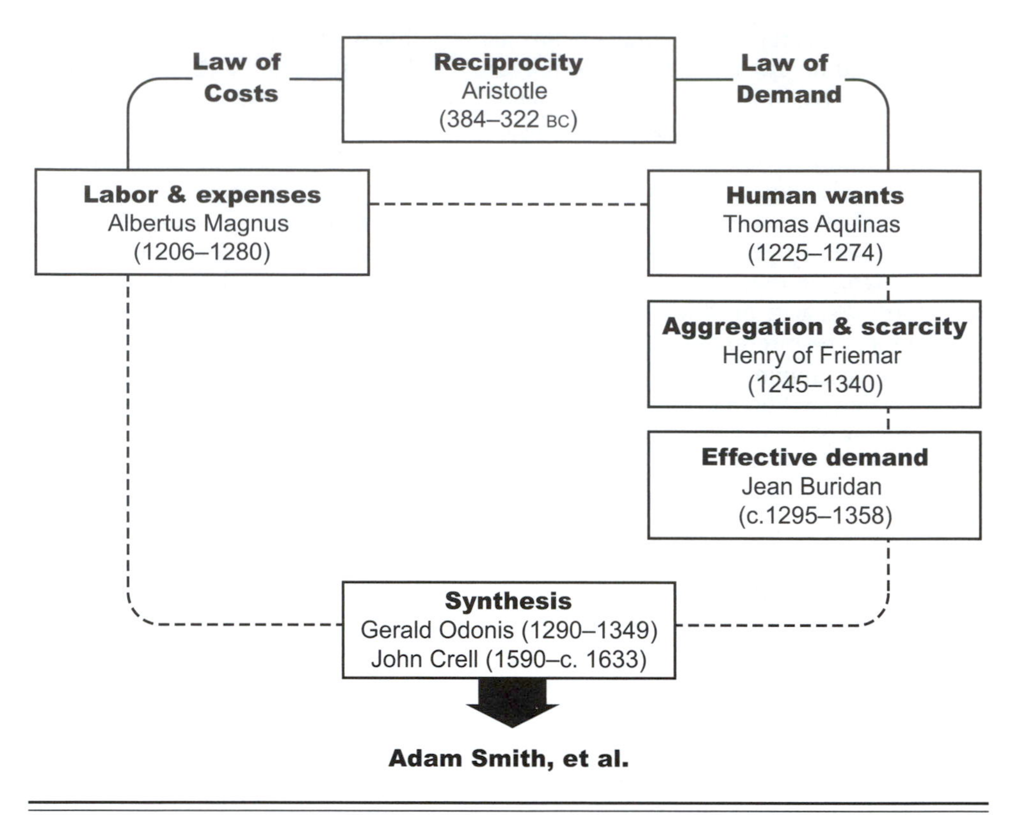

Figure 2-2 Aristotle, Aquinas, Albertus, Henry of Friemar, Buridan, Odonis, and Crell all helped lay the foundation for the development of value theory.

the ban an absolute prohibition, and for many centuries usury laws enjoyed widespread and official support. During the Middle Ages, usury and the doctrine of "just price" were the main economic topics that occupied the Scholastics.

In Latin, *usura*, from which the word "usury" derives, means payment for the use of money in a transaction that results in gain (i.e., net profit) for the lender; whereas *interesse*, from which the word "interest" derives, means "loss" and was recognized by ecclesiastic and civil law as a reimbursement for loss or expense. Interest was commonly regarded as compensation for delayed repayment or for loss of profits to the lender who could not employ his capital in some alternative use during the term of the loan. Risk was not generally considered as a justification for interest, because loans were usually secured by property worth many times the money advanced. Thus, the usury prohibition was not intended to curb the high profits of risk enterprise. For instance, the *societas* (partnership) was a recognized form of commercial organization dating back to Roman times. Its profit objective was officially sanctioned, and gains from trade were treated as earnings for effort and risk. The *census* was a kind of early financial instrument that combined elements of a mortgage and an annuity. Under the terms of this contract, the borrower incurred "an obligation to pay an annual return from fruitful property," usually a landed estate. By its nature, a *census* was not considered usurious.

In addition, bank deposits had become a form of investment by the thirteenth century. Merchant bankers paid interest on deposits. As early as the twelfth century, bills of exchange combined foreign exchange with credit, although interest was often concealed in a high exchange rate. In other words, during the Middle Ages, the Church doctrine on usury, existing alongside legitimate forms of interest taking, helped promote a double standard that became increasingly arbitrary over time, thereby creating opportunities for exploitation by those who made the rules.[9]

Over the years, medieval economic doctrine frequently came into conflict with medieval economic practice. Up to the thirteenth century, the sweeping condemnation of usury by the Church was accompanied by civil prohibitions, which varied widely from country to country. Yet, despite its widespread prohibition, usury was never entirely eradicated in any large part of Europe or for any important period of time. Professional pawnbrokers, though sometimes underground, probably always existed in medieval Europe. In fact, where they operated openly, they were licensed by the state, which received license fees.[10]

Because the Church's arguments in defense of usury make little sense in the context of modern economics, the whole topic is usually considered an analytical dead end. The chief flaws of the Scholastic analysis were its failure to recognize the productivity of money as an economic resource and its concomitant failure to recognize the time value of money. Some historians blame the Church's doctrine of usury for retarding the development of capitalism by suppressing the growth of credit markets. But up until recently, little research has been directed at explaining the anomalies between Church doctrine and Church policy on this subject.

In an attempt to break this pattern, Robert Ekelund, Robert Hébert, and Robert Tollison (see Notes for Further Reading) approached the subject by analyzing the medieval Church's behavior on the basis of its "monopoly" position among religious institutions. They conclude that it was in the Church's interest to selectively use the usury doctrine in order to keep its own cost of funds low, to prevent the entry of competing "firms," and to otherwise preserve its monopoly status. In the final analysis, therefore, the ultimate disappearance of the usury doctrine may have been a result of increased doctrinal competition in the wake of the Protestant Reformation rather than the effect of a systematic belief in the weakness of its underlying premises.

■ Theory Meets History: Economic Impact of Christianity and the Medieval Church

State and religion—and the combination's impact on economics—has been a feature of all ancient and modern societies. Temple civilizations, such as the Assyrian, Mesopotamian, and Egyptian cultures, were fundamentally a marriage of church and state where, in many cases, resources were directed, sometimes in mas-

[9] According to Raymond de Roover ("Scholastics, Usury and Foreign Exchange," p. 266), pawnbrokers and small moneylenders were the main victims of the church's campaigns against usury, "but the big bankers with international connections were left undisturbed. Far from being censured, they were called 'the peculiarly beloved sons of the Church' and prided themselves on being the Pope's exchangers."

[10] Before the Renaissance, the legal limits on personal loans from pawnshops ranged from a low of 10 percent in Italy to 300 percent in Provence, France. In the fourteenth century, the Lombards (Italian bankers) often charged 50 percent, although the most common legal pawnshop limit in effect was 43 percent. Monarchs, such as Emperor Frederick II (1211–1250), often paid interest of 30 to 40 percent to creditors, especially when collateral was not liquid. Commercial loans commonly fetched interest rates between 10 and 25 percent depending on the adequacy of commercial credits (see Sidney Homer, *History of Interest Rates*, pp. 89–103).

sive quantities (for example, the pyramids) to religious and "afterlife" ends. In the first century of the Common Era, a new religion emerged based upon the teachings of Jesus Christ. The resulting religion, Christianity, had to "out compete" other pagan and ethnic religions and used apostle-entrepreneurs such as St. Paul to offer a belief product with certain advantages compared to Judaism and Greco-Roman paganism. Multideity religions, such as Greco-Roman paganism, created large transaction costs for its "believers." Judaism blunted its monotheistic advantage by imposing costly rituals. By comparison Christianity offered a well-defined and happy afterlife contract with assurances of eternal salvation attached. It also propounded a "loving God" in place of a vengeful one. Moreover, its emphasis on social and charitable works and services quickened its spread throughout the East and large parts of Europe through the proselytizing efforts of disciples in enclaves within cities.

A problem emerged over the first three centuries of the Common Era: Christ did not return and multiple Christianities sprang up. The Emperor Constantine's call of the Council of Nicaea (325 CE) may be seen as the initial and principal element of the cohesiveness and "product" monopoly of the Christian religion. At Nicaea the template of Christianity was spelled out with the books of the New Testament, with competing Christianities labeled "heresy." Clear definition at Nicaea was necessary to avoid the emergence of alternative Christian "products" and to collect control rents (monetary returns) accruing to the legitimized Church and to civil governments as well. The council set in motion a long history of efforts by the Roman Catholic Church to expand and entrench its monopoly power in the West through reciprocity—one that gave civil governments and monarchs, such as the Merovingian and Carolingian rulers, Christian legitimacy in return for protection from all forces that challenged the Church or its properties. These developments, along with a high degree of voluntary and forced conversions at the lower geographic levels of Christian practice (Vikings were ultimately Christianized) and a lasting split with the Eastern Church (in the eleventh century) led to a high period of Church monopoly across much of Western Europe.

By all historical accounts, the medieval period marked a critical transition from the ancient world to the modern one, as we have already seen in this chapter with the inventions of Church-affiliated scholars. However, even a careful recitation of "who said what" provides an incomplete picture of this vital passage. It is widely agreed that the medieval Roman Catholic Church—the longest running institution of the West—played a pivotal role in the ultimate development of liberal capitalism, but opinions differ on whether the overall influence of the Church was favorable or not. In this final section, therefore, we review some of the issues that marked the transition from one age to the next.

Church Organization

After the twelfth century, Roman Catholicism faced only fringe religious competition from Jews and Moors, so it came to dominate large parts of Western Europe. Canon law (the legal system of the Church) was beginning to supplant and eventually dominate civil law in the loosely organized states and other political entities of the West. Ecclesiastical officials enacted laws respecting all aspects of the "supply" decision of various Church products, such as assurances of eternal salvation, political support of reigning monarchs, and various social services (e.g., hospitals, alms for the poor, etc.). The Church's web of influence was gradually extended to the establishment of marriage regulations, trade practices, and all manner of social and economic behavior. Kings, princes, and aristocrats owed much of their power to the approbation of the Roman Catholic authorities who, with an extensive coterie of clerical agents, helped rulers wage wars, maintain armies, and negotiate trade deals. The Church, moreover, was immensely wealthy and was a huge landholder during the medieval period. It collected revenues not only from voluntary contributions, but also from the sale of relics and indulgences, taxes, and land rents.

The organization of the medieval Church was analogous to what Oliver Williamson (*Markets and Hierarchies*, p. 137) calls an M-form corporation. This kind of firm is characterized by a central office that controls overall financial allocations and conducts strategic long-term planning (the Vatican) but allows divisions, usually regional, to have a high degree of autonomy in managing day-to-day operations (dioceses, or bishoprics). The pope assumed duties analogous to that of a CEO, and the Vatican had its own bank (the papal *camera*) and board of directors (the College of Cardinals). Its "retail" operations were extensive and widespread. The primary role of the Vatican central office was to provide doctrine and dogma relating to the essential principles of membership (e.g., interpretations of Holy Writ) and to collect rents from its many divisions and franchises. Downstream from the Vatican were the geographically dispersed purveyors of local Roman Catholicism, the monasteries, bishoprics, and parishes. While rents were collected at all levels, primary revenues came from these retail agencies of the downstream Church. Like all good corporations, the medieval Church set up enforcement policies and assigned jurisdiction to central and local authorities to prevent opportunistic behavior by its many agents.

Maintenance of the Church Monopoly and Doctrinal Manipulations

In order to preserve and protect its monopoly status, the medieval Church sought to prevent the entry of rival religions. Heretics were roundly condemned and shunned by Church leaders and Church members. Interdict, whereby the "sinner" was forbidden contact with other Christians, was one form of punishment. A more severe form of punishment was excommunication, which imposed total separation of the wrongdoer from the body Catholic and a sentence of eternal damnation if repentance was not made. Many heretics were put to death during warfare (e.g., the Crusades) or the dreaded Inquisition. Moreover, the medieval Church established an elaborate penal system for transgressors of all kinds.

In an attempt to protect its market dominance, the medieval Church also resorted to doctrinal manipulations in order to increase the demand for its services or to make consumer demand more inelastic. One manner of protection from rival firms in contemporary enterprise is product differentiation. Throughout the Middle Ages the Church manipulated the conditions attached to its chief product, assurances of eternal salvation. Marriage markets, mostly a matter of secular and civil concern prior to the Church monopoly, were invaded by the Church, which then issued regulations that allowed the Church a measure of control over dynastic families—one of the chief threats to its autonomy. Church officials practiced forms of price discrimination in meting out penance, establishing marriage policy, and selling indulgences. The doctrines of usury and just price were almost manipulated out of recognition. When the Church was a debtor, it seems, usury prohibitions were enforced, but not when it was a creditor. Similar manipulations extended to Church rules respecting monastery tithes and taxes, the granting of indulgences, jubilee attendance, and benefices granted to bishops and cardinals. Eventually the Church pushed its monopoly practices too far, encouraging doctrinal reforms that eventually coalesced in what we call the Protestant Reformation (see chapter 4).

A theory of rational behavior promotes understanding of the Church as an economic entity—one that benefited from increasing secularization of European society but also recognized that science, technology, and humanism would ultimately weaken the kind and form of product the Church was selling. If "belief in Christ and Christian principles" were the main issue, it would be difficult to explain how Church officials could wage war against other nations (the Crusades), or against other Christians (religious wars against Protestants), much less other Catholics (conflicts with the Eastern Orthodox Christian Church). Moreover, aggressive censorship of all kinds in the sixteenth and earlier centuries is also difficult to rationalize (e.g., the persecution of Galileo, a devout Catholic) except in an economic context, that is, the context of monopoly, market dominance, and profitability. Economists objectively viewing these policies and doctrines see them as examples of monopoly behavior and all that the model entails. Economic analyses of historical transformations approach the subject of institutional behavior on one of two grounds: public interest or private interest. If religious organizations, in this case the medieval Church, acted solely in the public interest, they would behave as a "good government"—one that provides the faithful with information, spiritual goods, and social goods at competitive prices (i.e., marginal cost). An economic examination of the behavior of the medieval Church provides little if any support for this view.

Protestantism was another transformative force of the medieval era. It emerged—significantly in northern Europe and England—mainly in response to opportunistic practices of the established Church. The net result was a lessening of the hold of the Roman Catholic version of Christianity in Europe. Some great scholars of the past found a force in the new creed that stimulated and encouraged the rise of capitalism (e.g., Max Weber, see Notes for Further Reading). The proponents of this view maintained that the Catholic Church's attack on excessive "money making" (an ancient idea as we have seen in the present chapter), on science, and on free thought, among other practices, retarded the development of liberal capitalism as espoused later by Adam Smith and the classical writers. But this view is far from universal. Other writers have insisted that the Catholic Church, despite its dogma and market dominance, encouraged economic development rather than retarded it. In short, the historical reasons for the emergence of liberalism are complex and varied and, at this distance in time, may never be fully understood. We shall revisit this issue in the next chapter, which examines yet another ideational and historical argument for the decline of authoritarian economies and the emergence of economic liberalism.

■ Conclusion

Although the period from Greek antiquity to the end of the Middle Ages constitutes roughly two thousand years, the fundamental economic structure of Western civilization changed little during that time. Both Greek antiquity and European feudalism were characterized by small, insular, self-sufficient economies with little capital and low levels of production. At the level of basic production, serfdom was akin to slavery, except for the legalistic difference that serfs maintained property rights over their own bodies. In effect, serfs were tied to the land, regardless of owner, whereas slaves belonged to a particular owner, regardless of whether or not the owner possessed land.

Throughout the first two millennia, isolated exchange in the East and the West predominated over what we now call market exchange. Consequently, the learned treatises of the day, whether derived from China, Arabia, or Europe, focused primarily on the question of fairness, not on the origin of prices. This focus was sustained in an intellectual tradition that stretched from Aristotle to the European Scholastics. The continuity of this tradition was preserved by Islamic nations, which served as a conduit for the reintroduction of ancient Greek ideas to the European continent.

In the seventeenth century, John Crell capped a Western tradition in value analysis that began with the early Scholastics four hundred years earlier. But it was a tradition within a tradition, so to speak. The Scholastic tradition in Europe was cohesive and tight-knit, because the Church in the Middle Ages enjoyed an intellectual monopoly on learning. Its scholars all spoke the same language, Latin. They were each trained by an educational system that was the same in every country. Each figure in that tradition professed the same fundamental beliefs and acknowledged the same authority of God and Church. Albert, Henry, and Crell were German; Aquinas was Italian; Buridan and Odonis were French. This heterogeneity was hardly noticed, however. As Schumpeter has said of the Scholastics: "Their country was Christendom, their state the Church" (*History*, p. 75). At the peak of this tradition, economic analysis was slowly being displaced by an early modern form of inquiry. The new economists of the eighteenth century, however, all had classical educations, so theirs was by no means a de novo approach to economic analysis.

From an institutional perspective, the Middle Ages were dominated by a single entity—the Roman Catholic Church—which had an enormous influence on secular states and society in general. Its practices were monopolistic in that it thwarted the entry of new religions by threat and by violence (e.g., excommunications, interdict, Crusades); by product differentiation (e.g., the invention of limbo, purgatory, and confession), and by taking control of fundamental social customs (e.g., law and marriage). Only when this monopoly began to break down in the sixteenth century did rival religions make serious inroads into the states of Western Europe. The interplay of religion, religious belief, political structures, and the self-interest of individuals and groups in late medieval and early modern societies combined to shift the economic axis of Western Europe. There is a kind of duality at work in major historical transformations that can be difficult to disentangle: Ideas shape events and have consequences, but events also mold ideas and help establish theories. The ideas that emerged from a "mercantile" economic organization and the consequences of economic self-interest that took place in the sixteenth and seventeenth centuries paved the way for another important transition from hegemonic mercantilism to economic liberalism, as we shall see in the following two chapters.

REFERENCES

Aristotle. *The Works of Aristotle*, 12 vols., W. D. Ross (ed.). Oxford: Clarendon Press, 1908–1952.

Chalk, Alfred F. "Schumpeter's Views on Philosophy and Economics," *Southern Economic Journal*, vol. 24 (January 1958), pp. 271–282.

Chang, J. L. Y. "History of Chinese Economic Thought: Overview and Recent Works," *History of Political Economy*, vol. 19 (Fall 1987), pp. 481–502.

Dempsey, Bernard W. "Just Price in a Functional Economy," *American Economic Review*, vol. 25 (September 1935), pp. 471–486.

de Roover, Raymond. "The Scholastics, Usury and Foreign Exchange," *Business History Review*, vol. 41 (1967), p. 266.

Friedman, David D. "In Defense of Thomas Aquinas and the Just Price," *History of Political Economy*, vol. 12 (Summer 1980), pp. 234–242.
Ghazanfar, S. M., and A. A. Islahi, "Economic Thought of an Arab Scholastic: Abu Hamid al-Ghazali (A.H. 450–505 / A.D. 1058–1111)," *History of Political Economy*, vol. 22 (Summer 1990), pp. 381–403.
Gomperz, Theodor. *Greek Thinkers: A History of Ancient Philosophy*, vol. 1, L. Magnus (trans.). New York: Humanities Press, 1955.
Gray, Alexander. *The Development of Economic Doctrine*, 2d ed. London: Longman, 1980.
Hessen, Robert. *In Defense of the Corporation*. Stanford: Hoover Institution Press, 1979.
Homer, Sidney. *A History of Interest Rates*, rev. ed. New Brunswick, NJ: Rutgers University Press, 1977.
Langholm, Odd. *Price and Value in the Aristotelian Tradition*. Bergen, Norway: Universitetsforlaget, 1979.
Lowry, S. Todd. *The Archaeology of Economic Ideas*. Durham, N.C.: Duke University Press, 1987.
———. "The Greek Heritage in Economic Thought," in *Pre-Classical Economic Thought*, S. Todd Lowry (ed.). Boston: Kluwer Academic Publishers, 1987.
Plato, *The Republic*, Henry Shorey (trans.). Cambridge, MA: Harvard University Press, 1977, vols. 1 & 2.
———. *Theaetetus*, Henry Shorey (trans.). Cambridge: Harvard University Press, 1977, vol 7.
Schumpeter, Joseph A. *History of Economic Analysis*, E. B. Schumpeter (ed.). New York: Oxford University Press, 1954.
Weber, Max. *The Protestant Ethic and the Spirit of Capitalism*. London: Allen & Unwin, 1930 [1904].
Wicksteed, P. H. *The Common Sense of Political Economy*. New York: A. M. Kelley, 1966.
Williamson, O. E. *Markets and Hierarchies: Analysis and Antitrust Implications*. New York: Free Press, 1975.
Xenophon. *Memorabilia and Oeconomicus*, E. C. Marchant (trans.). New York: G. P. Putnam's Sons, 1923.
———. *Scripta Minora*, E. C. Marchant (trans.). New York: G. P. Putnam's Sons, 1925.

Notes for Further Reading

The ancient world is practically a never-never land to most historians of economic thought, although there is a fairly large literature on the economics of the period. A sampler of original sources, including selections from Xenophon, Aristotle, Aquinas, Oresme, and Molina, can be found in A. E. Monroe, *Early Economic Thought* (Cambridge, MA: Harvard University Press, 1924). For more sweeping treatments of the period, see M. L. W. Laistener, *Greek Economics* (London: Dent, 1923); Moses I. Finley, *The Ancient Economy*, 2d ed. (Berkeley: University of California Press, 1985); Marshall D. Sahlins, *Stone Age Economics* (Chicago: Aldine-Atherton, 1972); J. J. Spengler, *Origins of Economic Thought and Justice* (Carbondale, IL: Southern Illinois University Press, 1980); and A. M. Andreades, *History of Greek Public Finance*, rev. ed., 2 vols. (Cambridge, MA: Harvard University Press, 1933). The latest, and arguably the best, analysis of the Greek tradition, however, is S. Todd Lowry's *The Archaeology of Economic Ideas* (see references), from which this chapter draws freely. For a complementary study emphasizing different themes, see Christos P. Baloglou, *The Economic Thought of the Ancient Greeks* (Thessaloniki: Historical and Folklore Society of Chalkidike, 1995). A useful overview of the entire period stretching from Greek to Roman to medieval economic thought is contained in Barry Gordon, *Economic Analysis before Adam Smith: Hesiod to Lessius* (New York: Harper & Row, 1975).

Much of the periodical literature on ancient economic thought centers on Aristotle, though not exclusively so. On some general topics, see A. H. M. Jones, "The Economic Basis of the Athenian Democracy," *Past & Present*, vol. 1 (February 1952), pp. 13–31; Kurt Singer, "Oikonomia: An Inquiry into the Beginnings of Economic Thought and Language," *Kyklos*, vol. 11 (1958), pp. 29–54; Cosimo Perotta, "The Legacy of the Past: Ancient Economic Thought on Wealth and Development," *The European Journal of the History of Economic Thought*, vol. 10 (Summer 2003), pp. 177–229; E. Simey, "Economic Theory among the Greeks and Romans," *Economic Review*, vol. 10 (October 1900), pp. 462–481; S. Todd Lowry, "The Archaeology of the Circulation Concept in Economic Theory," *Journal of the History of Ideas*, vol. 35 (July–September 1974), pp. 429–444; Gregor Sebba, "The Development of the Concepts of Mechanism and Model in Physical and Economic Thought," *American Economic Review, Papers and Proceedings*, vol. 43 (May 1953), pp. 259–271; and William Baumol's delightful excursus, "Economics of Athenian Drama: Its Relevance for the Arts in a Small City Today," *Quarterly Journal of Economics*, vol. 85 (August 1971), pp. 365–376.

The economic ideas of other writers who fit into the ancient scheme but whose ideas have not directly impinged on this chapter are examined by J. J. Spengler, "Herodotus on the Subject Matter of Economics," *Scientific Monthly*, vol. 81 (December 1955), pp. 276–285; William F. Campbell, "Pericles and the Sophistication of Economics," *History of Political Economy*, vol. 15 (Spring 1983), pp. 112–135; Stanley B. Smith, "The Economic Motive in Thucydides," *Harvard Studies in Classical Philology*, vol. 51 (1940), pp. 267–301; Panayotis Michaelides, Ourania Kardasi, and John Milios, "Democritus' Economic Ideas in the Context of Classical Political Economy," *The European Journal of the History of Economic Thought*, vol. 18.1 (2011), pp. 1–18.

The periodical literature on Plato's economic ideas is relatively sparse. William F. Campbell explores Plato's use of economic analogies in "The Free Market for Goods and the Free Market for Ideas in the Platonic Dialogues," *History of Political Economy*, vol. 17 (Summer 1985), pp. 187–197; C. B. Welles delves into the underpinnings of Plato's ideal society in "The Economic Background of Plato's Communism," *Journal of Economic History*, suppl., vol. 8 (1948), pp. 101–114; in a different vein, see Laurence C. Moss, "Platonic Deception as a Theme in the History of Economic Thought: The Administration of Social Order," *History of Political Economy*, vol. 28 (Winter 1996), pp. 533–557. Vernard Foley examines the parallels between Plato and Adam Smith in "The Division of Labor in Plato and Smith," *History of Political Economy*, vol. 6 (Summer 1974), pp. 171–191. For a critique of the conventional view that Plato's *Republic* endorses specialization, see Daniel Silvermintz, "Plato's Supposed Defense of the Division of Labor: A Reexamination of the Role of Job Specialization in the *Republic*," *History of Political Economy*, vol. 42 (Winter 2010), pp. 747–772. Silvermintz argues that Plato actually criticized specialization on grounds that it prevents individuals from achieving spiritual harmony and impedes philosophizing. Of course, Adam Smith, too, was of two minds regarding specialization (see Chap. 5).

The ideas of Protagoras have come to us mostly from the commentaries of Plato. See R. Hackforth, "Hedonism in Plato's Protagoras," *Classical Quarterly*, vol. 22 (1928), pp. 39–42, for a treatment of the hedonistic elements in Greek thought.

Aristotle's discussion of exchange has drawn the most attention from historians of economic thought. The problems of equality and proportion that concerned Aristotle are analyzed (without, however, mention of Aristotle) by L. B. Shaynin, "Proportions of Exchange," *Economic Journal*, vol. 70 (December 1960), pp. 769–782. Search for meaning in the cryptic passage of *The Nichomachean Ethics* continues to fan a lively debate among Aristotelian scholars. The following works trace the evolution of the debate in chronological order: Van Johnson, "Aristotle's Theory of Value," *American Journal of Philology*, vol. 60 (October 1939), pp. 445–451; Josef Soudek, "Aristotle's Theory of

Exchange: An Inquiry into the Origin of Economic Analysis," *Proceedings of the American Philosophical Society*, vol. 96 (1952), pp. 45–75; Karl Polyani, "Aristotle Discovers the Economy," in K. Polyani et al. (eds.), *Trade and Market in the Early Empires: Economies in History and Theory* (New York: Free Press, 1957), pp. 64–94; Whitney J. Oates, *Aristotle and the Problem of Value* (Princeton, NJ: Princeton University Press, 1963); Barry Gordon, "Aristotle and the Development of Value Theory," *Quarterly Journal of Economics*, vol. 78 (February 1964), pp. 115–128; S. Todd Lowry, "Aristotle's Mathematical Analysis of Exchange," *History of Political Economy*, vol. 1 (Spring 1969), pp. 44–66; and Ralph Dos Santos Ferreira, "Aristotle's Analysis of Bilateral Exchange: An Early Formal Approach to the Bargaining Problem," *The European Journal of the History of Economic Thought*, vol. 9 (Winter 2002), pp. 568–590. William Jaffé traces Aristotle's influence on the development of neoclassical price theory in "Edgeworth's Contract Curve: Part 2. Two Figures in Its Protohistory: Aristotle and Gossen," *History of Political Economy*, vol. 6 (Fall 1974), pp. 381–404. Scott Meikle, *Aristotle's Economic Thought* (Oxford: Clarendon Press, 1997), argues that Aristotle developed a coherent theory of economic value, wealth, exchange, and money, but it cannot be assimilated to what we call economics because its metaphysical foundation is incompatible with the Humean metaphysics on which economics rests. From an Aristotelian standpoint, ethics and economics are competitors over the same ground, as rival sources of reasons for decision making in the public realm, and they cannot be reconciled.

On the utilitarian premises of Aristotle's thought, see Kenneth D. Alpern, "Aristotle on the Friendships of Utility and Pleasure," *Journal of the History of Philosophy*, vol. 21 (July 1983), pp. 303–315. Aristotle's distrust of market activity is based on the supposed absence of constraints on acquisitive behavior. On this topic, see S. Todd Lowry, "Aristotle's 'Natural Limit' and the Economics of Price Regulation," *Greek, Roman and Byzantine Studies*, vol. 15 (1974), pp. 57–63; T. J. Lewis, "Acquisition and Anxiety: Aristotle's Case against the Market," *Canadian Journal of Economics*, vol. 11 (February 1978), pp. 69–90; William S. Kern, "Returning to the Aristotelian Paradigm: Daly and Schumacher," *History of Political Economy*, vol. 15 (Winter 1983), pp. 501–512; and the exchange between Kern and Spencer J. Pack in the same journal, vol. 17 (Fall 1985), pp. 391–394. "Unnatural" acquisition is also the basis for Aristotle's condemnation of usury. For a competent analysis of this complex issue, see Odd Langholm, *The Aristotelian Analysis of Usury* (Bergen, Norway: Universitetsforlaget, 1984).

Related matters, both general and specific, have attracted the attention of numerous other scholars. Moses I. Finley, "Aristotle and Economic Analysis," *Past & Present*, vol. 47 (May 1970), pp. 3–25, finds "not a trace" of economic analysis in Aristotle's *Ethics and Politics*; whereas Barry Gordon, "Aristotle and Hesiod: The Economic Problem in Greek Thought," *Review of Social Economy*, vol. 21 (1963), pp. 147–156, is more generous in his assessment. Additional facets of Aristotle's thought are explored by J. J. Spengler, "Aristotle on Economic Imputation and Related Matters," *Southern Economic Journal*, vol. 21 (April 1955), pp. 371–389; and Stephen T. Worland, "Aristotle and the Neoclassical Tradition: The Shifting Ground of Complementarity," *History of Political Economy*, vol. 16 (Spring 1984), pp. 107–134; see also the exchange between Worland and Richard Temple-Smith in *History of Political Economy*, vol. 18 (Fall, 1986), pp. 523–529. T. H. Deaton, R. B. Ekelund, and R. D. Tollison, "A Modern Interpretation of Aristotle on Legislative and Constitutional Rules," *Southern Economic Journal*, vol. 11 (February 1978), pp. 69–90, look at Aristotle in a public-choice perspective.

Ancient Jewish literature has rarely been mined for economic gems, but two prominent exceptions are Ephraim Kleiman, "Just Price in Talmudic Literature," *History of Political Economy*, vol. 19 (Spring 1987), pp. 23–45; and same author, "Opportunity Cost, Human Capital, and Some Related Economic Concepts in Talmudic Literature," *History of Political Economy*, vol. 19 (Summer 1987), pp. 261–287. The classic reference on

Roman social and economic history is M. Rostovtzeff, *Social and Economic History of the Roman Empire*, 2d ed., 2 vols. (London: Oxford University Press, 1957). Very little has been done on the history of economic analysis of the period, with the exception of Joseph Schumpeter's encyclopedic *History of Economic Analysis* (see references).

On the practical problem of price fixing in ancient economies, see H. Michell, "The Edict of Diocletian: A Study of Price Fixing in the Roman Empire," *Canadian Journal of Economics and Political Science*, vol. 13 (February 1947), pp. 1–12; and R. L. Schuettinger and E. F. Butler, *Forty Centuries of Wage and Price Controls* (Washington, DC: The Heritage Foundation, 1979). For some insights into early Christian economic thought, see Anastassios D. Karayiannis, "The Eastern Christian Fathers (AD 350–400) on the Redistribution of Wealth," *History of Political Economy*, vol. 26 (Spring 1994), pp. 39–68.

A brief summary of ancient Chinese economic thought is given by James L. Y. Chang (see references), as well as a useful bibliography that serves as a guide to further reading. Two translations into English of works that are especially serviceable in this respect are Guan Zhong, *Guan Zi*, 2 vols., W. Allyn Rickett (trans.) (Princeton, NJ: Princeton University Press, 1985 and 1998); and Hu Jichuang, *A Concise History of Chinese Economic Thought* (Beijing: Foreign Language Press, 1988).

On Islamic economics see Louis Baeck, "The Economic Thought of Classical Islam," *Diogenes*, No. 154 (Summer 1991), pp. 99–216; M. Y. Essid, "Islamic Economic Thought," in S. T. Lowry (ed.), *Pre-Classical Economic Thought: From the Greeks to the Scottish Enlightenment* (Norwell, MA: Kluwer Academic Press, 1987); Hamid Hosseini, "Understanding the Market Mechanism before Adam Smith: Economic Thought in Medieval Islam," *History of Political Economy*, vol. 27 (Spring 1995), pp. 539–561; and Timur Kuran, "The Discontents of Islamic Economic Morality," *American Economic Review*, vol. 86 (May 1996), pp. 438–442.

Ghazanfar and Islahi (see references) provide a detailed analysis of Ghazali's economic analysis. Other writers in the medieval Muslim tradition are covered in S. M. Ghazanfar (ed.), *Medieval Islamic Economic Thought: Filling the Great Gap in European Economics* (London: Routledge/Curzon, 2003). Also see J. D. Boulakia, "Ibn Khaldun: A Fourteenth-Century Economist," *Journal of Political Economy*, vol. 79 (Sept–Oct 1971), pp. 1105–1118; Abdol Soofi, "Economics of Ibn Khaldun Revisited," *History of Political Economy*, vol. 27 (Summer 1995), pp. 387–404; and J. J. Spengler, "Alberuni: Eleventh Century Iranian Malthusian?" *History of Political Economy*, vol. 3 (Spring 1971), pp. 92–104. For a modern treatment of economics and Islamism, see Timur Kuran, *Islam and Mammon: The Economic Predicaments of Islamism* (Princeton, NJ: Princeton University Press, 2004).

Even after Christendom reclaimed parts of Europe from the Moors, the Ottoman Empire continued to spread the sphere of Muslim influence from the late thirteenth century on. We cannot do justice to this tradition here, but the interested reader should consult two works by leading economic historians: Sevket Pamuk, *The Ottoman Empire and European Capitalism, 1820-1913: Trade, Investment Production* (Cambridge University Press, 2010); and Timur Kuran, "The Scale of Entrepreneurship in Middle Eastern History: Inhibitive Rules of Islamic Institutions," in David S. Landes, Joel Mokyr, and William J. Baumol (eds.), *The Invention of Enterprise: Entrepreneurship from Ancient Mesopotamia to Modern Times* (Princeton, NJ: Princeton University Press, 2010).

Many historians looking for important analytical developments in economics pass over medieval European thought in silence. Still, there are important writers who find great insights in medieval doctrine. For a trenchant survey, see J. A. Schumpeter, *History of Economic Analysis*, chap. 2 (see references); or Henry W. Spiegel, *The Growth of Economic Thought*, chap. 3 (Englewood Cliffs, NJ: Prentice-Hall, 1971), to which is appended an excellent bibliography on medieval economics. Oscar De-Juan and Fabio Monsalve, "Morally Ruled Behaviour: The Neglected Contribution of Scholasticism," *The*

European Journal of the History of Economic Thought, vol. 13 (Spring 2006), pp. 99–112, provide an overview of neglected contributions of Scholasticism to anthropological topics. The Scholastics provided alternatives to individualist and utilitarian economics. They argued that human beings are "morally ruled" by a sense of duty and that as social beings people compete and cooperate in order to achieve certain ends. Advantages are bestowed on market participants by special information or privilege, but these advantages should not be abused.

Odd Langholm has done more to mine the field of scholastic economics than any other writer; see, *Wealth and Money in the Aristotelian Tradition: A Study in Scholastic Economic Sources* (Bergen: Universitetsforlaget, 1983); same author, *Economics in the Medieval Schools* (Leiden: E. J. Brill, 1992); and again, *The Legacy of Scholasticism in Economic Thought: Antecedents of Choice and Power* (Cambridge: Cambridge University Press, 1998). Langholm scores again in "The German Tradition in Late Medieval Value Theory," *The European Journal of the History of Economic Thought*, vol. 15 (Spring 2008), pp. 555–570, which explores German economic thinking in regard to the Canon law requirement that goods should not be resold at a profit without some alteration, and explains how the Germans reinterpreted this principle to reflect the idea of "alteration in estimation" in the market rather than alteration in physical terms.

This chapter draws heavily on Langholm's work, as he is by far the most meticulous and convincing proponent of the view that modern value theory is a direct descendant from Aristotle. Much earlier the Scholastics were defended by Bernard W. Dempsey (see references) and Raymond de Roover, "The Concept of Just Price: Theory and Economic Policy," *Journal of Economic History*, vol. 18 (December 1958), pp. 418–438; and "Scholastic Economics: Survival and Lasting Influence from the Sixteenth Century to Adam Smith," *Quarterly Journal of Economics*, vol. 69 (May 1955), pp. 161–190. The same author has traced developments in monopoly theory back to the Church fathers in "Monopoly Theory Prior to Adam Smith: A Revision," *Quarterly Journal of Economics*, vol. 65 (November 1951), pp. 492–524. The thread of natural law that runs throughout medieval economics and beyond is reviewed by Jeffrey T. Young and Barry Gordon in "The Natural Law Tradition: Thomas Aquinas to Francis Hutcheson," *Journal of the History of Economic Thought*, vol. 14 (Spring 1992), pp. 1–17. Also see Barry Gordon's comparative analysis on Greeks and Scholastics, "Aristotelian Analysis and the Medieval Schoolmen," *History of Economics Review*, vol. 20 (Summer 1993), pp. 1–12. João César das Neves, "Aquinas and Aristotle's Distinction on Wealth," *History of Political Economy*, vol. 32 (Fall 2000), pp. 649–657, stresses Aquinas's independence from Aristotle on a key point in the development of medieval economics. Odd Langholm, "Buridan on Value and Economic Measurement," *History of Political Economy*, vol. 38 (Summer 2006), pp. 269–289, provides a closer look at the secular cleric commonly thought to represent the high point of medieval economic thought.

Some other noteworthy contributions to the understanding of just price and to the wider significance of medieval economics are John W. Baldwin, "The Medieval Theories of Just Price," *Transactions of the American Philosophical Society*, n.s., vol. 49, part 4 (Philadelphia, 1959); Albino Barrera, "Exchange Value Determination: Scholastic *Just Price*, Economic Theory and Modern Catholic Social Thought," *History of Political Economy*, vol. 29 (Spring 1997), pp. 83–116; E. A. J. Johnson, "Just Price in an Unjust World," *International Journal of Ethics*, vol. 48 (January 1938), pp. 165–181; Samuel Hollander, "On the Interpretation of the Just Price," *Kyklos*, vol. 18 (1965), pp. 615–634; and Stephen T. Worland, *Scholasticism and Welfare Economics* (Notre Dame, IN: University of Notre Dame Press, 1967). George W. Wilson extends Polyani's "status" interpretation of Aristotle's exchange model to Aquinas as well, in "The Economics of the Just Price," *History of Political Economy*, vol. 7 (Spring 1975), pp. 56–74, but his view has been challenged by Odd Langholm (see references) and by Stephen T. Worland in "Justium

Pretium: One More Round in an Endless Series," *History of Political Economy*, vol. 9 (Winter 1977), pp. 504–521; and in Worland's review of Langholm's book in the same journal, vol. 12 (Winter 1980), pp. 638–642. André Lapidus, "Norm, Virtue and Information: The Just Price and Individual Behavior in Thomas Aquinas' Summa Theologiae," *European Journal of the History of Economic Thought*, vol. 1 (Autumn 1994), pp. 435–473, returns to this timeless issue. Fabio Monsalve, "Economics and Ethics: Juan de Lugo's Theory of the Just Price, or the Responsibility of Living in Society," *History of Political Economy*, vol. 42 (Fall 2010), pp. 495–519, examines the thought of the "last great representative" of the Scholastics, particularly with regard to the just-price doctrine. Finally, on the dissolution of Scholasticism, see Wim Decock, "Lessius and the Breakdown of the Scholastic Paradigm," *Journal of the History of Economic Thought*, vol. 31 (March 2009), pp. 57–78.

The literature on usury itself is fairly extensive, but it sheds more economic heat than light. For historical perspective, see Carl F. Taeusch, "The Concept of 'Usury': The History of an Idea," *Journal of the History of Ideas*, vol. 3 (June 1942), pp. 291–318; and Raymond de Roover (see references, pp. 257–271).

Finally, a good perspective on the development of markets—especially in the period that marks the transition between the subject matter of this chapter and the next—can be found in two articles by R. H. Britnell: "English Markets and Royal Administration before 1200," *Economic History Review*, vol. 31 (May 1978), pp. 183–196; and same author, "The Proliferation of Markets in England, 1200–1349," *Economic History Review*, vol. 34 (May 1981), pp. 209–221. R. B. Ekelund, Jr., R. F. Hébert, and R. D. Tollison explore historical reasons for the emergence of liberalism and market economies as a response to religious change in several particular and general works, among them: "An Economic Model of the Medieval Church: Usury as a Form of Rent Seeking," *Journal of Law, Economics, and Organization*, vol. 5 (Fall 1989), pp. 307–331; "An Economic Analysis of the Protestant Reformation," *Journal of Political Economy*, vol. 110 (June 2002), pp. 646–671; and "The Economics of the Counter-Reformation: Incumbent Firm Reaction to Market Entry," *Economic Inquiry*, vol. 42 (October 2004), pp. 690–705.

A nontechnical overview of the impact of the medieval Church on economic development incorporating views just cited may be found in R. B. Ekelund, Jr., R. F. Hébert, R. D. Tollison, G. Anderson, and A. B. Davidson, *Sacred Trust: The Medieval Church as an Economic Firm* (New York: Oxford University Press, 1996). The impact of the Church on the medieval marriage market is developed in A. B. Davidson and R. B. Ekelund, Jr., "The Medieval Church and Rents from Marriage Market Regulations," *The Journal of Economic Behavior and Organization*, vol. 32 (February 1997), pp. 215–245. For more general treatments, see R. B. Ekelund, Jr., R. F. Hébert, R. D. Tollison, *The Marketplace of Christianity* (Cambridge, MA: M.I.T. Press, 2006); and R. B. Ekelund, Jr., and R. D. Tollison, *Economic Origins of Roman Christianity* (Chicago: The University of Chicago Press, 2011). Those who read French may consult Jean-Dominique Lafay, "L'Eglise médiévale sous le regard de l'analyse économique," *Sociétal*, vol. 26 (September 1999), pp. 108–111.

3 Mercantilism

Institutional changes underway in Western Europe by the beginning of the sixteenth century led to the decline of feudalism and the rise of an alternate set of socioeconomic institutions. The new era was distinguished by the emergence of stronger, more centralized nation-states and was encouraged and supported by a new doctrine. The term *mercantilism* is applied to the doctrine or policy that the economic interests of the nation as a whole are more important than those of individuals or parts of the nation; that a preponderance of exports over imports, with a corresponding accumulation of bullion, is desirable; and that agriculture, industry, and commerce should be directed toward this end. It was a policy that, not surprisingly, allowed the emergent nation-states to flex their newfound economic muscles.

By the nineteenth century, however, the intellectual and institutional environment had changed again to allow much more individual freedom and much less concentration of economic and political power. The term *capitalism* (coined by its chief antagonist, Karl Marx) came into use to describe the more decentralized economic organization of this new era. Thus, mercantilism refers to an intervening period between feudalism and economic liberalism. It describes an economic creed that prevailed at the dawn of capitalism, before the Industrial Revolution took hold.

There are two basic ways to analyze the economics of the system of thought called mercantilism. One way considers mercantilism to be a fairly cohesive, "static" set of ideas—that is, a body of thought summarized in the events of the day. We call this the *doctrinal* approach. Another approach sees mercantilism as an important historical *process*. It concentrates on the dynamics of competing interests and their role in defining economic and political institutions. We call this the *process* approach. Both approaches view mercantilism as a system of power, but the former features a set of distinctly mercantilist propositions, or "central tendencies," that characterize the thought of the age. In this approach, the propositions of mercantilism presumably withered away as mercantilism eventually was replaced by a competing set of ideas. The doctrinal approach suggests that humans and their ideas may be arranged on a continuum with "mercantile" at one extreme and "liberal" at the other. By contrast, the policy view spotlights those self-interested forces in the economic system that generate changes in power and wealth. It concentrates on the specific regulations of the mercantilist period and how each affected the competing groups of interests held by the monarch, parliament, courts, and producers. Compared to the doctrinal, or ideational, approach it emphasizes permanence because it assumes that the driving force of individual behavior in the mercantilist period is the same as the driving force of contemporary capitalism, namely, the self-interested pursuit of gain.

Despite a tendency to view these two approaches as rival theories, there is no reason why they cannot be treated as complementary. It is likely that our most complete understanding of mercantilism will come through the application of both approaches. For pedagogic reasons, however, we treat them separately in this chapter.

■ Mercantilism as Doctrine: The Economics of Nationalism

The term *mercantilism* was coined by Mirabeau in 1763 to describe that loose system of economic ideas that dominated economic discourse from the beginning of the sixteenth century to almost the end of the eighteenth century. Mercantilist writers were a disparate group. Many of them were merchants who simply espoused their own interests. Despite its international scope—mercantilism was a creed shared by England, Holland, Spain, France, Germany, Flanders, and Scandinavia—there was less consistency and continuity among mercantilists than among the Scholastics of the previous age. This lack of cohesion among mercantilist writers may be due to the absence of common analytical tools that could be shared and passed on to a generation of successors. Moreover, communication among mercantilists was poor or nonexistent, in contrast to the strong network of interrelations among modern economists. Nevertheless, mercantilism was based on several unifying ideas—doctrines and policy pronouncements that appear and reappear throughout the period.

An early, condensed summary of mercantilist principles was provided by Philipp Wilhelm von Hornick, an Austrian lawyer who published a nine-point mercantilist manifesto in 1684. Von Hornick's blueprint for national eminence emphasizes independence and treasure. Not all mercantilists accepted every point in von Hornick's program, but his nine points are sufficiently representative of the loose system of ideas that has come to be known as mercantilism.

Von Hornick's nine principal rules of national economy are:

1. That every inch of a country's soil be utilized for agriculture, mining, or manufacturing
2. That all raw materials found in a country be used in domestic manufacture, since finished goods have a higher value than raw materials
3. That a large, working population be encouraged
4. That all export of gold and silver be prohibited and all domestic money be kept in circulation
5. That all imports of foreign goods be discouraged as much as possible
6. That where certain imports are indispensable they be obtained at firsthand, in exchange for other domestic goods instead of gold and silver
7. That as much as possible, imports be confined to raw materials that can be finished at home
8. That opportunities be constantly sought for selling a country's surplus manufactures to foreigners, so far as necessary, for gold and silver
9. That no importation be allowed if such goods are sufficiently and suitably supplied at home

In the discussion that follows, we shall be concerned primarily with the general nature of these premises rather than with their elaboration by specific individuals. Readers should be mindful of the fact that the resulting characterization is a *simpli-*

fication and an idealization that may not apply specifically to any single mercantile nation. British, French, Dutch, and Spanish mercantilism differed in many essential respects, for instance. This disclaimer applies even more to individuals, a fact that may be easily verified by reading and comparing the writings of at least two mercantilists. (Some of the references provided at the end of this chapter may be consulted to that end.) No single individual held all the ideas that are expressed below as representing mercantilist thought, and what follows is only one of a number of possible characterizations of mercantilist ideas. The mercantilist period was one during which the threads of many ideas were being spun; as a consequence mercantilism as a set of ideas remains something of a patchwork quilt.

We will focus attention on several areas of interest: "real-world" ideas, views on international trade and finance, and examples of "dualism" in domestic policy. After an assessment of mercantilist ideas, we consider the historical process of mercantilism and its eventual role in the emergence of liberalism.

The Mercantilists and Real-World Ideas

Unlike writers from the feudal period, mercantilist writers showed less concern for moral issues (e.g., justice and salvation) and more concern for secular matters (e.g., wealth and power). On some issues a few writers of the mercantilist period looked backward, whereas others looked forward to laissez-faire, but en masse they were concerned with material, objective economic means and ends. And although their overall social goal of "state power" was subjective, their opinions on the workings of the economic system were a clear reflection of real-world habits of thought.

We have seen that the Scholastics built on the precept of divine law. As a rule, mercantilists rejected divine law in favor of natural law. Sir William Petty (see chapter 4), a trained physician, illustrated how conclusions about economic behavior could be drawn from analogies with natural sciences. In his best-known economic treatise, *Political Arithmetick*, Petty noted that:

> We must consider in general, that as wiser Physicians tamper not excessively with their Patients, rather observing and complying with the motions of nature, than contradicting it with vehement Administrations of their own: so in Politicks and Oeconomicks the same must be used. (*Economic Writings*, I, p. 60)

Though Petty wrote late in the mercantilist period, theories of social causation grounded in natural law appeared as early as the mid-sixteenth century. The idea of natural law grew into a fundamental tenet of the economic liberalism of the eighteenth century, providing, in one important respect, an almost seamless transition away from earlier preoccupation with the divine. As Eli Heckscher, a recognized authority on the period, emphasized: "There was little mysticism in the arguments of the mercantilists . . . they did not appeal to sentiment, but were obviously anxious to find reasonable grounds for every position they adopted" (*Mercantilism*, II, p. 308).

International Trade

These real-world concerns of the mercantilists were reflected in their intense focus on the material gain of the state. They saw society's material resources as a means to achieve the goals of national enrichment and well-being. They insisted that the nation's resources be used in such a way as to make the state as powerful as possible both politically and economically. Following the Age of Exploration, the sixteenth and seventeenth centuries witnessed the rise of great trading nations, as nation-states used exploration, discovery, and colonization to build power and influence. The major topic considered by mercantilist writers was, understandably, international trade and finance. Gold, and means to acquire it, was never far from the center of their concerns.

The Role of Money and Trade in Mercantilism. Money and its accumulation were prime concerns of the growing nation-states of the mercantilist era, because treasure was seen as a necessary element of national power. As already noted, a flourishing international trade followed the age of discovery and colonization, and gold bullion was the unit of international account. The acquisition of gold through trade and trade restrictions of many types were essential mercantilist ideas, and money, not real goods, was commonly equated to wealth.

Production and trade are vital steps to increased prosperity. To mercantilists, however, prosperity in the sense of increased per-capita income was secondary to the concentration of economic power in the hands of the state. National prosperity was to be accomplished through an export-import policy that led to a stockpiling of bullion. This stratagem, often referred to as "favorable balance-of-trade" policy, encouraged importation of (low-value) raw materials and exportation of (high-value) finished goods, thus assuring a net flow of money to the mercantilist country.

All this might sound quite reasonable if the mercantilists had been rationalizing preexisting comparative advantages within trading nations, but the disappointing truth is that many of them looked on trade and bullion accumulation as a zero-sum game, where more for country A meant less for countries B, C, and so forth. They did not appear to understand that increased total output and appropriate (dual) gains from trade might accrue simultaneously to trading partners. Given this zero-sum mentality, protectionism and "beggar-thy-neighbor" policies were justified as a means to increase national wealth, which would, in turn, increase national power and prestige.

International Trade and Specie Flow. Some writers, such as Gerard de Malynes (1586–1623), were confirmed bullionists, opposed to any export of specie (i.e., gold/silver coins) whatsoever. He condemned the practice of specie export by the East India Company, which was the leading avenue of Britain's trade with the East in the early seventeenth century. Although he had previously taken Malynes's position, Edward Misselden (1608–1654) attacked the extreme bullionist view, which amounted to an absolute prohibition of specie export even on individual transactions. Instead, Misselden advanced the notion that governmental policies should be directed to maximizing specie earnings on the basis of an overall balance of trade.

However contradictory and misdirected their orientation toward money seems to have been, the mercantilists produced the first real awareness of the monetary and political importance of international trade and, in the process, supplied a framework for international settlements that included both visible (products) and invisible (shipping expenses, insurance, etc.) items. In the course of attacking the bullionists, for example, Misselden developed the fairly sophisticated concept of a trade balance couched in terms of debits and credits. In *The Circle of Commerce* (1623), he actually calculated a balance of trade for England (from Christmas 1621 to Christmas 1622). He concluded, with disappointment, that it was a bad year.

> We see it to our griefe, that wee are fallen into a great Underballance of Trade with other Nations. Wee felt it before in sense; but now we know it by science: wee found it before in operation; but now we see it in speculation: Trade alas, faile's and faint's, and we in it. (*Circle of Commerce*, p. 46)

Misselden wished to emphasize the "scientific" nature of his calculations, and it is this fact, rather than the accuracy of his data, that sets his accounting apart from the mere collection of numbers, a practice that was widespread in early Egypt and Mesopotamia. Misselden arranged data for the purpose of understanding economic effects and promoting social ends, a more productive enterprise in a scientific sense.

One of the anomalies in mercantilist literature is the pervasive belief that wealth would be maximized through specie accumulation resulting from a trade surplus. Many mercantilists misunderstood the effects of an increase in the domestic money supply (monetization) that usually followed a trade surplus. One common error was the persistent belief that a favorable balance of trade—and thus specie accumulation—could continue over long and indefinite periods without adverse consequences. This error was fully exposed by David Hume (1711–1776), the philosopher-economist contemporary of Adam Smith. He identified a price-specie flow mechanism that linked the quantity of money in an economy to its prices, and alterations in prices to balance-of-trade surpluses and deficits.

Hume's idea, like most good ideas, appears simple in retrospect. Imagine a surplus in England's balance of trade. As a result, gold flows into England, but if all of the new gold is monetized (i.e., coined)—a distinct likelihood under a strict monetary gold standard—England's money stock increases in the same proportion. More money in circulation drives up domestic prices, including the prices of goods in the export sector of the economy, so that England's trading partners tend to buy fewer English goods in the face of higher prices. Faced with less money from the sale of exports, English consumers tend to buy fewer imports, so that in England the price of foreign goods falls relative to English goods. Foreign countries now buy fewer English goods and English consumers now buy more foreign goods. The result is to reverse the trade balance so that gold subsequently flows out of England and into the treasuries of its trading partners. In this manner, any initial trade *imbalance* tends to correct itself; and the misguided attempt to accumulate gold indefinitely becomes self-defeating. Hume's analysis deprived mercantilism of a key tenet of its logical foundation.

Hume expressed a more enlightened, and underappreciated, view of money: "'Tis none of the wheels of trade: 'Tis the oil," he wrote. Nevertheless Hume foresaw short-term salutary effects in the acquisition of specie. He wrote:

> In my opinion, 'tis only in this interval or intermediate situation, betwixt the acquisition of money and rise of prices, that the increasing quantity of gold and silver is favorable to industry. When any quantity of money is imported into a nation, it is not at first disperst into many hands; but is confin'd to the coffers of a few persons, who immediately seek to employ it to the best advantage. ("Of Money," in *Writings on Economics*, p. 38)

Hume believed that money is a "veil" that obscures the real workings of the economic system, and whether a nation's stock of money is large or small is of no great consequence after its stock of money adjusts to changes in the level of domestic prices.

The underlying principle behind Hume's specie-flow mechanism is the quantity theory of money, an idea anticipated by the political philosopher John Locke (1632–1704). The quantity theory of money poses a direct, predictable, and positive connection between the quantity of money in circulation and the domestic price level, such that increases in the money supply lead to increases in the price level. Most mercantilist writers, however, failed to understand the quantity theory of money. In most early expressions, the "theory" is no more than a tautology affirming that a given increase in money (say, a doubling) produces a given increase (doubling) of the price level. A more sophisticated variant equates the money stock multiplied by velocity (the number of times money turns over per year) to the price level multiplied by the number of income-generative transactions per year. In formulaic fashion, it is written as $MV = Py$. As a theory of the price level that identifies dependent variables (prices) and independent variables (money, velocity, and transactions), it is alternately expressed as $P = MV/y$ or, more generally, $P = f(M, V, y)$. When V and y are assumed to be constant, an increase in M leads to proportionate increases in P. Although this more sophisticated version did not appear until long after Locke and Hume (but see the discussion of Richard Cantillon in chapter 4), the mercantilists, to the detriment of their analysis, did not see even the simplest connection.

The Nation-State: Mercantilism as Domestic Policy

Many mercantilists feared the consequences of too much freedom, so they relied on the state to plan and control economic life. The list of policies specially designed to promote the interests of the nation-state was long and varied, consisting of many different regulations of the domestic and international economy. The domestic economy came under less scrutiny than the international economy and was subject to varying degrees of control; some sectors were heavily regulated, some only lightly so. Similarly, taxation and subsidization of particular industries, and measures restricting entry, varied widely across markets.

It was common practice during the mercantilist era for the state to establish legal monopolies in the form of franchises and patents. A franchise granted exclusive trading rights to a particular merchant or league of merchants, such as the East India Company. Some franchises also received massive subsidies from the king. The effect of all of this was a "mixed" economy, but with the mix far less on the side of individual freedom than was the case during the first half of the nineteenth century in England or in the United States. Some historians have treated the mercantilists as mere individual merchants pleading their own narrow interests. In a governing system in which the monarch controls virtually all property rights, perhaps the only way for a merchant class to develop is by an alliance of power between the monarch and the merchant-capitalist. The monarch depended on the merchant's economic activity to build up his or her treasury while the merchant depended on the authority of the monarch to protect his or her economic interests. Use of the political process to secure monopoly gains was by no means confined to that era, however. The practice is what economists now call *rent seeking*, where "rent" refers to the profits that are attributable to the existence of monopoly rather than to competitive advantage. In a later section, we shall probe more deeply into this particular idea as it relates to mercantilism.

"Ambiguity" in Mercantile Policies. From the very beginning we find mercantilist writings that on the one hand extolled international economic controls for society's enrichment but on the other hand presented eloquent pleas for domestic noninterference. In the doctrinal approach this dualism is somewhat of an embarrassment. At times, individual mercantilists could sound like impassioned economic liberals (in the nineteenth-century sense). An anonymous tract (attributed to John Hales) entitled *A Discourse on the Common Weal of This Realm of England* (1549) exhibited an early and prophetic distrust of the effectiveness of legislative controls in promoting society's welfare. Investigating the economic consequences of subdividing common land for individual ownership (i.e., the enclosure movement), the author argued that market forces are more efficient allocators of resources than government decree because profit provides the proper incentive to act. Underscoring the stupidity and futility of governmental regulation of grazing land, the author pointed out the difficulty of enacting such legislation (vested interests will inevitably arise to challenge it) and, if passed, the difficulty of enforcing the legislation (those who seek profits will find a way to subvert the law by one means or another). Moreover, economic regulations are often defeated by "natural" responses. For example, government-imposed price controls invariably give rise to black markets, regardless of when enacted. If Hales was indeed the writer in question, he made it clear by the following statement that self-interest is both natural and powerful: "everie man naturally will follow that wherein he seeth most profit." According to A. F. Chalk, "This is surely a very close approximation to Adam Smith's views concerning the self-interest motive in economic activity" ("Natural Law," p. 335).

The anonymous writer of 1549 was only one of many who advanced views during the mercantilist era advocating more liberal economic activity. Pleas for free internal trade became increasingly vigorous as the mercantile system devolved, especially in the writings of John Locke, Sir Dudley North, Charles Davenant, and Bernard de Mandeville. The emerging "liberal" beliefs relating to domestic policy not only stand in strong contrast to adamant mercantilist views on external trade restrictions, they represent a harbinger of persuasive challenges to state-controlled economies that reached an apex in Adam Smith's *Wealth of Nations*. A sympathetic assessment of mercantilism maintains that "what had begun as opportunistic and sporadic protests against commercial controls thus emerged, almost two centuries later, in the form of a systematized philosophy of economic individualism which proclaimed the beneficence of the laws of nature" (Chalk, "Natural Law," p. 347).

Labor and the "Utility of Poverty"

The interests of the moneyed merchant class and the landed aristocracy converged on the question of domestic policies toward labor and wages. Mercantilists considered the maintenance of low wages and a growing population as a means of national aggrandizement. The argument that labor should be kept at the margin of subsistence runs throughout the mercantilist age. In his classic work, *The Position of the Laborer in a System of Nationalism*, Edgar Furniss called it the "utility of poverty" argument. In the extreme it is premised on a belief that "suffering is therapeutic" and that, given the opportunity, menial workers would be lazy and improvident. It was believed that the generally low moral condition of the lower classes inclined them toward drunkenness and debauchery if wages were too high. In other words, if wages were beyond subsistence, the quest for physical gratification would lead workers to excess, vice, and moral ruin. On the other hand, workers facing poverty because of the high price of subsistence and/or low wages would be encouraged toward industry, which meant that they "lived better." Reflecting the common attitude of the era, Arthur Young noted in his *The Farmer's Tour Through the East of England* (1771): "Everyone but an idiot knows that the lower classes must be kept poor or they will never be industrious." The conventional wisdom of the day held that unemployment was simply the result of indolence.

Bernard de Mandeville (paradoxically, a "liberal" in other contexts) represents one extreme. He argued that children of the poor and orphans should not be given an education at public expense but should be put to work at an early age. Education ruins the "deserving poor," he argued, so that

> Reading, Writing and Arithmetick are very necessary to those whose Business requires such qualifications, but where People's livelihood has no dependence on these Arts, they are very pernicious to the Poor. . . . Going to School in comparison to Working is Idleness, and the longer Boys continue in this easy sort of Life, the more unfit they'll be . . . for downright Labour, both as to Strength and Inclination. (*Fable of the Bees*, p. 311)

Various proposals were put forward to limit debauchery and to make the poor industrious. In 1701, John Law proposed a tax on consumption in order to encourage frugality among the rich and industriousness among the poor. David Hume, who contributed to the liberal movement in other respects, supported "moderate" taxes to encourage industry, but he thought that excessive taxes destroyed incentives and provoked despair. These writers seemed to be aiming at a real wage that would support an "optimal level of frustration," one high enough to provide incentives for "luxuries" but low enough so that they could never be attained. As Furniss observed, it was of the utmost importance to mercantilist writers that

> the lowest ranks of the laboring classes be kept as full as possible, for upon the members of this group England relied for that economic power which was to bring her forth victorious from the struggle of nations after world supremacy. Thus, the nation's destiny was conditioned upon a numerous population of unskilled laborers, driven by the very competition of numbers to a life of constant industry at minimum wages: "submission" and "contentment" were useful characteristics for such a population and these characteristics could be fostered by a destruction of social ambition amongst its members. (*Position of the Laborer*, p. 150)

A Summary of Mercantilism as a System of Ideas. The major theoretical defects in mercantilist doctrine (always granting exceptions) were an inability to grasp the cyclical nature of international accounts and the linkage between domestic money supply and prices. In short, the mercantilists failed to integrate the Locke–Hume price-specie flow mechanism (or the quantity theory of money) into their analysis, which is ironic in view of their careful collation of trade statistics and systematic record keeping. Indeed, this penchant for assembling and keeping statistics on real-world quantities may well be the mercantilists' most important legacy to modern economics. Analytical insights in the mercantilist period, such as they were, sprang from careful empiricism. Mercantilists were among the first economic writers to be more concerned with actual experience than with metaphysical speculation. They brought economic questions to prominence, and in so doing, set the stage for advances made in the next period of economic thought.

In the meantime, economic processes within the mercantile economy (especially of England) were introducing institutional changes that taken together provide a cogent explanation for the historical rise and decline of mercantilism. This explanation pays little attention to what mercantilists said. It concentrates instead on what they did and why they did it.

■ Mercantilism as an Economic Process

The doctrinal approach to mercantilism gives us insight into how certain writers reacted to their environment in formulating a national creed, but it implies that only nationalistic ends were appropriate to mercantilist policies. What we call the process approach seeks to explain why and how mercantilism arose when it did and why it eventually gave way to a distinctly different economic system. This latter approach examines the economic motivations of individuals or coalitions within a national economy. It focuses on the gains to economic agents of using the state in order to acquire profits. Such profits, in the vernacular of modern economics, are called rents (i.e., monopoly returns). Thus, mercantilism is presented here as a form of rent seeking. Rather than rationalize a body of thought, this process view focuses on the factors that motivated historical change.

Some Basic Concepts in the Modern Theory of Regulation

In understanding the rise and fall of mercantilism, it is helpful to look forward for a mechanism to understand events of the past. Hence, a brief look at some contemporary ideas in the theory of economic regulation and politics is in order (a fuller explanation is contained in chapter 24). The term "rent seeking," conveys self-interested behavior of any or all parties to income distribution. When applied to the contemporary analysis of economic regulation, the idea is that, in *their own interests*, politicians (members of Parliament, Congress, state legislators, city councilors, etc.) will *supply* government monopoly privileges and regulations to individual businesspeople or merchants or to any group whose self-interest leads it to *demand* regulation. This self-interested activity does not (necessarily) mean that politicians will accept direct cash payments, although we shall see that such payments were far more common in the mercantilist era than they are today. The modern world involves more subtlety. Lobbyists can bestow favors on lawmakers outside of a strict cash nexus. Since most politicians are members of law firms, patronage via company retainer fees is a less obvious manner of accepting side payments. Contributions to electoral campaigns may be made at arm's-length from the candidate herself. Modern analysis seeks to explain the existence or absence of monopoly privileges in some realms of economic activity by examining the costs and benefits to the *individuals* engaged.

The formal specification of costs and benefits need not concern us here, but a couple of examples might help to understand how the process view works as an explanation. Consider "industry representatives," or lobbyists, as potential demanders of regulation. Their demand for monopoly privileges from government (e.g., entry control and/or subsidies) would obviously be related to how much profit they, or their clients, could expect from the privileges. For example, anything increasing the uncertainty of the duration of a monopoly privilege would reduce the value of the monopoly franchise to the industry. So would any costs imposed on the regulated firm (e.g., taxes and/or periodic inspections) as a quid pro quo for the franchise.

Now consider regulation from the supplier's side. Contemporary economics tells us that self-interested politicians will maximize their benefits (e.g., reelection and/or side payments) by supplying regulation in return for votes and/or money. People adversely affected by legislation face a major problem: the cost of organizing opposition. Large, diverse groups, such as retailers, may find it difficult to overcome the high costs of combining in order to establish an effective lobby. Small, narrow groups, such as undertakers, may find it easier to organize lobbying activities but may be unable to afford the expense of a successful lobby effort. The amount of regulation politicians will offer depends on the costs and benefits of doing so, as well as the coalition and organization costs necessary to actually supply the regulation. Ordinarily the larger the group required to pass special-interest legislation, the higher the coalition costs.

From an analytical standpoint, regulation may be treated as a "good" that is supplied and demanded like other goods in more conventional markets. A decrease in the net benefit to those who stand to gain from regulation would, other things being equal, lead to a reduction in the amount of regulation demanded. Likewise, an increase in the costs of supplying regulation—such as when the ability to supply regulation is transferred from a single individual (a monarch or dictator) to a group of individuals (a parliament or city council)—would, other things being equal, lead to a reduction in the supply of regulation.

In the mercantilist era, the prospect of obtaining a monopoly gave merchants a powerful incentive to seek regulation from the monarch. In this respect, the economic logic of mercantilism is the same as that driving much present-day politico-economic activity. Some groups (e.g., artisans then, telecommunications firms now) possess inherent organizational advantages in lobbying for state regulatory protection from competition (e.g., lobbying local justices of the peace responsible for enforcing the Statute of Artificers then, the Federal Communications Commission now) relative to other groups, such as consumers in general. Usually, then, the gains of successful interest groups consist of transfers of wealth from the consumers of regulated products to those who benefit from the regulations.

A particular kind of monopolistic activity takes place when firms combine to form a cartel, which is a formal combination of firms acting as a single monopolist under some form of central control. (OPEC, for example, is an international cartel run by the ministers of various oil-producing countries). Prices and/or output shares are ordinarily assigned to the members of the cartel, and their behavior is monitored or policed by an administrative board. Cartels may be privately or publicly organized, but in either case, strict entry controls are maintained. Private cartels are inherently unstable because there is a strong incentive to cheat on cartel price or output agreements if the cartel cannot be effectively policed. Most privately organized cartels are therefore unstable because enforcement is difficult. Cartels organized and/or sustained by governments, however, are more stable because governments have inherent advantages in enforcement. One of the advantages is that the cost of enforcement can be shifted to taxpayers. In instances where enforcement costs are a major consideration, therefore, certain firms may willingly submit to specific regulations as an inexpensive way to organize themselves into a virtual cartel. By putting themselves under the protection of government these firms relinquish direct control over entry, prices, or profits, but the other side of the bargain is that they gain protection from competitors, enjoy lower costs of enforcement, and are often able to influence the nature and substance of the regulations imposed.

Whether analyzing the old mercantilism of monarchical Europe or its more sinister twin in contemporary democracies, economic regulation can be seen as the outcome of a competitive process whereby interest groups seek the state's protection against rival interests. In the mercantilist setting, the relevant interest groups were most often local administrators, merchants, and laborers in the domestic economy, and import/export firms the international economy.

Entrepreneurship: Productive and Unproductive

Putting the concept of entrepreneurship in historical perspective underscores the fragile nature of entrepreneurism within the pantheon of economic ideas because culture and institutions determine whether entrepreneurial efforts result in the *creation* of wealth or its mere *distribution* (what economists today call rent seeking). What we call the "competitive process" may be focused on gaining special privileges from a central authority, or organizing the production and sale of goods to gain consumers' favor. In either case it is driven by a human actor motivated by profit. We call this actor an enterpriser, or *entrepreneur.*

Most likely entrepreneurial activity is as old as human history. But entrepreneurship takes on different guises depending on institutional and cultural context. In premarket societies property rights were concentrated in the hands of a tribal leader, and in later societies they were in the hands of the monarch. The nature of entrepreneurial activity conforms to the institutional makeup of society. Centralized authority and concentrated property rights give one form to entrepreneurship; highly dispersed property rights and highly developed markets give it another. Normatively speaking, enterprising behavior can be productive or unproductive. Unproductive entrepreneurship redistributes wealth but does not add to it; productive entrepreneurship adds to society's wealth.

William Baumol and Robert Strom remind us that unproductive entrepreneurship in bygone eras was a response to different institutional and cultural incentives:

> For much of human history there was no guarantee that the individual whose efforts enhanced the magnitude of the pie would reap rewards. Indeed, history is replete with examples of the opposite, as monarchs readily expropriated the property of others. In many cultures, the monarch theoretically owned everything, and in some societies, the king chose to transform this theory into reality quite often. Likelihood of expropriation is surely the ideal disincentive to productive effort. ("'Useful Knowledge' of Entrepreneurship," pp. 531–532)

In an age that takes its name, mercantilism, from the growing pool of merchants who engaged in buying and selling activities throughout the Western world, it would be surprising to find a low level of entrepreneurship. But what kind? The following hypothetical elaborates the issue within a mercantilist context.

Suppose a king or queen *gives* a grant to a favored courtier for the exclusive right to import and sell wine. The recipient will restrict output to what can be produced at the monopoly price, receiving monopoly profits (or rents) at the expense of consumers. One of the consequences of this action is that wealth is redistributed from consumers to suppliers. But suppose instead that the monarch puts the right to import and sell wine out for competitive bid. The winning bidder will be able to earn monopoly profits, but he will have to expend resources (lobbying the queen, engaging in legal pleadings, and so on) to obtain the right. In this case consumers lose as before, but there is an additional loss of resources expended by the winning bidder (as well as the losers, too). This kind of entrepreneurial activity, namely competition to secure exclusive privilege rather than to produce and sell what consumers want at an attractive price, is called *rent seeking*. It constitutes unproductive entrepreneurial activity. It may include bribery, larceny, and other forms by which rents and special privileges are sought.

During antiquity, cultural attitudes and practices placed a low value on productive entrepreneurial activity. The Age of Exploration opened up vast new markets and allowed commerce to expand at an accelerating pace, which gave entrepreneurs, a conspicuous part of the practical makeup of mercantilist society, expanded opportunities to engage in productive entrepreneurship. The explorers and their backers took unprecedented risks in the search for and development of new markets and resources. If successful, they increased the wealth of society at the same time they secured profits for themselves. Naturally the rent-seeking mode of wealth production was still operative. Monarchs, for example, were lobbied for the exclusive rights to import particular goods (for example, tobacco or spices). But productive entrepreneurship was, slowly but surely, gaining a foothold. Productive entrepreneurship, practiced by individuals engaged in enterprising activities that require independence of thought and action geared toward the acquisition of wealth, power, and prestige, *adds* net value to society. The key point that cannot be stressed enough is that the direction of entrepreneurial activity, at any particular time and in any particular place, depends heavily on the prevailing institutional arrangements and relative payoffs to activities that promote or retard economic growth.

In many societies today strong centralized governments have supplanted the monarchs of old. Not surprisingly, rent seeking is still commonplace. However, the cultural and institutional context is different than that associated with mercantilism. In contemporary society unproductive entrepreneurship may be exercised by persons who employ novel approaches to opportunistic, criminal, or socially damaging activities—opportunists who, rather than expand the economic pie by creating more wealth, seek to grab a larger slice of the pie for themselves by redistributing existing wealth. Individuals who worm their way into the bribe-taking bureaucracy, or attorneys who foment novel, potentially lucrative lawsuits, provide ready examples. Lobbying of politicians for privileges by industry (energy, agricultural, pharmaceutical) is an example of so-called "corporate capitalism" or unproductive entrepreneurship.[1]

The mercantilist era marked a kind of passage from medievalism to modernism. During this transition old attitudes and institutions weakened and the venues for productive entrepreneurship expanded. However, until about the time of the British Industrial Revolution the prevailing institutions in most countries encouraged redistributive activity by enterprising individuals, chiefly through rent seeking. During and after capitalism took root the structure of payoffs began to change again, as we shall soon see, putting entrepreneurship in a more positive light.

Internal Regulation in English Mercantilism

Unproductive entrepreneurship and rent seeking permeated both internal and external commerce in England over the fifteenth and sixteenth centuries, continuing to a degree in later centuries. Economic regulation at all levels of government took basically the same form in English mercantilism as it does in contemporary societies. Governments granted licenses, thereby offering the favored few protection from competitors. Important differences existed, however, between the conduct of institutions involving *local* as opposed to *national* regulation and monopoly. Local regulation of trades, prices, and wages in mercantilist times was vested in the medieval guild system. Enforcement of guild regulations in the Tudor period prior to Elizabeth I (1485–1558) was the responsibility of the guild bureaucracy, in combination with the town or shire administrative machinery. Elizabeth attempted to codify and strengthen these detailed regulations in the Statute of Artificers, a law that outlined the specific enforcement duties of local justices of the peace (JPs), aldermen, and local administrators. JPs and other administrative enforcers of local regulations were paid either very little or not at all for these services, a fact that led to local alignments of economic interests. These interests ultimately rendered the local provision of monopoly rights ineffective.

At the national level industrial regulation was created in three ways: (1) by statutes of Parliament, (2) by royal mandates, and (3) by decrees of the Privy Council of

[1] It must be noted that no type of entrepreneurship can take place without property rights establishment and enforcement—a central role of government in all but the most primitive societies. This role extended into the establishment of military installations to protect the great trading companies, partly established by the Crown in England (for example, the Africa Company, East India Company, and so on).

the king's court. It should be noted that merchants and monarchs alike stood to gain from rent seeking. The meshing of private interests of monarch and monopolist was firmly enshrined in English commerce as early as the fourteenth century, perhaps even earlier. The nature of this alliance was underscored in debate on the issue of monopoly in the House of Commons in 1601:

> First, Let us consider the word monopoly, what it is; *Monos* is *Unus*, and *Polis*, *Civitas*: So then the Meaning of the Word is; a Restraint of any thing Publick, in a City or Common-Wealth, to a Private Use. And the User called a Monopolitan; *quasi, cujus privatum lucrum esturbis et orbis Commune Malun*. And we may well term this Man, The Whirlpool of the Prince's Profits. (Tawney and Power, *Tudor Economic Documents*, II, p. 270)

These revealing definitions of monopoly and the monopolist remind us that the motives of economic actors are usually recognizable and have not changed over the centuries. But it would be a mistake to carry the analogy too far. Although the basic nature of mercantilism then and now is the same, there are important differences in the two rent-seeking environments. The most important difference for the purposes of the discussion here concerns the supply side of the market for regulatory legislation.

Mercantilist regulations at the national level were supplied by a single ruler, or monarch. Monarchy represents a uniquely low-cost opportunity for rent seeking, especially when compared with modern, democratic societies where the power to supply regulatory legislation is dispersed among various (sometimes conflicting) governmental powers. The consolidation of national power under the mercantile monarchies provides a logical explanation for the widespread rent seeking and economic regulation during this period of English history. We shall soon see how the growth and ultimate takeover of the power to supply regulatory legislation by Parliament dramatically altered the costs and benefits to buyers and sellers of monopoly rights in such a way as to lead to the decline of mercantilist regulation. But first we must consider the pattern and fate of local regulation.

The Enforcement of Local Economic Regulation

The legal framework for the enforcement of mercantilist economic regulation at the local level was set forth by the Elizabethan Statute of Artificers. This statute attempted to codify older rules for the regulation of industry, labor, and welfare, the important difference being that such regulations were to be *national* rather than *local* in scope. Some writers have pointed to the enormous increase in wages after the Black Death as the impetus to national regulation. The immediate economic reason was much more likely the inability of the towns to restrict cheating on local cartel arrangements. Towns petitioned the king to establish a nationally uniform system of regulation with the intent to protect local monopoly rights against encroachment, especially by outsiders. There were many attempts by self-interested merchants and town administrators to regulate economic activity and to prevent interlopers on local franchises. The city of London, especially, wished to restrict aliens and foreign technology that inhibited town profits. The solution most often proffered was to banish to the countryside aliens or those workers who did not meet "legal" qualifications for various trades. These sentiments are expressed in numerous Tudor documents.

The nationally uniform system of local monopolies was to be enforced by the JPs. In Eli Heckscher's words, "The Justices of the Peace were the agents of unified industrial legislation" (*Mercantilism*, I, p. 246). A primary feature of the system was that the JPs were not paid; and Heckscher argues that the absence of pay for the JPs led to lax enforcement through ineptitude and laziness. But it is more likely that low or no pay created a situation ripe for malfeasance by encouraging a self-interested pattern of enforcement—one suggesting both *sub rosa* activities and selective cartel enforcement of industries in which the JPs themselves had vested interests. Evidence suggests that the JPs' holdings in regulated enterprises increased as a consequence of the way the regulations were enforced. This could generally be accomplished either through preferential treatment—the firm in which a JP had an interest could be allowed to cheat on the cartel, while other firms could not—or through bribes made to minor enforcement personnel. The Queen's Council dictated that the JPs themselves be policed by high constables, who, having less civil authority than the JPs, were often on the receiving end of bribes. By the time of James I it was openly acknowledged that the JPs could be easily "bought." In 1620, the following testimony was given before Parliament by a Committee of Grievances:

> There are some patents that in themselves are good and lawful, but abused by the patentees in the execution of them, who perform not the trust reposed in them from his maj[esty]; and of such a kind is the Patent for Inns, but those that have the execution abuse it by setting up Inns in forests and bye villages, only to harbour rogues and thieves; and such as the justices of peace of the shire, who best know where Inns are fittest to be, and who best deserve to have licenses for them, have suppressed from keeping of alehouses; *for none is now refused, that will make a good composition* (Corbbett, *Parliamentary History*, pp. 1192–1193).

The reference to "a good composition" implied side payments by innkeepers in order to be granted licenses.

In every age it is difficult to find accurate records of illegal transactions because there is no incentive to report them. In the case of mercantilism, however, the testimony of contemporary observers seems to corroborate the view that the enforcers of internal mercantile regulations were self-interested parties. Thus, the claim that enforcers were indifferent and careless because they were not paid seems naive in retrospect. Modern economic theory leads us to *expect* malfeasance as the predictable response to low pay in occupations where an element of trust is dominant.[2] That is because the opportunity cost to the wrongdoer of being caught (and fired) is low. From this self-interested standpoint, the behavior of the JPs during the mercantilist era was quite efficient and predictable, given the constraints imposed by the Statute of Artificers.

Local Regulation and Resource Mobility. Another difficulty in enforcement of the Elizabethan system of local regulation is that those regulated could escape the jurisdiction of the law by moving outside the towns. Evidence exists that the rules were blatantly disregarded, despite attempts to limit mobility. Movement of artificers to the countryside was in fact blamed for the decay, impoverishment, and ruin of the cities (Tawney and Power, Tudor Economic Documents, I, pp. 353–365). As long as buyers and sellers could migrate to an unregulated sector in the suburbs and the countryside, the local cartel arrangements in the towns could be subverted. France, however, differed from England in this regard. According to Heckscher, "The most vital difference was that many important districts were set free from the application of the statutes in England, while in France nothing remained unregu-

[2] For example, see Gary Becker and G. J. Stigler, "Law Enforcement, Malfeasance, and Compensation of Enforcers."

lated in principle, apart from purely accidental exceptions or subordinate points" (Mercantilism, I, p. 266). It does not appear that the English countryside was "set free" in any conscious, deliberate act of policy. Instead economic resources merely responded to the incentives produced by a local pattern of enforcement pursued by the JPs. Movement out of the towns was simply a way for some artisans and merchants to lower their costs of operation.

Migration to escape local cartel regulations did not have to involve much distance. The suburbs of towns were filled with handicraftsmen who either could not get into the town guilds or wanted to escape their control. Because the nature of the trade involved was akin to that of a widely dispersed flea market, various efforts to bring these "cheaters" under control proved futile. Adam Smith illustrated this point nicely: "If you would have your work tolerably executed, it must be done in the suburbs where the workmen, having no exclusive privilege, have nothing but their character to depend upon, and you must then smuggle it into town as well as you can" (*The Wealth of Nations*, p. 313). Cheating on the local cartels thus became the economic order of the day, and the state's lack of success in dealing with enforcement problems is ample testimony to the inefficient nature of the Elizabethan cartel machinery.

Occasionally the crown struck back by creating institutional arrangements that made enforcement more efficient. For example, Elizabeth made a practice of granting to her favorite courtiers the right to collect fines for violations of the regulatory code. Eventually these rights came to be sold to the highest bidder, the successful bidder keeping for himself whatever he could collect. Enforcement remained uneven, and a sizable unregulated sector of the economy persisted, however, because some infringements (e.g., patents) were more lucrative to collect on than others. In the end the Statute of Artificers contained the seeds of its own destruction. The behavior of the unpaid or low-paid JPs and the ability of firms to escape regulation were the two major factors that helped undo *local* mercantilist regulation in the long run. We now turn to a consideration of the important part played by the mercantilist judiciary in the gradual demise of *national* economic regulation.

The Mercantilist Judiciary and the Breakdown of National Monopolies

In a system of national regulations, the only way to escape legal jurisdiction is to leave the country, which is more difficult and more costly than moving from city to suburb. Thus, the absence of a viable, unregulated alternative brought about more stable cartel arrangements in national markets than in local ones. The undoing of the national monopolies must therefore be explained by other factors, namely the changing constraints on economic activity in mercantilist England.

English Common Law and the Courts. The English judiciary system developed slowly and intricately. Basically, three common law courts evolved in the period between the Norman invasion and the mercantile era: the Court of King's Bench, the Court of Common Pleas, and the Court of Exchequer. These courts presided over civil matters, and all were initially under the crown's direct control, with the king often rendering decisions in the early period. During the thirteenth through the fifteenth centuries the courts grew increasingly independent of the crown, although the king retained the power to appoint and remove judges.

Up to the time of the Tudors, jurisdiction between the three courts was undefined and payment of judges depended in part on the collection of court fees. This led to a great deal of jurisdictional competition between the courts. Moreover, the functional separation of the branches of government toward the end of the fourteenth century intensified the division of interests between the King's Council, the Court of King's Bench, and Parliament: The Council identified and allied with the executive branch of government (monarch), the King's Bench united with the judicial branch, and Parliament became a legislative body, but with some vestiges of a judiciary (the House of Lords remains the highest appellate court in England). The separation of governmental functions brought with it a self-interested alignment between the common law courts and Parliament. The common law courts recognized Parliament as the source of laws that the courts were charged to enforce. In turn the many common lawyers in Parliament came to believe that errors in the judiciary should be corrected by Parliament, not by the King's Council.

This alliance between the common law courts and Parliament began centuries before the mercantilist period, by which time the courts had cartelized and established firm bureaucracies and jurisdictions. By 1550 the coincidence of interests between the courts and Parliament had intensified, owing principally to the rise of a competing legal system in the form of the *royal* courts that were established by the time of Elizabeth I.

The competing judicial system emerged from a tradition in Roman law (*curia regis*) that regarded the powers of the crown as outside normal legal jurisdictions, therefore, outside the common law courts. These other courts became entrenched in branches of the Royal Council, its subordinate court (the Court of Star Chamber), and in other parts of the executive branch of government, such as, the Court of Chancery. As the Court of Chancery and the Court of Star Chamber extended their jurisdictions into that of the common law courts, they met with fierce resistance from the judicial "cartel." Persistent attacks by the common lawyers successfully destroyed one of the courts of Chancery (Maitland, *Selected Historical Essays*, p. 115), and the confrontation served to cement the alliance between the common law courts and Parliament. In order for Parliament to enhance its power relative to the crown, it needed support for its legal actions, a support the common law courts were eager to provide. Besides its composition of individuals of similar training and interest, the common law courts were further drawn into Parliament's orbit because, inasmuch as the House of Commons could overturn any decision by a common law court, Parliament itself was regarded as simply another common law court. Interdependence was further motivated by the fact that whereas Parliament could control jurisdictional boundaries and other matters before the courts, it was dependent on the courts for the permanence and security of its legislation. This intertwined, complex judicial system formed the backdrop against which national mercantilist regulations were enacted and applied.

Effects of Judicial Competition on the Durability of Monopoly Rights

Competition between the king's courts and the common law courts created uncertainty over the durability of a monopoly right granted by a single governmental authority because a monopoly right valid in one court would not necessarily be considered valid in another. Hence, the security of monopoly privilege depended on the shifting fortunes of each court system, because monopoly rights become less valuable as they become less certain, and durable attempts by the crown to establish monopoly privileges met with less and less success over time.

Example 1. On grounds of national defense, Queen Elizabeth claimed regalian rights to the production of saltpeter and gunpowder in the 1580s. She granted a monopoly right to manufacture these products to George and John Evlyn. The Evlyn family subsequently enjoyed lucrative benefits from rent splitting with the crown for almost fifty years, but persistent counteraction by other merchants and the common law courts finally brought down the monopoly privilege, after which the manufacture of both saltpeter and gunpowder became the object of open competition.

Example 2. Elizabeth tried to imitate the French king's successful and lucrative salt tax but did not meet with the same success. Five years after a patent monopoly in salt was established, the patentees abandoned their investment, leaving huge salt pans rusting on the English coast. Private capitalists without any exclusive privileges thereafter entered the industry and profitably produced and sold salt over the next three decades, despite repeated attempts by the crown to reestablish monopoly rights.

Example 3. In 1588, a paper monopoly was granted to John Spilman, who claimed to have a new process for producing white paper. Ordinarily, patents issued to protect a new invention or process were unopposed by Parliament and the common law courts, but sometimes the patent was extended to enable its holders to "engulf" closely related products. Spilman gained this comprehensive benefit in 1597 when he was granted a monopoly over all kinds of paper manufactory. The monopoly proved impossible to enforce, however, and according to John Nef (*Industry and Government*, p. 106), within six years Spilman had to content himself with "such a share of the expanding market for papers as the efficiency of his machinery, the skill of his workmen, and the situation of his mills enabled him to command." Elizabeth's luckless experiences with franchising and rent-seeking activities ended in 1603, when, beseeched to grant a monopoly of playing cards, she personally declared that such patents were contrary to common law. Nevertheless, her successors often made new attempts to supply various regulations.

Example 4. During the monarchy of James I (1603–1625), successor to Queen Elizabeth I, the House of Commons and the common law courts consolidated their power and succeeded in blocking the establishment of enforceable, national monopolies that interfered with their interests or the profits of merchants aligned with them. This opposition to the crown's supposed right to supply regulation reached its zenith in 1624, when the celebrated Act Concerning Monopolies legally stripped the king of all means to monopolize industry.

Example 5. Upon the death of James I in 1625, his son, Charles I, ascended to the British throne and promptly tried to reassert regalian rights to grant monopoly by letters patent or by order of the Privy Council. With the aid of his powerful and persuasive minister, Sir Francis Bacon, he found a loophole in the 1624 statute and tried to make deals with large producers in many industries, particularly in alum and soap. Between 1629 and 1640 the alum patent brought in £126,000 and the soap patent an additional £122,000. King Charles's brazen move ultimately led to a head-to-head confrontation with Parliament and the constitutionalists, a battle that he ultimately lost, along with his head, in 1649.

These examples demonstrate that the returns from seeking national monopolies through the state fell drastically in the sixteenth and early seventeenth centuries as the conflict between Parliament and the crown intensified. History is unclear whether the conflict itself was motivated by monopoly policy, but regardless of origin, the conflict generated important side effects in the rent-seeking economy of England during the mercantilist era. Whereas the crown's concern for "public interest" may have played a role in the transition of power from the king to Parliament, the institutional facts of the centuries-old alliance between common law courts and Parliament plus Parliament's control over jurisdictional disputes between the two court systems suggest a very powerful, self-interested economic motivation. One important question remains, however: Why was Parliament unable to reinstitute and sustain mercantilist policies when it became the sole supplier of regulatory legislation?

The Decline of Mercantilism and the Rise of Parliament

The focal point of the conflict between Parliament and the crown in the struggle to supply monopoly rights concerned patents. Parliament wanted to restrain the unlimited power of the crown to grant monopoly privileges. The struggle was not over free trade versus government control but rather over who would have the power to supply economic regulations.

This became abundantly clear in 1624 when the House of Commons petitioned King James I to cease and desist from granting monopoly privileges in the form of letters patent. The petition was provoked by public controversy regarding a lighthouse on the English coast known as the Wintertonness Lights. Parliament had originally issued a patent to the master of Trinity House to erect and maintain the lighthouse. Under the provisions of this patent ships carrying coal past the lighthouse were to be charged sixpence for every 640 bushels of coal transported. In the meantime, Sir John Meldrum successfully petitioned King James I for a patent to the lighthouse, upon receipt of which he began to charge a rate for coal that was nearly seven times the rate allowed the master of Trinity House under the initial patent. Parliament was incensed, and invoked "public welfare" as the rationale for wresting economic control from the crown. Such displays of public virtue are, however, most often transparent attempts to gain control over a powerful means of patronage.

Although Parliament ultimately beat the crown at its own game and became the sole supplier of legislation in England, it was unable to consistently exploit its new power because of the high costs of multiparty decision making. It is invariably more costly to each individual for decisions to be made by many parties rather than by a single party, such as the monarch. Unable to delegate authority to an effective bureaucracy (which did not exist in this period), Parliament found it costly to legislate and even more costly to enforce economic regulations. It is a wry twist of history that after struggling long and hard with the crown for the right to operate a national system of economic regulation, Parliament discovered that the costs of sustaining the system were much larger than the pro rata benefits. On this fact, mercantilism ultimately floundered, and significant deregulation of the British economy subsequently ensued. Historically, mercantilism waned in the eighteenth century, only to resurface with more contemporary visages in the future. During antiquity, cultural attitudes and practices placed a low value on entrepreneurial activity.

The Force of Ideas: Mercantilism, American Style

Colonization was both an expression of mercantilism and an extension of it. All of the great nations of the sixteenth through the eighteenth centuries—Spain, Portugal, Holland, France, and England—engaged in colonizing activities around the globe. In the process of creating profits for Europeans, of course, great discoveries were made, including the modern discovery of the Americas. The desire to accumulate wealth and power (often through conquest) was a

(continued)

driving force in what we call mercantilism. The dominance of nation-states and the process of state building over the mercantilist period was, in large part, an expression of economic interests within those states. Supply and demand provides a ready explanation: Colonies provided a source of cheap raw materials and a ready market for the finished goods and services produced by the mother countries.

Mercantilist ideas, policies, and practices had an enormous impact on the history of the United States. The new overseas markets were relatively free and competitive, so that English and other European immigrants in the North American colonies were free to sell their wares to all demanders and to buy needed products (mostly finished goods) from any willing sellers. But as a legal extension of the English state, American colonists had to toe the line established by the mother country.

Practically from the beginning, the North American colonists were shackled with regulations that created profits (rents) for English economic interests. The Stuart kings claimed "regalian rights" over the economic development of the colonies and cut deals with, for example, the Virginia tobacco growers and merchants for a "take" in the form of taxes. Later, after England's constitutional revolution (1650–1660) and the restoration of the monarchy, Parliament gained new powers, so that both the monarchs and the Parliament regulated economic activities in the New World.

Although such rules were extensive, a small sample of them is illustrative of their impact.* Under a series of Navigation Acts (such as those passed in 1660, 1663, 1673, and 1696), American colonists were required to ship their exports in English-built ships. Particular exports of the colonists were "enumerated," that is, required by Parliament to be exported *only* to England or to English colonies. Tobacco, sugar, and indigo were on the list in 1660. The Navigation Act of 1663 benefited English merchants even more. It required that *all* European goods (with a few self-serving exceptions) transported to the colonies be shipped from England and on English-built ships. This had the effect of protecting British manufacturing and ship-building interests from foreign competition as well as allowing the crown to tax those goods that were excepted from the regulation.

Later, Parliament assigned customs officials in the colonies extraordinary powers of search and seizure and voided all colonial laws contrary to parliamentary decrees. English rulers, merchants, and politicians, as well as colonial governors, took advantage of the situation, and rent seeking became rife. One example makes clear the motives: The Hat Act passed Parliament in 1732 under pressure from London felt makers. Already facing French competition, London hat makers were fearful of the establishment of a hat industry in the North American colonies. The act prohibited the exportation of hats from one colony to another, required colonists wishing to enter the trade to undergo a seven-year apprenticeship, limited apprentices to two per shop, and barred the employment of Negroes in hat making altogether. A Molasses Act, passed the following year, had the same intent and purpose.

Naturally, these kinds of mercantilist policies had to be enforced, and the distance between colony and mother country made enforcement costly. Despite rampant piracy, smuggling, and privateering (capture of "enemy" ships during wartime), England's economic regulations were surprisingly effective, in part because independent colonial trade was hampered by a *legally* prescribed lack of money and credit institutions. Mercantilist laws and regulations forced a high degree of "self-sufficiency" on the American colonists, even though the colonists generally carried trade deficits with England. Rent-seeking activity in England finally created a huge reduction in the welfare of the average colonist, and rebellion was the inevitable outcome. Thus, the collision course with England, which ended in the Declaration of Independence and the birth of a new nation, was set much earlier in a course of action that taxed and regulated colonial trade and reduced the well-being of the average colonial citizen. This type of protectionism was (and remains today) associated with mercantilism and "neomercantilism."

* These examples are drawn from Richard B. Morris (ed.), *Encyclopedia of American History*, pp. 510–514.

Some historians emphasize the "dual" nature of mercantilist thought, which became increasingly manifest near the end of the mercantilist era. Many later mercantilists rejected domestic controls while they simultaneously defended protectionist measures in foreign trade. This apparent contradiction is less paradoxical if mercantilism is viewed as a form of rent-seeking activity. One particular incident, though small in itself, reveals that self-interested rent seeking was never far from the surface when mercantilist policies were shaped. King Charles I battled Parliament over his "ancient right" to customs duties, but lost his fight in 1641. Refusing to yield, the king reasserted his claim of absolute authority to levy taxes while Parliament was dissolved. Leaning on the support of Parliament, import merchants refused to pay customs to the king, who retaliated by seizing the merchants' goods. Some of the merchants resisted and were brought before the Privy Council. Merchant Richard Chambers brazenly declared that "merchants are in no part of the world so screwed as in England. In Turkey they have more encouragement" (Taylor, *Origin and Growth of the English Constitution*, p. 274).

■ Transition to Liberalism

Major historical turning points in the distant past are always difficult to pinpoint. Such is the case with the transition from a heavily regulated national economy to one of relatively free trade. In practice, no pure laissez-faire economy has ever existed, but significant structural changes in the British economy were detectable between the seventeenth and nineteenth centuries. To some extent, doctrinal and policy views of mercantilism offer different reasons for this transition.

The Doctrinal Transition: Mandeville

The doctrinal view maintains that mercantilism broke down because it lost intellectual respectability. In the century prior to 1776, liberal criticism of mercantilism reached a high pitch. One of the most effective proponents of the new liberalism during this period was Bernard de Mandeville.

Mandeville, who was mentioned previously as a sponsor of the mercantile doctrine of the utility of poverty, published an allegorical poem in 1705 entitled *The Grumbling Hive*; or *Knaves Turn'd Honest*. In this satirical work he argued that individual vices (self-interest) produce public virtues (maximize society's welfare), one of the central themes of Smith's *Wealth of Nations*. Later the poem was reprinted and enlarged in *The Fable of the Bees*, published in two parts (part I in 1714 and part II in 1729). The book was a sensation.

Rejecting a rationalist, metaphysical view of knowledge, Mandeville emphasized a theory of human nature based on the empirical proposition that sense impressions are all we can know of the world. Reasoning must come from facts, not from any rationalist or a priori considerations. In this important sense, he foreshadowed the liberal revolution, whose most effective voice was Adam Smith. Since sensations are the source of knowledge and since each individual receives different external stimuli, early empiricists argued that the optimal social organization would be one allowing a maximum degree of individual freedom.[3]

[3] Although he does not do so consistently, Mandeville suggests at several places in *The Fable* that man's central motivating force is pleasure. Thus, some may regard him as an anticipator of utilitarian thought (see chap. 6 of this text).

Mandeville thus rejected absolute criteria as the foundation for social systems or for individual behavior. He insisted that right and wrong are relative, and he wrote: "Things are Good and Evil in reference to something else, and according to the Light and Position they are placed in" (*Fable*, p. 367). This passage is reminiscent of Xenophon's earlier subjectivism (see chapter 2). Although Mandeville's empiricism and moral relativism were roundly attacked during his lifetime, his position gradually gained acceptance, popularizing the view (still current) that normative problems cannot be handled effectively by science.

Further, Mandeville's belief that despite being "full of vice" (or self-interest) individuals nevertheless promote public benefits was a clear anticipation of liberal thought. Humans are at base selfish creatures since they "give no Pleasure to others that is not repaid to their Self-Love, and does not at last center in themselves, let them wind it and turn it as they will" (*Fable*, p. 342). But as he pointed out, "Pride and Vanity have built more Hospitals than all the Virtues together" (*Fable*, p. 261).

Although Mandeville cannot be regarded as a consistent exponent of liberalism, he nevertheless presented a clear discussion of the philosophical underpinnings of nineteenth-century liberal thought. Even though he did not apply his system of self-interest to actual problems of commerce, as writers such as Richard Cantillon (see chapter 4) did, he nevertheless remains an important harbinger of economic liberalism.

The Institutional Transition

Regardless of which interpretation one applies to mercantilism, the system retarded economic growth as an unintended consequence of its principles and practices. The conventional, doctrinal interpretation emphasizes the misguided effort to accumulate gold and specie, whereas the process view underscores how societal wealth was dissipated through monopoly creation and rent seeking at different levels of government. According to the doctrinal view, mercantilism declined as its "errors" were slowly but surely exposed. The process view emphasizes the unintentional consequences of rent-seeking activity, which spawned institutional changes that gradually made rent seeking and internal regulation by the central government less feasible. Under either interpretation liberalism and free trade emerged as viable alternatives.

Pure laissez-faire never existed in England (or anywhere else) even after Parliament wrested the ability to supply regulation from the crown. The landed class retained control of Parliament and continued to pass legislation favorable to that class. But historians acknowledge that the deregulation of the British economy at this time was significant, even if their characterization of the dissolution of the old order has been willy-nilly. Whether deregulation eventually occurred because better ideas won out or because there was an increase in the cost to Parliament of supplying regulation, it should also be noted that the seventeenth and eighteenth centuries were periods of rapid technological advancement and that such quick-paced innovation in a reasonably competitive environment will tend to reduce the demand for legal cartels. This feature, too, may have played an important role in the decline of regulation in seventeenth-century England.

■ Conclusion

The analysis of mercantilism presented in this chapter has focused on the British economy. Intellectual and institutional forces interacted in the eighteenth century to nudge England and eventually other countries toward liberalism. Even at the height of its regulatory activity, however, the British economy was a pale reflection of its European counterpart—the French economy administered by Colbert, Louis XIV's finance minister. French mercantilism is often called "Colbertism," thus bearing the personal stamp of the man who shaped its policy. What made French mercantilism different was its very high degree of centralization and very efficient system of policing, factors that were never so great in England. The liberal reaction to French mercantilism reached its height in the writings of the Physiocrats, a group of French economists discussed in the following chapter.

References

Baumol, William, and Robert Strom. "'Useful Knowledge' of Entrepreneurship: Some Implications of the History," in D. S. Landes, Joel Mokyr, and W. J. Baumol (eds.), *The Invention of Enterprise: Entrepreneurship from Ancient Mesopotamia to Modern Times*. Princeton, NJ: Princeton University Press, 2010.

Becker, Gary, and G. J. Stigler. "Law Enforcement, Malfeasance, and Compensation of Enforcers," *Journal of Legal Studies*, vol. 3 (January 1974), pp. 1–18.

Chalk, Alfred F. "Natural Law and the Rise of Economic Individualism in England," *Journal of Political Economy*, vol. 59 (August 1951), pp. 330–347.

———. "Mandeville's *Fable of the Bees*: A Reappraisal," *Southern Economic Journal*, vol. 33 (July 1966), pp. 1–16.

Corbbett, W. *Parliamentary History of England*, vol. I. London: R. Bagshaw, 1966 [1806].

Furniss, Edgar S. *The Position of the Laborer in a System of Nationalism*. New York: Kelley and Millman, 1957.

Hales, John. *A Discourse of the Common Weal of This Realm of England*, E. Lammond (ed.). London: Cambridge University Press, 1929.

Heckscher, Eli. *Mercantilism*, 2 vols., Mendel Shapiro (trans.). London: G. Allen, 1935.

Holdsworth, Sir William. *A History of English Law*, 4 vols. London: Methuen, 1966 [1924].

Hornick, P. W. von. "Austria Over All If She Only Will," in A. E. Monroe (ed.), *Early Economic Thought*. Cambridge, MA: Harvard University Press, 1965.

Hume, David. *Writings on Economics*, E. Rotwein (ed.). Madison: University of Wisconsin Press, 1970.

Maitland, F. W. *Selected Historical Essays of F. W. Maitland*, Helen M. Cam (ed.). London: Cambridge University Press, 1957.

Mandeville, Bernard de. *The Fable of the Bees*, F. B. Kaye (ed.). London: Oxford University Press, 1924.

Misselden, Edward. "The Circle of Commerce," in Philip C. Newman, Arthur T. Gayer, and Milton H. Spencer (eds.), *Source Readings in Economic Thought*. New York: Norton, 1954, pp. 43–48 [1623].

Nef, John U. *Industry and Government in France and England, 1540–1640*. New York: Russell and Russell, 1968 [1940].

Morris, Richard B. (Ed.). *Encyclopedia of American History*. New York: Harper and Brothers, 1961.

Petty, William. *The Economic Writings of Sir William Petty*, 2 vols., C. H. Hull (ed.). New York: A. M. Kelley, 1963.

Smith, Adam. *The Wealth of Nations*. New York: Random House, 1937 [1776].

Tawney, R. H., and Eileen Power. *Tudor Economic Documents*, 3 vols. London: Longmans, 1924.

Taylor, Hannis. *The Origin and Growth of the English Constitution*, part II. Boston: Houghton Mifflin, 1898.

Young, Arthur. *The Farmer's Tour Through the East of England*, 4 vols. London: W. Strahan, 1771.

NOTES FOR FURTHER READING

The dominant the custom in economic literature has been to treat mercantilism as a set of ideas rather than as a set of individual and group interests spawned and shaped by prevailing institutions. Within this ideational/doctrinal view there have been two separate traditions, one "absolutist" in approach, the other "relativist." The absolutists tend to view the history of economics as a more or less steady progression from error to truth, whereas the relativists view past doctrines as justified within the context of their times. The former emphasize the presence of grave errors in mercantilist logic, errors exposed by David Hume and the classical economists. The primary instance of such faulty reasoning was the failure of mercantilist writers to recognize the self-regulating effects that the "specie-flow mechanism" imposed on attempts to realize a perennial trade surplus. The relativists, beginning with the German historical school and their English disciples, generally defend mercantilism as historically acceptable, given its aim of national power and wealth. Gustave Schmoller, *The Mercantile System and Its Historical Significance* (New York: Smith, 1931), represents the German historicist view. English disciples of the German Historicists include W. J. Ashley, *An Introduction to English Economic History and Theory*, vol. 1 (New York: Putnam, 1892); and W. Cunningham, *The Growth of English Industry and Commerce*, 2 vols. (New York: A. M. Kelley, 1968).

Jacob Viner is the clearest exponent of the absolutist view. His two classic papers on mercantilism were originally published in 1930 as "English Theories of Foreign Trade before Adam Smith," parts 1 and 2, *Journal of Political Economy*, vol. 38 (1930), pp. 249–301, 404–457, reprinted as the first two chapters of Viner's *Studies in the Theory of International Trade* (London: G. Allen, 1937). Viner viewed the mercantilists' trade theory as "objectionable from the point of view of modern doctrine," arguing that the "simplicity and brevity of the early analysis at least resulted in fallacies of comparable simplicity, but the later writers were able to assemble a greater variety of fallacies into an elaborate system of confused and self-contradictory argument" (*Studies*, p. 109). In a trenchant criticism of the relativist position, Viner wrote:

> The economic historians . . . seem to derive from their valid doctrine, that if sufficient information were available the prevalence in any period of particular theories could be *explained* in the light of the circumstances then prevailing, the curious corollary that they can also be *justified* by appeal to these special circumstances. There are some obvious obstacles to acceptance of this point of view. It would lead to the conclusion that no age, except apparently the present one, is capable of serious doctrinal error. It overlooks the fact that one of the historical circumstances that has been undergoing an evolution has been the capacity for economic analysis. More specifically, to be invoked successfully in defense of mercantilist doctrine it needs to be supported by demonstration that the typical behavior of merchants, the nature of the gains or losses from trade, the nature of the monetary processes, and the economic significance of territorial division of labor have changed sufficiently since 1550, or 1650, or 1750 to make what was sound reasoning for these earlier periods unsound for the present-day world. (*Studies*, pp. 110–111)

An interesting exploration of Viner's point is presented by W. R. Allen, "Modern Defenders of Mercantilist Theory," *History of Political Economy*, vol. 2 (Fall 1970), pp. 381–397.

Eli Heckscher's magisterial two-volume work, *Mercantilism*, published in Swedish in 1931 and translated into English (see references) and revised by the author in 1935, spans both the absolutist and relativist positions. Heckscher treats mercantilism as a coherent and interrelated system of power and economic controls in which attempts were made to maximize the well-being of the state. He argues that: "The state must have one outstanding interest, an interest which is the basis for all its other activities. What distinguishes the state from all other social institutions is the fact that, by its very nature, it is a compulsory corporation or, at least in the last instance, has the final word on the exercise of force in society" (*Mercantilism*, II, p. 15). Though Heckscher's interpretations are open to dispute on specific points, his book remains the essential work on the subject. On a more elementary level, Max Beer's *Early British Economists* (London: G. Allen, 1938) presents a less intricate discussion of mercantilism than Heckscher or Viner.

The original works of many of the major mercantilist writers, e.g., Gerard de Malynes, Thomas Mun, and Daniel Defoe, have been reprinted and published by A. M. Kelley. A rich lode of secondary materials exists focusing on mercantile doctrine and on individual mercantilists. R. C. Wiles discusses the shifting aims and analysis of mercantilist writers in "The Development of Mercantilist Thought," in S. Todd Lowry (ed.), *Pre-Classical Economic Thought* (Boston: Kluwer, 1987). The dualistic or "mixed" nature of mercantilist thought is emphasized in excellent papers by A. F. Chalk (see references) and W. D. Grampp, "The Liberal Elements in English Mercantilism," *Quarterly Journal of Economics*, vol. 66 (November 1952), pp. 465–501.

George D. Chosky focuses on the economic thought of a famous pair of mercantilists in "Previously Undocumented Macroeconomics from the 1680s: The Analytical Arguments and Policy Recommendations of Sir Dudley North and Roger North," *History of Political Economy*, vol. 24 (Summer 1991), pp. 515–532; and same author, "The Bifurcated Economics of Sir Dudley North and Roger North: One Holistic Analytic Engine," *History of Political Economy*, vol. 27 (Fall 1990), pp. 477–492. Marina Bianchi, "How to Learn Sociality: True and False Solutions to Mandeville's Problem," *History of Political Economy*, vol. 25 (Summer 1993), pp. 209–240, explores the thought of one of the most provocative writers of the era.

Three papers by E. A. J. Johnson probe mercantilist doctrine on the question of labor, unemployment, and the relation between labor intensity and international trade. As such, they form a useful accompaniment to the volume by Furniss cited in the references at the end of this chapter. See Johnson, "The Mercantilist Concept of 'Art' and 'Ingenious Labour,'" *Economic History*, vol. 2 (January 1931), pp. 234–253; "Unemployment and Consumption: The Mercantilist View," *Quarterly Journal of Economics*, vol. 46 (August 1932), pp. 698–719; and "British Mercantilist Doctrine Concerning the Exportation of Work and 'Foreign Paid Incomes,'" *Journal of Political Economy*, vol. 40 (December 1932), pp. 750–770. Also see D. Woodward, "The Background to the Statute of Artificers: The Genesis of Labor Policy, 1558–63," *Economic History Review*, vol. 33 (February 1980), pp. 32–44.

Some intellectual detective work into authorship and doctrinal influences is reflected in M. Dewar, "The Memorandum 'For the Understanding of Exchange': Its Authorship and Dating," *Economic History Review*, vol. 18 (April 1965), pp. 476–487; and G. H. Evans, "The Law of Demand: The Roles of Gregory King and Charles Davenant," *Quarterly Journal of Economics*, vol. 81 (August 1967), pp. 483–492. On the same subject, with an extension to classical economics, see A. M. Endres, "The King–Davenant 'Law' in Classical Economics," *History of Political Economy*, vol. 19 (Winter 1987), pp. 621–638.

Philosophy conditioned political, social, and economic thought in the mercantilist era and during the transition to liberalism. A reading of Thomas Hobbes's *Leviathan* (London: Dent, 1914) or Niccolo Machiavelli's *The Prince* (New York: Modern Library, 1950) exposes power as the central theme of the period. The amoral character of mercantilist thought is perhaps nowhere better expressed than in Machiavelli's advice to the prince: "Thus it is well to seem merciful, faithful, humane, sincere, religious, and also to be so; but you must have the mind so disposed that when it is needful to be otherwise you may be able to change to the opposite qualities" (*The Prince*, p. 65). The dualism in economic thought is explained partly by the philosophic dualism of the time. For an explanation of the impact of the "new" philosophies of Hume and Locke on liberalism and classical economics see Werner Stark, *The Ideal Foundations of Economic Thought* (New York: Oxford University Press, 1944), and Carl Becker, *The Heavenly City of Eighteenth-Century Philosophers* (New Haven, CT: Yale University Press, 1932).

Philosophers who developed certain theoretical tools of economic analysis also spurred the intellectual evolution of laissez-faire. In this regard, see Karen I. Vaughn, *John Locke: Economist and Social Scientist* (Chicago: University of Chicago Press, 1980); M. L. Myers, "Philosophical Anticipations of Laissez-Faire," *History of Political Economy*, vol. 4 (Spring 1972), pp. 163–175; and same author, *The Soul of Modern Economic Man* (Chicago: University of Chicago Press, 1983).

What we have called the process, or policy, view of mercantilism derives from the historical conception of Heckscher and the contemporary application of self-interested behavior and property-rights theory to understanding institutions and institutional change. Specifically, the policy view features economic and political "actors" maximizing individual self-interest. This view of mercantilism was suggested early on in Adam Smith's *Wealth of Nations* (see references), but it was more forcefully stated in reviews of Heckscher's *Mercantilism*. A highly regarded scholar, Heckscher nevertheless irritated economic historians by his generalized treatment of economic policy and his excessive emphasis on the cohesiveness of mercantilism as doctrine and policy unaffected by actual economic events. On this point, see C. H. Heaton, "Heckscher on Mercantilism," *Journal of Political Economy*, vol. 45 (June 1937), pp. 370–393.

Some historians charged that Heckscher's treatment, embedded as it was in ideas, practically ignored all reference to the political process through which the so-called unifying mercantilist policies were made. For example, D. C. Coleman, "Eli Heckscher and the Idea of Mercantilism," *Scandinavian Economic History Review*, vol. 5 (1957), pp. 3–25, concluded that the term mercantilism, as a label for economic policy, "is not simply misleading but actively confusing, a red herring of historiography. It seems to give a false unity to disparate events, to conceal the close-up reality of particular times and circumstances, to blot out the vital intermixture of ideas and preconceptions, of interests and influences, political and economic, and of the personalities of men" (pp. 24–25). Coleman argues that policy cannot be treated in a vacuum, nor can the role and interests of parties to the political process be ignored. Thus, the application of contemporary positive economic theory dealing with economic regulation and public choice goes far in filling this important gap in Heckscher's treatment.

This policy view as described in the present chapter is expanded by R. B. Ekelund, Jr., and R. D. Tollison, "Economic Regulation in Mercantile England: Heckscher Revisited," *Economic Inquiry*, vol. 18 (October 1980), pp. 567–599; and, same authors, "Mercantile Origins of the Corporation," *Bell Journal of Economics*, vol. 11 (Autumn 1980), pp. 715–720; elaborated further by B. Baysinger, R. B. Ekelund, Jr., and R. D. Tollison, "Mercantilism as a Rent-Seeking Society," in J. M. Buchanan et al. (eds.), *Towards a Theory of the Rent-Seeking Society* (College Station: Texas A & M University Press, 1980), which also includes other papers of interest on the subject. Ekelund and Tollison's views on mercantilism culminate in *Mercantilism as a Rent-Seeking Society* (College Station: Texas A&M University Press, 1981) and its extension, *Politicized Economies: Monarchy, Monopoly and Mercantilism* (College Station: Texas A&M University Press, 1997), where applications of property rights, rent-seeking theory, emergence of the modern corporation, and the neoinstitutional economic framework of the mercantilist economies of France, England, and Spain come under review. A similar approach along with extensions is found in D. C. North and B. R. Weingast, "Constitutions and Commitment: The Evolution of Institutions Governing Public Choice in Seventeenth-Century England," *Journal of Economic History*, vol. 49 (December 1989), pp. 803–832; and in H. L. Root, *The Fountain of Privilege: Political Foundations of Markets in Old Regime France and*

England (Berkeley: University of California Press, 1994), chapters 6 and 7. Some critics argue, albeit without supporting theory or evidence, that the neoinstitutional approach is inapplicable to mercantilism or that it neglects or downplays the importance of ideas. See, for example, Lars Magnusson (ed.), *Mercantilist Economics* (Boston: Kluwer Academic Publishers, 1993), which contains the following papers: Salim Rashid, "Mercantilism: A Rent-Seeking Society?" Cosimo Perrotta, "Early Spanish Mercantilism: The First Analysis of Underdevelopment," and A. W. Coats, "Concluding Reflections." Disparate, largely historiographic and ununified, views of mercantilism that focus on particular individuals or "theories" have emerged: see, for example, Lars Magnusson, *Mercantilism, The Shaping of Economic Language* (London: Routledge, 1993); and Cosimo Perrotta, "Is Mercantilist Theory of the Favorable Balance of Trade Really Erroneous?" *History of Political Economy*, vol. 23 (Summer 1991), pp. 301–336. However, as of yet, no positive theories of ideology or idea formation have emerged to set against an economic approach. The historiographic (chiefly scholastic) methodology employed in most attempts to capture the essence of something called "mercantilism" has not as yet produced much fundamental understanding of the main developments of the period. Indeed, one recent account of a single mercantilist (John Cary) and his translation into a number of languages argues (unconvincingly) that the empire- and power-building paradigm that mercantilism represents should be the starting point of a canon of economic theory. That canon would replace the trade-oriented market theory developed by Adam Smith that has served economics to the present day: see Sophus A. Reinert, *Translating Empire: Emulation and the Origins of Political Economy* (Cambridge: Harvard University Press, 2011). This argument will not bear scrutiny either with evidence or historical accuracy. Compare, for example, the evidence and conclusions concerning economic growth and ideational change over the English mercantile period in two works by Joel Mokyr: "Mercantilism, the Enlightenment, and the Industrial Revolution," in Ronald Findlay et al. (eds), *Eli Heckscher, International Trade, and Economic History* (Cambridge: Massachusetts Institute of Technology Press, 2006), pp. 269–303; and *The Enlightenment Economy: An Economic History of Britain, 1700-1850* (New Haven, CT: Yale University Press, 2010).

Details of the legal and political system that constituted mercantilism are given in a number of references in the present chapter. Maitland and Holdsworth provide the classic sources on the mercantilist judiciary. D. O. Wagner, "Coke and the Rise of Economic Liberalism," *Economic History Review*, vol. 6 (March 1935), pp. 30–44, presents a very interesting illustration of the duplicity with which common law jurists approached the subject of free trade. The fields of public choice and regulation, from which much of the process view of mercantilism takes its foundation, are the subject of chapter 24. However, there are several specific articles that are vital to understanding mercantilism as a process, especially Gary Becker and G. J. Stigler, "Law Enforcement, Malfeasance and Compensation of Enforcers," *Journal of Legal Studies*, vol. 3 (January 1974), pp. 1–18; Isaac Ehrlich and R. A. Posner, "An Economic Analysis of Legal Rule Making," *Journal of Legal Studies*, vol. 3 (January 1974), pp. 257–286; W. M. Landes and R. A. Posner, "The Independent Judiciary in an Interest-Group Perspective," *Journal of Law & Economics*, vol. 18 (December 1975), pp. 875–901; and G. J. Stigler, "The Theory of Economic Regulation," *Bell Journal of Economics and Management Science*, vol. 2 (Spring 1971), pp. 3–21.

4 The Dawn of Capitalism

Mercantilism arose as an economic creed against a backdrop of historical change. The seventeenth century brought its share of inventions, wars, and upheavals to Europe. During its term calculus and ice cream were invented, tea and coffee became popular in Europe, and central banking was introduced in France. Before mid-century the first permanent settlement was established in North America, the King James Version of the Bible was completed, Protestantism gained a foothold in Europe, the Thirty Years' War devastated Central Europe, the American Indian Wars began, and civil wars raged throughout France, Scotland, Ireland, and England. The Dutch tulip-mania bubble burst in 1637, ruining many family fortunes. In the second half of the century Protestantism was outlawed in France, the Dutch Republic went into decline, the Ottoman Empire continued its westward expansion, England became a constitutional monarchy following the Glorious Revolution, Sir Isaac Newton published his theory of gravitational forces, Peter the Great became tsar of Russia, and LaSalle claimed the Louisiana territory for France after exploring the length of the Mississippi River. In 1666 the Great Fire of London destroyed 373 acres inside the city walls and 63 acres outside, 87 churches (including St. Paul's Cathedral), and 13,200 houses. In 1672 the French went to war with the Dutch, and in 1692 the Salem witch trials were conducted in Massachusetts.

Medicine was enriched by William Harvey (circulation of blood); astronomy by Kepler and Galileo; mathematics by Newton and Leibnitz, co-inventors of calculus; philosophy by Bacon, Descartes, Hobbes, Locke, Pascal, and Spinoza; literature and dramatic arts by Shakespeare, Molière, Racine, Cervantes, Donne, and Milton; and art by Bernini and Rembrandt. All in all it was an era that greatly distanced itself from the Middle Ages and the Renaissance by its institutional changes, its challenges to authority, its preparation for the Enlightenment, and its cultivation of markets. Old ideas broke down at an accelerated pace, and new ideas quickly filled the void.

By the end of the seventeenth century, mercantilism, too, was in a state of flux. Sharp reactions to the regulatory state emerged where it was most firmly entrenched, in France and Spain. French writers like Pierre Boisguilbert (1646–1714) and Spanish writers like Pedro Rodriguez de Campomanes (1723–1702) held the state responsible for policies that retarded economic growth, and paved the way for economic reform in their respective countries. In England, Sir William Petty (1623–1687) joined a chorus of voices calling for economic and practical reform. And in France, an Irish expatriate, Richard Cantillon (1680?–1734?), took economics to new heights in the pre–Adam Smith era. The economics of this era was transitional, displaying a mixture of liberal and mercantilist elements, particularly on the question of money, the most sensitive of mercantilist subjects. In the middle of the seventeenth century, the first "school" of economists—later named the Physiocrats—reflecting the combined influences of Boisguilbert and Cantillon, broke cleanly with the old economic order. Their ideas represented a wholesale rejection of mercantilism and an important anticipation of laissez-faire. The ground for advances in economics that occurred during the emergence of capitalism in England and Europe was fertilized by the spread of the Enlightenment and the rise of Protestantism.

■ Sir William Petty

Petty lived in a period of emerging commercial capitalism, marked on the one hand by a nascent agricultural revolution and on the other by early signs of the incipient Industrial Revolution. He was many things—traveler, writer, adventurer, physician, academician, surveyor, businessman, and economist—but above all he was obsessed with the idea of fame and fortune. An episode from his brief medical career illustrates his flair for the sensational. As professor of anatomy at Oxford, he revived and nursed back to health a young woman hanged for infanticide in 1650. It created a sensation. Shortly afterward, an anonymous pamphlet appeared, entitled *News from the Dead*, possibly written (at least in part) by Petty himself, extolling his miraculous medical powers that defied death and the gallows. Many of Petty's efforts, including his forays into economics, were distinguished by such bravado.

Economic Method

Petty was a positivist before positivism became the dominant research criterion of the natural sciences. As a charter member of the Royal Society (London), he once proposed, in jest, that the group's annual meeting should be held on the feast day of St. Thomas the Apostle, known as "doubting Thomas," because he believed only in what he could see or touch. Petty named his method of inquiry "political arithmetic," a term calculated to express his conviction that the introduction of quantitative methods would produce a more rigorous analysis of social phenomena. The use of quantitative methods in the social sciences represented the ascendancy of material/mechanical conceptions over the Aristotelian syllogistic/deductive approach. Petty rejected the Aristotelian approach in favor of an approach advanced by Francis Bacon, who fused empiricism and rationalism into what we now call the *inductive method*. Bacon used the following metaphor to explain the new method.

> [Empiricists] are like the ant, they only collect and use; the reasoners resemble spiders, who make cobwebs out of their own substance. But the bee takes a middle course: it gathers its material from the flowers of the garden and of the field, but transforms and digests it by a power of its own. Not unlike this is the true business of philosophy; for it neither relies solely or chiefly on the powers of the mind, nor does it take the matter which it gathers from natural history and mechanical experiments and lay it up in the memory whole, as it finds it, but lays it up in the understanding altered and digested. (*New Organon*, p. 93)

The flight from the subjectivism and logico-deductivism of the ancient Greeks and the Scholastics toward empiricism and objectivism was later woven into British classical political economy, as we shall see in ensuing chapters. Petty recognized the novelty of the new approach, and hailed its advantages:

> The Method I take . . . , is not very usual; for instead of using only comparative and superlative words, and intellectual Arguments, I have taken the course (as a Specimen of the Political Arithmetick I have long aimed at) to express myself in Terms of Number, Weight, or Measure; to use only Arguments of Sense, and to consider only such Causes, as have visible Foundations in Nature; leaving those that depend upon the mutable Minds, Opinions, Appetites and Passions of particular Men, to the Consideration of others. (*Economic Writings*, p. 244)

Petty's method also attempted to separate morals from science. He claimed that moral problems arise only in the selection of *ends* that humans propose to attain by the use of science. But science does not exist to handle moral problems—it is simply a *means* to an end. However contemporary this may sound, Petty did not espouse a consistent economic philosophy based on this principle. Rather, he advanced numerous proposals for state intervention even as he supported liberal propositions of nonintervention. Moreover, because his economic writings were an integral part of his political and business activities, he was not above defending his own interests in the halls of power.

In the final analysis, Petty's investigations were not aimed at producing a general system of knowledge but rather at producing solutions to practical problems. He intended only to produce general guides for policy, which was the real basis of his political arithmetic. It was meant to collect the essential elements of the practical problem to be solved. It was not intended to be a perfect or a complete description of reality. Petty knew its limitations. Furthermore, he was aware that each economic problem confronted in the real world (whether a question of money, international trade, or whatever) must be treated not as an independent phenomenon but as an integral part of a larger whole. It is this "systemic" nature of his thought that lifts Petty above his contemporaries, and it is this same feature that led Karl Marx to proclaim him "the founder of modern political economy."

On Money

Petty recognized the three functions of money (standard of value, medium of exchange, store of value), but emphasized the second function over the others. He rejected the notion that money is an *absolute* measure of value, arguing correctly that its value varies with conditions of supply and demand. He was also aware of the fiduciary operations of banks, and the "artificial" nature of money as a commodity that merely facilitates trade. He used the following analogy to underscore his ideas about money and its role:

> Money is but the Fat of the Body-politick, whereof too much doth as often hinder its Agility, as too little makes it sick. 'Tis true, that as Fat lubricates the motion of the Muscles, feeds in want of Victuals, fills up uneven Cavities, and beautifies the Body, so doth Money in the State quicken its Action, feeds from abroad in the time of Dearth at Home; evens accounts by reason of its divisibility, and beautifies the whole, altho more especially the particular persons that have it in plenty. (*Economic Writings*, p. 113)

Like the mercantilists, Petty saw a relationship between the quantity of money and the level of productive economic activity, but he did not fully appreciate the relationship between the quantity of money and the level of prices, which lies at the heart of the quantity theory. He considered money to be an indirect cost of production, a cost that corresponds to the value of precious metals embodied in the stock of money. Thus, he viewed an excess of money as a waste because the surplus of precious metals could have been exchanged for means of production rather than being directly employed in the production process.

Petty's chief contribution to monetary theory was his use of the velocity-of-circulation concept to determine the optimum quantity of money. This makes him an important predecessor of John Locke and Richard Cantillon. He recognized that velocity of circulation quickens as the payment period (of wages) shortens, correctly underscoring the role of institutional factors such as the time intervals defining receipt of wages, rents, and taxes. True to his "positivist" declarations Petty argued, in contradistinction to the mercantilists, that the accumulation of money is a means to an end, not an end in itself. Although favorably disposed to the influx of money from a positive trade balance, he did not consider this an absolute priority. Moreover, he considered prohibitions on the export of money useless. What was important, he argued, was a high level of employment and economic activity, not the accumulation of mere treasure.

On Value

Petty is remembered often for certain economic slogans more than for his solid achievements in economic analysis. Chief among the slogans he popularized is his famous dictum "That Labour is the Father and active principle of Wealth, as Lands are the Mother" (*Economic Writings*, vol. 1, p. 63). Although this statement signals an early and profound recognition of the two "original factors of production," it contains little analytical merit. It certainly does not constitute a *theory* of value. Of much more importance was Petty's inquiries into a "natural par" between land and labor. He tried to relate the values of land and labor to each other by determining how much land is required to produce "a day's food of an adult man," taking the value of such output to be equivalent to the value of a day's labor. His objective was to establish a unit of measurement by which to reduce the available quantities of the two original factors, land and labor, to a homogeneous quantity of "productive power," which could then serve as the (land-labor) standard of value. Like all such efforts to find an absolute standard of value, this one, too, proved to be an analytical dead end, but it inspired Petty's successor, Richard Cantillon, to undertake similar research.

Despite the econometric flavor of Petty's economic studies, he did not produce a satisfactory theory of prices. In particular, he failed to recognize the importance of *relative* prices, which constitutes the core of modern microeconomics. And Marx's admiration for him notwithstanding, Petty did not develop a labor theory of value. If anything, Petty had a land theory of value, although it is misleading to call his achievement a genuine *theory* of value. What was missing was a fundamental mechanism capable of explaining exchange ratios between economic goods that are bought and sold.

Although Petty had the disposition of a theorist, his greatest accomplishment was providing a decisive new turn in economic method. His invention, Political Arithmetick, was a primitive form of econometrics, a field that was formalized in the 1930s and blossomed in the post–World War II era. As Joseph Schumpeter noted, Petty "was quite ready to fight for . . . [this methodological creed] and to start what would have been the first controversy on 'method.' But nobody attacked. A few followed. Many admired. And the vast majority very quickly forgot" (*History of Economic Analysis*, p. 211). Faced with the same issue a century later, Adam Smith chose safety over novelty, declaring in *The Wealth of Nations* (Book IV, chap. 5) that he had little faith in Political Arithmetick. Under Smith's guidance, classical economics reclaimed the logico-deductive method.

■ Nascent Liberalism in France: Boisguilbert, Cantillon, and the Physiocrats

France greeted the eighteenth century gripped in a long secular decline. Historians attribute its falling levels of output and national income to the costly wars and personal extravagances of Louis XIV. At least one writer, however, blamed his country's wretched state of affairs on its misguided mercantilist policies.

Boisguilbert (1646–1714)

Pierre le Pesant de Boisguilbert, a provincial magistrate in the city of Rouen, published five major works between 1665 and 1707, each directed toward the causes and cures of France's economic decline. He never attempted a systematic treatment of basic principles but aimed instead at solving specific economic problems, which he traced back to France's mercantilist policies.

Boisguilbert's attack on mercantilism was three-pronged. First, he rejected the mercantilist identity between money and wealth in favor of the notion that national wealth consists of goods and services. Money, he said, was merely the means of acquiring wealth; the proper goal of economic activity is the commodities useful to life (*Détail*, p. 198): "Gold and silver are not and never have been wealth in themselves, and are of value only in relation to, and in so far as they can procure, the things necessary for life, for which they serve merely as a gauge and an evaluation (in Cole, *French Mercantilism*, p. 242). Alongside Petty, Boisguilbert was one of the earliest writers to recognize the importance of circulatory velocity and of money substitutes, such as bills of exchange. He argued that it is not the quantity of money alone that is important but the amount of work money does. Accordingly, effective demand, not nominal money balances, is the key to national well-being. He adopted the distinctively Keynesian perspective that national income is determined by flows of money expenditure (see chapter 21 on Keynes).

The second aspect of Boisguilbert's critique focused on agriculture. He said that mercantilism produced national harm by directing resources away from agriculture toward manufacturing (especially luxuries). Trade restrictions, such as French minister Colbert's prohibition of grain exports, made matters worse. During times of plenty, the surplus grain could not find external markets, its price plunged, and lower prices drove down the income of farmers. The consequent decline in consumption spread from the farm sector throughout the economy, thus precipitating a general crisis. Boisguilbert proposed free trade as an antidote to Colbert's harmful policies. Free trade, he argued, would stabilize grain prices, expand agricultural production, and improve income distribution. Although apparently advocating laissez-faire, his true commitment to this principle was suspect because he proposed direct government action to support grain prices once they reached a "suitable" level (*Traité de la nature*, p. 369). Although he examined short-run cyclical movements of national income, Boisguilbert was more concerned with the long-run problem of secular decline. He estimated that between 1665 and 1695 the national income of France declined by about 50 percent (*Détail*, p. 163)—a direct consequence of the failure of aggregate demand dampened by an oppressive system of taxation.

The third aspect of Boisguilbert's critique of mercantilism focused on the French tax system. The specific taxes that came under his scrutiny were those known as the *taille*, the *aides*, and the *douanes*. The *taille* was a property tax, subdivided into a levy on real property and another on personal property. According to

Boisguilbert the problem was not so much with the taxes themselves as with their incidence. Nobility and clergy were exempt from tax, which meant that the full burden landed almost exclusively on the poorest proprietors. Under the Bourbon dynasty, administration of these property taxes was capricious, often depending on an arbitrary assessment of ability to pay and the aggressiveness and persistence of the local tax collector. Even in the same parish the effective tax rate could vary between 0.33 and 33 percent (*Détail*, p. 172).

To Boisguilbert the *aides* and the *douanes* were almost as damaging to consumption as the *taille*. The former were originally general sales taxes, but by the end of the seventeenth century they had become excise taxes, confined to a few products only, particularly wine. The wine tax became so oppressive that French workers practically stopped drinking wine (the ultimate sacrifice for a French person), foreign buyers turned elsewhere, and vineyards were taken out of cultivation. In 1779 the economist Le Trosne estimated that sales taxes *(aides)*, which brought in thirty million in revenue for the king, cost the people of France one-hundred-forty million of lost income. The *douanes* were nearly as bad. They consisted of duties on goods moving into or out of the kingdom as well as between provinces within the kingdom. The effect of these duties was either to restrict movement of goods altogether or to raise the prices of delivered goods to a prohibitive level, at least for the poor. Taken together, French excise taxes greatly restrained trade, both domestic and foreign. Boisguilbert blamed them for the destruction of France's foreign markets in wines, hats, playing cards, tobacco pipes, and whalebone (*Détail*, p. 196).

The Physiocrats (see below) later reacted strongly against the same oppressive tax system that roiled Boisguilbert and his contemporaries. But links between Boisguilbert and the Physiocrats are tenuous. The Physiocrats regarded Boisguilbert's reform measures as arbitrary, and they strove to substitute a natural system of finances in place of the existing one. Moreover, Boisguilbert did not anticipate the physiocratic concept of *net product* or their assertion regarding the exclusive productivity of agriculture. On matters of tax reform, however, the Physiocrats shared many of the same concerns as Boisguilbert, namely a desire to end the regressive nature of taxes and establish a more equitable distribution of the tax burden. Boisguilbert sought reform in order to liberalize consumption, whereas the Physiocrats aimed their tax reforms at the enhancement of capital accumulation and agricultural entrepreneurship.

■ Richard Cantillon

In 1755 a brief but remarkable book, *Essai sur la nature du commerce en général (An Essay on the Nature of Trade in General)*, was published under bizarre circumstances. Most likely printed in Paris, it carried the imprint of a London bookseller no longer in business. The subterfuge was probably designed to circumvent strict French censorship laws. The manuscript had been written more than two decades earlier; its author, Richard Cantillon, was a Paris banker and London merchant of Irish extraction. Some facts of his life and his influence are known, but the circumstances of his death (in 1734?) are shrouded in mystery. The popular account is that he was murdered in his sleep by a servant he had discharged weeks before. As the account goes, the disgruntled servant set his former master's house afire in order to make Cantillon's death appear accidental. Antoin Murphy (*Richard Cantillon*) has challenged this version of Cantillon's demise, making the case that Cantillon faked his own death in order to escape certain economic and political entanglements. We may never know what actually happened, but one way or the other, Cantillon disappeared from public life after 1734.

Cantillon's *Essai* represents state-of-the-art economics before Adam Smith (see chapter 5). It is a general treatise of penetrating insights and remarkable clarity, features that have not dimmed with the passage of time. Whereas Boisguilbert attacked the economic problems of French society, Cantillon focused on the discovery of basic principles. A checklist of his original contributions to economics underscores his importance. He was one of the first to:

1. Treat population growth as an integral part of the economic process
2. Develop an economic explanation of the location of cities and sites of production
3. Make a distinction between market price and intrinsic value (i.e., equilibrium price) and show how the two may converge over time
4. Demonstrate that changes in velocity are equivalent to changes in the stock of money
5. Trace the channels through which changes in the stock of money influence prices
6. Describe the mechanism by which prices adjust in international trade
7. Analyze income flows between major sectors of the economy

In addition to this impressive list of accomplishments what set Cantillon miles apart from the mercantilists was his Newtonian cast of mind, which is displayed on almost every page of *Essai*. Cantillon probed the economy much as Newton had probed the cosmos. Each writer viewed his subject as an interconnected whole made up of rationally functioning parts. For Cantillon this meant that the economy was constantly adjusting to basic changes in population, production, tastes, and so forth. The animus of this adjustment process was the self-interested pursuit of profit, a motive of such universal application that it takes the position in Cantillon's inquiry that Newton's "universal principle of attraction" (i.e., gravity) took in his.

Although Cantillon's manuscript circulated among a small cadre of writers in France and England before its eventual publication in 1755, its merit was quickly overshadowed by the power and influence of Physiocracy (see below). The full import of Cantillon's contribution was not appreciated until late in the nineteenth century, when the British neoclassical economist William Stanley Jevons (see chapter 15) rediscovered *Essai*. Jevons called it "the cradle of political economy," saying of its author that "the first systematic treatise on economics was probably written by a banker of Spanish name, born from an Irish family of the County Kerry, bred we know not where, carrying on business in Paris, but clearly murdered in Albermarle Street [London]" (see "Richard Cantillon," p. 360). Cantillon's work shows some concern for traditional mercantilist issues, but it is far more a disinterested inquiry into the workings of a nascent market economy. He drew on the works of prominent English writers such as Sir William Petty and John Locke, but his mantle of influence fell mostly on writers in his adopted country, France. Only later did his influence spread to such neoclassical writers as Jevons and to the neo-Austrian economists (see chapter 23).

In assessing Cantillon's place in the history of economic thought we emphasize three major themes of his work: (1) his view of the market and its operation, (2) the critical role and importance of the entrepreneur in economic activity, and (3) channels by which changes in the aggregate supply of money influence the economy.

The Market System

Cantillon conceived an economy as an organized system of interconnected markets that operate in such a manner as to achieve a kind of equilibrium. The inhabitants of the economy are bound together by mutual dependence, and the institutions of the system evolve over time in response to "need and necessity." The free play of self-interested entrepreneurs keeps the system in adjustment by their conduct of "all the exchange and circulation of the State" (*Essay*, p. 77). Considering the age in which Cantillon wrote, he assigns "the prince" a remarkably low profile, a fact underscoring his conviction that a market system works best *without* interference from government. Entrepreneurs, like other market participants, are bound together in reciprocity, as they "become consumers and customers one in regard to the other." Their number is therefore regulated by the number of customers, or total demand, for their services, and their decisions are made under conditions of uncertainty about the future.

Cantillon's economic system is hierarchical. Landlords sit atop the economic and social order and are represented as financially independent, although they derive income from the inhabitants of a state, who in turn rely on the proprietors to supply natural resources in production. Private property rights are deemed essential to the successful operation of a system of markets. Although entrepreneurs occupy the middle rank in Cantillon's hierarchy, their role is vital and pervasive. It is they who continually react to price movements in specific markets in order to bring about a tentative balance between particular supplies and particular demands.

Seeing the economy as a network of reciprocal exchanges, Cantillon provided one of the clearest early explanations of market price. His notion of intrinsic value (the measure of the quantity and quality of land and labor entering into production) underscores an early attempt to base price on some measure of "real" costs, at least insofar as equilibrium long-run values are concerned. When it came to short-run "market" price, however, Cantillon seemed ready to admit subjective assessments. He noted that "it often happens that many things which actually have this intrinsic value are not sold in the market at that value: that will depend on the humors and fancies of men and on their consumption" (*Essay*, p. 55). Another reason why market prices may be different from intrinsic values is that the plans of producers and their customers may be uncoordinated. Indeed, it would appear impossible always to achieve *perfect* coordination. Cantillon observed that "there is never a variation in intrinsic values, but the impossibility of proportioning the production of commodities and merchandise in a State to their consumption causes a daily variation, and perpetual ebb and flow of market prices" (*Essay*, p. 55).

The bargaining process described by Cantillon reflects the information possessed by market participants and the degree of coordination of individual plans. Disparate plans, he explained, tend to drive prices away from costs (i.e., intrinsic value):

> If the farmers in a State sow more wheat than usual, that is to say, much more than is needed for the annual consumption, the real and intrinsic value of the wheat will correspond to the land and labor which enter into its production; but as there is an over-supply and there are more sellers of wheat than buyers, the market price of wheat will necessarily fall below the cost or intrinsic value. If on the contrary the farmers sow less wheat than is needed for consumption there will be more buyers than sellers and the market price will rise above its intrinsic value. (*Essay*, p. 55)

One has only to substitute the word "natural" in place of "intrinsic" to appreciate how close this analysis comes to Adam Smith's (see chapter 5). If Cantillon had gone no further, he would have still provided an important description of the price mechanism. But he did go further, providing a rudimentary explanation of the network of price signals that link different markets. The following passage is rich in suggestions of self-interest as a motive force, relative prices as signals to adjust resource use, and opportunity costs as a basis of economic decision making:

> If some of the farmers sowed more grain than usual, they will feed fewer sheep and have less wool and mutton to sell. Consequently there will be too much grain and too little wool for the consumption of the inhabitants. Wool will be expensive, which will force the inhabitants to wear their clothes longer than usual, and there will be too much grain and a surplus for the following year. . . . If, however, next year they have too much wool and too little grain for the demand, they will not fail to change from year to year the use of the land, until they have arrived at proportioning their production to the consumption of the inhabitants. Thus a farmer who has appropriately proportioned his output to consumption will have part of his farm in grass, for hay, another for grain, wool, and so on, and he will not change his plan unless he sees some considerable change in demand. (*Essay*, pp. 80–81)

In this way Cantillon demonstrated how initially incompatible plans between buyers and sellers become mutually compatible over time by self-interested adjustments to changes in relative prices. The same sort of phenomenon manifests itself in the factor markets. Cantillon explained how labor adjusts itself naturally to the demand for it. When he described the tradition of raising sons in the same line of work as their fathers he stressed the natural forces at work allocating labor to different employments. If village workers bring up a number of their sons in one trade, "the surplus adults will have to leave in order to seek a livelihood elsewhere, which they generally find in cities. If some remain with their fathers—as they will not all find sufficient employment—they will live in great poverty and will not marry for lack of means to raise children" (*Essay*, p. 49). Although short-term changes in demand bring about higher or lower returns to various kinds of labor, Cantillon envisioned an eventual adjustment to equilibrium. He observed correctly that after out-migration and/or in-migration, "those who remain are always proportioned to the employment that suffices to maintain them. When there is a continuous increase of work, there are gains to be made and others will move in to share the business" (*Essay*, p. 50). Given a *permanent* increase in the demand for labor, Cantillon's statement of the allocative mechanism compares favorably with that developed by later neoclassical writers.

Competition and Entrepreneurship

As economic analysis matured in the nineteenth century, the notion of competition shifted gradually from a description of human activity involving risk and uncertainty to a set of finite conditions that defined one of several market structures. Some analytical precision was gained in the process, but at the cost of considerable realism. Cantillon developed the "old-fashioned" notion of competition, and he gave the entrepreneur a pivotal role in his theory of market adjustments. His economy consisted of socioeconomic classes—each class defined by a major economic function.

> [I]t may be established that, except for the prince and the property owners, all the inhabitants of a State are dependent. They can be divided into two classes, entrepreneurs and hired workers. The entrepreneurs are on unfixed wages while the others are on fixed wages as long as there is work, although their functions and ranks may be very unequal. The general who has his pay, the courtier his pension

> and the domestic servant who has wages, all fall into this last class. All the others are entrepreneurs, whether they are set up with capital to conduct their enterprise, or are entrepreneurs of their own labor without capital, and they may be regarded as living under uncertainty; even the beggars and the robbers are entrepreneurs of this class. (*Essay*, p. 76)

Clearly for Cantillon there are low entrance requirements to the entrepreneurial class, and just as clearly, entrepreneurs come and go, depending on the vicissitudes of the marketplace. As Cantillon described it, the essence of entrepreneurial activity is bearing risk. In the case of merchant-entrepreneurs, they buy goods at a known price in order to resell them "in large or small quantities at an uncertain price." The marketplace, therefore, is not for the fainthearted or the risk-averse. Cantillon wrote:

> These entrepreneurs never know how great the demand will be in their city, nor how long their customers will buy from them, since their rivals will try, by all sorts of means, to attract their customers. All this causes so much uncertainty among these entrepreneurs that every day one sees some of them go bankrupt. (*Essay*, p. 74)

Cantillon entertained a "general equilibrium" notion of how a market system works. That is to say, he recognized the interconnectedness between product markets and resource markets. Entrepreneurs are "allocated" according to the same mechanism that allocates laborers or goods:

> All these entrepreneurs become consumers and customers of each other, the draper of the wine merchant, and vice versa. In a State, they proportion themselves to the customers or their consumption. If there are too many hat makers in a city or on a street for the number of people who buy hats, the least patronized must go bankrupt. On the other hand, if there are too few, it will be a profitable business, which will encourage new hat makers to open shops, and in this manner, entrepreneurs of all kinds adjust themselves to risks in a state. (*Essay*, p. 75)

For various reasons presumably motivated by the objective of making economics more scientific, contemporary economic theory assigns a mere incidental role to the entrepreneur. Not so for Cantillon, who linked competition and entrepreneurship inevitably. Both were pervasive, and both defined the nature of economic markets. Hence he proclaimed confidently, "All the exchange and circulation of the State is carried on by the actions of these entrepreneurs" (*Essay*, p. 77).

The critical importance of entrepreneurship and its importance to capitalism must be underlined with what went before Cantillon's understanding of the concept. For example, James M. Murray (see references) writes paradoxically of medieval entrepreneurship without visible entrepreneurs in order to emphasize the point that medieval society could be entrepreneurial almost without anyone noticing. Feudal society was organized along strict, hierarchical lines of monarch, Church, lords, merchants, and peasants. The Church's spiritual lords (abbots, bishops, priests) behaved in an entrepreneurial manner by establishing monasteries, preserving and enhancing knowledge, and applying agricultural technology to augment the quantity of food and fiber. Temporal lords behaved in an entrepreneurial manner by mobilizing and sustaining labor (serfs) and applying agricultural technology to manor output. They invested in implements and draft animals necessary to till their fields. They provided capital and incentives to peasants in order to secure their labor for a variety of purposes, especially clearing forests to acquire more arable land.

Murray further points out that the first use of the word "entrepreneur" comes to us from the late Middle Ages, when the word (of undisputed French origin) was used to describe a battlefield commander. Only very gradually was the word extended to the battlefield of business. As urbanization occurred communities changed from seigniorial to merchant centers, so that "by the end of the medieval period, merchants came to direct many of society's 'productive forces' within cities and were subject to the corrective judgment of a society still bound to Christianity's mission to heal the rift between God and humanity and gain individual salvation for all the baptized" ("Entrepreneurs and Entrepreneurship," p. 88). Thus, even as Christianity's mission made the profit motive more opaque, it could not, and did not, fully impede the development of markets and entrepreneurial processes.

By Cantillon's time, a critical mass in the development of markets and networks had been reached, making qualitative as well as quantitative changes in the nature of commerce evident. Cantillon captured this transformation of enterprise better than anyone else, and he did so within an empirical/theoretical framework, thereby installing the entrepreneur as a vital cog in the market process. He recognized that the transformation of commerce was stoked by the gold and silver mines of Europe and the New World, but the interesting aspect of his analysis for the development of economic theory is the pivotal role he assigned to the entrepreneur, not to precious metals, in stoking economic growth.

The Effect of Money on Prices and Production

Despite Cantillon's impressive theoretical treatment of entrepreneurship, markets, and economic activity, his genius fully blossomed in the area of monetary theory. Cantillon originated the income approach to monetary theory, namely, the analysis of the causal chain that connects changes in the money stock to changes in aggregate expenditures, income, employment, and prices (see chapter 22 for a modern account of this theory). He starts with an account of the "three rents"—the income and expenditure streams of the agricultural sector. The farmer pays a rent to the proprietor; he makes a second expenditure for labor, livestock, and manufactured goods; and he earns a residual (the third "rent") that constitutes his net income. This rather crude notion of income flows by sector was refined by the French Physiocrat François Quesnay, in his *Tableau économique* (see below).

Displaying an empirical bent akin to Petty, Cantillon built on his three-rent concept by making estimates of the stock of money required to make the economy work smoothly. In the process he provided the first clear explanation of monetary velocity:

> In States where money is scarcer, there usually is more barter by valuation, than in those where money is plentiful, and circulation is more prompt and less sluggish than in those where money is not so scarce. Thus it is always necessary, when estimating the amount of money in circulation, to take into account the speed of its circulation. (*Essay*, p. 127)

Calling on the "quantity theory" of John Locke, which had become part of conventional wisdom, Cantillon recognized that in terms of the connection between money and prices Locke's theory did not go far enough:

> Everybody agrees that the abundance of money, or an increase in use in exchange, raises the price of everything. This truth is substantiated in experience by the quantity of money brought to Europe from America for the last two centuries. Mr. Locke lays it down as a fundamental maxim that the quantity of goods in proportion to the quantity of money is a regulator of market prices. . . . [However,] the great difficulty of this question consists in knowing in what way and in what proportion the increase of money raises the prices of things. (*Essay*, pp. 147–148)

Reflecting the age of Newton, Cantillon adorned his analytical principles with empirical research, collecting his data in a "statistical supplement" that was unfortunately lost to posterity. His statistical research convinced Cantillon that the relation between money and prices was not as simple and direct as was usually assumed by early adherents of the quantity theory. He had no trouble distinguishing between relative prices and a price *level*, and he reasoned correctly that the effect of monetary changes on relative prices depends on where new money enters the economy and into whose hands it passes first. If the increased money comes into the hands of spenders, they will raise expenditures on certain goods, driving up the prices of those items. Since some goods will likely be purchased more than others, "according to the inclination of those who acquire the money," relative prices will necessarily be altered. If, instead, the increase of money comes initially into the hands of savers who use it to increase the supply of loanable funds, the current rate of interest will be driven down, *ceteris paribus*, and the composition of total output will change in favor of investment goods (*Essay*, p. 178). The differential impact of increased money on different sectors of the economy became known subsequently as "the Cantillon effect," and it provided the germ of a distinctly Austrian theory of business cycles subsequently developed in the 1930s by Friedrich Hayek (see chapter 23).

Cantillon refused to separate monetary theory from value theory. He upheld a loanable-funds theory of interest, asserting that "the interest of money in a State is settled by the proportionate number of lenders and borrowers . . . just as the prices of things are fixed in the altercations of the market . . . by the proportionate number of sellers and buyers" (*Essay*, p. 198). With his focus on relative prices, Cantillon surveyed the effects of new money on interest rates and concluded once again that the demand-specific aspects are critical:

> If the abundance of money in a State comes from the hands of moneylenders, the increase in the number of lenders will probably lower the rate of interest. However, if the abundance comes from the hands of people who will spend it, this will have just the opposite effect and will raise the rate of interest by increasing the number of entrepreneurs who go into business as a result of this increased spending, and will need to supply their businesses by borrowing at all types of interest. (*Essay*, p. 178)

In effect, Cantillon saw very clearly what many writers of the next century ignored, namely, that an influx of precious metals can act in two ways: The output of the mines may be *lent*—which will tend to lower the rate of interest—or it may be *spent*—which will directly stimulate production, increase the demand for loans in anticipation of making a profit, and raise the rate that people are willing to pay for such loans.

Some historians of economics insist on placing Cantillon in the mercantilist camp, even though a close reading of his *Essai* provides weak support for this view. He retained some mercantilist notions concerning the balance of trade, and at times he seemed overly concerned with accumulation of specie, but as a banker his point of view was grounded more in contemporary business practices rather than in philosophy. Clearly Cantillon presented more theoretical substance than the mercantilists. His performance in this respect was solid. Though unpublished for many years, his manuscript circulated among a cadre of thinkers in France who emulated his effort and influenced the next generation of founders: the Physiocrats, and most likely through them, Adam Smith.

Physiocracy: "The Rule of Nature"

Every new science requires a philosophy, and the audacious philosophy of capitalism that Adam Smith would soon present to the world was already emerging, cocoonlike, by the middle of the eighteenth century. Two decades before Smith's magnum opus appeared a group of French writers laid claim to the name "economists." This group composed the first real "school of thought" in economics in the sense that it had a master and a group of like-minded disciples. After the word "economist" took on a more generic meaning, the group of French thinkers was renamed "Physiocrats." The term "Physiocracy" means "rule of nature." It is especially appropriate in this instance because the writers in question believed in natural law and in the primacy of agriculture.

The intellectual leader of the Physiocrats was François Quesnay, court physician to Madame de Pompadour and Louis XV. Quesnay and the small group of disciples he attracted pushed back the theoretical frontiers of the new science and infused it with an underlying philosophy. Physiocracy appealed to rational principles: It asserted that all social facts are linked together by inevitable laws, which would be obeyed by individuals and governments once they understood them. Adam Smith was an acquaintance of Quesnay, and physiocratic doctrine exerted a major influence on the venerable Scot, although he maintained his distance in some respects.

In this chapter we treat the Physiocrats as a group, although like mercantilists, they were a heterogeneous band. The publications of this group followed fairly closely on each other between 1756 and 1778. Its members included the Marquis de Mirabeau, Mercier de la Rivière, Dupont de Nemours, Guillaume-François Le Trosne, and Nicolas Baudeau. The French minister Turgot was sympathetic to physiocratic doctrine but did not consider himself a member of its inner circle.

King Louis XIV, and his successor Louis XV, ignored Boisguilbert's criticisms as France marched toward the nineteenth century under crushing debt, accumulated by numerous costly wars and court extravagance. The repressive system of French taxation required to support such royal profligacy weighed heavily of France's economy. Louis XVI, a reluctant monarch, inherited the debt, not the glamour, of his predecessors and was never able to right the ship of state. He ultimately became a high-profile victim of the French Revolution. Inasmuch as the Physiocrats' period of influence coincided closely with the reign of Louis XVI, they offered a last-ditch effort at economic reform before the monarchy was overthrown.

When the last Bourbon monarch ascended the throne, land values in France were falling because of declining agricultural output. Two thirds of French land was owned by clergy and nobility, who were exempt from taxation. Common farmers were required to pay a large share of their produce to the landlord and were heavily taxed on the remainder, making capital accumulation at the level of production virtually impossible for them. Domestic markets and personal income were further squeezed by the mercantilist policy of depressing wages and other production costs in an attempt to encourage exports. As Lewis Haney so aptly put it, "France was like a great railway or factory which has made no allowance for depreciation or depletion; her productive power was impaired and her credit shaken" (*History*, p. 176). The Physiocrats tried to come to the rescue, but ultimately failed. Yet, they left an important legacy to economic theory.

Physiocratic Economics

The Physiocrats were system builders, on a scale slightly larger than Cantillon but smaller than Adam Smith. In about 1750 Quesnay and his cohort, Vincent Gournay, asked themselves "whether the nature of things did not tend towards a science of political economy, and what the principles of this science were" (in Baur, "Studies," p. 100). Under Quesnay's leadership, Physiocracy devoted itself to the discovery of these principles. Its underlying philosophy was based on the medieval notion of *jus naturae* (natural law), but it added John Locke's concepts of *individual* rights and the justification of private property based on those rights. Although Physiocracy was basically a reaction against mercantilism, it bowed to expediency by not challenging the absolute authority of French monarchs; even as it advocated free trade and individual self-interest. The group drew the following description:

> The physiocrats . . . were a court party, though a radical one. The direct criticism of existing abuses and freedom of language were forbidden them. The only way open to reformers was to oppose to arbitrary power a higher one—the laws of nature. This, therefore, is the true origin of their *jus naturae*. (Baur, "Studies," p. 106)

Natural law, in other words, was part of the Physiocrats' scientific method. Contemporary methodology considers the concept of natural law outdated. Nevertheless, what the Physiocrats did is not very different from what economists do today: They proceeded from methodical observation of their world; they arranged and collated facts according to their causes; and they tried to form an analytical system based on a theoretical model—a system that agreed with the sound state of a highly civilized country. The embodiment of this method is Quesnay's *Tableau économique*, which was the heart and soul of physiocratic economics.

Physiocratic Theory. The Physiocrats argued that the best way to trace out the full effects of France's oppressive royal policies was to conceive the mutual-interaction economy in any one year as a circular flow of income and expenditure. (The idea of a circular flow was incipient in Cantillon's *Essai*). Any policy that had the effect of enlarging the circular flow was consistent with economic growth; whereas any that restricted it was inconsistent with economic growth. The same concept, considerably embellished and elaborated, is central to modern macroeconomic theory. Quesnay then picked out a key factor in the circular-flow process and analyzed the effects of various economy-wide policies by observing their impact on this key factor. (Note the familiar methodology, which economists continue to follow).

The key factor that Quesnay selected—and what stands today as the most outstanding fallacy of physiocratic doctrine—was the exclusive productivity of agriculture. In the *Tableau économique*, which was the name Quesnay gave to his visual representation of the circular flow, manufacturing and service industries are considered "sterile" in the sense that they contribute nothing to society's net product *(produit net)*, which is the true source of real wealth. To the Physiocrats, production meant creating a surplus: An industry is productive, therefore, if it makes more than is consumed in the process. According to the Physiocrats manufacturing merely changes the form of goods by converting inputs into outputs. They did not deny that such goods become more useful in the process, but they reasoned that only agriculture is capable of adding more to output than the mere sum of inputs. In other words, only agriculture is capable of creating a net product. If this unique meaning is kept in mind, however strange it may seem from a modern perspective, the doctrines of the Physiocrats will be more easily understood.

The original *Tableau* was an intricate numerical table that connected aggregate income flows between socioeconomic classes by zigzag lines. Rather than reproduce the cumbersome original diagram, we present a simpler graphical representation that nevertheless captures the essence of Quesnay's model. Figure 4-1 divides the economy into three classes, or sectors: (1) a productive class made up entirely of agriculturalists (perhaps also of fishermen and miners); (2) a sterile class consisting of merchants, manufacturers, domestic servants, and professional people; and (3) a proprietary class, including not only landlords but also those who have the slightest title to sovereignty of any kind. Income flows in clockwise motion, showing that the net product (i.e., net income, in money terms) is produced entirely by the first class and subsequently used to support its own activities or those of the other two classes.

Using Quesnay's figures and starting with a total wealth of five billion francs, which represents net product inherited from the previous production period, the flow chart shows that two billion francs is necessary for the upkeep of the productive class and its livestock during the year. In figure 4-1 this is represented as payments from the farm sector to the farm sector. This portion does not circulate. In addition, the farm sector spends one billion francs on manufactured goods (and services), which are also necessary to sustain the farmers during the year. The remaining two billion francs goes to the proprietors in the form of rents and taxes. This last two billion represents the net product, or surplus over necessary costs (rents and taxes were not considered necessary costs of production).

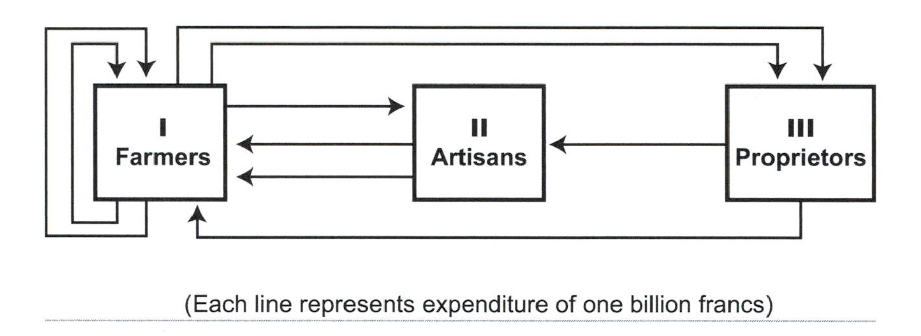

Figure 4-1 Each expenditure made by the farm sector for upkeep, manufactured goods, rents, and taxes is returned to the farm sector by the artisans, proprietors, and the farmers themselves.

The circuit is completed when the proprietors and those in the sterile class spend their income (proprietors: one billion for food and one billion for manufactures; sterile class: one billion for food and one billion for raw materials). In sum, the three billion francs originally spent by the agriculturalists returns to them, one billion coming from the proprietors and two billion from the artisans, and the process continues indefinitely. Note, however, that the agriculturalists are the only ones who produce a net product, that is, more than the costs of sustaining themselves and their agricultural activities.

Physiocratic Policy. At best this summary gives only a faint idea of the vast complexities involved in tracing the growth of revenues over time—which was the main concern of the Physiocrats. The circular flow model, however, gives us important insights into their policy prescriptions. The Physiocrats sought policies to encourage the accumulation of capital, which was retarded under the existing regime by an excessive tax burden on farmers. Thus, they argued for tax reform.

Quesnay had calculated the amount and productivity of capital necessary to attain a sound state of agriculture, and following Cantillon, he was convinced that the application of capital to agriculture was the only way of obtaining a taxable net product. The trick was to meet the needs of the treasury while at the same time doing away with a burdensome tax system that impeded agricultural development. The physiocratic solution to both problems was simply to tax the landlord instead of the farmer. The Physiocrats argued that tax collection in prerevolutionary France was highly inefficient because the tax was not levied on the group that ultimately paid the tax. They reasoned that since taxes can be paid only out of the net product, they should be levied against those who receive the net product.

Because landlords were responsible for improvements to their land, land rents constituted a potential source of capital accumulation for agricultural investment. Mercantilist restrictions on the free trade of agricultural products, however, kept farm prices (and therefore land rents) low by limiting demand. Thus, the Physiocrats argued for free trade. Removal of these restrictions, they felt, and a general "hands-off" policy by government, would allow capital to flow freely into the agricultural sector and enable the size of the circular flow to grow over time, in accordance with the "laws of nature."

It might be insinuated that the Physiocrats were antagonistic toward the landed class (nobility) because they wanted to shift the tax burden to them. This might have been the case if the Physiocrats were sympathetic to the revolutionists. But the Physiocrats neither showed animosity toward the nobility nor challenged the institution of private property. They considered landlords and their goodwill essential to the development process. After all, it was the proprietor who made the initial investment in clearing arable land and making certain improvements prior to turning the land over to the farmers for cultivation—and for this he was entitled to a share of the annual output. Later, Karl Marx, who was duly impressed with the physiocratic notion of surplus, but who freely inserted his socialist fervor into his economic writings, treated the landed proprietors as social parasites, even though this view was no part of physiocratic doctrine.

The Physiocrats presented a more enlightened view of landlords and their function. They believed that any immediate disadvantage to the proprietors caused by the tax would be more than offset in the long run by consequential increases in agricultural investment, net product, and rents. In short, although the landlords were a privileged class, their responsibilities were considered by the Physiocrats to be commensurate with their elevated position in society.

In the final analysis, it is perhaps as important to understand *how* the Physiocrats reasoned as it is to understand what they said. Like many social writers who succeeded them they conceived of the economy as fundamentally organic—an extremely complex and delicate amalgam of constituent parts, linked by the mechanism of market exchange, in which any disturbance to one part eventually communicated itself to all other parts through the process of interaction and reaction. Theirs might be called the first general-equilibrium analysis (see chapter 17). Much has been made of the analogy Quesnay drew between the operation of the economy and the performance of the human body. Anatomically, a disturbance to one part of the body—the stomach, for example—is sooner or later transmitted to other parts, which interact and react to compensate for the initial disturbance. In the economy, a disturbance in production brings about a disturbance in demand and vice versa, because of the interdependence of the two.

Criticisms of Physiocracy

Physiocracy attracted a fair amount of criticism in its heyday, but by and large, as a body of systematic principles it held sway for merely two decades before *The Wealth of Nations* made its appearance in 1776. The Italian economist, Galiani, reacting against Physiocracy, opposed both the idea of a natural order and the attempt to construct economic systems. The French philosopher Condillac correctly refuted the idea that manufacturers are sterile and helped establish a subjective theory of value, an issue that only tangentially concerned the Physiocrats, who were more interested in production and distribution than in the theory of exchange. But these complaints did not seriously threaten the prestige of the French economists.

Modern criticisms of Physiocracy usually take one of two forms: (1) their pure theory did not sufficiently accord with the facts of their day, or (2) their theory was overshadowed by normative considerations. The latter criticism implies that their doctrine can be reduced to a mere rationalization of class interests. Each argument has some merit.

The first argument centers on the charge that manufacturing is *sterile*. But what did the Physiocrats really mean by that term? As explained earlier, by "productive" they did not mean the mere capability of creating utility or adding value. Those actions that were looked on as productive by the Physiocrats certainly had this capability, but so, too, did most "sterile" occupations. According to Ronald Meek, "The real essence of a 'productive' occupation, according to the normal physiocratic use of the term, lay in the inherent capacity to yield a disposable surplus over necessary cost; and the real essence of a 'sterile' occupation lay in its inherent incapacity to yield such a surplus" (*Economics of Physiocracy*, p. 379).

The Physiocrats believed that manufacturing was sterile insofar as it was incapable of yielding a surplus only under conditions of free competition. They were perfectly willing to admit that under monopoly conditions, a value surplus over necessary costs might result from manufacturing. Contemporary economic theory tells us that under competitive conditions, long-run (equilibrium) price is just equal to average total costs of production. And in eighteenth-century France, this observation seemed in accord with the experience of the Physiocrats.

Where they erred badly was in maintaining that manufacturing is "naturally and inherently incapable of yielding a surplus over cost." They mistakenly concluded that because manufacturing *was* not yielding a value surplus over necessary costs under competitive conditions, it *never* could do so under competitive conditions (in the short run, for example). In this they were wrong, but their error was based on weak prophecy rather than deficient facts. And perhaps we ask too much if we demand that economists be seers as well as scientists.

Resolution of one question brings up another, however. If competition reduces the price of manufactured products to the level of necessary costs, why does it not do the same in agriculture, thus wiping out rent? At several points in their writings the Physiocrats seemed to toy with a monopoly explanation of land rent, but their answer was ambiguous. They regarded the net product as simply a gift of nature, or of God—a familiar argument in the early history of economic thought. While nature might explain a surplus of *physical* output in agriculture, it cannot explain the existence of a *value* surplus. The latter can be explained only by a general theory of value capable of explaining the determination of product and factor prices. The Physiocrats had certain notions of value, but they did not develop a theory of value. This task fell to Adam Smith, who responded awkwardly, as we shall soon see, but he at least directed attention to a serious void in economic theory.

The twentieth century produced two conflicting interpretations of Physiocracy, both of which are aimed at explaining class interests in eighteenth-century France. One view holds that the Physiocrats were merely neomedievalists, seeking to negate the tenets of mercantilism and repair the shortcomings of the old order (Beer, *Inquiry*). The other takes the contrary position that the Physiocrats were reformists seeking to serve the needs and interests of the newly established commoner-landowners (Ware, "Physiocrats").

There seems to be an element of truth in both. A more likely interpretation is that the Physiocrats looked in both directions—backward toward feudalism and forward toward capitalism. If this interpretation is correct, then their position in the history of economic thought is both pivotal and transitional. The Physiocrats sought to preserve the exalted position of the landlord (i.e., the nobility) and the institution of private property, remnants of feudalism, but they also attempted to create conditions favorable to the emergence of agricultural capitalism. In other words, they were cautious reformers, unwilling to eclipse the old order entirely but eagerly promoting a new one that promised expanded national output.

In the end, the Physiocrats' most permanent imprint on the development of economic analysis may have been their influence on Adam Smith. Smith became acquainted with the Physiocrats during his travels in France. He was attracted to their systematic turn of mind, which he cultivated in his own reflections and expressions. For lack of this same systematic turn of mind in others, a general theory of economics had not yet surfaced in England.

■ The Spanish Enlightenment: Iberian Economics

While France stood in awe of The Sun King (Louis XIV) and the splendor of Versailles, its neighbor to the south, Spain, was mired in down-at-the-heels decadence—plagued with stagnation, lagging food production, and persistent internecine and interregional struggles for political power. This sad state of affairs was in part the consequence of mercantilist policies, which served the interests of the monarch, the aristocracy, and the Church, and in part the consequence of other factors, such as periodic plagues and the out-migration of human capital.[1] Spanish mercantilism established internal and external regulation that promoted monopolies, distorted resource allocations, and retarded economic growth. An early and persistent example of aristocratic rent seeking involved the Mesta organization—a cartel of sheepherders that protected the Merino wool export monopoly. This cartel (which was not formally abandoned until 1836) obtained property rights to migratory sheep "roads" and to tax revenues from shepherding, shifted resources away from sedentary agriculture, and established limits on urban growth in Spain for over 600 years. Bad economic policy and ruinous expenditures on wars of conquest and other monarchical adventures eventually bankrupted the Spanish state, forestalling the introduction of the Industrial Revolution in Iberia, and limiting its economic growth.

Voices of protest and reform naturally arose. A "Spanish Enlightenment" grew and flourished over the last half of the eighteenth century and the first decade of the

[1] The Moors, who had occupied Spain for seven centuries, had made important contributions to agriculture, architecture, and Spanish culture (see chapter 3). In 1492, prejudice and religious intolerance led to the expulsion of the Jews and the Moors from Spain. Economically, the plan backfired since many of both groups were commercial and financial entrepreneurs who supported and enabled economic growth.

nineteenth.[2] Much of the literature associated with this enlightenment movement was understandably surreptitious because those who challenged established economic interests were always in danger of imprisonment or harm. The Holy Inquisition, very much in action in Spain at this time, opposed any ideas and policies that challenged the wealth or authority of the Catholic Church. Reform proposals had to be introduced very carefully in order to avoid the harsh punishment of the Inquisition. Carefully crafted and sometimes anonymous pamphlets circulated underground in the service of reform. Even these would not have been possible without the support of Spain's "enlightened despots," Charles III (1759–1788) and Charles IV (1788–1808), who wanted to make the state independent of the Church and who supported the idea of state-directed reform.

A number of important social scientists and reformers bubbled up from this dangerous intellectual stew,[3] among them Manuel Rubin de Celis (1743–?), Gaspar Melchor de Jovellanos (1744–1811), Francisco de Cabarrús (1752–1810), and Pablo de Olavide (1725–1803). One of the greatest of these reformers was Count Pedro Rodríguez de Campomanes (1723–1802), who allegedly wrote *Discurso sobre el fomento de la industria popular* in 1774, two years before *The Wealth of Nations* appeared.[4] Widely read in Spain and Latin America, Campomanes's book was one of the most influential economic works within the Spanish-speaking world. Schumpeter said in praise of its author that "in view of the date of Campomanes' *Discurso* (1774) it is not without interest to observe how little, if anything, he stood to learn from the *Wealth of Nations*" (*History*, pp. 172–173). The contributions made by Campomanes and his followers can be grouped into two interrelated areas of economic theory and policy: (1) ideas related to liberalism and free trade, and (2) practical reforms relating to economic sociology and economic education.

Liberalism and Free Trade

Campomanes and his contemporaries were insistent that greater economic welfare in Spain hinged on a thoroughgoing reform of the system of landholdings and property rights. Spanish landed estates were "entailed," meaning that they could not be broken up for sale on the death of their owner. Land entails were upheld, and large aristocratic family holdings were maintained by the practice of primogeniture, which directed inherited landed property to the eldest son. A second factor contributing to intense concentration of landed property was the vast accumulation of land holdings by the Catholic Church. Campomanes saw entails as an economic problem because they prohibited widespread ownership of property and discouraged the productivity that flows from individual ownership. (In England, Adam Smith railed

[2] Indeed, Physiocracy itself made inroads into Spanish thought, but as Vicent Llombart ("Market for Ideas") has shown, its impact was selective and limited. Spain did not spawn a cadre of professional economists who were dedicated single-mindedly to theory or scientific rigor. Most economic writers were lawyers, civil servants, merchants, or military officers who shared a common enthusiasm for economics as a "useful science" and who professed an "enlightened faith" in political economy as a basic instrument of economic progress.

[3] The discussion in this section is based extensively on the research of D. R. Street (see references and notes for further reading).

[4] Campomanes was the author of many other works, a number of which contained ideas similar to those presented in the *Discurso*. However, a lively debate arose on the authorship of the *Discurso* of 1774, with some evidence suggesting that the authorship should be assigned to Manuel Rubin de Celis, a writer and translator during the Spanish Enlightenment and an admirer of Campomanes. This debate is elaborated in Street (1986; 1991), and Llombart (1991) (see notes for further reading).

against similar problems regarding the "enclosures" and problems associated with the "commons.") Economic efficiency—output of products and services—could not be maximized when the economy was characterized by concentrated ownership in the hands of a few.

Campomanes also used the *Discurso* to argue for self-interest and free trade in input and product markets. Spanish mercantilism, like its other geographic variants, established an elaborate system of impediments to internal trade. The craft guilds instigated laws that restricted movements of persons, products, and inputs. Foreigners were prohibited from working in Spanish industries, thus limiting the introduction of new technologies and foodstuffs. Campomanes advocated free movement of all domestic inputs and outputs and supported free international trade with the Americas as well. He also condemned the price controls—so popular during food shortages throughout history—that had helped promote food riots during the eighteenth century. His cohorts, Jovellanos, Cabarrús, and Olavide, promoted similar ideas.

These writers also emphasized the twin villains in Spain's stagnation—regulation and high taxation. They roundly condemned the privileges of the Mesta and the high taxes extracted by the king. Campomanes and his cohorts argued for lower taxes on peasants and higher taxes on the aristocracy and the Church. Given the authoritarian regime in Spain, they made such arguments at considerable peril to themselves.

Economic Societies and Economic Education

In order to give liberalism a practical face, Spanish Enlightenment economists promoted economic societies and educational reforms. Among other things, slow growth in the Spanish economy was attributed to the failure of Church-sponsored education, most especially in the universities. As Don Street wrote: "The venturesome reformers in Spain were searching for pragmatic means to develop the country, an education which entailed something other than vapid philosophizing by undedicated and ignorant professors who required students to learn by rote and who had no use for experimentation" ("Spanish Enlightenment Economics," p. 33). A major reform advanced by Spain's liberal economists was to establish "economic societies"—specialized extra-university institutions that were dedicated to specific tasks that would foster economic growth.

The Spanish economic societies founded after 1775 were often based on foreign models. Some examples include the royal Spanish Academy, the Academy of History, the Academy of Fine Arts of Saint Ferdinand, the School of Mines in Almadén, and the Museum and Botany Garden at Madrid. Because Church-run universities often exhibited a fear of the (practical and theoretical) sciences, many of the new economic societies were scientifically oriented. The Basque Economic Society, for example, established what might be called Spain's first "land grant college," the Seminario Patriótico Vascongado in Vergara (see Street, "Spanish Antecedents"). Courses commonly taught there included chemistry, mineralogy, metallurgy, public architecture, agronomy, and political science. The societies also encouraged experiments in agriculture, along with new crops and plant culture, which helped increase the efficiency of Spanish farming.

The practical advantages of these new forms of education led to a belief among economic reformers that human capital was as important in increasing the productivity of the Spanish economy as real fixed capital. In the same year that Smith published *The Wealth of Nations*, Jovellanos argued that "the returns to labor, whatever its object of application, will not be in simple proportion to the number of hands employed in it, but in the combined proportion of this number and of the improvement applied to labor" ("Economia civil," p. 10, translated by Street, "Spanish Enlightenment Economics," p. 36). These ideas and technical advances swept across the Atlantic to the colonies, where they were absorbed by Benjamin Franklin and George Washington, to name a few.

Other reformers were even more radical. Cabarrús, who was indebted to the French Enlightenment philosophers Rousseau and Voltaire, advocated closing the Church-run educational system and replacing it with a scientifically based secular system. He was particularly incensed by the abysmal conditions of public health and burial practices in the Spanish economy, conditions that spread plague-borne disease such as smallpox. (His interest in such reforms clearly anticipated those of Edwin Chadwick in mid-nineteenth-century England—see chapter 10). Cabarrús also struck a modern note by condemning Church regulation of "implicit" markets, such as marriage and divorce. His "radical" beliefs, coupled with his staunch support of free speech, brought him into inevitable conflict with the Catholic Church and its Holy Inquisition. (See the box, The Force of Ideas: Economic Sociology in Enlightenment Spain).

The Force of Ideas: Economic Sociology in Enlightenment Spain

Nobel Prize (1992) winner Gary Becker pioneered the modern economic theories of human capital and economic sociology. Economic sociology draws an analogy between markets for goods and services such as beets or shoes and markets for such "sociological" phenomena as sex, marriage, polygamy, or psychological security. For example, marriage obviously occurs for numerous reasons, but whatever the reasons, the decision to marry can usually be expressed in terms of expected costs and benefits. When the net benefits of marriage exceed those of remaining single, people marry.

Given the specialized nature of the traditional woman's role, women have been particularly vulnerable to economic disadvantage within the family "production unit."* Thus, marriage can be seen as an institutional response to minimize certain gender risk. As Becker (*Treatise*, p. 38) puts the issue, "Marriage includes a contract that has protected specialized women with limited alternatives against abandonment, neglect, and other ill treatment by their husbands." Marriage, in the traditional contract, provides protection for women who are vulnerable because of (nonmarket) biological specialization. Hence, the Catholic Church's insistence on the indissolubility of marriage is particularly beneficial for women who want to maximize the degree of certainty of the marriage contract. Divorce results if there are obstacles to efficient pricing in the marriage market (leading to marriages of poorly matched spouses), and/or if recontracting is not permitted after marriage bonds are established. If divorce is not possible, a *substitute for divorce* will usually result. Utility of individuals is clearly reduced if such mechanisms are not available.

Almost two centuries before Becker, such ideas were recognized by the radical Spanish liberal Francisco de Cabarrús. Although "conservative" by profession (he was head of the Banco de San Carlos, the first National Bank of Spain), Cabarrús's writings were the most radical ideas that floated free of direct Church control. In a *carta* (position paper) written in 1792 but not published until 1808, Cabarrús defended civil dissolution of marriage on the intuitive ground that divorce was the only solution to "utility" reductions of the individuals involved, and on the practical basis that it would (indirectly) improve public health. Cabarrús argued that divorce was tantamount to recontracting when "mistakes" are made, that even Jesus Christ condoned divorce in instances of adultery, and that adultery was prevalent in Spain.

Cabarrús's arguments are compatible with Becker's modern views of utility maximization, but he went further in introducing a public health issue as well. Divorce would limit venereal disease by reducing the tendency of disgruntled husbands to purchase the services of prostitutes. (This assumes, of course, that prostitutes are at higher risk of venereal disease than the female population at large.) He must have felt strongly about this issue because Cabarrús argued that, as long as divorce was impossible, prostitution should be legalized as a means of disease control!

Cabarrús proposed that houses of prostitution in large population centers should be run under the direction of an elected official. Patrol squads with officers would be assigned to major streets to keep order and avoid problems. Any sign of disease would cause immediate removal of the prostitute to a hospital for treatment. Brothels should be scrupulously policed for cleanliness, and sanitation measures should be required to reduce the risk of contracting diseases. Prostitutes would be identified by a yellow feather worn on the head and would be required to remain in their own districts. In addition to identifying house numbers, brothels would be required to display a sign giving the names, ages, and hometowns of the tradeswomen in order to settle any complaints and put down any disorder. In sum, Cabarrús recognized that legalized divorce and prostitution would have two important social effects. First, the happiness of the individuals (if not their families) would be increased. Second, whether or not divorce was an option, husbands' flight to prostitutes would be made safer.

Whatever the merits of Cabarrús's arguments, they did not carry the day. Rather, his views got him (and his liberal cohorts) into deep trouble with the Spanish religious establishment and with the Holy Inquisition. Although the power of the Inquisition had weakened somewhat when his *cartas* were officially published in 1808, Cabarrús nevertheless had to be on constant guard for his life. He had already been thrown in prison briefly in 1790 as a "dangerous subject." After his death in 1810 his writings were officially "prohibited" by the Inquisition.

Cabarrús's "conceptions of morality" (interpreted through the modern prism of Becker's ideas) remind us of certain similarities between markets for economic goods and markets for social goods. Specifically, in the face of technological change and utility-maximizing behavior, artificial controls on marriage, divorce, and prostitution are likely to be as self-defeating in their sphere of behavior as quotas and price controls are in the market for traditional goods.

*This discussion is based on R. B. Ekelund, D. R. Street, and A. B. Davidson, "Marriage, Divorce, and Prostitution."

Beset on all sides by opportunists, power brokers, and privileged classes, and at great personal risk, the Spanish Enlightenment economists made important contributions to what might be called a "practical" theory of markets that operated on the principle of self-interest. Some of their contributions anticipated *The Wealth of Nations* of the same era. Like Smith, these Spaniards set forth practical remedies aimed at removing impediments to economic development and combating economic stagnation. Their most durable insights consisted of recognizing the importance and economic vitality of human capital acquisitions and the urgent need to reform the educational system in order to equip Spain for industrial development in the nineteenth century.

■ Capitalism at the Junction of Ideas and History

Even a cursory survey of the antecedents of economic liberalism makes it clear that ideas pertaining to the nature and operation of markets were around long before Adam Smith ever codified them. In various countries and within a number of alternative institutional settings, the framework of market exchange was gradually and persistently yielding to closer examination by writers in Britain and Western

Europe. The writers whose ideas comprise the subject of this chapter paved the way toward the full-scale avowal of free markets as a leading force of economic development. These ideas clearly had consequences for the course of history. Without question the various "enlightenment" movements of England, Scotland, France, and Spain were central moving forces of historical events. But we must not overlook the possibility of feedback—that historical events played a part, perhaps even a large part, in the formation of ideas—much as the way in which self-interested parties in mercantilist England helped create a set of institutions that made domestic regulations harder to establish and enforce. Before examining Adam Smith's seminal work on free trade in part II (chapter 5), we pause to collect some of the historical elements that contributed to the acceptance of free trade and the tenets of capitalism, knowing full well that (1) it is difficult to untangle ideas from history and history from ideas, and (2) it is quite possible that all of the factors mentioned in the preceding and ensuing chapters are intertwined and mutually dependent.

The Decline of Catholicism and the Rise of Protestantism

We have already alluded to the prominent role played by the medieval Catholic Church over the early and later Middle Ages (see chapter 2). The Church's attempts to forestall entry into the market for religion took the form of punishments (such as excommunication and the Crusades) on the one hand and doctrinal innovations aimed at retaining membership on the other. By the early part of the sixteenth century, however, events conspired to permit successful and sustained entry into the market for Christian religion. After being excommunicated by the Catholic Church in 1521, Martin Luther (1483–1546), a former Augustinian monk and theologian, established Lutheranism (through the Augsburg Confession) in 1530. Luther was followed by John Calvin and a number of other Protestants who gave life to new forms of Christianity in the ensuing years. Details of this breakaway are complex, but the introduction of Protestantism and the sixteenth-century religious movement known as the Reformation had an enormous impact on the way social scientists view the emergence of capitalism.

Weber's Thesis

First published in German in 1904–05, Max Weber's *The Protestant Ethic and the Spirit of Capitalism* (1930) inaugurated an ongoing debate about how capitalism took hold in the Western world. Weber's analysis of the relationship between religion and economic development placed more emphasis on broad religious imperatives than on the specific injunctions that each religion imposes on economic behavior. He formulated the concept of a "Protestant ethic," suggesting uniformity among Protestant religions that are, in fact, fragmented in terms of moral codes, beliefs, doctrines, and practices. He suggested a link between this Protestant ethic and the "spirit" of capitalism, a connection posited to explain why Western civilization proved such fertile ground for the Industrial Revolution and the development of capitalism.

Although the Protestant ethic is derived from fundamental religious principles, in Weber's treatment it is both "secular" and "worldly." It includes, or perhaps spawns, an economic ethic: "the *summum bonum* of this ethic [is] the earning of more and more money combined with the strict avoidance of all spontaneous enjoyment of life" (*Protestant Ethic*, p. 53). For Weber, the *spirit* of capitalism is antecedent to the *emergence* of capitalism, and both derive from the Protestant ethic.

Nowhere in his study does Weber define "the spirit of capitalism," but he conveys its meaning in terms of Benjamin Franklin's homespun philosophy on the utility of virtue. Weber wrote:

> Honesty is useful because it assures credit; so are punctuality, industry, frugality, and that is the reason they are virtues. . . . According to Franklin, those virtues, like all others, are only in so far virtues as they are actually useful to the individual, and the surrogate of mere appearance is always sufficient when it accomplishes the end in view. (*Protestant Ethic*, p. 52)

Within this ethic, making money is not only the highest good, it is a *duty*, one that is closely connected to the religious idea of a *calling*: "The earning of money within the modern economic order is, so long as it is done legally, the result and the expression of virtue and proficiency in a calling" (*Protestant Ethic*, pp. 53–54). By Weber's reasoning economic success is a measure of individual virtue. It is this idea that sets his analysis apart. Yet, he limits his thesis to Western Europe and America, for he is well aware that "capitalism existed in China, India, Babylon, in the Classic World and in the Middle Ages. But in all these cases . . . this particular ethos was lacking" (*Protestant Ethic*, p. 52).

Popular and naive perversions of Weber's thesis notwithstanding, he did not claim that the Protestant ethic alone was sufficient to bring about the capitalist system—in other words, he did not assert that religion *causes* capitalism. Nor did he champion the extreme position that modern capitalism would not have come into existence without the Protestant ethic. Instead he maintained the intermediate position that the Protestant ethic significantly fostered and accelerated the development of Western capitalism. He was well aware that forms of capitalism existed prior to the Reformation; and he was equally aware that only in Western Europe and America did capitalism "develop in a way and on a scale sufficient to bring about an Industrial Revolution and an industrial civilization" (Lessnoff, *Spirit of Capitalism*). For Weber, therefore, there was something special about the development of Western capitalism *after* the Reformation. He found that special factor in the Protestant work ethic and its strong element of asceticism.

Protestant theology tells us that salvation is attained by faith alone, but it also advocates forms of human behavior that are pleasing to God, such as good works. Luther, in particular, decisively altered the (pre-Reformation) Christian conception of good works by prescribing the fulfillment of duties in worldly affairs as the highest form of moral activity that an individual can perform (Weber, *Protestant Ethic*). Calvin complicated matters by adding the doctrine of predestination. Under Calvin's influence, good works became a reliable, objective sign of grace, so that those who practiced good works could have their doubts assuaged and their fears allayed. After Calvin, good works became not so much a toll on the highway to heaven but rather a way of lessening or banishing the fear of eternal damnation. It is easy to see how the combination of Lutheran virtue and Calvinist asceticism yielded an ethos that stimulated entrepreneurs and artisans alike to achieve economic success in their respective spheres. This ethic constituted a dramatic shift from the Christian ethic of the pre-Reformation era.

Weber's thesis suggests that the emergence of the Protestant ethic redirected societal tastes and preferences from consumption to saving—thereby augmenting funds for investment and economic growth. Protestantism also may have affected economic growth in Western Europe in other ways. Generally, for example, Protestant rituals were simpler, with less pomp and pageantry, and churches were less elaborate in construction and ritual. Compared to the great Roman Catholic cathedrals of Europe far fewer resources were devoted to Protestant churches. It is quite possible, moreover, that Protestantism's rejection of the numerous feast days on the Catholic calendar generated an increase in the number of work days, thereby increasing labor inputs under Protestant regimes. Additionally, the new religion expunged the Roman Catholic system of "indulgences for pilgrimages" to churches and holy places, a factor that also might have contributed to economic growth.

Not surprisingly Weber's thesis has provoked numerous challenges. Some critics emphasize that a nascent "capitalism" and an extensive use of markets in international trade existed in the Italian city-states long before Luther's entry. Furthermore, the Catholic Church's doctrine of usury, selectively enforced, may have made less impact on economic growth than commonly claimed. The possibility also exists that by eliminating cruder forms of heresy in the pre-Enlightenment period the Catholic Church facilitated the introduction of the "age of reason" and its encouraging effect on the development of markets and investments. On the other hand, the medieval Roman Catholic Church sometimes impeded the advance of science, which became a lodestone of capitalism.

Medieval Science and the Emergence of Capitalism

Science and technology were leading edges of capitalism in Western Europe. Low-level science and a spirit of open inquiry, especially in the form of agricultural technology, was fostered first in Spain and then spread throughout Europe. The influx of Arabian Muslim tribes into the Iberian Peninsula in the eighth century ushered in a period of high prosperity that continued through the monarchy of Ferdinand and Isabella. The Moors husbanded and developed natural and human resources, including those in agriculture, manufacturing, and commerce. New plants and trees were introduced, irrigation systems were developed, herding was carried on in a manner consistent with agriculture, mining flourished, and the weaving of silk and wool was celebrated all over the Western world. Relatively free trade reigned and customs duties were held to moderate levels. Moorish propagation, maintenance, and defense of learning, especially pertaining to mathematics, science, and architecture, also encouraged the development of Western Europe.[5]

Inasmuch as established religion is concerned, the role of Christianity was curiously ambivalent. Christian missionaries helped fuel the development of capitalist organizations in parts of Europe, particularly in the North. Monasteries became agricultural estates that contributed to our knowledge of crop rotation and ranch technology. Hard science, a product of Enlightenment, advanced steadily, if not always spectacularly, in the fifteenth, sixteenth, and seventeenth centuries. And just as meteorology reduced the demand for rain dance or rituals, medieval science began to offer better explanations for events, especially by adopting empiricism and the newly evolving "scientific method." But the Catholic Church sometimes sacrificed medieval science on the altar of doctrinal orthodoxy. Antagonistic actions against late medieval scientists, including John Hus (burned at the stake in 1415), Copernicus, Bruno Hildebrand (burned at the stake in 1600) and, most famously, Galileo, cropped up repeatedly. Galileo's most important and notable contribution was his *Dialogue Concerning the Two Chief World Systems—Ptolemaic & Coperni-*

[5] General religious tolerance of both Christians and Jews was practiced by the Moors also, a favor that was not repaid them by the later Christian monarchs who banished both Muslims and Jews from Spain in 1492.

can (1632) in which he demonstrated the superiority of the Copernican theory that the earth revolved around the sun. Aged and infirm, Galileo could not withstand the rigors of the Inquisition, which found his defense of the Copernican system "gravely suspect of heresy" and insisted on his repudiation of certain scientific views. Rather than face torture, Galileo capitulated, thus becoming for all time an icon of the tension between science and religion.[6]

Knowledge is a powerful economic force, most effective when widely disseminated. Therefore, the invention of the printing press by Johann Gutenberg (in the fifteenth century) was a major catalyst to the development of capitalism. The rapid dissemination of printing had earthshaking implications for the course of civilization, establishing the foundation for widespread literacy; aiding the development of a "permanent Renaissance" in science, philosophy, and literature and establishing the basis of the modern world. Less than seven decades after Gutenberg, the new science of printing also facilitated the spread of Luther's and Calvin's "new" Christian religion, ultimately conjoined with other sects as Protestantism. Despite early heresies that the Church managed to deflect, once the printing press became available as a mass medium to publicize Church abuses it was more difficult for it to repel market intruders.

Gutenberg's brilliant invention also transformed communications in the secular world. Treatises on trade and the dissemination of accounting principles in printed form helped propel *ideas* about trade. The whole debate regarding the pros and cons of controls under mercantilism by pamphleteers in England and on the Continent (see chapter 3) would not have been possible without the printing press. By expanding literacy across medieval Europe, the printing press helped to launch the "first" information revolution (equaling and perhaps exceeding the modern revolution in digital technology). The ability to establish and build on ideas concerning trade and commerce was a powerful force leading to the (ultimate) demise of absolute monarchies and regulations over domestic and international commerce.

Preconditions of Market Exchange

The decline of mercantilism in England and Holland and its staying power in France and Spain meant that capitalism evolved at different rates throughout Europe. The full flowering of capitalism, and the Industrial Revolution that propelled it, could only occur after legal codes had firmly established sound credit practices and secure property rights. Despite the checks to monarchical power introduced by Parliament and the establishment of common law after the Glorious Revolution of 1680, England did not reach the desired state of stability for another forty years. Instability reigned as long as the Catholic "Pretender" (Prince Charles Edward Stuart) to the English throne was given sanctuary by the French monarch. From time to time, rumors of his return (with an army) created bank runs and financial panics in England. Thus, the credible commitments required to establish a stable capitalist economy had to wait until the House of Hanover ascended to the English throne in 1720. Along the way, mercantilism declined bit by bit, paving the way for new investment and expanded markets.[7]

[6] Although the Inquisition was formally abolished in 1908, its function was folded into a Catholic institution called the Congregation of the Holy Office, which was renamed in 1965, the Sacred Congregation for the Doctrine of the Faith. Its role is to censor and issue pronouncements on certain contemporary books, other forms of communications, and elements of culture.

[7] For details of this process, see Wells and Wills, "Revolution, Restoration, and Debt Repudiation."

Another major transformation in European economies was triggered by the Black Death (i.e., bubonic plague) that ravaged Europe and Asia in the fourteenth century, killing millions of inhabitants. By some estimates, the plague reduced the population of Europe to somewhere between one-half to two-thirds of former levels. The surprising impact of this disastrous event was to change the relative prices of labor, land, and capital used in production. Wages rose as labor became scarce relative to land. The consequences were manifold. Land tenure systems developed in a manner that gave the laboring peasantry more secure rights in the land they worked. Greater security of property rights in turn stimulated increased productivity; in their own self-interest, land owners and producers "economized" on the scarce factor (labor) by making larger investments in capital, which brought about high returns to innovation and invention in agriculture and other areas. The handmaiden of invention was new forms of power—from animal and human to water, steam, and eventually electric power, which fueled the Industrial Revolution throughout Europe and ushered in the modern age.

■ Conclusion

Up to this point we have taken a necessarily brief look at the intellectual movements and historical changes that signaled the end of authoritarianism and highly controlled markets. The breakdown of old habits and traditions was slow in coming, but the pace quickened as the eighteenth century unfolded. Nevertheless, Adam Smith did not arrive, as Venus, on a shell from the sea. He was, in a real sense, the repository of the accumulated wisdom that preceded him. Previous ideas regarding demand, exchange, and production were central to the advent of capitalism. The replacement of centralized control in the hands of absolute monarchs by decentralized market exchange and secure individual property rights established incentives that spurred invention and efficiency like never before. All of these so-called "preconditions" for economic growth were recognized and expounded by individuals who rose above mundane observations, laying groundwork for the market theory that was to come.

Historical events obviously propel evolutionary change, but less obviously they are themselves shaped by ideas that vie for acceptance over time. Institutions critical to the emergence of capitalism evolved throughout the long expanse of history leading to today. Economic theory often assigns such forces to intellectual limbo as "exogenous" factors, thereby avoiding messy consequences that do not bend easily to empirical treatment. But analysts neglect such matters at their peril.

Christian religion and its changing forms undoubtedly played a critical role in the transformations that were to come in economic organization, first throughout northern Europe and then in the United States of America. Whether the arguments of Max Weber have merit, it seems clear that religious regime changes were at least *associated* with the capitalist spirit (*causation* is of course another matter). Problems of cause and effect, such as those presented by the nexus of religion and economics, are notoriously difficult to solve. We must not hasten to make "definitive" pronouncements about the cause of major historical and economic transformations, but we are on solid ground by recognizing that many factors—intellectual, historical, and institutional—combined to produce the Industrial Revolution and the new world it ushered in. One conclusion that can be drawn from this chapter is that all of the intellectual and historical elements of market operation were in place at the opening of the eighteenth century. Nevertheless, it was Adam Smith, a Scottish philosopher, who crystallized for all time the case for free markets and capitalism.

References

Bacon, Francis. *The New Organon and Related Writings*, F. H. Anderson (ed.), New York: The Liberal Arts Press, 1960.

Baur, Stephan. "Studies on the Origin of the French Economists," *Quarterly Journal of Economics*, vol. 5 (1890), pp. 100–107.

Becker, Gary. *A Treatise on the Family*. Cambridge, MA: Harvard University Press, 1981.

Beer, Max. *An Inquiry into Physiocracy*. New York: Russell & Russell, 1966 [1939].

Boisguilbert, Pierre. *Le detail de la France* [1695]. Reprinted in Daire.

———. *Traité de la nature, culture, commerce et interet des grains* [1707]. Reprinted in Daire.

Cantillon, Richard. *An Essay on Economic Theory: An English translation of Richard Cantillon's Essai sur la nature du commerce en general*, Chantal Saucier (trans.), Mark Thornton (ed.). Auburn, AL: Ludwig von Mises Institute, 2010 [1755].

———. *Essai sur la nature du commerce en général*, H. Higgs (ed.). London: Macmillan, 1931.

Cole, C. W. *French Mercantilism 1683–1700*. New York: Columbia University Press, 1943.

Daire, Eugene. *Economistes et financiers du 18e siècle*. Paris: Guillaumin, 1851.

Ekelund, R. B., D. R. Street, and A. B. Davidson. "Marriage, Divorce, and Prostitution: Economic Sociology in Medieval England and Enlightenment Spain," *European Journal of the History of Economic Thought*, vol. 3 (Summer 1996), pp. 1–17.

Haney, L. W. *History of Economic Thought*, 4th ed. New York: Macmillan, 1949.

Jevons, William Stanley. "Richard Cantillon and the Nationality of Political Economy," *Contemporary Review*, 1881. Reprinted in Richard Cantillon, *Essai sur la nature du commerce en général*, H. Higgs (ed.). London: Macmillan, 1931, pp. 333–360.

Jovellanos, G. M. "Economia civil," in M. Artola (ed.), *Obras*. Madrid, 1956 [1776].

Lessnoff, M. H. *The Spirit of Capitalism and the Protestant Ethic: An Enquiry into the Weber Thesis*. Aldershot, UK: Edward Elgar, 1994.

Llombart, Vicent. "Market for Ideas and Reception of Physiocracy in Spain: Some Analytical and Historical Suggestions," *European Journal of the History of Economic Thought*, vol. 2 (Spring 1995), pp. 29–51.

Meek, R. L. *The Economics of Physiocracy: Essays and Translations*. Cambridge, MA: Harvard University Press, 1962.

Murphy, Antoin E. *Richard Cantillon: Entrepreneur and Economist*. Oxford: Oxford University Press, 1986.

Murray, James M. "Entrepreneurs and Entrepreneurship in Medieval Europe," in D. S. Landes, J. Mokyr, and W. J. Baumol (eds.), *The Invention of Enterprise: Entrepreneurship from Ancient Mesopotamia to Modern Times*. Princeton, NJ: Princeton University Press, 2010.

Petty, William. *The Economic Writings of Sir William Petty*, 2 vols., C. H. Hull (ed.). New York: A. M. Kelley, 1963.

Schumpeter, J. A. *A History of Economic Analysis*. E. B. Schumpeter (ed.). New York: Oxford University Press, 1954.

Street, D. R. "The Economic Societies: Springboard to the Spanish Enlightenment," *Journal of European Economic History*, vol. 16 (Winter 1987), pp. 569–585.

———. "Spanish Antecedents to the Hatch Act Experiment System and Land Grant Education," *Agricultural History*, vol. 62 (1988), pp. 27–40.

———. "Spanish Enlightenment Economics," *SECOLAS Annals*. Statesboro: Georgia Southern University (1994), pp. 30–42.

Ware, N. J. "Physiocrats: A Study in Economic Rationalization," *American Economic Review*, vol. 21 (December 1931), pp. 607–619.

Weber, Max. *The Protestant Ethic and the Spirit of Capitalism*, Talcott Parsons (trans.), with foreword by R. H. Tawney. London: George Allen & Unwin, 1930 [1904–05].

Wells, John, and Douglas Wills. "Revolution, Restoration and Debt Repudiation: The Jacobite Threat to England's Institutions and Economic Growth," *Journal of Economic History*, vol. 60 (June 2000), pp. 418–441.

Notes for Further Reading

Sir William Petty's writings were collected and published together for the first time in 1899 by Charles Henry Hull (see references, Petty, *Economic Writings*). Hull prefaced the whole collection with a lengthy introduction on Petty's life and writings, including the issue of John Graunt's role in the development of statistics and his probable influence on Petty. A brief but able study of Petty's economics has been produced by Alessandro Roncaglia, *Petty: The Origins of Political Economy* (Armonk, NY: M. E. Sharpe, 1985). Tony Aspromourgos offers his retrospective on Petty in "The Life of William Petty in Relation to His Economics: A Tercentenary Interpretation," *History of Political Economy*, vol. 20 (Fall 1988), pp. 337–356. A. M. Endres examines Political Arithmetick in general and Petty's use of numbers in "The Functions of Numerical Data in the Writings of Graunt, Petty, and Davenant," *History of Political Economy*, vol. 17 (Summer 1985), pp. 245–264. On Petty and Cantillon together, see A. Brewer, "Petty and Cantillon," *History of Political Economy*, vol. 24 (Fall 1992), pp. 711–728. Marx drew inspiration from Petty's concept of surplus, but the idea has a more extensive pedigree. For a historical treatment of how early economists looked at the problem of producing enough agricultural product to sustain the population, and how to get that surplus to consumers, see Anthony Brewer, "The Concept of an Agricultural Surplus from Smith to Petty." *Journal of the History of Economic Thought*, vol. 33 (December 2011), pp. 487–505. Among others, Brewer considers the ideas of Petty, Cantillon, Hutcheson, Hume, Steuart, Mirabeau, and Smith.

The standard reference on Boisguilbert is Hazel Roberts's *Boisguilbert, Economist of the Reign of Louis XIV* (New York: Columbia University Press, 1935), but it is now dated somewhat. For a more recent assessment, see Gilbert Faccarello, *The Foundations of Laissez-Faire: The Economics of Pierre de Boisguilbert* (London: Routledge, 1999). See also J. J. Spengler, "Boisguilbert's Economic Views vis-à-vis Those of Contemporary Reformateurs," *History of Political Economy*, vol. 16 (Spring 1984), pp. 69–88. C. W. Cole (see references) devotes part of his work to Boisguilbert (pp. 231–267) as, in even larger measure, does J. H. Bast, *Vauban and Boisguilbert* (Groningen: P. Noordhoff, 1935). Boisguilbert's role as an early precursor of Keynes is discussed by S. L. McDonald, "Boisguilbert: Neglected Precursor of Aggregate Demand Theorists," *Quarterly Journal of Economics*, vol. 68 (August 1954), pp. 401–414.

The mystery surrounding Richard Cantillon does not stop with the man but extends to his *Essai* as well. Until at least the 1750s, a number of drafts survived of Richard Cantillon's *Essay on the Nature of Trade in General*, in different stages of completion. This is suggested by a paragraph-by-paragraph comparison between three versions of Cantillon's writings, namely the French *Essai* of 1755, fragments of Postlethwayt's *Universal Dictionary* (1752–1754), and Philip Cantillon's *Analysis of Trade* (1759). Richard van den Berg, "'Something Wonderful and Incomprehensible in Their Œconomy': The English Versions of Richard Cantillon's Essay on the Nature of Trade in General," *The European Journal of the History of Economic Thought*, vol. 19 (2012), pp. 868–907, claims that while numerous variations between the texts may be attributed to free translation practice or to interventions by later editors, others cannot; he suggests a comparative study of variations may provide us with insights into the development of the ideas of this masterful economic theorist.

The standard translation of Cantillon's *Essai sur la nature du commerce en général* by Henry Higgs (1931), though useful for several generations, has become less serviceable over time. A new English translation by Chantal Saucier, edited by Mark Thornton, has been published by the Ludwig Von Mises Institute with the title *An Essay on Economic Theory* (2010). Jevons hailed his rediscovery of Cantillon in "Richard Cantillon and the Nationality of Political Economy," *Contemporary Review* (January 1881), reprinted in Higgs (see references, Cantillon, *Essai*). An overview of Cantillon's work and his role in the history of economics is provided by J. J. Spengler, "Richard Cantillon: First of the Moderns," *Journal of Political Economy*, vol. 62 (August, October, 1954), pp. 281–295, 406–424. Cantillon's originality is also the theme of Mark Thornton, "Richard Cantillon and the Origins of Economic Theory," *Journal des Economistes et des Etudes Humaine*, vol. 8 (March 1998), pp. 61–74.

The Irish economist Joseph Hone, "Richard Cantillon, Economist-Biographical Note," *Economic Journal*, vol. 54 (April 1944), pp. 96–100, sought to establish 1697 as the date of Cantillon's birth, but this claim has been discredited by more recent research. The details of Richard Cantillon's life have long been shrouded in mystery, but a provocative biography by Antoin Murphy, *Richard Cantillon: Entrepreneur and Economist* (Oxford: Clarendon Press, 1986), sheds much light on this "mystery man" of economics. A major episode in Cantillon's banking career was his association with John Law's paper money scheme and his connection with the "Mississippi Bubble." For illuminating background on this period, see Earl J. Hamilton, "The Political Economy of France at the Time of John Law," *History of Political Economy*, vol. 1 (1969), pp. 123–149. Also, see Antoin Murphy, *John Law: Economic Theorist and Policymaker* (Oxford: Oxford University Press, 1997).

Cantillon's monetary theory is discussed briefly in relation to other preclassical theorists in Joseph Ascheim and C. Y. Hsieh, *Macroeconomics: Income and Monetary Theory* (Columbus: Merrill, 1969), pp. 144–146. A. M. Huq, "Richard Cantillon and the Multiplier Analysis," *Indian Journal of Economics*, vol. 39 (April 1959), pp. 423–425, emphasizes another macroeconomic theme in Cantillon's *Essai*. Antoin Murphy, "John Law and Richard Cantillon on the Circular Flow of Income," *European Journal of the History of Economic Thought*, vol. 1 (Autumn 1993), pp. 47–62, seeks to show that John Law had a prior claim to both Cantillon and Quesnay as the originator of the circular flow of income and expenditure.

The special role of land and its utilization in Cantillon's work is the subject of Hans Brems, "Cantillon versus Marx: The Land Theory and the Labor Theory of Value," *History of Political Economy*, vol. 10 (Winter 1978), pp. 669–678; Anthony Brewer, "Cantillon and the Land Theory of Value," *History of Political Economy*, vol. 20 (Spring 1988), pp. 1–14; and Tony Aspromourgos, "Cantillon on Real Wages and Employment: A Rational Reconstruction of the Significance of Land Utilization," *The European Journal of the History of Economic Thought*, vol. 4 (Autumn 1997), pp. 417–443. Other specific aspects of Cantillon's economics are treated in R. F. Hébert, "Richard Cantillon's Early Contributions to Spatial Economics," *Economica*, vol. 48 (February 1981), pp. 71–77; Renee Prendergast, "Cantillon and the Emergence of the Theory of Profit," *History of Political Economy*, vol. 23 (Fall 1991), pp. 419–430; Mark Thornton, "Cantillon on the Cause of the Business Cycle," *Quarterly Journal of Austrian Economics*, vol. 9 (Fall 2006), pp. 45–60; and same author, "Richard Cantillon and the Discovery of Opportunity Cost," *History of Political Economy*, vol. 39 (Spring 2007), pp. 97–120.

A divergence of opinion exists on whether Cantillon was a mercantilist. See Anthony Brewer, "Cantillon and Mercantilism," *History of Political Economy*, vol. 20 (Fall 1988), pp. 447–460; and two papers by Mark Thornton, "Was Richard Cantillon a Mercantilist?" *Journal of the History of Economic Thought*, vol. 29 (December 2007), pp. 417–435; and "Cantillon, Hume and the Rise of Anti-Mercantilism," *History of Political Economy*, vol. 39 (Fall 2007), pp. 453–480.

The Physiocrats helped pioneer the deductive method in economics while emerging as the first group of economic model builders. The logico-deductive background of eighteenth-century French thought is explored by Daniel Klein, "Deductive Economic Methodology in the French Enlightenment: Condillac and Destutt de Tracy," *History of Political Economy*, vol. 17 (Spring 1985), pp. 51–72; and Martin S. Staum, "The Institute Economists: From Physiocracy to Entrepreneurial Capitalism," *History of Political Economy*, vol. 19 (Winter 1987), pp. 525–550.

A penetrating study of the origins of Physiocracy, including the interaction between Quesnay and Mirabeau, can be found in E. Fox-Genovese, *The Origins of Physiocracy* (Ithaca, NY: Cornell University Press, 1976). Christine Théré and Loïc Charles, "The Writing Workshop of François Quesnay and the Making of Physiocracy," *History of Political Economy*, vol. 40 (Spring, 2008), pp. 1–42, provide a glimpse of the early days of the Physiocrats (before 1764), when Quesnay carefully controlled the research agenda of the group and it functioned more like a workshop than a distinct "school" of thought.

On Quesnay's liberal leanings versus his reliance on authority, see R. F. Hébert, "Authority Versus Freedom in Quesnay's Thought," *European Journal of the History of Economic Thought*, vol. 3 (Summer 1996), pp. 18–42. The standard general guide to Physiocracy for many years has been Henry Higgs, *The Physiocrats* (London: Macmillan, 1897), but it is now considered somewhat outdated. Also dated, but still accessible, is the treatment given the Physiocrats by Charles Gide and Charles Rist in their textbook *A History of Economic Doctrines from the Time of the Physiocrats to the Present Day*, R. Richards (trans.), 2d ed. (Boston: Heath, 1948). Much of the physiocratic literature is now available in English, thanks to Meek (see references). Stephan Baur (see references) examines the role of economic thought prior to the Physiocrats, as well as the influence of the Physiocrats on Adam Smith. As noted in the text, conflicting interpretations of Physiocracy exist between Beer (see references) and Ware (see references). D. C. Carbaugh attempted a reconciliation between the two opposing views in "The Nature of Physiocratic Society: An Attempted Synthesis of the Beer–Ware Interpretations," *American Journal of Economics and Sociology*, vol. 33 (April 1972), pp. 199–207. For a more recent review of the debate, see G. Schacter, "François Quesnay: Interpreters and Critics Revisited," *American Journal of Economics and Sociology*, vol. 50 (July 1991), pp. 313–322.

Some notable attempts to trace the origins of physiocratic thought are to be found in R. S. Franklin, "The French Socioeconomic Environment in the Eighteenth Century and Its Relation to the Physiocrats," *American Journal of Economics and Sociology*, vol. 21 (July 1962), pp. 299–307; O. H. Taylor, "Economics and the Idea of 'Jus Naturale,'" *Quarterly Journal of Economics*, vol. 44 (February 1930), pp. 205–241; and L. A. Maverick, "Chinese Influences upon the Physiocrats," *Economic History*, vol. 3 (February 1938), pp. 54–67. Along the same lines, see Bert Hoselitz, "Agrarian Capitalism, the Natural Order of Things: François Quesnay," *Kyklos*, vol. 21 (1968), pp. 637–662; and José Benitez-Rochel and Luis Roblels-Teigeiro, "The Foundations of the *Tableau Économique* in Boisguilbert and Cantillon," *The European Journal of the History of Economic Thought*, vol. 10 (Summer 2003), pp. 231–248. See also, Loïc Charles, "The Visual History of the *Tableau Économique*," *The European Journal of the History of Economic Thought*, vol. 10 (Winter 2003), pp. 527–550.

An attempt to explain Quesnay's nettlesome premise about the exclusive productivity of agriculture has been mounted by H. Spencer Banzhaf, "Productive Nature and the Net Product," *History of Political Economy*, vol. 32 (Fall 2000), pp. 517–551. Articles that explore the relationship of Quesnay to his contemporaries include W. Eltis, "L'Abbé Condillac and the Physiocrats," *History of Political Economy*, vol. 27 (Summer 1995), pp. 217–236; T. P. Neill, "The Physiocrats' Concept of Economics," *Quarterly Journal of Economics*, vol. 63 (November 1949), pp. 532–553; and same author, "Quesnay and Physiocracy," *Journal of the History of Ideas*, vol. 9, no. 2 (1948), pp. 153–173.

Mary Jean Bowman, "The Consumer in the History of Economic Doctrine," *American Economic Review*, vol. 41 (May 1951), pp. 1–18, discusses, among other things, the views of the Physiocrats. Their doctrines of foreign trade in relation to mercantilist and classical ideas are investigated by A. I. Bloomfield in "The Foreign Trade Doctrines of the Physiocrats," *American Economic Review*, vol. 28 (December 1938), pp. 716–735. P. Steiner, "Demand, Price and Net Product in the Early Writings of F. Quesnay," *European Journal of the History of Economic Thought*, vol. 1 (Spring 1994), pp. 231–251, explores the neglected role of demand in Quesnay's thought.

For different treatments of physiocratic tax proposals, see L. Einaudi, "The Physiocratic Theory of Taxation," in *Economic Essays in Honor of Gustav Cassel* (London: G. Allen, 1933); and G. B. Buurman, "A Comparison of the Single Tax Proposals of Henry George and the Physiocrats," *History of Political Economy*, vol. 23 (Fall 1991), pp. 481–496. W. J. Samuels looks at policy and institutions in physiocratic writings in two articles: "The Physiocratic Theory of Property and State," *Quarterly Journal of Economics*, vol. 75 (February 1961), pp. 96–111; and "The Physiocratic Theory of Economic Policy," *Quarterly Journal of Economics*, vol. 76 (February 1962), pp. 145–162.

The tableau as an analytical device has attracted the attention of several writers; see Almarin Phillips, "The *Tableau Economique* as a Simple Leontief Model," *Quarterly Journal of Economics*, vol. 69 (February 1955), pp. 137–144; I. Hishiyama, "The *Tableau Économique* of Quesnay," *Kyoto University Economic Review* (April 1960), pp. 1–46; T. Barna, "Quesnay's *Tableau* in Modern Guise," *Economic Journal*, vol. 85 (September 1975), pp. 485–496; and Lars Herlitz, "The *Tableau Économique* and the Doctrine of Sterility," *Scandinavian Economic History Review*, vol. 9 (1961), pp. 3–55; same author, "From Spending and Reproduction to Circuit Flow and Equilibrium: The Two Conceptions of the *Tableau Économique*," *The European Journal of the History of Economic Thought*, vol. 3 (Spring 1996), pp. 1–20; and in same journal and issue, Walter Eltis, "The *Grand Tableau* of François Quesnay's Economics," pp. 21–43.

J. J. Spengler offers some important insights as to how the physiocratic theory of consumption may have contributed to one of the cornerstones of classical economic theory in "The Physiocrats and Say's Law of Markets." *Journal of Political Economy*, vol. 53 (September 1945), pp. 193–211; and J. Johnson treads similar ground in "The Role of Spending in Physiocratic Theory," *Quarterly Journal of Economics*, vol. 80 (November 1966), pp. 612–632. A major reinterpretation of Quesnay and his system has been undertaken by W. A. Eltis, in two parts, "François Quesnay: A Reinterpretation," *Oxford Economic Papers*, vol. 27 (July and November, 1975), pp. 167–200, 327–351. See also A. C. Muller, "Quesnay's Theory of Growth: A Comment," *Oxford Economic Papers*, vol. 30 (March 1978), pp. 150–156; and the further comment by Eltis immediately following Muller's remarks.

In a series of papers spanning several years, Gianni Vaggi systematically explored key aspects of physiocratic thought. See, for example, "The Physiocratic Theory of Prices," *Contributions to Political Economy*, vol. 2 (March 1983), pp. 1–22; "A Physiocratic Model of Relative Prices and Income Distribution," *Economic Journal*, vol. 95 (December 1985), pp. 928–947; "The Role of Profits in Physiocratic Economics," *History of Political Economy*, vol. 17 (Fall 1985), pp. 367–384; and *The Economics of François Quesnay* (London: Macmillan, 1987).

Quesnay's Tableau Économique, Marguerite Kuczynski and Ronald L. Meek (eds.), London: Macmillan, 1972), reveals the extraordinary story of the disappearance and reappearance of successive editions of the *Tableau*. Joseph Schumpeter's *History of Economic Analysis* (New York: Oxford University Press, 1954), part II, chap. 4, deals with Petty and Cantillon as well as with the Physiocrats. Jean Cartelier, "Productive Activities and the Wealth of Nations: Some Reasons for Quesnay's Failure and Smith's Success," *The European Journal of the History of Economic Thought*, vol. 10 (Autumn 2003), pp. 409–427, highlights important differences between two writers whose production theories were very close to each other.

The writings of individual Physiocrats tend to be scattered and inaccessible. A notable exception concerns the most able of Quesnay's followers, Turgot. Most of Turgot's economic writings have been collected and translated by R. L. Meek, *Turgot on Progress*,

Economics and Sociology (London: Cambridge University Press, 1973); and by P. D. Groenewegen, *The Economics of A. R. J. Turgot* (The Hague: Martinus Nijhoff, 1977). See also, same author, "A Reappraisal of Turgot's Theory of Value, Exchange and Price Determination," *History of Political Economy*, vol. 2 (Spring 1970), pp. 177–196; and "A Reinterpretation of Turgot's Theory of Capital and Interest," *Economic Journal*, vol. 81 (June 1971), pp. 327–340. For a broader sweep of Turgot's ideas on progress and the emergence of institutions, see Philippe Fontaine, "Social Progress and Economic Behaviour in Turgot," *Perspectives on the History of Economic Thought*, vol. 7, S. T. Lowry, ed. (Aldershot, UK: Edward Elgar, 1992); and same author, "Turgot's 'Institutional Individualism,'" *History of Political Economy*, vol. 29 (Spring 1997), pp. 1–20. Anthony Brewer, "Turgot, Founder of Classical Economics," *Economica*, vol. 54 (November 1987), pp. 417–428, makes the case for Turgot as a classical economist rather than a Physiocrat.

For a summary of the economic writings of a Physiocrat who later expatriated to America, see J. J. McLain, *The Economic Writings of DuPont de Nemours* (Newark: University of Delaware Press, 1977). José Luis Cardoso, "Economic Thought in Late-Eighteenth Century Portugal: Physiocratic and Smithian Influence," *History of Political Economy*, vol. 22 (Fall 1990), pp. 429–441, establishes the reach of Physiocracy beyond France. Finally, for a broad sweep of French economic thought (including Cantillon) in the century prior to Adam Smith, see R. F. Hébert, "In Search of Economic Order: French Predecessors of Adam Smith," in S. Todd Lowry (ed.), *Pre-Classical Economic Thought* (Boston: Kluwer, 1987), pp. 185–210.

Comparatively little work has been done on the important contributions of Spanish Enlightenment economists in English. But see Louis Baeck, "Spanish Economic Thought: The School of Salamanca and the *Arbitristas*," *History of Political Economy*, vol. 20 (Fall 1988), pp. 381–408. For those who read Spanish, see Pedro Rodriguez de Campomanes, *Discurso sobre el fomento de la industria popular* (1774), Facsimile, Oviedo (1979); Francisco de Cabarrús, "Cartas" (1808), in J. A. Maravall (ed.), *Conde de Cabarrús* (1973). Authorship of the former is evaluated by D. R. Street, "The Authorship of Campomanes' *Discurso sobre el fomento de la industria popular:* A Note," *History of Political Economy*, vol. 18 (1986), pp. 655–660, and debated by Vicent Llombart, "The *Discurso sobre el modo de fomentar la industria popular* and the *Discurso sobre el fomento de la industria popular*, two editions of the same work by Campomanes: A Reply to D. R. Street," *History of Political Economy*, vol. 23 (1991), pp. 527–531, and Street's "Reply" (same issue), pp. 533–536. The Spanish Enlightenment and issues relating to retarded Spanish economic growth and its causes is treated in R. Herr, *The Eighteenth Century Revolution in Spain* (Princeton, NJ: Princeton University Press, 1958); and, by the same author, *Rural Change and Royal Finances in Spain* (Berkeley: University of California Press, 1989). An excellent overview is given by J. Vicens-Vives, *An Economic History of Spain* (Princeton, NJ: Princeton University Press, 1969). The particular and peculiar role of the Mesta guild of sheepherders in the Spanish economy is treated in J. Klein, *The Mesta: Study in Spanish Economic History 1273–1836* (Port Washington, NY: Kennikat Press, 1964 [reprint of 1920 edition]), and R. B. Ekelund, Jr., D. R. Street, and R. D. Tollison, "Rent Seeking and Property Rights Assignments as a Process: The Mesta Cartel of Mercantile Spain," *The European Journal of Economic History* vol. 26 (1997), pp. 9–35. In addition to works already mentioned by D. R. Street, see "The Human Capital Movement in the Spanish Enlightenment," *Midsouth Journal of Economics and Finance*, vol. 13 (1989), pp. 43–50, and "Jovellanos, An Antecedent to Modern Human Capital Theory," *History of Political Economy*, vol. 20 (1988), pp. 191–206.

Two excellent books on Spanish Enlightenment economics are Vicent Llombart, *Compomanes, economista y politica de Carlos III* (Madrid: Alionza Editorial, 1992); and L. Perdices, *Pablo de Olavide, El Ilustrado* (Madrid: Editorial Complutense, 1992).

Part II

The Classical Period

After 1776 the field of economics gathered steam, much like the Industrial Revolution that nurtured it. By giving organization to economics, Adam Smith focused the world's attention on the subject, and inspired a number of subsequent thinkers to turn their talents to this new field. Nowhere was this direction of effort more feverish than in England, where, in relatively rapid succession, David Ricardo, Robert Malthus, and John Stuart Mill laid important bricks in the mounting edifice of economic theory. So fertile was this age of economic analysis that the interval from 1776 to 1870 is now called the classical period.

Adam Smith was a key figure. His efforts to systematize economics and to construct a theory of economic development are presented in chapter 5. His ideas had a twofold effect: They discredited mercantilism as an economic creed and they set the pattern of future inquiry. Although there is a unifying thread running through classical macroeconomics, especially the British variant, there were also dissenting voices. Jeremy Bentham, a lawyer by training, developed a utilitarian creed that rejected Smith's theme of "natural harmony" and sought to promote an "artificial harmony" of interests in its place. Bentham's ideas are presented in chapter 6, and his influence, traced through Mill and his contemporary, Edwin Chadwick, is explored in Part III. Robert Malthus, whose population theory became an integral component of mainstream classical economics, nevertheless remained a maverick on several key points of macroeconomic theory, especially on the nature of aggregate demand (where he foreshadowed John Maynard Keynes). Malthus and his position on key issues are discussed in chapters 6 and 7. Departing slightly from Smith, Ricardo (chapter 7) sought to refocus economics on the issue of income distribution—but he did so within the analytical framework and macroeconomic focus established by Smith. Absorbing the intricacies of Ricardo's economics from an early age, Mill (chapter 8) attempted to synthesize and improve economic thought from Smith to his day.

5

Adam Smith
System Builder

That new dawn of capitalism that the Physiocrats so eagerly looked forward to had not yet arrived in 1776—when many Europeans were focused on the New World and the struggles of an emerging nation—but it was certainly on its way. And it was helped along, intellectually, by the publication in that year of a book that is still read and still published (not just by and for graduate students, incidentally): Adam Smith's *Inquiry into the Nature and Causes of the Wealth of Nations*. The prominence of this book in the development of economics gave its author the consensual title, "father of economics."

Adam Smith was born in Kircaldy, Scotland, in 1723. He was the only son of a father who died a few months before his birth and a mother who lived to the ripe old age of ninety. From his youth, Smith exhibited traits that we often attribute to "professorial" types. His biographers describe him as an apt pupil, although given to "fits of abstraction," which later in his academic life turned to fits of reverie that frequently unsettled his colleagues (when they observed him smiling to himself at religious services, for example). In one of his early morning reveries, clad in his nightgown, Smith walked fifteen miles before the church bells from a neighboring village "awakened" him. Absentmindedness seems to have been a feature of his character. On one occasion, engaged in a lively discourse while walking with a friend, and unaware of his whereabouts, he fell into a tanning pit! On another he is said to have absentmindedly dropped his bread and butter into boiling water. Moments later when he drank the concoction he declared it the worst cup of tea he had ever tasted.

A cameo portrait of Smith reveals an unhandsome visage marked by a protruding lower lip, a large nose, and bulging eyes. He was troubled all his life with a nervous affliction; his head shook, and he had a speech impediment. Yet, none of these flaws impaired his intellectual abilities, and his other charms endeared him to his friends and students. He described himself as "a beau in nothing but my books." To be sure, he was well versed in a wide array of subjects: He lectured not only on economics but also on broad philosophical issues and on literature. Students traveled from Russia and the Continent to attend his lectures. He was thoroughly acquainted with the writers of Greek and Roman antiquity as well as with the authors of his own day, especially his teacher Frances Hutcheson, his friend David Hume, and the eminent French philosopher, Montesquieu. During his travels in France he was introduced to Quesnay and his band of followers.

Smith cemented his reputation as a philosopher on the basis of his important work, *The Theory of Moral Sentiments*, first published in 1759. In this treatise Smith attempted to identify the origins of moral judgments, or moral approval and disapproval. Smith represented man as a creature of self-interest who nevertheless is capable of making moral judgments on the basis of considerations other than selfishness. This apparent paradox is resolved, Smith asserted, through the faculty of sympathy. That is, moral judgments are typically made by holding self-interest in abeyance and putting oneself in the position of a third-person, impartial observer. In this way, one reaches a sympathetic notion of morality rather than a selfish one, and morality actually transcends selfishness.

The Theory of Moral Sentiments and its problems attracted immediate interest and fame for its author. But some scholars regard its basic tenet as inconsistent with the importance Smith later placed on self-interest as a driving force in *The Wealth of Nations*. Informed opinion tends to view *The Wealth of Nations* as a logical extension of *The Theory of Moral Sentiments*, although that is not a unanimous judgment. Nineteenth-century German philosophers, who could not resolve the seeming contradiction between self-interest and sympathy, referred to it as *Das Adam Smith Problem*. Whether or not resolved to everyone's satisfaction, it is noteworthy that the progression in Smith's thought from an inquiry into justice (*The Theory of Moral Sentiments*) to an investigation of political economy (*The Wealth of Nations*) is fully consistent with the evolution of ideas exhibited by the Christian and Arabic Scholastics.

■ The Nature of Smith's Economic System

Adam Smith's prominent place in the history of economics owes much to the fact that he was a system builder. His system combined a theory of human nature and a theory of history with a peculiar form of natural theology and some hard-headed observations of economic life. In the narrow confines of the economic sphere, his system featured agriculture, manufacturing, and commerce. Exchange in this system is facilitated by the use of money, and production is characterized by the division of labor. The three main features of his central analysis are the division of labor, price and allocation, and the nature of economic growth.

Smith's focus on economics as an issue of moral philosophy gave the subject legitimacy and marked the beginning of what is called the classical period in economic thought. This period extends roughly from the appearance of *The Wealth of Nations* in 1776 to the death of John Stuart Mill in 1873. Although individual differences in ideas persisted among members of the classical school, commonly held principles included belief in natural liberty (laissez-faire) and the importance of economic growth as a means of bettering the condition of human existence.[1] Physiocracy, which is also based on these two premises, was rejected by Smith because it was too narrowly focused on agriculture as the source of wealth.

Natural Law and Property Rights

Unlike Cantillon, Smith made no attempt to segregate politics from economics, and as a result the subject that he pioneered in the eighteenth century came to be known as "political economy." The chief political and economic problems that Smith sought to define and resolve were the relation of the individual to the state and the

[1] Although he falls within the classical period, John Stuart Mill was somewhat of an exception on both these points (see chap. 8).

proper functions of the state in relation to its members. Smith's views on these matters were grounded in his system of natural theology, which he expounded at considerable length in *The Theory of Moral Sentiments* and carried forward, with some modifications, to *The Wealth of Nations*. That theology was none other than the Greek-Scholastic doctrine of natural law, albeit infused with Scottish common sense.

We have seen that the Physiocrats extolled a natural order based on natural law as opposed to positive law. For them, natural law reflected the mind of the creator, as inferred by human reason. It existed on a higher plane than positive law, which consisted of the mere proclamations of a legislative assembly. Because positive law was inferior to natural law, the less of it the better. This is one intellectual justification for laissez-faire. Both the Physiocrats and Adam Smith argued essentially in this vein.

In an attempt to illuminate the nature of natural law Sir Alexander Gray has pointed out that

> natural law is easier to talk about than to codify. But we come pretty near the core of things when we regard natural law as concerned with the personal property each individual has in himself, and as a groping effort to emphasize that there is a body of "Rights of Man" existing anterior to, and if need be against, the State. To express it in terms nearer our subject, "Natural Law" implies a restriction of the functions of government, in the interests of the liberty of the individual. ("Adam Smith," p. 155)

All through *The Wealth of Nations* and its predecessor, *The Theory of Moral Sentiments*, Smith explained how the divine government of the universe reacts on our immediate economic and political problems. The famous metaphor he used to drive home this point has come to known as the "invisible hand":

> Every individual necessarily labours to render the annual revenue of the society as great as he can. He generally, indeed, neither intends to promote the public interest, nor knows how much he is promoting it. By preferring the support of domestic to that of foreign industry, he intends only his own security; and by directing that industry in such a manner as its produce may be of the greatest value, he intends only his own gain, and he is in this, as in many other cases, led by an invisible hand to promote an end which was no part of his intention. Nor is it always the worse for the society that it was no part of it. By pursuing his own interest he frequently promotes that of the society more effectively than when he really intends to promote it. I have never known much good done by those who affected to trade for the public good. It is an affectation, indeed, not very common among merchants, and very few words need be employed in dissuading them from it. (*The Wealth of Nations*, p. 423)

This was both revolutionary and counter-intuitive to the ordinary eighteenth-century mind. If individuals are guided "naturally" by self-interest to promote the greater good of society, then there is no need for the kind of central planning that authoritative governments engage in. But Smith had already underscored the futility of central planning caused by the ineptness of bureaucrats and politicians in the *Theory of Moral Sentiments*:

> The man of system . . . is apt to be very wise in his own conceit; and is often so enamored with the supposed beauty of his own ideal plan of government, that he cannot suffer the smallest deviation from any part of it. He goes on to establish it completely, and in all its parts, without any regard either to the great interests, or

> to the strong prejudices which may oppose it. He seems to imagine that he can arrange the different members of a great society with as much ease as the hand arranges the different pieces upon a chess-board. He does not consider that the pieces upon the chess-board have no other principle of motion besides that which the hand impresses upon them; but that, in the great chess-board of human society, every single piece has a principle of motion of its own, altogether different from that which the legislature might choose to impress upon it. (pp. 380–381)

These passages underscore Smith's conviction that a natural harmony exists in the economic world that makes government interference in most matters both unnecessary and undesirable. The invisible hand, the doctrine of natural liberty, and the wisdom of God (seen even in the folly of men) are all part of the argument. But there is more than mere metaphysics at work here. Smith also advanced the empirical argument that government is *in fact* incompetent, and he emphasized the brazen impertinence of the bureaucrat who tells us what to do in areas where we clearly know our own interests much better than anyone else ever can. (Paradoxically, however, when Smith was presented the opportunity to become a regulator, he accepted—see the box, The Force of Ideas: Adam Smith as Regulator.)

The Force of Ideas: Adam Smith as Regulator

In *The Wealth of Nations* Adam Smith repeatedly attacked mercantilism and the intricate system of government regulations it spawned. It is therefore curious that two years after the appearance of his economic magnum opus Smith accepted an appointment as commissioner of Scottish Customs and the Salt Duties, a position he held until his death in 1790. In the eighteenth century, customs commissioners had broad enforcement powers: They were basically "import police," even maintaining their own small navy. The commission prosecuted smugglers and authorized the seizure and burning of their vessels, the breaking up of illegal liquor stills, and searches of private property. Chiefly, however, it functioned as a tax-collecting agency of British mercantilism, providing a major source of revenue for the royal government. In 1781, customs duties contributed almost one-fourth of total revenues collected in the United Kingdom.

How did the apostle of free trade spend his time as a regulator? Did he use the opportunity to reform customs administration, to deregulate a mercantilist agency, or did he behave as a hard-nosed regulator? The evidence is that Smith took his job seriously; that he worked diligently as a government regulator; and that he was more concerned with bureaucratic efficiency than philosophical principle during his tenure on the customs commission.* He expressed neither outrage nor boredom with his duties; nor did he seek to reform the agency or undermine its functions.

One would expect that the mundane job of collecting customs duties and enforcing customs law would be less intellectually stimulating than teaching at university or writing major philosophical tracts. Yet, Smith seemed to enjoy his role as an applied economist, even if it seems incongruous with his reputation as the prophet of economic liberalism. Does this episode tell us anything about the compelling force of self-interest that Smith put at the base of individual behavior?

When Smith took office as customs commissioner in 1788 he was fifty-five years old. His academic reputation was secure. He may have felt that his academic career had peaked. The job of customs commissioner paid £600 per year, a tidy sum in its day, but not much more than Smith could realize from alternative sources. Chances are he embraced the job of civil servant because (1) his family had a long history of employment as customs officials, and (2) he found the work interesting and challenging. Was he any less an economist for working on the side of the economic system he had railed against? Not unless one believes that the power of ideas is less than the power of individual action. Personal actions notwithstanding, published ideas are subject to large economies of scale. One clear and forceful idea in published form can reach and influence a large number of people at a relatively small cost. Moreover, ideas take time to form in people's minds and are influential only after a considerable lag. It is therefore far more likely that Smith would influence history by his written words than by his example in one small agency of a vast bureaucratic system. Adam Smith the deregulator—if he had chosen to exercise such a role—could never have been as much a force for economic liberalism as Adam Smith the teacher and author.

*See G. M. Anderson, W. F. Shughart, and R. D. Tollison, "Adam Smith in the Customhouse."

Human Nature

Smith's advocacy of natural liberty rested on, and was impelled by, human psychology. He was a hardheaded realist who took people as he found them and based his analysis of society on an unchanging human character. Smith attributed two innate features to the human psyche. The first is that as humans we are interested primarily in things nearest us, and much less so in things at a distance (in either time or space); thus, we are all of considerable importance to ourselves:

> Every man . . . is first and principally recommended to his own care; and every man is certainly, in every respect fitter and abler to take care of himself than of any other person. (*Theory of Moral Sentiments*, p. 359)

The second feature of human psychology, actually a corollary of the first, is the overwhelming desire of all individuals to better their condition:

> The desire of bettering our condition [is] a desire which, though generally calm and dispassionate, comes with us from the womb, and never leaves us till we go to the grave. In the whole interval which separates those two moments, there is scarce perhaps a single instant in which any man is so perfectly and completely satisfied with his situation, as to be without any wish of alteration or improvement of any kind. (*The Wealth of Nations*, pp. 324–325)

It is easy to confound self-interest (or Smith's preferred term "self-love") with unbridled selfishness, although Smith was careful to distinguish the two. A society that allows selfishness to run amuck is one that degenerates into chaos. Smith's "economic" man in *The Wealth of Nations* is not unlike his "moral" man in *The Theory of Moral Sentiments*. Both are creatures of self-interest, but their baser instincts are held in check by twin forces. In the moral sphere, *sympathy* is the faculty that holds self-interest in check; whereas in the economic sphere, *competition* is the faculty that restrains self-interest. Competition is the invisible hand that we identified earlier. In this way Smith was proposing a natural solution to "the Hobbesian dilemma," the belief expressed by Thomas Hobbes that a society without extensive government controls would devolve into chaos, making human life "nasty, poor, brutish and short." The key to understanding Smith's liberal philosophy is that an effective regulatory force (i.e., competition) exists in the nature of markets, making artificial (i.e., legislative) regulations unnecessary—and due to inherent governmental inefficiency—undesirable.

Monopoly, however, is the antithesis of competition and provides an avenue by which unbridled self-interest can destroy the economic welfare of society. Although all sellers of goods and services would like to charge the highest possible prices for their wares or skills, they generally cannot, unless they have some monopoly privilege, and in Smith's day, the source of monopoly privileges was (mercantilist) government. Some of Smith's most memorable passages contain invectives against monopoly privileges. (All of the excerpts from this point on are from Smith's *The Wealth of Nations*, unless otherwise noted.) In one place he wrote: "People of the same trade seldom meet together, even for merriment and diversion, but the conversation ends in a conspiracy against the public, or in some contrivance to raise prices" (p. 128). Elsewhere, he said: "Monopoly . . . is a great enemy to good management, which can never be universally established but in the consequence of that free and universal competition which forces everybody to have recourse to it for the sake of self-defense" (p. 147).

A Theory of History: Self-Interest and Economic Growth

In Adam Smith's view, the historical process of economic growth is driven by the interaction of self-interest, property rights, and the division of labor. The interplay of these forces in the proper institutional framework contributed to the coming of the "commercial age" and comprised the foundation of Smith's macroeconomics.

To Smith the history of civilization was characterized by four evolutionary stages. The first is characterized by hunting tribes; the second by pastoral pursuits; the third by sedentary farming; and the fourth by commerce. Each stage entails a different structure of property rights. A hunting culture does not recognize exclusive rights to property. All members of society stand on a relatively equal footing, both economically and socially, and there is little demand for a formal structure of civil government because the population is small and mobile. Leadership in such a culture is customarily provided by the old and the wise, whose direction is accepted by the rest of society in deference to their experience and superior intellect.

Over time, however, self-interest stimulates important sociopolitical evolution and economic growth. Civil society is a consequence of changing relations of private property and wealth. Speaking of an early transition in civil society, for example, Smith observed:

> Among nations of hunters, as there is scarce any property, or at least none that exceeds the value of two or three days labour; so there is seldom any established magistrate or any regular administration of justice . . . civil government is not so necessary.
>
> It is in the age of shepherds, in the second period of society, that the inequality of fortune first begins to take place, and introduces among men a degree of authority and subordination which could not possibly exist before. It thereby introduces some degree of that civil government which is indispensably necessary for its own preservation. . . . Civil government, so far as it is instituted for the security of property, is in reality instituted for the defense of the rich against the poor, or of those who have some property against those who have none at all. (p. 674)

In other words, in civil society a wealth hierarchy leads to a power hierarchy that establishes the rules of hereditary transfers of power, administration of justice, and so forth. In this way, security of property rights is assured and the stability that comes with secure property rights encourages production of more wealth.

Eventually, nomadic cultures tend to be replaced by stationary, agricultural communities. This settled life brings more stable food supplies, increased specialization, and larger population. In the Middle Ages, agricultural interests functioned within an institutional structure known as feudalism. Civil government under feudalism was greatly decentralized insofar as each of the manorial barons administered justice in his local domain. In Europe, this system lasted from the fall of the Roman Empire to about the end of the fifteenth century. Its structure is still approximated in some third-world nations today.

Just as self-interest explains the transition from nomadic to agricultural societies, so it explained for Smith the development of commercial society with its consequent growth of cities as trading centers. In the immediate period after the fall of Rome, urban tradesmen and mechanics were given equal tax treatment with their rural counterparts, the farmers. As city dwellers became more independent, however, merchants succeeded in getting a general exemption from certain "trading taxes." They therefore emerged as an early class of "free traders," and indeed, as the first capitalists. Townspeople, moreover, were usually allied with the monarch against their common foe, the land barons. The king often granted concessions to the cities in return for their allegiance against the feudal lords, and eventually fiscal independence could be obtained by the cities in return for a lump-sum tax paid to the king. These developments led to self-governance in the towns and the eventual establishment of a rule of law, which in turn provided a firm base for the expansion of trade, particularly in the coastal cities. Flourishing trade, in turn, made the cities even more independent of the manors. Ultimately towns became the haven of fledgling capitalists because city law protected runaway serfs, provided they had evaded capture for one year. Smith recognized this as a step in the accumulation of capital by the lower classes:

> If in the hands of a poor cultivator, oppressed with the servitude of villeinage, some little stock should be accumulated, he would naturally conceal it with great care from his master, to whom it would otherwise have belonged, and take the first opportunity of running away to a town. (p. 379)

Serfdom/villeinage/feudalism all describe the same thing: an institution in which peasants worked the land and were tied to it but did not own it. Serfs owed a certain amount of labor to the landlord, but once they accumulated small surpluses, they found that they could "buy back" this obligation by paying money rents to the landlords in lieu of labor services. First the surpluses were exchanged for money at the local grain markets; then the money was used to "commute" their labor obligation. This often resulted in a situation in which the peasant became very nearly an independent, small businessperson. He or she could rent from the lord, sell the produce to cover his rent, and keep the difference. The cumulative effect of this behavior was to erode the traditional ties of the manor and to substitute the market and the search for profits as the organizing principle of production. By the middle of the fourteenth century money rents exceeded the value of labor services in many parts of Europe.

The lords seemed willing to cooperate with the new institutional arrangements, in part because as their consumption patterns changed they required increasing amounts of cash to buy "trinkets" and luxuries from the town merchants. Before long, the lord of the manor was a mere landlord in the modern sense; soon a "market" in land emerged, based on an individual's right to own property, and was supported by the law of contract. From this point it was a short step to specialization and the division of labor—the hallmarks of the industrial age.

In sum, economic growth up to the appearance of the "commercial system" was a consequence of the interaction of self-interest, the evolution of property rights, and institutional change in the wider sense. By 1776, signs of the arrival of the commercial system were evident. Having observed this, Smith declared economic growth to depend in a critical way on the extension of specialization and division of labor. After reviewing the microeconomic foundations of Smith's growth theory we shall return to the central role of these twin principles.

The Wealth of Nations is a formidable book, and it is doubtful if even many economists have read it cover to cover. But it is a task that every serious student of economics should attempt (at least once). For the book contains much more than Smith's celebrated attack on mercantilism (monopolies) and his justification of natural liberty (laissez-faire), for which it is best known. Even by contemporary standards it is a marvelous work. And it was not a late-blooming classic, as were so many other economic treatises. It was widely read and quoted during Smith's lifetime.

A brief review of the contents of *The Wealth of Nations* reveals its breadth of treatment. Book I discusses the division of labor, the origin and use of money, and the determination of price, wages, profits, and rent, with a lively digression thrown in on variations in the value of silver. Book II contains Smith's oft-maligned theory of capital and interest. In Book III the reader is treated to a lengthy review of the economic development of Europe from ancient times to the eighteenth century. Book IV discusses different systems of political economy, including a scathing criticism of mercantilism and barriers to free trade. Book V concludes with a lengthy treatise on taxation and fiscal policy in eighteenth-century Britain. The final pages offer Smith's assessment of Britain's colonial policy and the wisdom of empire building.

In many ways the least-read parts of the book are the most delightful, as when Smith digresses on the history of education in the Middle Ages or the method of selecting bishops in the ancient Church. In fact, Smith's discussions of education and religion form points of departure for two related subfields of contemporary economic inquiry: the economics of education and the economics of religion. By a similar token, the field of public finance owes much to Smith's ample treatment in Book V. We cannot do justice to the full scope of Smith's contribution to the development of economics here; consequently we focus on the cornerstones of microeconomic and macroeconomic analysis presented in Books I–III.

■ Microeconomic Foundations of *The Wealth of Nations*

For all its diverse coverage of numerous economic topics, the central theme of *The Wealth of Nations* is economic development. Whereas the Physiocrats focused on growth of net product, Smith emphasized growth in national wealth (by which he meant, in today's terminology, national income). In one important respect, Smith succeeded where the Physiocrats did not. Smith established his macroeconomic theory of economic development on microeconomics, most notably the theory of value.

The Theory of Value

The chapter on value in *The Wealth of Nations* is preceded by a discussion of the advantages of division of labor and the use of money in advanced societies. Smith argued that the division of labor arises from a propensity in human nature to exchange, which requires that each trader have more goods than necessary to satisfy immediate needs (i.e., exchange requires a tradable surplus). Money enters the picture because it makes trade more flexible and convenient. Value then is determined by the rules that people naturally observe in exchanging goods for money or for one another. Smith posed the problem of value in terms of the following paradox:

> The word value . . . has two different meanings, and sometimes expresses the utility of some particular object, and sometimes the power of purchasing other goods which the possession of that object conveys. The one may be called "value in use"; the other, "value in exchange." The things which have the greatest value in use have frequently little or no value in exchange; and on the contrary, those which have the greatest value in exchange have frequently little or no value in use. Nothing is more useful than water: but it will purchase scarce anything; scarce anything can be had in exchange for it. A diamond, on the contrary, has scarce any value in use, but a very great quantity of other goods may frequently be had in exchange for it. (p. 28)

Smith did not resolve this riddle; he merely focused on the issue of value-in-exchange as central to his inquiry. So long as the significance of *incremental* valuations was overlooked this riddle was never adequately solved. Eventually the paradox yielded when the distinction was made and widely understood between total utility and marginal utility. Because water is plentiful, its value at the margin is low (reflecting low-priority uses); whereas because diamonds are scarce, their value at the margin is high (reflecting high-priority uses). Somehow this distinction (and its consequences) never quite crystallized in the minds of most classical economists as long as they remained preoccupied with the distinction between *value-in-use* and *value-in-exchange*. Smith set out to explain only exchange value, or relative price, and its changes over time.

Labor as a Measure of Value. Book I, chapters 5 to 7, of *The Wealth of Nations* contains the core of Smith's discussion of exchange value. It is a discussion that is marred by his tendency to treat simultaneously both the measure of value (price) and the cause of value. In chapter 5, for example, Smith writes that labor is the measure of value:

> The value of any commodity . . . to the person who possesses it, and who means not to use or consume it himself, but to exchange it for other commodities, is equal to the quantity of labour which it enables him to purchase or command. Labour, therefore, is the real measure of the exchangeable value of all commodities. (p. 30)

Smith seems to have acquired this idea, that what is bought with money (or with goods) is purchased by labor, from his friend David Hume, although the same idea was expressed earlier by Sir William Petty (see chapter 4). There are, however, certain practical and theoretical difficulties in a labor theory of value that Petty was unable to surmount. Smith revealed his awareness of these problems:

> It is often difficult to ascertain the proportion between two different quantities of labour. The time spent in two different sorts of work will not always alone determine this proportion. The different degrees of hardship endured, and of ingenuity exercised, must likewise be taken into account. There may be more labour in an hour's hard work than in two hours easy business; or in an hour's application to a trade which it cost ten years labour to learn, than in a month's industry at an ordinary and obvious employment. But it is not easy to find any accurate measure either of hardship or ingenuity. In exchanging indeed the different productions of different sorts of labour for one another, some allowance is commonly made for both. It is adjusted, however, not by any accurate measure, but by the higgling and bargaining of the market, according to that sort of rough equality which, though not exact, is sufficient for carrying on the business of common life. (p. 31)

Prices. Money is, of course, the most common measure of value, but Smith wanted to substitute labor in its place because he recognized that the value of money itself changes over time. He observed that everything has a real and a nominal price—the former unaffected by changes in the purchasing power of money. On this important distinction Smith wrote:

> Labour, like commodities, may be said to have a real and nominal price. Its real price may be said to consist in the quantity of the necessaries and conveniences of life which are given for it; its nominal price, in the quantity of money. The labourer is rich or poor, is ill or well rewarded, in proportion to the real, not the nominal, price of his labor. (p. 33)

It turns out that labor is an adequate measure of price only in a primitive economy ruled by barter. In Chapter 6, Smith finally makes it clear that when one leaves "that early and rude state of society which precedes both the accumulation of stock and the appropriation of land," labor alone cannot adequately explain market price. Capitalist economies are marked by capital accumulation and individual property rights in land and other resources. Thus, Smith asserts that in the more advanced societies market value is resolved into three component parts:

> Wages, profit, and rent are the three original sources of all revenue as well as of all exchangeable value. All other revenue [interest income, taxes, etc.] is ultimately derived from some one or other of these. (p. 52)

By this point in his exegesis, we can see that Smith is talking about the source of value and not merely its measure. By including profit as one of the necessary components of price, Smith demonstrated an understanding of the concept of opportunity costs, an idea also grasped by Cantillon. He observed:

> Though in common language what is called the prime cost of any commodity does not comprehend the profit of the person who is to sell it again, yet if he sells it at a price which does not allow him the ordinary rate of profit in his neighborhood, he is evidently a loser by the trade; since by employing his stock in some other way he might have made that profit. (p. 55)

Notice the natural development of ideas in these two chapters of *The Wealth of Nations*. Many writers before Smith had a labor-cost theory of value, and many writers after him attributed the same theory to Smith. But his explanation is really something else. It is one thing to charge that the true measure of value, in real terms, is labor time, and another to avow that the source of value is the necessary costs of production for each commodity. In short, Smith felt that labor theories of value were valid only for primitive societies where labor represents the main (if not the only) factor of production.

Market Price versus Natural Price. Chapter 7 of Book I is filled with what Mark Blaug called "the kind of 'partial equilibrium analysis' that has always been the bread and butter of economists" (*Economic Theory*, p. 39). In it, Smith discusses the natural and market price of commodities. Essentially, he set up a dichotomy between actual (i.e., market) price and natural (i.e., equilibrium) price. The former is determined by the interaction of supply and demand in the short run; the latter, by long-run costs of production. He wrote:

> The market price of every particular commodity is regulated by the proportion between the quantity which is actually brought to market, and the demand of those who are willing to pay the natural price of the commodity, or the whole value of the rent, labour, and profit, which must be paid in order to bring it thither. Such people

> may be called the effectual demanders, and their demand the effectual demand; since it may be sufficient to effectuate the bringing of the commodity to market. It is different from the absolute demand. A very poor man may be said in some sense to have a demand for a coach and six; he might like to have it; but his demand is not an effectual demand, as the commodity can never be brought to market in order to satisfy it. (p. 56)

More than a century later, Alfred Marshall (see chapter 16) presented a graphically explicit explanation of price that clarified Smith's distinction between natural and market price. Marshall's explanation is based on the now familiar concepts of supply and demand *schedules*, concepts that proved remarkably difficult for earlier writers to conceive and explain. It is not at all clear whether Smith thought of price and quantity adjustments in terms of shifting schedules of demand and supply or simply as movements along a given curve (or curves)—if, indeed, he thought of adjustments in this way at all. But we can use Marshall's analysis to interpret Smith and clarify his meaning.

Thus, in figure 5-1 (on the following page) assume some price—say, p_0—is equivalent to Smith's natural price. Furthermore, assume this price to be equal to the sum of the "natural rates of wages, rent, and profit," and to remain unchanged over time. Smith's concept of effectual demand suggests the existence of a downward-sloping demand curve. The poor beggar who would like to have a coach and six but cannot afford it would eventually purchase one, perhaps, if the price were low enough. Others of varying degrees of wealth might find their demands becoming "effective" at lower prices. Thus, in figure 5-1 assume the existence of demand curve D_0. Smith's effectual demand (i.e., quantity demanded at the natural price) is Q_0. Barring changes in tastes, incomes, prices of other goods, numbers of demanders and suppliers, and expectations about the future, p_0 and Q_0 would be the long-run equilibrium price and output in the industry under investigation. Let us now juxtapose Smith's commentary and figure 5-1:

> When the quantity of any commodity which is brought to market falls short of the effectual demand [Q_1], all those who are willing to pay the whole value of the rent, wages, and profit which must be paid in order to bring it thither, cannot be supplied with the quantity which they want [Q_0]. Rather than want it altogether, some of them will be willing to give more. A competition will immediately begin among them, and the market price will rise more or less above the natural price [to p_1, for example], according as either the greatness of the deficiency or the wealth and wanton luxury of the competitors, happen to animate more or less the eagerness of the competition. Among competitors of equal wealth and luxury the same deficiency will generally occasion more or less eager competition, according as the acquisition of the commodity happens to be of more or less importance to them. Hence the exorbitant price of the necessaries of life during the blockade of a town or in a famine. (p. 56)

The last sentence above is a clear reference to the importance of demand elasticity in the short run. Continuing in Smith's language, consider the reverse market situation:

> When the quantity brought to market exceeds the effectual demand [Q_2], it cannot be all sold to those who are willing to pay the whole value of the rent, wages, and profit, which must be paid in order to bring it thither. Some part must be sold to those who are willing to pay less, and the low price which they give for it must reduce the price of the whole. The market price will sink more or less below the natural price [to p_2, for example], according as the greatness of the excess

> increases more or less the competition of the sellers, or according as it happens to be more or less important to them to get immediately rid of the commodity. The same excess in the importation of perishable, will occasion a much greater competition in that of durable commodities. (p. 57)

The last sentence in the above passage is likewise a clear reference to the importance of supply elasticity in the short run.

Finally, Smith describes the conditions necessary to achieve balance in the marketplace:

> When the quantity brought to market is just sufficient to supply the effectual demand and no more, the market price naturally comes to be either exactly, or as nearly as can be judged of, the same with the natural price [p_0]. The whole quantity on hand can be disposed of for this price, and cannot be disposed of for more. The competition of the different dealers obliges them to accept of this price, but does not oblige them to accept of less. (p. 57)

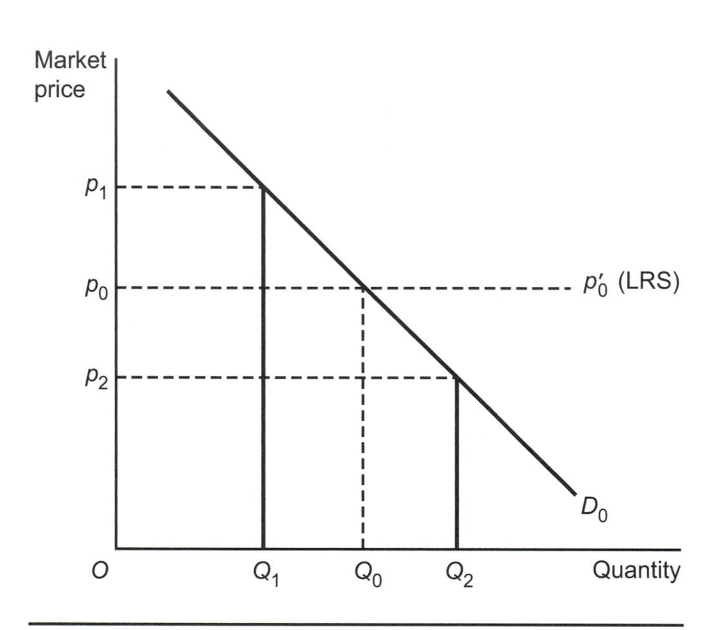

Figure 5-1 If Q_1 represents the quantity brought to the market, then the market price will rise above the natural price, from p_0 to p_1. A similar adjustment would occur if Q_2 were brought to market.

One can see in these passages the fundamental line of argument advanced by the medieval Scholastics (chapter 2). But Smith improved the earlier exposition by explaining how competitive forces work as a natural mechanism to drive buyers and sellers toward an equilibrium. He recognized that the economic realities of emergent capitalism made the doctrine of just price superfluous. In the "medieval" world markets were stunted and most trade did not take place under competitive conditions. Power was concentrated in the hands of few sellers. By contrast, Smith's "modern" world was one in which atomistic competition flourished, and economic power was thereby diffused. This diffusion of power, Smith argued, provided an automatic check to the individual *abuse* of power, which was a matter of great concern to the Scholastics. Smith's theory of natural price fulfilled the conditions for economic justice set forth by the Church doctors, but it did so not by appealing to moral codes but rather the natural forces of the competitive marketplace.

There is reason to believe, however, that Smith was not entirely comfortable with the abstract notions of price and equilibrium. Recall that in Scholastic economics (chapter 2) there were two competing "theories" vying for dominance: the supply side and the demand side. Each made its own claim to preeminence. The supply side argument maintained that since market price must cover costs of production over the long haul, value must be a function of the resources used in production. The demand side makes its own claim to being a determinant of value because people are willing to pay for something in proportion to the intensity of their desire. Smith noted that value can be influenced by utility (demand), but for reasons unknown he did not advance this side of the analysis. His contribution to demand theory is pretty much limited to a distinction between absolute demand (aggregate desire) and effectual demand (desire + purchasing power). Effectual demand is the demand of buyers who are willing to pay the "natural price," which is the price sufficient to cover production costs. Smith evidently felt that the "cost theory" of value needed further analysis, and he seemed to want to choose labor as the common denominator underlying the supply-side elements of value. He appeared, moreover, to be groping for an absolute and universal *measure* of value, but it was beyond his grasp. Smith's attempt to resolve the two sets of claims, supply and demand, led to the description of equilibrium outlined above.

There are two points that need to be emphasized regarding Smith's value theory. The first is that Smith represented the natural price as an equilibrium value (i.e., "the central price to which the prices of all commodities are continually gravitating") and as an *invariant* quantum over the long run. In modern parlance, he envisioned the long-run supply curve as horizontal (represented by the dashed line, p_0 p_0' in figure 5-1). Since this type of long-run supply curve exists only in industries characterized by constant (unit) costs of production, Smith's theory of value fits only a special case. Today economists recognize that many industries produce under conditions of increasing costs, and a few actually produce under conditions of decreasing costs.

The second point is that Smith was aware of the abstract nature of his model. He explained how real markets often deviate from the ideal:

> Though the market price of every particular commodity is in this manner continually gravitating, if one may say so, towards the natural price, yet sometimes particular accidents, sometimes natural causes, and sometimes particular regulations of police, may, in many commodities keep up the market price, for a long time together, a good deal above the natural price. (p. 59)

Smith's terminology needs to be appreciated for what it is. By "accidents" he meant events that cause information to be withheld from either sellers or buyers, such as trade secrets or clandestine production techniques. Examples of "natural causes" that push prices above the "natural" level include limited acreage of certain peculiar soils. Wine lovers know, for example, that all the land fit for producing Mouton-Rothschild clarets cannot supply the effectual demand, so that the price of this wine is many times its cost of production. Adam Smith felt that little could be done about the capriciousness of nature, and that trade and manufacturing secrets could not be kept for very long. But government intervention (i.e., "particular regulations of police") could keep actual prices above natural prices permanently. The British economy in Smith's day, rife with the institutional remnants of mercantilism, imposed restrictive practices that prevented many markets from reaching equilibrium, thereby limiting the volume of trade, internal and external, hindering the division of labor, and retarding economic development.

In a mercantilist economy, government is the source of monopoly privileges. Smith was quick to point out the parallel between government grants of monopoly privileges and trade secrets:

> A monopoly granted either to an individual or to a trading company has the same effect as a secret in trade or manufacturers. The monopolists, by keeping the market constantly understocked, by never fully supplying the effectual demand, sell their commodities much above the natural price, and raise their emoluments, whether they consist in wages or profits, greatly above the natural rate. (p. 61)

In the final analysis, Smith's model of market equilibrium was based on cause and effect, but he was careful to explain its abstract nature. Economic reality is different from theory because it entails conditions that slow or prevent smooth and certain adjustments to long-run equilibrium. On this score, it is instructive to compare Smith to the Physiocrats (see chapter 4), who viewed the *Tableau économique* as a rigid form of cause and effect. In their model, a given change in the primary income flows among the three socioeconomic classes of society created exact and continuing changes in national income. Despite his admiration for these "French men of system," Smith felt that the Physiocrats became unwitting captives of their own abstractions. Ever the Scottish realist, Smith regarded economic life as neither simple nor precise.

We must not overlook the fact that Smith had an enlightened view of the interdependence between product markets and factor markets, and that this interdependence is basic to his concept of long-run price adjustments. He noted, for instance, that if at any time the quantity of a good supplied exceeded the effectual demand:

> Some of the component parts of its price must be paid below their natural rate. If it is rent, the interest of the landlords will immediately prompt them to withdraw a part of their land; and if it is wages or profit, the interest of the labourers in the one case, and of their employers in the other, will prompt them to withdraw a part of their labour or stock from their employment. The quantity brought to market will soon be no more than sufficient to supply the effectual demand. All the different parts of its price will rise to their natural rate, and the whole price to its natural price. (p. 57)

In other words, according to Smith, product prices cannot be in long-run equilibrium unless factor prices are also in long-run equilibrium. The operation of all interdependent markets achieving simultaneous equilibrium constitutes what we now call general-equilibrium analysis, the formal mathematics of which were developed in the following century by the French economist Léon Walras (see chapter 17).

Smith's concept of natural value was an important clarification of advances made by earlier writers, but nevertheless it remains tautological. The theory of natural value explains price in terms of cost of production. But costs are themselves prices. They are payments made to purchase (or hire) the various factors of production. In essence, then, the theory of natural value explains prices by prices. A complete theory of value cannot stop here but must also explain the cause and determination of the payments to each factor of production.

Factors and Their Shares

Actually, Smith did not develop a satisfactory theory of the determination of wages, profit, and rent, but he did offer numerous important insights and contributions that were later expanded by his followers. It can be said that Smith offered as many as three explanations of wages, three explanations of rent, and perhaps two explanations of profit. In the discussion that follows we don't emphasize the analytical elegance of Smith's ideas so much as the wide range of penetrating insights that he entertained on the subject of income distribution.

Wages. Smith begins his discussion of wages as he did his discussion of value, by harking back to "that original state of things which precedes both the appropriation of land and the accumulation of stock." In a primitive society, wages are determined by productivity: "In that original state of things . . . the whole produce of labour belongs to the labourer. He has neither landlord nor master to share with him" (p. 64). But things change as institutions change. As soon as land becomes private property, the landlord demands his or her share of the annual produce, and as soon as capital accumulation occurs, the capitalist does likewise. Thus, the landlord and the capitalist share in the produce of labor, and Smith says that once this happens it becomes purposeless to trace further the possible effects of increased labor productivity on wages. Unfortunately this view retarded subsequent developments in the theory of income distribution, but nevertheless, it set the stage for Smith's development of the classical wages-fund concept, which played a prominent part in the refinement of Smith's theories by Ricardo, Malthus, and others. Smith's more refined theory of wages, such as it was, is contained in the wages-fund doctrine.

From an analytical standpoint the difficulty that confronts us so many years later is that the wages-fund was, simultaneously, a theory of wages *and* a theory of capital. The predominant view of wage payments throughout most of the eighteenth and nineteenth centuries can be summarized as follows: Accumulated capital makes it possible to employ labor and thus constitutes a fund for the maintenance of a working population. This fund consists of *advances to workers* for which the owner of the fund (i.e., the capitalist) expects, and is entitled to, a return. Although the notion of the wages-fund was not original with Smith, he gave the idea popular form:

> It seldom happens that the person who tills the ground has wherewithal to maintain himself till he reaps the harvest. His maintenance is generally advanced to him from the stock of a master, the farmer who employs him, and who would have no interest to employ him, unless he was to share in the produce of his labour, or unless his stock was to be replaced to him with a profit. (p. 65)

In this idea of a wages-fund, Smith brings together the essential ingredients of the economic growth process. The existence of a wages-fund is, simultaneously, a rationale for saving (i.e., accumulation), an explanation of wages and profit, and a determinant of population growth. The doctrine maintains that workers are dependent on capitalists to provide them with tools to work with and with food, clothing, and shelter (i.e., "wage goods of subsistence") in order to survive. The only way to increase the stock of wage goods is to induce capitalists to save, and the only way to do that is to increase profits, which, in Smith's view, constitutes the sole source of saving. In other words, savings must find an outlet in the production process—if used to hire more workers, the wages-fund grows, and so do the (average) payments to workers. Workers therefore spend more on wage goods, aggregate demand increases, and more is produced in the next period of production. In this system it is important to note that money is viewed as a medium of exchange only, not as a store of value. Hoarding appears irrational (i.e., costly), and therefore all savings are invested. That is, saving goes into the wages-fund. A particular variant of this view later came to be known as "Say's law," after the French economist and disciple of Smith, Jean-Baptiste Say.

In effect, the wages-fund represents capital earmarked for the hire of labor. In another place, however, Smith underscores the contractual nature of wages. Thus, he argues:

> What are the common wages of labour depends every where upon the contract usually made between those two parties, whose interests are by no means the

> same. The workmen desire to get as much, the masters to give as little as possible. The former are disposed to combine in order to raise, the latter in order to lower the wages of labour. (p. 66)

Thus, an individual wage, or wage level, is the result of a bargaining process. There is clearly a lower limit to wages, Smith continues, or to the combined activity of employers, since

> a man must always live by his work, and his wages must at least be sufficient to maintain him. They must even upon most occasions be somewhat more; otherwise it would be impossible for him to bring up a family, and the race of such workmen could not last beyond the first generation. (pp. 67–68)

As the wages-fund grows, then, it can support a larger population, so that as average wages rise sufficiently above subsistence, workers will propagate more and increase in number. Population growth cannot continue unrestrained, however, because larger populations place increasing burdens on the wages-fund. Thus, the long-run tendency may be toward subsistence levels of average wage rates. This constitutes yet a third theory, in which the long-run average wage is determined by subsistence.

Which one of these explanations represents Smith's theory of wages? The wages-fund, the contract theory, and the subsistence theory are not inconsistent with each other, and indeed, they may be collapsed into one. The size of the wages-fund explains the size of total wage payments, whereas individual or average wage rates are explained by supply-and-demand conditions. In the long run, Smith views wage rates as determined by costs of workers' maintenance and reproduction. The natural wage is a subsistence one, but "subsistence" simply means the minimum payment that workers insist on before they are willing to have children. In other words, labor, too, is produced at constant costs, so that the long-run supply curve of labor is horizontal at whatever wage is consistent with Smith's notion of subsistence. In the short run, however, wage rates may be above or below the long-run equilibrium wage, since short-run supply and demand may be affected by contractual arrangements, accidents of nature, legislation, and so on. On close examination, therefore, Smith subjects the price of labor to the same forces that determine the value of any good or service.

Whereas the distinction between short run and long run is a useful one in economic analysis, Smith's explanation allows that even in the long run, the trend in wages may be upward, since an increased demand for labor causes higher average wages and induces an increase in population, but with a sufficient time lag in the latter. In other words, in a growing economy, increases in labor supply may continually lag behind increases in labor demand. The practical limits to this process are something that concerned writers who succeeded Smith.

Aside from the question of the aggregate level of wages, Smith extended the discussion of "equilibrium wage differences," by which is meant the wage premiums occasioned by certain conditions of employment. Whereas the aggregate level of wages is an important macroeconomic variable, the notion of equilibrium wage differences is an important microeconomic consideration. Cantillon (chapter 4) was the first writer to broach this subject in a systematic way. Workers similarly trained and similarly situated in every other respect will nevertheless earn more or less according to the degree of time and expense in acquiring skills, the degree of risk and danger in employment, and the extent of trust required of employees. Cantillon opened this discussion with characteristic brevity:

> The crafts which require the most time in training or most ingenuity and industry must necessarily be the best paid. A skilful cabinet-maker must receive a higher price for his work than an ordinary carpenter, and a good clock and watchmaker more than a blacksmith.
>
> The arts and occupations, which are accompanied by risks and dangers, like those of foundry workers, sailors, silver miners, etc. ought to be paid in proportion to the risks. When skill is needed, over and above the dangers, they ought to be paid even more, such as ship pilots, divers, engineers, etc. When capacity and trustworthiness are needed the labor is paid still more highly, as in the case of jewelers, bookkeepers, cashiers and others. (*Essay*, p. 45)

In *The Wealth of Nations* (Book I, chap. 10, part 1), Smith elaborated these issues and broadened the discussion of "the inequalities of wages and profits arising from the nature of the employments themselves." A short summary of his main points follows. According to Smith:

1. *Wages vary in inverse proportion to the agreeableness of the employment.* ("The most detestable of all employments, that of public executioner, is, in proportion to the quantity of work done, better paid than any common trade whatever.")
2. *Wages vary in direct proportion to the cost of learning the business.* ("Education in the ingenious arts and in the liberal professions, is . . . tedious and expensive. The pecuniary recompence, therefore . . . , of lawyers and physicians ought to be much more liberal: and it is so accordingly.")
3. *Wages vary in inverse proportion to the constancy of employment.* ("No species of skilled labor . . . seems more easy to learn than that of masons and bricklayers. . . . The high wages of those workmen, therefore, are not so much the recompence of their skill, as the compensation for the inconstancy of their employment.")
4. *Wages vary in direct proportion to the trust that must be placed in the employee.* ("The wages of goldsmiths and jewelers are everywhere superior to those of many other workmen, not only of equal, but of much superior ingenuity; on account of the precious metals with which they are intrusted.")
5. *Wages vary in inverse proportion to the probability of success.* ("The counselor at law who, perhaps at near forty years of age, begins to make something by his profession, ought to receive the retribution, not only of his own so tedious and expensive education, but of that of more than twenty others who are never likely to make any thing by it.")

Profit and Interest. Smith declared that of the five factors affecting equilibrium wage differences only the first and the last affect equilibrium profit differences—namely "the agreeableness or disagreeableness of the business and the risk or security with which it is attended." Smith treated profit as a return to capital rather than a return to entrepreneurship, so his theory of profits is lacking by contemporary standards. In fact, it is overgenerous to attribute a theory of profit at all to Smith. Nevertheless, he offered useful insights into the profit-making process. The chief characteristic of profits, according to Smith, is their uncertainty:

> Profit is so very fluctuating that the person who carries on a particular trade cannot always tell you himself what is the average of his annual profit. It is affected, not only by every variation of price in the commodities which he deals in, but by the good or bad fortune both of his rivals and of his customers, and by a thousand other accidents to which goods when carried either by sea or land, or even when stored in a warehouse, are liable. It varies, therefore, not only from year to year,

> but from day to day, and almost from hour to hour. To ascertain what is the average profit of all the different trades carried on in a great kingdom, must be much more difficult; and to judge of what it may have been formerly, or in remote periods of time, with any degree of precision, must be altogether impossible. (p. 87)

What Smith suggested, therefore, is that whereas aggregate profits are not easily measured, interest may be viewed as a *proxy* for profit. He defined profit as "revenue derived from stock [i.e., capital] by the person who manages or employs it." He defined interest as revenue derived from stock "by the person who does not employ it himself, but lends it to another." Smith's conception of profit therefore emerges as the sum of two payments: (1) a return on capital advanced, and (2) a compensation for bearing risk. Interest alone cannot explain all profit, although it is a good indication of profit. Pushing this idea further, Smith wrote:

> According . . . as the usual market rate of interest varies in any country, we may be assured that the ordinary profits of stock must vary with it, must sink as it sinks, and rise as it rises. The progress of interest, therefore, may lead us to form some notion of the progress of profit. (p. 88)

Alert to the idea of opportunity costs, Smith added certain obiter dicta to the concepts of profit and interest. "The lowest ordinary rate of profit," he charged, "must always be something more than what is sufficient to compensate the occasional losses to which every employment of stock is exposed. It is the surplus only which is neat or clear profit." By the same token, Smith declared that: "The lowest ordinary rate of interest must . . . be something more than sufficient to compensate the occasional losses to which lending, even with tolerable prudence, is exposed. Were it not more, charity or friendship could be the only motives for lending" (p. 96). He also made it clear what effect competition would likely have on profits:

> The increase of stock, which raises wages, tends to lower profit. When the stocks of many rich merchants are turned into the same trade, their mutual competition naturally tends to lower its profit; and when there is an increase in stock in all the different trades carried on in the same society, the competition must produce the same effect in all. (p. 87)

It is generally accepted that Smith viewed profit as a residual, or surplus, perhaps because this was the view taken by Smith's leading British disciple, David Ricardo (see Chapter 7). However, the following excerpt from Smith's chapter on profit challenges this conventional wisdom:

> In reality high profits tend much more to raise the price of work than high wages. . . . Our merchants and master manufacturers complain much of the bad effects of high wages in raising the price, and thereby lessening the sale of their goods both at home and abroad. They say nothing concerning the bad effects of high profits. (pp. 97–98)

If, indeed, profit is a residual, it seems unlikely that it could be price determining, as the above passage suggests. But we shall leave it up to the reader to determine what Smith really meant on the matter of profit, a subject to which we shall return when we examine Smith's blueprint for macroeconomic growth.

Rent. Smith's discussion of rent hinges on three factors: (1) monopoly elements, (2) the residual surplus idea, and (3) alternative costs. Smith defined rent simply as "the price paid for the use of land," but he was emphatic that land rent "is naturally a monopoly price. It is not at all proportioned to what the landlord may have laid out upon the improvement of land, or to what he can afford to take; but to what the farmer can afford to give" (p. 145). Rent, like wages, is usually determined by contractual arrangement between landlord and tenant, but Smith clearly thought the bargain was uneven. He considered rent a monopoly return in part because the landlord had the upper hand:

> In adjusting the terms of the lease, the landlord endeavors to leave him [the tenant] no greater share of the produce than what is sufficient to keep up the stock from which he furnishes the seed, pays the labour, and purchases and maintains the cattle and other instruments of husbandry, together with the ordinary profits of farming stock in the neighborhood. This is evidently the smallest share with which the tenant can content himself without being a loser, and the landlord seldom means to leave him any more. (p. 144)

Other monopoly elements involved in the determination of rent include fertility and location. Thus, land fitted for a particular product may have a monopoly, such as the great wine-producing regions of the French Côte d'Or or the Champagne districts. In this case, Smith noted that the quantity of land devoted to wine production was too small to satisfy the effectual demand, so that the market price of French wines was higher than their natural price. He maintained that "the surplus of this price in this case, and in this case only, bears no regular proportion to the like surplus in corn or pasture, but may exceed it in almost any degree; and the greater part of this excess naturally goes to the rent of the landlord" (p. 155).

Smith also described rent as a residual payment. It is the part of annual produce remaining after all other costs of production, including ordinary profit, are realized. As such, rent is price determined rather than price determining. In Smith's own words, rent "enters into the composition of the price of commodities in a different way from wages and profit. High or low wages and profit are the causes of high or low price; high or low rent is the effect of it" (pp. 145–146).

Finally, Smith maintained that differential rents can be explained on the basis of alternative costs.

> In Europe corn[2] is the principal produce of land which serves immediately for human food. Except in particular situations, therefore, the rent of corn land regulates in Europe that of all other cultivated land. If in any country the common and favourite vegetable food of the people should be drawn from a plant of which the most common land, with the same or nearly the same culture, produced a much greater quantity than the most fertile does of corn, the rent of the landlord . . . would necessarily be much greater. (p. 159)

In other words, the rent of land in a particular use will depend greatly on the productivity of land in its next-best alternative use.

The Critical Role of the Entrepreneur

Some find it curious that Smith's theory of economic development allows a meager role to the entrepreneur. In this regard Smith's economics stands in stark contrast to Cantillon, who assigned the entrepreneur a pivotal role in the operation of a market economy. Perhaps the difference is explained in part by their backgrounds and objectives. Cantillon was a banker/businessman, who seemed more intent on writing a manual for businessmen/financiers. Smith was a philosopher/academic, who

[2] The term "corn" was at this time often used in the generic sense to mean virtually all edible grains, such as wheat, barley, oats, etc.

seemed more intent on writing a manual for statesmen/policy makers. Cantillon tried to exclude overt political considerations from his analysis, declaring them "no part of my subject." Smith may be fairly said to have integrated economics into politics to give birth to the subject henceforth known as "political economy."

Although Smith did not emphasize the role of the entrepreneur in *The Wealth of Nations*, he discussed entrepreneur-types earlier in *The Theory of Moral Sentiments* (1759). In *Wealth*, the entrepreneur is encountered in three different forms: the adventurer, the projector, and the undertaker. Smith speaks disparagingly of the first two and with unqualified approbation only of the undertaker, who he identified with "the prudent man"—a concept developed at length in *Moral Sentiments*.

According to Smith, adventurers are those who hazard their capital on the most difficult of enterprises, spurred on by unbounded confidence in their success, despite extraordinary risks. Smith attributed a measure of irrationality to this kind of behavior because although "the ordinary rate of profit always rises more or less with the risk, it does not . . . seem to rise in proportion to it, or so as to compensate it completely" (*Wealth*, p. 111). Adventurers, therefore, are not stable agents in a theory of economic development, because although a "bold adventurer may sometimes acquire a considerable fortune by two or three successful speculations," he "is just as likely to lose one by two or three unsuccessful ones" (*Wealth*, p. 114).

In Smith's day, the term "projectors" had a dual connotation. One type is cunning, lawless, scheming, and cheating; the other possesses ingenuity and integrity and engages in honest invention. Owing, perhaps, to the inconsiderable number of honest projectors, Smith was critical of the first class of projectors who devise "expensive and uncertain projects . . . which bring bankruptcy upon the greater part of the people who engage in them," like the "search after new silver and gold mines" (*Wealth*, p. 529). These projectors are injurious to society, Smith said, because "every injudicious and unsuccessful project in agriculture, mines, fisheries, trade, or manufactures, tends . . . to diminish the funds destined for the maintenance of productive labor" (*Wealth*, p. 324). Smith allowed, however, that some projectors are prudent businesspeople. Of the "prudent man" Smith said that "if he enters into any new projects or enterprises, they are likely to be well concerted and well prepared. He can never be hurried or drove into them by any necessity, but has always time and leisure to deliberate soberly and coolly concerning what are likely to be their consequences" (*Moral Sentiments*, p. 352). The prudent man, according to Smith, is frugal: He accumulates capital and is an agent of slow but steady progress.

By treating the entrepreneur as menace on the one hand and benefactor on the other, Smith left the concept of entrepreneurship muddled, for which he was derided by later scholars. Joseph Spengler characterized Smith's entrepreneur as essentially passive: "a prudent, cautious, not overly imaginative fellow, who adjusts to circumstances rather than brings about their modification" ("Adam Smith's Theory," pp. 8–9). Joseph Schumpeter, a leading analyst of the role of the entrepreneur in economic development (see chapter 23), was unsympathetic to Smith in many ways, not least of which was his treatment of the entrepreneur. According to Schumpeter, if pressed, Smith would have affirmed that no business runs by itself, yet

> this is exactly the over-all impression his readers get. The merchant or master accumulates "capital"—this is really his essential function—and with this "capital" he hires "industrious people," that is, workmen, who do the rest. In doing so he exposes these means of production to risk of loss; but beyond this, all he does is to supervise his concern in order to make sure that the profits find their way to his pocket. (*History*, p. 555)

Enzo Pesciarelli admits that Smith's works have to be mined carefully to find the few useful gems that comprise his contribution to the subject of entrepreneurship. Collecting the various hints sprinkled throughout the *Wealth of Nations*, and supplementing them with Smith's "prudent man" concept developed in *The Theory of Moral Sentiments*, Pesciarelli offers the following composite picture of Smith's entrepreneur ("Smith, Bentham, and Development," pp. 527–528):

- Smith's undertaker faces risk and uncertainty.
- Smith's undertaker formulates plans and projects in an effort to earn profit.
- Smith's undertaker seeks out the necessary capital for implementation of his planned undertaking.
- Smith's undertaker combines and organizes the productive factors.
- Smith's undertaker inspects and directs production.

What is missing from Pesciarelli's list of elemental characteristics is any explicit connection between entrepreneur and innovation. We know that Smith was very sensitive to the effects of innovation in a capitalist society. In fact, he was one of the first economic writers to recognize innovation as a professional activity. In a remark on inventions made by workmen, Smith noted that many improvements in manufacturing are made by workmen, but that a more learned class of men—"who are called philosophers or men of speculation"—also play a key role. Those who belong to this learned class, "whose trade it is not to do anything, but to observe everything . . . upon that account, are often capable of combining together the powers of the most distant and dissimilar objects." (*Wealth*, p. 10). Thomas Edison might easily fit into this group of "philosopher-inventors." This was a potentially fruitful line of inquiry, which, unfortunately, Smith did not develop to any measurable extent.

The eighteenth-century inventor (i.e., Smith's "philosopher" or "speculator") was an amateur by contemporary standards; yet, Smith's view of innovation as professional activity was ahead of its time. He held that innovation is the product of the division of labor, which in turn depends on the extent of the market. Innovation therefore appears first in markets that are enlarged by cheap transportation. Opulence and progress thereafter accompany the division of labor, and with this progress the innovator or inventor "becomes more expert in his own peculiar branch, more work is done upon the whole, and the quantity of science is considerably increased by it" (*Wealth*, p. 10).

Smith's Macroeconomics: Blueprint for Economic Development

Book I of *The Wealth of Nations*, devoted primarily to the microeconomic foundations of value and distribution, is a prelude to Smith's main objective: the nature and causes of economic development. His theory of economic development has to be pieced together because all of its essentials cannot be found in any one place in *The Wealth of Nations*. The starting point for all of Smith's macroeconomics is the division of labor. Joseph Schumpeter said that for Adam Smith the division of labor "is practically the only factor in economic progress" (*History*, p. 187).

Division of Labor

Despite some exaggeration Schumpeter's statement is very close to the mark. Smith's discussion of the division of labor in Book I provides an exceptionally lucid analysis of the gains from specialization and exchange—principles on which he based the theory of markets. In an oft-quoted passage, Smith described the gains from specialization and division of labor in a pin factory:

> A workman not educated to . . . the trade of the pin-maker . . . nor acquainted with the use of the machinery employed in it . . . could scarce, perhaps, with his utmost industry, make one pin in a day, and certainly could not make twenty. But in the way in which this business is now carried on, not only the whole work is a peculiar trade, but it is divided into a number of branches, of which the greater part are likewise peculiar trades. One man draws out the wire, another straights it, a third cuts it, a fourth points it, a fifth grinds it at the top for receiving the head; to make the head requires two or three distinct operations; to put it on, is a peculiar business, to whiten the pins is another; it is even a trade by itself to put them into the paper; and the important business of making a pin is, in this manner, divided into about eighteen distinct operations, which, in some manufactories, are all performed by distinct hands, though in others the same man will sometimes perform two or three of them. I have seen a small manufactory of this kind where ten men only were employed, and where . . . each person . . . [averaged] four thousand eight hundred pins in a day. But if they had all wrought separately and independently, and without any of them having been educated to this peculiar business, they certainly could not each of them make twenty, perhaps not one pin in a day. (p. 5)

From his discussion Smith concluded that there are three advantages of division of labor, each leading to greater economic wealth: (1) an increase in skill and dexterity of every worker, (2) the saving of time, and (3) the invention of machinery. Invention is a consequence of the narrow focus of a worker's attention on a particular object or task occasioned by the division of labor. As Smith explained: "Men are much more likely to discover easier and readier methods of attaining any object, when the whole attention of their minds is directed toward that single object, than when it is dissipated among a great variety of things" (p. 9).

Wealth, Income, and Productive and Unproductive Labor

We have already seen that Smith differed sharply with the mercantilists on the nature of a country's wealth. "High value of the precious metals," he observed, "can be no proof of the poverty or barbarism of any particular country. . . . It is a proof only of the barrenness of the mines which happened at that time to supply the commercial world" (p. 238). To Smith, national wealth was measured not by the value of precious metals but by "the exchangeable value of the annual produce of the land and labour of the country." Smith meant by the term "national wealth" essentially the same thing economists today mean by the term "national income" (or its common measure, GDP).

But Smith considered the essence of wealth to be the production of physical goods only, and this led in Book II to his unfortunate distinction between *productive* and *unproductive* labor. According to this distinction, productive labor is that which produces a tangible good of some market value. Unproductive labor, on the other hand, results in the production of intangibles, such as services performed by artisans or professionals. Smith characterized his own output (as a teacher) as essentially unproductive, since it did not result in tangible goods sold in the marketplace. He also categorized the services of lawyers, physicians, and other service-oriented workers in the same way.

This distinction between productive and unproductive labor has been much maligned. It is, of course, absurd to characterize the service industries as unproductive simply because they do not produce tangible goods. Yet, what Smith was driving at was the distinction between those activities that increase aggregate net investment, and thus serve the end of economic growth, and those activities that serve merely the needs of households. This latter distinction is a perfectly valid one in economic theory, although the terminology Smith chose is unfortunate. Despite the negative connotation, Smith did not consider unproductive workers useless; he simply did not regard their activities as furthering the goal of economic growth.

The Role of Capital

While division of labor—considered by Smith an inherent tendency in society—*starts* the growth process, capital accumulation is what keeps it going. Key elements in the growth process are the nature, accumulation, and employment of stock. By "stock," Smith meant *wealth* in modern terms, a part (or all) of which is reserved for consumption and a part of which may be reserved for deriving further revenue, through investment. The larger the last share, the greater the growth potential of any nation. Recall that capital accumulation enlarges the wages-fund, which in turn allows a larger number of workers to be engaged in productive activity, thereby increasing the size of national output.

Workers exhaust the wages-fund over time as they draw down advances for their subsistence during the production process. At the end of the production period, however, the goods produced are sold, ordinarily at a profit, so that the stock of wage goods (capital) is replenished, and even increased, by the amount of profit earned. In this manner, through profit accumulation, the stock of capital grows over time, thus supporting more workers and greater output in the next production period.

The complete chain of economic growth as represented by Smith is summarized in figure 5-2, in which growth is viewed as an ongoing process as long as the chain of causation remains unbroken. The line of causation proceeds in clockwise

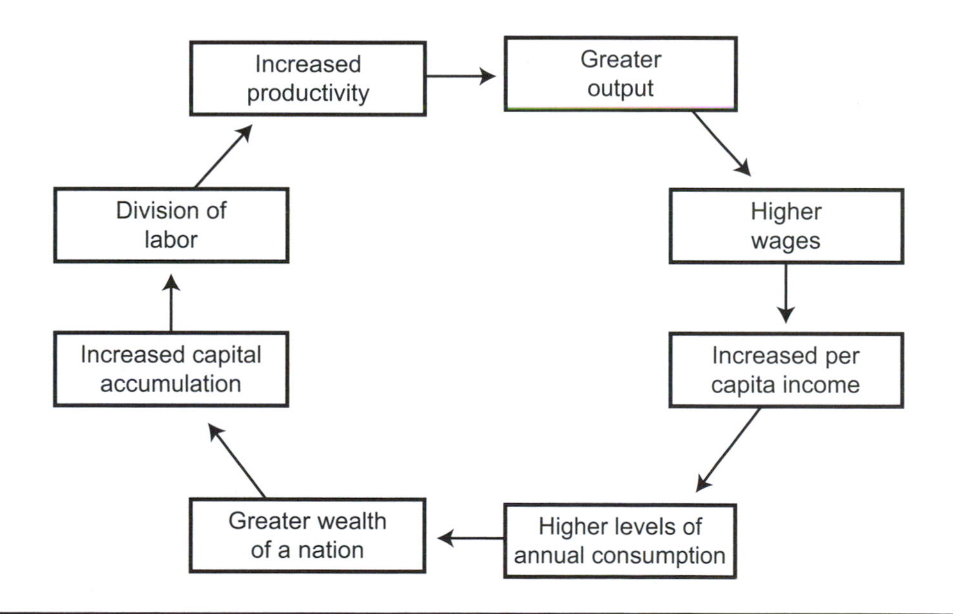

Figure 5-2 Smith's theory of economic growth is an ongoing process, with division of labor starting the growth process and proceeding in a clockwise fashion in the diagram.

fashion, starting at approximately the "ten-o'clock" position, with the division of labor. The ultimate constraint on the growth process is the increased difficulty of finding new and profitable investment outlets as the capital stock continues to grow over time.

■ Conclusion

From the Middle Ages to the mid-eighteenth century, Europe and Great Britain's populations and national outputs increased significantly. The Industrial Revolution was awakening when Adam Smith wrote *The Wealth of Nations*, causing a change in people's attitude toward trade and commerce. From a narrow concern with economic justice and the status quo typical of the Middle Ages, the predominant focus shifted to economic growth and change. This evolutionary shift, in turn, led to the dismantling of feudalistic and mercantilistic restraints of trade and commerce.

The reasons for this turnabout are not very obscure. In a society characterized by economic stagnation, such as medieval Europe, one person's gain is another's loss—hence the concern of the Church fathers for economic justice and their tendency to portray want minimization as the path to spiritual happiness and economic well-being. In the vernacular of contemporary game theory the writers of the medieval era tended to view economic activity as a "zero-sum game." When national output is expanding, however, economic activity becomes a "positive-sum game" where everyone can benefit at the same time. In the "positive-sum" arena people are less preoccupied with ethics and more intent on increasing economic wealth. Concerns about economic justice tend to melt away when each individual can get a larger slice of the (growing) economic pie without making someone else worse off. By 1776, the prospects of economic development made it possible, as well as desirable, to reduce restraints against individual profit seeking in an expanding economy.

The idea of a self-regulating economy operating within a market system was a new one in the mid-eighteenth century. Anticipations of the idea crept into early Continental economic literature before then, but clearly Adam Smith gave the idea its most timely and forceful expression. The perception of a natural social order, existing in the absence of any form of central planning, was one of the most liberating ideas ever to emerge in the history of economic thought. It shunted economic analysis onto a new path. Adam Smith led the way by providing a framework for analyzing the economic questions of income growth, value, and distribution. For practically the next century, economists worked largely within that framework to investigate the questions raised by the quiet Scottish philosopher. In this manner, Smith rightly came to be considered father of economics. He succeeded beyond measure in weaving together his own contributions plus those of his predecessors—who were many—into a systematic, comprehensive treatise that was greater than the sum of its parts.

Soon after its publication, Smith's book became many things to many people, a fact that accounts in no small measure for its immediate success. Businesspeople and workers alike could find passages in *The Wealth of Nations* to support their interests. Government bureaucrats were treated less kindly, although Smith reserved three important roles for the state: (1) to administer justice, (2) to provide for the national defense, and (3) to maintain certain enterprises in the public interest that could never be profitable if undertaken privately (i.e., the "public-goods" question). Now that we are into the twenty-first century, it seems obvious that each of these functions has weighed increasingly heavy on governments at every level.

References

Anderson, G. M., W. F. Shughart, and R. D. Tollison. "Adam Smith in the Customhouse," *Journal of Political Economy*, vol. 93 (August 1985), pp. 740–759.

Blaug, Mark. *Economic Theory in Retrospect*, 4th ed. London: Cambridge University Press, 1985.

Cantillon, Richard. *An Essay on Economic Theory: An English translation of Richard Cantillon's Essai sur la nature du commerce en général*. Chantal Saucier (trans.), Mark Thornton (ed.). Auburn, AL: Ludwig von Mises Institute, 2010 [1755].

Gray, Alexander. "Adam Smith," *Scottish Journal of Political Economy*, vol. 23 (June 1976), pp. 153–169.

Pesciarelli, Enzo. "Smith, Bentham and the Development of Contrasting Ideas on Entrepreneurship," *History of Political Economy*, vol. 21 (Fall 1989), pp. 521–536.

Schumpeter, Joseph A. *History of Economic Analysis*, E. B. Schumpeter (ed.). New York: Oxford University Press, 1954.

Smith, Adam. *An Inquiry into the Nature and Causes of the Wealth of Nations*, Edwin Cannan (ed.). New York: Modern Library, 1937 [1776].

———. *The Theory of Moral Sentiments*. Indianapolis: Liberty Classics, 1976 [1759].

Spengler, Joseph J. "Adam Smith's Theory of Economic Growth—Part II," *Southern Economic Journal*, vol. 26 (July 1959), pp. 1–12.

Notes for Further Reading

Inasmuch as the literature on Adam Smith is vast and varied, only a sampling can be presented here. For a glimpse of the large store of Smithiana, see Burt Franklin and F. Cordasco, *Adam Smith: A Bibliographical Checklist* (New York: Burt Franklin, 1950); and Henry W. Speigel's bibliography accompanying *The Growth of Economic Thought*, 3d ed. (Durham, NC: Duke University Press, 1991). The standard works on Smith's life and thought are John Rae, *Life of Adam Smith* (New York: A. M. Kelley, Publishers, 1965 [1895]); W. R. Scott, *Adam Smith as Student and Professor* (Glasgow: Jackson, Son & Co., 1937); and C. R. Fay, *The World of Adam Smith* (Cambridge: Heffer, 1960). On the first centenary of *The Wealth of Nations*, Walter Bagehot, an economist in his own right, wrote an interesting characterization of Smith, "Adam Smith as a Person," *Fortnightly Review*, no. 115 (July 1, 1876), pp. 18–42, reprinted in *Bagehot's Biographical Studies*, R. H. Hutton (ed.) (London: Longmans, 1881). More recent evaluations of Smith and his thought include E. G. West, *Adam Smith: The Man and His Works* (New Rochelle, NY: Arlington House, 1969); and Sam Hollander, *The Economics of Adam Smith* (Toronto: University of Toronto Press, 1973), a wholesale reinterpretation of Smith's significance as an economist.

A long-standing debate concerns the compatibility of intellectual arguments in Smith's *Theory of Moral Sentiments* and *The Wealth of Nations*. The preponderance of evidence seems to support the consistency thesis—there is no real conflict between the two works published almost twenty years apart. On this issue, see A. L. Macfie, "Adam Smith's Moral Sentiments as Foundation for His *Wealth of Nations*," *Oxford Economic Papers*, n.s., vol. 2 (October 1959), pp. 209–228; same author, "Adam Smith's *Theory of Moral Sentiments*," *Scottish Journal of Political Economy*, vol. 8 (1960), pp. 12–27; W. F. Campbell, "Adam Smith's Theory of Justice, Prudence, and Beneficence," *American Economic Review*, vol. 57 (May 1967), pp. 571–577; Ralph Anspach, "The Implications of the *Theory of Moral Sentiments* for Adam Smith's Economic Thought," *History of Political Economy*, vol. 4 (Spring 1972), pp. 176–206; R. L. Heilbroner, "The Socialization of the Individual in Adam Smith," *History of Political Economy*, vol. 14 (Fall 1982), pp. 427–439; J. T. Young, "The Impartial Spectator and Natural Jurisprudence: An Interpretation of Adam Smith's Theory of the Natural Price," *History of Political Economy*, vol. 18 (Fall

1986), pp. 365–382; same author, "Natural Jurisprudence and the Theory of Value in Adam Smith," *History of Political Economy*, vol. 27 (Winter 1995), pp. 755–773; and J. M. Evensky, "The Two Voices of Adam Smith: Moral Philosopher and Social Critic," *History of Political Economy*, vol. 19 (Fall 1987), pp. 447–468.

Some papers that explore the intersection between ethics and economics in Smith's work are as follows: R. E. Prasch, "The Ethics of Growth in Adam Smith's *Wealth of Nations*," *History of Political Economy*, vol. 23 (Summer 1991), pp. 337–352; Jerry Evensky, "Ethics and the Classical Liberal Tradition in Economics," *History of Political Economy*, vol. 24 (Summer 1992), pp. 61–77; same author, "Adam Smith on the Human Foundation of a Successful Liberal Society," *History of Political Economy*, vol. 25 (Fall 1993), pp. 395–412; and J. T. Young and Barry Gordon, "Distributive Justice as a Normative Criterion in Adam Smith's Political Economy," *History of Political Economy*, vol. 28 (Spring 1996), pp. 1–25.

The sesquicentennial of the publication of *The Wealth of Nations* in 1926 was followed fifty years later by a full-scale celebration of the bicentennial event. On the former, see J. M. Clark et al., *Adam Smith, 1776–1926* (Chicago: University of Chicago Press, 1928). In connection with the latter, see T. W. Hutchison, "The Bicentenary of Adam Smith," *Economic Journal*, vol. 86 (September 1976), pp. 481–492; G. J. Stigler, "The Successes and Failures of Professor Smith," *Journal of Political Economy*, vol. 84 (December 1976), pp. 1199–1214; and the entire Winter 1976 issue of *History of Political Economy*, which contains papers on Smith by Ronald Meek, H. W. Spiegel, E. G. West, and others. A major part of the bicentennial was the publication by the University of Glasgow of Smith's complete works and correspondence, accompanied by a new biography by I. S. Ross and two volumes of critical essays edited by A. S. Skinner and T. Wilson.

Smith's theory of history and his development of systematic inquiry is examined by Andrew S. Skinner in "Economics and History—the Scottish Enlightenment," *Scottish Journal of Political Economy*, vol. 12 (February 1956); "Adam Smith: The Development of a System," *Scottish Journal of Political Economy*, vol. 23 (June 1976), pp. 111–132; and "Smith and Shackle: History and Epistemics," *Journal of Economic Studies*, vol. 12 (1985), pp. 13–20; by G. Bryson in *Man and Society: The Scottish Inquiry of the Eighteenth Century* (New York: A. M. Kelley, 1968); and by Ronald L. Meek in "Smith, Turgot, and the 'Four Stages' Theory," *History of Political Economy*, vol. 3 (Spring 1971), pp. 9–27. Smith's theory of property rights is the subject of a note by David E. R. Gay, "Adam Smith and Property Rights Analysis," *Review of Social Economy*, vol. 33 (October 1975), pp. 177–179.

The starting point of Smith's theory of economic development is the division of labor. Despite its catalytic role in his theory of economic development Smith seemed of two minds on the subject. He recognized its benefits in Book I and its limitations in Book V. For a discussion of the issues, see E. G. West, "Adam Smith's Two Views on the Division of Labor," *Economica*, vol. 31 (February 1964), pp. 23–32; and Nathan Rosenberg, "Adam Smith on the Division of Labor: Two Views or One?" *Economica*, vol. 32 (May 1965), pp. 127–140. For historical antecedents of the concept, see Vernard Foley, "The Division of Labor in Plato and Smith," *History of Political Economy*, vol. 6 (Summer 1974), pp. 171–191. Alienation, the favorite theme of Karl Marx, has also been proposed as a specter for Adam Smith: see E. G. West, "The Political Economy of Alienation: Karl Marx and Adam Smith," *Oxford Economic Papers*, vol. 21 (March 1969), pp. 1–23; the critique of West by R. Lamb, "Adam Smith's Concept of Alienation," *Oxford Economic Papers*, vol. 25 (July 1973), pp. 275–285; and West's rejoinder, "Adam Smith and Alienation: A Rejoinder," *Oxford Economic Papers*, vol. 27 (July 1975), pp. 295–301. See also M. Fay, "The Influence of Adam Smith on Marx's Theory of Alienation," *Science and Society*, vol. 47 (Summer 1983), pp. 129–151. The concept of alienation arises again in J. P. Henderson, "Agency or Alienation? Smith, Mill and Marx on the Joint-Stock Company," *History of Political Economy*, vol. 18 (Spring 1986), pp. 111–131.

Smith's theory of economic development is explored by J. J. Spengler, "Adam Smith's Theory of Economic Development," *Science and Society*, vol. 23 (1959), pp. 107–132; by W. O. Thweatt, "A Diagrammatic Presentation of Adam Smith's Growth Model," *Social Research*, vol. 24 (July 1957), pp. 227–230; by V. W. Bladen, "Adam Smith on Productive and Unproductive Labor: A Theory of Full Development," *Canadian Journal of Economics and Political Science*, vol. 24 (1960), pp. 625–630; by Hla Myint, "Adam Smith's Theory of International Trade in the Perspective of Economic Development," *Economica*, vol. 44 (August 1977), pp. 231–248; by P. Bowles, "Adam Smith and the Natural Progress of Opulence," *Economica*, vol. 53 (February 1986), pp. 109–118; and by Gavin C. Reid, "Disequilibrium and Increasing Returns in Adam Smith's Analysis of Growth and Accumulation," *History of Political Economy*, vol. 19 (Spring 1987), pp. 87–106. Anthony Brewer, "The Concept of Growth in Eighteenth-Century Economics," *History of Political Economy*, vol. 27 (Winter 1995), pp. 609–638, argues that only Turgot and Hume anticipated Smith's view that continuing economic growth was the normal state of affairs. See also, Anthony Brewer, "Adam Ferguson, Adam Smith, and the Concept of Economic Growth," *History of Political Economy*, vol. 31 (Summer 1999), pp. 237–254, which argues that many of the main themes of Adam Smith's work were foreshadowed by Adam Ferguson, a leading figure of the Scottish Enlightenment.

On the origins of the exchange economy in Smith, see Andrew Skinner, "Adam Smith: The Origins of the Exchange Economy," *European Journal of the History of Economic Thought*, vol. 1 (Autumn 1993), pp. 21–46. James P. Henderson, "The Macro and Micro aspects of *The Wealth of Nations*," *Southern Economic Journal*, vol. 21 (July 1954), pp. 25–35, presents a balanced overview of Smith's economics. Smith's theory of value is explored by M. A. Stephenson, "The Paradox of Value: A Suggested Interpretation," *History of Political Economy*, vol. 4 (Spring 1972), pp. 127–139; David Levy, "Diamonds, Water and Z Goods: An Account of the Paradox of Value," *History of Political Economy*, vol. 14 (Fall 1982), pp. 312–322; Michael V. White, "Doctoring Adam Smith: The Fable of the Diamonds and Water Paradox," *History of Political Economy*, vol. 34 (Winter 2002), pp. 659–683; H. M. Robertson and W. L. Taylor, "Adam Smith's Approach to the Theory of Value," *Economic Journal*, vol. 67 (June 1957), pp. 181–198. Terry Peach, "Adam Smith and the Labor Theory of (Real) Value: A Reconsideration," *History of Political Economy*, vol. 41 (Summer 2009), pp. 383–406, argues that Smith meant the labor theory to apply to more than simple economies, and was more devoted to the principle than is commonly thought.

Almost all aspects of Smith's economics have drawn attention at one time or another. See, for example, Ronald L. Meek, "Adam Smith and the Classical Concept of Profit," *Scottish Journal of Political Economy*, vol. 1 (June 1954), pp. 138–153; Samuel Hollander, "Some Implications of Adam Smith's Analysis of Investment Priorities," *History of Political Economy*, vol. 3 (Fall 1971), pp. 238–264; P. E. Mirowski, "Adam Smith, Empiricism and the Rate of Profit in Eighteenth-Century England," *History of Political Economy*, vol. 14 (Summer 1982), pp. 178–198; R. F. Hébert and A. N. Link, "Adam Smith on the Division of Labor and Relative Prices," *History of Economics Society Bulletin*, vol. 9 (Fall 1987), pp. 80–84; David Levy, "Adam Smith's Case of Usury Laws," *History of Political Economy*, vol. 19 (Fall 1987), pp. 387–400; and C. E. Staley, "A Note on Adam Smith's Version of the Vent for Surplus Model," *History of Political Economy*, vol. 5 (Fall 1973), pp. 438–448. For more on the same issue, see H. D. Kurz, "Adam Smith on Foreign Trade: A Note on the Vent-for-Surplus Argument," *Economica*, vol. 59 (November 1992), pp. 475–481.

Adam Smith is widely referred to as the apostle of laissez-faire, though the term is of French, not British, origin. For a cross-section of Smith's views on the role of government and its policies, see Nathan Rosenberg, "Some Institutional Aspects of *The Wealth of Nations*," *Journal of Political Economy*, vol. 68 (1960), pp. 557–570; R. D. Freeman,

"Adam Smith, Education, and Laissez-Faire," *History of Political Economy*, vol. 1 (Spring 1969), pp. 173–186; Warren J. Samuels, "The Classical Theory of Economic Policy: Non-legal Social Control," *Southern Economic Journal*, vol. 31 (October 1973), pp. 123–137; G. J. Stigler, "Smith's Travels on the Ship of State," *History of Political Economy*, vol. 3 (Fall 1971), pp. 265–277; Donald Winch, "Science and the Legislator: Adam Smith and After," *Economic Journal*, vol. 93 (September 1983), pp. 501–520; H. H. Song, "Adam Smith as an Early Pioneer of Institutional Individualism," *History of Political Economy*, vol. 27 (Fall 1995), pp. 425–448; Edward J. Harpham, "The Problem of Liberty in the Thought of Adam Smith," *Journal of the History of Economic Thought*, vol. 22 (June 2000), pp. 217–237; Warren J. Samuels and Steven G. Medema, "Freeing Smith from the 'Free Market': On the Misperception of Adam Smith on the Economic Role of Government," *History of Political Economy*, vol. 37 (Summer 2005), pp. 219–226.

The issue of the invisible hand and its role in Smith's market system is explored by Stefano Fiori, "Visible and Invisible Order: The Theoretical Duality of Smith's Political Economy," *The European Journal of the History of Economic Thought*, vol. 8 (Winter 2001), pp. 429–448; S. Ahmad, "Adam Smith's Four Invisible Hands," *History of Political Economy*, vol. 22 (Spring 1990), pp. 137–144; J. R. Davis, "Adam Smith on the Providential Reconciliation of Individual and Social Interests: Is Man Led by an Invisible Hand or Misled by a Sleight of Hand?" *History of Political Economy*, vol. 22 (Summer 1990), pp. 341–352; Lisa Hill, "The Hidden Theology of Adam Smith," *The European Journal of the History of Economic Thought*, vol. 8 (Spring 2001), pp. 1–29; and Amos Witztum, "Interdependence, the Invisible Hand, and Equilibrium in Adam Smith," *History of Political Economy*, vol. 42 (Spring 2010), pp. 155–192, who asserts that there is a type of general equilibrium analysis in Smith, but it is different from that of contemporary economics. Michael E. Bradley, "Adam Smith's System of Natural Liberty: Competition, Contestability, and Market Process," *Journal of the History of Economic Thought*, vol. 32 (June 2010), pp 237–262, explores whether Smith's system of perfect liberty bears any traits of perfect competition, arguing that it does, but that it differs respecting rivalry between firms and the role of the entrepreneur. Bradley also contrasts Smith's view to neoclassical perfect competition, contestable markets theory, and the Austrian theory of competition.

It is possible that Galileo Galilei encountered and resolved the paradox of exchange value in a key methodological passage in his famous book on astronomy. Although his brush with this idea could not be termed "theoretical" or "economic" in any conventional sense, he understood that real price changes were related to scarcity. This astonishing point had been hitherto unrecognized. Adam Smith may have been influenced by Galileo on scientific method as revealed in Smith's *History of Astronomy*. Smith read and digested Galileo's famous works directly and through his careful study of his most important influence, Isaac Newton. Smith's failure to solve the paradox in the *Wealth of Nations* and to seek a measurement of constant change may have been, at least derivatively, an attempt to follow Galileo's methodological lead. See Robert B. Ekelund, Jr. and Mark Thornton, "Galileo, Smith and the Paradox of Value: The 'Connection' of Art and Science," *History of Economic Ideas*, vol. 19 (2011), pp. 85–101.

Here is a mélange of works on various aspects of Smith's thought that defies easy categorization: D. A. Redman, "Adam Smith and Isaac Newton," *Scottish Journal of Political Economy*, vol. 40 (May 1993), pp. 210–230; N. Rosenberg, "Adam Smith and the Stock of Moral Capital," *History of Political Economy*, vol. 22 (Spring 1990), pp. 1–18; J. A. Gherity, "Adam Smith and the Glasgow Merchants," *History of Political Economy*, vol. 24 (Summer 1992), pp. 357–368; Bruce Elmslie, "The Endogenous Nature of Technological Progress and Transfer in Adam Smith's Thought," *History of Political Economy*, vol. 26 (Winter 1994), pp. 649–663; and C. Nyland, "Adam Smith, Stage Theory, and the Status of Women," *History of Political Economy*, vol. 25 (Winter 1995), pp. 617–640. Neil De Marchi and Jonathan A. Greene, "Adam Smith and Private Provision of the Arts," *History of Political Economy*, vol. 37 (Fall 2005), pp. 431–454, provide reasons why Smith did not favor government intervention in the arts.

For conflicting interpretations of Smith's views on organized religion and economic incentives, see C. G. Leathers and Patrick. Raines, "Adam Smith on Competitive Religious Markets," *History of Political Economy*, vol. 24 (Summer 1992), pp. 499–514; and R. B. Ekelund, Jr., R. F. Hébert, and R. T. Tollison, "Adam Smith on Religion and Market Structure," *History of Political Economy*, vol. 37 (Winter 2005), pp. 647–660. Jerry Evensky, "Adam Smith's Moral Philosophy: The Role of Religion and Its Relationship to Philosophy and Ethics in the Evolution of Society," *History of Political Economy*, vol. 30 (Spring 1998), pp. 17–42, considers Smith's views on religion in a different context. Gavin Kennedy, "The Hidden Adam Smith in his Alleged Theology," *Journal of the History of Economic Thought*, vol. 33 (September 2011), pp. 385–402, criticizes the view that Smith was truly religious, arguing instead that his concessions to religion were simply conventional, and pronounced as safeguards against persecution. Kennedy also alleges that Smith was loathe to offend his mother's religious sensibilities, but he altered his works to make them less religiously oriented after her death.

Finally, on the relevance of Adam Smith's thought for the modern age, see S. Moos, "Is Adam Smith Out of Date?" *Oxford Economic Papers*, vol. 3 (June 1951), pp. 187–201; K. E. Boulding, "After Samuelson, Who Needs Adam Smith?" *History of Political Economy*, vol. 3 (Fall 1971), pp. 225–237; and R. H. Coase, "*The Wealth of Nations*," *Economic Inquiry*, vol. 15 (July 1977), pp. 309–325.

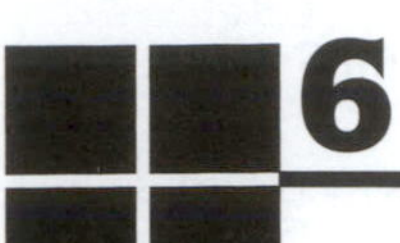

6

Classical Economics (I)
Utility, Population, and Money

Momentous change occurred during the era that produced classical economic literature. The quantifiable nature of this change is clouded today by the lack of reliable records and the passage of time, but economic historians have been able to give it an approximate face. In Great Britain income and population began to grow alongside each other in the mid-eighteenth century. From 1700 to 1871, national income in Britain increased eighteenfold. During the same time Britain's population increased almost fourfold. As one might expect, the volume of trade expanded, particularly after the liberalization of trade policy following the publication of *The Wealth of Nations*. At the same time, there was a fundamental change in the balance of the British economy. Agriculture, which accounted for 40–45 percent of national output during most of the eighteenth century, declined to only 14 percent by 1871. Manufacturing, which accounted for approximately 24 percent of national output in 1770, accounted for 38 percent a century later. The Industrial Revolution was clearly underway.

Adam Smith did more to establish economics as a scientific discipline than any writer before him. He established the foundations of classical value theory and provided a meaningful blueprint for economic growth. He also breathed into political economy an underlying philosophy based on the doctrine of utility, or self-interest. This philosophy maintains that the desire to improve one's position manifests itself in individual attempts to acquire benefits and avoid costs. The idea that self-interest was, if not the exclusive, at least the dominant influence on human activity gained ground very quickly in the eighteenth century. Smith was merely one in a long line of philosophers who espoused the principle, including David Hume, Smith's teacher and friend. Together they forged a philosophical framework that served as a touchstone for the new field of political economy.

Before the close of the eighteenth century, several key themes intruded on, and were embraced by, political economy. Although independently formulated, each of these themes was integrated into the newly recognizable subject. The first theme, utilitarianism, was implicit in Smith's writings but was given a much more forceful statement by Jeremy Bentham. The second theme, populationism, was embryonic in Cantillon's writing but was developed into a full-blown theory by Robert Malthus. The third theme, money, was resolutely shaped—under the influence of evolving banking theory and practice—into an axiom of classical macroeconomics.

■ Jeremy Bentham and Utilitarianism

Jeremy Bentham (1748–1832), a lawyer by training and a younger contemporary of Smith, formalized the doctrine of self-interest in terms of the *pleasure-pain principle*. In his *Introduction to the Principles of Morals and Legislation* (1789), Bentham wrote with confidence:

> Nature has placed mankind under the governance of two sovereign masters, *pain* and *pleasure*. It is for them alone to point out what we ought to do as well as to determine what we shall do. . . . The *principle of utility* recognizes this subjection. (p. 17)

From a policy standpoint there are two distinct ways in which the principle of utility (self-interest) has been interpreted. One rests on the belief in a *natural* identity of interests, the other on the belief in an *artificial* identity of interests. Adam Smith championed the natural identity thesis, which emphasized spontaneous order and harmony. He believed that in a free economy the individual self-interests of human nature harmonize of their own accord; consequently he advocated essentially a laissez-faire policy. Bentham, however, took a different tack, admitting that individuals are chiefly self-interested but denying any natural harmony of egoisms. Crime, for example, provides a case of self-interested behavior that violates the public interest. The very fact that crime existed was for Bentham sufficient proof that natural harmony did not. The central tenet of Bentham's philosophy, therefore, was that the interest of each individual must be identified with the general interest and that it was the business of the legislator to bring about this identification through direct intercession. Thus, it was in the form of the *artificial identity of interests* framework that Bentham first adopted the utility principle. His doctrine came to be known as *utilitarianism*.

Superficially, Bentham's doctrine bears a resemblance to the ancient Greek philosophy of hedonism, which also held that moral duty consists of the gratification of pleasure-seeking interests. But hedonism is individualistic; it prescribes individual actions without reference to the general happiness. Utilitarianism added to hedonism the ethical doctrine that human conduct *should* be directed toward maximizing the happiness of the greatest number of people. "The greatest happiness for the greatest number" became the watch phrase of the utilitarians—those who shared Bentham's philosophy. Among them were such personalities as the father–son combination of James and John Stuart Mill (see chapter 8) and Edwin Chadwick (see chapter 10). This group championed legislation plus social and religious sanctions that punished individuals for harming others in the pursuit of their own happiness. Bentham defined his principle in the following fashion:

> By the principle of utility is meant that principle which approves or disapproves of every action whatsoever, according to the tendency which it appears to have to augment or diminish the happiness of the party whose interest is in question . . . not only of every action of a private individual, but of every measure of government. (*Principles of Morals and Legislation*, p. 17)

This passage implies a very minimal distinction between morals and legislation. Bentham's self-appointed mission was to make the theory of morals and legislation scientific in the Newtonian sense. As Newton's revolutionary physics hinged on the universal principle of attraction (i.e., gravity), Bentham's theory of morals rested on the principle of utility. Newton's roundabout influence on the social sciences was widespread in the nineteenth century, which demonstrated a passion for measurement. Bentham rode the crest of this new wave in the social sciences. If pleasure and pain could be measured in some objective sense, then every legislative act could be judged on welfare considerations. This achievement required a conception of the general interest, which Bentham readily defined.

Bentham asserted that the general interest of the community is measured by the sum of the individual interests in the community. His utilitarian approach challenged class distinctions; it was both democratic and egalitarian. It mattered not whether one was a pauper or a king—each individual interest was to receive equal weight in the measurement of the general welfare. Thus, if something adds more to a peasant's pleasure than it subtracts from the happiness of an aristocrat, it is desirable on utilitarian grounds. Likewise, if government action of a certain kind enhances the happiness of the community more than it diminishes the happiness of some segment of it, intervention is thereby justified by Bentham's reasoning.

All of this presupposes a kind of "moral arithmetic," which Bentham saw as analogous to the mathematical operations required of Newtonian physics. The operations of moral arithmetic are not all of the same kind, however. The values of *different* pleasures are added for individuals, but the value of a *given* pleasure must be multiplied by the number of people who experience it, and the various elements that make up the value of each pleasure must also be multiplied by each other. This requires a rather complicated summing up. Facing the difficulties as best he could, Bentham chose money as an appropriate measure of pain and pleasure. Money, as we know, is subject to diminishing marginal utility: the more of it acquired, the less utility each additional unit conveys. Bentham recognized this fact, but he did not explore its consequences so as to more firmly establish consumer demand theory. It can be said fairly that Bentham was more of a utilitarian than a marginalist. Nevertheless, he exerted a major influence on one of the pioneers of neoclassical value theory, William Stanley Jevons (see chapter 15).

The Felicific Calculus

Bentham's attempt to measure economic welfare scientifically took the form of the felicific calculus, or summing up, of collective pleasures and pains. As early as 1789, in his *Introduction to the Principles of Morals and Legislation* (p. 30), Bentham described the circumstances by which the values of pleasure and pain were to be measured. For the community, they consist of the following seven factors:

1. The intensity of pleasure or pain
2. Its duration
3. Its certainty or uncertainty
4. Its propinquity or remoteness
5. Its fecundity, or the chance it has of being followed by sensations of the same kind (i.e., pleasure followed by more pleasure, or pain followed by more pain)
6. Its purity, or the chance it has of not being followed by sensations of the opposite kind (e.g., childbirth has a low index of purity because it represents a mixture of pain and pleasure)
7. Its extent, that is, the number of people who are affected by it

Bentham recognized that the fifth and sixth circumstances are not inherent properties of pain or pleasure itself but only of the act that produces pleasure or pain.

Therefore they serve only as indicators of the tendency of any act or event to affect the community.

After identifying the dimensions of pleasure/pain, Bentham spelled out the mechanics by which *welfare* calculations were to be made. "To take an exact account, then, of the general tendency of any act, by which the interests of the community are affected," he directed, "proceed as follows": Begin with any one person of those whose interests seem most immediately to be affected by it and take an account:

1. Of the value of each distinguishable pleasure which appears to be produced by it in the first instance.
2. Of the value of each pain which appears to be produced by it in the first instance.
3. Of the value of each pleasure which appears to be produced by it after the first. This constitutes the fecundity of the first pleasure and the impurity of the first pain.
4. Of the value of each pain which appears to be produced by it after the first. This constitutes the fecundity of the first pain and the impurity of the first pleasure.
5. Sum up all the values of all the pleasures on the one side, and those of all the pains on the other. The balance, if it be on the side of pleasure, will give the good tendency of the act upon the whole, with respect to the interests of that individual person; if on the side of pain, the bad tendency of it upon the whole.
6. Take an account of the number of persons whose interests appear to be concerned; and repeat the above process with respect to each. Sum up the numbers expressive of degrees of good tendency . . . in regard to . . . the whole: do this again with respect to each individual, in regard to whom the tendency of it is bad upon the whole. Take the balance; which, if on the side of pleasure, will give the general good tendency of the act . . . if on the side of pain, the general evil tendency with respect to the same community. (*Principles of Morals and Legislation*, pp. 30–31)

It is rather a tall order to follow this procedure for every act of public policy. Bentham admitted that he did not expect the felicific calculus to be followed pursuant to every moral judgment or legislative enactment, but he urged legislators and administrators always to keep the theory in view, for as close as the actual process of evaluation follows it, the nearer it will be to an exact measure.

An Evaluation of Utilitarianism

Bentham recognized some of the practical and analytical difficulties in his theory of welfare measurement and ignored others. One of the many problems confronting the theory is how to treat interpersonal comparisons of utility. To paraphrase an old cliché, one man's happiness may be another man's poison. The fact that different individuals have different tastes, different incomes, different goals and ambitions, and so forth, makes comparisons of utility (gained or lost) between individuals illegitimate by any objective criteria. Bentham admitted this obstacle, but he felt that such comparisons must be made, or else social reform is impossible. Hence his welfare theory is subjective (i.e., normative) rather than objective.

Another problem in Bentham's welfare theory concerns the weighting, if any, of qualitative pleasures. Should pleasures of the mind, for example, receive more or less emphasis than pleasures of the body? Although he was aware of this problem, Bentham was unable to resolve it. Like so many later economists, he settled on money as the best available measure of utility, even though money measures do not always register qualitative changes unambiguously.

Bentham was apparently unaware of the logical pitfall that economists call the *fallacy of composition*. This fallacy asserts that because something is true of a part, it is therefore true of the whole. Confident that the collective interest was a faithful representation of the individual interests that comprised it, Bentham represented the measure of collective interest as the sum of individual interests. While this assertion may be true in some instances, it is not necessarily true in all. A simple example may serve to illustrate this point. It is presumably in the general interest of American society to have every automobile in the United States equipped with all possible safety devices. However, a majority of individual car buyers may not be willing to pay the cost of such equipment in the form of higher auto prices. In this case, the collective interest does not coincide with the sum of the individual interests. The result is a legislative and economic dilemma. In other words, Bentham's basic assumption regarding welfare measurement may lead to inaccurate estimates of the general welfare.

On purely philosophical grounds, Bentham's view of human nature is essentially passive: people are "pushed" about by the search for pleasure and the avoidance of pain. Hence, in Bentham's view, there are no "bad" motives or "moral" deficiencies; there are only "bad" calculations regarding pleasure and pain. Bentham did not think it wrong to make a bad calculation; it may be stupid, but presumably stupidity can be corrected by education. Indeed, the utilitarians placed a great deal of emphasis on education as a means of social reform.

Utilitarianism is regarded by many as overly narrow in its approach to human behavior. Little or no room is given to behavioral motives other than the pursuit of pleasure and the avoidance of pain. But despite its inherent difficulties, Bentham felt that the felicific calculus was a useful, if unoriginal, theory. He believed that individual pleasure-pain calculations are made frequently, even if unconsciously. "In all this," he charged, "there is nothing but what the practice of mankind, wheresoever they have a clear view of their own interest, is perfectly conformable to" (*Principles of Morals and Legislation*, p. 32).

Bentham's search for an exact, quantitative measure of utility was bound to prove futile. Even to this day, welfare economists have never successfully solved the problem of interpersonal utility comparisons in such a way as to derive truly objective criteria on which to base welfare decisions. Nevertheless, the influence of Bentham's philosophy was transmitted through James Mill, a fellow utilitarian, to his son, John Stuart, particularly in the area of social reform. Moreover, the felicific calculus provided a foundation for Jevons's more profound insights into the marginal-utility theory of consumer behavior (see chapter 15).

Bentham's influence on economic policy was especially profound in the first decades following his death, when Edwin Chadwick and John Stuart Mill championed reforms based on utilitarian premises (see chapter 10). Even today Bentham's approach to economics inspires contemporary extensions of neoclassical theory into such areas as the economics of crime and the economics of franchise bidding (see the notes for further reading at the end of the chapter). In a general sense, Bentham was a master innovator of institutional and administrative reforms designed to alter economic incentives in compliance with the general will.

■ Thomas Robert Malthus and Population

A second cornerstone of classical economics was the population principle. The writer who gave classical population theory its definitive statement was Thomas

Robert Malthus (1766–1834). John Maynard Keynes, who later led a group of like-minded academicians at Cambridge University, called Malthus the "first of the Cambridge economists." At Cambridge Malthus studied for the ministry. Despite a congenital cleft palate, he won prizes for his declamations in Greek, Latin, and English. He graduated in 1788 and took holy orders the same year, but he remained at Cambridge as a graduate fellow until 1804, at which time he married, and according to the rules of the college, had to resign his fellowship.

Malthus's father befriended Jean-Jacques Rousseau and David Hume, both of whom are reputed to have been young Robert's (he went by his middle name) first visitors when he was an infant. Robert Malthus grew into an independent thinker, a trait that he later put to good use in establishing his reputation. In 1798 Malthus published, anonymously, *An Essay on the Principle of Population as It Affects the Future Improvement of Society, with Remarks on the Speculations of Mr. Godwin, M. Condorcet, and Other Writers*. Anonymity, however, quickly gave way to general recognition, and in due course, Malthus's name became a household word.

The full title of the *Essay* hints at its underlying motivation. Malthus reacted against the extreme optimism of the philosophers Godwin and Condorcet, who, inspired by the political euphoria of the French Revolution, forecast the elimination of social evils. They envisioned a society devoid of war, crime, government, disease, anguish, melancholy, and resentment, where every man unflinchingly sought the good of all. Malthus's answer to this utopian vision was deceptively simple: the perfectibility of human society is impossible, he stated, because the biological capacity of man to reproduce will, if left unchecked, outstrip the physical means of subsistence.

Malthus wrote his first *Essay on Population* without much evidential support. Afterward, and partly because of the furor it created, he began to add some empirical flesh to his bare-bones theory. Subsequent editions of the *Essay* appeared in 1803, 1806, 1807, 1817, and 1826. Finally, Malthus published *A Summary View of the Principle of Population* in 1830. By then the population principle he made famous had become a canon of classical economics. Despite numerous modifications through its several editions, the core thesis of the first *Essay* remained unchanged.

An Outline of the Theory

Malthus based his population principle on two propositions. The first asserted that "Population, when unchecked, increases in a geometrical progression of such a nature as to double itself every twenty-five years" (*A Summary View*, p. 238). He attempted to add precision to this principle by basing it on population experience in the United States. Available statistics were unreliable, however, and provided little real empirical support for Malthus's first postulate. Consequently, he acknowledged that this doubling of population every twenty-five years was neither the maximum growth rate of population nor necessarily the actual rate. But he insisted throughout that the potential growth rate of population always advanced in *geometric* progression.

The second postulate asserted that under even the most favorable circumstances, the means of subsistence (i.e., the food supply) cannot possibly increase faster than in arithmetic progression. The precision that Malthus attributed to this second assertion was unfortunate, since the arithmetic progression of the food supply could not be supported by fact, not even as loosely as the first assertion could about the growth of population. Nevertheless, the juxtaposition of these two postulates was jarring because it established an obvious discrepancy between the potential growth of population versus the food supply. In Malthus's own words: "The power of population being . . . so much superior, the increase of the human species can only be kept down to the level of the means of subsistence by the constant operation of the strong law of necessity, acting as a check upon the greater power" (*A Summary View*, p. 21).

This population dilemma posed theoretical and practical questions. The theoretical question centered on the identification of the actual checks to population growth; the practical question concerned solutions to the problem, namely, which checks should be encouraged over others. Malthus discussed both issues, beginning with the identification problem.

Positive and Preventive Checks. The ultimate check on population growth is limited food supply. But there are others, and Malthus classified various limiting factors into positive checks and preventive checks. The former, such as disease, increase the death rate; whereas the latter, such as contraception, lower the birthrate. A man of the cloth, Malthus held certain religious convictions. Hence, he favored neither contraception nor abortion as practical means to circumscribe population growth. In a carefully measured condemnation of the latter, he described abortion as "improper arts to conceal the consequences of irregular connection"! Although his views in this regard may be considered quaint by contemporary standards, the important issue for our purposes is the separation of theory and policy.

From a theoretical perspective the significance of Malthus's contribution lay in his ability to mold the procreative tendency and the checks to it into an analytical framework that focused attention on those forces tending to change the number of people on earth. The following summary is uppermost in Malthus's population theory:

Positive Checks on Population Growth: war, famine, pestilence
Preventive Checks on Population Growth: moral restraint, contraception, abortion

As theory, the population principle tells us that population will increase whenever the cumulative effect of the various checks is less than that of procreation; that it will decrease whenever the cumulative effect of the checks is greater than that of procreation; and that it will remain unchanged whenever the combined effects of the checks and of procreation are self-canceling. Viewed in this matter-of-fact way, the theory is value-free, and the analyst's job becomes that of determining the quantitative dimensions of the forces at play.

Theoretical Limitations. On the face of it, Malthus's population theory is neutral with respect to assumptions and conclusions. Given relevant empirical inputs as described above, the theory is capable of explaining all manner of population changes: growth, depopulation, or stagnation. But although the theory is quite general, Malthus advanced a specific outcome of the population–food supply struggle: he asserted that the inevitable result would be a subsistence economy. He believed that the tendency to procreate would in fact dominate the cumulative effect of the checks to population growth. This represents a departure from value-free science. It is an unfortunate departure for two reasons: (1) as prophecy, it has frequently proved wrong, and (2) the conclusion Malthus committed to is not at all inherent in his purely theoretical structure.

Does this tendency to draw a false conclusion invalidate the theory on which it rests? Not necessarily, for Malthus' theoretical structure is quite capable of yielding general conclusions regarding population and subsistence for different economies at different historical periods. What is required to make the theory operational in a predictive sense is reliable information about the magnitude of the tendencies embodied in his theoretical apparatus.

Malthus has been faulted for overlooking other checks that might forestall his gloomy conclusion. For one thing, he did not conceptually separate sex and procreation. Yet in a world of modern birth control techniques and other arts of family planning, the distinction is especially relevant. Many families limit the number of their offspring for reasons other than financial ones (e.g., a desire for personal freedom and mobility or a career). These additional checks overlooked by Malthus are capable of reducing the disparity between multiplication of the species and growth of the food supply.

A more serious shortcoming of Malthus's population theory was his tendency, shared by other classical writers, to underestimate the advance of agricultural technology. There was already the hint in the *Essay* that agriculture is subject to diminishing returns, a topic that Malthus later expanded in his theory of rent. As an economic law, however, diminishing returns hold only for a constant state of technology. And in advanced economies, rapid progress in technology has so far succeeded in forestalling the Malthusian specter of overpopulation and starvation. This does not, of course, deny the very real threat of subsistence in the developing world, where the Malthusian specter appears to be a genuine obstacle to economic growth and development. However, it is not at all clear that the problems of the developing world derive from natural calamities rather than the failure of government. (See the box, The Force of Ideas: Malthus, Birth Control, and Authoritarian Governments.)

The Force of Ideas: Malthus, Birth Control, and Authoritarian Governments

Malthus was somewhat ambivalent, but mostly pessimistic, concerning the relation between food supply and population. However, his population principle establishes that if the "checks" to population are sufficiently effective, it is possible to stave off population disasters and food crises indefinitely. Today there is more optimism in this regard because technological change has increased the effectiveness of Malthus's checks and brought new checks into existence. Persistent improvements in agricultural technology have raised the prospects of greater food supply. New and improved methods of birth control appear from time to time, reducing the prospects of excessive population growth. But in addition to factors overlooked by Malthus, such as changes in technology, economic theory has also matured to the point of offering additional explanations of population growth and decline.

In developed economies, income and wealth tend to grow as population expands. Contemporary economics tells us that income growth produces both income and substitution effects. As real income rises, so does the demand for most goods; as prices rise (alongside higher incomes), however, people tend to substitute relatively cheaper goods in place of relatively expensive ones. Children may be viewed as investment goods or as consumption goods. The tendency to treat children as investment goods is stronger in poor countries than in rich countries, for reasons that will be explained below. Nobel laureate Gary Becker (see chapter 26) and other economists have pointed out that when time costs are admitted, children are relatively expensive consumption goods. So in rich countries people tend to substitute relatively cheaper consumption goods—as measured by explicit and implicit costs—for relatively more expensive children. In other words, people buy more "stuff" and have fewer children. This phenomenon explains part of the reduction in population in the developed world, where fertility rates (i.e., number of live births per female) have been declining for some time, especially in Europe and North America. It also explains in part why population rates are high in poorer countries, where children are most often regarded as investment goods because on the one hand they provide labor resources to the family unit and on the other they provide a kind of "social security" for parents in their old age.

(continued)

Periodically we hear tragic news of massive starvation and high child mortality rates in poor countries, such as those in sub-Saharan Africa. Our first response is to invoke the ghost of Malthus to explain such misery. But the causes of starvation may lie elsewhere. Although differing in degree, income and substitution effects are in play everywhere. People who have limited means of accumulating wealth may regard children as a cheap means of "wealth" accumulation, driving population higher even in the face of poverty. We must also recognize that authoritarian governments may curtail economic growth by actions that reduce incentives to invest or adopt new technology. In other words, not all imbalances between population and food supply may be attributable to the factors that Malthus described.

■ Early Monetary Issues

For a time at least, Malthus's population theory seemed to settle an important question in classical economics, the issue of labor supply. After Malthus, population came to be the chief determinant of wages, and in subsequent explanations of labor's aggregate share of annual output, emphasis was placed on the wages-fund concept, which drew additional support from Malthus's population doctrine. An issue that proved more difficult to settle was the monetary question, namely what effect, if any, money has on economic activity.

Preclassical Monetary Theory

From roughly 1650 to 1776, monetary theory consisted primarily of two strands of thought. One argument advanced by John Law, Jacob Vanderlint, and (Bishop) George Berkeley was that "money stimulates trade." This argument stressed the effect of money on output and employment, largely ignoring the connection between money and prices. The other argument, made most forcefully by John Locke, Richard Cantillon, and David Hume, emphasized the connection between money and prices.

Like many early theories, the money-stimulates-trade argument was a useful first approximation. Underlying the theory was the idea that, given a volume of trade, there is an appropriate amount of money required to carry out exchange transactions. The element of truth in the money-stimulates-trade doctrine is that money is an important determinant of aggregate spending, which in turn determines the levels of output and employment. But this theoretical progression does not go far enough, especially in two critical respects. First, as previously noted, it ignores the possible effects of money on the price level. And second, it overlooks the role of expectations in the decision-making process. This last matter sharply divides Keynes (see chapter 21) from the money-stimulates-trade theorists of the seventeenth and eighteenth centuries. Unlike his forebears, Keynes did not assert that money is the key to solving unemployment. However, like them, he saw money as the key to *explaining* unemployment.

Although we have already discussed the mechanics of the quantity theory of money in chapters 3 and 4, we take this occasion to mention once again the name of David Hume (1711–1776), at whose hands the quantity theory of money took the form of its commonly accepted version. It was Hume who attempted a reconciliation of the money-stimulates-trade theory with the quantity theory of money. Moreover, it is in Hume's economic writings that the concept of neutral money emerges for the first time. As Keynes observed, "Hume had a foot and a half in the classical world" (*General Theory*, p. 343n).

Eighteenth-century attitudes toward money cannot be understood in a historical vacuum. The century opened with the monetary experiments of John Law, "who was inspired by the idea that an abundance of money is the royal road to wealth" (Rist, *History*, p. 103). After the collapse of Law's inflationary system in France, most of the enlightened men of that epoch—from Cantillon to Hume, from Quesnay and Turgot to Smith, and in the next century, from Thornton to Ricardo—deemphasized the importance of money, insisting instead that labor and natural resources are the fundamentals of wealth. Paradoxically, the business community continued to believe in a metallic currency even as the theorists argued against it.

Because Europe was ravaged by war throughout the eighteenth century, there was a great deal of pressure on the economies of Europe to expand the money supply. Scarcely had forced paper currency been established in England at the close of the century when everybody began to ponder ways and means of returning as quickly as possible to metallic currency. There may be some lessons for the present in this past experience. Adam Smith clearly taught that the only things that count in the advancement of wealth are the resources nature provides for man's activity and the use he makes of them through his labor and inventions. But this is not enough. It must be kept in mind that human beings live in society and that society is based on a set of reciprocal exchanges. The greater part of these exchanges takes place over extended periods of time, which introduces some uncertainty about the future. The goods that offer the best possibility of guarding against the uncertainties of time are precious, rare, durable, indestructible objects, such as gold.

In periods of increased uncertainty brought on by incipient inflation, controversies over "hard money" versus paper currencies are resurrected. Control of money supply is an important responsibility in every nation, and uncertainty waxes and wanes with volatility in stocks of money. What has been more durable as a theoretical issue is the controversy over money's "neutrality" or "nonneutrality." The neutrality of money refers to the fact that changes in the money stock have no effect on *relative* prices. In their zeal to discredit the mercantilist idea that money constitutes wealth, early monetary theorists gave the impression that money is a veil that hides the real forces of productivity, which alone account for genuine economic wealth. All that monetary changes do is change the *price level* in proportion to the change in money. Hume gave the classic exposition of this view:

> If we consider any one kingdom by itself, it is evident, that the greater or less plenty of money is of no consequence; since the prices of commodities are always proportioned to the plenty of money. . . . It is a maxim almost self-evident, that the prices of everything depend on the proportion between commodities and money, and that any considerable alteration on either has the same effect, either of heightening or lowering the price. (*Writings*, pp. 33, 41)

It is one thing to isolate the effects of money changes on the price level while ignoring the concomitant effects on relative prices, but it is quite another to deny that monetary shocks have any effect whatsoever on relative prices. Not all early monetary theorists were naive in this regard. Cantillon (see chapter 4) saw quite clearly the relative price effects of money, and Hume also worked out a domestic adjustment mechanism that described the short-run as well as the long-run effects of a change in money. He observed that an increase or decrease in money supply impacted not only prices but also employment, output, and productivity (Mayer,

"David Hume and Monetarism," p. 573). Finally, Gary Becker and William Baumol found virtually no support for the view that early monetary theorists unequivocally endorsed the "neutral money thesis." They thereby concluded that the whole idea was basically a "straw man" constructed for the convenience of neoclassical monetary theorists ("The Classical Monetary Theory," p. 376).

Classical Monetary Theory

Insofar as pure theory is concerned, most of the ground in monetary economics was broken in the eighteenth century. The nineteenth century had little more to do than adopt the monetary theory of Cantillon and Hume, which it did, sometimes adding more confusion than light.

The Bullion Report of 1810 provides the best summary statement of the period's monetary thought. As the eighteenth century came to a close England's attempt to check the imperialistic designs of Napoleon put a strain on the British banking system. In 1797 England stopped paying out funds in gold. At first Britain's switch to an inconvertible paper currency produced only a slight increase in the circulation of British bank notes and little change in exchange rates. But beginning in 1808 the increase in note issue began to make itself felt as prices climbed steadily and exchange rates fell. Certain sectors of the public expressed their concern, and early in 1810 Francis Horner, a member of Parliament, proposed in the House of Commons that a committee be appointed to investigate the high price of bullion. A number of witnesses were called to testify, after which a report drawn up largely by Horner, William Huskisson, and Henry Thornton was delivered to the Commons in June. It was not debated until the following year, however, when its conclusions were rejected.

The Bullion Report was the first official argument against discretionary monetary policy. It maintained that an excessive amount of note issue influenced the value of paper money and it attributed the high price of bullion (inflation) to this cause. Paradoxically, and contrary to prevailing evidence, the report maintained that Britain's monetary problems were not caused by a lack of public confidence in paper money. The committee's stance in this regard may have been staked by Thornton, who took a similar position in his book, *An Enquiry into the Nature and Effects of the Paper Credit of Great Britain* (1802). By the end of the report, however, the committee had practically reversed itself, for it concluded that the return to convertibility was the only way to "effectively restore general confidence in the value of the circulating medium of the kingdom" (Cannan, *Paper Pound*, p. 70).

The Bullion Report served as a pretext for David Ricardo's (see chapter 7) early pamphlets on monetary matters, which were published as commentaries on the report. In 1809, Ricardo issued his "Treatise on the Price of Bullion," and in 1816, his "Proposals for an Economical and Secure Currency." In both works Ricardo reaffirmed the quantity theory of money and advocated a return to convertibility. The concept of *quantity* completely dominated Ricardo's monetary theory. He maintained that both declines and rises in the price level are regulated by changes in the quantity of money. The idea of money as a store of value seems not to have occurred to him. He makes no mention of the demand for money. He defined money in the narrowest terms as a mere *regulator* of value. Ricardo either rejected or ignored the idea of money as a link between the present and the future by virtue of its imperishability and scarcity. His view of credit was also overly restrictive. For example, unlike Cantillon, he did not think of checks as instruments of circulation but as a means of economizing on the use of money. Since he did not regard checks as currency instruments, they could not affect prices. Taken together, Ricardo's ideas on money had the effect of changing the quantity theory of money into the *Ricardian* theory of money. His formulation was so one-sided and restrictive that it led many later economists to regard with suspicion any theory of money or prices in which quantity plays a part.

Published in 1823 after his death, Ricardo's *Plan of a National Bank* furthered the notion that paper money is an efficient substitute for metallic money because it requires fewer resources to maintain. All that is necessary is to fix the quantity of paper money once and for all. Ricardo devised a plan for this whereby the state would be granted the monopoly issue of paper money and would only be able to issue new notes against a backing of new gold from abroad. He introduced an element of currency elasticity, however, by allowing the central bank to engage in open-market operations: It would buy government securities when it desired to increase the quantity of money and sell them when it desired to decrease the quantity of money. These purchases and sales were to be determined by changes in the exchange rate, which would reflect the relation between the value of paper money and its metallic counterpart. Thus, it can be seen that the idea of such operations, while sometimes regarded as the height of modernism, is in fact very old. Moreover, it seems but a brief step from recognizing the legitimacy of such operations under a gold standard to the idea of a fully managed, fiat currency.

John Stuart Mill (see chapter 8), who represented classical economics at the height of its influence, also accepted the quantity theory but added qualifications to it, some of which served to correct Ricardo's excesses. For one thing, Mill recognized (as did Cantillon and Hume) that the rigid conclusions of the quantity theory were based on the assumption of an equiproportionate distribution of new money relative to initial money holdings. Any other distribution would upset the strict proportionality between money and prices. Furthermore, he believed that the strict quantity theory held only for metallic money. He said:

> When credit comes into play as a means of purchasing, distinct from money in hand, we shall hereafter find that the connection between prices and the amount of circulating medium is much less direct and intimate, and that such connection as does exist no longer admits of so simple a mode of expression. (*Principles*, p. 495)

Mill also recognized that an increase in bank credit under conditions of full employment could drive the interest rate down.

By far the brightest light among the classical monetary theorists was Henry Thornton, the British banker and parliamentarian mentioned above in connection with the Bullion Report of 1810. Thornton made two important contributions to monetary theory: (1) the distinction between the natural rate of interest and the bank (loan) rate of interest, and (2) the doctrine of "forced saving."

Regarding the first principle, Thornton correctly pointed out that the rate of return on invested capital (determined by thrift and productivity) regulates the bank interest rate on loans. If the bank rate is below the return on invested capital, competition for business loans will drive the bank rate up; if the bank rate is above the return on invested capital, the demand for bank loans will dry up, forcing banks to lower rates in order to make loans. Therefore, the question of determining the optimum quantity of bank loans depends on a comparison of the rate of return on capital (Thornton called this the "natural" rate) and the interest rate on bank loans. If investment and savings are determined by the real forces of thrift and productivity, then only a change in one or the other of these forces will shift the schedules depicted in figure 6-1. In this model, *SS′* represents the supply of savings as a function of the interest rate. Likewise, *II′* represents the demand for investable funds also as a function of the interest rate. The intersection of *SS′* and *II′* determines the natural rate (r). In monetary equilibrium, the loan rate (i) will be equal to the natural rate. But if monetary equilibrium is disturbed by an increase in paper money, the interest rate on bank loans will be driven down, say to i' (because of an increase in loanable funds). At the same time, *SS′* and *II′* would remain unchanged unless there was a change in the real factors of thrift and productivity, which would not be induced by a purely monetary phenomenon such as an increase in paper money.

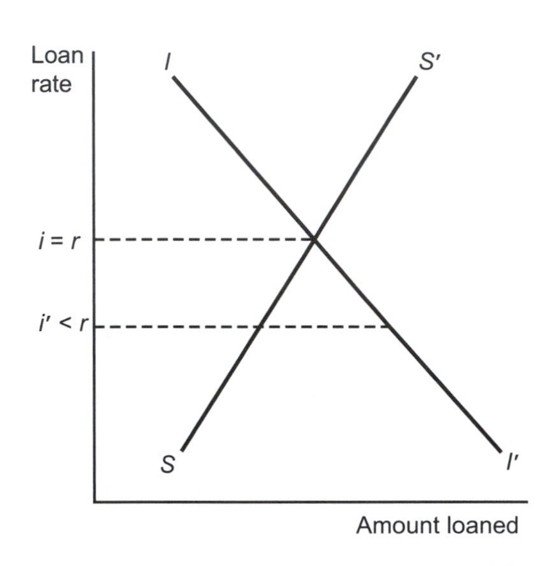

Figure 6-1 At monetary equilibrium, the loan rate is equal to the natural rate ($i = r$). With a monetary disturbance, the loan rate will diverge from the natural rate ($i \neq r$).

Thus, a gap would be created between the natural rate and the loan rate, and this gap would give rise to an insatiable demand for loans. The ensuing inflationary pressure would be eliminated only when the loan rate was again raised to its former level at r. In the process, however, prices would have climbed to a higher level. In this way, the quantity theory is vindicated: An increase in money leads to higher prices but not to a (long-run) change in the real interest rate.

Thornton's second contribution—the doctrine of forced saving—recognized that an increase in money brings about an increase in capital as well as an increase in prices. This would be the case as long as part of the new money went to entrepreneurs. If entrepreneurs converted this new money into capital, then output effects (forced capital accumulation) would accompany the higher prices associated with the increase in money; hence money would not be strictly neutral, as Hume maintained. In addition, Thornton suggested the possibility that an increase in bank notes under conditions of general unemployment would lead to an increase in output and employment rather than an increase in prices. Clearly, Thornton affirmed the neutrality of money only as a long-run proposition, and then only under certain circumstances.

■ Classical Economics and the Generators of Trade and Value

Classical economists, at least those writers reviewed in this chapter, placed little or no emphasis on entrepreneurism, with the exception of Jeremy Bentham, who was drawn into a discussion of the topic by his disagreement with Adam Smith on the subject of usury. Smith's advocacy of usury laws to prevent excessive financial resources from reaching prodigals and projectors struck a discordant note with Bentham, who considered it odd (as did many later economists) that the apostle of laissez-faire would advocate government intervention in financial markets. Smith established his position in a discussion of "sober people" (his offhand reference to entrepreneurs) in the *Wealth of Nations* (pp. 339–340):

> The legal rate [of interest] . . . , though it ought to be somewhat above, ought not to be much above, the lowest market rate. If the legal rate of interest in Great Britain, for example, was fixed so high as eight or ten per cent the greater part of the money which was to be lent, would be lent to prodigals and projectors, who alone would be willing to give this high interest. Sober people, who will give for the use of money no more than a part of what they are likely to make by the use of it, would not venture into the competition. A great part of the capital of the country would thus be kept out of the hands which were most likely to make a profitable and advantageous use of it, and thrown into those which were most likely to waste and destroy it. Where the legal interest, on the contrary, is fixed but a very little above the lowest market rate, sober people are universally preferred as borrowers, to prodigals and projectors. The person who lends money, gets nearly as much interest from the former, as he dares to take from the latter, and his money is much safer in the hands of the one set of people than in those of the other. A great part of the capital of the country is thus thrown into the hands in which it is most likely to be employed with advantage.

Bentham responded in his *Defence of Usury* (1787) that laws against usury limit the overall quantity of capital loaned and borrowed, and act to keep away foreign money from domestic capital markets. Both these effects tend to throttle the activities of successful entrepreneurs and impede economic development. He argued that interest rate ceilings discriminate against entrepreneurs of new projects, because, by their sheer novelty, such projects are more risky than those already proven profitable by experience. Moreover, legal restrictions such as usury laws are powerless to pick out bad projects from good ones.

Bentham pressed his argument further. He criticized Smith for underestimating the role of talented individuals whose imagination and inventiveness have been responsible for the progress of nations. He regarded innovation as the driving force behind the development of humanity, and viewed the projector as innovator. Hence, he reprimanded Smith for lumping prodigals and projectors together. For Bentham, the distinguishing feature of the latter is that they depart from routine patterns of behavior, break away from the common herd, discover new markets, find new sources of supply, and improve existing products or lower costs of production. Bentham asserted that to be a projector requires courage and genius ("Defence," p. 177), qualities to which we attribute "all those successive enterprizes by which arts and manufactures have been brought from their original nothing to their present splendor." Projectors create utility, Bentham argued, by bringing about improvements, whether such improvements "consist in the production of any new article adapted to man's use, or in meliorating the quality, or diminishing the expence, of any of those which are already known to us. It falls, in short, upon every application of the human powers, in which ingenuity stands in need of wealth for its assistant" ("Defence," p. 170). The affinity of this view to Schumpeter's (see chapter 23) is unmistakable.[1]

According to Pesciarelli ("Smith, Bentham"), Smith and Bentham each had a different view of human progress and consequently a different conception of the

[1] Pesciarelli ("Smith, Bentham," p. 531) points out that four of the five new combinations that comprise innovation emphasized by Schumpeter in his *Theory of Economic Development* were previously identified by Bentham.

entrepreneur. Bentham's entrepreneur is an exceptional individual, one above the common herd—a minority in society. Smith's entrepreneur is a common type—widespread in society, one who exercises self-control in the exercise of economic activity in order to receive the approbation of others. According to Pesciarelli, "The prudent man *unconsciously* promotes the interest of society because he *consciously* sets limits on the pursuit of his own interests. He is the *visible* promoter of the *invisible* hand; he is the *fulcrum* but also the *limit* of Smith's belief in the working of a self-adjusting mechanism" ("Smith, Bentham," pp. 534–535). Their divergent views led to different conceptions of economic development. For Bentham economic development is generated by discontinuous changes involving improvements (in the broadest sense) and resulting in a nonlinear path of progress. Smith's notion of economic progress is slow, gradual, uniform, and not subject to sudden variations.

By supporting the cause of projectors, Bentham was to some extent pleading his own case. He was a proponent of the Panopticon, the name he gave to his model prison, an architectural and institutional innovation. His brother, Samuel, devised the architectural idea behind the Panopticon, and it was first applied in Russia. This new prison consisted of a circular design in which all the cells were arranged concentrically facing a central pavilion, which contained an inspector, or at most a small number of inspectors. From his central vantage point the inspector could easily observe all the prisoners without being seen himself. Hidden by a system of blinds, prison administrators, even outside visitors, could inspect the prisoners while rendered invisible. Bentham thought that this would reform prisoners, because under constant scrutiny they would lose the will and the power to do evil. The idea was somewhat fanciful, and Bentham was never able to attract enough backers to make his model prison a reality. The site that he proposed for his novel construction was subsequently taken by the Tate Gallery in London.

Bentham's innovation on his brother's design was an administrative arrangement that established management by contract. The success of this arrangement was made to depend on the dynamic activities of the entrepreneur and the proper structuring of economic incentives. Bentham believed that true reform would occur in prisons only if the administrative plan simultaneously protected convicts against the harshness of their warders, on the one hand, and society against the wastefulness of administrators on the other. The choice, as he saw it, was between contract management and trust management. Elie Halévy explained the differences between these two administrative arrangements:

> Contract-management is management by a man who treats with the government, and takes charge of the convicts at so much a head and applies their time and industry to his personal profit, as does a master with his apprentices. Trust-management is management by a single individual or by a committee, who keep up the establishment at the public expense, and pay into the treasury the products of the convicts' work. (*Growth*, p. 84)

Bentham did not believe that trust management could establish the proper junction of interest and duty on the part of the entrepreneur because its success depended on "public interest" as a motivating factor. Like Smith, Bentham had much more confidence in individual self-interest as the spur to human action. But he had no confidence in spontaneous order. The beauty of contract management was that it brought about an *artificial* identity of interests between the public on the one hand and the entrepreneur on the other. In Bentham's scheme the entrepreneur is an independent contractor who "purchases," through competitive bid, the right to run the prison, thereby also acquiring title to whatever profits might be earned by the application of convict labor. Such an entrepreneur-manager could maximize his long-term gains by preserving the health and productivity of his worker-convicts. In this manner public interest became entwined with private interest.

In 1787, Bentham completed the idea of contract management by an additional administrative arrangement. He thought that life insurance offered an excellent means of joining the interest of one man to the preservation of a number of men. He therefore proposed that after consulting the appropriate mortality tables, the entrepreneur (prison manager) should be given a fixed sum of money for each convict due to die that year in prison, on condition that at the end of the year he must pay back the same sum for each convict who had actually died in prison. The entrepreneur would keep the difference as profit, thus providing economic incentive to lower the average mortality rate in his prison (*Works*, p. 53).

Bentham was virtually alone among British classical economists in his repeated emphasis on the entrepreneur as an agent of economic progress. Through contract management he recast the entrepreneur as government contractor, a franchisee who undertakes financial risk in order to obtain an uncertain profit. He also explicitly linked entrepreneurship to invention. He promoted contract management as a progressive (administrative) innovation that should therefore be rewarded accordingly, no less than an inventor is rewarded for a successful (product) invention (*Works*, p. 47).

■ Conclusion

The issues and concerns raised in this chapter combined to form the general backdrop against which classical economic analysis was staged in the nineteenth century. Self-interest became the dominant explanation of economic activity. Malthus's population theory entered economic analysis as an endogenous variable and became an integral part of the theory of aggregate income distribution. Finally, the quantity theory of money provided the analytical structure for understanding and explaining changes in the aggregate price level. With the exception of population theory, each of these propositions has remained within the corpus of mainstream economics. Neoclassical economics reclassified population changes as exogenous variables, that is, "outside" influences beyond the direct concern of the theorist. Smith recognized the role of the entrepreneur in society, but did not take full advantage of Cantillon's thoroughgoing insights regarding the centrality of the entrepreneur in the market economy. Whereupon, Bentham seized the opportunity to recast the entrepreneur as government contractor, but his idea remained fallow: the next generation of economists focused on other aspects of Smith's vision.

References

Becker, Gary, and William Baumol. "The Classical Monetary Theory: The Outcome of the Discussion," *Economica*, n.s., vol. 19 (November 1952), pp. 355–376.

Bentham, Jeremy. "Defence of Usury," in *Jeremy Bentham's Economic Writings*, vol. 1. W. Stark (ed.). London: George Allen & Unwin, 1952 [1787].

———. *An Introduction to the Principles of Morals and Legislation*. Oxford: The Clarendon Press, 1879 [1789].

———. *The Works of Jeremy Bentham*, vol. 4. J. Bowring (ed.). New York: Russell & Russell, 1962 [1838–1843].

Cannan, Edwin. *The Paper Pound of 1797–1821*. London: King, 1921.

Halévy, Elie. *The Growth of Philosophic Radicalism*, Mary Morris (trans.). London: Faber, 1928.

Hume, David. *David Hume: Writings on Economics*, E. Rotwein (ed.). Madison: University of Wisconsin Press, 1970.

Keynes, J. M. *The General Theory of Employment, Interest and Money*. London: Macmillan, 1936.

Malthus, T. R. *An Essay on the Principle of Population* and *a Summary View of the Principle of Population*, A. Flew (ed.). Baltimore: Penguin, 1970.

Mayer, Thomas. "David Hume and Monetarism," *Quarterly Journal of Economics*, vol. 95 (August 1980), pp. 89–101.

Mill, J. S. *Principles of Political Economy*, W. J. Ashley (ed.). New York: A. M. Kelley, 1965 [1848].

Pesciarelli, Enzo. "Smith, Bentham and the Development of Contrasting Ideas on Entrepreneurship," *History of Political Economy*, vol. 21 (Fall 1989), pp. 521–536.

Rist, Charles. *History of Monetary and Credit Theory*, Jane Degras (trans.). New York: Macmillan, 1940.

Smith, Adam. *An Inquiry into the Nature and Causes of the Wealth of Nations*, Edwin Cannan (ed.). New York: Modern Library, 1937 [1776].

Notes for Further Reading

General references to Bentham and his ideas include J. L. Stocks, *Jeremy Bentham* (Manchester, England: Manchester University Press, 1933); C. W. Everett, *Jeremy Bentham* (New York: Dell, 1966); D. J. Manning, *The Mind of Jeremy Bentham* (London: Longmans, 1900); and Elie Halévy (see references). From the standpoint of economics, perhaps the best original source on Bentham is his *Economic Writings*, 3 vols., W. Stark (ed.) (London: George Allen & Unwin, 1952–1954). *The Works of Jeremy Bentham*, 11 vols., J. Bowring (ed.) (New York: Russell & Russell, 1962), is more complete but ranges far beyond economics to morals, philosophy, and jurisprudence.

Two opposing views of Bentham's felicific calculus are presented by Lionel Robbins, *Bentham in the Twentieth Century* (London: University of London, Athlone Press, 1965); and John Plamenatz, *The English Utilitarians*, 2d ed. (Oxford: Blackwell, 1958). On the same subject, see W. C. Mitchell, "Bentham's Felicific Calculus," *Political Science Quarterly*, vol. 33 (June 1918), pp. 161–183, reprinted in *The Backward Art of Spending Money* (New York: McGraw-Hill, 1937). Bentham's welfare theory is examined by Antoinette Baujard, "A Return to Bentham's *Felicific Calculus*: From Moral Welfarism to Technical Non-welfarism," *European Journal of the History of Economic Thought*, vol. 16, (Summer 2009), pp. 431–453; and same author, "Collective Interest versus Individual Interest in Bentham's Felicific Calculus: Questioning Welfarism and Fairness," *European Journal of the History of Economic Thought*, vol. 17 (Fall 2010), pp. 607–634. Francophones should consult Nathalie Sigot, *Bentham et l'économique. Une histoire d'utilité* (Paris: Economica, 2001). On the impact of Bentham on the French Revolution and vice versa, see two articles by Marco Guidi, "The French Revolution and the Creation of Benthamism," *European Journal of the History of Economic Thought*, vol. 16 (Summer 2009), pp. 375–380; and same author, "Jeremy Bentham, the French Revolution and the Political Economy of Representation (1788–1789)," *European Journal of the History of Economic Thought*, vol. 17 (Fall 2010), pp. 579–605.

Other treatments include W. Stark, "Liberty and Equality, or: Jeremy Bentham as an Economist," *Economic Journal*, vol. 51 (April 1941), pp. 56–79, and vol. 56 (December 1946), pp. 583–608; Jacob Viner, "Bentham and J. S. Mill: The Utilitarian Background," *American Economic Review*, vol. 39 (March 1949), pp. 360–382; and T. W. Hutchison,

"Bentham as an Economist," *Economic Journal*, vol. 66 (June 1956), pp. 288–306. Also interesting is P. A. Palmer's "Benthamism in England and America," *American Political Science Review*, vol. 35 (October 1941), pp. 855–871; and E. G. West, "The Benthamites as Educational Engineers: The Reputation and the Record," *History of Political Economy*, vol. 24 (Fall 1992), pp. 595–622.

The standard reference on Malthus is James Bonar, *Malthus and His Work*, 2d ed. (New York: Macmillan, 1924). Another useful work is G. F. McCleary, *The Malthusian Population Theory* (London: Faber, 1953). See also, W. Petersen, *Malthus* (Cambridge, MA: Harvard University Press, 1979). James Bonar, C. R. Fay, and J. M. Keynes combined efforts to write "A Commemoration of Thomas Robert Malthus," *Economic Journal*, vol. 45 (June 1935), pp. 221–234, on the occasion of the centenary of Malthus's death. Keynes was also lavish in his praise of Malthus in his *Essays in Biography* (New York: Norton, 1963). For other appraisals, see Lionel Robbins, "Malthus as an Economist," *Economic Journal*, vol. 77 (June 1967), pp. 256–261; and R. L. Meek, "Malthus: Yesterday and Today," *Science and Society*, vol. 18 (Winter 1954), pp. 21–51.

Noteworthy treatments of Malthus's population theory include S. M. Levin, "Malthus's Conception of the Checks to Population," *Human Biology*, vol. 10 (1938), pp. 214–234; same author, "Malthus and the Idea of Progress," *Journal of the History of Ideas*, vol. 27 (January–March 1966), pp. 92–108; Kingsley Davis, "Malthus and the Theory of Population," in P. F. Lazarsfeld and M. Rosenberg (eds.), *The Language of Social Research* (New York: Free Press, 1955); J. P. Hubel, "The Demographic Impact of the Old Poor Law: More Reflections on Malthus," *Economic History Review*, vol. 33 (August 1980), pp. 367–381; David Collard, "Malthus, Population, and the Generational Bargain," *History of Political Economy*, vol. 33 (Winter 2001), pp. 697–716; J. M. Pullen, "Malthus on the Doctrine of Proportion and the Concept of the Optimum," *Australian Economic Papers*, vol. 21 (December 1982), pp. 270–285; same author, "Some New Information on the Rev. T. R. Malthus," *History of Political Economy*, vol. 19 (Spring 1987), pp. 127–140; P. Laslett, "Gregory King, Robert Malthus and the Origins of English Social Realism," *Population Studies*, vol. 39 (November 1985), pp. 351–362; and two articles by Samuel Hollander: "On Malthus's Population Principle and Social Reform," *History of Political Economy*, vol. 18 (Summer 1986), pp. 187–235; and same author, "Malthus's Vision of the Population Problem in the Essay on Population," *Journal of the History of Economic Thought*, vol. 12 (Spring 1990), pp. 1–26. Elise S. Brezis and Warren Young, "The New Views on Demographic Transition: A Reassessment of Malthus's and Marx's Approach to Population," *The European Journal of the History of Economic Thought*, vol. 10 (Spring 2003), pp. 25–45, explore the divergence of views regarding the family and labor market caused by different concepts of demographic transition. For an interesting account of where Malthus's population data came from, see Dean Peterson, "The Origins of Malthus's Data on Population: The Political and Religious Biases in the American Sources," *Journal of the History of Economic Thought*, vol. 19 (Spring 1997), pp. 114–126.

Correspondence between Senior and Malthus on the subject of population can be found in Nassau Senior's *Selected Writings on Economics* (New York: Augustus Kelley, 1966). Russell Dean, "Owenism and the Malthusian Population Question, 1815–35," *History of Political Economy*, vol. 27 (Fall 1995), pp. 579–597, draws a connection between Malthus and the Utopian Socialist, Robert Owen (see chapter 11). To celebrate the bicentennial of the first (anonymous) edition of Malthus's *Essay on the Principle of Population*, a mini-symposium was held that involved a number of Malthus scholars; see the papers and commentary by A. M. C. Waterman, Samuel Hollander, J. M. Pullen, and Donald Winch in *History of Political Economy*, vol. 30 (Summer 1998), pp. 289–363.

Monetary theory has an old and extensive history. On the preclassical period, see Douglas Vickers, *Studies in the Theory of Money: 1690–1776* (Philadelphia: Chilton, 1959); A. E. Monroe, *Monetary Theory before Adam Smith* (Cambridge, MA: Harvard

University Press, 1923); William Letwin, *The Origins of Scientific Economics* (Garden City, NY: Doubleday, 1964), which contains a reprint of Locke's early *Manuscript on Interest*; and Jacob Viner, *Studies in the Theory of International Trade* (New York: Harper & Row, 1937). F. Cesarano, "Monetary Theory in Ferdinando Galiani's *Della Moneta*," *History of Political Economy*, vol. 8 (Autumn 1976), pp. 380–399, provides insights into the early Italian contribution; Locke and Hume are the subjects of A. H. Leigh, "John Locke and the Quantity Theory of Money," *History of Political Economy*, vol. 6 (Summer 1974), pp. 200–219; J. A. Weymark, "Money and Locke's Theory of Property," *History of Political Economy*, vol. 12 (Summer 1980), pp. 282–292; M. I. Duke, "David Hume and Monetary Adjustment," *History of Political Economy*, vol. 11 (Winter 1979), pp. 572–587; and T. Mayer, "David Hume and Monetarism" (see references).

John Law (1671–1729), famous for his association with financial "bubbles," was one of the most controversial monetary theorists of all times. Economic historian Antoin Murphy has demonstrated how Law understood that monetary expansion could increase output and employment in an economy that is characterized by widespread unemployment. Moreover, Law was in full control of an understanding of the quantity theory, the circular flow of income, and a staple of microeconomic theory—the law of one price. See A. E. Murphy, ed., *John Law's Essay on a Land Bank* (Dublin: Aeon Publishing, 1994).

Adam Smith's ideas on money and monetary theory, which have not been aired in this chapter, are the subject of David Laidler's "Adam Smith as a Monetary Economist," *Canadian Journal of Economics*, vol. 14 (May 1981), pp. 185–200. C. N. Chen, "Bimetallism: Theory and Controversy in Perspective," *History of Political Economy*, vol. 4 (Spring 1972), pp. 89–112, discusses bimetallism within a general-equilibrium framework. An important nineteenth-century monetary economist was Thomas Tooke, whose ideas on the subject are explored by Carlo Panico, "Thomas Tooke and the Monetary Thought of Classical Economics," *European Journal of the History of Economic Thought*, vol. 19 (Fall 2012), pp. 679–683; Matthew Smith, "Thomas Tooke on the Bullionist Controversies," *European Journal of the History of Economic Thought*, vol. 15 (Winter 2008), pp. 49–84; and Arie Arnon, "The Transformation of Thomas Tooke's Monetary Theory Reconsidered," *History of Political Economy*, vol. 16 (Summer 1984), pp. 311–326.

For an examination of classical monetary theory in light of contemporary debate over the desirability of reinstituting the gold standard, see David Glasner, "A Reinterpretation of Classical Monetary Theory," *Southern Economic Journal*, vol. 52 (July 1985), pp. 46–67. See also, same author, "The Real-Bills Doctrine in Light of the Law of Reflux," *History of Political Economy*, vol. 24 (Winter 1992), pp. 867–894; and again same author, "Classical Monetary Theory and the Quantity Theory," *History of Political Economy*, vol. 32 (Spring 2000), pp. 39–59. Daniel Besomi, "Paper Money and National Distress: William Huskisson and the Early Theories of Credit, Speculation and Crises," *The European Journal of the History of Economic Thought*, vol. 17 (Winter 2010), pp. 49–85, explores the ideas of the third author of the Bullion Report of 1810.

For general surveys of the field of classical monetary theory, consult Charles Rist, *History of Monetary and Credit Theory* (see references), and F. W. Fetter, *Development of British Monetary Orthodoxy, 1797–1875* (Cambridge, MA: Harvard University Press, 1965). See also Wilfredo Santiago-Valiente, "Historical Background of the Classical Monetary Theory and the 'Real-Bills' Banking Tradition," *History of Political Economy*, vol. 20 (Spring 1988), pp. 43–63. David Ricardo's contributions to the theory of money and banking are scrutinized by R. S. Sayers, "Ricardo's Views on Monetary Questions," *Quarterly Journal of Economics*, vol. 67 (February 1953), pp. 30–49; by J. C. W. Ahiakpor, "Ricardo on Money: The Operational Significance of the Non-neutrality of Money in the Short-Run," *History of Political Economy*, vol. 17 (Spring 1985), pp. 17–30; and by A. Aaron, "Banking Between the Invisible and Visible Hands: A Reinterpretation of Ricardo's Place within the Classical School," *Oxford Economic Papers*, vol. 39 (June

1987), pp. 268–281, who argues that Ricardo's ideas paved the way for central banking. Jerome de Boyer des Roches, "Cause and Effect in the Gold Points Mechanism: A Criticism of Ricardo's Criticism of Thornton," *Economic Journal of the History of Economic Thought*, vol. 14 (Winter 2007), pp. 25–53, juxtaposes the ideas of two leading lights of the era.

G. S. Tavlas, "Some Initial Formulations of the Monetary Growth Rule," *History of Political Economy*, vol. 9 (Winter 1977), pp. 535–547, traces the evolution of the monetary rule to Jeremy Bentham and Henry Thornton. Neil T. Skaggs explores the ideas of yet another monetary writer of the day, in "John Fullarton's Law of Reflux and Central Bank Policy," *History of Political Economy*, vol. 23 (Fall 1991), pp. 457–480. But of all the early theorists, Henry Thornton was the most able. His major work, *An Enquiry into the Nature and Effects of the Paper Credit of Great Britain* [1802], has been reprinted, edited by F. A. Hayek (New York: Farrar & Rinehart, 1939). For more on Thornton, see Hayek, "Note on the Development of the Doctrine of 'Forced Saving,'" *Quarterly Journal of Economics*, vol. 47 (November 1932), pp. 123–133; and R. L. Hetzel, "Henry Thornton: Seminal Monetary Theorist and Father of the Modern Central Bank," *Federal Reserve Bank of Richmond Economic Review*, vol. 73 (July/August 1987), pp. 3–16. Jean-Stephane Mesonnier, "Interest Rate Gaps and Monetary Policy in the Work of Henry Thornton: Beyond a Retrospective Wicksellian Reading," *European Journal of the History of Economic Thought*, vol. 14 (Fall 2007), pp. 657–680, claims that Thornton's analyses offer a framework for regulating the value of money through adjustments to the bank rate. See also, Heinz D. Kurz, "The Genesis of Macroeconomics: New Ideas from Sir William Petty to Henry Thornton," *European Journal of the History of Economic Thought*, vol. 19 (Fall 2012), pp. 683–686.

Classical Economics (II)
The Ricardian System and Its Critics

We have seen that Adam Smith established the foundations of classical value theory and the first scientifically rigorous theory of economic growth. *The Wealth of Nations* fired the imagination of its readers, and the "new" field of political economy became a serious and timely topic of interest and debate. The pivotal nature of Smith's work is that it represented both a culmination of previous developments and a catalyst for future advances and refinements. One of those persons inspired by Smith to stretch the new science was David Ricardo (1772–1823).

Ricardo was born in London, the third of seventeen children of a Jewish immigrant stockbroker. With but a modicum of commercial education, he parlayed a modest stake into a sizable fortune by making shrewd investments in securities and real estate. In 1799, while on vacation and bored, he picked up Adam Smith's *Wealth of Nations* and soon became engrossed in it. Thus began a serious intellectual hobby. Ten years later he began writing pamphlets and arguing economic questions in the press, an avocation that morphed into a consuming intellectual pursuit. What ensured Ricardo's place in the history of economics was his ability to forge a general analytic system that yielded sweeping conclusions based on relatively few, basic principles. His "system" was a monument to the efficacy of deductive reasoning. He founded his analysis on three fundamental ideas that he borrowed from other writers: (1) classical rent theory, (2) Malthus's population principle, and (3) the wages-fund doctrine. Since the second and third propositions have already been examined in earlier chapters, we shall establish the first before proceeding to an explanation of the full Ricardian system.

The Classical Doctrine of Land Rent

The theory of rent played a pivotal role in the development of classical macroeconomics and in its "generalized" form is an important cog in contemporary economics. What began as a theory of land rent evolved into a more general theory of any (unearned) *surplus* that emanates from exclusive ownership or privilege. The generalized notion of *economic rent*, which is sometimes indistinguishable from the related concept of *profit*, will be explored again later, but it has already been used as an interpretive device in our treatment of mercantilism (see chapter 3). The "generalized" notion of rent emerged as a direct consequence of Ricardo's treatment.

Ricardo regarded rent as value in excess of real production—something caused by incident of ownership rather than by fundamental economic value imparted by free and equal trade. However, we should not get ahead of ourselves in this regard.

The first tract on land rent that could be called "classical" in the sense used here was written by James Anderson (1739–1808), a Scottish farmer and inventor. In 1777, Anderson published a pamphlet that clearly stated in embryonic form the principle of diminishing returns. This was followed by the more or less simultaneous and independent discoveries of basically the same idea in 1815 by Sir Edward West, T. R. Malthus, Robert Torrens, and David Ricardo. We knowingly overlook the differences between these writers in order to concentrate on a somewhat unified theory of rent that typifies the classical period. We focus on Ricardo even though he disclaimed originality and acknowledged his debt to both Malthus and West in this regard.

From Anderson to Ricardo, the immediate impetus for the development of the classical doctrine of rent was the Corn Laws controversy, which arose during the Napoleonic wars. Napoleon's embargo on British ports effectively kept foreign grain out of England, forcing British farmers to increase production of domestic grain in order to feed the population. Because costs of production were higher in England than abroad, the price of British grain rose. Between 1790 and 1810, British corn prices rose 18 percent per year on average. Not surprisingly land rents also increased; so much so landlords developed a vested interest in continuing to restrict grain imports. Parliament accommodated the landlords by passing protective legislation in the form of the Corn Laws of 1815. This very issue of agricultural protectionism and its effects on income distribution and economic growth stimulated the development of classical rent theory.

Malthus defined land rent as "that portion of the value of the whole produce which remains to the owner of land, after all the outgoings [i.e., costs] belonging to its cultivation, of whatever kind, have been paid, including the profits of the capital employed, estimated according to the usual and ordinary rate of the profits of agricultural stock at the time being" (*Inquiry*, p. 179). He understood that land rent is tied to the value of land's output, and that value is determined by the normal and necessary costs of production. But according to Malthus, rent does not affect agricultural prices in the same way as other costs. He said:

> The price of produce in every progressive country must be just about equal to the cost of production on land of the poorest quality actually in use; or to the cost of raising additional produce on old land, which yields only the usual returns of agricultural stock with little or no rent. (*Inquiry*, pp. 205–206)

In this passage Malthus established that there is a no-rent margin of production, at which the price of produce will cover all of the costs of land *excluding* rent. As regards this price, Malthus claimed:

> It is quite obvious that the price cannot be less; or such land would not be cultivated, nor such capital employed. Nor can it ever much exceed this price, because the poor land progressively taken into cultivation, yields at first little or no rent; and because it will always answer to any farmer who can command capital, to lay it out on his land, if the additional produce resulting from it will fully repay the profits of his stock, although it yields nothing to the landlord.
>
> It follows then, that the price of raw produce, in reference to the *whole quantity* raised, is sold at the natural or necessary price, that is, at the price necessary to obtain the actual amount of produce, although by far the largest part is sold at a price very much above that which is necessary to its production. (*Inquiry*, p. 206)

In other words, what Malthus was saying is that rent does not exist at the margin (i.e., on the worst land in cultivation) and arises on better lands only when poorer lands are brought into use. Ricardo was more explicit about this critical point. Describing land rent as "payment for the original and indestructible powers of the soil," he wrote:

> If all land had the same properties, if it were unlimited in quantity and uniform in quality, no charge could be made for its use, unless where it possessed peculiar advantages of situation. It is only, then, because land is not unlimited in quantity and uniform in quality, and because in the progress of population, land of an inferior quality, or less advantageously situated, is called into cultivation, that rent is ever paid for the use of it. When in the progress of society, land of the second degree of fertility is taken into cultivation, rent immediately commences on that of the first quality, and the amount of that rent will depend on the difference in the quality of these two portions of land. (*Works*, I, p. 70)

In this way, Ricardo identified rent at the *extensive* margin of cultivation (i.e., when more land is taken into cultivation). But he also recognized that because of diminishing returns on land *of the same quality* rent also arises on the *intensive* margin.

> It often, and indeed commonly happens, that before . . . the inferior lands are cultivated, capital can be employed more productively on those lands which are already in cultivation. It may perhaps be found, that by doubling the original capital employed on . . . [this land], though the produce will not be doubled . . . it may be increased . . . [by another magnitude], and that this quantity exceeds what could be obtained by employing the same capital, on [other] land.
>
> In such case, capital will be preferably employed on the old land, and will equally create a rent; for *rent is always the difference between the produce obtained by the employment of two equal quantities of capital and labour.* (*Works*, I, p. 71. Emphasis added)

By restricting the importation of grain the Corn Laws forced more intensive and extensive land cultivation in England. Ricardo showed that diminishing returns existed at both the intensive margin (more inputs applied to the same land) and the extensive margin (the same inputs applied to different types of land). Hence, agricultural protectionism raises land rents. Table 7-1 illustrates Ricardo's theory in numerical terms.

The first column in the table shows combined units of labor and capital, which are assumed to be added to production in fixed proportions (e.g., one man, one shovel). Lands of different fertility (but fixed amounts) are represented by different grades, such that No. 1 represents land of the highest fertility and Nos. 2 to 5 represent lands of lesser fertility, in descending order. The marginal product (MP) of capital and labor is the change in total product resulting from the addition of one more capital/labor input to production. In conformance with the law of diminishing returns, marginal product declines as more inputs are added to each type of land. As conventionally defined, and in this context, diminishing returns to labor occur only on the *intensive* margin. But experience also tells us that total product declines as production moves out to poorer lands. At the *extensive* margin, decreasing total output is due to differences in fertility.

Using Ricardo's definition of rent as "the difference between the produce obtained by the employment of two equal quantities of capital and labour," we may identify from table 7-1 the real rents paid at both the intensive and extensive margins. Thus, if only No. 1 land was cultivated, a real rent of 10 bushels would arise on

Table 7-1 Ricardo's Rent Theory Illustrated

Capital and Labor	Total and Marginal Products to Types of Land									
	No. 1	(MP_1)	No. 2	(MP_2)	No. 3	(MO_3)	No. 4	(MP_4)	No. 5	(MP_5)
0	0		0		0		0		0	
1	100	(100)	90	(90)	80	(80)	70	(70)	60	(60)
2	190	(90)	170	(80)	150	(70)	130	(60)	110	(50)
3	270	(80)	240	(70)	210	(60)	180	(50)	150	(40)
4	340	(70)	300	(60)	260	(50)	220	(40)	180	(30)
5	400	(60)	350	(50)	300	(40)	250	(30)	200	(20)

it after the introduction of the second "dose" of capital and labor (100 – 90 = 10). Introduction of a third dose of capital and labor on No. 1 land would subsequently raise total rent on that land to 30 bushels (100 – 80 + 90 – 80 = 30), and so on. At the extensive margin, rent is the difference between output on the best land and the worst land in cultivation for equal amounts of capital and labor applied to each. Thus, if No. 1, No. 2, and No. 3 land each receive three doses of capital and labor, rent on No. 1 land would be 60 bushels (270 – 210 = 60), and rent on No. 2 land would be 30 bushels (240 – 210 = 30). As always, there would be no rent at the margin of the last land in use.

Once information is known about the prices of inputs and outputs in table 7-1 the optimum allocation of total expenditures among types of land can be deduced. Suppose the price per bushel of corn was $1, so that the numbers in table 7-1 can be converted to revenues merely by placing dollar signs in front of them. It can be deduced from the table that if the price of each dose of capital and labor (per production period) was $100, production would take place only on No. 1 land. But if the price of the input was $60 per dose, it would be profitable to extend production to the point where marginal revenue (i.e., MP × price of corn) equals marginal input cost ($60). This would entail extending production to No. 5 land, employing five units of capital and labor on No. 1 land, four on No. 2, three on No. 3, two on No. 4, and one on No. 5 (to complete your understanding, verify this in table 7-1).

It should be pointed out that this theory explains agricultural rents only. In the classical theory of rent, it was assumed that land had no alternative uses. Either it was used to produce a homogenous commodity called "corn," or it lay fallow. Since the problem attacked by Malthus and Ricardo was that of determining the distribution of total output between rent versus wages and profits, they ignored the manufacturing sector, where rents were (assumed) negligible, and concentrated fully on agriculture, which was the major sector of the economy. Their theory allowed capital and labor to be perfectly mobile, not only between parcels of land but also between manufacturing and agriculture. Land, of course, was fixed in place and assumed merely to be brought into or out of agricultural production when economic circumstances warranted.

■ THE RICARDIAN SYSTEM

For reasons that will be explained momentarily, Ricardo had a far greater impact on the future direction of economic theory than Malthus, but each played an important part in the development of the other's analytical system. Malthus saw a close and direct link between the general level of wages and the price of corn. He argued in favor of the Corn Laws because he felt that free importation of grain would drive down domestic grain prices (and wages) and bring on a depression. Ricardo saw a close and inverse link between wages and profits. He argued against the Corn Laws because he believed they would drive wages up and profits down. Lower profits meant less capital accumulation and a threat to economic growth. In answering Malthus, Ricardo constructed an ingenious argument, built on the labor theory of value and the classical theory of rent.

The Labor Theory of Value: Empirical or Analytical?

Few misconceptions in the history of economics have been perpetuated as extensively as the simplistic version of Ricardo's theory of value. The interpretation that persists despite attempts to expunge it is a strict uncompromising theory that actually derives little or no support from Ricardo's writings. Ironically, it was not Ricardo's critics (e.g., Malthus and Samuel Bailey) but his ardent disciples who were mostly responsible for the misinterpretation. We prefer to characterize Ricardo's theory of value as a "real-cost" theory, which emphasizes the cost of labor but not to the exclusion of all other costs.

The central problem posed by Ricardo in his *Principles of Political Economy and Taxation* was how changes occur in the relative, aggregate-income shares of land, labor, and capital and what effect these changes have on capital accumulation and economic growth. The determination of rent was an integral part of this problem, but every theory of income distribution must rest on a theory of value, and Ricardo did not find Smith's value theory congenial to his particular concerns. Specifically, he pointed out certain deficiencies in Smith's doctrine of natural value. Smith argued that a rise in the price of one factor (e.g., wages) would increase the price of goods produced by that factor (e.g., labor). While this view explained changes in nominal prices, Ricardo found it incapable of explaining changes in *relative* prices.

Ricardo believed that Smith's restriction of the labor theory of value to a "primitive economy" was unnecessary because with certain modifications it provided the best general explanation of relative prices. To him the relation between value and labor time expended in production was straightforward: "Every increase of the quantity of labor must augment the value of that commodity on which it is exercised, as every diminution must lower it" (*Works*, I, p. 13). Although Ricardo never wavered from this basic position, he nevertheless added several qualifications required to make the theory more realistic. In the process, his theory of value ceased to be a pure labor theory. However, Ricardo consistently sidestepped his own qualifications in subsequent analysis and policy and made use of a simple labor theory in order to reach general conclusions.

The first exception to the above rule that Ricardo allowed was in the case of nonreproducible goods. "There are some commodities," he maintained, "the value of which is determined by scarcity alone. No labour can increase the quantity of such goods, and therefore their value cannot be lowered by an increased supply." The value of a Picasso painting or a bottle of a rare, exclusive vintage wine, in Ricardo's words, "is wholly independent of the quantity of labor originally necessary to produce them, and varies with the varying wealth and inclinations of those who are desirous to possess them." In a quantitative sense, however, this exception was unimportant to Ricardo, because "these commodities . . . form a very small part of the mass of commodities daily exchanged in the market" (*Works*, I, p. 12).

Ricardo pressed more important qualifications on the labor theory of value regarding the role and importance of capital, which he treated as "indirect" or "embodied" labor. Following Smith, Ricardo distinguished between fixed and circulating capital. Circulating capital "is rapidly perishable and requires to be frequently reproduced," whereas fixed capital "is of slow consumption." Value will therefore increase as the ratio of fixed to circulating capital increases and as the durability of capital increases. Ricardo explained:

> Suppose two men employ one hundred men each for a year in the construction of two machines, and another man employs the same number of men in cultivating corn, each of the machines at the end of the year will be of the same value as the corn, for they will each be produced by the same quantity of labour. Suppose one of the owners of one of the machines to employ it, with the assistance of one hundred men, the following year in making cloth, and the owner of the other machine to employ his also, with the assistance likewise of one hundred men, in making cotton goods, while the farmer continues to employ one hundred men as before in the cultivation of corn. During the second year they will all have employed the same quantity of labour, but the goods and machine together of the clothier, and also of the cotton manufacturer, will be the result of the labour of two hundred men, employed for a year; or rather, of the labour of one hundred men employed for two years; whereas the corn will be produced by the labour of one hundred men for one year, consequently if the corn be of the value of 500£ the machine and cloth of the clothier together, ought to be of the value of 1000£ and the machine and cotton goods of the cotton manufacturer, ought to be also of twice the value of the corn. But they will be of more than twice the value of corn, for the profit on the clothier's and cotton manufacturer's capital the first year has been added to their capitals, while that of the farmer has been expanded and enjoyed. On account then of the different degrees of durability of their capitals, or, which is the same thing, on account of the amount of time which must elapse before one set of commodities can be brought to market, they will be valuable, not exactly in proportion to the quantity of labour bestowed on them . . . but something more, to compensate for the greater length of time which must elapse before the most valuable can be brought to market. (*Works*, I, pp. 33–34)

We see from this passage that Ricardo recognized the two ways in which capital affects the value of goods: (1) capital used up in production constitutes an addition to the value of the product, and (2) capital employed per unit of time must be compensated (at the going rate of interest). Ricardo's insistence that time as well as labor is an important element of value constituted a genuine contribution to economics, for which he subsequently received little, if any, credit.

From an analytical standpoint, then, it is clear that Ricardo based value on the real costs of labor and capital. On conceptual grounds his theory differed from Smith's in that it excluded rent from costs. But on empirical grounds Ricardo argued that the relative quantities of labor used in production are the major determinants of relative market values. In terms of analytical method, Ricardo masterfully employed abstract, deductive reasoning. He preferred to base the principles of his analytical system on a single, dominant variable rather than on a number of lesser ones of dubious effect. To this end, he warned his readers (after noting the above effects of capital on value): "In the subsequent part of this work, though I shall occasionally refer to this cause of variation [i.e., time], I shall consider all the great variations which take place in the relative value of commodities to be produced by the greater or less quantity of labour which may be required from time to time to produce them" (*Works*, I, pp. 36–37). Whatever fault one finds with Ricardo's analysis, he cannot be accused of neglecting or hiding his assumptions.

Despite its rigor, Ricardo's value theory contained several deficiencies. In the first place, he did not deal adequately with qualitative differences in labor. Ricardo assumed that wage adjustments for qualitative differences in labor would occur in the marketplace and that once determined, these differences would vary little. Since he was seeking a measure of market value in the first place, this is a circular argument. In the second place, the exclusion of rent from costs can be justified only if land has no alternative uses (which Ricardo assumed, but unrealistically). Moreover, the Ricardian theory of value limited the influence of market demand to nonreproducible goods, which constitute a small number of goods traded in daily exchanges. In a more technical sense, Ricardo's theory was inadequate in the case where goods are not produced subject to constant average costs of production.

The Nature of Economic Progress: Toward the Stationary State

The theory of value, reduced to Ricardo's level of simplification, plus the theory of rent, provided the key to resolving the central problem of income distribution. It was, of course, necessary to relate the theory of value to the theory of prices in a complex economy. Ricardo did this by relating market price to the costs of production in the marginal (no-rent) firm. He noted:

> The exchangeable value of all commodities, whether they be manufactured, or the produce of the mines, or the produce of the land, is always regulated, not by the less quantity of labour that will suffice for their production under circumstances highly favorable, and exclusively enjoyed by those who have peculiar facilities of production; but by the greater quantity of labour necessarily bestowed on their production by those who continue to produce them under the most unfavorable circumstances. (*Works*, I, p. 73)

Ricardo recognized that there is no perfect measure of value, since any measure chosen varies with fluctuations in wages and profit rates. We noted earlier that different durabilities of capital, and different ratios of fixed to circulating capital, will affect market prices differently if wages change relative to profits. Thus, Ricardo devised an analytical gimmick—the "average firm"—in which both the ratio of capital to labor and capital durability are assumed equal to the economy average. Armed with these tools Ricardo set about solving the problem of income distribution and its changes over time.

Table 7-2 illustrates the nature of income distribution on no-rent land. Suppose that three doses of labor and capital on a given farm produce 270 bushels of corn per year. By virtue of being advanced from the wages-fund, the cost of each labor input constitutes an expenditure of circulating capital, and through annual depreciation the cost of each capital input constitutes an expenditure of fixed capital. By Ricardo's definition total profits each production period are equal to total revenues minus the sum of fixed and circulating capital expenditures. Now assume that the price per bushel of corn is $1, that the wage rate per worker is 10 bushels of corn and $10 of other necessities (the latter can be given in dollar terms because they are assumed to be produced under conditions of constant cost), and that the annual depreciation per unit of capital is $10. Profits on No. 1 land would be calculated as shown in table 7-2.

If all land were equally fertile, profits could continue at the same rate. But as capital and population increase, cultivation must be extended to No. 2 land, where three doses of labor and capital produce only 240 bushels of corn. Technically, more labor and capital are now needed to produce the same output on No. 2 land as on No. 1 land. Therefore, the price of corn must rise to $1.125 (i.e., 270/240 × $1.00 = $1.125). In Ricardo's system, this increase in the price of corn has the effect of raising money wages and aggregate rents and of lowering profits. The ensuing distributional pattern is illustrated in table 7-3.

Table 7-2 Income Distribution on No-Rent Land

Value of produce	= 270 × $1	= $270
Wage rate	= (10 × $1) + $10 =	20
Wage bill	= 3 × $20	= 60
Depreciation	= 3 × $10	= 30
Total profit	= $270 – $90	= 180
Rent		= 0

Table 7-3 demonstrates what we learned earlier—that rent arises on No. 1 land only when production with the same amount of capital and labor is extended to No. 2 land. The calculation of rent is, as Ricardo indicated, the value of the initial firm's output less the value of the marginal firm's output. This illustration can be extended to additional firms (i.e., types of land), of course, but the distributional effects of economic growth are already clear. Increased agricultural production leads to higher money wages but the same *real* wages. Invoking Malthus's population principle, Ricardo argued that wage rates would be at subsistence levels in the long run. On the other hand, higher nominal wage rates and increasing aggregate rents place a two-way squeeze on profits. Competition tends to equalize profits for all firms in a given industry, but profits are inevitably diminished as output increases. Eventually a minimum profit rate is reached, at which point additional capital accumulation and new investment ceases. Ricardo called this point the "stationary state." Theoretically, this minimum profit rate is zero; practically, however, it may be slightly above this level.

The process that Ricardo described may therefore be restated as a paradox: The logical result of economic growth is stagnation! Within the context of Ricardo's analytical system, this gloomy prospect is unassailable, but only because Ricardo uncritically accepted Malthus's population principle and did not allow for technological progress. In its final version the stationary state arises in the following manner: The average wage rate is determined by the proportion of fixed and circulating capital (i.e., the wages-fund) to the population. As long as profits are positive, the capital stock will increase, and the increased demand for labor caused by a growing wages-fund will temporarily increase the average wage rate. But when wage rates rise above subsistence, population increases. A larger population requires a greater food supply, so that, barring imports, cultivation must be extended to inferior lands. As cultivation pushes outward, aggregate rents increase and profits fall, moving the economy toward a long-run equilibrium, or stationary state.

Table 7-3 Income Distribution as Cultivation Expands

	No. 1 Land			No. 2 Land		
Value of product	270 × $1.125	=	$303.75	240 × $1.125	=	$270.00
Wage rate	(10 × $1.125) + $10	=	21.25	(10 × $1.125) + $10	=	21.25
Wage bill	3 × $21.25	=	63.75	3 × $21.25	=	63.75
Depreciation	3 × $10	=	30.00	3 × $10	=	30.00
Profits	$303.75 – 93.75 – 33.7	=	176.25	$270 – 93.75	=	176.25
Rent		=	33.75		=	0

Shortly after the appearance of Ricardo's *Principles*, a number of writers rallied to his doctrine and method. Perhaps the most able of these writers was John Ramsay McCulloch, a frequent contributor to *The Edinburgh Review*. McCulloch was joined by James Mill, the father of John Stuart (see chapter 8), and Thomas DeQuincey; together they formed a tight-knit band of Ricardians. But they were opposed by Malthus, now a member of the Royal Society and professor of political economy at the East India Company College, and Nassau Senior, who became the first professor of political economy at Oxford University in 1825.

■ The Ricardo–Malthus Correspondence

From their first meeting in 1811, there was little of fundamental importance in political economy that Malthus and Ricardo agreed on, a fact revealed in their lengthy correspondence with each other over two decades. Many disagreements were minor, but in 1815 their respective investigations of the Corn Laws put them on opposite sides of the free-trade issue.

The Corn Laws Controversy

Ricardo viewed rent as a *socially unnecessary payment* (i.e., a current payment made but not necessary to bring forth the available supply of land). Thus, when land rents rise (as Ricardo argued they would under the Corn Laws) they do so at the expense of profits. Because Ricardo saw profit as the engine that drove economic progress, he perceived in the Corn Laws a threat to economic growth, and therefore he argued vigorously in favor of free trade.

Malthus, however, argued that since workers' purchasing power was closely tied to the price of corn, higher corn prices benefitted workers.[1] As we noted earlier, it was common practice for classical writers on political economy to speak of "corn wages" in an attempt to describe real purchasing power. Therefore, a crucial question in the Corn Laws debate was whether or not higher corn prices meant higher *real* wages. Ricardo thought not, and he argued accordingly. Malthus took the opposite stand and argued in favor of the Corn Laws.

Their antagonism on this and other points of economics constituted merely the first of many famous disagreements that would ensue among future economists. George Bernard Shaw wryly expressed a common frustration among noneconomists when he said: "If you took all the economists in the world and laid them end to end, they still wouldn't reach a conclusion." Are there no permanent truths in economics?

Obviously, economists do disagree. And, as in the case of Malthus and Ricardo, disagreement is often based on interpretation, method, or policy rather than on theoretical principles. We have already seen that Malthus and Ricardo agreed on the basic theory of rent. Yet, debates on interpretation, method, and policy leave considerable room for value judgments, which in turn reduce the frequency of unanimity among participants of the debate.

Economic Method

One of the substantive disagreements between Malthus and Ricardo concerned economic method, as demonstrated in the Malthus–Ricardo debate on exchange value. Recall that Ricardo treated costs as the determinant of value but strove for

[1] For clarification on this point, see Grampp, "Malthus on Money Wages and Welfare."

simplification to the point that he treated a single variable (i.e., labor) as the only significant one. Malthus, on the other hand, less prone to abstractions, was more interested in economic principles "with a view to their practical application." He therefore insisted on incorporating Ricardo's cost analysis into a supply-and-demand framework. In retrospect it is hard to fault Malthus on this matter, but Ricardo's theory nevertheless dominated. The reasons for this are not entirely clear. There were two aspects of the value question that Malthus addressed. The first was an explanation of exchange value; the second was an explanation of the *measure* of value.

According to Malthus, the principle of supply and demand determines what Adam Smith called "natural price" as well as market price. He defined *demand* as the will combined with the power to purchase; and *supply* as the quantity of commodities for sale combined with the intention to sell them (*Principles*, p. 61). "But however great this will and these means may be among the demanders of a commodity," Malthus argued, "none of them will be disposed to give a high price for it, if they can obtain it at a low one; and as long as the means and competition of the sellers continue to bring the quantity wanted to market at a low price, the real intensity of the demand will not show itself" (*Principles*, p. 63). Malthus then correctly concluded that the causes of an increased price are "an increase in the number, wants, and means of the demanders, or a deficiency in the supply; and the causes which lower the price are a diminution in the number, wants, and means of the demanders, or an increased abundance in its supply" (*Principles*, p. 64).

As sensible as this now seems, Ricardo rejected Malthus's argument because he understood the term "demand" to mean something different. In fact, a comparative study of the works of both authors shows that Malthus and Ricardo often talked to each other at cross-purposes and that the whole confusion on the role of demand and supply could have been cleared up if they had each understood the difference between a change in quantity demanded (i.e., movement along a demand schedule) and a change in demand (i.e., shift of the schedule). The notion of supply and demand *schedules*, however, had not yet found its way, explicitly, into economic analysis. For his part, Ricardo viewed Malthus's efforts as an undue concern with trivia. In two letters to Malthus, he wrote:

> If I am too theoretical (which I really believe is the case), you I think are too practical. There are so many combinations and so many operating causes in political economy that there is a great danger in appealing to experience in favor of a particular doctrine, unless we are sure that all the causes of variation are seen and their effects duly estimated. (*Works*, VI, p. 295)

> Our differences may in some respects, I think, be ascribed to your considering my book as more practical than I intended it to be. My object was to elucidate principles, and to do this I imagined strong cases that I might show the operation of those principles. (*Works*, VIII, p. 184)

Their differences were not trivial. Ricardo's theory of value was oversimplified and long-run in its outlook, but it was the cornerstone on which his entire analytical system stood. If abandoned, the whole theoretical structure would collapse. Understandably, Ricardo resisted vehemently.

Compared with his views on the nature of exchange value, Malthus's ideas on the *measure* of value underwent many changes through his successive works. We are left with the impression that he was not quite sure of his mind on this subject, a failing that intruded on other parts of his economics as well. In the final analysis, this wavering aspect of Malthus's thought presented a weak defense against the onslaught of Ricardo's relentless logic. In the end, it may explain why Ricardo, not Malthus, had the greater influence on British classical economics.

Say's Law and Underconsumption

Disagreement over value theory bled into other analytical departures. Malthus challenged Ricardo's theory of profits as well. A major corollary of Ricardo's analysis was that the cost of producing food controls wages (directly) and profits (indirectly through the effect on wages). Higher corn prices lead to higher money wages and falling profits in the Ricardian system. Malthus, however, would not concede that higher food prices were the only or even the major reason for lower profits. Invoking Smith's distinction between "productive" and "unproductive" consumption, Malthus singled out insufficient aggregate demand as a cause of weak investment incentives and consequent reduction of profits.

Malthus's argument runs as follows: Aggregate demand is segregated into necessities and luxuries. That part of production devoted to the "necessities of life" creates its own demand, whereas the demand for that part devoted to "convenience and luxuries" depends on the consumption habits of the "nonproductive" elements of society (e.g., the landlords). Since the landlords do not always spend their incomes like other groups in society (i.e., on consumption goods), it is possible that an oversupply of commodities might exist. What is required to guarantee a steady expansion of output and to eliminate an oversupply of goods is a sufficient level of "effectual demand," and this, Malthus thought, would not be guaranteed by the mere importation of cheap food. Malthus presented his concept of effectual demand in a letter to Ricardo:

> Effectual demand consists of two elements, the power and will to purchase. The power to purchase may perhaps be represented correctly by the produce of the country whether small or great; but the will to purchase will always be the greatest, the smaller the produce compared with the population, and the more scantily the wants of society are supplied. When capital is abundant it is not easy to find new objects sufficiently in demand. In a country with little comparative capital the value of yearly produce may very rapidly increase from the greatness of demand. In short I by no means think that the power to purchase necessarily involves a proportionate will to purchase, and I cannot agree . . . that in reference to a nation, supply can never exceed demand. A nation must certainly have the power of purchasing all that it produces, but I can easily conceive it not to have the will. (*Works*, VI, pp. 131–132)

The classical idea that Malthus rejected in this passage took its name from a French expositor most closely connected with the notion that "supply creates its own demand," Jean-Baptiste Say. This short phrase, popularly known as Say's Law, does not do justice to the fundamental principle exposited by Say. More correctly, Say's Law maintains that in the process of production exactly enough income is generated to purchase the output produced, and it follows that—barring hoarding—all the income so generated will be spent to purchase that output. Few notions were so completely assimilated into the mainstream of classical economics as Say's Law. Malthus's criticism of Say's Law therefore indelibly marked him as a maverick among economists, a fact that nevertheless endeared him to that well-known pioneer of modern macroeconomic theory, and fellow graduate of Cambridge University, John Maynard Keynes (see chapter 21).

Although Malthus's assault on Say's Law had little effect on orthodox economics before Keynes, it contains at least one major insight into the savings-investment decisions that so concerned Keynes at a later date. The idea of an optimum propensity to save is inherent in Malthus's thought and is affirmed in the following passage from his *Principles*:

> If consumption exceed production, the capital of a country must be diminished, and its wealth must be gradually destroyed from its want of power to produce; if production be in great excess above consumption, the motive to accumulate and produce must cease from the want of an effectual demand. . . . The two extremes are obvious; and it follows that there must be some intermediate point, though the resources of political economy may not be able to ascertain it, where, taking into consideration both the power to produce and the will to consume, the encouragement to the increase of wealth is the greatest. (*Principles*, p. 7)

In other words, Malthus recognized that consumption expenditures represent demand and that savings represent potential demand (through investment), but that the latter by no means *guarantee* effective demand. In more modern jargon, *ex post* saving is always equal to *ex post* investment (a fact that Malthus apparently accepted), but *ex ante* saving need not always equal *ex ante* investment.[2] Thus, Malthus argued the possibility of a general glut.

Malthus's criticism of Say's Law was important in two respects, one immediate, the other postponed. The immediate effect was a challenge to Ricardo's theory of profit. The delayed effect was a stimulus to Keynesian analysis. In its own time, Malthus's analysis of aggregate saving had little impact, since he neither specified the market forces capable of maintaining the optimum rate of saving nor analyzed the purely monetary causes of overproduction. As a consequence, Say's Law was successfully defended by Ricardo and his followers, and it subsequently became an entrenched proposition of classical economics. (On the spread of economic theory, see the box, The Force of Ideas: "Marketing" Classical Economics.)

The Force of Ideas: Marketing Classical Economics

Classical economics, at least as presented by the great theorists reviewed in this chapter, was admittedly difficult to digest for the average reader. British academics and intellectuals might be expected to have mastered at least some of the arguments of the classical writers (especially Malthus's ideas on population), but literacy was still limited in nineteenth-century England and Europe, and books were expensive enough to be beyond the reach of the average worker and perhaps even some elements of the middle class. Learning the principles of political economy, then (and now), was not an easy task. Several writers tried to break through this wall of difficulty. James Mill's *Elements of Political Economy* (1812) and Jane Marcet's *Conversations on Political Economy* (1816) were both pitched to audiences of young middle-class readers.

Apparently the most successful of the popularizers of political economy was Harriet Martineau, the daughter of a Norwich textile manufacturer. An accomplished journalist and novelist, she pitched economics to working-class readers in a series of twenty-five novelettes of about 125 pages each, appearing monthly between 1832 and 1834. Like her contemporary writers of "serious fiction," Martineau had to support herself and her dependents in the periodical press. So she wrote for weighty journals, such as the *Edinburgh Review* and the *Westmin-*

(continued)

[2] This point is explained further in the Keynesian context in chap. 21.

ster Review, and published more than 1,600 articles in London's *Daily News*. Her enormously popular *Illustrations of Political Economy* (1832) was a great success and brought her financial independence in an era when women writers were uncommon, especially in the area of political economy. She followed her early success with another best seller, *Poor Laws and Paupers Illustrated* (1834).

Martineau mastered (at a workable level at least) the elements of political economy and was intent on providing contemporary illustrations of difficult concepts. Earlier treatments, as she pointed out in the preface to her first book, did "not give us what we want—the science in a familiar, practical form. They give us its history; they give us its philosophy; but we want its *picture*" (*Illustrations*, p. xi). Martineau's "pictures" consisted of fictional parables dealing with poverty, welfare policies also known as the Poor Law reforms, unionization, general relations between capital and labor, the factory acts, working conditions for women and children, and health. (Each book was followed with an enumeration of the principles to be learned from the story.)

Life in the Wilds (Book 1 of *Illustrations*) deals with a "primitive" community with plenty of labor but scarce capital. As capital accumulates in the community, little by little, the society begins to prosper. Martineau explains how, far from being antithetical to the interests of labor, capital cooperates with labor and creates leisure, opportunity, and, most of all, self-reliance. As she points out, "Labour was that of which there was the greatest deficiency in the community; and the means of shortening and easing labour was therefore the most valuable present which could be conferred" (*Illustrations*, p. 110).

Some of Martineau's most effective short novels also dealt with such "noneconomic" topics as the abolition of slavery (which she staunchly favored) and the status of women (she was an early "feminist"). Nevertheless, she held fast to the position that the application of classical economic principles would and could bring about a well-ordered society. In *The Hamlets* (1836) Martineau drew a clear lesson: Poor Laws welfare reforms proposed by Senior, Malthus, and the other classical writers deserved support because they redirected incentives toward industriousness and self-reliance. In other essays she emphasized the futility of labor unions in permanently increasing the wages of labor, and the negative impact of "factory legislation" on the fate of working women and children.

Martineau had her critics both in and out of the ranks of contemporary economists. The Romantics, who generally viewed capitalism and the Industrial Revolution with disdain, were particularly virulent in their criticisms of her suggestions for helping the poor. Charles Dickens, who agreed with Martineau on some matters, such as the abolition of slavery and the education of the deaf and blind, frequently attacked her economic views. The flavor of Dickens's antagonism is captured in his comment about Martineau's treatment of factory accidents. Dickens claimed it was impossible, as Martineau had attempted, "to justify, by arithmetic, a thing unjustifiable by any code of morals."* John Stuart Mill was another critic, alleging that Martineau had reduced laissez-faire to "an absurdity." Their dispute might have been "personal." At the height of her popularity, Martineau was selling 10,000 copies of her books per month, whereas in four years Mill sold only 3,000 copies of his *Principles of Political Economy*.†

Martineau clearly had an impact on the spread of political economy and on the society in which she lived. Always a champion of education as the primary means of bringing the poor out of poverty, she firmly rejected the idea that prosperity and a more just income distribution should be left to government. No one held a firmer belief that desirable social change could be brought about with a widespread inculcation of the principles of political economy.

*Quoted in Gillian Thomas, *Harriet Martineau*, p. 82.
†See Margaret G. O'Donnell, "Harriet Martineau," pp. 62–63.

Ricardo and Entrepreneurship

Ricardo was content to relegate the entrepreneur to a minor role (actually, almost no role). Fritz Redlich ("Toward the Understanding," p. 715) called this an "unfortunate legacy," because denying a central and pivotal role to the entrepreneur suggests that profit (meaning any return beyond mere replacement of capital) is not legitimate in a capitalist economy. By emphasizing the importance of capital and labor to the neglect of entrepreneurship Ricardo passed the "unfortunate legacy" on to Karl Marx, who extolled labor above all else, and created the capitalist bogey who sucks profit from the "industrious" people of the economy.

Classical economics in general had very little to say about the origin and nature of investment opportunities. This is especially true of Ricardo; he assumed that capitalists act rationally in seeking to maximize profits, but he ignored the trouble and risk involved in investing. Although he did not fall into the trap of assuming that all investment was profitable, like most classical economists, Ricardo treated innovation as mainly external to the economic system. Moreover, his theory of the stationary state supposes that as wealth increases, eventually all further opportunities for profitable investment disappear. This stands in marked contrast to the Schumpeterian view (chapter 23), which enlarged the scope and breadth of entrepreneurial activity and made it a centerpiece of his theory of economic development.

Ricardo failed entirely to pursue the suggestion of his contemporary, Jean-Baptiste Say, who formalized the term entrepreneur and defined it meaningfully some fourteen years before Ricardo's *Principles* appeared. At least one version of Say's work was available to Ricardo in English translation during this fourteen-year period. Yet, as Arthur Cole ("An Approach," p. 3) noted, "Not merely is the term [entrepreneur] itself absent in Ricardo's writings, but no concept of business leaders as agents of change (other than as shadowy bearers of technological improvements) is embraced in his treatment of economic principles." It is noteworthy that in the correspondence between Say and Ricardo, neither the nature nor the role of the entrepreneur is once mentioned, their usual discussion focusing instead on the topic of value. Entrepreneurship was thriving as Ricardo was writing his *Principles* to be sure, and a system of capitalism was well underway. But the pivotal roles of investment by capitalist-entrepreneurs was yet to be clearly described.

■ Nassau Senior and the Emergence of "Scientific" Economics

In the nineteenth century three Englishmen established the main steppingstones between Adam Smith and John Stuart Mill: Ricardo, Malthus, and Nassau Senior. Born in 1790 in Berkshire, Senior was the eldest son of the Vicar of Durnford. He was educated at Eton and later at Oxford, where he obtained a law degree in 1815, the same year Malthus, West, Ricardo, and Torrens published their pamphlets on rent. Law practice did not suit Senior's temperament or ambitions, however, and after some postgraduate work in political economy, he was named to the first endowed chair of political economy at Oxford in 1825. Appointed to various governmental commissions in the 1830s and 1840s, Senior was instrumental in shaping legislative reforms in education, factory conditions, and the Poor Laws (see chapter 9).

Chief among his published works was *An Outline of the Science of Political Economy*, first printed in 1836 and revised by Senior in 1850. Although criticized for lack of organization and consistency, Senior's *Outline* is an important milestone in the history of economics, not only for its criticism of Ricardian economics but also for its original contributions. Senior's contributions fall under two major headings: (1) his formulation of the scope and method of economic inquiry and (2) his important modifications of the Ricardian theories of value and costs.

Senior on Economic Method

An unexciting but necessary stage of development of any academic discipline is the identification and organization of basic principles, along axiomatic lines, to form a genuinely scientific framework. Senior was totally engrossed in this project, which qualifies him, in the view of Joseph Schumpeter, as the first "pure theorist" in economics. Certainly his subjective originality and his tireless attempts to unify and systematize economic theory entitle Senior to a more prominent place in the history of economics than he is generally accorded.

Senior began his *Outline* by defining the boundaries of economic inquiry. Political economy, he avowed, is "the science which treats of the nature, the production, and the distribution of wealth." He warned that other writers used the term "political economy" in a much wider sense—to include government, for example—but that the outcome of their efforts had been decidedly unscientific. He strove to make economic inquiry essentially positive (i.e., devoid of value judgments), because the province of the economist is "not happiness, but wealth" (*Outline*, p. 2). He affirmed his methodological position in no uncertain terms:

> [The economist's] premises consist of a very few general propositions, the result of observation, or consciousness, and scarcely requiring proof, or even formal statement, which almost every man, as soon as he hears them, admits as familiar to his thoughts, or at least as included in his previous knowledge: and his inferences are nearly as general, and, if he has reasoned correctly, as certain, as his premises.
>
> But his conclusions, whatever be their generality and their truth, do not authorize him in adding a single syllable of advice. That privilege belongs to the writer or statesman who has considered all the causes which may promote or impede the general welfare of those whom he addresses, not to the theorist who has considered only one, though among the most important, of those causes. The business of a Political Economist is neither to recommend nor to dissuade, but to state general principles, which it is fatal to neglect, but neither advisable, nor perhaps practicable, to use as the sole, or even the principal, guides in the actual conduct of affairs. . . . To decide in each case how far these conclusions are to be acted upon, belong to the act of government, an act to which Political Economy is only one of many subservient Sciences. (*Outline*, pp. 2–3)

The tendency of too many writers to confound the science of economics with the art of government was responsible, in Senior's view, for the unfavorable public prejudices in his day against political economy and political economists. Essentially, he believed economics should be an exercise in reasoning, not a fact-gathering expedition. He was prepared to state the facts on which the general principles of economics rest in a few sentences, "and indeed in a very few words." The difficulty of mastering economics, he said, lay not in observing and stating these few propositions but in reasoning from them correctly.

Those "few sentences" to which Senior alluded took the form of four basic postulates, or axioms, on which economic theory is based. Here are Senior's postulates in his own words (*Outline*, p. 26):

1. that every man desires to obtain additional wealth with as little sacrifice as possible
2. that the population of the world, or in other words, the number of persons inhabiting it, is limited only by a fear of a deficiency of those articles of wealth which the habits of the individuals of each class of its inhabitants lead them to require
3. that the powers of labour, and of the other instruments which produce wealth, may be indefinitely increased by using their products as the means of further production
4. that, agricultural skill remaining the same, additional labour employed on the land within a given district produces in general a less proportionate return, or, in other words, that though, with every increase of the labour bestowed, the aggregate return is increased, the increase of the return is not in proportion to the increase of the labour

The second and fourth postulates present, respectively, Senior's guarded affirmation of Malthus's population principle and the classic law of diminishing returns, but not without important modifications of each. Senior was willing to accept Malthus's population principle in the abstract, but he had little faith in its empirical validity. He added a check that has gained relevance with the passage of time. Individuals' desire to better their position in the world is at least as important as their sexual desire. By not realizing this, Senior argued, Malthus overlooked a strong, additional check to the growth of population.

Another reason for Senior's optimism on the population question as opposed to Malthus's pessimism relates to his interpretation of the laws of increasing and decreasing returns in industry and agriculture. In his fourth postulate, Senior gave precise expression (in the modern sense) to the law of decreasing returns by adding the proviso that technology must be held constant. Ricardo undoubtedly recognized that the validity of this law rests on the constant-technology assumption, but he never explicitly stated it. In explaining his fourth postulate, however, Senior voiced his conviction that the normal state of affairs in industry is *increasing* returns. He based this view on the questionable assumption that labor skills tend to increase in some sort of relation to increased population and capital, a view that runs counter to the orthodox Malthusian doctrine but that was nevertheless accepted by a surprisingly large number of writers in Senior's day.

Without downplaying the significance of Senior's modifications to the population principle, we turn our attention to his first and third postulates, because in the first instance Senior improved the classical and Ricardian theories of exchange value, and in the second he advanced a much improved theory of capital and interest.

Value and Costs

In terms of its impact on the subsequent development of economic theory, Senior's modifications of the Ricardian theory of value were more important than those introduced by Malthus. His major departures from Ricardo include: (1) substitution of a utility theory of value for Ricardo's "labor theory," and (2) refinements of Ricardo's production theory in light of monopolistic business practices.

Several Continental writers in the first half of the nineteenth century (e.g., Say and Condillac) perceived the fact that utility is more than a mere *condition* of value, as Ricardo had stated; it is a *cause* of value. However, they were unable to do anything analytically with this notion before Jules Dupuit, in 1844, presented his concept of marginal utility (see chapter 13); so utility theory accomplished nothing until much later. Senior did better than others in this respect, and was recognized by Léon Walras (see chapter 17), a paragon of neoclassical value theory, for his insightful treatment of utility and value. The chief adversary of the labor theory of value in the nineteenth century was always the supply-and-demand theory. Malthus, for example, went right to it and concentrated on it exclusively. Senior also adopted it, but in general he handled the demand-supply discussion better than Malthus. The higher flight of Senior's discussion was due to his recognition not only of the importance of relative utility but also of the *interdependence* between relative utility and relative scarcity.

Some economists think that Senior spent an inordinate amount of time and effort on definitions. Yet, his attention to detail has to be put in proper context. Particularly in the early stages of its development most of the confusion and disagreements in economics arose from imprecise or ambiguous use of terms. Sciences progress when they are able to narrow their focus and concentrate their attention on precise phenomena. Having earlier defined economics as the science of wealth, Senior took the next logical step, defining wealth, value, and utility. Wealth, he affirmed, includes all goods and services that (1) possess utility, (2) are relatively scarce, and (3) are capable of being transferred. This definition is at once broader than Adam Smith's—because it includes services as well as physical products—and very modern: It recognizes the pivotal importance of both demand factors (utility) and supply factors (scarcity).

Senior also "modernized" the definitions of value and utility. Value is "that quality in anything which fits it to be given and received in exchange; or in other words, to be lent or sold, hired or purchased." And utility "denotes no intrinsic quality in the things we call useful; it merely expresses their relations to the pains and pleasures of mankind" (*Outline*, p. 7). Finally, Senior clearly set forth the notion of diminishing marginal utility and its relation to relative scarcity in his discussion of humans' love of variety in consumption:

> Not only are there limits to the pleasure which commodities of any given class can afford, but the pleasure diminishes in a rapidly increasing ratio long before those limits are reached. Two articles of the same kind will seldom afford twice the pleasure of one, and still less will ten give five times the pleasure of two. In proportion, therefore, as any article is abundant, the number of those who are provided with it, and do not wish, or wish but little, to increase their provision, is likely to be great; and so far as they are concerned, the additional supply loses all, or nearly all, its utility. (*Outline*, pp. 11–12)

What stands out in this passage is Senior's clear recognition that both utility and scarcity *together* determine value. Surely Senior had in his grasp the key to unlock the classical paradox of value! But he didn't take the vital next step, which was to apply mathematical reasoning (i.e., differential calculus) to the matter. For the most part, British economists were either unable or unwilling to go this far. But in France, Antoine-Augustin Cournot and Jules Dupuit embarked on this path before very long (see chapter 13).

Monopoly. Ricardo's influence on Senior was considerable, even though they differed on several key points. Senior maintained, for instance, that "of the three conditions of value—utility, transferableness, and limitation of supply—the last is by far the most important" (*Outline*, p. 11). His discussion of value was therefore colored by a concern for those forces that affect costs of production and consequently limit supply. Chief among these forces was monopoly. Senior perceived monopoly in relative, not absolute, terms. He distinguished four degrees of monopoly and explained how each impacts supply (*Outline*, pp. 103–105):

1. A monopoly in which the producer does not have exclusive producing powers but in which he has exclusive facilities that he may use indefinitely with equal or increasing advantage (as in the case where exclusive patents are necessary to produce a certain product)
2. A monopoly in which the monopolist is the only producer but in which, because of the uniqueness of the product, he cannot increase the amount of his produce (as in the case of certain French vineyards, where increased output is impossible without destroying the unique properties of the wine produced)
3. A monopoly in which the monopolist is the only producer and can increase indefinitely, with equal or increasing advantage, the amount of his produce (as in the case of book publishing, where the product is protected by copyright, and the relative cost of publication diminishes as the number of copies published increases)
4. A monopoly in which the monopolist is not the only producer but has peculiar facilities which diminish and ultimately disappear as output is increased (as in most cases of economic production, including agriculture, where land or fertility must ultimately run out as output is increased)

These four cases are important because the effect of each case on production costs either establishes or does not establish an upper and lower limit to market price and therefore opens the way for varying degrees of demand to determine price. In the first case, for example, market price comes closer to the seller's cost of production than any other monopolized commodity, since competition among sellers without the exclusive facility (e.g., patent) will tend to keep prices in line with their costs of production. A patent monopolist may, of course, enjoy pure profits but is effectively barred from selling at a price above the nonpatented competition, although the actual price will depend on conditions of demand as well as on conditions of production.

The second case is that of completely inelastic supply, in which there is no upper limit on price except the level of demand, while the lower limit to price is equal to costs of production. The third case is the same as the first except that since the monopoly is absolute, there is no upper limit to price save that imposed by demand. The fourth case is the most general. It includes production under conditions of differential advantage and diminishing returns. This is really the Ricardian case, except that in Senior's formulation price depends not only on the production costs of the marginal firm but also on demand.

One has only to read Cournot (see chapter 13) and Senior side by side to realize how loose the theory of monopoly was before 1838. Nevertheless, by classifying the major cases of value the way he did, Senior succeeded in reconciling Ricardo's analysis with the supply-demand theory. A review of Senior's four cases reveals that cost of production is the controlling criterion in some cases and that demand is the controlling criterion in others, but the two are always interacting. It is true that Senior, having gotten this far, did not push the supply-demand analysis as far as he could have in evaluating the factors of production, but he certainly illuminated the path for those who came after him.

Capital and Interest. Senior also extended Ricardo's real-cost analysis by adding the cost of "abstinence" to the cost of labor. In the somewhat paradoxical statement of his third postulate, Senior hinted at the fact that in the long run roundabout methods of production are more productive than direct methods, a fact that the Austrian economist Eugen Böhm-Bawerk (see chapter 14) clarified a generation later.

"Roundaboutness" means postponing production of consumption goods by using labor and raw materials first to produce capital goods, which are then used along with additional labor and raw materials to produce more consumer goods than could have been produced with first producing the capital to be used with labor and raw materials. A classic example of increased efficiency from roundabout production is illustrated in the story of the fictional hero Robinson Crusoe. You undoubtedly know the story. Finding himself shipwrecked and stranded on a deserted island, Crusoe faces the economic necessity of survival. Let us assume that Crusoe's island contains an abundant supply of fish. The most direct method of production that Crusoe can adopt is to catch fish by hand, which is a clumsy means of production. But if he postponed fishing long enough to hew a pole and fashion a hook or make a bow and arrow (crude forms of capital goods), he would catch more fish at a faster rate than would be possible using the most direct, but least efficient, method.

The example is simple, but it illustrates a sophisticated principle, namely that capital accumulation requires postponement of consumption, or what Senior clumsily called, "abstinence." Abstinence is the name Senior gave to conduct necessary to generate profit. He meant it to convey two ideas: "Abstinence expresses both the act of abstaining from the unproductive use of capital, and also the similar conduct of the man who devotes his labour to the production of remote rather than immediate results" (*Outline*, p. 89). In this regard, abstinence constitutes a precondition for the production of "intermediate" goods (i.e., capital), and it provides the key to the third postulate: "that the powers of labour, and of the other instruments which produce wealth, may be indefinitely increased by using their products as the means of further production" (*Outline*, p. 26). Since human nature prefers instant gratification to delayed satisfaction, people are not inclined to postpone consumption unless they are compensated. The postponement of consumption is "abstinence;" the reward for this sacrifice is "interest."

Senior's description of interest as a return to abstinence was his most original contribution to economics, and it soon became assimilated into the mainstream of classical economic theory. In this regard he surpassed Smith, Malthus, and Ricardo, and his analysis of capital and interest stood as the most complete in British economics until William Stanley Jevons (see chapter 15) made further improvements. A retrospective view of Senior's performance must conclude, therefore, that in the process of formulating modifications of Ricardo's analysis, he made important contributions to the corpus of economic theory.

■ The Supremacy of Ricardian Economics

It is curious that although very little of pure Ricardian analysis remains in the mainstream of modern economics and very much of the analysis of his early critics does, Ricardo's influence on other economic writers was a dominant force through much of the nineteenth century. Always in a numerical minority, Ricardo and the Ricardians nevertheless carried the day in early British economics. Every major British economist of the nineteenth century, including John Stuart Mill (see chapter 8) and Alfred Marshall (see chapter 16), paid tribute to Ricardo, even while rejecting or reshaping some of his fundamental ideas.

The reasons for this phenomenon had as much to do with the nature of the Ricardian opposition as with the aggressiveness of Ricardo's disciples. Malthus's writings, for example, belie a theoretical looseness and an intellectual vacillation that undermined their effectiveness as a logical alternative to Ricardo's. Even Senior, whose method and analysis were more rigid than Malthus's, darted and swerved on a number of minor theoretical points. Moreover, Senior's failure to connect his modifications of Ricardo with the question of income distribution probably had an unfavorable effect on the ability of those contributions to attract a wider audience. As a result, Ricardo was in the peculiar position of being able to use impeccable logic to defend his system and simultaneously destroy opposing arguments, which were based on mere common sense rather than rigorous logic. The fact that Ricardo could do so convincingly and endear himself to other economists tells us much about his vast intellectual powers and also about the kind of people economists admire.

Moreover, there is something very positive about Ricardo's performance that must be noted, or else we fail to grasp what economics, as a science, is really about. The point is simply this: Ricardo's tightly reasoned analytical system—unmatched by his predecessors or his contemporaries—contained a *methodological consistency* that was of paramount importance to the successful development of a fledgling science. In retrospect it seems that Senior's overall performance and his specific attempts to give economics a scientific foundation, would have been improbable, if not impossible, without the prior performance of Ricardo. Hence, apart from the content of contemporary economics, Ricardo made a permanent and indelible contribution to the method economists follow in their intellectual pursuits.

■ The Elegant Dynamics of the Classical System

We now borrow a pedagogic tool from William J. Baumol (*Economic Dynamics*, chap. 2) in order to summarize the essence of classical economics in fairly concise terms. Those British economists who lived and wrote after Malthus and before Mill constitute the group whose economics are summarized here. A *synthesis* is all that is attempted, since there certainly was no unanimity of views on all economic topics among members of the classical school.

The major concern of the classical writers was, of course, economic growth, or the transition from a progressive state to a stationary state. The less desirable *stationary* state was viewed as the inevitable outcome of economic history. Classical (Ricardian) economic analysis was, therefore, long-run, based on a few simple (sometimes questionable) assumptions from which sweeping generalizations about economic development were made. Key elements in the process were (1) the Malthusian population principle, (2) the principle of diminishing returns in agriculture, and (3) the wages-fund doctrine.

The fundamental argument of classical growth theory follows simple lines. In an expanding economy, the level of investment and wages is high and growing. Capital accumulation proceeds apace. But high wages induce population growth, and the consequent pressures on the food supply—coupled with a fixed, existing quantity of fertile land—lead to diminishing returns to capital and labor in agriculture and the necessity of utilizing inferior grades of land to feed a growing population. Consequently, costs of production increase and profits fall. Falling profits cause a decrease in accumulation and investment as the stationary state is approached. Actual arrival of the stationary state could be postponed indefinitely through a series of highly productive inventions, but no classical writer denied its inevitability in the long run.

The process just described may be viewed graphically as a movement toward the stationary state over time—decades or perhaps even centuries. Consider figure 7-1. The size of the working population is measured on the horizontal axis. The vertical axis in figure 7-1 measures total product and total wages (in real terms) but

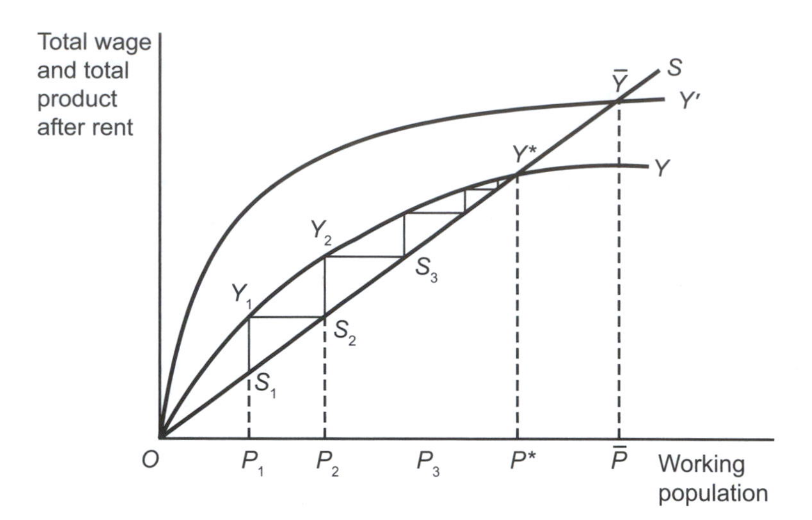

Figure 7-1 At population OP_1 total output is Y_1P_1 and total wages are S_1P_1. Profits of Y_1S_1 will increase the demand for labor and push wages up to Y_1P_1. Since wages are above subsistence at this level, population will increase to OP_2, thus tracing out the stepwise path to long-run equilibrium.

does not include total rent, which Ricardo treated as a mere transfer of income from one class to another. Thus, whenever profits fall—other things being equal—rents rise, and the stationary state is reached when profits fall to zero.

The slope of line OS in figure 7-1 is equal to the ratio of total subsistence wage payments to the size of the working population (e.g., Y^*P^* divided by OP^*). Although there is little evidence that Ricardo—or, for that matter, any of the classical economists—consistently regarded the subsistence wage as a constant proportion of total output, figure 7-1 assumes, for simplicity, that it is. Thus, at output level Y_1 and population P_1, the subsistence wage per worker would be equivalent to the ratio S_1P_1/OP_1. Likewise, at output and population levels Y_2 and P_2, respectively, the subsistence wage would be S_2P_2/OP_2. Moreover, since the level of subsistence as a proportion of output is assumed constant, $S_1P_1/OP_1 = S_2P_2/OP_2$.

Let us begin the analysis at an early stage of the classical economy, where population is small (say, OP_1) compared with other resources and where profits, the rate of accumulation, and wages are therefore all relatively high. It can be seen that the dynamic path to stationary-state equilibrium depends on the speed at which the population adjusts to changes in the level of market wages. At population OP_1, total output (after rent) would be Y_1P_1, and total wages would be S_1P_1. Given Ricardo's residual theory, total profits would equal Y_1S_1.

According to the wages-fund doctrine, the presence of accumulated profits leads to increased demand for labor, and the increased competition for labor eventually pushes wages up to Y_1P_1, at which point profits are squeezed out and accumulation ceases. But since wages are above subsistence at Y_1P_1, population begins to increase (to OP_2), and wages eventually return to subsistence at S_2P_2.

At OP_2, however, population is in temporary equilibrium only, for the increase in population to that level is accompanied by an increase in output from Y_1 to Y_2, thus opening up profits again in the amount of Y_2S_2. This new accumulation causes wages and population to rise again, thus tracing out the stepwise path in figure 7-1. The economy reaches the stationary state at population level P^*. Profits have disappeared from the system, wages are at the subsistence level, and rents on land of the highest fertility are at a maximum. In short, the dynamic working out of the classical theory—i.e., Malthusian population theory, diminishing returns in agriculture, the subsistence theory of wages, the classical theory of capital accumulation (the wages-fund doctrine), and the residual theory of profits—predicts a long-run, stationary-state equilibrium.

The stepwise adjustment path to stationary-state equilibrium in figure 7-1 assumes that population adjustments take place fairly rapidly, although this may not actually be the case. In reality, the adjustment path may follow (from below) the total-product curve *OY*. If population expands slowly, for example, then long before it reaches OP_2 some profit may reappear, propelling the process onward and keeping wages up above subsistence and near the total-product curve *OY*. Postponement of the stationary state is illustrated in figure 7-1 by an increase in productivity, brought about, perhaps, by improvements in technology. This increased productivity shifts the total-product curve upward to OY' and moves the point of stationary equilibrium to the right, to point $\bar{Y}$.

In this manner, the classical economists provided a sweeping analysis of the economic process. Their method is essentially deductive, although the classical dynamics is based on several empirical hypotheses that may or may not have been valid at the time (e.g., the assumption that all saving is automatically invested). Moreover, at least one of the hypotheses—the population principle—contained noneconomic variables that in contemporary analysis would be relegated to an exogenous role. Nevertheless, the classical dynamics represented a bold and striking approach to the policy problems of the time.

■ Conclusion

More than any other writer after Smith, Ricardo set forth the research paradigm of economics for the next generation of British economists. Ricardo treated political economy as an abstract discipline, a means to discover general laws of society—laws of equilibrium and laws of progress. Its practical consequences were of less concern. As a result, Ricardo's followers tended to view economic theory as detached from practice. Malthus and Senior fought against this detachment, but with limited success. Despite its abstract nature Ricardo's analytical system provided a powerful means by which to establish clear-cut policy proposals. British economists therefore rallied to its core. Generations later, Keynes had the sheer power of Ricardo's intellect in mind when he said: "Ricardo conquered England as completely as the Holy Inquisition conquered Spain" (*General Theory*, p. 32).

References

Baumol, W. J. *Economic Dynamics*, 3d ed. New York: Macmillan, 1970.

Cole, Arthur H. "An Approach to the Study of Entrepreneurship: A Tribute to Edwin F. Gay," *Journal of Economic History*, vol. 6 (1946), pp. 1–15.

Grampp, W. D. "Malthus on Money Wages and Welfare," *American Economic Review*, vol. 46 (December 1956), pp. 924–936.

Keynes, J. M. *The General Theory of Employment, Interest and Money*. London: Macmillan, 1936.

Malthus, T. R. *An Inquiry into the Nature and Progress of Rent, and the Principles by Which It Is Regulated*, reprinted in *The Pamphlets of Thomas Robert Malthus*. New York: A. M. Kelley, 1970 [1815].

———. *The Principles of Political Economy, Considered with a View to Their Practical Application*, 2d ed. New York: A. M. Kelley, 1951 [1836].

Martineau, Harriet. *Illustrations of Political Economy*. London: Charles Fox (1832).

———. *The Hamlets: A Tale*. Boston: James Monroe & Co. (1836).

O'Donnell, Margaret. "Harriet Martineau: A Popular Early Economics Educator," *Journal of Economic Education* (Fall 1983), pp. 59–64.

Redlich, Fritz. "Toward the Understanding of an Unfortunate Legacy," *Kyklos*, vol. 19 (1966), pp. 709–716.

Ricardo, David. *The Works and Correspondence of David Ricardo*, 10 vols., Piero Sraffa (ed.), with the collaboration of M. Dobb. London: Cambridge University Press, 1951–1955.

Schumpeter, Joseph. *History of Economic Analysis*, E. B. Schumpeter (ed.). New York: Oxford University Press, 1954.

Senior, N. W. *An Outline of the Science of Political Economy*. New York: A. M. Kelley, 1938 [1836].

Thomas, Gillian. *Harriet Martineau*. Boston: Twayne, 1985.

Notes for Further Reading

Murray Milgate and Shannon Stimson, *After Adam Smith: A Century of Transformation and Political Economy* (Princeton: Princeton University Press, 2009), provide an interesting account of an economy as an ordered social system "resembling a machine," an analogy suggested by Newtonian mechanics, and trace its effect on subsequent writers, including those found in this chapter and the next. Donald Winch reviews their book and its approach, "Review Essay: Politics and Political Economy *After Adam Smith*," *Journal of the History of Economic Thought*, vol. 33 (March 2011), pp. 119–129.

The closest thing to a full-scale biography of Ricardo is James P. Henderson, *The Life and Economics of David Ricardo* (Boston: Kluwer Academic Publishers, 1997), published by Henderson's colleagues after his death in 1995. Mark Blaug, *Ricardian Economics* (New Haven, CT: Yale University Press, 1958), presents an excellent and thorough study of Ricardo. An older, though not necessarily inferior, treatise is J. H. Hollander's *David Ricardo* (Baltimore: Johns Hopkins, 1910). Assistance in getting through the main parts of Ricardo's *Principles* is provided by Oswald St. Clair's *Key to Ricardo* (London: Routledge, 1957), which at one time was among the holdings of virtually every economics library in the country.

The influence of Ricardo on his contemporaries can be traced through articles by S. G. Checkland, "The Propagation of Ricardian Economics in England," *Economica*, vol. 16 (February 1949), pp. 40–52; Sam Hollander, "The Reception of Ricardian Economics," *Oxford Economic Papers*, vol. 29 (July 1977), pp. 221–257; R. L. Meek, "The Decline of Ricardian Economics in England," *Economica*, vol. 17 (February 1950), pp. 43–62; and F. W. Fetter, "The Rise and Decline of Ricardian Economics," *History of Political Economy*, vol. 1 (Fall 1969), pp. 370–387. Other retrospectives can be found in J. R. Hicks and Samuel Hollander, "Mr. Ricardo and the Moderns." *Quarterly Journal of Economics*, vol. 91 (August 1977), pp. 351–370, who discuss the rebirth of Ricardian economics in more modern dress; K. J. Arrow, "Ricardo's Work as Viewed by Later Economists," *Journal of the History of Economic Thought*, vol. 13 (Spring 1991), pp. 70–77; and L. E. Johnson, "Professor Arrow's Ricardo," *Journal of the History of Economic Thought*, vol. 15 (Spring 1993), pp. 54–71.

Two articles by Christophe Depoortère explore Ricardo's method: "On Ricardo's Method: The Unitarian Influence Examined," *History of Political Economy*, vol. 34 (Summer 2002), pp. 499–504; and same author, "On Ricardo's Method: The Scottish Connection Considered," *History of Political Economy*, vol. 40 (Spring 2008), pp. 73–110. This last article reconsiders Ricardo's stance on hypotheses and abstractions in economics, focusing on a possible connection between Ricardo and Dugald Stewart. See also, Sergio Cremaschi and Marcelo Dascal, "Malthus and Ricardo on Economic Methodology," *History of Political Economy*, vol. 28 (Fall 1996), pp. 475–511; and Sergio Cremaschi, "Ricardo and the Utilitarians," *The European Journal of the History of Economic Thought*, vol. 11 (Fall 2004), pp. 377–403, which rejects as myth the claim that Ricardo was dependent on Bentham and/or Mill. For more insights into what made Ricardo tick, see N. Churchman, "David Ricardo on Public Policy: The Question of Motive," *Journal of the History of Economic Thought*, vol. 17 (Spring 1995), pp. 133–152.

Ricardo's value theory is the subject of ongoing review, criticism, and reinterpretation. Two articles by G. J. Stigler have become "classic," both reprinted in Stigler, *Essays in the History of Economics* (Chicago: The University of Chicago Press, 1965): "Ricardo and the 93% Labor Theory of Value," *American Economic Review*, vol. 48 (June 1958), pp. 357–367; and "The Ricardian Theory of Value and Distribution," *Journal of Political Economy*, vol. 60 (June 1952), pp. 187–207. Francisco L. Lopes, "The Ricardo Puzzle," *History of Political Economy*, vol. 40 (Winter 2008), pp. 595–611, explains Ricardo's dogged adherence to a labor theory of value, despite his own doubts about its accuracy, as the only way for him to avoid Malthus's criticism. Giuliana Campanelli, "Ricardo's 'Curious Effect': A Mathematical Formulation," *History of Political Economy*, vol. 28 (Winter 1996), pp. 691–702, provides a mathematical presentation of Ricardo's main ideas on fixed capital and its effect on value. For a cross-section of views and various reinterpretations of Ricardo's theory of value, see M. J. Carlson, "The Epistemological Status of Ricardo's Labor Theory," *History of Political Economy*, vol. 30 (Summer 1998), pp. 293–334; and the much earlier assessment by J. M. Cassels, "A Reinterpretation of Ricardo on Value," *Quarterly Journal of Economics*, vol. 46 (May 1935), pp. 518–532. Ricardo was reinterpreted yet again by S. C. Rankin, "Supply and Demand in Ricardian Price Theory: A Reinterpretation," *Oxford Economic Papers*, vol. 32 (July 1980), pp. 241–262; L. E. Johnson, "Ricardo's Labor Theory of the Determinant of Value," *Atlantic Economic Journal*, vol. 12 (March 1984), pp. 50–59; A. Burgstaller, "Demand and Relative Price in Ricardo: An Examination of Outstanding Issues," *History of Political Economy*, vol. 19 (Summer 1987), pp. 207–215; and C. Casarosa, "A New Formulation of the Ricardian System," *Oxford Economic Papers*, vol. 30 (March 1978), pp. 38–63. R. H. Timberlake, "The Classical Search for an Invariable Measure of Value," *Quarterly Review of Economics and Business*, vol. 6 (Spring 1966), pp. 37–44, is worth reading.

The Ricardian theory of profits has been another lightning rod of controversy. See John Eatwell, "The Interpretation of Ricardo's Essay on Profits," *Economica*, vol. 42 (May 1975), pp. 182–187; Terry Peach, "David Ricardo's Early Treatment of Profitability: A New Interpretation," *Economic Journal*, vol. 94 (December 1984), pp. 733–751; Sam Hollander, "On a 'New Interpretation' of Ricardo's Early Treatment of Profitability," *Economic Journal*, vol. 96 (December 1986), pp. 1091–1097; R. Prendergast, "David Ricardo's Early Treatment of Profitability: A New Interpretation: A Comment," *Economic Journal*, vol. 96 (December 1986), pp. 1098–1104; and Peach's reply to his critics, "Ricardo's Early Treatment of Profitability: Reply," *Economic Journal*, vol. 96 (December 1986), pp. 1105–1112. Sam Hollander, *The Economics of David Ricardo* (Toronto: University of Toronto Press, 1979), touched off a virulent controversy by his wholesale reinterpretation of Ricardo's economics. The issue of profitability in Ricardo's writings is perhaps obscured by the shifting nature of profits in various editions of the *Principles*. In contrast to the preceding debate between Peach, Hollander, and others, see J. B. Davis, "Ricardo's Theory of Profit in the Third Edition of the *Principles*," *Journal of the History of Economic Thought*, vol. 15 (Spring 1993), pp. 90–108.

Ricardo's participation in political debate was related mostly to his wish to curb an expanding role of government. Nancy Churchman, "Public Debt Policy and Public Extravagance: The Ricardo-Malthus Debate," *History of Political Economy*, vol. 31 (Winter 1999), pp. 653–673, demonstrates that both his economic analysis and his political theory led Ricardo to conclude that government involvement in the economy should be confined to a narrow range of activities. William Dixon, "Ricardo: Economic Thought and Social Order," *Journal of the History of Economic Thought*, vol. 30 (June 2008), pp. 235–253, compares Ricardo's free-market liberalism with the work of Thomas Paine, emphasizing Ricardo's vision of a well-functioning economic order based on free trade and the extension of the franchise; and Timothy Davis, "David Ricardo, Financier and Empirical Economist," *The European Journal of the History of Economic Thought*, vol. 9 (Spring 2002), pp. 1–16, examines Ricardo's grounding in the "real world."

Here is a potpourri of articles and books on other topics in Ricardo's writings. Roy J. Ruffin, "David Ricardo's Discovery of Comparative Advantage," *History of Political Economy*, vol. 34 (Winter 2002), pp. 727–748; C. S. Shoup, *Ricardo on Taxation* (New York: Columbia University Press, 1960); Hans Brems, "Ricardo's Long-Run Equilibrium," *History of Political Economy*, vol. 2 (Fall 1970), pp. 225–245; M. J. Gootzeit, "The Corn Laws and Wage Adjustment in a Short-Run Ricardian Model," *History of Political Economy*, vol. 5 (Spring 1973), pp. 50–71; R. Brandis, "The Structure of Wages and Ricardian Wage Theory," *Journal of the History of Economic Thought*, vol. 12 (Spring 1990), pp. 76–80; A. Stirati, "Smith's Legacy and the Definitions of the Natural Wage in Ricardo," *Journal of the History of Economic Thought*, vol. 17 (Spring 1995), pp. 106–133; Sam Hollander, "Ricardo and the Corn Laws: A Revision," *History of Political Economy*, vol. 9 (Spring 1977), pp. 1–47; same author, "On the Endogeneity of the Margin and Related Issues in Ricardian Economics," *Journal of the History of Economic Thought*, vol. 13 (Fall 1991), pp. 159–174; and again, "The Development of Ricardo's Position on Machinery," *History of Political Economy*, vol. 3 (Spring 1971), pp. 105–135. An obscure contemporary of Ricardo who also discussed the issue of machinery and its effect on employment was John Tozer. See, Paola Tubaro, "Producer Choice and Technical Unemployment: John E. Tozer's Mathematical Model (1838)." *The European Journal of the History of Economic Thought*, vol. 15 (Fall 2008), pp. 433–454.

Some insights into Ricardo's mind-set and his reactions to Malthus's *Principles* can be gained from a study of vol. 2 of the masterful Sraffa edition of Ricardo's *Works* (see references), which reproduces Ricardo's notes and marginalia appended to his personal copy of Malthus's *Principles*. Sraffa's own interpretation of Ricardo is considered by some to be idiosyncratic. See, for example, Paul A. Samuelson, "Classical and Neoclassical Harmonies and Dissonances," *The European Journal of the History of Economic Thought*, vol. 14 (June 2007), pp. 243–271.

On the value debate between Malthus and Ricardo, see V. E. Smith, "Malthus' Theory of Demand and Its Influence on Value Theory," *Scottish Journal of Political Economy*, vol. 3 (October 1956), pp. 205–220; and Omar Pancoast, "Malthus versus Ricardo," *Political Science Quarterly*, vol. 58 (1943), pp. 47–66. The contentious nature of Malthus and his maverick standing among his contemporaries is discussed by W. D. Grampp, "Malthus and his Contemporaries," *History of Political Economy*, vol. 6 (Fall 1974), pp. 278–304. See also M. B. Harvey-Phillips, "Malthus' Theodicy: The Intellectual Background to His Contribution to Political Economy," *History of Political Economy*, vol. 16 (Winter 1984), pp. 591–608. Some historians contend that there are two Malthuses: the Malthus of the *Essay on Population* and the Malthus of *The Principles of Political Economy*. J. J. Spengler, "Malthus' Total Population Theory: A Restatement and Reappraisal," *Canadian Journal of Economics and Political Science*, vol. 2 (February, May 1945), pp. 83–110, 234–264, attempts to integrate the two. Malthus's position on the Corn Laws continues to be controversial. Grampp presents one view (see references), but J. J. Spengler, "Malthus the Malthusian vs. Malthus the Economist," *Southern Economic Journal*, vol. 24 (July 1957), pp. 1–11, presents another. For an earlier view on the same subject, see H. G. Johnson, "Malthus on the High Price of Provisions," *Canadian Journal of Economics and Political Science*, vol. 15 (May 1949), pp. 190–202.

Malthus may be gaining more respect as an economist than a populationist due to contributions by Takuo Dome, "Malthus on Taxation and National Debt," *History of Political Economy*, vol. 29 (Summer 1997), pp. 275–294; A. M. C. Waterman, "Hume, Malthus and the Stability of Equilibrium," *History of Political Economy*, vol. 20 (Spring 1988), pp. 85–94; and same author, "Reappraisal of 'Malthus the Economist,' 1933–97," *History of Political Economy*, vol. 30 (Summer 1998), pp. 293–334. G. Gilbert, "Economic Growth and the Poor in Malthus' Essay on Population," *History of Political Economy*, vol. 12 (Spring 1980), pp. 83–96, discusses the impact of economic growth on the working classes. Samuel Hollander claims to have uncovered an "about-face" by Malthus in his "Malthus's Abandonment of Agricultural Protectionism: A Discovery in the History of Economic Thought," *American Economic Review*, vol. 82 (June 1992), pp. 650–659. But the "discovery" provoked a mini-debate between J. M. Pullen, "Malthus on Agricultural Protection: An Alternative View," *History of Political Economy*, vol. 27 (Fall 1995), pp. 517–530; and Hollander, "More on Malthus and Agricultural Protection," *History of Political Economy*, vol. 27 (Fall 1995), pp. 531–538.

Several authors have explored Malthus's views on aggregate demand, economic growth, and business cycles. For a sampling, see W. A. Eltis, "Malthus's Theory of Effective Demand and Growth," *Oxford Economic Papers*, vol. 32 (March 1980), pp. 19–56; J. J. O'Leary, "Malthus and Keynes," *Journal of Political Economy*, vol. 50 (December 1942), pp. 901–919; same author, "Malthus' General Theory of Employment and the Post-Napoleonic Depression," *Journal of Economic History*, vol. 3 (1943), pp. 185–200; Samuel Hollander, "Malthus and the Post-Napoleonic Depression," *History of Political Economy*, vol. 1 (Fall 1969), pp. 306–335; L. A. Dow, "Malthus on Sticky Wages, the Upper Turning Point, and General Glut," *History of Political Economy*, vol. 9 (Fall 1977), pp. 303–321; and A. M. C. Waterman, "On the Malthusian Theory of Long Swings," *Canadian Journal of Economics*, vol. 20 (May 1987), pp. 257–270.

The tenor of the time can be judged by the works of other writers besides Malthus and Ricardo. Matthew Smith, "Thomas Tooke on the Corn Laws," *History of Political Economy*, vol. 41 (Summer 2009), pp. 343–382, examines Tooke's support of the classical liberal ideal of free trade and explains Tooke's conviction that the Corn Laws caused price instability, redistributed income to landlords from workers, and imposed serious difficulties on the lower income classes. A fine portrait of Sir Edward West that goes beyond his contribution to classical rent theory is presented by W. D. Grampp, "Edward West Reconsidered," *History of Political Economy*, vol. 2 (Fall 1970), pp. 316–343. A writer whose ideas were picked up by Malthus and used against Ricardo was James Maitland (1759–1839), the eighth Earl of Lauderdale, who published under that name. Although it was considered highly unorthodox in its day Lauderdale's *Inquiry into the Nature and Origin of Public Wealth* (1804) was a substantial analytical contribution. On the connection between Lauderdale and Malthus, see Morton Paglin, *Malthus and Lauderdale: The Anti-Ricardian Tradition* (New York: A. M. Kelley, 1961). Lauderdale has also been linked to Keynes. See Maurice Mann, "Lord Lauderdale: Underconsumptionist and Keynesian Predecessor," *Social Science* (June 1959), pp. 153–162; and P. Lambert, "Lauderdale, Malthus et Keynes," *Revue d'économie politique* (January–February 1966), pp. 32–56. B. A. Corry, *Money, Saving and Investment in English Economics, 1800–1850* (New York: St. Martin's, 1962), and R. G. Link, *English Theories of Economic Fluctuations, 1815–1848* (New York: Columbia University Press, 1959), provide a somewhat wider sweep of Lauderdale's contributions.

A number of British writers set themselves against Ricardo, especially in regard to his theories of value and rent. Among them were Samuel Bailey, John Craig, Richard

Jones, William F. Lloyd, Mountifort Longfield, and Robert Torrens. For the full force of these other arguments see R. M. Rauner, *Samuel Bailey and the Classical Theory of Value* (Cambridge, MA: Harvard University Press, 1961); B. W. Thor, "The Economic Theories of John Craig, a Forgotten Economist," *Quarterly Journal of Economics*, vol. 52 (August 1938), pp. 697–707; W. L. Miller, "Richard Jones's Contributions to the Theory of Rent," *History of Political Economy*, vol. 9 (Fall 1977), pp. 346–365; R. M. Romano, "William Forster Lloyd—A Non-Ricardian," *History of Political Economy*, vol. 9 (Fall 1977), pp. 412–441; L. S. Moss, "Mountifort Longfield's Supply and Demand Theory of Price and Its Place in the Development of British Economic Theory," *History of Political Economy*, vol. 6 (Winter 1974), pp. 405–434; and Lionel Robbins, *Robert Torrens and the Evolution of Classical Economics* (New York: St. Martin's, 1958). Against his challengers, Ricardo had the faithful and tireless J. R. McCulloch, who defended Ricardo against all comers. The standard work on McCulloch is D. P. O'Brien's *J. R. McCulloch: A Study in Classical Economics* (London: G. Allen, 1970).

Judging by the dearth of secondary literature, not everyone shares Schumpeter's high opinion of Nassau Senior as a theorist. Marian Bowley, *Nassau Senior and Classical Economics* (London: G. Allen, 1937), is the standard reference; but see also, S. L. Levy, *Nassau W. Senior: The Prophet of Modern Capitalism* (Boston: Humphries, 1943). Levy collected and edited some of Senior's previously unpublished writings under the title *Industrial Efficiency and Social Economy*, 2 vols. (New York: Holt, 1928). Finally, Say's Law and its importance for classical macroeconomics are treated extensively in Thomas Sowell, *Say's Law* (Princeton, NJ: Princeton University Press, 1972).

8

Classical Economics (III)
John Stuart Mill

John Stuart Mill (1806–1873) was both progeny and prodigy. His father was James Mill, economist, disciple of Jeremy Bentham, and author of the compendious *History of British India*. As an ardent follower of Bentham, James Mill believed in "home schooling." He undertook responsibility for the education of his eldest son, John Stuart, and started early on. In his *Autobiography*, John Stuart Mill recounted his unusual and exacting education: At the age of three he began to learn Greek and arithmetic; somewhat later he studied the histories of Hume, Gibbon, and Plutarch (works borrowed from Bentham's library); by the age of eight he had read the works of the great Greek philosophers (Herodotus, Xenophon, Plato, and Diogenes) in their native language and began a study of Latin.

When he was twelve, Mill embarked on studies in logic, reading classic treatises in English and Latin. The following year he read Ricardo's *Principles*, submitting himself daily to his father's grilling questions on political economy. Mill later opined: "I do not believe that any scientific teaching ever was more thorough, or better fitted for training the faculties, than the mode in which logic and political economy were taught to me by my father" (*Autobiography*, p. 20). By the tender age of fourteen, Mill had received the equivalent of a university education, and was dispatched to teach what he had learned to his younger brothers and sisters. Because Mill's father sheltered him from the usual childhood contacts, he approached adulthood unaware that his upbringing was extraordinary. In a reflective mood, he wrote:

> What I could do, could assuredly be done by any poor boy or girl of average capacity and healthy physical constitution: and if I have accomplished anything, I owe it, among other fortunate circumstances, to the fact that through the early training bestowed on me by my father, I started, I may fairly say, with an advantage of a quarter of a century over my contemporaries. (*Autobiography*, p. 21)

In 1823, Mill joined his father in the service of the East India Company, and he remained with that enterprise until his retirement thirty-five years later. His duties were not especially taxing and his mind kept teeming with ideas that found expression in articles he published on various philosophical and literary topics. His first major work, *A System of Logic*, published in 1843, was favorably received and ran to several editions, as did his very successful *Principles of Political Economy*, which appeared for the first time in 1848. These two works assured Mill's reputation as one of the outstanding thinkers of his day. He followed his early successes in fairly rapid succession with *On Liberty* (1859), *Considerations of Representative Government* (1861), *Utilitarianism* (1863), *Auguste Comte and Positivism* (1865), and *The Subjection of Women* (1869). Mill enriched four main areas of intellectual inquiry: (1) the problem of method in the social sciences, (2) clarification of the (Benthamite) principle of utility, (3) the nature and limits of individual freedom, and (4) the theory of representative government. However, his economic contributions concern us most.

Mill's Intellectual Transition

The rigors of Mill's early education and their weight on his young mind were a proximate cause of a prolonged period of mental depression that began when he was twenty years old. During his "blue" period, Mill concluded that none of the goals in life for which he had been trained were capable of bringing true happiness. He became aware of certain gaps and inadequacies in his upbringing and he turned to a group of Romantic writers for consolation.

Exposure to the Romantics

In an attempt to develop a more robust "internal culture," Mill read the works of the Romantic poets Coleridge and Wordsworth, and the ideas of the French philosophers of the Enlightenment. The writings of the poets, especially, not only gave Mill solace in his depression but also induced him to rethink certain ideas on the subject of economics. Coleridge and Wordsworth openly expressed their antagonism toward economics. They were later joined in their discontent by literary critics Thomas Carlyle,[1] Charles Dickens, and John Ruskin. Individually and as a group these authors held industrialism responsible for the decline of social sensibilities and the quality of life. Economics took the brunt of their criticism because they viewed political economy as *the science of industrialism.* Claiming to be protectors of the old order, the Romantics denied the efficacy of scientific inquiry. They judged economists guilty by association, failing to see that analysts do not necessarily give their stamp of approval to the existing order when they seek to explain it. Few economists of the day even took such bland criticism seriously. Mill was a prominent exception.

Mill and Comte

During his mental "crisis," Mill absorbed the ideas of Auguste Comte, the French philosopher and founder of sociology and positivism. Comte espoused a general *science of man*, which he named *sociology.*[2] He envisioned political economy as a branch of the general science of sociology but lamented its lack of empirical and historical relevance. He called for a new method as well as a new ordering of the social sciences. He called this new method *positivism*, by which he meant empiricism, or induction.

Mill reacted to diverse criticisms from Comte and the Romantics by reconstructing the philosophical and methodological foundations of his own views on political economy. He was sympathetic to Comte's attempts to construct a general science of humanity, but he nevertheless defended economics as a separate science, relevant to

[1] Having read Malthus on population, it was Carlyle who dubbed economics "the dismal science."

[2] Sociology, today, as a separate discipline, has become much more specialized than Comte's original vision of it. To Comte, sociology was to be an all-embracing study of humans, including economics, psychology, anthropology, history, and the like.

humans' social well-being. He also acknowledged the merits of the inductive method, but he defended the deductive method as inherently useful to a *social* science.

Mill maintained that the empirical, or inductive, method could not be relied on exclusively in the social arena because causes of social phenomena are often complex and interwoven, and effects are not easily distinguishable from one another. Deduction is a desirable check against the errors of casual empiricism, Mill believed, but it need not lead to dogmatic acceptance of ideas and theories that cannot be supported by fact. Thus, facts are a desirable check to pure deduction. In short, Mill achieved a delicate balance between the inductive–deductive extremes in economic method.

THE STRUCTURE OF MILL'S ECONOMIC INQUIRY

The delicate balance Mill sought between inductive and deductive reasoning is evident in his major economic work, *Principles of Political Economy*. In matters of theory he reaffirmed and enlarged the Ricardian framework, while simultaneously incorporating new ideas and new supportive evidence on numerous matters of political economy. Mill's *Principles* was a major success. Used as a text for almost sixty years (until replaced by Alfred Marshall's *Principles*), it was and is a complete treatise on classical economic theory, economic policy, and social philosophy. In this chapter we concentrate on the development and significance of Mill's economic theory; in the next we shall examine more fully his economic philosophy and policies.

The Character and Aim of *Principles*

The character and aim of Mill's *Principles* are best described by Mill himself:

> For practical purposes, Political Economy is inseparably intertwined with many other branches of Social Philosophy. Except on matters of mere detail, there are perhaps no practical questions, even among those which approach nearest to the character of purely economical questions, which admit of being decided on economical premises alone. And it is because Adam Smith never loses sight of this truth; because, in his applications of Political Economy, he perpetually appeals to other and often far larger considerations than pure Political Economy affords—that he gives that well-grounded feeling of command over the principles of the subject for purposes of practice. . . . It appears to the present writer that a work similar in its object and general conception to that of Adam Smith, but adapted to the more extended knowledge and improved ideas of the present age, is the kind of contribution which Political Economy at present requires. (*Principles*, pp. xxvii–xxviii)

From this passage one gets a glimmer of economics as a broad field of inquiry. Elsewhere Mill said that one is not likely to be a good economist if he is nothing else—reflecting, perhaps, Comte's perception that economics is a mere part of a larger "science of man." Clearly Mill emphasized the dual character of his work—theory and applications—from the outset. His goal was clear: to summarize and synthesize all the economic knowledge up to his day.

This methodological eclecticism gave the *Principles* a unique flavor. Through his contact with Auguste Comte and the Saint-Simonians (see chapter 11), he came to assert the now famous dichotomy between the economic laws of production and the social laws of distribution. The former, according to Mill, are unchangeable; they are governed by natural laws. Ricardo and his followers had perfected these laws, Mill thought, and taken together, they constituted economics in the narrow sense, as a separate science. But the laws of distribution, he insisted, are almost entirely a matter of human will and institutions, not determined by economics alone, but affected by changing values, mores, social philosophies, and tastes. The laws of distribution are therefore malleable, and to understand them fully one must look beyond economics to the historical laws that underlie economic progress.

Much of Comte's thought concerned the discovery of these historical laws. His celebrated view of history expressed in the "law of three stages" asserts that the development of the human intellect progresses through three separate and distinct stages: (1) the *theological* stage, in which human behavior and other phenomena are attributed to a deity, or to "magic"; (2) the *metaphysical* stage, in which the essence, or "nature," of a thing is substituted for divine personalities (e.g., natural law as an explanatory device); and finally (3) the *positive* stage, in which the scientific method is employed in finding truth. Comte attributed all social and economic progress to the perfection of the human intellect as it passes through these three stages.

Like many early treatises, Mill's *Principles* is divided into "books," or sections. The (immutable) economics of production, value, and exchange are generally confined to Books, I, II, and III, whereas Mill's (malleable) social views are aired in Book IV ("Influence of the Progress of Society on Production and Distribution") and Book V ("On the Influence of Government").

Mill on Production

Mill's ideas on production are firmly grounded in Ricardo's *Principles*, plus the (minimal) post-Ricardian refinements on that topic. The key roles in economic progress played by productive and unproductive labor, Say's Law, capital accumulation, the Malthusian population doctrine, and the wages-fund doctrine are all presented by Mill with great clarity. Like most economists in the post-Smith tradition Mill assigned a crucial role to capital and to capital accumulation in explaining production and economic development. He attached great importance to his "five fundamental propositions respecting capital," which restated the classical theory of economic progress.

In a nutshell Mill argued that, given Say's Law, employment and increased levels of output are dependent on the accumulation and investment of capital. Part of the investment in capital, the result of saving, is required to tide labor over a discontinuous production period. Although he later seemed to recant this idea, Mill revealed a clear understanding of the wages-fund doctrine:

> There can be no more industry than is supplied with materials to work up and food to eat. Self-evident as the thing is, it is often forgotten, that the people of a country are maintained and have their wants supplied, not by the produce of present labour, but of past. They consume what has been produced, not what is about to be produced. Now, of what has been produced, a part only is allocated to the support of productive labour; and there will not and cannot be more of that labour than the portion so allotted (which is the capital of the country) can feed, and provide with the materials and instruments of production. (*Principles*, p. 64)

Unemployment of resources—other than as a temporary state of affairs—was not considered possible because of Say's Law. Contrary to the Malthusian position, saving would automatically be turned into another form of spending (i.e., investment), and a general glut of goods from underconsumption was impossible. Mill, in short, never considered that there could be a lack of aggregate demand in the economic system. But as we shall see momentarily, Mill cleared up earlier confusions regarding Say's Law and the insufficiency of aggregate demand.

Mill on Economic Growth

Mill summarized and improved the classical theory of economic development. Like Ricardo, he believed the law of diminishing returns was a key factor limiting economic growth. Another limit was a declining incentive to invest. In general, however, Mill focused on the crucial variables of capital accumulation, population growth, and technology. Combining these principles with diminishing returns to agriculture, Mill offered a clear and comprehensive discussion of the classical theory of economic development.

Owing to diminishing returns and weakening incentives to invest, Mill argued that the economy was being propelled from a *progressive* state to a *stationary* state (see chapter 7). But Mill was one of the few, if not the only, classical economist to put forth a positive view of the stationary state. He regarded this long-run equilibrium position as a precondition for meaningful social reform. Only after the stationary state was reached could problems of equity in distribution be evaluated and social reforms proceed apace. Remember that distribution belonged to a set of economic relationships that were malleable in Mill's mind. What was required after the inexorable laws of economics had run their course was the enlightenment and wisdom of statesmen/legislators to enact meaningful reforms that would enhance social well-being. In light of subsequent developments in economics, especially the development of public choice theory (chapter 24) this stance by Mill is likely to be seen as naive. But setting aside for the moment his stance on distribution, Mill's statement of the dynamics of classical production theory achieved a depth of clarity and understanding of classical dynamics unsurpassed by any other writer of the classical era.

■ Mill's Theoretical Advances

The popular view of the *economist* John Stuart Mill is that he was a sophisticated synthesizer of little theoretical originality. Yet, this assessment is shortsighted. George Stigler ("The Nature and Role of Originality") argues persuasively that it would be difficult to point to a writer of greater theoretical originality than Mill. The purpose of this section is to elaborate on a few of Mill's more significant theoretical contributions. Though Mill himself did not emphasize the importance of these theoretical ideas (the theory of joint supply is found in a footnote, for example), they nevertheless indicate that he was more of a bridge between classical and neoclassical analysis than has commonly been perceived. The issues chosen for elaboration below are not exhaustive, but are selected to demonstrate the understated originality of Mill's contributions to economic analysis.

Supply and Demand

The first clear British contribution to static-equilibrium price formation in the modern sense was developed by John Stuart Mill. Utilizing purely verbal analysis, he advanced the theory of equilibrium price on several fronts. He fully recognized the analytical necessity of abstracting and simplifying the principles underlying the functional relation between price and quantity demanded and supplied. He noted, for example, that "in considering the exchange value scientifically, it is expedient to abstract from it all causes except those which originate in the very commodity under consideration" (*Principles*, p. 438). Having mastered the method of abstract reasoning exemplified in Ricardo, Mill was able to give a correct formulation of demand and supply as *schedules* showing the functional relation between price and quantity demanded and supplied, *ceteris paribus*.

Noting the terminological confusion that previous writers had exhibited, Mill proposed that the proper mathematical relation to express demand and supply is an *equation*, not a *ratio*, as had so often been supposed in economic literature (by Malthus, among others):

> A ratio between demand and supply is only intelligible if by demand we mean quantity demanded, and if the ratio intended is that between the quantity demanded and the quantity supplied. But again, the quantity demanded is not a fixed quantity, even at the same time and place; it varies according to the value; if the thing is cheap, there is usually a demand for more of it than when it is dear. (*Principles*, p. 446)

> The idea of a *ratio*, as between demand and supply, is [therefore] out of place, and has no concern in the matter: the proper mathematical analogy is that of an *equation*. Demand and supply, the quantity demanded and the quantity supplied, will be made equal. If unequal at any moment, competition equalizes them, and the manner in which this is done is by an adjustment of the value. If the demand increases, the value rises; if the demand diminishes, the value falls: again, if the supply falls off, the value rises; and falls if the supply is increased. (*Principles*, p. 448)

Most early formulations of value-and-demand theory relied on circular reasoning. Misunderstanding the correct nature of demand could lead to the allegation that demand depends in part on value but that value is determined by demand. Given Mill's distinction, however, if "demand increases" (or decreases) is read as a rightward (leftward) shift in demand, Mill's compact statement is almost entirely analogous to modern explanations of the mechanics of price changes. He therefore presented a perfectly adequate distinction between price-determined and price-determining changes in demand and supply. Mill's performance in this regard was not matched in England until Fleeming Jenkin presented a graphical exposition on supply and demand two decades later in his 1870 essay, "The Graphic Representation of the Laws of Supply and Demand, and Their Application to Labour." Mill was, moreover, one of Alfred Marshall's most important sources on the subject.

Joint Supply

Another contribution of importance to the technical advance of value theory was Mill's development of the theory of jointly supplied goods. Although Marshall is often given credit for the invention of the concept (he simply added the graphics), Mill stated the principle concisely in his *Principles* (his chapter entitled "Some Peculiar Cases of Value"):

> It sometimes happens that two different commodities have what may be termed a joint cost of production. They are both products of the same operation, or set of operations, and the outlay is incurred for the sake of both together, not part for one and part for the other. The same outlay would have to be incurred for either of the two, if the other were not wanted or used at all. There are not a few instances of commodities thus associated in their production: for example, coke and coal-gas are both produced from the same material, and by the same operation. In a more partial sense, mutton and wool are an example: beef, hides, and tallow: calves and dairy produce: chickens and eggs. Cost of production can have nothing to do with deciding the value of the associated commodities relatively to each other. It only decides their joint value. The gas and the coke together have to repay the expenses

of their production, with the ordinary profit. To do this, a given quantity of gas, together with the coke which is the residuum of its manufacture, must exchange for other things in the ratio of their joint costs of production. But how much of the remuneration of the producer shall be derived from the coke, and how much from the gas, remains to be decided. Cost of production does not determine their prices, but the sum of their prices. (*Principles*, pp. 569–570)

The Problem. The question raised by Mill in this regard is: Given a single cost function, how are profits from the two separate productions to be allocated to the jointly produced goods? Calculation of profits presupposes, of course, that prices can be determined for separate commodities. Mill's directions for determining a simultaneous equilibrium were explicit:

> Equilibrium will be attained when the demand for each article fits so well with the demand for the other, that the quantity required of each is exactly as much as is generated in producing the quantity required of the other. If there is any surplus or deficiency on either side; if there is a demand for coke, and not a demand for all the gas produced along with it; or vice versa; the values and prices of the two things will readjust themselves so that both shall find a market. (*Principles*, p. 571)

The Solution. Mill's solution to the joint-supply problem may be restated as follows: In the case where goods are produced jointly in fixed proportions, the equilibrium price of each product must be such as to clear its market, subject to the condition that the sum of the two prices equals their (average) joint costs. His apparently complete understanding of this special aspect of competitive pricing, without benefit of mathematical analysis, seems remarkable today.

Alfred Marshall (chapter 16) later enhanced our understanding of this complex problem by supplying graphics consistent with Mill's solution. These graphics are found in a footnote to chapter 6, Book V, of Marshall's *Principles of Economics*, and are replicated below in figure 8-1. The joint products in this application are beef and hides. Both products derive from steers but have different prices according to the demand in each submarket. *SS'* is a joint-supply, or *average-cost*, function for steers. The total demand for steers is represented by demand curve *DD'*, which is

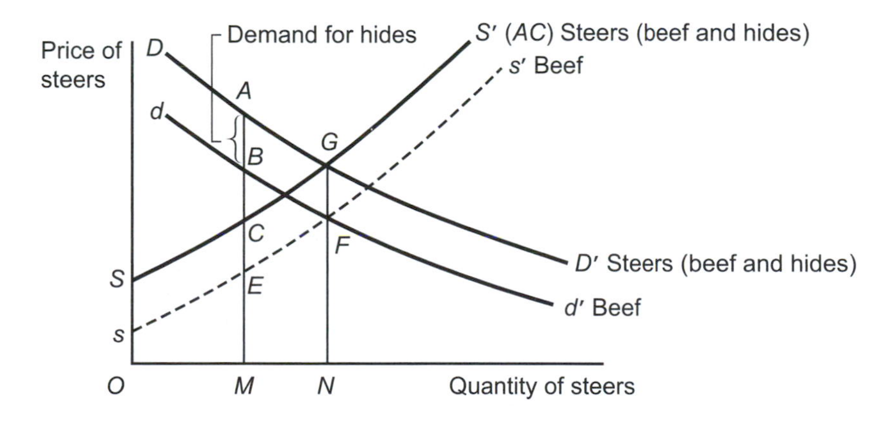

Figure 8-1 At competitive equilibrium *N*, the price of beef (*NF*) is determined by the intersection of *ss'* and *dd'*, and the price of hides (*GF*) is determined by subtracting *NF* from the total supply function.

the vertical summation of the separate demands for beef and hides. The demand function for beef is shown as *dd′*, so the demand for hides may be easily derived by vertically subtracting the demand for beef from the total demand for steers. Thus, at total quantity *M* of steers produced, *MB* represents the demand price for beef and *BA* represents the demand price for hides.

A special type of supply curve can be derived for beef, moreover. It is obtained by subtracting the demand price for hides from the supply price of the composite output, steers. As we have seen, the demand price for hides at quantity *M* is equal to *BA*. Subtracting *BA* from the total supply function yields a derived supply price for beef at quantity *M* of *ME* and thus a supply price for hides of *EC*. Following this procedure, the dashed supply function for beef (*ss′*) can be traced for each quantity.

Competitive equilibrium, as Mill clearly understood, is achieved when *N* steers are produced. At quantity *N*, the price of beef (*NF*) is achieved by the intersection of the supply-and-demand curves for beef (*ss′* and *dd′*). The price of hides is similarly determined (*GF*). The competitive market for both goods is in equilibrium when the quantity *N* is produced.[3] Several interesting characteristics of the Mill–Marshall model should be noted. First, an increase in the *demand* for one of the goods, say, hides, increases the *supply* of the other (in this case beef) and thus lowers its price. Second, an increase in average cost (*SS′*) raises the price of both the jointly produced goods. Moreover, these two results, as well as the construction of the Mill–Marshall analysis, depend on an assumption of fixity in the proportions of goods produced; i.e., an increase in steer production implies a proportionate increase in the production of beef and hides. Other models may be constructed on nonproportionality assumptions, of course, but do not reflect the "classic" formulation of the problem.

The peculiar case of joint supply may seem idiosyncratic in many product markets, but Mill's theory played an important part in trying to resolve problems in the areas of transportation and public-utility economics. More recently it has been used in public-goods models and in problems involving the supply of by-products, such as pollution. Mill's joint-supply theory was, in sum, a contribution of great significance for economic analysis.

The Doctrine of Alternative Costs

The issue of land rent as a necessary (or unnecessary) payment of production was left in a muddled state by Ricardo's unyielding treatment of rent as an inframarginal surplus. Recall that in the strict sense Ricardo's theory holds only if agricultural land has no alternative uses. Mill clarified the nature of rent by expositing the doctrine of alternative costs and applying it to land uses. In Book III, chapter 5 of his *Principles* he wrote:

> Land is used for other purposes than for agriculture, especially for residence; and when so used, yields a rent. . . . The ground rent of a building, and the rent of a garden or park attached to it, will not be less than the rent which the same land would afford in agriculture. . . . But when land capable of yielding rent in agriculture is applied to some other purpose, the rent which it would have yielded is an element of the cost of production of the commodity which it is employed to produce. (p. 475)

In other words, agricultural rent is not a cost of production when land has no alternative uses (Ricardo's case) but becomes a necessary cost of production once alternative uses are admitted.

[3] Note that at this point the sum of the two prices (*NF* + *FG*) equals their joint costs of production, *NG*.

The Economics of the Firm

As fascinating as Adam Smith's discussion of a pin manufactory was, it described a small-scale production process. With the passage of time, and the full flowering of the Industrial Revolution, manufacturing in Britain was undertaken on increasingly larger scales. Mill was sensitive to this development and alert to the consequences for economics—in his treatment of the laws of production he presented the first systematic discussion in a general treatise of the principle of economies of scale.

Smith correctly noted that the division of labor is one factor contributing to the growth of firms. Mill acknowledged that the division of labor is "one of the principle causes of large manufactories" (*Principles*, p. 132), but he also recognized the importance of scale. Another cause of firm growth, he said, "is the introduction of processes requiring expensive machinery. Expensive machinery supposes a large capital; and is not resorted to except with the intention of producing, and the hope of selling, as much of the article as comes up to the full powers of the machine" (*Principles*, p. 135).

Using the Post Office to illustrate his case of how a large, centralized enterprise scores efficiencies over small, decentralized business, Mill deduced the principle of economies of scale and proposed a simple test of whether or not such economies are present in any concrete case:

> As a general rule, the expenses of a business do not increase by any means proportionally to the quantity of business. . . . Whether or not the advantages obtained by operating on a large scale preponderate in any particular case over the more watchful attention, and greater regard to minor gains and losses, usually found in small establishments, can be ascertained, in a state of free competition, by an unfailing test. Wherever there are large and small establishments in the same business, that one of the two which in existing circumstances carries on the production at greatest advantage will be able to undersell the other. The power of permanently underselling can only, generally speaking, be derived from increased effectiveness of labour; and this, when obtained by a more extended division of employment, or by a classification tending to a better economy of skill, always implies a greater produce from the same labour, and not merely the same produce from less labour: it increases not the surplus only, but the gross produce of industry. If an increased quantity of the particular article is not required, and part of the labourers in consequence lose their employment, the capital which maintained and employed them is also set at liberty; and the general produce of the country is increased by some other application of their labour. (*Principles*, p. 134)

The Theory of Noncompeting Labor Groups

First Cantillon, then Adam Smith, recognized certain inequalities in wages because of the nature of the employments themselves and not because of any shortcomings of the laws of competition. Economists call these inequalities "equilibrium wage differences." Smith's discussion of equilibrium wage differences was based on the notion of full occupational mobility of the labor force in the long run. Mill, however, recognized an artificial barrier to labor mobility caused by the costs of education:

> If unskilled labourers had it in their power to compete with skilled, by merely taking the trouble of learning the trade, the differences of wages might not exceed what would compensate them for that trouble. . . . But the fact that a course of instruction is required, of even a low degree of costliness, or that the labourer must

> be maintained for a considerable time from other sources, suffices everywhere to exclude the great body of the labouring people from the possibility of such competition. . . . So complete . . . has hitherto been the separation, so strongly marked the line of demarcation, between the different grades of labourers, as to be almost equivalent to an hereditary distinction of caste; each employment being chiefly recruited from the children of those already employed in it, or in employments of the same rank with it in social estimation, or from the children of persons who, if originally on a lower rank, have succeeded in raising themselves by their exertions. (*Principles*, pp. 391–393)

Because the disparities that persist in certain labor markets cannot be explained by the principle of competition, these segments are called "noncompeting labor groups." Advanced training/education equips some workers with skills that cannot easily be duplicated, bestowing on affected workers a certain degree of monopoly power that can be exploited in the sale of their services. Professional football players do not compete (for wages) in any meaningful sense with insurance salesmen, for example.

The Theory of Market Gluts

Say's Law held broad sway over macroeconomic theory until John Maynard Keynes (chapter 21) totally discredited the idea. But the relationship between consumption and production was always nettlesome for the classical economists. The widespread view was that general overproduction of economic output cannot persist in the long run because market forces will correct temporary imbalances. Faced with oversupply, prices will fall in competitive markets, giving stimulus to more consumption, thus causing the surplus goods to be consumed. This is the principle that came to be known as "Say's Law" (see chapter 7). Mill was the earliest writer to recognize the limits to Say's Law and correctly state the condition for its validity. The key, Mill recognized, is understanding the role of financial instruments in the market economy:

> There can never, it is said, be a want of buyers for all commodities; because whoever offers a commodity for sale, desires to obtain a commodity in exchange for it, and is therefore a buyer by the mere fact of his being a seller. The sellers and the buyers, for all commodities taken together, must, by the metaphysical necessity of the case, be an exact equipoise to each other; and if there be more sellers than buyers of one thing, there must be more buyers than sellers of another.
>
> This argument [Say's law] is evidently founded on the supposition of a state of barter; and on that supposition, it is perfectly incontestable. When two persons perform an act of barter, each of them is at once a seller and a buyer. . . . If, however, we suppose that money is used, these propositions cease to be exactly true. . . . Interchange by means of money is . . ., as has been often observed, ultimately nothing but barter. But there is this difference—that in the case of barter, the selling and the buying are simultaneously confounded in one operation; you sell what you have and buy what you want, by one indivisible act, and you cannot do the one without doing the other. Now the effect of the employment of money, and even the utility of it, is, that it enables this one act of interchange to be divided into two separate acts or operations, one of which may be performed now, and the other a year hence, or whenever it shall be most convenient. ("Influence," p. 276)

It follows that at a given time people may wish to hurry sales of goods and postpone purchases—this is a period of general glut. But this glut may simply imply pent-up purchasing power held in the form of money or money substitutes. According to Mill:

> In order to render the argument for the impossibility of an excess of all commodities applicable to the case in which a circulating medium is employed, money must itself be considered a commodity. It must undoubtedly be admitted that there cannot be an excess of all other commodities, and an excess of money at the same time. ("Influence," p. 277)

Mill's "Neoclassical" Contributions

While Mill became the repository and grand master of classical thought, his role as a creative theorist who pointed the way to neoclassical economic analysis has been neglected. The list of contributions, discussed (however briefly) above, should be enough to dispel the notion of Mill as a slavish imitator/synthesizer of classical economics. His conceptualization and explanation of demand theory alone, including the "peculiar" case of joint supply and demand, places him in a direct line from Smith (chapter 5) to Marshall (chapter 16), and continues to inform contemporary branches of economic theory, including the theory and practice of economic regulation and the conditions surrounding the demands for public goods.

Moreover, Mill's purely theoretical achievements did not stop there. The role of price adjustments in establishing conditions of reciprocal equilibrium in several markets simultaneously was not a central theme in economic analysis until the neoclassical period and beyond. Major credit for this advance belongs to Léon Walras (chapter 17), who constructed a general equilibrium system of economic analysis in the generation that followed Mill. However, Mill's verbal model of reciprocal demand in the theory of international trade was a major building block in the construction of such a system.[4] In conception (if not in formalization and development) general equilibrium theory could justly be termed "Millian" as well as "Walrasian." In short, Mill's incisive contributions to value theory mark him as a bold and original pioneer during the high time of classical economics.

■ Mill's Normative Economics

Frequently regarded as the last great classical economist, Mill swam against the current of intellectual and socialist criticism of classical political economy by Romantics, socialists, and other heterodox thinkers. Being who he was, Mill could not help but be affected by this criticism. He often took even the most bizarre socialist critics more seriously than they deserved. For a time, he was almost a Saint-Simonian, although in his later life he found difficulties in the Saint-Simonian doctrine too elusive to resolve. Mill remained sympathetic to the *ideals* of socialism throughout his life, even though he found little force in the analysis of socialist writers. He was committed to social reform, but wished to promote it in a way that would preserve and enhance individual freedom and dignity as much as possible.

This humanistic concern for greater equality of wealth and opportunity sets Mill apart from other classical economists. He attempted, as we said before, a delicate balancing act. His theoretical adroitness displayed in the first three books of the *Principles* is counterpoised by his reformist élan displayed in the last two books. Books IV and V emphasize *applications* of political economy for the improvement of humanity, and Mill made it clear where he stood on the relation of theory versus practice in economics. He once wrote to a friend: "I regard the purely abstract investigations of

[4] Due to space constraints and the highly specialized nature of the subject, Mill's theory of international values is not explored in this book, but it can be found in Book III of his *Principles*.

political economy . . . as of very minor importance compared with the great practical questions which the progress of democracy and the spread of socialist opinions are pressing on" (*Letters*, I, seminar 170). It should be noted, however, that Mill never lost sight of the importance of theory as the proper foundation for taking policy positions. The last two books of the *Principles*, then, unlike the first three, are teleological (goal-oriented). They reveal Mill's concern for such social reforms as wealth redistribution, equality of women, workers' rights, consumerism, and education.

The Stationary State Revisited

The stationary state (chapter 7) as devised by Ricardo, and modified by Mill, was part of the teleological orientation of Books IV and V of the *Principles*. Mill broke with the Ricardian tradition, which viewed the stationary state as the end product of economic development. Mill made it the launching pad for an improved social system. To Mill, the stationary state became almost a kind of utopia, in which, having achieved affluence, the state could get on with solving the problems that really matter—namely, equality of wealth and opportunity.

Mill announced his break from the classical tradition in Book IV, where he attacked the idea of wealth accumulation merely for the sake of accumulation. Speaking in the first person, Mill said:

> I cannot . . . regard the stationary state of capital and wealth with the unaffected aversion so generally manifested towards it by political economists of the old school. I am inclined to believe that it would be, on the whole, a very considerable improvement on our present condition. I confess I am not charmed with the ideal of life held out by those who think that the normal state of human beings is that of struggling to get on. (*Principles*, p. 748)

In other places, too, Mill sounds remarkably modern—almost in league with those economists who denounce economic growth for its own sake.[5] But there is a word of caution from Mill for those who would "improve" society by first tearing it down:

> It is only in the backward countries of the world that increased production is still an important object: in those most advanced, what is economically needed is a better distribution, of which one indispensable means is a stricter restraint on population. Levelling institutions, either of a just or unjust kind, cannot alone accomplish it; they may lower the heights of society, but they cannot, of themselves, permanently raise the depths. (*Principles*, p. 749)

In this passage Mill reveals his conviction that true social reform does not consist merely in the destruction of oppressive institutions, but rather in "the joint effect of the prudence and frugality of individuals, and of a system of legislation favoring equality of fortunes, so far as is consistent with the just claim of the individual to the fruits, whether great or small, of his or her own industry" (*Principles*, p. 749).

Wealth Redistribution

Mill favored wealth redistribution, not income redistribution. The distinction between the two is not trivial. Mill did not wish to dampen productive incentives. As his father before him, he believed that individuals should be allowed to "reap the fruits of their own industry," which is to say that every person has a right to the

[5] Most vocal among later economists who joined this chorus are John Kenneth Galbraith (see chapter 19) and E. J. Mishan, *Costs of Economic Growth*.

income she or he *earns*. But neither James nor John Stuart sanctioned the accumulation of wealth as an end in itself. Both men believed that beyond a certain limit, further material gains are frivolous. In the younger Mill, this aversion to overaccumulation provoked a proposal to limit the size of bequests. He wrote:

> Were I framing a code of laws according to what seems to me best in itself, without regard to existing opinions and sentiments, I should prefer to restrict . . . what any one should be permitted to acquire, by bequest or inheritance. Each person should have power to dispose by will of his or her whole property; but not to lavish it in enriching some one individual, beyond a certain maximum, which should be fixed sufficiently high to afford the means of comfortable independence. The inequalities of property which arise from unequal industry, frugality, perseverance, talents, and to a certain extent even opportunities, are inseparable from the principle of private property, and if we accept the principle we must bear with these consequences of it: but I see nothing objectionable in fixing a limit to what any one may acquire by the mere favour of others; without any exercise of his faculties, and in requiring that if he desires any further, he shall work for it. (*Principles*, pp. 227–228)

Clearly, what Mill advocated was a world in which people are free from the pressing demands of economic necessity and open to improvements in the quality of life. He shared this idea with the Romantic poets, although he rejected their fulgent criticisms of political economy. But the kind of limits that Mill would impose on individual wealth involves value judgments and therefore belongs to the realm of normative economics. Issues of this sort cannot be resolved by positive economics, which confines itself to objective issues. Mill was quite emphatic about the stationary state as a good thing. Because of its liberating effect from the grinding necessities of economic survival, he saw in it expanded opportunities for human development:

> It is scarcely necessary to remark that a stationary condition of capital and population implies no stationary state of human improvement. There would be as much scope as ever for all kinds of mental culture, and moral and social progress; as much room for improving the Art of Living, and much more likelihood of its being improved, when minds ceased to be engrossed by the art of getting on. (*Principles*, p. 751)

Government and Laissez-Faire

A major part of Mill's normative economics concerns the proper role and influence of government, which he took up in Book V of the *Principles*. He began by distinguishing between the *necessary* functions of government and its *optional* functions. The necessary functions "are either inseparable from the idea of government or exercised habitually and without objection by all governments" (*Principles*, p. 796). Other functions, however, are not universally accepted, and therefore government action in these instances is controversial.

This distinction between necessary and optional functions is important only insofar as it enabled Mill at this stage of analysis to minimize discussions of the former and concentrate on the latter. Included in Mill's list of necessary government functions are the power to tax, coin money, and establish a uniform system of weights and measurements; protection against force and fraud; the administration of justice and the enforcement of contracts; the establishment and protection of property rights, including prescriptions on the use of the environment; protection of the interests of minors and mental incompetents; and the provision of certain public goods and services, such as roads, canals, dams, bridges, harbors, lighthouses, and sanitation.

Mill defended government activity in these areas with a lengthy digression on the economic effects of all manner of taxes, direct and indirect. His exhaustive treatment of these issues has endured through the ages. Nevertheless, it is a detour that threatens the continuity of Mill's narrative in Book V on the proper grounds for government action. Returning to this core issue in the final chapter of the *Principles*, Mill placed the burden of proof on those who would advocate government intervention. He himself stood squarely in the classical tradition by reaffirming the maxim that laissez-faire should be the rule and that any departure from it, "unless required by some great good, is a certain evil" (*Principles*, p. 950).

But just as Adam Smith was less doctrinaire on the matter of government interference than he is typically made out to be, John Stuart Mill was even less so. The key to Mill's philosophical position on the limits of the laissez-faire principle lies in his recognition that government interference under capitalism *could be required by some great good*. In this respect, Mill never shook off the early influence of Jeremy Bentham. Thus, Mill was able to list several exceptions to the doctrine of laissez-faire without compromising the basic principle. His exceptions allow government intervention in the areas of consumer protection, general education, preservation of the environment, selective enforcement of "permanent" contracts based on future experience (e.g., marriage), public-utility regulation, and public charity.

In short, Mill recognized, and in some cases enunciated for the first time, the majority of popular exceptions to laissez-faire that have become an integral part of modern capitalism, at least in the United States. The hundreds of watchdog agencies and regulatory commissions of government in the United States[6] are logical extensions of Mill's desire to make capitalism fairer and more humane. The specific details of Mill's policy concerns and proposals are considered in chapter 9. In fairness to Mill, he was very explicit about the caveats the state should employ in instituting such measures, and he would not necessarily approve of all existing amendments to the institutions of capitalism. Nevertheless, it is his willingness to make such amendments that underlines the transitional nature of his works and thoughts and that marks Mill as a modern economist in many respects.

■ Mill and the Decline of Classical Economics

John Stuart Mill was unquestionably a product of his intellectual environment, but he was also a molder of it. Fully within the classical tradition, he devoted his intellectual efforts to synthesizing and improving economic knowledge at a time when economics was beset on all sides by Romantic, social, and methodological criticism. He enriched economic theory by his own analytical contributions, and he did not hesitate to issue normative proclamations to underscore practical applications of economic knowledge. Mill skillfully displayed the interconnections between theory and policy, but he never confused the two. Wherever he advanced his normative views, he warned his readers of their arbitrariness. Even so, he revealed a spirit of disinterested inquiry by carefully presenting both the advantages and the disadvantages of any given proposition or course of action.

His influence on other economists and social thinkers was deep and long lasting. In his own century, Mill's concern for fundamental questions and his multifac-

[6] Professor Bauer-Romazani provides a short list of major regulatory agencies and commissions at http://academics.smcvt.edu/cbauer-ramazani/BU113/fed_agencies.htm. A complete list of U.S. government departments and agencies can be found at http://www.usa.gov/directory/federal/index.shtml.

eted talents as economist, philosopher, and logician insulated him against the attacks of lesser minds. (For a glimpse of Mill's contribution to economic method, see the box, Method Squabbles 2: Mill on Economic Method.) Indeed, Mill's legacy endures. As is true of most great thinkers, the questions he raised have proved more durable than the answers he gave. In this chapter we have concentrated on Mill's theoretical performance, with a few side glances at his policy proposals. In the next two chapters we shall see how Mill's ideas on policy, alongside those of his contemporary, Edwin Chadwick, became part of the political landscape of Great Britain.

Method Squabbles 2: Mill on Economic Method

In addition to his stellar contributions to economic theory and policy, John Stuart Mill was one of the first economists to state clearly what has become the dominant method of economic inquiry. While both Nassau Senior and David Ricardo made contributions to the establishment of a mainstream method for economists, Mill gave the nature of economic science its most effective expression in Book VI of his *A System of Logic* (1843). In simplified terms, Mill rejected methodological extremes and declared economics a science akin to chemistry or physics but dealing with a different, more complex subject matter—human nature. Therefore economics was a "social" science, not as advanced, perhaps, as more traditional sciences, but a science nevertheless.

Mill appealed to the physical sciences of his time in order to illustrate the *bona fides* of economics. Meteorology was, like economics, an imperfect science. In 1843 scientific inquiry had not yet succeeded in ascertaining the "order of antecedence and consequence" among meteorological phenomena so as to be able to predict the weather at any particular place and with any accurate degree of probability. (Indeed, such prediction is still imperfect, but it is much improved from Mill's day). But no one, said Mill, can doubt "that if we were acquainted with all the antecedent circumstances, we could . . . predict (except for difficulties of calculation) the state of the weather at any future time. Meteorology, therefore, not only has in itself every natural requisite for being, but actually is, a science; though, from the difficulty of observing the facts on which the phenomena depend (a difficulty inherent in the peculiar nature of those phenomena), the science is extremely imperfect."* Mill thought "tidology" (the study of tides) was a more "advanced" science, even though it too was in flux. The gravitational pulls of sun and moon in relation to the earth's gravitational field were clear determinants, but influences of a "local and causal nature" (the configuration of the ocean bottom, direction of the wind, etc.) also had to be accounted for. Unlike meteorology, tidology could be used to predict on the basis of known general laws; in other words, it was in a more advanced state of completion.

Like these natural sciences economic "science" was still a work "in progress," in Mill's opinion. It benefited from the use of both *inductive* (from specific experience to general cases) and *deductive* (from general laws to specific cases) reasoning. On the one hand Mill rejected the extreme methods of the "experimentalists" (inductivists), and on the other he declared the method of the "geometricians" (pure deductivists) inadequate. He maintained that the fundamental axioms on which economics was based were inductive—built up from empirical evidence in a continuous process of improving and modifying them. Like meteorology and tidology, the "laws" and axioms of political economy were in constant flux, based as they were on the evidence collected in their application. In sum, the act of deduction was required to draw valid conclusions based on inductively derived axioms.

Mill cautioned, however, that the social scientist always has to be on guard in the application of scientific "laws." If economics were not based on empirically derived axioms, he claimed, it would be like astronomy, in which "the data . . . are as certain as the laws them-

(continued)

selves." But in economics, "the circumstances . . . , which influence the condition and progress of society, are innumerable, and perpetually changing; though they all change in obedience to causes, and therefore to laws, the multitude of the causes is so great as to defy our limited powers of calculation."†

Mill therefore supported a determinist method for economics composed of inductive and deductive elements. The multitude of possible changes in human behavior and events, and the difficulty (only partially resolved today) of "testing" and data gathering, made prediction a perilous business. It is possible to discern tendencies—thus giving rise to the notion of economics as a science of tendencies—but a better understanding of these phenomena, which give rise to economic theory, is the true object of social science. In his day Mill was disappointed that economists had not amassed enough knowledge for anything like exact "prediction," although he did believe that there was enough for "guidance." Today, in a time when the Nobel Prize is routinely awarded in economic science, we know a bit more. However, the method Mill established for gathering knowledge remains much the same.

* J. S. Mill, *Logic*, pp. 30–31.
† *Logic*, p. 63.

Classical economics was, of course, never without its critics. The Malthusian population doctrine and the differential-rent theory, for example, underwent frequent attacks by radicals, socialists, and reformers throughout the nineteenth century. But in an 1869 issue of the *Fortnightly Review* a curious event took place within the classical orthodoxy of Great Britain that shook the foundations of the classical theoretical system. John Stuart Mill recanted the wages-fund doctrine.

The Wages-Fund Revisited

Recall from chapter 5 that the wages-fund doctrine held that during any given production period, a stock of circulating capital is advanced to laborers to tide them over to the next production period. This stock of circulating capital is determined by many variables, including the productivity of labor and capital accumulated in previous periods, the amount of capital invested in previous periods, and so forth. In crude terms, the doctrine indicated that at a macroeconomic level, the average wage rate over the period of production is determined by dividing the number of laborers into the stock of circulating capital. Thus, in *real terms*, a maximum real wage (that is, all the goods consumed by laborers) is established at the beginning of the production period. Properly stated, and given the assumption of a discrete time period of production, the wages-fund doctrine forms an integral and inextricable part of the dynamics of the classical system (see chapter 7).

Confusions Surrounding the Doctrine. Numerous confusions always surrounded the wages-fund doctrine. One of them concerns the introduction of money wage payments, which serve as the proxy for real wages. If the fund is understood as a money amount, then the amount going to labor could indeed be elastic and variable. But the stock of real wage goods on hand is nonaugmentable (at a given time), irrespective of the amount or variability of money wages paid. Money wages, then, are not the "capital" of the wages-fund theory. Even Adam Smith, who provided early and otherwise clear statements of the wages-fund theory, was not immune to the problem. As Frank Taussig pointed out with reference to Smith's treatment of the doctrine:

> Sometimes, indeed most commonly, this "stock" is conceived in terms of money or as consisting of funds in the hands of the immediate employer. Sometimes the money payments are described as of no essential importance, as only steps toward the distribution of real wages. The uncertainty and confusion which thus showed itself in Adam Smith continued to appear in almost all the discussions of wages for fully a century after his time. (*Wages and Capital*, p. 145)

Micro Theory versus Macro Theory. Another difficult problem concerned the attempt, by both defenders and critics, to read a microeconomic theory of wage determination into statements about the wages-fund. For example, Francis A. Walker, an American critic of the concept, argued that the wages-fund doctrine ignored the varying productivity of workers and therefore did not explain relative wage rates between different types of laborers or between laborers of different countries (e.g., the East Indians and the British). Walker was joined in this criticism by many others. Unfortunately, and in spite of misuse on the part of its proponents, the wages-fund doctrine was designed only as a rough-and-ready macroeconomic argument. It was not until the development of the marginal-productivity theory decades later that a satisfactory explanation of individual wage determination was broached.

Mill's Recantation[7]

All the main elements of the classical wages-fund doctrine were present in Mill's *Principles*, including the assumption of a point-input/point-output production process. Mill's *theoretical* view of the doctrine assumed that the present remuneration of labor was the consequence of past applications of capital and labor, and he held that a proportion of total output was destined for labor in advance of production. Moreover, Mill applied the doctrine at an *aggregate* level and in *real* terms.

By 1869, Mill had altered his views on the wages-fund doctrine, touching off a great deal of controversy. Some explanations given for Mill's recantation are based on extra-theoretical considerations. For example, since Mill recanted the doctrine in his review of a book by W. T. Thornton, some attribute his action to friendship with Thornton. Some believe Mill recanted because of his commitment to social reform. Others believe that Mill was influenced by his wife, Harriet Taylor—a staunch reformer—or by the philosopher Auguste Comte. While none of these influences should be discounted completely, a close examination of Mill's writings suggests that by 1869 he had changed his *theoretical* view of the wages-fund. For that reason we look to resolve this matter of shifting theoretical grounds.

The central issue in Mill's recantation concerned the fixity of the fund earmarked for the payment of labor. The idea of a fixed fund in the short run implied that in the aggregate, workers could claim no more in wage payments than an amount that would exactly deplete the fund. Thus, the doctrine of the wages-fund was frequently used to demonstrate the futility of efforts by labor unions to raise their aggregate compensation. The long run was a different matter—no classical economist argued that the fund was fixed over the long run. However, some advanced the argument that if labor unions were too aggressive in pushing their claims, profit expectations would decline, so that in the future less capital would flow into the fund, thereby reducing real wages eventually. In later life, Mill became sympathetic to labor unions, and this may have been the impetus that led him to reexamine the wages-fund theory, in particular the subject of its short-run fixity.

[7] This section follows closely the argument presented by R. B. Ekelund, Jr., "A Short-Run Classical Model of Capital and Wages."

In his 1869 review of Thornton's book *On Labour*, Mill rejected the popularly held assumption that the size of the fund is fixed. Of the aggregate amount that is spent on wages, Mill now asserted only that there is some upper limit. He wrote:

> There is an impassable limit to the amount which can be so expended; it cannot exceed the aggregate means of employing classes. It cannot come up to those means; for the employers have also to maintain themselves and their families. But, short of this limit, it is not, in any sense of the word, a fixed amount. ("Thornton on Labour," p. 516)

Mill refined the argument by dividing the employer-capitalist's means into two parts: capital and income on that capital. While the former is usually equated in classical economic nomenclature with the wages-fund, Mill argued that the capitalist could add to that amount by discretionary reductions of income. Capitalists, in other words, might respond to exogenous variables (e.g., union pressure, different profit expectations, etc.) by voluntarily reducing expenditures on themselves and their family in order to spend more on labor. In this way, Mill apparently thought that labor unions might be able to redistribute income in favor of the workers. Unfortunately, Mill's argument did not distinguish between money wages and real wages, or between short-run and long-run effects. Consequently, his recantation rests on dubious grounds.

A Short-Run Wages-Fund Model. In order to expose the deficiencies of Mill's recantation, we shall place it in the context of a short-run wages-fund model adhering to the usual classical assumptions. Those assumptions are:

1. Production takes place within a point-input/point-output production process.
2. The entire output of the economy is composed of fixed capital, wage goods, and capitalist consumables. There is, moreover, no transference of demands between markets; i.e., wage earners do not transfer demands from wage goods to capitalist consumables and vice versa.
3. Production in all industries is marked by a constant ratio of fixed to circulating capital.
4. Perfect competition (i.e., constant costs of production) exists everywhere.
5. The money supply is fixed for the term in question.
6. Population and productivity remain unchanged during the period in question.

Under these assumptions, the aggregate stock of goods in real terms during any period, say t_1 is determined by past production beginning at t_0 and cannot be increased during the interval, t_1 t_2. In real terms, consumption and investment decisions are made at the beginning of t_1 and the entire stock of goods is depleted by the end of the period (at the start of t_2), albeit at different rates of use. For example, consider figure 8-2, where the total stock of goods at t_1 is represented by OY_0, divided so that OM_0 is equal to fixed capital (e.g., machinery), M_0W_0 is equal to wage goods available for purchase by workers, and W_0Y_0 is equal to capitalist consumables. This tripartite division conforms to Mill's representation. Under the usual assumptions of the wages-fund theory, these various stocks are used up during the production period, so that at the end of t_1 each has fallen to zero.

Now let us examine the effects of a decision by the capitalist to reduce his or her own real income (W_0Y_0) in order to spend more on labor, the prospect Mill raised in his recantation. The effects of this redistribution of income are carried through in figures 8-3*a* and 8-3*b*. The former depicts the market for goods that are bought by workers, the latter the market for goods purchased by capitalists. Under the rigid supply conditions of the wages-fund model, output in each period is fixed and determined by the previous period. Thus, the supply curves in figures 8-3*a* and 8-3*b* are vertical lines. A voluntary reduction in real income by capitalists will cause the demand for capitalist consumables to shift to the left, lowering the average price of such goods from P_c *to* P'_c. In like manner, an increase in workers' real income will shift the demand for wage goods to the right, thereby raising the average price of those goods from P_w *to* P'_w.

The conclusion of this analysis is that under the assumptions of the classical wages-fund doctrine, the effects of any reallocation of funds by capitalists in favor of

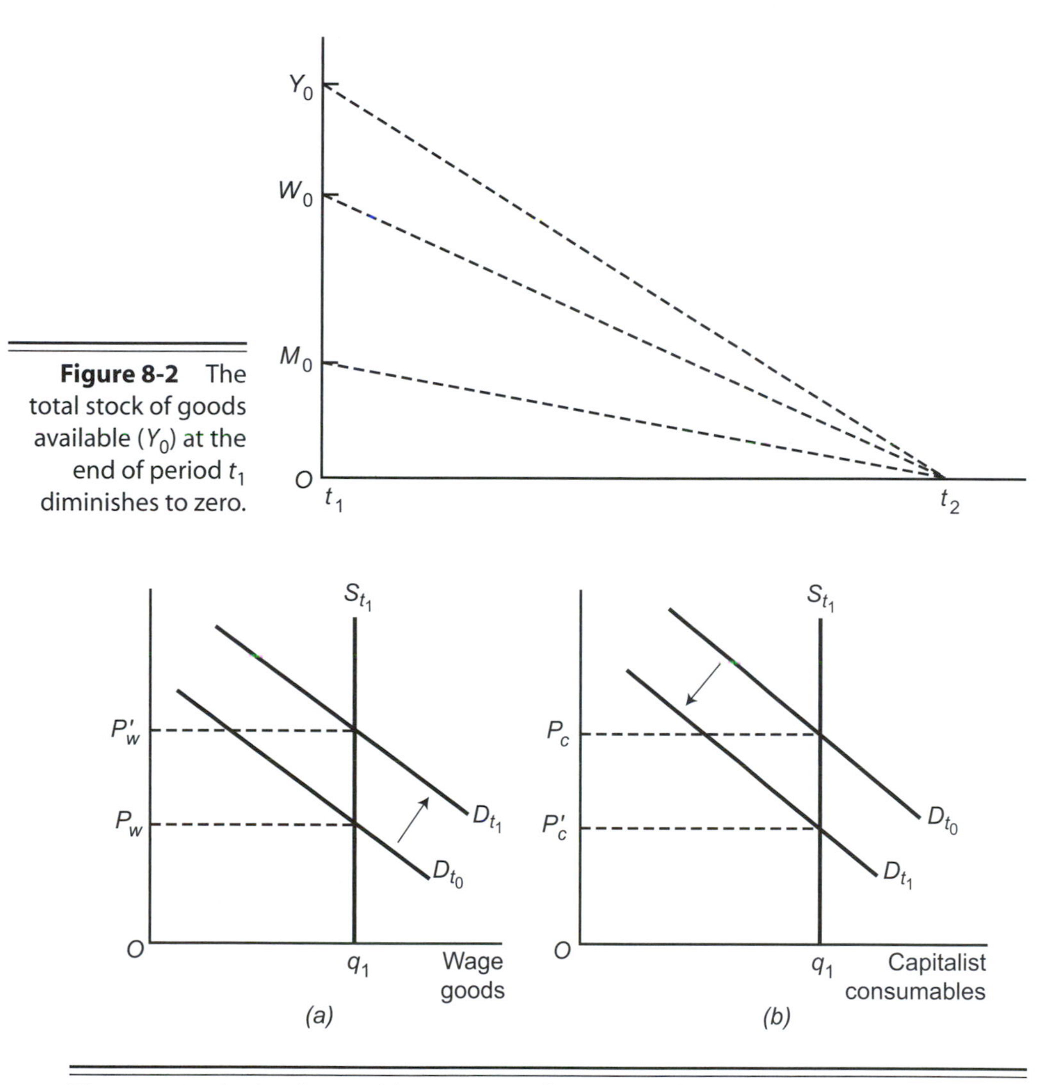

Figure 8-2 The total stock of goods available (Y_0) at the end of period t_1 diminishes to zero.

Figure 8-3 As the demand for wage goods increases from D_{t_0} to D_{t_1}, prices will rise from P_w to P'_w. In the long run, the entry of new firms will shift supply, causing prices to fall back to P_w. A similar effect will occur in the capitalist consumables market, in which a leftward supply shift will force prices back up to P_c. Over time, the quantities in both markets will also adjust.

labor are solely upon prices in the two markets. Furthermore, given a constant money stock and constant velocity, the price changes in the two markets will be proportionate in opposite directions, so that the aggregate price level will not be affected. More important from the standpoint of the laboring classes, the increase in money wages occasioned by the transfer of income from the capitalist class produces a price increase in wage goods that offsets the rise in money wages. Real wages remain unaffected by the transfer. Since Mill implied that workers would be better off under such a transfer, it seems clear that he confused *real wages* with *money wages*.

Long-Run Adjustments. The nature of the long-run adjustments that would accompany the kind of income redistribution just considered does not hold any brighter prospects for permanent increases in real wages. Given price changes in the two markets traced above, higher profits in the wage-goods industry would signal new firms to enter, whereas lower profits in the capitalist-consumables market would encourage some firms to exit. These long-run changes can be envisioned by shifting the vertical supply curve to the right in figure 8-3a and to the left in figure 8-3b. Under constant-cost conditions, price would tend to return to P_w in figure 8-3a and to P_c in figure 8-3b. The adjustments in each market might be lengthy, but the tendency would be for prices to return to the level they were before the suggested income transfer. The point that Mill seemed to forget (or deny) in his 1869 recantation is that in the classical world, permanent increases in real wages are traceable to real factors only, such as improvements in technology or some other increase in worker productivity.

Mill's recantation of the wages-fund doctrine and the subsequent confusion that it caused in the ranks of the classical orthodoxy is but one factor among a host of other possible reasons for the decline of classical economics. The rise of marginalism (see chapters 13 to 15) is often cited as a reason for this decline; another is the inroads made in the nineteenth century by historicist and socialist critics of economic orthodoxy (see chapter 11). Great policy debates, such as those over free trade, the rent issue, and trade unions, also played a role in the questioning of classical theory, especially in England and America. Presumably, all these developments contributed to the decline of classical economics as a dominant paradigm.

■ Entrepreneurism at the Classical Summit

John Stuart Mill's *Principles of Political Economy* is a watershed in British classical economics because it consists of a mature statement of the economic paradigm first developed by Smith and successively refined in Britain by Ricardo, Malthus, Senior, and others. It is also a kind of bridge between the economics of the old school (1776–1870) and the new (1871–1920). Yet, like his British forebears, Mill contributed little to the theory of entrepreneurship. He lamented the fact that "undertaker"—the English word popularly used to translate the French term *entrepreneur*—did not adequately convey the desired economic meaning (*Principles*, p. 406n). But throughout his economic works Mill treated entrepreneurs and their economic reward somewhat ambiguously. Echoing Say he identified the functions of entrepreneurs as direction, control, and superintendence. In one place he observed that the qualities of direction and superintendence are always in short supply (*Principles*, p. 108), and in another, he suggested that superior business talents always receive a kind of rent alongside ordinary profits (*Principles*, p. 476). But in the final analysis, he offered no clear-cut distinction between the capitalist and the entrepreneur, insisting that the return to the latter is composed of a risk premium and a wage of superintendence. He was, in the end, a mere caretaker of a notion that remained throughout classical economics pretty much in the shadow of Cantillon.

Schumpeter (*History*, p. 555) credits Say with the first distinct conceptualization of the entrepreneur apart from the capitalist; but even Say did not make full use of his own insight, nor did he see clearly all of its analytic possibilities. Among the English, Bentham "pushed the envelope", but he was more concerned with institutional reform (e.g., the Panopticon and other schemes) than with the development of core analytic principles that were strictly economic. Mill, of course, knew Bentham and read Say, but he followed up on neither one's suggestions where the entrepreneur was concerned. He kept the entrepreneur in the background of his distribution theory by focusing mainly on land, labor, and capital as agents of production. This suggests, at least by implication, that the entrepreneur is either a special laborer, or a combination of laborer and capitalist. It does not seem that Mill seriously entertained the idea of the entrepreneur as innovator. Where he discussed the labor of invention and discovery, for example, Mill treated its reward as merely a kind of wage.

Mill defined the capitalist's reward as the sum of an opportunity cost for postponing consumption (i.e., Nassau Senior's concept of "abstinence"), plus an indemnity for risk of capital, plus the "wages of superintendence." He asserted further that the wages of superintendence are not regulated by the same principle as workers' wages. Specifically, he maintained that the wages of superintendence are not advanced from capital, like the wages of other workers, but arise in profit, which is not realized until production is completed.

In Mill's time, the wages of labor were explained by the wages-fund doctrine, and in this view, the total amount that can be paid to labor is limited by the amount of capital previously accumulated. By separating the wages of superintendence from circulating capital Mill implied that there is no such limit on the wages of superintendence. But we are still left with a kind of functional "merger" between capitalist and entrepreneur in British classical economics that worked against a clear and unambiguous statement of the entrepreneur and his or her pivotal role in the competitive market process.

■ Conclusion

In terms of economic theory, John Stuart Mill represents the culmination of economic analysis begun by Adam Smith and extended by Malthus, Say, Ricardo and Senior. Dubbed "classical economics," this body of thought was cogent and logically correct. While its assumptions encompassed many broad and challengeable generalizations, its logic was sweeping and elegant. However, economists in the last third of the nineteenth century appeared to be asking questions that the classical theoretical system could not answer satisfactorily, if at all. The policy conclusions of classical theory simply were not acceptable to the majority of social scientists.[8] Increasingly attention turned away from macroeconomic issues to individual (microeconomic) behavior, and as it did economic analysis advanced in a new direction.

Can classical economics, then, have died in any meaningful sense? Though it is often easier to view intellectual history in terms of sharp breaks with past ideas, such a view would do a serious disservice to the classical economists and to their

[8] There were exceptions, of course. The American social critic Henry George, in his popular book *Progress and Poverty* (1879), rejected the wages-fund doctrine while recasting the Ricardian theory of differential land rents into a policy of urban-site value taxation.

theoretical structure. Old theories do not die, and unlike old soldiers, they don't even fade away. For instance, Alfred Marshall, the great neoclassical contributor to microeconomics, was very adamant in his admiration for, and use of, Ricardo's theory of cost in formulating partial-equilibrium analysis.

Marshall was one of many inheritors of the classical tradition who leaned heavily on Mill and his antecedents. It is difficult to improve on Marshall's description of the *transition* from the classical to the neoclassical. He wrote:

> The change may, perhaps, be regarded as a passing onward from that early stage in the development of scientific method, in which the operations of Nature are represented as conventionally simplified for the purpose of enabling them to be described in short and easy sentences, to that higher stage in which they are studied more carefully, and represented more nearly as they are, even at the expense of some loss of simplicity and definiteness, and even apparent lucidity. (*Principles*, p. 766)

Few episodes in the history of economic thought match the achievements of the classical economists in discovering and formulating the operations of an entire economic system. In addition, they established the method upon which modern economic reasoning is based. Although the assumptions of classical economics were in fact simplistic, its proponents attempted nothing less than global analysis of entire economies. One might legitimately wonder whether such large ends would or could be sought by contemporary economists. "Progress" and the quest for technical accuracy have probably robbed us of the will, but the classical theoretical structure remains as an inspiration for such an attempt. In struggling with the problems of economic development in developing nations, contemporary economists have returned on occasion to the simple analytics of classical dynamics. In other words, not only were classical ideas incorporated into neoclassical economics, they became the soil in which neoclassical economics grew.

References

Ekelund, R. B., Jr. "A Short-Run Classical Model of Capital and Wages: Mill's Recantation of the Wages-Fund," *Oxford Economic Papers*, vol. 28 (March 1976), pp. 66–85.

Marshall, Alfred. *Principles of Economics*, 8th ed. London: Macmillan, 1964 [1890].

Mill, J. S. "Thornton on Labour and Its Claims," *Fortnightly Review* (May, June 1869), pp. 505–518, 680–700.

———. *Letters of John Stuart Mill*, 2 vols., H. S. R. Elliot (ed.). London: Longmans, 1910.

———. *The Logic of the Moral Sciences*. LaSalle, IL: Open Court, 1988 [1843].

———. "Of the Influence of Consumption on Production," in *Essays on Some Unsettled Questions of Political Economy*, vol. 4 of *Collected Works of John Stuart Mill*, J. M. Robson (ed.). Toronto: University of Toronto Press, 1967 [1844].

———. *Autobiography of John Stuart Mill*. New York: Columbia University Press, 1924 [1873].

———. *Principles of Political Economy*, W. J. Ashley (ed.). New York: A. M. Kelley, 1965 [1848].

Mishan, E. J. *The Costs of Economic Growth*. London: Staples, 1967.

Schumpeter, Joseph. *History of Economic Analysis*, E. B. Schumpeter (ed.). New York: Oxford University Press, 1954.

Stigler, G. J. "The Nature and Role of Originality in Scientific Progress," *Economica*, n.s., vol. 22 (November 1955), pp. 293–302.

Taussig, F. W. *Wages and Capital*. New York: A. M. Kelley, 1968 [1896].

Thornton, W. T. *On Labour: Its Wrongful Claims and Rightful Dues, Its Actual Present and Possible Future*. London: Macmillan, 1869.

Notes for Further Reading

Insights into Mill's life and unusual upbringing are contained in frank detail in his *Autobiography* (see references), which was, according to his wishes, not published until the year of his death (1873). See also Alexander Bain, *John Stuart Mill, A Criticism: With Personal Recollections* (London: Longmans, 1882); Herbert Spencer et al., *John Stuart Mill: His Life and Works* (Boston: Osgood and Co., 1873); W. L. Courtney, *Life of John Stuart Mill* (London: Secker & Warburg, 1954); and Bertrand Russell, "John Stuart Mill," in *Portraits from Memory and Other Essays* (London: G. Allen, 1956).

Mill's multidimensional thought covers such fields as logic, philosophy, and economics. His contributions to the field of logic were epoch making. It is best to start with Mill himself. See J. S. Mill, *A System of Logic* (London: Longmans, Green, 1884); and same author, "On the Logic of the Moral Sciences," in H. M. Magid (ed.), *A System of Logic* (Indianapolis: Bobbs-Merill, 1965). Mill's classic essays, "On Liberty," "Utilitarianism," and excerpts from "Considerations on Representative Government," have been edited and reprinted by Marshall Cohen in *The Philosophy of John Stuart Mill* (New York: Modern Library, 1961). See also R. P. Anschutz, *The Philosophy of John Stuart Mill* (London: Oxford University Press, 1953). At one stage of his life, Mill was attracted by the positivist philosophy of Auguste Comte. See J. S. Mill, *Auguste Comte and Positivism* (London: Lippincott, 1865); and Mill's correspondence with Comte, *Lettres inédites de John Stuart Mill á Auguste Comte* (Paris: Felix Alcan, 1899), available only in French. R. B. Ekelund and Emilie Olsen, "Comte, Mill and Cairnes: The Positivist-Empiricist Interlude in Late Classical Economics," *Journal of Economic Issues*, vol. 7 (September 1973), pp. 383–416, explore the impact of Comte's positivism on Mill and Cairnes. For more on Mill's methodology see J. K. Whitaker, "John Stuart Mill's Methodology," *Journal of Political Economy*, vol. 83 (October 1975), pp. 1033–1050.

Considering Mill's economics in the more narrow sense, it is noteworthy that almost everything written on Mill by other economists has been collected under the editorship of John C. Wood, *John Stuart Mill: Critical Assessments* (London: Croom Helm, 1987). Pedro Schwartz, *The New Political Economy of John Stuart Mill* (Durham, NC: Duke University Press, 1973), reviews Mill's views on economic policy, demonstrating the relevance of Mill's thought for contemporary capitalism. The indefatigable Sam Hollander, *The Economics of John Stuart Mill* (Toronto: University of Toronto Press, 1985), has undertaken, in two volumes, a wholesale reinterpretation of Mill's economics in which he advances the controversial claim that there was no real intellectual break between classical and neoclassical (i.e., Marshallian) economics. However, Dimitris Sotiropoulos, "Why John Stuart Mill Should Not be Enlisted among Neoclassical Economists," *The European Journal of the History of Economic Thought*, vol. 16 (Fall 2009), pp. 455–473, maintains that Mill distanced himself from the utilitarianism of Bentham and the questionable assumptions underlying the felicific calculus, making his system different from the principles established by Jevons, Marshall, Walras, and Menger. A. Hirsch, "John Stuart Mill on Verification and the Business of Science," *History of Political Economy*, vol. 24 (Winter 1992), pp. 843–866, challenges Hollander's interpretation of Mill's view of science, arguing that Hollander subjugated Mill's *a priori* view of science to his "applications-style" empiricism.

G. J. Stigler defends Mill's originality as an economist in "The Nature and Role of Originality in Scientific Progress," *Economica*, vol. 22 (November 1955), pp. 293–302, reprinted in Stigler's *Essays in the History of Economics* (Chicago: University of Chicago Press, 1965), but on the issue of Mill's priority concerning the theory of joint cost, Stigler has been challenged by E. G. West, "Joint Supply Theory Before Mill," *History of Political Economy*, vol. 26 (Summer 1994), pp. 267–278. West contends that Adam Smith preceded Mill on this specialized topic, but his argument requires a somewhat strained reading of Smith. Other assessments of Mill in the large picture of economics include V. W. Bladen, "John Stuart Mill's *Principles*: A Centenary Estimate," *American Economic Review*, vol. 39, suppl. (May 1949), pp. 1–12; James Bonar, "John Stuart Mill, the Reformer: 1806–73," *Indian Journal of Economics*, vol. 10 (April 1930), pp. 761–805; W. D. Grampp, "Classical Economics and Moral Critics," *History of Political Economy*, vol. 5 (Fall 1973), pp. 359–374; Neil de Marchi, "The Success of Mill's *Principles*," *History of Political Economy*, vol. 6 (Summer 1974), pp. 119–157; same author, "Mill and Cairnes and the Emergence of Marginalism in England," *History of Political Economy*, vol. 4 (Fall 1972), pp. 344–363; and J. P. Platteau, "The Political Economy of John Stuart Mill, or, the Coexistence of Orthodoxy, Heresy and Prophecy," *International Journal of Social Economics*, vol. 12 (1985), pp. 3–26. A. L. Harris discusses Mill's ideas on freedom in two articles: "J. S. Mill on Monopoly and Socialism," *Journal of Political Economy*, vol. 67 (December 1959), pp. 604–611; and "Mill on Freedom and Voluntary Association," *Review of Social Economy*, vol. 18 (March 1960), pp. 27–44. See also, Elynor D. Davis, "Mill, Socialism, and the English Romantics: An Interpretation," *Economica*, vol. 52 (August 1985), pp. 345–358. In a recent spate of papers, E. Forget presents some interesting interpretations of Mill. In particular, see "John Stuart Mill's Business Cycle," *History of Political Economy*, vol. 22 (Winter 1990), pp. 629–642, in which the author argues that Mill suffused his analysis with institutional details, analyzing the rational behavior of market traders possessing varying degrees of imperfect information. Forget maintains that normal price provided the basis for Mill's business cycle theory.

The standard treatment of Mill's theory of international trade and reciprocal demand is Jacob Viner, *Studies in the Theory of International Trade* (New York: Harper, 1937), pp. 535–541. Mill's terms-of-trade argument was expanded by F. Y. Edgeworth in his *Papers Relating to Political Economy*, vol. 2 (London: Macmillan, 1925), p. 340ff; more recently by N. Kaldor, "A Note on Tariffs and the Terms of Trade," *Economica*, vol. 7 (November 1940), pp. 377–380; and again by H. G. Johnson, "Optimum Tariffs and Retaliation," *Review of Economic Studies*, vol. 21 (1953–1954), pp. 142–153. The possibility of "multiple equilibriums" in international trade and of Mill's alleged attempts to rule them out is discussed in two papers, one by D. R. Appleyard and J. C. Ingram, "A Reconsideration of the Addition to Mill's 'Great Chapter,'" *History of Political Economy*, vol. 11 (Winter 1979), pp. 459–476; and the other by J. S. Chipman, "Mill's Superstructure: How Well Does It Stand Up?" *History of Political Economy*, vol. 11 (Winter 1979), pp. 477–499. See also the reply by Appleyard and Ingram that follows Chipman in the same issue.

Mill's rendition of Say's Law may well have derived from his father, James Mill. On this matter, see B. Balassa, "John Stuart Mill and the Law of Markets," *Quarterly Journal of Economics*, vol. 73 (May 1959), pp. 263–274; and the comment by L. C. Hunter in the same journal, vol. 74 (May 1960), pp. 158-162. A clarification of Say's Law has been attempted by W. J. Baumol, "Say's (At Least) Eight Laws, or What Say and James Mill May Have Really Meant," *Economica*, vol. 44 (May 1977), pp. 145–162; but see also W. O. Thweatt, "Baumol and James Mill on 'Say's' Law of Markets," *Economica*, vol. 47 (November 1980), pp. 467–470.

On other specific aspects of Mill's economics, see L. C. Hunter, "Mill and Cairnes on the Rate of Interest," *Oxford Economic Papers*, vol. 11 (February 1959), pp. 63–97; J. H. Thompson, "Mill's Fourth Fundamental Proposition: A Paradox Revisited," *History of Political Economy*, vol. 7 (Summer 1975), pp. 174–192; Sam Hollander, "J. S. Mill on 'Derived Demand' and the Wage Fund Theory Recantation," *Eastern Economic Journal*, vol. 10 (January–March 1984), pp. 87–98; W. C. Bush, "Population and Mill's Peasant-Proprietor Economy," *History of Political Economy*, vol. 5 (Spring 1973), pp. 110–120; M. E. Bradley, "Mill on Proprietorship, Productivity, and Population: A Theoretical Reappraisal," *History of Political Economy*, vol. 15 (Fall 1983), pp. 423–429; Nathalie Sigot and Christophe Beaurain, "John Stuart Mill and the Employment of Married Women: Reconciling Utility and Justice," *Journal of the History of Economic Thought*, vol. 31 (September 2009), pp. 281–304; Sam Hollander, "Dynamic Equilibrium with Constant Wages: J. S. Mill's Malthusian Analysis of the Secular Wage Path," *Kyklos*, vol. 37 (1984), pp. 247–265; same author, "The Wage Path in Classical Growth Models: Ricardo, Malthus and Mill," *Oxford Economic Papers*, vol. 36 (June 1984), pp. 200–212; V. R. Smith, "John Stuart Mill's Famous Distinction between Production and Distribution," *Economic Philosophy*, vol. 1 (October 1985), pp. 267–284; and R. B. Ekelund, Jr., and Douglas M. Walker, "J. S. Mill on the Income Tax Exemption and Inheritance Taxes: The Evidence Reconsidered," *History of Political Economy*, vol. 28 (Winter 1996), pp. 559–581. An interesting exchange on Mill's "utility" theory is contained in the following papers: M. Bronfenbrenner, "Poetry, Pushpin and Utility," *Economic Inquiry*, vol. 15 (January 1977), pp. 95–110; M. S. McPherson, "Liberty and the Higher Pleasures: In Defense of Mill," *Economic Inquiry*, vol. 18 (April 1980), pp. 314–318; and the rejoinder by Bronfenbrenner, "Liberty and Higher Pleasures: A Reply," *Economic Inquiry*, vol. 18 (April 1980), pp. 319–320.

The wages-fund controversy and Mill's role in it were first capably summarized by F. W. Taussig, *Wages and Capital* (see references). Marshall's student and successor, A. C. Pigou, discusses the grounds of Mill's famous recantation in "Mill and the Wages Fund," *Economic Journal*, vol. 57 (June 1949), pp. 171–180. William Breit, "Some Neglected Early Critics of the Wages Fund Theory," *Southwestern Social Science Quarterly*, vol. 48 (June 1967), pp. 53–60, probed the early criticisms of the theory, and then examined the "first round" of the famous controversy, in which Longe, Thornton, and Mill figured prominently, in "The Wages-Fund Controversy Revisited," *Canadian Journal of Economics and Political Science*, vol. 33 (November 1967), pp. 523–528. Scott Gordon concentrates on the latter phase of the controversy in "The Wage-Fund Controversy: The Second Round," *History of Political Economy*, vol. 5 (Spring 1973), pp. 14–35. The interpretation of Mill's recantation utilized in this chapter is based on R. B. Ekelund, "A Short-Run" (see references), which has sparked a controversy of its own. For more on this subject, see J. Vint, "A Two Sector Model of the Wage Fund: Mill's Recantation Revisited," *British Review of Economic Issues*, vol. 3 (Autumn 1981), pp. 71–88; T. Negishi, "Mill's Recantation of the Wages Fund: Comment," *Oxford Economic Papers*, vol. 37 (March 1985), pp. 148–151; and R. B. Ekelund, "Mill's Recantation Once Again: Reply," *Oxford Economic Papers*, vol. 37 (March 1985), pp. 152–153. Yet another controversy has swirled around the issue of whether Mill used a "Malthusian" argument in support of trade unions. Arguing in favor of such a view, E. G. West and R. W. Hafer, "J. S. Mill, Unions, and the Wages-Fund Recantation: A Reinterpretation," *Quarterly Journal of Economics*, vol. 92 (November 1978), pp. 603–619, have challenged Ekelund's interpretation of Mill's recantation, but see the response by R. B. Ekelund and W. F. Kordsmeier, "J. S. Mill, Unions, and the Wages Fund Recantation: A Reinterpretation-Comment," *Quarterly Journal of Economics*, vol. 96 (August 1981), pp. 531–541.

The seemingly endless parade of opinions on Mill's recantation continues unabated. Two entries provide signposts to the directions taken by modern interpretations. J. Vint, *Capital and Wages: A Lakatosian History of the Wages Fund Doctrine* (London: Edward Elgar, 1994), renders a full-scale reinterpretation of the wages-fund doctrine from the perspective of Imre Lakatos's "methodology of scientific research programs." From this perspective, Vint concludes that the classical economists were rational to advocate the wages-fund idea, and that it was likewise rational of Mill both to reject it to the extent that he did and to maintain the doctrine in theory up to the final edition of his *Principles*. Given the logical problems within the Lakatosian theory itself, such results are ill-founded, particularly in its attempt to apply a theory (the wages-fund) within a theory (the whole of classical analytics). In a different direction (but in a similar normative vein), E. Forget, "J. S. Mill and the Tory School: The Rhetorical Value of the Recantation," *History of Political Economy*, vol. 24 (Spring 1992), pp. 31–59, exposes Mill as a "political animal," which he undoubtedly was, suggesting that Mill wanted to come down hard on the Tories and to "wrest political economy from the ideological stronghold of the middle and upper classes." Although this interpretation enlightens us to Mill's political proclivities, it does not resolve the mystery of Mill's recantation from the perspective of pure theory (a fact that Forget freely acknowledges). On pure theoretical grounds, the objections to the money-fund/real-fund confusion are spurious. The short-run *fixity* of the aggregate, average wage rate in the short run is logically assured by the economy-wide assumption of a discontinuous production function, with fixed-production coefficients. Moreover, the transference of demands between capitalist consumables (luxuries?) and goods consumed by the workers (wage-goods) is immaterial to the logic of the fixity of the fund, as well as to all other parts of Gross Domestic Product. But the controversy will not die; see Oskar Kurer, "Mill's Recantation of the Wages-Fund Doctrine: Was Mill Right, After All?" *History of Political Economy*, vol. 30 (Fall 1996), pp. 515–536.

A final issue that is related to the wages-fund debate relates to W. T. Thornton, disequilibrium theory, and to Thornton's supposed explosion of the laws of supply and demand. T. Negishi, "Thornton's Criticism of Equilibrium Theory and Mill," *History of Political Economy*, vol. 18 (1986), pp. 567–577, argues that Thornton had a view of equilibration, that it anticipated post-Walrasian "path-dependence," and that his specification of supply and demand should be respected. R. B. Ekelund, Jr., and S. Thommesen, "Disequilibrium Theory and Thornton's Assault on the Laws of Supply and Demand," *History of Political Economy*, vol. 21 (1989), pp. 567–592, argue that Thornton was considerably less sophisticated, having no intellectual basis for rejecting or establishing anything (see Negishi's "Reply" in the same issue). E. Forget, "John Stuart Mill, Francis Longe, and William Thornton on Demand and Supply," *Journal of the History of Economic Thought*, vol. 13 (Fall 1991), pp. 205–221, in a most interesting contribution, attempts (successfully) to reconstruct the analysis to which Thornton believed himself responding. Forget argues that Thornton was responding to popular fallacies concerning the wages-fund then extant, concluding (with Ekelund and Thommesen) that Thornton could not have been a "disequilibrium theorist" or much of a theorist at all. The debate, however, has not ended. For a dubious and strained resuscitation of Thornton's arguments, see Michael V. White, "'That God-Forgotten Thornton': Exorcising Higgling after *On Labour*," in N. De Marchi and M. S. Morgan (eds.), *Higgling: Transactors and Theory Markets in the History of Economics*, (Durham, NC: Duke University Press, 1994).

In certain quarters of the economics profession Thornton has been enlisted in an antitheoretical, antiorthodox barrage of criticisms. See, for example Phillip Mirowski, "Smooth Operator: How Marshall's Demand and Supply Curves made Neoclassicism Safe for Public Consumption, but unfit for Science," in R. Tullberg (ed.), *Alfred Marshall in Retrospect* (Aldershot: Edward Elgar, 1990). Robert B. Ekelund, Jr., "W. T. Thornton: Savant, Idiot, or Idiot-Savant?" *Journal of the History of Economic Thought*, vol. 19 (Spring 1997), pp. 1–23, rejects Mirowski's view. However, Thornton was not a one-trick pony. He made important early contributions to the theory of property rights and economic growth. See, in particular, his *A Plea for Peasant Proprietors* (originally published in 1848) in Philip Mirowski and Steven Tradewell (eds.), volume 3 of *The Economic Writings of William Thornton*, 5 vols., (London: Pickering & Chatto, 1999). Also see Robert B. Ekelund, Jr., and Mark Thornton, "William T. Thornton and Nineteenth Century Economic Policy: A Review Essay," *Journal of the History of Economic Thought*, vol. 23 (November 2001), pp. 513–531.

Part III

Responses to the Industrial Revolution—Orthodox and Heterodox

As the Industrial Revolution gathered steam, many sensibilities recoiled in horror at the conditions it encouraged: overcrowded cities, poor sanitation, long work hours, low wages, industrial accidents, and air and water pollution. Strident voices were raised against the "evils" of industrialism. Some of the criticism aimed at classical economics was based more on sentiment than on dispassionate analysis, but a few theoretical refinements nevertheless found their way into economics alongside the polemics and cries for reform.

France in particular harbored a number of reformers. It must be remembered that although the Enlightenment shone brightly there, France held on to mercantilism longer and embraced the Industrial Revolution later than England. Many of the dissenting voices in France therefore took aim at the monarchy and its sweeping powers, while others looked to government to correct the excesses of industrialism. The common theme, if there was one, was social reform, but not necessarily how to accomplish it. Before Marx entered the picture, reform was based on voluntarism—an appeal to humanity to willfully change the social system. Marx embarked on a new path by basing his economic theory on laws of history, so that change in his system was inevitable and inexorable.

England, as the force of the Industrial Revolution in the nineteenth century took hold, also experienced major problems as "side effects" of the great leap in technology and growth. Urbanization and poverty accompanied the Industrial Revolution. The class system made income and wealth distribution more rigid than it would have been in a more egalitarian society (which emerged at the beginning of the twentieth century). Chapters 9 and 10 consider British "orthodox" classical thinkers' approach to policy on critical social issues—some of which still affect contemporary society. Chapter 9 discusses the English distribution of income over the first half of the century and examines policies relating to welfare, including a discussion of the revision of the Poor Laws (England's welfare program at the time) and the Factory Acts affecting both adult and child labor. The obvious question arose, "Was it possible to raise people out of poverty?" The answer depends on the nature of human beings. The questions are the same as they are today: Is poverty a result of the environment or is it genetic; that is, is the nature and attitude of humans toward work malleable? This chapter deals with classical opinions on such matters.

Chapter 10 expands on these ideas and features the economic analysis through which two thinkers—John Stuart Mill and Edwin Chadwick—viewed the economic and social problems of the day. We give special emphasis to Mill's analysis of the English tax system and his advocacy of a progressive inheritance tax ("death duties"). While emphasizing the importance of incentives, Mill believed that such a tax might serve to address the class-driven distribution of income. But he discussed other tax measures as well. Edwin Chadwick analyzed social problems and collected statistics to support his views of reform. In chapter 10 we focus on Chadwick's views on disease, sanitation, and regulation of industries such as railroads. You will discover a unique and interesting approach to competition in Chadwick's worldview.

Policy prescriptions to eliminate income disparity and social distinctions came not only from within the classical world but from evolutionists, historicists, and socialist-communist writers as well. In chapter 11 you will learn about different criticisms of classical economics and platforms for social reform "outside" the economic orthodoxy. A brief survey of evolutionist thought, though incomplete, serves to convey the variety of attacks against classical economics. You will also be introduced to historicism, a critique of economic method that began in Germany but found adherents in England as well (as we shall see in part V). Chapter 12 deals with the economics of Karl Marx, which posed a different kind of challenge to classical economics because it was more systematic in content and more pervasive in impact. You will learn how Marx borrowed from German philosophy in his attempt to reshape classical economics into something that had remarkable appeal to "reformers" across the world in the twentieth century, from Vladimir Lenin to Fidel Castro.

9

Economic Policy in the Classical Period

Technology, Labor, and Poverty

While Ricardo and his followers pushed the abstract theory of classical macroeconomics to new heights, actual circumstances of the nineteenth century presented real (and frustrating) problems for the working classes. Poverty was not an abstraction. It engulfed the working classes and exacerbated social problems identified with an industrial economy, especially child labor, urban squalor, crime, and income distribution. In this chapter and the next we shall examine persistent economic and social problems of Western society and how economics and economists faced them. Many of the problems that accompanied the Industrial Revolution proved resistant to permanent solution, despite great advances in knowledge and technology. For example, clean air and water, occupational safety and health, and eradication of disease and poverty remain major concerns in many parts of the developed and developing world. Problems like these pose obstacles to economic growth, no less today than a century or more ago. Sanitation reform, for example, proved a key element in the improvement of labor productivity, the mitigation of poverty, and, ultimately, economic well-being. It should not surprise us, therefore, that the great minds of the day turned their attention and analyses to socioeconomic problems of the first magnitude.

In this chapter and the next we analyze some of these critical issues as treated by traditional economic thinkers. We briefly review the economic and social environment of the classical period, with emphasis on urbanization, technology, and health. We analyze the scope of the problem of income distribution in nineteenth-century England in order to provide insight into what the classical economists faced. We place *labor* and the attitudes of economists and thinkers toward the laboring poor at the core of our discussion. Part of that discussion is related to technologically driven change, which had an enormous impact on factory workers and child labor. The British Factory Acts are therefore central to a consideration of the issues under consideration.

Two names necessarily advance to the head of the practical reformers' list: Sir Edwin Chadwick (1800–1890), possibly the single most brilliant social and economic reformer of the century, and John Stuart Mill, one of the great classical economists and thinkers whose *theories* (in contrast to his policy views) we reviewed in the preceding chapter. As the last of Bentham's secretaries, Chadwick aligned his reforming zeal, as well as his policy prescriptions, with Bentham's utilitarianism. He was instrumental in writing and administering the English Poor Laws of the 1820s and 1830s. His authorship of the Sanitary Reports, submitted to Parliament in 1842 and 1843, further enhanced his standing among England's greatest social and economic reformers. Armed with mountains of data, mostly collected himself, Chadwick tackled problems—and offered solutions—to some of the most pressing problems of his day. John Stuart Mill, Chadwick's friend and ally in socioeconomic reform, may have been Chadwick's superior on matters of theory but always deferred to Chadwick on matters of fact. Together Mill and Chadwick presented important answers to the "radical" reforms posed by writers less steeped in conventional economic thought, such as those writers examined in chapter 11.

■ The "Real World" of Classical Economics

The nineteenth century was one of profound change. The technological landscape was transformed by the invention and development of the steam engine; applications of steam power to transportation and manufacturing; and new advances in chemistry, medicine, and biological sciences. These startling transformations occurred over an underbelly of social and economic change. The hereditary aristocracy, an artifact from medieval (feudal) and mercantile times, remained atop a class structure that skewed income against the middle and poorer classes. Cities, especially in England and the United States, began to grow at unprecedented rates. Urbanization proceeded apace as people moved from countryside to cities in search of jobs related to the burgeoning technologies. London grew from approximately a million people in 1800, to 2.5 million by 1850, and 6.7 million by the end of the century. But enormous problems haunted so much progress. Workers crowded each other in cities; housing and sanitation were inadequate; air and water were fouled; and crime, as well as poverty, became a persistent reality.

The transport revolution that railroads spawned had multiple effects on society—some good, some bad. Passengers on urban trolleys and railroads enjoyed lower "time costs," allowing the well-off to escape the dirty, noisy, crowded cities, but leaving the inner core of cities to deteriorate. Sanitary conditions worsened as urban cores were abandoned by the wealthy. Sewage was ubiquitous; in London alone, as many as a quarter of a million cesspools existed in 1825. Human waste and refuse was dumped in ditches and under the floorboards of houses. Disposal systems, such as they were, were often constructed with permeable brick, allowing leakage that rendered available water unfit to drink. Potable water was supplied through common-use pumps interspersed throughout the poorest and most dense parts of cities. Sometimes the water was filtered, and sometimes it was not. Underhouse cesspools created "night soil," the term used for decomposing human and other waste. These cesspools often overflowed, dumping contents into rivers that were commonly used as the "natural" conveyance for disposed waste. The Thames and its tributaries became germ infested and unwholesome.

Urban crowding and bad sanitation had predictable effects. Fear of random death became ingrained in the poor and disadvantaged. In the early part of the century one in three children did not reach the age of five years; the statistic later improved to only one in five. While the precise *source* of disease was not known in the early part of the century, owing partly to the relatively primitive state of science, people lived with the effects of disease and plague. Plagues of various kinds gained in frequency and virulence between 1820 and 1850. Influenza epidemics killed thousands of Londoners in 1831–1832, followed by a series of cholera, dysentery, and typhoid fever epidemics between 1836 and 1842. The city was struck repeatedly, with one of the worst typhus epidemics ravaging it in 1837–1838. Tens of thousands died—rich and poor alike.

Fear of the unknown can have a paralyzing economic effect. It can also endorse untested hypotheses. One such questionable supposition, perhaps understandable within the wretched urban environment, was that "miasmas," or airborne odors, caused the various plagues. Indeed, odors were so bad that Parliament temporarily closed its doors from a "great stink" that befell London in 1858. Even prescient observers such as Edwin Chadwick (chapter 10) subscribed to this theory, although, more than most, he was open to all evidence. It was not until 1854 and the so-called "Broad Street cholera outbreak" that Dr. John Snow demonstrated that cholera was waterborne. Given the slow pace of biological science the scientific community was reluctant to accept his results.[1] Eventually cause and effect were more tightly linked, as typhus came to be associated with lice, cholera and dysentery with waterborne bacteria, and so forth.

As the century developed, science advanced and longevity grew apace. The use of anesthesia and sterilization made surgery more effective in preserving human life. The discovery of bacteria and advances in chemistry likewise aided the cause. Improved public sanitation measures eventually broke through the veil of ignorance. The long struggle to tame disease and enhance economic productivity engaged economists and reformers who took stock of the society in their day and hailed its scientific advances. Their engagement, however, was conducted within the cultural determinants of a class structure that was in many respects an artifact of medievalism. The distribution of income and wealth within that class structure was a cultural lightning rod for the economists who took up the struggle.

■ Income Distribution in England

The exact dating of the Industrial Revolution in England may be a matter of debate, but it is clear that the effects were manifest from the mid-eighteenth century well into the nineteenth. All of the characteristics of that revolution—including a massive movement of people from country to urban environments—have been clear to historians for many years. The ultimate question for our purposes is: "How did that revolution have an impact on wealth and income levels of the entire population?" Though surprisingly good, the quality of statistics on wealth and income distribution in nineteenth-century England must necessarily be suspect. But even allowing for that, the flowering of the Industrial Revolution made the nineteenth century "England's century." Table 9-1 on the following page shows statistics on wealth and income during1700–1858. According to most accounts, progressive increases in aggregate income were translated into equally dramatic increases in *per capita* national income. Robert Dudley Baxter (*National Income*) claims that national income (from all sources) expanded threefold between 1801 and 1858. Leone Levi (*Taxation*) asserts that per capita income increased from £14.7 to £20.15 in the same interval.[2] However, per capita income statistics tell nothing of

[1] Using brilliant deduction, Snow plotted the incidence of cholera cases around the "potable" water pumps in London, finding a significantly higher incidence of the disease around the pump at Broad Street, thereby concluding that the disease was waterborne.

[2] Using statistics collected in France, Levi contrasted Britain's progress (£20.15 per capita in 1858) with that of France (£15 per capita) and Russia (£5 per head).

income distribution. The best statistics on income *distribution* tell a far different story, justifying the concern among economic and social reformers for the working poor and impoverished.

We acknowledge the data limitations inherent in such sources, but official accounts of the comparative income distributions of Great Britain (England and Scotland) in 1801 and again in 1848 are enlightening in several respects. Consider the following Lorenz curves[3] in figure 9-1, constructed from data collected by William Farr (*British Parliamentary Papers*, pp. 462–463). A persistent complaint

Table 9–1 Wealth and Income Estimates in United Kingdom (1700–1858)

Year	Population (Millions)	Wealth (Millions)	Per-Capita Wealth	Percentage Increase	Income (Millions)
1700	8	£0,600	£ 75	—	
1801	16	1,800	112	300	£220
1811	18	2,100	116	16	250 (1822)
1841	27	4,000	150	94	450
1858	29	6,000	206	50	600

Sources: Wealth estimate for 1700 by Gregory King, as reported by Evans ("Law of Demand"); other wealth estimates by Levi (*Taxation*, p. 6). Income estimates by Baxter (*National Income*, p. 66).

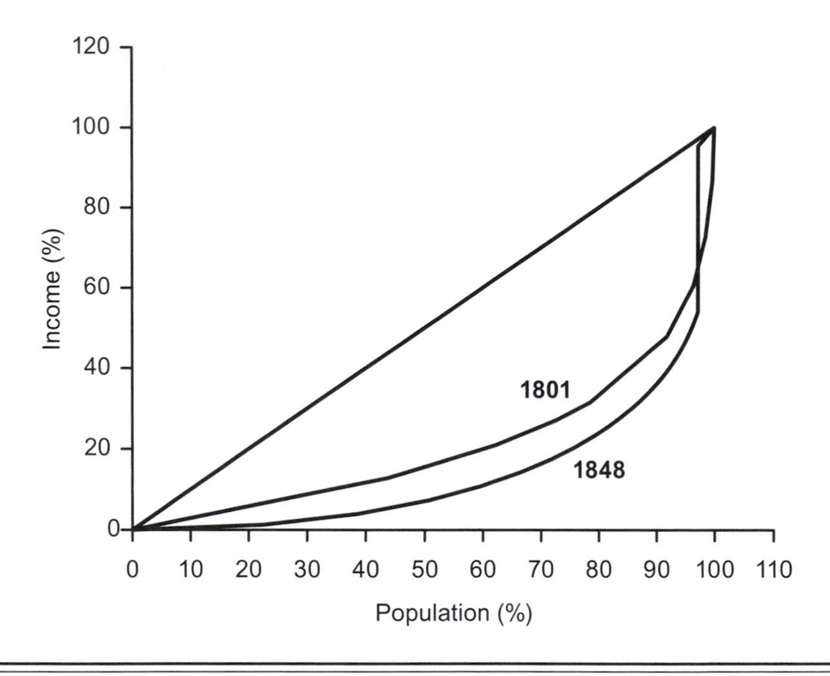

Figure 9-1 As a measure of income distribution, these Lorenz curves show that incomes in the United Kingdom were less equal in 1848 than in 1801—despite an increase in *average* income over the period.

[3] A Lorenz curve plots the actual cumulative distribution of income in percentages; usually compared with a curve showing a perfectly even distribution of income (the diagonal in figure 9-1).

among observers and compilers of tax statistics well into the nineteenth century was that income data is *self*-reported, leading to huge discrepancies between estimates of the number of returns reported and the income-earning population in various classes.[4] The dramatic inequality in income distribution among the self-reporters is obvious at a glance. By 1848, approximately 60 percent of the population earned just over 10 percent of the income of Great Britain. The lowest 22.5 percent earned only 1.3 percent of income while the upper 3 percent earned 45.5 percent of reported income. Reported income data was also affected by the fact that wages earned by manual labor was exempt from taxation and thus not recorded on income tax returns. Moreover, skewness of income distribution does not accurately reflect wealth distribution. Morton Peto presents evidence of massive undervaluations of property in addition to underreporting of income (*Taxation*, pp. 45–46).

Baxter shed additional light on the nature of income distribution in the United Kingdom in a paper read before the Statistical Society in 1868. Baxter divided income recipients into upper and middle class on the one hand and manual labor on the other. He further segmented each stratum into "independent" and "dependent." The latter included nonworking wives, homebound children and relatives, scholars, paupers, prisoners, vagrants, and manual laborers over 65 years old (*National Income*, p. 81). His population estimates are shown in table 9-2. Upper and middle classes (nonwage earners) comprised approximately 23 percent of Great Britain's population in 1867, whereas manual laborers made up approximately 77 percent. On this basis, wage earners in the United Kingdom outnumbered nonwage earners by approximately 3.5 to one. Drawing on Levi's companion data on wages and earnings of the working classes Baxter presented an estimate of income distribution for the year 1867.

The primary advantage of the Levi-Baxter calculations is that they incorporate the wage incomes of the working classes and the salaried incomes of the middle and upper income groups. By modern standards income distribution in England in 1867 was comparable to that of a developing country. By our calculations, taxes on

Table 9-2 Population Estimates by Class: United Kingdom (1867)

Upper and Middle Classes		
With Independent Incomes	2,759,000	
Dependent	3,859,000	
Subtotal		6,618,000
Manual Labour Class		
Earning Wages	10,961,000	
Dependent	12,130,000	
Subtotal		23,091,000
Total Estimated Population		29,709,000

Source: Baxter, *National Income*, p. 16.

[4] J. S. Mill argued that income taxes led to fraud and moral degeneration. Many others complained of cheating. The Draft Report to the Income Tax Committee of 1861, quoted by Baxter (*National Income*, p. 32), described the income from the trades and professions as dependent "on the conscience of the tax-payer, who often, it is feared, returns hundreds instead of thousands, and who is certain to decide any question that he can persuade himself to think doubtful, in his own favour." Also see Peto's elaboration and documentation of enforcement problems (*Taxation*, p. 49).

large incomes of £5,000 or more were assessed on 8,500 individuals, who received *average* income of £14,842. Those whose incomes fell below the minimum taxable amount (£100 in 1867) numbered 12,458,000 individuals, with *average* annual income of less than £33!

For the most part, the classical economists were acquainted with these facts. Even allowing generous room for error, British income distribution appeared, on its face, to be highly skewed in favor of the upper (aristocratic) class. (There wasn't much of a middle class yet in England, but some highly skilled workers and agriculturalists were moving toward that status.)

Apocalyptic predictions soon emanated from Marx and other heterodox writers of the mid-nineteenth century, forcing attention on the economic status of the laboring population. "Romantics," like novelist Charles Dickens, held the Industrial Revolution responsible for the denigration of the working class and, took to the literary stump to reform the economic system. Because economics was associated with the Industrial Revolution, economics itself became suspect and was often rejected outright by the zealots of reform. Classical economics, as we have seen, offered little room for reform because it emphasized, following Ricardo, "iron laws" and stationary (stagnant) equilibria. Adherence to Say's Law counseled patience in the face of temporary crises, because it established a self-correcting mechanism that would restore the economy to health in the long run. Laborers, in this theoretical framework, had little to look forward to, as they were relegated to a subsistence wage despite their best efforts. As a consequence, cries for reform grew ever louder. Prominent economists, like Mill, Chadwick, and Senior, were not swept away by the rising tide of criticism but rather sought to find solutions to social problems within the "orthodoxy" of the classical canon.

■ Early Reforms: The Poor Laws and Factory Acts

Conscious attempts to mitigate poverty in Great Britain were undertaken as early as 1601, when Parliament began to enact a series of "Poor Laws" designed to relieve the economic stress on the poor. By John Stuart Mill's time the nation had more than two centuries of legislative experience confronting the problem. Relief was organized at the local level, with churches given responsibility for administering poor relief on a parish-wide basis. Revenues were initially raised by an income tax on parish inhabitants, but over time the system came to be funded by property taxes instead. Sir Edward Knatchbull's Act of 1722–23 enabled workhouses to be established either singly or in combination with other parishes.

The actual running of workhouses was not necessarily undertaken by the parish itself. Management could be, and sometimes was, contracted out to a third party who would undertake to feed and house the poor, charging the parish a weekly rate for each inmate. The contractor would also provide the inmates with work and could keep any surplus income generated. This system was known as "farming" the poor. The contract was usually awarded to the bidder offering the best price for the job, which might take a variety of forms: comprehensive maintenance of all the paupers in a parish; managing just the workhouse or just a particular group of paupers, such as infants and children; keeping lunatics under control; or providing medical relief. In 1796, eager to promote his system of "contract management," Jeremy Bentham (chapter 6) promulgated a grandiose scheme for "Pauper Management"—an early example of privatization that proposed the formation of a National Charity Company that would construct a chain of 250 enormous workhouses, financed by a large number of small investors. Each workhouse would hold around two thousand inmates who would be put to profitable work and fed a Spartan diet. Like many of Bentham's privatization schemes, this one, too, was not undertaken.

The condition of the laboring poor was a special concern of J. S. Mill; he devoted two chapters of Book II of his *Principles* to remedies for the low wages of workers. His laissez-faire convictions, belief in the allocative merits of economic incentives, and concern for social justice are clearly evidenced in his opinions on the Poor Laws. He thought it "right that human beings should help one another; and the more so, in proportion to the urgency of the need" (*Principles*, Robson [ed.], p. 960). He supported the findings of the Royal Commission on Poor Law Reform (whose members included Senior and Chadwick) on the grounds that the absence of relief would have grave social consequences for the disabled poor—the blind, the aged, the sick, the very young, and so forth. The problem was to design a system of relief that would care for the destitute but discourage the able-bodied from becoming wards of the state. This was clearly a matter of structuring economic incentives. Mill wrote in the *Monthly Repository* of 1834:

> The condition of a pauper must cease to be, as it has been made, an object of desire and envy to the independent labourer. Relief must be given; no one must be allowed to starve; the necessaries of life and health must be tendered to all who apply for them; but to all who are capable of work they must be tendered on such terms, as shall make the necessity of accepting them be regarded as a misfortune. . . . To this end, relief must be given only in exchange for labour, and labour at least as irksome and severe as that of the least fortunate among independent Labourers. ("Proposed Reform," p. 361)

Implicit in Mill's statement is the assumption that subsidies would make the working poor indolent and unproductive, a result that policy must guard against. Efficiency of this able-bodied army of paupers could only be obtained within the workhouses, since the decentralized program of parish relief was fraught with inefficiencies and outright bribery. Mill felt that the parish relief system imposed "fatal consequences" on the industry and prudence of the poor, whereas the workhouse offered "the means by which society may guarantee a subsistence to every one of its members, without producing any of the fatal consequences to their industry and prudence" that the outdoor parish relief system provided ("Lord Brougham's Speech," p. 597). Despite his concern for social justice and his support of the Poor Laws, Mill did not take a leading role in their establishment. He was, however, definitely concerned with the design of an optimum system to alleviate, and ultimately eliminate, poverty. His writings and correspondence on this issue, as we will see in this chapter and the next, reflect a lifelong concern with the means of achieving three interrelated goals pertaining to poverty and income distribution: aid for the destitute, provision of the right kind of work incentives for the able-bodied unemployed, and use of government policy as a vehicle for altering income distribution. Whether anyone today would defend Mill's means to attain these goals is less important than the fact that he attempted to blend a concept of social justice with market economics. He did not, however, advocate improvement based merely on environmental changes, as some other reformers did.

After 1802 the British Parliament passed a series of increasingly stringent acts regulating the employment of children, adolescents (those under eighteen years of age), and adult women. Early legislative efforts were modest, but in 1833 the first effective act was passed under the sponsorship of Lord Althorp. Althorp's Act banned employment of children under nine years of age and restricted the hours and conditions of work for those between the ages of nine and eighteen. The act also provided an enforcement mechanism, which had been missing from earlier factory acts. Reformers generally hailed Althorp's Act as a great step forward in social policy. Nassau Senior, economist and consultant administrator, was at the center of the discussion concerning this early capitalist reform measure, and his role in this timely debate gives us insight into the policy implications of classical economics.

Senior was called into government service to assess the economic implications of the Factory Acts. He accepted the general provisions of Althorp's Act but argued that the cost structure of the typical textile mill (England's chief industry of the period) was such that further reductions of hours worked would eliminate the mill's margin of profit. His argument proceeded along the following lines: The average net profit per firm in the competitive cotton industry was 10 percent, which Senior took to be the normal rate of return in the industry. His research showed that the average firm in the industry was spending £4 on fixed capital (plant and equipment) for every £1 on working capital (raw materials). Thus, he argued that a reduction in the workday by one hour would reduce variable costs (and output) but not fixed costs. In effect, reduced hours of work would lower output, force plant and equipment into idleness, and increase the fixed-cost burden per unit of output (because output would fall but fixed costs would not). Senior felt that because of the disproportionate share of fixed costs in the total costs of manufacturing, the increase in per-unit costs by reducing the workday would wipe out the normal rate of return of the textile mills.

Until recently, Senior's argument has been evaluated chiefly on the quality of his empirical research, which has been questioned by many writers. But there is a sound analytical principle in Senior's analysis that has sometimes been overlooked. He argued that restrictions on labor contracts that render capital idle reduce the marginal efficiency of capital, thereby diminishing the efficiency of resource allocation. Writing in 1843, Senior made it clear that a legislated reduction in the marginal efficiency of capital (which lowers the rate of return on capital investment below what could be earned in other industries) would cause higher-cost producers to leave the industry, thereby reducing employment and granting a competitive advantage to foreign producers who were not subject to the same restrictions (*Industrial Efficiency*, p. 309). In other words, Senior advised Parliament that the Factory Acts served to hand foreign competitors an increased share of the domestic textile market, an important lesson that is no less meaningful for contemporary debates about global competition. Therefore even though Senior's argument is incorrect that eliminating the "last hour" of work would destroy normal profit—indeed, it has often been the subject of ridicule by later writers—there is nevertheless merit in his analysis.

The Poor Laws and Factory Acts represent early attempts to address poverty among the indigent and working poor. They may be viewed therefore as a kind of "laboratory experiment" designed to utilize the self-interest, natural-law axiom of Adam Smith in order to channel the "natural" incentives of the poor toward desired ends. These natural incentives were taken as given by human nature. With few exceptions, there was no clear plan for altering the "natural" incentives of the poor and the laboring classes; nor was there any mechanism for improving class mobility. Fundamentally, most of the classical writers accepted the profile of labor that changed little from the mercantilist period, although most writers rejected Mandeville's characterization of them as "brutes." Eventually, more enlightened views of labor began to emerge.

The Force of Ideas: Senior's Interest-Group Theory of Economics

A more subtle aspect of Senior's analysis of the Factory Acts has been largely ignored, and this aspect seems to foreshadow a basic principle of the contemporary theory of public choice (see chapter 24). Senior recognized that Althorp's Act imposed an economic loss on the parents of children under nine who were prohibited from working in the textile mills and a similar loss on the parents of children between the ages of nine and thirteen whose hours were restricted by the act. He also noted a corresponding gain on the part of workers (or their parents) over thirteen whose hours were not restricted by the act. This led him to question the motives of those seeking to restrict the length of the workweek. He concluded that the Factory Acts were not inspired by the "public interest" so much as the interest of the (adult male) factory operatives who sought to raise their own wages. In a closely reasoned passage, Senior argued:

> [The workers'] original object was to raise the price of their own labour. For this purpose the spinners, who form . . . a very small . . . but a powerful body among them, finding that they could not obtain a limitation of the hours of work to ten by combination, tried to effect it through the legislature. They knew that Parliament would not legislate for adults. They got up therefore a frightful, and (as far as we have heard and seen) an utterly unfounded picture of the ill treatment of the children, in the hope that the legislature would restrain all persons under 18 years old to ten hours, which they knew would, in fact, restrict the labour of adults to the same period. (*Selected Writings*, p. 19)

At the heart of this issue is whether or not young workers and female workers were in direct competition with adult male workers for jobs and pay. While this question has not been settled by contemporary historians of economic thought, strong evidence exists to support the notion that child labor and female labor were *substitutes* for adult male labor rather than complements. (Senior himself treated them mostly as complements and probably erred in doing so.) By reducing the physical exertion required on the job, technological advances (e.g., invention of the spinning mule, etc.) made it possible for adolescents and women to enter the workforce. The same technological advances threatened job security of the spinners (mostly adult males), who possessed the necessary brawn and had acquired the necessary skills under earlier technology. Senior was alert to the self-interests involved and interpreted the movement toward a ten-hour workweek on the basis of small-group interests. Threatened by gradual reductions in wages and employment due to technological advances in the textile industry, spinners supported "ten hours" legislation. Unable to get a ten hours bill passed, they tried indirectly to reduce the elasticity of demand for their services by lobbying against the employment of children, adolescents, and females.

For the historical record, the spinners were successful in achieving their objectives. The Factory Act of 1833 led to a significant reduction in child labor. The number of workers under fourteen years of age in the textile industry was reduced by 56 percent between 1835 and 1838, and this reduction occurred while overall employment within the industry was growing rapidly. Flush with this success, the adult male textile operatives gained additional restrictions on the hours and work conditions of females in the Factory Act of 1844. It goes without saying that Senior showed that *private* incentives could work against the improvement of the poor and laboring classes.*

*While the "correct" interpretation of this historical episode involving the British Factory Acts remains controversial, Senior's role in the policy debates of his day is enlightening in several respects. For one thing, it reveals in a meaningful way how economic theory can be brought to bear on important social issues. For another, it pits the informed economist against the less-informed (at least in economics) social reformers who frequently agitate for change. Whether right or wrong in all parts of his analysis, Senior showed that he was alert to the lessons of Adam Smith—namely that the self-interest axiom applies to coalitions of private-interest groups and to politicians as well as to businesspeople. These ideas are explored more fully in Anderson et al. (see references).

■ Labor as a Utilitarian Policy Issue

Owing to its downtrodden circumstances, the position of labor in the economy became a critical and central issue of classical economics, both in its *microeconomic* and *macroeconomic* conceptualizations. As part of a medieval inheritance these views leeched into policy discussions of the nineteenth century and gave them a peculiar shape. In chapter 3 we saw that certain mercantilists either took an extremely dim view of human nature or succumbed to the interests of the moneyed merchant class when dealing with the poor. That practice persisted into the nineteenth century. The "utility of poverty" idea is incipient in the wages-fund theory, which postulated that if the laboring poor received wages in excess of the barest subsistence, they would be lazy and slothful and little better than animals; if they received less, they would not survive due to overpopulation and starvation. From there it is a short step to postulating an "optimum" level of poverty. Mandeville (chapter 3) even argued that poor and orphaned children should not be given an education because it would "ruin" them for productive work. While these arguments seem insensitive and backward today, they fit the tenor, and the class structure, of the times.

This bleak assessment of progress for the poor and laboring classes was a stimulant to growing awareness of labor and its role in production as well as a catalyst to more enlightened economic policy. Poor relief was the first line of attack. Poor relief at the parish level was widely considered a disaster. The program was haunted by nagging questions without easy answers. Should social relief be "indoors" in workhouses or "outdoors," administered by government functionaries? Should workhouses use the "carrot" (provide education, sanitary housings, and so on) or the "stick" (punishment for sloth and/or malingering)? And the biggest question of all haunted even the most considerate reformers: Can any reasonable measures to change the plight of the poor have the intended effect?

■ The Big Question: Can the Poor Be Lifted out of Poverty?

Some classical writers like Adam Smith and John Ramsay McCulloch clearly did not condemn the poor outright in the manner of Mandeville, but their analytics left plenty of room for the self-interested attitudes held by the wealthier classes toward the poor. The class structure of nineteenth-century England was fairly rigid, but most of the classical writers did believe in a "bootstrap theory" of upward mobility. Few went beyond the idea that progress was possible only if workers and the poor acquired (somehow) a "taste for capitalism." One important exception was Edwin Chadwick who, ironically, was vilified by the poor for his advocacy of the workhouse under the Poor Laws.

Chadwick sometimes slipped backward into the mercantile view of labor, but he ultimately adopted a very different perspective than most of the classical writers regarding the possibilities for the laboring population and the dependent or indigent poor. He was a thoroughgoing utilitarian (in the Benthamite sense), and all of his reform proposals reflected that fact. But he also believed that man's character is strongly and effectively changed by *environmental influences*. In talking about laborers engaged in railway construction, he wrote: "Many of the men are reckless, but what is the cause? No man cares for them; they labour like degraded brutes; they feed and lodge like savages; they are enveloped in vice as with an atmosphere;

the sensual only is present" (*Papers*, p. 49). Elsewhere he said: "I do not deny the force of hereditary conditions and habits which countenance such superficial generalisations, but I have seen that those conditions and habits may be *much sooner and more effectually altered*, than is commonly supposed" ("Improvements," p. 77, emphasis added).

Chadwick's approach to reform, therefore, represents a combination of these (empirically based) propositions into a theoretical structure that posited utility maximization subject to environmental and institutional constraints. His great familiarity with the human condition convinced him that altered constraints were the key to economic and social mobility, which, in turn, defined the potential for success of the laboring and poor classes.[5] He remonstrated those who promoted the idea that poverty is inexorable: "The Mandevillians have brutalized millions of human beings, and brought them to a state in which they are ready to rush on to the injury of themselves, and the destruction of all around them" ("Taxes," pp. 246–247).[6] He argued instead that the state of the workers and the poor was due not to any inherited failure or character flaws but rather to environmental constraints. The solution to poverty, therefore, was to develop social, economic, and political institutions designed to foster bourgeois characteristics in the lower classes. John Stuart Mill became his willing ally in the mission to improve the lot of the working poor.

Mill's open rejection of the paternalistic view of class structure established a corollary to Chadwick's rejection of the mercantilist attitude toward the poor. Mill cast the problem in terms of two opposing worldviews: "The one may be called the theory of dependence and protection, the other that of self-dependence" (*Principles*, Ashley [ed.], p. 759). The former takes the position that the upper classes have the duty and responsibility to care for the lower classes (what the French call *noblesse oblige*) and in return the lower classes owe allegiance to their employers. Mill argued that this view was mutually destructive: "If the rich regard the poor, as by a kind of natural law, their servants and dependents, the rich in their turn are regarded as a mere prey and pasture for the poor; the subject of demands and expectations wholly indefinite, increasing in extent with every concession made to them." This situation, he continued, leads to "the total absence of regard for justice or fairness in the relations between the two, [which] is as marked on the side of the employed as on that of the employers" (*Principles*, Ashley [ed.], p. 761). A more lasting solution, Mill thought, was to raise the working poor to the same footing as middle-class English society, although the scope of his policy program was less ambitious than Chadwick's.

Of course there are other ways to address the issues of poverty and skewed income distribution, and we shall visit alternative approaches in chapters 11 and 12. But it is worth noting at this juncture that many of the so-called "utopian socialists"

[5] Despite his best efforts Chadwick was unable to rid himself completely of mercantile preconceptions. In his later life he argued that "it may be maintained as a principle of political economy that a poor man must make a poor master, and that he had better serve a rich one, a capitalist, i.e., a work finder and a wage finder; that a poor man never works for so bad a master as when he works for himself" (*Evils of Disunity*, p. 26). Chadwick had an unfortunate proclivity to moralize, which is evident in his discussion of the use of "common labourers" as locomotive engineers in the construction of railroads: "High wages, with such a class of men, only increase the danger [of construction accidents]; for it generally leads to an increase in drinking" (*Papers*, p. 25).

[6] As we noted in chapter 3, Mandeville (*Fable*, p. 311) is the best source of this extreme attitude: "Abundance of hard and duty Labour is to be done, and coarse Living is to be complied with: Where shall we find a better Nursery for these necessities than the Children of the Poor? none certainly are nearer to it or fitter for it."

shared Mill's and Chadwick's emphasis on environmental constraints, though not their emphasis on the efficacy of economic incentives. Robert Owen, for example, was the most forthright: "Any general character, from the best to the worst, from the most ignorant to the most enlightened, may be given to any community, even to the world at large, by the application of proper means; which means are to a great extent at the command and under the control of those who have the influence in the affairs of men" ("Address to the Inhabitants of New Lanark," p. 14). But Owen may more properly be considered a socialist, whereas Mill merely flirted with socialism, and Chadwick did not believe that the government could run anything well.

■ Technology, Labor, and Poverty: Classical Perspectives

The Industrial Revolution was at base a technological transformation that dominated the nineteenth-century social and economic landscape. But for the most part, the classical writers only dimly understood the long-term impact of technology. They were aware that technology could "shock" the economic system, but their analysis was mostly of a *macroeconomic* nature. They allowed that there would be an "upward drift" in aggregate real wages through time—with cultural rather than biological revisions to the notion of subsistence—but their main concern was the impact of machinery on employment. When they considered the microeconomic consequences they focused chiefly on the impact of machinery on labor in the short and long run rather than on the social dimensions of poverty. The narrow analysis of the employment effects of labor-saving machinery has become known as the "Compensation Controversy," which figured prominently in both classical and Marxian economic doctrine. Chadwick took the position that the introduction of machinery would result only in temporary unemployment, a view he shared with McCulloch, Mill, and Malthus.

In the cotton industry, where mechanization was progressing swiftly, Malthus argued that the end result of the introduction of machinery was likely to be an increase in employment because the product was, in the contemporary vernacular, one of elastic demand (see O'Brien, *Classical Economists,* p. 227). It followed, therefore, that new machinery could lead to a reduction of poverty for certain workers. McCulloch maintained that machinery caused only temporary, "frictional" unemployment (see O'Brien, *Classical Economists*, pp. 302–306). Mill's analysis of the Compensation Controversy was somewhat less, but he reached the same conclusion. He wrote: "all increases of fixed capital, when taking place at the expense of circulating, must be, at least temporarily, prejudicial to the interests of the labourers" (*Principles*, Ashley [ed.], p. 93). He then detailed the circumstances wherein laborers are injured by mechanization. From a practical standpoint, however, Mill asserted that the substitution of fixed for circulating capital is not an ordinary occurrence. Rather, "improvements are always introduced very gradually, and are seldom or never made by withdrawing circulating capital (wages to hire labor) from actual production, but are made by the employment of the annual increase" (*Principles*, Ashley [ed.], p. 97). Mill argued that in a growing economy, mechanization is financed from the net increase in national output, leaving the wages-fund, and hence, the demand for labor, unchanged (in a macroeconomic sense). On this basis Mill was in agreement with Chadwick, Malthus, and McCulloch. He stated: "I do not believe that, as things are actually transacted, improvements in production are often, if ever, injurious even temporarily, to the labouring classes in the aggregate"

(*Principles*, Ashley [ed.], p. 97). He was, however, like virtually all of the classical writers, responding to a *macroeconomic* situation.[7]

The classical writers, almost without exception, encased their views on labor within the abstract context of the wages-fund theory, a staple of classical macroeconomics. Chadwick followed the other classical writers to a point, but also provided a unique assessment of labor markets that featured actual empirical observations. He *observed* the behavior of individuals who were technologically unemployed. While investigating the direct effects of the institution of labor-saving machinery on the pauper rolls and Poor Laws administration, Chadwick concluded that technological improvement was *not* a contributing factor to pauperism. He presented evidence to back his claim, again drawn from relentless personal investigation. According to Chadwick:

> In one instance, where, by the introduction of Mr. Whitworth's street-sweeping machine into a large town district, the labour of the entire body of sweepers by hand had been displaced. I confidently expected that that class, at least, who were of the lowest labourers, and the least capable of changing the object on their labour, would be found, as a class, on the destitute relief list; but as a class, they were not there. ("Extracts," p. 806)

With dogged determination, Chadwick tried to locate the displaced street-sweepers. He found that 8 percent had since died (a percentage that Chadwick noted was not significantly different from expected mortality), 6 percent were unaccounted for, and the rest had found employment elsewhere. Chadwick attributed their re-employment to the initiative of the individuals: "Under the stimulus of an extraordinary necessity they had found for themselves miscellaneous services, for which, under that stimulus, they qualified themselves, which services no one else could have anticipated or found out for them . . . and none had fallen below their former position, which indeed was scarcely possible" ("Extracts," p. 806). Chadwick also allowed that the uncontrolled effect of market pressures may result in laborers actually improving their situation, hypothesizing that markets may be efficient in making adjustments to equilibrium disturbances.

Chadwick also recognized another advantage to the introduction of labor-saving machinery: increased job security. He believed that mechanical operatives were less likely to be subject to cyclical unemployment if displacing them was *marginally* more costly than retaining skilled workers. His argument was that if workers cannot be safely dismissed because of difficulty of finding suitable replacement, the

[7] The Compensation Controversy began when Ricardo added a chapter entitled "On Machinery" in the third edition of *The Principles of Political Economy and Taxation*, where he concluded that mechanization might be prejudicial to labor. Explaining his change of heart from previous editions Ricardo wrote: "I am convinced that the substitution of machinery for human labor is often very injurious to the interest of the class of labourers" (*Principles*, p. 388). Mark Blaug explained Ricardo's analysis as follows: "The basic argument is that if the introduction of machinery involves the diversion of labor previously required to produce wage goods, if instead of new machines being financed out of retained earnings they are financed by drawing down the wages fund, then output may fall for a time and produce unemployment" (*Economic Theory*, pp. 137–138). It should be noted that Ricardo based his analysis on the assumption that circulating capital (the wages-fund) is converted into fixed capital, which J. S. Mill later rejected. Ricardo's analysis of mechanization was taken by Karl Marx and became a central element in Marx's "Laws of Capitalistic Motion" (see chap. 12 of our text). Marx also made mechanization a driving force behind his "Law of a Growing Industrial Reserve Army," which posits that the permanent dislocation of labor by machinery creates a growing unemployed class as technological improvement advances.

costs of maintaining an idle machine (i.e., maintenance and interest on borrowed capital) is a "penalty on the owner of the machine for every day he omits to find work and keep the artisan employed at these high wages. Under these circumstances, the owner becomes, to a greater extent than may be supposed, the servant of the operative" ("Extracts," p. 804). He might have added that employers may be less likely to temporarily discharge workers if the cost of rehiring them is high. As usual, Chadwick's investigations probed behind the obvious and superficial, shining light on the complexity of many economic decisions.

Labor Conditions and the Business Cycle

Chadwick observed a close association between mechanization and the business cycle, advancing the counter-intuitive belief that manufacturing distress was beneficial to labor in the long run. Manufacturing distress, he argued, led to technological improvements and the introduction of labor-saving capital, which in turn had net beneficial effects on the laboring poor. Acknowledging detrimental short-run effects, he nevertheless confidently argued that recessions often had a *positive* effect on innovation! As always, for him it was a matter of submitting hypotheses to empirical investigation.

Commenting on the effects of the blockage of cotton shipments to British textile manufacturers during the American Civil War, Chadwick noted: "It was an axiom of the late Mr. John Kennedy, who was called the father of the cotton manufacture, that no manufacturing improvements were ever made except on 'threadbare profits'" ("Improvements," p. 3). Chadwick considered it axiomatic that when profits are low, entrepreneurs have the greatest incentive to innovate; whereas, "When the trade is doing well, the axiom is, that they cannot be better than well, and they remain as they are" ("Opening Address," p. 3). In a manner of speaking, Chadwick adumbrated the "crucible theory" of entrepreneurship: When profits are falling and inventories of unsold goods rising, the entrepreneur's

> nerves are strained, as much as any officer's in a military command, and his mind is tasked, even with the aid of new divisions of labor, of brokers to buy his raw material, and of agents to have an outlook and sell his produce. Being under heavy penalties for every day he fails to find work and wages for his corps, he is driven to his wits' end to exercise invention, and listens greedily to any which bids fair to cheapen production, lower prices and stimulate consumption. ("Improvements," p. 3).[8]

Labor, Technology, and Human Capital

As previously mentioned, Chadwick was aware of the temporary unemployment that resulted from manufacturing distress. However, since he predicted that recessions led to higher wages and increased stability of demand by dint of entrepreneurs' adjustments, he was more concerned with alleviating the short-run costs of the business cycle rather than eliminating them completely. Labor, too, can adjust to the adverse consequences of recession. Chadwick suggested that laborers could mitigate the short-run, personal disadvantages of recessions by investment in human capital and diversification; or, in the broadest sense, education.

[8] On the "crucible theory" see Janet Nixdorff and George Solomon ("Role of Opportunity Recognition"). We note here that Chadwick's view of invention is opposed to that advanced by Schumpeter (see chap. 23), who argued that product research and development takes its greatest stimulus from monopoly profits (*Capitalism, Socialism and Democracy*, p. 106). Schumpeter's thesis is controversial and unverified, primarily because such empirical evidence that exists is inconclusive as to which form of market structure is most conducive to effective market innovation.

Chadwick was one of the earliest writers to understand that a general system of education for the poor and laboring classes had both public and private benefits. The public benefits are mostly in the nature of an externality. Education creates public (human) capital, which benefits society in various ways: Raising society's general level of intelligence will result in greater social stability, he argued, through encouragement of a lower propensity to violence and through generating more and better informed voters. A critical aspect of the educational scheme should be to improve public *knowledge of the legal structure* and the penalties entailed therein. Hence, Chadwick lobbied for all manner of skill and literacy enhancements and against what he called "taxes on knowledge," that is, excise taxes on newsprint.

On the issue of diversification, he was very straightforward. Having warned cotton manufacturers against dependency on only one source of a vital factor of production (e.g., American cotton) Chadwick counseled laborers not to put too many "eggs" in one basket: "There is a lesson on domestic prudence, on the like principle [diversification], the expediency of which, for families of the wage classes, ought to be strongly impressed upon them, namely to avoid, as much as they can, having all the working members of the same family engaged in the same manufacture" ("Improvements," pp. 10–11). Thus, by spreading the family's sources of income across several industries, a household would be less susceptible to the vagaries of manufacturing distress. The same principle, of course, is now widely recognized as a principle of risk and portfolio management in the world of finance.

The pauper and lower classes were kept that way in part by ignorance, with the complicity of the upper classes, which controlled government. Chadwick was scathing in his criticism: "In fact, the measures of government, whether by design or not, keep the immense mass of people in the state of ignorance which predisposes them to extravagant action, while it fosters and gives power to the fanaticism which takes the lead among them" ("Taxes," p. 115). He thought a major, immediate corrective would be "the entire removal of the obvious taxes on knowledge. The reduction of the stamp duty, proposed by ministers, will benefit only the press and the middle classes; as regards the labouring classes it is paltry; and will keep the larger channels of public information as far out of their reach as before. Every penny of duty retained is a bounty on ignorance." Pressing further, Chadwick asserted: "There can be no safety from the most fearful outrages against life and property but in the intelligence and moral feelings of the labouring classes." ("Real Incendiaries," p. 116). But, more than as a protection of life and property, Chadwick felt that a literate population would provide a form of human capital that would mitigate poverty and encourage economic growth. The poor and illiterate were dupes of the upper, ruling classes, he said, whether by design or by accident. The antidote to this situation is knowledge:

> A habit of reading the public journals, cannot fail to gradually loosen the authority of a certain class of ignorant popular leaders, whose governing motives are less sympathy for the sufferings of the people and a desire to advance social happiness than insatiable vanity and love of power, and whose only claims to authority are reckless confidence and incessant action, which never waits, or allows others to wait, for evidence or deliberations. To such men as to the priests who sway an ignorant people, divided attention is divided power. ("Taxes," p. 246)

Despite the public benefits of improved education, Chadwick identified the greatest benefits in private terms. He treated expenditures on education as a form of capital investment necessary to the improvement of labor's condition. Specifically, he expected education to increase wages and job security. On these two points, he was unequivocal. Discussing the effects of steam power on agriculture, Chadwick blamed lapses in education as an obstacle to economic advance: "Unfortunately, in the present state of education in the agricultural districts, if higher wages were offered, the men were not to be found to do the work with the greatest amount of economy, and in order to attain this end, their education must be improved" ("Forces," p. 63).

In other words, he viewed education as a vital component of economic efficiency, especially when used in conjunction with (then) modern machinery. It might be hard to sustain Chadwick's enthusiasm today, when the quality of education in many countries is questioned on all sides, but he was unswervingly confident in his own judgment, declaring:

> If the principles of economical and social science which I have indicated in their relation with the means of intellectual, moral, and physical improvement, be duly regarded and applied, the conditions of the manufacturing population, instead of being deplorable, will, with the increased and increasing stages derivable by the people from the extraordinary improvements in the mechanical arts for which they are required as ministers and the servants, be brought up to a high state of moral and social advancement. ("Opening Address," p. 27)

In addition to increased employment opportunities generated by education, the increased choice set of available jobs serves to lessen the effect of the business cycle. Education breeds self-reliance, such that "the better educated, who can write and inquire for themselves, and find out for themselves new outlets and sources of productive employment which no one else can find out for them, and who can read for themselves, and act upon written or printed instructions. The really well-trained, educated, and intelligent, are the best to bear distress" ("Opening Address," p. 12). The comparative advantage at bearing distress comes about not only because of the relative efficiency at job search but also because the worker is better suited to learning new manufacturing skills.

Mark Blaug said of the classical economists as a group that they "favored education more for purposes of moral improvement than for the development of productive skills" (*Economic Theory*, p. 226), but Chadwick had a broader vision that laid primary stress on the human capital aspects of education. He and Mill were in total agreement on this point. They shared a philosophical foundation, utilitarianism, which can be traced to their mentor, Bentham. Despite occasional lapses into the jaded propositions about workers that beset the mercantilist period, both Mill and Chadwick took seriously the economic analysis of the condition of the laboring poor. Where they differed was in the minor nuances that defined the relative importance of environment versus incentives in regard to human nature.

■ Conclusion

The multitalented and energetic John Stuart Mill was a giant in the development of economic theory and is accorded his rightful place in that history. In his own right, Chadwick was equally talented and energetic, but his contributions consisted more in the elaboration of institutions and how they affected economic incentives. When probed in full, the contributions of Mill and Chadwick to economic policy convey a sharp and slightly kaleidoscopic "answer" to the sometimes shrill and emotional criticisms of economics and industrialism launched by the "utopian socialists" (chapter 11) and Marx (chapter 12). Recognizing lack of theoretical underpinnings in the popular criticisms of the former group, Marx tried to distance himself from them. Though probably understood by few who read his works, and despite its flaws, Marx's theoretic apparatus surpassed that of the "utopians" in the public arena.

This chapter has presented some dimensions of the "orthodox" (as opposed to the Marxian) assault on the economic and social climate of the time. Some writers in the classical tradition made a conscious effort through English politics to alter the condition of the laboring poor. The first fruit of this effort was the early passage of British Poor Laws and a series of Factory Acts, but these palliatives affected only a part of the population and they contained, at least implicitly, a (fatalistic) view of the poor and laboring classes that was noticeably beginning to wither under increased scrutiny. The old view said that Providence created poor and rich, lower and upper classes and little could be done about it, a view that was a holdover from the medieval and mercantile periods when it was considered axiomatic that maintenance of a large body of poor workers was necessary for a great nation to function.

The altered circumstances of labor and production introduced by the Industrial Revolution provoked new concerns by economists and social thinkers. The effects of technology on labor and wages could not be ignored in the new circumstances. John Stuart Mill and Edwin Chadwick were in the vanguard of economists awakening to the economic transformations taking place. Mill was willing to flex economic theory to make room for the heightened concerns. Edwin Chadwick held social and economic institutions under a microscope in order to identify palliatives driven by economic incentives. Both writers believed the nature and condition of the poor and the working poor *could* be changed for the better by harnessing the power of economic incentives. The rigid English class structure did not yield easily; consequently the mobility of labor was retarded unnecessarily.

Nevertheless, once it was admitted that the poor were in nature like everyone else, the door opened to means for changing their environment and for utilizing and altering incentives to provide avenues for progress in income distribution. Mill and Chadwick led the charge among classical economists in scaling the castle walls of intellectual inflexibility. Their respective roles in this regard are discussed further in the next chapter.

References

Anderson, G. M., R. B. Ekelund, Jr., and R. D. Tollison. "Nassau Senior as Economic Consultant: The Factory Acts Reconsidered," *Economica*, vol. 56 (February 1989), pp. 71–82.

Baxter, Robert Dudley. *National Income: The United Kingdom*. London: Macmillan, 1868.

Blaug, Mark. *Economic Theory in Retrospect*, 3rd ed., Cambridge: Cambridge University Press, 1978.

British Parliamentary Papers, vol. I, Irish University Press Series of British Parliamentary Papers, (Shannon: Irish University Press, 1968).

Chadwick, E. "The Real Incendiaries and Promoters of Crime," *The Examiner*, no. 1203 (1831), pp. 114–116.

———. "The Taxes on Knowledge," *Westminster Review*, vol. 20 (1831), pp. 238–267.

———. "Improvements in Machinery—Races of Workmen—Nominally Low-Priced Labour," *Journal of the Royal Society of Arts*, vol. 5 (1856), pp. 77–78.

———. "On the Forces Used in Agriculture," *Journal of the Royal Society of Arts*, vol. 8 (1857), pp. 62–63.

———. "Opening Address of the President of the Department of Economy and Trade, at the Meeting of the National Science, Held at York in September 1865," *Journal of the Statistical Society of London*, vol. 28 (1865), pp. 1–33.

———. *On the Evils of Disunity in Central & Local Administration Especially with Relation to the Metropolis and Also on the New Centralisation for the People Together with Improvements in Codification and in Legislative Procedure*. London: Longmans, Green, 1885.

Evans, G. H., Jr. "The Law of Demand—The Role of Gregory King and Charles Davenant," *Quarterly Journal of Economics*, vol. 81 (1967), pp. 483–492.

Levi, Leone. *On Taxation: How It Is Raised and How It Is Expended*. London: John W. Parker and Son, 1860.

Mandeville, Bernard de. *The Fable of the Bees*, B. F. Kaye (ed.). London: Oxford University Press, 1734 [1924].

Mill, J. S. "Lord Brougham's Speech on the Poor Law Amendment Bill." *Monthly Repository*, vol. 7 (1834), p. 597.

———. "The Proposed Reform of the Poor Laws," *Monthly Repository*, vol. 8 (1834), p. 361.

———. *Principles of Political Economy*, W. J. Ashley (ed.). New York: A. M. Kelley, Publishers, 1965 [1848].

———. *Principles of Political Economy*, J. M. Robson (ed.), *Collected Works*, vols. 2 and 3. Toronto: University of Toronto Press, 1966 [1848].

Nixdorff, Janet and Solomon, George. "Role of Opportunity Recognition in Teaching Entrepreneurship," http://sbaer.uca.edu/research/icsb/2005/paper148.pdf.

O'Brien, Denis. *J. R. McCulloch: A Study in Classical Economics*. London: George Allen & Unwin, 1970.

———. *The Classical Economists*. Oxford: Clarendon Press, 1975.

Owen, Robert. "An Address to the Inhabitants of New Lanark." *A New View of Society and Other Writings of Robert Owen*, G. D. H. Cole (ed.). London: Dent, 1821 [1927].

Peto, Morton. *Taxation: Its Levy and Expenditure, Past and Future: Being an Enquiry into Our Financial Policy*. New York: D. Appleton, 1863.

Ricardo, David. *Principles of Political Economy and Taxation. Volume I: The Works and Correspondence of David Ricardo*, Pierro Sraffa, (ed.). London: Cambridge University Press, 1969 [1817].

Schumpeter, J. *Capitalism, Socialism and Democracy*, New York: Harper and Row, 1942 [1962].

Senior, N. W. *Industrial Efficiency and Social Economy*, vol. 2. New York: Henry Holt, 1928.

———. *Selected Writings on Economics*. New York: A. M. Kelley, 1966.

Smith, Adam. *An Inquiry into the Nature and Causes of the Wealth of Nations*. New York: Modern Library, 1776 [1937].

Notes for Further Reading

Lionel Robbins's *The Theory of Economic Policy in English Classical Political Economy* (London: Macmillan, 1965) provides a good general introduction to classical economic policy. Robbins's interpretations are pristine and get to the heart of important matters. For example, on Mill's so-called socialist leanings he writes: "Mill is very typical. It is this vision of the future, rather than that of central collectivism, which has usually captured the fancy of lovers of liberty who, for one reason or another, have wished to transcend the society based on private property and the market" (p. 160). Also see Robbins's comments on the contrast between the precision suggested by Bentham's "felicific calculus" and the rough-and-ready *marginal* alterations in economic policies actually recommended by Bentham's disciples (p. 181). Another valuable introduction to classical economic theory is D. P. O'Brien's *The Classical Economists Revisited* (Princeton, NJ:

Princeton University Press, 2004). Chapters 6, 9, and 10 are especially good, as are the bibliographies that follow them. For the view that Bentham was a collectivist and Mill essentially a Benthamite, see J. B. Brebner, "Laissez-Faire and State Intervention in Nineteenth Century Britain," *Journal of Economic History*, vol. 8, supp. (1948), pp. 59–73. On the influence of economists on nineteenth-century legislation, see two contributions by F. W. Fetter: "The Influence of Economists in Parliament on British Legislation from Ricardo to John Stuart Mill," *Journal of Political Economy*, vol. 83 (October 1975), pp. 1051–1064; and his longer treatment *The Economists in Parliament, 1780–1868* (Durham, NC: Duke University Press, 1979).

The medieval and philosophical origins of the concept of laissez-faire are discussed by Jacob Viner, "The Intellectual History of Laissez-Faire," *Journal of Law & Economics*, vol. 3 (October 1960), pp. 45–69. Contributors to the Romantic and literary criticism of economics that had some impact on Mill are reviewed by W. D. Grampp, "Classical Economics and Moral Critics," *History of Political Economy*, vol. 5 (Fall 1973), pp. 359–374. There is an extensive literature dealing with individual policy issues in classical economics. On the Factory Acts in particular, see K. O. Walker, "The Classical Economists and the Factory Acts," *Journal of Economic History*, vol. 1 (1941), pp. 170–191; L. R. Sorenson, "Some Classical Economists, Laissez-Faire, and the Factory Acts," *Journal of Economic History*, vol. 12 (1952), pp. 101–117; D. P. O'Brien, *The Classical Economists* (*supra*), pp. 277–279; and Mark Blaug, "The Classical Economists and the Factory Acts—A Reexamination," *Quarterly Journal of Economics*, vol. 72 (May 1958), pp. 211–226. On a related topic, see W. D. Grampp, "The Economists and the Combination Laws," *Quarterly Journal of Economics*, vol. 93 (November 1979), pp. 501–522. In his analysis of the Factory Act of 1833, H. P. Marvel, "Factory Regulation: A Reinterpretation of Early English Experience," *Journal of Law & Economics*, vol. 20 (October 1977), pp. 379–402, concluded that "this innovation in industrial regulation was not enacted and enforced solely out of compassion for the factory children. It was, instead, an early example of a regulated industry controlling its regulators to further its own interests." Thus, Marvel describes the very same process of rent seeking in representative democracy that we elaborated in chapter 3. The implication is that other forms of early nineteenth-century social controls may also constitute examples of rent seeking, although these other forms have not yet been subjected to such analysis. For a similar conclusion, see Clark Nardinelli, "Child Labor and the Factory Acts," *Journal of Economic History*, vol. 15 (1980), pp. 739–755.

The public-choice ramifications of Senior's analysis of the Factory Acts are explored by G. M. Anderson, R. B. Ekelund, Jr., and R. D. Tollison, "Nassau Senior as Economic Consultant: The Factory Acts Reconsidered," *Economica*, vol. 56 (February 1989), pp. 71–81. On the confused issue of Senior's "last hour" analysis, see Orace Johnson, "The 'Last Hour' of Senior and Marx," *History of Political Economy*, vol. 1 (Fall 1969), pp. 359–369; J. B. DeLong, "Senior's 'Last Hour': Suggested Explanation of a Famous Blunder," *History of Political Economy*, vol. 18 (Summer 1986), pp. 325–333; and the dialogue between DeLong and J. M. Pullen in *History of Political Economy*, vol. 21 (Summer 1989), pp. 299–312. E. G. West has written extensively on education in classical economics, see West, "Private versus Public Education, A Classical Economic Dispute," *Journal of Political Economy*, vol. 72 (October 1974), pp. 465–475; same author, "Resource Allocation and Growth in Early Nineteenth-Century British Education," *Economic History Review*, vol. 23 (April 1970), pp. 68–95. Also see Margaret O'Donnell, *The Educational Thought of the Classical Political Economists* (London: University Press of America, 1985). On classical views of "appropriate" policy toward emergent corporate forms of business organization, see C. E. Amsler, R. L. Bartlett, and C. J. Bolton, "Thoughts of Some British Economists on Early Limited Liability and Corporate Legislation," *History of Political Economy*, vol. 13 (Winter 1981), pp. 774–793. Agrarian economic organization and population incentives are examined by W. C. Bush, "Population and Mill's Peasant-Proprietor Economy," *History of Political Economy*, vol. 5 (Spring 1973), pp. 110–120.

The critical distinction between Bentham's "artificial" identity of interests and Smith's "natural" identity of interests is discussed by Elie Halévy, *The Growth of Philosophical Radicalism*, Mary Morris (trans.) (Boston: Beacon Press, 1955). Chadwick's role in the history of public administration is well-known. The astonishing range of social causes in which he was embroiled, highlighted in this chapter and the next, is outlined in his massive vita. See R. A. Lewis, *Edwin Chadwick and the Public Health Movement, 1832–1854* (London: Longmans, 1952), pp. 380–395. Chadwick's actions on behalf of Poor Laws reform made him one of the most hated public figures of his day, and his personality did not ease the situation. In what seems a majority opinion, Lewis described him as follows: "He was a bore, a really outstanding specimen of bore in an age when the species flourished. He was too keenly aware of his own merits; while, on the other hand he had no patience with fools, and his definition of a fool was a very wide one, taking in, as it did, nearly everybody who disagreed with him. With a wholesome suspicion of power wielded by others he managed to combine a boundless confidence in the benefits of power in his own strong hands, and every scheme drawn up by Edwin Chadwick seemed to contain a provision at some point for giving more power to Edwin Chadwick. . . . He stirred up a great deal of mud, and it is a tribute not a reproach that so much of it was thrown back at him by his critics." For another biographical treatment of Chadwick, see S. E. Finer, *The Life and Times of Sir Edwin Chadwick* (London: Methuen, 1952). Additional secondary sources on Chadwick and his pregnant ideas can be found in "Notes for Further Reading" at the end of chapter 10.

10

J. S. Mill and Edwin Chadwick on Taxation and Public Economics

Major economic transformations like the Industrial Revolution usually wind up as a mixed blessing. We saw in the last chapter that despite the tremendous spur to economic development by technological advance, adverse side-effects inevitably followed, creating a dilemma for economists and policy makers alike. The old order of mercantilism was sustained by strong centralized government and authoritarian market controls. The new order, industrialism, required a liberating philosophy that allowed market-based incentives relatively free sway. Adam Smith supplied the philosophy of limited government that the new industrial order required. But second-generation classical economists were constantly balancing the need to limit government, on the one hand, with the practical necessity to use it as a vehicle for socio-economic improvement, on the other. This chapter examines those areas in which Mill and Chadwick performed a delicate balancing act between proactive and reactive government action in the emergent market economy.

The second half of the nineteenth century was a victory for laissez-faire and economic freedom inasmuch as public institutions were gradually and progressively constrained in a way that provided marginal gains for free trade, both domestically and internationally. Two especially noteworthy constraints on government typified the age of nineteenth-century laissez-faire. The first was a fairly rigid adherence to a monetary gold standard, which denied the central government access to the printing press (fiat money), thereby limiting the amount of government spending for war or social programs. The second was the limits placed by a conservative government (then led by Prime Minister Robert Peel and Chancellor of the Exchequer William Gladstone) on the amount and types of taxation the government could levy. Gladstone in particular promoted a number of policies designed to produce a balanced withdrawal of government from the private sector. Among them were the repeal of the Corn Laws (finally accomplished in 1846), the reduction of income taxes, and the prohibition of sales and excise taxes. The calculated effect of Gladstone's policies of public finance was less government and a practical realization of laissez-faire, but in this context laissez-faire consisted mainly of legal limitations on the tax base available to the government.[1] The straightforward policy was

[1] Baysinger and Tollison ("Chaining Leviathan") argue that the implementation of Gladstonian financial and economic policies in mid-nineteenth-century England marked the official end of mercantilism. The question of when mercantilism actually declined, however, depends on how the terms "mercantilism" and "laissez-faire" are defined and understood.

to "starve the beast."[2] The state would necessarily be kept small in terms of its sphere of influence because it could not "afford" to intervene on a large scale.

Against this backdrop of shrinking government, Mill and Chadwick agitated for improvement of the working class. They clearly understood the value of open, competitive markets (although Chadwick would have attenuated private property rights along with a competitive bidding system) and the actual and potential gains from trade. But they were also attuned to the *negative* impacts of the Industrial Revolution. Problems of income inequality, urbanization, and especially urban poverty of the working and dependent segments of the population were much on their minds. Following Bentham, they understood that "incentives mattered" and that while laissez-faire had produced marvels in terms of aggregate economic growth, the generally low condition of labor was a drag on a healthy economy. The question then was: *Can the mobility of labor and its well-being be altered by changing tax structures, the physical environment of the poor, and public policy?* Both Mill and Chadwick thought so, but each invoked a different *modus operandi*.

■ Social and Economic Policies of J. S. Mill

John Stuart Mill, economist, philosopher, humanitarian, and Member of Parliament, was in the vanguard of those espousing progressive policies regarding education, welfare, trade unions, and the equality of women. He and Chadwick alike adopted the Benthamite model of social reform, namely proper arrangement of incentives to achieve desired ends. Mill's sociological and philosophical treatment of society's "ends" underwent considerable change over time, but his reform proposals were consistently grounded in "market" measures. That is to say, Mill recognized the nature and importance of economic incentives as a guide to human action. We will see that Chadwick espoused the same objectives but was far more apt to invoke government intervention than his great friend Mill.

Nature and Scope of Economic Policy

An ardent defender of liberty, Mill nevertheless kept an ever-watchful eye on the conditions of the poor. Committed to both commercial and individual freedom, he would sometimes countenance exceptions to the former in order to nurture the latter. In his view, personal liberty required equality of *opportunity*, not equality of income or talents. Thus, he noted that

> many, indeed, fail with greater efforts than those with which others succeed, not from difference of merits, but differences of opportunities; but if all were done which it would be in the power of a good government to do, by instruction and by legislation, to diminish this inequality of opportunities, the difference of fortune arising from people's own earnings could not justly give umbrage. (*Principles*, Robson [ed.], p. 811)

To Mill the essential element of liberty is that individuals "all start fair," and he conceded to government the basic role of establishing social and economic policies that promote equality of opportunity.

[2] This does not mean that certain artifacts of the mercantile system did not remain. Internal mercantilism began to decline as early as the seventeenth century due to institutional change (see chapter 3), but external control of international trade and the associations with empire building were a large part of the British economy. Particularly in the agricultural sector, Mokyr establishes that rent-seeking interest groups influenced trade subsidies and restrictions into the twentieth century (*Enlightened Economy*).

Mill divided government interventions into two types: (1) "authoritative" interventions that prohibit or restrict market forces and (2) "supportive" interventions that augment market forces. These two types of interventions might also be thought of in terms of the concepts of *ex ante* and *ex post*. *Ex ante* equality refers to those interventions designed to ensure that individuals start fairly, for example, all runners begin at the same mark. *Ex post* equality refers to those interventions such as taxation that attempt to impose some criterion of fairness in the actual outcome of social processes involving risk and uncertainty. *Ex ante* in this context relates to prospects. *Ex post* relates to results. Both types of equality may result from the same social policy, but in general this division is useful for analyzing Mill's several policy positions. In golf, for example, handicapping is used to equalize competition in the sense of making the contest more level and "fair" at the start, but the data for handicapping are derived from average scores in previous contests. In the same sense, taxation over time blends the *ex ante* and *ex post* concepts of equality.

Taxation and Poverty

As we learned in chapter 8, Mill was sensitive to the distinction between income distribution and wealth distribution. He did not wish to interfere greatly with the former because of the adverse effect that income redistribution has on incentives. However, wealth was a different matter. Inherited wealth, in particular, represented a means to perpetuate unequal distribution among the classes. Mill looked, therefore, to various means of taxation to eliminate wide disparities in wealth and alleviate the meager condition of the working class. Like Smith, Mill was a general advocate of proportional taxation. He stressed "equality of sacrifice," but he also expressed concern for the effects of taxation on the condition of the poor. He sponsored three different tax policies aimed at alleviating poverty: The first involved a minor adjustment to the income tax; the second involved a graduated inheritance tax; and the third involved certain sumptuary restrictions.

Income Tax. To Mill, the least objectionable of all taxes was a "fairly assessed" income tax. He wanted tax rates to be proportional at all income levels, with a built-in exemption for all incomes below a certain amount. In 1857 he suggested that this minimum be set at £100, although he allowed that the controlling factor must be whatever amount is required to purchase the "necessaries of the existing population." At the time, the vast majority of the English population earned well below that amount (see chapter 9). Mill supported his argument by defending a low tax rate on the next increment of income (between £100 and £150) on the grounds that existing indirect taxes were regressive and fell hardest on individuals earning between £50 and £150 (*Principles*, Robson [ed.], p. 830).

Although he believed that, in principle, proportional income taxes would be the most equitable, Mill thought it inadvisable to rely solely on income taxes as a source of government revenue. Attempts to strictly enforce income taxes would inevitably lead to tax evasion, fraud, and collection irregularities, in his view. "Commercial dishonesty," he pointed out, was "the certain effect of Sir Robert Peel's income tax; and it will never be known for how much of that evil product the tax may be accountable, or in how many cases a false return was the first dereliction of pecuniary integrity" (*Essays*, p. 702). Despite these weighty objections, Mill justified an income tax so that the rich would pay their share of taxation.

Mill did not have in mind a minimum-income program because his income tax proposal did not guarantee everyone an income of £100; it merely exempted from taxation those whose incomes fell below this level. He wanted to build into the tax system individual incentives to work; hence, the exemption was important in removing marginal disincentives to earn among the poorest classes of society. As for the rich, proportional taxes were preferable to progressive income taxes for the same reason. Mill noted: "To tax the larger incomes at a higher percentage than the smaller, is to lay a tax on industry and economy; to impose a penalty on people for having worked harder and saved more than their neighbors. It is not the fortunes which are earned, but those which are unearned, that it is for the public good to place under limitations" (*Principles*, Ashley [ed.], p. 808).

Inheritance Tax. Adam Smith was opposed to the inheritance tax not only because it did not conform to his canons of taxation, but also because it transferred capital to the state, which generally proved inept at the use of capital. Mill parted ways with Smith by denying any right of inheritance, and he contended that both individuals and society would be better off if no one received large fortunes that freed them from the necessity of working. He took the view that, except for near relatives, inheritances should be abolished, the amount of bequests should be limited, and rates should be progressive. Mill believed that inheritances were the chief impediment to greater income equality over time, and inheritance taxes should be used to redress extreme inequalities of wealth and to encourage a situation in which all start fairly. As always in matters of taxation, the key for Mill was the impact of any tax on incentives. Whereas he favored proportionality in income taxation for reasons mentioned above, he did not object to progressively higher rates on inheritances, because incentives are not adversely affected in the case of bequests and because the tax base is comprised of unearned rather than earned wealth.

Mill's reasoning was borrowed from Bentham, who rejected "natural law" in favor of utilitarianism. Declaring natural law "sheer nonsense," Bentham expressed utter contempt for those who would use it as the foundation for public policies.[3] Bentham always focused on incentives, and in this he was followed by his two famous protégés, Mill and Chadwick. He favored inheritance tax because he thought it would produce revenue with minimum sacrifice. He defended the (virtually) painless inheritance tax on collateral legatees (distant relatives) because he reasoned that those who received unexpected "windfalls" would not see their utility diminished if they did not receive the unexpected. At the same time, inheritance taxes could be used to lighten the burden of taxes on the poor and working classes of society (*Supply without Burden*). Death, in other words, constituted a limitation on property rights unlike deprivations of the living.[4]

On occasion Mill has been labeled a "socialist" for his views on inheritance taxation, but he only countenanced limits on individual property rights after a person's

[3] Bentham wrote: "Who is this . . . Queen '*Nature*,' who makes such stuff under the name of laws? . . . In what year of her own, or any body else's reign, did she make it, and in what shop is a copy of it to be bought, that it may be burnt by the hands of the common hangman. . . . It being supposed, in point of *fact*, that the children have or have not a right, of the sort in question, given them by the *law*, the only rational question remaining is, whether, in point of *utility*, such a right *ought* to be given them or not? To talk of a *Law of Nature*, giving them, or not giving them a *natural right*, is so much sheer nonsense, answering neither the one question nor the other" (*Supply without Burden*, pp. 93–94).

[4] A similar argument was advanced in another connection—the rights to one's burial plot—in Chadwick's appendage to the 1842 Sanitary report (*Report on the Sanitary Conditions*, 1843). Chadwick, the utilitarian practitioner, appended a brief exposition of the English law with respect to perpetuities in public burial grounds. A ruling judicial interpretation proclaimed that rights consisted in a balancing between those of the dead and those of the living.

death. He relied on population control and strict rules regarding inheritance limits to redistribute wealth and to provide for *ex ante* equality in British society, resisted politically by a hereditary aristocracy. Nevertheless, changes were slow in coming. Legacy and succession duties remained low in Britain throughout the nineteenth century. The Stamp Act of 1815 set the basic rates of inheritance duties, until it was amended by the Finance Act of 1910. Moreover, real-estate wealth remained beyond the reach of these "stamp duties," which included a (regressive) probate tax on all inheritances and a legacy (and succession) duty that varied by kinship between legator and legatees.[5] Gladstone tried to levy new death duties on freehold and hereditary landed properties in 1853, but according to Morton Peto the results were minimal in a statistical sense (*Taxation*, pp. 118–120). Factors contributing to the failure of reforms included assessment problems and ease of tax evasion and the political resistance of the landed aristocracy.

As a *percentage* of property bequeathed, large increases and massive levies of death duties did not occur until the twentieth century. Nevertheless, the revenue raised by death duties rose during Mill's lifetime and afterward, due in part to population growth, increased coverage, more accurate reporting, and persistent governmental emphasis on direct versus indirect taxation. According to Peto death-duty receipts from probate and bequests grew from about £2 million in 1851 to £3.4 million in 1859 (*Taxation*, pp. 135–136). Alfred Soward and W. E. Willan report that dramatic increases in the gross capital value of properties subject to estate duties pushed the tax "take" to more than £31.7 million in 1918 (*Taxation of Capital*, pp. 338–339; 343). Death duties as a percentage of total government revenue also rose over the last half of the nineteenth century, indicating that the kind of redistribution Mill envisioned was actually underway prior to the massive expansion of the state in England at the turn of the century. At this point many landed estates were dispersed and reformers of various stripes (as we will see in the following two chapters) were successful in greater government participation in the British economy.

Excise and Sumptuary Taxes. According to Mill indirect taxes bore disproportionately on the poor, especially since many excise duties were on "necessities." He advocated selective discrimination in setting import duties and excise rates so that the burden of taxation would not fall unduly on the poor. He did not object to the appropriateness or legitimacy of these levies but to their relative burden:

> The duties which now yield nearly the whole of the customs and excise revenue, those on sugar, coffee, tea, wine, beer, spirits, and tobacco, are in themselves, where a large amount of revenue is necessary, extremely proper taxes; but at present grossly unjust, from the disproportionate weight with which they press on the poorer classes. . . . It is probable that most of these taxes might bear a great reduction without any material loss of revenue. (*Principles*, Robson [ed.], p. 872)

Mill's concern for equality of opportunity among the poor also explains his support of sumptuary taxes, especially those on luxury goods. He singled out "snob" goods for special attention, declaring that expenditure by the rich not "for the sake of the pleasure afforded by the things on which the money is spent but from regard to opinion, and an idea that certain expenses are expected from them, as an

[5] Despite some variations, rates prior to 1910 were as follows: husband or wife (0%); lineal ancestors or issue (1%); brothers or sisters or their descendants (3%); brothers or sisters of the father or mother or their descendants (5%); brothers or sisters of a grandfather or grandmother or their descendants (6%); other collaterals or strangers (10%). In 1910 rates rose, with a charge (1%) added to husband and wife (see Soward and Willan, *Taxation of Capital*, pp. 323–324).

appendage of station . . . is a most desirable subject of taxation" (*Principles*, Ashley [ed.], p. 869).

Taking all these proposals together and recognizing the financial requirements of the state, Mill sought to promote equality of opportunity by providing incentives to work, by reducing the regressive burden of indirect taxes on the poor, and by offsetting the remaining burden on the poor with a high and progressive inheritance tax. His integrated approach to economic policy thus suggested an antipoverty program based on tax relief. Income distribution consistent with equality of opportunity could and should be altered, in Mill's view, by legislative power. But indirect support through tax relief was not sufficient in itself. Mill designed a more direct form of support as well.

Income Redistribution in Theory and Practice

Mill's 1845 essay "The Claims of Labour" (see *Essays*) outlined a program for public policy that exemplified clearly the distinction in economics between "normative" and "positive" that he made in his earlier work, *On Logic*. Noting the gathering momentum of socialist agitation for income redistribution, Mill affirmed the desirability of policies that redistribute income to the poor. Once again, however, he insisted that the question was one of means, not ends. Mill was unimpressed by the proposals of the socialists and the Romantics. For the most part, they sought to improve the condition of the poor by merely raising wages—a program Mill found dangerous because its advocates refused to attach population limits to their wage proposals. Good Malthusian that he was, Mill concluded that an increase in the birthrate would wipe out the gains in wages advocated by the socialists. What was needed was a change in the living habits of the working class. He wrote: "If the whole income of the country were divided among them in wages or poor-rates, still, until there is a change in [laborers] themselves, there can be no lasting improvements in their outward condition" (*Essays*, p. 375). Mill had nightmarish visions of large classes of people becoming dependents of the state, citing the Irish and French experiences in this regard (*Later Letters*, p. 44). He regarded welfare dependence as a most pernicious form of evil and, unhappily, a lesson that the poor learn more easily than any other.

Having rejected socialist and Romantic proposals for income redistribution as being at odds with the nature of human beings, Mill championed instead a system of self-help based on education and proper economic incentives. Like Bentham, he advocated public education. He supported Chadwick's proposal that government pay for the education of pauper children, but the measure was defeated by the House of Lords in 1834. Mill conceived education as learning in the broad sense, and he customarily backed changes that would cultivate "a taste for capitalist values" among the laborers. One such measure was a plan of government loans to the poor for improving their living accommodations. Certain programs, Mill felt, needed government impetus to get off the ground but, once established, should be capable of sustaining themselves without further help.

Indeed, this idea is consistent with Mill's support of a minimum income for the laboring poor. He stressed that public assistance should always be a tonic rather than a sedative. Public assistance should never dispense with, or replace, self-help. Care must always be taken in designing programs to allow a person's own labor, skill, and prudence to flourish, thereby affording each worker a better hope of attaining success by legitimate means. This, in fact, became a test to which all plans of philanthropy and benevolence should submit, Mill argued, whether intended for the benefit of individuals or of classes, and whether conducted on the voluntary or on the government principle (*Principles*, Robson [ed.]). He was unwilling to rely entirely on private charity, however, because Mill considered *it uneven in its bestowal of benefits*. Besides, he argued, poverty has external effects (i.e., costs) on the wider community (e.g., crime, beggary) and so should be solved by public policy rather than by private charity.[6]

The above mentioned measures provide positive inducements to raise up the poor, but Mill also recommended the removal of present discouragements to the lower classes. He chided government for failure to build the right kind of economic and legal incentives into the social structure, arguing that it was the government's responsibility to remove every impediment that legal and fiscal systems place on attempts of the poor to better themselves. For example, he advocated removal of defects in the common law of partnership, which restrained the poor from experimenting with joint-stock companies. Even more interesting is Mill's proposal to revamp the tax system on land transactions. The Stamp Office taxed land transactions of even the smallest amount, whereas legal fees were the same regardless of the size of transaction. The result was to suppress incentives to invest on the part of the poor peasant. Should the poor manage to save, Mill argued, economic constraints within the legal system shut off investment outlets for their savings. The land tax system was therefore of negative value in establishing opportunities for redistribution. In sum, Mill wished to use government policy to implement a minimum-income plan that utilized market forces to maintain work incentives. He clearly believed that the "low moral condition" of the poor could be improved by public assistance, provided that "while available to everybody, it leaves to everyone a strong motive to do without it if he can" (*Principles*, Robson [ed.], p. 961).

A Brief Summary of Mill's Approach

Mill's approach to social reform was closely aligned with his overall view of "justice." Justice meant equal opportunities "at the start" but not (necessarily) equal results "at the finish." This maxim makes very good sense in the abstract, but it is difficult policy to put into practice. The problem is an intergenerational one. How, in an ever-growing and changing population, could a beginning and an end be identified? Mill's answer to this question was to reward earners and entrepreneurs who produced value for society and to tax away "unearned incomes" from hereditary fortunes, many of them originating in medieval fiefdoms from a bygone era and passed down to successive generations. To Mill, property rights ended at the coffin.

However one views Mill's argument respecting inheritance as a means to distributive justice, he could never abandon his "Ricardian" roots. He clearly defended incentives, free markets, and innovation as the essential goads to progress. He believed that minimal government, generally of the Gladstonian type, was preferred but that incentives to progress could be built into programs. Government had a role, especially in redressing the "opportunity disparities" in a class-structured society, but that role was "indirect" and minimalist in character. His good friend Edwin Chadwick went much further than Mill was willing to go in his quest to change the constraints affecting the poor. Chadwick had few reservations about extending the power of centralized authority.

[6] Moreover, a "free-rider" problem would exist when no private individual has any incentive to provide charitable contributions because he or she assumes that others would. This is, for instance, the classic argument for government's provision of national defense.

■ The Political Economy of Sir Edwin Chadwick

There is some disagreement about the extent to which J. S. Mill was a collectivist, owing mainly to his views on inheritance, but it is clear that he was greatly influenced by the political thought of Jeremy Bentham and the economic analysis of David Ricardo. He defended private property, personal liberty, and decentralized government, even though he sometimes seemed willing to compromise these ends to the utilitarian ethic of the greatest good for the greatest number. His friend and ally, Edwin Chadwick, bowed more deeply at the utilitarian altar, and his persistence as the quintessential bureaucrat had a far-reaching impact on British social and economic policy. As one writer said of him, Chadwick had his insistent fingers in practically every interventionist pie during his administrative career.

Chadwick's domineering personality made him hated by many and feared by some, but his boundless energy was evident to all. Actively involved in the design and implementation of English social and economic legislation for over thirty years, Chadwick is credited as the driving force behind improvements in the Poor Laws, municipal water supply, drainage, sewage treatment, public health, civil service, school architecture, education of pauper children, and many other programs considered progressive in his day. With Bentham, he was also the leading proponent of a "competitive principle" that has found resurgence in our own day. Unlike Mill, however, he had few credentials as a serious economist, although he understood and accepted the four macroeconomic cornerstones of the classical system. In keeping with this, his biographers have represented him as a lawyer and civil servant. Be that as it may, it would be almost impossible to find anyone in the nineteenth century who saw more clearly the variety and kinds of economic problems that confront the modern policy maker or who was more at home in "classical" economic theory than Chadwick.

Law, Economics, and the Artificial Identity of Interests

Chadwick was trained in law, but he gave up the life of a barrister for a career in civil service. He was sympathetic to Bentham's "worldview" and, in particular, to his belief in legislation grounded in utilitarianism. He was also versed in Ricardian economics, though not as steeped in the subject as Mill. This combined intellectual heritage of Bentham and Ricardo reinforced Chadwick's conviction that individual initiative is the mainspring of social progress. Throughout his life he remained a vocal defender of this principle and often advocated change in the existing social structure that would preserve and/or enhance the free play of individual initiative.

What Chadwick brought to Benthamism was administrative genius that straddled utilitarian theory and bureaucratic practice. Bentham rejected Adam Smith's doctrine of the *natural* identity of private and public interests and sought to replace it with an *artificial* identity of interests, achieved through administrative arrangements. His public policy goal was to arrange obligations and punishments in such a way that the incentive to cause public harm through private action was removed, or at least blunted. But the practical implementation of this idea required a clear conception of the public interest. Bentham's personal view that the public interest is the summation of individual interests was fraught with analytical difficulties because it involved grandiose assumptions and interpersonal utility comparisons (see chapter 6). Chadwick simplified the idea of public interest by redefining it in terms of economic efficiency: Anything that reduced economic waste was found to be in the public interest. Under this banner, Chadwick advocated sweeping administrative reforms in the provision of both private and public goods.

One famous example will serve to illustrate Chadwick's approach to institutional reforms through incentive manipulation. Confronted with the problem of reducing the mortality of British criminals transported to Australia, Chadwick noted that on embarkation from a British port the British government paid a flat fee to the ship's captains for each convict transported. The captains, of course, found that they could maximize profits by taking on as many prisoners as could be carried safely without endangering the ship and by minimizing expenditures (for food and drink, etc.) on the prisoners en route. Survival rates among the prisoners under this incentive system were as low as 40 percent, and English clerics complained bitterly about the inhumanity of the system. After a quick assessment of the situation, Chadwick changed the payment system so that the ships' captains received a fee for each live convict that *disembarked* in Australia. Within a short time the survival rate increased dramatically to 98.5 percent (Chadwick, "Opening Address"). All that was needed was to give the ships' captains an incentive to protect the health of their human cargo—thus creating an artificial identity between the public interest (i.e., the health of the prisoners) and the private interests (i.e., the shipper's profit). This same principle guided all of Chadwick's policy research.

Economics of Crime and the "Preventive Principle"

In England the poor were not only perpetrators of crime but the primary victims of a badly constructed administration of criminal justice. Chadwick saw an opportunity to induce social reform by engaging the combined elements of Bentham's utilitarianism and Ricardo's economics. As usual he focused on incentives, which he traced to existing institutional arrangements.

The Common-Pool Problem. A common-pool resource (also called a common-property resource) presents special problems for economists because the size or characteristics of the resource make it costly (but not impossible) to exclude potential (nonpaying) beneficiaries from its use. Unlike pure public goods, in which individuals cannot be effectively excluded from use, and use by one individual does not reduce availability to others, common-pool resources face problems of congestion or overuse, because they are subtractable. A common-pool resource typically consists of a stock variable, or core resource (e.g. water or fish), and a flow variable (i.e., extractable, renewable, noncore units that can be consumed without decimating the core resource). The object of public policy in this regard is to protect and preserve the core resource in a way that allows for continuous harvest and consumption of the noncore units. Chadwick's analysis of crime and criminal behavior emphasized the open-access, common-pool aspects of the enforcement and prosecutorial sides of the British criminal justice system. He recognized free-rider problems within the system and lobbied Parliament to change received institutions in a manner that would prevent crime and encourage more efficiency in law enforcement.

At the beginning of the eighteenth century, law enforcement in England was conducted by unpaid parish constables and magistrates or justices-of-the-peace (JPs). Larger towns added night watchmen and the beadle (i.e., constable's assistant). This system soon broke down under increases in population and human mobility; as a result, metropolitan parishes moved to a system of pay to encourage more people to work as night watchmen. But Chadwick believed that the change ignored serious supply-side problems, such as time, transactions, and information costs.

Chadwick's Preventive Principle. In 1829 Chadwick released his study of a proposal to establish a municipal police force in the city of London. Prepared for Sir

Robert Peel's[7] Select Committee, his report on police was a brilliant application of Benthamite principles and an effective means of emphasizing Chadwick's "preventive principle," which became a key element of so many of his later reforms. This principle maintains that the surest way to reduce waste is not to alleviate inefficiencies after the fact but to keep them from occurring beforehand. Chadwick was a fanatic on the principle of prevention, and he always implied that preventive measures were generally accompanied by large pecuniary economies, most particularly in the areas of crime and police.

An avid believer in the primacy of statistical research, Chadwick commonly conducted "field inquiries" on problems that required administrative solutions. His direct questioning of criminal offenders produced the following behavioral profile: Thieves, he learned, are impatient with steady labor, dislike physical exertion, enjoy leisure, are not easily deterred by the threat of punishment, and value the prospect of uninterrupted success. He learned that criminals make rational "career" choices based on pecuniary gain. Typical of the responses Chadwick got from his interviews was the retort of one Frenchman to the question of why he chose a life of crime. The perpetrator replied: "I keep myself within bounds of moderation: yet as a thief, I realise eighteen francs a day. But at my trade as a tailor I only earn three. I put it to you—would *you* be honest only on that?" ("Préçis," p. 391).

Chadwick concluded that individuals calculate the expected benefits and costs of committing crimes against property, and that for any given booty obtained, the *expected* gain will be greater the higher the probabilities of apprehension and conviction. He did not reject earlier claims by Bentham and others that there are trade-offs between the severity of punishment (for example, death for stealing food) and its certainty, but Chadwick's research indicated that severe punishment was a relatively weak deterrent. From his empirical studies he learned that: (1) existing police administration and jurisprudence placed the risk-costs associated with crime at very low levels, although the punishments were very severe, and (2) a high probability of capture and conviction was the stronger deterrent to crime.

In its basic approach and elements, Chadwick's calculations find a modern parallel in the writings of Isaac Ehrlich, George Stigler, and Gary Becker. He argued that the (probability-adjusted) marginal benefits and costs of criminal behavior could be altered by certain administrative actions that would deter property crimes. In other words, property crimes could be deterred by lowering marginal benefits or raising marginal costs, or both. Some actions could be taken by potential victims, such as arming themselves against thieves; installing locks, home alarm systems, safes; and so forth. From the perspective of the perpetrator, however, Chadwick recognized that the marginal cost of crime was a compound probability of being apprehended, convicted, and punished. He therefore favored administrative arrangements that would improve the probabilities of each of these procedural elements.

Police Effectiveness. Chadwick maintained that crime prevention was the joint responsibility of police and the public, but he identified disincentives for individuals to cooperate with public sector law enforcement that could be traced back to the common-pool problem. Inasmuch as victims were denied compensation, it was difficult to secure their cooperation, or that of witnesses. In a general sense, existing institutional arrangements induced private individuals to underinvest in the

[7] British police to this day are called "bobbies" in honor of Sir Robert, Britain's prime minister who successfully established a metropolitan police force in 1829—over many strenuous objections.

maintenance of public benefits and overinvest in the generation of private, internalized benefits. Chadwick complained:

> By allowing no compensation, and making parties pay the expense of all proceedings for the recovery of stolen property, they are taught to view the crime as a matter with which they may act as best suit their own interests, without reference to the public, which can claim of them no sacrifice, since, in this instance, at least, it [the public] has failed to perform its first duty of giving protection. ("Preventive Police," p. 273)

For their part, the police had no incentive to collect or supply information on theft. As Chadwick noted, in cities where "no reward can be hoped for, no exertion will take place, and . . . no profit can be derived by them [police] from the prevention of the great mass of depredation" ("Preventive Police," p. 277). Crime is encouraged, Chadwick concluded, by the rational behavior of victims and police, when jointly confronted by the common-pool problem.

In order to make the police a more efficient *preventive* force, Chadwick focused on police compensation and administrative economies. He found a close connection between the quality of law enforcement and the compensation of enforcers. His research indicated that police wages were so low in Britain as to encourage as many thefts of high-valued property as possible, "in order that large rewards may be offered for its recovery" ("Preventive Police," p. 254). A solution to the wage problem was to base police wages on productivity, but inability to measure the real services of prevention barred a "final" solution. As a second-best solution Chadwick suggested an adjustment of wages based on the comparison of crimes committed in one police jurisdiction with those committed in other jurisdictions where property was similarly situated. Distortions caused by discrepancies between actual and reported crimes or in the rate of reporting crimes would, of course, remain in such a system, and Chadwick recognized that only improvements in the collection and accuracy of crime data could correct those deficiencies. For this reason he harped on the desirability of a centralized bureau for collecting and disseminating crime data, including descriptions of stolen property.

On most matters of administrative economy Chadwick was a centrist. He challenged specialization and division of labor as principles of preventive efficiency, arguing that where deterrence is the objective, maximum efficiency is promoted by the geographical dispersion of preventive "inputs." Hence he argued for consolidation of functions in cases where public benefits are likely to occur. For example, because it is easier to extinguish fires (and thereby reduce property loss) if detection and extinction occur soon after combustion, Chadwick advocated the consolidation of police and firemen, which places more preventive agents in the field and consequently reduces the time lag in detecting and extinguishing fires. He drove home his point with the force of a scientific rule: "The force of one man for fire service at half a mile is worth four men at three quarters of a mile, worth six men at a mile, and worth eight men at a mile and a half" ("Police and the Extinction of Fires," p. 426). An additional benefit of consolidation would be improved efficiency in the detection of arson. Chadwick viewed this as no small consequence, since reliable estimates put the number of intentional fires in the London metropolis at one-third of the total.

The Economics of Justice. Among the costs faced by lawbreakers is not only the probability of capture but also the probability of conviction. Again Chadwick recognized that in each case the probability of punishment is not a single value but rather the compound result of a series of separate probabilities that arise at each stage of the judicial procedure. Besides the chance of being discovered, pursued, or detected, all governed by the state of police, Chadwick identified corresponding elements of judicial procedure; in particular: (1) the chance, if detected and apprehended, of being indicted; (2) the chance of error in framing the indictment; (3) the chance of dismissal of a bill of indictment by the grand jury; and (4) a number of contingent chances in the trial process, such as the exclusion of evidence; the quality of witnesses, lawyers, judges, and juries; etc.

Chadwick's most vicious attack on existing institutions was on the grand jury system, which he labeled "the stronghold of perjury," a system that gives to delinquents "all the chances (of escape) arising from the ignorance and want of skill both in the jurymen and the witness" ("Preventive Police," p. 298). He estimated that criminals go free more often because of a lack of expertise among jurors than because of improper action taken by judges, and he called for the elimination of the grand jury system as one way of raising costs to the guilty without simultaneously endangering the innocent. In addition to reforms that would streamline court procedures, Chadwick favored institutional arrangements that would lower the individual costs of prosecuting crimes or of providing information necessary to court proceedings.

Chadwick's centralization schemes did not find a sympathetic reception among segments of British society. Fearing loss of individual liberties, the English were highly suspicious of a centralized police. Some feared that a highly centralized police would lead to a replication of the much despised French system of spies in the service of police. Past experience with a judiciary tightly linked to the monarchy also fed resistance. Fear that the police would be used to enforce workhouse incarceration in new versions of the Poor Laws was a major concern among the workers. And many entrenched narrow-interest groups did not want to change the status quo. Politicians and magistrates of the landed gentry opposed Chadwick's plan because it would transfer the "contractual powers" and wealth of the proprietors to a centrally managed national police force. The sharpest opposition, which Chadwick belatedly identified, came from the entrenched, rent-seeking interests of the local JPs, their associated bureaucracies, and the legal profession.

Ultimately, a public police force *was* adopted in England. By 1900, 179 separate police forces had been established in England and Wales, but there was little consolidation of police administration until the twentieth century, when rising crime levels followed armistice from wars, and union agitation helped to break down resistance to change. However, the retention of judicial procedures that made private participation in the justice system costly then, remains to the present day, despite technological improvements and the institution of regular, paid police.

The institutions Chadwick described and attempted to change are imbedded in the modern U.S. system of law enforcement and jurisprudence, making his analysis timely even at this late date. Although technology has reduced information costs, the incentive problems in policing, in prevention, and in the legal system itself are essentially the same. The same rent-seeking interest groups that resisted Chadwick's reforms continue to coalesce against contemporary legal and jurisprudential reforms. In some respects, Chadwick was a man for all seasons.

Disease, Sanitation, and Living Conditions of the Poor

The consensus view is that sanitation reform was Chadwick's greatest achievement. But rather than considered independently, the most striking element of Chadwick's legacy was how the roles that sanitation reform and his prior investigations into English poverty shaped Chadwick's analysis of the entire structure of the British economy, especially concerning the environmental constraints that determined the conditions and behavior of the poor. Chadwick's goal of "sanitizing" England was far from an isolated event; moreover, his efforts in this regard had implications beyond the narrow concerns of public health.

Building on his long involvement in matters of socioeconomic reform, especially regarding the condition of the poor, Chadwick championed sanitation in a concerted attempt to enhance the economic condition and productivity of labor and hence the overall economy. In short, sanitation reform and centralized control were for him the keys to improvement of labor productivity, the elimination of poverty, and, ultimately, economic growth. As before, his argument for centralized provision of sanitation and other social and economic projects was premised on his belief, after diligent study, that local governments were unable to promote productive activities.

Chadwick was alert to the many dimensions of poverty. His early investigations on the condition of the working poor convinced him of the value of human capital—investments in education in particular—as one means to improve the permanent condition of labor and the poor. He also noted that nineteenth-century improvements in medical science had actually improved life expectancy among middle- and upper-class citizens from the previous century. This conundrum—increased life expectancy on average, but wretched conditions and early death amongst the low-income working poor and the destitute (the "dependent class")—was a major motivation for Chadwick's research into sanitation and its effects.

Chadwick's 1842 sanitary report investigated every corner of the United Kingdom and every facet of sanitary conditions. His research led him to the following two generalizations: (1) life expectancies had increased, and (2) substantial benefits would be realized through *restructuring sanitary provision and administration.* As proof of the first proposition, Chadwick cited insurance company life tables, compiled as early as 1828 ("On the Means of Insurance, pp. 384–421). He compiled and compared statistics from Northampton and Sweden. For more than three decades, most British insurance companies used life expectancy from Northampton as the basis for calculating insurance premiums. Statistics on life expectancies in other regions were based on more current data compiled by medical and governmental authorities and a major insurance company (the Equitable table). Chadwick recognized that in almost every category, life expectancy had increased.

Chadwick's campaign for sanitary reform gathered steam after he became aware that there were apparent differences in life expectancies for individuals *in different circumstances*, which led him to question the underlying circumstances that promote sickness and death. As was his custom, Chadwick compiled a mountain of data on the matter.[8] He began by separating the death statistics by county and by source (disease vs. nondisease, the former considered preventable). Then, using his general knowledge of the physical conditions of the counties, he concluded that a substantial portion of all illness was caused by environmental factors. Areas with the highest death rate from disease were those with the most deplorable physical conditions, such as inadequate supplies of fresh water, excess ground moisture, and inadequate waste removal. He found that the number of deaths due to respiratory problems and epidemics of various kinds dwarfed the number from

[8] In this connection Chadwick argued that the poor might take extra measures in the presence of moral hazard created by insurance. (See the box, "Force of Ideas: "Chadwick on Insurance and Infanticide as Moral Hazard.")

other sources. Most importantly, the number of deaths from these two sources alone produced the greatest number of orphans, imposing a high social cost on the state, and a detriment to labor productivity and to economic growth.

The Force of Ideas: Chadwick on Insurance and Infanticide as Moral Hazard

Because death is an obvious certainty for everyone in all classes and in all ages, many people tend to "put away" something during their lives to cover funeral expenses when they inevitably occur. The laboring poor and middle class in mid-nineteenth-century London were no exception. But Chadwick found burial "insurance" sold by undertakers to be riddled with fraud. And in analyzing the situation he discovered an important and modern economic principle: moral hazard.

Chadwick marshaled available statistics to bolster his claim that, from an actuarial perspective, and regardless of the age group involved, burial insurance premiums were excessive. But he looked beyond mere monetary consequences. In his day, workers typically congregated in "public houses" (drinking establishments), which became the logical place to promote burial "clubs" or the sale of burial "insurance." Sensing a profit opportunity, the owners of such establishments became sponsors of burial insurance, sometimes offering a weekly beer allowance to patrons in return for their dues.* Chadwick quickly concluded that monetary incentives of this sort created deviations from acceptable behavior, the most egregious of which was infanticide.

As was his practice, Chadwick conducted field studies. In Manchester he found that children, especially (less valued) females, were put at risk by multiple registrations in burial clubs. The actual cost of burying a child was between 30s. to £1, but the death benefits in Manchester were set at £3–5. Perverse incentives and the high cost of acquiring information (about multiple registrations) led to moral hazard, and unintended consequences. The clerk of the Manchester Union gave testimony regarding seven children in a particular family who died by starvation. Sordid evidence from other English locales confirmed more starvations, poisonings, and maltreatment. Hoping to collect more than once, parents insured their children in as many as nineteen clubs and societies, a practice that proved difficult to limit and/or police. Some of these societies adopted rules that alleviated moral hazard (and adverse selection), much as life insurance companies later adopted the common exclusion for suicide. "Yet," Chadwick said, "frauds are occasionally committed by persons who much know that they have not long to live" (*Report on Sanitary Conditions*, p. 68).

Life insurance coverage up to but not exceeding the amount of insurable interest was the rule among the best life insurance companies, and Chadwick thought that the principle—stated legislatively during the reign of George III—should be applied to burial insurance as well. Ever the economist, Chadwick thought that a collateral means of preventing infanticide was to *lower the expense* of funerals, which would, in turn, reduce "the temptations to crime constituted by the apparent expedience of the insurance of the payment of large sums to meet that expence" (*Report on Sanitary Conditions*, p. 69). In other words, perverse incentives could be addressed by changing rules and regulations affecting specific markets.

*Death announcements were often signals of a forthcoming "celebration." As part of his investigation Chadwick directed a question to the secretary of one of the better organized burial societies regarding how the insurance proceeds were used. Mr. Gardner, the secretary, answered: "'The family provide themselves with drink, and the friends coming also drink. I have known this to be to such excess, that the undertaker's men, who always take whatever drink is given them, are frequently unfit to perform their duty, and have reeled in carrying the coffin. At these times it is very distressing. The men who stand as mutes at the door, as they stand out in the cold, are supposed to require most drink, and receive it most liberally. I have seen these men reel about the road, and after the burial we have been obliged to put these mutes and their staves into the interior of the hearse and drive them home, as they were incapable of walking. After the return from the funeral, the mourners commonly have drink again at the house. This drinking at the funeral is a very great evil" (*Report on Sanitary Conditions*, p. 60).

The same official testified that the child of a laboring family "had been entered in at least ten burial clubs; and its parents had six other children, who only lived from nine to eighteen months respectively. They had received £20 from several burial clubs for one of these children, and expected to receive at least as much on account of this child" (*Report on Sanitary Conditions*, p. 64). Testimony was given in a criminal proceeding from an acquaintance that "she was a fine fat child shortly after her birth" but that she soon became quite thin and did not get a sufficiency of food. In spite of the testimony, the case was dismissed by the jury due to a lack of evidence concerning the exact cause of death (*Report on Sanitary Conditions*, p. 65).

Chadwick proposed changes in sanitary engineering and administration to reduce these costs and eliminate disease-promoting factors. His favored solution was to establish an integrated water and sewer system to which every house was connected, a system that he sought to show was privately profitable as well as socially efficient. The old system allowed all manner of water contamination. Much illness could be traced to water-borne and air-borne contaminants generated from existing burial practices (i.e., "graveyard externalities"). Disposal of human excrement, primitive by modern standards, was another source of disease and contamination. Chadwick believed that renovated and modernized water delivery systems would work to eliminate disease and water-borne epidemics, and that the resulting full price to consumers would constitute an incentive for these improvements.

Changing Economic Constraints

Chadwick's investigations led him to conclude that the condition of the laboring classes was being held in check by disease and debilitation caused by environmental factors that could be willfully changed by introducing proper sanitation and hygiene. The problems to be corrected were not merely local but national in scope. They included overcrowding, excessive dampness, and accumulation of the by-products of human existence. To eliminate these problems, Chadwick proposed a multidimensional program, all facets of which were designed to encourage the development of sanitary habits by lowering the full cost of hygiene. The first matter was to remove waste from the individual inhabitants and then to remove it from the vicinity of the larger population. Next it was necessary to instill habits of personal hygiene in every inhabitant. Finally, it was necessary to improve housing and working conditions. Chadwick put the onus for the first two squarely on the government.

The first public action consisted of the installation of a water and sewer system with complete connectivity to every household. Chadwick was adamant on the inclusion of a water supply to all buildings not only for personal use but also for the immediate removal of waste. He noted that "it will be manifest that for an efficient system of house cleansing and sewerage, it is indispensible that proper supplies of pure water should be provided" (*Report on the Sanitary Condition*, p. 135). With the installation of the water and sewer system, "the chief obstacles to the immediate removal of decomposing refuse of towns and habitations," namely "the expense and annoyance of the hand labour and cartage requisite for the purpose" would be eliminated (*Supplementary Report*, p. 423). Chadwick estimated that costs would be reduced to one-twentieth or one-thirtieth of the former costs and at the lower price, a greater quantity of public hygiene would result.

Along with the reduced cost of removing waste, Chadwick asserted that the delivery of water to every household would promote personal hygiene. Under the old system of cisterns located in each neighborhood; "the minor comforts of cleanliness are of course foregone, to avoid the immediate and greater discomforts of having to fetch the water" (*Report on the Sanitary Condition*, p. 141). Incentives matter, of course, to individuals in every social class. "Even with persons of a higher condition, the habits are greatly dependent on the conveniences, and it is observed, that when the supplies of water into the houses of the middle class are cut off by the pipes being frozen, and when it is necessary to send for water to a distance, the house-cleansings and washings are diminished by the inconvenience" (*Report on the Sanitary Condition*, p. 141). In contemporary terms Chadwick was arguing that the full-cost (including time costs) of cleanliness has an effect on the quantity of cleanliness consumed. Chadwick recognized that the *full*-cost of water was the sum of its purchase price plus the opportunity wage rate per hour times the number of hours it took to fetch the water for home use. To provide the appropriate economic incentive for improved personal hygiene he called for a reduction in the full-cost of water by having it home-delivered. Once again, the solution to a public problem required the creation of an artificial identity of interest. The desired (public) result of home sanitation could be ensured by the proper structuring of economic incentives. To this end he pointed out that "if the labourer or his wife or child would otherwise be employed, even in the lowest paid labour or in knitting stockings, the cost of fetching water by hand is extravagantly high" (*Report on the Sanitary Condition*, p. 142).

Beyond the public provision of water and sewer systems, Chadwick saw opportunities where employers could greatly improve the conditions of the poor and the working class simply by changing the constraints they faced. The provision of suitable housing is a case in point. Chadwick called for capitalists to undertake "the erection of dwellings of a superior order" (*Supplementary Report*, p. 298). Although he appealed to benevolence initially, his research led him to conclude that the benefits to employers would in most cases exceed their costs. He cited as evidence the experience of one entrepreneur who, strictly out of benevolence, invested in improved housing and provided schools for the children of his employees. Yet, he "was surprised by a pecuniary gain ground in the superior order and efficiency of his establishment, in the regularity and trustworthiness of his work people" (*Supplementary Report*, p. 301). Chadwick believed that proper housing would improve worker productivity by providing greater proximity to place of work and by reducing "all the attacks of disease, occasioned by exposure to wet and cold and the additional fatigue in traversing long distances to and from his home to the place of work" (*Supplementary Report*, p. 299).

Besides the provision of housing, Chadwick maintained that the health of the working population was greatly affected by their work environment and that factories could be designed to promote the well-being of the workforce. He cited the case of a cotton mill engineered with the health of the workers in mind. The factory was designed to provide an abundance of fresh air and a means of controlling the climate. Moreover, the machinery was installed in a manner that maximized protection against industrial accidents. Ever mindful of costs and benefits Chadwick observed that "the first expense of such a building is higher than a manufactory of the old construction, but it appeared to possess countervailing economic advantages to the capitalist" (*Supplementary Report*, p. 307). He clearly believed that the laborers' condition could be altered by changing the constraints faced by workers and that promoting benevolence only goes so far, but appeals to the profit motive can be ultimately effective.

Sanitation and the Economy

Chadwick clearly envisioned sanitation as a public good, to be supplied, when possible, through the franchise-bidding process. His defense of the sanitary principle has had a lasting impact on advanced economies. Water supply and sewage disposal systems are almost everywhere the consequence of public expenditure today, sometimes with, and sometimes without, franchise bidding. Chadwick saw an economic link between government outlays on improved sanitation and the benefits to be expected from implementing sanitation reform. He thought that part of the social benefit equation was a prolonged average life span. Although he investigated the difference in death rates between and within rural and urban districts, Chadwick based his arguments concerning mortality, correctly as it turns out, on class differences.[9]

Chadwick considered it axiomatic that early mortality was preventable by improved sanitation—in particular by providing means of pure water delivery and reduced-cost waste disposal. Lower costs to the *individual* of personal hygiene saved lives by preventing the creation and spread of disease. Among the lower classes particularly, these improvements meant greater labor productivity and lower death rates. But these *private* benefits had spillover effects on the *public* economy. Lower death rates, as suggested in table 10-1 (on the following page), reduced the number of widows and orphans that were destined to become wards of the state. Thus, the cost of sanitation reform—at least partly provided by the government—had to be weighed against the benefits to government (cost saving) from reduced welfare and Poor Laws relief to the lower and destitute segments of society. When private benefits—greater worker productivity and business profits (a net gain)—are added to the social savings, Chadwick considered sanitation reform as a winning proposition. Preventable early mortality clearly supported utilitarian goals. Critically, Chadwick, as had Bentham, appealed to private (net benefit producing) incentives as well as to public provisions to promote these ends.

Public Goods and Institutional Forms of Competition

The idea that public policy consists of altering the institutional arrangements of society so as to induce self-interested individuals to behave in a way conducive to the public good is a decidedly Benthamite notion. But the practice of Benthamite politics is facilitated best by concentrating the ownership and control of property rights in the hands of a central authority, thus infusing this view with a certain "despotic" flavor.[10] Chadwick almost seemed to view centralized control as a *prerequisite* for eliminating waste, and he was so committed to this principle that he reformulated the notion of competition to accommodate it to the exigencies of central authority.

After thirty years of investigating, designing, and reformulating myriad public policies, Chadwick consolidated his views on the proper mode of government interventions and presented them in a "position paper" to the Royal Statistical Society. Citing the coexistence of sound and unsound principles of competition, Chadwick contrasted the orthodox view (which assumed large numbers of rival firms that shared the market) with a "new" concept of competition that assumed rivalry

[9] On the adequacy of the statistical component of Chadwick's *Report on the Sanitary Conditions*, James Hanley argues that Chadwick was correct in his conclusions, despite contemporary criticisms to the contrary ("Edwin Chadwick").

[10] It is precisely on this point that Mill and Chadwick parted company on the matter of economic policy. Chadwick was an avowed centralist, whereas Mill distrusted the centralized concentration of power.

Table 10-1 The Chief Causes of Death Producing Orphanage

Diseases, etc.	Manchester Union Deaths	Whitechapel Union Deaths	Bethual Green Parish Deaths	Strand Union Deaths	Oakham-Upingham Unions Deaths	Alston, with Garrigill Parish Deaths	Bath Union Deaths	Avg. Age of Deceased	TOTALS	
									Deaths	No. of Orphans
Respiratory	500	212	147	95	69	47	40	51	1,110	2,218
Epidemic, Endemic, Contagious	146	65	73	28	34	9	4	46	359	862
Other	129	68	104	32	36	7	8	54	384	694
Violent Deaths	94	44	20	16	23	13	5	46	215	508
Nervous	74	41	38	17	25	3	5	55	203	296
Undescribed	63	40	7	9	6	NA	2	47	127	171
Digestive	60	16	10	10	14	5	3	54	118	180
Old Age	84	104	46	13	47	5	NA	74	299	56
Total	1,150	590	445	220	254	89	67	53	2,815	4,985

among several bidders to win an *exclusive* right to serve the entire market. Chadwick labeled the orthodox notion "competition within the field" and his "new" principle "competition for the field." Describing his strong support for the latter, Chadwick declared:

> As opposed to that form of competition [within the field], I proposed as an administrative principle, competition "for the field," that is to say, that the whole field of service should be put on behalf of the public for competition—on the only condition on which efficiency, as well as the utmost cheapness, was practicable, namely the possession, by one capital or by one establishment, of the entire field, which could be most efficiently and economically administered by one, with full securities towards the public for the performance of the requisite service during a given period. ("Results of Different Principles," p. 385)

Possessed of an early notion of "public goods"—those that provide benefits external to the immediate user—Chadwick vigorously sought to apply the principle of competition within the field to this class of goods. He considered it wasteful to implement or enforce a competitive system based on decentralized property rights, so he proposed an alternative system in which government, representing society, would buy out competing suppliers and bid out the exclusive right to supply the public good. Chadwick called this principle "contract management."

Illustrating Contract Management. Figure 10-1 sets out Chadwick's principle in more modern dress. The negatively sloped cost curves are those of a public utility, transportation firm, or natural monopoly. An unrestrained profit-maximizing monopolist would produce quantity Q_p and sell it at price P_p. Chadwick's point is that given certain conditions and alternative property rights assignment, the existence of natural monopoly need not imply monopoly price and profits. Specifically,

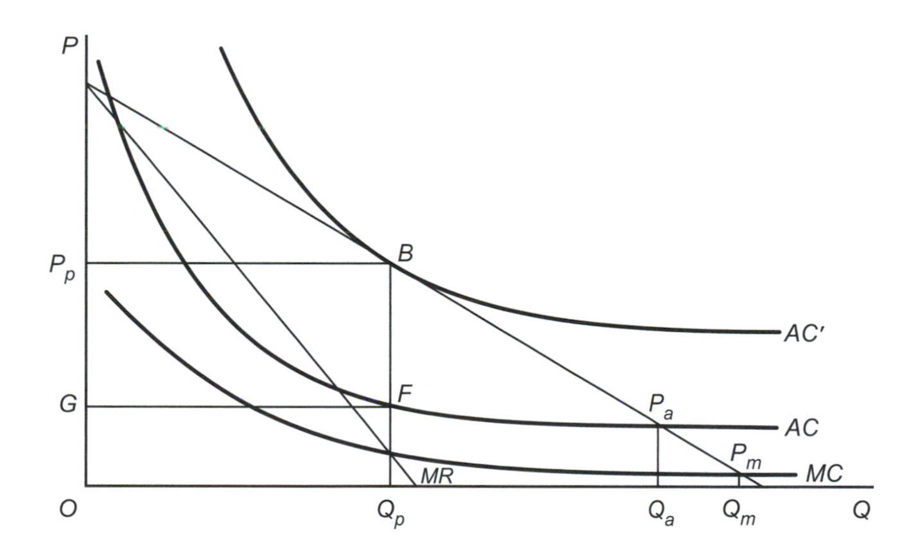

Figure 10-1 In the absence of price and/or quantity contract specifications, average cost will increase from *AC* to *AC′*, resulting in a transfer of welfare from the monopolist to society by GP_pBF. If the government specifies some quantity Q_a to be supplied, bidding will continue until price reaches P_a.

given that an elastic supply of competitive bidders exists and that the costs of collusion among bidders are high enough, the government could purchase the small number of competing firms and let out for bid the exclusive right to supply the good or service in question.

A number of institutional and contractual arrangements are possible in this context. The government may or may not provide fixed plant and capital equipment. The contract period may be of fixed duration, or it may be reopened at the discretion of the government. Certainty and/or perfect information may or may not be assumed on the part of some or all parties. For example, treatment of windfall gains and losses may be made part of the model. Solutions will, of course, vary according to the nature of the assumptions made.

Some possible solutions may be shown with the aid of figure 10-1. Assume that certainty and perfect information exist on the part of the government and bidders and that the government supplies the fixed capital. The problem, then, is to investigate how the nature of the contract specifications alters the solution. If price and/or quantity are not specified in the terms of the contract, the maximum bid made by suppliers to the government does not change the solution except for a transfer of welfare from the monopolist to society. Such a transfer is depicted in figure 10-1 by the amount GP_p/BF. It would in effect raise the average cost to the successful supplier to AC', resulting in a Chamberlinian "tangency solution" (see chapter 20) between AC' and the demand curve at price P_p.

The more usual case—the one that Chadwick featured in the case of railroads—is the situation in which the government contractually specifies some minimum quantity (and/or quality) to be offered and lets potential suppliers engage in a bidding process. If, for example, the government contractually specifies some quantity Q_a to be supplied, bidding will proceed to price P_a, at which only normal profits are being earned. The important point is that Chadwick's principle makes the attainment of a "competitive" solution (where average revenue equals average cost and economic profit is zero) a possibility through public ownership and private operation. Chadwick favored this approach, among other reasons, because he did not believe that the government could operate anything efficiently. All this implies that the competitive bidding process, given altered property-rights assignment, might approximate at least some of the results of the orthodox model of competition, where competition is defined as a market structure of many rival, independent firms. Whether or not this is a practical result depends on numerous institutional forces, including the mode of consolidation, design of contracts, cost of acquiring information, and so on.

Applications of Contract Management. In the 1860s, Chadwick became the leading British proponent of the nationalization of railroads. His argument did not support government operation of the railways but rather consolidation under the principle of contract management. In Chadwick's view, railroads were a natural monopoly characterized by fractious management and wasteful competition. However, he did not think that government ownership and operation would be an improvement. On the surface, he appeared to be in the best tradition of laissez-faire when he argued that "the Government is utterly incapable of any direct management of manufactures, or of anything else of an administrative character" ("Proposal," p. 202). Nevertheless, his proposal called for concentration of authority in the hands of a central administration. By 1860, moreover, Chadwick could cite the government's successful implementation of a contract management scheme for the provision of postal services.

Chadwick's investigation into the conditions of water supply and public health in London revealed that the problem was one of natural monopoly.[11] Thus, he regarded competition within the field as inappropriate. He found the field of service currently divided among seven separate companies, several of which had become multiform monopolies, duplicating one another's facilities, so that two or three sets of pipes ran down many streets, doling out insufficient supplies of water of inferior and often unwholesome quality. Chadwick estimated that consolidation under the principle of contract management could save £100,000 per year, which could then be used for exploration and development of new water supplies.

Chadwick noted also that municipal gas companies in the city of Paris competed initially under an almost identical situation of natural monopoly. A study by the French government into the cost and supply conditions of several independent gas companies found the charges excessive. The city then undertook consolidation according to Chadwick's principle, with the result that customer charges declined 30 percent, the quality of gas supplied improved, and the value of shareholders' assets increased by 24 percent ("Results of Different Principles," p. 388). Chadwick presented additional evidence of two gas companies in northern England whose prime cost of supplying gas dropped by almost two-thirds after the kind of consolidation he championed.

Chadwick attributed the rejection of his proposed administrative reform of London water to the vigorous protests of vested interests. Undeterred, he asserted that the traditional form of competition over the decade of the 1850s burdened consumers with higher prices, imposed more risk on stockholders, and inflicted on the public inadequate water quality and delivery systems. He had little trouble coming up with a never ending list of possibilities for contract management. The provision of beer, bread, and public taxis were candidates. Importantly, however, he seems often to have been describing markets in disequilibrium. In such circumstances almost any market could be shown to contain inefficiencies, thus becoming a candidate for subrogation of property rights. This is a severe deficiency in Chadwick's theory of "competition for the field" inasmuch as it may provide "efficiency" at the cost of free enterprise and inviolable property rights.

A Brief Summary of Chadwick's Approach

Clearly, sanitation reform—which in the West is appropriately credited to Edwin Chadwick—was a central element of the utilitarian agenda in nineteenth-century England. Other reforms—mostly financed by taxation and local assessments—in the fields of education, health, and crime prevention rounded out the program. Chadwick was an energetic, driving force spearheading all these reforms. His favoritism for centralized authority to effect reforms was greeted with mistrust in certain quarters, but inasmuch as his arguments were always empirically based and innovative, he deserved to be taken seriously, as J. S. Mill, for one, did. Invention and application of the concept of franchise bidding was only one example of Chadwick's innovativeness and perspicacity. He understood the principle and consequences of asymmetric information, the nature of common-pool problems, time costs, and many other "modern" microanalytic principles, which he applied to economic issues and to the utilitarian agenda.

[11] A natural monopoly is said to exist when it is technically more efficient to have a single producer or enterprise. In some cases, the survival of a single firm is the natural outcome of competition among several firms.

Conclusion

Both Mill and Chadwick shared Bentham's belief in utilitarianism, the critical nature and importance of incentives, the efficacy of creating artificial identities of interest, and the philosophic acceptance of the "opportunity" principle—best enunciated by Mill as the proposition that "all start fair." This last principle understood that differences in genetics, ambition, and energy would allow for differential end results but maintained that each generation should start out with equal access to education, good health, and other opportunities. This idea of equal opportunity, though enshrined in the United States Declaration of Independence, represented a major departure for nineteenth-century Britain. Both writers believed that the goal could be approached and the class system eventually dismantled. Mill advocated high or prohibitive death taxes, for example, as a means to that end.

Despite agreement regarding the aims of economic policy, Mill and Chadwick worked two different sides of the utilitarian street. Mill defended inter vivos gifts but essentially argued that property rights cease upon death. He therefore supported a high and progressive inheritance tax on the estates of the dead. Like Chadwick he was keen to build incentives into government programs, but he rejected the kind of centralization espoused by his friend and colleague. Mill championed income distribution supportive of a strong middle class that functioned within a market-oriented, private-property system. He based his support of the Poor Laws on social justice, but he worried that income assistance, without an adequate quid pro quo extracted from its recipients, would inevitably "enslave" a segment of society in a permanent, counterproductive welfare system. Chadwick had similar concerns regarding "outdoor" relief for the poor but burrowed into the underlying problems—education and sanitation—which helped create the demand for poor relief.

Empirical investigations were a core practice of Chadwick's utilitarianism but made little impact on Mill's agenda. Mill always deferred to Chadwick on matters of fact, as we have already mentioned. His early education in Ricardian economics channeled his mind toward abstract deduction, not empirical investigations. He reviewed and admired Chadwick's voluminous writings and offered advice to his friend along the way, but his reluctance to endorse Chadwick's plan to nationalize industries (railroads) or socialize property rights (for example, funeral and cabriolet markets) was not deterred by Chadwick's evidence. Although neither writer was a socialist in any traditional sense, Chadwick did countenance market interventions when his studies indicated a positive net utility outcome from designated policies. He wanted to eliminate waste from many particular markets, believing that a transfer of property rights from open competition to a government-created contract-letting body of "experts" could and would maximize utility.

References

Baysinger, Barry, and Tollison, R. D. "Chaining Leviathan: The Case of Gladstonian Finance," *History of Political Economy*, vol. 12 (Summer 1980), pp. 206–213.

Bentham, Jeremy. *Supply without Burden: or Escheat vice Taxation*. London: J. Debrett, 1795.

Chadwick, Edwin. "On the Means of Insurance," *Westminster Review*, vol. 9 (1828), pp. 384–421.

———. "Preventive Police," *London Review*, vol. 1 (1829), pp. 252–308.

———. *On an Inquiry into the Sanitary Condition of the Labouring Population of Great Britain*. London: W. Clowes and Sons. Reprinted as *Report on the Sanitary Condition*

of the Labouring Population of Great Britain, M. W. Flinn (ed.). Edinburgh: Edinburgh University Press, 1965 [1842].
———. *Report on the Sanitary Conditions of the Labouring Population of Great Britain: A Supplementary Report on the Results of a Special Inquiry into the Practice of Interment in Towns*. London: W. Clowes and Sons, 1843.
———. "Results of Different Principles of Legislation and Administration in Europe; Of Competition for the Field, as Compared with Competition within the Field of Service," *Royal Statistical Society Journal*, vol. 22 (1859), pp. 381–420.
———. "Opening Address," *Journal of the Royal Statistical Society of London*, vol. 25 (1862).
———. "On the Proposal That the Railways Should Be Purchased by the Government," *Journal of the Society of Arts*, vol. 9 (February 1866), p. 203ff.
———. "The Police and the Extinction of Fires," in B. W. Richardson (ed.), *The Health of Nations: A Review of the Works of Edwin Chadwick*, vol. 2. London: Longmans, 1887.
———. "Précis of Preventive Police," in B. W. Richardson (ed.), *The Health of Nations: A Review of the Works of Edwin Chadwick*, vol. 2. London: Longmans, 1887.
Hanley, James. "Edwin Chadwick and the Poverty of Statistics," *Medical History*, vol. 46 (2002), pp. 21–40.
Mill, J. S. *Principles of Political Economy*, W. J. Ashley (ed.). New York: A. M. Kelley, Publishers, 1965 [1848].
———. *Principles of Political Economy*, in *Collected Works of John Stuart Mill*, J. M. Robson (ed.), vols. 2 and 3. Toronto: University of Toronto Press, 1966 [1848].
———. *Essays on Economics and Society*, in *Collected Works of John Stuart Mill*, J. M. Robson (ed.), vols. 4 and 5. Toronto: University of Toronto Press, 1967.
———. *The Later Letters of John Stuart Mill, 1848–1873*, in *Collected Works of John Stuart Mill*, F. E. Mineka and D. N. Lindley (eds.), vols. 14–17. Toronto: University of Toronto Press, 1972.
Mokyr, Joel. *The Enlightened Economy: An Economic History of Britain, 1700-1850*. New Haven, CT: Yale University Press, 2010.
Peto, Morton. *Taxation: Its Levy and Expenditure, Past and Future: Being an Inquiry into our Financial Policy*. New York: D. Appleton, 1863.
Soward, Alfred W. and Willan, W. E. *The Taxation of Capital*. London: Waterlow and Sons, 1919.

Notes for Further Reading

J. S. Mill's many policy views are featured in the masterful and very accessible collection of his writings in the Toronto series. See especially Mill's *Essays on Economics and Society* (see references). There is some debate as to whether Mill was in the vanguard of those supporting progressive policies regarding income distribution, the equality of women, trade unions, public education, and welfare programs. On this matter see Pedro Schwartz, *The New Political Economy of J. S. Mill* (Durham, NC: Duke University Press, 1972); and R. B. Ekelund, Jr., and R. D. Tollison, "The New Political Economy of J. S. Mill: The Means to Social Justice," *Canadian Journal of Economics*, vol. 9 (May 1976), pp. 213–231. A contrasting view is presented by E. G. West, "J. S. Mill's Redistribution Policy: New Political Economy or Old?" *Economic Inquiry*, vol. 16 (October 1978), pp. 570–586, who asserts that Mill was a Victorian moralist, a blatant Malthusian with regard to the prospects of the poor, and an elitist supporter of labor unions; but see the rejoinder by Ekelund and Tollison that follows West's article.

For more on Mill's policy views, see Samuel Hollander, *The Economics of John Stuart Mill*, vol. 2 (Toronto: University of Toronto Press, 1985). Hollander (pp. 897–899) lends his support to the idea that Mill was motivated by concern for the working poor. In Hollander's wake, some curious and idiosyncratic interpretations have floated to the surface, especially one advanced by Oskar Kurer: "John Stuart Mill and the Welfare State,"

History of Political Economy, vol. 23 (Winter 1991), pp. 713–730, in which Mill is advanced as a champion of "modern welfare-state legislation." See also, same author, "John Stuart Mill: Liberal or Utilitarian?" *The European Journal of the History of Economic Thought*, vol. 6 (Summer 1999), pp. 200–215, in which Kurer states that Mill was not a liberal in the classical sense; rather he linked the theory of government intervention to the principle of utility through a social welfare function.

Semantics are of limited interest, but Mill's view of tax policy as a tool to effect short-term and long-term economic reform is an issue of far greater importance. In this regard, even though Mill devised his views in the context of nineteenth-century British economic and social conditions, they are clearly and distinctly "modern," which is the position advanced by R. B. Ekelund, Jr., and Doug Walker, "J. S. Mill on the Income Tax Exemption and Inheritance Taxes: The Evidence Reconsidered," *History of Political Economy*, vol. 28 (Winter 1996), pp. 559–581. The issues regarding inheritance that Mill raised are still debated and unresolved. See, for example, John Cunliffe and Guido Erreygers, (eds.), *Inherited Wealth, Justice and Equality* (New York: Routledge, 2012).

Notwithstanding the debate over the "newness" of Mill's policy views, Pedro Schwartz (The *New Political Economy*) has made a very good case for his conclusion that the critiques of laissez-faire by Cairnes, Sidgwick, Marshall, and Pigou would have been unthinkable without Mill's earlier efforts. Schwartz concludes: "From Mill stemmed the neoclassical (one might say, the Cambridge) tradition of critical evaluation of the working of the market" (p. 151). More than once Mill argued that interventions were necessary in the case of natural monopoly. As an advocate of government ownership of waterworks (production and distribution) and gas companies, Mill argued for municipal purchase and administration of these companies where possible. As Schwartz has shown with respect to Mill's views on the regulation of the London water supply, however, Mill was very concerned that a centralized board not be given power to consolidate water services; see P. Schwartz, "John Stuart Mill and Laissez-Faire: London Water," *Economica*, vol. 23 (February 1966), pp. 71–83. In spite of his earlier advocacy of centralization in the case of the Poor Laws administration, Mill (under the possible influence of de Tocqueville) came to distrust centralized concentration of authority. Provision of telegraph and railway services may have been an exception, however; see the appendix to R. B. Ekelund, Jr., and E. O. Price, "Sir Edwin Chadwick on Competition and the Social Control of Industry: Railroads," *History of Political Economy*, vol. 11 (Summer 1979), pp. 213–239.

Although Chadwick was the quintessential economic policy maker of the nineteenth century, relatively little has been written of his policy exploits by economists. Some notable exceptions are R. A. Lewis, "Edwin Chadwick and the Railway Labourers," *Economic History Review*, vol. 3 (1950), pp. 107–118; and R. F. Hébert, "Edwin Chadwick and the Economics of Crime," *Economic Inquiry*, vol. 16 (October 1977), pp. 539–550. Some of Chadwick's policy views were presented by E. O. Price, "Contributions of Sir Edwin Chadwick to Economic Policy," unpublished PhD dissertation (College Station: Texas A & M University, 1979). Chadwick's policy and theoretical arguments have now been collected and extended by Robert B. Ekelund, Jr. and Edward O. Price, III, *The Economics of Edwin Chadwick: Incentives Matter* (Cheltenham: Edward Elgar, 2012).

Two recent papers address particular gaps in our knowledge of the extent of Chadwick's utilitarian approach to economic policy. For a survey of the breadth of Chadwick's approach see A. W. Dues, "The Scope of Chadwick's Bidding Scheme," *Journal of Institutional and Theoretical Economics*, vol. 150 (September 1994), pp. 524–536. See also, R. B. Ekelund, Jr., and G. S. Ford, "Nineteenth Century Urban Market Failure? Chadwick on Funeral Industry Regulation," *Journal of Regulatory Economics*, vol. 12 (July 1997), pp. 27–52, which underscores Chadwick's enduring ability to combine rhetoric and economic argument in support of a regulatory apparatus aimed at controlling funeral services and cemetery plots.

After a long hiatus, the Bentham–Chadwick plan of contract management has been recast as the "Chicago Theory of Regulation." Harold Demsetz, "Why Regulate Utilities?" *Journal of Law & Economics*, vol. 11 (October 1968), pp. 55–65, explicated a principle of competition whose origin he attributed to Edwin Chadwick; but see W. M. Crain and R. B. Ekelund, Jr., "Chadwick and Demsetz on Competition and Regulation," *Journal of Law & Economics*, vol. 19 (April 1976), pp. 149–162. It is important to note that practical implementation of the "Chadwick plan" may engender many problems not anticipated by Chadwick or his modern defenders. Critics argue that the design and implementation of optimal contracts may present as many or more difficulties than those found in more traditional forms of regulation. The problems of contract management vary with the technical and competitive characteristics of the industry and must be developed in the context of a case study. For an interesting example of the latter, see O. E. Williamson, "Franchise Bidding for Natural Monopolies—In General and with Respect to CATV," *Bell Journal of Economics*, vol. 7 (Spring 1976), pp. 73–104.

Despite possible impediments and misgivings, the "Chadwick plan" of franchise bidding for the exclusive right to service is alive and well. Strong and vigorous support for such plans has emerged in Europe, Asia, and the United States. With respect to waterworks in particular, see Steven H. Hanke and J. K. Walters, "Privatizing Waterworks: Learning from the French Experience," *Journal of Applied Corporate Finance*, vol. 23 (2011), pp 30–35. More generally see Steve H. Hanke (ed.), *Prospects for Privatization*. New York: The Academy of Political Science, 1987.

An appreciation of Chadwick's incredible foresight and creativity in the policy analysis of economic problems can be gleaned from the comparison of his views on crime with the "latest word" by economists on the subject. See Hébert, "Chadwick and the Economics of Crime"; G. S. Becker, "Crime and Punishment: An Economic Approach," *Journal of Political Economy*, vol. 76 (March/April 1968), pp. 169–217; G. S. Becker and G. J. Stigler, "Law Enforcement, Malfeasance, and Compensation of Enforcers," *Journal of Legal Studies*, vol. 3 (January 1974), pp. 1–18; and G. J. Stigler, "The Optimum Enforcement of Laws," *Journal of Political Economy*, vol. 78 (May/June 1970), pp. 526–536.

On the common-pool problem and how Chadwick's recognition of it fit into his reform scheme, see Bruce Benson, "Are Public Goods Really Common Pools? Considerations of the Evolution of Policing and Highways in England," *Economic Inquiry*, vol. 32 (April 1994), pp. 249–271; and R. B. Ekelund, Jr., and Cheryl Dorton, "Criminal Justice Institutions as a Common Pool: The 19th Century Analysis of Edwin Chadwick," *Journal of Economic Behavior and Organization*, vol. 50 (March 2002), pp. 1–24. In some areas of thought Chadwick was neither unknown nor elusive. So linked was he in the public mind with sanitation reform that he became known to his contemporaries as "Drains" Chadwick. For a discussion of his sanitation reforms from the standpoint of engineering and public health, see Maurice Marston, *Sir Edwin Chadwick, 1800-1890* (Boston: Small, Maynard and Company, 1925); Anthony Brundage, *England's "Prussian Minister": Edwin Chadwick and the Politics of Government Growth, 1832–1854* (University Park, PA: Pennsylvania State University Press, 1988). Christopher Hamlin, *Public Health and Social Justice in the Age of Chadwick, Britain: 1800–1854* (Cambridge: Cambridge University Press, 1998), provides an engaging and stimulating perspective on the politics surrounding Chadwick's public sanitation campaign and the rise of science as an apparent neutral authority in policy making. Hamlin carefully retells the story of the foundations of public health in Industrial Revolution Britain not as the triumph of responsible government over urban filth but as a politically savvy choice to undermine the potential of public medicine to provide a basis for radical criticism of laissez-faire capitalism.

Although cloaked in controversy, Chadwick's role in the development of public health in the United Kingdom is prodigious. The one hundredth anniversary of his death (1990) and the one hundred and fiftieth anniversary of the first Public Health Act (1998) was an occasion for serious and deserved plaudits for him in the U.S. and abroad.

11

Nineteenth-Century Heterodox Economic Thought

In previous chapters we saw how classical economics was previewed by Richard Cantillon and the Physiocrats, formed by Adam Smith, and reshaped by Bentham, Malthus, Ricardo, Say, Senior, and J. S. Mill, among others. By the middle of the nineteenth century "political economy" was a reasonably unified, coherent body of analysis that represented a fledgling science. As part of its maturation process, classical economics became an orthodox discipline. But from the very beginning it was subject to many attacks. This chapter surveys some of the dissident voices raised against classical economic orthodoxy. Even though strident and diverse in nature, criticism did not defeat or replace classical political economy and its central doctrines of economic development and income distribution. Nevertheless, the writers surveyed in this chapter had an impact on the formation of economic thinking. Indeed, the tradition of heterodox thought within the corpus of economic theory and analysis continues to this very day.

Between the major accomplishments of Smith (1776) and Mill (1848) momentous events of social, economic, and political significance transpired on both sides of the Atlantic. In North America, the Declaration of Independence signaled the birth of a new nation in the same year that Smith published *The Wealth of Nations*. Peopled mainly by European emigrés, the new nation faced many problems in its initial drive toward decolonization and economic self-sufficiency. But the United States of America was rich in territory and natural resources, requiring only a steady stream of people, which turmoil in other parts of the world promoted. In Europe, the French Revolution led to social and economic reorganization, as the *ancien régime* melted away. Great Britain oversaw the incubation of industrialism and the rise of the factory system—what historians refer to as the Industrial Revolution. These transformations posed different challenges to different nations and provoked different criticisms by different writers.

In England an early protest against the dire predictions of Ricardo was raised by Thomas Hodgskin and William Thompson, leaders of a group that came to be known as "Ricardian Socialists." This group offered an antidote to classical economics, which was able to withstand the assault of the dissenters by virtue of the theoretical elegance of the Ricardian system. In France, the early promise of the French Revolution was severely tested by the Reign of Terror that followed. Those who heralded the passing of the old regime as the triumph of reason over privilege saw their hopes dashed by the aftermath of the revolution. And in Germany, a country splintered by numerous political and economic boundaries, philosophical forces, quite distinct from the British or French variants, were at work. For its part, the United States of America, though flush with the reality of its recent independence, remained a net importer of ideas.

Global social and intellectual ferment was fanned by several philosophic winds. On the one hand British industrialism was propelled by a high degree of pragmatism, which led to practical augmentations of productive capacity. On the other, Continental society was entrenched in Cartesian rationalism, which rejected material things in the search for inner truth. In contrast to their British counterparts European philosophers placed more emphasis on group than individual activity. Rousseau, for example, though aware that property rights are conducive to individual and social progress, argued that there are desirable *social* uses of property. And Hegel viewed freedom, not in the Lockian sense as a relation between individual and group, but in terms of *associations* with others, such as family, church, and state. The major attacks on classical economics came from Continental writers, though not exclusively.

■ Romanticism

Romanticism arose to smite classic rationalism. Its themes were exalted fantasy, unrepressed passion, and depth of feeling. It found adherents throughout Europe, and in England it was targeted mainly against utilitarianism. Occasionally cloaked in individualistic guise, Romanticism mainly fostered a collectivist outlook. As the favorite form of collectivism, socialism arose initially from a combination of three factors: the pre-Romantic conception of the bourgeoisie and its class struggle against privileged groups, the supposition of common ownership of land and tools in primitive society, and Rousseau's idea of the equality of men.

With the exception of Rousseau, all the great philosophers of the French Enlightenment viewed history as a steady progression of humans toward reason and truth. In the economic arena, this view seemed to be affirmed by the rapid expansion of production and productive capacity in the first half of the nineteenth century. But many people considered economic development uneven. The working class generally received low wages, worked long hours, and toiled under adverse factory conditions. This led throughout the nineteenth century to "unorthodox" attempts (i.e., opposed to the efforts of Mill and Chadwick) by champions of the working class to "socialize" economics. These attempts ranged from the paternalism of Robert Owen (1771–1858), a wealthy British industrialist, to the fantasies of Charles Fourier (1772–1837), a French visionary who advocated free love and communal living. Some of these socialist schemes were not easily distinguishable from capitalism—such as Saint-Simon's (1760–1825) program of industrial administration—whereas others, such as P. J. Proudhon's (1809–1865) proposed reforms, bordered on anarchy. All of these early plans for social and economic reorganization, however, had one thing in common—they relied on a *voluntary* appeal to human nature. In this sense, they were all products of the Enlightenment. And in this sense also, they were to Karl Marx, all "utopian."

The Force of Ideas: Romantic Critiques of Classical Political Economy

The system promulgated by Adam Smith and his followers that championed markets, economic growth, and the progress spawned by the Industrial Revolution was attacked passionately by critics and naysayers in the nineteenth century. A leading source of criticism came from the so-called "Romantics." The Romantic Movement, so beautifully expressed in literature by the likes of Byron, Keats, Coleridge, and Shelley, emphasized the power of nature to transform humanity, which was itself part and parcel of nature.

Essayists picked up these ideas. Perplexed by the complexity of the industrial age, Henry David Thoreau (who was both anticapitalist and antigovernment), advised: "We may believe it, but never do we live a quiet, free life . . . but are enveloped in an invisible network of speculations. Our progress is only from one such speculation to another, and only at rare intervals do we perceive that it is no progress" (*Writings*, p. 61). To Thoreau and others, the practical effects of the Industrial Revolution were unpleasant: increased urbanization and overcrowding; more poverty, filth, disease; and lack of public services. But rather than emulate John Stuart Mill's focus on trying to establish the *ex ante* conditions for equality of opportunity (or what we now call "access"), the Romantics mounted an *ex post* attack on the progenitors of wealth and "injustice." They regarded the wicked capitalists and greedy bankers as enemies of the poor.

One of the Romantics, John Ruskin, reacted to political economy on two fronts: (1) he changed the focal point from production to consumption; and (2) he made the science normative instead of descriptive. Ruskin the moralist opposed Mill the theorist. He claimed that his principles of political economy were summed up thusly: "Government and co-operation are in all things and eternally the laws of life; anarchy and competition eternally and in all things, the laws of death" ("Modern Painters," p. 207). Some of the Romantics did not believe any sort of ultimate equality was possible. They often equated white "wage slavery" with Negro slavery*

The Romantics closed their eyes and minds to the prospect that capitalism in a democratic society could and would supply antidotes to the problems they identified. Charles Dickens, a great novelist but a poor social scientist, refused to acknowledge that a market system could provide means to lift people out of poverty. Moreover, he failed to compare the plight of the rural poor of the past with the urban poor of his day. Opportunities still exist for "rags to riches" experiences to unfold within capitalist societies. Moreover, Thoreau's choice to "become one with nature" is a choice that is routinely made even under conditions of modern capitalism. (The westward movement of many U.S. citizens in the nineteenth century can be explained in part by the "lure of nature").

Foundationally the Romantics emphasized the costs of progress while ignoring or minimizing its benefits. In the main, change is always unsettling because it imposes costs on some and benefits on others. Those who endure new costs will protest and attempt to maintain the status quo—through government (or even violence) if possible. The real questions are nettlesome: What is the alternative to change? Should we obstruct scientific and technological progress in an attempt to lower "social costs"? Are comparisons meaningful between earlier medieval forms of rural poverty and the conditions faced by lower classes in an expanding urban and industrial environment? In the end, it would appear that the "Romantics" failed to understand the possibilities of how advancing economies would deal with social and economic problems, especially under democratic forms of government.

*Recent research contends that those who tagged economics as "the dismal science" were themselves racist. Ruskin believed in the "impossibility of equality" and Dickens (in his seldom- read classic *Hard Times*) argued that slavery was a tool to increase blacks' intellectual development and make them fit for freedom. By contrast, virtually all economists of the time were egalitarians in this regard. So, it is an open question whose philosophy was more "dismal" (see the provocative book by David M. Levy, *How the Dismal Science Got its Name*).

European Evolutionary Thought

The idea that society evolves through a succession of stages, each more advanced than the former, is a historical strand of thought woven through much Western philosophy. This evolutionary idea was evident in Smith's vision of a natural, societal progression through three stages: agricultural, industrial, and finally, "trading" (commercial). Whereas Smith used the stadial theory to establish the benefits of atomistic markets, socialists used it to justify collectivism.

The idea of progressive "stages" of historical and economic development was the centerpiece of several socialist doctrines. Here we explore the ideas of Nicolas de Condorcet (French), Henri Saint-Simon (French), J. C. L. Simonde de Sismondi (Swiss), and Friedrich List (German). Taken together, these writings provide a cross-sectional illustration of the historical, evolutionary approach to economics.

Condorcet and the Laws of History

One of the earliest proponents of the evolutionary approach in Europe was the French philosopher Condorcet (1743–1794), who believed that historical development is subject to general laws and that the task of the historian is to discover these laws by which humans progress "toward truth and well-being." Condorcet called for a new science, based on history, that would "predict the progress of the human species . . . direct it and . . . accelerate it" (*Esquisses*, p. 4). The French Revolution, motivated by the rationalist philosophy of the Enlightenment, demonstrated in its bloody aftermath that social perfection was not the result of reason alone, as had been optimistically assumed. Thus, Condorcet regarded the revolution as part of the errors of the past, a mere transitional stage on the road to ultimate social perfection. His new science of history relied on empiricism in place of rationalism. "Observations on what man has been and what he is today," wrote Condorcet, "lead immediately to the ways of assuring and accelerating the further progress for which man's nature permits him to hope" (*Esquisses*, p. 4).

Condorcet understood that the development of social progress is more uneven than the perfection of human knowledge. He attributed the lag in social development to the fact that history, until his day, had always been the history of *individuals* rather than the history of the *masses*. As a result, the needs and well-being of society had been sacrificed to those of a few people. He sought to rectify this by recasting history as the study of the masses. Condorcet therefore originated two important themes that in some measure underlie almost all nineteenth-century criticism of capitalism: the idea of "natural" laws of historical development, and the "collectivist" view of history as the study of the masses.

Saint-Simon: Pixilated Prophet of Industrialism

Claude Henri de Rouvroy, Comte de Saint-Simon (1760–1825), was a member of the French nobility who renounced his title during the early stages of the French Revolution but was nevertheless imprisoned as an enemy of the state during the Reign of Terror. He somehow escaped execution and gained his freedom after the fall of Robespierre in 1794. Like another famous Frenchmen—the Marquis de Lafayette—he fought on the side of the colonists in the American Revolution. By virtue of his contribution to the defeat of General Cornwallis at Yorktown, Saint-Simon boasted: "I can thus consider myself as one of the founders of liberty in the United States, because it was this military operation which determined the peace and established irrevocably the independence of America" (*Oeuvres*, vol. 18, p. 140).

Egotistical and possibly delusional, Saint-Simon nevertheless was a visionary in many respects.[1] He was a leading advocate of canals, proposing to the Viceroy of Mexico in 1783 a canal to join the Atlantic and the Pacific, and another to connect Madrid to the Atlantic in 1787. One of his disciples led the construction of the Suez Canal in Egypt and attempted, but failed, to replicate that success in Panama. (The Panama Canal was completed in 1913 by the United States after the French abandoned the project.) He inspired a number of followers, often described as *technocrats*, and he influenced a number of important philosophers, including Auguste Comte, John Stuart Mill, and Karl Marx.

Saint-Simon's utopian vision of society reflected the influence of the French Enlightenment, which extolled reason. The refinement of reason, and its ability to direct economic production, was, in his view, a product of the evolutionary progress of history. According to Saint-Simon history moved through ascending stages of development. The first stage, typified by prerevolutionary France, was based on military force and the uncritical acceptance of religious faith. During this stage, the monarch and the Church dominated the production and distribution of wealth. The second stage, characterized by post-revolutionary France, was based on industrial capacity and scientific knowledge. The third stage was based on science and industry, which Saint-Simon extolled as the hallmarks of the modern age. He devoted his efforts to social reorganization schemes that would remove impediments to the development of both. In Saint-Simon's bold new world, science became the handmaiden of industry—a means to provide better living conditions for all. Indeed, he blurred the distinction between science and industry by talking more and more about the science *of* industry, by which he meant directing science and technical expertise toward ever-increasing amounts of production. The "production of useful things," he wrote, "is the only reasonable and positive end that political societies can set themselves" (*Oeuvres*, vol. 18, p. 13). According to Saint-Simon the old order must be swept away in order for society to reach the highest level of economic progress:

> The prosperity of France can only exist through the effects of the progress of the sciences, fine arts and professions. The Princes, the great household officials, the Bishops, Marshals of France, prefects and idle landowners contribute nothing directly to the progress of the sciences, fine arts and professions. Far from contributing they only hinder, since they strive to prolong the supremacy existing to this day of conjectural ideas over positive science. (*Oeuvres*, vol. 20, p. 24)

Saint-Simon proposed to reorganize government so that industrial administration replaced existing forms of social control. He opposed government in the traditional sense, in which a privileged few exercised power over the unprivileged many. "Government always harms industry when it mixes in its affairs," he wrote, ". . . even in instances where it makes an effort to encourage it" (*Oeuvres*, vol. 18, p. 186). Saint-Simon wanted to replace traditional government (monarchy) with an industrial parliament. Details were not lacking in Saint-Simon's fertile imagination. His industrial parliament, patterned in part after the British system, consisted of three bodies. The first—the Chamber of Invention—would be made up of 300 members: 200 civil engineers, 50 poets, 25 artists, 15 architects, and 10 musicians. Its primary duty would be to draw up a plan of public works that would be designed and

[1] Saint-Simon claimed that his ancestor, Charlemagne, appeared to him while he was imprisoned and gave him the task of saving the French Republic from the excesses of the revolution. Once freed from prison, he claims to have instructed his servant to awaken him each day with the same phrase: "Arise, Monsieur le Comte, you have great things to do today."

undertaken to increase France's wealth and improve the conditions of its inhabitants. The second—the Chamber of Examination—would likewise be made up of 300 members, the majority consisting of mathematicians and physical scientists. Its job would be to draw up a master plan for education and to evaluate the desirability and feasibility of projects proposed by the first chamber. The third body—the Chamber of Execution—would consist of an unspecified number of representatives of each branch of industry. It would levy taxes and exercise veto power over all projects proposed and approved by the first two chambers.

Saint-Simon's goal was to displace the parasitic class by raising the productive class. But he did not identify or explain the process by which this transformation was to take place. He seemed unconcerned about how power would be transferred from the ruling class to the ballot box. He ignored deep-seated antagonisms among different social classes, insisting instead that as civilization advanced, different interests would be drawn together into a common zeal for social and economic betterment. He did not share Adam Smith's trust in self-interest and limited government to accomplish economic growth and development. In place of the invisible hand he advocated the loose fist of mutual cooperation. At base, Saint-Simon's new society rested on cooperation. Naively, he trusted the advance of reason to enlighten individuals to their true interest. It is this aspect of Saint-Simon's system that provoked Karl Marx to refer to his system and others like it as "utopian."

Some later writers interpreted Saint-Simon's industrial parliament as a blueprint for a fully planned economy. However, in Saint-Simon's new industrial society central planning was confined to the production of public works—which does not represent a radical departure from Adam Smith's notion of limited government. As we saw in chapter 5, Smith justified certain government functions; in particular,

> those public institutions and those public works, which, although they may be in the highest degree advantageous to a great society are, however, of such a nature, that the profit could never repay the expense to any individual or small number of individuals, and which it therefore cannot be expected that any individual or small number of individuals should erect or maintain. (*Wealth of Nations*, p. 681)

There is, nevertheless, a major difference between Smith and Saint-Simon. Smith envisioned a *harmony* of (class) interests springing from the natural order of a market economy. Saint-Simon envisioned an *identity* of interests evolving from enlightenment and reason. His optimism was undeterred by the messy clash of individual or class interests. He persisted in the belief that all people had a stake in the outcome of the production process, hence all new forms of social organization "must conform directly to the interests of the greatest majority of the population; they must be considered as a general political consequence deduced from the divine moral principle; *all men must regard themselves as brothers; they must concern themselves with helping one another*" (*Oeuvres*, vol. 22, pp. 116–117). In the final analysis, Saint-Simon put his trust in education, broadly speaking; whereas Smith relied on human nature and the predictability of economic incentives. A cynic might say that Saint-Simon called on people's higher nature to guide economic development, whereas Smith relied on people's lower nature to produce the same result.

While unfolding his stadial view of history, Saint-Simon maintained that the hallmark of the "modern age" is the displacement of religious thought by science and reason. However, in the third, most advanced stage of history he argued that religion reappears in a higher form, which he called "physicism." Physicism rejects deism, somehow unifies mind and matter, and treats all phenomena, mental as well as material, as explicable by scientific laws. In this manner Saint-Simon completed the formulation of his "Law of Three Stages" (i.e., polytheism, theism, physicism)—that his secretary, Auguste Comte, later claimed as his own. For Saint-Simon, as for Comte, the stadial theory was a way of explaining how the sciences pass from the conjectural to the positive.[2] He accurately charted the future direction of capitalism in many important respects. The concept "technocracy," if not the term, traces back to him. He anticipated the successive development of specialization and expertise—backed by one scientific advance after another—and its transformative effect on modern corporations. His ideas and influence are readily traceable in the works of the twentieth-century economist John Kenneth Galbraith (see chapter 19).

In his later years, Saint-Simon's writings wandered aimlessly into physics and physiology,[3] which induced his followers to espouse a kind of bizarre mysticism. Some of his disciples became notorious for their socially "radical" views, and they modified Saint-Simon's doctrine almost beyond recognition. Nevertheless, their perversion came to be known, however inappropriately, as *Saint-Simonism*.

Simonde de Sismondi Rejects Say's Law

Born in Geneva as J. C. L. Simonde, this Swiss economist changed his surname to Simonde de Sismondi (1773–1842) in 1800 after learning that he was descended from a noble Italian family by that name. He is therefore known to history as Sismondi. Though trained as a historian, Sismondi acquired practical experience in business and finance in France while he was young. His first venture into economics, *De la richesse commerciale* (1803) was intended as a systematic exposition of the ideas of Adam Smith combined with an "absolutely new" way of looking at changes in aggregate output. Applying arithmetic and algebra to the task, Sismondi represented output in any given year as a function of investment in the previous year. He then showed how output varied in a closed economy (without international trade) versus an open economy (with international trade); and how an open economy produced different results when it had an export surplus as compared to an import surplus. But the book drew little notice, so it made no direct contribution to the development of economics. Sixteen years later, Sismondi presented his own theory of aggregate equilibrium income in his major economic work, *Nouveaux principes d'économie politique* (1819). This work marks his entry into the controversy over Say's Law and the theory of market gluts.

According to Sismondi, the utility of output must be balanced against the disutility of work, an idea that W. S. Jevons later transformed into a microeconomic theory of labor supply (see chapter 15). Sismondi argued that whenever the disutility of labor exceeds the utility of output in a given period, output will subsequently decline until balance is restored. When the discrepancy between utility of output and disutility of labor is reversed, output in subsequent periods will increase until balance is again restored. In a complex economy, however, different people make balancing decisions in isolation from one another, so that aggregate balance is not always assured. The germ of this theory can be found in physiocratic literature (see chapter 4), but Sismondi transformed the idea into a theory of aggregate equilibrium, thus challenging the prevailing view (i.e., Say's Law) that there could not be a general glut in the aggregate economy.

[2] Turgot (see chapter 4) sketched out, briefly, a three-stage theory of history before Smith (in 1750) and Condorcet followed suit in 1795. But Saint-Simon was the first to adumbrate the version that led to Comte's "positive" program based on historical evolution.

[3] He argued at length, for example, that the industrious beaver, not the idle monkey, is the highest creature next to man.

Sismondi's view was attacked immediately by the reigning British economic orthodoxy, but the following year, another maverick, T. R. Malthus (see chapter 6) entered the fray on his side. In his *Principles of Political Economy* (1820), Malthus expressed ideas he had long defended in correspondence with Ricardo; so Marx's portrayal of Malthus's book as simply the "English translation" of Sismondi is not fair. The debate over Say's Law raged on for a decade or more, and was resurrected in the twentieth century after a period of dormancy. More recent debates on Say's Law revolve around macroeconomic monetary controversies, however, which were not Sismondi's concern. British classical economists of the nineteenth century acted as if Sismondi and Malthus were arguing about secular stagnation rather than temporary disequilibrium, and the distinction between short-run and long-run effects became blurred until revisited by Keynes in the 1930s. Along with Malthus, Sismondi may rightfully be considered a precursor of Keynes (see chapter 21). He may also be considered a precursor of Marx (see chapter 12), who appropriated (without acknowledgement) Sismondi's emphases on "proletarians," increasing concentration of capital, recurring business cycles, technological unemployment, and economic dynamics in general.

The Flaws of Capitalism. Like other children of the Enlightenment, Sismondi was affected by the dramatic social and economic shifts brought about by the French Revolution. To his way of thinking, the new era aroused conflicts of interest between capital and labor, thus displacing the economic cooperation of the guild system with a new, less stable industrial regime. Improvements in living conditions lagged seriously behind the increases in wealth ushered in by the machine age. Rather than serve to increase social welfare Sismondi believed that unrestrained competition produced universal rivalry, large-scale production, and oversupply. Overproduction, in turn, precipitated commercial crises and economic depression.

Some fifty or so years before Marx, Sismondi anticipated the class struggle between labor and capital that Marx emphasized in *Das Kapital*. Whereas Saint-Simon believed that economic cooperation and organization were the inevitable outcomes of economic progress, Sismondi blamed the class struggle on the very institutions of capitalism. But unlike Marx, he did not regard the class struggle as a permanent feature of the new economy. Inasmuch as the class struggle was a consequence of existing institutions, he believed it could be eliminated by appropriate institutional amendments. What escaped Sismondi, however, was the realization of precisely which factors constitute the driving force of historical change.

One of Sismondi's most telling attacks on classical economics concerned machinery. On balance, classical economics viewed the introduction of machinery as beneficial because it lowers average costs of production and product prices, and thus increases consumer welfare. Sismondi felt that the benefits of machinery were more than offset by the technological unemployment that followed its introduction on a large scale. It is self-evident that the introduction of labor-saving machinery displaces workers. Sismondi argued that each worker so displaced finds his or her income drastically reduced even as output is increased by the same machinery that displaced him or her. He therefore argued that overproduction and economic crisis inevitably follow the widespread introduction of machinery. Moreover, because machinery is expensive, only the largest firms can afford it; hence the accumulation of machinery in large firms gives them a decided advantage over small firms and tends to drive many small manufacturers out of business, causing unemployment on a second front. The adverse effects foretold by Sismondi are not inevitable, however. The use of machinery has the capacity to increase the demand for labor as well as decrease it. Sismondi was either unwilling or unable to see that the growth of output brought about by machinery sometimes creates additional employment opportunities.

Machinery evoked many violent emotions among workers in the nineteenth century. The infamous Luddite Revolts—in which workers attacked and destroyed the "evil" machines that stole their jobs—shows just how passionate, and wrongheaded, reactions could be.[4] In this regard it is important to note that Sismondi's criticism was not aimed at machinery per se but at the social organization that subjected workers to the vagaries of competition. His summary statement on this matter is explicit:

> Every invention in the arts, which has multiplied the power of man's work, from that of the plough to the steam engine, is useful. . . . Society had made progress only through such discoveries; it is through them that the work of man has sufficed for his needs. . . . It is not the fault of the progress of mechanical science, but the fault of the social order, if the worker, who acquires the power to make in two hours what would take him twelve to make before, does not find himself richer, and consequently does not enjoy more leisure, but on the contrary is doing six times more work than is demanded. (*Nouveaux principes*, p. 349)

Theory and Method. Sismondi's complaint against classical economics was based less on theoretical principles than on its method, aims, and conclusions. Unlike Nassau Senior (see chapter 7) who strove to make economics more scientific by removing normative elements from it, Sismondi treated economics as a subset of the science of government. Whereas Saint-Simon wanted to replace government with industrial administration, Sismondi held that government and economics are inseparable. He considered economics a moral science:[5] "The physical well-being of man," he declared, "insofar as it can be the work of his government, is the object of political economy" (*Nouveaux principes*, p. 8). A science that concerns itself solely with the means of increasing wealth without studying the purpose of such wealth was, in Sismondi's view, a false science.

In a subtle attack on the theory of self-interest, Sismondi pointed out that in the struggle to achieve personal gain, not every individual force is equal. Hence, "Injustice can often triumph . . . being backed by public force which is believed to be impartial, but which, in fact, without examining the cause, always places itself on the side of the stronger" (*Nouveaux principes*, p. 408). In a phrase, exercise of individual self-interest does not always coincide with the general interest.

> It is to the interest of one to rob his neighbor, and it is to the interest of the latter to let him do it, if he has a weapon in his hand, in order not to be killed; but it is not to the interest of society that one should use force and the other should give in. The entire social organization presents to us at every step a similar compulsion, not always with the same sort of violence, but always with the same danger of resistance. (*Nouveaux principes*, p. 200)

Sismondi especially rejected the abstract, deductive method of Ricardo and his followers, preferring instead the comparative, historical method. In his telling description of economics he indicts classical political economy and defends his own method:

[4] The Luddites—who took their name from (mythical?) leader, Ned Lud—were armed rebels who clandestinely attacked textile mills in England and destroyed textile machinery during 1811–1812. While the motivation for these attacks was complex and multifaceted, historians agree that a major source of discontent was unemployment caused by machines displacing labor.

[5] Many nineteenth-century writers, from Bentham onward, did not see a contradiction in fusing the terms "moral" and "science." This was especially true in France.

> [Economics] is not founded on dry calculations, nor on a mathematical chain of theorems, deduced from some obscure axioms, given as incontestable truth. . . . Political economy is founded on the study of man and men; human nature must be known, and also the condition and life of societies in different times and in different places. One must consult the historian, and the travelers; one must look into one's self; not only study the laws, but also know how they are executed; not only examine the tables of exportation and importation, but also know the aspect of the country, enter the bosom of families, judge the comfort or suffering of the masses of the people, verify great principles by observation of details, and compare ceaselessly science with daily practical life. (*De la richesse commerciale*, I, p. xv)

Sensing the complexity of the industrial era, Sismondi felt that the abstract theories propounded by the classical economists were inadequate for the modern age. He blamed the reigning orthodoxy for drawing too many loose observations that applied only to England, and for misleading people by declaring principles universal when they are, in fact, rooted in weak foundations. Sismondi also protested the tendency of the abstract theorists to reduce habits and customs to mere calculations; and he criticized "those who wished to see man isolated from the world, or rather who considered abstractly the modifications of his existence, and always arrived at conclusions that are belied by experience" (*Études*, p. 4).

Sismondi the historian was interested in those periods of transition that characterize the passing of one regime and the beginning of another. In practice he was concerned with ameliorating the condition of the proletariat (a term Marx borrowed from him) during this transition. He was particularly influential in France where he originated the line of inquiry that the French call *économie sociale* (social economy). Sismondi influenced a number of writers who were not outright socialists but who protested the evils of unrestrained laissez-faire. Along with him, these writers sought some happy halfway house between capitalism and socialism that would retain the principle of individual liberty as much as possible. In retrospect his criticism of the classical school may have been justified by historical experience, but his theoretical reasoning was marred by a logical flaw. Marx revived his theory of economic crises and his concern for the working class, but in his theory of overproduction, which posited that useful production must always be preceded by increased demand, Sismondi did not admit the possibility that increased production could itself create additional demand.

List and National Political Economy

History, coupled with nationalism, also rallied a distinct group of German economists in the nineteenth century. The peace treaty that ended Germany's participation in the Napoleonic Wars left the country divided into thirty-nine different states, most of which were individual monarchies acting more or less independently. A complex system of interstate tariffs that impaired the free and easy exchange of goods internally produced economic isolation and retarded economic development. Yet, the German states imposed no import duties on foreign goods, thus inviting British surplus products and those of other countries to enter German markets where they were sold at extremely low prices. These circumstances threatened the very existence of German manufacturing and commercial interests so badly that by the 1830s a general clamor arose for economic unity and uniform tariffs.

Unification of the German states was the goal of many German nationals. One of the earliest advocates of nationalism was Friedrich List (1789–1846), the son of a

German leatherworker who gave up an academic career to become active in German politics. In 1819 he became the leader of the General Association of German Manufacturers and Merchants, a group seeking to confederate the disunited German states. He subsequently became the face of the movement to develop a system of national economy and was the forerunner of a peculiar Germanic strain of economic thought that eventually formed the German Historical School (see below).

List strenuously objected to those aspects of classical economics that stressed absolutism and universalism. He rejected the idea that classical economic principles hold for all time and for all countries. Principles that might apply to England were not relevant to Germany, which stood at another level of development and faced different economic problems. In the final analysis, List subordinated economics to politics, but he bequeathed to Marx the view that industry is more than the mere combination of labor and capital—it is primarily a *social* force that itself creates and improves capital and labor. Industry not only shapes present production, but gives direction and form to future production. In other words, there is a dynamic about it that was missing from classical economics.

Protectionism and Economic Development. List applied a method of inquiry originated by Saint-Simon: the idea that an economy must pass through successive stages before it reaches maturity. The historical stages of development identified by List were: (1) barbaric, (2) pastoral, (3) agricultural, (4) agricultural-manufacturing, and (5) agricultural-manufacturing-commercial. Like Saint-Simon and Sismondi, List focused more on the transition between stages of economic development than on the end result. He argued that free trade would speed passage through the first three stages of development but that protection was required to facilitate transition between the last two. Once the final stage was reached, free trade is warranted once again. The system of protection that List advocated was designed to be temporary and remedial, because not every nation advances at the same pace. He gave eloquent expression, for example, to the argument for protection of "infant industries":

> In nations . . . which possess all the necessary mental and material conditions and means for establishing a manufacturing power of their own, and of thereby attaining the highest degree of civilization, and development of material prosperity and political power, but which are retarded in their progress by the competition of a foreign manufacturing Power which is already farther advanced than their own—only in such nations are commercial restrictions justifiable for the purpose of establishing and protecting their own manufacturing power; and even in them it is justifiable only until that manufacturing power is strong enough no longer to have any reason to fear foreign competition, and thenceforth only so far as may be necessary for protecting the inland manufacturing power in its very roots. (*National System*, p. 144)

By List's reckoning Great Britain was the only country to have attained the final stage of economic development. While the Continental and American nations struggled to reach this level, cheap British imports were thwarting the development of domestic manufacturing. According to List international competition could not exist on an equal footing until all nations reached the final stage of development. Hence he advocated protective tariffs for Germany until it could reach its final stage. It is important to note that List was not an outright protectionist. He felt that protection was warranted only at critical stages of history. His writings are replete with examples borrowed from history and experience showing that economic protection is the only way for an emerging nation to establish itself. He pointed to America's experience as vindication of his views. Not surprisingly he found ready support among U.S. protectionists, particularly Alexander Hamilton and Henry Carey.

The Flaws of Classical Economics. List rejected the absolutism and cosmopolitanism of classical political economy. Against the classical view he argued that economic principles do not hold for all nations at all times. His own method was historical and nationalistic. His stadial theory of economic development, for example, was calculated to demonstrate the inability of classical economics to recognize and reflect the variety of conditions existing in different countries, and most especially, in Germany.

Like Sismondi, List subordinated economics to politics in general. He maintained that it was not enough for the statesman to know that the free interchange of products will increase wealth (as demonstrated by the classical economists); he must also know the ramifications of such action for his own country. Consequently he held that free trade is undesirable if it harms domestic workers or industries. Moreover, he was not willing to sacrifice the future for the present. He argued that the crucial economic magnitude in economic development is not wealth—as measured by exchange value—but *productive power.* "The power of producing wealth," he said, "is infinitely more important than the wealth itself" (*National System*, p. 108). Therefore economic resources must be safeguarded in order to assure their future existence and development. This view was used by List to further justify his protectionist arguments. It also lies at the root of the popular "infant-industry" argument in support of protective tariffs.

List's originality in economic theory and method consisted in his systematic use of historical comparison as a means of demonstrating the validity of economic propositions, and in his persistent emphasis on the social character of economic activity. In this respect he not only influenced Karl Marx but provided a methodological rallying point for the economists of the German Historical School.

■ The Utopian Socialists

Although socialism remains an active force in many areas of the globe, the concept itself is very vague. The word socialism conjures up a number of meanings: public ownership of economic enterprise, subjugation of individual freedom to collective interests, elimination of private property, redistribution of wealth from rich to poor, centralized direction of economic activity, and so on. In practice, socialism is rarely the clear-cut alternative to capitalism it is reputed to be. Every capitalist economy today possesses some socialist elements and vice versa. Moreover, many past writers who are deemed socialist today can be distinguished from one another by significant philosophical and/or methodological differences. Nevertheless, there is sufficient common ground among nineteenth-century writers to group them outside the orbit of the classical economists. This is particularly true of that coterie of writers that Marx called "utopian socialists."[6]

The utopian socialists regarded capitalism as irrational, inhumane, and unjust. They repudiated the idea of laissez-faire and the doctrine of the harmony of interests. They believed in the perfectibility of humans and society through the proper construction of the social environment. And they all developed reform schemes that

[6] Marx used this phrase to distinguish his brand of socialism from other theories not based on dialectical materialism. It is debatable whether Marx's own theory was significantly less utopian than the theories he disdained; nevertheless, the phrase is useful in a categorical sense.

appealed to voluntary action rather than inexorable historical "laws." In this section we will examine the ideas of Robert Owen (Welsh), Charles Fourier (French), and Pierre Joseph Proudhon (French).

Owen's Grand Experiment

Born in obscurity to Welsh parents, Robert Owen (1771–1858) worked his way up the ladder of success in the textile industry to achieve fame and fortune by his thirtieth year. Owen was especially alert to the changes in economic and social life brought about by the introduction of machinery. The mechanical marvels of Arkwright (spinning frame), Crompton (spinning mule), and Hargreaves (spinning jenny) transformed the textile business in England and helped make Owen a wealthy man, but their impact on the working class was not so apparently beneficial. Owen repudiated the popular social view that poverty is the just consequence of the sins of the working class. In *A New View of Society* (1813) he turned traditional social theory upside down by asserting that an individual's character is formed *for* him, not *by* him. In other words, rather than accept the conventional wisdom that the wretched are poor because they are wretched, Owen argued that the poor are wretched because they are poor! Improve a man's social environment, he argued, and you improve the man. This single precept lay at the center of his social philosophy. He embellished it by stating his "true principles" which he set forth in his "Report to the County of Lanark" in 1821 (in Morton, pp. 58–59):

1. Character is universally formed *for* and not *by* the individual.
2. *Any* habits and sentiments may be given to mankind.
3. The affections are *not* under the control of the individual.
4. Every individual may be trained to produce far more than he can consume, while there is sufficiency of soil left for him to cultivate.
5. Nature has provided means by which population may be at all times maintained in the proper state to give the greatest happiness to every individual, without one check of vice or misery.
6. Any community may be arranged, on a due combination of the foregoing principles, in such a manner as not only to withdraw vice, poverty, and, in a great degree, misery from the world, but also to place *every* individual under such circumstances in which he shall enjoy more permanent happiness than can be given to *any* individual under the principles which have heretofore regulated society.
7. That all the assumed fundamental principles on which society has hitherto been founded are erroneous, and may be demonstrated to be contrary to fact.
8. That the change which would follow the abandonment of these erroneous maxims which bring misery to the world, and the adoption of principles of truth, unfolding a system which shall remove and forever exclude that misery, may be effected without the slightest injury to any human being.

Shortly after his marriage to the owner's daughter in 1800, Owen began to manage New Lanark Mills in Scotland, which served as a proving ground for his social theories. The workforce at New Lanark was an intemperate and immoral bunch, given to frequent bouts of drunkenness and debauchery. It was a tough task for a young, new manager, but Owen approached his job with reformist zeal. He set out to prove his theory that a worker's character is determined by his social environment. He wished to test the premise that a contented workforce was a more efficient workforce. At New Lanark he restricted the labor of children and devoted much time and money to their education. He improved housing conditions for the workers and their families, raised wages, shortened work hours, and made other provisions to enrich the lives of the community's inhabitants.

To the amazement of his skeptical fellow industrialists, the mills that Owen managed continued to earn substantial profits after his reforms were introduced. Nevertheless, his success was short-lived. He was eventually forced out of New Lanark by business partners who resented his program. This bitter experience convinced him that private initiative could not be relied on to bring about lasting social and economic reform. He therefore advocated a larger role for government. He sought laws promoting factory reforms, aid to the unemployed, and, eventually, a national system of education. He lived to see a second social experiment launched at New Harmony, Indiana, but it failed within three years of its establishment. Although many of the reforms he championed are now commonplace in industrial societies, Owen did not live to see his suggested reforms legislated into action.

Fourier's Shattered Dream

In his saner moments Charles Fourier (1772–1837) was more than a little eccentric; in his wilder moments he was probably more than a bit insane. In between these poles, he displayed a mastery of the smallest detail and an uncanny power of prediction. Like Saint-Simon and List, he believed that civilization passes through certain stages of development. However, his vision of the world was so fanciful almost no one took him seriously. He asserted that nineteenth-century France was in its fifth stage of advance, having passed already through (1) confusion, (2) savagery, (3) patriarchalism, and (4) barbarity. He predicted that after passing through two more stages, society would approach the upward slope of harmony—the final stage of utter bliss—which would endure for eight thousand years. Then, history would reverse itself and descend back through each stage to the beginning.

In apocalyptic fashion Fourier detailed the earthly changes that would accompany the final stage of harmony: six new moons would replace the one in existence; a halo, showering gentle dew, would circle the north pole; the seas would turn to syrup (e.g., oceans of Coca-Cola?); and all violent and repulsive beasts of the earth would be replaced with their opposites, which would be tame and serviceable to humanity—anti-lions, anti-whales, anti-bears, anti-bugs, and anti-rats, for example. To top it all off, the life span of humans in the final stage of history would stretch to 144 years, of which 120 years would be devoted to the unrestrained pursuit of sexual love.

It is tempting to dismiss all this as the pure frenzy of a madman—except for one thing: Despite its fantastic nature Fourier devised a plan for reorganizing society that captured the imagination of others who shared his distress over the evils of capitalism. His plan was a forerunner of the twentieth-century commune. He proposed multiple "garden cities" (*phalanstères*) modeled after a grand hotel, where ideally fifteen hundred people would live in common. No restrictions would be placed on individual liberty, nor would income be forcefully redistributed. Fourier did not believe in income or wealth redistribution of the leveling kind; he maintained that poverty and income inequality "are of divine ordination, and consequently must forever remain, since everything that God has ordained is just as it ought to be" (*Nouveau monde industriel*, 1848, in Gide and Rist, p. 256). He did not object to private property per se, only to its *abuse*, as when income is earned without work. Residents of the *phalanstère* would be able to purchase hotel-like accommodations suitable to their individual tastes and pocketbooks. Individual property would not be confiscated but transformed into fully participating common-stock shares of the *phalanstère*. Cooperation would replace self-interest so that economic production would be undertaken collectively. Fourier promised high returns to wealthy capitalists who invested in his scheme but was ultimately disappointed. It is said that in his old age he stayed home at appointed times each day to receive potential investors, but no one ever came.

Fourier regarded the conflict of individual interests as the main evil of capitalism. Hence, he designed the *phalanstère* to eliminate conflicts of interests by making each member a cooperative *owner* as well as wage earner. Hence, each member was to be given an active voice in the management of the *phalanstère*. As worker/investor/owner, each resident would receive income from three sources: wages of labor, interest of stock, and salary of management. Fourier posited the precise division of profits: four-twelfths to capital, five-twelfths to labor, and three-twelfths to management. Because he foresaw economies through communal living Fourier's *phalanstère* promised maximum comfort at minimal cost. Collectivity was the rule. Even unpleasant household tasks were to be undertaken collectively, thereby eliminating much individual drudgery. Fourier would assign such tasks to children, who, perversely, but by their very nature, delight in getting themselves dirty. Adults would restrict themselves to work they enjoyed, and Fourier mused that a kind of friendly competition would emerge in the form of contests to see who could do his or her job best. It is easy to see how Fourier's plan could appeal to dreamers, especially after Owen's more practical ideas bore little fruit. It is also easy, among the more sober-minded, to dismiss Fourier out of hand. Fantasy notwithstanding, however, he was a pioneer of the cooperative movement.

Proudhon: "Scholastic Anarchist"

Pierre Joseph Proudhon (1809–1865) is usually considered a French socialist even though he criticized socialism as vehemently as he did capitalism. It is more appropriate to represent him as a libertarian in the extreme. The most distinguishing features of his thought were a rejection of all authority and an almost medieval concern for economic justice in exchange. Because these combined themes pervade his work, we have tabbed him a scholastic anarchist.

Criticism of Authority. Proudhon railed against all forms of authority. In 1840 he published a sensational essay entitled "What is Property?" His answer—"property is robbery!" His inflammatory pamphlet brought him notoriety not only for its radical views, but also because he was charged with conspiracy by the French government. Proudhon refused to back down. He stubbornly defended his position in this passage:

> If I were asked the following question: What is slavery? and I should answer in one word, *It is murder*, my meaning would be understood at once. No extended argument would be required to show that the power to take from a man his thought, his will, his personality, is a power of life and death; and that to enslave a man is to kill him. Why then to this other question: What is property? may I not likewise answer, *It is robbery*, without the certainty of being misunderstood; the second proposition being no other than a transformation of the first. ("What is Property," in Manuel and Manuel, p. 363)

In actuality what Proudhon renounced is not ownership of property per se but the consequences of private property in a market economy. He was opposed to certain attributes of property, namely what he considered unearned income in the form of rent, interest, or profit. In the next chapter we shall see a similar strain in Marx's thought. Like Saint-Simon, Proudhon felt strongly that everyone should work. Like Marx (who also spent his life in abject poverty), he had little choice.

Proudhon complained that the French Revolution of 1789 had lost its direction. Rather than focus on sweeping the political system away, the heirs to the revolution merely sought to *reform* it. Aware that political powers always tended toward concentration and centralization, he argued that tyranny was inevitable. Proudhon had a passion for liberty—he wanted liberty to be absolute, everywhere, and forever. Of the tripartite values of the French Revolution, "liberty, equality, fraternity," it is clear that liberty was uppermost in his mind. In places he sounds almost Saint-Simonian, even though he generally deprecated Saint-Simon's ideas. In discussing industrial organization, a favorite theme of Saint-Simon, Proudhon expressed a mutual desire to eliminate government functionaries:

> To live without government, to abolish all authority, absolutely and unreservedly, to set up pure *anarchy* seems to [some] ridiculous and inconceivable, a plot against the Republic and against the nation. What will these people who talk about abolishing government put in place of it? they ask.
>
> We have no trouble in answering. It is industrial organization that we will put in place of government. . . . In place of laws, we will put contracts. . . . In place of political powers, we will put economic forces. In place of the ancient classes of nobles, burghers, and peasants, or of business men and working men, we will put the general titles and special departments of industry: Agriculture, Manufacture, Commerce, etc. In place of public force, we will put collective force. In place of standing armies, we will put industrial associations. In place of police, we will put identity of interests. In place of political centralization, we will put economic centralization.
>
> Do you see how there can be order without functionaries, a profound and wholly intellectual unity? ("General Idea," in Manuel and Manuel, p. 371)

Proudhon also shared Saint-Simon's faith in a higher order of social unity than what he saw around him in his day. He declared that truth and reality are essentially historical and that progress is inevitable. Science rather than authority holds the key to the future, he wrote, and it alone, rather than self-interest, is the chief motivator of progress:

> What no monarchy, not even that of the Roman emperors, has been able to accomplish; what Christianity, that epitome of the ancient faiths, has been unable to produce, the universal Republic, the economic Revolution, will accomplish, cannot fail to accomplish. It is indeed with political economy as with the other sciences: it is inevitably the same throughout the world: it does not depend upon the fancies of men or nation: it yields to the caprice of none. . . . Truth alone is equal everywhere: science is the unity of mankind. If then science, and no longer religion or authority, is taken in every land as the rule of society, the sovereign arbiter of interests, government becoming void, all the legislation of the universe will be in harmony. ("General Idea," in Manuel and Manuel, pp. 374–375)

Paradoxically, Proudhon was attracted to the cosmopolitanism of classical political economy and its opposition to excessive government intervention. Above all else, he sought protection of individual freedom. He wished to preserve economic forces and economic institutions, unlike the socialists he knew; at the same time, like them, he wanted to suppress existing conflict between these forces. He did not endorse the socialist plea to eliminate private property, but he did advocate its universal distribution. He wanted everyone to have property, which he considered the greatest guarantor of liberty. However, he put no faith in the state to accomplish this end. He thought the widespread possession of property would be achieved through a process of rationalization, or enlightenment. It is probably for this reason that Marx considered his ideas "utopian." In contrast to Marx, Proudhon's thought was evolutionary rather than revolutionary.

Justice and Exchange. Despite his affinity for the philosophy of classical political economy, Proudhon refuted the arguments of the classical economists in order to distance his position from theirs. He detected a false promise in classical liberalism that defeated its conclusions. Proudhon was convinced that the price mechanism—which classical liberalism relied on to accomplish social ends—was just as oppressive as law and other government actions. In the final analysis, he judged a major assumption of classical economics untenable—the premise that economic power is more or less equally diffused in the marketplace. The law of supply and demand, he claimed, is a "deceitful law . . . suitable only for assuring victory of the strong over the weak, of those who own property over those who own nothing" (cited in Ritter, p. 121). Presumably, if each market participant had an equal chance to benefit from the vagaries of supply and demand, Proudhon would accept the market as a method of organizing society. But he did not believe that all traders were equally subject to the market; hence he thought the market incapable of fulfilling its promise to protect each individual's freedom to pursue his or her own goals.

In retrospect Proudhon's criticism of economic liberalism is misplaced, since what he objected to was monopoly, not competition. In fact, Proudhon gloried in the notion of competition. Declaring the market oppressive, he nevertheless said that competition is "the spice of exchange, the salt of work," adding that "to suppress competition is to suppress liberty itself" (cited in Ritter, p. 123). Proudhon acknowledged that competition encourages creativity and on that account should be maintained. As he saw it, the task of the economist is to create a more appropriate environment for competition so that its benefits could be realized.

In Proudhon's ideal society the social fabric is held together by mutual respect rather than authority. Economic exchange in his world "imposes no obligation on its parties but that which results from their personal promise . . . it is subject to no external authority. . . . When I bargain for some good with one or more of my fellow citizens, it is clear that then it is my will alone that is my law" (cited in Ritter, p. 124). In order to protect bargainers from being exploited in market exchange, Proudhon strove to equalize power among market participants. This is what lies behind his proposals for the universalization of property and the creation of interest-free loans for all customers. To protect against trade stalemates that might result from the leveling of economic power, he encouraged social diversity, which he thought would stimulate competition and, at the same time, be consistent with individual liberty. Social diversity, he maintained, tends to prevent economic deadlocks by increasing traders' incentives to compromise. Nonmarket disputes (e.g., over ideology), moreover, cannot arise under true mutualism.

Proudhon's mutualism offers yet another parallel to Saint-Simon. Neither writer trusted the egoistic practice of self-interest to spontaneously establish social harmony, as Adam Smith proclaimed. Saint-Simon suggested replacing traditional government with a hierarchy of experts who are able to discern and promote the public interest. Proudhon rejected all forms of law, government, and hierarchy in favor of the mutualist principle of commutative justice. The duty of all traders in Proudhon's marketplace is to exchange goods with one another of equal, real value. Thus, he imposed the same basic rule of trade as that of Aristotle or Aquinas (see chapter 2). The problem with such maxims of trade, as we have seen, is that their purely subjective nature does not guarantee the viability of mutual exchange. In fairness to Proudhon, he recognized this shortcoming of his theory of exchange, but he never could adequately resolve this issue in a manner consistent with his libertarian principles.

German Historicism

Although most of the critics surveyed in this chapter up to now anchored their ideas to an evolutionary, progressive theory of history, we reserve the term *historicism* for a different brand of heterodoxy that surfaced in the nineteenth century. In this context, historicism refers to the role of history in defining the proper *method* of economic inquiry, not necessarily its premises, theorems, and conclusions. There were two nineteenth-century variants of historicism that encroached on economics, a German variant and a British variant. In this chapter we focus on German historicism. In a later chapter we introduce British historicism as a backdrop to neoclassical British economics and American institutionalism (see chapter 19). German historicism, which in the nineteenth century constituted a somewhat milder form of criticism than Marxist economics, appears here as a stage for Karl Marx's singular contribution to the social sciences, which is the subject of the next chapter.

The core question raised by historicists is whether economics can be legitimately studied apart from its political, historical, and social milieu—an issue that is still debated among social scientists. Both William S. Jevons (see chapter 15) and Alfred Marshall (see chapter 16) made important concessions to the historicist point of view. Moreover, a number of the organizers of the American Economic Association (founded in 1886), especially its first secretary, Richard T. Ely, were educated in Germany under the tutelage of the historicists. The significance of the historicist movement, therefore, should not be taken lightly, even if major methodological issues raised by them were sometimes based on a misunderstanding of logical processes.

The German Historical School is often divided into two groups of writers: the "older," less extreme school, and the "younger," more dogmatic members who propounded rigid and extreme views on economic method. Members of the older school include its founder, Wilhelm Roscher, as well as Karl Knies and Bruno Hildebrand. The younger school was dominated by the tenacious Gustav Schmoller.

Dating the precise origin of ideas is always difficult, if not impossible. Writers who combined economics with historical research may be found throughout the history of ideas, but a distinctive grouping of them emerged in Germany around 1840. Several reasons exist for the rise of historicists to supremacy in Germany. First, that country provided a suitable and favorable environment for historical economics to impose itself. Theoretical economics had not become entrenched in Germany. On the contrary, Germany harbored something of a hostile attitude toward it. Second, German philosophy had always stressed an "organic" rather than an individualistic approach to economic and social problems. Thus, men of the caliber of Roscher, Knies, and Hildebrand, spurred partly by the philosophy of Hegel and by the organic jurisprudence of Frederick Karl von Savigny, were drawn into the search for broad economic and cultural laws that would explain the world in which they lived. Hegel's emphasis on evolving ideas as the motive for changes in social organization is implicit in most German literature of the era, including the historicist movement. Hegelian influence figures prominently in List's doctrine of the succession of states, for example, which he developed as early as 1845. In fact, Hegel's philosophy permeated practically all aspects of German social thought in the nineteenth century, including that of Marx and the Romantics.

Wilhelm Roscher

Time and a dubious reputation as extraneous cast a shadow over the mass of historicist literature. Most historians of economics pass over the field in silence, while others deride the famous (and some would say, pointless) *methodenstreit* (literally "battle of methods") that pitted Gustav Schmoller against Carl Menger, leader of the Austrian School (see chapter 14). This neglect is particularly regrettable in the case of the founder of the "older historical school," Wilhelm Roscher. Like his colleagues, Roscher incorporated Hegelian ideas on history in his work on economics.

Born at Hanover in 1817, Roscher studied jurisprudence and philosophy at the universities of Göttingen and Berlin from 1835 to 1839. In 1848 he became professor of political economy at the University of Leipzig. Although he began his work on economic history as early as 1838, his magisterial grasp of history and historical methods was put on full display in 1854, with the publication of his major economic treatise, *System des Volkswirschaft* (*Principles of Political Economy*). This encyclopedic work matched the scope of J. S. Mill's classic treatise and established Roscher as a scholar of the first rank. He did not want to abandon Ricardian economics altogether; he merely wanted to supplement and complete it. The historical method that he outlined for this purpose sought to combine organic, biological analysis—the study of living, breathing human beings—and statistics to discover the laws of economics. In other words, economics could not be entrusted exclusively to the abstract, deductive method. Roscher wrote:

> That which is general in Political Economy has . . . much that is analogous to the mathematical sciences. Like the latter, it swarms with abstractions. . . . It also supposes the parties to the contract to be guided only by a sense of their own best interest, and not to be influenced by secondary considerations. It is not, therefore, to be wondered at, that many authors have endeavored to clothe the laws of Political Economy in algebraic formulae. [But] . . . the advantages of the mathematical model of expression diminish as the facts to which it is applied become more complicated. This is true even in the ordinary psychology of the individual. How much more, therefore, in the portraying of national life! . . . The abstraction according to which all men are by nature the same, different only in consequence, is one which, as Ricardo and von Thünen have shown, must pass as an indispensable stage in the preparatory labors of political economists. It would be especially well, when an economic fact is produced by the cooperation of many different factors, for the investigator to mentally isolate the factor of which, for the time being, he wishes to examine the peculiar nature. All other factors should, for a time, be considered as not operating, and as unchangeable, and then the questions asked, What would be the effect of a change in the factor to be examined, whether the change be occasioned by enlarging or diminishing it? But it never should be lost sight of, that such a one is only an abstraction after all, for which, not only in the transition to practice, but even in finished theory, we must turn to the infinite variety of real life. (*Principles*, p. 105)[7]

[7] This kind of cautionary signal about the dangers of abstraction continues to echo down through the centuries; see, for example, Nobel laureate Wassily Leontieff's "Theoretical Assumptions and Nonobserved Facts," in which it is argued that the weak and all too slow-growing empirical foundations of economics cannot support the proliferating superstructure of pure economic theory.

History and the recording of it (data) were essential for Roscher because he rejected the idea of economics as a set of normative, value-loaded prescriptions. He set as his goals the faithful description of what has come to pass and the explanation of how social and national life came to be as it is. He said:

> Our aim is simply to describe man's economic nature and economic wants, to investigate the laws and the character of the institutions which are adapted to the satisfaction of these wants, and the greater or less amount of success by which they have been attended. Our task is, therefore, so to speak, the anatomy and physiology of social or national economy. (*Principles*, p. 111)

Roscher expected the historical path of discovery to lead to broad laws of historical (economic) development that would allow comparisons within and between nation-states. He argued that classical economics—especially the Ricardian variant—did not, and could not, provide the whole story. Underscoring the advantages of this historical method, Roscher stressed that its use in economics would establish "a firm island of scientific truth, as universally recognized as truth as are the principles of mathematical physics by physicians of the most various schools" (*Principles*, p. 113).

Joined in this task by Karl Knies and Bruno Hildebrand, Roscher devoted his lifework to establishing the historical method. In a prolific stream of publications that included the one-thousand-page *Principles*, he set out to integrate economics and other phenomena. But when it came to treating the theory of traditional topics—money, wages, values, and so forth—Roscher accepted, in the main, the analyses of John Stuart Mill. In later editions of his *Principles*, Roscher even incorporated W. S. Jevons's contributions to utility and statistics. What was different about Roscher's work was not any overt antagonism to classical political economy but his incredible display of historico-statistical virtuosity aimed at enlarging and elucidating received economic theory. Roscher's passion for history and statistics led him into side excursions on the construction of price indexes and other topics including population, international trade, and protectionism. The history of prices in turn led to a study of economic institutions such as slavery, church, money, and insurance. Many of these themes still repay careful reading, but in the end, despite his best efforts, Roscher was unable—even with the assistance of Knies and Hildebrand—to reorient the dominant method of economics. When the more extreme "younger" school took over, the tide turned toward antagonism.

Gustav Schmoller

The younger historical school, led by the indomitable Gustav Schmoller, pushed Roscher's historicism to extremes. Schmoller argued that all received economic analysis, especially Ricardo's, was not only useless but downright pernicious. Rather than repeat the errors of the abstract, deductive method, the younger historical school set out to study economics de novo as an organic subject. Schmoller seriously proposed that due to the unrealism of its assumptions, its degree of theoretical abstraction, and its neglect of interrelated and relevant facts, existing economic theory be discarded completely. In its place he would substitute historical laws of development, laws that Schmoller attempted to establish in numerous publications, including his compendious *Grundriss der Allgemeine Volkswirtschaftslehre* (roughly translated as *Outline of General Economic Theory*), an ambitious attempt to capture sweeping historical laws in a single, systematic treatise.

Published between 1900 and 1904, Schmoller's *Grundriss* was described by Wesley Clair Mitchell as a "treatise of beginnings" (*Types of Economic Theory*, p.

574). For Schmoller and his followers economic laws were not discoverable by mere logical deductions, but rather they were found in the study of society in the broadest possible context. Thus, the younger historical school combined history and ethnology (i.e., a branch of anthropology that deals with the study of cultures) to explore such topics as medieval institutions (especially the guild system), urban development, banking, and various industry studies. As Joseph Schumpeter remarked, Schmoller was essentially a historically minded sociologist.

Thus, while the older historical school questioned the abstractedness and absolutism of classical economic theory, the younger school rejected theory altogether. Schmoller established sharp lines of demarcation in the ensuing debate over method: He wished to replace the abstract-deductive method with the historico-inductive method. Such theoretical antagonisms were bound to stir up controversy sooner or later, and when it came, it is no surprise that the bitterness was hottest and heaviest in Germany. The first blow came from neighboring Austria, where Carl Menger (see chapter 14) was in the midst of reforming classical economics by preserving its theoretical roots.

In 1883, Menger published a book on methodology (*Investigations into the Method of the Social Sciences with Special Reference to Economics*) that launched a frontal attack on Schmoller by vindicating the use of economic theory as a legitimate procedural device in the social sciences. What followed was a protracted and heated debate that has come to be known as the *methodenstreit*, or battle of methods. In retaliation Schmoller wrote an unfavorable review of Menger's *Investigations*. Menger counterattacked in a pamphlet entitled *Errors of Historicism* (1884); which elicited a predictable rebuttal from Schmoller, and so on. The bitter quarrel that provoked these exchanges involved personalities and intellectual preferences as well as methodological substance. Because the debate was largely a matter of precedents and the relative merits of theory versus history, much of the fight amounted to "tilting at windmills."

The issue of the proper method to employ in economics, as in each social science, is not a trivial one. But the extreme to which Schmoller took the historicist doctrine made it antirationalist: It refused to derive any general rules from reason, insisting instead on recording unique events in almost infinite historical variation. No doubt facts are extremely important, but the jumble of facts that present themselves in everyday life must be steered by something if they are to be meaningful and useful. Schmoller's historicism offered no principles to guide or restrain human action. Thus, it was a well without a spring to feed it. It may be that Joseph Schumpeter—who was trained in the Austrian tradition opposed to Schmoller and his followers—issued the last word on the matter. He said that "since there cannot be any serious question either about the basic importance of historical research in a science that deals with a historical process or about the necessity of developing a set of analytic tools by which to handle the material, the controversy, like all such controversies, might well . . . have been wholly pointless" (*History of Economic Analysis*, p. 814).

■ Heterodoxy and Entrepreneurism

This chapter presents (non-Marxian) heterodox economic thought as it emerged in England and Western Europe in the nineteenth century. The record shows that France (and to a lesser extent England) provided fertile ground for early socialist thought. The strain was more prevalent in France, probably because England escaped the upheaval of the French Revolution. The entrepreneur is a key actor in a market-exchange economy, which is antithetical to the aspirations of socialist economies. Since socialism stresses collective action, its proponents are not likely to be much concerned about the role and significance of entrepreneurism.

German historicism, however, presents another story. Despite the predominant tendency among historians of economic thought to treat historicism as an unfortunate detour in the development of economic science, one may justifiably expect to find discussions of entrepreneurship in a discipline that emphasizes living, breathing persons and historical experience. Roscher treated the subject in much the same way as J. B. Say and J. S. Mill, representing entrepreneurial activity as a special form of labor, and profit as a special form of wage. Earlier German economists such as J. H. von Thünen and H. K. von Mangoldt hammered out theoretical innovations in the treatment of entrepreneurism, but their ideas are reserved for chapter 14, where they fit into the backdrop of Carl Menger, founder of the Austrian School.

Schmoller's contribution is easy to overlook because it is subtle, not wedded closely to economic theory, and indiscriminately infused with normative propositions. He showed that entrepreneurship and leadership resemble each other—a theme commonly associated with Wieser (see chapter 14), who impressed on Schumpeter the importance of the "sociology of leadership."[8] Schmoller recognized the creative role of exceptional individuals as an internal factor of the development process. The major characteristics of entrepreneurship he identified—initiative, risk, leadership—resemble common basics of a theory of entrepreneurship, but his antagonism toward theory in the conventional sense did not incline him to invest entrepreneurism with theoretical substance. He was content to emphasize that those best endowed with will power and motivational drive, the "born leaders" of society, would become the most successful entrepreneurs (*Grundriss*, vol. 2, p. 434). He defined the entrepreneur in unambiguous terms as the person who is the center and head of an enterprise, the one who takes the initiative and bears the risks (*Grundriss*, vol. 1, p. 413).

Unfortunately Schmoller slipped easily into making normative statements, whether due to his aversion to theory or his general character is uncertain. He portrayed entrepreneurs who manage the challenges of large enterprises as not only highly energetic, but also ruthless (*Grundriss*, vol. 1, p. 430). On that account he observed that economic improvements such as rising productivity and living standards attributable to entrepreneurism might be accompanied by the spread of antisocial attitudes, such as greed. To safeguard the effects of entrepreneurship, he argued that it needs to be embedded in a framework of political regulations and customary institutions. Such statements were not grounded in a solid, theoretic approach, since he did not explore the function of the entrepreneur by means of an elaborate theory of entrepreneurship. But aside from his normative "errors" Schmoller (and later, Werner Sombart) tilled the ground for Schumpeter's influential perspective by emphasizing the institutional embeddedness of entrepreneurship as a historical fact of the exchange economy.

[8] Schmoller's influence on Schumpeter's treatment of entrepreneurial activity (see chapter 23) as the central element in his theory of economic development has not been widely appreciated; but see Ebner, "Institutional Analysis of Entrepreneurship."

Conclusion

Even as British classical economics was consolidating its position and becoming an orthodox body of thought in the nineteenth century it was subject to various criticisms from different quarters. Evolutionists, historicists, radicals, reformers, and Romantics all weighed in against what historian Thomas Carlyle injudiciously dubbed "the dismal science." It is not easy to gauge the full effect of these criticisms even as far removed as we are today. Yet, at least two things are clear from the historical record: First, dissent has been part of the history of economics from its beginning (and we shall encounter dissent of various kinds in later sections of this book). Second, the missing element in nineteenth-century heterodox economic thought was a truly scientific "engine of analysis" that could propel economics toward the resolution of pressing problems. Near the middle of the century, Karl Marx undertook to fill this void.

As we approach the next chapter it is worth noting that Hegelian philosophy formed a common root of German historicism and Marxian economics. Hegel considered history the proper guide to the science of society, a theme echoed by Marx and the historicists alike. However, Marx rejected Hegel's peculiar view of liberty, which involved submission to the state. For his part, Marx anticipated the withering away of the state. Inasmuch as most of the German historicists exalted the nation and the role of government they were better Hegelians than Marx in this regard. On the practical side, German historicists promoted a social policy of ameliorating the condition of the working class. They envisioned a kind of "people's capitalism" in which workers obtained a proprietary interest in industry. Their views were therefore compatible with the welfare state that Otto von Bismarck undertook to construct when he came to power near the end of the century. The failures of the group were not so much of the practical as the intellectual kind. Not only were they unable to discover the universal laws of historical development, they also failed to convince the next generation of theoretical economists to embrace the historicist method—a method that has and continues to have gravitas in economics. They may have struck a chord by extolling fact-finding, but their quantitative data were not assembled in a manner that could verify economic theory. Because their facts had to speak for themselves, they underestimated the extent to which meaningful measurement depends on a theoretical framework to organize and interpret observations.

The issue of proper balance between theory and facts is a delicate one that requires attention to context and detail. A clear lesson that can be drawn from the historicist interlude in the history of economics is that some theories, though elegant, may be "empty" in the sense that they have no empirical content or grounding in fact. Although the younger historical school rejected Roscher's moderate approach to historicist economics, he was acutely aware of the symbiotic relationship between theory and facts. He wrote:

> It is evident that, of statistics in general, economic statistics constitute a chief part, and precisely the part most accessible to numerical treatment. As these economic statistics need to be always directed by the light of Political Economy, they also furnish it with rich materials for the continuation of its structure, and for the strengthening of such foundations as it already has. They are, moreover, the indispensable condition of the application of economic theorems to practice. (*Principles*, pp. 94–95)

This passage could be taken as a warning that contemporary economic theory may yet have to pay dearly for ignoring the saner and less extreme messages of the historicist doctrine. At the very least the historicist movement is an expression of the desire to preserve basic insights into the historical and changing nature of economic and social phenomena against the onslaught of oversimplified and mechanistic views of the "laws" of rational behavior. In this sense, it was an important step in the development of related disciplines, especially sociology.

References

Condorcet, Marquis de Marie-Jean. *Esquisses d'un tableau historique des progrès de l'esprit humain*. Paris, 1795.

Ebner, Alexander. "The Institutional Analysis of Entrepreneurship: Historicist Aspects of Schumpeter's Development Theory," in J. G. Backhouse (ed.), *Joseph Alois Schumpeter: Entrepreneurship, Style and Vision*, Boston: Kluwer, 2003.

Gide, Charles, and Charles Rist. *A History of Economic Doctrines from the Time of the Physiocrats to the Present Day*, 2d ed., R. Richards (trans.). Boston: Heath, 1948.

Leontieff, Wassily. "Theoretical Assumptions and Nonobserved Facts." *American Economic Review*, vol. 61 (March 1971), pp. 1–7.

Levy, David M. *How the Dismal Science Got its Name: Classical Economics and the Urtext of Racial Politics*. Ann Arbor: The University of Michigan Press, 2001.

List, Friedrich. *The National System of Political Economy*, S. S. Lloyd (trans.). New York: Longmans, 1928 [1841].

Morton, A. L. *The Life and Ideas of Robert Owen*. New York: Monthly Review Press, 1963.

Mitchell, Wesley Clair, *Types of Economic Theory*, vol. 2. New York: A. M. Kelley, 1969.

Proudhon, Pierre-Joseph. "What is Property," in F. E. Manuel and F. P. Manuel, (eds.), *French Utopias: An Anthology of Ideal Societies*. New York: Free Press, 1966.

———. "The General Idea of the Revolution in the Nineteenth Century," in F. E. Manuel and F. P. Manuel (eds.), *French Utopias: An Anthology of Ideal Societies*. New York: Free Press, 1966.

Ritter, Allan. *The Political Thought of Pierre-Joseph Proudhon*. Princeton, NJ: Princeton University Press, 1969.

Roscher, Wilhelm. *Principles of Political Economy*, vol. 1, J. J. Lalor (trans.). New York: Henry Holt, 1877 [1854].

Ruskin, John. "Modern Painters," in E. T. Cook and Alexander Wedderburn (eds.), *The Works of John Ruskin*, vol. 5. London: George Allen, 1905.

Saint-Simon, C. H., and Prosper Enfantin. *Oeuvres complètes de Saint-Simon et Enfantin*, 47 vols. Aaelen: Otto Zeller, 1963 (the writings of Saint-Simon are in volumes 15, 18–23, 37–40).

Schmoller, Gustav von. *Grundriss der allgemeinen Volkswirtschaftslehre*, vols. 1 & 2. Munich and Leipzeig: Duncker & Humblot, 1900 and 1904.

Schumpeter, J. A. *History of Economic Analysis*, E. B. Schumpeter (ed.). New York: Oxford University Press, 1954.

Sismondi, J. C. L. Simonde de. *De la richesse commerciale, ou principes* d'économie politique appliquées à la *législation du commerce*, 2 vols. Geneva, 1803.

———. *Nouveaux principes* d'économie politique, vol. 1. Paris: Delaunay, 1827.

———. Études sur l'économie politique. Paris, 1836.

Smith, Adam. *The Wealth of Nations*, Edwin Caanan (ed.). New York: Modern Library, 1937.

Thoreau, David. *The Writings of Henry David Thoreau*, vol. 7. Boston: Houghton-Mifflin, 1906.

Notes for Further Reading

The following three articles from *History of Political Economy* provide an overview of the kind of criticism leveled at classical economics: W. D. Grampp, "Classical Economics and Its Moral Critics," vol. 5 (Fall 1973), pp. 359–374; T. E. Kaiser, "Politics and Political Economy in the Thought of the Ideologues," vol. 12 (Summer 1980), pp. 141–160; and C. C. Ryan, "The Friends of Commerce: Romantic and Marxist Criticisms of Classical Political Economy," *History of Political Economy*, vol. 13 (Spring 1981), pp. 80–94. Some helpful general surveys of socialist thought are: Alexander Gray, *The Socialist Tradition: Moses to Lenin* (London: Longmans, 1946); G. D. H. Cole, *A History of Socialist Thought*, 5 vols. (New York: St. Martin's, 1953–1960); and George Lichtheim, *The Origins of Socialism* (New York: Praeger, 1969). Gray is particularly strong on the economic aspects of socialist thought; Lichtheim concentrates on socialist thought before Marx. Robert Heilbroner's ever-popular and readable *The Worldly Philosophers*, 7th ed. (New York: Touchstone, 1999), contains a delightful chapter on the utopian socialists. Biographical details of individual dissenters may be found in Philip Arestis and Malcolm Sawyer (eds.), *A Biographical Dictionary of Dissenting Economists*, 2d ed. (Cheltenham, UK: Edward Elgar, 2000).

Henryk Grossman's two-part article, "The Evolutionist Revolt against Classical Economics," *Journal of Political Economy*, vol. 51 (October, December 1943) discusses the ideas of Condorcet, Saint-Simon, Sismondi, James Steuart, Richard Jones, and Karl Marx. For more on Condorcet, see Keith M. Baker, *Condorcet: From Natural Philosophy to Social Mathematics* (Chicago: University of Chicago press, 1975); and Emma Rothschild, *Economic Sentiments: Adam Smith, Condorcet, and the Enlightenment* (Harvard University Press, 2001). The intermediate ground between the progressive philosophy of history of Condorcet and the regressive philosophy of Rousseau was occupied by Condillac. See Arnaud Orain, "Decline and Progress: The Economic Agent in Condillac's Theory of History," *The European Journal of the History of Economic Thought*, vol. 10 (Autumn 2003), pp. 379–407.

Saint-Simon's original works appeared in French, but fragmentary translations are contained in F. M. H. Markham (ed.), *Social Organization, the Science of Man and Other Writings* (New York: Harper & Row, 1964), which also contains a useful introduction. Additional English translations appear in G. G. Iggers (trans.), *The Doctrine of Saint-Simon: An Exposition. First Year, 1828–1829* (Boston: Beacon Press, 1958). Saint-Simon's influence is discussed in Elie Halévy's *Era of Tyrannies*, R. K. Webb (trans.) (Garden City, NY: Anchor Books, Doubleday & Co., 1965), and is the subject of full-length treatment by sociologist Émile Durkheim, *Socialism and Saint-Simon*, A. W. Gouldner (ed.) and C. Sattler (trans.) (Yellow Springs, OH: Antioch Press, 1958), and by historian Frank Manuel, *The New World of Henri Saint-Simon* (Cambridge, MA: Harvard University Press, 1962). A leading twentieth-century specialist in industrial organization, E. S. Mason, "Saint-Simonism and the Rationalisation of Industry," *Quarterly Journal of Economics*, vol. 45 (August 1931), pp. 640–683, emphasized the relevance of Saint-Simon's ideas to modern capitalism. Some of the same themes are repeated by Niles Hansen, "Saint-Simon's Industrial Society in Modern Perspective," *Southwestern Social Science Quarterly*, vol. 47 (December 1966), pp. 253–262. F. A. Hayek provides a distinctly unsympathetic treatment of Saint-Simon and his influence in *The Counter-Revolution of Science: Studies in the Abuse of Reason* (New York: Free Press, 1955).

Most of Sismondi's works (e.g., *Nouveaux principes*) are available in French only, but a collection of his essays has been translated into English; see J. C. L. Sismondi, *Political Economy and the Philosophy of Government* (New York: A. M. Kelly, 1965 [1847]). See also, H. W. Spiegel (ed.), *The Development of Economic Thought* (New York: Wiley, 1952), pp. 253–268. Secondary literature on Sismondi is rather sparse, but see Mao-Lan Tuan, *Simonde de Sismondi as an Economist*, (New York: Columbia University Press, 1927); and Thomas Sowell, "Sismondi: A Neglected Pioneer," *History of Political Economy*, vol. 1 (Spring 1968), pp. 62–88. Lenin sought to refute Sismondi's ideas in *A Characterization of Economic Romanticism* (Moscow: Foreign Languages Publishing House, 1951 [1897]).

Rousseau's ideas and political philosophy became embedded in European society. His notion of envy is contrasted with modern notions by Claire Pignol, "Rousseau's Notion of Envy: A Comparison with Modern Economic Theory," *The European Journal of the History of Economic Thought*, vol. 9 (Fall 2012), pp. 529–549. Pignol maintains that envy functions as a kind of criticism of self-interest, but tension exists between the modern theory and different concepts of envy expressed by Rousseau.

Henry David Thoreau was the major "Romantic" voice in the United States, but has not drawn much attention from economists. An exception is Christian Becker, "Thoreau's Economic Philosophy," *The European Journal of the History of Economic Thought*, vol. 15 (Spring 2008), pp. 211–246. Becker represents Thoreau as a critic of classical political economy, especially Say's work. Thoreau was concerned that through the modern economy human beings can become alienated from themselves and nature. David A. Spencer, "Work in Utopia: Pro-work Sentiments in the Writings of Four Critics of Classical Economics," *The European Journal of the History of Economic Thought*, vol. 16, (Winter 2009), pp. 97–122, examines how Fourier, Carlyle, Ruskin, and William Morris thought work would be done in their utopian societies. Each believed that the disutility of labor was a product of capitalist society and could be overcome in utopia, where work would be a positive activity rather than a drudge.

Robert Owen, *A New View of Society and Other Writings* (New York: Everyman's Library, Dutton, 1927) provides an introduction to the mind of the master of New Lanark Mills. The standard biography of Owen is Frank Podmore, *Robert Owen: A Biography* (New York: Appleton, 1906). E. R. A. Seligman's *Essays in Economics* (New York: Macmillan, 1925) includes an essay entitled "Owen and the Christian Socialists." An Internet resource, The History Guide: Lectures on Modern European Intellectual History, offers an introduction to the ideas of Fourier (http://www.historyguide.org/intellect/lecture21a.html), and Owen and Saint-Simon (http://www.historyguide.org/intellect/lecture22a.html).

Few of Fourier's works have been translated into English. See Julia Franklin (trans.), *Design for Utopia: Selected Writings of Charles Fourier* (New York: Schocken Books, 1981); and J. Beecher and R. Bienvenu (eds. and trans.), *The Utopian Vision of Charles Fourier: Selected Tracts on Work, Love, and Passionate Attraction* (Boston: Beacon Press, 1971). N. V. Riasanovsky, *The Teachings of Charles Fourier* (Berkeley: University of California Press, 1970), provides good coverage of Fourier's ideas; and E. S. Mason, "Fourier and Anarchism," *Quarterly Journal of Economics*, vol. 42 (1928), pp. 228–262 repays careful reading, even at this late date. John Cunliffe and Guido Erreygers, "The Enigmatic Legacy of Charles Fourier: Joseph Charlier," *History of Political Economy*, vol. 33 (Fall 2001), pp. 459–484, tentatively demonstrate that perhaps Fourier's influence was not negligible after all.

Is anarchy more provocative than passionate attraction? Why else has Proudhon been translated more than Fourier? See, P. J. Proudhon, *What Is Property?*, B. R. Tucker (trans.) (New York: H. Fertig, 1966); P. J. Proudhon, *General Idea of the Revolution in the Nineteenth Century*, J. B. Robinson (trans.) (London: Freedom Press, 1923); and P. J. Proudhon, *System of Economic Contradictions: or the Philosophy of Poverty*, B. R. Tucker (trans.) (Princeton, NJ: B. R. Tucker, 1888). P. J. Proudhon, *Proudhon's Solution of the Social Problem*, Henry Cohen (ed.) (New York: Vanguard, 1927), comprises a group of articles on banking and other topics. For biographical details on Proudhon's life, see George Woodcock, *Pierre-Joseph Proudhon* (New York: Macmillan, 1956); and J. H. Jackson, *Marx, Proudhon and European Socialism* (New York: Macmillan, n.d.). This last book details the relation between the two leading socialists of the mid-nineteenth century. Proudhon's ideas have provoked a variety of responses. For two dramatic reactions, see J. S. Shapiro, "Pierre Joseph Proudhon: Harbinger of Fascism," *American Historical Review*, vol. 50 (July 1945), pp. 714–737; and Dudley Dillard, "Keynes and Proudhon," *Journal of Economic History*, vol. 2 (May 1942), pp. 63–76. For a brief glimpse of "America's Proudhon" see B. N. Hall, "Josiah Warren, First American Anarchist," *History of Political Economy*, vol. 6 (February 1974), pp. 95–108.

The broad sweep of nineteenth-century German economics is explored by historian David F. Lindenfeld, *The Practical Imagination: The German Sciences of State in the Nineteenth Century* (Chicago: University of Chicago Press, 1997). See also, Keith Tribe, *Strategies of Economic Order: German Economic Discourse, 1750-1950* (Cambridge University Press, 1995), for an overview of two hundred years of German economic thought from the *Staatswissenschaften* of the eighteenth century to National Socialism and the Social Market of the nineteenth. T. W. Hutchison discusses both the "older" and "younger" German historical schools in his *Review of Economic Doctrines, 1870–1929* (Oxford: The Clarendon Press, 1953), chaps. 8 and 12; and again in "Some Themes from Investigation into Method," in J. R. Hicks and W. Weber, *Carl Menger and the Austrian School of Economics* (London: Oxford University Press, 1973). Joseph Schumpeter provides a useful and perceptive overview of the stage and its actors in his *History of Economic Analysis* (see references), pp. 800–824. Those especially interested in methodology should consult Felix Kaufman, *Methodology of the Social Sciences* (New York: Oxford University Press, 1944).

Friedrich List's ideas were favored by American protectionists in the nineteenth century, but the American position had already been staked out much earlier by Alexander Hamilton in his *Report on the Subject of Manufactures* (1791), reprinted in A. H. Cole (ed.), *Industrial and Commercial Correspondence of Alexander Hamilton* (New York: A. M. Kelley, 1968). Margaret E. Hirst, *Life of Friedrich List and Selections from His Writings* (London: Smith, Elder and Company, 1909) contains excerpts from List's *Outlines of American Political Economy*, which was written on behalf of the American protectionists during List's visit to the United States. H. W. Spiegel, *The Growth of Economic Thought*, 3d ed. (Durham, NC: Duke University Press, 1991) contains additional references to List's works.

Noting the cursory treatment usually accorded to the German Historical School in standard textbooks, H. K. Betz, "How Does the German Historical School Fit?" *History of Political Economy*, vol. 20 (Fall 1988), pp. 409–430, seeks to define the group's contributions to the theory of economic policy and pattern modeling. Haim Barkai examines money and monetary issues in German historical thought in "The Old Historical School: Roscher on Money and Monetary Issues," *History of Political Economy*, vol. 21 (Summer 1989), pp. 179–200; and again in "Schmoller on Money and the Monetary Dimension of Economics," *History of Political Economy*, vol. 23 (Spring 1991), pp. 13–39.

Yuichi Shionoya (ed.), *The German Historical School: The Historical and Ethical Approach to Economics* (London: Routledge, 2001) contains thirteen essays (some slightly anomalous) on various members of the older and younger schools and their impact on Japanese economists. Same author, *The Soul of the German Historical School* (Berlin: Springer, 2005) contains methodological essays on Schmoller, Weber, and Schumpeter. H. H. Nau and Bertram Schefold (eds.), *The Historicity of Economics: Continuities and Discontinuities of Historical Thought in 19th and 20th Century Economics* (Berlin: Springer, 2002) consists of six conference papers that deal with the legacies of historical economics since Schmoller. This volume seeks to establish a link between the German Historical School and the New Institutional Economics on grounds of a common concern for institutions and path dependency. The very existence of the German Historical School has been called into question by Heath Pearson, "Was There Really a German Historical School of Economics?" *History of Political Economy*, vol. 31 (Fall 1999), pp. 547–562. Bruce Caldwell, "There Really *Was* a German Historical School of Economics: A Comment on Heath Pearson," *History of Political Economy*, vol. 33 (Fall 2001), pp. 649–654, defends the distinction; but see Pearson's rejoinder following Caldwell's article.

On Schmoller and the later historicists, see Nicholas Balabkins, *Not by Theory Alone . . . The Economics of Gustav von Schmoller and Its Legacy to America* (Berlin: Duncker und Humblot, 1988); Ben B. Seligman, *Main Currents in Modern Economics* (New York: Free Press, 1962), chap. 1; and W. C. Mitchell, *Types of Economic Theory* (New York: A. M. Kelley, 1969), chap. 19. Mitchell's assessment of the *methodenstreit* is especially informative. For a different and more contemporary view of the famous controversy, see Sam Bostaph, "The Methodological Debate Between Carl Menger and the German Historicists," *Atlantic Economic Journal*, vol. 6 (September 1978), pp. 3–16. Closer to the heat of the moment, Menger's position in the *methodenstreit* was chronicled by his disciple, Eugen Böhm-Bawerk, "The Historical vs. the Deductive Method in Political Economy," *Annals of the American Academy of Political and Social Science*, vol. 1 (October 1890), pp. 244–271.

Erik Grimmer-Solem, *The Rise of Historical Economics and Social Reform in Germany, 1864–1894* (Oxford: Clarendon Press, 2003) attempts to revise the prevailing hackneyed view of the younger historical school, but before delving into Grimmer-Solem's book, see Heath Pearson's review of it in *History of Political Economy*, vol. 37 (Summer 2005), pp. 395–397. Helke Peukert, "The Schmoller Renaissance," *History of Political Economy*, vol. 33 (Spring 2001), pp. 71–116, analyzes the revival of interest in Schmoller in the late twentieth century. Heino H. Nau, "Gustav Schmoller's Historico-Ethical Political Economy: Ethics, Politics and Economics in the Younger German Historical School, 1860–1917," *The European Journal of the History of Economic Thought*, vol. 7 (Winter 2000), pp. 507–531, contributes to this revival. For a sympathetic view of the historical school and its contributions, in particular the positive accomplishments of a single member of the younger school, see A. Schweitzer, "Typological Method in Economics: Max Weber's Contribution," *History of Political Economy*, vol. 2 (Spring 1970), pp. 66–99.

12

Karl Marx
Historical Determinism vs. Utopian Socialism

Whether understood or misunderstood it would be hard to find a more influential writer in the history of social thought than Karl Marx. Despite the decline of Marxist-inspired economies throughout the world today, the man and his system of thought captured the imagination of intellectuals the world over. Marx influenced many fields: philosophy, sociology, psychology, and political theory. But his major work, *Das Kapital* (*Capital*), is about economics above all. What set him apart from so many other economists was his ability to weave together the philosophical, historical, sociological, psychological, political, and economic threads of argument into a coherent whole.

Born in Trier, Prussia, in 1818, Marx was the son of middle-class Jewish parents who later converted to Christianity. As a youth he was popular with his playmates and enjoyed an amicable relationship with his parents. At the age of seventeen, he entered the University of Bonn as a law student, but despite a sharp mind, his studies suffered from the distractions of youth. He attended class rarely, indulging instead in the good times and high jinks of college life. His father grew tired of his son's poor academic performance, withdrew him from the University of Bonn after his first year, and enrolled him at the University of Berlin, an institution less tolerant of nonacademic distractions. During the continuance of his training in jurisprudence and political economy at Berlin, Marx came under the influence of Georg Wilhelm Friedrich Hegel and Ludwig Andreas von Feuerbach, whose ideas helped shape his own views of history, religion, and society.

Marx switched schools again, and after completing his PhD dissertation at the University of Jena in 1841, he moved back to Bonn, hoping to secure a teaching position at the university he had formerly attended. He abandoned this hope in 1842, at which point he assumed the editorship of the *Rheinische Zeitung*, a German newspaper in which he could air his unorthodox ideas and indulge his taste for the literature of the French socialists. After strict censorship was imposed on the *Rheinische Zeitung* in 1843 Marx resigned as editor. In June of the same year he married his childhood sweetheart (Jenny von Westphalen) and moved to Paris, where he founded a new journal—the *Deutsch-Französische Jarbucher.* All the while Marx continued to write, though mostly on philosophical topics. In Paris, however, he began a systematic study of economics, especially of Smith and Ricardo. There, too, he studied the materialist philosophers, including Locke; he became acquainted with Proudhon; and he began to distill most of his major ideas. His most active literary decade was yet to come, but in 1844 Marx wrote a number of manuscripts, which were later collected and published as *Economic and Philosophic Manuscripts of 1844*.

In the meantime, Marx had become an outcast in his native country. The Prussian government declared him guilty of treason in 1844 for his articles in the *Jarbucher*, making it impossible for him to return to his homeland. The following year, prodded by Prussia, he was also expelled by France. He fled to Brussels, where, in due course, his *Theses on Feuerbach* (1845), *The German Ideology* (1846, with Engels), and *The Poverty of Philosophy* (1847) were published—the last a scathing critique of Proudhon's earlier *Philosophy of Poverty*. In 1847 Marx gave a series of lectures, which were later published as *Wage Labour and Capital* (1849). *The Communist Manifesto* followed in 1848, and in 1849 Marx and his family settled in London, where he spent the remainder of his life, a great part of which was spent writing and studying economics in the library of the British Museum. In 1851, Marx entered a ten-year period as occasional contributor to the *New York Daily Tribune*, whose fees helped sustain his family's meager existence.

Marx began a feverish period of writing and publishing in 1857. In that year alone he prepared a lengthy critique of political economy that was to serve as an outline for his later magnum opus. Now known as the *Grundrisse*, these manuscripts were undiscovered and unpublished until World War II. Marx began *A Contribution to the Critique of Political Economy* in 1858 and finished it the following year. By 1863, he had also completed *Theories of Surplus Value*. The first volume of *Capital* appeared in 1867, but he had not completed the second and third volumes by his death in 1883. These last two volumes appeared under the editorship of Marx's lifetime friend and collaborator, Friedrich Engels, who died in 1895, a year after the publication of the third and final volume.

Marx's personal life was marked by all kinds of adversity, including abject poverty and political repression. Certainly, Marx could be bitter about his personal trials. He made no effort to hide his bitterness when, near the end of his life, he wrote acidly: "I hope the bourgeoisie will remember my carbuncles all the rest of their lives!" Possibly this bitterness explains why Marx is frequently portrayed as a sullen, brooding genius. But this characterization obscures one of the most remarkable things about the man—his extraordinary success, despite adversity, in the personal relationships that matter most. His love for his wife, and hers for him, was enduring and uncompromising. His children adored him, reflecting the same filial love that Marx had bestowed on his own father. Carbuncles notwithstanding, Karl Marx had, by several criteria, a very fruitful life.

■ Overview of the Marxian System

Marx's mature thought provides a theory of historical processes, based on material and economic forces, culminating in social and economic change of the existing order. In contrast to the overt, intellectual specialization of a later day, Marx's thought ranged over philosophy, history, and economics. As a philosopher and historian he was steeped in, but not a part of, the German tradition. As an economist he was likewise steeped in, but not a part of, the British classical tradition.

Hegel, Feuerbach, and German Philosophy

The dominant figure in German philosophy during the nineteenth century was Georg Hegel (1770–1831), whose ideas influenced not only Marx but also the German historicists (see chapter 11). The aspect of Hegel's philosophy that most influenced Marx was his theory of progress. Hegel claimed that history holds the key to the science of society. He viewed history not as a sequence of accidental occurrences or a collection of disconnected stories but rather as an organic process guided by the human spirit. It is not smoothly continuous but instead is the outcome of opposing forces. According to Hegel historical progress occurs when one force is confronted by its opposite. In the struggle, both are annihilated and are transcended by a third force. This so-called dialectic has frequently been summarized, conceptually, by the interplay of "thesis," "antithesis," and "synthesis." The Hegelian dialectic maintains that at some point in history an idea, or thesis, is confronted by an opposing idea, or antithesis. In the ensuing battle of ideas, neither one remains intact, but both are synthesized into a third, and this is how all general knowledge, as well as history, advances.

Although Marx found fault with some elements of Hegel's philosophy, he adopted the Hegelian dialectic, then modified it to accommodate Ludwig Feuerbach's doctrine of materialism. Feuerbach, another leading German philosopher, was every bit as Hegelian as Marx, but in *The Essence of Christianity* (1841), written ten years after Hegel's death, he added "materialism" to Hegel's concept of "self-alienation." Materialism to Feuerbach meant that humans are not only "species beings," as Hegel asserted, but also sensuous beings, so that sense perception must therefore become the basis of all science. Feuerbach maintained that all history is the process of preparing humans to become the object of "conscious," rather than "unconscious" activity.

According to Feuerbach, one area where unconscious activity predominates is religion. Religion is the mere projection of idealized human attributes onto an otherworldly object (i.e., God). This supernatural object is then worshipped by humans as all-powerful, all-knowing, and all-perfect. Claiming to be a "realist," Feuerbach argued that religion is unreal. He regarded the attributes of the divinity as nothing more than the *idealized* attributes of humans, which, of course, cannot be realized in this imperfect world. Humans are willing to accept their imperfect, earthly existence only because they unconsciously promise themselves perfection in another world. In other words, religion makes life bearable. And it is for this reason, proclaimed Feuerbach, that religion is such a universal phenomenon.[1]

From this perch it is a short step to reason that religion is a form of self-alienation. Feuerbach and Marx both used the term "alienation" to refer to a process—and a result—of converting the products of individual and social activity into something apart from themselves, both independent of them and dominant over them. However, whereas Feuerbach confined his analysis to the way in which humans alienate themselves in religion and in philosophy, Marx applied the concept to all manner of political and economic activity, including the very institutions of capitalism. In Marx, for the first time, the state joins hands with God as an "alien" being. The state derives its power and its existence from the fact that human beings are either incapable or unwilling to face head-on the problems that confront them in daily social interactions with one another. Over time, this monolithic structure called the "state" increases its power over people's lives, simply because they allow it to do so.

[1] Marx's acceptance of this view underlies his description of religion as "the opiate of the masses."

Marx's Economic Interpretation of History

The philosophical backdrop of Hegel and Feuerbach is essential to understanding the innovative character of Marx's thought. Grafting Feuerbach's materialism to Hegel's dialectic, Marx developed a "dialectical materialism," which was uniquely his own. He then extended this idea to the economic realm. Marx considered the prime mover of history to be the way in which individuals make a living, that is, the way in which they satisfy their material needs. This is important because unless their material needs are satisfied, human beings would cease to exist. In Marx's words, "Men must be able to live in order to 'make history.' . . . [Therefore] the first historical act is . . . the production of the means to satisfy these needs, the production of material life itself" (*German Ideology*, in Marx, *Writings*, p. 419). Showing his understanding and appreciation of the interrelations between economics and history, Marx declared production both a historical and an economic act. He made production the focal point and driving force among the mutually conditioning forces of production, distribution, exchange, and consumption. For Marx, economics became the *science of production*.

Production is a social force insofar as it channels human activity into useful ends. But Marx asserted that methods of production help to shape human nature itself. In one of his earlier works he wrote:

> The way in which men produce their means of subsistence depends first of all on the nature of the actual means they find in existence and have to reproduce. This mode of production must not be considered simply as being the reproduction of the physical existence of the individuals. Rather it is a definite form of activity of these individuals, a definite form of expressing their life, a definite *mode of life* on their part. As individuals express their life, so they are. What they are, therefore, coincides with their production, both with what they produce and with *how* they produce. The nature of individuals thus depends on the material conditions determining their production. (*German Ideology*, in Marx, *Precapitalist*, p. 121)

Like Adam Smith, Marx recognized that the development of productive forces in every economy depends on the degree to which the division of labor is carried. Whereas Smith anticipated natural harmony, Marx saw conflict of interests as the logical outcome of the progressive division of labor. Conflict arises, he said, in a series of events. The division of labor leads first to the separation of industrial and commercial labor from agricultural labor, and hence to the separation of town and country. Next it leads to the separation of industrial from commercial labor, and finally to a division among workers within each kind of labor. Conflict continues as individual interests contradict community interests and each worker becomes "chained" to a specific job. Eventually (à la Feuerbach) labor becomes an alien power, opposing the worker and enslaving him.

According to Marx the conflict between individual interests and community interests encourages the rise of the state as an independent power, a power divorced from the real interests of the individual and the community, even though it owes its being to the social classes already determined by the division of labor. Each class in power seeks to promote its own interest as the general community interest. But the community perceives the resulting class interest as an alien force that it cannot control. The situation becomes intolerable when two conditions are fulfilled. First, the great mass of humanity is rendered propertyless in a world of wealth and culture. This will only happen after production reaches a high level of productive power and a high degree of development, as under mature capitalism. Second, the development of productive forces must be universal. As a practical premise, the phenomenon of the "propertyless" class must reach worldwide proportions; otherwise, revolution and communism could exist only as local events, not as global realities.

Static versus Dynamic Forces in Society

What Marx called the "forces of production," developed through rational application of division of labor, are essentially dynamic. They consist of land, labor, capital, and technology, each of which is constantly changing in quantity and/or quality as a result of changes in population, discovery, innovation, education, and so on. During the course of their social lives, however, humans enter into certain definite relations that are independent of their will but indispensable to their lives as productive beings. These relations of production correspond to a worker's developmental stage of skill and productivity. Taken together, they constitute the "rules of the capitalist game." They are essentially static and consist of two types: *property* relations and *human* relations. Property relations exist between people and things; human relations exist between people. According to Marx, the sum total of these relations constitutes the economic structure of society, on which is superimposed a legal and political superstructure corresponding to definite forms of social consciousness. Every aspect of the socioeconomic structure owes its origin to the relations of production simply because institutions exist in order to make humans conform to the relations of production.

Figure 12-1 provides a simple schematic summary of Marx's theory of society. As the division of labor is pushed to its logical conclusion, labor becomes increasingly fragmented. The ensuing conflicts of interest are further aggravated by the

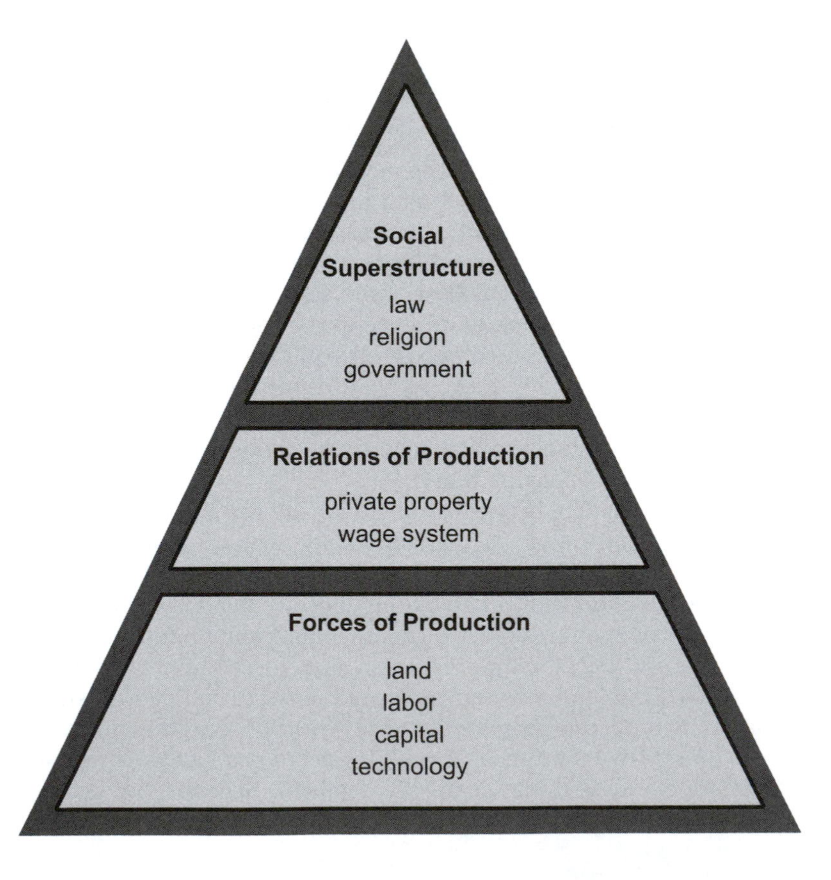

Figure 12-1
Marx's "social pyramid," in which the structure of society owes its origin to the basic facts of economic production.

institution of private property, which ensures the splitting up of accumulated capital among different owners and thus the division between capital and labor. In terms of figure 12-1, the dynamic *forces* of production come into conflict with the static *relations* of production. Once this conflict reaches a sufficient pitch, class struggle and revolution occur, and the social pyramid crumbles, from top to bottom. Marx succinctly summarized the dynamic process of social change determined by the forces of production in his preface to *A Contribution to the Critique of Political Economy*:

> The mode of production of material life determines the character of the social, political, and spiritual processes of life. It is not the consciousness of men that determines their existence, but on the contrary, their social existence that determines their consciousness. At a certain stage of their development, the material forces of production in society come in conflict with the existing relations of production, or—what is but a legal expression for the same thing—with the property relations within which they have been at work before. From forms of development of the forces of production these relations turn into their fetters. Then comes the period of social revolution. With the change of the economic foundation the entire immense superstructure is more or less rapidly transformed.
>
> No social order ever disappears before all the productive forces, for which there is room in it, have been developed; and new higher relations of production never appear before the material conditions of their existence have matured in the womb of the old society. . . . The bourgeois relations of production are the last antagonistic form of the social process of production—antagonistic not in the sense of individual antagonism, but of one arising from conditions surrounding the life of individuals in society; at the same time the productive forces developing in the womb of bourgeois society create the material conditions for the solution of that antagonism. (pp. 20–21)

All of this is, of course, more than a theory of economics; it is a theory of history, politics, and sociology as well. In his iconic work, *Capital*, Marx used his more-or-less integrated theory of social behavior to analyze *capitalism*, not socialism or communism. That being said, a full understanding of the dynamics of his analysis would be extremely difficult without familiarity of Marx's view of how social change comes about.

■ Marx's Early Writings on Capitalist Production

Das Kapital was the result of many years of investigation by Marx into the laws of history, economics, and sociology. These years of study and contemplation produced gems that were all but lost after Marx launched his major work in 1867. Revisiting Marx's early writings adds dimension to his mature thought and provides insights into the intellectual path of his feverish mind.

The Economic and Philosophical Manuscripts of 1844

Marx began a critical study of political economy shortly after he moved to Paris in 1843. The following year he completed several manuscripts that were apparently intended to be a major part of a forthcoming book. The book never materialized, however, and the manuscripts remained unpublished for more than eighty years. When a full edition of these extant works was published in 1932 under the title *Economic and Philosophic Manuscripts of 1844*, the occasion generated much excitement among Marxian scholars and some reinterpretation of Marx's later works.

Contrary to some interpretations, we find a basic continuity between Marx's early writings and *Capital*. However, by the time he wrote the latter, Marx had abandoned the purely metaphysical concepts that he had initially acquired from the German philosophers in favor of a more empirical analysis.

The central theme of the *Manuscripts* is that once capitalism became a dominant force in Western civilization history became the saga of alienation in people's lives as producers. Marx represented communism, therefore—achieved through a revolution against private property—as the final escape from alienation. Although he had not yet worked out the labor theory of value by this time, Marx already expressed in the *Manuscripts* the idea that labor is the source of all wealth. He had already made the empirical observation that the worker gets only a small part of this wealth, barely enough to continue working. The lion's share of the product of labor goes to the capitalist, and this leads to a bitter struggle between capital and labor. Marx reasoned that in this struggle the capitalist has all the advantages, and aims to keep wages to a minimum. Capitalism, therefore, turns labor into a mere commodity and reduces all human relations to money relations. The capitalist inevitably is enriched by these relations at the expense of the worker, who settles into a subsistence-level existence.

In an early analysis of profit, also contained in the *Manuscripts*, Marx noted a trend toward monopoly concentration of capital into fewer and fewer hands. This trend leads to an increase in total profits and an increase in the total misery of the working class. Marx theorized that eventually the contradictions within the capitalist system would lead to its demise, thus opening the way for humans to become truly free. All these ideas reappear in Marx's more mature works; although, as might be expected, they are worked out with more precision and detail the second time around.

What the *Manuscripts* of 1844 do not contain is a penetrating analysis of the basic contradictions of capitalism—one must look to *Capital* for that. But they do contain a fairly mature statement of methodological criticism aimed at political economy. For example:

> Political economy starts with the fact of private property, but it does not explain it to us. It expresses in general, abstract formulas the *material* process through which private property actually passes, and these formulas it then takes for laws. It does not *comprehend* these laws, i.e., it does not demonstrate how they arise from the very nature of private property. Political economy does not disclose the source of the division between labor and capital, and between capital and land. When, for example, it defines the relationship of wages to profit, it takes the interest of the capitalists to be the ultimate cause; i.e., it takes for granted what it is supposed to explain. Similarly, competition comes in everywhere. It is explained from external circumstances. As to how far these external and apparently accidental circumstances are but the expression of a necessary course of development, political economy teaches us nothing . . . exchange itself appears to it to be an accidental fact. The only wheels which political economy sets in motion are *greed* and the *war amongst the greedy—competition*. (*Manuscripts*, pp. 106–107)

Clearly, Marx criticized economists for not explaining (understanding?) the underlying *causes* of capitalism. In his view it was simply not enough to understand the mere workings of markets; one must also know how the market mechanism came about and where it is going. Marx felt it essential to grasp the connection between, as he put it: "private property, greed, and the separation of labor, capital, and landed property; between exchange and competition, value and the devaluation of men, monopoly and competition, etc.—the connection between this whole estrangement and the *money* system" (*Manuscripts*, p. 107).

Moreover, Marx criticized political economy on the basis of social contradictions that he had empirically observed. The basic contradiction he cited is that "the worker becomes all the poorer the more wealth he produces . . . [he] becomes an ever cheaper commodity the more commodities he creates" (*Manuscripts*, p. 107). The devaluation of workers, in other words, proceeds in direct proportion to the increasing value of commodities, and in the process workers confront the objects of their labor (commodities) as things outside themselves, things that, once completed, they have no control over or ownership of—as *alien* things, a power independent of its producer. This idea, of course—that labor is by its very nature the externalizing of a human capacity—Marx got from Hegel. But he now criticized economics for concealing the alienation inherent in the nature of labor by not considering the direct relation between the worker and production. This relationship, so assiduously analyzed by Marx, is the hallmark of Marxian economics and is the feature that distinguishes it most from classical economics.

The *Grundrisse* (1857–1858)

Marx's *Manuscripts of 1844* represent an initial foray into economic criticism by a young radical. They do not have the polish or incisiveness of his magnum opus published more than two decades later. But in the ensuing years, Marx perfected the tools of analysis he inherited from the classical economists, and persistently worked them into his dialectic. By 1858 he had accumulated a number of manuscripts that collectively might be considered an outline and draft version of the technical arguments later used in his magnum opus, *Capital*. This collection of papers bears the title *Grundrisse der Kritik der Politischen Ökonomie* (*Outlines of the Critique of Political Economy*). Only fragments of the *Grundrisse* have been translated into English, but they reveal some things that are not included in *Capital*, such as a discussion of precapitalist systems and a study of the interrelations of the component parts of capitalism (e.g., production, distribution, exchange, and consumption).

Marx upbraided the classical economists for their basically ahistorical view of production. In the *Grundrisse*, he sought to relate the process of production to the stage of social development. He particularly took issue with Mill's position that production—as opposed to distribution—is subject to immutable laws independent of history (see chapter 8). His own view was that production takes place within a social context and only by individuals who are at a certain stage of social development. Moreover, every form of production creates its own legal relations and forms of government. Marx concluded that the so-called general conditions of production espoused by the classical economists were nothing more than abstract concepts that together did not make up any real stage in the history of production.

These abstract concepts make it impossible, said Marx, for economics to deal with the true nature of capitalist production—which involves the study of labor as basic to productive enterprise, the analysis of the historical bases of capitalist production, and the examination of the fundamental conflict between bourgeoisie and proletariat. Marx began to weave together these ideas in his *Grundrisse*. He finalized his labor theory of value and his theories of surplus value, and of money. The following year, in *A Contribution to the Critique of Political Economy*, Marx unveiled his thesis that conflict between the development of the productive forces and the relations of production provides the driving force of social revolutions. Thus, by

1860, the foundation was set for Marx's crowning achievement. The first volume of *Capital* appeared in 1867. (On the comparative frameworks of Smith and Marx, see the box, Method Squabbles 3: Invisible Hand or Heavy Fist?)

Method Squabbles 3: Invisible Hand or Heavy Fist?

When economics was still a fledgling science, Adam Smith carefully elaborated his vision of a productive economy that achieves economic growth and prosperity by relying on individual initiative and limited government. His implicit acceptance of the revolutionary slogan, "that government governs best which governs least" rests on his belief that coordination and harmony will come about in a market economy through the free play of competition.

Marx claimed that Smith merely parroted the interests of the ruling capitalist class, which he referred to as the *bourgeoisie*. In contrast to Smith, he characterized the market process as a disorganized, uncoordinated system, in which producers typically overproduce and consumers exercise no choice over their purchases. According to Marx, the main feature of capitalism was "the anarchy of production." He denounced capitalists as thieves who robbed the workers by paying them less than the full value of their services, a situation he termed the *exploitation of labor*.

To Marx, it made no sense to describe the market as organized economic activity because there was no organizer. He maintained that coordination of economic activity required conscious, centralized control. Thus, he proposed an alternative social system whose goal would be to eliminate exploitation and increase the efficiency of production. In the end, all society would be turned into one immense factory, directed by workers themselves, who would be liberated from the shackles of capitalism. Marx denigrated Smith's "invisible hand" as a euphemism for the existing chaotic order, in which "chance and caprice have full play in distributing the producers and their means of production among the various branches of industry."

At base, a fundamental point of method separates Smith from Marx. Whereas Smith reflected the Enlightenment emphasis on the primacy of the individual, Marx mirrored the German ideology of group supremacy. It is as though, for Marx, the workers have no individual faces or interests; instead they are defined by their membership in a common body, which Marx called (borrowing Sismondi's term), the *proletariat*. Identity does not exist apart from this group. Marx would not admit that any meaningful gains for the proletariat could arise from economic growth in the existing capitalist regime. Thus, meaningful revolutionary reform for Marx simply meant displacing one group of rulers (the bourgeoisie) with another (the proletariat).

By not looking beyond the problems of collective decision making (no matter who the rulers), Marx put a far greater burden than did Smith on the innate goodness of mankind. Smith may not have approved entirely of the human behavior he observed, but he took mankind as he found it. For his part, Marx believed in the perfectibility of society because he believed in the perfectibility of human nature. After more than a century of experience with Marxist schemes of collective organization, we appear to be no closer to his ultimate "reality."

■ The Nature of Capitalism

At this point in our review of Marx it should be clear that by the time he was ready to write *Capital*, he had certain clear-cut objectives in mind—objectives that were consistent with his dialectical view of history. Specifically, he wanted to show (1) how the commodity form of market exchange leads to class conflict and exploitation of the labor force, (2) how the commodity system will be thwarted eventually, and fail to operate because of its own inherent contradictions, and (3) why class conflict under capitalism, unlike class conflicts under earlier economic systems, will ultimately lead to rule by the exploited rather than by a new ruling class.

Marx conceived capitalism as an economic system in which people make a living by buying and selling things (i.e., commodities). Commodities, he said, are distinguished by four characteristics. They are: (1) useful, (2) produced by human labor, (3) offered for sale in the market, and (4) separable from the individual who produced them. In *Capital*, Marx set out to analyze the production and distribution of commodities. Any such explanation would be empty without a theory of value. For inspiration and authority, he turned to Smith and Ricardo on this point.

The Labor Theory of Value

After a careful review of classical economic literature, Marx determined that labor is the essence of all value. To him, value was an *objective* property of each and every commodity. It therefore had to be rooted in something more substantial than the purely "superficial" market forces of supply and demand. In fact, Marx could not abide purely subjective valuations (by utility comparisons, for example) because he was a materialist who held that material relations alone determine value. He also believed that these relations determine value *prior* to the determination of price, so that price reflects merely a value caused by the purely objective element common to all commodities, which is to say, labor.

Contradiction in Classical Value Theory? We have seen that classical economics contained not one but two theories of exchange value: the short-run determination of price by supply and demand and the long-run theory of "natural price," or cost of production. Marx sensed a contradiction in this conventional presentation. The theory of natural price holds that price is invariant in the long run, whereas even casual observation tells us that market prices fluctuate constantly. If such fluctuations are the result of mere chance, then so, too, are economic crises. Marx could not admit this prospect without denying his theory of dialectical materialism, so it is no surprise that he rejected classical value theory. In *Wage Labour and Capital* he wrote: "It is solely in the course of these fluctuations that prices are determined by the cost of production. The total movement of this disorder is its order" (*Marx–Engels Reader*, p. 175).

Seemingly contradictory statements like this animate Marx's dialectic, while stirring consternation among the uninitiated. "What does he mean?" The answer is that Marx recognized, as did the classical economists, that under competition market prices do not fluctuate randomly but revolve around a definite point. If the selling price of a commodity falls below its cost of production for too long, its producer is forced out of business. If the selling price exceeds the cost of production, excess profits arise, which attract competitors and lead temporarily to overproduction, driving prices down. Consequently, the point around which competitive market price fluctuates is cost of production. To Marx, however, this meant labor costs and labor costs alone. Thus, he saw value as being determined not by the "laws of the market" but by production itself.

Murray Wolfson, a prominent Marxian scholar, has explained the matter in another way. Market prices are ideal (i.e., subjective) estimates of the ratios of exchange by potential buyers and sellers. But competition forces these ideal estimates to conform to the material reality of the labor consumed in their production.

One might, of course, explain prices directly by the interaction of these ideal estimates until the subjective valuations are in equilibrium. Marx's materialism, however, closed that avenue. The direction of causation cannot be from the *ideal* valuation to the *objective* exchange ratio. To conform to Marx's belief system a scientific explanation must go from the material to the ideal. Hence, Marx's labor theory of value is unique because it is rooted in materialist philosophy.

Wages and Capital. Having settled on an objective labor theory of value, Marx faced Ricardo's problems anew: (l) If labor is the essence of exchange value, what is the exchange value of labor? (2) How is the value of goods produced by machinery determined? Marx approached the first problem this way. The value of labor power may be divided into an amount necessary for the subsistence of labor and an amount over and above that. The former, which Marx called "socially necessary labor," determines the exchange value of labor itself—its wage. The latter, termed "surplus value," is appropriated by the capitalist. Marx made it clear that capitalism could not exist unless the worker produced a value greater than his or her own subsistence requirements:

> If a day's labor was required in order to keep a worker alive for a day, capital could not exist, for the day's labor would be exchanged for its own product, and capital would not be able to function as capital and consequently could not survive. . . . If, however, a mere half-day's labor is enough to keep a worker alive during a whole day's labor, then surplus value results automatically. (*Grundrisse*, p. 230)

Marx asserted that surplus value arises in production, not exchange. Thus, the capitalist turns to labor to get surplus value from each worker engaged in production, a process described by Marx as "exploitation of labor." Exploitation exists because the extra value contributed by labor is expropriated by the capitalist. Surplus value arises not because workers are paid *less* than they are worth but because they *produce more* than they are worth. Since this extra amount is expropriated by the owners of land and capital, surplus value may be regarded as the sum of the nonlabor shares of income (i.e., rent, interest, and profit) that comprise the price of final goods.

Marx touted the concept of surplus value as his main achievement, and it is an integral part of his central theme of class conflict and revolution. Two classes emerge under capitalism, with one class being forced to sell its labor power to the other in order to earn a living. This contractual arrangement transforms labor into a commodity alien to the worker. Without the difference between the exchange-value of labor (i.e., its subsistence wage) and its use-value (value of labor's output), the capitalist would have no interest in buying labor power; hence, it would not be salable and its commodity-like character would disappear. So for Marx the ingredients for social conflict—alienation and polarization of classes—are inherent in the nature of capitalism.

Ricardo had proffered labor as the best *measure* of value, though not necessarily as the sole *cause* of value. Marx trumped Ricardo. He saw labor as both the measure and the cause of value. Moreover, he held that only labor—not machines—can produce surplus value. How, then, does one value machinery? Ricardo fumbled awkwardly with this question. Marx answered that machines are "congealed labor" and therefore equal in value to the cost of the labor that produced them. This is a forced answer, because it denies that machines are productive in themselves and should therefore be valued in excess of the labor that has gone into their production. Nevertheless, Marx was so committed to the labor theory of value that he either ignored this objection or relegated it to minor importance.

The "Great Contradiction." Some of Marx's critics raised a serious objection to the labor theory in the form of what has come to be known as the "great contradiction," which was posed in terms of the following question: If the exchange value of commodities is determined by the labor time they contain, how can this be reconciled with the empirically observed fact that the market prices of these commodities frequently differ from their labor values? Or to put it another way: Inasmuch as competition guarantees a uniform rate of profit throughout the economy, how do we account for the different capital/labor ratios that exist across industries? A Marxian theory of value (i.e., labor alone creates surplus value) holds that profits are higher in labor-intensive industries, but empirically this is not the case. Thus, since capital/labor ratios differ while the rate of profit remains uniform, it cannot be true, Marx's critics argued, that value is determined by payments to labor alone.

Marx may have anticipated this problem in his early writings, but his celebrated rebuttal to his critics is contained in the third volume of *Capital*, published posthumously by Engels. Marx invoked the theory of the competition of capitals, which operates to establish a uniform rate of profit for all firms engaged in production. He then added the aggregate, average profit so-derived to the (different) costs of production in different industries, and found that the individual deviations of market prices from true (labor) values tend to cancel out (in the aggregate). Lo and behold! Problem solved! Marx's "solution" is demonstrated below in the discussion of the transformation problem. However, the solution requires the use of peculiar Marxian terms, which we now attempt to explicate.

Some Marxian Definitions. Marx's "solution" to the great contradiction utilized certain terminology that he borrowed from classical economics and other terms of his own invention. What follows is a thumbnail sketch of his terms, including their "mathematical" notation.

Constant capital (c)	=	charges on fixed capital (i.e., depreciation plus the cost of raw-material inputs)
Variable capital (v)	=	total wages paid to labor
Outlay (k)	=	cost of production (excluding profit), or $c + v$
Surplus value (s)	=	contribution of workers for which they are not paid, or excess of gross receipts over the sum of constant and variable capital
Rate of surplus value (s')	=	ratio of surplus value to variable capital employed, or s/v
Rate of profit (p')	=	ratio of surplus value to outlay, or $s/(c + v)$
Organic composition of capital (O)	=	ratio of capital to labor employed in production

Although the terminology is peculiar to Marx, the concepts employed are familiar to contemporary students. For example, in terms of national income accounting it could be said that GNP $= c + v + s$ and NNP $= v + s$.

The Transformation Problem. On Marx's behalf, and citing his authority in Volume 3 of *Capital*, Engels presented Marx's "solution" to the great contradiction with the aid of an illustration replicated on the following page as table 12-1. Marx's analysis and discussion rest on three major assumptions: (1) different commodities are produced with different organic compositions of capital (i.e., different capital/labor ratios) and use up constant capital at different rates in production; (2) for con-

Table 12-1 Transformation of Values into Prices

(1) Commodity	(2) Capitals	(3) Capital Used Up	(4) Cost	(5) Surplus Value	(6) Labor Value	(7) Average Profit	(8) Sales Price	(9) Deviation of Price from Value†
A	$80c + 20v$	50	70	20	90	22	92	+2
B	$70c + 30v$	51	81	30	111	22	103	−8
C	$60c + 40v$	51	91	40	131	22	113	−18
D	$85c + 15v$	40	55	15	70	22	77	+7
E	$95c + 5v$	10	15	5	20	22	37	+17
Totals	500*	202	312	110	422	110	422	0

*This total includes a combination of "stocks" and "flows" (c + v) and is used to determine the average profit in column 7.

†Although the sales price (column 8) and labor value (column 6) differ for each commodity, column 9 shows the algebraic sum of individual differences is zero.

venience, the rate of surplus value is taken to be 100 percent; and (3) competition will tend to equalize the rate of profit among industries at the "average rate," that is, the ratio of aggregate surplus value to aggregate outlay.

Marx noted that the organic composition of capital in any single industry will depend on the technical relation of labor power to other means of production. But for purposes of illustration, the ratios of constant capital to variable capital in table 12-1 are arbitrarily chosen. Five different commodities are represented in column 1, each produced with different capital/labor ratios, as revealed in column 2. Commodity A, for example, is produced with 80 units of constant capital and 20 units of variable capital. For simplicity assume that 80 and 20 are dollar expenditures so that the heterogeneous units of "capital" and "labor" can be summed to determine outlay in each of the five industries. It can be noted, therefore, that outlay equals $100 in each industry and that the aggregate outlay of the simple economy is $500. Column 3 shows the units of constant capital used up in the production process for each of the five industries. The dollar cost of each commodity is determined in column 4 by adding wage costs (variable capital) to column 3. Land is left out of the illustration as a means of production but can easily be accommodated along with constant capital. Column 5 shows surplus value in each industry, entered at 100 percent of expenditures on variable capital. Column 6 reveals the "true" value (labor value) of each commodity according to Marx's labor theory. The values in this column are determined by adding cost (column 4) to surplus value (column 5).

According to Marx, the cost of a commodity differs from its sales price by the average amount of profit, which is added to cost (column 4) in order to determine the sales price (column 8). Column 7 is the average profit for each industry and is uniform across industries because of the law of competition. The profit rate in Marxian terms is $s/(c + v)$, or $110/500 = 0.22$, which, when multiplied by the outlay in each industry ($100), yields the dollar amounts shown in column 7. A comparison of columns 8 and 6 shows that market price differs from labor value for each commodity, as the critics contended, but column 9 reveals that the algebraic sum of the individual differences is zero. Marx concluded: "The deviations of prices from values mutually balance one another by the uniform distribution of the surplus value, or by the addition of the average profit of 22 percent of advanced capital to the respective cost-price of the commodities" (*Capital*, vol. 3, p. 185).

This so-called transformation of values into prices supports Marx's contention that in the aggregate, labor is the true source of value, and in his preface to the third volume of *Capital*, Engels touted it as a triumph over Marx's critics. The truth is, however, that few economists today are willing to accept the transformation problem as a valid substantiation of the labor theory of value. Ingenious as it is, Marx's solution denies that machinery is productive over and above the amount of labor congealed in it, a view that modern economists find counterintuitive and empirically invalid.

It should be noted that in the final analysis, the mechanics of value theory was of relatively minor importance to Marx, who was more interested in the construction of a quasi-Ricardian model of the development of an entire socioeconomic system. The narrower subject of value theory gained importance after Marx's death because of an emphasis on price determination in neoclassical economics. Moreover, debates over the transformation problem have been more intense among neoclassical economists than among neo-Marxians.

The Laws of Capitalist Motion

The dynamics of Marx's theory—what he called "the laws of capitalist motion"—represents a major departure from classical economics and reflect Marx's emphasis on technological change as the driving force of his economic theory. Adam Smith was a preindustrial writer who understood progress in terms of rational human behavior rather than in terms of technical advance. David Ricardo had very limited industrial experience; it was never his intention to recast political economy as a theory of technological change. If anything, he saw the economic challenge to society as an agricultural problem. John Stuart Mill was more open to the prospects of technological change, yet he did not make it a core element of his theory as Marx did. Marx described five laws, or general tendencies, inherent in capitalism. Each stemmed from the dynamic nature of the economy, and each was rooted in the conflict between the dynamic "forces of production" and the static "relations of production."

The Law of Accumulation and the Falling Rate of Profit. Under capitalism, business people try to acquire more surplus value in order to increase their profit. By Marx's definition surplus value is derived from labor. Thus, we might expect capitalists to seek out labor-intensive production methods in order to maximize their profits. In fact, however, entrepreneurs continually strive to substitute capital for labor. Marx spelled out the incentive:

> Like every other increase in the productiveness of labour, machinery is to cheapen commodities, and, by shortening the portion of the working day, in which the labourer works for himself, to lengthen the other portion that he gives, without equivalent, to the capitalist. In short, it is a means for producing surplus value. (*Capital*, vol. 1, p. 405)

The individual capitalist can profitably substitute capital for labor because it takes time to adjust to new methods of production. This gives the first capitalist to introduce labor-saving machinery a differential advantage. Mechanized firms will be able to produce at lower costs than the average market price that is determined by productive conditions of more-mechanized and less-mechanized firms.

However, what is true for the individual is not true for all. If every capitalist introduces more machinery, the organic composition of capital rises, surplus value falls, and so does the average rate of profit. (Verify this from table 12-1.) Hence, the collective result of each capitalist's drive to accumulate more capital and more profit tends to drive down the average rate of profit. Another reason why the rate of profit might fall over time is that workers may push for higher wage rates. If realized, this prospect will drive up production costs, while prices will still be determined by "socially necessary labor." Ricardo recognized this prospect, but he felt that such a development would be checked by the Malthusian population trap. But Marx was no Malthusian; he maintained that population is culturally and socially determined. Therefore, higher wages will not necessarily be forced down again by rapid population growth.

The Law of Increasing Concentration and the Centralization of Industry. The drive for profit described above eventually and inevitably leads to a greater substitution of capital for labor and transforms small-scale industry into large-scale enterprises with greater division of labor and far more output capacity. This increase in production and productive capacity, Marx felt, would lead to general overproduction, thus driving prices down to the point where only the most efficient producers would survive. The less efficient firms would be driven out of business by this process, and their assets then gobbled up by the survivors. As a result, industry would become more and more centralized, and economic power would be increasingly concentrated in the hands of a few.

The Law of a Growing Industrial Reserve Army. The dynamic change caused by technological innovation and capital-labor substitution has a drastic effect on the working class, namely unemployment. In the passage below, note how Marx turns into a curse the division of labor that Smith hailed as an economic blessing:

> The self-expansion of capital by means of machinery is directly proportional to the number of workers whose means of livelihood have been destroyed by this machinery. The whole system of capitalist production is based upon the fact that the worker sells his labour power as a commodity. Thanks to the division of labour, this labour power becomes specialised, is reduced to skill in handling a particular tool. As soon as the handling of this tool becomes the work of a machine, the use-value and the exchange-value of the worker's labour power disappear. The worker becomes unsalable, like paper money which is no longer legal tender. That portion of the working class which machinery has thus rendered superfluous . . . either goes to the wall in the unequal struggle of the old handicraft and manufacturing industry against machine industry, or else floods all the more easily accessible branches of industry, swamps the labor market, and sinks the price of labour-power below its value. (*Capital*, vol. 1, p. 470)

Marx maintained that this displacement of workers by machines creates a "growing industrial reserve army of unemployed," one of the inherent contradictions he attributed to capitalism. As the foregoing discussion illustrates, this unemployment is of two types: (1) technological unemployment (caused by the substitution of machinery for labor) and (2) cyclical unemployment (caused by overproduction, which in turn is caused by increasing concentration and centralization).

The Law of Increasing Misery of the Proletariat. Marx claimed that the collective misery of the proletariat increases as the industrial reserve army grows. To make matters worse, capitalists will try to offset a falling rate of profit by lowering wages, imposing longer workdays, introducing child and female labor, and so forth, all of which contributes to the absolute misery of the working class.

The first effect of this reactive widespread use of machinery is to bring women and children into the labor force, because slight muscular strength can be amplified by the use of machines. Instead of selling only his own labor power, therefore, the worker is forced to sell that of his wife and children. Hence, Marx says, the worker "becomes a slave trader." Increased exposure to the rigors of factory life leads to high child mortality rates and to moral degradation among women and children. Marx cited public health reports in Britain in an attempt to confirm these allegations.

Because it is the most powerful means for shortening the working time required to produce a commodity the machine also becomes the most powerful means for prolonging the workday, allowing the capitalist to appropriate more surplus value. Because specialized and costly machinery left idle even for short periods is expensive to capitalists, they strive to minimize the length of idle machine time. The results of adding capital inputs, therefore, are longer workdays, less leisure time, and more misery for the laborer. Longer workdays and intensification of work effort sap the strength and endurance of the working class.

From a historical standpoint, this seems the least valid of Marx's arguments. In strictly economic terms, Marx's doomsday prophecy has not come to pass. Of course it is unclear whether the working class has made great economic strides *because* of Marx's influence or *despite* his prediction of increasing misery. At any rate, his formulation of the increasing-misery doctrine does not lend itself readily to empirical testing. Some Marxists have attempted to reconcile actual working conditions with this part of Marx's theory by asserting that the *relative* misery of the working class has increased—they point to the dehumanizing effects of today's automated production, or to the increasing alienation and polarization of workers and ethnic minorities. But it is fair to say that such arguments have not proved persuasive to non-Marxists.

The Law of Crises and Depressions. Marx linked the explanation of business cycles to investment spending. In this he anticipated Keynes (see chapter 21) and other economists of a later generation. He noted that capitalists will invest more at some times than at others. When the army of unemployed grows and wages fall, capitalists will tend to hire more labor and invest less in machinery and equipment. But when wages rise capitalists will substitute machines for workers, bringing about unemployment and depressed wages, precipitating periodic crises. He tied these periodic crises to his increasing-misery doctrine. The mere *occurrence* of crises was not enough; Marx had to show capitalism's susceptibility to crises of *increasing* severity. He did this by stressing the never-ending drive of the capitalist to accumulate. But this drive to accumulate is, for Marx, self-contradictory because it leads to the *overproduction of capital*, and thus to repeated crises:

> As soon as capital would have grown to such a proportion compared with the labouring population, that . . . the increased capital produces no larger, or even smaller, quantities of surplus-value than it did before its increase there would be an overproduction of capital. That is to say, increased capital $C + \Delta C$ would not produce any more profit . . . there would be a strong and sudden fall in the average rate of profit . . . due to a change in the composition of capital. (*Capital*, vol. 3, pp. 294–295)

The falling average rate of profit occasioned by the introduction of more machinery signals the impending crisis. Over time, Marx argued, these crises would become more severe; that is, they would affect more people (because of increases in population over time), and last longer. Marx maintained there would be a tendency toward *permanent* depression because the industrial reserve army gets larger as the crises become more severe. The logical outcome of such a tendency is social revolution. Eventually the proletariat must unite, throw off their chains, and take over the means of production.

The End of Capitalism and Beyond

According to Marx the classical economists misrepresented the economic system insofar as they considered money a mere medium of exchange. Commodities rarely trade for other commodities directly; instead, they are sold for money, which is then used to purchase other commodities. Symbolically, the classical representation of production and exchange is $C–M–C'$, where C stands for commodities and M stands for money. But Marx held that in a capitalist economy, the process is $M–C–M'$, where $M' > M$. In other words, money (capital) is accumulated to purchase (or produce) commodities, which are then sold for an even greater sum of money. M' is M plus profit (surplus value). We have seen that in the Marxian system the drive to accumulate surplus value involves the kind of internal contradictions that lead to the demise of the capitalist economy.

Marx's writings leave no doubt that he believed in a global revolution, although he rarely discussed the nature of the post-capitalist world. We know that the new society he envisioned was to be a communist one in which bourgeois private property would no longer exist, because he speaks of:

> communism as the *positive* transcendence of *private property*, or *human self-estrangement*, and therefore as the real *appropriation of the human* essence by and for man; communism therefore as the complete return of man to himself as a *social* (i.e., human) being—a return become conscious, and accomplished within the entire wealth of previous development. This communism, as fully developed naturalism, equals humanism, and as fully developed humanism equals naturalism; it is the *genuine* resolution of the conflict between man and nature and between man and man—the true resolution of the strife between existence and essence, between objectification and self-confirmation, between freedom and necessity, between the individual and the species. Communism is the riddle of history solved, and it knows itself to be this solution. (*Manuscripts*, p. 135)

In *The Communist Manifesto*, Marx spoke of communism as a revolutionary new mode of production and described a ten-point communist agenda that he envisioned for advanced economies (pp. 31–32):

> These measures will of course be different in different countries. Nevertheless in the most advanced countries the following measures will be generally applicable.
>
> 1. Abolition of property in land and application of all rents of land to public purposes
> 2. A heavy progressive or graduated income tax
> 3. Abolition of all right of inheritance
> 4. Confiscation of the property of all emigrants and rebels
> 5. Centralization of credit in the hands of the state, by means of a national bank with state capital and an exclusive monopoly
> 6. Centralization of the means of communication and transport in the hands of the state

7. Extension of factories and instruments of production owned by the state, the bringing into cultivation of wastelands, and the improvement of the soil generally in accordance with a common plan
8. Equal obligation of all to work; establishment of industrial armies, especially for agriculture
9. Combination of agriculture with manufacturing industries; gradual abolition of the distinction between town and country by a more equitable distribution of the population over the country
10. Free education for all children in public schools; abolition of children's factory labor in its present form; combination of education with industrial production, etc.

This ten-point program raises a number of questions regarding implementation and operation, but Marx stopped short of giving his followers a blueprint for implementation. Obviously he saw his task as the *analysis* of capitalism and its internal contradictions, and apparently he preferred to leave the building of new societies to others. Consequently, after Marx's death the door was left ajar for considerable controversy and disagreement over the *applied* aspects of his political economy. A bitter battle near the turn of the century between moderate revisionists, such as Eduard Bernstein, and the militant Marxists/Leninists ensued. Bernstein admirably summed up the genius and the pitfalls of Marx's ideas this way:

> A dualism runs through the whole monumental work of Marx . . . the work aims at being a scientific inquiry and also at proving a theory laid down long before its drafting. Marx had accepted the solution of the Utopians in essentials, but had recognized their means and proofs as inadequate. He therefore undertook a revision of them, and this with the zeal, the critical acuteness, and love of truth of a scientific genius. . . . But as Marx approaches a point when that final aim enters seriously into question, he becomes uncertain and unreliable. . . . It thus appears that this great scientific spirit was, in the end, a slave to a doctrine. (*Evolutionary Socialism*, pp. 209–210)

■ Conclusion

Marx had a profound influence on the twentieth century, and it is a testimonial to his far-ranging intellect that his influence surpassed the boundaries of economics. Even within the narrow discipline of economics, however, Marx's reach extended far beyond the small group of economists who were Marxist in the strict sense—people such as Paul Sweezy, Maurice Dobb, Paul Baran, and Ernest Mandel, to name a few. Any economist who reasons from the primacy of production in explaining economic relations may be said to have felt the influence of Marx. (Piero Sraffa is perhaps the leading example of a later generation). The same can be said for those who embrace the dialectical method, whether or not they accept the ultimate conclusions of Marx's analysis.

In Marx's time, the dialectical method, especially its Hegelian variant, permeated the Continent, whereas the English-speaking world remained aloof, more influenced by the empiricism of Locke and Hume. As a result, scientific thought in general has been empirical in nature while social, political, and theological thought, especially with its roots on the Continent, has tended to be dialectical. This has led to very different perspectives, which explains the observed lack of understanding and tolerance between the different intellectual traditions.

Modern Marxists have ostensibly rallied around the essential core of humanism in Marx's thought. The complexities of mass production and the "third world" deprivation of various groups and nations have made the kind of alienation Marx described seem very real to a large segment of society. Even those who decry the necessity of violent revolution for meaningful social change are often spurred by a Marx-like humanism to seek alternative forms of social reform. In the end, this may prove to be the most durable part of Marx's legacy.

References

Bernstein, Eduard. *Evolutionary Socialism: A Criticism and Affirmation*, E. C. Harvey (trans.). New York: Schocken Books, 1965.

Feuerbach, Ludwig Andreas. *The Essence of Christianity*, Marian Evans (trans.). London: John Chapman, 1854.

Marx, Karl. *A Contribution to the Critique of Political Economy*, S. W. Ryazanskaya (trans.). Moscow: Progress Publishers, 1970.

———. *Capital*, Ernest Untermann (trans.) and F. Engels (ed.). 3 vols. Chicago: Charles Kerr, 1906–1909.

———. *Grundrisse der Kritik der Politischen Ökonomie*, 2 vols. Berlin: Dietz-Verlag, 1953.

———. *Economic and Philosophic Manuscripts of 1844*, Martin Milligan (trans.) and D. J. Struik (ed.). New York: International Publishers, 1964.

———. *Precapitalist Economic Formations*, J. Cohen (trans.) and E. J. Hobsbawm (ed.). New York: International Publishers, 1965.

———. *Writings of the Young Marx on Philosophy and Society*, L. D. Easton and K. H. Guddat (eds. and trans.). Garden City, NY: Anchor Books, Doubleday, 1967.

———, and F. Engels. *The Communist Manifesto*, Samuel H. Beer (ed.). New York: Appleton-Century-Crofts, 1955.

———. *The Marx–Engels Reader*, R. C. Tucker (ed.). New York: W. W. Norton, 1972.

Wolfson, Murray. *A Reappraisal of Marxian Economics*. New York: Columbia University Press, 1966.

Notes for Further Reading

The standard source of biographical information on Marx is Franz Mehring's *Karl Marx: The Story of His Life*, Edward Fitzgerald (trans.) (London: G. Allen, 1936). Two other sources worth mention are E. H. Carr's *Karl Marx: A Study in Fanaticism* (London: Dent, 1934); and Robert Payne's more recent *Marx* (New York: Simon & Schuster, 1968). The personal side of Marx is explored by Edmund Wilson in *To the Finland Station* (Garden City, NY: Doubleday, 1940). See also David McLellan, *Karl Marx* (New York: Viking, 1975).

Ernest Mandel has written several interpretative works on Marx's economics. *An Introduction to Marxist Economic Theory* (New York: Pathfinder Press, 1970) is a brief and highly readable introduction to Marxian economics for student and professor alike. Thomas Sowell, *Marxism* (New York: William Morrow, 1985) presents another lucid and carefully reasoned account. *The Formation of the Economic Thought of Karl Marx*, Brian Pearce (trans.) (New York: Monthly Review Press, 1971), is more difficult but nevertheless very instructive. Finally, Mandel's two-volume work, *Marxist Economic Theory*, Brian Pearce (trans.) (New York: Monthly Review Press, 1968), challenges the most ardent Marx enthusiast. For another view on the development of Marx's economics, see Roman Rosdolsky, *The Making of Marx's "Capital"* (London: Pluto Press, 1977). The impact of Marx's ideas, both as originally propounded and as interpreted and reformulated over the years, is the subject of David McLellan (ed.), *Marx: The First 100 Years* (New York: St. Martin's Press, 1983).

Two works that compare and contrast Marx to other major thinkers are Spencer Pack, *Aristotle, Adam Smith and Karl Marx: On Some Fundamental Issues in 21st Century Political Economy* (Cheltenham, U.K.: Edward Elgar, 2010); and Heinz D. Kurz, "Technical Progress, Capital Accumulation and Income Distribution in Classical Economics: Adam Smith, David Ricardo and Karl Marx," *The European Journal of the History of Economic Thought*, vol. 17, (December 2010), pp. 1183–1222, which discusses how the classical authors developed a sophisticated typology of forms of technological change that can be analyzed in terms of an inverse movement of wages and profits. Ferdinando Meacci, "Different Divisions of Capital in Smith, Ricardo and Marx," *Atlantic Economic Journal*, vol. 17 (December 1989), pp. 13–21, provides a different kind of comparison between Marx and Ricardo involving divisions of capital.

The development and continuity of Marx's thought has been discussed by later writers, both in regard to Marx's overall thought and in regard to specific aspects of his analytical system. See, for example, Murray Wolfson, "Three Stages in Marx's Thought," *History of Political Economy*, vol. 11 (Spring 1979), pp. 117–146, in which he argues that Marx was successively an empiricist, a humanist, and a materialist, and that his conception of the ideal society changed with each successive stage. Regina Roth, "Marx on Technical Change in the Critical Edition," *The European Journal of the History of Economic Thought*, vol. 17, (December 2010), pp. 1223–1251, examines Marx's fascination with technological progress, both in terms of its negative effects on the working class and its revolutionary power to transform society.

The following articles stress Marx's early thought on various aspects of his mature theory: J. E. Elliot, "Continuity and Change in the Evolution of Marx's Theory of Alienation: From the *Manuscripts* through the *Grundrisse* to *Capital*," *History of Political Economy*, vol. 11 (Fall 1979), pp. 317–362; Allen Oakley, "Aspects of Marx's *Grundrisse* as Intellectual Foundations for a Major Theme in Capital," *History of Political Economy*, vol. 11 (Summer 1979), pp. 286–302; and Arie Arnon, "Marx's Theory of Money: The Formative Years," *History of Political Economy*, vol. 16 (Winter 1984), pp. 555–576. Arnon shows, for example, how Marx's monetary theory evolved from a Ricardian starting point but wound up against Ricardo on the side of Thomas Tooke. Suzanne Brunhoff, *Marx on Money*, M. J. Goldbloom (trans.) (New York: Urizen Books, 1976), presents a mature view of Marx's monetary theory, which Arnon supplements by his historical work. For more on the subject of Marx's monetary theory, see Don Lavoie, "Marx, the Quantity Theory, and the Theory of Value," *History of Political Economy*, vol. 18 (Spring 1986), pp. 155–170, who accuses Marx of being a "closet" quantity theorist; and Murray Wolfson, "Comment: Marx, the Quantity Theory, and the Theory of Value," *History of Political Economy*, vol. 20 (Spring 1988), pp. 137–140, who explains the dualism in Marx's thought that underlies Lavoie's interpretation. Eckhard Hein, "Money, Interest and Capital Accumulation in Karl Marx's Economics: A Monetary Interpretation and Some Similarities to Post-Keynesian Approaches," *The European Journal of the History of Economic Thought*, vol. 13 (Winter 2006), pp. 113–140, argues that many elements of Marx's economics are comprised of monetary analysis rather than real analysis. He claims that Marx's theory of value, his rejection of Ricardo on Say's law, and his theories of credit and interest fit this pattern.

The influence of classical economics on Marx's thought and the extent to which his analysis emulated earlier economists has been a subject of repeated discussion. See G. S. L. Tucker, "Ricardo and Marx," *Economica*, vol. 28 (August 1961), pp. 252–269; and Bela Belassa, "Karl Marx and John Stuart Mill," *Weltwirtschaftliches Archiv*, vol. 83 (1959), pp. 147–163. Although the answer seems obvious on the surface, the question of how close Marx's value theory was to Ricardo's continues to crop up. One important source of ideas on Marx's theory of value is I. I. Rubin, *Essays on Marx's Theory of Value* (Toronto: Black Rose Books, 1972). The proposition that labor alone is the source of surplus value is explored by Stephen Merrett, "Some Conceptual Relationships in *Capital*,"

History of Political Economy, vol. 9 (Winter 1977), pp. 490–503. Shalom Groll, "The Active Role of 'Use Value' in Marx's Economic Analysis," *History of Political Economy*, vol. 12 (Fall 1980), pp. 336–371, advances the unconventional view that demand played an important role in Marx's theory of value and that Marx's concept of demand is closer to modern theory than to Ricardo's. On this subject, see also Steve Keen, "Use-Value, Exchange Value, and the Demise of Marx's Labor Theory of Value," *Journal of the History of Economic Thought*, vol. 15 (Spring 1993), pp. 107–121, who asserts that if Marx had been consistent in applying his own logic, he could not have advocated a labor theory of value. J. S. Dreyer, "The Evolution of Marxist Attitudes toward Marginalist Technique," *History of Political Economy*, vol. 6 (1974), pp. 48–75, explains how marginalist techniques of pricing have crept into Marxian economics. The subject of value in Marxian economics continues to draw attention and to spur revision. See, for example, Samuel Bowles and Herbert Gintis, "The Marxian Theory of Value and Heterogeneous Labour: A Critique and Reformulation," *Cambridge Journal of Economics*, vol. 1 (June 1977), pp. 173–192; Ian Steedman, "Heterogeneous Labour, Money Wages, and Marx's Theory," *History of Political Economy*, vol. 17 (Winter 1985), pp. 551–574, who concludes that Marx's concept of abstract labor is of little or no use and that his concept of value is essentially no different from the classical concept of a quantity of labor; and David Leadbeater, "The Consistency of Marx's Categories of Productive and Unproductive Labour," *History of Political Economy*, vol. 17 (Winter 1985), pp. 591–618, who defends Marx's use of the categories and finds them consistent and effective for analyzing the determinants and limitations of capitalist accumulation. See also Robert Chernomas, "Productive and Unproductive Labor and the Rate of Profit in Malthus, Ricardo, and Marx," *Journal of the History of Economic Thought*, vol. 12 (Spring 1990), pp. 81–95.

Although the phrase "laws of capitalist motion" is uniquely Marxian, Marx drew freely on classical economics, especially in formulating those "laws" relating to the behavior of profits and wages. On Marx's profit theory, see Angus Walker, "Karl Marx, the Falling Rate of Profit and British Political Economy," *Economica*, vol. 38 (November 1971), pp. 362–377; M. A. Lebowitz, "Marx's Falling Rate of Profit: A Dialectical View," *Canadian Journal of Economics*, vol. 9 (May 1976), pp. 232–254; and Shalom Groll and Z. B. Orzech, "Technical Progress and Values in Marx's Theory of the Decline in the Rate of Profit: An Exegetical Approach," *History of Political Economy*, vol. 19 (Winter 1987), pp. 591–614, which challenges the dominant view that Marx attributed the falling rate of profit to changes in the organic composition of capital. For a logical (not empirical) attempt to show that the tendency of the rate of profit to fall is not unique to capitalism, see E. L. Khalil, "The Implication for Socialism of Marx's Theory of the Tendency of the Rate of Profit to Fall," *Journal of the History of Economic Thought*, vol. 16 (Fall 1994), pp. 292–309.

Marx's wage and employment theories are matters of continuing debate. On Marx's conviction that overproduction would be a frequent occurrence under capitalism, see Bernice Shoul, "Karl Marx and Say's Law." *Quarterly Journal of Economics*, vol. 71 (November 1957), pp. 611–629. Immiserization (Marx's term for the worsening conditions of the proletariat) may spring from a number of causes: low wages, long hours, unemployment, alienation, exploitation, and so forth. Murray Wolfson, Z. B. Orzech, and Susan Hanna, "Karl Marx and the Depletion of Human Capital as Open-Access Resource," *History of Political Economy*, vol. 18 (Fall 1986), pp. 497–514, have explored the possibility of exploitation in terms of external costs rather than in terms of Marx's main theoretical formulation based on the labor theory of value. They conclude that there may be more exploitation in the former sense than in the latter. The causes of immiserization, and the historical accuracy of Marx's prophecy that it will increase over time, are discussed by Thomas Sowell, "Marx's 'Increasing Misery' Doctrine," *American Economic Review*, vol. 50 (March 1960), pp. 111–120; F. M. Gottheil, "Increasing Misery of the Proletariat: An Analysis of Marx's Wage and Employment Theory," *Canadian Journal of Economics and Political Science*, vol. 28 (February 1962), pp. 103–113; R. L. Meek, "Marx's Doctrine of Increasing Misery," *Science and Society*, vol. 26 (1962), pp. 422–441; and D. Furth, A. Heertje, and R. Van Der Veen, "On Marx's Theory of Unemployment," *Oxford Economic Papers*, vol. 30 (July 1978), pp. 253–276.

The possible link between immiserization and the Malthusian population problem is the subject of a series of papers in the *American Economic Review*. W. J. Baumol, "Marx and the Iron Law of Wages," *American Economic Review*, vol. 73 (May 1983), pp. 303–308, touched off the debate by claiming that Marx did not subscribe to the view that wage levels must fall toward subsistence under mature capitalism, a position emphatically rejected by Sam Hollander, "Marx and Malthusianism: Marx's Secular Path of Wages," *American Economic Review*, vol. 74 (March 1984), pp. 139–151; but defended by M. D. Ramirez, "Marx and Malthusianism: Comment," *American Economic Review*, vol. 76 (June 1986), pp. 543–547. Reacting to the Baumol/Ramirez versus Hollander debate, Allin Cottrell and W. A. Darity, Jr., "Marx, Malthus, and Wages," *History of Political Economy*, vol. 20 (Summer 1988), pp. 173–190, have taken the middle ground—they argue that Baumol/Ramirez fail to establish that Marx rejected the falling-wage doctrine but that Hollander went too far in ascribing to Marx the consistent position that wages must be driven downward. Cottrell and Darity find that immiserization of the proletariat need not be linked to a secular decline in real wages. Outside this debate, but on the same general subject, Michael Perelman, "Marx, Malthus, and the Organic Composition of Capital," *History of Political Economy*, vol. 17 (Fall 1985), pp. 461–490, advances the notion that Marx viewed the "Malthusian problem" as merely one of the many internal contradictions of capitalism. For more on the nature of wages in the Marxian system, see Francis Green, "The Relationship of Wages to the Value of Labour-Power in Marx's Labour Market," *Cambridge Journal of Economics*, vol. 15 (June 1991), pp. 199–214.

The sparks of controversy have been ignited once again by Sam Hollander on yet another issue, namely whether or not Marx's economics may be characterized as general equilibrium theory. Hollander argues the affirmative in "Marxian Economics as 'General Equilibrium' Theory," *History of Political Economy*, vol. 13 (Spring 1981), pp. 121–155; but his claim has been challenged by Dusan Pokorny in "Karl Marx and General Equilibrium," *History of Political Economy*, vol. 17 (Spring 1985), pp. 109–132, who finds no textual evidence in Marx to support Hollander's claim.

The most famous critique of Marx's economics in the nineteenth century, designed to be the definitive repudiation of Marxian analysis, was launched by the Austrian economist Eugen Böhm-Bawerk, *Karl Marx and the Close of His System*, Paul Sweezy (ed.) (New York: A. M. Kelley, 1949). Joining Böhm-Bawerk in his attack on Marx was the Russian economist Ladislaus von Bortkiewicz, "The Transformation of Values into Prices in the Marxian System," reprinted in the volume by Böhm-Bawerk referred to above; and same author, "Value and Price in the Marxian System," *International Economic Papers*, no. 2 (1952). Together, these works touched off a long debate, which is still raging, on the validity of Marx's solution to the "transformation problem." The following works represent a cross-section of the issues in this protracted debate: J. Winternitz, "Values and Prices: A Solution of the So-Called Transformation Problem," *Economic Journal*, vol. 58 (June 1948), pp. 276–280; K. May, "Value and Prices of Production: A Note on Winternitz's Solution," *Economic Journal*, vol. 58 (December 1948), pp. 596–599; Francis Seton, "The Transformation Problem," *Review of Economic Studies*, vol. 24 (June 1957), pp. 149–160; and Ronald Meek, "Some Notes on the Transformation Problem," *Economic Journal*, vol. 66 (March 1956), pp. 94–107.

After a brief hiatus, the debate was revived in 1971 by Paul Samuelson, "Understanding the Marxian Notion of Exploitation: A Summary of the So-Called Transformation Problem between Marxian Values and Competitive Prices," *Journal of Economic*

Literature, vol. 9 (June 1971), pp. 399–431. Samuelson's article drew additional comment from Joan Robinson and Martin Bronfenbrenner in the December 1973 issue of the same journal. Furthermore, the debate continued with interpretations and commentary by W. J. Baumol and Michio Morishima and a "final word" by Samuelson in the March 1974 issue of the *Journal of Economic Literature*. Nevertheless, see the article by Allen Oakley, "Two Notes on Marx and the 'Transformation Problem,'" *Economica*, vol. 43 (November 1976), pp. 411–418. For an important, albeit analytically complex attempt to illuminate the basic Marxian premises concerning value, see Murray Wolfson, "The Transformation Problem: Exposition and Appraisal," *Journal of the History of Economic Thought*, vol. 12 (Fall 1990), pp. 179–195.

Surprisingly little has been written about Marx's vision of communism or about the relative economic merits of socialism versus competition from a strictly Marxian perspective. Perhaps this is because Marx spent far more time analyzing the weaknesses of capitalism than sketching out the postcapitalist society. Several articles skirt these issues. See J. E. Elliot, "Marx and Contemporary Models of Socialist Economy," *History of Political Economy*, vol. 8 (Summer 1976), pp. 151–184; same author, "Marx and Engels on Communism, Scarcity, and Division of Labor," *Economic Inquiry*, vol. 18 (April 1980), pp. 275–292; and same author again, "Marx and Schumpeter on Capitalism's Creative Destruction: A Comparative Restatement." *Quarterly Journal of Economics*, vol. 95 (August 1980), pp. 45–68.

M. C. Howard and J. E. King, "Marxian Economists and the Great Depression," *History of Political Economy*, vol. 22 (Spring 1990), pp. 81–100, detail how the Great Depression was viewed by Marxists. Same authors, "Karl Marx and the Decline of the Market," *Journal of the History of Economic Thought*, vol. 30 (June 2008), pp. 217–234, explore Marx's thought regarding the long-run tendencies of capitalism and show how his views were misunderstood by his followers who believed that capitalism in the nineteenth and twentieth centuries was in the midst of its final stages.

T. W. Hutchison, "Friedrich Engels and Marxian Economic Theory," *Journal of Political Economy*, vol. 86 (April 1978), pp. 303–320, suggests that Engels's contributions to Marx's economics are much more important than has been generally recognized, specifically Engels's account of the essential functions of the competitive-price mechanism. See also Øyvind Horverak, "Marx's View of Competition and Price Determination," *History of Political Economy*, vol. 20 (Summer 1988), pp. 275–298, who tries to bring Marx's theory of competition into sharper relief by contrasting it with the neoclassical concept of competition. Finally, Joan Robinson, *Essay on Marxian Economics* (London: Macmillan, 1966), attempts to reconcile Marxian and orthodox economics. Among other things, she contends that Marx's argument regarding the fate of capitalism does not depend crucially on the labor theory of value. But old habits die hard, and the debate over Marx's labor theory of value rages on. For additional sparks in this old tinderbox, see Jean Cartelier, "Marx's Theory of Value, Exchange and Surplus Value: A Suggested Reformulation," *Cambridge Journal of Economics*, vol. 15 (September 1991), pp. 257–270; Chai-on Lee, "Marx's Labour Theory of Value Revisited," *Cambridge Journal of Economics*, vol. 17 (December 1993), pp. 463–478; and Stephen Pratten, "Structure, Agency, and Marx's Analysis of the Labour Process," *Review of Political Economy*, vol. 5 (October 1993), pp. 403–426.

The fall of the Berlin Wall in 1989 sent many Marxists into retreat. Several years later a mini-symposium was organized around the question: "With Marxian economics in disarray as a touchstone for actual economies (in Eastern Europe, the former Soviet Union, etc.), is it now time for historians of economics to reclaim their interest in Karl Marx?" See the keynote paper by Anthony Brewer and ensuing comments from John Elliot, Duncan Foley, Samuel Hollander, M. C. Howard, J. E. King, Takashi Negishi, Alessandro Roncaglia, Margaret Schabas, and Ian Steedman in *History of Political Economy*, vol. 27 (Spring 1995), pp. 109–206.

Part IV
The Neoclassical Era

Mill's recantation of the wages-fund doctrine and Marx's mounting challenge to the market system undoubtedly stirred much soul-searching about the adequacy of classical economics. But the new departure we now call neoclassical economics was spurred by more than doubt and criticism. After all, classical economics was macroeconomic in its orientation. It was, therefore, ill-equipped to handle the microeconomic problems of efficiency and resource allocation, which came increasingly to the fore as the nineteenth century wore on. Even before Mill's *Principles* appeared in 1848, certain French economists and engineers began to raise questions about individual demand, consumer welfare, profit maximization, and efficient allocation of resources, primarily in the context of providing those public goods that Smith had consigned to government, such as roads, bridges, canals, and later, railways. The introduction of the railroad, in particular, focused attention on fixed and variable operating costs, return on investment, and the location of market activity, all firm-specific issues that classical macroeconomics largely ignored.

This next part of the book traces the development of early neoclassical economics. It begins with certain writers who lived in the midst of the classical period but pioneered the new approach ahead of their time. It then considers the multiple founders of neoclassical theory, stressing the more or less simultaneous discovery of the new analytics by English, German, and French writers. You will learn that neoclassical economics is united by its focus (the firm and/or the individual rather than the entire economy) and its embrace of subjective over strictly objective considerations in its formulation of value. It is diverse, moreover, in its tolerance of several different methods. For example, mathematics began to encroach on economic analysis with more and more vigor during the neoclassical period, but different writers had far different views on the nature, role, and adequacy of mathematics as a tool of economic inquiry. There were also major differences among the pioneers of neoclassical economics on the extent to which subjectivism should replace objectivism in the formulation of the new theories.

13

Proto-Neoclassical Economics in France

Cournot and Dupuit

We concluded chapter 7 with a classical macroeconomic model built on principles established by Ricardo and other classical writers. This model utilized the basic tenets of classical economic theory (population doctrine, wages-fund theory, etc.) to make deductions and generalizations about aggregate output, income distribution, and population. While British political economy was consolidating and extending its sphere of influence in the first half of the nineteenth century, great strides of a different sort in the establishment of formal economic analysis were being made outside Britain. The subject of these efforts was not the macroeconomic variables of income, output, population, profits, and wages (as distributive shares) but rather the behavior of microeconomic quantities such as prices, quantities offered and demanded, and profits connected with *specific* commodities or services. Writers in this parallel tradition developed theories about the effects of various forms of economic organization (monopoly, for example) on prices and outputs, and investigated the effects of transport costs, rents, and transport pricing schemes on the location of industries. Because many of the issues considered by these writers involved public or quasi-public goods that were supplied by government entities, important tenets of public finance and welfare economics were advanced in this period, and the theories of price discrimination and product differentiation took root. When viewed in retrospect, the era was one of the most fertile in the history of economic analysis. Whereas the pioneers of the macroeconomic foundations of economics were British, the leading analysts of its microeconomic foundations were French. French economic orthodoxy, however, was ambivalent, if not hostile, to its contributions.

A. A. Cournot (1801–1877)

One of the most original minds ever to attack economic theory, Antoine-Augustin Cournot faced tragedy and disappointment at several turns. Born in 1801 in Haute-Saône, France, Cournot received his early education at local schools before entering the École Normale in Paris at the age of twenty, where he studied mathematics. Despite an ominous (and ultimately fulfilled) presentiment of impending blindness, Cournot indulged his insatiable appetite for books (scientific and otherwise) throughout his youth. When he graduated from the École Normale Cournot remained in Paris, where, after a period of relative poverty, he obtained work as the secretary to one of Napoleon's generals, Marshall Gouvion Saint-Cyr. He completed his doctorate at the University of Paris during this period (1823 to 1833) and came into contact with leading intellectuals of the day, many of them physical scientists and engineers. During his tenure as a university student, Cournot published several mathematical articles as well as Marshall Saint-Cyr's military memoirs.

Cournot's papers on mathematics attracted the attention of the great physicist and statistician Poisson, who helped him secure a position in 1834 as professor of mathematics at Lyons, where he taught differential calculus and completed the initial work on his book on probability (*Exposition de la théorie des chances et des probabilités*). The next year Cournot was appointed school superintendent at Grenoble, and within a few months he assumed additional responsibilities as inspector general of education (succeeding Ampère, the renowned student of electrical science). In 1838, Cournot married and also published his seminal work on microeconomics, *Recherches sur les principes mathématiques de la théorie des richesses* (*Researches into the Mathematical Principles of the Theory of Wealth*). He was also made a traveling inspector general of education, based in Paris.

Trouble with his vision forced Cournot to take a leave of absence in 1844, which he spent in Italy. He became superintendent of the Dijon Academy in 1854, where he remained until his retirement in 1862, at which time he returned to Paris. Throughout this period and during his retirement in Paris, Cournot continued to publish books on social philosophy and on economics. Probably as a result of his piecemeal loss of sight, the character of his work altered. His two later books on economics, *Principes de la théorie des richesses* and *Revue sommaire des doctrines économiques*, published in 1863 and 1877, respectively, do not employ mathematics to treat economic questions, and they do not add significantly to Cournot's original work on economic theory, which he published decades earlier. Cournot died suddenly in 1877, never having achieved due recognition in his native country or elsewhere for his contributions. The importance of his work was later extolled by Léon Walras, which eventually brought him belated recognition. Cournot would probably be more than a little surprised and pleased at the course of microeconomic analysis in the post-1877 period because his impact and influence now permeate the very core of modern economic theory.

Cournot on Method

Cournot's ideas on the proper method in political economy are of great importance in assessing his role in theory development. Defending the use of mathematics as a kind of shorthand for expressing complex ideas, Cournot evaluated the earlier efforts of Smith, Say, and Ricardo:

> There are authors, like Smith and Say, who, in writing on Political Economy, have preserved all the beauties of a purely literary style; but there are others, like Ricardo, who, when treating the most abstract questions, or when seeking great accuracy, have not been able to avoid algebra, and have only disguised it under arithmetical calculations of tiresome length. Any one who understands algebraic notation, reads at a glance in an equation results reached arithmetically only with great labor and pains. (*Researches*, p. 4)

Cournot's chief criticism of past writers was, "They imagined that the use of symbols and formulas would have no other end than that of leading to numerical calculations" and they did not see that the object of mathematical analysis was to "find relations between magnitudes which cannot be estimated numerically and between *functions* whose law is not capable of being expressed by algebraic symbols." This view of method persists in his later works also. "Science," he wrote in 1863, "is not obliged to await empirical laws . . . in order to draw certain and useful consequences from general characteristics which they can supply, or certain relationships which can exist between them and upon which reason, alone, sheds light."[1] Accordingly, he championed the use of mathematics, specifically differential and integral calculus, in expressing arbitrary functions, provided that certain conditions are met. An example—the law of demand—familiar to all students of economics, illustrates Cournot's method.

As most students know, the law of demand states that quantity demanded is a function of price, or $D = F(P)$. The quantity demanded at each price is, moreover, related to a number of other variables (e.g., income, wealth, tastes, etc.), but these are assumed constant when drawing up an individual demand schedule. According to conventional analysis, a change in one of the nonprice determinants causes the entire demand curve to shift, which connotes a change in demand. A change in quantity demanded, by contrast, occurs along a given demand curve when price changes, all other determinants remaining constant. Cournot understood perfectly the value of the *ceteris paribus* assumption, or "other things equal" condition. This is evident in his *Principes de la théorie des richesses*, where he noted that the *loi de débit*, or law of sales ("sales" being synonymous with "demand"),

> rests essentially on population, on the distribution of wealth, on general well-being, on tastes, on the habits of the consuming population, on the multiplication of markets, on the extension of the market resulting from transport improvements. All these conditions relative to demand remain the same; if we suppose that production conditions change (i.e., that costs rise or fall, that monopolies are restricted or suppressed, that taxes are increased or lightened, that foreign competition is prohibited or allowed) prices will vary and the corresponding variations in demand, provided that prices are actually raised, will serve for the construction of our empirical tables. If, to the contrary, prices change because the law of demand has itself changed, due to a change in causes which no longer influence production but consumption, the construction of our tables will be made impossible, since they must show how demand changes by virtue of a change in price and not by virtue of other causes.

It is clear from his explicit treatment of demand that Cournot expressed the idea as a mathematical function, so that demand meant a price–quantity relationship (i.e., change in price leads to change in quantity demanded) whereas a change in any other demand variable (e.g., income) leads to a change in the price–quantity relationship itself (i.e., a shift of the function or schedule). This method of analysis is so common today that the modern theorist would not think of expressing complex ideas in verbal form alone, but at the time Cournot wrote, verbal expression was the common tack of the economic theorist. He was, therefore, a pioneer in the true sense of the term.

What, we may ask, did Cournot hope to accomplish by this line of inquiry? What kind of theory did he seek to develop with mathematical tools? Did it have practical consequences or was it out of touch with reality, a common complaint against economic theory today? The answer to these questions reveals the bril-

[1] Quotations without page references in this chapter are from unpublished translations made by the authors of this text. Original French texts are cited in the references at the end of the chapter, but where translations exist, English titles are substituted for the French.

liantly dual nature of Cournot's approach to method. Economic analysis, he argued, needs to be *grounded* in empirical observation and in facts. He rejected purely "speculative" foundations for his demand function, such as utility, and affirmed an empirical approach. The title of the chapter on demand in the original *Recherches*, "De la loi du débit," or "The Law of Sales," hints at this empirical approach, and Cournot quickly set the record straight. He noted: "Sales or demand increase when price decreases." He acknowledged that prices and the law of demand could fluctuate during a year, so he expressed his curve as a relation between *average* annual price, P, and "the quantity sold *annually* in the country or in the market under consideration," $F(P)$. Hence, $D = F(P)$ is a curve connecting time-series data on sales and the prices at which these sales are realized over the course of a year.

Cournot's theoretical specification of demand (a continuous, negatively sloped function) resulted from his own observation and from simplifications and observations of the relations between price and quantity. Theory may then be lifted from these facts and manipulated in order to arrive at deductions based on certain assumptions. But theory needs to be derived and specified in the first instance from actual observed facts—not from caprice. The tools derived this way possess a usefulness and a generality that far transcend the empirical facts that spawned them. It was part of Cournot's genius to have been able to recognize and explain how facts, theory, and model construction are intertwined.

Cournot's Micro Models

Cournot turned this empirical method into the creation of numerous models of firm behavior based on the demand curve. We shall consider his two most enduring models: (1) the monopoly model and (2) the duopoly (two producers) model.

A Monopoly Model. In chapter 5 of the *Researches*, Cournot erected a monopoly model of business behavior on the principle of profit maximization. The basic facts of the (illustrative) model are that a proprietor has sole ownership of a mineral spring that has healthful qualities unlike any other. Hence this is a strong monopoly both because of exclusive ownership and unique product. Rather than charge the highest obtainable price—which by virtue of the law of demand would probably result in few sales—Cournot argued that the proprietor will adjust his price so as to get the greatest net revenue. In the case of zero costs, he demonstrated mathematically that the monopolist's best outcome is to maximize gross receipts. Assuming a demand function $D = F(p)$ that is always negatively sloped (i.e., $dD/dp < 0$), the proprietor will adjust p such that total revenue, $pF(p)$, is at a maximum. The quantity of sales that will produce this maximum is found by applying differential calculus. Sales will reach a maximum when the extra revenue from an additional unit sold is zero, i.e., when marginal revenue is zero. When costs are present, Cournot showed that profit maximization occurs when marginal cost equals marginal revenue (or when the slope of a profit function, $\pi = TR - TC$, equals zero).

Cournot's monopoly model may be presented graphically, as in figures 13-1*a* and 13-1*b*. Assume the linear demand curve in figure 13-l*a* to represent Cournot's law of demand. (Ignore curve *MC* for the present.) The (zero-cost) proprietor will adjust his sales of mineral water such that he sells quantity Q_n at price P_n since at quantity Q_n the addition to total revenue (i.e., marginal revenue) is equal to the addition to total cost (i.e., marginal cost). That is, $MR = MC$ at quantity Q_n. Alternatively, but equivalently, the zero-cost proprietor simply maximizes total revenue, as seen at quantity Q_n in figure 13-1*b*. In the zero-cost case, the *TR* curve *becomes* the profit function, π_0.

This "marginal principle," derived by applying differential calculus, eventually became the central organizing principle of microeconomic theory. It allowed Cournot (and anyone else after) to solve the basic questions faced by each firm—what quantity to produce and what price to charge? Cournot gave a straightforward solution. Assuming that $\varphi(D)$ was equal to the cost of making a number of liters equal to D, Cournot's profit equation becomes $\pi = pF(p) - \varphi(D)$. Profit maximization requires that the slope of the profit function equal zero—or, in Cournot's notation, that $D + dD/dp \{p - d[\varphi(D)]/dD\} = 0$. In plainer language, profit maximization takes place where $MR - MC = 0$. As Cournot put it, "Whatever may be the abundance of the source of production, the producer will always stop when the increase in expense exceeds the increase in receipts" (*Researches*, p. 59).

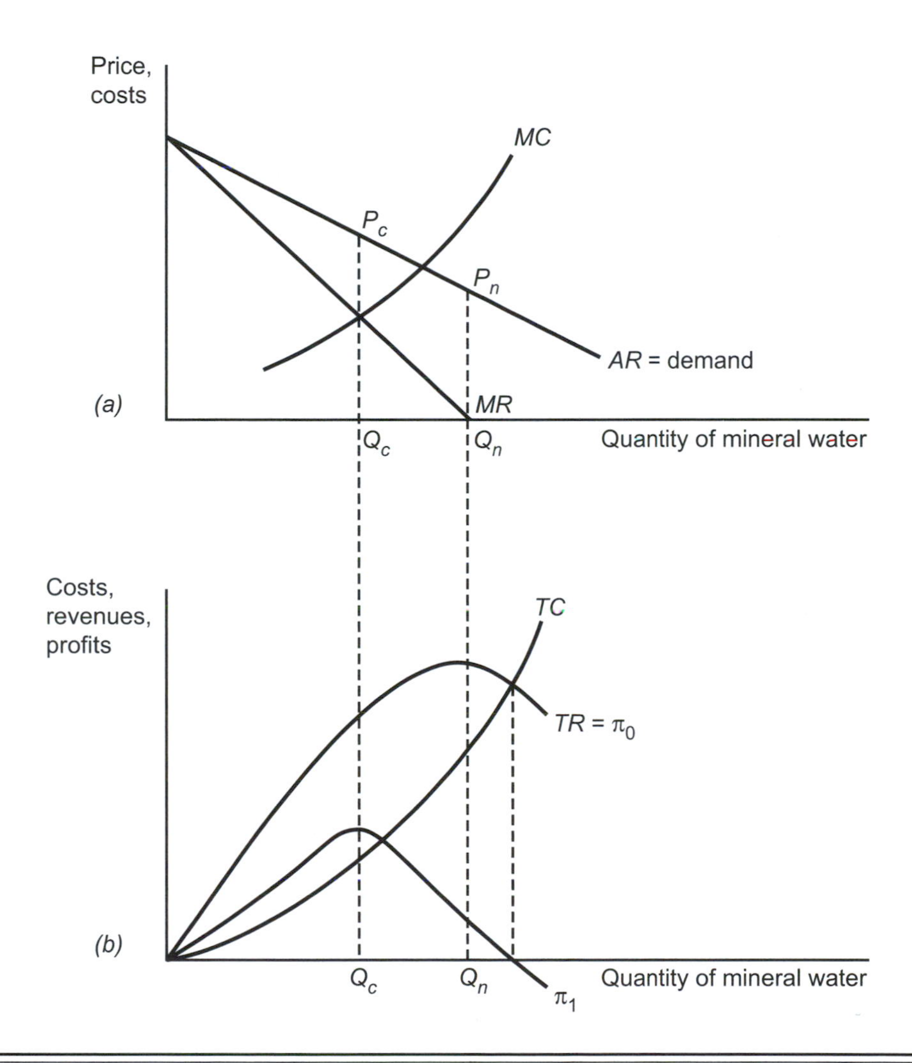

Figure 13-1 In a zero-cost situation, the firm will sell Q_n at P_n. With positive costs, quantity Q_c will be sold at P_c, following the marginal principle. Note that at Q_c, the profit function π_1 is at a maximum.

In reference to figure 13-1*a*, Cournot established that profits are at a maximum where $MR = MC$. Output produced will be Q, and price will be P_c; further, Q_c will be lower and P_c will be higher than in the case of zero costs. Figure 13-1*b* is an alternative way to treat the problem and its solution using the mineral-springs proprietor's *total* cost, revenue, and profit functions. Verify that the proprietor will cease production at Q_c in figure 13-1*b*, where the profit function π_1 is at a maximum (Cournot included a second condition—that the slope of the profit function be zero at Q_c and, further, that profits decline with either increases or decreases in quantity). Note that the mineral spring is not operated to maximize gross returns at Q_n but to maximize *net* returns at Q_c. The geometrically inclined reader will see that at Q_c, the slope of the *TC* function is equal to the *slope* of the *TR* function, or $MC = MR$, as in figure 13-1*a*. Cournot's development of the theory of monopoly would, in short, compare most favorably with that of any modern textbook writer, for it is precisely Cournot's theory that modern writers on monopoly are explicating.

Duopoly Analysis. Perhaps the most famous theory developed by Cournot relates to his second model, in which he introduced an additional seller of mineral water. In a profoundly original theoretical conception, Cournot's duopoly (two sellers) analysis laid the groundwork for many other ideas of importance to economics, such as imperfect competition (see chapter 20) and game theory (see chapter 25). Although Cournot's theory of duopoly was later altered and refined (notably by the English economist Francis Y. Edgeworth and the French mathematician Joseph Bertrand), its originality endures.

Cournot considered two sellers, *A* and *B*, who both sell the same product and know the total (aggregate) demand curve for their perfectly homogeneous product, mineral water. Otherwise, they are completely ignorant of each other's actions, to the extent that *A* thinks that *B* will keep his quantity constant no matter what *A* does, and *B* thinks the same thing about *A*'s quantity. Unrealistically, both sellers continue to make this assumption no matter how much experience they have *to the contrary*. In the language of duopoly, this assumption is called a *zero-output conjectural variation*, i.e., a conjecture that *B* will have no output reaction to *A*'s actions. Cournot further assumed that either *A* or *B* could supply all the mineral water demanded and, moreover, that mineral-water production is costless. He analyzed the problem of output and price determination both mathematically and graphically in the *Researches*, but our explanation emphasizes the graphical approach.

Cournot developed a new tool, *reaction curves*, to illustrate the optimal solution to the duopoly problem. Figure 13-2 depicts a concave reaction function *AA*, which reveals *A*'s choice of outputs with respect to *B*'s choice of outputs. Specifically, it shows the outputs that firm *A* will select in order to maximize profits, *given B*'s selection of outputs. For example, if *B* selects output b_0, then in order to maximize profits *A* will want to charge a certain price for its output a_0. If, on the other hand, *B* produces quantity b_1, *A* will be led by the profit motive to produce a lower quantity a_1, and so on for all other quantities *B* might produce. Whatever quantity *B* chooses, moreover, *A* "thinks" that it will be permanent, and so *A* acts to maximize his or her profits with this in mind.

What quantity will *A* and *B* end up producing? Clearly, the problem cannot be solved without adding *B*'s reaction function, so that we may see the kind of responses *B* will make to *A*'s output. The two functions are combined in figure 13-3, where *B*'s reaction function is defined in the same manner as *A*'s was above.

Suppose *B* decides to produce some output—say, b_0—on the assumption that *A* will keep output at level a_0. *B* would then be maximizing his or her profits at output

b_0. On the assumption that B would hold output at level b_0, A would maximize profits by producing output a_1. Such a move would cause B to reassess the situation and to increase his or her output to b_1, which maximizes his or her profits when A sells a_1. However, the assumption is constantly violated (though sellers A and B never catch on), and the process of output variation to maximize profits goes on as traced by the arrows in figure 13-3.

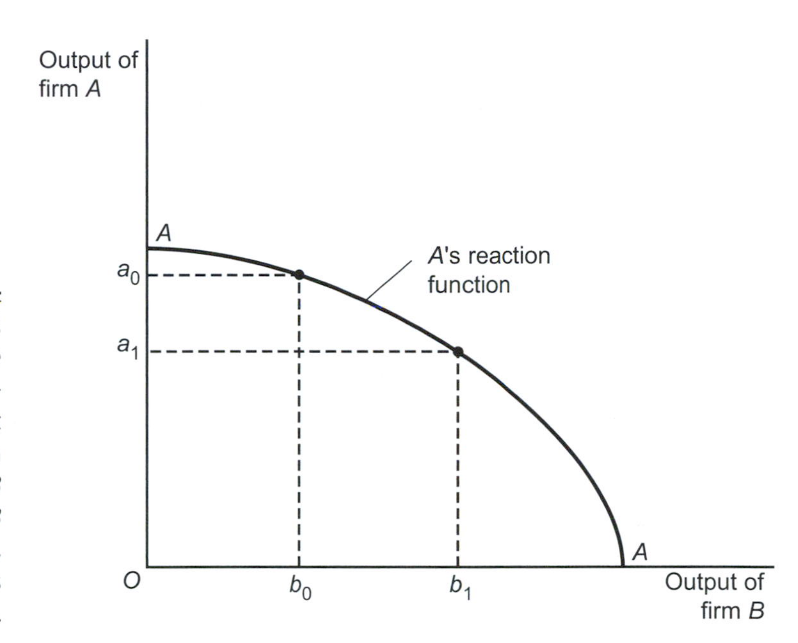

Figure 13-2
A's reaction curve describes the profit-maximizing output level for *A* given each level of output that *B* chooses. Thus when *B* chooses to produce b_0, *A* will maximize profits by producing a_0.

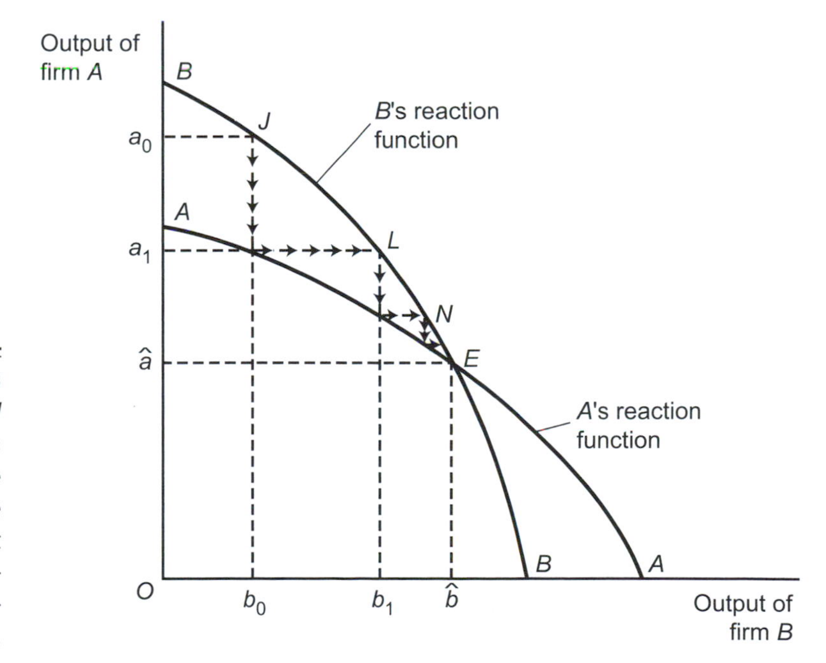

Figure 13-3
Beginning at point *J* (when *B*'s output is b_0), the arrows trace the path to stable equilibrium (point *E*) through successive output adjustments by *A* and *B*.

Point E (figure 13-3) represents an equilibrium solution for firms A and B. What this means is that if each firm moves away from point E, it will always return. At point E the duopolists both share profits (Cournot expressed this amount mathematically) and charge a common price that is lower than the price that would result under simple monopoly (a fact that Cournot himself noted) but higher than the one that would be charged under full and open competition. To be precise, duopoly output would be two-thirds the output produced if the market were competitive. The generalized result is that output would be $n/(n + 1)$ times competitive output. Thus, if there were five sellers, quantity sold would be five-sixths of competitive output. If there were 2,000 sellers, output would clearly approach the competitive amount. In this manner Cournot related his duopoly theory to the competitive model in which the number of sellers is large.

Cournot: An Evaluation

Besides duopoly theory, Cournot provided many other important theoretical insights. Among them were (1) a clear statement of the simple competitive model; (2) a very advanced model of composite and derived demand (for copper and zinc to produce brass); and (3) last but not least, a full-blown discussion of the *stability* of various economic equilibriums, which considers the possibility of wild variations in quantity and price. (The reader may gain some notion of the third issue by *reversing* the reaction curves or by switching the labels of the axes in figure 13-3.) Cournot's book was, in short, filled with new ideas.

Still, Cournot's contributions to method and to monopoly-duopoly theory have dominated the attention of theorists. And these ideas, especially those related to duopoly, attracted several critics. As previously mentioned, Edgeworth and Bertrand tinkered with Cournot's duopoly model, altering many of his assumptions. Why, for example, should a duopolist consider the quantity and not the price of his rival constant? More pointedly, how can A (for example) continue to assume that B's output will remain constant in spite of *repeated* evidence to the contrary? What if there was an output limit on one or both of the duopolists? And so on.

Many of these issues have been resolved but it is part of the continuing fascination of Cournot's model that the solution of one issue brings up two more. Cournot-like models have inspired theoretical offshoots such as oligopoly models, bilateral bargaining, and alternative assumptions concerning conjectural variation in modern game theory. His simple model was, and continues to be, the font of many ideas in economic theory (see, for example, the box on the following page, The Force of Ideas: Game Theory, The Brainchild of Cournot). His powerful ideas should place Cournot among the first rank of economic theorists. Moreover his vision of what economic theory could be was sweeping and ultimately, influential. He conceived economic theory as a box of tools, rooted in empiricism, which would comprise the organizing principles in analyzing myriad economic problems. This cognizance, so tragically ignored by his contemporaries, carried him to a pinnacle of achievement seldom reached in the history of economic theory.

■ Jules Dupuit (1804–1866)

While Cournot was working out the foundations of microeconomics, a venerable French institution—the École des Ponts et Chaussées (School of Civil Engineering)—nurtured a man who would combine micro tools with a theory of utility to

The Force of Ideas: Game Theory, the Brainchild of Cournot

Game theory, one of the most interesting and robust tools of modern economic analysis, was spawned in the nineteenth century and matured in the twentieth. The formal foundations of the idea are ascribed to the great twentieth-century mathematician John von Neumann and to the economist Oskar Morgenstern who collaborated on *The Theory of Games and Economic Behavior*, published in 1944. But the idea was clearly anticipated by Cournot.

Initially applied to such topics as politics and military strategy, many of the applications of game theory are currently in use in economics. Von Neumann and Morgenstern pointed out that Cournot's duopolists played a kind of "game" in that each made some independent conjecture about the other's output decision. As discussed in this chapter, one duopolist conjectured or believed that the other would hold output constant in the face of profit-maximizing adjustments in his or her own output. Given Cournot's assumptions, neither of the duopolists learned that this conjecture was unrealistic, so the outcome of the rivalry is that each seller shares the market equally and together they produce a level of output in equilibrium, equal to two-thirds the level of output that would be produced under competitive conditions (see text).*

Modern game theory incorporates less naive behavioral conjectures than Cournot's original model, inasmuch as it considers the payoffs associated with *alternative* conjectures. Consider the following problem, which is attributed to the mathematician A. W. Tucker. Suppose that two kidnappers are caught in the act but that the police only have hard evidence to convict them for a lesser offense. In an attempt to improve their evidence, the police sequester the prisoners separately and try to get confessions from them in the following manner. Each kidnapper is separately informed that (1) if one confesses, that one goes free and the other gets the death penalty; (2) if neither confesses, both will receive the lighter penalty that accompanies the lesser crime; (3) if both confess, both will receive a severe penalty but one less than death. Given the payoffs and the uncertainty, the expected solution is that both kidnappers confess.

This famous example is called the *prisoner's dilemma*. Its relevance to war games and to many kinds of economic behavior is fairly obvious. Advertising strategies between competing firms, for example, fit this model, as does any situation where strategic actions between individuals are *interdependent*. The prisoner's dilemma is a radical simplification because the prisoners are isolated and unable to communicate with each other so that they cannot collude in formulating a response to the police. Other "games" might be structured to allow cooperation or collusion, and all sorts of strategies might be evaluated. Its many applications have made game theory a valuable tool of economic analysis in evaluating competitive strategies and the various forms of industrial organization.

*Cournot's formal model was outfitted with other assumptions later in the nineteenth century by French mathematician Joseph Bertrand (who added the conjecture that the duopolist holds price constant) and by the neoclassical economist F. Y. Edgeworth (who conjectured that the duopolist holds quantity constant but with an output limit on each). See the notes for further reading at the end of this chapter.

establish the foundations of demand theory, public finance, public-goods theory, and welfare economics. Like Cournot, this brilliant French engineer practiced economics as an avocation, not a profession; and like Cournot, he brought keen practical insight to his analysis of economic problems.

Arsène-Jules-Étienne Juvenal Dupuit was born on May 18, 1804, in Fossano, Italy, when the region was ruled by France. He returned to France with his parents at the age of ten. There he continued his education in the secondary schools at Versailles, at Louis-le-Grand, and at Saint-Louis, where he finished brilliantly by winning a physics prize in a large competition. In 1824 he entered the famed French School of Civil Engineering (the École des Ponts et Chaussées). As a newly certified civil engineer he was put in charge of roadway and navigation projects in the department of Sarthe in 1827. He married in 1829 and in 1836, two years before Cournot published his *Researches*, Dupuit was promoted to the rank of first-class engineer.

Dupuit concerned himself with problems of economic interest throughout his illustrious career as an engineer. His experiments on the deterioration of roadways led to his *Essay and Experiments on Carriage Hauling and on the Friction of Rotation* (1837). A subsequent contribution on the same subject earned him a gold medal, awarded by vote of fellow engineers. Eventually he received France's crowning glory, induction to the Legion of Honor, on May 1, 1843.

The floods of the Loire in 1844 and 1846 stimulated Dupuit's *Theoretical and Practical Studies on the Movement of Running Water* (1848), and his classic *Floods: An Examination of the Means Proposed to Prevent Their Return* (1858). In 1850, Dupuit was called to municipal duty in Paris as director and chief engineer. There he studied municipal water distribution and supervised the construction of sewers. In December of 1855, Dupuit was named Inspector-General of Civil Engineering, the highest rank in the corps. He was, in short, one of the most distinguished engineers in France at the time. But political economy was Dupuit's hobby and the object of his passionate attention, and his career as an engineer afforded him opportunities to indulge his taste for economic questions. Unfortunately, a projected book entitled *Political Economy Applied to Public Works*, to which Dupuit referred as early as 1844, was never brought to completion (death intervened in 1866). With the exception of his short plea for free trade, *Commercial Freedom*, published in 1861, Dupuit's reputation as an economist must stand with a considerable number of journal contributions to economic policy and theory.

Dupuit's Unique View of Economics

Dupuit's special insights into economic analysis were the combined result, on the one hand, of his technical and scientific training in calculus and functions and, on the other, of his keen observation and utilization of the mountain of statistics on public-works revenues and costs gathered by himself and his fellow engineers. In economics, Dupuit was self-taught; he read Smith, Ricardo, and Say, the French expositor of classical economics. He was also influenced by Say's successor at the Collège de France, Pellegrino Rossi (see chapter 18). However, Dupuit's economics marks a clear departure from the old school. Classical economists such as Smith, Say, Malthus, and Ricardo undoubtedly influenced Dupuit's opinions on *macroeconomic* issues. But the one writer who could have helped him most in the area of microeconomics—Cournot—was apparently unknown to him. And, at one point, both lived and worked in Paris simultaneously!

Dupuit's contributions relate primarily to his engineering interests. According to one of his biographers, "Political economy, which attracts at every turn the engineer's interest, had also been the object of his constant study, and he was no less learned in that science than in that of public works." But it was the *combination* of these interests that produced Dupuit's special genius for theory and concept formation. His analytical tools were forged by three considerations. He focused on: (1) subjects of economic interest and importance; (2) relevant, observed facts and statistics abstracted from these subjects; and (3) mathematical analysis—deductive logic and graphical depiction—to organize and reorganize relations suggested by these facts and statistics. Theories conceived and derived in this manner, could be confronted with new facts and data for confirmation or alteration.

In other words, Dupuit's method treated political economy as a combined science of reason and observation. Cournot also combined the two, but with far less emphasis on empirical support and its correspondence to theory. Dupuit realized that unorganized statistics are meaningless. "To better see the facts, to better observe them, one must clarify them by light of reason," he wrote. His major effort in economic analysis was directed toward a real-world problem—measuring public utility, the *social welfare* produced by public goods and services. In keeping with this goal he made seminal discoveries in the theoretical areas of marginal utility, demand, consumer surplus, simple and discriminating monopoly, and marginal-cost pricing. In each case, the issue of chief concern was to understand the optimum price and output policies of public goods.

Marginal Utility and Demand

Dupuit was the first economist to present a cogent discussion of the concept of marginal utility and to relate it to a demand curve. Fully utilizing his powers of observation and abstraction, Dupuit was able to show, as early as 1844, that the utility that an individual (and a collection of individuals) obtains from a homogeneous stock of goods is determined by the use to which the last units of the stock are put. In doing so, he clearly pointed out that the marginal utility of a stock of some particular good diminishes with increases in quantity taken. Based on observation Dupuit established that each consumer "attaches a different utility to the same object according to the quantity he can consume." He illustrated his point with a practical example of a technological improvement in how water is supplied to a hillside town:

> Water is distributed in a city which, situated on a height, could procure it only with great pains. There was then such a value that the hectoliter per day was 50 francs by annual subscription. It is quite clear that every hectoliter of water consumed in these circumstances has a utility of at least 50 francs.

He posited that each unit of a given quantity of water will have a different utility and continued his argument by focusing on the effect of reductions in water's price. He supposes that as a result of the installation of pumps, costs of procuring water in the town drop by 20 francs:

> What happens? First, the inhabitant who consumed a hectoliter will continue to do so and will realize a benefit of 20 francs on his first hectoliter; but it is highly probable that this lower price will encourage him to increase his consumption; instead of using it parsimoniously for his personal use, he will use it for *needs less pressing, less essential*, the satisfaction of which is *worth more than 30 francs*, since this sacrifice is necessary to obtain water, but is worth *less than 50*, since at this price he relinquished this consumption. ("Utility and Its Measure")

Each increment of the same commodity carries a different utility because additional units will allow "less pressing, less essential" needs to be met. Therefore the additional utility derived from additional units of the same commodity must decline.

Elaborating this point, Dupuit supposed that when the price fell to 20 francs, the individual would demand 4 hectoliters "to be able to wash his house every day; give them to him at 10 francs, he will ask for 10 to be able to water his garden; at 5 frs. he will ask for 20 to supply a water font; at 1 franc he would want 100 to have a continuous flow [i.e., a fountain]," and so on. Dupuit clearly and unambiguously as-

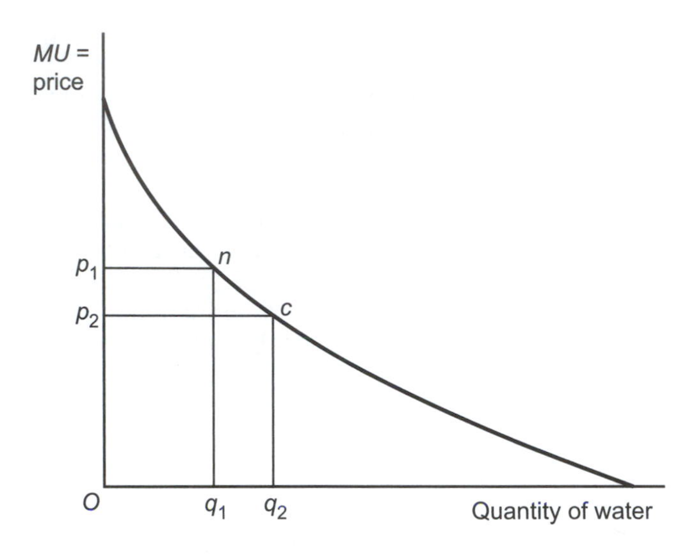

Figure 13-4 As the price of water declines from p_1 to p_2, the consumer will begin to satisfy less pressing wants. Therefore the consumption of water will increase from q_1 to q_2.

serted that it is the least pressing need for a commodity, not its most pressing need that defines the exchange value of the *entire* stock of goods. He affirmed this argument by a graphical representation, as shown in figure 13-4.

Assume that the consumer is originally in equilibrium when the price of water is at p_1 and the quantity taken is q_1. Now assume with Dupuit that the price of water falls to p_2. At the lower price for water the individual is in disequilibrium at point c. The marginal utility of the last unit of the consumer's existing stock is greater than the now-lower marginal utility of water represented by the lower price. In terms of price, what the consumer would pay for q_1 of water is greater than the price he or she *must* pay for quantity q_1. The same quantity of water (q_1) could be bought at a lower total expenditure, but Dupuit assumed that the consumer would not do this. Attached to each incremental unit of water between quantity q_1 and quantity q_2 is a marginal satisfaction greater (albeit diminishing) than that which would obtain for the incremental unit corresponding to price p_2. Thus, in an effort to maximize total satisfaction, the individual will increase purchases of water up to, but not beyond, quantity q_2.

As suggested by the labeling of the vertical axis (marginal utility = price) of figure 13-4, the marginal-utility curve is Dupuit's demand curve (*courbe de consommation*), and although most of his examples are concerned with transportation and communication, he maintained that the same laws apply to all goods and services. He provided explicit directions for the construction of such a curve in his article entitled "Tolls," which appeared in the 1852–53 French *Dictionary of Political Economy*:

> If, in a table of two columns, one inserts in the first all the prices, from 0, the one which corresponds to the greatest consumption, up to the price that stops all consumption, and in the second, regarding the price, the corresponding quantity consumed, we will have the exact representation of what we call the law of consumption.

In a paper entitled "On the Measurement of the Utility of Public Works," Dupuit constructed such a demand curve in 1844, six years after Cournot's *Researches* was published.

Like Cournot, Dupuit gave the equation for the curve of consumption as $y = f(x)$ or, alternatively, $Q_d = f(p)$. Additionally, Dupuit (as Léon Walras and other economists were to do later) placed the independent variable, price, on the x axis and the dependent variable, quantity, on the y axis. For reasons that will be explained later, Alfred Marshall (see chapter 16) reversed the axes, and thereafter, most economists adopted Marshall's practice (if not always his procedure, which treated marginal-demand price as a function of quantity). Dupuit's construction is reproduced as figure 13-5. He described it as follows:

> If . . . [we supposed that] along a line *OP* the lengths *Op*, *Op'*, *Op"* . . . represent various prices for an article, and that the verticals *pn*, *p'n'*, *p"n"* . . . represent the number of articles consumed corresponding to these prices, then it is possible to construct a curve *Nnn'n"P* which we shall call the curve of consumption. *ON* represents the quantity consumed when the price is zero, and *OP* the price at which consumption falls to zero. ("Measurement of the Utility of Public Works," p. 106)

It is obvious that this curve is identical in conception to that of figure 13-4; that is, Dupuit's demand curve is a marginal-utility curve. Dupuit made his meaning clear, with reference to figure 13-5, by stating, "The utility of . . . *np* articles is at least *Op* and . . . for almost all of them the utility is greater than *Op*."

The relation that Dupuit posited between price, marginal utility, and quantity was, a "fact of experience," he said, that "has been verified statistically." It was a theory of powerful originality, for in linking the demand curve with utility Dupuit established a new subset of economic analysis—welfare economics. Specifically, Dupuit maintained that the total area under the demand curve of figure 13-5 (area *OPN*) represents the total utility produced by the commodity. At some price—say, *Op"*—there is some amount that consumers would be *willing* to pay for the commodity over and above what they must pay. The amount that they *must* pay is represented by area *Op"n"r"* in figure 13-5, and it represents the firm's receipts (ignore for the present the other price-output combinations). In the case of zero costs (assumed in

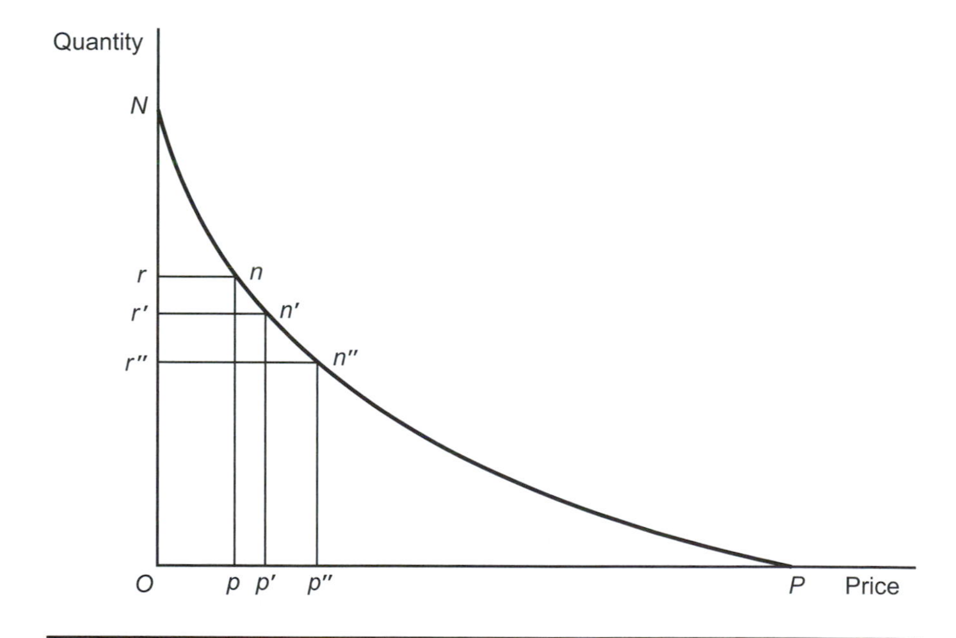

Figure 13-5 The area inside *OPN* represents the total utility derived from a commodity having the demand curve *PN*. At price *Op*, consumers pay an amount equal to *Ornp* and receive a surplus utility equal to *nPp*.

figure 13-5) areas $Op''n''r''$ may be called "producer surplus" or "producers' rents." The amount that consumers would be willing to pay over and above what they must pay is area $p''n''P$. In Dupuit's terms this is "utility remaining to consumers," but Alfred Marshall later renamed the concept "consumer surplus." Dupuit's numerical examples of these concepts (presented in the following section) illustrate their theoretical importance; but even more noteworthy they demonstrate Dupuit's analytical craftsmanship in developing theories of monopoly and price discrimination.

Consumer Surplus, Monopoly, and Price Discrimination

In the course of his economic writings, Dupuit was led to investigate some of the factors that give rise to monopoly pricing. Conditions existing among French railroad companies were of particular interest to him because the circumstances of that market did not fit easily into received economic models. He noted that "the interest of ordinary capitals is regulated by the law of supply and demand . . . while the means of transportation are monopolies." Thus, generally speaking, "ways of communication," or forms of transportation, are sheltered from competition.

To illustrate his point Dupuit compared the economic principles that determine house rents with those affecting transport rates. The degree of existing competition matters. Exorbitant rents for lodging, according to Dupuit, could not exist for very long because, "if it was known that house rental yields a revenue superior to the rental of other capitals, speculation would focus very quickly on the construction of houses and equilibrium would be established." Thus, the entry of new firms in the face of supranormal profits keeps monopoly rents from persisting over the long run in the housing market. But as Dupuit indicated, freedom to enter the railroad industry is inhibited by certain factors indigenous to that industry. Enormous amounts of capital, in the first instance, restrict the possibility of entry to a limited number of firms. Also, Dupuit recognized that because of the uniqueness of the first enterprise, a "new one can survive only at the expense of the first and . . . the profit which is sufficient for one is not sufficient for two."

With the exception of Cournot, whose work was unknown to him, Dupuit broke new ground by addressing the principles on which the simple monopolist (as constituted above) behaves. He formulated the rule of monopoly profit maximization in the course of his discussion of the effects on utility of tolls and transport charges. Table 13-1, reproduced from an 1849 article, illustrates Dupuit's early conception of this well-known principle.

The data in table 13-1 refer to a tariff or rate that a monopoly railroad may charge for passage. In this instance Dupuit was considering the case of an unregulated monopolist free to charge a rate that would maximize profits. He declared: "If the road or bridge or canal is private property, the owner company has only one aim, and that is to get the largest possible income from the toll." Thus, the monopolist facing the demand schedule derived from the data in table 13-1, with no costs of production, would charge a rate of 5 francs in order to maximize gross receipts. Dupuit then extended the example to include costs of production. He said that the "cost of traction" could be represented by 2 francs per unit of passage. These traction costs are variable, rising as distance increases. Dupuit continued:

> The rate which maximizes net yield is not the same as that which maximizes gross yield. The latter rate was 5, the former is 6, and it would grow indefinitely with the cost. It follows that when traction cost diminishes, the toll must diminish to yield maximum receipts. ("Tolls and Transport Charges," p. 20)

By focusing on net revenue, Dupuit correctly stated the principle of profit maximization and pointed out that if the level of traction costs increased, the profit-maximizing tariff would increase and output would decrease. The net receipts, additionally, are net only of variable expenses. Fixed costs, such as "certain administrative expenses, interest on construction expenditures, etc.," must also be covered in the long run. Consequently, Dupuit's net receipts are not long-run profits, as are his gross receipts (without costs of production). Dupuit, referring to the data in table 13-1, said, "If fixed costs were more than 104 [francs] and it were possible to charge only one uniform rate, the railroad would be a losing proposition with any tariff."

Table 13-1 A Monopoly Demand and Utility Calculation

			Yield of the Tariff	
Tariff	**Number of Passengers**	**Utility**	**Gross**	**Net**
0	100	445	0	–200
1	80	425	80	–80
2	63	391	126	0
3	50	352	150	50
4	41	316	164	82
5	33	276	165	99
6	26	234	156	104
7	20	192	140	100
8	14	144	112	84
9	9	99	81	63
10	6	69	60	48
11	3	36	33	27
12	0	0	0	0

In addition to an analysis of profit maximization, Dupuit's early treatment of monopoly contained another important analytical tool, which was later used by Alfred Marshall. Specifically, both investigations posited a relation between monopoly revenue and consumer surplus, given, of course, the constancy of the marginal utility of money. Making an implicit identification of the demand curve with a utility function, Dupuit supplied a utility calculation for his railroad example (see column 3, table 13-1). In this case the price that maximized net revenue would be a tariff of 6 francs, and the total utility (consumer surplus, producer surplus, and costs) produced by this tariff would be 234 francs.

According to Dupuit, total utility always breaks down into three parts: lost utility, producer surplus, and consumer surplus. At the 6 franc tariff the total utility of 234 francs divides as follows: Assuming fixed costs are nonexistent, the lost utility equals 52 francs, the total variable costs of carriage (i.e., 2 francs × 26 passengers). The producer surplus is identical to the net receipts of 104 francs. The consumer surplus is the residual of 78 francs (i.e., 234 – 52 – 104).

If we momentarily depart from Dupuit's presentation and assume that the fixed cost is exactly 104, then monopoly revenue disappears. In the short run the 104 francs accruing to the owner of the railway is of the nature of an economic rent (i.e., producer surplus) on fixed investment, but as Dupuit succinctly pointed out, these fixed costs must ultimately be met by the monopolist. Thus, under the assumption that the fixed costs are 104 francs there would be no monopoly revenue. A consumer surplus is produced, however, in the amount of 78 francs.

Price Discrimination and Welfare: Numerical Analysis

Dupuit was the first to present a cogent analysis of how consumer surplus could be decreased or increased by a policy of price discrimination. He explained this result with the aid of tables 13-2 and 13-3. Table 13-2 utilizes the same demand data as table 13-1 but adds a fixed cost of 110 francs. The result of adding fixed costs is that there now exists no single tariff that will maximize profit. A tariff of 6 francs will, however, minimize losses. Dupuit demonstrated that profits are nevertheless possible if price discrimination is allowed. Suppose 14 passengers could be induced by some means of differentiation to pay a tariff of 8 francs while 12 continued to pay 6 francs. The same 26 passengers would then yield gross revenue of 184 francs and profit of 22 francs. Consumer surplus, however, would decline from 78 to 50 francs.

Table 13-3 shows these results and the effects of various other combinations of dual pricing. Using a two-class tariff of 4 and 7 as an example, Dupuit showed how consumer surplus could be increased over the single tariff case. From table 13-2 we know that 41 passengers are willing to buy tickets at a price of 4 francs. Dupuit assumed it possible to distinguish 20 passengers from this group who would be will-

Table 13-2 Monopoly Demand, Utility, and Costs

			Costs			Revenue	
Tariff	Number of Passengers	Total Utility	Variable	Fixed	Total	Gross	Net
0	100	445	200	110	310	0	–310
1	80	425	160	110	270	80	–190
2	63	391	126	110	236	126	–110
3	50	352	100	110	210	150	–60
4	41	316	82	110	192	164	–28
5	33	276	66	110	176	165	–9
6	26	234	52	110	162	156	–6
7	20	192	40	110	150	140	–10
8	14	144	28	110	138	112	–26
9	9	99	18	110	128	81	–47
10	6	69	12	110	122	60	–62

Table 13-3 The Two-Class Tariff

	Single Tariff	Two-Class Tariff				
	(6)	(6,8)	(5,10)	(4,7)	(3,7)	(2,6)
Number of passengers	26	(12,14)	(27,6)	(21,20)	(30,20)	(37,26)
Total utility	234	234	276	316	352	391
Gross revenue	156	184	195	224	230	230
Total costs	162	162	176	192	210	236
Net revenue	–6	22	19	32	20	–6
Consumer surplus	78	50	81	92	122	161

ing to pay a price of 7 francs for the journey. In this case discrimination would yield gross receipts of 224 francs [(20 × 7) + (21 × 4)]. Subtracting total costs of 192 francs leaves net receipts to the monopolist of 32 francs. The consumer surplus is calculated as the difference between total utility and gross receipts, a value of 92 francs.

Discrimination: Dupuit's Graphics

Dupuit also expressed these ideas graphically. In figure 13-6, suppose *OM* is the profit-maximizing price. The utility produced by the commodity or service depicted by the demand curve of figure 13-6 would be distributed in the following manner: the monopoly revenue would equal the area *OMTR*; the consumer surplus (or the utility remaining to consumers, in Dupuit's terminology) would equal area *TMP*; finally, the lost utility, *utilité perdue*, would equal the triangle *RTN*.

Under conditions of competition this lost utility would result from scarcity of resources. However, since Dupuit assumed zero costs of production in this instance, lost utility in his example can only be attributable to restrictions of output under monopoly. The significance of Dupuit's theory of price discrimination is that he showed how economic welfare could be increased (i.e., lost utility could be reduced) by differential pricing. He explained with reference to figure 13-6:

> When the consumers can be placed in several categories [by separating markets or differentiating products or services] each of which attributes a different utility to the same service, it is possible, by a certain combination of taxes, to increase the product of the toll [the sum of consumer surplus and monopoly revenue] and to diminish the loss of utility. ("Measurement of the Utility of Public Works," p. 108)

Thus, if the monopolist faced with the demand curve of figure 13-6 was able to increase the total quantity sold to *Or* via discrimination, the *total utility* (the sum of consumer surplus and monopoly revenue in the no-cost case) would equal the area *OPnr*, which is greater than *OPTR* by *RTnr*. The increase in monopoly receipts would clearly depend on the number of submarkets that the monopolist would be able to establish and invade. As Dupuit correctly pointed out:

> If from among the *pn* consumers at price *Op* you can distinguish the number *pq* who would consume at the price *OM*, and from among the latter the number *Mq'* who would consume at price *Op'*, and can oblige them by various combinations to pay those prices, then the yield . . . will be the sum of the three rectangles *Ornp* + *pqTM* + *Mq'n'p'*; the utility to consumers [consumer surplus] will be the three triangles *nqT* + *Tq'n'* + *n'p'P*; while the loss of utility is merely that due to the lowest price, the triangle *Nrn*. ("Measurement of the Utility of Public Works," pp. 108–109)

It can readily be seen that monopoly profits under discrimination (assuming no costs) increase considerably over those that result from the simple monopoly price *OM*. Specifically, profits increase by *Mp'n'q'* + *Rqnr*, and it is important to note that they can be increased without increasing output beyond that established under the simple monopoly output *OR*. In other words, price discrimination could affect the *distribution* of welfare without affecting the *total* utility produced. But Dupuit believed that discrimination was desirable only if it increased quantity beyond that obtained under a single-price, simple monopoly system, for only in that event would lost utility (*utilité perdue*) be reduced.

With respect to figure 13-6, Dupuit knew that output would increase if only one of the markets could be served at the simple monopoly price but more than one could be served with price discrimination. The market in which price *Op'* is charged

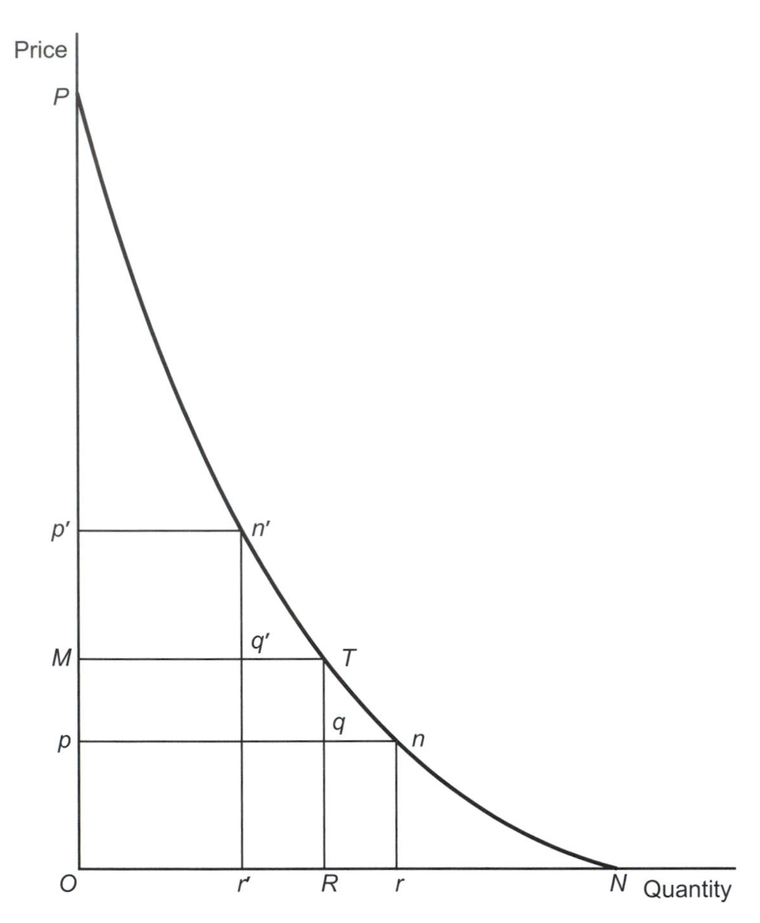

Figure 13-6 In addition to price *OM*, a lower price, *Op*, will enlarge the seller's revenue and the consumers' surplus by reducing lost utility. A higher price, *Op′*, will enlarge the seller's revenue but lower the consumers' surplus.

would have been served in any event, given the simple monopoly profit-maximizing price *OM*. But the relatively weaker market delineated by price *Rq* would not have been entered at the simple monopoly price *OM*. Dupuit's implicit suggestion that output would increase (by *Rr*) if discrimination allowed the monopolist to enter markets not entered at the simple monopoly price was only much later given scientific treatment by A. C. Pigou and Joan Robinson (see chapter 20). Yet it is certainly clear that as early as 1844 Dupuit was at the threshold of output analysis under price discrimination, which finally yielded to Robinson's expert treatment almost a century later.

Dupuit and Entrepreneurship

As one of the first writers in economics to closely analyze product quality and its impact on markets, Dupuit was naturally led into a discussion of the role of the entrepreneur. He associated the entrepreneur's role with demand discovery, which he conceived as a two-stage process: The first stage emphasizes innovation; the second stresses calculation and judgment. Both functions are complex and subtle.

In the first instance, the entrepreneur must devise winning combinations of characteristics that make up a desirable product or service. Dupuit therefore linked entrepreneurship to product differentiation. He recognized that some product variations are natural and some are contrived, but he did not consider the distinction crucial. The important thing in his judgment was whether product differentiation creates value *in the subjective judgment of the consumer.* He was aware that different elasticities of demand enter the calculation and that shrewd entrepreneurs will seize the opportunities that present themselves in this regard. He cited product labeling as a case in point:

> The same merchandise, disguised in different stores under various forms, is often sold at very different prices to the rich, the well-to-do, and the poor. There is the fine, the very fine, the extra fine, and the super fine, which, although drawn from the same barrel, present no real difference other than a better label and a higher price. Why? Because the same thing has a very different utility value for the consumer. If the goods were sold merely at the average price, all those who attached less utility than the price would not buy, and thus would incur a loss; and the seller would lose because many of his customers would be paying for only a very small part of the utility they receive ("Utility and Its Measure," p. 177).

In the second instance, the entrepreneur must estimate the utility that consumers attach to a particular good or service in order to devise an optimal pricing scheme. The most important issue for Dupuit was the combined and simultaneous effect of product differentiation on the entrepreneur's profits and the consumers' utility. He took it for granted that consumers' total utility would rise if the sales of goods and services increased, and he saw price/product differentiation as a means to increase total sales by inducing marginal consumers who would otherwise be "priced out" of a single product, single price market to enter a price/product differentiated market. It is up to the entrepreneur to motivate this process. Because all exchange involves transaction costs, Dupuit said that the entrepreneur must account for such aspects as convenience, location, and waiting (time). In transport markets, for example, he advised that nominal rates (e.g., train tickets) might be lowered to offset the transaction costs imposed by slow-moving trains, inconvenient departure/arrival schedules, traffic congestion, and the opportunity costs associated with alternative modes of transport. In other words, entrepreneurial responsibilities extend to attempts to accommodate customers' opportunity costs by adjusting *nominal* price to *real* demands.

Ultimately the quest for entrepreneurial profits, which is the essence of dynamic competition, requires intuition, inventiveness, and judgment. It is much more complex than merely selling the same good at the same price as one's rivals, or even at different prices imposed by natural market divisions. Dupuit looked beyond these simple constraints and raised the notion of competition to a situation in which entrepreneurs constantly tinker with ideas that eventually take form in various attributes that alter the utility-producing nature of a product or a service. The idea that the entrepreneur produces and/or sells a single product at a single price never fit comfortably into economic analysis because there are too many examples to the contrary. Yet, neoclassical analysis embraced the idea, warts and all, in an attempt to manage change and improve theoretic precision. At a time when microeconomics was still embryonic, Dupuit emphasized economic *activity* rather than market *structure*. This brought him into close contact with the Austrian variant of neoclassical economics (see chapter 23) rather than its British counterpart.

Benefit-Cost Analysis: The Early Application of Price Theory to Public Goods

Although Dupuit deserves credit as the first writer to analyze the optimum provision of public goods and public works from a welfare standpoint, belated research has shown that he was but one of a long line of French engineer-economists interested in these problems. The French engineers Joseph Minard and Henri Navier, for example, were working on similar questions before Dupuit. Nevertheless, Dupuit's invention of the marginal-utility function enabled him to give much improved estimates of the benefits derived from governmentally supplied goods, and it is his formulation that has inspired contemporary research on these issues.

Dupuit's general rule for the provision of public goods, such as highways, water distribution, and public transport, was that the government should provide these goods if a pricing scheme could be devised to cover the total annual cost associated with the good while simultaneously producing "net utility." In other words, the good should be provided if the marginal annual receipts of an enterprise could cover the marginal costs (including capital costs) to be amortized annually over a specified number of years.

Dupuit's theory of the optimum provision of public goods may be illustrated utilizing the model of price discrimination developed above. His analysis of discrimination was completely general in its description of the pricing technique. Specifically, he recognized that a public monopoly, in contrast to a private monopoly, may follow a policy of constrained discrimination. In Dupuit's view, government ownership finds its *raison d'être* in society's decisions concerning the distribution of real income. If the public interest is an overriding consideration in the provision of a good or service, the government should operate the enterprise in such a manner as to maximize the consumer surplus. Whereas the size of the consumer surplus is of no significance to a private monopolist, it is of prime importance to a government concerned with the distribution of income. As Dupuit noted:

> The conduct of a monopoly raises a series of important questions. . . . Is the largest possible profit to be earned? Is the yield to be a fixed sum and the loss of utility reduced to a minimum? ("Tolls and Transport Charges," p. 31)

The government would likely seek to maximize the consumer surplus under the full-cost constraint, which Dupuit presumably invoked as an allocative criterion. This could be accomplished by using a single price, and in several examples the single price was suggested. However, Dupuit did not overlook the value of a policy of price discrimination by a government-operated monopoly.

Table 13-3 illustrates one situation in which price discrimination by a government monopoly can increase public utility (i.e., aggregate welfare). To make his case, Dupuit first described the solution that a private company would take. Assuming unconstrained profit maximization, he wrote that "the tariff (4,7) yields decidedly more than the other combinations, and that is the one which a private company would adopt." (Note that this profit-maximizing two-class tariff nevertheless results in an improvement in consumer surplus over the simple monopoly rate of 6; output would increase, and average [simple] price would decline as well.) The two-class tariff does not maximize consumer surplus, however, and should the government assume ownership of the enterprise, some sort of alternative pricing scheme could be established to augment the consumer surplus. Dupuit pointed out with reference to table 13-3:

> The tariff (2,6) maximizes utility [net utility, or producer surplus and consumer surplus], though it does involve the railway in a loss of 6; but this loss can be avoided by raising the second-class price just a little above 2, which would reduce utility to about 260 and passengers to 60. This is the tariff which the government would adopt, because it would cover all costs. The railway operated by a private

> company would serve only forty-one passengers and give them a utility of 92; if operated by the government, it would serve 60 passengers and give them a utility of about 160. ("Tolls and Transport Charges," pp. 22–23)

Thus, Dupuit's welfare measure (consumer surplus) provided a mechanism for analyzing the effects of discriminating monopoly under alternative property and institutional arrangements. His early and original insights into welfare theory, nurtured as they were by an economic and empirical tradition among French engineers engaged in public service, provided the necessary backdrop against which an important and fruitful area of modern economics is being enacted. The clear enunciation and application of the utility principle and the demonstration that society's welfare could be improved by public action in a private economy when conditions of competition are not ubiquitously effective leave Dupuit unchallenged as the most important early precursor of modern doctrine and practice in the field.

■ Engineers and Cross-Fertilization of Economic Ideas

A thorough examination of Cournot's and Dupuit's contributions to economic analysis demonstrates that a sophisticated economic theory of the firm was underway with surprising momentum before 1850, especially in France. A later giant in microeconomic theory, Alfred Marshall (see chapter 16) paid tribute to the special genius of French engineers in his *Industry and Trade* (p. 117):

> Frenchmen are especially fitted for certain large enterprises by their talent for engineering. From early times French cathedrals and fortifications, French roads and canals have borne evidence to high creative faculty. Since the Revolution the engineering profession has been held in special honour in France: there is perhaps no other country in which the ablest lads are so generally inclined towards it.

To be sure, French institutions exalted engineering studies and facilitated the training of able personnel. Napoleon reformed French higher education into a two-tiered system: the universities and the *grandes écoles*. The latter, which persist to this day, are institutions of higher learning of limited size and scope, concentrating on rigorous, functional, and specialized training, and restricting admissions to only the brightest students.

Cournot and Dupuit were products of the *grandes écoles*, Cournot of the École Normale and Dupuit of the École des Ponts et Chaussées. Schooled in mathematics, committed to scientific rigor, and alert to intellectual opportunities, these "residual economists" pioneered important aspects of the modern theory of the firm in precisely those areas left underdeveloped by the British tradition: the evaluation of investment plans, the consequences of fixed and variable costs for pricing decisions, the rudiments of product differentiation, the conditions for successful price discrimination, and other implications of profit maximizing behavior in imperfectly competitive markets.

At the École des Ponts et Chaussées in particular, an impressive and lengthy oral and written tradition in economic inquiry accumulated from the inception of the school in 1747. By the 1830s Henri Navier (1785–1836), Joseph Minard (1781–1870), and Charlemagne Courtois (1790–1863) were plumbing the depths of benefit-cost analysis in the evaluation of public works. Civil engineers like them paved the way for Dupuit's pioneer analysis. Moreover, the influence of the *grandes écoles* extended beyond national borders. The École des Ponts et Chaussées had a policy of accepting foreign students, and one of the most capable who entered in 1830 was an American, Charles Ellet (1810–1862), whom Jacob Viner ranked "with Cournot and Dupuit as a pioneer formulator of the pure theory of monopoly price in precise terms" (*Long View*, p. 388). And there were others: Alphonse Belpaire from Belgium, and Wilhelm von Nördling from Austria, who improved the statistical specification and discovery of railway cost functions.

This French engineering tradition that spawned Dupuit developed momentum that carried it into the twentieth century, encouraging further innovations by Émile Cheysson (1836–1910), René Tavernier (1853–1932), and Clément Colson (1853–1939). But France was not the only country with a strong engineering tradition that spilled over into economics. The earliest foundations of a parallel German tradition are not as clear, but one practitioner in particular contributed to economic theory at a high level. Wilhelm Launhardt (1832–1918), the successor in Germany of J. H. von Thünen and H. K. von Mangoldt, taught engineering at the Hanover Technical School where, like at the École des Ponts et Chaussées, the focus of economic inquiry was on the provision of public goods. Launhardt's *Mathematische Begrundung der Volkwirtschaftslehre* (1885), translated in 1993 as *Mathematical Principles of Economics*, is an excursion into the central problem of exchange, which in some respects builds on Walras's earlier analysis (see chapter 17), and in some respects anticipates Marshall (see chapter 16). Launhardt's emphasis throughout the *Mathematical Principles* on the comparison of both competitive and monopoly outcomes with the arrangement that maximizes total utility is also evocative of Dupuit's path-breaking contribution.

In England, where the engineering tradition was more practical and less theoretical, two engineers in particular did work that compares favorably to the French and Germans: Dionysius Lardner (1793–1859) and Fleeming Jenkin (1833–1885). Lardner especially influenced W. S. Jevons (see chapter 15) to forge ahead with the development of microeconomic theory. In sum, nineteenth-century engineers from different cultures and countries were alert to certain economic problems outside the net of classical economics and were actively seeking solutions to those problems. The global intellectual landscape of economics in the nineteenth century was neither provincial nor myopic, even though the contemporary "keepers of truth" were not always receptive to contributions from allied disciplines. Insularity is, in large measure, the enemy of progress in economic theory. A review of the material in this chapter should serve to demonstrate that economists stood to gain from the efforts of the engineers, and it is entirely possible that the reverse is also true. Specialization and division of labor, in intellectual pursuits as well as in the economic theory of production, have definite advantages, but these advantages can be diluted by overspecialization and close-mindedness. Economists, no less than other specialists, must therefore guard against slavish efforts to protect their own turf at all costs.

■ Conclusion

Engineers are mainly *practitioners* who daily face the necessity of getting things done. Finding no analytical precedent in classical economics for the problems that confronted them, French engineers and their counterparts in other countries were stimulated to forge new analytical tools. Sadly, because their expertise was considered "too technical" (i.e., mathematical) by the reigning, orthodox economists, their contributions were not always embraced. Such was the fate of Cournot (though not an engineer he rationalized a method that engineers could readily identify and implement) and Dupuit, in France, and of Launhardt in Germany. The fact that these writers received belated recognition after so many years is testimony to the vigilance required to repel intellectual arrogance and myopia—a vigilance which, if not maintained, condemns us to the continuous rediscovery of earlier truths at potentially high costs.

REFERENCES

Cournot, A. A. *Researches into the Mathematical Principles of the Theory of Wealth*, N. T. Bacon (trans.). New York: A. M. Kelley, 1960 [1838].

———. *Principes de la théorie des richesses*. Paris: Librarie Hachette, 1863.

Dupuit, Jules. "On the Measurement of the Utility of Public Works," in R. H. Barback (trans.), *International Economic Papers*, no. 2. London: Macmillan, 1952, pp. 83–110 [1844].

———. "On Tolls and Transport Charges," in E. Henderson (trans.), *International Economic Papers*, no. 11. London: Macmillan, 1962, pp. 7–31 [1849].

———. "Tolls," in Charles Coquelin (ed.), *Dictionnaire de l'économie politique*, vol. 11. Paris: Guillaumin, 1852–1853.

———. "On Utility and Its Measure," *Journal des Economistes*, 1st ser., vol. 35 (July–September 1853), pp. 1–27. Reprinted in Mario de Bernardi, *De l'utilité et de sa mesure: Écrits choisis et republiés*. Torino: La Riforma Sociale, 1933.

Marshall, Alfred. *Industry and Trade*, 3d ed. London: Macmillan, 1920.

Viner, Jacob. *The Long View and the Short: Studies in Economic Theory and Policy*. New York: Free Press, 1958.

NOTES FOR FURTHER READING

An article that does not bear directly on Cournot or Dupuit, but nevertheless raises interesting questions about the influence of mechanics on economics, is Ivor Grattan-Guinness, "How Influential Was Mechanics in the Development of Neoclassical Economics? A Small Example of a Large Question," *Journal of the History of Economic Thought*, vol. 32 (December 2010), pp. 531–581. Grattan-Guinness presents an overview of several specific ideas from mechanics that influenced economics in the second half of the nineteenth century. By examining the analogies between mechanics and economics in the work of a series of neoclassical economists, the author concludes that the influence of mechanics is milder than is commonly thought. Another article that "sets the table" for the approaching "feast" of public economics is Gilbert Faccarello, "An 'exception culturelle'? French Sensationist Political Economy and the Shaping of Public Economics," *The European Journal of the History of Economic Thought*, vol. 13 (Spring 2006), pp. 1–38, which after surveying some ideas in public economics from Turgot and Condorcet to Say, concludes that French economists devised the first theory of the optimal level of government expenditure.

Although Cournot's microeconomics received a great deal of attention from twentieth-century theorists, a very small number of assessments of his work exists in English. For those who read French, see Claude Ménard, *La formation d'une rationalité économique: A. A. Cournot* (Paris: Flammarion, 1978); and François Vatin, *Économie politique et économie naturelle chez Antoine-Augustin Cournot* (Paris: Presses Universitaires de France, 1998). A review of Ménard's book, in English, by R. F. Hébert appears in the *History of Economic Thought Newsletter*, vol. 23 (Autumn 1979), pp. 21–23. Other French sources are Émile Callot, *La philosophie biologique de Cournot* (Paris: 1960); Georges Loiseau, *Les doctrines économiques de Cournot* (New York: 1970); François

Bompaire, *Le principe de liberté économique dans l'oeuvre de Cournot et dans celle de l'École de Lausanne* (Paris: 1931); and two articles by René Roy, "L'Oeuvre économique d'Augustin Cournot," *Econometrica*, vol. 7 (April 1939), pp. 134–144; and "Cournot et l'école mathematique," *Econometrica*, vol. 1 (1933), pp. 13–22. An interesting account of Cournot's life is given by A. J. Nichol, "Tragedies in the Life of Cournot," *Econometrica*, vol. 6 (July 1938), pp. 193–197; and by Irving Fisher, "Cournot and Mathematical Economics," *Quarterly Journal of Economics*, vol. 12 (January 1898), pp. 119–138, 238–244.

The empirical nature of Cournot's demand theory is documented in C. L. Fry and R. B. Ekelund, Jr., "Cournot's Demand Theory: A Reassessment," *History of Political Economy*, vol. 3 (Spring 1971), pp. 190–197. The relationship of Cournot to his contemporaries, and the hostile reception accorded his theory, as well as Cournot's multiple efforts to gain recognition, are explored by R. B. Ekelund, Jr., and R. F. Hébert, "Cournot and His Contemporaries: Is an Obituary the Only Bad Review?" *Southern Economic Journal*, vol. 57 (July 1990), pp. 139–149. On the same subject, see also R. D. Theocharis, "A Note on the Lag in the Recognition of Cournot's Contribution to Economic Analysis," *Canadian Journal of Economics*, vol. 23 (November 1990), pp. 923–933. R. W. Dimand, "Cournot, Bertrand, and Cherriman," *History of Political Economy*, vol. 24 (Fall 1995), pp. 563–578, discovered an enthusiastic early adherent of Cournot in the person of Canadian economist W. B. Cherriman.

A clear and relatively timeless discussion of the Cournot, Bertrand, and Edgeworth solutions to the duopoly problem is presented by Fritz Machlup in his *Economics of Sellers' Competition* (Baltimore: Johns Hopkins University Press, 1952); but see Jean Magnan de Bornier, "The 'Cournot–Bertrand Debate': A Historical Perspective," *History of Political Economy*, vol. 24 (Fall 1992), pp. 623–656, for an attempt to correct widespread misunderstandings about Cournot vis-à-vis Bertrand. Clarence Morrison, "Magnan de Bornier on Cournot–Bertrand," *History of Political Economy*, vol. 33 (Spring 2001), pp. 161–165, took issue with de Bornier, who responded in the same issue, pp. 167–174. Bruce Larson and Claire Childers, "Operationally Meaningful Theorems in Light of Cournot," *History of Political Economy*, vol. 24 (Winter 1992), pp. 895–908, trace a part of Cournot's legacy through the subsequent contributions of Edgeworth and Samuelson. Nicola Giocoli, "'Conjecturizing' Cournot: The Conjectural Variations Approach to Duopoly Theory," *History of Political Economy*, vol. 34 (Summer 2003), pp. 175–204, opens the "Pandora's Box" of conjectural-variations reasoning inaugurated by Cournot.

Among other things, Cournot had a major impact on the development of game theory, the branch of economics pioneered by John von Neumann and Oskar Morgenstern in *The Theory of Games and Economic Behavior* (Princeton, NJ: Princeton University Press, 1944). The pre-1944 literature on the development of two-person zero-sum games is examined by R. W. and M. A. Dimand, "The Early History of the Theory of Strategic Games from Waldegrave to Borel," *Toward a History of Game Theory*, Annual Supplement to Volume 24, *History of Political Economy*, ed. E. R. Weintraub (Durham, NC: Duke University Press, 1992), pp. 15–27.

The economic writings of Dupuit are composed largely of journal contributions in the *Annales des Ponts et Chaussées* and in the *Journal des Économistes*. A collection of Dupuit's major articles (in French), published in Italy under the editorship of Mario de Bernardi, is entitled *De l'Utilité et sa mesure: Écrits choisis et republies* (Torino: La Riforma Sociale, 1933). Two of these articles are in published translation (see references). At long last, a compendium of Dupuit's collected works has been assembled and carefully edited, but in French only; see, Jules Dupuit, *Oeuvres économiques complètes*, 2 vols., Yves Breton and Gérard Klotz (eds.) (Paris: Economica, 2009). For reviews of this collection and its significance to the history of economic thought, see Manuela Mosca, "Œuvres économiques complètes," *The European Journal of the History of Economic Thought*, vol. 18 (Spring 2011), pp. 296–306; and R. B. Ekelund, Jr., and R. F. Hébert,

"The Intellectual Legacy of Jules Dupuit: A Review Essay," *History of Political Economy*, vol. 44 (Fall 2012), pp. 493–504.

Long obscured in the Anglo-Saxon tradition of history of economic thought, the French econo-engineering approach was exposed by R. B. Ekelund, Jr., and R. F. Hébert, *Secret Origins of Modern Microeconomics: Dupuit and the Engineers* (Chicago: University of Chicago Press, 1999). Jean-Pascal Simonin and François Vatin (eds.), *L'oeuvre multiple de Jules Dupuit (1804–1866): Calcul d'ingénieur, analyse économique et pensée sociale* (Angers: Presses Universitaire de Angers, 2002), have assembled papers by several authors in an attempt to establish the full range of Dupuit's influence. Dupuit's contributions to utility theory and to other facets of economic analysis are assessed in the following works: G. J. Stigler, "The Development of Utility Theory," *Journal of Political Economy*, vol. 58 (August, October 1950), pp. 307-327, 373–396, reprinted in Stigler, *Essays in the History of Economics* (Chicago: The University of Chicago Press, 1965); R. W. Houghton, "A Note on the Early History of Consumer's Surplus," *Economica*, n.s., vol. 25 (February 1958), pp. 49–57; R. B. Ekelund, Jr., "Jules Dupuit and the Early Theory of Marginal Cost Pricing," *Journal of Political Economy*, vol. 76 (May–June 1968), pp. 462–471; R. B. Ekelund, Jr., "A Note on Jules Dupuit and Neoclassical Monopoly Theory," *Southern Economic Journal*, vol. 25 (January 1969), pp. 257–262; R. B. Ekelund, Jr., "Price Discrimination and Product Differentiation in Economic Theory: An Early Analysis," *Quarterly Journal of Economics*, vol. 84 (May 1970), pp. 268–278; Arnaud Diemer, "Jules Dupuit et la discrimination par les prix," in Pierre Dockès, et al. (eds.), *Les traditions économiques françaises 1848–1939* (Paris: CNRS Éditions, 2000); and R. B. Ekelund, Jr., and W. P. Gramm, "Early French Contributions to Marshallian Demand Theory," *Southern Economic Journal*, vol. 36 (January 1970), pp. 277–286. See also R. B. Ekelund, Jr., and Mark Thornton, "Geometric Analogies and Market Demand Estimation: Dupuit and the French Contribution," *History of Political Economy*, vol. 23 (Fall 1991), pp. 397–418. The early French tradition in public finance, of which Dupuit was a part, is discussed in two articles by R. B. Ekelund, Jr., and R. F. Hébert: "Dupuit and Marginal Utility: Context of the Discovery," *History of Political Economy*, vol. 8 (Summer 1976), pp. 266–273; and "French Engineers, Welfare Economics and Public Finance in the Nineteenth Century," *History of Political Economy*, vol. 10 (Winter 1978), pp. 636–668. Also on Dupuit, see Alan Abouchar, "A Note on Dupuit's Bridge and the Theory of Marginal Cost Pricing," *History of Political Economy*, vol. 8 (Summer 1976), pp. 274–277; Bernard Grall, "De l'entretien des routes à la mesure de l'utilité: le calcul de substitution chez Dupuit (1842–1844)," in Pierre Dockès, et al. (eds.), *Les traditions économiques françaises 1848–1939* (Paris: CNRS Éditions, 2000); and R. B. Ekelund, Jr., and Y. N. Shieh, "Dupuit, Spatial Economics and Optimal Resource Allocation: A French Tradition," *Economica*, vol. 53 (November 1986), pp. 483–496. The history of the concept of consumer surplus, beginning with Dupuit's seminal contribution, is traced up to the first half of the twentieth century by R. B. Ekelund, Jr., and R. F. Hébert, "Consumer Surplus: The First Hundred Years," *History of Political Economy*, vol. 17 (Fall 1985), pp. 419–454. Dupuit was also surprisingly advanced in his views of consumer behavior and the role of the entrepreneur in satisfying consumer demands, especially in light of Kelvin Lancaster's work on "characteristics-based" demand. See R. B. Ekelund, Jr., and R. F. Hébert, "Dupuit's Characteristics-Based Theory of Consumer Behavior and Entrepreneurship," *Kyklos*, vol. 44, Fasc. 1 (1990), pp. 19–34. R. B. Ekelund, Jr., "The *Economist* Dupuit on Theory, Institutions, and Policy: First of the Moderns?" *History of Political Economy*, vol. 32 (Spring 2000), pp. 1–38, makes the case for Dupuit as a complete economist in the modern sense.

Yves Breton and Gérard Klotz, "Jules Dupuit, *Société d'économie politique de Paris* and the Issue of Population in France (1850–66)," *The European Journal of the History of Economic Thought*, vol. 13 (Summer 2006), pp. 337–363, presents Dupuit's thoughts on population and Malthusian problems in an attempt to establish him as more than merely a brilliant engineer-economist. Philippe Poinsot, "The Foundations of Justice in Jules Dupuit's Thought," *The European Journal of the History of Economic Thought*, vol. 17 (December 2010), pp. 793–812, argues that the dispute between Dupuit and the French liberals was not strictly about public utility versus natural rights. For Dupuit, justice is based on welfare and hence, public utility, although natural rights are not necessarily excluded from consideration.

The recurrent theme in Ellet's work is that business decision making could and should be based on mathematically derived principles, which Ellet called "the Laws of Trade." See Charles Ellet, Jr., *An Essay on the Laws of Trade in Reference to the Works of Internal Improvement of the United States* (New York: A. M. Kelley, 1966); and same author, "The Laws of Trade Applied to the Determination of the Most Advantageous Fare for Passengers on Railroads," *Journal of the Franklin Institute*, vol. 30 (1840), pp. 369–379. With few exceptions, Ellet has been passed over by historians of economic thought. The notable exceptions are C. D. Calsoyas, "The Mathematical Theory of Monopoly in 1839: Charles Ellet, Jr.," *Journal of Political Economy*, vol. 58 (April 1950), pp. 162–170; an unpublished dissertation by C. H. Shami, *Charles Ellet, Jr., Early American Economist and Econometrician 1810–1862: An Analytical Exposition of His Theories* (New York: Columbia University, 1968); R. B. Ekelund, Jr., and D. L. Hooks, "Joint Demand, Discriminating Two-Part Tariffs and Location Theory: An Early American Contribution," *Western Economic Journal*, vol. 10 (March 1972), pp. 84–94; and C. R. Bell, "Charles Ellet, Jr., and the Theory of Optimal Input Choice," *History of Political Economy*, vol. 18 (Fall 1986), pp. 485–495.

The lively interest in applied economic questions at the École des Ponts et Chaussées is amplified by examining the contributions of a number of its famous students. See R. B. Ekelund, Jr., and R. F. Hébert, "Public Economics at the École des Ponts et Chaussées: 1830–1850," *Journal of Public Economics*, vol. 2 (July 1973), pp. 241–256. Besides Ellet, who was enrolled at the École as an *externe*, R. D. Theocharis, "C. Courtois: An Early Contributor to Cost-Benefit Analysis," *History of Political Economy*, vol. 20 (Summer 1988), pp. 265–274, has added the name of Charlemagne Courtois to the list of pioneering engineer-economists.

Émile Cheysson's contributions to economics have been analyzed by R. F. Hébert in several articles: "Émile Cheysson and the Birth of Econometrics," *Économies et Sociétés*, vol. 20 (October 1986), pp. 203–222; "A Note on the Historical Development of the Economic Law of Market Areas," *Quarterly Journal of Economics*, vol. 86 (November 1972), pp. 563–571; "Wage Cobwebs and Cobweb-Type Phenomena: An Early French Formulation," *Western Economic Journal*, vol. 11 (December 1973), pp. 394–403; and "The Theory of Input Selection and Supply Areas in 1887: Émile Cheysson," *History of Political Economy*, vol. 6 (1974), pp. 109–113. Wilhelm Nordling's statistical research on railway cost curves is preserved in Elizabeth Henderson's translation, "Note on the Cost of Railway Transport," *International Economic Papers*, no. 10 (1960), pp. 64–70. Cheysson incorporated Nordling's statistics into his "econometric" model of railway profit maximization.

For an English translation of Launhardt's pioneer *Mathematische Begrundung der Volkwirtschaftslehre*, see Launhardt, *Mathematical Principles of Economics*, John Creedy (trans.) (Aldershot, UK: Edward Elgar, 1994), which exposes the full range of Launhardt's "general-equilibrium" approach to exchange and value, as well as his substantial contributions to spatial economics. A brief extract from this same work was translated earlier and included in W. J. Baumol and S. M. Goldfeld (eds.), *Precursors in Mathematical Economics: An Anthology* (London: London School of Economics and Political Science, 1968). For those who read German, the standard early reference on Launhardt's spatial economics is E. Schneider, "Bemerkungen zu einer Théorie der Raumwirtschaft," *Econometrica*, vol. 3 (1935), pp. 70–105.

British engineers who helped pioneer advances in nineteenth-century microeconomics include Dionysius Lardner and Fleeming Jenkin, who both fit into the story of William Stanley Jevons (see chapter 15). Lardner's book, *Railway Economy*, resides in the library at the École des Ponts et Chaussées, but it is not known whether there was any direct filiation between French and English engineers on microeconomic ideas. D. L. Hooks, "Monopoly Price Discrimination in 1850: Dionysius Lardner," *History of Political Economy*, vol. 3 (Spring 1971), pp. 208–223, explores Lardner's contribution to the theory of monopoly price and the concept of demand for a product over economic distance. Jenkin's economic writings have been collected and reprinted under the title *The Graphic Representation of the Laws of Supply and Demand, and Other Essays on Political Economy, 1868–1884* (London: London School of Economics and Political Science, 1931). For an assessment of Jenkin and his work, see A. D. Brownlie and M. F. L. Prichard, "Professor Fleeming Jenkin, 1833–1885: Pioneer in Engineering and Political Economy," *Oxford Economic Papers*, vol. 15 (November 1963), pp. 204–216. An excellent commentary on Lardner and Jenkin is provided by R. M. Robertson, "Jevons and His Precursors," *Econometrica*, vol. 19 (July 1951), pp. 229–249.

14

Microeconomics in Germany and Austria
Menger, Wieser, and Böhm-Bawerk

German economics in the nineteenth century may be viewed in the literal sense, as spawned by Germany's native sons, or it may be treated as the collective wisdom of economists who expressed themselves in the German language. In the literal sense, the peak analytical achievements of the nineteenth century were relatively few, although powerfully original. Several key German writers anticipated the marginalist revolution in economic analysis, and their work is on a par with Cournot and Dupuit. J. H. von Thünen, H. H. Gossen, and H. K. von Mangoldt contributed to an analytical tradition that was rich in theoretical insight but was underappreciated by the German historical school (see chapter 11). As the historicists gained the upper hand in the universities of late nineteenth-century Germany, the seat of theoretical economics shifted to Austria, a country politically apart from Germany but joined to its sister state by a common language and culture.

This chapter deals primarily with the economics of the three writers who together made up the Viennese school. The founder of this group was Carl Menger (1840–1921). He was joined by two younger but able disciples: Friedrich Wieser (1851–1926) and Eugen Böhm-Bawerk (1851–1914). Together they established a systematic approach to economic analysis that persists today as an alternative to mainstream (i.e., Anglo-American) neoclassical economics. Many of their students and their students' students became prominent twentieth-century economists, especially Joseph Schumpeter, Ludwig von Mises, Friedrich Hayek, Fritz Machlup, Gottfried Haberler, and Oskar Morgenstern (see chapter 23).

German Proto-Neoclassicists

In order to stress the continuity of Germanic ideas, we turn first to the pioneers—those writers who blazed the way for theoretical economics in Germany and Austria. The contributions of J. H. von Thünen, H. H. Gossen, and H. K. von Mangoldt form an analytical backdrop for the Viennese school.

J. H. von Thünen

Johann Heinrich von Thünen (1783–1850) was a successful farmer and brilliant theorist who worked in isolation on his agricultural estate in Mecklenburg, Germany. He understood, as few economists have before or since, the proper relation between theory and facts—which is the hallmark of any scientific investigation. It was this characteristic of his thought that endeared him to Alfred Marshall (see chapter 16), who claimed to have "loved [him] above all my masters" (*Memorials*, p. 360). One of the things Marshall learned from von Thünen was how to apply the principle that all forms of expenditure should be carried to the point at which the product of the last unit equals its cost: the total product is maximized only when resources are allocated equimarginally.

Von Thünen is credited with a number of important and original anticipations of modern economic theory, such as the concepts of economic rent, diminishing returns, opportunity costs, and the marginal-productivity theory of wages. Above all else, however, he was a pioneer in the economic theory of location; so we will examine his contribution to marginal analysis primarily in that context. Like Ricardo, von Thünen recognized that differences in the cost of producing agricultural products result from utilization of land of different quality. Whereas Ricardo focused on differences in soil fertility, von Thünen concentrated his analysis on differences in land location (i.e., distance from a central selling point). At the same time, he recognized that those products that are bulky in relation to value are more costly to transport than those that are less so, and that perishability of some farm products prevents long periods in transit.

The problem, therefore, was to devise the best (most profitable) system of land utilization. Von Thünen's solution was so carefully worked out that he rightfully deserves the distinction of being called the father of location theory in economics. His argument was couched in a theoretical construction, or model, which has the following characteristics: A large town (market) is situated in the center of a fertile plain that has neither canals nor navigable rivers. The only means of conveyance is by horse-drawn wagon or a similar means of transport. All land within the plain is of equal fertility, and there are no other comparative advantages of production between plots. At a considerable distance from the city, the plain ends in an uncultivated wilderness. The town draws its produce from the plain, the inhabitants of which it supplies with manufactured products. There is no trade with the outside world.

A model developed by Melvin Greenhut (*Plant Location*, see references) shows how the boundaries of production are determined for two competing crops once the costs of production and transportation are known. In figure 14-1 assume that *O* is the central market point in the middle of a homogeneous plain. *OA* is the cost of producing a dollar's worth of potatoes and *A′S* is the cost of transporting the potatoes over a distance of *OJ* miles. Similarly, *A″T* and *OK* represent an identical cost and distance in the opposite direction. *AS* and *AT* show the gradual increase in transport costs (and total costs) as the distance from *O* increases. On the other hand, *OB* represents the cost of producing a dollar's worth of wheat, and *B′M* represents its transport cost for distance *OX′*. (The same relationship exists for cost *B″N* and distance *OX*). The freight rate is assumed to be higher on potatoes than on wheat because the former yields a greater bulk per acre than the latter.

Von Thünen's assumption of a uniform, homogeneous plain means that labor and capital are equally productive at all locations and that the cost of production per acre of output is everywhere the same. From figure 14-1 it will be seen that at a dis-

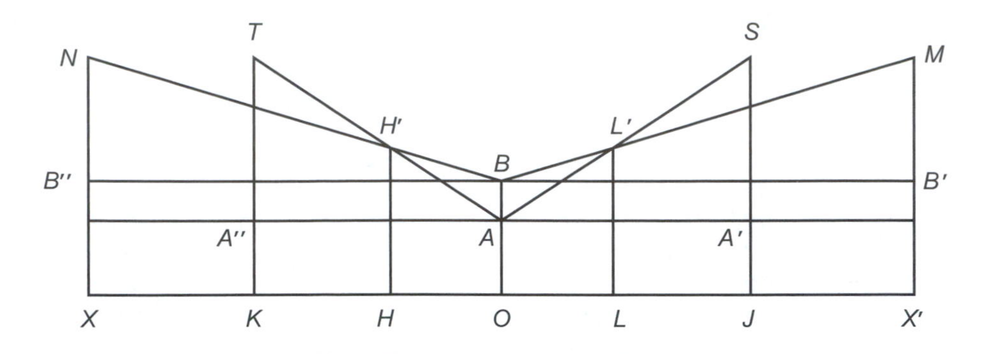

Figure 14-1 The delivered cost of a dollar's worth of potatoes (*AS* or *AT*) exceeds the delivered cost of a dollar's worth of wheat (*BM* or *BN*) to the east of *L* and to the west of *H*. Therefore potato producers will locate in the *OL* and *OH* regions, and wheat will be grown in the *LX'* and *HX* regions.

tance beyond *OL*, the delivered cost of a dollar's worth of potatoes (cost line *AS*) exceeds the delivered cost of a dollar's worth of wheat (cost line *BM*). Therefore, producers of potatoes will tend to locate to the west of *L* and to the east of *H*, whereas wheat producers will locate to the east of *L* and to the west of *H*. Furthermore, if transport costs are the same in every direction, *OL* becomes the radius of a circle within which potato production will take place. In other words, von Thünen's model gives us the least-cost location for each crop within the isolated state. It also illustrates the principle of equimarginal allocation. Resources should be allocated to potato production only up to the point where the cost of producing a dollar's worth of potatoes equals the cost of producing a dollar's worth of wheat. Finally, the model can be generalized to include more than two crops.

Von Thünen's theory deals with the classical problem in location analysis, namely, the location of producers over an area that serves consumers at a central point. Although its assumptions are restrictive, it nevertheless marked a significant beginning in locational analysis and in mathematical economics. Moreover, Greenhut has shown that the analysis is not limited to agricultural locations but can be adapted to the locational decision of manufacturing concerns as well.

H. H. Gossen

The first writer who developed a full-fledged theory of consumption grounded in the marginal principle was Hermann Heinrich Gossen (1810–1858), also a native of Germany. He served as a tax assessor for the Prussian government but had retired from this position by the time he wrote his one great work in 1854, a book entitled *Development of the Laws of Human Relationships and of Rules to Be Derived Therefrom for Human Action*. Despite Gossen's high expectations, the book passed almost unnoticed. In bitter disappointment, he recalled all of the unsold copies from the publisher (who had published it on commission only) and destroyed them. Afflicted with tuberculosis soon afterward, Gossen died in 1858, convinced that his ideas, original and valuable as they were, would never bring honor to his name. So ended in personal tragedy a life that had much to give theoretical economics but that received even less recognition in his native country than Cournot had in his.

Technically speaking, Gossen's work shares certain traits with the work of Dupuit, Jevons, Walras, and, to a somewhat lesser extent, Menger. Yet, more than anyone else—with the possible exception of Jevons—Gossen's economics seems to be rooted in an attempt to mathematize Bentham's hedonic calculus. Gossen viewed economics as the theory of how people as individuals and as groups realize the maximum of pleasure with the minimum of pain. He insisted that mathematical treatment was the only sound way to handle economic relations and applied this method throughout his work to determine maxima and minima.

Gossen's book was organized in two parts of about equal length. The first, devoted to pure theory, has attracted the most (belated) attention for its early formulation of the two laws that have come to bear Gossen's name. Gossen's first law formulated the principle of diminishing marginal utility and gave it graphical expression. His second law described the condition for utility maximization: To maximize utility a given quantity of a good must be divided among different uses in such a manner that the marginal utilities are equal in all uses. Also included in this first part of his work are Gossen's laws of exchange (accompanied by complicated geometrical representation) and his theory of rent. The second part of his book is devoted to applied theory, including the "rules of conduct pertaining to desires and pleasures," and the refutation of certain "social errors" concerning education, property, money, and credit. Philosophically, Gossen was a utilitarian and a classical liberal; he was opposed to government intervention, especially in those instances when individual initiative and free competition suffice as guiding principles of the economic order.

The neglect of Gossen's work was a setback for the progress of economic theory. He was rediscovered by Jevons in 1879, but only after independent discoveries of the same magnitude had been made in economics by Jevons, Menger, and Walras. Important contributions to the subjective theory of value and the marginal principle preceded Gossen's, of course (Dupuit's contribution appeared a decade earlier, for example), but no work carried either idea as far as Gossen did until after 1870. His bitter disappointment at the neglect of his work was understandable, but he was also naive. He boasted that his work did for economics what Copernicus had done for astronomy—a pretentious claim, but one that Léon Walras (see chapter 17) nevertheless took for understatement. But then we must remember Walras's own disappointment when he did not receive the Nobel Peace Prize after nominating himself. As for Gossen, perhaps the most encouraging thing that can be said of his personal tragedy is that the future was on his side.

H. K. von Mangoldt

Unlike von Thünen and Gossen, Hans Karl Emil von Mangoldt (1824–1868) operated from an academic base. He received his doctorate in 1847 from the University of Tübingen, then studied for two years under Roscher at the University of Leipzig, and for a short time with Georg Hanssen[1] at the University of Göttingen. In between he pursued a journalistic career that he was forced to abandon in 1854 because of his liberal beliefs. Mangoldt got permission to teach on the basis of his first book, *Die Lehre vom Unternehmergewinn*, a study of entrepreneurial profits, published in 1855. Seven years later he was elected to the chair vacated by Karl Knies at the University of Freiburg. In 1863, Mangoldt published his second book,

[1] Georg Hanssen (1809–1894) held a faculty position at Göttingen where he was known primarily for his empirical work, but he also did much to draw attention to the work of von Thünen.

Grundriss der Volkswirthschaftlehre, a small treatise that had its origin in his lecture notes but also contained some highly original theoretical innovations. T. W. Hutchison called it "a distant infant cousin of Marshall's Principles" (*Review of Economic Doctrines*, p. 134). Mangoldt died of a heart attack in 1868, after a short life.

Mangoldt's theoretical work is divided into two parts. His first book, which developed the theory of profit and the role of the entrepreneur, shows the combined influence of Roscher and von Thünen (through Hanssen). It was probably inspired in part by the challenge of socialism, which induced Mangoldt to take a fresh look at how factor rewards are distributed. Mangoldt was one of a few early writers who separated the entrepreneur from the capitalist and linked entrepreneurial profit to risk taking. Specifically, he characterized entrepreneurial profits as the reward for a range of activities, including finding particular markets, acquisition of productive agents, skillful combination of factors of production on the right scale, successful sales policy, and in the final analysis, innovation. Frank Knight found Mangoldt's profit theory "a most careful and exhaustive analysis" (*Risk, Uncertainty and Profit*, p. 27).

The second part of Mangoldt's work (*Grundriss*) consists of a reworking of the main parts of economic theory from a curiously ambiguous perspective, one that combined aspects of classical and neoclassical analysis. Despite this ambiguity, the list of original contributions by Mangoldt is fairly impressive, considering the fact that Mill's *Principles* represented the state of the discipline in Mangoldt's day. This list includes a "Marshallian" treatment of supply and demand, embryonic notions of elasticity and economies of scale, a discussion of multiple equilibriums, the generalization of von Thünen's (marginal productivity) principle of distribution (especially a generalized concept of rent), and a graphical analysis of price formation under conditions of joint supply and demand. Mangoldt's subjective theory of value must be added to the small but growing list of such treatments before 1871, but the subjective viewpoint did not permeate his analysis as it did the later work of the Austrians.

The purpose of this section has not been to link von Thünen, Gossen, and Mangoldt with the Austrian school in any overt sense but merely to indicate the depth and breadth of Teutonic economic thought in the nineteenth century. This sets the stage for an appreciation of the Austrian contribution. We wish to note, however, that a retrospective view of the writings of early German theorists gives new force and meaning to Alfred Marshall's statement that "the most important economic work that has been done on the Continent in this century [19th] is that of Germany" (*Principles*, p. 66).

■ Carl Menger (1840–1921)

The fundamental details of Menger's life can be set forth simply. He was born in 1840 in Galicia, then part of Austria, descended from a family of Austrian civil servants and army officers. Menger studied law at the universities of Prague and Vienna, and in 1867 he turned to economics, perhaps because of an interest in stock market prices (he covered the stock market for a time as a writer for the Vienna *Zeitung*). Menger published his carefully written *Grundsätze* (translated as *Principles of Economics*) in 1871, and his fame began to spread soon thereafter. He received an appointment to the University of Vienna, where he remained on faculty until his retirement in 1903. Between 1876 and 1878 he served as tutor to Crown Prince Rudolf.

At first blush, Menger appears to have been the epitome of the plodding, pedantic academic. But in fact he was the leader of a veritable theoretical revolution, the founder of a school of thought, and a verbal scrapper par excellence against what he regarded as the excesses of German historicism. By his own volition, he became a major protagonist in the *methodenstreit* (method struggle) with historicist Gustav Schmoller (see chapter 11). Menger entered the fray by attacking Schmoller in his *Untersuchungen über die Methode des Sozialwissenschaften* (1883) in which he defended the deductive method against Schmoller's extreme historicism. Emphasizing all-important subjective factors, Menger defended self-interest, utility maximization, and complete knowledge as the elemental foundations of economics. He considered aggregative, collective ideas useless, unless they were firmly grounded in individual behavior.

Schmoller defended the historical method as the only method relevant for analyzing the social organism. In Schmoller's view, the Austrians, by focusing on the individual's behavior under constraints, were leaving out the most important things—dynamic institutions. In the end, the debate became personal and, in consequence, pointless. Schmoller and his followers (effectively, it would seem) boycotted Austrian professors at German universities, and it was a long while before Germany produced theorists of the first rank. In the end, however, the steady influence of Menger's *Principles*[2] and the work of his disciples began to overcome historicist criticism, and the controversy ended with the Austrians getting the upper hand. Austrian economics picked up adherents in England (William Smart and James Bonar), and the principle of subjective utility analysis eventually carried the day. For that reason, Menger's *Principles* took on a leading role in the development of Austrian economics.

Menger and Economizing Man

Menger's economic theory is characterized by careful logic beginning at the most fundamental levels. He began his investigation into value theory, for example, with a lengthy and systematic discussion of goods, which he distinguished from what he called "useful things." In order for a thing to possess goods-character, four conditions must be met simultaneously: (1) the thing must fulfill a human need, (2) it must have properties that would establish a causal connection between it and the satisfaction of the need, (3) there must be a recognition of this causal connection, and (4) there must be command of the thing sufficient to direct it to the satisfaction of the need. If one of these conditions was missing, a person would have a useful thing, but not a commodity in the market sense.

Armed with a basic definition of an economic good, Menger proceeded to distinguish goods by order. Goods of the first order are capable of satisfying human needs directly, while higher-order goods (capital, production goods) derive goods-character from their ability to produce lower-order goods. Higher-order goods can satisfy human needs only indirectly, for as Menger pointed out with reference to the production of bread, "What human need could be satisfied by a specific labor service of a journeyman baker, by a baking utensil, or even by a quantity of ordinary flour?" (*Principles*, pp. 56–57).

Menger emphasized the *complementarity* of higher-order goods in establishing their "goods character." The ability of higher-order goods to satisfy human needs requires command over complementary goods of higher order. He illustrated the

[2] Ironically, Menger dedicated his *Principles* to Wilhelm Roscher, founder of the older historical school. As noted in chapter 11, Roscher was far less extreme in his (historicist) critique of economic theory than Schmoller.

causal connection between first-order goods and higher-order goods with an example in which he hypothesized what would happen if the demand for tobacco disappears. According to Menger:

> If, as the result of a change in tastes, the need for tobacco should disappear completely, the first consequence would be that all stocks of finished tobacco products on hand would be deprived of their goods-character. A further consequence would be that the raw tobacco leaves, the machines, tools, and implements applicable exclusively to the processing of tobacco, the specialized labor services employed in the production of tobacco products, the available stocks of tobacco seeds, etc., would lose their goods-character. The services, presently so well paid, of the agents who have so much skill in the grading and merchandising of tobaccos in such places as Cuba, Manila, Puerto Rico, and Havana, as well as the specialized labor services of the many people both in Europe and in those distant countries, who are employed in the manufacture of cigars, would cease to be goods. (*Principles*, p. 65)

It is the causal sequence, i.e., the notion that the value (and goods-character) of first-order goods is transmitted or imputed to higher-order goods, which so typifies Austrian economics. Menger also emphasized a basic complementarity and interdependence of all goods we consume. This complementarity, which Menger so belabored with respect to consumption, was also, as we shall see, carried over to the theory of production by the Austrians.

Economic Goods and the Valuation Process

Having established the fundaments of the things that are traded in a market, Menger set out to show how humans, on the basis of a knowledge of available supply and demand, direct the available quantities of goods to the greatest possible satisfaction. He maintained that the origins of human economy were coincident with the origins of economic goods. *Economic goods* are defined as those whose requirements are greater than the available supply. *Noneconomic goods*, conversely, are those, such as air or water, whose supply exceeds requirements. And here Menger makes an interesting point—that the basis for property is the protection of ownership of economic goods. (By contrast, communism is founded on noneconomic relations.) Of course, there is nothing inherent in goods that make them economic or noneconomic; their character can change with changes in supply or demand.

According to Menger, a good is said to have value if economizing humans perceive that the satisfaction of one of their needs (or the greater or lesser completeness of its satisfaction) depends on their command over the good. Utility is the capacity of a thing to satisfy human needs, and as such it is a prerequisite of goods-character. Of course, noneconomic goods may also possess utility since the subjective valuation between use and need (one's need for air or water, for instance) relates to a specific quantity; but economic goods, Menger pointed out, presuppose scarcity.

Menger's distinctions call to mind Smith's water–diamond paradox. Smith, it will be recalled, was puzzled by the fact that water, which has so much value in use, has no value in exchange, while diamonds, which have practically no value in use, are expensive. Menger argued that both water and diamonds undisputedly possess utility, the difference being that diamonds are scarce relative to the demand for them. Further, the subjective valuation between use and need for water could not be related to a specific quantity, and water therefore cannot possess use value. Use value presupposes scarcity, and economic goods alone possess use value.

The Equimarginal Principle

Although Gossen has priority in this regard, Menger nevertheless presented one of the first clear discussions of the equimarginal principle of welfare maximization. He first emphasized that satisfactions have different degrees of importance to people:

> The maintenance of life depends neither on having a comfortable bed nor on having a chessboard, but the use of these goods contributes, and certainly in very different degrees, to the increase of our well-being. Hence there can also be no doubt that, when men have a choice between doing without a comfortable bed or doing without a chessboard, they will forgo the latter much more readily than the former. (*Principles*, p. 123)

In other words, there is a subjective factor in an economizing individual's valuation process, and this subjective element establishes the extent to which different satisfactions have different degrees of importance. Menger emphasized that within the same class of goods, satisfactions may vary in importance. People try to satisfy their more urgent before their less urgent needs, but they will also combine the more complete satisfaction of more pressing wants with the lesser satisfaction of less pressing wants.

Menger explained his theory with the use of a table, replicated below as table 14-1. The Roman numerals depict ten classes of wants, represented in descending order so that want III is less urgent than want II, want IV is less urgent than want III, and so on. To drive home his point, Menger assumed that an individual is able to rank satisfactions in a cardinal manner, i.e., assign number indices to them. Thus, the individual can say that consumption of the first unit of commodity I (e.g., food) yields 10 units of satisfaction, while the first unit of commodity V (e.g., tobacco) gives but 6. To derive valid conclusions we must assume that satisfactions from consuming, say, goods IV and VII (or any other two goods) are independent. Furthermore, we assume that some other resource (other than goods I to X) is being used to obtain units of these ten goods, and that additional units of each commodity may be obtained with an equal expenditure of this resource (for convenience, we call this other resource "money," and we assume that the unit price of each good purchased is $1).

According to Menger an economizing person would behave in the following manner. If the individual possessed a limited budget of $3 and spent it all on the commodity of highest importance (I), he or she would obtain 27 units of satisfaction (i.e., 10 + 9 + 8). In this instance, however, the individual would seek to combine satisfactions obtained from commodities I and II. Buying 2 units of commodity I and 1 unit of commodity II, the individual would obtain 28 units of satisfaction (i.e., 10 + 9 + 9). With, say, $15 at his or her command, the individual would allocate expenditures so that, *at the margin*, the satisfaction

Table 14-1 The Theory of Value

I	II	III	IV	V	VI	VII	VIII	IX	X
10	9	8	7	6	5	4	3	2	1
9	8	7	6	5	4	3	2	1	0
8	7	6	5	4	3	2	1	0	
7	6	5	4	3	2	1	0		
6	5	4	3	2	1	0			
5	4	3	2	1	0				
4	3	2	1	0					
3	2	1	0						
2	1	0							
1	0								
0									

obtainable from commodities I through V would just equal 6, as can easily be verified from table 14-1.[3] Thus, Menger established an equimarginal principle. That is, given scarce means (dollars, in our example), the individual will arrange his or her various consumptions so that at the margin, satisfactions are equal. In doing so, Menger's economizing individual maximizes total satisfaction. Paradoxically, Menger established the importance of being unimportant.

> Accordingly, in every concrete case, of all the satisfactions secured by means of the whole quantity of a good at the disposal of an economizing individual, only those that have the least importance to him are dependent on the availability of a given portion of the whole quantity. Hence the value to this person of any portion of the whole available quantity of the good is equal to the importance to him of the satisfactions of least importance among those assured by the whole quantity and achieved with an equal portion. (*Principles*, p. 132)

Thus, it is the least urgent satisfaction obtainable from a given stock of goods that gives value to that good. For example, imagine a given quantity of water available to an individual. He or she puts the available stock to many uses, from the most urgent (maintaining life) to the least (watering his or her flower garden). The determination of the value of any portion of water is in this case subjective—it is in its least important use, gardening. Any given portion of the good could stand for any other portion, of course.

In extending value theory this way, Menger also considered the impact of differences in the quality of goods on their value. He presented a theory of exchange and its limits, concluding that under certain cases, "If command of a certain amount of A's goods were transferred to B and if command of a certain amount of B's goods were transferred to A, the needs of both economizing individuals could be better satisfied than would be the case in the absence of this reciprocal transfer" (*Principles*, pp. 177–178). His examples of isolated exchange are copious, eschew mathematical expression, and are often cumbersome—but they broke new ground. In addition, Menger analyzed the effects of competitive and monopoly structures on price. Like Jevons, but unlike Dupuit, he did not relate utility (satisfactions, in Menger's terms) to the demand curve. Thus, along with Jevons, he ignored consumer surplus. Yet, a survey of Menger's overall contributions to utility and value theory reveals a contribution of clear originality in breadth and exposition. Moreover, his originality persisted in his theory of production.

Imputation and Factor Values

One of Menger's most interesting and important contributions relates to his attempt to determine the value of productive resources, or what he called "higher-order goods." When discussing the value of consumer goods Menger put *opportunity cost* at the center of his analysis. The value of a particular good to an individual is equal, he said, "to the importance he attaches to the satisfactions he would have to forgo if he did not have command of it" (*Principles*, p. 162). This same principle extends to the valuation of higher-order goods as well. Menger approached the problem by means of a thought experiment.

[3] What would the economizing individual do if he or she possessed $16 rather than $15? Another expenditure of $1 on an additional unit of goods I through VI would yield only 5 units of satisfaction, and satisfactions would then not be equal at the margin. Unless units of all commodities were infinitely divisible (an assumption of mathematical continuity), the individual would be in disequilibrium. The result is a consequence of Menger's discrete ordering.

Suppose a given amount of labor, capital, and land combines to produce some output (x). On what does the value of any unit of productive resources—say, a unit of labor—depend? The value of a unit of labor is determined by the net loss of satisfaction resulting from the reduction in final output attributable to the unit of labor. The reduction in output depends, of course, on the degree to which the productive resources are substitutable. Productive relations are generally of two sorts: (1) *variable proportions*, in which the proportions of different higher-order goods can be altered to produce a given output, and (2) *fixed proportions*, in which a fixed amount of one resource must be combined with a fixed amount of another resource to produce a given output. An example of the former might be the ability to alter proportions of fertilizer and land to produce a given amount of agricultural output. Fixed-proportion relations might be typified by the necessary proportions of hydrogen and oxygen required to produce water. Menger clearly understood the importance of both types of productive relations and their significance for the valuation of higher-order goods, and, unlike his followers, Wieser and Böhm-Bawerk, he emphasized the very wide range within which proportions could be varied.

Returning to our example, how would Menger evaluate a unit of labor? He gave explicit directions:

> Assuming in each instance that all available goods of higher order are employed in the most economic fashion, the value of a concrete quantity of a good of higher order is equal to the difference in importance between the satisfactions that can be attained when we have command of the given quantity of the good of higher order whose value we wish to determine and the satisfactions that would be attained if we did not have this quantity at our command. (*Principles*, pp. 164–165)

In the case of variable proportions, the reduction in a unit of labor would mean that the output of $x(x^0)$ would be reduced to some level, say x^1. The remaining labor, capital, and land still produce x. The value of the unit of labor would then be the difference in total satisfaction when x^0 was produced and when x^1 was produced (or $x^0 - x^1$). This theory, original to Menger, might be characterized as a *marginal-value-productivity* theory of input valuation.

But if productive relations are arranged in rigidly fixed proportions, the reduction of a unit of labor would mean that no x would be produced. Would the value of a unit of labor (or of any of the other inputs), then, be the whole output of x? Assuming that resources are originally combined to produce goods for maximum satisfaction, a recombination of the remaining labor, capital, and land could produce a *different* good—say, y—but it would result in lower total satisfaction. Thus, Menger reasoned that the value of a unit of labor would be the difference between total satisfaction when the unit was used to produce $x(x^0)$ and total satisfaction when all resources but that unit were used to produce some other good, y. Unfortunately, it is difficult to develop a concept of marginal productivity under such circumstances, and Wieser and Böhm-Bawerk all but ignored Menger's insistence on the applicability of variable proportions. Wieser, however, tackled this same problem with a different effect, as we shall soon see.

■ FRIEDRICH VON WIESER (1851–1926)

Friedrich von Wieser was born in Vienna in 1851 of aristocratic parents. He entered the University of Vienna to study law at the age of seventeen. After graduating in 1872, Wieser was briefly employed in government service, but his strong intellectual interests pulled him back into academics, this time to study economics. Armed with a travel grant and joined by his boyhood friend (and later brother-in-law), Eugen von Böhm-Bawerk, Wieser studied economics under Karl Knies at the university of Heidelberg, and he studied at the universities of Jena and Leipzig. Already much impressed with Menger's *Principles*, Wieser wrote a seminal paper on value that formed the foundation for his later ideas. In 1884, he was appointed professor of economics at the German University in Prague. In 1903, he inherited Menger's position at the University of Vienna. He became Austrian minister of commerce in 1917, but owing to the collapse of the Austro-Hungarian Empire, later returned to teaching. A man of wide-ranging intellect, Wieser maintained his broad interests (among other interests he was a great fan of opera) by writing on varied topics and by creating, in his own home, a forum for artistic and intellectual communication.

Wieser's most important theoretical work was *Natural Value (Der naturliche Werth)*, published in Vienna in 1889, a book that further probed the themes set forth by Menger. In a second book, *Social Economics*, he combined economic theory and institutional analysis, already foreshadowing his later interests in sociology. His great sociological study and final work, *Das Gesetz der Macht* (1926) was an exhaustive analysis of numerous societal organizations. Despite an incredible range of interests, Wieser maintained his focus on economics, and he is famous chiefly for his extensions of Menger's ideas on utility, value, and input-output valuations. As it turned out, his emphasis on purely theoretical ideas detoured interest in his later and seminal work on the interrelationships of economics and institutions. We shall try to restore some balance in this regard, beginning with a discussion of some of the major theoretical ideas of *Natural Value* and proceeding to a review of some of his "institutional" ideas.

Value Theory

Although the idea of marginal utility was at the center of Menger's analysis, it was Wieser who coined the actual term "marginal utility" (*grenznutzen*). Wieser's basic statement of the general law of value expanded on Menger's earlier model. With the aid of an arithmetic example (see table 14-2) set forth below, Wieser explained the law in the following fashion. In this table the numbers in each row interact with the respective numbers in its column. The first row, for example, depicts the number of goods purchased at alternative prices specified on the second row (Wieser called these prices "units of value"). Total utility from consuming alternative quantities is calculated by adding up successive units of value. Thus, when the individual is consuming 2 units of the commodity, total enjoyment is 19 utility units, the sum of 1 unit at 10 and 1 unit at 9. The addition of a third unit of consumption adds a marginal utility of 8 for a total of 27 units. Note that Wieser, as Dupuit had earlier, identified a good's price (or units of value) with the marginal utility it conveys.

Table 14-2 Ascending and Descending Branches of Utility

(I)	Goods	0	1	2	3	4	5	6	7	8	9	10	11
(II)	Prices	0	10	9	8	7	6	5	4	3	2	1	0
(III)	Total utility	0	10	19	27	34	40	45	49	52	54	55	55
(IV)	Total value	0	10	18	24	28	30	30	28	24	18	10	0
(V)	Total utility minus total value	0	0	1	3	6	10	15	21	28	36	45	55
		Ascending branch						Descending branch					

Row IV of the example shows the amount of total value or gross receipts, which is determined by multiplying the quantity of goods sold by its price (i.e., row I times row II). Given the negatively sloping demand function, total receipts initially rise, reach a maximum, and then decline. Row V shows the value lost from indifference, and it is the difference between total utility and total receipts. Recall that Menger argued that it is the use to which the *last* unit of a stock of goods is put that represents the value of any unit of a homogeneous stock. Wieser argued that the total value of the stock increases by *less* than the price paid for *additional* units of the good. In adding the second unit of the stock, for example, the individual experiences a 9-unit increase in total utility, but now both units possess a valuation of 9. Wieser reasoned that since it is the marginal unit that represents value to the consumer, he or she would be unwilling to pay more than 9 for both units. In a competitive market, moreover, only one price for homogeneous goods can prevail. Thus, total *receipts* will increase as long as the incremental addition to total utility exceeds the incremental loss. Wieser called this situation (purchases of goods 0 to 5 in his numerical example) the "upgrade" (or ascending) branch of value, and the opposite situation the "downgrade" (or descending) branch of value.

The Antinomy of Value: Graphics. A simple graphical model will illustrate these elementary but crucial points (though Wieser did not provide graphics). Figure 14-2a depicts total revenue and total utility, while figure 14-2b depicts the corresponding demand, marginal-revenue, and marginal-utility functions. Total revenue and total utility rise between O and x as quantity consumed increases; and marginal

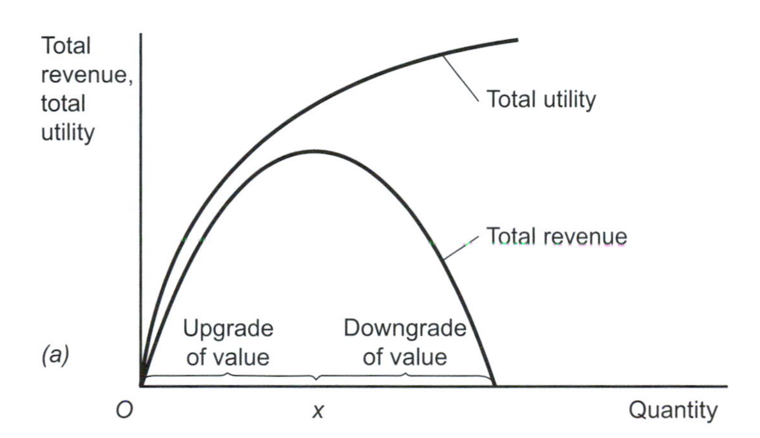

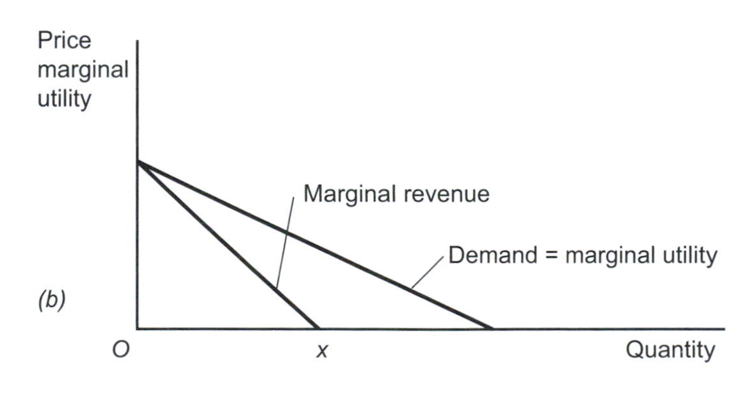

Figure 14-2 The upgrade of value is over the range where total utility and total revenue are rising and marginal revenue is positive. The downgrade of value is over the range of output where total utility is still rising but total revenue is declining and marginal revenue is negative.

revenue is positive (but declining) in this range, which characterizes the upgrade of value. Beyond quantity x, total utility continues to rise because marginal utility is still positive, but total revenue begins to decline (i.e., marginal revenue is negative).[4] This range constitutes the downgrade of value.

Wieser drew the following conclusions from his value theory. He thought that for the most part society's production was on the upgrade of value—that is, total revenue and utility increased together—but he stressed the antinomy (opposition) between exchange value and utility in the downgrade (i.e., beyond quantity x), when total utility is still rising but total revenue is falling. Wieser set forth the reasons for this antinomy between value and utility in the downgrade:

> In every self-contained private economy utility is the highest principle; but, in the business world, wherever the providing of society with goods is in the hands of [entrepreneurs] who desire to make a gain out of it, and to obtain a remuneration for their services, exchange value takes its place. The private [entrepreneur] is not concerned to provide the greatest utility for society generally; his aim is rather to obtain the highest value for himself—which is at the same time his highest utility. Utility approves itself as the first principle in the [entrepreneur's] economy; but, just because of this, in the conflict between exchange value and social utility, it is exchange value which is victorious—so far at least as the [entrepreneur] has power to act according to his own interest. (*Natural Value*, p. 55)

In this fashion Wieser described the deleterious effects of monopoly on social utility. The antinomy held only insofar as the entrepreneur possessed economic power. Under free competition, as Dupuit indicated earlier, social utility would be maximized, and no antinomy between value and utility would exist. In fact, Wieser concluded that the "economic history of our own time is rich in examples which prove that competition can press prices far on the down grade of exchange value" (*Natural Value*, p. 56).

But what of those cases where competition does not prevail? Though he believed that those instances were too few to justify a full-fledged socialist economy, Wieser advocated selected governmental interferences. He also noted another important breakdown in the real economy. In a self-contained, idealized economy, value in use depends on utility, and goods are produced according to the rank of their value. In this instance exchange value is the measure of personal acquisition. But in a real economy exchange value depends not only on utility but also on purchasing power. Exchange value in the real world does *not* necessarily measure value in use, or utility. In such a world, production is determined not only by "simple want" but also by the superior means of a part of the populace. Cognizant of the radical implications of applying utility theory to a real economy, Wieser wrote:

> Instead of things which would have the greatest utility, those things are produced for which the most will be paid. The greater the differences in wealth, the more striking will be the anomalies of production. It will furnish luxuries for the wanton and the glutton, while it is deaf to the wants of the miserable and the poor. It is therefore the distribution of wealth which decides how production is set to work, and induces consumption of the most uneconomic kind: a consumption which wastes upon unnecessary and culpable enjoyment what might have served to heal the wounds of poverty. (*Natural Value*, p. 58)

The disparity of purchasing power between demanders leads to yet another anomaly. The price of some commodities, such as bread, is determined by the valuation of

[4] It might be worthwhile to compare Wieser's model with Dupuit's (see chap. 13) on these points.

the weakest buyers, usually the poorest. But because of "the importance of being unimportant" wealthy people don't pay their maximum demand price for bread, only that price determined by the weakest buyer's valuation. Wieser claimed, "It is only where the rich compete among themselves for luxuries . . . that they pay according to their own ability, and are measured according to their own personal standard." Real-world prices, in other words, do not ordinarily reflect the marginal-utility valuations that would exist if the marginal utility of purchasing power were the same for all individual demanders (such a condition would not require equality of income distribution).

Natural Value. In order to bring these ideas into focus, Wieser constructed an idealized model of value as it would exist in a communistic state. Natural value would exist where goods were valued simply by the relation between the amount of the stock and marginal utilities. It would not be disturbed by "error, fraud, force, change," or the existence of private property and the consequent disparities in purchasing power. Utility, or value in use, would be the sole guide to the allocation of scarce resources in the production of goods. Production decisions would be determined by highest marginal-utility valuations and not by fragmented income distribution.

Although Wieser's model is highly abstract, its use led to an important practical conclusion, which communistic economies have been slow to learn: namely, that prices play a crucial role in establishing optimum allocation of scarce resources. Land rent is a case in point. In defense of his theory, Wieser said:

> Land rent is, perhaps, the formation of value that is most frequently attacked in our present economy. Now I believe our examination will show that, even in the communistic state, there must be land rent. Such a state must, under certain circumstances, calculate the return from land, and must, from certain portions of land, calculate a greater return than from others: the circumstances upon which such a calculation is dependent are essentially the same as those which today determine the existence of rent, and the height of rent. The only difference lies in this, that, as things now are, rent goes to the private owner of the land, whereas, in a communistic state, it would fall to the entire united community. (*Natural Value*, pp. 62–63)

Thus, the formation of natural value, even in a communistic state, requires a market-system type of allocation. Rents and "natural" returns to all factors have to be recognized in order to ensure an economic distribution of resources. These returns, however, do not have to be privately received, and even if they are, they could be taxed away by government.[5]

In sum, what Wieser demonstrated and argued is that the formation of value is a neutral phenomenon. An understanding of natural value provides evidence neither for nor against a socialist organization of society (so that presumably the case has to rest on other grounds). This neutral precept is the foundation for exchange value in *all* societies, irrespective of the fact that natural value is overlaid with many other factors (such as controls, regulations, fiat, monopoly, and vast differences in purchasing power). Wieser was the first economist to point out the generality of the theory of utility valuation and to make explicit the usefulness of the market system in allocating resources irrespective of social organization. Nevertheless, social organization remained an abiding concern of Wieser (see the box, The Force of Ideas: Power, Leadership, and the Social Economy).

[5] Henry George, an American economist, said as much in his *Progress and Poverty* (1879). George advocated the taxation of urban site rents in order that "productive" factors (labor and capital) might be encouraged.

The Force of Ideas: Power, Leadership, and the Social Economy

Menger showed an early interest in the evolution of economic institutions, but it was his disciple, Wieser, who made a concerted effort to integrate economic analysis with role and function of institutions. Despite his concern with the collective goal of economic welfare, Wieser rejected the collectivist approach in favor of an individualistic one. He maintained that institutions form part of the economic process once they become imbedded in the social structure, and as such, they subsequently define the constraints on individual decision making. Consequently, Wieser bridged the ideas of Menger and Veblen (see chapter 19).

Wieser argued that each individual maximizes his or her utility subject to the constraints imposed by institutions that represent the collective results of individual human action. These institutions, although created and destroyed by individual action, acquire power to constrain individual behavior in recognized and unrecognized ways—and these constraints become society's "natural controls." For Wieser, true freedom lies in the recognition that such controls (e.g., law, morals, contracts, property rights, habits, and customs) are the basis for further development, progress, and preservation. If society is ruled by tyrants, however, these "natural controls" produce discord and repression. Therefore, leadership is a vital social trait.

Wieser saw progress as the consequence of inventive spirit and action; therefore leadership is manifest by economic, political, and moral entrepreneurship. In a market economy, entrepreneurship takes place within a dynamic process of competition that pits rival against rival. This process takes inequality for granted. Entrepreneurs are people of superior abilities and creativity who are better able to utilize the competitive process to the betterment of themselves and their customers. They are followed by the masses of imitators, who emulate their successes. The social economy encourages certain alliances, however, in which power groups perform pivotal roles. These groups, which Wieser described as monopoloidal, stand in stark contrast to the atomistic economic units of Adam Smith (see chapter 5) and Alfred Marshall (see chapter 16).

Monopoloidal interest groups emerge as the intermediate result of a competitive process in *disequilibrium*. According to Wieser, various power groups form monopoloidal organizations, which "have in fact traits of monopoly; they confer monopolistic power. But at the same time they are subject, in other directions, to the pressure of competition or are otherwise restricted. They are . . . intermediate forms, lying midway between monopoly and competition. Neither the theory of pure monopoly nor the theory of pure competition, least of all the theory of attribution, will do them entire justice" (*Social Economics*, p. 221)

It is tempting to trace the otherwise novel views of E. H. Chamberlin (see chapter 20) on "mixed" forms of competition to this passage, written almost two decades before Chamberlin's *Theory of Monopolistic Competition* (1933). But the key point Wieser emphasized is that the welfare-enhancing effects of rivalrous competition do not depend on the number of firms but rather on the relative economic power of opposing groups. Thus, long before J. K. Galbraith (see chapter 19), who is most readily identified with this argument of "countervailing power," Wieser welcomed labor unions as an opposing force against monopoloidal employers. No monopoloidal organization, unless protected by legal barriers to entry, is immune from the rigors of competition, Wieser argued.

In the final analysis, Wieser elevated competition to the highest level among social principles. Competition provides the breeding ground for society's leaders, who, in turn provide the model for others to emulate. "In no other of the great fields of human activity," he wrote, "where men strive for supremacy through rival efforts, do they find broader scope for self-assertion. . . . No economic order, without suffering very great disadvantages, may dispense with the use, in one way or another, of the supreme power of competition towards social success" (*Social Economics*, pp. 210–211).

In this passage and in others derived from his theory of social economy, Wieser affirmed that a noncoerced competitive system acts better than any other to create a fluid environment within which entrepreneurship works as the modus operandi of economic progress. His great insight, shared by a younger Austrian of later renown, Joseph Schumpeter (see chapter 23), was that self-interested, utility-maximizing individual behavior creates and alters institutions along fairly predictable lines, and that these institutions constrain future economic actors until forward-looking and creative leader-entrepreneurs are able to break existing molds and change institutions once more.

Factor Valuation: Wieser's Theory of Imputation

Wieser admired Menger's earlier treatment of imputation and clearly built his system of input and output valuation on it, although he tried to repair a critical weakness he discovered in his mentor's approach. Menger had argued that the value of a complementary production good (i.e., higher-order good) might be determined by removing it from its highest-valued use and observing the resulting drop in utility. In the case of fixed proportions, removal of one of the inputs required the recombination of the others to produce a different product. The value of the removed factor (which Menger termed the "share dependent upon cooperation") was then determined by the difference in value terms between the old product (before the factor was removed) and the alternative product (made remaining inputs after the factor is removed). The problem, as Wieser plainly saw, was that this technique made *overvaluation* possible.

Wieser's simple example makes his criticism clear. Suppose the total value produced by three inputs in their best alternative (highest-marginal-utility product) is 10 units of value. Taking away one of the inputs and recombining the other two might generate a product with 6 units of value. The value of the removed input is then 4. The problem, which Wieser recognized, was that all the inputs could be valued in the same way, giving 12 as the sum of their separate values. But their value in combination was only 10! Consequently, Menger's method could lead to overvaluation of inputs.

The Simultaneous Solution. As an alternative method, Wieser suggested that the productive contribution of the input be the modus operandi of the valuation process. As Wieser put it, "The deciding element is not that portion of the return which is lost through the loss of a good, but that which is secured by its possession" (*Natural Value*, p. 85). In order to arrive at this deduction, Wieser assumed that all production goods (inputs) are actually employed in an optimum fashion. Returning to Menger's example, he assumed that resources are combined in fixed proportions (although he clearly recognized the existence of variable proportions in the real world). A hunter, for example, depends on both rifle and cartridge to kill a tiger that is about to spring on him or her. Valued together, Wieser argued, the value of rifle and cartridge is the success of the shot. Taken singly, however, the value of each cannot be calculated. As Wieser pointed out, there are two unknowns (x and y) and one equation, $x + y = 100$, where 100 is the value of the successful result.

With more unknowns than equations, the problem cannot be solved. But Wieser's ingenious solution was to determine the contribution of combined productive factors in every industry and to set this contribution out in equations. As he directed:

> It is possible not only to separate these effects approximately, but to put them into exact figures, so soon as we collect and measure all the important circumstances of the matter; such as the amount of the products, their value, and the amount of

> the means of production employed at the time. If we take these circumstances accurately into account, we obtain a number of equations, and we are in a position to make a reliable calculation of what each single instrument of production does. (*Natural Value*, pp. 87–88)

As an example of his calculation of the contribution of cooperating productive inputs, Wieser presented three industry equations with three unknown input values:

$$x + y = 100$$
$$2x + 3z = 290$$
$$4y + 5z = 590$$

Here x, y, and z are productive inputs, and the right-hand side of the equality is the total value produced by the *combined* inputs (the combinations are, of course, fixed). Solving simultaneously, the values of the inputs are determined: $x = 40$, $y = 60$, and $z = 70$. Each input is thus ascribed a definite share in producing total value. This approach takes account of the interdependencies among inputs, whereas Menger's "subtractive" solution did not. Moreover, in a system of simultaneous equations, the resulting values exactly exhaust the total product.

Resource Allocation. Wieser's simultaneous solution may be viewed in a slightly different manner, which illustrates the Austrian view of the whole valuation process. The issue might be put in the form of a question: Assuming that resources are properly allocated and that the system is in equilibrium (as we did in the equations above), what is the value of each input, and how are resources allocated?[6] Given that an input is used in the production of a number of final or consumer goods, its value will be determined by the least valuable good that it produces. This value is determined at the margin, by the marginal utility of the last unit of the least valuable good the input is producing. Input value is imputed, and the value of the input, thus derived, establishes the opportunity cost of utilizing it in all other industry productions requiring it. Given fixed-proportions production functions in all industries and the rational (profit-maximizing) allocation of resources, the supplies of all other goods utilizing the input will be determined. Given the marginal utilities for these other goods, values are determined.

It is important to note that Wieser's solution to the problem of input and output valuation, while typical of the Austrian approach, is not like that found in the standard economics textbook of today or even like that set forth in Marshall's *Principles*. Wieser (and the Austrians generally) did not develop the determinants of demand and supply that interact to determine value. Rather they emphasized the role of the marginal utility of final goods as the primary determinant of value. They assigned supply no independent role in establishing values. Inputs are valued by imputation in strict, cause-and-effect fashion. Through opportunity cost, values of inputs and outputs are then determined in the entire system.[7]

[6] Wieser referred to these inputs as "cost means" of production. He contrasted these cost means with cost-specific means of production. Cost-specific means are those inputs that are scarce or those that are suited only to the production of one product or a limited number of products. Cost means of production, on the other hand, are distributed over the entire productive process. As a general rule, Wieser thought that labor and capital should be regarded as cost means, while land should usually be classed as cost-specific means.

[7] It has been argued that, in at least one sense, this system is circular because it assumes the thing to be proved. Critics contend that one begins by assuming an optimum distribution of resources and then, via opportunity cost, "explains" value and the optimum distribution of inputs. On this point, see G. J. Stigler, *Production and Distribution Theories* (see references).

In sum, the marginal utility of final output is presented as the *source* of value by Austrian economists. In addition, they discovered a very special kind of input productivity theory, one that might best be described as a marginal-utility-product theory of input valuation. In other words, the value of an additional unit of input applied to production is determined by the marginal utility of the additional units produced ($MUP_i = MP_i \times MU_x$) rather than by the traditional marginal-*value* product, which is found by multiplying the firm's marginal *revenue* by the input's marginal product ($MVP_i = MP_i \times P_x$). Conceptual differences in approach aside, however, it is clear that Austrian value theory reached a high point in Wieser's *Natural Value*.

■ EUGEN BÖHM-BAWERK (1851–1914)

Eugen Böhm-Bawerk, friend and brother-in-law of Friedrich Wieser, was the third of the great founders of Austrian economics. Some writers consider Böhm-Bawerk the premier capital theorist of economics. Surely his impact on neoclassical and postneoclassical theorists, such as Knut Wicksell and Friedrich Hayek, has been of vast importance. But Böhm-Bawerk enjoyed a variety of achievements besides being a principal developer of Austrian capital theory.

Born in Brünn, Austria, in 1851, Böhm-Bawerk was the son of a highly placed government official. He entered government service briefly after graduating from law school at the University of Vienna, but he soon was attracted to a study of economics. Like Wieser, Böhm-Bawerk began his economic studies in Germany, where he studied under Karl Knies. He was appointed professor of economics at the University of Innsbruck in 1881, and there he completed his first book, which concerned the value of patents as abstract, legal claims. In 1884, Böhm-Bawerk published the first volume of his three-volume magnum opus, collectively entitled *Capital and Interest* (*Kapital and Kapitalzins*). The first volume is entitled *History and Critique of Interest Theories* (1884), the second (and very likely the most important) is *The Positive Theory of Capital* (1889), and the third, which is a collection of appendixes to the third edition of *The Positive Theory of Capital*, is entitled *Further Essays on Capital and Interest* (1909–1912). All three volumes have been translated into English.

Böhm-Bawerk also distinguished himself as a statesman. In 1889 he was called to the Ministry of Finance for the purpose of preparing taxation and currency reform. He served as Austrian Minister of Finance on three occasions over a span of almost ten years. His tenure in the position is associated with great stability and progress in Austrian financial management, an accomplishment achieved without being associated with any political party. In 1904, he resigned and resumed his academic career, this time at the University of Vienna.

Though Böhm-Bawerk was a tireless scholar, his economic writings were often interrupted by civil duties and show signs of undue haste. Thus, his work—difficult reading at any level of expertise—has been criticized as incomplete or ambiguous. Assessments differ, however. Böhm-Bawerk's prize pupil, Joseph Schumpeter (see chapter 23) compared him to Ricardo and declared that his *Positive Theory of Capital* "was an effort to scale the greatest heights that economics permits, and that the achievement actually reached a level where only a few lofty peaks are to be found" (*Ten Great Economists*, p. 153). By contrast, George Stigler (chapter 24) was less effusive but admitted that Böhm-Bawerk's influence on later economists outstripped even that of Menger and Wieser. Moreover, his fame persists in the field of capital and interest theory. Many contemporary capital theorists believe, not without some justification, that neoclassical capital theory takes its start from Böhm-Bawerk. Our survey therefore, focuses on his theory of capital and interest. But first, we shall explore his "subjective" credentials as a member of the Austrian school. We turn to his lucid exposition of the role of subjective factors in establishing exchange value.

Subjective Value and Exchange

Böhm-Bawerk may have considered that there was little to add to the advances in value theory made by Menger and Wieser. He and Wieser adopted Menger's value theory, and Böhm-Bawerk readily assimilated most of Wieser's improvements. For the most part, his assumptions are identical to those made by Wieser, including the ones concerning fixed-proportions production functions, the theory of imputation, and an assumption of rigidly fixed supplies of productive inputs.[8] Despite his lack of originality in these areas, Böhm-Bawerk contributed interesting nuances on themes originally developed by Menger and advanced by Wieser. One of Böhm-Bawerk's most interesting and successful variations on the subjective-value theme is of prime importance both for its clarity and its ingenuity. In *The Positive Theory of Capital*, Böhm-Bawerk demonstrated the determination of price with two-sided competition. His famous example is predicated on ten buyers and eight sellers of horses in a free market. All the horses offered for sale are assumed of equal quality, and all parties to the exchange possess perfect knowledge of the market situation.

Böhm-Bawerk set up a table representing ten buyers (A_1–A_{10}) and eight sellers (B_1–B_8) of horses and their *subjective* valuations of each horse. An adaptation of Böhm-Bawerk's table is presented here as table 14-3. From the table we see that buyer A_1 places a $300 subjective valuation on a horse so that he will demand a horse at any price *at or below* $300.[9] In like fashion, seller B_6 places a $215 valuation on the horse he has for sale, meaning that he will sell his horse *at or above* $215. Böhm-Bawerk designated the strength of buyers as *decreasing* from A_1–A_{10}, and the strength of sellers as *increasing* from B_1–B_8. Thus, seller B_1 is the weakest in that he places the lowest of the minimum subjective evaluations on horses, and buyer A_{10} is the weakest in that he has the *lowest* of the maximum subjective valuations upon horses.

How is exchange value determined? Suppose we arbitrarily start with a bid of $150. What would happen in an auction market? At this bid price all ten willing buyers remain in the market, but only three willing sellers; that is, because of subjective evaluations, only sellers B_1, B_2, and B_3 would be willing to offer one horse each at an exchange value of $150. Obviously, the market does not clear since there are ten buyers and only three sellers at $150. As price rises above $150, however, the horse market begins to adjust. Weaker buyers—those with lower subjective evaluations—are eliminated from the market, and as price rises, sellers are added. As price rises to $210, for example, four buyers are eliminated from the trading (weak buyers A_7–

[8] Böhm-Bawerk mentions an interesting exception to rigidly fixed supplies in *The Positive Theory of Capital*. Adopting Jevons's theory of labor supply, he admitted that the disutility of work might enter as an independent determinant of input supply. But he minimized this independent determinant on the grounds that Jevons's theory requires a piece-rate system, which, Böhm-Bawerk's casual empiricism told him, was unimportant in the modern economy.

[9] Note that Böhm-Bawerk expressed the subjective valuations of buyers and sellers in terms of objective dollar valuations, without alluding to some of the possible theoretical problems raised thereby.

A_{10}), and five sellers remain (B_1–B_5). But there is still a disparity between six willing buyers (A_6–A_1) and five willing sellers (B_5–B_1), so the market does not reach equilibrium at this price. If price rises by \$5 to \$215, buyer A_6 drops out of the market, but seller B_6 enters. Thus, at this price there are five buyers and six sellers. The market cannot clear at \$215.

By now the problem should be obvious. How might one drop buyer A_6 from exchange without simultaneously including an additional seller (in this case B_6)? The answer is simple. Price must rise above \$210 to exclude A_6, but not as high as \$215, so that B_6 is not included. Thus, given the data of table 14-3, the price limits will be set as follows: price must be greater than \$210 but less than \$215. A price of \$213 or any intermediate value would therefore clear the market. In this way, Böhm-Bawerk underscored one of the determining factors in exchange value, the influence of *marginal pairs* of buyers and sellers in determining price. In this example the main characters that determine price are the successful pair, buyer A_5 and seller B_5, coupled with the unsuccessful pair, buyer A_6 and seller B_6. Alternatively, we might say it is the evaluations of the weakest of successful buyers (A_5) and the strongest of successful sellers (B_5) coupled with the evaluations of the strongest of unsuccessful buyers (A_6) and the weakest of unsuccessful sellers (B_6) that set the limits to exchange value.

Table 14-3 Böhm-Bawerk's Horse Market

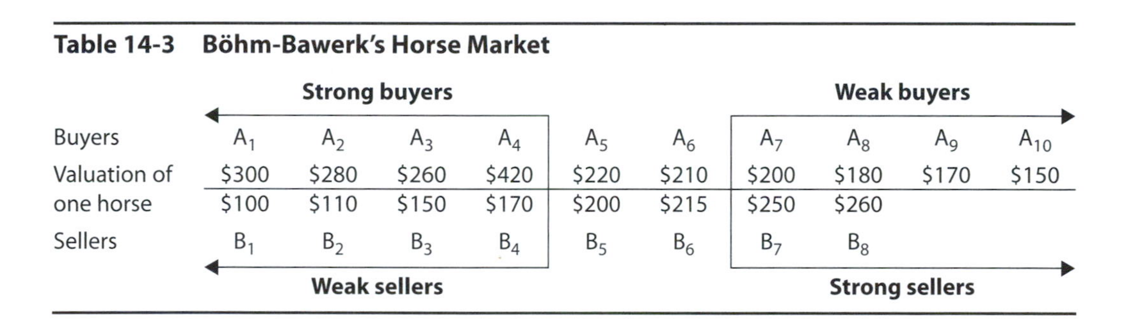

	Strong buyers						Weak buyers			
Buyers	A_1	A_2	A_3	A_4	A_5	A_6	A_7	A_8	A_9	A_{10}
Valuation of	\$300	\$280	\$260	\$420	\$220	\$210	\$200	\$180	\$170	\$150
one horse	\$100	\$110	\$150	\$170	\$200	\$215	\$250	\$260		
Sellers	B_1	B_2	B_3	B_4	B_5	B_6	B_7	B_8		
	Weak sellers						Strong sellers			

In this manner Böhm-Bawerk established that it is these marginal pairs of buyers and sellers—and these marginal pairs alone—that determine price. Outside these limits, buyers and sellers might be added indefinitely without affecting equilibrium price. The addition of buyers or sellers with subjective evaluations *within* the limits set by the marginal pairs has the effect of narrowing the upper and lower limits to price. An infinitely large addition of buyers and sellers would make the supply and demand functions look like the typical and smooth Marshallian ones we generally posit today. But Böhm-Bawerk wished to emphasize the discrete and discontinuous nature of the functions (imagine stair-step demand and supply functions from the data of table 14-1). Real-world market situations, in Böhm-Bawerk's view (and in the typical Austrian paradigm), were not characterized by smooth and continuously differentiable demand and supply functions, including infinite numbers of buyers and sellers. Rather, in the Austrian view, any practical exchange situation included only a finite number of traders, and the discrete nature of buyer and seller evaluations must be accounted for. This typically Austrian assumption is a major point of contrast with the prevailing Marshallian view, which assumes continuity. The latter (and prevailing) approach is far easier to deal with mathematically, which might account for some of its success. But Austrians would challenge the assumptions of the Marshallian view as unrealistic and would argue that economic analysis should account for this fact.

It is clear that the Austrians had a point. The continuity of many economic functions is taken for granted but may not have much basis in fact. Böhm-Bawerk was determined to explicate the nature of price determination in a world of discrete numbers of buyers and sellers. Moreover, the role of subjective evaluations in exchange was never more clearly described. Though Menger and Wieser had worked out the essentials of Austrian value theory, Böhm-Bawerk helped to clarify the process of exchange.

Capital Theory

Perhaps the most important contribution made by Böhm-Bawerk was his poignant introduction of time considerations into economic analysis. His central and simple premise was that the production of final (consumers') goods takes time and that roundabout methods of producing these goods are more productive than direct methods. This gain in production, however, is partially offset by the time-consuming nature of roundabout production methods. Böhm-Bawerk explained that original means of production (raw materials, resources, labor) could be used in immediate production (as fictional hero, Robinson Crusoe did, for instance) or could be used to produce capital (which he called "produced means"), which, combined with labor, could then be used to produce consumers' goods. Böhm-Bawerk thought that the latter method, though it takes longer, was more effective because it allowed the productivity of capital to be added to the productivity of labor. Moreover something more than mere additivity is at work. As hinted at by the imputation problem, combinations of capital and labor are likely to be more effective when operating together than like amounts operating separately. In other words, there are interdependencies to consider among combined factors of production. This means that the longer the productive period (which means using a more roundabout and capital-intensive method), the higher the total product would be. In the Austrian theory of production time itself becomes an input, and the length of the production period of consumers' goods is itself a variable.

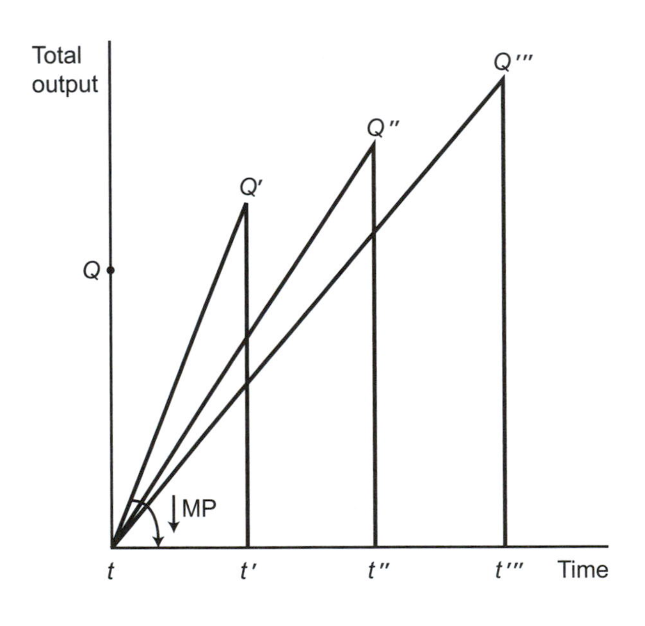

Figure 14-3 As "roundaboutness" increases from *t* to *t*′, etc., total output also increases, but at a decreasing rate. The slope of the ray *tQ*′ is the marginal product of capital during period *tt*′.

These points are illustrated in figure 14-3. Time is measured on the horizontal axis, and total output (*Q*) is measured on the vertical axis. The production period is represented on the time axis. Period tt'' is longer than period tt', for instance, and period tt''' is greater than period tt''. It can be seen that total output grows absolutely with the extension of the period of production, whereas marginal output declines with these extensions. Why did Böhm-Bawerk argue that longer periods of production are more productive? Consider what happens when the production period is extended. As the production period lengthens, more capital is used, the ratio of capital to labor increases, and final output is enlarged, albeit at a decreasing rate.

The Discontinuous Production Period. Böhm-Bawerk's model has certain affinities to the classical wages-fund doctrine, but there are also some peculiarities that command our attention. Whereas both models employ a discontinuous production period of variable length, the classical model assumed a discontinuous production period of fixed duration. Böhm-Bawerk's period-of-production model is characterized by continuous inputs and point outputs. That is, inputs are added in a flow, but outputs "ripen" at some discrete point of time. The important question that immediately arises concerns the length of the production period. At one point Böhm-Bawerk suggested that an absolute period of production might be used, but he soon realized an obvious problem. Assume that a point output produced today is a silver drinking cup. What is the absolute period of production? Conceivably, the silver input used in producing the cup might have been mined in Roman times. The concept of determining a production period for any point output is therefore intractable. Therefore Böhm-Bawerk proposed an alternative approach, the average production period, in which inputs are weighted according to their proximity to point outputs. Inputs are weighted by the number of periods used, and the sum of these weighted inputs is then divided by the number of inputs in order to obtain an average production period.

Unfortunately, Böhm-Bawerk's second approach also contains grave deficiencies. One of the chief objections is rather obvious. Inputs are simply not homogeneous; yet, Böhm-Bawerk made no provisions for this fact—he simply assumed that they were. Second, perhaps more importantly, there is the question of assigning the proper "period" weights. Is output attributable to the most recent inputs or to inputs from a more distant past? Although these problems were serious, Böhm-Bawerk retained the assumption of an average period of production as a workable theoretical constraint.[10]

Aside from these issues, both the classical wages-fund model and Böhm-Bawerk's period-of-production model employed the same immediate determinant of the length of the production. Böhm-Bawerk's novel contribution in this area lay in his close investigation of the interest rate as the major determinant of the size of the subsistence fund.

The Interest Rate. Böhm-Bawerk regarded interest as a payment for the use of capital, and the use of capital, as we have seen, means intermediate products (i.e., roundaboutness). Because roundaboutness involves longer time engaged in production, interest must be related to time in some logical way. Böhm-Bawerk based his interest theory on what we now call positive time preference, which maintains that present goods are worth more than future goods. He offered three "proofs" for this fundamental proposition.

[10] One of Böhm-Bawerk's "students" in capital theory, Knut Wicksell, at first adopted the average period of production but later abandoned it as unworkable.

The first cause of the difference in value between present and future goods derives from the immediacy of present wants. We are not indifferent to the future, but we live in the present. Future wants are almost always perceived as less pressing than immediate wants. In general, people find themselves in one of two circumstances. Those who are less well provided for in the present than in the future judge present goods to be more valuable. Those who find themselves better provided for in the present than they are likely to be in the future still have command over future goods by the possession of present goods (especially money), which they can store up as a reserve for the future.

The second cause for the difference in value between present and future goods is that people systematically undervalue future wants and the means to satisfy them. Böhm-Bawerk's argument on this point rests on three corollaries: (1) since we can't know the future with certainty, the imaginary picture that we construct of our future wants will always be fragmentary and incomplete; (2) most people suffer from a general lack of willpower—faced with the choice between "now" and "then," few will postpone gratification of a present want; and (3) given the uncertainty and shortness of human life, people do not wish to postpone something that they may never get to enjoy.

The third cause for the difference in value between present and future goods is the technical superiority of present goods over future goods as a means of satisfying human wants. This corollary rests on the principle of roundaboutness established earlier by Böhm-Bawerk. It simply recognizes that present goods (including money) can be put into production *sooner* than future goods, so that the flow of output that will emerge from intermediate products will always be larger, if started now rather than later.

Of these three causes, Böhm-Bawerk placed the greatest emphasis on the third, which he claimed was independent of the other two and, moreover, was capable of explaining positive time preference on its own. More protracted methods of production are always more productive than less protracted methods of production, and therein lies the technical superiority of present goods. From this general discussion, it was a fairly short leap to the idea that interest is the premium people pay for present goods over future goods. From the perspective of the lender, of course, interest is the compensation required to postpone the higher enjoyment conveyed by present goods.

It is noteworthy that Böhm-Bawerk's theory of interest and capital is deeply rooted in the subjectivism of Austrian value theory. Indeed, it was on this basis that he distanced himself most from the classical approach to the subject. With a few notable exceptions (e.g., Lauderdale and Senior) classical economic theory treated capital as subservient to labor because it was itself the product of labor. This idea (which was also held in the extreme by Karl Marx) proved to be a major stumbling block to meaningful analytical progress in the theory of interest. The fault of classical interest theory is that it refused to admit that capital was productive apart from labor. Senior saw the error of this argument, but he remained a "classical" economist by encasing his new insights within the cost-of-production theory of value. Thus, Böhm-Bawerk, who credited Senior with overturning certain false ideas about capital and interest, also criticized him for neglecting time preference and opportunity costs, two cornerstones of the new subjectivism. In the final analysis, however, Böhm-Bawerk used Senior's foundation to build a new edifice rather than scrap all past ideas to begin anew.

■ Entrepreneurism in German and Austrian Economics

German and Austrian economists of the nineteenth century did more to revive and nurture the subject of entrepreneurship in economic theory than their counterparts in other European countries. By 1814, J. B. Say's *Treatise* had been translated into German and began to circulate among scholars in German and Austrian universities, giving impetus to an attempt to establish entrepreneurial profit as a distinctive, functional share in the theory of income distribution. Major advances were made by von Thünen, Mangoldt, Gottlieb Hufeland (1760–1817), Friedrich Hermann (1795–1868), and Adolph Riedel (1809–1872).

In 1815, Hufeland generalized the idea that every wage contains a premium for scarcity to explain entrepreneurial profit as a special kind of wage consisting of the rent of ability. Hermann's theoretical economics undermined the British, classical wages-fund theory by asserting that all factor returns are ultimately paid from consumers' income. Like Hufeland, he generalized the concept of rent to all factors, including the entrepreneur. And like Say, he viewed the entrepreneur as one who organizes production within the institutional structure of a firm. Riedel extended Cantillon's conception of the entrepreneur as the economic agent who takes on uncertainty so that others may escape risk (e.g., through the establishment of fixed-price contracts). He perceived that uncertainty is inevitable in the acquisition of income and that the entrepreneur provides a useful service to income earners who are risk-averse and who would therefore willingly trade uncertainty for the security of a "sure thing." As a supplier of "certainty," the entrepreneur is rewarded for his foresight or penalized for lack of it. If he sells goods at a price above his contracted fixed-input costs, he gains; if not, he loses. Riedel also explored the notion of the entrepreneur as innovator, and as organizer of "team production." By connecting the problems of the organization of firms with the entrepreneurial function of reducing income uncertainty for certain inputs, he anticipated (along with Mangoldt) the nature of transaction costs later expounded by Ronald Coase (see chapters 16 and 26).

Although best known for his location theory, set forth in the first volume of *The Isolated State* (1826), it was in the second volume (1850) that von Thünen put forth an explanation of profit that clearly distinguished the return of the entrepreneur from that of the capitalist. What he labeled "entrepreneurial gain" is profit minus (1) interest on invested capital, (2) insurance against business losses, and (3) the wages of management. This residual represents a return to entrepreneurial risk, which von Thünen identified as *uninsurable*, insofar as "there exists no insurance company that will cover all and every risk connected with a business. A part of the risk must always be accepted by the entrepreneur" (*Isolated State*, p. 246). He was also alert to the relationship between uninsurable risks and opportunity costs. He wrote:

> He who has enough means to pay to get some knowledge and education for public service has a choice to become either a civil servant or, if equally suited for both kinds of jobs, to become an industrial entrepreneur. If he takes the first job, he is guaranteed subsistence for life; if he chooses the latter, an unfortunate economic situation may take all his property, and then his fate becomes that of a worker for daily wages. Under such unequal expectations for the future what could motivate him to become an entrepreneur if the probability of gain were not much greater than that of loss? (*Isolated State*, p. 247)

Moreover, von Thünen clearly appreciated the difference between management and entrepreneurship. He maintained that the effort of an entrepreneur working on his own account was different from that of a paid substitute (i.e., "manager"), even if they have the same knowledge and ability. The entrepreneur is forced to bear the anxiety and agitation that accompanies his business gamble; he spends many sleepless nights preoccupied with the single thought of how to avoid catastrophe; whereas the paid substitute can sleep soundly at night, secure in the knowledge of having performed his (minimal) duty. Anyone who has nursed along a new enterprise knows the anxiety to which von Thünen referred.

What is especially interesting about von Thünen's treatment is how he turns the discussion from the trials of the entrepreneur into a kind of "crucible" theory of the development of entrepreneurial talent. The sleepless nights of the entrepreneur are not unproductive; it is then that the entrepreneur makes plans and arrives at solutions for avoiding business failure. Adversity in the business world thereby becomes a training ground for the entrepreneur. "Necessity is the mother of invention," von Thünen wrote, "so the entrepreneur through his troubles will become an inventor and explorer in his field." As such, the entrepreneur supplies "greater mental effort in comparison with the paid manager," for which he deserves "compensation for his industry, diligence, and ingenuity" (*Isolated State*, p. 248). This extra reward is a justifiable payment to the entrepreneur, no less than that surplus which accrues to the inventor of a new and useful machine.

What makes this a significant step forward in the theory of entrepreneurship is the fact that von Thünen successfully married the separate strands of entrepreneurial theory that heretofore, on the one hand, characterized the entrepreneur as risk bearer (Cantillon) and, on the other, portrayed him as innovator (Bentham). He was quite explicit about the fact that there are two elements in entrepreneurial income: a return to entrepreneurial risk and a return to ingenuity. The sum of these two comprise "business profit," he said, and drew a sharp distinction between entrepreneurship and the mere use of capital:

> Capital will give results, and is in the strict sense of the term capital, only if used productively; on the degree of this usefulness depends the rate of interest at which we lend capital. Productive use presupposes an industrial enterprise and an entrepreneur. The enterprise gives the entrepreneur a net yield after compensating for all expenses and costs. This net yield has two parts, business profits and capital use. (*Isolated State*, p. 249)

Hans von Mangoldt, professor at the universities of Göttingen and Freiburg, pushed farther. Joseph Schumpeter (see chapter 23) judged his work on entrepreneurship "the most important advance since Say" (*History*, p. 556*n*). Mangoldt attempted to reform Hermann's theory, which sought the essential characteristic of entrepreneurship in the personal activity of entrepreneurs. Hermann maintained that entrepreneurship entails a certain kind of labor, and if these (entrepreneurial) tasks are delegated to anyone else, the delegator ceases to be an entrepreneur. Among these tasks Hermann listed the assembling of capital, the supervision of business, the securing of credit and trade connections, and the assumption of risk connected with the prospect of irregular gains.

Mangoldt discarded Hermann's first three entrepreneurial tasks as inessential to a "pure" notion of entrepreneurship. He argued that although entrepreneurs customarily participate in their own enterprises with their own capital and personal supervision, these services could be furnished just as well by salaried labor. What remains from Hermann's theory after jettisoning the first three elements is risk bearing. Mangoldt concluded: "That which alone is inseparable from the concept of the entrepreneur is, on the one hand, owning the output of the undertaking—control over the product brought forth, and, on the other hand, assuming responsibility for whatever losses may occur" ("Precise Function of the Entrepreneur," p. 41).

Thus, Mangoldt's theory of entrepreneurship was production-oriented and risk-centered. He distinguished between "production to order" and "production for the market." The former is safe because service and payment are simultaneous, a circumstance that eliminates the uncertainty of changing market conditions between the start of production and sale of the final product. The latter is speculative because the product is destined for exchange on a market of uncertain demand and unknown price. Even thought this distinction is imprecise, Mangoldt found it useful because, strictly speaking, "every possibility of a change in the subjective estimate of the service, or the remuneration [of it], offers such an uncertainty," and "since such a possibility is excluded only by a perfect simultaneity of service and payment, every business which needs for its carrying through any time whatever, could not, in the strictest sense of the word, be undertaken to order" ("Precise Function of the Entrepreneur," p. 37).

Mangoldt's distinction provides a framework for discussing degrees of risk that confront the entrepreneur. By his reckoning those enterprises that require the longest time to bring their products to the point of final sale involve the most uncertainty, whereas those that involve the shortest time require the least amount of entrepreneurship. Risk and uncertainty go to the heart of the matter. The distinctiveness of the entrepreneur is that he assumes the burden of the fluctuations in expenditure that must be made in any business, and ultimately in its success or failure. In this respect Mangoldt stood squarely in the tradition begun by Cantillon.

Following Hufeland and Hermann, Mangoldt represented the entrepreneur as a separate factor of production, and established entrepreneurial profit as the rent of ability. He divided entrepreneurial income into three parts: a premium on uninsurable risks; an amount to compensate the entrepreneur for interest and wages (including only payments for special forms of capital or productive effort that did not admit of exploitation by anyone other than the owner); and entrepreneur rents, that is, payments for differential abilities or assets not held by anyone else. Alfred Marshall took special note of this last item, citing Mangoldt approvingly in his development of the principle of quasi-rent (see chapter 16).

Mangoldt's theory did not concentrate on an ideal type of entrepreneur but rather on decisions an entrepreneur must make in an uncertain, competitive environment: the choice of techniques, the allocation of productive factors, and the marketing of production. He acknowledged successful innovation as part of entrepreneurship, but he was more interested in the allocative function of the entrepreneur. Therefore, his contribution was consistent with a static theory of resource allocation but mute on the role of the entrepreneur in a dynamic theory of growth and development.

Wieser closed this gap by stressing the leadership qualities of the entrepreneur. He tried to bring everything connected with the theory and practice of enterprise under his umbrella-like definition. He spoke of entrepreneurs as the "great personalities" of capitalism: "bold technical innovators, organizers with a keen knowledge of human nature, farsighted bankers, reckless speculators, the world-conquering directors of the trusts" (*Social Economics*, p. 327). On the subject of entrepreneurship Wieser painted with a broad brush, incorporating sociological as well as economic elements in his treatment. Not only is Wieser's multifarious entrepreneur required to be multitalented, "he must [also] possess the quick perception that seizes new terms in current transactions as his affairs develop; [and] he must possess the independent forcefulness to regulate his business according to his views." Finally, Wieser's entrepreneur must have the courage to accept risk and be spurred onward by "the joyful power to create" (*Social Economics*, p. 324). Later we shall see how Wieser's student, Joseph Schumpeter (see chapter 23), absorbed his master's ideas and painted on an even broader canvas, making the entrepreneur the pivotal figure in the theory of economic development.

■ Conclusion

The analytical performance of the Austrians, and indeed of all the neoclassical writers, amplifies at least one important point. Their ideas demonstrate that the dawning of neoclassical analysis was a lengthy process. Microanalysis was born in several countries and in the writings of quasi-isolated individuals, many of which did not belong to the standard contingent of academic economists. If anything, neoclassical economics was an international invention greatly nurtured by contributors from allied fields. However, the pace of microanalytic work quickened in the early 1870s, and the noontime of the neoclassical age was about to arrive in France and England.

References

Böhm-Bawerk, Eugen. *The Positive Theory of Capital*, in George D. Huncke (trans.), *Capital and Interest*, vol. II. South Holland, IL: Libertarian Press, 1959 [1889].

George, Henry. *Progress and Poverty*. New York: Cosimo, 2005 [1879].

Greenhut, M. L. *Plant Location in Theory and Practise*. Chapel Hill: The University of North Carolina Press, 1956.

Hutchison, T. W. *A Review of Economic Doctrines, 1870–1929*. Oxford: Clarendon Press, 1953.

Knight, F. H. *Risk, Uncertainty and Profit*. New York: Harper & Row, 1965 [1921].

Marshall, Alfred. *Principles of Economics*, 2d ed. London: Macmillan, 1891.

———. *Memorials of Alfred Marshall*, A. C. Pigou (ed.). London: Macmillan, 1925.

Mangoldt, H. K. E., von, *Die Lehre vom Unternehmergewinn: ein Beitrag sur Volkswirthschaftlehre*. Leipzig: Teuber, 1855. [A fragment of this work has been translated as: "The precise function of the entrepreneur and the true nature of entrepreneur's profit," in F. M. Taylor (ed.), *Some Readings in Economics*. Ann Arbor, MI: George Wahr, 1907].

———. *Grundriss der Volkswirthschaftlehre*. Stuttgart: Maier, 1863. [A chapter was translated as: "The Exchange Ratio of Goods," *International Economic Papers*, vol. 11].

Menger, Carl. *Principles of Economics*, James Dingwall and Bert F. Hoselitz (trans.). Glencoe, IL: Free Press, 1950 [1871].

Schumpeter, J. A. *History of Economic Analysis*, E. B. Schumpeter (ed.). New York: Oxford University Press, 1954.

———. *Ten Great Economists: From Marx to Keynes*. New York: Oxford University Press, 1951.

Stigler, George J. *Production and Distribution Theories: The Formative Period*. New York: Macmillan, 1941.

Thünen, J. H. von. *The Isolated State in Relation to Agriculture and Political Economy*, Vol. 2, in B. W. Dempsey, *The Frontier Wage*. Chicago: Loyola University Press, 1960.

Wieser, Friedrich, von. *Natural Value*, A. Malloch (trans.) and William Smart (ed.). New York: Kelley and Millman, 1956 [1889].

———. *Social Economics*, A. Ford Hinrichs (trans.). New York: A. M. Kelley, 1967 [1914].

Notes for Further Reading

Eighteenth century German economic thought was associated most closely with cameralism, a theory in which public revenue was the sole measure of economic prosperity. As such, it lagged behind classical economics in building a theoretic core on which to erect the scaffolding of political economy. For some background on cameralism and its chief architect, see Hans-Christoph Schmidt am Busch, "Cameralism as 'Political Metaphysics': Human Nature, the State, and Natural Law in the Thought of Johann Heinrich Gottlob von Justi," *The European Journal of the History of Economic Thought*, vol. 16 (Summer 2009), pp. 409–430. Owing to the spreading of Smith's and Say's ideas through Germany in the nineteenth century, economics took a more theoretic turn.

Kiichiro Yagi, *Austrian and German Economic Thought: From Subjectivism to Social Evolution* (London: Routledge, 2011), uses unpublished and archival material collected over three decades to explore facets of economic thought of leading Austrian and German economists of the nineteenth century. T. W. Hutchison, *Review of Economic Doctrines, 1870–1929*, chap. 8 (see references), provides a more limited, but nevertheless useful, overview of German economics in the nineteenth century. Von Thünen's work has been translated into English piecemeal, and is now available in two separate volumes: vol. 1, *Von Thünen's Isolated State*, Carla Wartenberg (trans.) and Peter Hall (ed.) (Oxford: Pergamon, 1966); and vol. 2 *The Isolated State in Relation to Agriculture and Political Economy*, is reprinted in B. W. Dempsey, *The Frontier Wage* (see references). Various assessments of particular aspects of von Thünen's economics include but are not limited to E. Schneider, "Johann Heinrich von Thünen," *Econometrica*, vol. 2 (January 1934), pp. 1–12, reprinted in *The Development of Economic Thought*, H. W. Spiegel (ed.) (New York: Wiley 1952); A. H. Leigh, "Von Thünen's Theory of Distribution and the Advent of Marginal Analysis," *Journal of Political Economy*, vol. 54 (December 1946), pp. 481–502; H. L. Moore, "Von Thünen's Theory of Natural Wages," parts I and II, *Quarterly Journal of Economics*, vol. 9 (April, July 1895), pp. 291–304, 388–408; Colin Clark, "Von Thünen's Isolated State," *Oxford Economic Papers*, n.s., vol. 19 (November 1967), pp. 370–377; M. L. Nerlove and Efraim Sadka, "Von Thünen's Model of the Dual Economy," *Journal of Economics*, vol. 54 (1991), pp. 97–124. B. F. Kiker, "Von Thünen on Human Capital," *Oxford Economic Papers*, n.s., vol. 21 (November 1969), pp. 339–343; H. D. Dickinson, "Von Thünen's Economics," *Economic Journal*, vol. 79 (December 1969), pp. 894–902; and Andreas Grotewold, "Von Thünen in Retrospect," *Economic Geography*, vol. 35 (October 1959), pp. 346–355. Mark Blaug provides a useful guide to von Thünen's life and influence in his introduction to a new Italian translation of von Thünen's *Isolated State*, included in the IRPET Classics of the Regional Science Series.

Gossen's *Entwicklung der Gesetz des menschlichen Verhehrs, und der daraus fliessenden Regeln für menschliches Handeln* (1854) has been translated into English as *The Laws of Human Relations and the Rules of Human Action Derived Therefrom*, R. C. Blitz (trans.) (Cambridge, MA: MIT Press, 1983), with an introduction by Nicholas Georgescu-Roegen. For an enthusiastic endorsement of Gossen by Léon Walras, written in the first blush of discovery, see "Walras on Gossen," in *The Development of Economic Thought*, H. W. Spiegel (ed.) (New York: Wiley, 1952), pp. 471–488. Also see Spiegel's entry on Gossen in the *International Encyclopedia of the Social Sciences*, vol. 6, pp. 209–210; and the later entry by Jürg Niehans in *The New Palgrave: A Dictionary of Economics*, J. Eatwell, M. Milgate, and P. Newman (eds.) (London: Macmillan, 1987), vol. 2, pp. 550–554.

Other secondary sources on Gossen are as rare as a first edition of his *Entwicklung*, but glimpses of his originality can be found in the preface to W. S. Jevons, *The Theory of Political Economy*, 2d ed. (London: Macmillan, 1879); and in Maffeo Pantaleoni, *Pure Economics*, T. B. Bruce (trans.) (London: Macmillan, 1898). Also see W. Jaffé, "The Normative Bias of the Walrasian Model: Walras versus Gossen," *Quarterly Journal of Economics*, vol.

91 (August 1977), pp. 371–388. Albert Jolink and Jan van Daal, "Gossen's Laws," *History of Political Economy*, vol. 30 (Spring 1998), pp. 43–50, argue that Gossen's theoretical construction (i.e., postulates, theorems, and auxiliary assumptions) leads to a suboptimal outcome. Philippe Steiner, "The Creator, Human Conduct and the Maximisation of Utility in Gossen's Economic Theory," *The European Journal of the History of Economic Thought*, vol. 18, (Summer 2011), pp. 353–379, examines Gossen's emphasis on mathematical reasoning in conjunction with his consistent religious references. Steiner concludes that Gossen's religious views were vital for his historical and theoretical understanding of utility maximization and the government of rational, selfish human beings.

Translations of Hans von Mangoldt's works have been made in dribs and drabs. See Mangoldt, "The Exchange Ratio of Goods," *International Economic Papers*, vol. 11 (1962), pp. 32–59; "On the Equations of International Demand," *Journal of International Economics*, vol. 5 (1975), pp. 55–97; and "The precise function of the entrepreneur and the true nature of entrepreneur's profit" (see references). Erich Schneider, "Hans von Mangoldt on Price Theory: A Contribution to the History of Mathematical Economics," *Econometrica*, vol. 28 (1960), pp. 380–392, attempted to "rescue Mangoldt's work from oblivion" by exposing his analysis of price formation using joint supply and demand, but Schneider's effort was judged incomplete by John Creedy, "Mangoldt and Interrelated Goods," *Journal of the History of Economic Thought*, vol. 13 (Spring 1990), pp. 99–108, who tried to repair omissions by reinterpreting Mangoldt's pioneer analysis of price determination in interrelated markets. For a balanced perspective on Mangoldt's place in the history of economics, see K. H. Hennings, "The Transition from Classical to Neoclassical Economic Theory: Hans von Mangoldt," *Kyklos*, vol. 33 (1980), pp. 658–682.

For critical reviews of the thoughts of Menger, Wieser, and Böhm-Bawerk, see G. J. Stigler's *Production and Distribution Theories*, chaps. 6–8 (see references); and T. W. Hutchison's *Review of Economic Doctrines, 1870–1929*, chaps. 9–12 (see references). As always, J. A. Schumpeter, *History of Economic Analysis* (see references), pp. 843–855, 924–932, is a valuable reference. A. M. Endres, "Menger, Wieser, Böhm-Bawerk, and the Analysis of Economizing Behavior," *History of Political Economy*, vol. 23 (Summer 1991), pp. 279–299, explores the process of choice and the goals of economizing behavior in Austrian value theory from the standpoint of biological, ethical, and psychological precepts; see also, same author, "Carl Menger's Theory of Price Formation Reconsidered," *History of Political Economy*, vol. 27 (Summer 1995), pp. 261–287. Endres weighs in yet again on the founding Austrians as neoclassical economists rather than separatists, in *Neoclassical Microeconomic Theory: The Founding Austrian Version* (London: Routledge, 1997). But see Gilles Campagnolo, *Criticisms of Classical Political Economy: Menger, Austrian Economics and the German Historical School* (London: Routledge, 2009), for an appraisal of the role of the German Historical school in Menger's thought. Menger's founding role in the development of the Austrian school is also discussed by Frank Knight in his introduction to the Dingwall translation of Menger's *Principles*. Also see F. A. Hayek, "Hayek on Menger," in *Development of Economic Thought*, Henry W. Spiegel (ed.), cited previously, pp. 526–567; H. S. Bloch, "Carl Menger: The Founder of the Austrian School," *Journal of Political Economy*, vol. 48 (June 1940), pp. 428–433; and J. A. Schumpeter, *Ten Great Economists* (see references), which contains essays on Böhm-Bawerk and Wieser as well as on Menger. The entire issue of the Atlantic *Economic Journal*, vol. 16 (September 1978), is devoted to papers on Menger and Austrian economics; see especially the papers by Lawrence Moss, Israel Kirzner, and Ludwig Lachmann.

The (in)famous *methodenstreit* between Menger and Schmoller has drawn scant attention in the secondary literature. Many writers regard it solely as an *academic* "war of ideas," but Gary M. Anderson, Robert B. Ekelund, Jr., and Robert D. Tollison, "*Methödenstreit*: The Economics of Competing Interests," *The European Journal of Political Economy*, vol. 8 (1992), pp. 401–418, investigate interest-group concerns that may have motivated the debate (i.e., Austrian economists were trying to enter the German academic cartel managed by Schmoller).

On the development of utility theory in general, see G. J. Stigler, "The Development of Utility Theory," *Journal of Political Economy*, vol. 58 (August–October 1950), reprinted in *Essays in the History of Economics* (Chicago: The University of Chicago Press, 1965); Jacob Viner, "The Utility Concept in Value Theory and Its Critics," *Journal of Political Economy*, vol. 33 (August–September 1925), pp. 369–387, 638–659, reprinted in Viner, *The Long View and the Short* (New York: Free Press, 1958); R. S. Howey, *The Rise of the Marginal Utility School, 1870–1889* (Lawrence: The University Press of Kansas, 1960); Emil Kauder, *A History of Marginal Utility Theory* (Princeton, NJ: Princeton University Press, 1965); and the entire issue of *History of Political Economy*, vol. 4 (Fall 1972), especially the articles by Blaug, Howey, Streissler, Stigler, and Shackle. An important article for understanding the differences between the three cofounders of the marginal utility tradition is William Jaffé, "Menger, Jevons, and Walras De-homogenized," *Economic Inquiry*, vol. 14 (December 1976), pp. 511–524. See also W. N. Butos, "Menger: A Suggested Interpretation," *Atlantic Economic Journal*, vol. 13 (July 1985), pp. 21–30.

Two useful sources of information on Menger's "institutional" economics include A. M. Endres, "Institutional Elements in Carl Menger's Theory of Demand: A Comment," *Journal of Economic Issues*, vol. 18 (September 1984), pp. 897–902; and G. P. O'Driscoll, Jr., "Money: Menger's Evolutionary Theory," *History of Political Economy*, vol. 18 (Winter 1986), pp. 601–616. See also, Gilles Campagnolo, "Carl Menger's 'Money as Measure of Value," *History of Political Economy*, vol. 37 (Summer 2005), pp. 233–261, which contains an introduction and English translation of an article written by Menger in 1892 on the theoretical aspects of money (previously available only in French). Mikael Stenkula, "Menger and the Network Theory of Money," *The European Journal of the History of Economic Thought*, vol. 10 (2003), pp. 587–606, shows that Menger was aware of the network characteristic of money and some of the problems associated with this.

Wieser's social economics is described in vol. 2 of W. C. Mitchell's *Lecture Notes on Types of Economic Theory* (New York: A. M. Kelley, 1969); and in R. B. Ekelund, Jr., "Power and Utility: The Normative Economics of Friedrich von Wieser," *Review of Social Economy*, vol. 28 (September 1970), pp. 179–196. An instructive description of Wieser's system (and of the Austrian system generally) of input and output pricing can be found in chap. 12 of M. Blaug's *Economic Theory in Retrospect*, 4th ed. (London: Cambridge University Press, 1985). The Austrian system also spread to England. See William Smart, *An Introduction to the Theory of Value* (New York: A. M. Kelley, 1966).

Böhm-Bawerk's theory of value and capital is capably explicated by Klaus H. Hennings, *The Austrian Theory of Value and Capital. Studies in the Life and Works of Eugen von Böhm-Bawerk* (Cheltenham, UK: Edward Elgar, 1997), which also contains correspondence between Böhm-Bawerk and Wicksell (see chap. 22) previously unpublished. Beginning with an interchange between Böhm-Bawerk and J. B. Clark in the *Quarterly Journal of Economics* in the 1890s and early 1900s, Böhm-Bawerk's theory of capital and interest has been the subject of continual debate. The original debate is the subject of an unpublished doctoral dissertation by David E. R. Gay entitled *Capital and the Production Process: A Critical Evaluation of the Böhm-Bawerk–Clark Debate and Its Relation to Current Capital Theory* (College Station: Texas A & M University, 1973). For another assessment of Böhm-Bawerk in light of his engagement with several contemporaries on the theory of interest, see Jürg Niehans, "Böhm-Bawerk versus John Doe: The Interest Controversies," *History of Political Economy*, vol. 23 (Winter 1991), pp. 567–586. Among the economists Niehans considers in regard to Böhm-Bawerk are Alfred Marshall, J. B. Clark, T. N. Carver, F. A. Fetter, Adolphe Landry, Ladislaus von Bortkiewicz, and Irving Fisher. An overview of Böhm-Bawerk's period-of-production model based on a subsistence fund and its role in capital theory is presented in Donald Dewey, *Modern Capital*

Theory (New York: Columbia University Press, 1965); and F. A. Lutz, *The Theory of Capital*, chap. 1 (London: Macmillan, 1965).

Avi J. Cohen, "The Kaldor/Knight Controversy: Is Capital a Distinct and Quantifiable Factor of Production?" *The European Journal of the History of Economic Thought*, vol. 13 (Winter 2006), pp. 141–161, examines the capital-theory dispute between Nicholas Kaldor and Frank Knight (see chapter 15), in light of Böhm-Bawerk's problem. Cohen argues that this controversy is important for understanding disputes regarding periods of production vs. production functions on the one hand, and roundaboutness vs. diminishing returns on the other. According to Cohen the Kaldor/Knight dispute underscores Knight's role as a "precursor" of new growth theory and Kaldor's turning point in his interest in Austrian theory.

The mechanics of Böhm-Bawerk's theory of interest is analyzed graphically and mathematically by Robert Dorfman, "A Graphical Exposition of Böhm-Bawerk's Interest Theory," *Review of Economic Studies*, vol. 26 (February 1959), pp. 153–158; J. Hirshleiffer, "A Note on the Böhm-Bawerk/Wicksell Theory of Interest," *Review of Economic Studies*, vol. 34 (April 1967), pp. 191–200; and D. E. R. Gay, "The Aggregate Factor-Price Frontier in Böhm-Bawerk's Period of Production Capital Model: A Graphical Derivation," *Eastern Economic Journal*, vol. 3 (July 1975), pp. 205–211. It should be noted, at least in passing, that Böhm-Bawerk's protégé, Knut Wicksell, attempted to clarify Böhm-Bawerk's theory of capital in *Value, Capital and Rent* (New York: A. M. Kelley, 1970).

A. M. Endres, "The Origins of Böhm-Bawerk's Greatest 'Error': Theoretical Points of Separation from Menger," *Journal of Institutional & Theoretical Economics*, vol. 143 (June 1987), pp. 291–309, explores Böhm-Bawerk's departure from Menger. In a similar vein, Endres again, "Some Microfoundations of Austrian Economics: Böhm-Bawerk's Version," *The European Journal of the History of Economic Thought*, vol. 3 (Spring 1996), pp. 84–106, attempts to establish "precisely what was distinctive about Böhm-Bawerk's version of Austrian microeconomic theory."

In addition to everything else, Böhm-Bawerk was a formidable historian of economic thought. His *History and Critique of Interest Theories*, first published in 1884, is an unmatched masterpiece. The first English translation, by William Smart, appeared in 1890; it has been re-translated by George D. Huncke and Hans F. Sennholz (South Holland, IL: Libertarian Press, 1959). Like Wieser, Böhm-Bawerk was interested in the sociology of power and its effects on production and exchange. See, "Control of Economic Law," in R. Mez (trans.), *Shorter Classics of Eugen von Böhm-Bawerk*, vol. I (South Holland, IL: Libertarian Press, 1962 [1914]). See also Emil Lederer, "Social Control versus Economic Law: An Old Dogma and a New Situation," *Social Research*, vol. 51 (Spring/Summer 1983), pp. 91–110.

The Austrian tradition was carried on by a second generation of writers, including Oskar Morgenstern and Joseph Schumpeter. But F. A. Hayek and Ludwig von Mises, in particular, carried the seeds to England and America, where they fell on somewhat rocky soil. More detail on this subject will have to wait until chapter 23.

15

Microeconomics in England and America
W. S. Jevons and J. B. Clark

The climate of economic opinion in England was of a distinctly stormy nature in the late 1850s, 1860s, and 1870s. Mill's recantation of the wages-fund doctrine in the *Fortnightly Review* in 1869 (see chapter 8) was thought by many to be the death knell of classical economics. But, in truth, the reasons for the decline of credence in the classical paradigm may be laid at many doors. An interest in labor problems, socialist and "progressive" philosophies, and Darwinian evolutionist ideas, as well as the historicists' reactions to classical political economy (see chapter 11) and Mill's eleventh-hour misgivings about laissez-faire, all contributed to rising doubt of the adequacy of classical economics in England. If widespread dissatisfaction with an old paradigm is, as many intellectual historians believe, the prerequisite for the emergence of a fundamentally new (but not necessarily contradictory) system of thought, then a ready explanation for the emergence in England of Jevons's *Theory of Political Economy* in 1871 is at hand. Furthermore, while Jevons and other economists in England and Europe were cementing the foundation of neoclassical economics, the American economist John Bates Clark was independently discovering the marginal-utility and marginal-productivity theories of value and distribution.

W. S. Jevons

William Stanley Jevons (1835–1882) was one of the most interesting and enigmatic characters in the history of British economic thought. A man of rare (often esoteric) powers of analysis, he was also one of the most practical professional economists who ever lived. Although his ideas were profound and original, he had no students or disciples of consequence—in spite of the fact that he held a major university post in political economy (at Manchester).

Jevons was born in England and raised in an educated (but nonacademic) Unitarian environment in which economic and social problems were often discussed.[1] At the age of eighteen, he moved to Australia, where a remunerative job offer as assayer at the Sydney Mint promised to alleviate family financial problems at home. He remained there for five years, during which time his biographer, J. M. Keynes, claims he was struck with all the original ideas on economics that he later developed and expanded on his return to England.

With his interest in political economy awakened by his experiences at the mint, Jevons returned to England in 1859 to continue his studies at the University of London, where he obtained a degree in 1865. Besides political economy, his early training was technical (including mathematics, biology, chemistry, and metallurgy), and the subjects it encompassed permeated his entire intellectual career. This early period was especially fecund for Jevons. In 1862, in several communications to the British Association, he outlined (1) the skeletal structure of utility theory (*Notice of the General Theory of Political Economy*) and (2) the scenario for his statistical studies of fluctuations (*On the Study of Periodic Commercial Fluctuations, with Five Diagrams*), both of which are discussed in this chapter. In 1863 Jevons published a book entitled *Pure Logic* (one of the most significant and presently neglected areas of his interests), and in 1865 he published *The Coal Question*, a book that brought him to prominence in economic circles.

The Coal Question was based on a questionable analogy between the role of corn in Malthus's theory of population and that of coal in the industrial progress of Britain. Nevertheless, the book attracted a good deal of attention in political and intellectual circles, including that of Prime Minister Gladstone. From this point onward, Jevons's interests fluctuated from pure logic to economics and back again. His economic interests ran the gamut from statistical analyses of prices and gold (and significant institutional studies of money markets) to pure theory and commercial fluctuations, of which his controversial sunspot theory was one (*The Solar Period and the Price of Corn* [1875]). In 1871 Jevons published his most enduring work, *Theory of Political Economy*, a book based on his early ideas on utility theory communicated to (but ignored by) the British Association in 1862.

In 1876, after numerous bouts of nervous and physical exhaustion (at the age of thirty-six he was obliged to give up all work for a time), Jevons left Manchester for a professorship in political economy at University College in London. He resigned this post in 1880 due to a return of ill health and a pressing desire to complete a massive treatise tentatively titled *Principles of Economics*. Although fragments remain, this last work was never completed. In August 1882 an enfeebled Jevons, just short of his forty-seventh birthday, drowned while swimming off the south coast of England.

Jevons's untimely death deprived the world of an original economic mind. But this assessment has been formed mostly in retrospectives of his work. During his life and immediately afterward, Jevons seems to have had little impact on the course of economics. As noted above, he left no serious students or disciples. His books did not sell well. (J. M. Keynes calculated that by 1936 only 39,000 copies of

[1] A lifelong music lover, Jevons became enchanted, following an early devotion to Beethoven, with the experimental music of Berlioz and Wagner, who he believed were writing the "music of the future." His knowledgeable and laudatory descriptions of the innovative nature of these composers are clear evidence that the quest for rearrangement and changes in form was a deeply engrained habit of his thought. It is interesting to note that Jevons's early conviction about his own genius and originality almost exactly parallels Wagner's.

Jevons's nine major works in economics and logic had been sold!). Moreover, the person who came to dominate British economics near the end of the century, Alfred Marshall, displayed an ungenerous attitude toward him.

How might one account for the distinctly mediocre impact of a writer whose powers of originality have been favorably compared to Marshall's? A retrospective by one of his admirers, John Maynard Keynes, gives us some insights into Jevons's character.

> What sort of man was Jevons in himself? There is no strong personal impression of him which has been recorded, and 54 years after his death it is not easy to find a definite imprint on the minds of the few now left who knew him. My belief is that Jevons did not make a strong impression on his companions at any period of his life. He was, in modern language, strongly introverted. He worked best alone with flashes of inner light. He was repelled, as much as he was attracted, by contact with the outside world. He had from his boyhood unbounded belief in his own powers; but he desired greatly to influence others whilst being himself uninfluenced by them. He was deeply affectionate towards the members of his family but not intimate with them or with anyone. ("*William Stanley Jevons,*", p. 304)

This character portrayal by one who was anything but introverted is reinforced by Jevons's self-assessment, as expressed in a letter to his beloved sister Lucy.

> I cannot say of course that my disposition for reserve and loneliness was originally intentional on my part; it probably originated in bashfulness, which other people think, and which, no doubt, is, a very silly thing. Yet I ascribe to this disposition almost everything I am, and believe that a certain amount of reserve and solitude is quite necessary for the information of any firm and original character. This is in fact almost self-evident, for if any one were brought up in continual intercourse with the thoughts of a number of other people, it follows almost necessarily that his thoughts will never rise above the ordinary level of the others. . . . Solitude, no doubt, produces one class of minds and characters, and society another; the latter may give quickness of thought and some other showy qualities, but must tend to interrupt longer and more valuable trains of thought, and gradually destroy the habit of following them, while solitude promotes reflection, self-dependence, and originality. These, I believe, I possess to a greater or less extent, and I therefore, on principle, do not altogether regret that my habits have been as you know them. (*Letters and Journal*, pp. 85–86)

So Jevons defended his aloofness. He bragged to Lucy that, with one "slight exception," he had never gone to a party; and that he had at last succeeded in "impressing upon all friends the fact that it is no use inviting me." Traits that would be considered weaknesses in others were regarded as strengths by Jevons.

From an early age Jevons was confident that he would revolutionize the science of economics. In 1858 he wrote from Australia to his sister Henrietta (who was reading Adam Smith's *The Wealth of Nations* at the time):

> There are a multitude of allied branches of knowledge connected with man's condition; the relation of these to political economy is analogous to the connection of mechanics, astronomy, optics, sound, heat, and every other branch more or less of physical science, with pure mathematics. I have an idea, which I do not object to mention to you, that my insight into the foundations and nature of the knowledge of man is deeper than that of most men or writers. In fact, I think that it is my mission to apply myself to such subjects, and it is my intention to do so. You are desirous of engaging in the practically useful; you may feel assured that to extend and perfect the abstract or the detailed and practical knowledge of man and society is

> perhaps the most useful and necessary work in which any one can now engage. . . . There are plenty of people engaged with physical science, and practical science and arts may be left to look after themselves, but thoroughly to understand the principles of society appears to me now the most cogent business. (*Letters and Journal*, p. 101)

Despite his clearly perceived mission, however, Jevons's "habits" of isolation, shyness, aloofness, and social inhospitality carried over into his later academic life. Keynes quotes Jevons's colleague, Professor Herbert Foxwell, as saying that "'There never was a worse lecturer, the men would not go to his classes, and he worked in flashes and could not finish anything thoroughly,' and then after a pause with a different sort of expression [Foxwell continued], 'the only point about Jevons was that he was a genius'" ("*William Stanley Jevons*," p. 307). A look at Jevons's entire lifework bears out Foxwell's opinion. Jevons's legacies to economics are indeed fragmentary, but they are the leavings of genius.

■ Jevons's Theory of Value

Jevons's major contribution to economic theory was to establish consumer behavior on the basis of utility judgments. From this foundation he constructed a theory of exchange and a theory of labor supply and capital. Many of these ideas, which were expressed chiefly in his *Theory of Political Economy*, were not new. Indeed, Jevons very generously noted that many of the features of his economic theory had been developed previously by others. Two of his most important precursors were Dionysius Lardner, who developed a theory of the firm in his *Railway Economy* of 1850, and Fleeming Jenkin, who established a graphical presentation of the laws of supply and demand in 1870. (See the box, The Force of Ideas: Engineers as Precursors). Nevertheless, many of Jevons's theoretical contributions were original and important. His discovery of marginal utility was made independently of all other writers, and thus reflects his original cast of mind.

The Force of Ideas: Engineers as Precursors

Unlike many an economic pioneer, Jevons was perennially gracious in mentioning his precursors. Two writers, both engineers, are mentioned in the first edition of Jevons's *Theory of Political Economy* as having directly influenced his thought: Dionysius Lardner (1793–1859) and Fleeming Jenkin (1833–1885). Lardner was an engineer, astronomer, and essayist on numerous scientific topics, but he often ventured into other fields. *Railway Economy* (1850; see references), his only work that relates to economics, was filled with facts, but it also exposed a theory that drew Jevons's attention. Jevons read the book in 1857 and claimed that it inspired him to investigate economics in mathematical terms.

Based on empirical studies of railroad costs and revenues, Lardner developed a fully formed theory of a profit-maximizing railroad. He depicted the point of optimal profit by means of a diagram. In this diagram Lardner made "price" (in the form of a railway rate) the independent variable (the one free to change), and "quantity" the dependent variable. He showed that unit costs fall (up to some point) with the amount of traffic carried. But fixed costs are invariant, and would remain to be paid even if the price were so high as to eliminate all traffic. Total costs are thus the sum of fixed and variable costs. Lardner's diagram also showed a railway total revenue function, which he expressed mathematically. Indeed, the mathematical expression of total revenue by Lardner may have been the stimulus to Jevons's interest in using mathematics to express economic theory.

Lardner's function took the following simple form. Let r = the tariff imposed by the railroad per mile on each ton carried; D = the average distance in miles to which each ton of goods is carried; N = the number of tons booked; and R = the gross receipts from goods transport. It follows that total receipts may be expressed as $R = NDr$. As the tariff is lowered, the average distance of each ton of freight carried, D, and the number of tons booked, N, increase. Total receipts will increase to some maximum and then (due to increasing elasticity of demand unnoted by Lardner) decline to zero at a zero tariff rate. In effect, Lardner identified the profit maximizing quantity as that output at which marginal cost equals marginal revenue. The precise effect this kind of theorizing had on Jevons is difficult to know, but it is curious that Jevons did not take the logical step of deriving a demand curve from Lardner's total receipts expression, nor did he present a model of profit maximization in his own writings.

A second, and possibly more direct, influence on Jevons came from Fleeming Jenkin, an engineer whose 1870 publication, "The Graphic Representation of the Laws of Supply and Demand," induced Jevons to hurry his *Theory of Political Economy* into print. Jenkin set out to refute W. T. Thornton's bizarre assault on the wages-fund theory and the laws of supply and demand (see chapter 8). In the process he presented a persuasive, but wholly graphical, explanation of the principles of supply and demand in his essay, exposing the circularity of many previous discussions of price determination. He claimed that both demand and supply "may be said to be functions of price," and he correctly represented demand as identifying the "quantity which, then and there [i.e., at a price], buyers would purchase at that price."* Jenkin defined supply in essentially the same way, so that he presented both quantity demanded and quantity supplied as functions of price. His graphical representation clearly established equilibrium price and quantity at the junction of his demand and supply schedule. In fact, his explanation of how market equilibrium is established by competitive forces would compare favorably with any modern textbook discussion of the subject.

Although Jenkin had a clear understanding of the equilibrating market process, he muddled his analysis of what caused changes in the two curves or functions. For example, he identified no income parameter when discussing demand. It therefore appears that Jenkin's theoretical statement of the demand function did not surpass earlier expositions (Mill's for instance) in terms of completeness or importance, even though he alluded to the concept of elasticity of demand and suggested the possibility of establishing statistical demand estimations (which he did not undertake). It may have been Jenkin's penchant for graphical exposition of economic principles that influenced Jevons (and Alfred Marshall). Be that as it may, Jenkin's essay remains, at least for its day, a benchmark in the development of the graphics of partial equilibrium price analysis in England.

It is another curious episode in the history of economic ideas that Jevons, who had a clear appreciation for both Lardner's and Jenkin's work, did not undertake a formal analysis of the profit-maximizing firm or of supply and demand. He skipped over the mutual interdependence of supply and demand even though the idea was there for the taking in his predecessors' work. Nevertheless, the force of graphical presentation to clarify economic principles was manifest in Lardner and Jenkin, and once adopted by Jevons, passed into the mainstream of economic analysis.

*"Graphic Representation," p. 77.

Utility Theory

The actual discovery of utility theory, and specifically marginal-utility theory, was made by Jules Dupuit, as we have seen in chapter 13. There had been essentially adventitious statements of the same principle by Nassau Senior, William Lloyd, and Montifort Longfield. Dupuit, however, had developed the theory in an empirical milieu and had based his argument on empirical facts. Jevons, although possibly looking to the practical concerns of Lardner for inspiration, based his reasoning partially on physiological theory. In this connection Jevons specifically noted the Weber–Fechner studies of stimulus and response.

In his establishment of utility theory, Jevons's background in science and scientific measurement was much on his mind. He considered economics fortunate in that some of its important quantities (prices and so forth) were capable of exact measurement. He had early and unbounded faith in the future of mathematics and statistics as indispensable aids to discovery in economics. Yet, he placed a *subjective* maximand—utility—in the starring role in economic analysis. Jevons admitted that the calculus of pleasure and pain (or utility theory) had subjective features, although he expressed hopes that the *effects* of utility might somehow be ascertained in a scientific sense. In 1871 he wrote:

> A unit of pleasure or of pain is difficult even to conceive; but it is the amount of these feelings which is continually prompting us to buying and selling, borrowing and lending, labouring and resting, producing and consuming; and *it is from the quantitative effects of the feelings that we must estimate their comparative amounts*. We can no more know nor measure gravity in its own nature than we can measure a feeling; but, just as we measure gravity by its effects in the motion of a pendulum, so we may estimate the equality or inequality of feelings by the decisions of the human mind. (*Theory of Political Economy*, p. 11)

Immediately, then, Jevons acknowledged that one could, at best, obtain only ordinal *estimates* of the quantity around which the entire economic system revolves. In his *Theory* (unless otherwise noted, all citations for *Theory* refer to the 1871 edition), Jevons noted that utility is basically introspective, and he recognized explicitly that interpersonal comparisons from one individual or group to another are impossible (although he may have failed to heed his own warnings in the concept of a "trading body," as we shall see). Nevertheless, despite all these difficulties, Jevons set out the new core of economics in utility terms.

Marginal Utility. Following Bentham's lead (see chapter 6), Jevons maintained that the value of pleasure and pain varies according to four circumstances: (1) intensity, (2) duration, (3) certainty or uncertainty, and (4) nearness or remoteness. Jevons discussed each of these at length. Pain is simply the negative of pleasure, and in individual calculations the algebraic sum (i.e., net pleasure) is the meaningful quantity. Like Bentham before him, Jevons injected a probabilistic element into economic analysis when he discussed the ways in which the uncertainty of future events and future "anticipated feelings" affect behavior. In one especially telling passage, Jevons suggested how time preference and anticipation permeate economic quantities:

> The cares of the moment are but ripples on the tide of achievement and hope. We may safely call that man happy who, however lowly his position and limited his possessions, can always hope for more than he has, and can feel that every moment of exertion tends to realize his aspirations. He, on the contrary, who

> seizes the enjoyment of the passing moment without regard to coming times, must discover sooner or later that his stock of pleasure is on the wane, and that even hope begins to fail. (*Theory*, p. 35)

Paradoxically, however, Jevons never incorporated this all-important element directly into his theory of utility.

The object of economics, Jevons asserted, is maximization of pleasure, or in his own words, humans seek to procure the "greatest amount of what is desirable at the expense of the least that is undesirable" (*Theory*, p. 37). However, he strove to make this proposition more objective by attaching it to something concrete, such as *commodities*.

According to Jevons a commodity is an "object, substance, action, or service which can afford pleasure or ward off pain; and *utility* is the abstract quality whereby an object serves our purposes, and becomes entitled to rank as a commodity" (*Theory*, p. 38). Eschewing any pretensions of direct measurability, Jevons claimed that individual behavior would reveal a person's utility and preferences and that the investigator must accept these without making value judgments. As he clearly noted, "Anything which an individual is found to desire and to labour for must be assumed to possess for him utility" (*Theory*, p. 38). Thus, flagpole sitters, astronauts, kamikaze pilots, heroin addicts, and suicides might simply be regarded as maximizing utility (under certain constraints, of course).

Jevons's theory of marginal utility is basically simple and straightforward, and he used elementary arithmetic and geometry to illustrate the basic nature of his argument. Unlike any of his predecessors, he clearly specified that a utility function is a relation between the commodities an individual consumes and an act of individual valuation. Utility is not an *intrinsic* or inherent quality that things possess. Instead, utility has meaning only in the act of valuation.

Jevons's vast improvements over Bentham's utility theory consist in the following features of his formal utility analysis: (1) his clear distinction between total utility and marginal utility, (2) his discussion of the nature of marginal utility, and (3) his establishment of the equimarginal principle, as it relates to alternative uses of the same commodity and to choices *between* commodities. By clearly distinguishing between total utility and what he called the "degree of utility," Jevons resolved Adam Smith's water–diamond paradox. For our purposes, Jevons's "degree of utility" may be regarded as identical to marginal utility. Both total and marginal utilities were related to the quantities of goods possessed, and only to those quantities.

Graphical Analysis. In algebraic notation, Jevons's utility function is expressed as $U = f(X)$, which should be read as "the utility of commodity X (food) is a function of the quantity of X the individual holds." It should be noted that all other goods are left out of the picture; that is, it may be assumed that either they are nonexistent or their quantities are held constant. Assuming that one could add tiny portions of food to the individual's store—that is, "continuously," in the language of arithmetic—one might derive a utility function as depicted in figure 15-1a (on the following page). Here the total utility of food (the quantities of other things held constant) may be seen to rise as quantities are added up to X_0, reach a maximum at that point, and then decline. But the utility of an additional unit of food, which Jevons called the "degree of utility," declines as units of food are added to the individual's consumption. Mathematically, Jevons wrote du/dx, to be read as "the ratio of a small change in utility to a small change in X (food)." Figure 15-1b, which is derived from figure 15-la, demonstrates this idea. Further, he assumed that the mar-

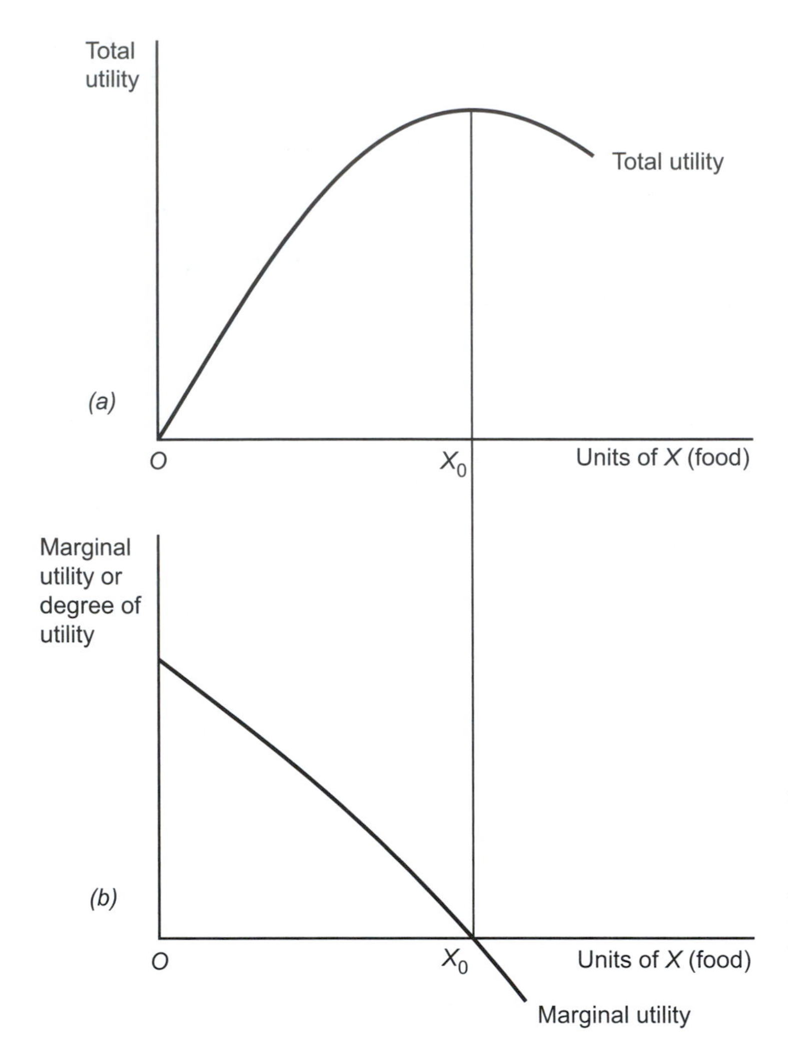

Figure 15-1 Total utility rises continuously up to X_0 units of food, but marginal utility declines continuously as additional units of food are consumed per unit of time.

ginal utility (used synonymously with "degree of utility") of food was declining after the very first unit taken, although he was undoubtedly aware that this might not always be the case. Jevons's law may then be stated as follows: The degree of utility for a single commodity varies with the quantity possessed of that commodity and ultimately decreases as the quantity of that single commodity increases.

The Equimarginal Principle. Jevons presented a clear understanding of the individual's maximizing behavior in discussing a person's allocation of any given commodity among alternative uses. If an individual starts with a fixed stock S of a commodity X, and the uses of that commodity are represented by x and y, then the stock must be divided up between those uses such that $S = x + y$. Now Jevons, in effect, asks the question: How does an individual decide how to allocate his fixed stock among the two uses? The simple and intuitively logical answer is that the quantity of X should be allocated to the two uses so that the increase in utility from adding an additional unit of X in use x just equals the increase in utility from adding an additional unit of X in use y. In Jevonian terms, the equimarginal condition implies that

$$\frac{du}{dx} = \frac{du}{dy} \quad \text{or} \quad MU_x = MU_y$$

where MU_x stands for the degree of utility of commodity X in use x, and similarly for y.

The equimarginal principle, first clearly explained by Jevons, also holds for the allocation of scarce, fixed means (say, income) among all goods in the individual consumer's budget. If x represents number of beers and z represents packs of cigarettes, then the consumer will allocate scarce income y such that the $MU_x = MU_z$, assuming that beers and cigarettes are the same price and that all y is expended on these two goods. A more general formulation of the equimarginal principle, one that does not appear in Jevons but that accounts for different prices of n goods, is the one familiar to every student of basic economics:

$$\frac{MUx}{P_x} = \frac{MUz}{P_z} = \frac{MUn}{P_n}$$

In order to ensure that all income is allocated among the individual's consumptions (which could include a savings account), an additional condition is needed:

$$P_xX + P_zZ + \ldots + P_nN = Y$$

where P_xX represents the individual's expenditure on X, P_zZ represents the expenditure on Z, etc. The sum of all these expenditures equals income Y. Although Jevons did not work out the details, his argument underlies the whole development of the theory of individual maximization behavior, which is at the core of contemporary theory.

Theory of Exchange

Jevons developed a theory of exchange (i.e., an explanation of why and how goods trade between individuals in a market) by combining the theory of utility discussed in the previous section with his *law of indifference*. The law of indifference states that in any free and open market, at any given time, there cannot be more than one price for the same (homogeneous) commodity. Another element of his exchange theory is the idea of a "trading body," a concept that, as we shall see, is not without some difficulties. By a trading body Jevons meant "any body of either buyers or sellers," which could mean anything from two individuals to an entire population. Jevons insisted that every trading body "is either an individual or an aggregate of individuals, and the law in the aggregate must depend upon the fulfillment of the law in the individuals" (*Theory*, pp. 88–89). Neglecting, for the moment, any problems with the concept, let us assume, with Jevons, that there is one trading body (A) possessing a stock of beef (a) and another trading body (B) possessing a stock of corn (b). How does exchange take place? Jevons presented a graphical and symbolic solution.

Let the marginal-utility functions for corn and beef be represented as in figure 15-2 (on the following page), which we here adapt, with slight alterations, from Jevons's own diagram.

Let an increase (decrease) in the quantity of corn (beef) be read from left to right on figure 15-2 and an increase (decrease) in the quantity of beef (corn) be read

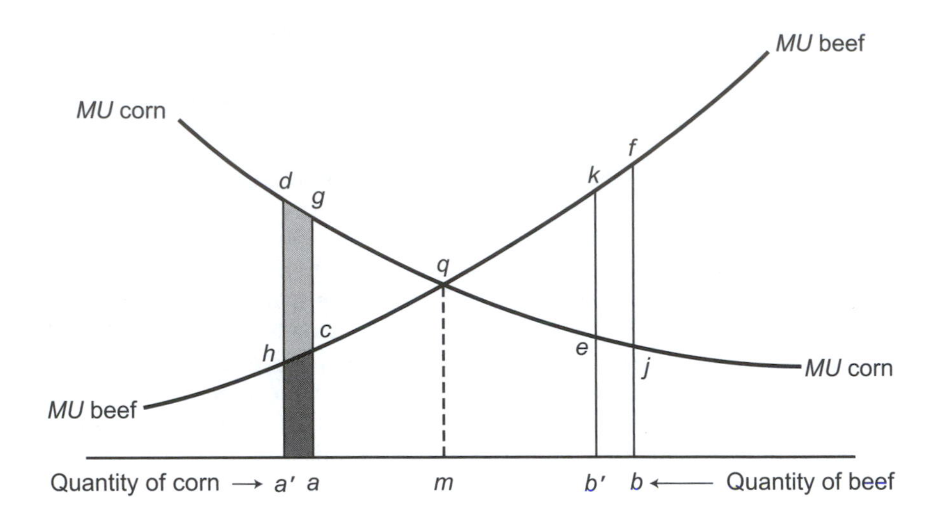

Figure 15-2 If trader A has an initial endowment of a′ corn and beef, he can improve his situation by exchanging beef for corn with trader B. At all points to the left of *m*, trader A receives a net gain of utility by exchanging beef for corn, whereas at all points to the right of *m*, trader B receives a net gain of utility by exchanging corn for beef.

from right to left in the same figure. Units of both commodities must be represented by equal lengths, of course.

Consider trading body A and assume that it holds a quantity a' of corn. An *increase* in A's holding of corn, represented by the little line aa', simultaneously represents a decrease in A's holdings of beef. But the important point is that A *gains* by the trading of beef for corn. Why? Because it would gain more utility by acquiring corn (i.e., $a'dga$) than it would lose by giving up beef (i.e., $a'hca$). With reference to figure 15-2, A would receive a *net gain* of area *hdgc*.

A would continue to trade until equilibrium is reached at point *m*, which represents, in this simple case, the intersection of the marginal-utility curves. B does the same. (It is left for the reader to trace out B's maximizing behavior.) At *m*, no further gains from trade can be realized by either trading body, and trade ends.[2] Thus, Jevons concluded that freedom of exchange, projecting these results, must be to the advantage of all. Laissez-faire thus received a boost from this aspect of utility theory.

Theory of Labor Supply

One of Jevons's most interesting applications of utility theory was to the theory of *labor supply.* With labor, as with all other activities, two quantities were of primary importance to Jevons in explaining behavior: cost incurred and utility gained (proxies for pain and pleasure). Jevons defined labor as "any painful exertion of mind and body undergone partly or wholly with a view of future good" (*Theory*, p. 168). The

[2] Jevons also expressed the condition arithmetically. If we let MU_a^A represent the final degree of utility of trading body A for commodity a (corn) and so on, then Jevons's equilibrium equations of exchange may be expressed as

$$\frac{MU_a^A}{MU_b^A} = \frac{MU_b^B}{MU_b^B} = \frac{a \text{ (total quantity of beef retained)}}{b \text{ (total quantity of corn retained)}}$$

reader may object that many people at least claim to like their work. Jevons, however, was thinking of some concept of *net* pain—a balance of the painfulness and the pleasure of working. He also implicitly assumed that workers were on a piecework system and that they could alter the amount of work performed. This latter assumption, except perhaps over a long-run period, does not present a very accurate picture of present conditions or even of those that existed in Jevons's time. Nevertheless, his idea has some applicability wherever the conditions he assumed are relevant.

In analyzing the work decision, Jevons focused on three quantities: net pain from work, amount of production, and amount of utility gained. Graphically, the combination of these quantities may be analyzed as in figure 15-3. In a piecework system the worker's real wage and income depend on his or her rate of production. The curve *pq* may be regarded as the degree of utility weighted by the worker's production or output. The *reward* for labor, in other words, may be regarded as the product of the rate of production and the degree of utility. The *costs* of labor are represented by the curve traced out by *ed*. Here Jevons assumed that the act of beginning work is onerous (getting up in the morning for some of us?) and produces net *pain*. But as work continues, it becomes more and more pleasurable on balance, until a point is reached where painfulness begins to overwhelm the pleasure of working. Thus, the net-pain-of-labor curve peaks out and turns downward, becoming negative.

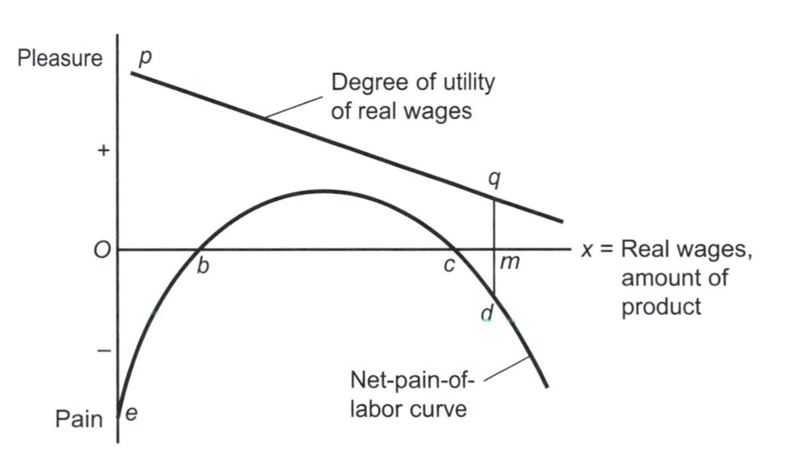

Figure 15-3 In this analysis based on hedonic calculus, a worker will offer labor services in the amount *m*, because at that point the cost of working, *md*, equals the reward of work, *mq*.

Applying the equimarginal principle in this context means that the worker will stop producing when the net pain of working is equivalent to the degree of utility of the real wages produced. That occurs at point *m* in figure 15-3. At point *m*, where the cost of working *md* (net pain) equals the reward from working *mq* (the utility reward), the worker would cease work. To go beyond this point would bring greater costs than rewards. Thus, Jevons established a theory of labor supply based on his notions concerning utility.

■ Jevons as a Pure Theorist

Our investigation of some of Jevons's purely theoretical ideas is necessarily incomplete. For example we have not reviewed in detail his theory of rent and his productivity theory of capital and interest. However, our discussion of his utility approach to value, exchange, and labor should leave little doubt in the reader's mind that Jevons was an innovative, original thinker.

Although utility theory revolutionized value theory, Jevons's own ideas on exchange value were curiously lopsided. Though he never relied on supply and demand curves, he was aware of Fleeming Jenkin's effective use of these concepts in explaining market value. He conceded, therefore, that "Our theory is perfectly consistent with the laws of supply and demand; and if we had the functions of utility determined, it would be possible to throw them into a form clearly expressing the equivalence of supply and demand" (*Theory*, p. 101). Yet, he seemed targeted on deeper origins of value, noting that, "The laws of supply and demand are thus a result of what seems to me the true theory of value or exchange" (*Theory*, p. 101). It wasn't results that interested him so much as root causes. He zeroed in almost exclusively on *utility* as the source of value and aptly summarized his "final" position in the form of a catena that spells out the chain of connections between important economic variables:

> Cost of production determines supply;
> Supply determines final degree of utility;
> Final degree of utility determines value. (*Theory*, p. 165)

Hence, labor value, and presumably the value of *all* inputs, is determined by the utility or value of the product it produces, and not vice versa. Independent alterations in supply due to alterations in costs of productive inputs are not taken into account. Supply of goods, as in the theory of exchange shown in figure 15-2, is presumed *fixed*.

Jevons believed that utility theory effectively refuted the labor theory of value, which he (erroneously) identified as *the sole* determinant of value in Ricardo's *Principles*. His independent discovery of utility analysis led him to reject the earlier cost-of-production emphases of classical writers such as Smith and Mill as well. What Jevons failed to recognize in his economic analysis was that supply and demand *mutually* determine prices. Fleeming Jenkin had suggested as much in 1870 or earlier, but it was Alfred Marshall (see chapter 16) who most clearly and completely set forth the co-impact of independently determined supply and demand upon price determination two decades later.

In spite of this fundamental criticism of his value theory, Jevons's decision not to formally link demand curves with marginal-utility curves has been lauded by many economists, most notably by Léon Walras (see chapter 17). As we have seen, Jevons looked forward to the day when these "functions of utility" could be empirically determined, at least in an ordinal (ranking) sense. But until that day, he was unwilling to link demand and utility functions in partial equilibrium, as Dupuit had done before him and as Marshall was to do later.

Very restrictive assumptions must be imposed for the demand curve of even a single individual to represent a utility measure (i.e., for price and marginal utility to be equated, as Dupuit did—see figure 13-4). The marginal utility of money must be held constant with respect to the prices or quantities of all other goods; goods in the consumer's budget must be assumed to be unrelated; and so forth. These conditions are not apt to be met in any real-world case, and it is to Jevons's credit that he recognized this important point.

As befits his ambivalent nature, however, Jevons erred in a related matter. Recall that he had defined a trading body as any body of buyers and sellers. We discovered in connection with his theory of exchange that Jevons presumably believed that an aggregate degree-of-utility function could be constructed in order to analyze trade. Such a construction is manifestly illegitimate, however, since it would require the summing up of different individuals' degree-of-utility functions for some good. Since incomes, tastes, and preferences vary, there is no reason to expect that the *MU*'s of these individuals would be comparable. The fact that Jevons required only ordinal ranking is of no help to him in this dilemma. An interpersonal summation of rankings would not avoid the problem.

In the final analysis Jevons's theoretical apparatus contains several ambiguities. His analysis of utility was pathbreaking, and it contains an essential key to value theory, but his performance on the microeconomic stage lacked the sophistication and the completeness of Marshall's. Still, many pioneering bits of analysis are contained in his *Theory of Political Economy*. Had he lived to complete his projected *Principles*, Jevons might have left economic science far richer; however, as it stands, his contributions to pure theory, though piecemeal, were solid. Keynes (Alfred Marshall's most renowned student) described Jevons's *Theory* as "simple, lucid, unfaltering, chiseled in stone where Marshall knits in wool" ("William Stanley Jevons," p. 284).

■ Jevons and Statistical Science

Jevons's pioneer efforts in utility analysis were more than matched by his efforts in empirical and statistical science. In 1862, after publishing early works on scientific meteorology, Jevons set out to apply scientific principles to commercial statistics.[3] He sent his first statistical paper, "On the Study of Periodic Commercial Fluctuations," to the British Association in 1862, along with his earliest theoretical paper on utility. In it Jevons analyzed variation in the following magnitudes: average rate of discount, 1845 to 1861 and 1825 to 1861; total number of bankruptcies, 1806 to 1860; average price of government bonds, 1845 to 1860; and average price of wheat, 1846 to 1861. Jevons presented his data diagrammatically, and concluded that data should be arranged in such a way as to best elucidate the most interesting aspects for the purposes of the investigator. As an early discoverer of *seasonal fluctuations*, Jevons noted:

> Every kind of periodic fluctuation, whether daily, weekly, monthly, quarterly, or yearly must be detected and exhibited, not only as a subject of study in itself, but because we must ascertain and eliminate such periodic variations before we can correctly exhibit those which are irregular or non-periodic, and probably of more interest and importance. (*Investigations*, p. 4)

Thus, Jevons offered various explanations for the seasonal fluctuations in his various data, applying the process of scientific abstraction used in his theoretical work.

Price Series and Index Numbers

One of Jevons's most important statistical papers was "A Serious Fall in the Value of Gold Ascertained and Its Social Effects Set Forth" (1863). In it Jevons applied the general proposition "that an article tends to fall in value as it is supplied

[3] Most of Jevons's statistical studies were collected after his death by his wife, Harriet, and published by his friend Foxwell. These studies can be found in Jevons's *Investigations in Currency and Finance*.

more abundantly and easily than before" to the then-recent gold discoveries in Australia and California. The French economist Michel Chevalier had predicted such a fall, but others, including William Newmarch and John Ramsay McCulloch, had doubted Chevalier's argument.

In order to understand Jevons's achievement better it must be recognized that economists of this period had only vague and ambiguous notions of what a fall in value was. Thus, Jevons had to begin with an introductory lesson in logic applied to statistics. He had to explain the meaning of an average rise of prices, and, most importantly, the method of constructing price indexes. In this latter effort, he was clearly a pathbreaker. He discussed at length the compilation of price tables, computation of arithmetic and geometric means, the problem of weighting, and the selection of the sample commodities. Then with statistics gathered from various periodicals, including *The Economist*, the *Gazette*, and *The Times*, Jevons constructed an average annual price of thirty-nine commodities for the years 1845 to 1862. After assessing the statistics and painstakingly plotting them, he concluded:

> It is hardly necessary to draw attention to the permanent elevation of prices since 1853. . . . The lowest average range of prices since 1851 has indeed happened in the last year 1862; but prices even then stood 13 percent above the average level of 1845–50. . . . *Examine the yearly average prices at any point of their fluctuations since 1852, and they stand above any point of their fluctuations before then within the scope of my tables.* There is but one way of accounting for such a fact, and that is by supposing a very considerable permanent depreciation of gold. (*Investigations*, pp. 44–45)

Jevons also discussed the depreciation of silver and the *rate* of fall in the value of gold, relating the total fall in gold value to the quantity in use.

Finally, Jevons investigated the *effects* of gold depreciation (price increase) on debtors, creditors, and various other classes. Throughout he displayed a keen practical knowledge of credit institutions and commerce. He concluded that creditors, those injured by gold depreciation, have no equitable claim to compensation, but he failed to discuss the distributional effects of gold depreciation. He recognized, however, the *indirect* effects of gold discovery, such as the creation of new colonies, the dissemination of the English people and language, and the invigoration of commerce.

Several years later, Jevons continued and expanded his statistical study of price movements in "The Variation of Prices and the Value of the Currency Since 1782," published in the *Journal of the Statistical Society of London* (June 1865). In this paper Jevons reduced data from Tooke and Newmarch's *History of Prices* into price indexes of all commodities and individual classes of commodities. He evaluated the theoretical foundations of all commonly used price indexes, favoring the geometric mean over the arithmetic mean and the harmonic mean. On the merit of these alternative calculations, Jevons observed, "It is probable that each of these is right for its own purposes when these are more clearly understood in theory" (*Investigations*, p. 114). The geometric mean presented some calculational advantages, such as the ability to correct results by the continual use of logarithms. Also, Jevons wanted a ratio that would *underestimate* variations by comparison with the arithmetic mean.

As in his previous paper, Jevons meticulously explained his construction of the index from Tooke's data, including methods for "correcting" the data over various intervals and for the classifications of commodities. For example, the price data between 1800 and 1820 had to be corrected to reduce prices and their variations to a gold standard, because the Bank of England sponsored a paper standard during this period (see chapter 6). The quality of Jevons's study, in short, was extremely high, and the results, multiple price indexes between 1782 and 1865, mark the most important early attempt at systematic price indexing in economic literature. Jevons's instinct for order and his readiness to raise questions concerning the quality of his raw data and his statistical methods make his contributions to price-index construction not only above the level of his time but considerably ahead of his time.

Sunspots and Commercial Activity

Jevons's romance with statistical investigations carried him to the most fanciful and, ultimately, the most ridiculed idea of his life—the explanation of commercial crises on the basis of the periodic alteration of spots on the sun. The "sunspot theory" integrated Jevons's earlier work on prices with his lifelong interest in astronomical and meteorological phenomena. In "The Solar Period and the Price of Corn" (1875), he put the matter succinctly:

> If the planets govern the sun, and the sun governs the vintages and harvests, and thus the prices of food and raw materials and the state of the money market, it follows that the configurations of the planets may prove to be the remote causes of the greatest commercial disasters. (*Investigations*, p. 185)

From his meteorological research Jevons initially calculated the length of the sunspot cycle at 11.11 years. Parts of James E. Thorold Rogers's great work, *A History of Agriculture and Prices in England*, had begun to appear, giving Jevons a source of raw data. But in 1875, Jevons was not convinced that the information he had in hand justified a firm belief in a causal relation between sunspots and commercial activity. Still, in noting that the electric telegraph was a favorite dream of sixteenth- and seventeenth-century physicists, Jevons pointed out:

> It would be equally curious if the pseudo-science of astrology should, in like manner, foreshadow the triumphs which precise and methodical investigations may yet disclose, as to the obscure periodic causes affecting our welfare when we are least aware of it. (*Investigations*, p. 186)

In 1878 Jevons returned to the subject of sunspots with renewed vigor, first in a paper to the British Association ("The Periodicity of Commercial Crises and Its Physical Explanation") and then in an article in *Nature* ("Commercial Crises and Sun-Spots"). At this time Jevons was convinced by new evidence that the duration of the sunspot cycle was 10.44 years instead of 11.11, a dating that more closely correlated with the commercial cycle of crises. The coincidence was just too much for Jevons, and he leaped to a conclusion:

> I can see no reason why the human mind, in its own spontaneous action, should select a period of just 10.44 years to vary in. Surely we must go beyond the mind to its industrial environment. Merchants and bankers are continually influenced in their dealings by accounts of the success of harvests, the comparative abundance or scarcity of goods; and when we know that there is a cause, the variation of the solar activity, which is just of the nature to affect the produce of agriculture, and which does vary in the same period, it becomes almost certain that the two series of phenomena, credit cycles and solar variations, are connected as effect and cause. (*Investigations*, p. 196)

Did Jevons allow mere coincidence to drag him into an untenable and rigid position? How were alterations in harvests *transmitted* into commercial cycles? Although he had dealt with European experience in the earlier paper, Jevons now argued that the impact on money and commercial markets in England was exerted through foreign trade with India and the Orient. Periodic crises in Indian harvests would alter prices of raw produce and the nature of England's trade balance. In his 1875 paper, Jevons had emphasized the "psychic" determinants—optimism, despondency, panic, and so forth—of the trade cycle, and he had tried to relate them to oscillations in the price of food. Now Jevons abandoned these psychic effects in explaining the "transmission mechanism" and emphasized merely the *coincidence* of high prices in India and commercial crises in England. But Jevons admitted the major problem with such an argument: that if the cause of commercial crises in England was the high price of agricultural produce in India, a lag between high prices and crises would be expected or even required. None could be observed. In short, some explanation of the relation or transmission was needed, but Jevons offered none. The theory he deduced from his study of the available data was simply incomplete. Astronomers returned to an 11.11–year sunspot cycle, moreover, and while the idea probably had some merit in primarily agrarian societies, it is now believed that the determinants of the trade cycle are far more complex than Jevons (or other early writers) thought.[4]

In spite of the "sunspot episode," Jevons's overall statistical work deserves very high marks. The scientific spirit manifest in the attempt to discuss the causes of economic phenomena permeates Jevons's empirical work, and his study of price series will forever stand as a monument and as an example to those concerned with economics and empiricism. In fact, Jevons is recognized as one of the spiritual forefathers of nonprobabilistic econometrics.

■ Jevons and the International Spread of Economic Ideas

Jevons's contributions to economic theory and statistics are almost matched by his role in the *spread* of economic analysis. Seldom has a writer been more generous in acknowledging the priority of other writers, both previous and contemporary. In May of 1874 a correspondence began between Jevons and the French economic theorist Léon Walras (see chapter 17). Walras published his *Elements of Political Economy* in that year, setting out a framework of utility and general equilibrium analysis. In the interest of propagating his ideas, Walras initiated a monumental correspondence with a large number of economists from all over the world. The result of that correspondence, among other mutual benefits, was the establishment of a list of "mathematico-economic" works drawn up by Jevons and later amended by Walras. In his preface to the second edition of his *Theory of Political Economy*, Jevons described this list:

> With the progress of years, however, my knowledge of the literature of political economy has been much widened, and the hints of friends and correspondents have made me aware of the existence of many remarkable works which more or less anticipate the views stated in this book. While preparing this new edition, it occurred to me to attempt the discovery of all existing writings of the kind. With this view I drew up a chronological list of all the mathematico-economic works known to me, already about seventy in number, which list, by the kindness of the editor, Mr. Giffen, was printed in the *Journal of the London Statistical Society* for June 1878. (p. xix)

[4] It is interesting to note here that another famous scientist, Newton, spent years trying to convert base metals into gold, a process known as alchemy.

Jevons forwarded this list to all the leading economists of the time, and Walras had it published in Paris in the *Journal des Économistes*.

Jevons used his 1879 preface to promote his confidence in the mathematical approach to economic analysis; and for this reason he brought to the attention of other economists the theoretical efforts of Cournot, Dupuit, Ellet, Gossen, Auguste and Léon Walras, von Thünen, Jenkin, and Lardner, together with a host of other lesser-known writers, such as Beccaria, Lang, Bordas, Minard, and Boccardo. Many of these writers remain virtually unknown today, and some deservedly so, but at the seed time of neoclassical analysis, the recognition and critical evaluation of the work of other theorists were of profound importance.

In the process of classifying and identifying earlier writings, Jevons realized and admitted that his own work was not very original. Cournot had pioneered in mathematical expression; Cournot, Lardner, and Dupuit established the theory of the firm; and Dupuit and Gossen discovered utility theory, the latter going so far as to establish clearly the equimarginal principle. But in spite of the obvious disappointment Jevons must have felt on making these discoveries, he graciously recognized and honored those he considered his predecessors, however small the prior contributions might have been. In doing so, he set a sterling example of what a scholar should be, and at the same time he encouraged an open-door policy on economic ideas, which eventually enriched the neoclassical tradition in England and elsewhere.[5]

■ John Bates Clark and Marginalism in America

American economic theory in the nineteenth century generally lagged behind that of England and Europe. In 1880, the British economist T. E. Cliffe-Leslie observed that "American political economy is in the main an importation from Europe, not an original development" (in Hollander's *Economic Essays*, p. 2). But in the years following Leslie's remark, a group of able young scholars returned from post-graduate study in German universities and sparked a new awakening in American economic thought. Among these young scholars was John Bates Clark (1847–1938), who, prior to traveling to Germany and studying under Karl Knies, graduated from Amherst College in 1875. On his return, Clark taught economics, history, and other subjects at Carleton, Smith, and Amherst Colleges and Johns Hopkins University. In 1895, he obtained a position as a professor of political science at Columbia University, where he was also editor of *Political Science Quarterly*.

The young American scholars returning from Germany were inclined toward the historical, inductive method of the German historical school (see chapter 11). Consequently, they aimed their investigative efforts at concrete problems. Among other matters, they considered American protectionism, fiscal studies, the labor movement, the development of transportation, and public finance. Clark was an exception, however. His mind was more inclined toward deductive reasoning. While his colleagues were collecting and interpreting statistics on economic and social problems, Clark systematically thought his way through mass and detail. The result was a stellar contribution to economic theory and a unified philosophy that had hitherto been absent from American economic thought. Jacob Hollander paid tribute:

[5] T. W. Hutchison, in an interesting paper on the international flow of ideas, "Insularity and Cosmopolitanism in Economic Ideas" (see references), suggests that this new door was slammed shut in England mainly by the hegemony and dominance of Marshall's *Principles*. After 1890, in other words, insularity, if not downright chauvinism, again characterized British economic thought.

> Clark began his systematic work at a time when Roscher and Jevons, from quite different directions, had given shattering blows to the classical theory. Even after a quieting interval, the effect of the impact was to revive in acute form the old opposition in economic approach, extending as far back as the controversies of Malthus and Ricardo. . . . Marshall [see chapter 16] in England and Clark in the United States adjusted the situation in fine spirit of scientific continuity. (*Economic Essays*, p. 5)

Clark's economic analysis was essentially static, although it was he who introduced the division of "statics" and "dynamics" into economics, thereby giving future economists a convenient taxonomy to partition their work. Clark himself hoped to further the development of economic dynamics, but unfortunately he got no further than comparative statics. His (static) system of theory was based on five postulates that, taken together, ally him with the philosophy of utilitarianism and also bind him to a fairly rigid set of assumptions. His five postulates (reproduced here from Homan, *Contemporary Economic Thought*, pp. 35–36) are:

1. Private property is a basic social institution.
2. Individual freedom of activity operates through active competition in all gainful pursuits.
3. Government interferes in the economy only for the protection of property, enforcement of contracts, and maintenance of competition.
4. Capital and labor are freely mobile.
5. Economic activity is motivated by man's attempt to satisfy wants.

The Marginal-Utility Theory of Value

Clark's mature views on value and distribution are contained in *The Distribution of Wealth* (1899), although he formulated his marginal-productivity theory ten years earlier. His theory of value, based on the primacy of the marginal-utility principle, dates back to a series of articles and monographs appearing between 1877 and 1882. This series was eventually published in 1886 as *The Philosophy of Wealth*. In his private correspondence, Clark admitted that his theory of value was essentially the same as Jevons's, although he approached the problem from a different angle and worked independently of the earlier marginalists. In comparing his own theoretical advances to Jevons's, Clark observed:

> The Jevons theory assumes that increments of some commodity are offered in succession to a consumer and that, as his desire for them is gradually satiated, he attaches less and less importance to them, and the last or "final" increment consumed is the one that figures in the adjustment of values. I had not myself made use of just this supposition, but had thought of the consumer as measuring the importance to himself of different articles already in his possession and adjusting his purchases in such a way that articles of the same cost have the same "effective utility" to him and this may be measured, either by working to replace one that is worn out or lost, or by going without it and measuring the reaction on his enjoyments so occasioned. It amounted to a final utility theory, but was cast in a somewhat different form. (in Dorfman, *Economic Mind*, Appendix, p. iii)

Clark did, however, expand the marginalist theory of value by considering the effects of *qualitative* increments rather than merely quantitative increments in consumers' goods and in producers' goods. In an analysis that is reminiscent of Dupuit (see chapter 13), he contended that most economic goods and services are not simple utilities but "bundles of utilities." Each good is made up, in other words, of a composition of different elements, one or more of which enter into the purchaser's preference pattern. The following passage elaborates:

> What a man does, as his means increase, is, before anything else, to demand new qualities in the articles that he uses. Often he does not add at all to their number; but he causes them to be made of finer material or to be larger and handsomer. He adds to his wealth for consumption, not new things, but new utilities; and these are mainly attached to things of the kind formerly consumed. . . . The literal effect of spending his last dollar consists in the substituting of a good article for the cheap one, with which he would have contented himself if his available means had been smaller. (*Distribution of Wealth*, p. 214)

This view is one of Clark's most important insights, because it goes further than the earlier theories of marginal utility in singling out the "proper" increment that adjusts value. In essence, Clark focuses on how price is determined by increments within increments. The last increment of a good does not alone determine price in every instance, but an increment of quality in that incremental good usually does. Secondly, and perhaps most presciently, Clark recognizes that goods possess multiple qualities, and in different proportions. Driving an old heap of a car might provide basic transportation, but driving a new Jaguar or Mercedes provides transportation plus prestige, status, and so forth. Some contemporary microeconomists, such as Kelvin Lancaster (see chapter 26), have built consumer theory around the fact that individuals do not demand market goods per se, but rather the characteristics and attributes provided by market goods. Additionally, Clark seemed to be teetering on the brink of a statement of the role of product differentiation in the theory of price. However, he didn't go that far, and economics waited for many decades for the pivotal importance of product differentiation and the "demand for qualities" to become a part of microeconomic theory.

The Marginal-Productivity Theory of Distribution

Ricardo provided the first great economic treatise on income distribution, and in it, he established the theory of land rent based on the marginal productivity of land. Ricardo's theory maintains that land rent is determined by the productivity of the last unit of land in cultivation (see chapter 7). Therefore, he might be considered an "incumbent marginalist," in possession of a vital principle, but not fully aware of its possibilities. Oddly enough, despite all the feverish activity of a so-called "marginal revolution" in value theory around 1870, economists were extremely slow in generalizing the marginalism inherent in Ricardo's rent theory to factors of production other than land. Clark deserves credit for correcting this oversight, although he shares that credit with Philip Wicksteed (1884–1927), an Englishman, and Knut Wicksell (1851–1926), a Swede. These three showed that wages and interest are likewise determined by the same principle as Ricardo's rent, whereas the fourth factor payment, profit, generally disappears under conditions of pure competition.[6]

Throughout *The Distribution of Wealth*, Clark affirmed and reaffirmed the principle that final productivity is the regulator of the value of each factor of production. For example, in chapter 7 of that work he observed that marginal workers set the

[6] Clark defined "profit" as a residual income (i.e., the remaining share after rent, interest, and wages are paid). His definition is synonymous with the modern concept of pure profit, which, of course, is driven to zero under conditions of free and open competition. Normal profits, in Clark's view, were simply another form of wage and therefore would be included in labor's share of total income.

standard for wages, just as marginal bushels of wheat set the standard for the value of the total crop. In chapter 8 of *Distribution* he explained why competition produces this result:

> It is by assuming perfectly free competition among employers that we are able to say that the man on the intensive margin of an agricultural force of laborers will get, as pay, the value of his product. When such a man offers himself to an employer, he is virtually offering an addition to the farmer's crop. If one farmer will not pay the market price of the additional produce, another will pay it, provided that competition does its work quite perfectly. (*Distribution of Wealth*, pp. 99–100)

Clark also assumed a homogeneous workforce and active competition among workers for jobs, so that the wage received by one worker of a given type would be the same as that received by all workers of the same type. He extended the same principle of marginal productivity to capital and to land as well.

Using Clark's principle of factor-price determination, we may now show graphically the distribution of total product between rent and wages, when land is fixed in supply. Since we are limited to two dimensions in the following figure, assume that land and labor are the *only* two productive factors in use. In figure 15-4, let *BC* represent the marginal product of land, and *AD* the number of laborers added to land. *BC* is downward-sloping because of the law of diminishing returns. The area under the marginal-product curve represents total product (*ABCD*).

To Ricardo, rent was a differential surplus. In figure 15-4, rent may be identified as the difference between the value of the total product (*ABCD*) and the share of total product going to labor. Since each laborer receives the value of the last worker's marginal product as his wage (that is, *CD*), the total wage bill is *AECD*. Thus, the differential surplus, called "rent," is equal to *EBC*. This is derived as follows: Value of total product *ABCD* minus payments to labor *AECD*, so that *ABCD* – *AECD* = *EBC*, or rent.

Clark recognized that the returns to labor and to capital could also be expressed as a differential surplus. In figure 15-5, for example, let *BC* be the mar-

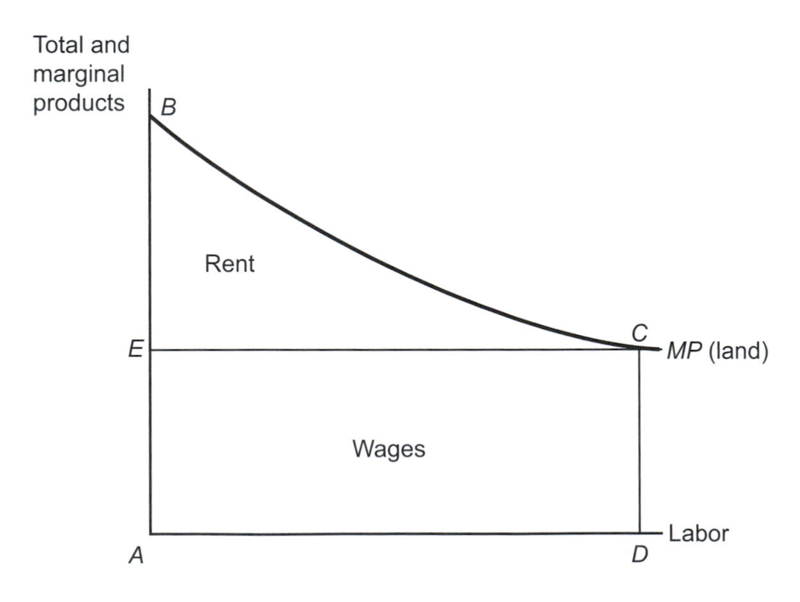

Figure 15-4 Rent is the differential return when labor and land are the only two factors in use and units of labor are added to production.

ginal product of capital instead of land. Once again the wage bill for *AD* workers will be *AECD*, and *EBC* will now be the differential surplus that goes to capital in the form of interest. Finally, in figure 15-6, let *BC* be the marginal product of labor, and *AD* the number of capital inputs in production. According to Clark's marginal-productivity theory of factor returns, each capital input will receive *CD* as payment. The total return to capital in the form of interest will therefore be *AECD*, with labor receiving the differential surplus *EBC*. In other words, the same principle of marginal productivity determines each factor return.

In this way, Clark succeeded in integrating the theory of distribution with the theory of value. He established the fact that the same marginal principle is perfectly capable of explaining the valuation of goods and of factors. The Austrians, it will be

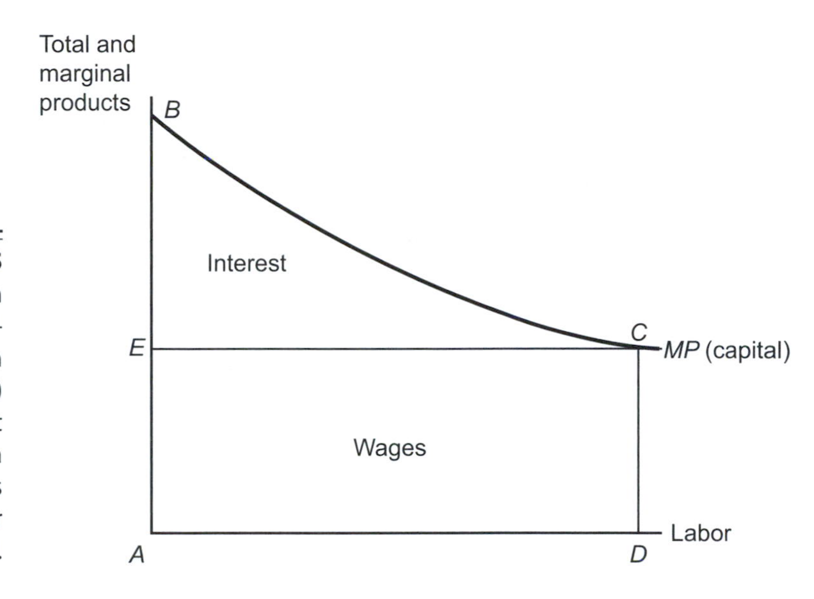

Figure 15-5 Interest, the return to capital, is the difference between total product (*ABCD*) and the amount paid to labor when production inputs are limited to labor and capital.

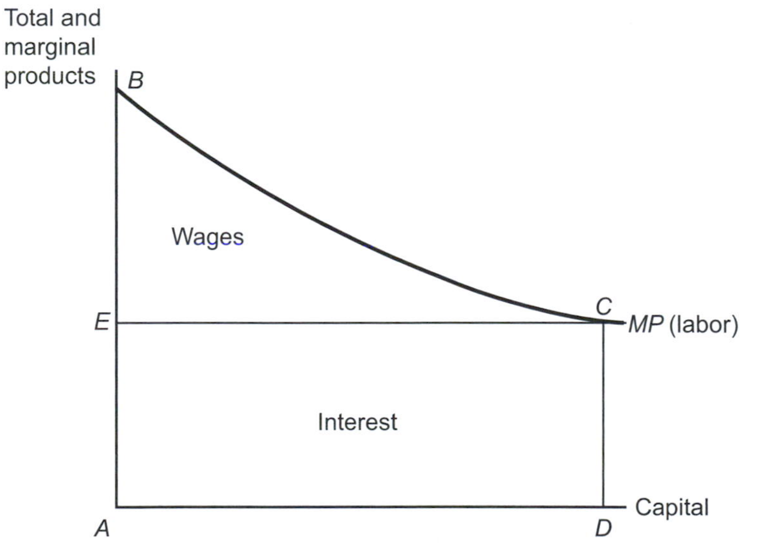

Figure 15-6 If *BC* is the marginal product of labor and *AD* is the number of capital units used in production, wages may be calculated as the difference between total product at *AD* and the cost of capital.

remembered, especially Menger and Wieser, had taken the first step toward such integration with their theories on imputation (see chapter 14). The imputation principle was a straightforward extension of Menger's subjective value theory insofar as the value of higher-order goods was attributed to the contribution made by those goods to consumer utility.

By contrast, in Clark's analysis marginal-productivity theory is an extension of the Ricardian rent principle. It asserts that the value of each factor in production is determined by its marginal contribution to total output. It is based on the principle of diminishing returns and a full recognition that *any* factor, not just land, may be the fixed factor.

■ Assessing Clark's Contribution

Clark's principle of marginal productivity is useful in explaining employment decisions by an individual competitive firm, but as a theory of factor-price determination it leaves something to be desired. It is not a supply-and-demand theory of price. In fact, its independence from considerations of supply and demand constitutes a major weakness. As microeconomic theory, the principle of marginal productivity explains that a competitive firm will hire factors up to the point where each factor's marginal product is just equal to its income payment. But in so doing, the theory accepts the supply of the named factor as given. It does not relate the price of the factor to supply; nor does it relate the price of the factor to the demand for goods. The Austrians, at least, were on the right track in this respect because their theory of imputation recognized the interdependence between product demand and factor demand. By itself, therefore, the marginal-productivity principle is not a satisfactory explanation of factor price.

In addition, Clark worked out his theory under purely static, competitive conditions where uncertainty and risk are absent. In 1921, another American, Frank Knight, offered an alternative explanation of factor pricing under conditions of uncertainty. Knight maintained that uncertainty on the part of the entrepreneur about the demand for and price of his product induces him to hire factors of production on the basis of the *expected value* rather than actual value of each factor's marginal product. While Knight's argument is not a criticism of Clark per se, it nevertheless underscores the limited applicability of the marginal productivity principle in its naive formulation.

Inexplicably, Clark chose to wrap his marginal-productivity theory in normative clothing. He implied in no uncertain terms that there is something inherently just in each factor's receiving no more and no less than the value of its marginal product. As a result, he used the marginal-productivity theory to justify income distribution under competition. Clark was severely criticized for injecting ethical principles into his theory, and even his son, John Maurice Clark—an eminent economist in his own right—rejected this part of the theory while defending the core principle of marginal-productivity. However, Clark's normative judgments need not detain us here, since they are in no way central to the theoretical principle he established.

■ Clark on Entrepreneurship

Having studied in Germany, Clark was familiar with Mangoldt's work and accepted the idea that "men do not hazard their capital for an amount of annual gains that in a long term of years will just offset their losses. They demand more than this and they get it" ("Insurance," p. 45). However, Clark refused to accept that risk-bearing is part of the entrepreneurial function, arguing (as Schumpeter did at a later date) that all risk is borne by the capitalist. Clark used the term entrepreneur "in an unusually strict sense, to designate the man who coordinates capital and labor without in his own proper capacity furnishing either of them." It was his view that "the entrepreneur, as such, is empty-handed," a phrase evocative of Israel Kirzner's (chapter 23) "pure and penniless entrepreneur" ("Insurance," pp. 45–46). In other words, the entrepreneur cannot risk anything because he has nothing to risk.

In later works, Clark couched his discussion in terms of statics and dynamics, giving support to the distinction that inclined Schumpeter (chapter 23) to a more dynamic view of entrepreneurship. In Clark's analysis the static state is a situation where demand, capital, and technology are given. Static conditions do change over time, however: populations grow, wants change, and improved production technologies are discovered and implemented. But in Clark's world, departures from static-state equilibria are evolutionary. The mobility of labor and capital is requisite to the restoration of new, albeit temporary, equilibria.

In the dynamic economy Clark made the entrepreneur responsible for the coordination that restores the economy to an equilibrium position.[7] According to Clark (*Essentials*, pp. 82–83), this coordinator (entrepreneur) may perform several functions: "He may, for example, both labor and furnish capital, and he may, further, perform a special coordinating function which is not labor, in the technical sense, and scarcely involves any continuous personal activity at all, but is essential for rendering labor and capital productive." This notion of the entrepreneur as the dynamic force that moves the economy back to equilibrium after some disturbance is still very much alive in contemporary theory, but it was challenged in the twentieth century by Schumpeter's counter claim that the entrepreneur is the agent that *causes* disequilibrium. On the related matter of insurance, Clark recognized the differences between insurable and uninsurable risks (which he termed "static" and "dynamic"), but he did not go so far as to integrate this distinction into a general theory that based profit on risk as well as dynamic change. That task fell onto the shoulders of Frank Knight.

Despite its shortcomings, Clark's contribution was substantial, particularly on the American scene, where he rose to prominence as the leading economic theorist of his day. As such, he provided inspiration and leadership to a growing cadre of competent American economists. He was active in forming the American Economic Association in 1885, and he served as its third president. Even at this late date, John Bates Clark is one of the most honored and revered of early American economists.[8] He provided a powerful impetus to the eventual acceptance of marginalism, lending support in the Anglo-Saxon world to Jevons's pioneering contributions.

[7] On the deficiencies of the argument that the entrepreneur is a mere coordinator, see Hawley (1900, pp. 84–89).

[8] The John Bates Clark Award, given every other year to the most distinguished economist under 40 years of age, is granted by the American Economic Association. Clark was also blessed with brilliant students—Thorstein Veblen, for example (see chapter 19). The fact that Veblen rejected the type of economic inquiry that Clark helped advance did not lessen the sense of pride Clark felt in his prize pupil.

■ CONCLUSION

The prescient insights of Jevons and J. B. Clark (joined by a chorus of insights from Cournot, Dupuit, von Thünen, Menger, and others in Europe) set the stage for a growing consensus of what constituted economic theory. Multiple and diverse elements constituted the expansive, multifaceted body of microeconomics. Utility theory as a basis for consumer behavior, productivity theory as the foundation for a generalized theory of rent, and marginalism as the glue to hold it all together, were the necessary elements for the construction of a holistic partial equilibrium analysis by Alfred Marshall and general equilibrium theory by Léon Walras. Importantly, the neoclassical paradigm, one that remains a guide to economic investigation, did not arrive in a neat package as the contribution of a single individual. It was, as most advancement in human thought, the product and evolution of many minds. It is also useful to remember that the evolution of economic ideas did not end with neoclassical economics but continues as a process that builds on a fruitful and complex past.

REFERENCES

Clark, J. B. "Insurance and Business Profits," *Quarterly Journal of Economics*, vol. 7 (October 1892), pp. 45–54.

———. *The Distribution of Wealth*. New York: Macmillan, 1899.

———. *Essentials of Economic Theory*. New York: Macmillan, 1907.

Dorfman, Joseph. *The Economic Mind in American Civilization*, vol. 3. New York: The Viking Press, 1949.

Hawley, F. B. "Enterprise and Profit," *Quarterly Journal of Economics*, vol. 15 (November 1900), pp. 75–105.

Hollander, J. H. (ed.). *Economic Essays Contributed in Honor of John Bates Clark*. New York: The Macmillan Company, 1927.

Homan, Paul T. *Contemporary Economic Thought*. New York: Harper, 1928.

Hutchison, T. W. "Insularity and Cosmopolitanism in Economic Ideas, 1870–1914," *American Economic Review*, vol. 45 (May 1955), pp. 1–16.

Jenkin, Fleeming. "The Graphic Representation of the Laws of Supply and Demand, and Their Application to Labour," in *The Graphic Representation of the Laws of Supply and Demand, and Other Essays on Political Economy, 1868–1884*. London: London School of Economics and Political Science, 1931 [1870].

Jevons, W. S. *Theory of Political Economy*. New York: Kelley and Millman, 1957 [1871].

———. *Theory of Political Economy*, 2d ed. New York: Kelley and Millman, 1879.

———. *Letters and Journal*, H. A. Jevons (ed.). London: Macmillan, 1886.

———. *Investigations in Currency and Finance*, H. S. Foxwell (ed.). London: Macmillan, 1909.

Keynes, J. M. "William Stanley Jevons, 1835–1882: A Centenary Allocution on His Life as Economist and Statistician," *Essays in Biography* (New York: W. W. Norton, 1963). Originally published in *Journal of the Royal Statistical Society*, vol. 99 (1936), pp. 516–548.

Lardner, Dionysius. *Railway Economy*. New York: A. M. Kelley, 1968 [1850].

NOTES FOR FURTHER READING

Bert Mosselmans, *William Stanley Jevons and the Cutting Edge of Economics* (London: Routledge, 2006), attempts to situate Jevons within the history of economic thought in relation to his logic, ethics, religion, and aesthetics. But perhaps the best source on Jevons is Jevons himself. Few economists have led more interesting, albeit truncated, lives. Furthermore, Jevons had few peers as an observer of life and a commentator on ideas. His *Letters and Journal*, capably edited by his wife, Harriet, is a must in gaining an appreciation of Jevons's incisive views on every conceivable subject from himself to science, music, statistics, political economy, and a multitude of other topics. In letters to his sister Lucy, his brother Herbert, and many others, Jevons chronicled his sojourn in Australia and his travels to the United States in 1859. These letters also tell of his growing interest in social science and of his decision to apply mathematics to economics. His life and entire career are laid bare in his correspondence with members of his family and with other economists, including his friends H. S. Foxwell and Léon Walras. For a look at Jevons through his personal correspondence, see R. D. C. Black (ed.), *Papers and Correspondence of William Stanley Jevons*, (New York: A. M. Kelley, 1977). Additional biographical material is contained in H. W. Jevons, "William Stanley Jevons: His Life," *Econometrica*, vol. 2 (July 1934), pp. 225–231; and H. S. Jevons, "William Stanley Jevons: His Scientific Contributions," *Econometrica*, vol. 2 (July 1934), pp. 231–237.

Jevons's *Theory of Political Economy*, *Coal Question*, and *Investigations in Currency and Finance* are indispensable in reconstructing his contributions to economic theory and statistics. His theories of labor, capital, rent, and interest are forthrightly analyzed by G. J. Stigler in *Production and Distribution Theories: The Formative Period* (New York: Macmillan, 1941). On Jevons's methodology, see his trenchant essay entitled "Economic Policy," read before Section F (on statistics) of the British Association for the Advancement of Science, reprinted in R. L. Smyth (ed.), *Essays in Economic Method* (New York: McGraw-Hill, 1962).

Jevons's debt to Bentham and the means by which Bentham's notion of utility was transmitted into neoclassical economics are discussed by Tom Warke, "Mathematical Fitness in the Evolution of the Utility Concept from Bentham to Jevons to Marshall," *Journal of the History of Economic Thought*, vol. 22 (March 2000), pp. 5–27. Rhead S. Bowman, "Jevons's Economic Theory in Relation to Social Change and Public Policy," *Journal of Economic Issues*, vol. 23 (December 1989), pp. 1123–1147, explores the intersection between Jevons's ideas on theory and policy, emphasizing Jevons's view of economics as social ethics. In a second article, "Policy Implications of W. S. Jevons's Economic Theory," *Journal of the History of Economic Thought*, vol. 19 (Fall 1997), pp. 196–221, Bowman concludes that Jevons believed that he had essentially established the theoretical foundation for public-sector analysis. Sandra J. Peart, "W. S. Jevons's Methodology of Economics: Some Implications of the Procedures for 'Inductive Quantification,'" *History of Political Economy*, vol. 25 (Fall 1993), pp. 435–460, probes Jevons's views on determinism and the connection of his methodology to Mill's. For a more comprehensive study, see same author, *The Economics of W. S. Jevons* (London: Routledge, 1996).

J. M. Keynes, "William Stanley Jevons, 1835–1882," written on the occasion of the centennial of Jevons's birth and reprinted in Keynes's *Essays in Biography* (London: Macmillan, 1933), provides penetrating insights into Jevons's life and talents. See also Lionel Robbins, "The Place of Jevons in the History of Economic Thought," *The Manchester School of Economics and Social Studies*, vol. 7 (1936), pp. 1–17; and R. D. C. Black, "W. S. Jevons and the Foundation of Modern Economics," *History of Political Economy*, vol. 4 (Fall 1972), pp. 364–378. Also by Black, see "Jevons, Marginalism and Manchester," *The Manchester School of Economics and Social Studies*, vol. 40 (March 1972), pp. 2–8. This entire issue of *The Manchester School* contains a compendium of papers devoted to Jevons on the 100th anniversary of the publication of his *Theory of Political Economy.*

John Creedy, "Jevons's Complex Cases in the Theory of Exchange," *Journal of the History of Economic Thought*, vol. 14 (Spring 1992), pp. 55–69, extends Jevons's simple case of two trading bodies to the more complex case of three traders and three goods. On a narrower topic, the affiliation of Jevons and the eminent astronomer George Darwin, see K. H. Hennings, "George Darwin, Jevons and the Rate of Interest," *History of Political Economy*, vol. 11 (Summer 1979), pp. 199–212. The affinity between Jevons and Böhm-Bawerk regarding interest and capital theory is explored by Klaus Hamberger, "Böhm-Bawerk, Jevons and the 'Austrian' Theory of Capital: 'A Quite Different Relation,'" *The European Journal of the History of Economic Thought*, vol. 8 (Spring 2001), pp. 42–57.

The academic and intellectual milieu in England before and after Jevons is the subject of discussion by S. G. Checkland, "Economic Opinion in England as Jevons Found It," *The Manchester School of Economics and Social Studies*, vol. 19 (May 1951), pp. 143–169; N. B. deMarchi, "The Noxious Influence of Authority: A Correction of Jevons's Charge," *Journal of Law & Economics*, vol. 16 (April 1973), pp. 179–190; and T. W. Hutchison, "The Marginal Revolution and the Decline and Fall of English Classical Political Economy," *History of Political Economy*, vol. 4 (Fall 1972), pp. 442–468. Ian Steedman, "Jevons's *Theory of Political Economy* and the 'Marginalist Revolution,'" *The European Journal of the History of Economic Thought*, vol. 4 (Spring 1997), pp. 43–64, attempts to put Jevons's main economic treatise within the context of the marginalist revolution.

Cournot's influence on Jevons's theory of demand is raised by Sam Bostaph and Y. N. Shieh in "W. S. Jevons and Lardner's *Railway Economy*," *History of Political Economy*, vol. 18 (Spring 1986), pp. 49–64, which also serves as an excellent introduction to Lardner's work. The same authors further amplify this theme in "Jevons's Demand Curve," *History of Political Economy*, vol. 19 (Spring 1987), pp. 107–126, which contrasts Jevons's performance with that of Fleeming Jenkin. Finally, an alternative interpretation of Jevons's formulation of value theory is given by R. B. Ekelund, Jr., and Yeung-Nan Shieh in "Jevons on Utility, Exchange, and Demand: A Reassessment," *Manchester School of Economics and Social Studies*, vol. 57 (March 1989), pp. 17–33. Ekelund and Shieh argue that Jevons worked out certain partial and general equilibrium concepts independently of Marshall and Walras and that he was far more creative in both of these areas than is commonly thought. Michael V. White, "Strange Brew: The Antinomies of Distribution in W. S. Jevons' *Theory of Political Economy*," *The European Journal of the History of Economic Thought*, vol. 2, (Fall, 2005), pp. 583–608, tries to explain why Jevons abandoned much of his explanatory framework in the second edition of his *Theory*. Same author, "In the Lobby of the Energy Hotel: Jevons's Formulation of the Postclassical 'Economic Problem,'" *History of Political Economy*, vol. 36 (Summer 2004), pp. 227–271 argues that the key contours of Jevons's theory of value and distribution can be reformulated in terms of the conservation of energy.

Jevons's mathematical approach to microeconomic theory originally met with stiff resistance. Margaret Schabas, "Some Reactions to Jevons' Mathematical Program: The Case of Cairnes and Mill," *History of Political Economy*, vol. 17 (Fall 1985), pp. 337–354, maintains that Cairnes and Mill first stood together against the use of mathematics in economic theory but eventually came around to Jevons's position. The same author presents a more in-depth study of Jevons's contributions to mathematical economics in *A World Ruled by Number: William Stanley Jevons and the Rise of Mathematical Economics* (Princeton, NJ: Princeton University Press, 1990), which details how Jevons parlayed beginning studies on logic into economics and the prominence he gave to inductive inference and probability in his theory. Jevons's early and skillful attempts to introduce statistical techniques to economic analysis are appraised by John Aldrich, "Jevons as Statistician: The Role of Probability," *Manchester School of Economics and Social Studies*, vol. 55 (September 1987), pp. 233–256, who concludes that although Jevons did not contribute materially to the development of theoretical statistics per se, he set the pattern for the economist as consumer of statistical techniques.

One of the few authors to take Jevons's sunspot theory seriously, S. J. Peart, "Sunspots and Expectations: W. S. Jevons's Theory of Economic Fluctuations," *Journal of the*

History of Economic Thought, vol. 13 (Fall 1991), pp. 243–265, concludes that periodicity, not meteorology, was the central issue of Jevons's concern, and that the transmission mechanism (from sunspots to economic cycles) is more sophisticated than Jevons's critics realize.

For an assessment of J. B. Clark by his economist son, see John Maurice Clark, "John Bates Clark," *International Encyclopedia of the Social Sciences*, vol. 2 (New York: Macmillan, 1968). For an older appraisal, see J. M. Clark's article on J. B. Clark in H. W. Spiegel (ed.), *The Development of Economic Thought* (New York: John Wiley & Sons, 1952). See also A. H. Clark and J. M. Clark, *John Bates Clark: A Memorial* (New York: Columbia University Press, 1938). The standard reference on Clark's marginal-productivity theory is G. J. Stigler, *Production and Distribution Theories* (New York: Macmillan, 1941). Frank Knight offered criticism and alternative formulations in *Risk, Uncertainty and Profit* (New York: Harper & Row, 1965 [1921]). Four letters from Alfred Marshall to J. B. Clark, expressing Marshall's admiration for the American's work, appear in Alfred Marshall, *Memorials of Alfred Marshall*, A. C. Pigou, ed. (New York: A. M. Kelley, 1966), pp. 412–418.

Until recently Clark was pretty much ignored by historians of economics. Making partial amends for this neglect are: John Henry, *John Bates Clark: The Making of a Neoclassical Economist* (New York: St. Martin's Press, 1995); Mary Morgan, "Marketplace Morals and the American Economists: The Case of John Bates Clark," in *Higgling: Transactors and Their Markets in the History of Economics*, Neil de Marchi and Mary Morgan (eds.), *History of Political Economy*, vol. 26 (1994) Supplement, pp. 229–252; Joseph Persky, "The Neoclassical Advent: American Economics at the Dawn of the 20th Century," *Journal of Economic Perspectives*, vol. 14 (Winter 2000), pp. 95–108; and Thomas C. Leonard, "Clark as a Pioneering Neoclassical Economist," *History of Political Economy*, vol. 35 (Fall 2003), pp. 521–558.

16

Alfred Marshall and the Neoclassical Synthesis

The foundations of neoclassical economics were clearly established in England and Europe by 1870, as the abundance of evidence presented in the last three chapters suggests. But the consolidation of piecemeal efforts to replace classical economics was not yet at hand until the nineteenth century neared its end. It was then that the seminal and cohesive works of Alfred Marshall (1842–1924) and Léon Walras (1834–1910)—the twin founders of modern neoclassical analysis—made their impact. Fundamental differences in the scope and method in the approach of these two writers are detailed in the following chapters and will help to place each in perspective. Since there is a clear progression between the ideas of Jevons and Marshall, however, we begin our discussion of neoclassicism with Marshall, and follow it in the next chapter with Walras.

Alfred Marshall was born in Clapham, England, in 1842. Many of his ancestors were clerics, and Alfred's father, William, though a career banker, wanted his son to follow in the ancestral tradition. William Marshall was a stern disciplinarian who often pushed his intelligent though overworked son to his mental and physical limits. It was not at all uncommon for him to drill young Alfred on his schoolwork until almost midnight. Later, Alfred recalled that only annual summer visits to a distant aunt saved him in his youth from mental and physical exhaustion. At prep school Marshall acquired the name "Tallow Candles" for his pallor, ill dress, and overwrought appearance. He did not make friends easily, and his two most enjoyable intellectual pursuits—mathematics and chess—were forbidden by his authoritarian father. In 1861, a rebellious Marshall refused a scholarship at Oxford (which would have led to the ministry) because, as he put it, he could not abide further study of dead languages. His father could not afford to send him to college without scholarship, but with the help of a wealthy uncle, Marshall was able to enroll at Cambridge University, where he indulged his taste for mathematics and distinguished himself as an honor student.

Marshall's passion for mathematics served him well in two respects. First, he saw it as an expression of independence from his domineering father. Second, the money he earned from tutoring in mathematics enabled him to support himself at Cambridge and repay his uncle. After satisfying the debt to his uncle Marshall wrote: "Mathematics had paid my arrears. I was free for my own inclinations" (*Memorials of Alfred Marshall*, p. 5). Those inclinations ultimately led him to political economy in 1867, but only after several detours, which he later described in his memoirs.

> From Metaphysics I went to Ethics, and thought that the justification of the existing condition of society was not easy. A friend, who had read a great deal of what are now called the Moral Sciences, constantly said: "Ah! if you understood Political Economy you would not say that." So I read Mill's *Political Economy* and got much excited about it. I had doubts as to the propriety of inequalities of opportunity, rather than of material comfort. Then, in my vacations I visited the poorest quarters of several cities and walked through one street after another, looking at the faces of the poorest people. Next, I resolved to make as thorough a study as I could of Political Economy. (*Memorials*, p. 10)

Having settled on economics, Marshall approached its study with a personal dedication that he maintained to the end—a dedication that in no small measure accounts for his sizable contributions to economic analysis.

While his father still vainly hoped that his son would take holy orders, Marshall married a former student, Mary Paley, in 1877. Rules of his fellowship at Cambridge forced him to resign his fellowship upon marriage. The Marshalls left Cambridge for Bristol, where both Alfred and Mary lectured on political economy at newly founded University College, and collaborated on *The Economics of Industry*, which was first published in 1879. Their years at Bristol were spent happily enough, save for an extended period of illness on Marshall's part. In 1884, when a faculty position at his former school opened up, Marshall returned to Cambridge with his health restored. There the Marshalls spent the rest of their years in what Alfred called "a small cultured society of great simplicity and distinction."

Fifty years of writing by Alfred Marshall yielded eighty-two publications, including books, articles, lectures, conferences, and testimony before three Royal Commissions. His immensely popular and influential *Principles of Economics* (1890) has gone through nine editions to date; *Industry and Trade* (1919) through five editions; and *The Economics of Industry* (1879) through two editions and ten printings. Only his *Money, Credit and Commerce* (1923), which was published a year after his death, has not appeared in multiple editions.

Marshall's biographers agree, however, that his impact on economics cannot be measured by his publications alone. Much more important for the progress of economic theory was his practice of transmitting his original ideas to a generation of able students long before those ideas appeared in print. The strong oral tradition that Marshall began at Cambridge constitutes an extremely important chapter in the history of economic analysis, particularly in monetary theory (see chapter 22). As early as 1888, Herbert Foxwell wrote of Marshall: "Half the economic chairs in the United Kingdom are occupied by his pupils, and the share taken by them in general economic instruction in England is even larger than this" ("Economic Movement," p. 92). Marshall's students and protégés, among whom were J. M. Keynes (see chapter 21) and A. C. Pigou, nurtured this "Cambridge tradition" and extended it in many directions.

Marshall's incessant delay in putting his ideas into print was a frequent source of frustration to students and friends alike. To his credit, Marshall was an extremely cautious and meticulous writer who hesitated to publish anything until he had thought through the implications of its content and perfected its presentation. The same caution caused Marshall to be a late expositor of marginal-utility analysis, although historical evidence indicates that he derived the principle of marginal utility independently of Jevons, Menger, and Walras, and at about the same time. As a better mathematician, moreover, Marshall rose above Jevons and Walras. Despite his mathematical skill and proclivity for the subject, his approach to the use of mathematics in economics remained circumspect. In his youth he had translated the works of Ricardo and Mill into mathematical symbols, but apparently he did so as a matter of personal convenience. Later, in the preface to his famous *Principles*, Marshall justified the use of mathematics in economics as a kind of personal "shorthand":

> The chief use of pure mathematics in economic questions seems to be in helping a person to write down quickly, shortly and exactly, some of his own thoughts for his own use. . . . It seems doubtful whether anyone spends his time well in reading lengthy translations of economic doctrines into mathematics, that have not been made by himself. (*Principles*, pp. x–xi)

In *Principles*, Marshall confined his use of diagrams and other mathematical notations to footnotes and appendixes so as not to allow the mathematics to detract from the economics. He was interested above all in plain communication—with businesspeople as well as with students. Moreover, he was acutely aware that overreliance on mathematics "might lead us astray in pursuit of intellectual toys, imaginary problems not conforming to the conditions of real life: and, further, might distort our sense of proportion by causing us to neglect factors that could not easily be worked up in the mathematical machine" (*Memorials*, p. 84).

Had Marshall in fact foreseen the subsequent development of mathematical economics in all its intensity, he might have wished to publish his own rules on the subject in a more conspicuous place than in a letter to his friend and colleague, Arthur Bowley. On February 27, 1906, Marshall offered this retrospective:

> I had a growing feeling in the later years of my work at the subject that a good mathematical theorem dealing with economic hypotheses was very unlikely to be good economics: and I went more and more on the rules—(1) Use mathematics as a shorthand language, rather than as an engine of inquiry. (2) Keep to them till you have done. (3) Translate into English. (4) Then illustrate by examples that are important in real life. (5) Burn the mathematics. (6) If you can't succeed in 4, burn 3. This last I did often. (*Memorials*, p. 427)

Marshall's doubts as to the usefulness of the techniques of theoretical mathematics and statistics should not, however, be misinterpreted. He continuously counseled deep historical and statistical knowledge of any matter under investigation. He considered command of empirical facts a prerequisite to reasonable conclusions. In sum, Marshall was a master economist because he possessed a *combination* of talents. Keynes best underscored Marshall's gifts when he wrote:

> His mixed training and divided nature furnished him with the most essential and fundamental of the economist's necessary gifts—he was conspicuously historian and mathematician, a dealer in the particular and the general, the temporal and the eternal, at the same time. (quoted in Marshall, *Memorials*, p. 12)

Finally, Marshall was an economist's economist—an acknowledged and undisputed leader of colleagues and students alike. He believed that economics required the cooperation of many people with many different talents. Like his contemporary Walras, Marshall helped advance the professionalization of economics. The difference was that Marshall was able to exert his influence from the firm footing of a long-standing tradition at Cambridge University, whereas Walras was forced to operate from a lonely outpost in Switzerland.

■ MARSHALL AND HIS METHOD

It is in the way Marshall viewed things that we find some of his most interesting and enduring contributions to economic science. In other words, the key to Marshall's partial equilibrium approach to economic theory and to applied economics is contained in his statements on method. Although Marshall's method was derived from several interrelated ideas, we shall discuss them separately. First, we shall consider Marshall's definition of economics and economic laws. Next we shall describe his brilliant conception of the role of time in economic analysis. Finally, we shall discuss how Marshall related time to markets and market processes. These themes pave the way for a discussion of his famous conception of competitive equilibrium.

Marshall's Definition of Economics

In the first place, Marshall viewed the science of economics circa 1890 as merely an extension—really a *continuation*—of the ideas espoused by Adam Smith. He believed that neoclassical economics was a modern version of old classical doctrines. A new age and new problems changed the emphasis of economic analysis, but he believed that the relatively simple analyses of Ricardo and Mill were still relevant. Marshall "filled in" where the gaps in classical economics were greatest, helping to build a body of microeconomic analysis to complement the macroeconomics of his forebears. But what is the nature of economic science, as he saw it?

Again and again, throughout *Principles*, Marshall explicated his conception of economic science. In defining the scope and purpose of his book, he noted in the preface to the first edition that:

> In accordance with English tradition, it is held that the function of the science is to collect, arrange and analyse economic facts, and to apply the knowledge, gained by observation and experience, in determining what are likely to be the immediate and ultimate effects of various groups of causes; and it is held that the Laws of Economics are statements of tendencies expressed in the indicative mood, and not ethical precepts in the imperative. Economic laws and reasonings in fact are merely a part of the material which Conscience and Common-sense have to turn to account in solving practical problems, and in laying down rules which may be a guide in life. (*Principles*, pp. v–vi)[1]

Marshall's method, then, rests essentially on refined common sense. Economic science is but the working out of rational behavior refined by organized analysis and reason. Facts and history are essential to the economic theorist, but as Marshall noted, facts alone teach us nothing. Given institutional and ethical constraints regularities and tendencies of human actions must be observed and extracted from historical and empirical data. Analysis, in this view, is shorthand for common sense: if given sufficient regularities, it allows general rules or theories to be developed and applied in particular situations.

One of the central reasons many historical and other heterodox thinkers rejected traditional economic analysis is because it allegedly neglected the complexity of human actions. Aware of the vulnerability of economics to this criticism,

[1] Unlike certain writers in the classical tradition, Marshall did not adhere to an extreme view of economic man, i.e., one uninfluenced by altruistic motives. Indeed, one of the unique characteristics of his book is that Marshall *is willing* to take ethical forces into account, provided they occur with sufficient regularity within economic life.

Marshall provided brilliant defenses. He compared the abstract method of economics to the method of the physical and natural sciences:

> Economic laws are statements with regard to the tendencies of man's action under certain conditions. They are hypothetical only in the same sense as are the laws of the physical sciences: for those laws also contain or imply conditions. But there is more difficulty in making the conditions clear, and more danger in any failure to do so, in economics than in physics. The laws of human action are not indeed as simple, as definite or as clearly ascertainable as the law of gravitation; but many of them may rank with the laws of those natural sciences which deal with complex subject-matter. (*Principles*, p. 38)

Economic theory, Marshall thought, was facilitated because the economic facts of human behavior could be segmented from general facts. Economics was concerned with *measurable motives*, that is, money and prices. Though not a perfect measure, "With careful precautions money affords a fairly good measure of the moving force of a great part of the motives by which men's lives are fashioned" (*Principles*, p. 39).

Time and *Ceteris Paribus*

Roughly, then, Marshall's method consisted of commonsense abstraction from economic facts and behavior through general analysis and reason. The science of economics resulting from the application of this method, moreover, had the twin purposes of knowledge for its own sake and use in solving practical problems. But of what, precisely, did this method consist? If nature's riddles are complex and the human mind is limited, as Marshall asserted, how can we acquire knowledge about economic subjects? Specifically, for a particular market, how can we adequately analyze prices and profits when tastes, income, technology, and costs are continuously changing through time?

In reality, time enters the analysis of economic facts and quantities at every step, and it was perhaps one of Marshall's greatest contributions to recognize its importance. Even better, he worked time into his entire method of approaching economic analysis, noting at the start that it was the "centre of the chief difficulty of almost every economic problem" (*Principles*, p. vii). Marshall explained how time is to be handled in economic analysis by means of his famous discussion of normal demand-and-supply equilibrium.

> The element of time is a chief cause of those difficulties in economic investigations which make it necessary for man with his limited powers to go step by step; breaking up a complex question, studying one bit at a time, and at last combining his partial solutions into a more or less complete solution of the whole riddle. In breaking it up, he segregates those disturbing causes, whose wanderings happen to be inconvenient, for the time in a pound called *Ceteris Paribus*. The study of some group of tendencies is isolated by the assumption *other things being equal:* the existence of other tendencies is not denied, but their disturbing effect is neglected for a time. The more the issue is thus narrowed, the more exactly can it be handled: but also the less closely does it correspond to real life. Each exact and firm handling of a narrow issue, however, helps towards treating broader issues, in which that narrow issue is contained, more exactly than would otherwise have been possible. With each step more things can be let out of the pound; exact discussions can be made less abstract, realistic discussions can be made less inexact than was possible at an earlier stage. (*Principles*, p. 366)

Thus, Marshall proposed to handle the problem of continuous change (time) through the judicious use of *ceteris paribus* assumptions, or conditioning clauses. Other writers had *implied* "other things being equal" in constructing theories, but it was Marshall who explicitly outlined the procedure and consistently applied it throughout his microeconomic studies, including cost-of-production analysis and value theory.

Time and Markets

The use of *ceteris paribus*, necessitated by inevitable effects of time on economic quantities, is a most useful fiction for modern microeconomics. Perhaps nowhere is this better illustrated than in Marshall's example of how the market for fish operates. Marshall considered three hypothetical circumstances or problems that would affect the fishing trade. First, there are very quick changes, such as vagaries of the weather, which cause very short-term fluctuations in the price of fish. Second, Marshall posited changes of moderate length, such as an increase in the demand for fish owing to an extended cattle plague that reduces the supply of beef (a substitute good). Finally, he formulated a long-period problem for the fishing trade over a whole generation, perhaps caused by a change in consumer tastes.

When considering short-run market conditions, the very quick day-to-day changes in demand and supply can be neglected. Temporary changes in the catch of fish, in the weather, or in the availability of substitutes or complements for fish obviously cause temporary oscillations around what Marshall called the *normal* short-term price of fish. Very short-term shifts in supply and demand—some of them canceling out—can easily be imagined. But the key to understanding Marshall's method lies in the relation between changing demand and production conditions through time and the concept of normal price. In order to get a clear understanding of Marshall's method, we must first look at the effects of time on the production conditions of the firm (in this case, a fishing firm).

The Short Run. Marshall posited the existence of a representative, or average, firm operating in a competitive market. The concept is ambiguous, even by Marshall's own definition: "Our representative firm must be one which has had a fairly long life, and fair success, which is managed with normal ability, and which has normal access to the economies, external and internal, which belong to that aggregate volume of production; account being taken of the class of goods produced, the conditions of marketing them and the economic environment generally" (Principles, p. 220). Mark Blaug attributes this invention to Marshall's "restless quest for realism," but in fact the representative firm "is an abstraction; it is neither an arithmetic average, nor a median, nor even a modal firm. It is representative, not with respect to size, but with respect to average costs" (*Economic Theory in Retrospect*, p. 391). Aside from the difficulties associated with the concept, such a firm might be depicted as in figure 16-1a on the following page. (Ignore for the moment the curves of figure 16-lb.) Specifically, figure 16-1a depicts the short-run production conditions of the representative fishing firm. In the short run (one or two years in Marshall's view) the ability of the fishing industry to supply fish is not indefinitely expansible. In figure 16-1a, this limit to additional production is represented by the rising marginal-cost and average-cost functions beyond quantity q_i. The fishing firm, in other words, cannot alter all its inputs in a short period of time, and some of its inputs must be regarded as fixed. It takes time, for example, to build new boats and to train a new and larger generation of fishermen. The firm can, of

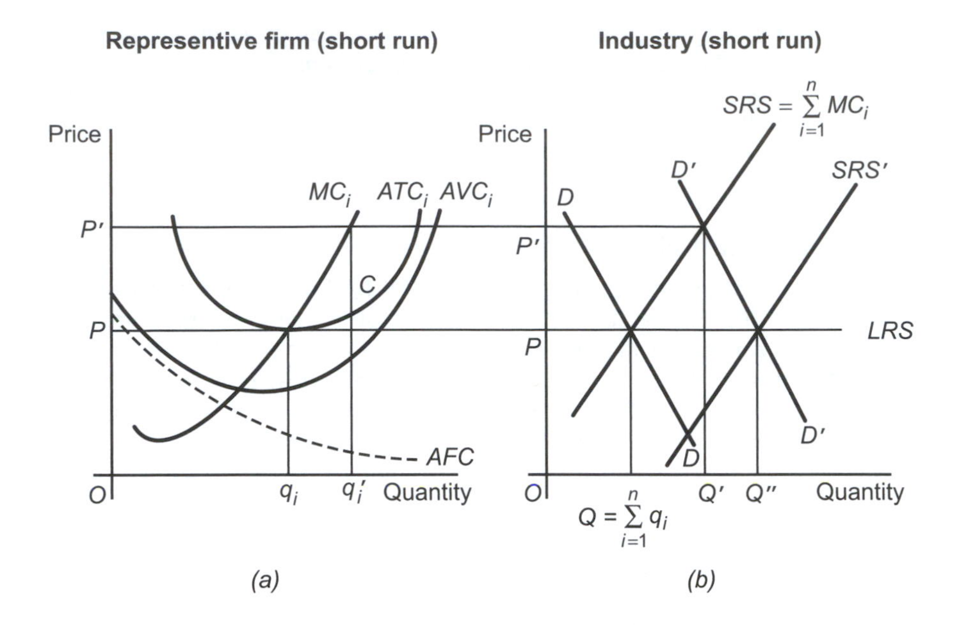

Figure 16-1 A short-run increase in market demand from *DD* to *D′D′* raises the market price from *P* to *P′* and industry output from *Q* to *Q′*. Each firm will earn economic profits because the average revenue *P′* exceeds average costs *C* at quantity q_i'. In the long run, as new firms enter the industry, the supply curve will shift to the right, from *SRS* to *SRS′*, pushing the equilibrium price back to *P*, but there will be more output, *Q″*.

course, increase other inputs. In the short run, which assumes the existence of fixed or quasi-fixed capacity, when a firm adds more variable inputs, its average total costs and average variable costs will diverge from each other. The difference between average total cost and average variable cost is average fixed cost, which declines over the whole range of output (the dashed function in figure 16-1a). This difference between the AVC_i and AFC functions would not exist but for fixed costs. If all inputs are variable, then average total cost and average variable cost would be identical at all levels of output.

It is also important to note the reason why the average-cost functions of figure 16-1*a* are U-shaped. As variable inputs—say, fishermen, deckhands or nets—are added to the "plant" capacity of fishing boats, returns in the form of the number of fish caught per unit of input increase. Average costs, both total and variable, decline. But as variable units are added, average productivity of those inputs in terms of fish caught will decline beyond a point. Therefore, the average cost of supplying fish declines over some range of output but must inevitably rise. Likewise, the marginal cost to the fishing firm, that is, the change in total cost as output is increased one unit, may fall at first but must inevitably rise. Clearly, as a result of a simple law of arithmetic, marginal cost must equal average total cost when the latter is at a minimum.

We now turn our attention to the effect of Marshall's long-run/short-run distinction on the condition of market *demand*. Marshall posited an increase of moderate length in the demand for fish due to a cattle plague and used the *ceteris paribus* tool to predict the resulting price and output in the fish market. Now included in *ceteris paribus* are variations that affect the fishing industry but whose effects take place too slowly to have an appreciable influence in the short run. This left Marshall free to focus on the factors that would affect the market for fish given a short-run increase in demand. Thus, he wrote:

> We give our full attention to such influences as the inducements which good fishing wages will offer to sailors to stay in their fishing homes for a year or two, instead of applying for work on a ship. We consider what old fishing boats, and even vessels that were not specially made for fishing, can be adapted and sent to fish for a year or two. The normal price for any given daily supply of fish, which we are now seeking, is the price which will quickly call into the fishing trade capital and labour enough to obtain that supply in a day's fishing of average good fortune; the influence which the price of fish will have upon capital and labour available in the fishing trade being governed by rather narrow causes such as these. This new level about which the price oscillates during these years of exceptionally great demand will obviously be higher than before. Here we see an illustration of the almost universal law that the term normal being taken to refer to a short period of time, *an increase in the amount demanded raises the normal supply price.* (*Principles*, p. 370)

The example perfectly illustrates Marshall's method. Very short-run and long-run factors affecting the fishing trade are ignored or assumed constant, while those influences having direct bearing on the market over the relevant time period are given full play in explaining market price and quantity. Marshall put operational time, not chronologic time, at the center of the analysis. The "capital and labour available in the fishing trade" are obviously a function of different variables in the short and long run since it takes time to construct new capacity and to induce additional workers to enter the fishing trade. As a result, normal supply price will differ in both periods, as we shall see presently.

Competitive Equilibrium. Competitive equilibrium occurs over time as the forces described by Marshall come into play. Supply decisions follow demand changes to propel competitive markets to new equilibria. Again, consider figure 16-1. The fishing-industry demand and supply curves are depicted in figure 16-1b, where, under purely competitive conditions the positively sloped short-run supply function (*SRS*) is simply the horizontal summation of all the marginal-cost curves of the firms constituting the industry. Initially the industry demand function for fish is *DD*, and industry equilibrium exists at the intersection of *SRS* and *DD*, resulting in equilibrium values of price and output at *P* and *Q* (the sum of the quantities produced by all the firms). The representative firm is a price taker under competitive conditions. We assume that, initially, price *P*, or average revenue, is equal to minimum average total costs of production, and that total costs ($q_i \times ATC_i$) equal total revenue ($q_i \times P$). Thus, no economic profits exist in the industry before the alteration in demand.

Now consider Marshall's supposition that a cattle plague causes a temporary increase in the demand for fish, so that demand shifts to *D′D′*. After a period of adjustment (during which demand price exceeds supply price), the price of fish rises to *P′* and industry output rises to *Q′*, which is the summation of the now larger outputs (q_i') of the individual firms. The firms are maximizing profits at output q_i' since marginal cost is equal to marginal revenue (in competition, *price* is equal to marginal revenue). Thus, as Marshall explained, the short-term *normal* supply rises with an increase in the demand for fish.

The important point is that, given sufficient information on the part of potential competitors, a price of P' could not ordinarily persist in the fish market. At quantity q_i each firm earns economic profits because average revenue (P) exceeds average cost (C). If the increase in fish demand becomes permanent because of a change in tastes (a long-run adjustment), then normal supply price will be governed by a different set of causes. In short, a permanent long-term increase in the demand for fish engenders long-term production adjustments by firms in the industry. In a regime of competition economic profits (or losses) signal that a long-term adjustment is in order. The nature of the adjustment can vary, however, and in a passage of brilliance and clarity Marshall described the possibilities:

> The source of supply in the sea might perhaps show signs of exhaustion, and the fishermen might have to resort to more distant coasts and to deeper waters, Nature giving a Diminishing Return to the increased application of capital and labour of a given order of efficiency. On the other hand, those might turn out to be right who think that man is responsible for but a very small part of the destruction of fish that is constantly going on; and in that case a boat starting with equally good appliances and an equally efficient crew would be likely to get nearly as good a haul after the increase in the total volume of the fishing trade as before. In any case the normal cost of equipping a good boat with an efficient crew would certainly not be higher, and probably be a little lower after the trade had settled down to its now increased dimensions than before. For since fishermen require only trained aptitudes, and not any exceptional natural qualities, their number could be increased in less than a generation to almost any extent that was necessary to meet the demand; while the industries connected with building boats, making nets, etc. being now on a larger scale would be organized more thoroughly and economically. If therefore the waters of the sea showed no signs of depletion of fish, an increased supply could be produced at a lower price after a time sufficiently long to enable the normal action of economic causes to work itself out: and, the term Normal being taken to refer to a long period of time, the normal price of fish would decrease with an increase in demand. (*Principles*, pp. 370–371)

Long-Run Conditions. Returning to figure 16-1, consider Marshall's second possibility, i.e., that additional capital and labor applied to the fishing trade would yield a proportionate increase in the catch. Economic profits might cause firms to react in several ways: Existing firms might increase their scale of operations to increase output, and/or new fishing firms might join the market. If for convenience we eliminate the first possibility, the short-run industry supply curve will shift to the right (to *SRS'*) with the entry of new firms. Since we are assuming that the normal cost of "equipping a good boat with an efficient crew" remains the same as at lower levels of total output, the representative firm's cost functions do not shift. After all adjustments take place, the market is again in long-term equilibrium with zero economic profits at price P but at a higher level of output. The long-run supply price of fish is constant (at P in figure 16-1), and the long-run supply function (*LRS*) may be traced out by connecting the two intersections of supply and demand after all adjustments have taken place. If the *LRS* function is horizontal, as in figure 16-1, we say that fishing is a constant-cost industry. Proportionate increases in inputs of capital and labor yield proportionate increases in output of fish.

Actually, we have been assuming that the fishing firm was in long-run equilibrium *before* the increase in demand took place. Figure 16-1*a* does not depict a long-run equilibrium for the firm, however. The long-run situation of the representative firm after all adjustments have taken place is as shown in figure 16-2. Since there are no *fixed* costs in the long run, all costs to the firm are variable. This is reflected

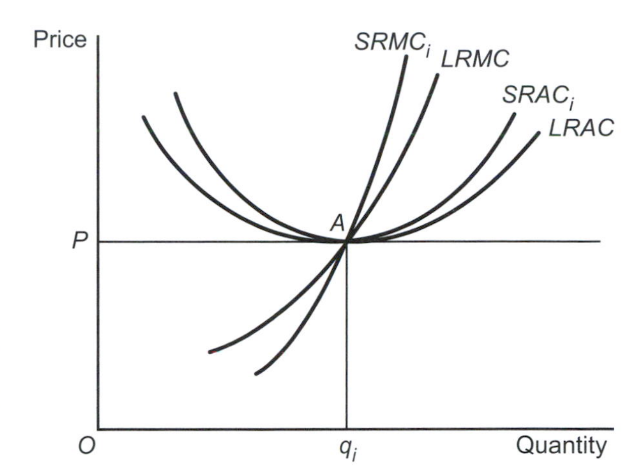

Figure 16-2 Long-run equilibrium for the firm is where the lowest point of the *LRAC* and a particular *SRAC* curve are tangent to the market price.

in figure 16-2 by the fact that there is no distinction between average total cost and average variable cost. The long-run average-cost curve is commonly called an "envelope" or a "planning" curve, and it was first developed by Jacob Viner, not by Marshall (see notes for further reading at the end of this chapter). The envelope curve is really drawn as a series of tangencies of many possible short-run curves. Only one of these short-run curves ($SRAC_i$) is tangent at the point of minimum long-run average cost (point *A* in figure 16-2). It is the same average cost (ATC_i) we assumed in figure 16-1*a*. Given price *P*, the representative fishing firm will produce output q_i. At this long-run equilibrium for the firm, quantity q_i is produced with an optimum scale of plant, i.e., at minimum long-run average costs. Quantity q_i is also an optimum rate of output in that the scale of plant represented by $SRAC_i$ is utilized at its most efficient level, i.e., at minimum costs. The important point is that competition and freedom of entry or exit in the fishing industry guarantee that output (given the cost conditions assumed) will be produced at minimum long-run average costs.

Thus, a review of Marshall's fishing example yields insights into his method of utilizing time-period analysis and *ceteris paribus* assumptions. The same example provides a springboard for discussing Marshall's concept of competitive equilibrium and market adjustments. So far we have considered only the most common representation of competitive market adjustment: the constant-cost case. We now turn to two other cases alluded to by Marshall in his discussion of the fishing trade, i.e., the increasing- and decreasing-cost-industry cases. We shall see that the latter concept was the more important and controversial since it shaped some of Marshall's other ideas, especially those on welfare economics, which in turn shaped the course of twentieth-century microeconomics.

Industry Supply and the Economics of Production

It is a simple matter to demonstrate the two other long-run supply conditions implied by Marshall in his example of the fishing trade. Unfortunately, some of the concepts usually associated with these supply conditions are not clear in the *Principles* and caused difficulties for the theory of competition, as we shall see in chapter 20. Graphically, however, cases of increasing and decreasing cost may be depicted simply. Consider figures 16-3 and 16-4, for example, in which only industry curves are represented.

Increasing and Decreasing Costs

In the increasing-cost case, contrary to the one described by figure 16-1, the firm's cost curves rise as industry output expands. That is, with reference to figure 16-3, the *LRS* function is positively sloped. Full long-run adjustment to the increase in demand (e.g., from *D* to *D′*) will take place only at higher costs (at *B*). In the fishing example, for instance, Marshall noted the possibility that the supply of fish in the sea might become somewhat depleted, so that fishermen would have to resort to fishing in more distant areas. Such activity would become more costly in that proportionate applications of homogeneous capital and labor would yield less than proportionate returns in the catch.

But Marshall noted a more interesting possibility—that of a downward-sloping long-run supply function for the industry. With reference to figure 16-4, decreasing *LRS* implies that additional output will be produced at lower unit costs to the firm. Here, an increase in demand (from *D* to *D′*), which increases firm output, causes the

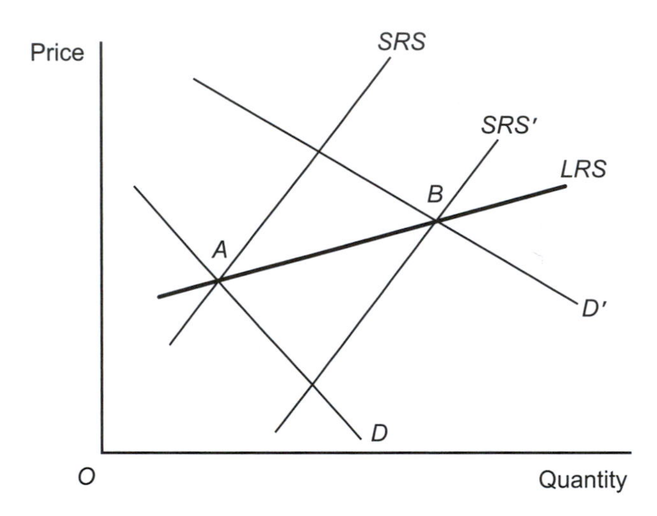

Figure 16-3 Increasing long-run supply costs result when a representative firm's unit costs rise as a consequence of output expansion to meet an increase in market demand.

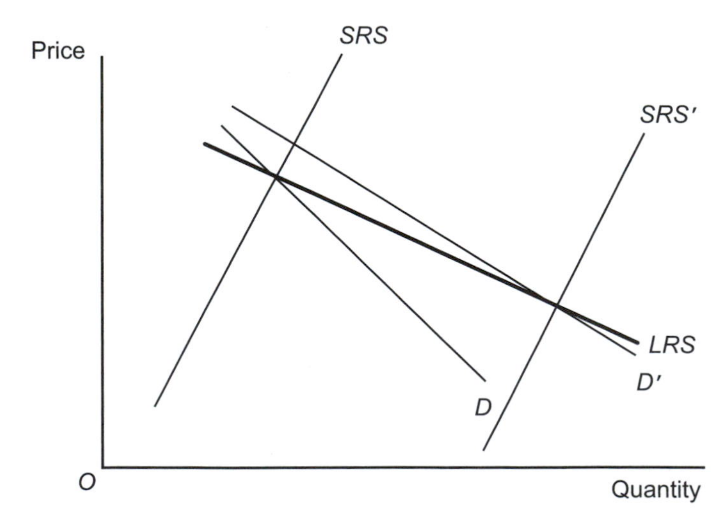

Figure 16-4 Decreasing long-run supply results when a representative firm's unit costs decline as a consequence of output expansion to meet an increase in market demand.

short-run supply function (*SRS'*) to intersect the new demand curve at a price lower than at the previous output level. This would happen if the firm's average-cost curves shift downward as output increases, which could occur, Marshall suggested, because of lower input prices. Better organization and larger operations in boat-building and net making could drive down factor prices resulting in lower unit costs to the fishing firm. If this happened, the long-run industry supply of fish would be negatively sloped as in figure 16-4.

Internal and External Economies. Although Marshall did not develop a full-blown theory of a firm's cost functions,[2] he discussed two types of economies in production that might explain industry supply behavior. Specifically, he divided economies associated with increased production into those external to the firm and those internal to the firm. Marshall defined external economies as those "dependent on the general development of the industry" and internal economies as those dependent on the organization and efficiency of the management within the individual firms.

An increase in output may generate internal economies from the division of labor and improved use of machinery within the firm. Some capital (e.g., specialized machinery) is indivisible and can be utilized only in large-scale production, so that full economic efficiency of both capital and labor can be attained only with increases in production. As output expands, long-run average cost declines, but after some level of output, average cost must again rise owing to inefficiencies of management and the difficulties of marketing the product. Internal economies and diseconomies are simply an explanation for the typical U-shaped long-run average-cost curve.

External economies occurring with increased output, as Marshall identified them, are production economies that are external to the firm but internal to the industry. Marshall linked external economies to the location of industry, but his discussion contains very few examples. Among others, he mentions the following external economies from the agglomeration of firms in a given locale:

1. Better information and skills
2. Availability of skilled labor
3. Economies in the use of specialized machinery

In explaining the first, Marshall (somewhat cryptically) noted that, after an industry has chosen a locale, "The mysteries of the trade become no mysteries; but are as it were in the air, and children learn many of them unconsciously." Moreover:

> Good work is rightly appreciated, inventions and improvements in machinery, in processes and the general organization of the business have their merits promptly discussed: if one man starts a new idea, it is taken up by others and combined with suggestions of their own; and thus it becomes the source of further new ideas. And presently subsidiary trades grow up in the neighborhood, supplying it with implements and materials, organizing its traffic, and in many ways conducing to the economy of its material. (*Principles*, p. 271)

Additionally, Marshall argued that localized industry provides a "constant," orderly market for skilled and specialized labor. Presumably, industries are attracted to regions where scarce labor inputs (in the firm's production functions)

[2] In his famous paper entitled "Cost Curves and Supply Curves" (see notes for further reading at the end of this chapter), Jacob Viner developed the envelope, or long-run, cost curve for the firm.

are readily available. Simultaneously, of course, labor is attracted to regions where the demand for its services is high. As the industry "grows up" in a given area, the availability of specialized labor is expanded and enhanced.

Marshall suggested that as an industry matures, economies in the use of specialized machinery become realizable. He also hinted that the growth of supportive, subsidiary industries creates external economies for firms within the industry.

> The economic use of expensive machinery can sometimes be attained in a very high degree in a district in which there is a large aggregate production of the same kind, even though no individual capital employed in the trade be very large. For subsidiary industries devoting themselves each to one small branch of the process of production, and working it for a great many of their neighbors, are able to keep in constant use machinery of the most highly specialized character, and to make it pay its expenses, though its original cost may have been high, and its rate of depreciation very rapid. (*Principles*, p. 271)

External Economies, Graphically Considered. In figure 16-5, the costs and revenues of the representative firm are depicted in figure 16-5*a*, and the industry curves are shown in figure 16-5*b*. Initial industry and firm equilibriums occur at price *P*, formed by the intersection of short-run industry supply *SRS* (which equals ΣMC) and short-run industry demand *DD*. If we assume that demand increases from *DD* to *D′D′*, short-term economic profits accrue to firms within the industry (note that these profits are not shown in figure 16-5, but the process is totally analogous to that described in reference to figure 16-1). Each firm's rate of output is increased (as always, up to the point where price equals marginal cost of production), but profits signal the entry of new firms into the market. As new firms enter, external economies are realized. The economies, which shift the long-run cost

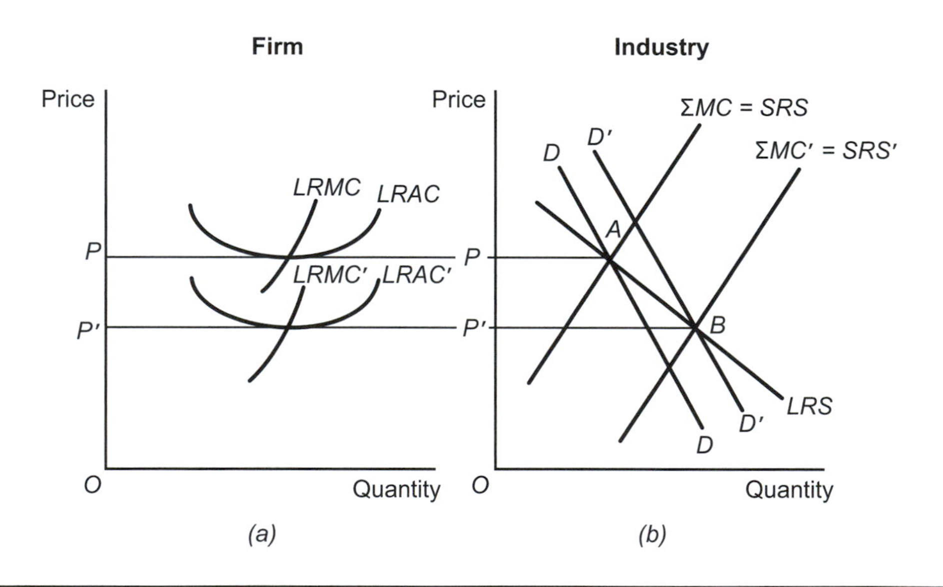

Figure 16-5 A short-run increase in market demand, from *DD* to *D′D′*, causes expansion of output by existing firms and attracts new firms to the industry. The presence of external economies lowers the *LRAC* and *LRMC* of each firm, and the result is a long-run downward-sloping supply curve (*LRS*).

curves of each of the firms downward, are, by definition, external to each of the firms but internal to the industry.

Thus, the positions of the long-run cost curves of the firm are not independent of changes in industry output, as they are in the constant-cost case.[3] With reference to figure 16-5, the firm's long-run cost curves shift downward to *LRAC′* and *LRMC′* when new firms enter the industry. A new industry equilibrium is reached at price *P′* (point *B*), where short-run supply *SRS′* (or $\Sigma MC'$) is equal to the new industry demand *D′D′*. Connection of the loci of the two equilibrium sets of price and quantity (represented at points *A* and *B* in figure 16-5) traces out a downward-sloping long-run industry supply curve.[4] The decreasing function *LRS* appears to represent the analytical substance of what Marshall meant by the term "decreasing-cost industry," although there could be some debate on the issue. Clearly, the concept is fraught with difficulties, not only in interpretation but also in substance. However, far from being simply a theoretical curiosity, Marshall's discussion of external economies and decreasing costs is of prime importance on several counts. First, the limitations of his partial equilibrium method are exposed by the concept of the decreasing-cost industry. Second, a whole new area of microanalysis—the study of imperfect competition—was in large part initiated in the 1920s and 1930s through a questioning of the compatibility of decreasing costs with the theory of competition.[5] Before discussing Marshall's analytical use of his alternative-cost assumptions, it will be instructive to look at each of these issues briefly.

Long-Period Supply: Analytical Difficulties

The limits of Marshall's method—which he clearly understood—are revealed in the case of external economies and decreasing costs. We have argued that the long-period supply function, as depicted in figure 16-5*b*, is negatively sloped as a result of external economies. One might argue that the long-run costs curves of the firm shift downward because of a fall in input prices with increases in industry output. Unfortunately, as Mark Blaug has suggested (*Economic Theory in Retrospect*, p. 381), such reasoning merely shifts the explanation a step away. Why, for instance, do input prices fall? If the fall is due to external economies in the supplying industries, we are still at pains to describe the nature of these economies. Consequently, we have left a fall in input prices off our list of external economies.

But we encounter difficulties even when confronted with the list Marshall described (better use of machinery, better methods, etc.). Specifically, it becomes extremely doubtful whether partial equilibrium analysis, such as that described by figure 16-5, can handle the problem. The long-run supply curve is drawn up on the assumption that technology is constant. A change in technology would cause a shift in the curve. In the list of external economies given by Marshall, it would be difficult to find a single economy that did not, in some way, alter technology. This is especially true as the period considered lengthens.

[3] We skirt the more complex question of whether the representative firm's rate of output (q_i in figure 16-1*a*) will be larger, smaller, or the same with changes in industry output.

[4] The short-run supply functions of figure 16-5*b* are positively sloped, nevertheless, since they are the sum of positively sloped firms' marginal-cost functions.

[5] Marshall's concept of external economies and diseconomies was generalized by his successor, A. C. Pigou, into a theory relating to "uncompensated services or disservices." Pigou also related these externalities to competitive market failure, but the force of his arguments has been considerably diluted by the modern theory of externalities developed by Frank Knight and Ronald Coase (see text below and notes for further reading at the end of this chapter).

One important question related to the analysis, then, concerns the reversibility of the long-run supply curve. Economies and/or technological advances in an industry are ordinarily not destroyed when demand declines in that industry. Therefore, the long-run industry supply curve (as in figure 16-5) would not be reversible. If economies are not reversible and alterations in technology occur, partial equilibrium analysis may be used only as a very rough approximation in explaining prices and conditions in the market. Marshall himself recognized and pinpointed these difficulties. As he incessantly warned:

> Violence is required for keeping broad forces in the pound of Ceteris Paribus during, say, a whole generation, on the ground that they have only an indirect bearing on the question in hand. For even indirect influences may produce great effects in the course of a generation, if they happen to act cumulatively; and it is not safe to ignore them even provisionally in a practical problem without special study. Thus, the uses of the statical method in problems relating to very long periods are dangerous; care and forethought and self-restraint are needed at every step. The difficulties and risks of the task reach their highest point in connection with industries which conform to the law of Increasing Return; and it is just in connection with those industries that the most alluring applications of the method are to be found. (*Principles*, pp. 379–380n)

But, significantly, Marshall was unwilling to throw out the baby with the bath water. Noting that it is true that his method treated "variables *provisionally* as constants," he correctly indicated that it is also the case that his method is the only one "by which science has ever made any progress in dealing with complex and changeful matter, whether in the physical or moral world" (*Principles*, p. 380n).

A second point concerns the compatibility of decreasing-cost conditions and the existence of competitive equilibrium. Far from being a matter of esoteric interest, this issue spawned debate that was a major factor leading to the development of the theory of imperfect competition in the 1930s (see chapter 20). Briefly stated, can perfect competition coexist with external economies and decreasing costs? A moment's reflection clearly reveals that it cannot. Given that the firm's long-run cost curves are inversely related to industry output (as would exist at least for increases in output when external economies are present), any firm would have the incentive to purchase all other firms because any single firm would wish to *internalize* the external economies within the industry. A monopoly, with multiplant production, would be the likely outcome. Clearly, one must choose between the theory of competitive equilibrium and the theory of decreasing costs. The recognition of this fact by several of Marshall's disciples led to the extensive development in the twentieth century of a theory of imperfect competition.

Thus far we have examined Marshall's theory of competitive equilibrium, a theory that employs his partial equilibrium method. We have also examined his discussion of external economies and decreasing costs, as well as some of the theoretical difficulties that these concepts present. Before returning to these concepts and to the analytical use to which Marshall put them, we must look at another side of his massive contribution to competitive analysis, i.e., the theory of demand and consumer surplus.[6]

[6] Some of Marshall's contributions to value theory have already been previewed, i.e., the Mill–Marshall theory of joint supply presented in chapter 8.

■ Demand and Consumer Surplus

In our discussion of competitive equilibrium we have assumed the existence of an industry demand function. Just what is a demand function, how is it constructed, and what is it used for? More than any other economic theorist before or since, Marshall provided lengthy, though not always clear, answers to these questions. He was influenced, perhaps even to a large extent, by the demand analyses of Cournot and Dupuit, and it is clear that J. S. Mill's formulation of demand theory (see chapter 8) left its mark. As we have seen, Marshall added a clear graphical treatment of Mill's concepts of joint supply and reciprocal demand. But in the case of demand theory, Marshall enlarged the concept significantly—so significantly, in fact, that the adjective "Marshallian" is often used to denote a whole tradition in demand theory. One of the reasons for Marshall's great emphasis on demand in his *Principles* was to counteract the classical emphasis on costs of production as the sole determinant of value.

Marshall's Demand Curve Specification

Marshall stated the law of demand in the following manner: "There is then one general law of demand: The greater the amount to be sold, the smaller must be the price at which it is offered in order that it may find purchasers; or, in other words, the amount demanded increases with a fall in price, and diminishes with a rise in price" (*Principles*, p. 99). However, Marshall, unlike most of his predecessors, recognized that before one can draw up a demand schedule, a number of assumptions must be specified. Marshall's *ceteris paribus* assumptions that support the functional relation between price and quantity demanded may be summarized as follows:

1. The time period for adjustment
2. The subject's tastes, preferences, and customs
3. The amount of money (income or wealth) at the subject's command
4. The purchasing power of money
5. The price and range of rival commodities

Time in Demand Analysis. As he did in the case of his treatment of cost, Marshall applied time and the ceteris paribus method to demand theory. Time is a necessary element in demand theory because "time is required to enable a rise in the price of a commodity to exert its full influence on consumption" (*Principles*, p. 110). As we learned in the example of the fishing trade, tastes may change over time and tastes are related to use. People can acquire a taste for something with repeated use. This presents a problem for demand theory, of which Marshall was fully cognizant. Given that time is required to obtain the full effects on quantity demanded of a price change and that protracted use of a substitute good may alter tastes for both the original good and its substitute, doesn't this change one of the bases on which a demand schedule is drawn up? Marshall replied:

> While a list of demand prices represents the changes in the price at which a commodity can be sold consequent on changes in the amount offered for sale, *other things being equal;* yet other things seldom are equal in fact over periods of time sufficiently long for the collection of full and trustworthy statistics. There are always occurring disturbing causes whose effects are commingled with, and cannot easily be separated from, the effects of that particular cause which we desire to isolate. This difficulty is aggravated by the fact that in economics the full effects of a cause seldom come at once, but often spread themselves out after it has ceased to exist. (*Principles*, p. 109)

Marshall's solution to the problems time introduced to demand theory was to specify a parameter in demand theory for the time period of adjustment. Because alteration of the time period of adjustment (say, the duration of the cattle plague) could change the demand curve significantly, it is essential to specify a period for which the demand function is constructed. He was aware of the need to place human tastes or customs, as well as the price of closely related goods, in his pound of *ceteris paribus*:

> The demand prices in our list are those at which various quantities of a thing can be sold in a market *during a given time and under given conditions*. If the conditions vary in any respect the prices will probably require to be changed; and this has constantly to be done when the desire for anything is materially altered by a variation of custom, or by a cheapening of the supply of a rival commodity, or by the invention of a new one. (*Principles*, p. 100)

The Income Parameter. When the price of a good falls, two things happen. First, the good is cheaper relative to all other goods in the consumer's budget, and the consumer will substitute that good for others (the substitution effect of a price change). Second, the consumer's real income rises as the purchasing power of money increases, causing the consumer to buy more of all normal goods in his or her budget (the real-income effect of a price change).[7] Because the introduction of a real-income effect rotates the demand function, Marshall had to indicate the kind of income he wished to hold constant along the demand curve. Although one can find statements that offer a contrary interpretation, in the main it appears that he wished to ignore alterations in the purchasing power of money. In his analysis of marginal diminishing price, Marshall invoked a constant-real-income assumption:

> The larger the amount of a thing that a person has the less, other things being equal (i.e., the purchasing power of money and the amount of money at his command being equal), will be the price which he will pay for a little more of it: or in other words his marginal demand price for it diminishes. (*Principles*, p. 95)

Marshall underscored the necessity of correcting for changes in the purchasing power of money. Whether the Marshallian demand curve falls into the category of the modern constant-money-income or the modern constant-real-income formulation depends on the interpretation given to the assumed constancy of the purchasing power of money and the importance that is attached to it. According to Milton Friedman's interpretation, the only way the purchasing power of money can remain constant as the price of the good under analysis changes is for the purchaser to be compensated by changes in money income or countermovements in the prices of other goods he or she consumes to maintain the constancy of real income in utility terms ("Marshallian Demand Curve," pp. 463–465). However, the traditional interpretation proffered by J. R. Hicks (and others) claims Marshall's assumption of the constancy of the purchasing power of money is a simplifying tactic that is, in rigorous terms, inconsistent with the rest of his formulation (Hicks, *Theory of Wages*, pp. 38–41).

Viewed in retrospect, both interpretations appear correct, though each refers to a different point on a continuum of Marshall's levels of abstraction. The possibility of two distinct interpretations results from Marshall's failure to specify explicitly at what level of abstraction he was operating in various facets of his analysis. In the

[7] A normal good is one whose consumption increases as income increases (steak, for example); consumption of an inferior good (beans, perhaps) declines as income increases.

theoretical formulation of the demand curve, Marshall's exposition fits the constant-real-income classification, and Friedman's interpretation appears valid. In practical applications such as consumer surplus, the constant-money-income interpretation, which assumes that Marshall simply ignored changes in the purchasing power of money, seems more fitting. The apparent ambiguity can be resolved to some extent by remembering that Marshall intended his *Principles* to be not only a clarifying exposition of economic analysis but also of practical use in everyday life.

Consumer Surplus

In terms of operational concepts (i.e., those that are useful in the real world), the most important of Marshall's principles may be his notion of consumer surplus. Marshall's measure has been in and out of favor with economists, and it is certain that there are many difficulties connected with it. But whether Marshall's measure (or refurbishments of it) surmounts these difficulties is not really relevant. Many policy decisions require a measure of the benefits produced by goods (and particularly by public goods in cost-benefit calculations), and consumer surplus is among the best that economics offers. Moreover, the concept of consumer surplus exists irrespective of whether a Marshallian demand curve measures it correctly. At any rate, Marshall applied the concept to analyze several real-world problems, such as monopoly and taxation.

The concept of consumer surplus originated with Jules Dupuit (see chapter 13), who also applied it in innovative ways, especially to public goods. But Marshall popularized the concept and gave it the name we now attach to it. He described consumer surplus as follows:

> The price which a person pays for a thing can never exceed, and seldom comes up to that which he would be willing to pay rather than go without it: so that the satisfaction which he gets from its purchase generally exceeds that which he gives up in paying away its price; and he thus derives from the purchase a surplus of satisfaction. The excess of the price which he would be willing to pay rather than go without the thing, over that which he actually does pay, is the economic measure of this surplus satisfaction. It may be called consumer's surplus. (*Principles*, p. 124)

The Case of Tea. To further understand this concept and its operational significance, Marshall provided a numerical example. He posited a consumer's demand schedule for an unimportant commodity (i.e., one that accounts for a small portion of his total expenditures), such as tea. Table 16-1 replicates Marshall's example.

Let us suppose that the consumer purchases 1 pound of tea at a price of 20 shillings. According to Marshall this establishes that the consumer's total enjoyment or satisfaction derived from consuming that amount is "as great as that which he could obtain by spending 20s. on other things" (*Principles*, p. 125). Now suppose that the price falls to 14s. The buyer could still purchase 1 pound of tea, obtaining a surplus satisfaction of 6s., or a consumer surplus of *at least* 6s. But if he buys an additional pound, the utility of this additional amount must be at least equivalent to 14s., so that he now obtains for 28s. a quantity of tea

Table 16-1 Price of Tea per Pound

Shillings	Quantity Demanded
20	1
14	2
10	3
6	4
4	5
3	6
2	7

that is worth to him at least 34s. (20s. + 14s.). Thus, consumer surplus, in Marshall's calculation, is at least 6s.

We may view the situation graphically as in figure 16-6, which depicts the consumer's demand for tea. Successive price declines clearly increase the surplus utility that the individual receives from consuming tea, so that when the price falls to 2 shillings, he buys 7 pounds, which "are worth to him not less than 20, 14, 10, 6, 4, 3, and 2s. or 59s. in all." This sum of 59 shillings measures the total utility to the consumer (*utilité absolue*, in Dupuit's terms) of the 7 pounds of tea. But the consumer must pay only 14 shillings for 7 pounds, so that he receives a sum of utility equivalent to (at least) 45 shillings from consuming 7 pounds of tea. Marshall called this amount "excess satisfaction" as consumer surplus.

Figure 16-6 As price declines from 20s. to 2s., the total utility of the consumer increases to a value of 59s. (20 + 14 + 10 + 6 + 4 + 3 + 2). Since the consumer must pay only 14s. for 7 pounds, his consumer surplus is equivalent to 45s.

The Marshallian Measure. The concept of consumer surplus is clear and logical, but problems arise when the surplus is measured by an area under the Marshallian demand curve. In order to appreciate this let us suppose that the demand curve of figure 16-6 is Marshallian in the sense that it is drawn up under the assumptions listed earlier in this chapter. It will be recalled that one of those assumptions is the constancy of the purchasing power of money. But as price falls for our consumer of tea, the purchasing power (real value) of his or her money will increase, and an increase in the purchasing power of money is equivalent to an increase in the consumer's real income. The problem is that as real income increases its marginal utility decreases, just as the marginal utility of any good decreases as its quantity increases. With respect to the consumption of tea this means that a shilling is not a shilling in utility terms as the consumer moves down his or her demand curve. The marginal utility of shillings is not the same when the consumer is buying 1 pound at

20s. as when he or she is buying 7 pounds at 2s. Marshall expressed consumer surplus in money terms, but the units of money (say, 45s. when 7 pounds at 2s. are consumed) do not carry the same utility value because the real income of the consumer is altered. Without getting into unnecessary complexities, we can confidently state that the Marshallian (constant-money-income) demand curve will either overestimate or underestimate the surplus.

Marshall tried to avoid being cornered by the constant-marginal-utility-of-money assumption. One reason he selected tea, an "unimportant" commodity, is because real-income changes would be negligible for small purchases. But even though it can be minimized, the problem does not go away in any rigorous theoretical treatment of consumer surplus. The ambiguity of Marshall's "final" position left the theory in some disarray, but in all likelihood he was merely seeking a rough approximation to guide certain kinds of public policy. He declared that his purpose in devising the notion of consumer surplus was primarily to provide "an aid in estimating roughly some of the benefits which a person derives from his environment" (*Principles*, p. 125).[8]

Before turning to specific applications Marshall gave to consumer surplus, it is necessary to clear up a different kind of ambiguity. Note that throughout the text we have used the generalized term *consumer surplus,* which can apply to one or more individuals. But Marshall, on the one hand, wrote of *consumer's* surplus, while on the other, he developed *market* demand curves that summed up the functions of many individuals and attempted to determine *consumers'* surplus. We might call it the "problem of the apostrophe"—when demands (as utility functions) of many individuals are added up, we speak of consumers' surplus and treat the monetary value of the surplus as a utility value. But clearly, individuals' incomes, tastes, and preferences must differ, so that 5 pounds of tea at 4 shillings for individual A does not necessarily convey the same utility as 5 pounds at 4 shillings for individual B. To be sure, money demands can be added up to form market demand curves, but illegitimate interpersonal comparisons of utility are involved when these money amounts (areas under the market demand curve) are used to express utility. Nevertheless, certain assumptions could be invoked (such as equal income of the separate demanders) that would make approximations more plausible. Importantly, Marshall was aware of most of the difficulties. But, after acknowledging them, he proceeded to put his imperfect approximation to use in discussions of monopoly and optimum public policies of taxation and subsidization.

■ Marshall on Optimum Pricing and Monopoly

Utilizing a market demand curve as an approximation of the utility produced by a commodity, Marshall embarked on a theoretical excursion that allowed government interference in free markets in order to promote maximum social satisfaction. Coupling his marginal-utility/demand curve with the theories of long-run supply, Marshall sought to determine whether social welfare (i.e., aggregate utility) could be improved by a system of government taxes or subsidies. He considered the welfare effects of taxes and "bounties" (subsidies) on industries characterized by decreasing, increasing, and constant long-run supply functions.

[8] Some (but not all) of the problems of utility measurement are avoided by using ordinal (indifference-curve) analysis. The ordinal approach requires the consumer to indicate more or less satisfaction rather than to make a numerical specification in cardinal (1, 5, 20, etc.) terms.

The Increasing-Cost Case

Marshall analyzed the effects of taxing or subsidizing an increasing-cost industry in graphical terms, as depicted in figure 16-7. Output for the increasing-cost industry originally takes place at quantity *OH* (and at price *OC*), where demand curve *DD′* intersects industry supply *SS′*. At this quantity consumer surplus is represented by *CDA*, the total area under the demand curve (*ODAH*) less the amount that consumers actually pay (*OCAH*). Now suppose that the government enacts a per-unit tax on production in the amount *TA* per unit of output. The effect of this tax would be to shift the market supply curve (which, remember, is the summation of each firm's marginal-cost functions) to the left by the amount of the tax. In our case, the supply function decreases to *ss′*. After the tax is levied, the quantity of the commodity sold is reduced to *Oh*, and price rises to *Oc* (determined at the intersection of *ss′* and *DD′*). Now consumers pay *Ocah* for a quantity of the commodity that yields them *ODah* in utility. Consumer surplus is reduced to *cDa*. The government's proceeds from the tax are equal to the amount of the tax *aE* (= *TA*) multiplied by the output produced after the tax, *FE* (= *Oh*). In other words the tax produces revenue equal to *FcaE*.

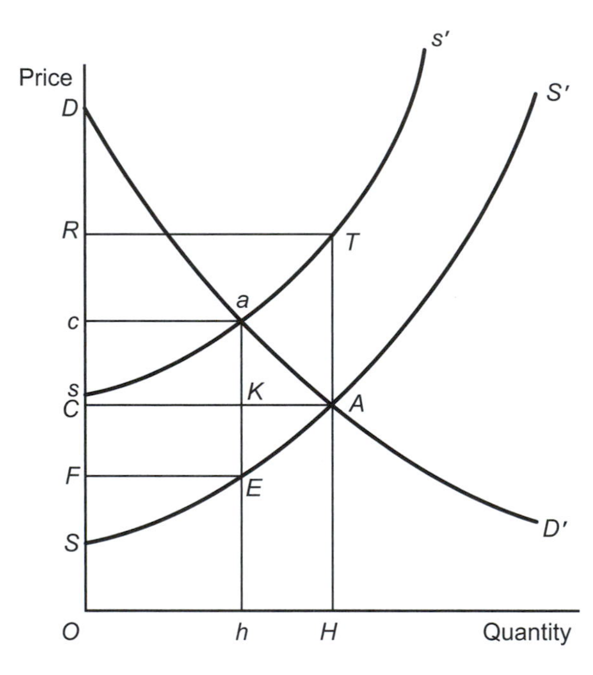

Figure 16-7 At initial equilibrium *A*, consumer surplus is the area *CDA*. A per-unit tax in the amount *TA* will reduce consumer surplus to the area *cDa* and bring in tax revenue in the amount *FcaE*. Since the area *FCKE* is greater than the triangle *aKA*, the government will increase welfare by spending the tax proceeds on public goods.

In order to judge the welfare effects of the tax Marshall compared the consumer surplus lost to the tax revenue gained. To be conclusive, this requires an assumption that the utility created by government expenditure of tax receipts is equal, dollar-for-dollar, to the utility lost due to higher prices paid by consumers. In figure 16-7, the critical issue is whether area *FcAE* exceeds area *CcaA*. If it does, then the government could increase welfare by taxation.[9]

[9] As Blaug pointed out in his *Economic Theory in Retrospect* (p. 388), the argument does not necessarily hold when losses in producer surplus are included.

Reversing the argument, Marshall concluded that subsidization of an increasing-cost industry would cause a reduction in consumer welfare. This point may also be demonstrated in figure 16-7, assuming in this case that *ss′* is the original supply curve and that price and quantity are originally *Oc* and *Oh*, respectively. Should the government subsidize the industry in the amount *TA* (or *aE*) per unit, the supply function would shift rightward toward *SS′*, increasing the equilibrium of output and price to *OH* and *OC*. The total amount of the subsidy required will be the unit amount *TA* multiplied by the new equilibrium quantity produced, *OH* (= *CA*). The cost of the subsidy would therefore be represented by the area *CRTA*. Because the subsidy results in a lower price, consumer surplus would increase from *cDa* to *CDA*, an increase of *CcaA*. If this increase in consumer surplus is less than the cost of the subsidy (which, in this case, it clearly is), then on utility grounds, at least, subsidizing the industry reduces consumer welfare.

Subsidies and Decreasing Costs

In a second, analogous case, Marshall argued that, on theoretical grounds, decreasing-cost industries should be subsidized in order to promote maximum welfare. The essentials of the argument are often invoked in contemporary discussions of electrical utilities and other utilities that are assumed to be characterized by decreasing costs. Figure 16-8 demonstrates graphically that welfare may be increased by subsidizing decreasing-cost industries. Assume that the original industry supply and demand functions are *DD′* and *ss′*, establishing price *Oc* and output *Oh*. Now, what if the government decided to subsidize the industry in order to increase total output to *OH*? The subsidy required would equal *TA* (or *aE*) per unit of output. The supply curve would, in effect, shift downward to *SS′*, and at the new equilibrium *OH* would be produced at price *OC*. Consumer surplus increases from *cDa* (at output *Oh*) to *CDA* (at output *OH*), an increase of *CcaA*. The total subsidy,

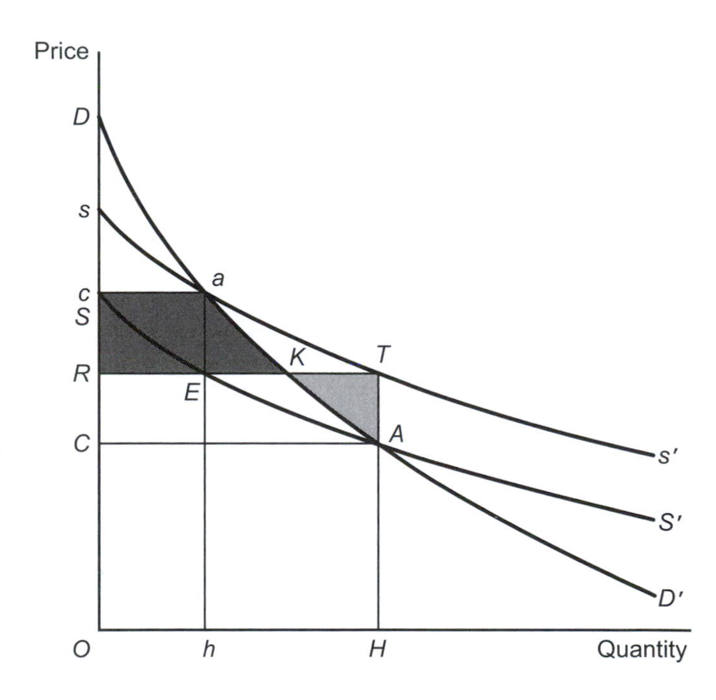

Figure 16-8 A subsidy in the amount of *TA* per unit of output will increase consumer surplus from *cDa* to *CDA*. Since the increase in consumer surplus exceeds the cost of the subsidy, consumer welfare is increased.

as in the increasing-cost example of figure 16-7, is equal to the per-unit amount of *TA* multiplied by the number of units sold, *OH* (= *CA*), or a total subsidy equal to area *CRTA*. For the subsidy to create an increase in welfare, it is necessary that the increase in consumer surplus *CcaA* be greater than the government's subsidy *CRTA*. This will be the case, referring to figure 16-8, since area *KTA* is less than area *RcaK*. In this way, Marshall demonstrated that welfare could be improved by subsidizing decreasing-cost industries.[10]

By extending the same lines of argument to constant-cost industries, of the kind described in figure 16-1, Marshall showed as well that constant-cost industries should be neither taxed nor subsidized, because either a tax or a subsidy would produce smaller changes in consumer surplus than their corresponding changes in tax receipts.

Some of the theoretical problems associated with Marshall's use of the demand curve as a welfare measure have already been discussed. But it is to Marshall's credit that he pointed out a particularly important difficulty where taxation and subsidization are involved. In his words, the "doctrine of maximum satisfaction . . . assumes that all differences in wealth between the different parties concerned may be neglected, and that the satisfaction which is rated at a shilling by one of them, may be taken as equal to one that is rated at a shilling by any other" (*Principles*, p. 471). Any statement imputing utility levels to individuals or groups is, strictly speaking, nonscientific. In the tax-subsidy analysis, there are clearly gainers and losers. Is the utility lost by the losers (those taxed) greater than, equal to, or less than the utility received by the gainers (consumers of decreasing-cost-industry products)? A positive or negative answer to the question requires a value judgment, and Marshall did not flinch from making a few, one of which was that "The happiness which an additional shilling brings to a poor man is much greater than that which it brings to a rich one" (*Principles*, p. 474). When speaking of policies in which there are gainers and losers, some such assumption must be made, and Marshall was, *as a first approximation*, ready to make it.

Marshall's treatment of the doctrine of maximum satisfaction provides us with more examples of the dichotomy between his theoretical and operational concerns. The theory and its conclusions are tentative in that they require certain nonscientific assumptions concerning the summation of utilities of gainers and losers. But Marshall proceeded anyway, issuing warnings all along the way and concluding that his propositions "do not by themselves afford a valid ground for government interference." In his own view, he simply identified a problem, noting that much remained to be done, especially in the area of statistical estimates of supply and demand. The problem of devising policies to maximize welfare did, in fact, engender a great deal of interest among Marshall's disciples and others in the Cambridge tradition, though progress has been piecemeal and incomplete.[11] But Marshall was asking important questions, always with a view to the applications of economic analysis.

Monopoly and Economic Welfare

One other important example of Marshall's concern for the usefulness of utility theory can be found in the area of simple monopoly analysis. He went to great

[10] By reverse argument he also showed that welfare would be reduced if these industries were taxed.

[11] The problem of empirical identification of increasing- and decreasing-cost industries was tackled by A. C. Pigou, J. H. Clapham, and D. H. Robertson, with small success. The problem of scientific estimation of welfare or "benefit" transfers has beguiled many economists, who have had even less success (see notes for further reading at the end of this chapter).

lengths to point out the implications of the distinction, originally stated by Dupuit (see chapter 13), between monopoly revenue and consumer surplus. Again, as in the case of the consumer surplus argument, Marshall enlarged the analytical value of the tool by probing the implications of the monopolist's net revenue. Specifically, Marshall showed that because of various economies of scale and the ability to finance technological improvement, both associated with monopoly market structure, "The supply schedule for the commodity, if not monopolized, would show higher supply price than those of our monopoly supply schedule" (*Principles*, pp. 484–485). Marshall went further and stated that if the monopolist had unlimited command over capital, equilibrium quantity under free competition would be less than that for which demand price is equal to supply price under monopoly.

On some of the most interesting pages of the *Principles*, Marshall analyzed the possibility of a short-run "altruistic entrepreneur" who might regard a gain in consumer surplus as coequal with a gain in monopoly revenues. He called the money sum of consumer surplus and monopoly revenue "total benefit." In a variation on this theme, the theory of "compromise benefit," the monopolist would calculate and maximize the sum of (1) monopoly revenue to be obtained at any given price and (2) some percentage (one-half, one-third, etc.) of the corresponding consumer surplus. Marshall thought that such principles could be applied by a government interested in increasing consumers' welfare through the supply of public goods (e.g., bridges, water, and gas), although he strongly indicated that it should do so only under the constraint of equating total revenue with total costs. But, ever practical, Marshall pointed out:

> Even a government which considers its own interests coincident with those of the people has to take account of the fact that, if it abandons one source of revenue, it must in general fall back on others which have their own disadvantages. For they will necessarily involve friction and expense in collection, together with some injury to the public, of the kind which we have described as a loss of consumers' surplus. (*Principles*, p. 488)

In the limiting case of government ownership or operation there would be no compromise; consumer surplus would be maximized subject only to the provision that full costs be covered.

Thus, on the issues of governmental policy toward business, Marshall's utility theory (coupled with his theoretical views on long-run supply functions) led him to some rather unorthodox and even radical suggestions. Although the type of utility theory on which his analysis is based has been largely out of favor for many years, the problems Marshall attacked (determining optimum public policies toward market enterprise) are still very much with us. It is noteworthy, moreover, that modern attempts to measure social welfare have not advanced much beyond Marshall's "welfare triangles."

The Case of Externalities

One of Marshall's applications that has loomed large in contemporary economic analysis concerns the general area of "externalities," property rights, and "market failure." Marshall's discovery and elaboration of the concept of external economies proved to be fertile ground for the development of new theoretical principles in the field of public economics. Above we saw that Marshall identified something called "external economies," by which the effects of certain types of industry development and expansion lowered the cost curves of firms within industries—a positive "externality" to the firm.

Apart from Marshall's very practical identification of an externality, a philosophical tradition of welfare maximization stemming from Benthamite utilitarianism (see chapter 6) continued through J. S. Mill and through one of Marshall's Cambridge colleagues, Henry Sidgwick. In this tradition, economists discovered that providing the greatest good for the greatest number *solely* through market means contained a hitch—the market might "fail" to accurately reflect costs and benefits if externalities existed. An example of negative externalities might be a steel factory belching smoke and slag into the surrounding area, damaging houses, lungs, and drinking water downstream. A positive externality might result if one individual maintains a garden that neighbors enjoy but for which no practical means of charging the beneficiaries can be devised. Similar problems arise today whenever we discuss "environmental" issues.

A. C. Pigou, who was Marshall's protégé and handpicked successor at Cambridge (in 1910), greatly expanded this idea and proposed a "Marshallian" solution. In 1912, in his *Wealth and Welfare* and in an expanded "second edition" entitled *The Economics of Welfare* (1920), Pigou discussed the possibility of market failure. Consider the problem of water pollution, an example of a negative externality. A negative externality exists if the marginal *social* costs of pollution exceed the marginal *private* costs of pollution (by an amount equal to the marginal pollution damage). Figure 16-9 depicts the marginal private cost (*MPC*), marginal social cost (*MSC*), and demand curves for such an activity. If the polluting firm is able to escape the social costs of pollution, it makes its decision based on the *MPC* curve. Quantity Q_0 is produced, and society is forced to bear marginal pollution costs of AP_0. There is "too much" output of this good from society's point of view.

Pigou's solution was to impose a *tax* on the offending industry so that the *MSC* curve would represent the cost of production perceived by the firm. In this case, the firm would bear the *full* cost (private + social) of producing this good and output would be restricted to Q_1 (with a higher price than before). Following Marshall, Pigou chose taxes and subsides as means to address market failures. In this context, Pigou contemplated an *expanded* role for government, in the form of legislative or regulatory action. An extension of this idea from a different perspective emphasiz-

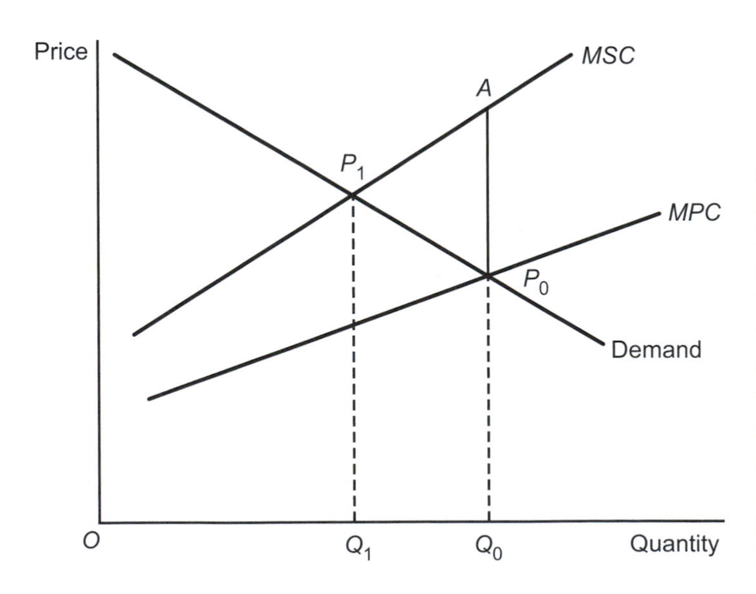

Figure 16-9 If the polluting firm can ignore the social cost of production, it will produce output Q_0, forcing society to bear the cost AP_0. One way to raise the marginal private cost to the level of marginal social cost is by taxing the polluting firm according to the difference between *MSC* and *MPC*.

ing private, contractual solutions rather than government intervention, was pioneered by another Marshallian, Ronald Coase (see the box, The Force of Ideas: The Coasian Revolution in Property Rights).

The Force of Ideas: The Coasian Revolution in Property Rights

A twentieth-century economist steeped in the Marshallian tradition made seminal contributions that address the "external effects" problem. In 1960 Ronald Coase drew attention (as had Bentham and Chadwick before him) to the incentive effects that particular assignments of property rights have on economic activity. In "The Problem of Social Cost," a work representative of the contributions that earned him the Nobel Prize in Economic Science in 1991, Coase challenged Pigou's assumption that externalities are unidirectional in nature (see the discussion surrounding Figure 16-9 in this chapter). Coase emphasized the reciprocal (or bilateral) nature of externalities. A cigarette smoker cannot cause an externality if individuals do not put themselves in his or her proximity. Water polluters would not have created an externality if there had been no downstream population settlement.

How does the Coase argument work? Consider an example of air pollution—a factory belching smoke over a nearby community. While harmful to the community, these "spillover effects" create benefits to the firm. As the output of the firm rises, however, the firm's marginal benefits of pollution decline because the rate of return on additional production generally declines. On the cost side, the marginal cost of pollution is measured by the harm created by the smoke, which is an increasing function of production, since more production means more smoke. In Coase's conception, the marginal costs of pollution (to the community) must be balanced against its marginal benefits (to the firm).

What often prevents a market solution is the absence of clearly defined property rights. Who has a right to fresh air? Coase argued that a market solution will result if we simply assign legal ownership rights over air quality to one of the other parties. If homeowners in the surrounding neighborhood hold the rights to clean air and if free exchange is allowed, the firm could buy the right to pollute from its neighbors. It would want to do so, so long as its excess profits from polluting exceed the additional costs it would have to pay the people in the neighborhood. Marginal benefits to the firm (additional profits from polluting) would decline as marginal costs (increasing degrees of pollution) rise. At some level of production, the firm would not be willing to buy pollution rights. The argument is symmetrical in that if firms get the pollution rights, the same analysis would apply. In this instance the homeowners would buy pollution reductions from the firm, but only up to the point where the marginal cost to them was equal to the marginal benefits they receive. That point is exactly the same as the one where the firm would have been unwilling to buy rights when homeowners had them. This is the central insight offered by the Coase theorem: In a world in which bargaining costs nothing, the assignment of legal liability to a particular party *does not matter.* A certain equilibrium level of output and its resulting level of pollution will exist regardless of whether firms or consumers own the air.*

Under the conditions of the Coase theorem, as described above, government interventions (pollution guidelines, tax penalties, etc.) cannot improve on a settlement negotiated by those parties who are directly involved with the externality problem. The theorem can be used to analyze a number of real-world externality problems so long as bargaining and transaction costs are zero or negligible. Coase argued that if the judicial system makes a proper assignment of liabilities (to the low-cost participant to the externality), market forces and incentives may be sufficient to generate efficient solutions to externality problems. Their presence, in other words, provides no prima facie case for governmental interferences of a legisla-

(continued)

tive type (such as the Occupational Safety and Health Administration or the Environmental Protection Agency in the United States).

What if transaction costs (i.e., the costs of defining and enforcing a system of ownership) are significant in particular situations? In this event, a number of "solutions" have been tried. These include taxing or subsidizing externalities (as in the Pigovian solution described in the text); the government sale of "pollution rights" to offending firms, which could theoretically get the offenders to reduce pollution to optimal levels; or direct regulation that requires firms to install certain types of pollution-control equipment and other regulating devices. Because these "solutions" are generally pursued in the arena of politics, practical outcomes are not likely to be optimal. Sometimes just leaving the imperfect market solution alone may achieve the best outcome in a variety of imperfect solutions. At any rate, the Coase theorem provides a benchmark for analyzing externality problems.

*A whole new (post-1960) field of economics was originated by the Coase theorem. Called "law and economics," it studies the impact of legal rules and institutions on the economy. Many law schools have specialized fields in law and economics, and two journals (the *Journal of Law and Economics* and the *Journal of Legal Studies*) publish a consistent flow of literature on the subject.

■ Marshall on Elasticity, Factor Demand, and Optimal Resource Allocation

Elasticity

One of the most useful tools in the microeconomist's tool kit is the concept of elasticity. Like many ideas refined by Marshall, the concept of elasticity can be found in the works of earlier writers. Jenkin, for example, alluded to it in 1870. But it was Marshall who gave the concept its mathematical character and its contemporary standing.

Elasticity is a general concept that finds application in many circumstances. It can be applied to the study of demand, supply, production, and so forth. In its generalized form it simply measures the responsiveness of one variable to changes in another variable. Armed with an understanding of the concept one can measure price elasticity of demand, price elasticity of supply, input elasticity, output elasticity, income elasticity, and so forth. We choose to examine Marshall's use of price elasticity of demand with the understanding that the concept has widespread application in other circumstances as well.

As Marshall put it, "The *elasticity* (or *responsiveness*) of demand in a market is great or small according as the amount demanded increases much or little for a given fall in price, and diminishes much or little for a given rise in price" (*Principles*, p. 102). "Much" or "little" are inexact terms, so Marshall gave the notion more precision. Price elasticity of demand is defined simply as the percentage change in quantity demanded divided by the percentage change in price. Algebraically, $N_D = [\Delta Q_D / Q_D] \div [\Delta P / P]$.[12] Demand is considered elastic if N_D is greater than 1, inelastic if less than 1, and of unit elasticity if equal to 1.

[12] Marshall also applied the basic concept to supply. Later, a "cross-elasticity" concept was developed. Cross-elasticity is defined as the responsiveness of the quantity demanded of a commodity A to a change in price of another commodity B.

Marshall recognized the circumstances that determine elasticity in each instance and gave numerous practical examples. Basically, he argued that *ceteris paribus* demand is more *elastic:*

1. The greater the proportion of an individual's total budget that expenditures on the commodity represent (salt, for instance, is a necessity and also represents a small expenditure for both rich and poor people)
2. The longer the price change is in effect (time again)
3. The larger the number of substitutes
4. The larger the number of uses to which the commodity can be put

For good measure, Marshall discussed how elasticity differed between rich, middle-class, and poor buyers. In a passage clearly revealing his Victorian preoccupation with classes, he noted the effect of acquired tastes on the demand for meat:

> In the ordinary working class districts the inferior and the better joints [of meat] are sold at nearly the same price: but some well-paid artisans in the north of England have developed a liking for the best meat, and will pay for it nearly as high a price as can be got in the west end of London, where the price is kept artificially high by the necessity of sending the inferior joints away for sale elsewhere. (*Principles*, p. 107)

Always alert to modes of fashion and social standing, Marshall noted, "Part of the demand for the more expensive kinds of good is really a demand for the means of obtaining a social distinction, and is almost insatiable" (*Principles*, p. 106).

The usefulness of price and income elasticity of demand estimates, made possible by Marshall's brilliant discussion of the concept, is fairly obvious in budget analysis and all aspects of consumption theory. But, in a common display of his broad vision and acute perceptiveness, Marshall extended the notion of elasticity *and* its usefulness beyond its realm in the theory of consumer behavior into the theory of producer behavior—the demand for factor inputs (i.e., labor, capital, land).

Factor Demand[13]

The study of factor demand (derived demand for productive inputs) and factor-demand elasticity was presumably initiated by Marshall, and subsequently advanced further by A. C. Pigou and John R. Hicks. However, at least by the eighth edition of the *Principles*, Marshall credited both Böhm-Bawerk and Irving Fisher with related developments, and it seems fairly clear that Cournot was tinkering with a similar concept as early as 1838.

Marshall's discussion of the determinants of derived-factor-demand elasticity is found chiefly in Book V of his *Principles*, in chapter 6 entitled "Joint and Composite Demand, Joint and Composite Supply" (and in his mathematical notes XIV and XV, pp. 852–854). Characteristically, rather than present an abstract, general theoretical argument Marshall used homely examples involving plasterers employed in housing construction and knife handles used in making knives. Also characteristically, Marshall did not make his underlying assumptions specific. Yet, he did make one explicit statement that subsequent writers apparently overlooked, a statement that places Marshall somewhat outside the frame of analysis of writers who followed his lead. J. R. Hicks, R. G. D. Allen, and others interested in derived demand have

[13] This section draws heavily on the treatment of factor demand in S. C. Maurice, "On the Importance of Being Unimportant" (see references).

almost uniformly assumed long-run competitive equilibrium. Marshall, however, clung to the short run:

> The period over which the disturbance extends being short, and the causes of which we have to account as re-adjusting demand and supply being only such as are able to operate within that short period . . . we should notice that, referring as it does to short periods, it is an exception to our general rule of selecting . . . cases in which there is time enough for the full long-period action of the forces of supply to be developed. (*Principles*, p. 382)

In his example involving plasterers' labor, Marshall seems generally to assume variable-proportions production, or something very much like it. But like Carl Menger (see chapter 14), he was undecided in this area. His statement, "A temporary check to the supply of plasterers' labour will cause a *proportionate* check to the amount of building" suggests fixed proportions, at least as far as plasterers' labor is concerned, and his results seem consistent with the assumption of fixed proportions; paradoxically, Marshall implied variable factor proportions throughout his discussion. Variable proportions enter chiefly through commodity demand, that is, through a change in the product. Marshall wrote that

> an increased difficulty in obtaining one of the factors of a finished commodity can often be met by modifying the character of the finished product. Some plasterers' labour may be indispensable; but people are often in doubt about how much plaster work it is worthwhile to have in their houses, and if there is a rise in its price they will have less of it. (*Principles*, p. 386)

Whether proportions are fixed or not, Marshall stated the fundamental law of derived demand in clear terms: "The demand schedule for any factor of production of a commodity can be *derived* from that for the commodity by subtracting from the demand price of each separate amount of the commodity the sum of the supply prices for corresponding amounts of the other factors" (*Principles*, p. 383). Blades and handles are used in fixed proportions to make knives. Knowing the supply of blades and the demand for knives, the problem Marshall posed was that of determining the derived demand for handles. He treated the problem both graphically and mathematically. Marshall's graphic model is reproduced as figure 16-10, in a figure that is related to the Mill–Marshall joint-supply model (and constructed in the same manner as figure 8-1).

Here the demand for knives *DD′* is given, as are the supply functions for knives and handles *SS′* and *ss′*, respectively. Now the problem is to derive a demand function for handles, and Marshall uses the following conventions. Take a quantity *OM* of knives. *MP* is the demand price for *OM* knives. The supply price of *OM* knives is *MQ*, and the supply price of the handles for *OM* knives is *Mq*. The difference, *Qq*, is the supply price of *OM* blades. Now in order to obtain the demand price for handle inputs (to produce quantity *OM*), Marshall simply subtracted the supply price of blades (*Qq*) at *OM* from the demand price for knives (*MP*) at *OM*. A demand price *Mp* (*MP* – *Qq*) is thus obtained for handles. It can be seen that *Qq* equals *Pp*. An identical procedure is followed for all other quantities of knives, and a demand function *dd′* for handles may thereby be traced out. The demand price for blades is simply the difference between the total-knife-demand price and the derived-demand price for handles. The supply price for blades is given objectively by the difference between the two supply functions *SS′* and *ss′*.

Equilibrium, in the model described by figure 16-10, takes place when quantity *OB* of knives is produced at price *BA*. The derived demand for handles *dd′* inter-

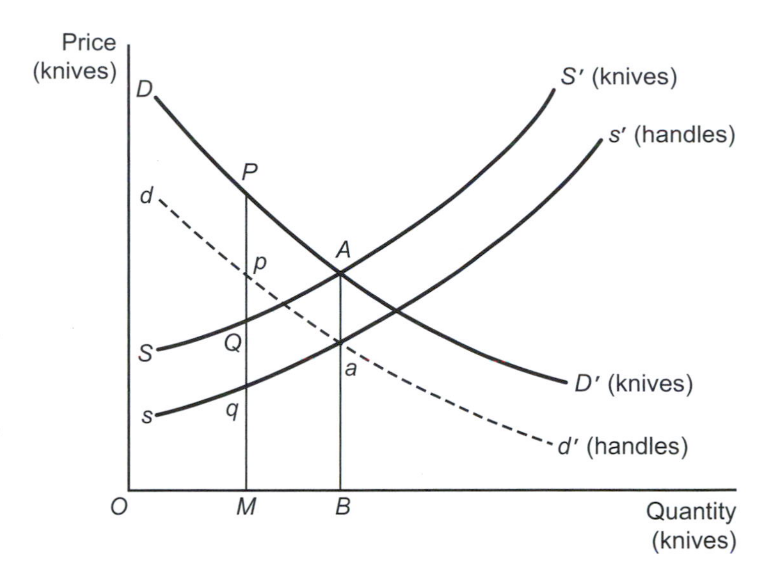

Figure 16-10 At equilibrium *A*, the price of handles, *Ba*, is determined by the intersection of *ss′* and *dd′*, and the price of blades, *aA*, is determined by subtracting *Ba* from the supply of knives.

sects the handle-supply function at a, and the equilibrium price paid for handles is Ba; whereas the equilibrium price paid for blades is established at Aa. (Obviously, $Ba + aA = BA$.) The demand for any input can be derived, then, if one knows the supply prices of the other factors and the demand for final output.

Resource Allocation and the Distribution of Product

In his theory of derived demand Marshall allowed fixed input proportions as a first approximation. His statements are not well organized, but at least in the short run Marshall adhered to a marginal-productivity theory of distribution. At various points in the *Principles*, Marshall asserted that for the most efficient allocation of resources, all inputs should be hired up to the point where their marginal product equals their marginal cost. The following passage is a summary statement of Marshall's famous "principle of substitution."

> Every agent of production, land, machinery, skilled labour, unskilled labour, etc., tends to be applied in production as far as it profitably can be. If employers, and other businessmen, think that they can get a better result by using a little more of any one agent they will do so. They estimate the *net product* (that is *the net increase of the money value of their total output after allowing for incidental expenses*) that will be got by a little more outlay in this direction, or a little more outlay in that; and if they can gain by shifting a little of their outlay from one direction to another, they will do so.
>
> Thus, then the uses of each agent of production are governed by the general conditions of demand in relation to supply: that is, on the one hand, by the urgency of all the uses to which the agent can be put, taken together with the means at the command of those who need it; and, on the other hand, by the available stocks of it. And equality is maintained between its values for each use by the constant tendency to shift it from uses in which its services are of less value to others in which they are of greater value, in accordance with the principle of substitution. (*Principles*, pp. 521–522)

In a number of chapters (*Principles*, Book VI, chaps. 1–13), replete with practical examples, Marshall described the returns to the several factors of production. Rent is a return to inputs absolutely fixed in supply and without alternative opportunities, but Marshall also introduced the notion of "quasi-rent," a return to *temporarily* fixed factors devoted to production in the short run. Quasi-rent, as conceived by Marshall, is of the nature of "sunk capital." According to George Stigler, Marshall's statement is "merely another way of saying that only prime or variable costs are price-determining in the short run" (*Production and Distribution Theories*, p. 95). In the long run, returns to these fixed investments must be covered by market price, or capital will exit the industry. In other words, only in the short run is quasi-rent (the difference between total cost and variable cost) not a necessary payment in order for output to be produced.

Marshall's treatment of the returns to labor typifies the new microeconomic approach to an age-old problem. Under the new paradigm the demand for labor depends on its marginal productivity, as does the demand for any factor input. But the conditions governing the supply of labor differ markedly in the two Marshallian market periods. In the short run, Marshall adopted a theory of labor supply very much like the one propounded by Jevons (see chapter 15). Jevons had focused on the intersection of the marginal disutility of labor and the marginal utility of real income (represented by the marginal utility of the money wage). In Jevons's model, laborers stop working when the marginal utility of their wage is equal to the marginal disutility of work. Although he admitted exceptions, Marshall believed that as a general rule, the supply of labor was positively related to the reward for labor in both long-run and short-run situations.

Marshall held that labor supply in the *long run* was governed chiefly by the cost of producing labor. Classical economists said as much and argued that long-run wages would tend toward subsistence. But in view of the fact that wages exceeded subsistence in England, Marshall was compelled to explain why wages were higher than the cost of producing labor. His explanation focused on both the physical *and* the mental powers of the worker. In anticipation of what was to become known later as the "human capital" theory, Marshall recognized the cost of acquiring certain marketable skills. Often, those who pay the cost of acquiring skills do not reap the rewards, as for example, when parents pay for their children's education. In such matters the profit motive may not be a reliable guide. Parents would presumably educate their children in occupations in which the reward-to-expense ratio is greatest. But the lag between investment and return is quite long, often fifteen to twenty years. Prediction over a period of this length is often impossible. Moreover, incomes of parents differ, which means that expenditures (or investments) in rearing and educating labor will be significantly different. According to Marshall these and other rigidities explained the widely differing wage rates observed in England at the time.

■ Marshall on Capital and Entrepreneurship

Marshall explained the returns to capital (interest) and entrepreneurship (profits) in the same manner, thus displaying the sweeping application of marginal analysis. The demand for capital, which is subject to diminishing returns, is its marginal productivity, and Marshall clearly indicated that capital would be applied up to the point where its marginal value product equaled the rate of interest (*Principles*, p. 520). But in the long run, assuming a perfectly competitive system, the real return to capital would be determined, as is the case for all factors of production, by its cost of production.

Overall, Marshall's treatment of distribution relied heavily on his Anglo-Saxon heritage, and it is particularly reminiscent of Smith's and Ricardo's handling of the question. It may well be that he placed too much emphasis on cost of production as an explanation for factor returns, as did his classical academic forebears. His discussion is also often criticized for general lack of rigor, which is undoubtedly the case. All this notwithstanding, Marshall was perhaps never so close to practical wisdom as when he analyzed, through numerous examples, the reasons for wage and profit differentials or the impact of risk on rate of return. His practical knowledge of business behavior and actual markets was phenomenal, all of which makes his discourse on distribution one of the most enjoyable and profitable parts of the *Principles*. Also, his adherence to the popular theories of the day, most particularly the evolutionary biology of Darwin and Wallace, gave his ruminations on the subject a distinctively "modern" flavor. The peculiar skill of the entrepreneur, Marshall argued, is shaped by an economic struggle for survival in the competitive marketplace.

To the extent that they entertained the subject at all, many early neoclassical writers, with the exception of the Germans, approached entrepreneurship as a cog in the theory of income distribution. That is to say, they were more interested in explaining the reward to the entrepreneur as a factor return than investigating the role of the entrepreneur as a motivating force of economic development or as an equilibrating/disequilibrating force in a market system. Marshall paid more attention than his colleagues to the nature and function of entrepreneurship because he was heavily influenced by the German tradition on the one hand and the principles of biological evolution expounded by Charles Darwin and Alfred Wallace on the other. It would be misleading to claim a theory of entrepreneurship on Marshall's behalf, but at the same time he was more devoted to the subject than many of his contemporaries.

Marshall argued that profit represents a payment for business ability, a slippery concept, but one that opened a more promising avenue than Mill's rather limited idea that profits are "the wages of superintendence." Marshall accepted Mill's explanation up to a point, but followed Mangoldt (chap. 14) in treating entrepreneurial profit as a kind of "rent of ability." The analogy to rent, he claimed, is more appropriate because entrepreneurial talents tend to be in limited supply (like land) and unique to individuals who are capable of exercising imagination and shrewd judgment. How did Marshall reconcile the contrasting views of Mill and Mangoldt? He thought of entrepreneurs both as individuals and as a class. As a class, Marshall posited that entrepreneurs' rewards are commensurate with the levels of human capital they acquired; but as individuals, he maintained that entrepreneurs receive a differential return, akin to rent, and hence equal to their marginal productivity.

> The class of business undertakers contains a disproportionate number of persons with high natural ability; since, in addition to the able men born within its ranks it includes also a large share of the best natural abilities born in the lower ranks of industry. And thus while profits on capital invested in education is a specially important element in the incomes of professional men taken as a class, the rent of rare natural abilities may be regarded as a specially important element in the income of businessmen, so long as we consider them as individuals. (*Principles*, p. 623)

In *Industry and Trade*, more so than in *Principles*, Marshall reserved a special place for the human agent that directs rather than follows economic circumstances. He described the elements of "business genius" as alertness, sense of proportion, strength of reasoning, coordination, innovation, and willingness to take risks (*Industry and Trade*, pp. 356, 358). He argued that this combination of abilities could be acquired through experience, but not taught by formal education. He divided entrepreneurs into two classes, active and passive. Active entrepreneurs are "those who open out new and improved methods of business," whereas passive entrepreneurs are "those who follow beaten tracks" (*Industry and Trade*, p. 597). He attributed "wages of superintendence" to the latter group of passive entrepreneurs and "rent of ability" to the former group of active entrepreneurs, whose reward is subject to risk. The venturesome entrepreneur cannot avoid risk because he directs capital and labor to an uncertain end. In order to be successful, therefore, he must be capable of conceiving "wise and far reaching policies, and . . . carry[ing] them out calmly and resolutely" (*Industry and Trade*, p. 606).

At bottom, Marshall's entrepreneur was a business manager, although he used the term management to mean more than mere superintendence. Following Darwin, Marshall argued that professional business managers emerge as a special group from an evolutionary process that is driven by specialization and division of labor. This "Darwinism" may explain Marshall's inability or unwillingness to tie the entrepreneur to a single function or set of abilities. The concept itself seems to evolve endlessly in Marshall's writings, but in the final analysis, he placed more emphasis on the existence and necessity of business ability than on anything else.[14]

In his early work, Marshall stressed duty as an important stimulus to human action. But his faith in the widespread application of this Victorian virtue dwindled during the 1880s. After 1890, Marshall placed the chief responsibility for the economic and moral progress of society on the restless, farsighted, pioneering, but unsung entrepreneur. By 1907, duty had receded farther into the background, and Marshall was extolling the entrepreneur for his imagination as well as his leadership:

> Men of this class live in constantly shifting visions, fashioned in their own brains, of various routes to their desired end; of the difficulties which nature will oppose to them on each route, and of the contrivances by which they hope to get the better of her opposition. This imagination gains little credit with the people, because it is not allowed to run riot; its strength is disciplined by a stronger will; and its highest glory is to have attained great ends by means so simple that no one will know, and none but experts will even guess, how a dozen other expedients, each suggesting as much brilliancy to the hasty observer, were set aside in favour of it. (*Memorials*, pp. 332–333)

In a purely analytical sense, the most important contribution Marshall made to the theory of entrepreneurship was to extend Mangoldt's notion of rent-of-ability, though he did not, as Schumpeter points out, restrict the idea to the entrepreneur (*History*, p. 894). Freeing himself from the analytical impediments of the classical wages-fund doctrine, Marshall attempted to cut through the amorphous nature of "labor" to capture the uniqueness of individual ability. Observation and experience told him that "business genius" was unevenly distributed and that unique skills received a kind of surplus, or rent.

Despite the fact that Marshall wrote during the high tide of competitive capitalism, his theory of entrepreneurship gave little prominence to invention and innovation. Also, despite his lip service to evolution as a vital force in economics, he

[14] In a parallel vein, Marshall made the simple declaration, "Knowledge is our most powerful engine of production"—an insight that is especially resonant in the digital age, which is often referred to as "the knowledge economy."

devoted his intellectual energies mainly to advancing the theory of comparative statics and partial equilibrium. For the most part, his students and disciples followed suit.

■ Conclusion

Alfred Marshall's *Principles* was, in a significant sense, a benchmark in the development of economics. But as we have seen, a number of important writers contributed to the corpus of neoclassical microanalysis before the publication of Marshall's classic work. (We return to this theme again in the following chapter.) Cournot, Dupuit, Jevons, and Walras, to mention only the most seminal contributors, antedated Marshall's concerns. On separate points of doctrine (e.g., consumer surplus, demand, monopoly, joint supply, and marginal productivity), Marshall's inventions were upstaged by the aforementioned writers and by John Stuart Mill. Objectively, on a doctrine-by-doctrine basis, Marshall does not rank extremely high on originality, although it is true that he developed many ideas independently and with more intensity and unusual clarity.

On what basis, then, does Marshall's great (and largely untarnished) reputation lie? As in the case of Adam Smith, his fame is due principally to the fact that he wrote a book that caught the academic spirit of the time. He did so, moreover, by directing his appeal to the intelligent layperson. In modern parlance, he "put it all together"; Marshall synthesized classical and neoclassical analyses of cost and utility, producing one cogent engine of far-reaching economic analysis.

But, as we have seen, Marshall was much more than a mere synthesizer. His partial equilibrium method became a kind of glue that bound all the various branches of economic theory together. The use of conceptual time, which was at the heart of this method, was a massive and original contribution to modern economic theory and policy. In addition to numerous original theoretical inventions, Marshall never touched a "received" concept without extending or improving it.

There is little doubt that Marshall was a great theorist, but we tend to lose sight of the fact that he was also a very practical man. A probable reason for the subsequent emphasis on the theoretical aspects of his work is that Marshall's students (whose names almost form a litany of great twentieth-century British theorists) chose to work on and refine the theoretical concepts of the *Principles*. In other words, there appears to be a large and unfortunate gap between Marshall's interests in economics and those of the Marshallians, his students and disciples. The Marshallians viewed their task as clarifying and developing the *analytical* areas of the *Principles*, while simultaneously ignoring and dismissing the practical context in which Marshall encased his ideas. Thus, Marshall has often been accused of making ambiguous statements of certain theoretical ideas. But many of these criticisms are misdirected, for they fail to treat Marshall's theory as he often treated it himself—as a tool for attacking practical social and economic problems. As indicated in the present chapter, an understanding of the several levels of abstraction he used in dealing with demand curves might have forestalled the protracted debate over the nature of the formal specification of demand in the *Principles*. Marshall's "ambiguities," moreover, apparently have not forced other theorists to view all sides of economic questions, as he strove to do.

If Marshall were alive today, his quest for an economic analysis that could be used in practical economic problems might even lead him to characterize the theoretical developments that sprang from the *Principles* as "overelaborate." The complex process of mathematizing economic analysis, which the discipline has been undergoing for many decades, appears alien to the concept of the nature and purpose of economics. Marshall demanded empirical, or at least imaginable, referents to all his analytical tools. Many subsequent theorists of high reputation—some claiming to be disciples of Marshall—have been equally as adamant in demanding none.

Marshall, of course, was always ready to point out the gaps and deficiencies in his analytical constructs. But his conception of the nature of economics was focused on suggested *applications*, making allowance for the analytical deficiencies that inevitably accompany a social science. He would probably be the first to laud the development of theoretical improvements, but he would as surely criticize the cleavage between theory and actual events that marks a great deal of contemporary economics. The kernel of Marshall's genius lay in his ability to learn from economic and social problems and, in turn, to contribute toward their solution.

References

Blaug, Mark. *Economic Theory in Retrospect*, 4th ed. London: Cambridge University Press, 1985.

Coase, Ronald. "The Problem of Social Cost," *Journal of Law and Economics*, vol. 3 (October 1960), pp. 1–44.

Friedman, Milton. "The Marshallian Demand Curve," *Journal of Political Economy*, vol. 57 (December 1949), pp. 463–495.

Hicks, John R. *The Theory of Wages*. London: Macmillan, 1932. Revised 1968.

Foxwell, H. S., "The Economic Movement in England," *Quarterly Journal of Economics*, vol. 2 (October 1887), pp. 84–103.

Marshall, Alfred. *Principles of Economics*, 8th ed. London: Macmillan, 1920.

———. *Industry and Trade*, 3rd ed. London: Macmillan, 1920.

———. *Memorials of Alfred Marshall*, A. C. Pigou (ed). London: Macmillan, 1925.

Maurice, S. C. "On the Importance of Being Unimportant: An Analysis of the Paradox in Marshall's Third Rule of Derived Demand," *Economica*, vol. 42 (November 1975), pp. 385–393.

Pigou, A. C. *Wealth and Welfare*. London: Macmillan, 1912.

———. *The Economics of Welfare*. London: Macmillan, 1920.

Stigler, George J. *Production and Distribution Theories*. New York: Macmillan, 1941.

Notes for Further Reading

The University of Florence (Italy) publishes a *Marshall Studies Bulletin*, devoted to studies on Alfred Marshall's economics and, more generally, to the history of economic ideas in Britain from the nineteenth to the twentieth century. An electronic version of this bulletin is available online at http://www.dse.unifi.it/CMpro-v-p-121.html. John Sutton's *Marshall's Tendencies: What Can Economists Know?* (Boston: MIT Press, 2000) is essential reading for understanding the "standard paradigm" of economics and Marshall's role in its construction. For some serious fun, especially for mystery buffs, see a series of books by Marshall Jevons: *Murder at the Margin* (Princeton: Princeton University Press, 1978); *The Fatal Equilibrium* (New York: MIT Press, 1985); and *A Deadly Indifference* (New York: Carroll and Ampersand Graf Publishers, 1995). These are riveting "whodunits" in which master-sleuth, Henry Spearman, employs Marshallian analysis to solve murders. "Marshall Jevons" is the pen name of economists William Breit and Kenneth G. Elzinga.

The secondary literature on Marshall and his ideas is enormous and growing. On Marshall himself, the most comprehensive single source is Peter Groenewegen, *A Soar-*

ing Eagle: Alfred Marshall, 1842–1924 (Aldershot, UK: Edward Elgar, 1995). See also, J. M. Keynes, "Alfred Marshall," *Economic Journal*, vol. 34 (September 1924), pp. 311–372, reprinted in Keynes's *Essays in Biography* (London: Macmillan, 1933). Keynes's *Essays* also contains a memoir on Marshall's wife, "Mary Paley Marshall (1850–1944)." R. H. Coase, "Alfred Marshall's Mother and Father," *History of Political Economy*, vol. 16 (Winter 1984), pp. 519–527, rounds out the family portraits. The *Memorials of Alfred Marshall*, edited by his student A. C. Pigou (see references), should not be missed. For later assessments of Marshall's work by Marshallians, see G. F. Shove, "The Place of Marshall's *Principles in Economic Theory*," and C. W. Guillebaud, "The Evolution of Marshall's *Principles*," both appearing in the *Economic Journal*, vol. 52 (December 1942), pp. 294–329, 330–349. T. W. Hutchison's *Review of Economic Doctrines 1870–1929*, chap. 4 (Oxford: Clarendon Press, 1953), contains a brief interpretive account of Marshall.

For an interesting, though not exhaustive, discussion of Marshall's method, see R. H. Coase, "Marshall on Method," *Journal of Law and Economics*, vol. 18 (April 1975), pp. 25–31; H. Brems, "Marshall on Mathematics," *Journal of Law and Economics*, vol. 18 (October 1975), pp. 583–585; E. F. Beach, "Marshallian Methodology," *International Journal of Social Economics*, vol. 14 (1987), pp. 19–26; Stephen Pratten, "Marshall on Tendencies, Equilibrium, and the Statical Method," *History of Political Economy*, vol. 30 (Spring 1998), pp. 121–163; and Andrew Vasquez, "Marshall and the Mathematization of Economics," *Journal of the History of Economic Thought*, vol. 17 (Fall 1995), pp. 247–265.

David Reisman has authored a trilogy on Marshall in which he examines, respectively, the different aspects of Marshall's thought: economics, politics, and ethics. See, in order, *The Economics of Alfred Marshall* (London: Macmillan, 1986); *Alfred Marshall: Progress and Politics* (New York: St. Martin's, 1987); and *Alfred Marshall's Mission* (New York: St. Martin's, 1990). R. D. C. Black, "Jevons, Marshall and the Utilitarian Tradition," *Scottish Journal of Political Economy*, vol. 37 (February 1990), pp. 5–17, provides additional insight into Marshall's tendency to treat economics as applied ethics. Among other things, Black concludes that although Jevons was a thoroughgoing Benthamite, Marshall was not. Marshall famously said that he wanted to use economics as a vehicle for social reform, i.e., doing "good." For evidence that he really did want to "do good" see Rhead S. Bowman, "Marshall: Just How Interested in Doing Good Was He?" *Journal of the History of Economic Thought*, vol. 26 (December 2004), pp. 493–518.

An excellent and detailed overview of Marshall's contributions to analysis may be found in chaps. 9 and 10 of Mark Blaug's *Economic Theory in Retrospect* (see references). Milton Friedman's essay entitled "The Marshallian Demand Curve" (see references) offers a persuasive case for identifying the Marshallian demand curve with a constant-purchasing-power-of-money assumption. Other Marshallian writers, such as Hicks, disagree. See the classic paper by J. R. Hicks and R. G. D. Allen, "A Reconsideration of the Theory of Value," *Economica*, n.s., vol. 1 (February, May 1934), pp. 52–76, 196–219. See also M. J. Bailey's comment on Friedman's paper, "The Marshallian Demand Curve," *Journal of Political Economy*, vol. 62 (June 1954), pp. 255–261. For a sketch of developments related to the Marshallian demand curve, see R. B. Ekelund, Jr., E. G. Furubotn, and W. P. Gramm, *The Evolution of Modern Demand Theory*, chap. 2 (Boston: Heath, 1972). Also useful is John Aldrich, "The Course of Marshall's Theorizing About Demand," *History of Political Economy*, vol. 28 (Summer 1996), pp. 171–217. Marshall's "Giffen Paradox," which posits the possibility of a positively sloped demand curve, is analyzed by G. J. Stigler in "Notes on the History of the Giffen Paradox," *Journal of Political Economy*, vol. 55 (April 1947), pp. 152–156. But for a more recent assessment of Stigler's position, see William P. Gramm, "Giffen's Paradox and the Marshallian Demand Curve," *The Manchester School of Economic and Social Studies*, vol. 38 (March 1970), pp. 65–71.

The firm's envelope or planning curve, which simplifies Marshall's long-run analysis, was developed by Jacob Viner in his classic paper, "Cost Curves and Supply Curves,"

Zeitschrift fur Nationalökonomie, vol. 3 (September 1931), pp. 23–46. Marshall's fiction of the representative firm is severely criticized in Lionel Robbins, "The Representative Firm," *Economic Journal*, vol. 38 (September 1928), pp. 387–404. The whole area of Marshall's theories of production and distribution is brought under skillful and critical review in chap. 4 of Stigler's *Production and Distribution Theories* (see references). On the suffusion of Marshall's time period method into his theory of distribution, see H. M. Robertson's "Alfred Marshall's Aims and Methods Illustrated from His Treatment of Distribution," *History of Political Economy*, vol. 2 (Spring 1970), pp. 1–64. Likewise, see G. L. S. Shackle, "Marshall's Accommodation of Time," in *Epistemics and Economics* (London: Cambridge University Press, 1972); and P. C. Dooley, "Alfred Marshall: Fitting the Theory to the Facts," *Cambridge Journal of Economics*, vol. 9 (September 1985), pp. 245–255.

Marshall's fundamental contribution to time-period analysis in market exchange is also the subject of P. L. Williams, "A Reconstruction of Marshall's Temporary Equilibrium Pricing Model," *History of Political Economy*, vol. 18 (Winter 1986), pp. 639–653. In the same broad vein, see J. M. Gee, "Marshall's Views on 'Short-Period' Value Formation," *History of Political Economy*, vol. 15 (Summer 1983), pp. 181–205; O. F. Hamouda, "On the Notion of Short-Run and Long-Run: Marshall, Ricardo and Equilibrium Theories," *British Review of Economic Issues*, vol. 6 (Spring 1984), pp. 55–82; and Michel De Vroey, "Marshall on Equilibrium and Time: A Reconstruction," *The European Journal of the History of Economic Thought*, vol. 7 (Summer 2000), pp. 245–269, which tries to sort out the differences between Marshallian and Walrasian concepts of equilibrium.

R. B. Ekelund, Jr., and R. F. Hébert, "The Dupuit–Marshall Theory of Competitive Equilibrium," *Economica*, vol. 66 (May 1999), pp. 225–240, compare Dupuit's method with Marshall's and conclude that they shared a vision of how economic markets work, as well as how scientific inquiry on the subject is to be conducted. Marshall's theory of exchange has also been reviewed by D. A. Walker, "Marshall's Theory of Competitive Exchange," *Canadian Journal of Economics*, vol. 2 (November 1969), pp. 590–597. The following two articles by D. A. Walker on Marshall's long-run and short-run concepts of labor supply should be read in tandem: "Marshall on the Long-Run Supply of Labor," *Zeitschrift für die Gesamte Staatswissenschaft* (October 1974), pp. 691–705, and "Marshall on the Short-Run Supply of Labor," *Southern Economic Journal*, vol. 41 (January 1975), pp. 429–441. Joseph Persky, "Marshall's Neo-classical Labor Values," *Journal of the History of Economic Thought*, vol. 21 (September 1999), pp. 257–268, establishes that Marshall did not entirely forsake key classical concerns.

The related issues of external economies and increasing returns (decreasing costs) have probably been responsible for more debate than any others discussed in Marshall's *Principles*. As we saw in the text of the present chapter, A. C. Pigou translated the concept of external economies into a divergence between marginal social costs and marginal private costs. The Pigovian solution was to levy a tax (or a subsidy in the opposite case) on the industry. In 1924, however, Frank Knight challenged Pigou's discussion on several crucial points, demonstrating that competition does not lead to excessive investment as Pigou (and others) had alleged. See Knight, "Some Fallacies in the Interpretation of Social Costs," *Quarterly Journal of Economics*, vol. 38 (August 1924), pp. 582–606.

The important connection between Pigou's welfare economics and the earlier work of Henry Sidgwick is established by Margaret G. O'Donnell in "Pigou: An Extension of Sidgwickian Thought," *History of Political Economy*, vol. 11 (Winter 1979), pp. 588–605. Roger Backhouse, "Sidgwick, Marshall and Cambridge," *History of Political Economy*, vol. 38 (Spring 2006), pp. 15–44, maintains that Sidgwick's influence went beyond Pigou and attempts to overcome the marginalization of Sidgwick's role in the development of the broader Cambridge tradition.

The modern Coasian criticism has created an entirely new area of economics—the economics of property rights. A good place to start in this vast literature is the survey by

E. G. Furubotn and S. Pejovich, "Property Rights and Economic Theory: A Survey of Recent Literature," *Journal of Economic Literature*, vol. 10 (December 1972), pp. 1137–1157. Nahid Aslanbeigui and Steven Medema, "Beyond the Dark Clouds: Pigou and Coase on Social Cost," *History of Political Economy*, vol. 30 (Winter 1998), pp. 601–625, attempt to narrow the differences between the Pigovian and Coasian approaches.

On the subject of consumer surplus and particularly Marshall's role in its development, see P. C. Dooley, "Consumer's Surplus: Marshall and His Critics," *Canadian Journal of Economics*, vol. 16 (February 1983), pp. 26–38, and R. B. Ekelund, Jr., and R. F. Hébert, "Consumer Surplus: The First Hundred Years," *History of Political Economy*, vol. 17 (Fall 1985), pp. 419–454.

The question of the existence and, indeed, of the usefulness of the concepts of industries of constant, increasing, or decreasing returns was raised by J. H. Clapham in a delightful paper, "Of Empty Economic Boxes," *Economic Journal*, vol. 32 (September 1922), pp. 458–465, and D. H. Robertson extended the criticism of the concept in "Those Empty Boxes," *Economic Journal*, vol. 34 (March 1924), pp. 16–31. The incompatibility of competitive equilibrium and a condition of decreasing costs (increasing returns), which led partly to the development of the theory of imperfect competition, was brought out in a brilliant paper by Piero Sraffa, "The Laws of Returns under Competitive Conditions," *Economic Journal*, vol. 36 (December 1926), pp. 535–550. The Viner, Knight, Clapham, Pigou, Robertson, and Sraffa papers mentioned here are reprinted in *Readings in Price Theory*, George J. Stigler and Kenneth E. Boulding (eds.) (Homewood, IL: Irwin, 1952). R. Prendergast, "Increasing Returns and Competitive Equilibrium—The Content and Development of Marshall's Theory," *Cambridge Journal of Economics*, vol. 16 (December 1992), pp. 447–462, deals with this "reconciliation problem," emphasizing Marshall's reliance on biological conceptions. See also N. Hart, "Increasing Returns and Marshall's Theory of Value," *Australian Economic Papers*, vol. 59 (December 1992), pp. 234–244.

Marshall as "historicist-evolutionist" and the influence of Darwin on his thought are discussed by the prominent sociologist Talcott Parsons in two classic papers: "Wants and Activities in Marshall," *Quarterly Journal of Economics*, vol. 46 (November 1931), pp. 101–140, and "Economics and Sociology: Marshall in Relation to the Thought of His Time," *Quarterly Journal of Economics*, vol. 46 (February 1932), pp. 316–347. On this important issue, see Marshall's own statements in "The Old Generation of Economists and the New," *Quarterly Journal of Economics*, vol. 11 (January 1897), pp. 115–135, reprinted in *Memorials of Alfred Marshall*, A. C. Pigou, ed. Several writers have continued to explore this nebulous idea up to the present time. See, for example, Tiziano Raffaelli, *Marshall's Evolutionary Economics* (London: Routledge, 2003); same author, "Whatever Happened to Marshall's Industrial Economics?" *The European Journal of the History of Economic Thought*, vol. 11 (Summer 2004), pp. 209–229; A. A. Awan, "Marshallian and Schumpeterian Theories of Economic Evolution: Gradualism vs. Punctualism," *Atlantic Economic Journal*, vol. 14 (December 1986), pp. 37–49; A. L. Levine, "Marshall's *Principles* and the Biological Viewpoint: A Reconsideration," *Manchester School of Economic and Social Studies*, vol. 51 (September 1983), pp. 276–293; and N. B. Niman, "Biological Analogies in Marshall's Work," *Journal of the History of Economic Thought*, vol. 13 (Spring 1991), pp. 19–36. Niman examines Marshall's (not entirely successful) attempt to build an economic theory based on the foundations of natural science.

For more evidence of Marshall's sociology and his tendency to blend it with his economics, see T. Levitt, "Alfred Marshall: Victorian Relevance for Modern Economics," *Quarterly Journal of Economics*, vol. 90 (August 1976), pp. 426–444; M. A. Pujol, "Gender and Class in Marshall's *Principles of Economics*," *Cambridge Journal of Economics*, vol. 8 (September 1984), pp. 217–234; R. M. Tullberg, "Marshall's Tendency to Socialism," *History of Political Economy*, vol. 7 (Spring 1975), pp. 75–111; A. Petridis, "Alfred Marshall's

Attitudes to the Economic Analysis of Trade Unions," *History of Political Economy*, vol. 5 (Spring 1973), pp. 165–198; and J. D. Chasse, "Marshall, the Human Agent and Economic Growth: Wants and Activities Revisited," *History of Political Economy*, vol. 16 (Fall 1984), pp. 381–404. The latter explores the relations Marshall developed between income distribution, the standard of living, and economic growth. P. C. Dooley, "Marshall's Parable of the Meteoric Stones: Rent, Quasi-Rent and Interest," *American Journal of Economics and Sociology*, vol. 50 (April 1991), pp. 197–206, explores special assumptions required to reconcile the classical theory of distribution with the neoclassical theory. Peter Groenewegen, "Marshall's Treatment of Technological Change in *Industry and Trade*," *The European Journal of the History of Economic Thought*, vol. 17 (December 2010), pp. 1253–1269, examines Marshall's view of the causes of technological change and its implications for firm size. Technological change is also an important part of the section of Marshall's *Industry and Trade* (see references) dealing with changes in business organization.

The growing professionalism of economics in his day and particularly Marshall's contribution to it are the subjects of J. Maloney, "Marshall, Cunningham and the Emerging Economics Profession," *Economic History Review*, vol. 29 (August 1976), pp. 440–451; and R. F. Hébert, "Marshall: A Professional Economist Guards the Purity of His Discipline," in R. V. Andelson (ed.), *Critics of Henry George* (London: Associated University Presses, 1979). Katia Caldari, "Alfred Marshall's Critical Analysis of Scientific Management," *The European Journal of the History of Economic Thought*, vol. 14 (March 2007), pp. 55–78, examines Marshall's views on scientific management, both critical and affirmative. For more on Marshall's views of entrepreneurship, see Laurence Moss, "Biological Theory and Technological Entrepreneurship in Marshall's Writings," *Eastern Economic Journal*, vol. 8 (January 1982), pp. 3–13.

Finally, some of the best and most interesting recent work on Marshall is that of John K. Whitaker, especially on the matter of the early development of Marshall's thought. See Whitaker's "Alfred Marshall: The Years 1877 to 1885," *History of Political Economy*, vol. 4 (Spring 1972), pp. 1–61; and same author, "Some Neglected Aspects of Alfred Marshall's Economic and Social Thought," *History of Political Economy*, vol. 9 (Summer 1977), pp. 161–197. Professor Whitaker has also edited two volumes containing the early writings of Marshall: *The Early Economic Writings of Alfred Marshall, 1867–1890* (New York: Free Press, 1975).

The year 1990 marked the centennial of Marshall's *Principles* and spawned a number of centenary tributes. For two broad retrospectives, see *Centenary Essays on Alfred Marshall*, J. K. Whitaker (ed.) (Cambridge: Cambridge University Press, 1990); and *Alfred Marshall in Retrospect*, R. M. Tullberg (ed.) (Brookfield, VT: Edward Elgar, 1990). D. P. O'Brien's contribution to *Centenary Essays* should be read in conjunction with G. Argyrous, "The Growth of Knowledge and Economic Science: Marshall's Interpretation of the Classical Economists," *History of Political Economy*, vol. 22 (Fall 1990), pp. 529–537. For more retrospectives, see the *Scottish Journal of Political Economy*, vol. 37 (February 1990), an issue devoted mainly to Marshall. Especially noteworthy are the articles by D. P. O'Brien, "Marshall's Industrial Analysis," pp. 61–84, R. D. C. Black (*op. cit.*), and J. Creedy, "Marshall and Edgeworth," pp. 18–39.

17

The Mantle of Léon Walras

Having seen the brilliance of Cournot and Dupuit in France (see chapter 13), it is tempting to conclude that Léon Walras (1834–1910) was the heir-apparent to the French econo-engineering tradition. But the actuality is far more complicated, involving peculiar institutions and complex human interactions. Although Walras eventually scaled the heights of economic analysis, his path to the top was long and bumpy. Unable to secure a university post in his native France, he struggled to gain a voice from a lonely educational outpost in Switzerland. By contrast, Alfred Marshall reached a position of dominance in a leading English university, Cambridge, surrounded and supported by able colleagues and disciples. But such differences aside, it would be difficult to overestimate the collective impact of Walras and Marshall on economics and those that practice it. The framework of contemporary mainstream developments in microeconomics, as well as key developments in macroeconomics (monetary theory, for instance), is either Walrasian or Marshallian in character. For these reasons and for many others, Walras and Marshall are rightfully regarded as two of the most important economic theorists who ever lived.[1]

Contrasts between Marshall's and Walras's Approaches

Because their joint, though independent, influence on economics was so strong and vital, it is appropriate to highlight certain fundamental differences between these two giants of neoclassical economics. Two more dissimilar and diverse contributors to the mainstream of contemporary economic analysis can hardly be imagined. They were contemporaries, but Walras was the elder statesman in terms of age and priority of publication. Their great works—Walras's *Elements of Pure Economics* (1874) and Marshall's *Principles of Economics* (1890)—published almost twenty years apart, each had a resounding impact on economics. Yet, each work, like each man, was different. The most instructive contrasts between them are to be found in the scope and method of their respective theoretical achievements.

[1] This statement is not meant to imply that Walras and Marshall were the only contributors to the neoclassical paradigm. The small army of writers considered in chaps. 13–15 were of a neoclassical ilk, and indeed the neoclassical age (c. 1870 to 1920) produced other great economists (e.g., Knut Wicksell and a whole Swedish tradition, F. Y. Edgeworth, P. H. Wicksteed, Vilfredo Pareto, and Irving Fisher), some of whom will be considered subsequently in this book. Nevertheless, Walras and Marshall are of such significance as to deserve special treatment.

Partial Equilibrium versus General Equilibrium

Both writers were concerned essentially with the microeconomic foundations of price formation. That is, they—along with Cournot, Dupuit, and other predecessors—viewed the equilibrating process of prices and quantities as the result of market exchange (though, as we shall see, their views of the method of price and quantity adjustment differed). The essential difference between Walras and Marshall involves the scope of the subject under analysis. Marshall, and virtually all writers on microeconomics before him, utilized an approach to particular markets that is now called *partial equilibrium analysis*. Walras, on the other hand, developed a broader and more complex method of looking at (interconnected) markets, called *general-equilibrium analysis*.

The important distinction between Marshall and Walras on this point is simple, although it sometimes gets lost in the complexity of analytical twists and turns. Basically, when a market is analyzed according to Marshall's partial equilibrium method it is considered in quasi-isolation. For instance, take the market for any commodity—such as coffee. In both Marshallian and Walrasian views, the equilibrium price and quantity of coffee are determined by the intersection of the demand function and the supply function (French economists typically called the latter an "offer curve"). Where Marshall and Walras differed was in regard to the *determinants* of the supply and demand curves and the nature and process of market equilibration.

If he were specifying the individual demand function for coffee, Marshall would make demand a function not only of the price of coffee but also of the prices of goods closely related to coffee (substitutes and complements) and of the income and tastes of consumers. All the other factors influencing the demand for coffee (the prices of distantly related goods, market interactions vis-à-vis changes in the price of coffee, etc.) are held constant or ignored altogether. As we saw in the previous chapter, Marshall used *ceteris paribus* assumptions in dealing with individual and market demand and supply curves for any particular good. He was impelled to ignore or to hold in abeyance seemingly unrelated or distantly related determinants of the price and quantity of any particular good so that the main features of the individual market could be isolated for examination. This partial equilibrium method had been employed before him by Cournot, Dupuit, and Jenkin, among others.

By contrast, Walras was more interested in the *interdependencies* between markets. In his view, all markets are interrelated because the valuation process necessarily occurs in all markets simultaneously. Thus, according to Walras, anyone who has not maximized his or her satisfactions will have excess demands (to be defined below) for some goods, including coffee, and excess supplies of others. Utility maximization—the object of exchange—means disposing of excess supplies in order to eliminate excess demands. Therefore, *every* act of exchange influences the values of *all* goods in the economic system. By the same perspective, Walras viewed the production and input side of economic activity as interrelated. Indeed, the interdependence of the entire system of production and consumption was the focus of Walras's *Elements*.

How, then, would Walras describe the market for coffee? He would argue that Marshall's *ceteris paribus* assumption was inappropriate because other things are *not* equal. Because the whole system is interconnected an increase in demand for coffee necessarily means that there are excess suppliers of other goods in the system. Consequently, any price change in coffee will have further effects on other markets (e.g., haircuts) that react back on the coffee market and produce further changes. These basic interconnections of all markets, which Marshall chose to ignore, constitute the heart of Walras's system. Thus, at an abstract, theoretical level, Walras argued that an analysis of the market for coffee—in isolation from all variables in the system—was inappropriate.[2] In contrast to Marshall's partial equilibrium approach, Walras's method was a general-equilibrium approach.

Doctrinal Antagonism over Method

All this is not to imply that Marshall and Walras were unaware of—or incapable of using—each other's system. In fact, in elaborating Mill's doctrine of reciprocal demands (see chapter 8), Marshall produced an elegant two-commodity, two-country general-equilibrium model that explained international values. In his *Principles*, however, he consciously chose partial equilibrium analysis as the appropriate method for dealing with selected markets in a complex world. Even so, he never denied the correctness of Walras's system.

For his part, Walras was adamant—even rude—in pointing out what he perceived to be Marshall's major errors. Although Walras was not opposed to the use of demand curves for *particular* goods, he objected to the use of such curves if they excluded the interdependencies of utilities and demands for all goods. He also vehemently rejected the tacit identification of marginal utility with demand, a practice that Dupuit had originated. In fact, Walras's salvos were often directed jointly at Dupuit and Marshall. In a letter to his Italian contemporary Maffeo Pantaleoni, for example, Walras pointed out that his analysis of exchange considered demand functions containing many independent variables and that this was the basic difference between his own concept of demand and those of Dupuit, Marshall, and two prominent Austrian theorists, Rudolph Auspitz and Richard Lieben (*Correspondence*, letters 379 and 465). Walras identified Marshall's demand formulation with that of Dupuit (see chapters 13 and 16), and he held that Dupuit and Marshall illegitimately attempted to explain demand curves in terms of (marginal) utility curves. As for his own role in value theory, he considered himself to have been the first to show the interactions between Cournot's demand apparatus (without utility accoutrements) and Jevons's theory of the final degree of utility (see chapters 13 and 15). Yet, most of Walras's objections to the Dupuit–Marshall demand theory were ill-founded, for in this instance he failed to appreciate the convenience (and usefulness) of the *ceteris paribus* convention in partial equilibrium theory.

Curiously, Walras was almost always in a pique when speaking of Marshall. He seemed always ready to find merit in Continental economists' work but, with the exception of Jevons, he launched biting attacks against English writers. For example, while exonerating Jevons and Gossen from criticism because they did not attempt to deduce demand curves from utility curves, he called Marshall the "great white elephant of political economy" and attacked him and his brilliant colleague F. Y. Edgeworth for jealously and obstinately attempting to defend Ricardo's and Mill's theory of price (*Correspondence*, letter 1051).

Part of this divisiveness stems from the fact that Walras and Marshall developed their analyses and wrote their respective books for two very different audiences. Marshall's avowed purpose in writing *Principles* was to inform the intelligent layperson, and particularly the businessperson, of the fundamental tools and uses of economic analysis. Consequently, most of his formal analysis appears either in foot-

[2] This is true irrespective of the fact that Walrasians are forced to utilize partial equilibrium conventions in dealing with practical questions.

notes or in appendixes. Walras, however, was clearly writing for his professional colleagues. It is doubtful whether more than a handful of leading world theorists in 1874 readily digested Walras's mathematical treatment of exchange (although Marshall was probably one of them), but its formal elegance was sure to impress a few. These differences of form and substance may help us understand the relative acceptance of the two works by the profession. But what is not so easy to understand is the almost total lack of communication between Marshall and Walras. Cultural and theoretical differences aside, it is imperative that we understand the ideas of the men who have come to be appreciated as two of history's greatest economic theorists. (See the box, Method Squabbles 4: The Hedgehog and the Fox.)

Method Squabbles 4: The Hedgehog and the Fox

Some regard as excessive Schumpeter's judgment that Walras was, in matters of pure theory, "the greatest of all economists,"* but most agree that few theorists left a more lasting imprint on subsequent generations. Walras's enduring legacy has established a framework for organizing ideas and for looking at the economic system in a way that avoids mistakes in logic. In assessing that contribution, we should note, however, that Walras was more of an architect than a builder.

A decade before the appearance of Mill's *Principles of Political Economy*, Cournot (1838) wrote:

> In reality the economic system is a whole of which all the parts are connected and react on each other. . . . It seems, therefore, as if, for a complete and rigorous solution of the problems relative to some parts of the economic system, it were indispensable to take the entire system into consideration. But this would surpass the powers of mathematical analysis and of our practical methods of calculation, even if the values of all the constants could be assigned to them numerically.†

Walras's lasting achievement was to have constructed a mathematical system displaying in great detail precisely the interrelationships stressed by Cournot. Despite his boldness, however, Walras did not provide the "complete and rigorous solution" alluded to by Cournot. Instead, he provided a solution "in principle," making no pretense that it could be used directly in numerical calculations. The difference is important, for it is a matter of form over content.

Emphasis on form is important in economics. On the one hand it helps us to avoid mistakes in logic. By translating vague statements into symbolic form and using elementary mathematics, Walras was able to jettison much irrelevant material, show that some statements are mutually contradictory, and demonstrate the validity of others. On the other hand, it provides a language, or classificatory scheme for organizing analytical materials—like labels for the compartments of a filing box. Walras's general-equilibrium scheme offers us a bird's-eye view of the economy as a whole and prods us to be ever mindful of the interconnectedness of its constituent parts. But form alone is not sufficient for fruitful economic theory. Meaningful economic theory requires content as well. Economists need more than the right kind of language; they also need something to say.

Marshall and Walras each had much to say, even if they set their message in different channels. The two giants of early neoclassical economics had different conceptions of economic theory. The difference is only palely reflected in the familiar dichotomy between "partial equilibrium" and "general equilibrium." Marshall was devoted to economic theory as a means of solving practical problems. He repeated often the expression that economic theory is "an engine for the discovery of concrete truth," and his wryly written "rules" for the use of mathematics in economic analysis (see chapter 16) belie the same concern. It was Marshall's contention that:

> Facts by themselves are silent. . . . In order to be able with any safety to interpret economic facts. . . . We must know what kind of effects to expect from each cause and

> how these effects are likely to combine with one another. This is the knowledge which is got by the study of economic science.... The economist... must stand fast by the more laborious plan of interrogating facts in order to learn the manner of action of causes singly and in combination, applying this knowledge to build up the organon of economic theory, and then making use of the aid of the organon in dealing with the economic side of social problems.‡

According to an ancient Greek poet, "the fox knows many things, but the hedgehog knows one big thing." By this analogy, Léon Walras was the hedgehog of economic theory and Alfred Marshall the fox.

*Joseph Schumpeter, *History of Economic Analysis*, p. 827.
†Augustin Cournot, *Researches*, p. 127.
‡Alfred Marshall, "The Present Position of Economics," in Pigou's *Memorials*, pp. 166, 168, 171.

■ Léon Walras: Sketch of His Life and Work

Léon Walras was born in 1834 in Normandy, France. He retained the citizenship of his birthright even though he spent most of his adult life in neighboring Switzerland. Like John Stuart Mill, he was fathered by an economist, though his early education was not nearly as rigorous as Mill's. His father, Auguste, was the only teacher of economics he knew. Later, when his reputation surpassed that of his parent, Walras revealed the influence of his father in many matters of economic policy.

Auguste Walras had been a classmate—and probably an admirer—of Cournot at the École Normale Supérieure in Paris. Other than this we know little of possible filiations between Auguste Walras and Cournot. But we do know that Walras senior introduced Walras junior to Cournot's *Mathematical Principles of the Theory of Wealth* early on. Eventually, Léon Walras, more than any other writer, called the world's attention to the merits of Cournot's mathematical economics. But despite his brilliance, Cournot had retreated from the problem of general-equilibrium analysis, declaring it beyond the powers of mathematical competence. Undaunted, Walras not only surpassed Cournot in this regard but became the acknowledged founder of general-equilibrium analysis.

Walras gave little indication in his youth that he would become a great economist. He received an ordinary education, taking two baccalaureate degrees—one in letters and one in science. Yet, he flunked the mathematics section of the entrance exam to the École Polytechnique—France's elite *grande école*, and chief preparatory school for civil engineers. Walras might have made a poor engineer, for he showed little interest in subsequent engineering studies undertaken at the École des Mines—an engineering school of lesser rank than the École des Ponts et Chaussées, where Dupuit had excelled. In 1858 he turned to literary pursuits, publishing a mediocre novel in that year and a hardly more noteworthy short story the following year. Somewhat chastened by these two disappointing forays into literature, Walras promised his father that he would make economics his life work. Before he could obtain an academic position in his chosen field, however, he fathered twin girls out of wedlock, edited a short-lived monthly review, and worked for a railroad company and two banks. While he was seeking an academic post he was nevertheless studying economics in his spare time and doing some writing on the subject.

Walras's unpopular ideas—which in his youth were approximately the same as his father's (both favored land nationalization, mathematical economics, and a subjective theory of value, in contrast to Ricardo's cost-of-production theory)—barred him from securing an academic post in France, but in 1870 he was finally named—over the objections of almost half of the selection committee—to a professorship in the faculty of law at what later became the University of Lausanne (Switzerland).[3] At Lausanne Walras prospered intellectually, even if not financially. He was never financially secure until his marriage to a rich widow in 1884, five years after the death of his first wife. But at Lausanne he began the feverish activity that eventually led to the publication of all his best-known works in economics.

In 1874 and 1877 he published the two parts of his *Élements d'économie politique pure*, a seminal work on the marginal-utility theory of value and on general-equilibrium analysis. He followed this in 1881 with the *Théorie mathematique de bimétallisme* and, in fairly rapid succession, he published *Théorie mathematique de la richesse sociale* (1883) and *Théorie de la monnaie* (1886). He had always planned to write two systematic treatises on applied economics and social economics to accompany his 1874 work on pure theory, but his strenuous pace at Lausanne sapped much of his energy. He quit teaching in 1892 and later was content to publish his collected papers (rather than the systematic works he had earlier envisioned) under the respective titles *Études d'économie sociale* (1896) and *Études d'économie politique* (1898).

In the heyday of his career at Lausanne, Walras corresponded with just about every economist of any repute throughout the civilized world. In part, he did so out of frustration, for his law students at the university showed little interest in, or taste for, economics. Deprived of stimulating colleagues or students (at least in economics), Walras sent his prepublished manuscripts to other economists abroad for critical review. This practice eventually blossomed into a vigorous campaign to spread his ideas globally.

Intellectual frustration was not the only likely cause of Walras's tireless correspondence. The assembled record of that correspondence reveals his fervent zeal to persuade, beseech, cajole, or otherwise enlist the aid of other economists in spreading the mathematical method of analysis as it applied to economic theory. Regardless of his motives, Walras succeeded on a large scale in advancing the international dissemination of ideas so essential to rapid progress in any science.

In sum, Walras cast a broad shadow over the entire field of economics. His strong suit, of course, was pioneering new frontiers in economic analysis. In the words of William Jaffé, his main biographer:

> This was the achievement of Walras, a lonely, cantankerous savant, often in straitened circumstances, plagued with hypochondria and a paranoid temperament, plodding doggedly through hostile, uncharted territory to discover a fresh vantage point from which subsequent generations of economists could set out to make their own discoveries. ("Léon Walras," p. 452)

He had a keen sense of the importance of building strong foundations on which other advances could be erected. In a cunning assessment of his own approach to scientific inquiry, Walras wrote to a friend: "If one wants to harvest quickly, one must plant carrots and salads; if one has the ambition to plant oaks, he must have the sense to tell himself: my grandchildren will owe me this shade" (cited in Schumpeter, *History*, p. 829).

[3] Lausanne followed the practice common in France (the result of a reorganization plan of Napoleon) of offering all economics courses in the major universities in the school of law.

■ Walras and Marshall on the Market Adjustment Mechanism

One of the most instructive contrasts between Walras and Marshall concerns the so-called law of markets, also referred to as the "adjustment mechanism" in microeconomic discussions of markets. In discussing this topic, Walras and Marshall emphasized the concepts of excess demand/supply and the stability properties of equilibrium. Because they are closely related, we treat these issues together, though the concept of excess demand will be extended further in the following section on general equilibrium.

Price Adjustments versus Quantity Adjustments

Insofar as the market adjustment mechanism is concerned the basic difference between Walras and Marshall is that Walras regarded price as the adjusting variable when markets are in disequilibrium whereas Marshall focused on quantity as the adjusting variable. Stated symbolically and somewhat naively, Walras viewed demand and supply equations (or functions) in the following (mathematical) form:

$$\text{(a)} \quad Q_{d_x} = f(p_x)$$

$$\text{(b)} \quad Q_{s_x} = f(p_x)$$

Marshall, on the other hand, viewed functional relations the other way around:

$$\text{(c)} \quad D_{p_x} = f(q_x)$$

$$\text{(d)} \quad S_{p_x} = f(q_x)$$

Both these formulations require additional explanation. First, the demand and supply equations are said to be "functions" since, in Walras's case, quantity demanded and quantity supplied of some commodity *x*—the left-hand side of equations (a) and (b)—are said to be functions (*f*) of the price of *x*—the right-hand side of equations (a) and (b). Marshall, in contrast, related the demand and supply price of some commodity *x* to the quantity of *x* demanded and supplied.

The variable described in parentheses on the right-hand side of all equations is called the "independent variable" (or price in Walras's case, and quantity in Marshall's). Changes in the independent variable cause the dependent variable—the left-hand side of equations (a)–(d)—to take on different values. Simply stated, Walras indicated that quantity demanded and supplied depends in some way on prices, whereas Marshall indicated that demand price and supply price depend in some way upon the quantity of the good.[4]

Figure 17-1 on the following page attempts to clarify these matters. Focus first on figure 17-1*b*, which assumes that price is the independent variable and depicts the supply and demand functions for some good.[5] Conceptually, one might imagine

[4] Obviously, we are neglecting a host of other independent variables in the demand-and-supply relations, such as income, prices of substitutes and complements (indeed, all other goods in Walras's estimation), utility, the production function, and prices of inputs.

[5] It is customary (except in economics) to display a two-variable function with the independent variable always on the horizontal axis. Thus, a literal depiction of Walrasian functions would display price on the horizontal axis. Through force of habit, and the dominant influence of Marshall, economists generally portray price on the vertical axis, even when it is assumed to be the independent variable, as in this case. This modern eccentricity is undoubtedly due to the practice of Marshall, who displayed the variables as shown in fig. 17-1*b*. However, Marshall adhered to accepted mathematical practice, because he considered quantity to be the independent variable, not price (see the discussion below).

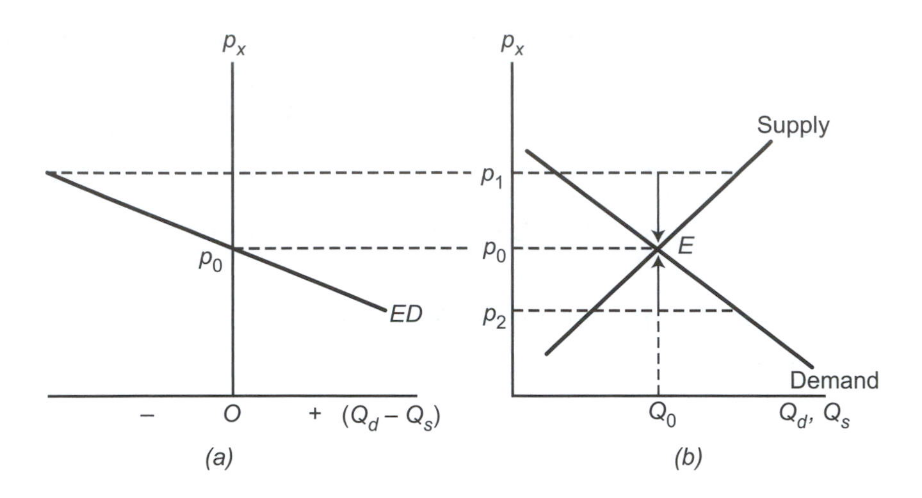

Figure 17-1 If market price is too high for equilibrium (for example, p_1,), negative excess demand (i.e., excess supply) will drive price down toward its equilibrium value. If price is too low for equilibrium (p_2), excess demand will drive price upward toward its equilibrium value.

presenting demanders and suppliers with a list of prices to which they would declare the quantities they would offer and demand at alternative prices. Point *E* in figure 17-1*b* represents the equilibrium price and quantity that competition will produce in the market. If, for some reason, price were established below equilibrium, say at p_2, quantity demanded at that price would exceed quantity supplied, and a shortage would result. This shortage induces competition among buyers, which in turn bids up price. As price rises, some demanders are excluded from the market, and some sellers are included. There are market forces, in other words, causing price and quantity to return to the equilibrium point *E*. Similarly, should price happen to be above equilibrium, a surplus of the good would result, and competition among suppliers would lower price, thereby increasing the number of demanders in the market and decreasing the number of suppliers. In other words, price is the adjusting force (the independent variable), so that once equilibrium is displaced by any cause, price adjustments will cause a return to equilibrium. For this reason, the system described in figure 17-1 is said to be *stable* in the Walrasian sense.

Walras's Excess-Demand Function. Alternatively, stability can be described in terms of excess demand and its consequences. Excess demand is defined simply as the difference between quantity demanded and quantity supplied at any given price, or symbolically as $ED = (Q_d - Q_s)$. An excess-demand schedule can be drawn up as in figure 17-1*a*, which traces out these differences. For example, the excess demand at price p_1 is a negative amount since $Q_d - Q_s$ at that price is negative. Thus, a negative excess demand can be regarded as positive excess supply. Excess demand is zero at the equilibrium price and positive at prices below equilibrium. In order for a Walrasian system to be stable, the *ED* function must be negatively sloped, as drawn in figure 17-1.

Now let us look at the adjustment mechanism and stability properties as represented by Marshall. Figure 17-2 again reproduces the situation one normally

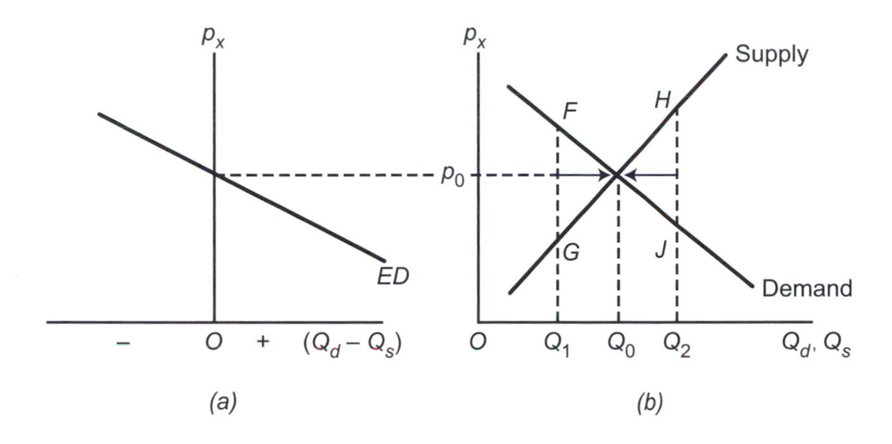

Figure 17-2 If output is below its equilibrium value (for example, Q_1), the presence of economic profits will encourage greater output. If output exceeds its equilibrium value (Q_2), the ensuing economic losses will encourage lower output.

expects to encounter in real markets—a positively sloped supply function and a negatively sloped demand curve, the same as those shown in figure 17-1. The conceptual difference between Walras and Marshall is that Marshall would draw the demand and supply curves by presenting a list of alternative quantities to suppliers and demanders and asking them to list maximum demand and supply prices that would be assigned to those quantities. The adjustment that takes place in the market (when demand and supply are not in equilibrium) is therefore not a *price* adjustment, as Walras assumed, but a *quantity* adjustment.

The Marshallian quantity adjustment can be visualized in figure 17-2. Assume that quantity for some reason is less than the equilibrium quantity Q_0. At quantity Q_1, for example, demand price (point *F* on the demand curve) is greater than supply price (point G on the supply curve). In Marshallian terms, when $D_p > S_p$, firms in the competitive industry are earning economic profits. Output will therefore increase, bringing the market back into equilibrium at Q_0.[6] Similarly, if output should exceed the equilibrium level, as at quantity Q_2 in figure 17-2, supply price for that output (point *H*) will be greater than demand price (point *J*), and economic losses will induce firms to reduce output, and equilibrium will be reestablished at Q_0. Thus, as the arrows in figure 17-2 indicate, the Marshallian equilibrium is stable. Given disequilibrium, in other words, underlying forces in the system will guarantee a return to equilibrium. Likewise, in terms of the excess-demand function developed by Walras, the Marshallian functions are seen to be stable.[7] Given positively sloped supply curves and negatively sloped demand functions, Marshallian *and* Walrasian stability each require a negatively sloped excess-demand function such as that in figures 17-1 and 17-2.

[6] The increase in output occurs for two reasons: (1) existing firms increase output, and (2) there is entry of new firms in the industry.

[7] Actually, to be consistent, some excess-price function should be developed in figure 17-2*a*. For convenience, however, we present the inverse of the Marshallian supply and demand functions so that a Marshallian excess-demand function can be compared with the one generated by Walras. Marshall never bothered to do this, however.

Backward-Bending Supply

Although the respective approaches of Walras and Marshall to market adjustment differ, there is no tension between the two as long as supply curves assume their traditional upward slope. However, the approach chosen becomes critical in the case of backward-bending supply curves.[8] Such instances are unusual, but two examples readily come to mind. First, as practically all mercantile writers clearly perceived, the supply curve of labor might bend backward if workers trade off additional income from work for more leisure, so that they actually work less at higher wages. Second, backward-bending supply curves may exist in markets for foreign exchange, as shown by W. R. Allen ("Stable and Unstable Equilibrium"). So the issue holds more than mere academic interest. In the presence of a backward-bending supply curve the analyses of Walras and Marshall diverge rather than converge, as the following discussion demonstrates.

Assume a market (say, for labor) in which the demand curve intersects only the backward-bending portion of the supply curve, as depicted in figure 17-3. At demand price p_0 quantity demanded equals quantity supplied. The excess-demand function shown in panel (*a*) remains as shown in figures 17-1 and 17-2. It can be shown that the system is stable in Walrasian terms because a price displacement from equilibrium engenders competitive forces that will guarantee a return to equilibrium.

But the system described in figure 17-3 is *unstable* in Marshallian terms. In panel (*b*) assume some quantity Q_1 that is less than the equilibrium quantity Q_0. At Q_1, supply price G is clearly greater than demand price *F*. In that event Marshall envisioned economic losses and a reduction in output supplied. Any reduction in output from Q_1 would magnify the gap between demand and supply. Equilibrium, in short, would never be reached. Any departure from point *E* would be followed by

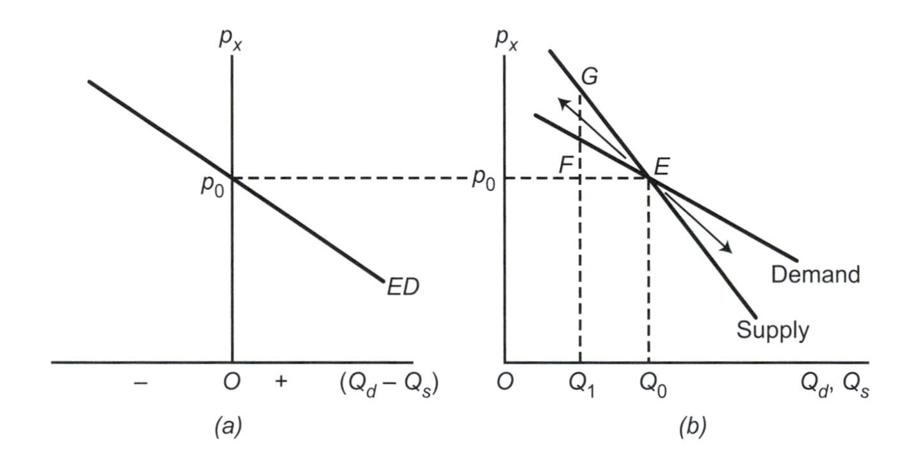

Figure 17-3 The market described in (*b*) is stable in a Walrasian sense (i.e., price is the independent variable), but unstable in a Marshallian sense (i.e., quantity is the independent variable).

[8] Milton Friedman and Peter Newman offer alternative resolutions of the difference between Walras and Marshall on the question of stability and backward-bending supply functions (see notes for further reading at the end of this chapter).

explosive market disturbances if Marshallian adjustments take place. In this case, then, a negatively sloped excess-demand function implies Walrasian stability but Marshallian instability!

With a little more effort you can grasp the implications of a situation in which the labeling of the demand and supply curves of figure 17-3 is reversed. In this case the demand curve would intersect the supply curve from above. The excess-demand function corresponding to these curves would be positively sloped. The system would be unstable in the Walrasian sense because quantity demanded would exceed quantity supplied at all prices above equilibrium price p_0. Competition would force price to ever-higher levels, pushing the system further from equilibrium. However, Marshallian adjustment in this case would produce stability, because demand price would exceed supply price at quantities below equilibrium quantity Q_0, and thus produce a return to equilibrium. In sum, the positively sloped excess-demand function (which accompanies negatively sloped supply and demand schedules) expresses instability in Walras's system and stability in Marshall's. In terms of excess demand, stability is symmetrical in both systems for normally sloped demand and supply schedules, but asymmetrical when demand and supply curves are both negatively sloped.

How Important Is Market Stability?

At first blush the notion of stability might seem esoteric and irrelevant. It could be argued, for instance, that the issue of instability vanishes in the face of market experience. If by unstable markets we mean price and quantity "explosions" away from equilibrium, there is little empirical evidence to support such phenomena. Nevertheless, the issue is far from being irrelevant. It may be that real-world constraints (e.g., futures markets and/or arbitrage in international finance) prevent markets from exploding. Moreover, even if markets are stable always and everywhere, it is nevertheless important to be able to discern the process by which equilibrium is displaced and the manner in which it is restored. And even though the question of market equilibrium is, strictly speaking, a different matter from that of stability, the adjustment processes of Walras and Marshall force attention to the problems of stability and instability of market systems.

The practical importance of stability in markets has probably been overshadowed by an academic interest in the subject. Following the leads of Walras and Marshall, contemporary economic theorists have demonstrated a persistent interest in discussing the stability properties of their analytical models. It has not been considered enough to describe a model; rather, it is important to show that the model has properties that make it viable and stable. Many of the most important contributions to modern macroeconomic and monetary theory, for example, deal with displacement of market equilibrium and the process by which equilibrium is restored.

Yet, there is a practical side to the issue as well. Conditions of stability or instability become paramount when a dynamic element is introduced into the static processes of Walras and Marshall. The so-called *cobweb theorem*, well known to agricultural economists since it applies principally to goods with long production processes, is one such model. Lagged-variable models of the cobweb type have many crucial implications for stability in real-world agricultural markets, and perhaps in other markets as well.[9]

[9] Evidence indicates that the complexities of cobweb-type models may not have escaped earlier economists of the nineteenth century. (See R. F. Hébert, "Wage Cobwebs.")

Walras called this rather complex process of dynamic market adjustment *tâtonnement*—a groping for equilibrium—and in contemporary analysis his concept has been of consummate usefulness in numerous models of microeconomic and macroeconomic behavior. Don Patinkin, a leading macroeconomist of the twentieth century, and Nobel Prize winners, Sir John R. Hicks and Kenneth Arrow, have devoted a great deal of time to questions such as: Is a competitive equilibrium possible, and if there is a displacement, will the system return to equilibrium? Walras's contribution to this subject is therefore of a high order. Whereas earlier writers (Cournot, for example) only hinted at the importance of this issue, Walras and Marshall (particularly the former) made stability a vital part of their analyses.

As an interesting historical footnote, both Walras and Marshall claimed priority in the development of stability analysis. The issue of priority was raised in correspondence between Marshall and Jevons (Walras, *Elements*, p. 502, n. 5). Marshall claimed to have developed the issue of stability in 1873, but as William Jaffé noted, Marshall's treatment of the subject was little more than suggestive. In his privately printed *Pure Theory of Foreign Trade* (1879) Marshall defined stable equilibrium in reference to reciprocal-demand curves, but Walras had done so in print as early as 1874 and therefore clearly had priority. Far more important than this issue of priority (which is a difficult one to settle) is the fact that through the course of the discussion, neither Walras nor Marshall, but particularly Marshall, seemed to have had any appreciation of the other's analysis. Simple jealousy might explain a debate on priority, but Marshall's failure to understand Walras correctly is something else again. Nevertheless, an aura of dissonance seemed to envelope the two giants of the neoclassical era.

■ The Role of the Entrepreneur in Walrasian Economics

Walras's economics shows us a state of ultimate and timeless adjustment maintained by the competitive self-interest of the individual suppliers of productive services. In this world each productive service contributes technically and essentially to the production, transport, and sale of goods, thereby earning each day that amount by which the withdrawal of one such productive unit would reduce the daily output of the system as a whole. Furthermore, in his analytic system the total of all the payments to the suppliers of productive services exactly exhausts their total product. Theoretically, the entrepreneur takes his place alongside the other suppliers of productive services.

Outwardly Walras considered the entrepreneur an important figure. In his *Elements of Pure Economics* (1874), he carefully delineated four classes of productive factors, thus setting the mode of modern practice. His disquisition is reminiscent of Cantillon's three-class presentation of landowners, workers, and entrepreneurs, with the important difference being that Walras recognized the capitalist apart from either the landowner or the entrepreneur. He was quite explicit about the separation and distinction of economic factors of production. After dispensing with the usual categories of landowner, laborer, and capitalist, Walras wrote:

> In addition, let us designate by the term entrepreneur a fourth person, entirely distinct from those just mentioned, whose role it is to lease land from the landowner, hire personal faculties from the laborer, and borrow capital from the capitalist, in order to combine the three productive services in agriculture, industry or trade. It is undoubtedly true that, in real life, the same person may assume two, three, or

> even all four of the above-defined roles. In fact, the different ways in which these roles may be combined give rise to different types of enterprise. However that may be, the roles themselves, even when performed by the same individual, still remain distinct. From the scientific point of view, we must keep these roles separate and avoid both the error of the English economists who identify the entrepreneur with the capitalist and the error of a certain number of French economists who look upon the entrepreneur as a worker charged with the special task of managing a firm. (*Elements*, p. 222)

Walras's argument with the English economists concerned a point of scientific method. He argued that although in practice the functions of capitalist and entrepreneur may frequently be merged, in theory they must be treated separately in order to advance clear thinking about the nature and consequences of each. Surprisingly, he reserved his harshest criticism in this regard for his own countrymen. He accused Say of misunderstanding the nature of the entrepreneurial function, declaring that "this person [the entrepreneur] is absent from his theory" (*Elements*, pp. 425–426). He justified his own position by excluding the activities of coordination and supervision from the entrepreneur's functions. Those activities, he argued repeatedly, are part of routine management and are therefore rewarded by the payment of the wages of management.[10]

A study of Walras's correspondence shows that he maintained his position on the entrepreneur consistently over a long period of time. In his *Elements* he characterized the entrepreneur as an intermediary between production and consumption, an equilibrating agent egged on by profit opportunities in the marketplace that arise whenever selling price is greater than costs of production. Thus, it would appear that the entrepreneur operates in an arena of disequilibrium. Walras's explanation was evocative of Cantillon:

> If the selling price of a product exceeds the cost of the productive services for certain firms and a profit results, entrepreneurs will flow towards this branch of production or expand their output, so that the quantity of the product [on the market] will increase, its price fall, and the difference between price and cost will be reduced; and, if [on the contrary], the cost of the productive services exceeds the selling price for certain firms, so that a loss results, entrepreneurs will leave this branch of production or curtail their output, so that the quantity of the product [on the market] will decrease, its price will rise and the difference between price and cost will again be reduced. (*Elements*, p. 225)

In 1887, Walras wrote to the American economist Francis Walker that "the definition of the entrepreneur is, in my opinion, the thing that binds all of economics together." He persistently argued against the admixture of economic functions, declaring the entrepreneur to be "exclusively . . . the person who buys productive services on the market for services and sells products on the market for products, thus obtaining either a profit or a loss" (*Correspondence*, vol. 2, p. 212). He repeated his position on the entrepreneur several years later, in a letter to his disciple, Vilfredo Pareto, explaining how he differed from Alfred Marshall on the subject: "Marshall reasons mainly by assumption that the owner of services is a worker who takes it upon himself to make goods and sell them," whereas, "I interpose the entre-

[10] In listing his criticisms of past writers Walras's distinction between the "English" and "French" was somewhat artificial: Turgot was guilty of the same "error" as the English classical economists (i.e., not separating capitalist and entrepreneur), and Mill was guilty of the same "error" as Say (i.e., identifying entrepreneurship with the coordination and supervision of productive factors).

preneur as a distinct person whose role is essentially that of demanding services and selling products" (*Correspondence*, vol. 2, p. 629).

We may take this evidence as confirmation of the fact that the entrepreneur held a prominent place in Walras's view of the world as it actually operates. The extent to which he integrated the function of the entrepreneur into the core of his analytical system is another matter, however. At issue is the idealized nature of Walras's theoretic model and whether it bears any resemblance to real-world practice. This issue was debated back and forth in the twentieth-century by prominent economists, but neither side took a clear victory. Walras obscured matters by introducing the "zero-profit entrepreneur" into his static, general-equilibrium system, a model devoid of time or uncertainty. Since the entrepreneur neither gains nor loses in competitive equilibrium, his *raison d'etre* disappears in that state. In order to bring his general-equilibrium system to a determinate mathematical solution, Walras expunged all of the things from his model that give meaning to the entrepreneur. Mathematical nicety and practical necessity inevitably clashed, and Walras was not able to reconcile the two. This explains why there are very few mathematical models that formally analyze entrepreneurial behavior within a closed economic system. Enmeshed in this dilemma and seeing no way out, Walras developed a theoretic construct of an economy that worked like a predictable, impersonal, and frictionless machine. In G. L. S. Shackle's phrase, it was an "inhuman model," incapable of conveying the full range of economic activity (*Uncertainty in Economics*, p. 91). On this account, Schumpeter concluded that Walras's contribution to the theory of entrepreneurship was essentially negative (*History*, p. 893).

Michio Morishima (*Walras' Economics*) defended Walras by reasserting the centrality of the entrepreneur in Walras's theoretic model, but he was roundly criticized by Jaffé ("Walras' Economics," p. 535), who insisted that "in his whole theoretical construct, Walras deliberately abstracted from uncertainty." This explains the absence of the entrepreneur, *qua* entrepreneur, from the Walrasian model in its "normal" operation. Jaffé concluded that "as for the role of the entrepreneur in Walras's analytical model, the *Elements* restricted it to that of arbitrageur, and nothing else" ("Walras' Economics," pp. 529–530). But Jaffé's position was challenged by his former student, Donald Walker, who asserts that Walras made important and lasting contributions to the theory of the entrepreneur and that Schumpeter built his own novel concept of the entrepreneur on a Walrasian foundation ("Walras' Theory," p. 18).

Because the debate produced no clear consensus, ambiguity and diversity of opinion continue to beset Walras's contribution to the theory of entrepreneurship. On the one hand it appears that Walras had an unambiguous notion of real-world entrepreneurs and that he assigned them great importance in the practical world of business. On the other hand his chief scientific achievement, the mathematical general-equilibrium model, systematically eliminated—by assumption (and perhaps by necessity)—the centrality of the entrepreneur. As theory goes, Walras's general-equilibrium system was a momentous contribution. But as a suitable showcase for the essentiality of the entrepreneur it was a total void.

■ Pareto, General Equilibrium, and Welfare Economics

Walras's legacy, perceived at first as insignificant in France, was amply reflected in the work of his Italian disciple, Vilfredo Pareto (1848–1923). Pareto adopted Walras's general-equilibrium framework and used it to improve key areas of economics, including methodology (see notes for further reading at the end of this chapter). In his *Cours d'économie politique* (1896–1897) and his *Manuel d'économie politique* (1906), Pareto explored the conditions in exchange and production that comprise the foundations of modern welfare economics. Unlike the English (Marshall–Pigou) tradition in welfare theory, which was cast in a partial equilibrium framework, Pareto built his system on Walrasian general-equilibrium precepts. Although Pareto did not derive all the conditions for a global welfare maximum, those relating to production and consumption now bear his name.

A Pareto Maximum in Consumption

Borrowing from both British and French traditions, Pareto established the conditions for welfare maximization in exchange. He applied ordinal utility analysis to Walrasian general equilibrium, engaging F. Y. Edgeworth's consumer "indifference curves" (*Mathematical Psychics*, 1881) to show that in exchange of a fixed supply of goods, a welfare optimum would occur when no individual could benefit from trade without injuring someone else. Pareto's argument can be made more concrete by identifying a *marginal rate of substitution* in exchange. For any individual the marginal rate of substitution between any two commodities—say, x and y—measures the number of units of y that must be sacrificed per unit of x so that the level of satisfaction remains the same. (The marginal rate of substitution is the slope of the indifference curve.)

A Pareto optimum in exchange requires that the marginal rate of substitution between *any* pair of consumer goods must be the same for any two individuals (selected at random) who consume both goods. If this is not the case, then one or both parties could gain from exchange. In other words, exchange is Pareto optimal as long as at least one of the parties to the trade is made better off without leaving the other party worse off.[11] Once trade reaches a point where one party can benefit only at the expense of another, any further statements concerning exchange require additional specification. In fact, a whole area of modern welfare economics centers on the attempt to specify the conditions under which a value-free answer can be given when policy changes involve gainers and losers. It is perhaps too early to decide whether or not the quest for a value-free social welfare function is illusory, but it is certain that Pareto, at least implicitly, inaugurated the attempt.

Paretian Factor Substitution

In the theory of production, the concept analogous to the consumer's marginal rate of substitution between any two goods is the firm's *marginal rate of technical substitution* between any two inputs. The marginal rate of technical substitution measures the number of units of an input i that can be substituted for another input j in such a way as to maintain a constant level of output. Thus, as with an indifference curve, one might construct a curve (convex to the origin) depicting the manner in which one input may be substituted for another while output is held constant. In microeconomic theory, this curve is called an *isoquant*, and its slope is the marginal rate of technical substitution.

Although Pareto did not develop isoquants, he did state the conditions necessary for the optimum distribution of resources, given a *fixed supply* of inputs. The

[11] Traditionally, Paretian welfare theory is presented with the aid of an Edgeworth "box diagram," which is a useful graphical technique for illustrating the relations between two economic activities with fixed inputs. See C. E. Ferguson, *Microeconomic Theory* (in the references) for a lucid exposition of general equilibrium and welfare economics utilizing box diagrams.

Pareto condition is that the marginal rate of technical substitution between any pair of inputs must be the same for all producers (chosen at random) who use both inputs. If this were not the case, reallocation of inputs could result in larger total output without a reduction in the output of any single commodity. An optimum further implies that each factor receives a wage equal to the value of its marginal product, a state of affairs that occurs under perfect competition. Analysis of this issue is a staple in undergraduate courses in microeconomic theory. Thus, Walras and Pareto contributed to the principles of optimality in exchange and production.

Welfare and Competition

There are many serious problems connected with Pareto's development of welfare theory, including the possibility of deriving a nonnormative social-welfare function. Another severe limitation is the assumption of nonaugmentable supplies of inputs and outputs. In addition, models focused on *static* equilibrium disregard the effects of uncertainty and a host of other factors. Beyond these problems, however, Pareto's welfare theory, which rests on the maximizing behavior of individuals, adds a great deal of support to the assertion (made by Adam Smith) that a freely competitive system leads to optimal social welfare. Consumers, in an attempt to maximize satisfaction, are led to trade until their marginal rates of substitution between goods are equal. Producers, in their attempt to maximize profits, are led to hire inputs up to the point where their marginal rates of technical substitution are equivalent. Pareto's demonstration, assuming that "externalities" do not exist (see chapter 16), places the case for competition on a more objective basis. His emphasis on the *effects* of maximizing behavior is in sharp contrast to the somewhat metaphysical premises that many other proponents of competitive theory relied on. Consequently, Pareto helped to quicken the acceptance of Walras's general-equilibrium analysis.

■ Walras's Correspondence and Its Impact on Economics

Léon Walras was a passionate believer in the system that he developed, and with the fervor of a religious zealot, he attempted to proselytize economists and policy makers all over the globe. Between 1857 and 1909, he communicated with virtually every major economist in the world. The definitive collection of Walras's extraordinary correspondence was published in 1965 under the editorship of William Jaffé. With meticulous care and incredible scholarship, Jaffé selected, edited, and commented on almost eighteen hundred letters (from a still larger correspondence) in which Walras discussed an enormous array of topics with other economists and interested parties. A review of this correspondence—which spans fifty years and five different languages—reveals the many sides of Walras: his petty debates over the priority of theoretical ideas; his general contempt for English economists (especially Mill and Marshall); his personal lobbying for a Nobel Peace Prize in recognition of his scientific discoveries and their alleged application to society and social problems; his protestations against critics; and his pleadings on behalf of mathematical economics as the mainspring of social reform.[12] Mainly, however, we find Walras marketing, advertising, and hawking his general-equilibrium system—here lobbying shamelessly with journal editors for summaries of his system to be printed, there on the offensive, attacking partial equilibrium analysis.

[12] A favorite subject of Walras the socialist was land nationalization. The revenues derived therefrom, he argued, could be used to finance government expenditures.

It is clear from his correspondence that Walras was willing to make herculean efforts to spread his conception of economic science. He was concerned not only that the errors he perceived in others' writings be corrected but also that his own place be established in the profession. In a letter of April 11, 1893, to his student Vilfredo Pareto, Walras noted that it would give him

> great pleasure (if I am still there to enjoy it) to have others eventually recognize that only Gossen, Jevons, and I have conceived the degree of utility as the central element in valuation and that I, alone, have demonstrated the *proportionality* of the final degrees of utility to all exchanges, prices, or values to the state of general equilibrium and production. And as for Dupuit, Menger, Wieser, Böhm-Bawerk, Auspitz and Lieben, Marshall, Edgeworth, and *all the rest*, they have confused price and the final degree of utility through identification of the curve of utility and the demand curve. (*Correspondence*, vol. 2, letter 1123)

Walras did not try to mask his Anglophobe sentiments. With the single exception of William Stanley Jevons, who with Walras's help added a large appendix on mathematical writings in economics to the 1879 edition of his *Theory of Political Economy* (see chapter 15), Walras had very little good to say about traditional British political economy or economists. He never missed an opportunity to take a swipe at Ricardo, Edgeworth, or Marshall, the latter being regarded in the "English tradition." In a letter (May 25, 1877) to his friend Jevons, he even noted that J. S. Mill "is as poor a logician as he is a mediocre economist"—in spite of the incredible pains, Walras added, that Mill took to avoid giving proofs.[13]

In more general terms, Walras's correspondence is a shimmering mirror of a most unusual man, his era, and the human spirit that yearns for recognition in light of accomplishment. Through his correspondence Walras was an international ambassador for the discipline of economics. Although some of the issues taken up in the *Correspondence* seem trifling, they are nevertheless issues that helped shape the modern profession of economics. Walras's unflinching attempt to sell economics as a science was a seminal force in molding the character of the discipline in the twentieth century. The barriers of national interests and separate languages tended to fall away with the increasingly mathematical character of the science. More than any other single economist, Léon Walras established and "sold" an analytical method whose cultivation transcended national boundaries. How he did so—with incessant but often rewarding debates and arguments—is not really the main point, but it certainly flavors the historical record, which has now established Walras among the giants of the field of economics.

■ Conclusion

Walras's most original contribution to economics was his mathematical specification of a general-equilibrium system. Such a system stresses the vast and intricate web of interrelations in a modern economy. It may be contrasted with partial equilibrium analysis, which ignores such interrelations in order to focus on specific firms or individuals. Before Walras, Cournot had pointed out that a complete and rigorous solution of the problems relative to specific parts of the economic system requires consideration of the entire system and its interconnections. Even before

[13] In fairness, Walras was only agreeing with Jevons's own assessment of the value of Mill's writings on logic (see *Correspondence*, vol. 1, letter 379). Jevons was ready to identify Richard Cantillon, and not Adam Smith, as the first great developer of liberal economic doctrine!

Cournot, Cantillon and Quesnay had presented a clear vision of the economy consisting of many interconnected parts. But Cournot thought the problem of general equilibrium was beyond the reach of mathematical analysis, Cantillon applied his notion of reciprocity to an emergent market system, and Quesnay never got as far as a mathematical specification of microeconomic relations. Walras's genius lay in his grasp of the problem anticipated by Cantillon, Quesnay, and Cournot, and in his demonstration that the problem was solvable, at least in principle.

It is generally held by most economists that Walras's contribution was one of form more than of substance. Clearly there is an architectonic quality to Walras's general-equilibrium system. The pattern of the system is precise, but Walras did not undertake the vast statistical research necessary to provide concrete solutions to each of the equations in the system. There are, in fact, tremendous problems in specifying the relevant equations in precise terms and in gathering data on such a large scale. The recognition of such problems is not meant to diminish the importance of Walras's contribution. Himself a mediocre mathematician, Walras nevertheless demonstrated the power of mathematics in solving complex theoretical problems. He made it possible, moreover, to see that equilibrium of the household and the markets for final goods was consistent with equilibrium of the firm and factor markets. The attempts of Jevons and the Austrians to find a simple causal relation between marginal utility, input prices, and goods prices seem naive and unsophisticated by comparison.

References

Allen, William R. "Stable and Unstable Equilibrium in the Foreign Exchanges," *Kyklos*, vol. 7 (1954), pp. 395–408.

Cournot, A. A. *Researches into the Mathematical Principles of the Theory of Wealth*, N. T. Bacon (trans.). New York: A. M. Kelley, 1960 [1838].

Ferguson, C. E. *Microeconomic Theory*, 3d ed. Homewood, IL: R.D. Irwin, 1972.

Hébert, R. F. "Wage Cobwebs and Cobweb-Type Phenomena: An Early French Formulation," *Western Economic Journal* (December 1973), pp. 394–403.

Jaffé, William. "Léon Walras," in *International Encyclopedia of the Social Sciences*, vol. 16. New York: Macmillan, 1968, pp. 447–552.

———. "Walras' Economics as Others See It," *Journal of Economic Literature*, vol. 18 (1980), pp. 528–549.

Morishima, Michio. *Walras' Economics: A Pure Theory of Capital and Money*. Cambridge: Cambridge University Press, 1977.

Patinkin, Don. *Money, Interest and Prices*, rev. ed. New York: Harper & Row, 1965.

Pigou, A. C. *Memorials of Alfred Marshall*. London: Macmillan, 1925.

Schumpeter, J. A. *History of Economic Analysis*, E. B. Schumpeter (ed.). (New York: Oxford University Press, 1954).

Shackle, G. L. S. *Uncertainty in Economics*. Cambridge: Cambridge University Press, 1995.

Walker, Donald A. "Walras' Theory of the Entrepreneur," *De Economist*, vol. 134 (1986), pp. 1–24.

Walras, Léon. *Elements of Pure Economics*, William Jaffé (trans.). Homewood, IL: Irwin, 1954 [1874].

———. *Correspondence of Léon Walras and Related Papers*, William Jaffé (ed.), 3 vols. Amsterdam: North-Holland, 1965.

Wicksell, Knut. *Value, Capital and Rent*. New York: A. M. Kelley, 1970.

Notes for Further Reading

Until his death in 1980, William Jaffé was the leading authority on the life and writings of Léon Walras. In addition to his translation of Walras's *Elements*, Jaffé collected and edited the voluminous *Correspondence* (see references), a product that ranks as one of the great contributions to research in the history of economic thought. Virtually every major and minor figure of the neoclassical period is presented or discussed in the *Correspondence*, and Jaffé's comments and annotations are invaluable and exhaustive. It is a must, not only for any serious researcher on Walras but also for research on almost any facet of neoclassical economics. Some idea of the content of the *Correspondence* may be obtained from the following review articles: S. C. Kölm, "Léon Walras' Correspondence and Related Papers: The Birth of Mathematical Economics," *American Economic Review*, vol. 58 (December 1968), pp. 1330–1341; D. A. Walker, "Léon Walras in the Light of His Correspondence and Related Papers," *Journal of Political Economy*, vol. 78 (July/August 1970), pp. 685–701; and Vincent Tarascio, "Léon Walras: On the Occasion of the Publication of His Correspondence and Related Papers," *Southern Economic Journal*, vol. 34 (July 1967), pp. 133–145.

Before his death, Jaffé was engaged in writing a comprehensive biography of Walras, a project cut short by his demise. Jaffé's literary leavings were collected by his student, Donald Walker, and published posthumously; see William Jaffé, "The Antecedents and Early Life of Léon Walras," *History of Political Economy*, vol. 16 (Spring 1984), pp. 1–57, which emphasizes the influence of Auguste Walras on his more famous son. In a series of articles stretching over an academic lifetime, Jaffé explored many aspects of Walras's economics. See, for example, William Jaffé, "A. N. Isnard, Progenitor of the Walrasian General Equilibrium Model," *History of Political Economy*, vol. 1 (Spring 1969), pp. 19–43; "The Birth of Léon Walras's *Elements*," *History of Political Economy*, vol. 9 (Summer 1977), pp. 198–214; "Léon Walras's Role in the 'Marginal Revolution' of the 1870's," *History of Political Economy*, vol. 4 (Fall 1972), pp. 379–405; "The Walras-Poincaré Correspondence on the Cardinal Measurability of Utility," *Canadian Journal of Economics*, vol. 10 (May 1977), pp. 300–306; "The Normative Bias of the Walrasian Model: Walras versus Gossen," *Quarterly Journal of Economics*, vol. 91 (August 1977), pp. 371–388; and "Léon Walras: An Economic Adviser Manqué," *Economic Journal*, vol. 85 (December 1975), pp. 810–823.

Donald Walker has taken up the mantle left by his mentor Jaffé. In *Walras's Market Models* (Cambridge: Cambridge University Press, 1996) Walker distinguishes three stages in Walras's economic thought—juvenile, mature, and decline. In *Walrasian Economics* (Cambridge: Cambridge University Press, 2006) Walker examines the foundations of Walras's works and the influence he has had on other theorists. Walker has become virtually a one-man industry on Walras. See, for example, D. A. Walker, "Is Walras' Theory of General Equilibrium a Normative Scheme?" *History of Political Economy*, vol. 16 (Fall 1984), pp. 445–469, which raises anew a question posed by Jaffé in 1977; same author, "Walras and His Critics on the Maximum Utility of New Capital Goods," *History of Political Economy*, vol. 16 (Winter 1984), pp. 529–554, which attributes to Walras an adumbration of the marginal conditions for a Pareto optimum in the market for capital goods; same author, "The Structure of Walras's Mature Model of Capital Goods Markets," *The European Journal of the History of Economic Thought*, vol. 3 (Summer 1996), pp. 254–274, which attempts to clarify "Walras's finest work on the subject of capital"; same author, "Walras's Theory of the Entrepreneur," (see references), which tries to rescue Walras from "the misunderstandings and decades of neglect" surrounding his treatment of the entrepreneur in economic theory. For even more Walker on Walras, see "Walras's Theories of Tâtonnement," *Journal of Political Economy*, vol. 95 (August 1987), pp. 758–774; "Edgeworth versus Walras on the Theory of Tâtonnement," *Eastern Economic Journal*, vol. 13 (April/June 1987), pp. 155–165.

Outside of the Jaffé–Walker circle, see Milton Friedman, "Léon Walras and His Economic System," *American Economic Review*, vol. 45 (December 1955), pp. 900–909, for an evaluation of Walras's work on the occasion of the first English translation of the *Elements*; David Collard, "Léon Walras and the Cambridge Caricature," *Economic Journal*, vol. 83 (June 1973), pp. 465–476, gives an assessment from within the Marshallian tradition; and R. J. Rotheim, "Equilibrium in Walras's and Marx's Theories of Capital Accumulation," *International Journal of Social Economics*, vol. 14 (1987), pp. 27–43, presents the socialist perspective. For a side of Walras not often explored, see Albert Jolink, *The Evolutionist Economics of Léon Walras* (New York: Routledge, 1996). Also see Jolink and Jan van Daal, *The Equilibrium Economics of Leon Walras* (London: Routledge, 1993), which traces Walras' serial development of general-equilibrium models through the five editions of his *Elements*, arguing that in a broader context these models should be considered instrumental in Walras's design for optimal economic order.

A brief nontechnical discussion of Walras and Marshall on stability is provided by Axel Leijonhufvud, "Notes on the Theory of Markets," *Intermountain Economic Review*, vol. 1 (Fall 1970), pp. 1–13. Milton Friedman has also proposed a resolution of the Walras–Marshall stability paradox in his *Price Theory: A Provisional Text*, rev. ed. (Chicago: Aldine, 1962), p. 93. Peter Newman, *The Theory of Exchange* (Englewood Cliffs, NJ: Prentice-Hall, 1965), pp. 106–108, argues that the Marshall–Walras models are not comparable because the Marshallian stability conditions were designed for production theory, while the Walrasian ones were devised for a theory of exchange. Akira Takayama, *Mathematical Economics* (Hinsdale, IL: Dryden Press, 1974), pp. 295–301, presents a nonmathematical summary of Newman's argument, enlarges on it, and concludes that both "Marshall and Walras clearly recognized that there are these two types of adjustments and they both used them in the proper context." Michel De Vroey, "A Marshall-Walras Divide? A Critical Review of the Prevailing Viewpoints," *History of Political Economy*, vol. 41 (Winter 2009), pp. 709–736, evaluates the viewpoint that Marshall's theory is at least partly a proto-general-equilibrium one, and discusses conflicting views about whether Marshall and Walras are complementary or alternative theorists. Same author, "Marshall and Walras: Incompatible Bedfellows?" *The European Journal of the History of Economic Thought*, vol. 19 (October 2012), pp. 765–783, compares Marshall and Walras on a number of points where they arguably conflict: the purpose of economic theory, the use of mathematics in economics, their different methods of handling complexity, their conceptions of equilibrium, and their presuppositions about trade organization.

A number of nontechnical expositions of Walrasian general equilibrium exist. J. R. Hicks's "Léon Walras," *Econometrica*, vol. 2 (October 1934), pp. 338–348, may still be read profitably. A graphical description of general equilibrium and Paretian welfare theory is contained in C. E. Ferguson, *Microeconomic Theory*, 3d ed., chaps. 15 & 16 (Homewood, IL: Irwin, 1972). A more advanced and thorough discussion is presented in Don Patinkin, *Money, Interest and Prices* rev. ed. (New York: Harper & Row, 1965). On Walras's capital theory as the basis for a theory of economic growth, see W. D. Montgomery, "An Interpretation of Walras's Theory of Capital as a Model of Economic Growth," *History of Political Economy*, vol. 3 (Fall 1971), pp. 278–297. Jan van Daal, "From Utilitarianism to Hedonism: Gossen, Jevons and Walras," *Journal of the History of Economic Thought*, vol. 18 (Fall 1996), pp. 271–286, compares the Frenchman's pioneer efforts with his German forebear.

Some comparative questions of method are discussed by A. N. Page, "Marshall's Graphs and Walras's Equations: A Textbook Anomaly," *Economic Inquiry*, vol. 18 (January 1980), pp. 138–143; and D. Pokorny, "Smith and Walras: Two Theories of Science," *Canadian Journal of Economics*, vol. 11 (August 1978), pp. 387–403. Andrea von Witteloostuijn and J. A. H. Maks, "Walras on Temporary Equilibrium and Dynamics," *History of Political Economy*, vol. 22 (Summer 1990), pp. 223–237, seek to correct some of the "textbook" misconceptions of Walras's economics, especially with regard to uncertainty and disequilibrium.

Michael H. Turk, "The Fault Line of Axiomatization: Walras' Linkage of Physics with Economics," *The European Journal of the History of Economic Thought*, vol. 13 (June 2006), pp. 195–212, examines the impact of physics on Walras's attempts to mathematize economics. Walras's failure to resolve certain issues in this respect poses serious problems that have persisted to the present day. Same author, "The Mathematical Turn in Economics: Walras, The French Mathematicians, and the Road not Taken," *Journal of the History of Economic Thought*, vol. 34 (June 2012), pp 149–167, argues that ideas germinating in nineteenth-century French mathematical literature might have significantly altered the way in which economics became formalized after Walras.

Walras's theory of money has not drawn as much attention as other aspects of his thought, but see S. G. F. Hall, "Money and the Walrasian Utility Function," *Oxford Economic Papers*, vol. 35 (July 1983), pp. 247–253; and Renato Cirillo, "Léon Walras' Theory of Money," *American Journal of Economics & Sociology*, vol. 45 (April 1986), pp. 215–221. See also, same author, "The True Significance of Walras' General Equilibrium Theory," Revue européenne des sciences sociales, *vol.* 14 (1976), pp. 5–13.

Maurice Allais and Talcott Parsons give an overview of Pareto and his thought in D. L. Sills and R. K. Merton (eds.), "Vilfredo Pareto," *International Encyclopedia of the Social Sciences*, vol. 2 (New York: Free Press, 1968). Luigino Bruni, *Vilfredo Pareto and The Birth Of Modern Microeconomics* (Cheltenham, UK: Edward Elgar, 2002), reveals Hicks's debt to Pareto and concludes that Pareto's revolution in choice theory is better understood in the context of his own philosophical framework.

Pareto's *Manuel* (the French edition was published in 1906) has been translated, but the translation has stirred controversy. See William Jaffé, "Pareto Translated: A Review Article," *Journal of Economic Literature*, vol. 10 (December 1972), pp. 1190–1201; and the exchange between J. F. Schwier, Ann S. Schwier, William Jaffé, and Vincent Tarascio in the *Journal of Economic Literature*, vol. 12 (March 1974), pp. 78–96. Vincent Tarascio has published widely on Pareto's scientific methodology and welfare theory. See Tarascio, *Pareto's Methodological Approach to Economics: A Study in the History of Some Scientific Aspects of Economic Thought* (Chapel Hill: The University of North Carolina Press, 1968); same author, "Vilfredo Pareto and Marginalism," *History of Political Economy*, vol. 4 (Fall 1972), pp. 406–425; same author, "Pareto on Political Economy," *History of Political Economy*, vol. 6 (Winter 1974), pp. 361–380; and again, "Pareto: A View of the Present through the Past," *Journal of Political Economy*, vol. 84 (February 1976), pp. 109–122. Luigino Bruni and Francesco Guala, "Vilfredo Pareto and the Epistemological Foundations of Choice Theory," *History of Political Economy*, vol. 33 (Spring 2001), pp. 21–49, trace the development of Pareto's views on the foundations of economic theory and seek to clarify the curious combination of ordinalism and operationalism that Pareto introduced. See also Christian E. Weber, "Pareto and the 53 Percent Ordinal Theory of Utility," *History of Political Economy*, vol. 33 (Fall 2001), pp. 541–576.

Vincent Tarascio, "Paretian Welfare Theory: Some Neglected Aspects," *Journal of Political Economy*, vol. 77 (January–February 1969), pp. 1–20, attempts to clarify some long-standing issues regarding Pareto's welfare theory. See also Michael McLure, "Pareto, Pigou and Third-party Consumption: Divergent Approaches to Welfare Theory with Implications for the Study of Public Finance," *The European Journal of the History of Economic Thought*, vol. 17 (October 2010), pp. 635–657, argues that the differences between Pareto's and Pigou's ideas on economic and social welfare in the case of third-party consumption go beyond the difference between ordinal and cardinal representations of utility and can be traced to fundamentally different characterizations of science. For a condensed but useful overview of the development of welfare economics and some of its persistent problems, see R. F. Hébert and R. B. Ekelund, "Welfare Economics," in John Creedy and D. P. O'Brien (eds.), *Economic Analysis in Historical Perspective* (London: Butterworth, 1984), pp. 46–83.

18

Hegemony of Neoclassical Economics

Most history of economic thought textbooks establish a demarcation in the 1870s between classical economics and neoclassical economics. Considering the preceding chapters in this section, the following picture easily emerges. Neoclassical economics was a tripartite development, launched in England by William Stanley Jevons in 1871; in Austria by Carl Menger in 1871; and in France by Léon Walras in 1874. Alfred Marshall codified and extended the basic principles of neoclassical theory for modern economists in his *Principles of Economics*, first published in 1890. Cournot and Dupuit paved the way for the transition from classical macroeconomics to neoclassical microeconomics, but their efforts were largely neglected. This is the conventional wisdom.

The problem is that this potted history grossly simplifies actual developments in the history of economic thought and ignores many other threads that were woven into what became the fabric of neoclassical economics. In this chapter we present a more sophisticated interpretation by elaborating two important and significant facts. First, the tools of neoclassical analysis were widely available across Europe well before 1870, making the notion that neoclassical economics experienced a tripartite "immaculate conception" around 1870 naive. Second, the popular interpretation of events undervalues the key contribution of Alfred Marshall, who put an indelible stamp on neoclassical economics by defining the appropriate method of economic inquiry. When we refer to neoclassical economics today, we usually mean the collection of tools of economic knowledge available to (and invented by) Marshall, channeled and directed into uses dictated by his view of economic science. Admittedly, not all contemporary economists who regard themselves as neoclassicists follow Marshall's path. Some "high-brow" theorists prefer to adopt Cournot's view that economics is rational mechanics. Others maintain that connection to the real world is unimportant in theoretical research. But the bulk of the profession accepts Marshall's method of economic inquiry, and it is his brand of neoclassicism that forms the core of contemporary neoclassical economics. Of course, like all giants in a field, Marshall absorbed much from his predecessors.

The Proto-Neoclassicists before 1870

The essence of neoclassical economics is far from settled in the history of economic thought. Some writers emphasize the increasingly mathematical character of economic thought after 1870. Others point to marginalism as the hallmark of neoclassical economics. Others plant the roots of neoclassical economics in the subjectivism of utility theory. Still others stress the static analysis of efficient allocation as the distinguishing feature of neoclassical economics.

There is a grain of truth in all of these claims. But in more ways than are commonly appreciated, the economist's tool kit was rapidly filling in the decades before 1870. Many writers of different nationalities contributed to the assemblage of microeconomic principles. For example, in Great Britain (see table 18-1) William Whewell applied mathematics to Ricardian economics in 1829 and the ensuing years. He based his economic studies on the twin beliefs that mathematics could render economics simpler, clearer, and more systematic and that it could help avoid the danger of drawing false conclusions from the assumptions that had to be made. William Forster Lloyd gave a series of lectures at Oxford University between 1832 and 1837 in which he explained a theory of value based on the principle of marginal utility. Mountifort Longfield propounded similar ideas at Trinity College in Dublin. His lectures, published in 1834, established a complete demand and supply theory, supplemented by utility analysis, and he espoused a marginal productivity theory of distribution. John Stuart Mill, generally regarded as a classical economist (see chapter 8), has also been proclaimed an important proto-neoclassical by Nobel laureate, George Stigler ("Nature and Role of Originality").

One of the most distinctive "neoclassical" contributions of the era was made by Dionysius Lardner, an astronomer and railway engineer. His book *Railway Economy* (1850) brimmed over with suggestions regarding the "neoclassical" theory of

Table 18-1 British Proto-Neoclassical Contributors

Name	Profession	Writings	Contributions
William Whewell (1799–1866)	Scholar	*Mathematical Exposition of Some Doctrines of Political Economy* (1829–31)	Developed mathematical analysis of Ricardian economics; developed fixed capital model and one dealing with input substitution between labor and machinery
Mountifort Longfield (1802–1884)	Scholar, Jurist	*Lectures on Political Economy* (1834)	Established complete demand-supply theory supplemented by elements of utility analysis; marginal productivity theory of distribution
W. F. Lloyd (1794–1852)	Scholar	*Lectures on Population, Value, Poor Laws, and Rent* (1837)	Lectured on marginal-utility theory of value
J. S. Mill (1806–1873)	Scholar	*Principles of Political Economy* (1848)	Developed theory of noncompeting groups, joint products, alternative costs, economics of the firm, supply and demand
Dionysius Lardner (1793–1859)	Engineer	*Railway Economy* (1850)	Analyzed railroad pricing structures; developed simple and discriminating monopoly analysis; analyzed monopoly firm in terms of total cost and total revenue, both mathematically and graphically (with an implicit demand curve)

the firm, especially the pricing of transport services, the behavior of simple and discriminating monopolies, the location of firms, and the theory of profit maximization. Lardner developed a graphical model that implied a demand curve, but he did not explicitly sketch one.

These isolated and scattered contributions within Britain do not constitute a "school of thought" in the usual sense, but they demonstrate that certain building blocks were being put into place not long after Adam Smith's death. Outwardly, the overlap with the classical school was minimal, yet in the first half of the nineteenth century British writers were already prominently featuring certain elements of economic theory—like mathematical models and marginal analysis—that were to become part of the body of neoclassical economics. The process of inventing and collecting analytical tools had begun, even though the guiding force that would direct those tools to greatest effect did not materialize until the next generation.

Our focus on German historical economics in chapter 11 obscures the fact that a trend toward "neoclassical" economics was established in Germany during the nineteenth century as well (see table 18-2). In Germany, as in France, engineers paved the way for soon-to-be economists by raising issues not addressed by classical economics. A generation before Dupuit, the German engineer Claus Kröncke

Table 18-2 German Proto-Neoclassical Contributors

Name	Profession	Writings	Contribution(s)
Claus Kröncke (1771–1843)	Engineer	*Versuch einer Theorie des Fuhrwerks, mit Answendung ouf den Strassenbau* (1802)	Early "cost-benefit" calculations of roads and canals; benefits associated with cost and price reductions of improved transport
G. Graf von Buquoy (1781-1851)	Engineer	*Die Theorie der Nationalwirthschaft* (1815)	Used differential calculus to choose optimum technique in agriculture; grasped decreasing returns and increasing (marginal) cost, but failed to understand the "benefits" side of the calculation
Gottlieb Hufeland (1783–1850)	Jurist	*Neue Grundlegung der staatswirthschafskunst, durch Prüfung und Berichtigung ihrer Hauptbegriffe von Gut, Werth, Preis, Geld und Volksvermögen mit ununterbrochener Rücksicht auf die bisherigen Systeme* (1807)	Provided early subjective theory of value and elements of a productivity theory of distribution, based not merely on physical productivity but on value productivity as well, which emerged in the process of price formation
J. H. von Thünen (1783–1850)	Agronomist	*Der isolierte Staat in Beziehung aut Landwirtschaft und Nationolökonomie* (1826–50)*	Developed theory of rent, location, and resource allocation based on principle of marginal productivity, along lines of comparative statics
K. H. Rau (1792–1870)	Scholar	*Grundsätze der Volkswirthschaftlehre* (1826; 1841)	Developed marginal productivity theory of value simultaneously with von Thünen; treated all prices in the same demand-supply framework; saw distribution as part of price theory; drew supply and demand curves after 1840

Table 18-2 German Proto-Neoclassical Contributors *(cont'd)*

Name	Profession	Writings	Contribution(s)
F. B. W. Hermann (1795–1868)	Scholar, Statistician	*Staatwirthschaftliche Untersuchungen* (1832)	Recognized, contra Ricardo, that production costs are demand dependent and used "opportunity cost" approach to demand, but without marginal utility as basis for evaluation; anticipated later Austrian approach to output and input valuation.
C. W. C. Schüz (18??–18??)	Scholar	*Grundsätze der Nationalökonomie* (1843)	Developed theory of marginal-product pricing of factors (VMP) suggested by Hermann
H. H. Gossen (1810–1858)	Law clerk, Businessman	*Entwicklung der Gesetze des menschlichen Verkehrs, und der daraus fliessenden Regeln für menschliches Handeln* (1854)*	Developed utility functions related to time, not quantity; made optimal allocation of resources dependent on equalization of marginal utilities; moved constrained optimization into the center of value and allocation theory
W. G. F. Roscher (1817–1894)	Scholar	*Die Grundlagen der Nationalökonomie: Ein Hand und Lesebuch für Geschäftsmanner und Studierende* (1854)*	Proposed subjective theory of value and theory of noncompetitive pricing; wrote standard textbook for generation of German economists nurtured on Rau
H. K. E. von Mangoldt (1824–1868)	Scholar	*Die Lehre vom Unternehmergewinn* (1855)* *Grundriss der Volkswirthschaftlehre* (1863)*	Developed partial-equilibrium, mathematical theory of prices that extended beyond Cournot; used comparative statics to analyze multiple equilibria, as well as joint-supply and demand; derived demand curves from underlying utilities in cases of variable quantities
K. G. A. Knies (1821–1864)	Scholar, Statistician	"Die nationalökoenomische Lehre vom Werth" (1855)	Put principle of diminishing marginal utility at core of value theory; rejected Marx's theory of value because it denied utility
Peter Mischler (1824–1864)	Scholar	*Grundsätze der Nationalökonomie* (1857)	Menger's teacher; used utility to measure aggregate welfare, prices to measure individual utility; anticipated Gossen on key points
A. E. F. Schäffle (1831–1903)	Scholar	*Das gesellschaftliche System der menschlichen Wirthschaft* (1867)	Advanced subjective theory of value; emphasized purpose and causal relationship of goods typical of Menger, but did not recognize von Thünen's marginalism; Menger's predecessor at University of Vienna

*Translated into English

introduced "cost-benefit" calculations of roads and canals. Another German engineer, G. G. von Buquoy, used differential calculus to solve economic problems in agriculture. The subjectivist tradition in German economics (in which utility considerations were granted a prominent role) began with Gottlieb Hufeland (1807) and was continued by practically every important writer before Menger. Karl Rau (1826), a leading textbook writer of the first half of the nineteenth century, insisted that *all* prices be treated with the same demand-supply framework, and he drew demand and supply curves from 1841 on. Friedrich Hermann (1832) did not employ marginal-utility analysis, but he used an opportunity-cost approach to demand, and he anticipated the input-valuation procedure later introduced by Menger (see chapter 14). C. W. C. Schüz (1843) extended Hermann's analysis by developing the theory of factor pricing based on the value of marginal product.

Wilhelm Roscher (1854) (see chapter 11) discussed the theory of noncompetitive pricing and advocated a subjective theory of value in his textbook, which eventually supplanted Rau's popular text. Karl Knies (1855) put the principle of diminishing marginal utility at the core of his value theory. Hans von Mangoldt (see chapter 14) elaborated the utility foundations of demand and developed a partial equilibrium, mathematical theory of prices that surpassed Cournot. Menger's teacher, Peter Mischler (1857), defended utility as a measure of economic welfare and anticipated the equimarginal principle of utility. And Menger's predecessor at the University of Vienna, Albert Schäffle (1867), emphasized subjective evaluations and relationships in much the same manner as Menger.

Two German writers whose writings were "neoclassical" in everything but name were Johann von Thünen and Hermann Heinrich Gossen (see chapter 14). Von Thünen practically invented location theory in 1826 and he later established a workable microeconomic theory in which economic decisions and economic evaluations are made at the margin in a constrained optimization model. He borrowed from the physical sciences, especially in the use of differential calculus, to solve economic problems. He stands today as the "father" of the comparative statics model. Gossen did for the theory of consumption what von Thünen did for the theory of production. He was one of the earliest writers to work out the formal theory of consumer behavior based on the principle of marginal utility. He also borrowed from the physical sciences in order to introduce more precision and clarity into economic analysis. Gossen's utility functions relate to time rather than quantity—which technically puts them outside the strict neoclassical mold—but his originality in using mathematics and diagrams to explain the principles of constrained maximization is nevertheless striking and original. Taken together, the contributions of von Thünen and Gossen provide a fairly complete neoclassical theory of optimal allocation of economic resources.

Cournot and Dupuit (see chapter 13) brought the econo-engineering tradition to fruition in France, but French contributions to neoclassical economics can be traced back to Condillac (1776), who established the subjective theory of value the same year that *The Wealth of Nations* appeared (see table 18-3). A. N. Isnard (1781) anticipated Léon Walras on many essential points and is an important predecessor of the general-equilibrium approach to neoclassical economics. Demand theory advanced at the hands of Germain Garnier (1796) and J. B. Say (1828), who developed an income-stratified notion of demand that Dupuit later incorporated into his pioneer work. From his classroom at the École Nationale des Ponts et Chaussées in the early 1830s, Charles Minard (1850) demonstrated the richness of economic inquiry and its anchor in the concept of utility. Cournot, of course, practically invented the neoclassical theory of the firm in 1838. In his personal tribute, Alfred

Table 18-3 French Proto-Neoclassical Contributors

Name	Profession	Writings	Contributions
E. B. de Condillac (1714–1780)	Philosopher, Cleric	*Le commerce et le gouvernement considérés relativement l'un à l'autre* (1776)*	Established subjective theory of value; Roscher's pet source for notions on utility
A. N. Isnard (1749–1803)	Engineer	*Traité des richesses* (1781)	Established mathematics of exchange equilibrium, production, capital, interest, and foreign exchange; anticipated general equilibrium approach of Walras
Germain Garnier (1754–1821)	Aristocrat	*Abrégé élémentaire des principes de l'économie politique* (1796)	Established income stratification of demand (i.e., the pyramid of wealth)
J. B. Say (1767–1832)	Industrialist, Scholar	*Traité d'économie politique pratique* (1803)* *Cours complet d'économie politique pratique* (1828)	Related utility to demand; Dupuit inspired by Say's confusion to establish marginal utility theory of demand; pyramid of wealth; launching pad for Dupuit's theory of demand
Charles Minard (1781–1870)	Engineer	"Notions élémentaire d'économie politique appliquée aux travaux publics" (1830/1850)	Developed cost-benefit analysis based on discounted value of time; influential teacher at École National des Ponts et Chaussées
A. A. Cournot (1801–1877)	Mathematician, Philosopher	*Recherches sur les principes mathématiques de la théorie des richesses* (1838)*	Derived mathematical theory of demand and supply; applied marginal analysis to the theory of the firm, under monopoly and competitive conditions; developed theory of duopoly based on quantity conjectures; based demand curves on "observation"; adopted a rational and mechanical theory of markets
A. E. J. Dupuit (1804–1866)	Engineer	"De la mesure de l'utilité des travaux publics" (1844)* "De l'influence des péages sur l'utilité des voies communication" (1849)* "De l'utilité et de sa mesure: De l'utilité publique" (1853)	Advanced utility-based analysis of demand; first modern cost-benefit approach to markets; calculation of net benefit under alternative market conditions and pricing structures (e.g., competition, monopoly, price discrimination); identified time period of adjustments in market model; established economics as theoretical and empirical science with a "Marshallian" methodology; analyzed impact of property rights assignments and interest groups, public-choice models; graphical treatment of price-quantity and price-quality determination

*Translated into English

Marshall wrote: "Cournot was a gymnastic master who directed the form of my thought" (*Memorials*, p. 360).

In the eighteenth century, Italy produced four major economists who displayed "neoclassical" tendencies (see table 18-4). The father figure of Italian neoclassicism was Ferdinando Galiani (1751), who based value theory on utility and scarcity,

Table 18-4 Italian Proto-Neoclassical Contributors

Name	Profession	Writings	Contributions
Ferdinando Galiani (1728–1787)	Scholar, Statesman	*Della Moneta* (1751)*	Established value theory based on utility and scarcity; equilibrium as a result of interdependence between price and quantity; resolved paradox of value
C. B. Beccaria (1712–1769)	Scholar, Administrator	*Dei delitti e delle pene* (1764)* *Elementi de economia publica* (1771)*	Embraced utility as principle of economic action; discovered idea that underlies modern indifference analysis; established mathematical economics; influenced Bentham
Antonio Genovesi (1712–1794)	Scholar, Cleric	*Lezioni de Commercio ossia di Economia Civile* (1765)	Made a comprehensive presentation of utilitarian welfare economics. Derived value from demand, based on utility; linked quality to value
Pietro Verri (1728–1797)	Scholar, Administrator	*Degli elementi del commercio* (1760) *Meditazioni sull'economia politica* (1771)*	Offered a clear conception of economic equilibrium based on the "calculus of pleasure and pain"; developed a constant outlay demand curve; argued that supply and demand determine all prices, including interest
L. M. Valeriani (1758–1828)	Scholar	*Del prezzo delle cose tutte mercantili* (1806)	Made astute use of demand and supply functions
Francesco Fuoco (1774–1841)	Scholar	*Saggi economici* (1825–27)	Focused on subjective theory of value; idea of "public happiness" as a state of equilibrium
Pellegrino Rossi (1787–1848)	Scholar, Statesman	*Cours d'économie politique* (1840)	Applied subjective theory of value; successor to Say at Collège de France; influenced Dupuit
Gerolamo Boccardo (1829–1904)	Scholar, Statesman	*Trattato teorico-pratico di economia politica* (1853)	Treated value as exchange ratio and market price as outcome of demand and supply; argued that reduction in price uncovers lower levels of demand (i.e., anticipated elasticity)
Francesco Ferrara (1810–1900)	Scholar, Statesman	"Lezioni di economia politica" (1856–58)	Developed a sophisticated theory of value based on subjective factors, i.e., a psychological cost-benefit analysis of alternative choices; anticipated the "marginal revolution"

*Translated into English

established economic equilibrium as a result of interdependence between price and quantity, and resolved the paradox of value before Smith even posed it.

Cesare Beccaria (1764; 1771) also embraced utility as the principle of economic action, anticipated modern indifference analysis and championed the mathematical method in economic investigation. Antonio Genovesi (1765) put forth a comprehensive program of utilitarian welfare economics and derived value from demand, which he based on the concept—if not the name—of marginal utility. Pietro Verri (1760; 1771) offered a clear conception of economic equilibrium based on the "calculus of pleasure and pain." He developed a constant-outlay demand curve and asserted that demand and supply determine *all* prices, including interest (the price of loans).

In the nineteenth century, Luigi Valeriani, Francesco Fuoco, Pellegrino Rossi, Gerolamo Boccardo and Francesco Ferrara continued the Italian tradition. Joseph Schumpeter said of Valeriani (1806), "he could have taught Senior and Mill how to handle supply and demand functions" (*History*, p. 511). Fuoco (1825–1827) advocated a subjective theory of value and advanced the idea that "public happiness" is a state of equilibrium. Rossi (1840) propounded a subjective theory of value at the Collège de France, where he succeeded J. B. Say. Dupuit cited Rossi frequently. Boccardo (1853) explained market price as an exchange ratio—the outcome of demand and supply—and in his arguments about the effect of lower prices on quantity demanded he anticipated the principle of elasticity that Marshall later popularized. Ferrara (1856–1858) developed a sophisticated theory of value based on psychological cost-benefit considerations.

U.S. economists lagged behind their European cohorts during the nineteenth century, with one notable exception. Charles Ellet, Jr., studied at the École Nationale des Ponts et Chaussées in Paris—which was then the world's leading postgraduate institution of engineering studies—and brought that school's brand of economic analysis to North America. In the same year that Cournot published his major economic work, Ellet published his book, *An Essay on the Laws of Trade with Reference to the Works of Internal Improvement in the United States* (1839). For more than a century, economists on both sides of the Atlantic overlooked the merits of this book, a virtual incubator of "neoclassical" ideas. Its recurrent theme is that business decisions could and should be based on mathematically derived principles. Ellet forged a number of new analytical tools, including mathematical models of monopoly and price discrimination, a theory of optimal input selection, and a duopoly model that is, in some respects, superior to Cournot's.

Regardless of geographic origin, practically all of these proto-neoclassical contributions were based on economic rationality formulated in terms of the "marginalism" inherent in downward-sloping demand curves. Admittedly many of these contributions were fragmented and isolated. But four writers rose above the rest: von Thünen, Gossen, Cournot, and Dupuit. In these four writers the fundamental tools of neoclassical analysis, expressed verbally, graphically, or mathematically, may be found in clear and original fashion by 1860. Thus, the so-called "marginal-utility revolution" was not so much a revolution as an evolution.

For example, in the matter of demand theory, Dupuit, Cournot, and Gossen established downward-sloping demand curves based on the rational behavior of individual consumers confronting a schedule of costs and benefits. Dupuit went so far as to invent the principle of consumer surplus as a means of testing the wisdom of public policy. This group of writers firmly established the importance of maximizing subject to constraints. Gossen found equilibrium for individuals subject to an expenditure constraint where the marginal benefits were equal. Von Thünen discussed selection of inputs based on their marginal productivity; Gossen looked at the choice of labor inputs based on labor's productivity. Cournot and Dupuit discussed the concept of price elasticity of demand, although it had not yet been given that name. Gossen also constructed exchange models based on utility considerations, and Dupuit advanced a model of international exchange that employed Marshallian-like periods of adjustment (i.e., short-run versus long-run).

Cournot, Dupuit, and Gossen established a framework of market equilibrium based on conceptions of supply and demand. In turn, Cournot and Dupuit showed how this framework established the underlying profit-maximizing principles for monopolists and competitors, and Dupuit further discussed the conditions and consequences of price discrimination. Cournot created a theory of oligopoly and duopoly with mutual interdependence, and Dupuit applied this theory to product differentiation by quality in markets. Von Thünen and Dupuit brought the implications and effects of time, technology, space, and property rights into economic theory.

If the theoretical tool kit that appears in Marshall's *Principles* is taken as a benchmark for principles that constitute neoclassical microeconomics, there is very little that cannot be found in the works of Cournot, Dupuit, Gossen, and von Thünen. Indeed, in a number of areas such as duopoly, price discrimination, and spatial competition, Marshall's analysis is less accomplished than his predecessors'.

■ Lessons to Be Learned

Several overall points emerge from this overview of early developments in neoclassical economics. First, there is a pronounced Continental dominance in the development of the "new" themes. In terms of sheer numbers, Germany and Italy dominated (see tables 18-2 and 18-3); yet, the proto-neoclassical tradition in other countries also made serious headway. Erich Streissler ("Influence of German Economics") exposed the rich heritage of neoclassical spirit among German writers who preceded Menger, and Robert Ekelund and Robert Hébert (*Secret Origins of Modern Microeconomics*) revealed the obscure origins of French economic theory before Walras. But the Italian contribution remains largely neglected outside that country, and in England the proto-neoclassicists have been overshadowed by the almost exclusive focus on the usual major figures of the classical era.

Second, many new analytical techniques emerged from practitioners like engineers, agronomists, and merchants, not just from academicians. In Great Britain, Germany, and Italy, the writers who consistently probed "neoclassical" themes came primarily from within the academy, but in France and the United States it was chiefly engineers who broke new ground (see tables 18-4 and 18-5). Germany's most original economists, von Thünen and Gossen, were outliers. Von Thünen was an agronomist while Gossen was a law clerk and businessman. Lardner (Great Britain) was an astronomer and engineer. Whewell (Great Britain) and Cournot (France) were mathematicians. Condillac (France) and Genovesi (Italy) were clerics.

Third, if history is a proper guide, economic theory is not mathematics, nor is mathematics the same as economic theory. Gossen, for example, was a mediocre mathematician but seems to have invented modern diagrammatic economics. New insights in economic theory are sometimes expressed in mathematical terms, but they are also often expressed with verbal or graphical tools and only later translated into mathematics.

Table 18-5 American Proto-Neoclassical Contributor

Name	Profession	Writings	Contributions
Charles Ellet, Jr. (1810–1862)	Engineer	*An Essay on the Laws of Trade in Reference to the Works of Internal Improvement in the United States* (1839)	Developed elaborate mathematical models of monopoly and price discriminating firms; invented duopoly theory in same year as Cournot; developed theory of optimal input selection and joint inputs

The final point is that except for Dupuit, none of the proto-neoclassical writers who have been discussed so far shared the Marshallian vision of economics as an engine of scientific discovery—a vision that had a preponderant impact on the way economists practice economics.

■ WHAT DID MARSHALL KNOW AND WHERE DID HE LEARN IT?

It is difficult to know what sources Alfred Marshall drew from for his *Principles* and how he came to know of them. The most thorough attempt to trace the influences on Marshall's thought to date can be found in Groenewegen (*Soaring Eagle*, ch. 6). By his own testimony, Marshall read Cournot in 1868; von Thünen, Hermann, Roscher, Rau, and von Mangoldt around 1869–70; Jenkin in 1870; Jevons in 1871; and Dupuit in 1873 or sometime after. How these influences impinged on his thinking remains somewhat obscure, but on some points the connections are clear. For example, Marshall adopted Hermann's classification of internal and external wants, acknowledged his anticipation of quasi-rent, and cited his notion of capital (*Principles*, pp. 55*n*, 432*n*, 788*n*). It is even plausible, as Streissler ("Influence," pp. 32–33) contends, that Marshall might have gotten the general structure of the *Principles* from earlier German writers, but we do not believe that he got his ideas on demand, marginal utility, consumer surplus, and general competitive equilibrium from them. Marshall told John Bates Clark that von Thünen inspired his distribution theory (*Memorials*, pp. 412–413). Furthermore, he said that his opinions derived more substance from von Thünen than Cournot (p. 360).

It is widely recognized that Marshall drew on earlier sources in assembling the components of neoclassical microeconomics, and we have long known that Marshall did not regard his contributions as revolutionary. What is new is the claim that many of the tools in his kit existed before Menger, Jevons, and Walras and that Marshall had some awareness of the earlier proto-neoclassicists. But discussions of neoclassical economics often underestimate the extent to which it consists of a scientific method, as well as a set of tools, and the extent to which Marshall was instrumental in laying the groundwork for that method. Indeed, there are indications that Marshall considered the lack of a proper scientific basis for economics to be the most pressing problem confronting the discipline.

Marshall affirmed his belief that economic science is a procedure for scientific discovery in Book I, chapter 3 of his *Principles*. He noted similarities between economics and all other sciences: "It is the business of economics, as of almost every other science, to collect facts, to arrange and interpret them, and to draw inferences from them" (*Principles*, p. 29). However, economic analysis faces certain limitations that may not apply in all the other sciences. In sciences like physics or astronomy, the variables used in the theory can include most of the important causes and effects, so that an empirical test can be matched closely to the theory. Economic theory often fails in this regard because, by necessity, human sciences rely on theories that do not include all of the variables that are relevant at a specific time and place.

Although Marshall focused on static equilibrium, a concept borrowed from physics, he denied explicit analogies between the laws of physics, astronomy, or mechanics and those of economics. Instead, Marshall compared economics to meteorology.

> The laws of economics are to be compared with the laws of the tides, rather than the simple and exact law of gravitation. For the actions of men are so various and uncertain, that the best statement of tendencies, which we can make in a science of human conduct, must needs be inexact and faulty. . . . And since we must form to ourselves some notions of the tendencies of human action, our choice is between forming those notions carelessly and forming them carefully. (*Principles*, pp. 32–33)

John Sutton explains, "The key to Marshall's view lies in his claim that economic mechanisms work out their influences against a messy background of complicated factors, so that the most we can expect of economic analysis is that it captures the 'tendencies' induced by changes in this or that factor" ("Marshall's Tendencies," p. 4). Thus, Marshall accepted mathematical models and static equilibrium theory as helpful organizing principles for understanding the functioning of actual markets. But he insisted that tendencies produced by self-interested, rational human behavior yield predictable results only within the limited confines of "disturbing causes," which must be examined one at a time using the *ceteris paribus* assumption. Marshall's methodology is one in which not all factors are specified within a theory (nor can they be) and where some of the unspecified factors may measurably alter predicted results. This latter approach encouraged the development of modern methods of econometrics in order to determine, probabilistically, which factors do and which do not alter results.

In the battle over induction (from theory) versus deduction (from evidence), Marshall occupied the middle ground. He told Edgeworth that because "theory alone was empty, while empirical investigations without theory were suspect; hence only the interweaving of theory and evidence constituted 'economics proper'" (Sutton, "Marshall's Tendencies," p. 13). In his evaluation of Marshall's impact, Sutton argues: "What the birth of the standard paradigm brought into economics was a new insistence on the importance of formulating rival views in the guise of sharply defined theories that could be evaluated by reference to clear empirical tests. It is this, rather than any rigid recipe for research, that remains its enduring legacy" ("Marshall's Tendencies," pp. 105–106).

Although Marshall was lavish in his praise of von Thünen and Cournot, he borrowed their theories, not their methods. Von Thünen did not attempt to encase his theory in a strict methodological framework. In an article written about Gossen, Jurg Niehans claims that von Thünen made the farm his economic paradigm (*New Palgrave*, II, pp. 550–554). Peter Groenewegen asserts that von Thünen's method gave Marshall "greater awareness of the importance of gathering facts and experimentation for scientific activity," which is probably true (*Soaring Eagle*, p. 152). However, von Thünen's method was of a different order than Marshall's (and Dupuit's). Von Thünen collected facts with which to verify theory. This constitutes a version of the "scientific method" as we know it, but it is a method that belongs to the realm of arithmetic, whereas the method that Marshall proposed for economics appears to be "statistical" in the probabilistic sense.

Cournot, while widely regarded as the precursor of economic statistics, actually rejected empiricism when it came to economic science. He took refuge in what Claude Ménard calls "rational mechanics," displaying a curiously ambivalent attitude toward statistics ("Three Forms of Resistance to Statistics," p. 533). This view of science is verified throughout Cournot's *Researches*, where all of the scientific analogies are to "hard" sciences such as mechanics, physics, astronomy, and "motion." Only once did Cournot admit empiricism into his analysis, in the formulation of his demand curve, where he based the inverse relation between price and quantity on observation. This single insertion is best viewed as a stalking horse for a mechanical and purely mathematical science of economics. Cournot's goal was in fact to fashion economics along the lines of an "abstract science" like hydrostatics. Ditto for Gossen, who believed: "It is impossible to present the true system of economics without the aid of mathematics—a fact that has long been recognised in the case of pure astronomy, pure physics, mechanics and so forth" (Theocharis, *Development of Mathematical Economics*, p. 198): With proper caveats, virtually the same mechanical approach was employed by the rest of the proto-neoclassicists. The single exception was Dupuit.

Dupuit was undaunted by the uncertain or "capricious" nature of utility as a foundation for the demand curve, and he explained its negative slope on the basis of diminishing marginal utility, which could be measured in monetary terms.[1] He envisioned economic science as a combination of both theory and empiricism. From the very beginning of his economic investigations, Dupuit combined empiricism—hypothetical or actual observation—with demand, producing actual estimations of demand curves and consumer surplus ("On the Measure of Utility," p. 104). In addition to his empirically based demand curves, Dupuit proffered other examples of actual or "anecdotal" empirical referents to economic theory, including analysis of bridges, rock quarries, and canals; population; and water distribution. These discussions show the use of a recognizably modern scientific method involving *a priori* theorizing, testing, and reformulating "missing" elements in the original theory.

When Dupuit is compared to Marshall, especially on key points of theory and method, he stands in the vanguard of the "new" approach. We find Dupuit expounding economic method in 1860 in a fashion exactly analogous to Marshall's exposition 30 years later. In discussing the usefulness of mathematical abstraction in the search for solutions to economic problems, Dupuit cautioned that because of the complexity of economic events they require empirical verification so as to enrich and inform "provisional laws." The following passage makes it clear that Dupuit regarded economics as a process of discovery. The parallel between his argument and Marshall's analogy between economics and tides is striking.

> There are times when throngs of curiosity-seekers flock to the seaside to see a hundred-year tide. Science, which has discovered what causes tides, can tell us that on a certain day the sun and moon will be so aligned as to cause the water level to rise far above normal, nevertheless it may happen that the tide does not behave as predicted. Is this cause to doubt the reigning theory? Does it mean that the influence of the sun and moon on the tides was suspended for a day? No, of

[1] Marshall's defense of welfare measures in terms of money (*Principles*, Book I, ch. 2, pp. 15–22 and following) is identical to that of Dupuit ("On the Measure of Utility," pp. 102–107). Dupuit always argued that there is no "utility other than what people will pay for" and that "political economy, speculating on wealth and on the sacrifices which we are disposed to make in order to obtain it, must necessarily take into account the energy of the will by its expression in money" ("De l'utilité et de sa mesure," p. 14).

> course not; this great disappointment simply indicates that the height of the tides depends on regular actions that we know how to calculate and on another action that still eludes science. On the day when the phenomenon was anticipated, an action that could not be predicted, such as a shift in wind direction, could have produced effects contrary to what was calculated. The same is true of economic events. (*La Liberté commerciale*, p. 138)

Moreover, Dupuit encased his methodological argument in the context of a "periods-of-adjustment" (short-run versus long-run) model of competitive equilibrium—a hallmark of Marshall's theoretical presentation of competitive markets, and a staple of every introductory economics text thereafter. Expounding on the effect of a tariff reduction on the relative prices of English iron and French wine, Dupuit argued:

> Economics might predict that free trade would lower the price of iron in France to 170 francs within a few years; but if the price falls to 120 francs instead, due to improvements in metallurgical processes, or the discovery of more abundant new minerals; or on the contrary, if the price rises to 300 francs because of the influx of gold and silver from California or Australia, these events do not refute basic principles. Of course, doubting Thomases, swayed by mere appearances and overcome by their great disdain [for abstract theory], can marshal facts in opposition to the theory, but surely intelligent people will not be convinced by their attacks. (*La Liberté commerciale*, p. 138)

Likewise, on the usefulness of *ceteris paribus* Dupuit anticipated Marshall root and branch, as his writing demonstrates:

> When an effect depends on many causes, it can only be calculated exactly if every condition is taken into account simultaneously. Nevertheless, it is defensible for science to isolate each of these causes and to calculate their effects separately; indeed it is the only way for it to investigate and to discover knowledge. (*La Liberté commerciale*, p. 138)

These passages, which Dupuit amplified considerably in their original context, present clear and unequivocal evidence that the primary method by which economists study economic phenomena today was explicitly outlined a generation before Marshall. Marshallian neoclassical economics parallels Dupuit's method and not Cournot's, or von Thünen's, or any of the other proto-neoclassical writers.

Whether this remarkable parallel constitutes evidence of a genuine connection between Marshall and Dupuit or a mere instance of historical serendipity is not really the issue. Marshall could have formed his views on scientific method—as well as his theoretical insights on utility, demand, and consumer surplus—independently of Dupuit, or through other intellectual connections. For example, Marshall knew the work of Jevons, who also mentioned tides in his discourse on economic method, although Jevons ultimately adopted a "harder" view of economic science.[2] The issue

[2] Marshall was also quite familiar with the work of John Stuart Mill, who elaborated a view of economic method that anticipated Dupuit and Marshall in several key respects. Mill admitted the complexity of economics, recognized the uncertainty introduced to it by disturbing causes, distinguished between social sciences and physical sciences, and outlined the necessity of *ceteris paribus*. Later, however, Mill appeared to argue that *ceteris paribus* is only a logical convention in reasoning, not a method of discovery to the extent that each causal element is brought in one at a time empirically to explain effects within a theory and possibly to change its nature (*A System of Logic*, Book VI, ch. 2, parts 1 and 2). For his part, Dupuit asserted that empirical methods are useful for discovering general principles as well as verifying their existence, whereas Mill rejected the role of *a posteriori* methods as a discovery mechanism ("On the Definition of Political Economy," p. 331).

instead is that both Marshall and Dupuit espoused the same method—the method practiced today—which has progressively stimulated improved econometric and statistical techniques. Hence, Marshall transmitted many of Dupuit's ideas, either wittingly or unwittingly. This means that his central importance to economics consists not so much in the originality of his ideas but in his ability to persuade the bulk of the profession of the efficacy of the new paradigm.

The Force of Ideas: Fame and Notoriety in Economics

Reflecting on fate, the Roman emperor, Marcus Aurelius (AD 121–180), noted that all is *ephemeral*, including fame. Life is short; nothing lasts forever. But no matter how transitory, it is interesting to reflect on how fame is achieved in the first place. In many fields of endeavor, true creativity is not easily recognized, and fame often eludes those who later prove to be masters of a subject. The Augustinian monk, Gregor Mendel (1822–1884), discovered the basic principles of genetics with his pea-growing experiments only to bury his results in an obscure agricultural journal, where they were ignored until rediscovered a century later. It took thirty-four years for the rest of the scientific community to catch up to it. Johann Sebastian Bach—now recognized as one of the greatest musical composers of all time—lapsed into virtual obscurity after his death only to be elevated to his rightful place many decades later. Many great creative minds are never recognized. So it was with the economists who anticipated neoclassical economics. Many wrote piecemeal contributions "above their time," out of their time, before their time, and generally before microeconomics and its mathematical emphasis came to be recognized as a central paradigm.

This chapter has focused on a large number of "anticipators" of neoclassical economic theory—figures from many disciplines and from many countries, who, by virtue of their writings, may be deserving of a certain amount of fame or recognition. There may well be others who have escaped recognition altogether. Despite these piecemeal contributions of economic creativity, we have argued that two French writers (Cournot and Dupuit) and two German writers (von Thünen and Gossen) were, taken together, the authors of the whole paradigm of neoclassical theoretical thinking. None were trained as "economists" but each contributed greatly to traditional modern price theory.

Of these four pioneers, only Dupuit and Cournot attempted to "market" their ideas. An engineer, Dupuit met with only limited success in selling his "neoclassical" theory and method to economists committed to traditional modes of thought. Cournot attempted three times (in 1838, 1863, and 1877) to persuade the economics profession of the superiority of his "scientific" conception of economics as rational mechanics. Was he ignored? Shunned is a better word. His second effort of 1863 received reviews of mixed praise and constructive criticism. But Cournot stubbornly persisted in believing that his brilliant theoretical system supported a nascent socialist system of economic organization—a belief rejected by the reigning French liberals of his day.*

Luck seems to play a large role in determining whether one receives lasting fame. Over the long haul, as Aurelius suggested, fame is fleeting. But, in the short run, ideas must be aggressively marketed and reviews written. Indeed, over the short run, it may well be true that the only bad review is an obituary. Or, as saucy screen actress Mae West said: "It's better to be looked over, than overlooked."

*See Robert B. Ekelund, Jr., and Robert F. Hébert, "Cournot and His Contemporaries" (in the reference section).

Conclusion

A genuine, functioning tool kit for neoclassical microeconomics existed long before Marshall's *Principles* in 1890 and well before the legendary triumvirate of Menger, Jevons, and Walras came on the scene around 1870. The argument could be made that neoclassical/marginalist ideas that floated about prior to 1870 were merely scattered pieces in a great intellectual puzzle. In some individual cases, that may have been true. It is also true that neoclassical microeconomics does not appear to have evolved in a neat or linear way, or in an intellectual battle between "systems" or "schools." But the quantity and quality of the achievement of the proto-neoclassicists is too great for their work to be set aside as isolated, fragmentary, or incomplete.

Jules Dupuit, in particular, managed to assemble a complete paradigm with demand/utility specifications, marginalism with respect to inputs, cost conceptions based on time periods of production, welfare calculations under alternative market structures, graphical and mathematical analysis and illustrations, and a well-stated and well-formed method for establishing microeconomic science. Dupuit anticipated Marshall in most of the key ingredients that came together to form neoclassical microeconomics.

Alfred Marshall was an accomplished theorist, but more importantly, he was at the center of a "synthesizing community." He shaped his theoretical tools with a single purpose in mind: to make economics an engine of scientific discovery. Furthermore, by specifying its methodological framework, he channeled the new tools of economic theory into what has become the traditional neoclassical paradigm. The Marshallian method, which combined inductive theory and deductive empiricism, ultimately shaped the modern practice of economics and spurred the twentieth-century development of econometrics.

References

Beccaria, Cesare B. *Dei delitti e delle pene*. English translation, *An Essay on Crime and Punishment*. London: J. Almon, 1767.

———. *Elementi de economia publica*, in *Cesare Beccaria Opere*, S. Romagnoli (ed.). Florence: Sansoni, 1958. English translation, *A Discourse on Public Economy and Commerce*. New York: Burt Franklin, 1970.

Boccardo, Gerolamo. *Trattato teorico-practico di economia politica*. Torino: Dalla Società Editrice della Biblioteca dei Comuni Italiani, 1853.

Buquoy, G. Graf von. *Die Theorie der Nationalwirthschaft*. Leipzig: Breitfopf & Härtel, 1815.

Condillac, E. B. de. *Le Commerce et le gouvernement considérés relativement l'un à l'autre*. Paris: Jombert et Cellot, 1776. English translation, *Commerce and Government Considered in Relation to Each Other*, Shelagh Eltis (trans.), S. M. Eltis and W. Eltis (eds.). Aldershot, UK: Edward Elgar, 1998.

Cournot, A. A. *Researches into the Mathematical Principles of the Theory of Wealth*, Nathaniel Bacon (trans.). New York: Macmillan, 1929.

Dupuit, Jules. "De la mesure de l'utilité des travaux publics," *Annales des Ponts et Chaussées: Mémoires et documents*, 2d ser., vol. 8, no. 2 (1844), pp. 332–375. English translation, "On the Measure of Utility of Public Works," R. M. Barback (trans.), *International Economic Papers*, vol. 2 (1952), pp. 83–110.

———. "De l'influence des péages sur l'utilité des voies communication," *Annales des Ponts et Chaussées: Mémoires et documents*, 2d ser., vol. 17, no. 1 (1849), pp. 207–248. English translation, "Tolls," Elizabeth Henderson (trans.), *International Economic Papers*, vol. 11 (1962), pp. 7–31.

———. "De l'utilité et de sa mesure: De l'utilité publique," *Journal des économistes*, vol. 36 (1853), pp. 1–27. Reprinted in *De l'utilité et de sa mesure: Écrits choisis et republiés par Mario de Bernardi*. Torino: La Riforma Sociale, 1933.

———. *La liberté commerciale: Son principe et ses consequences*. Paris: Guillaumin, 1861.

Ekelund, Robert B., and Robert F. Hébert, "Cournot and His Contemporaries: Is an Obituary the Only Bad Review?" *Southern Economic Journal*, vol. 57 (July 1990), pp. 139–149.

———. *Secret Origins of Modern Microeconomics*. Chicago: University of Chicago Press, 1999.

Ellet, Charles. *An Essay on the Laws of Trade in Reference to the Works of Internal Improvement in the United States*. Richmond, VA: P. D. Bernard, 1839. Augustus Kelley reprint, 1966.

Ferrara, Francesco. "Lezioni di economia politica," in B. R. Ragazzi (ed.), *Le opera complete di Francesco Ferrara*. Rome: Bancaria Editrice, 1955.

Fuoco, Francesco. *Saggi economici*, 2 vols. Pisa: Sabastiano Nistri, 1825–1827.

Garnier, Germaine. *Abrégé élémentaire des principes de l'économie politique*. Paris: H. Agasse, 1796.

Galiani, Ferdinando. *Della moneta* (1751). English translation, *On Money*, P. R. Toscano (ed.). Ann Arbor: University of Michigan Press, 1971.

Genovesi, Antonio. *Lezioni di Commercio ossia di Economia Civile*, 2 vols. Napoli: Fratelli Simone, 1765–1767.

Georgescu-Roegen, Nicholas. "Hermann Heinrich Gossen: His Life and Work in Historical Perspective," in H. H. Gossen, *The Laws of Human Relations and the Rules of Human Action Derived Therefrom*. R. C. Blitz (trans.). Cambridge, MA: MIT Press, 1983.

Gossen, H. H. *Entwicklung der Gesetze des menschlichen Verkehrs, und der daraus fliessenden Regeln für menschliches Handeln*. Berlin: R. L. Brager 1889 [1854].

Groenewegen, Peter. *A Soaring Eagle: Alfred Marshall, 1842-1924*. Aldershot, UK: Edward Elgar, 1995.

Hermann, F. B. W. *Staatswirthschaftliche Untersuchungen*. Munich: Anton Weber, 1832.

Hufeland, Gottlieb. *Neue Grundlegung der Staatswirthschaftskunst, durch Prüfung und Berichtigung ihrer Hauptbegriffe von Gut, Werth, Preis, Geld und Volksvermögen mit ununterbrochener Rücksicht auf die bisherigen Systeme*. Giessen & Wetzlar, 1807.

Isnard, Achylle-Nicolas. *Traité des richesses*, 2 vols. Lausanne and London: François Grasset, 1781.

Knies, Karl. "Die nationalökonomische Lehre vom Werth," *Zeitschrift für die gesamte Staatswissenschaft*, vol. 11 (1855), pp. 421–475.

Kröncke, Claus. *Versuch einer Theorie der Fuhrwerks, mit Anwendung auf den Strassenbau*. Giessen, 1802.

Lardner, Dionysius. *Railway Economy*. London: Harper & Brothers, 1850. New York: Augustus Kelley reprint, 1968.

Lloyd, William F. *Lectures on Population, Value, Poor Laws and Rent* (1837). New York: Augustus Kelley reprint, 1968.

Longfield, Mountifort. *Lectures on Political Economy, delivered in Trinity and Michaelmas Terms, 1833*. Dublin: R. Milliken & Son, 1834. Reprinted in *The Economic Writings of Mountifort Longfield*. R. D. C. Black (ed.). New York: A. M. Kelley, 1971.

Mangoldt, Hans K. E. von. *Die Lehre vom Unternehmergewinn: Ein Beitrag zur Volkswirthschaftlehre*. Leipzig: Teuber, 1855.

———. *Grundriss der Volkswirthschaftlehre*. Stuttgart: Maier, 1863.

Marshall, Alfred. *Memorials of Alfred Marshall*, A.C. Pigou (ed.). London: Macmillan, 1925.

———. *Principles of Economics*, 8th ed. London: Macmillan, 1920.

Ménard, Claude. "Three Forms of Resistance to Statistics: Say, Cournot, Walras," *History of Political Economy*, vol. 12, no. 4 (1980), pp. 524–541.

Mill, John Stuart. "On the Definition of Political Economy; and on the Method of Philosophical Investigation in that Science" (1836). In J. M. Robson (ed.), *Collected Works of John Stuart Mill*. Toronto: University of Toronto Press, 1967, pp. 309–339.

———. *A System of Logic*. London: John W. Parker, 1843.

———. *Principles of Political Economy, with some of their applications to Political Philosophy*, 2 vols. London: John W. Parker, 1848.

Minard, Charles Joseph. "Notions élémentaire d'économie politique appliquées aux travaux publics," *Annales des Ponts et Chaussées: Mémoires et Documents*, 2d ser., vol. 19, no. 1 (1850), pp. 1–125.

Mischler, Peter. *Grundsätze der Nationalökonomie*. Vienna, 1857.

Niehans, Jürg. *The New Palgrave: A Dictionary of Economic Theory and Doctrine*. J. Eatwell, M. Milgate and P. Newman (eds.). London: Macmillan, 1987, vol. 2, pp. 550–554.

Rau, Karl Heinrich. *Grundsätze der Volkswirthschaftlehre*. Heidelberg: C. F. Winter, 1826.

———. *Grundsätze der Volkswirthschaftlehre*, 4th ed. Heidelberg: C. F. Winter, 1841.

Roscher, Wilhelm. *Die Grundlagen der Nationalökonomie: Ein Hand und Lesebuch für Geschäftsmanner und Studierende*. Stuttgart: Cotta, 1854. English translation, *Principles of Political Economy*, J. J. Lalor (trans.). New York: Henry Holt, 1878.

Rossi, Pellegrino. *Cours d'économie politique*. Paris: Joubert, 1840.

Say, Jean-Baptiste. *Traité d'économie politique*. Paris: Crapelet, 1803. English translation, *A Treatise on Political Economy*, C. R. Prinsep (trans.). New York: A. M. Kelley, 1971.

———. *Cours complet d'économie politique pratique*. Paris: Rapilly, 1828.

Schäffle, Albert E. F. *Das gesellschaftliche System der menschlichen Wirthschaft*. Tübingen: Laupp, 1867.

Schumpeter, Joseph A. *History of Economic Analysis*, E. B. Schumpeter (ed.). New York: Oxford University Press, 1954.

Schüz, Carl W. C. *Grundsätze der Nationalökonomie*. Tübingen, 1843.

Stigler, George J. "The Nature and Role of Originality in Scientific Progress," *Economica*, vol. 22 (November 1955), pp. 293–302.

Streissler, Erich W. "The Influence of German Economics on the Work of Menger and Marshall," in B. J. Caldwell (ed.), *Carl Menger and His Legacy in Economics*. Annual Supplement to Volume 22, *History of Political Economy*. Durham, NC: Duke University Press, 1990, pp. 31–68.

Sutton, John. *Marshall's Tendencies: What Can Economists Know?* Cambridge, MA: MIT Press, 2000.

Theocharis, Reghinos D. *The Development of Mathematical Economics from Cournot to Jevons*. London: Macmillan, 1993.

Thünen, J. H. von. *Der isolierte Staat in Beziehung auf Landwirtschaft und Nationalökonomie* (1826–1863). English translation, *The Isolated State*, vol. 1, Carla Wartenberg (trans.). Oxford: Pergamon Press, 1966. Volume 2 appears in *The Frontier Wage*, B. W. Dempsey (trans.). Chicago: Loyola University Press, 1960.

Valeriani, Luigi M. *Del prezzo delle cose tutte mercantili*. 1806.

Verri, Pietro. *Degli elementi del commercio* (1760). In P. Custodi (ed.), *Scrittori classici italiani di economia politica*, parte moderna. Milan: G. G. Destefanis, 1803–1805.

———. *Meditazioni sull'economia politica* (1771). English translation, *Reflections on Political Economy*, B. McGilvray (trans.), P. Groenewegen (ed.), *Reprints of Economic Classics*, Series 2:4. Sydney: University of Sydney, 1986.

Whewell, William. *Mathematical Exposition of Certain Doctrines of Political Economy*. New York: A. M. Kelley, 1971.

Notes for Further Reading

The idea that marginalism constitutes the essence of neoclassical economics has been defended by T. W. Hutchison, *A Review of Economic Doctrines, 1870–1929* (Oxford:

Clarendon Press, 1953), p. 16, and by a host of contributors to "Papers on the Marginal Revolution in Economics," *History of Political Economy*, vol. 4 (Fall 1972). Emilia di Patti, "Francesco Ferrara and Subjective Value Theory," *History of Political Economy*, vol. 33 (Summer 2001), pp. 315–344, finds the roots of neoclassical economics in the subjectivism of utility theory; whereas Klaus Hennings, "The Transition from Classical to Neoclassical Economic Theory: Hans von Mangoldt," *Kyklos*, vol. 33 (1980), pp. 658–681, insists on the static analysis of efficient allocation as the distinguishing feature of neoclassical economics. Lawrence Birken, "From Macroeconomics to Microeconomics: The Marginalist Revolution in Sociocultural Perspective" *History of Political Economy*, vol. 20 (Summer 1988), pp. 251–264, concludes that "the emergence of marginalism was part of a larger cultural redefinition that occurred during (and may have been shaped by) the transition from a proto-industrial to an industrial culture."

The standard reference on Whewell and his mathematical school is James P. Henderson, *Early Mathematical Economics: William Whewell and the British Case* (Lanham, MD: Rowman & Littlefield, 1996). See also, Jinbang Kim, "The Technique of Comparative-Static Analysis in Whewell's 'Mathematical Exposition,'" *History of Political Economy*, vol. 33 (Winter 2001), pp. 843–854. Menachem Fisch and Simon Schaffer (eds.), *William Whewell: A Composite Portrait* (Oxford: Oxford University Press, 1991), have assembled a collection of papers on this famous British polymath. See especially the article by Gerd Buchdahl, "Deductivist versus Inductivist Approaches in the Philosophy of Science as Illustrated by Some Controversies Between Whewell and Mill," pp. 311–344. Along the same lines, see E. W. Strong, "William Whewell and John Stuart Mill: Their Controversy over Scientific Knowledge," *Journal of the History of Ideas*, vol. 16 (1955), pp. 209–231. E. R. A. Seligman, "On Some Neglected British Economists," *Economic Journal*, vol. 13 (September–December, 1903), first called attention to the British "marginal-utility" school. Richard M. Romano, "William Forster Lloyd—A Non-Ricardian," *History of Political Economy*, vol. 9 (Fall 1977), pp. 412–441; and Laurence S. Moss, "Mountifort Longfield's Supply and Demand Theory of Price and Its Place in the Development of British Economic Theory," *History of Political Economy*, vol. 6 (Winter 1974), pp. 405–434, provide further embellishments on Lloyd and Longfield. Lardner's contributions to microeconomic theory have been explored by Donald M. Hooks, "Monopoly Price Discrimination in 1850: Dionysius Lardner," *History of Political Economy*, vol. 3 (Spring 1971), pp. 208–223; see also the extensive discussion of Lardner in R. B. Ekelund, Jr., and R. F. Hébert, *Secret Origins of Modern Microeconomics* (Chicago: University of Chicago Press, 1999).

Aside from von Thünen, secondary literature on the German writers reviewed in this chapter is scarce. On the prominence of von Thünen in economic theory, see Mark Blaug, "The German Hegemony of Location Theory: A Puzzle in the History of Economic Thought," *History of Political Economy*, vol. 11, no. 1 (1979), pp. 21–29; and Heinz D. Kurz, "Thünen's Contribution to Location Economics and Marginal Productivity Theory," in *Industry, Space and Competition: The Contributions of Economists of the Past*, Michel Bellet and Corine L'Harmet (eds.) (Aldershot, UK: Edward Elgar, 1998), pp. 25–48. Erich W. Streissler, "Rau, Hermann and Roscher: Contributions of German Economics Around the Middle of the Nineteenth Century," *The European Journal of the History of Economic Thought*, vol. 8 (Autumn 2001), pp. 311–331, focuses on three prominent German economists. For more on Hermann, see Heinz D. Kurz, "Friedrich Benedikt Wilhelm Hermann on Capital and Profits," *European Journal of the History of Economic Thought*, vol. 5 (Spring 1998), pp. 85–119. On von Mangoldt, see Hennings' article in *Kyklos* cited above. Kosmas Papadopoulos and Bradley W. Bateman, "Karl Knies and the Prehistory of Neoclassical Economics: Understanding the Importance of *Die Nationaloekonomische Lehre vom Werth*" (1855)," *Journal of the History of Economic Thought*, vol. 33 (March 2011), pp 19–35, evaluate Knies's role in anticipating marginal value theory.

Gossen's preeminence is justifiably proclaimed by William Baumol and Stephen M. Goldfeld, *Precursors in Mathematical Economics: An Anthology* (London: London School of Economics and Political Science, 1968); by Nicholas Georgescu-Roegen, "Hermann Heinrich Gossen: His Life and Work in Historical Perspective," in H. H. Gossen, *The Laws of Human Relations and the Rules of Human Action Derived Therefrom*, R. C. Blitz (trans.) (Cambridge, MA: MIT Press, 1983); and by R. D. Theocharis, *The Development of Mathematical Economics from Cournot to Jevons* (London: Macmillan, 1993). Georgescu-Roegen and Theocharis agree that Gossen invented graphical analysis in economics.

Shelagh Eltis has translated Condillac's key economic contribution as *Commerce and Government Considered in their Mutual Relationship* (Cheltenham, UK: Edward Elgar, 1997). The introduction to this translation, written by Shelagh and Walter Eltis, lends support to the claim that Condillac was an important proto-neoclassical in France. See also Walter Eltis, "France's Free Market Reforms in 1774–6 and Russia's in 1991–3: The Immediate Relevance of l'Abbé de Condillac's Analysis," *The European Journal of the History of Economic Thought*, vol. 1 (Autumn 1993), pp. 5–19; and Arnaud Orain, "'Preferring that which You Desire Less': A Condillacian Approach to Choice Under Uncertainty," *The European Journal of the History of Economic Thought*, vol. 18, (Fall 2011), pp. 321–352, examines Condillac's probabilistic theory of choice.

In the twentieth century French economics came to be dominated by Walras and his disciples, but as William Jaffé, "A. N. Isnard, Progenitor of the Walrasian General Equilibrium Model," *History of Political Economy*, vol. 1, no. 1 (1969), pp. 19–43, has shown, Isnard was an important precursor. Almost nothing has been written on Germain Garnier, despite his indirect influence on Say and Dupuit. But see Yves Breton, "Germain Garnier, L'économiste et l'homme politique," in Gilbert Faccarello and Philippe Steiner (eds.), *La Pensée Économique pendant la Révolution Française*. (Grenoble: Presses Universitaires de Grenoble, 1990). Cournot, Dupuit, and, to a lesser extent, Say, are treated in detail by Ekelund and Hébert in *Secret Origins* (cited above). See also notes for further reading following chapter 13 in this text. Stephen Stigler, *The History of Statistics: The Measurement of Uncertainty Before 1900* (Cambridge, MA: Harvard University Press, 1986), contains an excellent treatment of Cournot and his tenuous relationship with statistics.

Outside of Italy there is very little secondary literature on the writers presented in this chapter. Rossi's influence within France is discussed by Martin S. Staum, "French Lecturers in Political Economy, 1815–1848: Varieties of Liberalism," *History of Political Economy*, vol. 30 (Spring 1998), pp. 95–120. For those who read French, see László Ledermann, *Pellegrino Rossi, L'Homme et l'économiste, 1787–1848* (Paris: Sirey, 1929). On Ferrara, see di Patti (cited above); and Antonio Guccione, "Ferrara's Theory of Value and the Cost of Reproduction Principle," *History of Political Economy*, vol. 25 (Winter 1993), pp. 677–696. Some sense of Galiani's economic reforms is conveyed by Gilbert Faccarello, "Galiani and Necker on Economic Reforms," *The European Journal of the History of Economic Thought*, vol. 1 (Autumn 1994), pp. 519–550. Pierre Luigi Porta and Roberto Scazzieri explore Verri's ideas in "Pietro Verri's Political Economy: Commercial Society, Civil Society, and the Science of the Legislator," *History of Political Economy*, vol. 34, (2002), pp. 83–110.

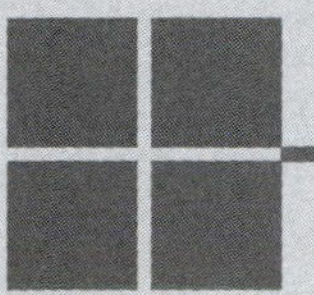

Part V

Twentieth-Century Paradigms

The heyday of early neoclassical economics ran from about 1870 to about 1920. However, Marxism was gaining ground, especially among underdeveloped nations anticipating a leap into the industrial age, even while the new science was being assembled by Jevons, Menger, Walras, and Marshall. Other challenges to the existing orthodoxy mounted as well. In America—a country that tolerated dissent even as it embraced capitalism and individual freedom—a new, heterodox school of thought arose called *institutionalism*, which harbored a distinctly antitheoretical bias. Moreover, as orthodox economic theory fended off the challenge of institutionalism, it was redirecting itself back toward macroeconomics, especially after the onslaught of the Great Depression. Periods of economic upheaval inevitably encourage reexamination of fundamental economic premises, and the Great Depression was no exception. Modern macroeconomics was born in the midst of this global economic catastrophe, mainly through the efforts of John Maynard Keynes. The early part of the twentieth century may therefore be characterized as a period of considerable upheaval. This section brings together multiple strands of thought, from the stridency of American institutionalism against neoclassical economics (chapter 19), to the reaffirmation of neoclassical economics expressed in the new political economy of the postwar era (chapter 24).

Leadership in economic theory shifted to America after World War II, aided in large part by the emigration of many European scholars to the United States. Restoration of world peace and the relocation of much of the world's intelligentsia unleashed extensive creative activity. Economists on both sides of the Atlantic began to rethink the respective roles of competition and monopoly, as well as hybrid forms, in economic theory (chapter 20). In the post–World War II period Keynesian macroeconomics (chapter 21) rose to a position of dominance but confronted challenges from new classical theorists (chapter 22) that led to many modifications and refinements. Austrian economics (chapter 23), which was repressed in the onslaught of Keynesian theory, began to reassert itself after disaffection mounted with the Keynesian legacy. And "political economy"—that sphere of human activity where the economic and the political intersect—enjoyed a resurgence as the second half of the century got underway (chapter 24), driven in part by the study of how economic policy can be perverted by democratic institutions.

19

British Historicism, Thorstein Veblen, and American Institutional Economics

We saw in chapters 11 and 12 that the nineteenth-century intellectual landscape was strewn with vociferous and sometimes shrill critics of classical theoretical economics. Criticism from certain quarters did not abate with the advent of neoclassical economics. Like theory, criticism possesses a tradition of its own—a tradition that is alive and well in contemporary assessments of capitalism and the capitalist process.

The present chapter features the "institutional economics" of Thorstein Veblen (1857–1929), a twentieth-century critic of received theoretical economics. Although influenced to some extent by British Historicists, Veblen created the only uniquely American school of economics. In very much the same spirit as their German counterparts, British historicists at the turn of the century touted a method of economic study that emphasized the search for broad laws of historical development, use of inductive empirical generalizations rather than deductive logic, and the general irrelevance of accepted economic science. Veblen's work also projected a mood of large-scale dissatisfaction with British neoclassical economics, and like some British historicists, he adopted a "Darwinian" view of the capitalist process. However, Veblen went far beyond the British historicists in terms of methodology and cohesiveness. Indeed, it is essentially Veblen's methodology that made its permanent mark on economics. We begin, therefore, with a statement of the leading British historicists' "case against economic method" as a springboard to our investigation of Veblen's contributions.

Nineteenth-Century British Historicism

As late as the 1840s, intellectual conditions in England had decidedly solidified around Ricardian economics, a situation that strongly contrasted to the intellectual "anarchy" on the Continent. Eric Roll noted that "The legacy of Ricardo was considered sacrosanct; and even as late as 1848 John Stuart Mill regarded himself in matters of theory as little more than a proponent of pure Ricardianism" (*History*, p. 299). J. R. McCulloch, James Mill, and Harriet Martineau (who penned moralistic fairy tales replete with "lessons" from classical economics) turned out to be effective popularizers of what they thought to be the Ricardian legend. The charisma surrounding Ricardian abstraction grew to formidable proportions.

Ironically, however, a cohesive historicist revolt originated on British soil. In 1831 the Reverend Richard Jones, sometimes regarded in economics as the first institutionalist, published *An Essay on the Distribution of Wealth and on the Sources of Taxation*. In it he complained that the matrix of the Ricardian analysis was far too narrow to be of practical use. He felt that economic assumptions should be historically determined and empirically justifiable. In his words, the Ricardians "confined the observations on which they founded their reasonings to the small portion of the earth's surface by which they were immediately surrounded" (p. xxiii). But his lonely voice was drowned in a sea of Ricardian dogma. Still, methodological criticism of classical economics resurfaced in England from time to time.

Bagehot, Spencer, and Darwin

Walter Bagehot (1826–1877), banker, author of *Lombard Street*, and editor of the conservative periodical, *The Economist* (which was founded by his father-in-law, James Wilson), espoused the heretical cause in 1876 in the *Fortnightly Review*, a journal that became the unofficial mouthpiece of the British historicists. The claim by Lord Bryce that Bagehot was "the most original mind of his generation," is difficult to sustain based on his scattered economic writings, but his intellectual versatility was never in doubt (Buchan, *Spare Chancellor*, p. 260). He saw connections between economics, politics, psychology, anthropology, and the natural sciences, and therefore refused to draw natural boundaries between most of these subjects and "literary studies." Initially a follower of Ricardo, Bagehot later pressed the necessity of integrating institutional structures with economic theory. By ignoring institutions, Bagehot claimed, economic theory was guilty of the pretentious and fallacious claim of overgeneralization. He maintained that the Smith–Ricardo British tradition in political economy suffered from three major defects. First, it was too culture-bound; it took things for granted that did not apply to other countries. Hence, orthodox classical economics was practically useless in understanding economic development outside Great Britain, since the institutional backdrop was seldom the same in other countries. Second, British economics dealt with "imaginary" people, not "real" ones. By ignoring the aforesaid connections between economics, politics, psychology, anthropology, and the natural sciences, economics dealt with a mere narrow facet of human behavior. Third, considered as a body of knowledge, British political economy claimed a certainty that did not accord with the facts of human experience.

Despite his interest in methodology, Bagehot did not push his criticism very far. He failed to draw out the implications of his behaviorist and institutionalist approach to economics. He left no school of disciples, nor did he provide an agenda for future political economists. But in certain circles his style of argument was extremely persuasive and he inspired others to carry the same torch.

Awakening intellectual despair over the alleged uselessness of classical economic postulates was due in large measure to philosophical ferment. Herbert Spencer, himself subeditor of *The Economist* from 1848 to 1853, was partly responsible for this agitation, although he in no way condoned it. Spencer's first love was biology, but his writings clearly spelled out the relation between biological and social evolution, even before Darwin. He sketched this relationship in clear and vibrant prose:

> A social organism is like an individual organism in these essential traits: that it grows; that while growing it becomes more complex; that while becoming more complex, its parts acquire increasing mutual dependence; that its life is immense

> in length compared with the lives of its component units . . . that in both cases there is increasing integration accompanied by increasing heterogeneity. (*Autobiography*, vol. 2, pp. 55–56)

Along with other social sciences, economics was being interpreted in the light of this type of analysis. In England, increasing economic interdependence manifested itself in the growing division of labor and burgeoning British trade. Spencer's concept of integration provided one explanation for the rapidly declining atomism of firms and their drift toward monopoly and oligopoly.

This philosophical stew of ideas was stirred immensely by the appearance of Darwin's *Origin of Species* in 1859. To the orthodox economist, and of course to the extremely individualistic Spencer, Darwin's work merely reiterated what had been known all along about the "inevitable" forces of laissez-faire. But the British historicists, eclectic in their appraisal of Spencer and Darwin, added biological evolution to their theories of institutional and social development. Bagehot even applied Darwinian principles of natural selection to the political struggles of nation-states. And, importantly, one of the strongest and most vigorous foundations of Veblen's institutional economics—his theory of change—finds its origin in the Spencer–Darwin conceptions of "process" and "evolutionary and quasi-random change." However, the British historicists did not apply Spencerian–Darwinian evolutionist principles to economic institutions in any significant and cohesive manner, either individually or as a group. Rather, they looked to other "deterministic" theories of change in forming their concepts of economics.

Comte, Ingram, and Cliffe-Leslie

One of the leading philosophers of the nineteenth century was the French positivist, Auguste Comte, whose ideas were very much in vogue among certain British intellectuals. One British historicist in particular, John Kells Ingram (1823–1907), reflected Comte's views. Ingram's whole professional career was spent at Trinity College in Dublin. A man of ubiquitous interests, he accepted much more than his mentor's views on social and economic progress; he became the leading British expositor of Comtian thought, going to the extremes of writing sonnets on the "religion of humanity." Comte's "social dynamics" infused Ingram's *History of Political Economy*—British historicism's only full-length critique of economic theory. But Comte's use of this phrase clashes with the modern economic meaning of the term and even more so with the Darwinian conception of evolution. Comte's "social dynamics" imply a necessary and continuous movement of humanity toward a teleological and predictable end. Relating as it does to the development of society, Comte's concept derives its basic data from history and is, therefore, the science of history. Ingram eagerly co-opted this notion in setting forth what he conceived to be the proper method of economic inquiry. In 1888 he maintained:

> These [Comte's] general principles affect the economic no less than other branches of social speculation; and with respect to that department of inquiry, they lead to important results. They show that the idea of forming a true theory of the economic frame and working of society apart from its other sides is illusory. (*History*, pp. 193–194)

Ingram was not being entirely original, because John Stuart Mill's work also reflects the influence of Comte, especially in Book IV (on social reform) of his *Principals of Political Economy* (1848). But Ingram was not impressed by Mill's treatment. Speaking for the historicists, he declared that this part of Mill's *Principles* "appears to us one of the least satisfactory portions of his work" (*History*, p. 194).

Moreover, Mill did not represent the dominant view. Mill's contemporary, John Elliot Cairnes (1823–1875), believed that infiltration of Comtian ideas offered little promise for political economy, even though he acknowledged that the subject "has no panacea to offer for the cure of social evils" and that "practical application of scientific principles are . . . not the proper fruit, but the accidental consequence of scientific knowledge" ("M. Comte and Political Economy," p. 602). Cairnes thought that Mill's pet idea, the subordination of political economy to the more general field of sociology, would be a barren endeavor, at least until cognate social sciences were brought up to a like stage of advancement.

Minority view or not, the historicists used Comte's and other deterministic philosophies of change as a starting point for their assault on the "vicious abstraction" and attachment to the deductive method of the British classical economists. Ingram was influenced partly by his contemporary, T. E. Cliffe-Leslie (1826–1882), who joined the chorus of wages-fund criticisms and categorically attacked wanton deduction. Cliffe-Leslie presented a case for "positive economics" regarding statistical verification of all laws and assumptions as crucial to social theory. The British historicists argued that the formal incorporation of empiricism with economic science had the great advantage of forcing the economist to use much neglected and ever-changing facts. The alternative was metaphysics. They attacked unverified abstraction as alien to the very conception of a social science.

Some historicists simply felt that the existing body of theory was untenable. Cliffe-Leslie proposed a purge of all heuristic postulates from the science, hoping to clear the air for new "theory." Arnold Toynbee, uncle of the famous historian by the same name, more circumspect in his appraisal of existing abstraction, proposed a symbiotic relationship between history and theory and felt that "Ricardo becomes painfully interesting when we read the history of his time" (*Lectures*, p. 28). Toynbee abandoned the attempt to discover a universal body of economic truths, however, feeling that economics is necessarily relativistic. Historicists generally believed that theories would be derived by placing political economy on a broader base, such as making it a branch of sociology. Ingram underlined this point in an analogy comparing society to the human body, and the economist to the physician:

> The physician who had studied only one organ and its function would be very untrustworthy even in the therapeutics of that organ. He who treats every disease as purely local, without regard to the general constitution, is a quack; and he who ignores the mutual action of the physique and the moral in disease, is not properly a physician, but a veterinary. These considerations are just as applicable, *mutatis mutandis* to the study of society, which is in so many respects kindred to biology. ("Present Position," p. 50)

In the historicist paradigm, economics was regarded as a science, but one that assigned a minor role to logical deduction and rejected *a priori* abstractions. Historicists maintained that theory should be derived by induction and by historical processes. Subjects worthy of study could be found by comparing the successive states of society in order to discover the laws of social affiliation—a process similar in principle to the comparison of organisms at different stages of biological development. Society and social facts could not be studied apart from their history. History was therefore seen as the mainspring from which the science of economics would emerge.

The Impact of British Historicism

All of this had noteworthy practical effects. Although the attempts to make economics a branch of sociology and to derive a body of theory via historical processes failed, the writings of Bagehot, Cliffe-Leslie, Ingram, and Toynbee left their mark on major British theorists of the day. Influenced by Cliffe-Leslie, William Stanley Jevons (see chapter 15) judged the historicists' orientation to be "indispensable," and qualifiedly repudiated the laissez-faire principle. However, he continued to defend the deductive method. Indeed, Jevons considered deduction to be a necessary element in the process of induction. He grew to believe that statistical verification was required to rescue economics from public hostility as well as from the more basic status of idle speculation. Although he agreed with the general methodological prescriptions of Cliffe-Leslie and Ingram, and although he thought that their criticism could "hardly fail to overcome in the end the prestige of the false old doctrines," (*Theory of Political Economy*, p. xxi) Jevons nevertheless remained suspicious of the attempt to supplant orthodox theory with the historical approach. To do so, he thought, would be to make of political economy a barren and occult science.

At the pinnacle of nineteenth-century neoclassicism Alfred Marshall (see chapter 16) praised the work of the historicists, finding it "one of the great achievements of our age; and an important addition to our real wealth" (*Principles*, p. 70). Somewhat later he affirmed his alliance to the "new generation" of economists, those propounding a less didactic and modified orthodoxy. In many respects, Marshall's *Principles* reflect economists' growing concern for social reform, and his plea for an "evolutionary" approach to economics may have been a direct result of his brush with historicism. Marshall's contemporary, John Neville Keynes, father of John Maynard and the foremost methodologist of his day, said that the "study of economic history plays a distinct and characteristic part in the building up and perfecting of political economy" (*Scope and Method*, p. 314), but he, along with Jevons and Marshall, thought that the study of history and the "inductive" method should supplement, not replace, economic theory. With the passage of time, even though ideas on appropriate methodology continued to clash, neoclassical theoretical economics ultimately provided the accepted training ground for economists in England, and economic history (with the emphasis on the noun) largely became, in England and the United States, a subfield of general economics.

■ Thorstein Veblen and American Institutionalism

Conditions within the economics profession in late-nineteenth-century America were markedly different from those in Britain and Europe. Eclecticism had always been the hallmark of American economists. From Thomas Jefferson and Alexander Hamilton to Henry Carey and Henry George, English and Continental ideas were filtered through the uniquely American experiences and institutions. Pragmatism permeated both philosophy and economics well into the twentieth century. Classical and neoclassical *theoretical* analysis consequently never had the hold on American economists that it did on English economists.[1] Some classical theoretical ideas were

[1] American Nobel laureate Kenneth Arrow reports that, as late as his graduate student days at Columbia University (1940–1942), no required course in price theory was offered, though Veblenian economics was prominently featured. Further, Arrow notes, "The corrosive skepticism of Veblen towards 'received' theory had, belatedly and even posthumously, undermined the never-very-secure hold of neoclassical thought on the teaching of American economics" ("Thorstein Veblen as an Economic Theorist," p. 5).

turned on their heads in order to fit them to the American situation by economists such as Henry Carey and Francis A. Walker. The ideas of historicists were able to take root in such a freewheeling intellectual environment. Richard T. Ely and E. R. A. Seligman, along with the more orthodox F. A. Walker, all founders of the American Economic Association (AEA) in 1886, were sympathetic to the historicist cause. (Ely was educated in Germany under the aegis of historicists.) In many respects, these writers represented a left wing of the AEA and its professional economists. In the preface to Ely's *Introduction to Political Economy*, J. K. Ingram heralded the growing acceptance of historicist views, declaring, "A more humane and genial spirit has taken the place of the old dryness and hardness which once repelled so many of the best minds from the study of economics" (pp. 5–6). Into this very receptive milieu stepped a formidable American critic and iconoclast, Thorstein Veblen. Although he was influenced by philosophical and intellectual forces (including those of the historicists) from abroad, Veblen's ideas on economics may nevertheless be clearly stamped "Made in U.S.A."

The Critic's Life and Preconceptions

Thorstein Bunde Veblen was born in Wisconsin and was of Norwegian ancestry (his first name means "son of Thor," the Norse god of thunder). At the age of eight he moved to a large farm in Minnesota. In 1874 he entered Carleton College, a religious training school, where he quickly demonstrated his brilliance along with a calculatingly critical attitude toward everything, including religion. Veblen also studied at Johns Hopkins University, where he was greatly influenced by J. B. Clark, and at Yale University, where he received a PhD in philosophy in 1884. Unable to secure an academic position, he returned to his father's farm. For seven years he was a voracious and eclectic reader of social science literature, including economics. In 1890 Veblen entered Cornell University as a graduate student, but soon thereafter he joined the faculty of the University of Chicago, where he became editor of the *Journal of Political Economy*.

During his twelve-year tenure at Chicago and afterward, Veblen became the most visible and highly regarded social and economic critic of his time. In numerous journal contributions and books, including the iconic *Theory of the Leisure Class* (1899), he assessed problems in then-existing social institutions and scathingly criticized classical and neoclassical economic analysis. Veblen's prestige as a thinker and academician (by all accounts he was an awful teacher) was not sufficient to overcome his flagrant and frequent violations of social mores and his biting attacks on businesspeople supporting the university—and he was asked to leave in 1904.

After leaving Chicago, he took positions at Stanford University, at the University of Missouri, and at the New School for Social Research, never rising above the rank of assistant professor. In 1927 he returned to California, where he died on August 3, 1929, a few months before the great stock market crash (which in a sense he had predicted, and probably would have enjoyed a great deal). His brilliant student, Wesley C. Mitchell, penned the following epitaph:

> A heretic needs a high heart, though sustained by faith that he is everlastingly right and sure of his reward hereafter. The heretic who views his own ideas as but tomorrow's fashion in thought needs still firmer courage. Such courage Veblen had. All his uneasy life, he faced outer hostility and inner doubt with a quizzical smile. Uncertain what the future had in store, he did the day's work as best he might, getting a philosopher's pleasures from playing with ideas and exercising

> "his swift wit and his slow irony" upon his fellows. However matters went with him, and often they went ill, he made no intellectual compromises. (*What Veblen Taught*, p. xlix)

Despite the relatively simple facts of his life, Veblen was a complex intellectual. Throughout his very productive life he was uncannily able to view the real world and the world of ideas (circa turn-of-the-century America) from the outside. He once attributed the intellectual and scientific predominance of European Jews to their *lack* of contemporary preconceptions and to their initial immersion in a culture stamped "B.C." Like them, and perhaps because of the essentially Nordic cultural background of his youth, Veblen was able to view society in much the way a pathologist approaches an autopsy. He was insatiably curious about what makes social and economic processes "tick" and especially about the mode and method of how societies—as the totality of cultural and technological institutions—change.

The formative forces that shaped Veblen's preconceptions were manifold. His views on human nature were shaped by behaviorism and, specifically, by theories of instincts and habits, which stood in strong contrast to the rationalistic and utilitarian conceptions of the classical and neoclassical writers. The Spencer–Darwin view of social and biological evolutionary change had a major impact on Veblen's "worldview," as did the instrumentalist philosophy of William James. Veblen also much distrusted mathematics and statistics as tools of science, sarcastically labeling those who resorted to such calculations as "animated slide-rules." (Were he alive today he might call them "computer jockeys.")

Veblen's thoughts on particular subjects are often hard to decipher because they appear in statements that are piecemeal, scattered, and often contradictory. An appreciation of his "system" is not rendered easier by the fact that his writings are peppered with polemical speculation, personal prejudices, gratuitously normative statements, cynicism, and wry humor. His brilliant command of the English language has sent more than a few readers running to the dictionary. The study of Veblen is akin to a ride on a Ferris wheel. Categorically, it matters not where one gets on, for the rider always returns to the same spot. The essentials of Veblen's theory were formed early and remained virtually unchanged throughout his life. Indeed, one might say that his later works were merely extensions and elaborations of a central thesis set forth earlier. We begin our analysis with Veblen's views on human nature and his ideas on the method of economics.

Human Nature and Economic Method

In part II of this book we saw how the classical economists regarded people as rational calculators of pleasures and pains. Natural law, or its extension, the "invisible hand," kept people on course and in general promoted the greatest social good for the greatest number. Veblen denounced this belief as superficial nonsense. He argued that humans are significantly more complex creatures, led by particular instincts and characterized by instinctive behavior and habits.[2] People aren't "lightning fast calculators" of pleasures and pains but rather are curious beings who, *by nature*, hit on new ways of doing things. In sum, people are creatively curious and are creatures of acquired propensities and habits.

[2] Veblen's instinct-habit psychology and its interactions with human propensities of thought have been criticized as one of the less satisfactory parts of his work. We do not take a position on this issue, but interested readers may wish to consult notes for further reading at the end of the chapter for more information.

In an anthropological study of human culture, Veblen concluded that certain instincts, such as the "instinct of workmanship" (the title of one of his most interesting books) applied to all humans in all societies. Veblen concluded that the most significant factor in determining human propensities and preconceptions is the material circumstances in which people find themselves. Material circumstances (including technology) shape a person's or a society's worldview, which, in turn, give rise to relations between humans and property, humans and the legal-political system, humans and philosophy, humans and religion, and so on. A *worldview* is thus premised on the material conditions of any particular age. Institutions—ways of doing things, thinking about things, and distributing the rewards for work, and so forth—arise to support a set of material circumstances. Most beings are indelibly stamped with a set of preconceptions unique to their particular time and place, preconceptions that are bestowed by a given technological system. Veblen posited that interactions between technological institutions, on the one hand, and ceremonial institutions, on the other, constitute the mainsprings of change in his system.

All this should sound somewhat familiar to anyone versed in the ideas of Marx (see chapter 12). Marx's views of human nature and the impact of technology on culture were partially analogous to Veblen's, but without the Darwinian influence. Veblen's theory of cultural and institutional change follows the Darwinian theory of biological evolution in which "ends" are not exactly predictable. The application of evolutionary principles to human culture was, in Veblen's view, even more critical since human *biological* evolution and mental capacity had been essentially *fixed* for thousands of years, while cultural evolution has progressed at a much more rapid pace. In other words, the imprint of evolution is almost exclusively cultural. Thus, the basic difference between Marx and Veblen concerns the theory of change each advanced. This is also an essential difference between Veblen and practically *all other* economic writers, including the classical economists. A fuller appreciation of this important concept of economic and cultural change resides in what Veblen considered the "proper" method of economic study.

"Matter of Fact" versus Animistic Preconceptions

Veblen attacked the philosophical foundations of economic orthodoxy in a long and brilliant critical essay entitled "The Preconceptions of Economic Science" (first published in the *Quarterly Journal of Economics* in 1899–1900). He argued that Adam Smith was, in part, possessed of a matter-of-fact, empirical preconception, though he was guilty of fostering an "animistic" view of the world in economic science. In an animistic preconception, perceptions of reality are guided by deistic notions (i.e., God or Nature), so that life has a teleological, or natural, outcome. Thus, we find Smith (and other classical economists) discussing a natural or equilibrium price, which, when disturbed, would return through an assumed natural order (see chapter 5). According to Veblen:

> The animistic preconception enforces the apprehension of phenomena in terms generically identical with the terms of personality or individuality. As a certain modern group of psychologists would say, it imputes to objects and sequences an element of habit and attention similar in kind, though not necessarily in degree, to the like spiritual attitude present in the activities of a personal agent. The matter-of-fact preconception, on the other hand, enforces a handling of facts without imputation of personal force or attention, but with an imputation of mechanical continuity, substantially the preconception which has reached a formulation at the

> hands of scientists under the name of conservation of energy or persistence of quantity. Some appreciable resort to the latter method of knowledge is unavoidable at any cultural stage, for it is indispensable to all industrial efficiency. All technological processes and all mechanical contrivances rest, psychologically speaking, on this ground. This habit of thought is a selectively necessary consequence of industrial life, and, indeed, of all human experience in making use of the material means of life. It should therefore follow that, in a general way, the higher the culture, the greater the share of the mechanical preconception in shaping human thought and knowledge, since, in a general way, the stage of culture attained depends on the efficiency of industry. ("Preconceptions," p. 141)

Veblen said that the utilitarianism of Bentham and Mill simply substituted hedonism ("self-interest") for achievement of purpose as a ground for legitimacy. The result was that utilitarian philosophy made economics a science of wealth, in which the individual is inert, because human will and institutions are basic assumptions, and values are therefore eliminated. Economics became (and remained, in Veblen's view) a deterministic and categorical discipline that attributed all good things to a beneficent, but functionless and static, competitive system (i.e., good = normal = right). Based on an incessant quest for monetary gain, the competitive system yields predictable outcomes when interfered with, or when interferences are removed.[3] One of Veblen's persistent themes was that the instincts and habits emerging from pecuniary hedonism characterized American society *both on the supply and on the demand sides*. Absentee ownership and conspicuous consumption and leisure were the expected responses to a pervasive utilitarian preconception that created a "consumption economy." (We shall return to this matter below.)

Veblen's methodological critique may be summarized as follows. First, he argued that the orthodox neoclassical view of the economic system, and the theoretical superstructure it supported, was sterile and essentially useless. But he did *not* argue, as is sometimes supposed, that neoclassical analysis was invalid, given its assumptions. One difficulty was its simplistic view of human nature—Bentham's concept of "pecuniary rationality"—rather than an instinct-habit conception, and another was its outmoded concept of change. Second, in a positive vein, Veblen based his own theory on (1) an implicit hypothesis that historical events (social, economic, and political) are determined and best described by *group* characteristics formed by the sum of instinct-habitual human behavior, and (2) a Darwinian (evolutionary), not a deterministic, view of change is the appropriate tool for dealing with social and economic phenomena.

Even today many dissident writers share Veblen's assumption regarding group behavior. His Darwinian view of change, an insight of genuine originality, is motivated by a *causal sequence* or process. Consider a movement from situation A to situation B. The determinist would argue that if A represents a competitive equilibrium, its displacement would either cause equilibrium to be restored once the disturbing factor was removed or cause equilibrium to change in some predictable way if the disturbing factor was allowed to persist for a long period of time. That is, assuming that fundamental economic data (utility functions, costs, institutions, etc.) do not change from A to B, the *effects* of a single disturbing change may be analyzed with considerable precision. (See the Marshallian method of *ceteris paribus* discussed at length in chapter 16.)

[3] This type of competitive system was described by numerous neoclassical writers, including the Austrians and Alfred Marshall. But it must be remembered that Wieser and Marshall exhibited strong undercurrents of dissent from this method.

In Veblen's concept of causal sequence, the mere cessation of interference with the system, or the introduction of a single, permanent change at state A, will not leave the outcome the same as if no interference had taken place. The effects of single changes at A are not predictable; nor are states A and B comparable in any meaningful way as long as tastes, technology, and institutions are constantly changing. By employing a deterministic method orthodox economic analysis requires that the underlying data of the system remain the same over the period of analysis. However, Veblen proposed a system of constant and ineluctable change. To him, economics was most accurately described as a process, or as a "proliferation."

The Interaction of Ceremony and Technology

Veblen put these methodological concepts and his instinct-habit psychology at the core of a positive theory of economic change. His analysis may be applied to specific institutions, as we shall soon see, but the overall design of his theory incorporates a grand view of economy-wide institutional change. Figure 19-1 represents a schematic attempt to portray Veblen's concept of economic change.

Veblen identified two groups of institutions, "technological" and "ceremonial," each of which is in a constant state of flux. The existence and characteristics of these two sets of institutions are determined by the unchangeable characteristics of human nature on the one hand, and the anthropological and historical processes they engender, on the other. Institutions are shaped over time by human instincts—Veblen specifically emphasized the instincts of workmanship and the innate "idle curiosity" of human beings—which manifest themselves in a certain technology. The technology of the modern age is characterized by a "machine process," which is instrumental in establishing ceremonial institutions: a characteristic set of property rights, social and economic structures, habits of thought, and so on. The technological institutions (i.e., machine process) is the dynamic force in Veblen's society, whereas ceremonial institutions tend to be static. Thus, the social and economic institutions characteristic of a "long primitive stage" of society are inextricably

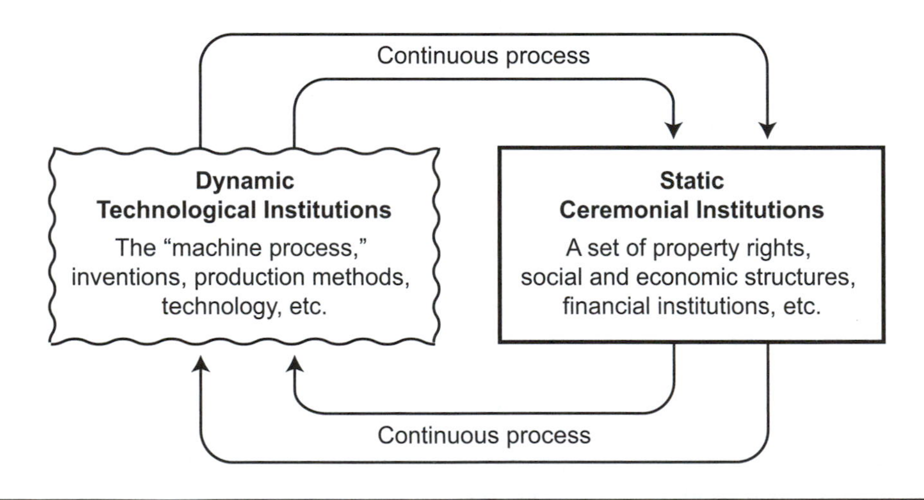

Figure 19-1 The interrelation of technological and ceremonial institutions is based on unchangeable characteristics of human nature and the anthropological and historical processes.

bound to the nature (and growth) of technology over that period. Feudal social and economic institutions were as essentially characteristic of the technology extant over the Middle Ages as contemporary "ceremonial" institutions were characteristic of the more advanced production methods of the nineteenth and twentieth centuries.

Two aspects of the institutional process described in figure 19-1 must be expanded because: (1) the relations between the two types of institutions are not quite as simple as described above, and (2) certain forms of social and economic behavior, as well as associated mental preconceptions that characterize humans throughout their development, have been *amplified* under a given "machine process."

In the first place, ceremonial institutions, including property rights, not only are the product of the machine process of any given period but also impinge on technology, thwarting or encouraging it as the case may be. This interrelation could last only over a "short" period of time (perhaps several hundred years), however, since in the long run a technology based on idle curiosity and the human ability to invent must be *dynamic*. Stated differently, ceremonial institutions can constrain the machine process, but only temporarily. In the long run, according to Veblen, technological institutions will shape social and economic relations.

In the second place, certain preconceptions or behavioral characteristics may be common to humans *throughout* their entire development but may be emphasized by a particular state of technology. Thus, as we shall see, conspicuous consumption and leisure, while very much in evidence over a certain stage in development, rest on certain *general* behavioral characteristics of humans typical to them since the beginning of time. Humans are born with certain instincts and with a set of preconceptions about the way in which the world works. For example, emulation is a behavioral characteristic of humans, especially in societies that embrace a pecuniary culture. Likewise, a pecuniary culture is the *product* of a technology that permits and even fosters the divorce between ownership and management; between proprietary accumulation and the actual productive process; between "business" and enterprise.

Early in the twentieth century Veblen viewed the capitalist process as one that generates an indigenous business cycle, but the institutional framework that supersedes it is always the product of past and present interactions of ceremonial and technological institutions. Ceremonial institutions regarding private property, like economic science itself, are increasingly characterized by a love of money. Advancing technology permits a separation of production from finance. "Making goods" becomes very different from "making money." In this well-known distinction Veblen noted that, after the Industrial Revolution, the functions of owner-producers and managers became increasingly separated. Businesspeople and *captains of finance* attempted to subvert the progress of technology, reducing output and increasing pecuniary returns through monopoly measures. Making money, not goods, became the object of the game. (Note the augmentation of certain Marxian themes.) According to Veblen, acquisition of money through subversion and "warlike traits" are characteristic of businesspeople. (Veblen's infamous attacks on the role of businesspeople in commerce were pitiless.) At the same time workers and engineers—those close to the machine process—tend to reject old technology and develop new (and presumably cheaper) means of production.

Economics Meets Sociology: Conspicuous Consumption

Veblen's envisioned outcome of the dynamic process of technological change and the cyclical forces that it produces are near at hand. But first we must digress to examine an important aspect of the social process—conspicuous consumption. Veblen's most subtle and famous idea juxtaposed psychology, economics, and sociology.[4] In *The Theory of the Leisure Class* he launched a detailed study of the formation of tastes and the act of consumption. Neoclassical economists had assigned utility functions to individuals on the assumption that utility derived from any given expenditure was independent of the utility from any other expenditure, either by the same consumer or by any other. (In more formal jargon, utility functions are said to be additive.) Veblen claimed that this was defective theory because it neglected an *essential* part of the economic process—study of the formation of tastes and consumption patterns. In other words, the neoclassical economists took as given one of the most fundamental parts of the analysis.[5] Veblen's critique was vivid:

> The hedonistic conception of man is that of a lightning calculator of pleasures and pains, who oscillates like a homogeneous globule of desire of happiness under the impulse of stimuli that shift him about the area, but leave him intact. ("Why," p. 389)

As a practical matter Veblen recognized the prime importance of higher consumption to the maintenance of aggregate demand in a pecuniary economy. But he insisted that consumption be treated as an inextricable part of the ceremonial institutions of capitalism. Moreover, his view was rooted in a theory of *pecuniary emulation* rather than in that of simple utility maximization.

In Veblen's conception, the instinct to emulate others was second in strength only to the instinct of self-preservation. In his lengthy anthropological study of the "emulatory instinct" (*Theory*, pp. 22–34), Veblen argued that property acquisition became the conventional basis for social esteem early in the history of humankind. Most property was initially acquired through plunder, but over the long path of history, it became "more honorable" to acquire wealth *passively* rather than through predation. In addition to the "honor" of passively acquired wealth, a person's status is determined by how well one's holdings compare with those of his or her immediate peer group and with the group immediately above. In a sense, therefore, acquisitiveness drives economic activity:

> In any community where goods are held in severalty it is necessary, in order to his own peace of mind, that an individual should possess as large a portion of goods as others with whom he is accustomed to class himself; and it is extremely gratifying to possess something more than others. But as fast as a person makes new acquisitions, and becomes accustomed to the resulting new standard of wealth, the new standard forthwith ceases to afford appreciably greater satisfaction than the earlier standard did. The tendency in any case is constantly to make the present pecuniary standard the point of departure for a fresh increase of wealth; and this in turn gives rise to a new standard of sufficiency and a new pecuniary classification of one's self as compared with one's neighbours. (*Theory*, p. 31)

Veblen's theory of pecuniary emulation recognizes the nonsatiability of human wants as much as neoclassical economics does. "More is better than less" in both paradigms. But in emphasizing the basic human "instinct of workmanship" as the motor of pecuniary achievement, Veblen asserts that ironically, in the acquisitive society productive work becomes a mark of infirmity and leisure becomes evidence

[4] The idea of "conspicuous consumption" may be judged to have originated during mercantile times by Bernard de Mandeville and revisited later in the classical period by John Rae. However, Veblen raised the concept to its highest expression.

[5] In a wry twist, critics of academic economists have often accused them of enjoying "the leisure of the theory class."

of pecuniary strength. Leisure itself becomes a consumption good, and conspicuous consumption and conspicuous leisure are thus two sides of the same coin. Although there is a distinguishable, elite "leisure class," every class in society is subject to the same strivings.[6]

The bulk of Veblen's book is composed of wide-ranging (and largely sociological) applications of this bold generalization. With disregard for common disciplinary boundaries, he extended his theory into the realm of sociology to investigate the consumption of "immaterial goods by leisure-class gentlemen: quasi-academic, quasi-scholarly pursuits, awards, and trophies" that stand in evidence of unproductive leisure. Veblen also brought within the fold of his analysis such matters as gift giving, fashion, the leisure activities of middle-class wives, the social status of athletics, manners, and higher learning.[7] He concluded that conspicuous consumption is a waste of goods and conspicuous leisure is a waste of time. Just what Veblen would do about these matters is not clear, but the avoidance of productive work and the enjoyment of conspicuous waste were part and parcel of contemporary society as he saw it.

While Veblen's brilliant analysis of consumption brings a certain delight to iconoclasts, his ideas did not permeate twentieth-century orthodox analysis. Nevertheless, some features have been incorporated by degrees into both macroeconomic and microeconomic studies. Harvey Leibenstein attempted to reconcile Veblen's analysis with neoclassical theory in his 1950 article "Bandwagon, Snob, and Veblen Effects in the Theory of Consumers' Demand." Leibenstein identified a "Veblen good" as one whose utility derived not only from the direct use of the good but also from the price paid for it. Thus, a conspicuous price is the price that a consumer believes other people think he or she paid for a commodity. It is this price that determines a good's "conspicuous consumption utility." Quantity demanded may then be regarded as a function of a good's money price, P, and its *expected* conspicuous price, P'. This kind of behavior may be illustrated by figure 19-2 (on the following page), which is adapted from Leibenstein. In the diagram, alternative demand curves for consumers are derived by changing the money price on the assumption that some expected conspicuous price is constant. Thus, demand curve D_1 is derived varying the money price and assuming that expected conspicuous price P_1 is constant. In a perfect market with perfect information, equilibrium occurs when expected conspicuous price and actual real price are equal, where $P_1 = P'_1$, $P_2 = P'_2$, and so forth. If the expected conspicuous price increases, the demand curve shifts to the right for every money price. Alternative possible equilibriums may then be traced out as points A, E, F, yielding an *upward-sloping* Veblenian demand curve (not to be confused with the Giffen good of orthodox neoclassical theory).

A *Veblen effect* may be isolated, moreover, by supposing a decline in price from equilibrium at P_2 to P_1. In the absence of any changes in expected conspicuous price,

[6] Veblen relates two anthropological episodes to galvanize his point. The first involves Polynesian chiefs who, "under the stress of good form, prefer to starve rather than carry their food to their mouths with their own hands." The second involved a French king who died through an excess of moral stamina in the observance of good form: "In absence of the functionary whose office it was to shift his master's seat, the king sat uncomplaining before the fire and suffered his royal person to be toasted beyond recovery. But in so doing he saved his Most Christian Majesty from menial contamination" (*Theory*, pp. 42–43).

[7] Among other Veblenian gems is his treatment of children as conspicuous waste, i.e., as a consumer good. Says Veblen: "The conspicuous consumption, and the consequent increased expense, required in the reputable maintenance of a child is very considerable and acts as a powerful deterrent. It is probably the most effectual of the Malthusian prudential checks" (*Theory*, p. 113).

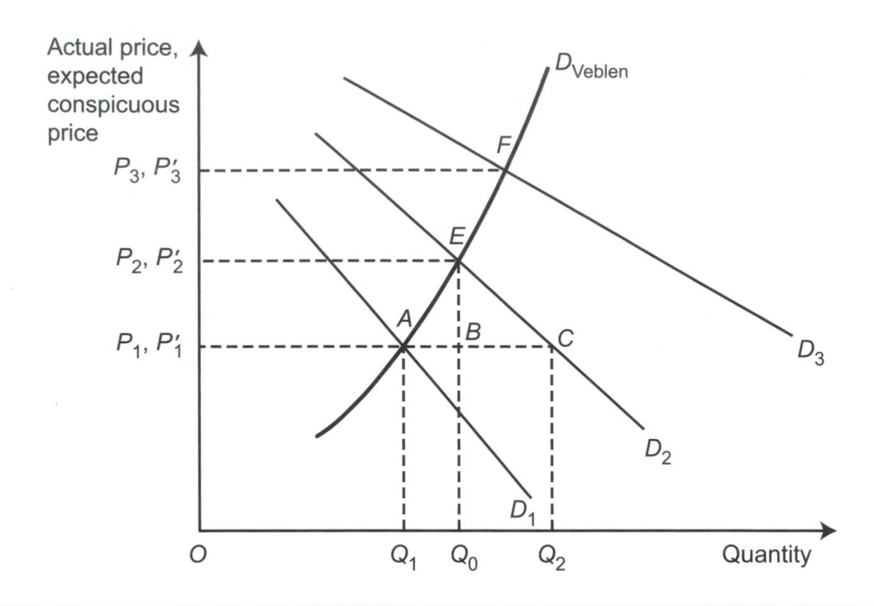

Figure 19-2 As the expected conspicuous price rises from P'_1 to P'_2 to P'_3, the demand curve shifts to the right, from D_1 to D_2 to D_3. Tracing out the alternative equilibriums, *A, E, F* yields an upward-sloping Veblenian demand curve.

quantity demanded would expand along demand curve D_2 from Q_0 to Q_2. But when expected conspicuous price falls to P'_1, output thereby declines by an amount Q_2Q_1. Thus, the pure price effect is positive, Q_0Q_2, and the Veblen effect is negative, Q_2Q_1, producing a net negative effect on quantity of Q_0Q_1. Price reduction of a Veblen good may produce a reduction in quantity if the Veblen effect outweighs or overbalances the price effect. The point of this discussion is that although the consumption concepts propounded by Veblen are complex and subtle, they may have relevance for, and be integrated within, the neoclassical framework of microeconomics.

Economic Change and the Future of Capitalism

In a number of studies, including the *Theory of Business Enterprise* (1904) and a set of essays entitled *The Engineers and the Price System* (1921), Veblen expanded his theory of institutional change under capitalism. In the process, he spelled out a theory of the business cycle and a prognosis for the capitalist system.

Veblen saw economic and social change as the result of interaction between technological and ceremonial institutions. This interaction is made more concrete by identifying the two institutions with certain groups in the process of change. Whereas Veblen identified "captains of industry," corporate financiers, investment bankers, absentee owners, and businesspeople as part of the ceremonial process, he lumped technicians, engineers, and certain workers into his definition of technological institutions. Originally, the functions of directly overseeing the "machine process" and the management of the firm were one and the same. This melding of functions created the preconditions for maximum production, which was Veblen's goal. As the pecuniary aspects of culture began to dominate, however, and as specialized knowledge grew apace, the two functions were divorced. Veblen described this split:

> A new move in the organization of business enterprise has come in sight, whereby the discretionary control of industrial production is shifting still farther over to the side of finance and still farther out of touch with the requirements of maximum production. The new move is of a twofold character: (a) the financial captains of industry have been proving their industrial incompetence in a progressively convincing fashion, and (b) their own proper work of financial management has progressively taken on a character of standardized routine such as no longer calls for or admits any large measure of discretion or initiative. They have been losing touch with the management of industrial process. (*Engineers*, p. 41)

In their pursuit of profits, businesspeople face two alternative courses of action: lower production costs or restrict output (in monopoly fashion). According to Veblen, businesspeople had in the main followed the latter practice because, among other reasons, it required less familiarity with the workings of the machine process. But this is shortsighted, he argued, because by choosing to "make money" rather than "make goods" businesspeople mismanage resources and even sabotage the technological-productive process, all the while catering to the vested interests of investment bankers, stockholders, and so forth.

Technicians, engineers, and workers close to "the machine process" generally have a different mind-set. Their goal is to encourage and devise means and machines for maximizing real output. Though they work for the businesspeople–corporate financiers, Veblen argued that they were becoming increasingly aware of the utter wastes of business enterprise. Thus, it was the industrial experts, not the businesspeople, who finally began to criticize this "unbusinesslike" mismanagement and neglect of the ways and means of industry:

> Two things have been happening which have deranged the regime of the corporation financier: industrial experts, engineers, chemists, mineralogists, technicians of all kinds, have been drifting into more responsible positions in the industrial system and have been growing up and multiplying within the system, because the system will no longer work at all without them; and on the other hand, the large financial interests on whose support the corporation financiers have been leaning have gradually come to realize that corporation finance can best be managed as a comprehensive bureaucratic routine. (*Engineers*, pp. 44–45)

Veblen therefore looked to the engineers and other industrial experts to reorder the system of production, a role that fit more conveniently into his theory of the business cycle.

Like Marx (see chapter 12), Veblen believed that business cycles were *endogenous* to capitalism, and for many of the same reasons. While he did not ground his theory of business cycles on a labor theory of value, Veblen explained recession and prolonged depressions along Marxian lines. He maintained that there were two basic factors leading to recession: (1) banker uncertainty after a period of new capitalization and expansion of industry and (2) technological displacement by new and more efficient inventions and productive processes.

In the first instance businesses accumulate debt as a result of increased business capitalization during a boom. The banker-lender becomes uncertain as to repayment and begins to call in loans (or not renew them). Possibly due to its maturity structure, the holders of existing debt are unable to meet banker demands, and as more and more uncertainty develops, the entire system becomes vulnerable and foments a recession.

In the second instance the technological displacement of old firms by new firms induces recession. Cost-reducing inventions are typically adopted by new competitors. Rates of return are thereby driven down on the older assets of existing firms, causing lower-than-anticipated profits or, at the limit, bankruptcies. Investment falls, and the psychology of recession leads to a downturn of business activity.[8]

Thus, depression results both from instabilities in the financial system and from technological displacement caused by new inventions. After a depression phase, the cycle "bottoms out" as the overhead burden is "worked off." Financial expansion takes place along with increases in employment and new capital investment. Rising prices and overexpansion occur, once more precipitating a new cycle.

A number of aspects of the Veblenian cycle are of interest. Veblen characterized the expansion phase of the cycle as one of overproduction and overcapitalization. Overproduction is the consequence of *underconsumption* in Veblen's theory of the cycle. Joining such underconsumptionists as Malthus before him (see chapter 7) and J. M. Keynes after him (see chapter 21), Veblen believed that the business cycle was exacerbated by the saving and investment motives of financiers and owners of business enterprises. Though the instinct to emulate and to consume conspicuously was operative in all classes, Veblen apparently thought it insufficient to maintain aggregate demand. Consequently, underconsumption and the psychological effect of falling prices and redundant capital were factors leading to prolonged recession.

Whereas Marx attributed business cycles to the inner contradictions of capitalism, Veblen emphasized the failings of human nature. He believed that the businessperson's attempt to avert crises caused by declining profit rates led to business concentration and to other forms of (inadvertent) "sabotage." Consolidations of industry took place in order to avoid reductions in total business capitalization. Thus, after progressive cycles, capitalist industry became more and more consolidated in the same manner as premised in Marx's laws of "increasing concentration" and the "falling rate of profit" (see chapter 12).

But the sabotage might be pervasive. In an argument that clearly anticipates an important contemporary idea, Veblen charged that businesspeople would attempt to "capture" the government's regulatory apparatus and use it for orderly and organized sabotage against the public. One example of the incestuous relationship between government and business that is encouraged by capitalism is the matter of tariffs and external trade restrictions. Veblen wrote:

> Where the national government is charged with the general care of the country's business interests, as is invariably the case among the civilized nations, it follows from the nature of the case that the nation's lawgivers and administration will have some share in administering that necessary modicum of sabotage that must always go into the day's work of carrying on industry by business methods and for business purposes. The government is in a position to penalize excessive or unwholesome traffic. So, it is always considered necessary, or at least expedient, by all sound mercantilists, as by a tariff or by subsidies, to impose and maintain a certain balance or proportion among the several branches of industry and trade that go to make up the nation's industrial system. (*Engineers*, pp. 18–19)

In a brilliantly incisive passage Veblen turned his "capture theory" loose on internal regulation and restrictions:

> Of a similar character, in so far that in effect they are in the nature of sabotage—conscientious withdrawal of efficiency—are all manner of excise and revenue-

[8] Contemporary writers have amplified Veblen's point and argued that initial investment problems caused by anticipated technological innovations lead to government regulation or to "administered controls" (see notes for further reading).

> stamp regulations; although they are not always designed for that purpose. Such would be, for instance, the partial or complete prohibition of alcoholic beverages, the regulation of the trade in tobacco, opium, and other deleterious narcotics, drugs, poisons, and high explosives. Of the same nature, in effect if not in intention, are such regulations as the oleomargarine law; as also the unnecessarily costly and vexatious routine of inspection imposed on the production of industrial (denatured) alcohol, which has inured to the benefit of certain business concerns that are interested in other fuels for use in internal-combustion engines; so also the singularly vexatious and elaborately imbecile specifications that limit and discourage the use of the parcel post, for the benefit of the express companies and other carriers which have vested interest in traffic of that kind. (*Engineers*, pp. 20–21)

As these passages reveal, Veblen saw, correctly, that the aim of much regulation, especially that which endorses legalized cartels and legitimizes monopolies, was the protection of vested interests at the expense of the public interest.[9]

These examples of "sabotage" comprise what Veblen called a conscientious withdrawal of efficiency by business. All such withdrawals attempt to subvert the productive process—to reduce output to the most profitable levels. This subversion of the productive process brings on business cycles of increasing severity. Veblen tells us that the representatives of technological institutions could be expected to resist the imbecile activities of businesspeople, but from where would the resistance come, and what sort of institutions would eventually triumph?

Marx had argued that propertyless workers would coalesce in common cause to challenge and overthrow the propertied bourgeoisie, but Veblen believed that organized labor exercised its *own* conscientious withdrawal of efficiency in order to keep its returns above the "competitive level" earned by the "common man." He therefore opposed the American Federation of Labor (AFL), a frequent target of his criticism. American labor organizations, he asserted, were vested interests in their own right, always ready to do battle for their own privilege and profit. Union leaders dominated the politics of the AFL, but the benefits to its rank-and-file workers were dubious at best.

> The rank and file assuredly are not of the kept classes, nor do they visibly come in for a free income. Yet they stand on the defensive in maintaining a vested interest in the prerogatives and perquisites of their organization. They are apparently moved by a feeling that so long as the established arrangements are maintained they will come in for a little something over and above what goes to the common man. (*Vested Interests*, p. 165)

Far from placing trust in the labor movement, Veblen lumped business and organized labor together in their efforts to subvert the productive process. Therefore, if capitalism was to be saved, it would have to be by the efforts of engineers and industrial managers. Although this class of people represented less than 1 percent of the population, Veblen nevertheless believed it could alter the industrial

[9] Veblen also recognized that government perversions of the system extend to the financial sector as well. At a time when the Federal Reserve System was a new creature of government, Veblen objected: the "process of pooling and syndication that is remaking the world of credit and corporation finance has been greatly helped on in America by the establishment of the Federal Reserve System. . . . That system . . . has very conveniently left the substantial control in the hands of those larger financial interests into whose hands the lines of control in credit and industrial business were already being gathered. . . ." (*Engineers*, pp. 50–51). How many times since Veblen penned these words has the Fed been accused of favoring big business interests at a high cost to workers, small-business owners, and investors?

order of finance capitalism. Engineers and other industrial-production personnel were trained largely at public expense, and they alone would be competent to run the system. Veblen often hinted that nonaligned workers, the "common man" (and even the rank and file), were becoming more aware of the profitable abuse of technology perpetrated by business and organized labor. Eventually, therefore, a struggle must ensue, but Veblen was never clear about the nature of the struggle or its outcome. Presumably some type of socialism was the likely result, but whereas Marx could issue precise predictions within his system, Veblen could not. The fact that he consistently maintained an evolutionist's outlook on the prospects of capitalism meant that he could never be certain of the outcome, and in the end he could only speculate. His intriguing speculation was that capitalism, particularly American capitalism, was at a turning point:

> In effect, the progressive advance of this industrial system towards an all-inclusive mechanical balance of interlocking processes appears to be approaching a critical pass, beyond which it will no longer be practicable to leave its control in the hands of businesspeople working at cross purposes for private gain, or to entrust its continued administration to others than suitably trained technological experts, production engineers without a commercial interest. What these men may then do with it all is not so plain; the best they can do may not be good enough; but the negative proposition is becoming sufficiently plain, that this mechanical state of the industrial arts will not long tolerate the continued control of production by the vested interests under the current businesslike rule of incapacity by advisement. (*Engineers*, p. 58)

A Brief Assessment of Veblen's Economics

Veblen's prognostication of social upheaval certainly appeared to be vindicated when the stock market crashed in 1929. Although the causes of the onset and the severity of the Great Depression are still being debated, there is no argument about the extent of the financial collapse and the human and resource unemployment that followed in its wake. Was this the "critical pass" Veblen spoke of in referring to the probable collapse of the capitalist system? The question is problematic, but the answer may be informed by considering Veblen's analysis of the capitalist system from both the theoretical and the practical side.

First, consider Veblen's theoretical scenario. The Great Depression did not bring on an "age of engineers" or an end to the price system of resource allocation and distribution. Veblen failed to perceive that self-interested behavior would have extended to *any* group of individuals in control of the productive process. Engineers and the "common man" were not "philosopher kings" any more than businesspeople, financiers, and organized labor were. The ascendance of the engineers would simply have created new "vested interests" in money making. To be sure, institutional changes occurred in American capitalism after the Depression but they did not result from the development of a new elite class of technological superiority.

Second, Veblen's analysis suggested that engineers, or some technical elite, would maximize production *without regard to prices* in a hazily conceived type of socialism or quasi-socialistic system. But, empirically, no communistic or socialistic state has survived in the modern era without some recourse to a price system. Some form of prices (either explicit prices or shadow prices) are necessary in socialist systems in order to obtain efficient allocations of resources. As F. A. Hayek so forcefully argued, prices convey necessary information in a market system (see chapter

23). If you eliminate the market system, you eliminate the informational data necessary to achieve efficiency. Both Veblen and Marx were naive in their understanding of markets. To date nothing has proved superior to prices as providers of economic information in the marketplace.

Third, from a more practical point of view, Veblen underestimated the ability of the system to adjust. His strong disdain of businesspeople led him to the erroneous belief that virtually all output markets were characterized by monopoly or oligopoly. Veblen never appreciated the fact that real competition constrains the attempted "withdrawal of efficiency" by businesspeople in most instances. Fourth, he underestimated the role of government and the legal system in addressing problems of social costs and externalities. For good or evil, the government instituted numerous interventions to alter income distribution in the post-1930s era. At least some of these interventions have sometimes acted as a political filter between "vested interests" and the "common man."

We have observed before that economists typically don't make good prophets. Veblen is no exception. But although his speculations may be easily criticized or dismissed, his economics commands serious attention. Deficiencies aside, Veblen tried to construct a theory of human behavior outside the utilitarian mold. However questionable his success may be, he probed issues that refuse to go away, especially those that pertain to economic development and to the nature and consequences of property rights.

While the Veblenian paradigm has never substituted for the usefulness of neoclassical economic analysis (as perhaps Veblen thought it should), it is not necessary to choose one or the other. His long-run institutional studies may be used to supplement short-run price theoretical analysis. Surely there is room for discussion within the economics profession along the lines of Veblen's "grand vision." If for no other reason, Veblen may be read for the gainful reminder that economics is a *social* science, not a mere branch of mathematical inquiry. (On the possible intersections between institutional economics and neoclassical economics, see the box, The Force of Ideas: Evolutionary Economics, Then and Now.)

The Force of Ideas: Evolutionary Economics, Then and Now

Economics has always been used to analyze and explain past institutions and, hopefully, to predict the directions of quantities that matter to humans (e.g., wages, prices, GDP, employment, and so on). That quest is the object of all economists, Veblenian and neoclassical, those who use statics or dynamics. Economists, in other words, have always been interested in how institutions and economies modify and change. That was, as noted in this chapter, certainly Veblen's objective, and it is a fair question to ask how far his views have come in achieving this end.

The key to understanding economic growth involves understanding the "motor" that propels institutional change. The essential propellants for Veblen were "habits" or "instincts." He believed that each society and each stage of society can be identified by its own set of habits and institutions—the latter evolving to meet "instinctual" human ends. However, although he recognized a specific sociological-anthropological variant of "economizing," Veblen did not identify how a cost-benefit mechanism applied to utility-maximizing behavior could explain change.*

Neoinstitutional economics is the result of applying modern microeconomic analysis to institutions and institutional change.† It makes the good old-fashioned neoclassical theory of economizing through behavioral calculation of costs and benefits the motor of institutional

(continued)

change. It stems from the proposition that rational choice (under particular constraints) creates and alters institutions such as property rights structures, law, contracts, government structures, and regulation. These institutions and the organizations they help create provide incentives or establish costs and benefits that, for a time, govern economic activity and economic growth. But through time institutions are themselves altered by economic activity due to either "feedback" mechanisms or because particular institutions create economic incentives for change. Within such a model, any change in an "exogenous" variable (i.e., external shock) could alter the configuration of property rights or costs and benefits, creating institutional change. Laws surrounding marriage, administrative regulation, or the form of religious or fiscal institutions may (and have been) analyzed using neoinstitutional economics.

Thus, neoinstitutional economics has strayed from the original intent of Veblen, whose antagonism toward businesspeople led him to disdain market economics. Even so, Veblen's emphasis on institutional change had a poignant effect. Neoinstitutionalists have profitably employed cost-benefit analysis in producing an evolutionary approach to society and culture. This has served to disrupt the almost exclusive emphasis by neoclassical economists on a static and (sometimes) institutionless world. There is more than a touch of irony in the fact that a blend of neoclassical and institutional traditions is producing an entirely new and enriched area of contemporary economics.

*See R. W. Ault and R. B. Ekelund, "Habits in Economic Analysis," pp. 431–445. The fact that Veblen argued that pecuniary behavior was responsible for creating institutions such as the corporation, the stock market, and corporate finance generally does not mean that he produced an economizing theory of endogenous habit formation (see the Raines and Leathers paper in "Notes for Further Reading," this chapter).

†Neoinstitutional economics has been advanced most vigorously by 1993 Nobel Prize winner Douglass North.

■ Second-Generation Veblenians

Veblen's ideas, unlike those of Adam Smith or Alfred Marshall, were not so easily cultivated by his successors. Although it may be said that Veblen had a theory of economic and social development, there was far less specificity and cohesiveness about his work than that exhibited in the neoclassical paradigms of Alfred Marshall or Léon Walras. Moreover, whereas Marx was orderly in arranging his (often obscure) ideas, Veblen was not. A research program for future scholars is difficult to flesh out of his turgid, rambling prose.[10] In addition, as noted at the beginning of this chapter, Veblen wore different hats, sometimes that of the economic scientist, sometimes that of the iconoclastic polemicist and social critic. Some of the theoretically inclined followers of Veblen have imitated him by studying the role of specific institutions and processes, while others have pursued more practical studies. In order to impart the eclectic flavor of Veblen's legacy, in this section we briefly review the ideas of three Veblenians (a much looser term than "Marshallians")—J. R. Commons, W. C. Mitchell, and C. E. Ayres—prior to a more detailed discussion of a third-generation Veblenian, John Kenneth Galbraith, in a separate section. Although each is recognized as an American institutionalist, one could hardly imagine a more disparate group of individuals.

[10] That sardonic wit and acerbic pundit H. L. Mencken was so exasperated by Veblen's writings that he remarked in response to one of Veblen's essays: "What is the sweating professor trying to say?"

John Rogers Commons (1862–1945)

Commons was born in Ohio, did graduate work at Johns Hopkins University, and was probably the foremost scholar at the University of Wisconsin for almost three decades (1904–1932). He was less of a theoretician than an adamant champion of social and economic reform, pursued through legislation. Along with Wisconsin's liberal governor Robert M. LaFollette, Commons wrote and sponsored labor, antitrust, and public-utility regulations for the state. Wisconsin's enactments of his legislative proposals established a model from which federal regulations of similar activities were later drawn. Commons's numerous publications are a potpourri of criticism; demand for social reform; historical-empirical information; and classical, socialist, and marginalist ideas. He was not a pure institutionalist of the Veblenian stripe, choosing instead to focus on the operation of man-made institutions (such as regulatory or antitrust agencies) and how they are affected by private property, legislation, and court decisions.

In the *Legal Foundations of Capitalism* (1924) Commons emphasized law and the courts as constraining elements in the economic system, an idea that is very much alive today in the economics of government regulation (see notes for further reading at the end of the chapter). But in his multivolume (and practically incomprehensible) *Institutional Economics* (1934) Commons took the definition of institutionalism beyond Veblen's original vision. To Commons, markets and their effects could be judged good or bad through (admittedly normative) criteria of efficiency and justice. A just and efficient system therefore could be devised and implemented through optimal legislative regulations and judicial action. He clearly did not share Veblen's skepticism about government's ability to raise the general welfare through institutional change. Although Commons was unable to effect any fundamental reorientation of economics, he did have a profound impact on a number of his students at Wisconsin.

Wesley Clair Mitchell (1874–1948)

Wesley Clair Mitchell was a student of Veblen, professor at the University of Chicago from 1922 to 1940, and one of the two or three most famous American economists of his generation. Mitchell gave economics in general, and institutional economics in particular, a statistical foundation. He established the National Bureau of Economic Research in 1920, an institution thriving to this day. It is difficult to overestimate the importance of Mitchell's pioneering attempts to quantify simple economic concepts such as "money," "prices," and "income," but it is fair to say that Jevons's earlier pathbreaking analyses of index-number construction and statistical studies of price series (see chapter 15) came to life under Mitchell's able supervision. In his monumental book, *Business Cycles* (1913), Mitchell analyzed booms and depressions from the nineteenth century through the monetary panic of 1907, utilizing masterfully reconstructed data on bond prices and yields, wages, commodity prices, the money stock (a central variable in Mitchell's interpretation), and monetary velocity. His approach to economic analysis—theory interrelated with empirical explanation—had a profound impact on the direction taken by economic studies in twentieth-century America. Due in large measure to his efforts, studies in GNP accounting, business-cycle analysis, growth, antitrust, and industrial organization can now be accompanied by empirical referents. In sum, Mitchell established a program for the collection and use of empirical data that, together with subsequent mathematical and statistical analysis, has given much of modern economics its particular character.

But how did Mitchell's great contribution relate to his mentor's institutionalism, especially since Veblen vigorously denounced as unproductive mathematical and statistical complements to economic theory? Whereas Veblen sought to establish the cultural and psychological bases for certain types of institutions and for institutional change, Mitchell aimed to objectify pecuniary institutions and business fluctuations. As such, Mitchell's work was an extension of Veblen's, but one that Veblen himself did not pursue or find extremely useful. As in the case of Commons, Mitchell's "institutional economics" took a direction that was somewhat askant from Veblen's original conception.

Clarence Edwin Ayres (1892–1972)

Of all the American institutionalists Clarence Edwin Ayres remained closest to Veblen's original theoretical conceptions. Educated at Brown University and at the University of Chicago, Ayres spent practically his entire academic career (1930–1968) at the University of Texas. Indeed, owing to the influence of Ayres, the University of Texas became the locus of the institutionalist school in America over these years. In a number of important publications, including *The Theory of Economic Progress* (1944) and *Toward a Reasonable Society: The Value of Industrial Civilization* (1961), Ayres reworked the theoretical concerns of Thorstein Veblen. Like Veblen, Ayres was steeped in philosophy, being particularly oriented to John Dewey's pragmatist-instrumentalist approach. In terms of economic policy, Ayres advocated pragmatic, liberal modifications of capitalism, akin to those championed by Commons. But he rejected socialism and fascism. An underconsumptionist like Veblen and J. M. Keynes, Ayres supported modified economic planning and economic regulation as a palliative for what he judged the excesses of capitalism.

In terms of theory, however, Ayres was a technological determinist. He believed that technology is an absolute value toward which society should be gravitating. He spoke of a life process to which institutions either did or did not contribute. The goal of Ayres's system was "full production," which included maximization of human creativity, artistic pursuits, and so forth, in addition to material well-being. Ayres contrasted institutional values with technological values, indicating that "true" and "false" institutional values could be judged on the basis of their "contribution to the life process."[11] In his view technology was an ultimate value since it alone was independent of cultural considerations. In effect, Ayres made institutional economics a study of technology and of technological change. Unlike Veblen, he did not totally repudiate the value of markets and the price system, but he did argue that prices and markets were less important than technology and institutions in determining the direction of "full production." Like Veblen, however, Ayres was unable to provide a consistent and cohesive framework within which to analyze the momentum and life history of economic societies. In spite of Ayres's very creative work, there are numerous gaps and contradictions in the institutionalist theoretical paradigm that remain to be filled and resolved by others.

■ John Kenneth Galbraith: The Institutionalists' Popularizer

Even a cursory review demonstrates that institutional economics took several divergent paths after Veblen. Mitchell added an inductive-statistical component; Com-

[11] During the 1960s the authors of this book attended a lecture by Ayres in which he attacked Coca-Cola as a "false" value, i.e., one detracting from the "life process."

mons translated institutional economics into a program for social (chiefly legislative) reform; and Ayres extended Veblen's conception into a theory of technological values. The concerns of modern institutionalists reflect all these diverse interests and many others. But, perhaps more than any other writer of institutionalist leanings, John Kenneth Galbraith cornered the interest of social scientists and the reading public.

Galbraith (1908–2006) is one of the best-known social critics of twentieth-century America. His long and active life took him down many avenues: Harvard faculty member, economic adviser to the president, novelist, and U.S. ambassador to India, among others. He has also written numerous influential and heretical books on the social and economic system. In part, Galbraith's work is a modern repository of heterodox thought. His thought reveals many traces from varied sources, but his ideas invariably align with those of Veblen. We choose here to focus on two ideas that are distinctly Galbraithian: (1) the process of *countervailing power* and (2) the identification of a *social imbalance* within the context of an affluent society.

As early as 1952, in his book *American Capitalism*, Galbraith was concerned with the traditional (i.e., orthodox *Marshallian*) explanation of "how things work" in the American economic system. He was already arguing that affluence (which he called "unseemly opulence") was a mixed blessing. Most particularly, he charged that orthodox economic theory was unrealistic, since any acquaintance at all with the facts of the real world would negate the relevance of the competitive model—the stock-in-trade of Marshallian economics. Galbraith was not afraid to issue certain value judgments that, when placed in a dynamic theory of social behavior, provided a springboard for his criticism of static, orthodox political economy. Thus, he argued that income inequality "distorts the use of resources," since "it diverts them from the wants of the many to the esoteric desires of the few—if not from bread to cake at least from Chevrolets to Cadillacs" (*American Capitalism*, pp. 104–105). He maintained as well that unnecessary inequality of income—unnecessary in the sense that it does not reward differences in intelligence, application, or willingness to take risks—may also impair economic stability.

Countervailing Power

Galbraith baldly declared that the competitive model of neoclassical economics was academic hokum. Modern markets do not operate smoothly and continuously to establish and maintain competitive equilibria. Competition had broken down, he said, creating concentration and monopoly power and destroying the self-regulating tendencies of many markets. Yet, this one-sided development did not dissolve all restraints. What the economic orthodoxy overlooked, according to Galbraith, was the existence of countervailing power and its effect on market outcomes.[12] In other words, new restraints on private power arise in monopolistic markets to replace competition, constraints that

> were nurtured by the same process of concentration which impaired or destroyed competition. But they appeared not on the same side of the market but on the opposite side, not with competitors but with customers and suppliers. It will be convenient to have a name for this counterpart of competition and I shall call it countervailing power. (*American Capitalism*, p. 111)

At first blush, "countervailing power" appears to be a manifestation of the standard, neoclassical theory of bilateral monopoly. But Galbraith rejects this idea; he

[12] This concept can be traced back to Wieser's *Social Economics* (see chapter 14).

argues that the presence of bilateral monopoly is a mere "adventitious occurrence," whereas countervailing power is a process that develops in response to private economic power that emerges from the original breakdown of competition. In other words, Galbraith envisions countervailing power as a process in the *Veblenian* sense. Moreover, Galbraith advanced the concept as an important explanation for many developments, including trade unionism, retail cooperatives, chain stores, and the like. His concepts of market and product go beyond the narrow confines of traditional theory, approaching E. H. Chamberlin's treatment of differentiated products in monopolistic competition (see chapter 20).

Galbraith maintained that the existence or nonexistence of countervailing power has great relevance for public policy. Specifically, the failure of countervailing power to restrain monopoly forces is *a raison d'être* for government intervention in a private economy. As he wrote in 1952:

> Without the phenomenon itself being fully recognized, the provision of state assistance to the development of countervailing power has become a major function of government—perhaps the major domestic function of government. Much of the domestic legislation of the last twenty years, that of the New Deal episode in particular, only becomes fully comprehensible when it is viewed in this light. (*American Capitalism*, p. 128)

To further punctuate his argument, Galbraith wrote:

> The groups that sought the assistance of government in building countervailing power sought that power in order to use it against market authority to which they had previously been subordinate. (*American Capitalism*, p. 136)

Galbraith also argued that antitrust policy should be modified to permit the implementation of those policies that encourage the development of countervailing power so as to check monopoly power wherever possible. Moreover, he asserted that where government intervention has occurred, it has been the result not of competition but of a breakdown in countervailing power.

There are, however, gaps of a serious nature in Galbraith's theory of countervailing power. If it is to be used as a tool of public policy, one must be able to determine *original* as opposed to *generated* countervailing power. In *American Capitalism*, Galbraith identified two categories of monopoly: (1) original monopoly that emerges as a result of the breakdown of competition and (2) countervailing monopoly that develops in response to existing market power. He might well have added a third category (which, in fact Veblen anticipated), namely that which arises because of industry demands for regulation—in the form of assistance, subsidies, and contracts, not to mention control over entry.

In a more fundamental sense, Galbraith's theory lacks a cogent explanation of how power emerges in the first place and how it affects market processes and the political system, all of which are interesting and legitimate concerns of the economist as social scientist. One wonders how countervailing power is supposed to affect prices and the distribution of income, a subject that should be of high interest in Galbraith's socialist state. When does the government step in to socialize or control areas of the economy (e.g., low-cost housing)? How long do we wait for market processes to develop in "defenseless" areas of the economy before the government steps in? Unfortunately, Galbraith's theory does not give us the answers to these queries. Nevertheless, his discussion may provide a starting point for an eventual neoinstitutionalist synthesis.

Social Imbalance

In *The Affluent Society* (1958), a book that has sold more copies than Adam Smith's *The Wealth of Nations*, Galbraith seemed to object to American society because it is rich and because its values are misdirected. This time Galbraith took on the orthodoxy through the theory of consumer demand. He maintained that (1) to its detriment the received theory has disallowed "any notion of necessary versus unnecessary or important as against unimportant goods" (*Affluent Society*, p. 147); and (2) having neglected certain implications of diminishing marginal utility, economists have been unable to see that more of certain goods—through time—is not better than less. This is, of course, normative stuff. In his critique of positive economics, Galbraith wrote:

> Any notion of necessary versus unnecessary or important as against unimportant goods was rigorously excluded from the subject. . . . Nothing in economics so quickly marks an individual as incompetently trained as a disposition to remark on the legitimacy of the desire for more food and the frivolity of the desire for a more elaborate automobile. (*Affluent Society*, p. 147)

With scholarly impertinence, Galbraith asserted that consumer sovereignty is a myth and that in modern times the chain of cause and effect runs from production to consumption, not the other way around. In order to maintain an affluent society, one in which production and income are growing, new wants must be manufactured. Thus, Galbraith focused on the crucial role of advertising in creating and manipulating wants for new consumer goods, which are provided at the expense of social goods. He denounced the social imbalance that results.

In the tradition of another American maverick, Henry George, Galbraith maintained that economic problems lead to social ills. "The more goods people procure, the more packages they discard and the more trash that must be carried away. If the appropriate sanitation services are not provided, the counterpart of increasing opulence will be deepening filth. The greater the wealth, the thicker will be the dirt" (*Affluent Society*, p. 256). Here's another example of Galbraith at full throttle. Commenting on the rebellion of youth, he said: "Schools do not compete with television and the movies. The dubious heroes of the latter, not Miss Jones, become the idols of the young" (*Affluent Society*, p. 257).

Galbraith details a whole litany of social ills that result from a breakdown of the economic forces of competition and a value system that encourages wasteful private consumption at the expense of public goods. At the heart of this "inappropriate" value system is the fact that advertising and emulation work primarily on the creation of private wants. In fact, a large part of Galbraith's theory rests on Veblen's concept of conspicuous consumption, as described earlier in this chapter. In order to redress social imbalance, Galbraith proposes increased government taxation at all levels and redirection of government expenditures (away from national defense, to be sure). In *The New Industrial State* he asserted: "In the absence of social intervention, private production will monopolize all resources" (p. 310). Hence he argued vigorously that government must take a more active role to assure that social balance is engendered and preserved in the process.

Some Comments on Galbraith's System

Though a Canadian by birth, John Kenneth Galbraith is a lineal intellectual descendant of former American heterodox thinkers, especially Henry George and

Thorstein Veblen. There is a commonality among these writers insofar as they make group behavior the focal point of analysis. Moreover, like Veblen, Galbraith takes an institutional approach in his attempt to provide a theory of the unfolding process of modern capitalism. But Galbraith's ideas—like those of his distinguished predecessors—lack specificity. There are many gaps, moreover, in his theory of the evolutionary process of capitalism. A case in point relates to the government's redress of social imbalance. Galbraith argues that "affirmative action" on the part of the government is required, but he does not spell out how social needs and their magnitudes are to be assessed. One wonders whether it is to be on the basis of conjecture, special pleading, or value judgments. Principles of modern public finance (which developed within the orthodoxy) such as benefit-cost analysis are admittedly imperfect, but they appear to be incomparably more useful as a guide to policy than those suggested by Galbraith and his camp.

Galbraith's disregard of the individual, and especially of the individual's intellectual independence and preferences, predisposed him to conclude that individuals cannot discern what is in their own best interests. He is unimpressed by the usefulness of the price system in allowing individuals to register their choices between economic and social alternatives (for example, to choose less costly gasoline and more pollution rather than more costly gasoline and less pollution). His frustration with the distribution of income and the level of social-goods provision determined by free will and market led him to champion the extension of government as a palliative. There is no question that social goods must be provided. Modern economists who defend the neoclassical theory of markets are at least as interested as Galbraith in the problem of the provision of public goods. The debatable issue, of course, is the method of provision and the theory and philosophy behind it.

■ Conclusion

The fate of a *pure* institutionalist paradigm remains uncertain. No one, not even a self-proclaimed institutionalist, pretends to have established a single, cohesive, and consistent body of thought. Should we identify the "system" of Veblen, or some combination of the writings of Veblen, Commons, Mitchell, Ayres, and Galbraith, as the foundation for a school of neoinstitutionalism? "Institutional economics" appears to be an open-ended inquiry.

There is a strong and growing recognition within the traditional body of contemporary American economics that institutions, and specifically property-rights institutions, must be integrated into economics in a meaningful way. In other words, a property-rights literature is developing that highlights the interactions of legal institutions, economic behavior, and economic outcomes. Major beneficiaries of this broader approach have been theories of economic growth and development, law and economics, comparative economic organization, and economic regulation. At a time when a large segment of American economists have retreated from policy matters and forced economic theory into tighter mathematical straitjackets, others have been expanding economic theory and policy in very interesting and fruitful ways (see, for example, chapter 26). Institutional economics may yet have much to contribute to this expansive development.

In short, we might regard institutional economics as an umbrella under which many significant and productive ideas may be sheltered. As a separate inquiry, the "school" has largely consisted of an organon for strident criticism of neoclassical economics. Progress may well require compromise with more traditional strains of

American economic thought. Compromise and eclecticism are, after all, distinctly American characteristics.

References

Ault, R. W., and R. B. Ekelund, Jr. "Habits in Economic Analysis: Veblen and the Neoclassicals," *History of Political Economy*, vol. 20 (Fall 1988), pp. 431–445.

Arrow, Kenneth. "Thorstein Veblen as an Economic Theorist," *American Economist*, vol. 19 (Spring 1975), pp. 5–9.

Buchan, A. *The Spare Chancellor: The Life of Walter Bagehot*. London: Chatto & Windus, 1959.

Cairnes, J. E. "M. Comte and Political Economy," *Fortnightly Review*, vol. 7 (1870), pp. 579–602.

———. "Political Economy and Laissez-Faire," *Fortnightly Review*, vol. 10 (1871), pp. 80–97.

Ely, Richard T. *Introduction to Political Economy*. New York: Hunt and Eaton, 1891.

Galbraith, J. K. *American Capitalism: The Concept of Countervailing Power*. Boston: Houghton Mifflin, 1952.

———. *The Affluent Society*. Boston: Houghton Mifflin, 1958.

———. *The New Industrial State*. Boston: Houghton Mifflin, 1967.

Ingram, John K. *History of Political Economy*. London: A. & C. Black, 1915 [1888].

———. "The Present Position and Prospects of Political Economy," in R. L. Smyth (ed.), *Essays in Economic Method*. New York: McGraw-Hill, 1963 [1898].

Jevons, W. S. *The Theory of Political Economy*, 5th ed. New York: A. M. Kelley, 1965 [1879].

Jones, Richard. *Essay on the Distribution of Wealth and on the Sources of Taxation*. London: John Murray, 1831.

Keynes, J. N. *The Scope and Method of Political Economy*. New York: A. M. Kelley, 1963 [1890].

Leibenstein, Harvey. "Bandwagon, Snob, and Veblen Effects in the Theory of Consumers' Demand," *The Quarterly Journal of Economics*, vol. 62 (May 1950), pp. 183–207.

Marshall, Alfred. *Principles of Economics*, 4th ed. London: Macmillan, 1899.

Mitchell, W. C. (ed.). *What Veblen Taught: Selected Writings of Thorstein Veblen*. New York: A. M. Kelley, 1964.

Roll, Eric. *A History of Economic Thought*, 4th ed. Homewood, IL: Richard D. Irwin, 1974.

Smyth, R. L. (ed.). *Essays in Economic Method*. New York: McGraw-Hill, 1963.

Spencer, Herbert. *Autobiography*, 2 vols. New York: Appleton, 1904.

Toynbee, Arnold. *Lectures on the Industrial Revolution of the Eighteenth Century in England*. London: Longmans, Green, 1890.

Veblen, Thorstein. "Why Economics Is Not an Evolutionary Science," *Quarterly Journal of Economics*, vol. 12 (July 1898), pp. 373–426; vol. 14 (February 1900), pp. 240–269.

———. "The Preconceptions of Economic Science," *Quarterly Journal of Economics*, vol. 13 (January 1899), pp. 121–150, (July 1899), pp. 396–426; vol. 14 (February 1900), pp. 240–269.

———. *The Theory of the Leisure Class*. New York: Modern Library, 1934 [1899].

———. *The Vested Interests and the Common Man*. New York: Capricorn Books, 1969 [1919].

———. *The Engineers and the Price System*. New York: Viking, 1921.

Notes for Further Reading

Two excellent summaries of the historical movement are T. W. Hutchison, *A Review of Economic Doctrines, 1870–1929*, chaps. 8, 12 (Oxford: Clarendon Press, 1953); and Ben B. Seligman, *Main Currents in Modern Economics*, chap. 1 (New York: Free Press, 1962).

Social Darwinism was an important influence on the philosophical and social thought of the time. In this regard, see William Graham Sumner, *Social Darwinism: Selected Essays* (Englewood Cliffs, NJ: Prentice-Hall, 1963); and the brilliant overview by Richard Hofstadter, *Social Darwinism in American Thought*, rev. ed. (Boston: Beacon Press, 1955).

On British historicism and its development, see R. B. Ekelund, Jr., "A British Rejection of Economic Orthodoxy," *Southwestern Social Science Quarterly*, vol. 47 (September 1966), pp. 172–180; and A. W. Coats, "The Historicist Reaction in English Political Economy, 1870–1890," *Economica*, vol. 21 (May 1954), pp. 143–153. John Neville Keynes's *Scope and Method of Political Economy* (see references) is still one of the most penetrating contributions to economic methodology in the literature. With incredible skill and thoroughness Keynes sorted out the issues and the supposed conflicts between the orthodox methods of Mill and Cairnes and those defended by the German and British historicists. In the process, the elder Keynes produced a work of lasting significance.

An interesting and growing literature exists on specific members of the British historical school demonstrating their eclecticism vis-à-vis orthodox political economy and their great diversity of interests. Cliffe-Leslie's interest in Irish and English social reform and his role in the origins of the historical movement are the subject of G. M. Koot's "T. E. Cliffe-Leslie, Irish Social Reform and the Origins of the English School of Economics," *History of Political Economy*, vol. 7 (Fall 1975), pp. 312–316. See also, R. D. C. Black, "The Political Economy of T. E. Cliffe-Leslie (1826–82): A Reassessment," *The European Journal of the History of Economic Thought*, vol. 9 (Spring 2002), pp. 17–41. Ingram's affinity to Comte is explored by Gregory C. Moore, "John Kells Ingram, the Comtean Movement, and the English Methodenstreit," *History of Political Economy*, vol. 31 (Spring 1999), pp. 53–78. A leading doctrinal opponent of orthodox laissez-faire principles regarding labor and union policy in the mid-Victorian period is considered in P. Adelman, "Frederic Harrison and the Positivist Attack on Orthodox Political Economy," *American Journal of Economics & Sociology*, vol. 31 (July 1972), pp. 307–317. The most extensive study of the methodological and philosophical underpinnings of the British historical movement is contained in Craig Bolton, *The British Historical School in Political Economy: Its Meaning and Significance* (unpublished PhD dissertation, Texas A & M University, 1976). The Reverend Richard Jones's actual use of induction is the subject of W. L. Miller's "Richard Jones: A Case Study in Methodology," *History of Political Economy*, vol. 3 (Spring 1971), pp. 198–207. Miller's careful studies of the evolutionist and economist-social scientist Herbert Spencer may be consulted with profit. See, for example, his treatment of Spencer's conception of public policy in the "static" state of society: "Herbert Spencer's Theory of Welfare and Public Policy," *History of Political Economy*, vol. 4 (Spring 1972), pp. 207–231.

The joy and pleasure of reading Veblen in the original should not be missed by any student of economic and social thought. In addition to the works listed in the references of this chapter, all of Veblen's major works have been reprinted by A. M. Kelley and are generally accessible. The secondary literature on Veblen is vast and kaleidoscopic. For someone unfamiliar with Veblen a good place to start is Stephen Edgell, *Veblen in Perspective: His Life and Thought* (Armonk, NY: M. E. Sharpe, 2001). Arguably, the best biographical study of Veblen and his times remains Joseph Dorfman's *Thorstein Veblen and His America* (New York: A. M. Kelley, 1961 [1934]). John Patrick Diggins, *Thorstein Veblen: Theorist of the Leisure Class* (Princeton University Press, 1999), originally published as *The Bard of Savagery*, is a critical biography that attempts to unravel the riddles that surround Veblen's reputation and to assess his varied and important contributions to modern social theory. See also the brief but incisive paper by Kenneth J. Arrow, "Thorstein Veblen as an Economic Theorist" (see references). Excellent overviews of Veblen's economic system and his economic critique of capitalism are contained in two essays:

Thomas Sowell, "The Evolutionary Economics of Thorstein Veblen," *Oxford Economic Papers*, n.s., vol. 1 (July 1967), pp. 177–198; and, especially, Donald A. Walker, "Thorstein Veblen's Economic System," *Economic Inquiry*, vol. 15 (April 1977), pp. 213–237. Phillip A. O'Hara, "Veblen's Critique of Marx's Philosophical Preconceptions of Political Economy," *The European Journal of the History of Economic Thought*, vol. 4 (Spring 1997), pp. 65–91, judges the correctness of Veblen's criticisms of Marx and Marxism. On the connections between American and British institutionalists, see Malcolm Rutherford, "American Institutionalism and its British Connections," *The European Journal of the History of Economic Thought*, vol. 14 (2007), pp. 291–323. Rutherford argues that the connections between the two camps are far more extensive than is commonly thought, and he ponders why the British institutionalists never formed a unified school of thought.

Veblen's concept of conspicuous consumption is echoed in some twentieth-century economic analysis, as Leibenstein's microeconomic formulation suggests. In a macroeconomic context, see James S. Duesenberry's *Income, Saving and the Theory of Consumer Behavior* (Cambridge, MA: Harvard University Press, 1949). A modern reaffirmation of the "given tastes" assumption of neoclassical microanalysis—one that Veblen challenged—is found in G. J. Stigler and G. S. Becker, "De Gustibus Non Est Disputandum," *American Economic Review*, vol. 67 (March 1977), pp. 76–90.

That there is a genetic component or predisposition in habit formation is indisputable, and Veblen may have very well appreciated the fact. Beyond a possible awareness of the role of evolution and genetics, however, Veblen focused on the inexact forces of "expedience, adaptation and concessive adjustments" in his explanation of the role of habits in economic change. Richard W. Ault and Robert B. Ekelund, Jr., (see references) argue that a blending of Veblen's anthropological view of habits with a neoclassical cost-choice framework, wherein habits are considered endogenous to the choice process, yields a more cogent and satisfactory analysis of economic and institutional change than either produces individually. Ault and Ekelund also believe that Veblen's analysis suffered from his refusal to view economizing and habit formation in the manner of neoclassical economics (i.e., as largely endogenous to economic processes). On the mischief caused by making institutional change an endogenous factor, see Olivier Brette, "Thorstein Veblen's Theory of Institutional Change: Beyond Technological Determinism," The *European Journal of the History of Economic Thought*, vol. 10 (Autumn 2003), pp. 455–477.

The combination of Veblen's views on habits and habit formation and neoclassical cost-choice theory yields something very much like the new institutionalist analysis of economic history and change; see D. C. North and R. P. Thomas, *The Rise of the Western World* (London: Cambridge University Press, 1973). This view has been rejected by Malcolm Rutherford in *Institutions in Economics: The Old and the New Institutionalism* (Cambridge: Cambridge University Press, 1994), although he compares W. C. Mitchell's work favorably with North and Thomas in a later paper; see Rutherford, "An Introduction to 'Money Economy and Modern Civilization,'" *History of Political Economy*, vol. 28 (Fall 1996), pp. 317–328, where he argues that Veblen was only "inexact," that his "theory" of habit formation was in fact endogenous, and that his ideas were "formative" in producing a theory of institutional change. But it is Veblen's "theory" that is constantly outdistanced by the neoclassical theory and evidence of economizing behavior. Further, as noted in this chapter, pecuniary values were not associated with material progress. For example, J. P. Raines and C. G. Leathers, "Evolving Financial Institutions in Veblen's Business Enterprise System," *Journal of the History of Economic Thought*, vol. 15 (1993), pp. 249–264, showed that Veblen argued "pecuniary behavior" was primarily responsible for creating institutions such as the corporation, common and preferred stock, and corporate finance generally. This is not, however, as Raines and Leathers themselves pointed out, a general theory of endogenous habit formation, and Veblen did not or was incapable of describing a utility-maximizing view of institutional change outside of an ill-understood "pecuniary context."

Veblen's prediction of a technical revolution led by engineers is a matter of some controversy. Malcolm Rutherford, "Thorstein Veblen and the Problem of the Engineers," *International Review of Sociology*, vol. 3 (1992), pp. 125–150, and Donald Stabile, "Veblen and the Political Economy of the Engineer: The Radical Leader and Engineering Leaders Came to Technocracy at the Same Time," *American Journal of Economics & Sociology*, vol. 45 (January 1986), pp. 41–52, agree on Veblen's long-standing interest in the opportunities faced by engineers in a technical society, whereas Rick Tilman, "Veblen's Ideal Political Economy and Its Critics," *American Journal of Economics & Sociology*, vol. 31 (July 1972), pp. 307–317, and same author, "Incrementalist and Utopian," *American Journal of Economics & Sociology*, vol. 32 (December 1973), pp. 155–169, suggest Veblen's interest was an aberration from his early work. Janet Knoedler and Anne Mayhew, "Thorstein Veblen and the Engineers: A Reinterpretation," *History of Political Economy*, vol. 31 (Summer 1999), pp. 255–272, attempt to set the record straight on where Veblen actually stood on this matter.

J. E. Biddle, "Twain, Veblen and the Connecticut Yankee," *History of Political Economy*, vol. 17 (Spring 1985), pp. 97–108, draws a tenuous link between Mark Twain and Thorstein Veblen, particularly the shared view that human actions are motivated more by custom and habit than by reason. On the other hand, divergence between Veblen and Commons on how to treat a specific form of business property is the subject of A. M. Endres, "Veblen and Commons on Goodwill: A Case of Theoretical Divergence," *History of Political Economy*, vol. 17 (Winter 1985), pp. 637–650.

Veblen's judgment that classical-neoclassical economics was pre-Darwinian and that his analysis provided a new evolutionary theory is disputed in a paper by L. B. Jones, "The Institutionalists and *On the Origin of Species*: A Case of Mistaken Identity," *Southern Economic Journal*, vol. 52 (April 1986), pp. 1043–1055. On the basis of information recently come to light in Darwin's early diaries, Jones argues that it was Adam Smith's theories of competition and the division of labor that led Darwin to develop the theories of speciation and natural selection. The prior conventional wisdom held that Malthus was the source of Darwin's evolutionary concepts. Stephen Edgell and Rick Tilman, "The Intellectual Antecedents of Thorstein Veblen: A Reappraisal," *Journal of Economic Issues*, vol. 23 (December 1989), pp. 1003–1026, maintain that Darwin was the major influence on Veblen; see also same authors, "John Rae and Thorstein Veblen on Conspicuous Consumption: A Neglected Intellectual Relationship." *History of Political Economy*, vol. 23 (1991), pp. 167–180. G. M. Hodgson, "Thorstein Veblen and Post-Darwinian Economics," *Cambridge Journal of Economics*, vol. 16 (September 1992), pp. 285–301, tries to explain what Veblen meant when he referred to economics as an "evolutionary science." William Waller and Ann Jennings, "The Place of Biological Science in Veblen's Economics," *History of Political Economy*, vol. 30 (Summer 1998), pp. 189–217, establish the specific and restricted role of biology in Veblen's social theories, despite his frequent use of biological terminology. Alain Marciano, "Economists on Darwin's Theory of Social Evolution and Human Behaviour," *The European Journal of the History of Economic Thought*, vol. 14 (2007), pp. 681–700, provides an overview of how economists have looked at Darwin (that is, how they mention or quote him). Only recently, he argues, has economics begun to incorporate both the social and biological aspects of Darwin's thinking on evolution.

Veblen applied the concept of technological displacement and the reduction of capital values to business cycles, and Commons used the idea in a regulatory framework that has been buttressed with a modern (neoinstitutionalist) defense of the regulatory process by Victor Goldberg; see his "Regulation and Administered Contracts," *Bell Journal of Economics*, vol. 7 (Autumn 1976), pp. 425–448. The writings on capitalist dynamics of another great "evolutionist," Joseph A. Schumpeter, are contrasted with Veblen's in L. A. O'Donnell's "Rationalism, Capitalism and the Entrepreneur: The Views of Veblen and

Schumpeter," *History of Political Economy*, vol. 5 (Spring 1973), pp. 199–214. An interesting paper contrasts the contemporary "radical critique of economics" (mainly of 1960s' origin with Marxian overtones) with the theoretical structure of Veblenian economics, showing why Veblen has had so little influence on the radicals; see J. E. Pluta and C. G. Leathers, "Veblen and Modern Radical Economics," *Journal of Economic Issues*, vol. 12 (March 1978), pp. 125–146. Leathers has also compared Veblen and Hayek, concluding that Veblen's theory of cultural evolution was one of institutional drift, whereas Hayek's theory was one of efficient selection of institutions; see C. G. Leathers, "Veblen and Hayek on Instincts and Evolution," *Journal of the History of Economic Thought*, vol. 12 (Fall 1990), pp. 162–178. On the continuing relevance of Veblen beyond his time, see Doug Brown (ed.), *Thorstein Veblen in the Twenty-First Century: A Commemoration of the Leisure Class* (Cheltenham, UK: Edward Elgar, 1998), a collection of twelve articles on various aspects of Veblen's work.

On Commons, see Jeff Biddle, "Purpose and Evolution in Commons's Institutionalism," *History of Political Economy*, vol. 22 (Spring 1990), pp. 19–47. The renaissance of interest in Commons-type legal analysis is discussed in Victor Goldberg's "Commons, Clark, and the Emerging Post-Coasian Law and Economics," *The Journal of Economic Issues*, vol. 11 (December 1976), pp. 877–893. A real insight into the theoretical structure of Commons (and into his substantial ego) may be sifted from his autobiography, *Myself*.

Mitchell was the "economist's economist" of his generation. Jeff Biddle, "A Citation Analysis of the Sources of Wesley Mitchell's Reputation," *History of Political Economy*, vol. 28 (Summer 1996), pp. 137–169, found that from about 1915 to 1930 Mitchell was among the economists most frequently cited in the journal literature. That he was a superb historian of thought is reflected in his lecture notes, edited by Joseph Dorfman in the two-volume *Types of Economic Theory* (New York: A. M. Kelley, 1967). Kelley has also reprinted a number of Mitchell's works, including *The Backward Art of Spending Money and Other Essays* [1937], which is a very fine Mitchell "sampler." One of Mitchell's specialties was monetary economics, and an essay by Abraham Hirsch brings out the interrelations of Mitchell's unique views of theory, policy, and economic verification in this area; see "Mitchell's Work on the Causes of the Civil War Inflations in His Development as an Economist," *History of Political Economy*, vol. 2 (Spring 1970), pp. 118–132. Hirsch also examines Mitchell's ambivalence toward methodology and his use of mainstream economic theory in "The A Posteriori Method and the Creation of New Theory: W. C. Mitchell as a Case Study," *History of Political Economy*, vol. 8 (Summer 1976), pp. 152–206. Perhaps the best assessment of Mitchell as an economist and quantity theorist is the tribute of his admirer Milton Friedman; see "Wesley C. Mitchell as an Economic Theorist," *The Journal of Political Economy*, vol. 58 (December 1950), pp. 465–493. Also see Eli Ginzberg, "Wesley Clair Mitchell," *History of Political Economy*, vol. 29 (Fall 1997), pp. 371–390, for an evaluative essay written by one of Mitchell's admiring students in 1931. An institutionalist-labor theorist contemporary of Mitchell at Chicago, Robert F. Hoxie, is discussed in P. J. McNulty's essay, "Hoxie's Economics in Retrospect: The Making and Unmaking of a Veblenian," *History of Political Economy*, vol. 5 (Fall 1973), pp. 449–484. Hoxie and others influenced by Veblen's ideas were somewhat influential in forming FDR's economic policies over the Depression years. FDR's "brain trust" was heavily influenced by institutionalist ideas.

C. E. Ayres's full and quietly rebellious life is aptly chronicled by W. L. Breit and W. P. Culbertson in "Clarence Edwin Ayres: An Intellectual's Portrait," *Science and Ceremony* (Austin: University of Texas Press, 1976). In addition to the Coats essay on Ayres, this volume contains essays on Ayres by a number of leading social and economic scholars, including Talcott Parsons, James M. Buchanan, Gordon Tullock, Joseph J. Spengler, and Alfred F. Chalk (the epistemology of Ayres is clearly revealed in Chalk's essay). While most of these papers do not concern Ayres's thought per se, they are very much in the spirit of the broad inquiries he sponsored. Three other papers on Ayres provide helpful background: W. L. Breit, "The Development of Clarence Ayres' Theoretical Institutionalism," *Social Science Quarterly*, vol. 54 (September 1973), pp. 244–257; D. A. Walker, "The Institutionalist Economic Theories of Clarence Ayres," *Economic Inquiry*, vol. 17 (October 1979), pp. 519–538; and, same author, "The Economic Policy Proposals of Clarence Ayres," *Southern Economic Journal*, vol. 44 (January 1978), pp. 616–628. In the latter paper Ayres is shown to have become a rather commonplace "liberal" with respect to policies designed to alter income distribution, although his "minimum income proposal" contained a negative income tax provision. The influence of John Dewey on Ayres is chronicled by Floyd McFarland, "Clarence Ayres and His Gospel of Technology," *History of Political Economy*, vol. 18 (Fall 1986), pp. 617–637.

Some works by Galbraith not cited in this chapter are *The Great Crash, 1929* (Boston: Houghton Mifflin, 1955); *A Theory of Price Control* (Cambridge, MA: Harvard University Press, 1952); *Economics and the Art of Controversy* (New Brunswick, NJ: Rutgers University Press, 1955); *The Liberal Hour* (Boston: Houghton Mifflin, 1960); and *Economics and the Public Purpose* (Boston: Houghton Mifflin, 1973). For an insightful assessment of Galbraith's "system" see Scott Gordon's "The Close of the Galbraithian System," *Journal of Political Economy*, vol. 76 (July/August 1968), pp. 635–644; and Galbraith's reply, "Professor Gordon on 'The Close of the Galbraithian System,'" *Journal of Political Economy*, vol. 77 (July/August 1969), pp. 494–503. Veblen and Galbraith are compared and contrasted by C. G. Leathers and J. S. Evans, "Thorstein Veblen and the New Industrial State," *History of Political Economy*, vol. 5 (Fall 1973), pp. 420–437, while Harold Demsetz makes a provocative attempt to discover and test the empirical content of Galbraith's theory in "Where Is the New Industrial State?" *Economic Inquiry*, vol. 12 (March 1974), pp. 1–12. Finally, lucid overviews of Galbraith and Veblen are contained in W. L. Breit and Roger Ransom, *The Academic Scribblers* (New York: Holt, 1982).

20

Competition Revised
Chamberlin and Robinson

Of the numerous directions taken in twentieth-century microeconomics, perhaps the most important one has been the search for models descriptive of actual markets. Alfred Marshall, as we recall from chapter 16, devoted the lion's share of his attention to models of perfect competition on the one hand and pure monopoly on the other.

Perfect competition is a model premised on a large number of sellers that produce a homogeneous product. Because the number of firms is indefinitely large, no one seller can affect the price and profits of other firms; that is, the actions of one firm have no effect on the price and output decisions of other firms. Since the model assumes complete freedom of entry and exit, neither long-run economic profits nor economic rents exist. In contrast, the monopoly model, first accurately described by Cournot and Dupuit and subsequently expanded by Marshall and others, is characterized by a single firm with exclusive control over the output of the good in question. Economic profits are greater under this market structure than under any other because economic power is greater and more concentrated than under any market structure that includes more than one seller.

These two models, the essentials of which had been worked out fairly early in the nineteenth century, are polar extremes. Although he displayed some awareness of a middle ground between the two extremes, Marshall perpetuated the cultivation of these two diverse models of the firm, and economists through 1933, with a few important exceptions, did not bother to analyze price and output equilibriums of firms whose decisions had an effect on one another's policies. But in 1933 two important (and independently written) books appeared in America and England whose titles and central themes addressed this very problem: Edward H. Chamberlin's *Theory of Monopolistic Competition* and Joan Robinson's *Economics of Imperfect Competition*. Their ideas were spawned by the thinking and debates of others, which we discuss next.

Duopoly Analysis

Augustin Cournot was probably the first writer to analyze an imperfect market. In Cournot's case of duopoly (see chapter 13), there were two sellers whose profit-maximizing behavior depended upon each thinking the other's output would remain constant. Cournot found a solution, but it was dependent on this rather naive assumption. Cournot stimulated other writers to take up the issue, but only after a lag of almost fifty years. Chief among the early writers to formulate alternative models of duopoly were Joseph Bertrand in 1883 and F. Y. Edgeworth in 1897. Bertrand, a French mathematician, argued that given the assumption that the prices of the rival seller are assumed constant (by each of the sellers), price and output will reach competitive levels. Edgeworth, on the other hand, placed output constraints on each of his duopolists, producing an indeterminate range over which prices and outputs of the two sellers oscillate.

The Cournot-Bertrand and Edgeworth results depended on the special assumptions that each made concerning the behavior of the duopolist/competitors. Perhaps it was this tenuousness of result that led Alfred Marshall to avoid contributing to duopoly theory (though he was certainly aware of Cournot's solution). Nonetheless, Marshall unwittingly encouraged other economists to pursue the matter. Recall that in the *Principles*, Marshall discussed the possibility of the existence of industries characterized by increasing returns, or decreasing costs. A debate ensued principally in the 1920s, involving several important disciples of Marshall, over whether competitive equilibrium was compatible with increasing returns.

Sraffa and Imperfect Competition

Marshall's successor at Cambridge, A. C. Pigou, participated in this fresh debate, but Cambridge economist Piero Sraffa defined the issues clearly in 1926 in an article entitled "The Laws of Returns under Competitive Conditions." Sraffa had proved elsewhere that decreasing-cost conditions were indeed incompatible with long-run Marshallian competitive equilibrium. One or the other had to be given up. But in 1926 he noted a significant gap in economic theory attributable to the exclusive cultivation of the market models of competition and monopoly. Sraffa concentrated on market imperfections that defenders of the competitive model dismissed as "frictions." He denied that these obstacles are frictions, declaring that they "are themselves active forces which produce permanent and even cumulative effects" on market prices and outputs. Establishing the groundwork for models of imperfect competition, Sraffa further argued that these obstacles to competition "are endowed with sufficient stability to enable them to be made the subject of analysis based on statistical assumptions" ("Laws of Returns," p. 542).

Sraffa also suggested some obstacles that might affect monopoly strength or the elasticity of the demand curve faced by the imperfectly competitive seller: possession of unique natural resources, legal privileges, the control of a greater or lesser proportion of the total production, and the existence of rival commodities. Thus, out of a contradiction in Marshall's analysis of competition, Sraffa teased a new approach to market theory. In 1933, Joan Robinson (another important Cambridge economist) explicitly credited Sraffa and the increasing-returns controversy as the impetus to her analysis of imperfect markets. For his part, E. H. Chamberlin's development of monopolistic competition was not directly influenced by Sraffa, but by Cambridge economist A. C. Pigou—more specifically, by an imbroglio over the explanation of railway rates generated by a debate between Pigou and American economist Frank Taussig.

Taussig and Pigou on Railway Rates

The Taussig–Pigou controversy centered on the question of whether the observed pattern of multiple railway rates could best be explained by the Mill–Marshall theory of joint supply (see chapter 8), which was Taussig's position, or by the presence of high railway common costs and corresponding ability to price-discriminate between buyers (Pigou's position).

In 1891, scarcely a year after the publication of Marshall's *Principles*, F. W. Taussig of Harvard University attempted to explain multiple railway rates in the United States by means of the joint-cost argument, an integument of orthodox competitive theory. Taussig entered the debate over railway rates in order to thwart the widely accepted notion that the government should own the railroads, an idea encouraged by the belief that monopoly and discriminatory rates were inherent in, and exclusive to, any system of private control. Against this sentiment, Taussig argued because a railroad's expenses are preponderantly joint, varying rates for rail service would persist even under government ownership.

The essentials of Taussig's supportive reasoning may be set out simply. First, Taussig noted (correctly) that railroads have high fixed costs that do not change with the level of traffic, a feature that sets railroads apart from most other firms. Taussig asserted:

> We have here [on the railroads] commodities produced in part at least, at joint cost. For the explanation of the values of commodities produced under such conditions, the classic economists developed a theory which they applied chiefly to cases like wool and mutton, gas and coke, where practically the whole of the cost was incurred jointly for several commodities. But obviously it also applies, *pro tanto*, to cases where only part of the cost is joint. The conditions for its application exist in any industry in which there is a large plant, turning out, *not one homogeneous commodity*, but several commodities, subject to demand from *different quarters with different degrees of intensity*. ("Contribution," p. 443, italics supplied)

Consequently, the "law of one price," an element of the competitive model, clearly does not apply to railroads; this fact, however, does not constitute prima facie evidence of monopoly. Taussig insisted that railroads were conforming to the theory of competitive joint supply by asserting that: (1) the unit of output offered by a railroad is heterogeneous, not homogeneous, and (2) different demand elasticities for rail service contribute to, or are the sole cause of, this heterogeneity.

He concluded that, excepting a small element of direct costs, demand price for the separate transport services offered by a railroad inevitably must allocate the *joint costs* of all outputs, just as a competitive market sets prices for wool and mutton. Different rates would persist for the transport of copper and coal under a regime of competition, and although such price differences would be magnified within monopolistic market structures, they could not be eliminated by government ownership or regulation because monopoly is not the prime source of differential rates. These principles, Taussig concluded, explain pricing in many other industrial operations as well, but railways "present on an enormous scale a case of the production at joint cost of different commodities" ("Contribution," p. 453).

A. C. Pigou rejected the view that rates could be explained on the basis of joint cost, and he blamed Taussig for the persistence of this error (*Wealth and Welfare* 1912). Devoting an entire chapter to the issue of railway rates, Pigou argued that: (1) Taussig was mistaken in identifying rail costs as preponderantly joint, and (2) he was led to this error by regarding the transport service supplied as a heterogeneous unit of output. Pigou was convinced that multiple rail rates were explained instead by monopoly, coupled with the presence of the necessary conditions for price discrimination. He maintained that the large mass of railway common costs were allocated by differing demand elasticities for the *homogeneous* unit of output.

Although it is generally conceded that Pigou won the debate and that price discrimination is the essential explanation for rail rates, F. W. Taussig's reasoning concerning the heterogeneity of railroad output encouraged E. H. Chamberlin to revise the theory of competition. In a 1961 essay, Chamberlin attributed the origin of his theory of imperfect competition to the Taussig–Pigou controversy. He admitted that Pigou had the upper hand in the debate but argued that "a very slight element of monopoly" would have supported Taussig's position. This slight element of monopoly—some ability to control price—may be the result of the ability to differentiate products. In the course of the debate Taussig said: "We speak of railways and the like industries as 'monopolies.' Yet they are far from being industries to which the strict theory of monopoly price can be applied" ("Railway Rates," p. 383). Railroads are subject to degrees of competition, from other railroads and from other modes of transportation. But the degree of product differentiation in existing markets was something worthy of more investigation.

■ Chamberlin's Quest for a New Theory

Chamberlin presented his new theory as "monopolistic competition," which is a bit of an oxymoron. But the core idea is sound. The new theory emphasized that in many markets elements of monopoly and competition combine in ways that don't fit the definition of either pure competition or pure monopoly. On the one hand, markets composed of many sellers, typically characterized as competitive, may be marked by degrees of monopoly to the extent that products can be differentiated in a way to make each product unique in some manner. On the other hand, markets composed of a single seller may be marked by degrees of competition to the extent that barriers to entry are not absolute.

Product Differentiation

One of the most important insights of Chamberlin's new theory of monopolistic competition was that most firms engage in nonprice competition as well as price competition. Though a large number of firms might exist in a market (the competitive element), each was viewed by Chamberlin as having a unique product or advantage that gave it some control over price (the monopoly element).

Sraffa had already anticipated this development in a general way, but Chamberlin specifically noted that products achieve some degree of "uniqueness" by copyrights, trademarks, brand names, and location (i.e., in economic space products might be identical but buyers, because of the distances involved, may have locational allegiances). Chamberlin clearly perceived the duality of many markets:

> In this field of "products" differentiated by the circumstances surrounding their sale, we may say, as in the case of patents and trademarks, that both monopolistic and competitive elements are present. The field is commonly regarded as competitive, yet it differs only in degree from others which would at once be classed as monopolistic. In retail trade, each "product" is rendered unique by the individuality of the establishment in which it is sold, including its location (as well as by trademarks, qualitative differences, etc.); this is its monopolistic aspect. Each is subject to the competition of other "products" sold under different circumstances and at other locations; this is its competitive aspect. Here, as elsewhere in the field of differentiated products, both monopoly and competition are always present. (*Theory*, p. 63)

Many examples of Chamberlin's theory come to mind. Aspirin is the generic name for acetylsalicylic acid, but goes by many different brand names: Anacin, Bayer, Ecotrin, Excedrin, and many others. Through advertising and packaging, each brand is established and differentiated, thus creating a market of buyers who demand a *specific* product. Depending on the size and intensity of demand in each case, the seller can charge a (monopolistic) price that may differ from that of his or her competitors. Although a large number of substitutes compete for the consumer's aspirin dollar, price differentials can, and do, exist.

These differences can persist even though the chemical compound that constitutes aspirin is the same in all aspirin products. Consumers may be persuaded or convinced that differences exist, even if they do not. Aware of this, sellers attempt to engender brand loyalty, or customer allegiance, so that purchasers will not be deterred if the seller charges a price slightly higher than a competitor's brand. In this manner, profits can be increased (in the short run, at least).

Location may also be used to differentiate products that are otherwise the same. Suppose, for example, five drugstores exist in a large city and further assume they are alike in service and range of offerings. Each drugstore may offer the same physical product, but Chamberlin recognized that particular store locations might convey special advantages, thus differentiating the product. The degree of monopoly and the degree of freedom with which any store can price its products will depend on the number and dispersion of drugstore demanders, as well as on the location of competing sellers. Store location is then part and parcel of product differentiation.[1]

A multiplicity of other examples of differentiation could be cited. Automobiles are differentiated, but substitutability still exists. Markets for furniture, toothpaste, fine china, groceries, fitness centers, clothing, and so on, are all differentiated somehow. Chamberlin's point was well made and may be summarized as follows: There exists practically no market that is not characterized by monopoly elements. These monopoly elements are manifested by some form of differentiation: product, location, or service, for example. This fact means that each seller has some control over price, however small. When much (little) substitutability exists, the demand for the product is more (less) elastic, giving the individual seller less (more) control over price. Whereas Marshall regarded price as the sole variable under analysis in value theory, Chamberlin regarded both price and the product itself as variables under the control of firms in markets characterized by elements of both competition and monopoly. This was a fundamental and critical departure from standard microeconomic orthodoxy.

Advertising as a Means of Differentiation

A little reflection will reveal that competitive advertising is largely unnecessary under either pure competition or pure monopoly (a single seller with no substitutes). In fact, because it would reduce profits, it would be counterproductive. By definition, the purely competitive firm produces and sells a homogeneous product and is able to sell all of its output at the given market price. Under these conditions, brand loyalty is not an issue. There would be no need to advertise, and by doing so a firm would increase its costs without changing its revenues. The perfectly competitive model assumes that wants are given and known to all market participants.

[1] One of the authors lives in a city that has three different (chain) drugstores across from each other at a major four-way intersection. Is this a conscious attempt among competitors to eliminate each other's locational advantage?

Firms therefore have no incentive to discover or change consumers' wants. Likewise by definition, a pure monopolist faces no competitors and no substitutes; it would not need to advertise and would reduce profits by doing so.

Chamberlin recognized, however, that advertising is the modus operandi of monopolistic competition, and he lumped advertising with other measures into what he called "selling costs." Of such costs he said: "Advertising of all varieties, salesmen's salaries and the expense of sales departments, margins granted to dealers (retail and wholesale) in order to increase their effort in favor of particular goods, window displays, demonstrations of new goods, etc., are all costs of this type" (*Theory*, p. 117). The purpose of all these costs is clear: to alter the position and/or elasticity of the demand function facing the individual firm.

The individual entrepreneur's reasons for advertising are obvious: "to shift to the right the demand curve for the advertised product by spreading knowledge of its existence, by describing it, and by suggesting utilities it will provide the purchaser" (*Theory*, p. 119). Chamberlin claimed that advertising affects demands by manipulating wants. Some ads are simply not informative at all, in other words, but are competitive in attempting to rearrange wants.[2] Today, such advertising is common fare on television, radio, and the Internet, as well as on billboards. Its intent is to shift the demand curve of the advertised good to the right, at the expense of substitute goods in the product group. In this way advertising allocates demand among competing sellers, but unless the consumer's total expenditures rise (i.e., saving is reduced), it does not increase aggregate demand. Advertising, in sum, plays a crucial role in establishing and maintaining product differentiation in the monopolistically competitive firm.

Chamberlin's Two Demand Curves

Let us consider now the demand situation facing the monopolistically competitive firm. Chamberlin suggested that the product-differentiated firm faces two demand curves, although he behaved as if only one is relevant. Figure 20-1 depicts two demand functions, *DD* and *dd*, which intersect at point *C*. Both of these functions are negatively sloped because the firm is assumed to have some control over price. Suppose that the firm, which is assumed to be in a monopolistically competitive market, is charging price P_M and selling quantity Q_M. How does the firm (whose product faces a large number of competing substitute products) view the situation? Given that all firms in his product group produce substitutable goods, the seller believes that he could increase sales considerably by lowering his price below P_M. However, *the seller also believes that a marked reduction in sales will result from raising his price above* P_M, because he believes that none of his competitors will follow. Thus, assuming that the seller believes that his action will go unnoticed by his rivals, the demand curve facing the firm would be *dd*.

The problem is that such an assumption is unwarranted. If our representative seller can profit from a price reduction, so can any of his rivals, assuming, as Chamberlin did, that costs for all firms are identical. Thus, it is reasonable to expect that *all* monopolistic competitors would have an incentive to reduce prices. If every firm in the product group followed the price cut of our representative seller, sales would ex-

[2] Social unrest in underdeveloped countries is often said to rest on a "demonstration effect." The advertisement of expensive automobiles, household conveniences, and luxury goods in these countries is said to alter the individual's "utility function" or want pattern. Finding such goods unobtainable under the constraints of existing institutions, individuals take steps to alter these institutions.

pand for each firm only from the general price reduction and not at the expense of rival firms. *DD* depicts the demand curve, given that rival firms follow the price actions of any one firm.

Both curves *dd* and *DD* are drawn under the assumption that advertising expenditures are at a constant level for each firm. Should the firm under consideration increase its amount of competitive advertising, given that other firms do not react similarly, the demand functions facing the firm in figure 20-1 would shift to the right, and profits could be increased. Advertising expenditures would be optimized for the firm when $1 of additional selling costs added exactly $1 to the firm's receipts.

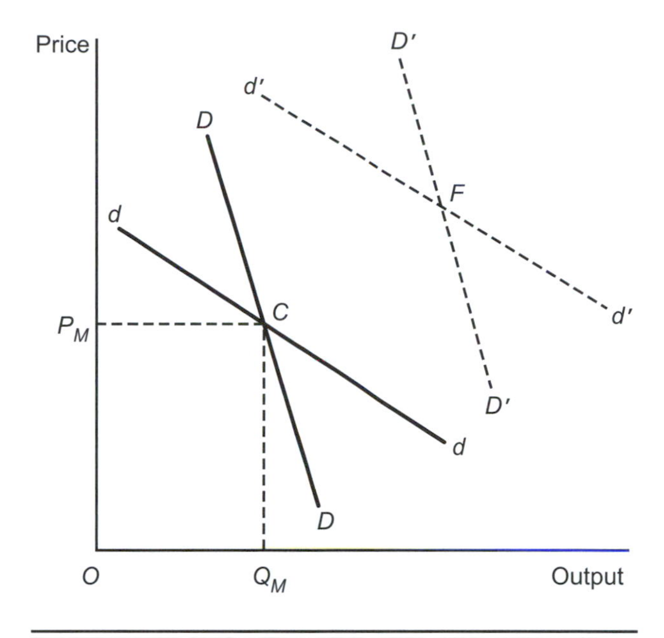

Figure 20-1 A monopolistically competitive firm can increase its sales along demand curve *dd* by reducing its price below P_M. However, if rival firms follow the price actions of any one firm, the demand curve will change to *DD*.

Long-Run Equilibrium in a Chamberlin Regime

We are now in a position to discuss Chamberlin's famous "tangency solution" to the market model of monopolistic competition. Once his solution is described, its conclusions may then be contrasted to those of the perfectly competitive Marshallian model. First let us collect the assumptions of the model. Chamberlin focused on a single firm in an industry composed of many sellers producing and selling closely related and substitutable products.[3] Each seller has some control over price, and since he is in a large group of sellers, he assumes that his price actions will not provoke any reaction from competitors. He would, in short, view his demand curve as *dd* or *d'd'* of figure 20-1, and assuming that the degree of product differentiation had been determined, he would manipulate prices in order to increase profits. Like Marshall, Chamberlin made use of the "representative firm" fiction, so that every firm's cost and demand were treated as identical.

Figure 20-2 on the following page shows a model replicating demand curves *dd*, *d'd'*, and *DD* from Figure 20-1, as well as a long-run average cost *LRAC*, which closely follows Chamberlin's presentation (*Theory*, p. 91).[4] Let the representative

[3] It is perhaps worth repeating that products or product groups do not have to have similar physical characteristics. A new boat may be highly substitutable for a vacation in Hawaii. Although the two are obviously not physically similar, they could constitute a product group in Chamberlinian terms.

[4] See Ferguson, *Microeconomic Theory*, chap. 10, for a discussion of the dynamics of this equilibrium.

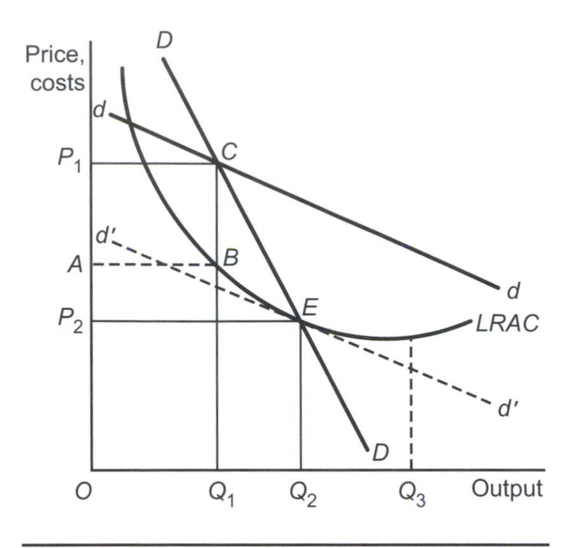

Figure 20-2 At price P_1, and output Q_1, each seller will make profits of $ABCP_1$. If a seller lowers the price below P_1 and rival sellers follow suit, the *dd* function will slide down the *DD* function until it (new schedule *d′d′*) intersects *DD* at point *E*.

seller (in a field of, say, 100 sellers) find herself at the intersection of curves *dd* and *DD* (point *C*), charging price P_1 and producing quantity Q_1. Each firm will produce the same price and quantity, and each will earn profits of $ABCP_1$. Now consider the manner in which any one of the firms views its situation. The seller believes, erroneously it turns out, that she may increase her profits by lowering price; i.e., she believes that demand curve *dd* is relevant because her rivals will not reduce prices when she does. But each rival does in fact reduce prices, and instead of expanding along curve *dd*, the firms expand along *DD*.

Each seller continues to believe that he or she could increase profits by lowering price, and each one does so. The *d′d′* function continues sliding down the *DD* function until it (now *d′d′*) intersects *DD* at point *E*. Here the firm's demand curve is tangent to the long-run average costs, and economic profits are eliminated. If the *d′d′* function fell *below* its position in figure 20-2, losses would ensue and price would subsequently increase. In short, the tangency equilibrium is stable. Quantities greater than Q_2 would produce a loss to the firm since long-run average cost would be greater than average revenue or demand.[5] Chamberlin's equilibrium exists uniquely at the tangency of *d′d′* with *LRAC* and simultaneously at the intersection of *d′d′* and *DD*.

Monopolistic Competition: A Waste of Resources?

A charge often leveled at monopolistic competition is that its economic effects are inefficient compared with those of perfect or pure competition. Specifically, it is alleged that excess capacity exists at a monopolistically competitive equilibrium such as point *E* in figure 20-2. Let us look into the nature of this charge.

Figure 20-3 abstracts some of the functions of figure 20-2, including the *dd* demand function and the long-run average-cost function. The *LRAC* function, as the reader might recall from chapter 16, is often called an "envelope" or "planning" curve. It is composed of a series of tangencies of points on the short-run average-cost curve. $SRAC_1$ and $SRAC_2$ are two such short-run curves, and for simplicity assume that between any two short-run U-shaped curves, another could be drawn for a slight alteration in scale of plant. The firm is producing an *optimum rate of output* when it utilizes the existing scale of plant (i.e., existing resources invested) to produce at the lowest average cost of production. Given a scale of plant characterized by $SRAC_1$, this optimum rate of output would be Q_m^1. Since, from the point of view of the firm, output Q_m

[5] The total number of sellers was kept constant throughout the analysis. See Chamberlin's *Theory*, p. 92.

is a profit-maximizing equilibrium state, from *society's* viewpoint the plant is being underutilized in that Q_m^1 is not being produced.

A second reason proffered for the inefficiency of monopolistic competition is that it does not produce a competitive rate of output, i.e., one that achieves an optimum scale of plant from society's point of view. Recall that under perfect competition, firms' demand curves are horizontal, or infinitely elastic. Such a demand curve is represented in figure 20-3 as the horizontal line $P_c d_c$. The long-run output for the purely competitive firm would be Q_c, corresponding to both an optimum rate of output and an optimum scale of plant from society's point of view. Thus, it is alleged, waste exists for two reasons: (1) because the monopolistically competitive firm does not utilize its existing resources to produce a socially optimum rate of output and (2) because a socially optimum scale of plant is rendered impossible as a result of product differentiation, which creates a negatively sloped demand function. "Excess social capacity" is then measured as $Q_m Q_c$.

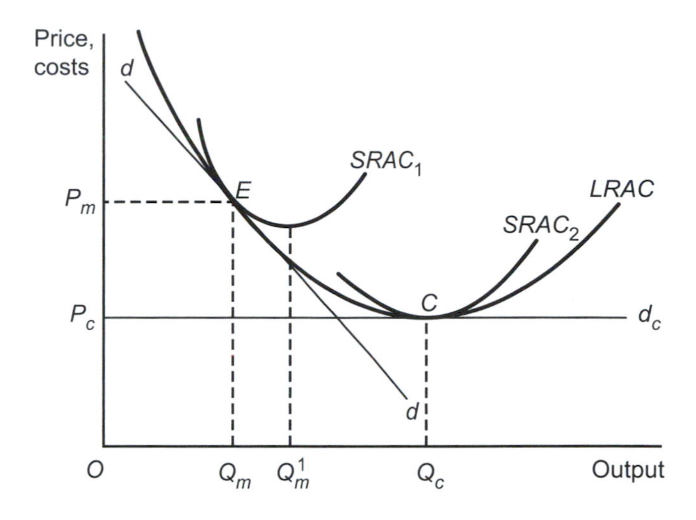

Figure 20-3 A monopolistically competitive firm will maximize profits at price P_m and output Q_m, but given the scale of plant represented by $SRAC_1$, the optimum rate of output from society's point of view will be Q_m^1. "Excess social capacity" is measured by $Q_m Q_c$, where Q_c is the competitive rate of output.

Chamberlin did not agree with this conclusion, however. Product differentiation, he argued, introduces variety and expands the continuum of the consumer's choices, factors that must be taken into account in any comparison of social benefits delivered by pure competition versus monopolistic competition. Variety might be utility-enhancing for its own sake but would not be possible in a regime of perfect competition in which every firm offers a homogeneous product. The increased social welfare from variety that monopolistic competition represents may well be greater than the loss in terms of excess social capacity that the market model necessitates. The theorist can only speculate.[6]

Chamberlin: A Tentative Evaluation

Chamberlin's *Theory of Monopolistic Competition* was an important benchmark in the development of value and a provocation for development of the theory of

[6] The whole foundation of monopolistic competition has been questioned in a number of important recent contributions (see notes for further reading at the end of the chapter). The substance of this modern argument is that what may appear to be excess capacity is simply a competitive market's working out of a means to reduce transaction costs, "waiting time," or other time-associated costs.

industrial organization. A great deal of interest developed in models of monopolistic competition in the 1930s, 1940s, and 1950s. Fritz Machlup, Robert Triffen, William Fellner, Arthur Smithies, and many others built on Chamberlin's work. Practically every text in first-level economics and in intermediate microeconomic analysis devotes space to Chamberlin and his ideas.[7] Chamberlin devoted his entire life to the selling of his theory. In article after article he amplified, corrected, expanded, and contrasted issues surrounding monopolistic competition, and many of these appeared as appendixes to successive editions of *The Theory of Monopolistic Competition* (it went through seven editions).

Although a number of theorists continue to work Chamberlinian "realism" into value theory, a large and ever-growing coterie of writers has come to defend an expanded model of perfect competition as a more consistent and useful approach to microeconomic problems. Why? Not because the assumptions of perfect competition seem more realistic, but because a modified competitive analysis seems to yield very fruitful predictions concerning the behavior of price and quantity in individual markets. At the time, however, Chamberlin struck a responsive chord in economic analysis by emphasizing monopolistic elements in the competitive process. He thereby stimulated interest in the market conditions of specific industries, which in turn gave impetus to industry studies and to the field of industrial organization. Many of his ideas have raised questions that are still relevant to economic analysis. Chamberlin's major achievement, then, seems to have spawned interesting new paths of analysis rather than to have provided economics with a well-cultivated and finished alternative to the competitive model. As such, his contributions are noteworthy, substantial, and important for the future of economic theory. (On the filiation of ideas between Chamberlin and Austrian/Chicago approaches, see the box, The Force of Ideas: Imperfect Competition Meets Industrial Organization.)

■ Joan Robinson and Imperfect Competition

The history of science is replete with situations in which multiple discoveries of the same principle occur more or less simultaneously. An example of this in economics is provided by the cotemporaneous contributions of E. H. Chamberlin and Joan Robinson. Robinson's early training in Marshallian economics at Cambridge University, reflecting the influence of A. C. Pigou and Piero Sraffa, led her to a comparative analysis of monopolistic and competitive markets that culminated in a work called *The Economics of Imperfect Competition*. Published in 1933, Robinson's *Economics of Imperfect Competition* is an analytical tour de force. In the main, she contributed little to the roles of product differentiation and advertising as elements of monopolistic markets, but her book introduced and used, in her own invented phrase, a "set of tools" that has become valuable in the partial-equilibrium analysis of markets and market structures. Specifically, Robinson reintroduced Cournot's untitled concept of marginal revenue into the theory of the firm and gave it form under different types of market structure.

Fully cognizant of the fact that *degrees* of monopoly exist, Robinson chose the pure monopoly model as a proxy for all those intermediate structures that Cham-

[7] The reader is encouraged to read Chamberlin's *Theory of Monopolistic Competition* and to remember that the ideas presented here are only a sample. His assessments of the duopoly models of Cournot, Bertrand, Edgeworth, and Hotelling are particularly recommended.

The Force of Ideas: Imperfect Competition Meets Industrial Organization

E. H. Chamberlin stands on the cusp of not one but two approaches to the contemporary study and practice of industrial organization. One might call these two approaches the "old" and the "new" views of industrial organization. The "old" view emphasized the conduct, structure, and performance of real-world markets within a static, Marshallian context. The practical import of this old view is that it encased industries within a rigid taxonomy that categorized a single firm as "least competitive"; a three-firm oligopoly as a bit more competitive; large numbers of firms as most competitive; and so on. This approach has led to the characterization of real-world industries, such as autos and pharmaceuticals, in terms of "concentration" ratios, the idea being that the degree of competition or lack thereof can be made formulaic. The Federal Trade Commission and the U.S. Justice Department have approved or denied mergers between firms on the basis of measured concentration ratios. Chamberlin's perceived contribution to this paradigm was the invention of a method of market taxonomy wherein market structures between the extremes of "competition" and "monopoly" could be classified and arrayed.

For many years Chamberlin's contribution was considered to have exerted a profound effect on the early development of industrial organization theory and practice. Much of this development took place at Harvard University, where Chamberlin taught for many years.* However, the alignment of Chamberlin with the Harvard paradigm is misguided. Chamberlin was primarily concerned with such essentially dynamic market phenomena as product differentiation and advertising. As a consequence he attempted to develop a "rivalrous" theory of competition, which placed major importance on products, product qualities, information, and other elements of "full price" in assessing market performance. This "new" theory of rivalrous competition does not identify competitiveness with *numbers* of competitors. Two competing rivals may be as "competitive" in terms of results as 1,000 competitors.

Economists in the Austrian tradition had long looked at markets as a process of entrepreneurial activity. Starting with Menger and Wieser (see chapter 14), and continuing through Mises and Hayek (see chapter 23), this tradition has flourished, despite being regarded by many as outside the mainstream. At the University of Chicago, however, Frank Knight gave these concerns incipient legitimacy by expanding the concept of entrepreneurship and establishing the institutional backdrop that encouraged expanded ideas about competition. Led by heirs apparent George Stigler and Gary Becker, these "new" neoclassicists pioneered the economics of information, adding several important nonprice elements to the standard theories of consumption and production (see chapter 26).

The unifying theme of this Chicago tradition in industrial organization theory resides in Chamberlin's original assertion that quality variability, aided and abetted by advertising, and other measures that may appear to be anticompetitive, are indeed the very things that comprise the dynamic, competitive process. Ironically, the new industrial organization theory, nurtured by a combination of Austrian and Chicago influences, is more in keeping with the basic contribution of Chamberlin than the old version pioneered at Harvard University.

Chamberlin himself recognized unresolved problems occasioned by the attempt to place the dynamic notions of product differentiation and advertising into the static mold of Marshallian economics. Neglect of these analytical shortcomings led his followers to emphasize structure, conduct, and performance rather than to confront the complexities of product differentiation. Had his theory been properly interpreted, Chamberlin's work might have led to a more timely understanding of the competitive process in which quality, product, distance, time, and other competitive dimensions must be included in order to produce a correct and full understanding of what comprises an industry, as well as how competition works within it.

*See, in particular, E. G. Mason, "Price and Production Policies of Large-scale Enterprise," pp. 61–74; J. S. Bain, *Barriers to New Competition*; and R. E. Caves, *American Industry*.

berlin had begun to classify.[8] In this sense, Robinson's approach was both more traditional and more general than Chamberlin's. Nevertheless, within the confines of her method of analysis she was able to make first-rate contributions to the theory of the firm under all imperfectly competitive market structures. Her analysis was especially penetrating on the nature and role of monopoly and price discrimination.

Pigou, Robinson, and the Theory of Price Discrimination

In chapter 13, Dupuit's analysis of price discrimination was discussed at some length. We saw that his contribution was concerned primarily with the welfare advantages of price discrimination over simple monopoly pricing. In other words, it had a distinct policy focus, albeit outside Marshall's sphere of influence, yet closely aligned with it. Following in the footsteps of Marshall, A. C. Pigou and Joan Robinson refined and developed the purely theoretic foundations of price discrimination. We caution the reader that their detailed analyses might perhaps best be left to specialists in the field of economic theory, but we nevertheless present a verbal overview of the Pigou–Robinson theory.[9]

Price discrimination is an activity carried on by a firm with monopoly power because it is profitable. Essentially it involves the selling of identical units of a commodity to different individuals and groups of individuals at *different* prices. Discussion of its causes and effects begins with recognition of the formal conditions necessary for price discrimination to exist.

Conditions Necessary for Price Discrimination. First, a degree of monopoly power is required. The firm need not be a single seller, but it must face a downward-sloping demand curve for its product. Any firm (including the whole range from monopolistically competitive to pure monopoly) that has any degree of control over the price of its product possesses one of the prerequisites for price discrimination. Second, the firm must be able to discern (or artificially create) more than one market for its product. These markets must be separable and customers must be assigned to separate markets. For example, age allows movie theatres to charge one price for children, another for adults, and another for "seniors." Retrading between consumers in the several markets must not occur, either because it is too costly or impossible. In the movie example, tickets cannot be interchangeable between age groups. (Such retrading might be effectively disallowed by the use of different-colored tickets and/or by an age check at the theater door.) A third prerequisite for price discrimination is that the relative profitability in the separate markets must be different, measured at simple monopoly price. Specifically, the elasticities of demand, or the ratios of simple monopoly price to marginal revenue, must be different in two (or more) markets facing the monopolist. This condition makes good economic sense. If a monopolist is selling some given quantity X and if he or she can identify and separate two markets, one of which will yield a higher addition to revenue for every unit sold, it will be profitable for the monopolist to transfer units of output from the market yielding lower revenues to the one producing higher revenues. Transfers of this type will continue until marginal revenue in each market reaches the same level.

Figure 20-4 is a model that illustrates the basic principles of Robinson's price-discrimination analysis. Here we are presented with demand curves of two separa-

[8] Chamberlin's classifications of market structures (polypoly, etc.) were expanded by Fritz Machlup and others. See the references at the end of this chapter.

[9] We direct the reader interested in the intricate details to Robinson's *Economics of Imperfect Competition*, chaps. 15 and 16, or to other sources listed in the references at the end of this chapter.

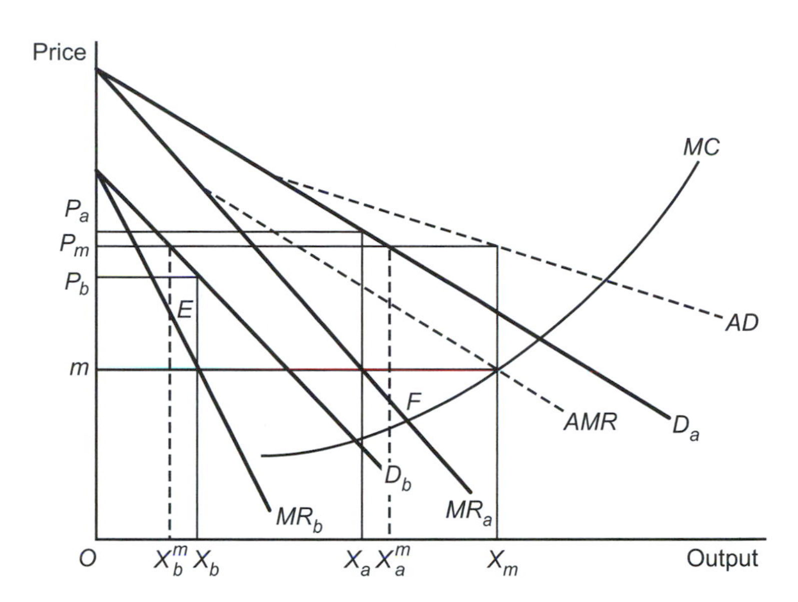

Figure 20-4 A single-price monopolist will produce output X_m and charge price P_m, selling output X_b^m and X_a^m in the two markets. A discriminating monopolist will equate the single-value marginal cost to the marginal revenue in each market, and produce output X_a for market A at price P_a, and output X_b for market B at price P_b.

ble markets, represented by D_a and D_b. The aggregate demand and marginal revenue facing the monopolist are found by summing (horizontally) the demand and marginal revenue functions of the two separable markets. These two aggregate functions are represented by the dashed curves *AD* and *AMR*, respectively. These are the only curves relevant for a monopolist who charges only *one* price, and under this system he or she would produce output X_m, which corresponds to the equating of marginal cost (*MC*) with aggregate marginal revenue *AMR*. In the single price case, price would be equal to P_m (read off *AD* at output X_m). Total output X_m would be allocated in the two markets from the demand curves D_a and D_b. In other words, if price P_m is charged for the product, X_b^m will be sold in market B, and output X_a^m will be sold in market A, yielding a total monopoly output of X_m.

The Discriminating Monopolist. We can now evaluate the situation facing the monopolist. If the necessary conditions exist for price discrimination in the situation represented in figure 20-4 (i.e., segmented markets, etc.) the monopolist can increase his or her profits by transferring sale units from market A to market B! Why? Because the addition to revenue from an additional sale in market B is greater than that in market A. Figure 20-4 verifies this point. At simple monopoly price P_m the marginal revenue of sales in market B corresponds to some value, *E*, and the marginal revenue in market A corresponds to value *F*. Since $E > F$, the transfer of a unit of output from A to B would add more to the firm's revenue (*E*, approximately) than the firm would lose by doing so (*F*, approximately). Thus, the profit-maximizing monopolist would find it in his or her interest to adjust sales and price in the two markets so that the revenues produced there were exactly the same. This result is accomplished by equating *MC* and *AMR* as before, but also by equating this single value *MC* to the marginal revenues in the two separate markets. Graphically, in figure 20-4, this single value of *MC* is shown as the line drawn to point m on the vertical axis from the point where $MC = AMR$. Discriminating outputs and prices are determined by the intersection of this line with the *MR*'s in the separate markets. Output X_a for market A is produced and sold at price P_a, and output X_b is sold at price P_b in market B. Note that output is increased in market B by the same amount as it is decreased in market A. Thus, in the case described in figure 20-4, total output remains unchanged, irrespective of whether the monopolist discriminates. However, monopoly profits are clearly increased by price discrimination.

Output Effects: Robinson's Contribution

With the model of figure 20-4 firmly in hand we are in a position to evaluate Robinson's contribution to price discrimination. Pigou had clearly described this model as early as 1912 in his *Wealth and Welfare* (a revised version entitled *The Economics of Welfare* was published in 1920). In the case depicted in figure 20-4, the simple monopolist redistributes utility to itself from consumers by way of price discrimination. This utility redistribution takes the form of increased profits and decreased consumer surplus. This is so because the total quantity sold remains the same before and after a two-price system is employed.[10]

One of the most frequent arguments raised against monopoly in the economic literature (by Dupuit, Wieser, Marshall, and many others) is that it reduces economic welfare by reducing output below levels that would result under competitive conditions. If we seek to apply the same comparative criterion within monopoly, we find that the case depicted in figure 20-4 does not provide any objective social basis for choosing simple monopoly structures over discriminating monopoly structures, or vice versa. Output remains the same in either case. Possibly the redistribution achieved through price discrimination outrages a popular sense of equity; but on pure economic grounds it is hard to justify a definitive stance against price discrimination on the basis of Pigou's analysis.

However, we should point out that in his analysis of price discrimination Pigou used only *linear* curves (like those in figure 20-4) in concluding that the introduction of price discrimination leaves output unchanged. Robinson demonstrated that the linear-curve situation was only a special case. She showed that compared to simple monopoly pricing price discrimination could result in greater or less output depending on circumstances. Her proof of this crucial point is fairly complex, but the method and conclusions of her analysis are fairly straightforward. Basically, whether or not output changes is a question that hinges on the concavity of the demand curves in the separate markets. Concavity relates to the change in the *slope* of the demand curves. In succinct terms, Robinson established that price discrimination will result in more output than simple monopoly pricing if the demand curve in the more elastic market is relatively more concave, and smaller if the demand curve in the more elastic market is relatively more convex than the demand curve in the less elastic market.[11] If the demand curves are linear, as in Pigou's case (i.e., figure 20-4), Robinson demonstrated that the curves are of *equal* concavity and that output remains unchanged by price discrimination.

Because the theoretical models employed by Robinson are complex and somewhat esoteric, one might justifiably wonder whether the whole issue is of purely academic interest. Stated differently, does her difficult theoretical analysis of relative concavities in monopoly have anything to do with the real world? The answer, as with many economic questions, depends on the empirical evidence respecting the shapes of demand curves in noncompetitive markets. But in light of government pol-

[10] At this point the reader might profit from rereading those sections of chap. 13 dealing with price discrimination.

[11] The concavity of the demand curves in the two markets is to be evaluated at simple monopoly price.

icies against prima facie price discrimination, the issue takes on practical significance. An unequivocal ban against all forms of price discrimination may reduce social welfare if price discrimination does in fact produce higher outputs than simple monopoly. Robinson cited international trade as one arena where this might be true:

> This is probably a common case where the more elastic market is an export market in which the exported goods are in competition with those produced locally. It will often happen that only a small amount can be exported at relatively high prices but that as the price of the exported goods approaches and falls below the price of the local rival goods the demand for them increases very rapidly—in short the demand curve is highly concave. (*Economics of Imperfect Competition*, p. 205)

Other instances in which the relevance of Robinson's analysis might apply include the transportation and public-utilities sectors, where price discrimination on the basis of different elasticities of demand might well result in increases in output.

There is a large body of legislation in the United States that outlaws price discrimination without establishing any kind of welfare "test" that Robinson's analysis could afford. The Clayton Act of 1914, and its extension, the Robinson-Patman Act of 1936,[12] prohibit certain types of price discrimination on the premise that price discrimination is prima facie harmful to the public interest. Indeed, prohibitions against price discrimination have become one of the most important parts of antitrust legislation. Since antitrust legislation is designed to deal with monopoly market structures wherein discrimination or the expansion of discriminatory pricing is a possibility, these laws deny the welfare gains of potential output increases. In short, informed analysis of the type pioneered first by Dupuit and later by Robinson suggest that the traditional presumption against price discrimination in antitrust enforcement should be reevaluated whenever the policy alternatives are between single-rate monopoly pricing and multiple-pricing schemes. Only careful empiricism can sort out the probable results in any particular case.

This chapter has considered only a few of the unique features of Joan Robinson's book, and at only a superficial level. Her discussions of rent and comparisons of monopoly and competitive output, for example, are important parts of received microanalysis. Her book, like Chamberlin's, was destined to become a classic in the annals of economic theory.

■ Knight, Chamberlin, Robinson, and Entrepreneurism

We saw in chapter 13 that Dupuit linked the entrepreneur to the process of product differentiation early in the nineteenth century but the idea did not gain much traction thereafter until Chamberlin and Robinson brought product differentiation into mainstream neoclassical economics. Robinson and Chamberlin showed that profits may be earned and retained by entrepreneurs who achieve a privileged monopolistic position in the selling market or, in the case of Robinson, a monopsonistic position in the factor market. But it was Frank Knight (1885–1972) who created an eclectic theory of profit a decade earlier, which integrated all the previous theories of profit and entrepreneurship. Knight treated profit as a residual return earned by the entrepreneur as a consequence of correct decisions taken in the present to bear fruit sometime in the uncertain future. His theory rests on a sharp dis-

[12] The surname "Robinson" attached to this legislation bears no relation to the author of *The Economics of Imperfect Competition*. Yet it is ironic that legislation bearing the same surname as Joan Robinson was formulated in complete disregard of her contribution.

tinction between risk and uncertainty. Risk exists when the future outcome of a present action is unknown but adequate data exist to make a probability calculation. For example, a businessperson can insure against fire or flood loss in order to protect her factory. Certain risks can be insured against because there is a sufficient historical sample of previous incidents to permit an actuarial calculation. Apart from insurable risk Knight defined uncertainty as a situation involving uninsurable risk. A person confronts uncertainty when she takes a present decision under conditions that do not permit a probability calculus. In such instances the decision maker must rely on her own judgment, intuition, and whatever data she may accumulate.[13] Knight's rational, profit-maximizing entrepreneur will reduce the area of uncertainty as much as she can by insuring against risk, making forward contracts wherever possible, and accumulating as much data as possible. Nevertheless, there always remains an area in which true uncertainty persists. It may be some element of costs that is incalculable; more likely, the strategies of competitors cannot be determined. It is in the face of this kind of uncertainty that the entrepreneur proves her mettle.

In the end Knight's theory frees the entrepreneur from (insurable) risk, but assigns her the difficult task of decision making under (uninsurable) uncertainty. In a market economy, the entrepreneur's good decisions are rewarded by profit; bad decisions are penalized by loss. Profits may result from decisions concerning the state of the market, decisions that result in increasing the degree of monopoly, decisions about the forward holding of liquid stocks that give rise to windfall gains or decisions about introducing new techniques or innovations that, if successful, give rise to profits. In the final analysis all types of profits, whether they originate in the market structure; in general movements of the price level; in changes in government, commercial, fiscal, or monetary policy; or in successful innovation, may be subsumed in this general concept of profit as the entrepreneur's reward for successful decision making under conditions of uncertainty. Persistent losses mean that the entrepreneur is not likely to continue in her decision-making capacity.

Although Chamberlin and Robinson did not make entrepreneurship the focal point of their analyses, they inevitably shifted attention that way because it is hard to imagine product differentiation, price discrimination, attempted demand manipulation (through advertising), and other strategies of imperfect competition without assigning a prominent role to the entrepreneur. Because of Knight, Chamberlin, and Robinson, the entrepreneur began to move steadily away from "manager" toward a "unique and vital cog" in the theory of market behavior.

■ Conclusion

Taken as a broad reorientation of economic theory, the fate of the imperfect competition movement remains uncertain. One presumably unintended consequence was to narrow and harden the legacy concept of competition. Israel Kirzner, for example, complained: "The perfectly competitive model was never dominant in neoclassical economics until E. H. Chamberlin and Joan Robinson brought us imperfect competition. Then, they retroactively attributed perfect competition to

[13] Some mathematicians maintain that the difference between risk and uncertainty is not of kind but of degree, depending only on the amount of data available to inform a probability calculus. The point cannot be debated here, but we believe our discussion in this section can be sustained without definitive resolution of the debate.

those that preceded them" ("Between Mises and Keynes"). This criticism echoed earlier in Chamberlin's assessment of Robinson's work.

> *Imperfect Competition* followed the tradition of competitive theory, not only in identifying a commodity (albeit elastically defined) with an industry, but in expressly assuming such a commodity to be homogeneous. Such a theory involves no break whatever with the competitive tradition. The very terminology of "imperfect competition" is heavy with implications that the objective is to move towards "perfection." ("Product Heterogeneity," p. 87)

Chamberlin regarded his own work as more revolutionary and spent much of his remaining career trying to distance his work from Robinson's despite the economics profession's tendency to lump them together. We find that despite important differences between the two approaches to imperfect competition, there is less continuity between Marshall and Robinson than implied by Chamberlin—and less rupture between Chamberlin and competitive theory than we might be led to believe. Marshall and the Marshallians had, of course, studied monopoly as an extreme in value theory. But Robinson's insistence on the pervasiveness of monopoly and degrees of monopoly power certainly departs from Marshall's general characterization of markets. Though she did not view monopolistic competition or anything approaching it as a norm or as a general theory of value (as Chamberlin did), it is clear that she accepted the inevitability of a continuing world of monopolies. Thus, she recommended policies (minimum-wage legislation, etc.) that would soften their impact or partially increase welfare (allowance of price discrimination when output increased over simple monopoly). Such attitudes are hardly traditional, because it made monopoly, not competition, the key subject of analysis. All in all, it would perhaps be best to combine Chamberlin's and Robinson's approaches, calling the whole mélange "imperfect competition." Apart from a distinct difference in emphasis, and in levels of analysis, the two works do in fact have a single message: The competitive model is, in the main, inappropriate for describing observable pricing structures. In its stead, monopoly models are what economists should develop and expand.

Notwithstanding the initial surge of interest in models of imperfect competition, more recently the focus of many economists has turned back to the competitive model. It would, of course, be an overstatement to suggest that the nadir of such models is at hand, but it is the case that realism in model building often brings complexities that theory and empiricism cannot handle. Such is probably the case in some areas of imperfect competition. Indeterminacies in duopoly-oligopoly models of the type suggested by Chamberlin have repelled some theorists interested in firm behavior. The competitive model and its accoutrements, on the other hand, offer appealing and simple explanations of firm behavior. Many economists are attracted to simple, analytically satisfying, models. (Perhaps this is why Robinson has fared better than Chamberlin, since her tool kit was more like Marshall's.)[14] Still, Chamberlin's and Robinson's theoretical contributions have become staples of contemporary books and courses on price theory. It is probably much too soon to judge the outcome of the value revolution. But whether it is viewed as a simple skirmish within the neoclassical tradition or as a full-fledged flight from that tradition, the Chamberlin–Robinson reorientation continues to play a major role in contemporary economic thought.

[14] As for herself, Robinson questioned the value of most of partial-equilibrium price theory, including her own! (See Robinson, "Imperfect Competition Revisited.")

References

Bain, Joseph S. *Barriers to New Competition*. Cambridge, MA: Harvard University Press, 1956.

Caves, Richard E. *American Industry: Structure, Conduct, Performance*. Englewood Cliffs, NJ: Prentice-Hall, 1967.

Chamberlin, Edward H. "Product Heterogeneity and Public Policy," *American Economic Review*, vol. 40 (May 1950), pp. 85–92.

———. *The Theory of Monopolistic Competition: A Re-orientation of the Theory of Value*, 8th ed. Cambridge, MA: Harvard University Press, 1962.

Ferguson, C. E. *Microeconomic Theory*, 3d ed. Homewood, IL: Irwin, 1972.

Kirzner, I. M. "Between Mises and Keynes," *The Austrian Economics Newsletter*, vol. 17, no. 1 (Spring 1997). Retrieved from http://mises.org/journals/aen/aen17_1_1.asp.

Machlup, Fritz. *The Economics of Sellers Competition*. Baltimore: Johns Hopkins, 1952.

Mason, Edward G. "Price and Production Policies of Large-scale Enterprise," *American Economic Review*, vol. 29 (1939), pp. 61–74.

Pigou, A. C. *Wealth and Welfare*. London: Macmillan, 1912.

Robinson, Joan. *The Economics of Imperfect Competition*. London: Macmillan, 1933.

———. "Imperfect Competition Revisited," *Economic Journal*, vol. 63 (September 1953), pp. 579–593.

Sraffa, Piero. "The Laws of Returns under Competitive Conditions," *Economic Journal*, vol. 36 (December 1926), pp. 535–550.

Taussig, Frank. "A Contribution to the Theory of Railway Rates," *Quarterly Journal of Economics*, vol. 5 (1891), pp. 438–465.

———. "Railway Rates and Joint Cost Once More," *Quarterly Journal of Economics*, vol. 27 (1913), pp. 378–384.

Notes for Further Reading

E. H. Chamberlin was not the first or the only important American "eclectic" to emerge over the early Marshallian period in America. We have already seen that Veblen (chapter 19) was one of these. But a number of others might be mentioned, including Arthur Twining Hadley (1856–1930). Hadley, whose "principles" textbook, *Economics: An Account of the Relations Between Private Property and Public Welfare* (New York: G. P. Putnam's Sons, 1896), was very influential at American universities early in the century, was the inventor of a number of important ideas that were to influence the course of economics in the twentieth century. In this and in an earlier book on railway economics, *Railway Transportation: Its History and Its Laws* (New York: G. P. Putnam's Sons, 1885), Hadley (1) established property rights as the organizing principle of economic behavior and theory in a Coasian framework; (2) developed a process notion of competition that includes limit pricing and the concept of contestable markets; (3) recognized that politics and bureaucracy were endogenous to the system; (4) made advances in the theory of the firm; and (5) presented a complete development of business cycles under capitalism featuring the lack of efficient property rights as a chief element in the process of competition. These kinds of contributions laid the basis for the dominance of American economics over the twentieth century. With regard to Hadley and others, see A. B. Davidson and R. B. Ekelund, Jr., "America's Alternative to Marshall: Property, Competition, and Capitalism in Hadley's *Economics* of 1896," *Journal of the History of Economic Thought*, vol. 16 (Spring 1994), pp. 1–26; Melvin Cross and R. B. Ekelund, Jr., "A. T. Hadley on Monopoly Theory and Railway Regulation: An American Contribution to Economic Analysis and Policy," *History of Political Economy*, vol. 12 (Summer 1980), pp. 214–233; and, same authors, "A. T. Hadley: The American Invention of the Economics of Property Rights and Public Goods," *Review of Social Economy*, vol. 39 (April 1981), pp. 37–50.

A good place to start delving into the subject of imperfect competition is J. J. Gabszewicz and J.-F. Thisse, (eds.), *Microeconomic Theories of Imperfect Competition: Old Problems and New Perspectives*, (Cheltenham, U.K.: Edward Elgar, 1999), a collection of 44 articles, dating from 1838 to 1988. The collection provides a broad overview of the major theoretical concepts in the field and includes contributions from W. J. Baumol, J. P. Benassy, E. H. Chamberlin, A. Cournot, A. Dixit, F. Y. Edgeworth, J. Stiglitz, J. Tirole, and others. Today there exist a number of alternative theories of imperfect competition, depending on the premises established and the market to be analyzed. Fritz Machlup, *The Economics of Sellers Competition* (see references), and William Fellner, *Competition among the Few* (New York: A. M. Kelley, 1960), provide excellent treatments of monopolistic competition, imperfect competition, and oligopoly theory, along with many theoretical extensions. The question of efficiency and monopolistic competition is discussed in a number of papers by Harold Demsetz. See, for example, "The Nature of Equilibrium in Monopolistic Competition," *Journal of Political Economy*, vol. 67 (February 1959), pp. 21–30. Also see A. S. DeVany, "An Analysis of Taxi Markets," *Journal of Political Economy*, vol. 83 (February 1975), pp. 83–94, for an extension of the theme of monopolistic competition in a particular market, that of taxicabs.

A neglected pioneer in the development of monopolistic competition theory is Heinrich von Stackelberg, a German economist. See his *Marktform and Gleichgewicht* (Vienna: Julius Springer, 1934), published just one year after the appearance of Chamberlin's and Robinson's works. Von Stackelberg developed a Cournot-type graphic technique to analyze the market results from various types of conjectural assumptions on the part of competitors. Concluding that instability and disequilibrium characterize many markets, von Stackelberg urged state intervention. His book is reviewed in Wassily Leontief's "Stackelberg on Monopolistic Competition," *Journal of Political Economy*, vol. 44 (August 1936), pp. 554–559. This article provides a mathematical treatment of von Stackelberg's theory. The best nontechnical exposition of his alternative models may be found in Fellner, *Competition among the Few* (*op cit*). Von Stackelberg geometry has been put to use in analyzing certain aspects of public-goods theory. See William L. Breit, "Public Goods Interaction in Stackelberg Geometry," *Western Economic Journal*, vol. 6 (March 1968), pp. 161–164. Von Stackelberg's *Theory of the Market Economy* has been translated by A. T. Peacock (London: William Hodge, 1952).

An even earlier pioneer in duopoly/oligopoly analysis must also be mentioned. In 1929 the American economist Harold Hotelling, in "Stability in Competition," *Economic Journal*, vol. 39 (March 1929), pp. 41–57, constructed a model wherein location of firms itself is a variable. He demonstrated the quasi-monopolistic power of each firm to set price on the basis of locational advantages (akin to product differentiation). Paul Sweezy utilized Chamberlin's two-demand curve analysis (see figure 20-1) to discuss the alleged rigidity of oligopoly prices in his "Demand under Conditions of Oligopoly," *Journal of Political Economy*, vol. 47 (August 1939), pp. 68–73. One of the most exciting developments in twentieth-century economic theory can be applied to the analysis of duopoly-oligopoly behavior. John von Neumann and Oskar Morgenstern's *Theory of Games and Economic Behavior* (Princeton, NJ: Princeton University Press, 1943) combined the considerable talents of a mathematician and an economist to produce a mathematical theory of business and social organization. The far-reaching implications of the book extend to decision strategies on the part of duopolist/oligopolist competitors.

The early history of the theory of price discrimination, so closely tied to product differentiation and imperfect competition, is analyzed by Robert B. Ekelund, Jr., "Price Discrimination and Product Differentiation in Economic Theory: An Early Analysis," *Quarterly Journal of Economics*, vol. 84 (May 1970), pp. 268–278. Along with Dupuit, Pigou, and Robinson, F. Y. Edgeworth also pioneered in the theory of price discrimination; see his "Contribution to the Theory of Railway Rates," *Economic Journal*, vol. 22

(June 1912), pp. 198–218. An outstanding survey of the contemporary theory of price discrimination is contained in Louis Phlips, *The Economics of Price Discrimination* (Cambridge: Cambridge University Press, 1981). Among other things, this survey reveals the richness of modern theory with its emphasis on quality variations, an innovation that may be traced to Dupuit. On this last point, see T. R. Beard and R. B. Ekelund, Jr., "Quality Choice and Price Discrimination: A Note on Dupuit's Conjecture," *Southern Economic Journal*, vol. 57 (April 1991), pp. 1155–1163.

Two articles by C. P. Blitch trace the influence of the neglected economist Allyn Young (Chamberlin's dissertation director) on the development of Chamberlin's theory of monopolistic competition. See Blitch, "Allyn A. Young: A Curious Case of Professional Neglect," *History of Political Economy*, vol. 15 (Spring 1983), pp. 1–24; and same author, "The Genesis of Chamberlinian Monopolistic Competition Theory: Addendum," *History of Political Economy*, vol. 17 (Fall 1985), pp. 395–400. A somewhat different view, which is highly speculative and does not fit the historical evidence, is offered by T. P. Reinwald, "The Genesis of Chamberlin's Monopolistic Competition Theory," *History of Political Economy*, vol. 9 (Winter 1977), pp. 522–534; and same author, "The Genesis of Chamberlinian Monopolistic Competition Theory: Addendum—A Comment," *History of Political Economy*, vol. 17 (Fall 1985), pp. 400–402. Two articles by A. S. Skinner delve more deeply into the origins of Chamberlin's analysis: "The Origins and Development of Monopolistic Competition," *Journal of Economic Studies*, vol. 10 (1983), pp. 52–67; and "Edward Chamberlin: *The Theory of Monopolistic Competition*: A Reorientation of the Theory of Value," *Journal of Economic Studies*, vol. 13 (1986), pp. 27–44. In the latter appraisal, Skinner explores Chamberlin's reaction to the Marshallian perspective. Nahid Aslanbeigui and Guy Oakes, "Hostage to Fortune: Edward Chamberlin and the Reception of *The Theory of Monopolistic Competition*," *History of Political Economy*, vol. 43 (Fall 2011), p. 471–512, describe Chamberlin's hostility toward Joan Robinson's theory and why he believed it different from, and inferior to, his own. They also examine the reception of Chamberlin's work, and his failure to convince others regarding Robinson. R. B. Ekelund, Jr., and R. F. Hébert, "E. H. Chamberlin and Contemporary Industrial Organisation Theory," *Journal of Economic Studies*, vol. 17 (1990), pp. 20–31, trace the filiations of Chamberlinian theory to Austrian economics and the concerns of the Chicago School. R. D. Peterson, "Chamberlin's Monopolistic Competition: Neoclassical or Institutional?" *Journal of Economic Issues*, vol. 13 (September 1979), pp. 669–686, explores Chamberlin's debt to Veblen (see chapter 19) and the affinity of monopolistic competition to institutional economics.

Several edited volumes of essays in honor of Joan Robinson have been written. For a collection of assessments by an international team of economists who analyze various aspects of Robinson's thought, including her contribution to the development of the Keynesian tradition at Cambridge University, her works on the economics of the short period, and her critique of Pigou, see Maria Cristina Marcuzzo, Luigi Pasinetti, and Alessandro Roncaglia (eds.), *The Economics of Joan Robinson* (London: Routledge, 1996). In the same vein, G. R. Feiwel (ed.), *Joan Robinson and Modern Economic Theory* (New York: New York University Press, 1989), collected essays, some critical, some laudatory, from across a wide spectrum of economic theorists in relation to Robinson's philosophy, methodology, macroeconomics, and economic theory and specifically the notions of equilibrium, time, capital and growth, and unemployment and the theories of general equilibrium, trade, imperfect competition, games, credit markets, and finance. I. H. Rima (ed.), *The Joan Robinson Legacy* (Armonk, NY: M. E. Sharpe, 1991), presents a mixed collection of essays, mostly by persons who would style themselves "post-Keynesian," on various aspects of Robinson's many contributions to economic doctrine and method. A bit more biographical is M. S. Turner, *Joan Robinson and the Americans* (Armonk, NY: M. E. Sharpe, 1989); and A. A. Asimakopolous, "Joan Robinson and the Americans," *Journal of Post-Keynesian Economics*, vol. 13 (Fall 1990), pp. 111–124.

A sampling of the periodical literature on Robinson includes F. G. Hay, "The Joan Robinson Legacy: A Review Article," *American Journal of Economics and Sociology*, vol. 51 (October 1992), pp. 399–400; G. C. Harcourt, "Joan Robinson's Early Views on Method," *History of Political Economy*, vol. 22 (Fall 1990), pp. 411–428; same author, "Joan Robinson 1903–1983," *Economic Journal*, vol. 105 (September 1995), pp. 1228–1243; and again, "Joan Robinson and Her Circle," *History of Economic Ideas*, vol. 9 (2001), pp. 59–71; Vivian Walsh, "The Economics of Joan Robinson," *Science and Society*, vol. 65 (Summer 2001), pp. 229–235; J. E. King, "Your Position is Thoroughly Orthodox and Entirely Wrong: Nicholas Kaldor and Joan Robinson, 1933–1983," *Journal of the History of Economic Thought*, vol. 20 (December 1998), pp. 411–432; Zohreh Emami, "Joan Robinson's Views on Teaching Economics," *History of Political Economy*, vol. 26 (Winter 1994), pp. 665–680. Andrea Maneschi, "The Place of Lord Kahn's *Economics of the Short Period* in the Theory of Imperfect Competition," *History of Political Economy*, vol. 20 (Summer 1988), pp. 155–171, contends that Richard Kahn's 1929 doctoral dissertation at Cambridge University (though never published in English) "represents a significant stage in the development of the theory of imperfect competition which began with the pioneering paper by Piero Sraffa (1926) and culminated in the *magna opera* of Joan Robinson (1933) and Edward Chamberlin (1933)."

John Maynard Keynes and the Development of Modern Macroeconomics

One of the most compelling developments in twentieth-century economic analysis has been the resurgence of the classical economists' interest in aggregate economics—that is, in both monetary and macroeconomic theory. For well over two hundred years the quantity theory of money was the chief mechanism for organizing economists' thoughts about the aggregate economy. But events both internal and external to the discipline led to the emergence of a different approach to the macroeconomy in the mid-1930s. This movement, encompassing both economic theory and economic policy, took on the name of its leader, the British economist John Maynard Keynes. For decades, beginning in the 1950s and 1960s, Keynesian thought dominated fiscal policy in the United States and many other Western nations. However, with the emergence of strong inflationary pressures in the 1970s and 1980s, the policy emphasis shifted once again to money and to the reassertion of the underlying principles of the quantity theory. The *theoretical* shift to monetarism occurred even earlier. Both paradigms coexist in contemporary thought on aggregate economics. We cannot hope to air all of these views in detail here. We seek only to survey some major ideas in contemporary macroeconomics in this chapter and the next. This chapter is devoted to Keynes and Keynesian theory, and the following one considers the twentieth-century development of quantity-theory/monetarist thought.

Overview of Keynes and His Economics

John Maynard Keynes was one of the most famous and influential economic theorists of the twentieth century. While many economists today would minimize the analytical importance of his contribution, probably none would deny that his impact inside and outside the profession has been as great as Ricardo's, Mill's, or even Keynes's mentor, Alfred Marshall. Modern fiscal policy—the manipulation of government taxation and expenditures to affect prices, employment, and income—owes much to Keynes. His importance as a thinker is thus undeniable, and so we devote an entire chapter to an introduction to Keynesian theory and policy. But readers need to be aware of certain features and limitations of our treatment of Keynes in the present chapter.

First, although Keynes's magnum opus, *The General Theory of Employment, Interest and Money* (which we refer to as the *General Theory*), is popularly thought to represent a great break with past ideas, it is more likely that Keynes's ideas on economic theory evolved over a fairly long period of time. This chapter focuses solely on the Keynesian economics that appeared in the *General Theory* and neglects the transitional aspects of his thought.

Second, our treatment is based on a standard and popular version of what Keynes "really" said in the *General Theory*. This standard version is known as the "income-expenditure model," and it has been a staple of Keynesians almost since the *General Theory* was published. The main popularizers of this model have been Nobel laureate John R. Hicks and Harvard economist Alvin H. Hansen. Both writers were early propagators of Keynesian ideas, and the graphs used to depict these ideas are often called Hicks–Hansen diagrams. Our discussion derives much from the Hicks–Hansen approach to Keynes, but the reader is forewarned that several studies published after Hicks's and Hansen's have provided alternative interpretations of Keynes's intent in the *General Theory*.[1]

Third, the reader should also be aware that the Keynesian legend has a distinct policy theme. The legend has it that Keynes was the first (at least with respect to the Great Depression of the 1930s) to advise governments to engage in discretionary spending and taxation (budget deficits) to cure depression and unemployment. But the policy legend has been open to question. It has even been convincingly demonstrated that typically Keynesian advice regarding compensatory spending was forthcoming in the *early* 1930s, but from economists at the University of Chicago and elsewhere who have, in the lore of economic thought, been pictured as extreme defenders of orthodox, neoclassical, and monetarist government policies (see J. Ronnie Davis, *The New Economics and the Old Economists*). Our discussion, owing to space constraints, perpetuates the (inaccurate) legend of a typically Keynesian policy, however.

Fourth, the reader may well wonder how Keynes's ideas could still be the subject of so much debate. One might think that what Keynes really thought should be well settled by now. At least two important factors contribute to modern controversy. The first is the fact that Keynes's own statements of his ideas were often ambiguous. Moreover, he left many lines of analysis undeveloped or underdeveloped. A second, related point is that interpretations of Keynes's ideas by influential post-Keynesians have fixed opinions about what Keynes thought, rendering his fate not unlike that of Ricardo, whose ideas were and are the subject of debates. The reader should always bear in mind the simple fact that there may be vast differences between Ricardo and Ricardians, Saint-Simon and Saint-Simonians, Keynes and Keynesians, and so on. Naturally, all this implies that a definitive assessment of Keynes and Keynesian economics or history of economic thought is not yet possible. Here we seek only to provide a simple introduction to basic Keynesian thought and policy. In order to orient ourselves, however, let us first consider Keynes's very interesting life.

[1] For the most interesting of these alternative interpretations, the serious student should consult Axel Leijonhufvud's *On Keynesian Economics and the Economics of Keynes*. Leijonhufvud argues that Keynes's chief concern was a presentation of a macroeconomic quantity adjustment model rather than an analysis of unemployment equilibrium per se, which has been the traditional interpretation of Keynes's interests.

■ J. M. Keynes, Dilettante and Economic Theorist

John Maynard Keynes (1883–1946) was born ten years after Mill's death and seven years before Alfred Marshall published his *Principles of Economics*. If heredity has an important impact on mental achievement, John Maynard was certainly as fortunate as John Stuart Mill. His father, John Neville, and his mother, Florence Ada, were both intellectuals. John Maynard's father was a famous logician and writer on economic methodology best known for his work, *The Scope and Method of Political Economy*, published in 1890. John Maynard inherited from his parents a great intellectual curiosity and a lifelong love for the arts, especially the theater. His devotion to his father, who outlived him (J. N. Keynes died in 1949), was poignant and lasting.

Keynes was educated at Eton, arguably the most prestigious of English prep schools. He was alternatively immersed in classical literature, logic, mathematics, dramatics (he once played Hamlet), and in the high jinks of school life. He carried over his frenetic intellectual activity to King's College, Cambridge, where he received his university education. In a letter to his good friend B. W. Swithenbank Keynes described his collegiate pace:

> Immediately after hall I went to a Trinity Essay Society and heard a most brilliant satire on Christianity. From there I went to an informal philosophical debating society of interesting people where I stayed till nearly twelve; I then went to see Monty James where I stayed till one; from there I went on to another man with whom I talked till half past four. At half past seven I got up and read the Lesson in Chapel. I had four hours' work that morning, and rowed half a course in the afternoon. In the evening I went as a visitor to the Political Society to hear a paper on the Jesuits. (Harrod, *Life*, p. 68)

And so it was during his whole career, first as a student and then as an author, government official, and fellow at King's College.

Keynes was always surrounded by individuals of similar interests. Friendship was very important to him, and as a member of the famous Bloomsbury group (named for a London neighborhood), he was in intimate and stimulating contact with leading British intellectuals. In addition to Keynes, the original Bloomsbury group included Leonard and Virginia Woolf, Duncan Grant, Clive and Vanessa (Virginia Woolf's sister) Bell, E. M. Forster, and, perhaps its most influential member, Keynes's good friend Lytton Strachey. Anti-Victorian and bohemian, the Bloomsbury group considered all issues (philosophy, social convention, art, literature, and music) with the utter frankness and conceit generated by a firm belief in their own intellectual superiority. Although his major interest and achievements were to depart significantly from those of the Bloomsbury set, Keynes clearly contributed to, and drew cultural sustenance from, the group.

Economics had always interested him. He took courses from Alfred Marshall, and in 1905, Marshall wrote of his pupil to J. N. Keynes: "Your son is doing excellent work in Economics. I have told him that I should be greatly delighted if he should decide on the career of a professional economist. But of course I must not press him" (Harrod, *Life*, p. 107). Marshall probably did not find it necessary to press much, for Keynes's interest grew steadily. He was a natural. And, moreover, he knew it. Keynes's precociousness and wide range of activities carried over into his entire brilliant career, which by 1906 was leading him toward civil service as well as economics. In that year, Keynes passed the civil service examination and was assigned to a position in the Indian office. Quickly bored with his administrative duties, Keynes devoted ever more of his time to a study of probability theory, which culminated in his *Treatise on Probability* (1921), highly praised by Bertrand Russell and others.

In 1911 Keynes joined F. Y. Edgeworth as co-editor of the *Economic Journal*, the official organ of the Royal Economic Society, a position he retained until 1945. In 1913 he published *Indian Currency and Finance*, a work on international finance related to the gold exchange standard. Rapidly gaining fame as a monetary expert, Keynes entered the treasury department in 1915 and remained there until the end of World War I. He served as British treasury representative to the peace treaty conference of Versailles. With grave forebodings concerning the terms of European recovery, he resigned from the treaty conference. He later attacked the conditions of the treaty, and Prime Minister Lloyd George's policies, in *The Economic Consequences of the Peace* (1919). Keynes urged the victors to moderate their pressing demands on defeated Germany—a position that made the book an immense critical success.[2]

During the 1920s, Keynes taught at King's College, Cambridge. He was an enthusiastic and successful lecturer, but he soon reduced his teaching load in order to engage in a multitude of other activities. Keen to be independent of salaried employment, he began speculating in the foreign exchanges and amassed a fortune of approximately half a million pounds by 1937. He later served as chairman of the board of the *Nation*, a liberal weekly; and assumed the duties of bursar (financial analyst and manager) of King's College, for which he received, at the outset, £100 per year.

In 1923, Keynes published his *A Tract on Monetary Reform*, which was a polemic in favor of discretionary management of the internal money stock and against the gold standard as a capricious determinant of the internal economy. In 1925, he married a Russian beauty, Lydia Lopokova, one of the great Diaghilev's prima ballerinas. With his marriage, Keynes's interests between economics and the Bloomsbury group began to separate, and thereafter economics became and remained the major focus of his life. In 1930 Keynes published a book that he intended to crown his lifework in the field of money. His *Treatise on Money* was only a "still" picture of his ideas at that time; yet, it anticipated and even developed some of the mature ideas that were later displayed in the *General Theory*. Specifically, the *Treatise* explores the key roles of saving and investment in influencing the level of income—ideas that owe much to the influence of Keynes's friend and colleague Dennis H. Robertson. After 1930 Keynes ramped up his output even more. In addition to his magnum opus, *The General Theory of Employment, Interest and Money*, he displayed his pedagogical and persuasive skills in *Essays in Persuasion* (1931), and again in *Essays in Biography* (1933), both of which can still be read for enlightenment and enjoyment. In addition to his writing during this time, Keynes continued his lecturing, civil service, and college duties.

In the late 1930s Keynes became increasingly concerned with the financial burdens imposed by the impending war with Germany. He tackled the problems of reordering wartime resource priorities and the ensuing excess demand it creates in *How to Pay for the War* (1940). Between 1941 and 1946, he negotiated wartime lend-lease financing, and in 1946 he was instrumental in arranging loans to Great Britain under the U.S. Marshall Plan of reconstruction. That same year Keynes was made a vice president of the World Bank, at which he took a leadership position, along with

[2] In other ways, Keynes had turned a handsome profit from his wartime experience. While Big Bertha was shelling Paris, Keynes was at an art auction representing London's National Gallery. (The auction was to improve France's exchange position.) On that occasion, he acquired a number of fine pieces for the gallery, but he bought a Cézanne and an Ingres for himself. As Keynes's biographer Harrod reports, the shelling depressed prices.

Harry Dexter White, in formulating plans to restore the international monetary system (which led to the Bretton Woods Agreement). This dizzying array of activities took its toll on a heart, weakened by a previous attack, and in the summer of 1946, Keynes died at the age of sixty-three. The world lost a mind that probably could have reached high flights of achievement in any one of a number of areas, but Keynes himself chose economics.

■ Theoretical Outline of the *General Theory*

As noted earlier, the actual writing of the *General Theory* took place in the midst of the Great Depression. From the beginning of the 1930s, Keynes had been much concerned about the employment crisis, which was deepening drastically in the United States and England. He voiced concern in several communiqués to President Roosevelt, including a famous open letter to him in *The New York Times*. Keynes's advice was to make vigorous use of fiscal policy (government tax and expenditure policy) to supplement the private-sector economy, which, in Keynes's view, was failing to confront the employment problem. Roosevelt appeared to follow Keynes's advice, but guardedly. Whatever other meaning the episode had, it clearly indicates that the environment of the early 1930s was much on Keynes's mind prior to writing the *General Theory*.

As an independent discipline economics was experiencing internal pressures in the 1930s. Marshallian microeconomics was going through some radical extensions, including the revisions of E. H. Chamberlin and Joan Robinson (see chapter 20). Keynes himself had raised questions concerning the adequacy of neoclassical monetary theory in his *Treatise on Money*, and several of his colleagues were focusing on the importance of expenditures in aggregate output determination. Richard Kahn had developed a concept of an investment multiplier, and he, along with other leading Cambridge economists (Joan Robinson, R. G. Hawtrey, and R. F. Harrod), was steadily engaged in discussions of departures from standard economic theory. A general rethinking of neoclassical economic theory, and specifically Marshall's economics, must have contributed to Keynes's seminal work. Thus, a confluence of internal and external pressures led him to offer an alternative to neoclassicism. Keynes firmly believed that he was making a significant departure, but it was not an easy one. He spoke of a "long struggle of escape" from traditional methods of thought and expression, and he was at pains to explicate and emphasize these differences.

Keynes's Reaction to the Classics

In an attempt to dramatize his break with the past, Keynes used the term classics to refer to a long line of orthodox writers from Smith and Ricardo through Marshall and Pigou (Keynes treated his senior colleague, Pigou, as the repository of the entire orthodox tradition). Moreover, in Keynes's frame of reference classical economics was reduced to an idealized model not unlike the one considered in chapter 7 of this book.[3] He promptly rejected this idealized model of classical macrotheory even though he freely acknowledged several anticipators of his ideas.[4]

[3] Refer back to the section entitled "The Elegant Dynamics of the Classical System" at the end of chapter 7.

[4] Keynes's anticipators were, for the most part, dissenters from the classical tradition. A superb historian of thought, Keynes reviewed and evaluated these heretics in chap. 23 of the *General Theory*, "Notes on Mercantilism." In this connection, see chap. 3 of the present book.

Keynes's essential break with the classics was over the notion of Say's Law, which, broadly and naively stated, holds that supply creates its own demand. Say's Law (with all its accoutrements) implied that as a long-term proposition unemployment could not be permanent because the free enterprise economy was self-adjusting; any disturbances from a full-employment-full-production equilibrium would be only temporary. The classics had reasoned that in real terms the economy functioned much like a barter system. Goods were exchanged for goods, and money represented simply a standard of value and a medium of exchange. In Pigou's words, money was a "veil." It hid the *real* workings of the economy. It was the grease of trade, not the wheel.[5]

An equivalent way of stating Say's Law is to say that aggregate savings (income removed from the expenditure stream) will always equal investment (income returned to the expenditure stream) at full employment. As Böhm-Bawerk stressed, people generally prefer present consumption to future consumption, but given that savings is a function of the reward for savings, or a rate of interest, they can be induced by a positive rate of interest to hold more assets in the form of savings. Thus, the classics reasoned that the amount of savings was positively related to the rate of interest.

Investment, however, is negatively related to the interest rate because, among other reasons, the productivity of given investments decline with incremental increases in investment expenditure (technology being constant, of course). These relationships are summarized in figure 21-1, in which economy-wide saving and investment schedules are represented as functions of the rate of interest. The classics reasoned that at interest rate r_0 savings equaled investment, which meant that what is not spent on consumption goods (saved) was invested (spent on capital goods). A flexible interest rate mechanism guaranteed this result. Flexibility in this context means that if investment exceeds savings, say, at interest rate r_1, the rate of interest would be bid up to r_0 by investors. Conversely, if savings are greater than investment, savers will bid the interest rate down to r_0.

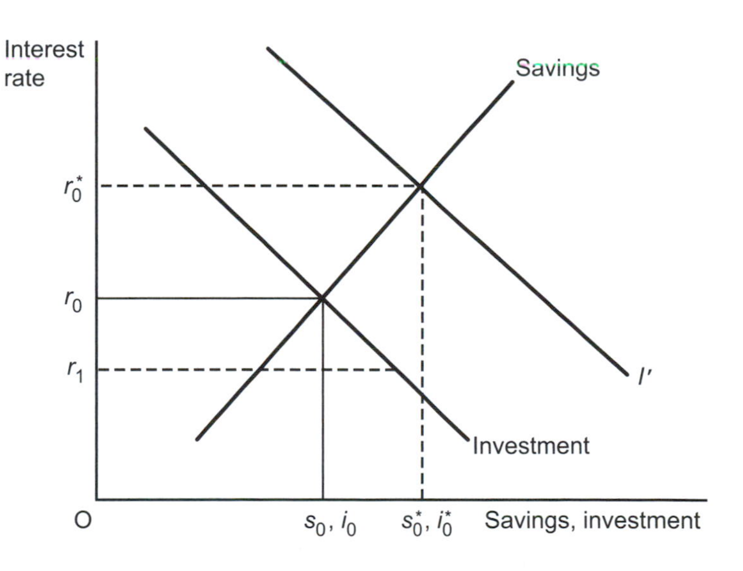

Figure 21-1 At interest rate r_0, savings equal investment. If investment increases from I to I', the new equilibrium rate of interest rises to r_0^* and the amount of savings and investment increases to s_0^* and i_0^*, respectively.

[5] Again, refer back to chap. 6, which dichotomizes the real from the monetary aspects of the macroeconomy.

The classical model reasoned that an increase in investment (which might have resulted from inventions or innovations) caused an upward shift in the investment schedule (shift to I' in figure 21-1), causing the level of investment to increase and the level of consumption to *decrease*. Society is induced to save more (and consume less) by a rising rate of interest. At the new equilibrium the rate of interest rises to r_0^*, and the amount of savings and investment increases to s_0^* and i_0^*, respectively. The real increase in savings ($s_0^* - s_0$) represents the decrease in consumption, but the decrease in consumption caused thereby is exactly matched by the increase in investment ($i_0^* - i_0$). In equilibrium the economy would neither overproduce nor underproduce. Given free markets, general laissez-faire, and rapid interest rate responses, Say's Law was a sure thing. A ready demand for goods (consumption and investment) could always be depended on. The market would always clear at full employment.

The interest-rate-adjustment mechanism provided one assurance of the validity of Say's Law. Another was the classical proposition of flexible wages and prices in the economy. If, for some reason, the economy was sluggish in adjusting to fundamental changes in savings and investment (say, as a result of a massive change in the desire to save), flexible prices and wages would guarantee a smooth short-term adjustment. With a dearth of aggregate demand, money, wages, and prices would fall such that full employment and full production would be resumed. Entrepreneurs would be willing to accept lower prices in order to sell their goods, and workers would be willing to take lower money wages, provided prices fell in the same proportion. Any disturbance that caused unemployment and output reductions was bound to be temporary since the competition in labor and product markets would always adjust the real variables of the system to equilibrium.

Keynes flatly and boldly rejected these classical adjustment mechanisms. In his two-pronged attack on Say's Law he maintained: (1) that the equilibrium of savings and investment did not depend solely on the interest rate but was determined instead by a complex host of additional factors, meaning there was no guarantee that the two would necessarily be equal at a level of economic activity that produced full employment; (2) rigidities in the economy such as seller monopolies and labor unions thwarted the fluid movement of wages and prices, thus preventing the smooth adjustment assumed by the classical model. Keynes believed that laborers operated under "money illusion," meaning their behavior was related to the money wage (W) rather than to the real wage (W/P) they received. Because workers would *refuse* to take cuts in their money wages, he reasoned, the self-equilibrating tendencies of the classical model would not work. Because the level of employment was *inversely* related to the real wage rate (on this Keynes and the classics agreed), the refusal of laborers to take money wage cuts was a direct denial of the classical wage-rate-adjustment mechanism.

Keynes pushed the argument further, arguing that even if workers were prepared to take cuts in their money wages, such wage cuts meant lower real wages and increased employment (a movement down the demand curve for labor) if and only if prices remained constant. But prices could not remain constant in the face of falling money wages since lower wage incomes mean less demand for goods and services, which in turn forces prices down. Now if prices fall at the same time that wages fall, real wages (and therefore employment) might not change (unless the Keynes effect, which we shall consider later on, was operative). In other words, Keynes felt that the adjustment of money wage rates was ineffective in reducing unemployment.

Keynes believed that unemployment could be efficiently attacked only by manipulating aggregate demand. Given stable money wage rates workers would be willing to accept increases in prices that resulted from an increase in demand. Such increases would *lower* real wages, thereby stimulating employment. Keynes turned the classical proposition around. Employment is not increased by lowering real wages, but real wages will fall when employment increases due to greater aggregate demand. A more complete explanation of this important point will be given later in this chapter, but in order to understand Keynes's critique of classical employment theory, we must first look at some distinctly Keynesian inventions that laid the groundwork for his system. First we look at a concept to which we have already alluded, aggregate demand.

Aggregate Demand

In reformulating the concept of aggregate demand Keynes turned away from the quantity-theory-of-money framework favored by the classics and embarked on a new approach that stressed the component parts of aggregate expenditures. The first major component he analyzed was aggregate consumption, which took the name of *consumption function*. A consumption function relates the consumption of all private goods and services to the aggregate level of income in a positive way. It is conveniently expressed as $C = f(Y)$, to be read as consumption (C) is a function of aggregate income (Y). Consumption, as Keynes well knew, is related to a host of other factors—price expectations, the utility of saving for future consumption versus present consumption, income expectations, institutions, habits, and so on. But Keynes wished to hold these other variables in abeyance in order to look at the close connection of consumption and income. Aggregate income is generated by returns to the factors of production (i.e., wages, interest, rent, and profits) and as such may be consumed or saved. It follows, therefore, that saving, too, is a function of income in the same manner as consumption. Figure 21-2 gives graphic representation to these Keynesian functions.

The assumptions Keynes made with respect to these functions are as follows. The *average propensity to consume* (i.e., total consumption divided by total income) declines as income falls. However, the *marginal propensity to consume*, or the ratio of a change in consumption to an incremental change in income (i.e., $\Delta c/\Delta y$)

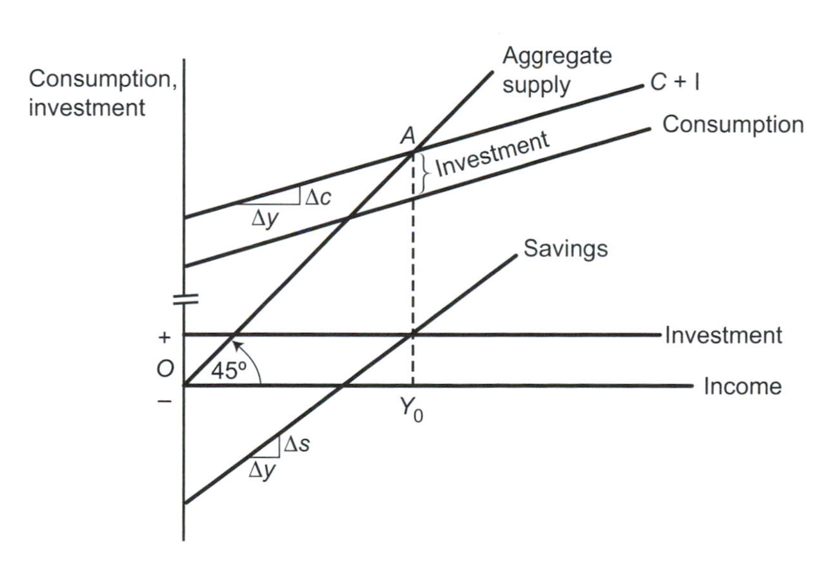

Figure 21-2 The intersection of aggregate demand and aggregate supply schedules (point *A*) determines an equilibrium level of income, Y_0. If income exceeds Y_0, then aggregate supply will exceed aggregate demand.

remains constant. Any alteration in the marginal propensity to consume would create alterations (shifts or rotations) in the consumption and savings functions. Any of the aforementioned nonincome determinants of consumption (tastes, price, and income expectations) would have this effect.

Keynes defined an aggregate supply function as the aggregate supply price of output from employment of N workers, or $Z = \varphi(N)$ in functional notation. This function is represented by a 45° line in figure 21-2, so that the demand for goods at given prices exactly equals the supply of goods.[6] In addition to consumption, the total aggregate demand for goods and services in the private sector also includes investment (i.e., demand for plant, equipment, etc.). Keynes believed that for the most part (at least in the short run) investment spending could be regarded as autonomous, or independent of the level of income. This assumption might be reasonable if large businesses make long-term investment commitments irrespective of purely short-term income conditions. Autonomous investment assumes the shape of a horizontal line, as shown in figure 21-2. When added to the consumption function, total demand takes the form of $C + I$, which represents the vertical sum of consumption and investment at each level of aggregate income.

If we confine our analysis to a closed (no external trade), private-sector (no government) economy, we can identify equilibrium level of income Y_0 at the intersection of aggregate demand ($C + I$) and aggregate supply (45° line). At point A the aggregate sale proceeds of Y_0 level of output precisely equal the aggregate cost (factor payments) of producing output Y_0. If the level of income were greater than Y_0, aggregate supply would exceed aggregate demand. In other words, the aggregate cost of producing that higher level of output would exceed the receipts obtainable from consumption and investment expenditures at that level. This is so because consumption would not increase sufficiently to absorb the increased supply. Barring price changes (which are ignored in this simple model), unsold inventories would pile up, and entrepreneurs would cut back production to Y_0. For the opposite and analogous reason, output would increase to Y_0 should it temporarily fall below Y_0. The aggregate output level is thus considered stable. A central element in Keynes's theory is that the economy could reach a stable equilibrium output level, such as Y_0, but it would not necessarily constitute a full-employment level of national output. An economy could be, Keynes concluded, in an "unemployment equilibrium." This conclusion was totally at odds with classical economic theory.

The Role of Investment

The simple Keynesian model outlined in the preceding section ignores two major sectors of a modern economy: government and international trade. Keynes kept things simple at the outset in order to establish the essential working components of his "new" theory. Of the two components of aggregate demand recognized so far, Keynes viewed investment demands as by far the more volatile. Investment demands are determined by a host of factors besides the interest rate, including expected future returns. Indeed, a well-known Keynesian concept, the *marginal efficiency of capital* (actually investment), relates the cost of investment capital to the expected returns over the life of investment projects. Expectations, often volatile and dependent on capricious psychological factors, have direct, important effects on investment and hence on income.

[6] This representation departs from standard theory in which aggregate supply is a function setting output produced against alternative *price levels* of output.

A more fundamental problem at the heart of Keynes's alternative theory is that expenditures have multiple (repetitive) effects on income. A change in investment expenditures, for example, does not result in a "one-shot" change in income by the amount of the spending change but, rather, by some multiple. Keynesian macroeconomics therefore sought to account for these multiplier effects. In order to grasp the basic principle of a spending multiplier, consider figure 21-3, which is similar to the one preceding it. The initial spending level, $C + I$, determines an equilibrium level of income Y_0. This level is stable in the sense described in the previous section. Now, suppose that one of the determinants of investment changes—say, expectations—and that investment increases from I to I' by an amount labeled ΔI. The effect on total expenditures causes an upward shift in the aggregate demand function to the level $C + I'$, causing a new equilibrium to be reached at Y_1.

The multiplier effect is theoretically predictable because it depends on the numerical value of the marginal propensity to consume. The dependence is easily explained. The initial injection of investment (ΔI) is received as income by factor-share recipients. That means that income is increased by ΔI. These recipients have marginal propensities to consume and save that, of necessity, add up to 1. Imagine that the marginal propensity to consume is 75 percent, in which case 75 percent of the initial new receipt of income is spent. At this point income is generated in the amount $\Delta I + 3/4(\Delta I)$. But the process does not stop there. The $3/4(\Delta I)$ spent by the initial recipients is received as income by other factors, who spend a portion and save a portion.

Multiple rounds of spending are thereby touched off by a single injection of expenditure into the system. When the process approaches the limit, the change in income ΔY is equal to $1/(1 - MPC)$, or, in our example, $1/(1 - 3/4) = 4$, *times* the initial investment increase. If the initial investment injection was $10 billion, the ultimate change in income would be $40 billion. The value of the multiplier is obviously 4. If we designate this multiplier as k, then it follows that $k = \Delta Y/\Delta I$.

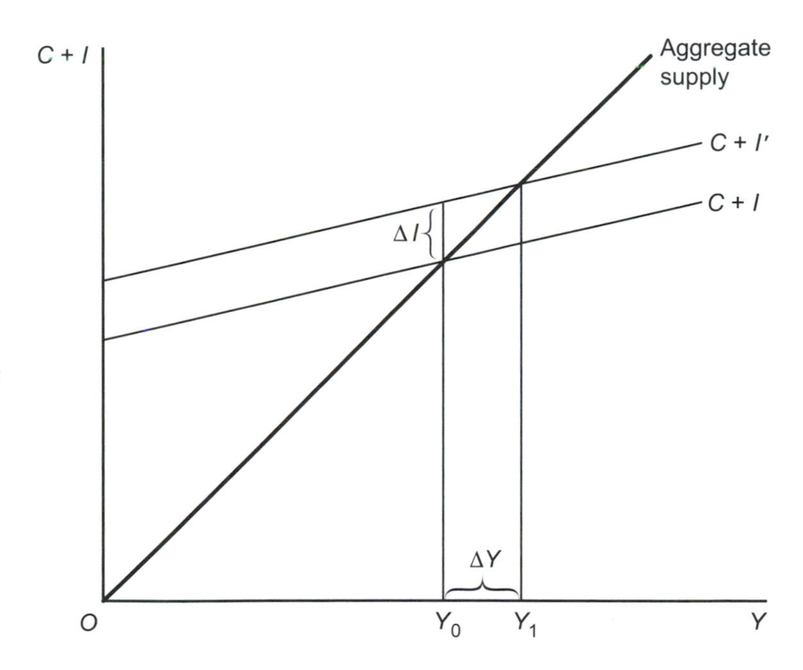

Figure 21-3
If investment increases from I to I', the aggregate demand function will shift upward by ΔI. Income will also increase from Y_0 to Y_1.

It can be seen, therefore, that following Keynesian logic, the capriciousness of private investment, coupled with its multiplier effects on income, means that prediction of aggregate income is complex and difficult. But even if income levels and changes could be predicted with a high degree of accuracy, such levels would only be full-employment levels *by accident*. To see why, we delve a bit deeper into Keynes's theory.

Unemployment Equilibrium

The classical writers believed that the demand for labor was equivalent to the marginal productivity of labor and that labor supply was an increasing function of the real wage. This classical view of labor functions is reproduced in figure 21-4*a*. Equilibrium real wage $(W/P)_0$ produces full employment of labor inputs N_0. Should the equilibrium real wage be displaced, say, to $(W/P)_1$, unemployment would occur in the amount *AB*. Workers would competitively bid the money wage down and reestablish full employment at N_0.

We have already seen that Keynes rejected this hypothesis. He argued that laborers could be involuntarily unemployed. Theoretically, Keynes accepted the classical notion of the demand for labor as determined by labor's marginal product. But he insisted workers were motivated to supply labor by the money wage offered, not the real wage. And because workers suffered from money illusion they would not take cuts in their prevailing money wage. These premises are incorporated into figure 21-4*b*, where money wage W_0 is a floor. The employment level N^* represents full employment of labor, and the labor demand functions D_N and D'_N are now the value of the marginal product of labor (because the demand is set against the money wage instead of against the real wage).

The question is whether there could be any involuntary unemployment in the economic system. The classical economists recognized that at an equilibrium real wage, such as $(W/P)_0$ in figure 21-4*a*, voluntary and frictional unemployment could exist. Unemployment could be voluntary in the sense that certain amounts of labor would choose to exempt themselves from the labor force at wage $(W/P)_0$. But Keynes viewed the matter differently. In figure 21-4*b*, labor would supply quantity

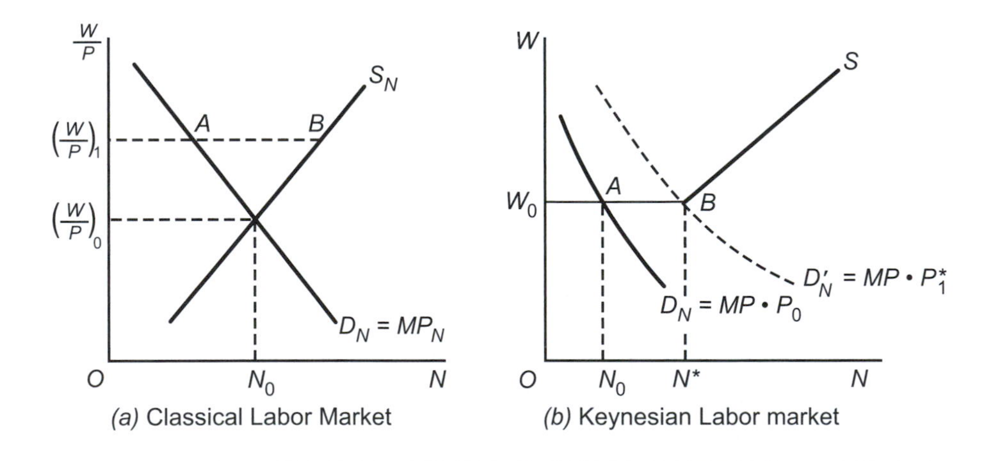

Figure 21-4 The classical labor market automatically adjusts itself to full employment, whereas the Keynesian labor market does not automatically adjust.

N^* at money wage W_0, but demand might be such that only a lesser quantity N_0 would be demanded at real wage $(W/P)_0$. The result would be what Keynes called "involuntary unemployment." Here we have the anomalous effect that labor is involuntarily unemployed in the amount *AB*, and yet the labor market is in equilibrium in the sense that no automatic tendency for employment to change from N_0 could be expected. No unique full-employment level of output could be presupposed, therefore. Economy-wide equilibrium could be achieved at any labor utilization level. Laborers, in the first place, would not take money wage cuts, thereby reducing the real wage rate for increased employment. In the second place, even if they did, prices would likely fall in the same proportion, causing the labor demand function to shift to the left and leaving the unemployment level unchanged.

Thus, a situation like that described in figures 21-5*a* and 21-5*b* might be observed. Outputs Y_0 and Y^* are functions of inputs (labor and capital). An equilibrium occurs at input and output levels N_0 and Y_0, but at these levels involuntary unemployment exists in the amount *AB*. Aggregate demand would have to increase by *MN* in order to bring the economy to full employment. Keynes believed that private investment alone would not be likely to bring this about, and he suggested compensatory government expenditures and taxation (fiscal policy) in order to relieve unemployment and underproduction. We will discuss these aspects of Keynesian policy later, but before that we must probe further into Keynes's beliefs about individuals' motivations for holding money and how they respond to monetary changes.

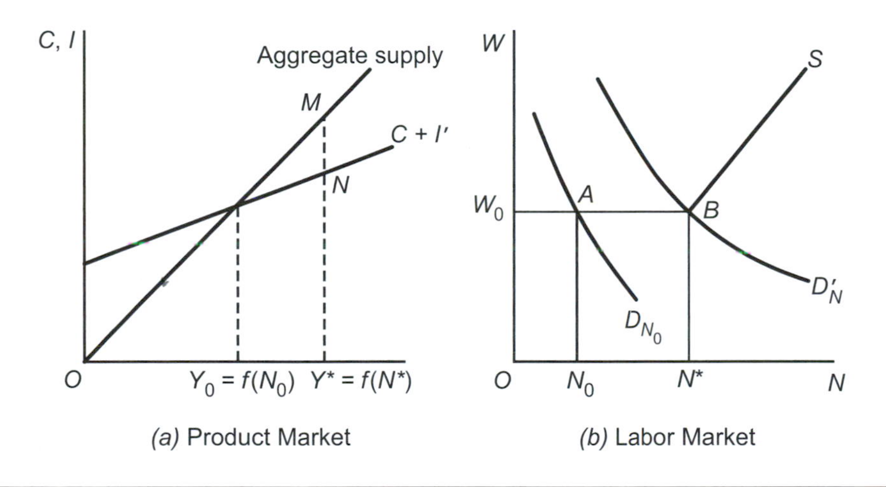

Figure 21-5 At equilibrium levels N_0 and Y_0, involuntary unemployment exists in the amount *AB*. Aggregate demand would have to increase by *MN* to bring the economy to full employment.

Liquidity Preference and the Role of Money in the Keynesian System

The neoclassical economists adhered to a long-established and well-known theory about money, the so-called quantity theory of money. The oldest version of the theory was given shorthand expression by the equation, $MV = PY$, where *M* stands for the stock of money, V for velocity (annual turnover of the money stock), P for the price level, and Y for some index of aggregate output. Keynes himself had adhered to the Cambridge version early in his academic life. The Cambridge equation, $M = kPY$, is a simple mathematical transformation of the older version but emphasizes holding money for transaction purposes (k is the *reciprocal* of velocity and represents the demand for transactions balances). In the typical treatment, people were assumed to hold a constant proportion of their income as cash to finance transactions. As incomes rise, people hold more cash, but the cash-balance proportion of higher incomes remains the same. An increase in transactions demand for money, or an increase in the average amount of cash balances individuals hold as a percentage of income, means that velocity, or the turnover of the average dollar facilitating national income, is reduced.

Economists before Keynes did not regard velocity as a strict numerical constant, but they did assert that it was relatively stable and predictable. If true, the implications for economic theory and policy are clear. If V is constant or predictable, M is controllable, and P is (relatively) stable up to full employment, then M can be adjusted to produce changes in income (Y) when there are unemployed resources in the economy.[7] Keynes accepted the premise that people hold money for transactions purposes and that the transactions demand for money is related to income. He argued, however, that individuals hold money for other reasons as well and that an important reason to hold money is to speculate in the bond market. In other words, while the classical economists considered that individuals hold money for transactions and even for precautionary (saving for a rainy day) motives, Keynes argued that they would hold money as an alternative to holding bonds. He called this "liquidity preference" and asserted that the chief determinant of speculative money balances is the interest rate, not income. This is because the interest rate represents the opportunity cost of holding cash balances.

Figure 21-6 shows a typical liquidity preference function, L_S. In this representation the only alternative to holding money is to hold bonds. Keynes theorized that at high interest rates (i.e., low bond prices) individuals would prefer to hold bonds rather than money because the opportunity cost of holding money is relatively high. As the interest rate falls, however, bond prices rise, pushing down their yields and making bonds less attractive to buy. But now *selling* bonds becomes more attractive because of the rise in bond prices (capital gains). Thus, as the interest rate falls individuals will choose to hold more of their assets in the form of money and less in the form of bonds. This inverse relationship between interest rates and money holdings is traced out by L_S in figure 21-6.

Keynes's demand for money function has a unique feature, namely the liquidity trap, which is represented by the horizontal portion of the liquidity preference function. Keynes's followers emphasized this feature far more than Keynes himself, but the argument is clearly his. He had argued in the *General Theory* that the interest rate might fall so low (price of bonds so high) as to induce all investors to withdraw from the bond market. Everyone, in short, would want to hold the *more liquid asset*, money. If this were indeed the case, it means that there is a kind of floor to interest

[7] At all other times, of course, the classical economists viewed money as having a stabilizing role and as oiling the wheels of trade. Proposals by Milton Friedman and others, related to a rule of a constant growth rate in the money stock, reflect this traditional concern; see chapter 22 for more details.

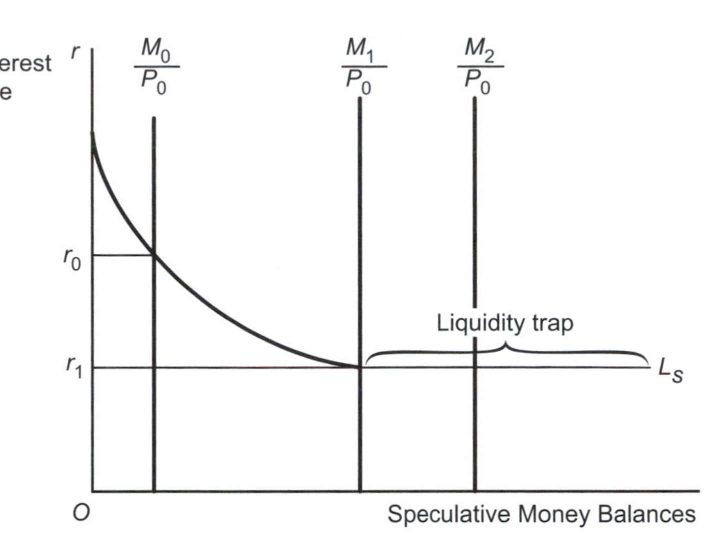

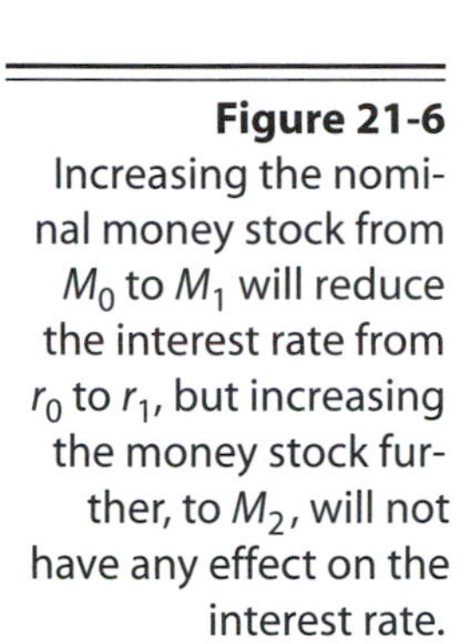

Figure 21-6
Increasing the nominal money stock from M_0 to M_1 will reduce the interest rate from r_0 to r_1, but increasing the money stock further, to M_2, will not have any effect on the interest rate.

rates so that below that level, no further reductions in the interest rate can induce more capital investment via the bond market.[8]

What has all this to do with monetary policy and its effectiveness? Keynes argued that although the rate of interest was determined by a combination of real and monetary factors in the economic system, the existence of the speculative demand for money meant that the mechanism by which money influenced income and employment in the economic system was not as simple and predictable as the classical economists believed. Specifically, one of the major impacts of money on spending, income, and employment was through its effect on interest rates. Lower interest rates ordinarily meant, *ceteris paribus*, higher levels of investment and consumption (since lower interest rates made present consumption more attractive relative to future consumption, i.e., saving). Typically, monetary policy might lower the interest rate and thereby increase spending to a full-employment level.

Consider a liquidity trap in place, as in figure 21-6. If there is unemployment at the prevailing interest rate r_0 the standard economic argument is that increasing the real money stock (M/P) drives down the equilibrium interest rate and stimulates more business investment. If prices remain the same, the real money stock can be increased by increasing the nominal money stock (M). Hence the increase from M_0 to M_1, assuming that prices remain constant, reduces the interest rate from r_0 to r_1. So far, so good. But if unemployment exists at interest rate r_1, the same policy will not work. Increases in the real money supply from that point (e.g., from M_1/P_0 to M_2/P_0) do not lead to a change in the interest rate because the return on investment is considered too low to be worth the risk. Hence, society will hold all the new assets in the form of money balances. Since the interest rate does not fall, investment and consumption—for this reason at least—will be unaffected. Given the liquidity trap, Keynes concluded that monetary policy designed to work through interest rate changes is helpless in the face of widespread unemployment and a depressed economy.

[8] Sir Dennis Robertson once provided an amusing description of the liquidity trap: "The rate of interest is what it is because it is expected to become other than it is; if it is not expected to become other than it is, there is nothing left to tell us why it is what it is" (*Essays*, p. 174).

Prices: Flexible or Inflexible?

Did the liquidity trap exist? Keynes and many of his followers believed that the monetary and psychological conditions accompanying the Great Depression suggested the existence of such a trap. (Subsequent empirical evidence does not support the existence of a trap.) For this reason and a bevy of other reasons, Keynes rejected a policy that relied solely on monetary measures and supported a strong fiscal policy instead to promote economic stabilization. Whether intended or not, his stance then created a bias toward fiscal policy to combat recessions ever since.

We turn now to theoretical matters regarding prices and stabilization. We saw earlier that Keynes regarded prices as fairly inflexible downward, which he attributed to resistance maintained by monopoly elements and collusive practices in several segments of the economy. But what if prices were flexible downward? As a theoretical proposition, Keynes agreed that falling prices could improve the situation faced by a depressed economy. In fact, this phenomenon has taken the name of the *Keynes effect*. If the money stock is held constant, a reduction in prices would increase the real stock (M/P) of money. As is easily seen from figure 21-6, the interest rate would fall with a constant M and a lower P. If the economy does not face a liquidity trap and investors and consumers are in fact responsive to lower interest rates, a greater stock of real money would have the effect of raising the level of aggregate demand, income, and employment (as, indeed, the classics argued).

While Keynes agreed in theory, he chose to stress the practical effects of falling prices. He appeared to believe that a declining price level would have other, opposite, and harmful effects on the economy. For example, falling prices would have the effect of raising the real level of fixed business indebtedness. Moreover, falling prices could be extremely detrimental to business expectations regarding future profits. Because he believed that aggregate investment is conditioned largely by price and profit expectations, a rapid decline in the price level may, practically speaking, reduce the level of investment even in the face of declining interest rates. Bankruptcies and adverse business conditions would almost certainly follow falling prices. In sum, Keynes did not believe that economic catastrophe could be averted merely by a flexible and falling price level.

Fiscal versus Monetary Policy

As the whole tenor of our discussion reveals, Keynes did not regard the economic mechanisms of the private sector as infallible guards against prolonged unemployment. He believed an economy could be stuck in an unemployment equilibrium. The existence of downwardly flexible wages and prices could not be assured and, even if it could, it would not guarantee full employment. Because of other limitations established by the investment function and the liquidity trap, monetary policy was not reliable as a corrective measure. How, then, might the unemployment gap in aggregate demand (see *MN* in figure 21-5*a*) be bridged?

If one is convinced that solutions will not come from the private sector or from the monetary authorities, where else do you look except the government sector? Backed by his theoretical arguments, Keynes asserted the government should use its powers to tax and spend in order to influence the business cycle. Government spending is a direct injection of public investment into the income stream. Government spending could be financed by taxation (which would reduce consumption, but by less than the amount of the tax), by the sale of bonds to the Federal Reserve, or by some other means. The income- and employment-generative effects of all these alternatives could then be assessed and action taken to achieve economic stability.

Keynes did not believe that single injections, or "pump priming," would be enough to correct a seriously depressed economy. What was required was a full-scale and planned program of discretionary fiscal policy as well as a strengthening of built-in stabilizers (such as progressive taxation). The government must stand ready, in short, to provide the conditions for full employment. Keynes's basic message is clear. He believed in fiscal activism. (For a challenge on this posture from one of Keynes's contemporaries, see the box, Method Squabbles 5: Twentieth-Century Titans, Keynes vs. Schumpeter.)

Method Squabbles 5: Twentieth-Century Titans, Keynes vs. Schumpeter

Joseph A. Schumpeter (1883–1950) and John Maynard Keynes (1883–1946) were born only a few months apart. But each was schooled in a different tradition, and both may, for very different reasons, be justly viewed as the most important and influential economists of the twentieth century.

Keynes, as we have seen in this chapter, was a "Cambridge man" all the way—ensconced within the great English neoclassical tradition identified with Alfred Marshall. Although he later rejected the Marshallian mode of "equilibrium theorizing," Keynes cannot be understood apart from the Cambridge tradition. His great insight rested on the central abstraction of aggregate demand. Keynes believed, unlike his Cambridge predecessors, that insufficient demand (i.e., aggregate spending) by consumers and investors would leave the economy in a kind of perverse equilibrium, stagnating permanently below full employment. In consequence, as discussed in this chapter, Keynes focused on means to increase demand through government policies and interventions in the economy. How far Keynes would go to achieve these results is uncertain, although today's governments in the Western World have embraced deficit finance as a way of life. We know that Keynes himself was distrustful of central planning, although he most certainly underestimated the strength of bureaucratic and political incentives.*

Schumpeter was different on all counts. Steeped in the Austrian tradition of Carl Menger, Frederick von Wieser, and Eugen Böhm-Bawerk, Schumpeter wrote a brilliant doctoral dissertation in 1911, *The Theory of Economic Development* (see chapter 23), which, later translated into English, brought him worldwide attention as a leading economic theorist. After World War I, Schumpeter served as Austria's finance minister, and throughout the 1920s, he lectured across Europe, with a protracted stay in England. In 1932 he emigrated to the United States to escape Nazi persecution. He joined the faculty at Harvard University, where he remained until his death in 1950.

Both theorists had their eyes on macroeconomics. Whereas Keynes might be said to have played the role of economist-tinkerer in rescuing a stagnant economy, Schumpeter elevated the entrepreneur's role to the prime mover of economic development. Keynes viewed the economy chiefly as an abstraction wherein individuals could be cleverly manipulated by government actions designed to produce full-employment equilibrium. Schumpeter, in contrast, viewed the economy from "below"—from the perspective of individuals whose risk-taking and profit-seeking behavior spurred innovations and new growth opportunities. Accordingly, Schumpeter looked for ways to ensure free enterprise, not to manage it. In Austrian fashion he understood the essence of capitalism as a process that held the keys to prosperity. Stationary state equilibria did not interest him. Schumpeter said: "The problem that is usually being visualized is how capitalism administers existing structures, whereas the relevant problem is how it creates and destroys them."†

(continued)

To Schumpeter, the tendency of an economy to fall below levels of full employment resulted from shrinking opportunities to earn profits. As breakthroughs in technology or production occur they inspire new investment and greater opportunities for profit, thus generating economic development. In such a dynamic economy, government intervention and central control are impediments to the growth process. Far more mistrustful than Keynes of the results of fiscal management, Schumpeter argued that tyranny would inevitably follow government intervention. In his mind, the first victim of such tyranny would be the entrepreneurial spirit.

The opposing views of Keynes and Schumpeter have shaped virtually all twentieth-century thinking, debate, and policy regarding the role of government in the economy. Moreover, these debates continue. They rage on a daily basis in various guises in newspapers, on TV talk shows, and in blogs. As such, the essential concerns of both Keynes and Schumpeter live on.

*He wrote the following in response to criticisms by economist Friedrich Hayek that an overplanned economy represents tyranny: "Moderate planning will be safe enough if those carrying it out are rightly oriented in their own minds and hearts to the moral issue [of tyranny]" (quoted in Robert Heilbroner, *The Worldly Philosophers*, p. 244). This opinion is visionary but dubious in a world where Marshallian self-interest applies to both politicians and bureaucrats. Empirically, we know that extreme forms of planning have not worked in Eastern Europe and the (former) Soviet Union.

†See Joseph A. Schumpeter, *Capitalism, Socialism, and Democracy*, p. 81.

Eventually, all these ideas became part of a new economic orthodoxy. Even the most academically untrained legislator in today's advanced economies is at least aware of Keynesian policy prescriptions, if not of their theoretical underpinnings. Keynes's ideas eventually permeated most institutions of higher learning in the United States and elsewhere during the postwar period. They were commonplace in the United States thanks to their relatively early introduction into one of the most successful contemporary textbooks since Alfred Marshall's *Principles*—Paul Samuelson's *Economics* (1st ed., 1948).

Of course Keynesian economic analysis has been continuously tinkered with, refined, remolded, criticized, and/or maligned. There is even an academic journal, the *Journal of Post-Keynesian Economics* devoted to the mission of refining and extended Keynesian ideas. Nevertheless, as we shall see in the next chapter, monetarism reemerged, especially in the 1970s and early 1980s, as a substantive and significant challenge to the Keynesian vision. Just as Marshall's *Principles* was the subject of heated discussion after its publication in 1890, so Keynes's *General Theory* has undergone a similar fate.

■ Paradigm Shift or Paradigm Realignment?

In a seminal work entitled *The Structure of Scientific Revolutions*, Thomas Kuhn explained that the introduction of new paradigms of thought, such as the Keynesian model, occurs when old paradigms are no longer capable of providing good answers to the questions posed to them. But old paradigms are often firmly entrenched, and their defenders frequently rise to protect them and show that a paradigm that is considered new may really be just a subset of an old one (thereby, of course, renewing and rejuvenating it). It appears that, to a certain extent, Kuhn's theory of the nature of ideational progress fits the case of John Maynard Keynes.

Recall that Keynes used A. C. Pigou's *Theory of Unemployment* as his straw man in attacking the classical model. But one of Pigou's ideas, widely known as the "Pigou effect" and later as the "real-balance effect," continues to haunt Keynesian theory. Keynes had argued that prices and wages were not flexible downward because of the agglomeration of monopoly power on both the input and the output sides of the market. But he argued further that price and wage declines would likely not increase income and employment because declining wages would lead to declining prices (since declining wage income means reduced demand for final output), which would mean that the real wage would not be reduced appreciably. The Keynes effect, discussed above, was a theoretical possibility, but its impact was limited by the inelasticity of the investment function and by the liquidity trap, discounting all the practical difficulties with falling prices.

Pigou, however, had identified another effect of falling prices. When prices fall, individuals' real balances rise—that is, the real value of their money holdings (M/P) increases—thereby creating a wealth effect that serves to stimulate consumption. In short, consumption will increase with increases in real balances. A beach bum with $1 to his name can become a millionaire (in real terms) if the price level falls low enough. The theoretical conclusion is inescapable. With falling prices the Keynes effect might be rendered impotent by the liquidity trap and an inelastic investment function, but the Pigou effect would kick in. A falling price level, therefore, should be capable of generating increased expenditures that would push the economy toward full employment.

As a theoretical proposition, then, the Pigou effect saves neoclassical theory. Don Patinkin reached this conclusion in his doctoral dissertation at the University of Chicago in 1947. Patinkin published his elegant and systematic analysis in 1956 in an important book, *Money, Interest and Prices*. Utilizing a Walrasian general-equilibrium model comprised of three markets (money, commodities, and bonds), a Keynesian expenditure approach (in the commodity market), and an expanded Pigou effect, Patinkin persuasively demonstrated the theoretical consistency of neoclassical macroeconomics.

Patinkin's analysis is at a high theoretical level that puts it beyond the reach of nonspecialists, but his conclusions are clear—namely: (1) given the classical assumptions of full employment and price flexibility, and the absence of money illusion, the conclusions of the quantity theory of money are valid; (2) Keynes's analysis of the speculative motive for holding money was a genuine contribution but its introduction (unless money illusion is introduced) does *not* upset the conclusions of neoclassical macroeconomic theory; and (3) because of the stickiness of prices and wages in an actual economic system, Keynesian policy prescriptions have merit. Though Patinkin's contribution was promptly dubbed "Much Ado about Pigou," its importance lies in its thoroughness and in its clear exposition of the assumptions by which Keynes obtained his results. Patinkin demonstrated how the speculative demand for money along with the expenditure approach to national income, as well as other Keynesian ideas, could be worked under the umbrella of neoclassicism, thereby exposing the alleged weakness of naive neoclassical economics.

■ Conclusion

The emergence of the Keynesian paradigm (in modern dress) as a preferred model is problematic because so much depends on empirical estimates of the elasticities of the theoretical functions in question—estimates that are difficult and sometimes impossible to obtain. Price declines of the type required by the Pigou effect for full employment are not within our historical experience, and even if feasible, they may present the same practical difficulties required for the Keynes effect. Thus, the Keynesian model itself rests in limbo, but there are strong indications that the rejuvenated neoclassical model is beginning to win the day theoretically. It is no secret that in matters of policy, Keynesian ideas on compensatory finance became the reigning economic orthodoxy in the twentieth century. Orthodox Keynesians viewed the Employment Act of 1946 as a victory, but it was merely a beginning. Keynesian ideas continue to permeate the highest policy echelons of government, especially during Democratic administrations. Most presidential economic advisers have been schooled in the tradition of Keynes. As a by-product, mountains of data on unemployment, income, and expenditures have been built up for use by the policy makers.

Where, then, does Keynes belong in the history of economic thought? As noted in the introduction, only a tentative assessment is possible at such close distance, but several facts do stand out. At the very least, Keynes is, and probably will continue to be, an important figure in the history of economic thought. Apart from the charismatic quality of Keynesian ideas, out of which a veritable modern legend has developed, Keynes was an influential economist. Between the ridiculous excesses of certain Keynesians and the apologetics of certain neoclassicists (who refuse to find anything of value in Keynes), there is at least a minimum legacy. This legacy is one of focus on macroeconomic theory and the policy issues it engenders inside and outside the professional discipline of economics. In many ways, Keynes was a catalyst. The tremendous resurgence of interest in monetarism (and in other macroeconomic concepts) might not have been possible without the counterpoint of Keynesian thought and policy. He did not live to see the massive influence of his ideas, but politicians, economists, citizen-taxpayers, and historians of economic thought have been subjected to his influence. In season and out, Keynes stirred the waters of economic ideas.

References

Davis, J. Ronnie. *The New Economics and the Old Economists*. Ames: The Iowa State University Press, 1971.

Hansen, Alvin H. *A Guide to Keynes*. New York: McGraw-Hill, 1953.

Harrod, R. F. *The Life of John Maynard Keynes*. New York: Harcourt, Brace, 1951.

Heilbroner, Robert. *The Worldly Philosophers*, rev. ed. New York: Simon & Schuster, 1961.

Hicks, J. R. "Mr. Keynes and the 'Classics': A Suggested Interpretation," *Econometrica*, vol. 5 (April 1937), pp. 147–159.

Keynes, John Maynard. *The General Theory of Employment, Interest and Money*. London: Macmillan, 1936.

Leijonhufvud, Axel. *On Keynesian Economics and the Economics of Keynes*. New York: Oxford University Press, 1968.

Patinkin, Don. *Money, Interest and Prices*, 2d ed. New York: Harper & Row, 1965.

Pigou, A. C. *The Theory of Unemployment*. London: Macmillan 1933.

Robertson, Dennis. *Essays in Money and Interest*. London: Fontana Library, 1966.

Schumpeter, Joseph. *Capitalism, Socialism, and Democracy*, 3d ed. New York: Harper & Row, 1950.

Notes for Further Reading

Although a large and detailed literature exists on Keynes and his ideas, only a small sample can be mentioned here. We shall not attempt to capture all of the post-Keynesian amendments and interpretations of the master's work. Several biographies have been written about Keynes. The standard biography, by someone who knew Keynes personally, is R. F. Harrod, *The Life of John Maynard Keynes* (see references). Also see D. E. Moggridge, *Maynard Keynes: An Economist's Biography* (London: Routledge, 1992), which traces Keynes's career on all its many levels; and Vincent Barnett, *John Maynard Keynes* (London: Routledge, 2012), who argues controversially that a main but often neglected feature of *The General Theory of Employment, Interest and Money* was allowing psychology a much greater role within economics and that Keynes's policy writings were more concerned with Britain's national interest than is sometimes recognized. Barnett also recounts the story of Keynes's colorful private life as a member of the Bloomsbury group of artists and intellectuals. Craufurd D. Goodwin, "The Bloomsbury Group as Creative Community," *History of Political Economy*, vol. 43 (Spring 2011), pp. 59–82, adds background by recognizing the organization of the Bloomsbury group as akin to a policy think tank. Goodwin describes the group's approach to discussions of several social problems, including the place of the arts in developed economies, how to improve the situation of women and minorities, and how to solve environmental problems.

The record on what Keynes was really like still makes interesting and somewhat titillating reading. See Michael Holroyd, *Lytton Strachey: A Critical Biography*, 2 vols. (New York: Holt, 1968), which contains a considerable amount of information on Keynes; E. S. Johnson and H. G. Johnson, *The Shadow of Keynes: Understanding Keynes, Cambridge, and Keynesian Economics* (Chicago: University of Chicago Press, 1978); C. H. Hession, *John Maynard Keynes: A Personal Biography of the Man Who Revolutionized Capitalism and the Way We Live* (New York: Macmillan, 1984); and R. J. A. Skidelsky, *John Maynard Keynes* (New York: Viking, 1986).

Gardner Ackley, *Macroeconomic Theory* (New York: Macmillan, 1961), is a helpful source on traditional Keynesian economics and post-Keynesian developments in cycle, growth, investment, and inflation theory. For an abbreviated summary of aggregate analysis before the *General Theory* see James L. Cochrane, *Macroeconomics before Keynes* (Glenview, IL: Scott Foresman, 1970), who utilizes a model of behavior appropriate to physiocratic, classical, Marxian, and neoclassical macroeconomics, emphasizing anticipators of Keynesian ideas.

The British economist Richard Kahn anticipated Keynes's multiplier analysis, and it now seems clear that a number of Swedish authors, including Erik Lundberg and John Akerman, were toying with ideas very similar to those of Keynes, especially in the field of monetary theory. Otto Steiger, "Bertil Ohlin and the Origins of the Keynesian Revolution," *History of Political Economy*, vol. 8 (Fall 1976), pp. 341–366, plays up the independence of the Stockholm school's writings, which proceeded, according to Steiger, within a neo-Wicksellian framework (see ch. 22 on Wicksell). Michaël Assous, "Kalecki's 1934 Model vs. the IS-LM Model of Hicks (1937) and Modigliani (1944)," *The European Journal of the History of Economic Thought*, vol. 14 (2007), pp. 97–118, argues that Kalecki's 1934 work produced many of the conclusions of neoclassical theory, along with an explanation of unemployment, before the *General Theory* and that Kalecki explained the difference between classical and Keynesian theories without reference to either liquidity preference or the rigidity of wages.

The origins of a stock-in-trade of (what has been thought to be) Keynesian fiscal theory—the balanced budget multiplier—is explored in two early papers by William A. Salant and Jørgen Gelting, with commentaries by Walter S. Salant, Bent Hansen, and Paul Samuelson: see "Origins of the Balanced-Budget Multiplier, I–IV," *History of Politi-*

cal Economy, vol. 7 (Spring 1975), pp. 3–55. J. Ronnie Davis, *The New Economics and the Old Economists* (see references), argues that Keynes was "scooped" by Chicago economists of the early thirties in regard to fiscal policy. See also B. L. Jones, "Lauchlin Currie and the Causes of the 1937 Recession," *History of Political Economy*, vol. 12 (Fall 1980), pp. 303–315. According to R. T. Nash and W. P. Gramm, "A Neglected Statement of the Paradox of Thrift," *History of Political Economy*, vol. 1 (Fall 1969), pp. 395–400, John M. Robertson, an underconsumptionist and pre-Keynesian philosopher, stated the paradox of thrift as early as 1892.

Of special interest in appreciating Keynes's differences with classical writers is John R. Hicks (see references). In a similar vein, see B. T. McCallum, "On the Observational Inequivalence of Classical and Keynesian Models," *Journal of Political Economy*, vol. 87 (April 1979), pp. 395–402. For an ambitious attempt to explain the logic of Keynes's rejection of the classical model, see Michel Rosier, "The Logic of Keynes' Criticism of the *Classical* Model," *The European Journal of the History of Economic Thought*, vol. 9 (Winter 2002), pp. 608–643. Alessandro Roncaglia, "Keynes and Probability: An Assessment," *The European Journal of the History of Economic Thought*, vol. 16 (2009), pp. 489–510, presents an overview of Keynes's contributions to probability theory, particularly in light of the classical and frequentist theories of probability and the criticisms they received.

Important post-Keynesian developments in the area of economic dynamics include P. A. Samuelson, "Interactions between the Multiplier Analysis and the Principle of Acceleration," *Review of Economics and Statistics*, vol. 21 (May 1939), pp. 75–78; and J. R. Hicks, *A Contribution to the Theory of the Trade Cycle* (London: Oxford, 1950). Also see M. Fisher, "Professor Hicks and the Keynesians," *Economica*, vol. 43 (August 1976), pp. 305–414; and Paul Mizen and J. R. Presley, "Keynes, Hicks, and the Cambridge School," *History of Political Economy*, vol. 30 (Spring 1998), pp. 1–16. Keynes's emphasis on consumption as the major component of total spending initiated a number of alternative formulations of consumption. For example, see J. S. Duesenberry, *Income, Saving, and the Theory of Consumer Behavior* (Cambridge, MA: Harvard University Press, 1949); and Milton Friedman, *A Theory of the Consumption Function* (Princeton, NJ: Princeton University Press, 1957).

Detailed assessments of Keynesian economics abound. A provocative place to begin is T. D. Togati, "Keynes as the Einstein of Economic Theory," *History of Political Economy*, vol. 33 (Spring 2001), pp. 117–138. Luigi Pasinetti and Bertram Schefold (eds.), *The Impact of Keynes on Economics in the Twentieth Century* (Cheltenham, UK: Edward Elgar, 1999), explore Keynes's legacy to economics. On the genesis and subsequent evolution of Keynes's ideas, see D. E. Moggridge, "From the *Treatise* to the *General Theory*: An Exercise in Chronology," *History of Political Economy*, vol. 5 (Spring 1973), pp. 72–88; D. Patinkin, "John Maynard Keynes: From the *Tract* to the *General Theory*," *Economic Journal*, vol. 85 (June 1975), pp. 249–271; Robert W. Dimand, *The Origins of the Keynesian Revolution: The Development of Keynes's Theory of Employment and Output* (Aldershot, UK: Edward Elgar, 1988), which also traces the development of Keynes's monetary theory as it progressed from the *Tract* through the *Treatise* to the *General Theory*. Other treatments of a similar nature include Harry G. Johnson, "Keynes' *General Theory*: A Revolution or War of Independence?" *Canadian Journal of Economics*, vol. 9 (November 1976), pp. 580–594; Maria Cristina Marcuzzo, "The Collaboration Between J. M. Keynes and R. F. Kahn From the *Treatise* to the *General Theory*," *History of Political Economy*, vol. 34 (Summer 2002), pp. 421–447, who concludes on the basis of correspondence that relations between these two authors were strong, continuous, and fertile, with the student (Kahn) playing the inverted role of correcting, testing, and refining the master's ideas.

Numerous assessments of Keynesian economics appeared in the 1960s as Keynes's influence in the United States grew. Three are mentioned here: Harry G. Johnson, "The *General Theory* after Twenty-Five Years," *American Economic Review*, vol. 51 (May

1961), pp. 1–17; Robert Lekachman (ed.), *Keynes' General Theory: Reports of Three Decades* (New York: St. Martin's, 1964); and, in a much more critical vein, David McCord Wright, *The Keynesian System* (New York: Fordham University Press, 1961). On the relevance of Keynes for successive generations, see James Tobin, "How Dead Is Keynes?" *Economic Inquiry*, vol. 15 (October 1977), pp. 459–468; and for a glimpse of Keynes's thought in his later years, see John B. Davis, "Keynes's Later Philosophy," *History of Political Economy*, vol. 27 (Summer 1995), pp. 237–260.

Some elaborations and/or clarifications of Keynes's work include: Volker Caspari, "A Marshallian Perspective of Keynes's *General Theory*," *Metroeconomica*, vol. 40 (June 1989), pp. 101–118; A. A. Asimakopulos, "The Nature and Role of Equilibrium in Keynes's *General Theory*," *Australian Economic Papers*, vol. 28 (June 1989), pp. 16–28; M. E. Brady, "The Mathematical Development of Keynes's Aggregate Supply Function in the *General Theory*," *History of Political Economy*, vol. 22 (Spring 1990), pp. 167–172; Bill Gerrard, "Beyond Rational Expectations: A Constructive Interpretation of Keynes's Analysis of Behaviour Under Uncertainty," *Economic Journal*, vol. 104 (March 1994), pp. 327–337; S. A. Drakopolous, "Keynes's Economic Thought and the Theory of Consumer Behavior," *Scottish Journal of Political Economy*, vol. 39 (August 1992), pp. 318–336; and Kevin D. Hoover, "Relative Wages, Rationality, and Involuntary Unemployment in Keynes's Labor Market," *History of Political Economy*, vol. 27 (Winter 1995), pp. 653–685. Nicola Meccheri, "Wage Behaviour and Unemployment in Keynes' and New Keynesians' Views: A Comparison," *The European Journal of the History of Economic Thought*, vol. 14 (2007), pp. 701–724, compares two strands of New Keynesianism in light of Keynes's own work, concluding that although all parties agree that involuntary unemployment is a central problem, the New Keynesians' views on real and nominal wages and their effects on employment represent a significant departure from the idea developed in the *General Theory*.

Don Patinkin, "A Study of Keynes' Theory of Effective Demand," *Economic Inquiry*, vol. 17 (April 1979), pp. 155–176, touched off a mini-debate on the proper interpretation of Keynes's demand theory. B. Littleboy and G. Mehta, "Patinkin on Keynes's Theory of Effective Demand," *History of Political Economy*, vol. 19 (Summer 1987), pp. 311–328, contend that the theory of effective demand is more completely developed by Keynes in his *Treatise on Money* than Patinkin gives him credit for. Patinkin's rejoinder is contained in *History of Political Economy*, vol. 19 (Winter 1987), pp. 647–658. On the same issue, see also Claudio Sardoni, "Marx and Keynes on Effective Demand and Unemployment," *History of Political Economy*, vol. 18 (Fall 1986), pp. 419–441; and R. X. Chase, "Keynes's Principle(s) of Effective Demand: Redefining His Revolution," *Journal of Economic Issues*, vol. 26 (September 1992), pp. 865–891. Although American post-Keynesians claim to be the most literal interpreters of Keynes, Jochen Hartwig, "Keynes vs. the Post Keynesians on the Principle of Effective Demand," *The European Journal of the History of Economic Thought*, vol. 14 (2007), pp. 725–739, argues that significant differences exist between post-Keynesian versions of the principle of effective demand and Keynes's formulation; he offers an alternative model more in line with Keynes's own views.

Much of Keynesian macroeconomics deals with the theory of investment. The effect of Keynes's notion of uncertainty on calculations of expected yields on investments is discussed by Mark Stohs, "Uncertainty in Keynes' *General Theory*," *History of Political Economy*, vol. 12 (Fall 1980), pp. 372–382, who claims that Keynes rejected the idea of numerical measures of prospective yields but believed some kind of nonnumerical calculation is possible. This interpretation has been questioned by C. A. Garner, "Uncertainty in Keynes' *General Theory*: A Comment," *History of Political Economy*, vol. 15 (Spring 1983), pp. 83–86, followed by Stohs's rejoinder, in which he argues for a modified Cartesian approach to economics. S. F. LeRoy, "Keynes' Theory of Investment," *History of Political Economy*, vol. 15 (Fall 1983), pp. 397–421, tries to elucidate what Keynes "really meant" by his theory of investment. Among other things, LeRoy claims that Keynes had in mind a temporary, general-equilibrium, two-sector model with nonshiftable capital, and that this is at variance with practically all previous interpretations of Keynes's investment theory. The curious diffusion of the idea of the investment multiplier is recounted by Daniele Besomi, "On the Spread of an Idea: The Strange Case of Mr. Harrod and the Multiplier," *History of Political Economy*, vol. 32 (Summer 2000), pp. 347–379.

After Hayek (see chap. 23) joined the faculty at the London School of Economics (LSE), he became the chief intellectual rival of Keynes and his Cambridge coterie. On Keynes's personal and professional relations with LSE in 1920–1946, see Susan Howson, "Keynes and the LSE Economists," *Journal of the History of Economic Thought*, vol. 31 (September 2009), pp. 257–280, which deals mostly with the LSE economists' reactions to Keynes, as opposed to Keynes's opinions of them. Howson claims that Hayek briefly "inoculated" the LSE against Keynes's ideas. Nicolò De Vecchi, "Hayek and the General Theory," *The European Journal of the History of Economic Thought*, vol. 13 (2006), pp. 233–258, surveys Hayek's criticisms of Keynes, especially the relations between consumption and investment, the ideas surrounding liquidity preference, and Keynes's theory of interest. De Vecchi finds that Hayek's arguments were already answered implicitly in the *General Theory*. For a comparison of how Keynes and Hayek viewed aggregate price adjustments, see George Selgin, "Hayek versus Keynes on How the Price Level Ought to Behave," *History of Political Economy*, vol. 31 (Winter 1999), pp. 699–721.

Another issue is the entrepreneur's motivation in initiating new investments. Don Patinkin, "New Materials on the Development of Keynes' Monetary Thought," *History of Political Economy*, vol. 12 (Spring 1980), pp. 1–28, argued that Keynes's entrepreneur based his decision to expand output on the fact that aggregate receipts exceed aggregate variable costs; but Harold Dickson, "How Did Keynes Conceive of Entrepreneur's Motivation? Note on Patinkin's Hypothesis," *History of Political Economy*, vol. 15 (Summer 1983), pp. 229–248, claimed that said decisions are based, instead, on whether or not the expansion of output is expected to increase profits.

Monetary issues in Keynes's work come to the fore in Jörg Bilbow, *Keynes on Monetary Policy, Finance and Uncertainty: Liquidity Preference Theory and the Global Financial Crisis* (New York: Routledge, 2009), which illustrates how Keynes's methodology inspired his economic theorizing and how this led to fundamental insights concerning the role of money that contrasted with orthodox closed-system modeling. For a review of Bilbow's book see Ingo Barens, "Keynes on Monetary Policy, Finance and Uncertainty," *The European Journal of the History of Economic Thought*, vol. 19 (2012), pp. 488–490. On a related monetary issue, P. G. McGregor, "Keynes on Ex Ante Saving and the Rate of Interest," *History of Political Economy*, vol. 20 (Spring 1988), pp. 107–118, defends Keynes's post-*General Theory* view of interest rates against charges of confusion and inconsistency.

Although Keynes was not very sympathetic to Marx, several writers have emphasized affinities between the two. See Peter Kenway, "Marx, Keynes and the Possibility of Crises," *Cambridge Journal of Economics*, vol. 4 (March 1980), pp. 23–36; and Dudley Dillard, "Keynes and Marx: A Centennial Appraisal," *Journal of Post-Keynesian Economics*, vol. 6 (Spring 1984), pp. 421–432. Michael Hudson, "German Economists and the Depression of 1929–1933," *History of Political Economy*, vol. 17 (Spring 1985), pp. 35–50, shows how German economists, particularly Wilhelm Lautebach (the "German Keynes"), employed Keynesian public policy during the Depression. The Keynesian model depicted in figure 21-3 of this chapter has become the staple of beginning textbooks, and yet it is considered by some to be analytically weak and unsophisticated. D. R. Fusfeld, "Keynes and the Keynesian Cross: A Note," *History of Political Economy*, vol. 17 (Fall 1985), pp. 385–390, defends the Keynesian cross diagram against its supposed shortcomings and claims that Keynes himself explicated the strengths of the model, although he never documented them in his writings.

Disputes on the real nature of Keynes's system continue among post-Keynesians as well as among historians of economic thought. On the spread of the Keynesian system and particularly the role of John R. Hicks in popularizing the Keynesian model, see Farhad Mahloudji, "Hicks and the Keynesian Revolution," *History of Political Economy*, vol. 17 (Summer 1985), pp. 287–308. Leijonhufvud's interpretation of the Keynesian system (see references) remains the most provocative, but the entire *Journal of Post-Keynesian Economics* is devoted to grappling with interpretative issues of this sort. Those who would allow Keynes to speak for himself should consult his own summary of the *General Theory*, namely Keynes, "The *General Theory* of Employment," *Quarterly Journal of Economics*, vol. 51 (September 1937), pp. 209–223.

Keynes was a brilliant biographer and historian of thought as well as a first-rate theorist. See his *Essays in Biography*, rev. ed. (New York: Norton Library, 1951); and Donald A. Walker, "Keynes as a Historian of Economic Thought: The Biographical Essays on Neoclassical Economists," *History of Political Economy*, vol. 17 (Summer 1985), pp. 159–186. For those more interested in Keynes's philosophy than his economics, see J. B. Davis, *Keynes's Philosophical Development* (Cambridge: Cambridge University Press, 1994), which traces the changes in Keynes's philosophy after he began to concentrate his energies on economics; and B. W. Bateman and J. B. Davis (eds.), *Keynes and Philosophy: Essays on the Origin of Keynes's Thought* (Brookfield, VT: Edward Elgar, 1991). R. E. Backhouse and B. W. Bateman, "Keynes and Capitalism." *History of Political Economy Winter*, vol. 41 (Fall 2009), pp. 645–671, analyze what Keynes meant by capitalism, especially in regard to its definition, fragility, and morality, and how his views relate to the Bloomsbury group.

Contemporary Macroeconomics
Monetarism and Rational Expectations

Despite a few notable exceptions discussed in chapter 6, money in the aggregate sense was often seen by classical economists as an impediment to proper economic reasoning. There were important debates about money, such as the bullionist and currency school arguments, but in such controversies the chief concern was about the institutions affecting the supply of money. The classical economists wanted to cut through pure monetary phenomena in order to link the determinants of the wealth of a nation to *real* factors involving thrift and productivity. To them, the stock of money determined the general price level, but as an aggregate variable, it was incapable of explaining *real wealth* or *relative* prices. Moreover, most industrial nations supported gold or specie standards that were viewed as "self-regulating." Inflations could and did occur, but they were attributed to wars and other disasters (during which the gold standard was usually suspended) or to the money-printing tendencies of improvident governments or politicians. In classical theory, then, a dichotomy existed between value theory on the one hand and monetary theory on the other. The former was determined by real forces; the latter by monetary considerations.

This dominant view began to change in the twentieth century as neoclassical writers—particularly Irving Fisher, Knut Wicksell, and A. C. Pigou—attempted to put aggregate monetary theory on a par with value theory. The transmission mechanism from money to prices, the determinants of the velocity of circulation and of the demand for money, and the general role of interest rates in the process of monetary expansions and contractions were all matters of concern to these writers. All the elements of a rather sophisticated version of the quantity theory were on hand well before Keynes penned the *General Theory*. But Keynes spurned the existing body of monetary theory in his attempt to revolutionize macroeconomics. Money mattered very little or not at all in his revised neoclassical view.

The lack of faith in monetary policy as a central stabilizing device in the macroeconomy persisted through the 1960s. But the Keynesian message introduced a pernicious bias into policy making spawned in a political arena. Keynesian suggestions about deficit spending were easily followed during periods of recession, whereas the ideas of budget surpluses or balanced budgets (suggested by Keynes during periods of inflation) proved politically unpopular and extremely rare. The very Keynesian principles that made the economy deflation- or depression-proof, in other words, may have made it inflation-prone. Events of the 1960s, especially the (largely) deficit-financed Vietnam War, led to large increases in the money stock, which was accompanied by serious and persistent problems with inflation. Predictably, these events led to a confrontation with Keynesian economics and to a real and practical resurgence of interest in "monetarism," which is based on a refinement of the classical quantity theory. (In theoretical terms, the quantity theory was never absent from the economic intellectual scene.) The purpose of this chapter is to chronicle twentieth-century developments that became incorporated into contemporary macroeconomics.

■ Monetary Theory Goes Neoclassical

Despite a noticeable lack of unanimity in early formulations of the quantity theory, each representation established a more or less direct relation between money and prices. With a few notable exceptions, such as John Locke and Henry Thornton, no classical writer assigned an explicit role to the interest rate as an important determinant of economic activity. On the other hand, the quantity theory was not purely mechanical, since increases in the quantity of money were seen by Cantillon, Thornton, Ricardo, and Mill as affecting the demand for commodities and, through greater demand, as raising prices. Whereas classical writers often discussed the forces that would preserve (or destroy) a new equilibrium, they did not explore the adjustment process in the transition from one equilibrium to the next, nor did they analyze the stability conditions of new equilibriums following monetary disturbances. A large part of this void was initially filled by neoclassical writers Irving Fisher and Knut Wicksell.

Irving Fisher and the Equation of Exchange

In 1911, Yale University professor Irving Fisher (1867–1947) followed a lead from John Stuart Mill and derived a mathematical framework for expounding the workings of the quantity theory. Fisher wrote: $MV + M'V' = PT$, where M is the stock of currency in circulation; V is currency's annual velocity of circulation, or the rate at which currency changes hands; M' is the volume of demand deposits held by banks; V' is annual demand-deposit velocity of circulation; P is the aggregate price level; and T is an index of the physical volume of transactions. Since our modern definition of money includes bank demand deposits, the above equation can be rewritten more simply as $MV = PT$, hereafter referred to as Fisher's Equation of Exchange.

Fisher's mathematical expression finds its verbal antecedent in Mill, who wrote:

> If we assume the quantity of goods on sale, and the number of times those goods are resold, to be fixed quantities, the value of money will depend upon its quantity; together with the average number of times that each piece changes hands in the process. . . . Consequently, the amount of goods and transactions being the same, the value of money is inversely as its quantity multiplied by what is called the rapidity of circulation [velocity]. And the quantity of money in circulation is equal to the money value of all the goods sold, divided by the number which expresses the rapidity of circulation. (*Principles*, p. 494)

Fisher realized that his equation of exchange was an accounting identity, therefore a truism. But that does not render it useless from the standpoint of economic theory. In fact, Fisher used it to assert once again the proportionality between increases in M and increases in P. With certain assumptions the equation of exchange subsequently became a mathematical expression of the quantity theory. Fisher's assumptions were that velocity (V) and the volume of trade (T) were independent of the money supply and that the price level was a passive rather than an active variable. Hence he affirmed the strict proportionality between M and P as a long-run proposition. His specification of the determinants of V and T was incredibly complete. In essence, V and T were assumed determined by real factors (habit and custom, technology and institutional arrangements), so that changes in the stock of money did not cause changes in any of the real determinants of V and T.

A Missing Link: The Real-Balance Effect. More important than his mathematical rendition of the strict quantity theory was Fisher's identification of the connection between an increase in the quantity of money and the ensuing increase in prices. The missing link that ensures the stability of monetary equilibrium is the real-balance effect. It can be explained this way. An increase in individual money holdings disturbs the optimum relation between an individual's cash balances and his or her expenditures. In Walrasian terms, more money at the existing price level creates an excess supply of money balances in individual hands. Thus, individuals seek to reduce their excess money balances by increasing expenditures. Furthermore, if output remains unchanged (as Fisher assumed), the increased money demand will push prices up until they have risen in the same proportion as the increase in money. In this way a new equilibrium is reached and maintained because individual money balances are returned to their optimal level.

This idea was absent from earlier formulations of the quantity theory, although having discovered it, Fisher did not exploit the real-balance effect fully. He never showed, for example, how excess money balances could be used to purchase securities, thereby pushing security prices up and the interest rate down. In other words, Fisher never demonstrated how an increase in money could cause increased output indirectly through lower interest rates (we shall see, momentarily that Wicksell stepped into this breach). Instead, Fisher turned to the interrelation between inflation, interest rates, expectations, and the holdings of real-cash balances.

Inflation and the "Fisher Effect." In seminal works such as *The Purchasing Power of Money* (1911) and *The Theory of Interest* (1930), Fisher explored the ramifications of actual and expected inflation and its interactions with nominal interest rates and the demand for real balances. First consider the demand for real-money balances, which may be expressed as follows:

$$m_d = f(y, i)$$

where m_d, the demand for real balances, is a function of y, real income, and i, the nominal rate of interest. Money demand is the reciprocal of velocity. Although Fisher did not elaborate this functional form of money demand as completely as A. C. Pigou and Milton Friedman, two writers considered later in this chapter, he did discover the important process through which the *nominal* interest rate, which is the *opportunity cost of holding money*, is determined.

In a flash of practical wisdom Fisher saw that the *nominal* interest rate was the product of two factors: (1) the *real* rate of interest, which reflects the basic underlying forces of borrowing and lending in the economy, or what the classics called thrift and productivity, and (2) the *expected* inflation rate at some point of time. In some sort of "global equilibrium"—i.e., with constant rates of inflation—the actual rate equals the expected rate. In general, simplified terms, Fisher's concept may be expressed as follows:

$$i = r + P^*$$

where i is the nominal rate of interest, r is the real rate of interest, and P^* is the *expected* rate of inflation. Naturally, when the expected rate equals the actual rate of inflation, the nominal interest rate is equal to the real rate.

The logic of Fisher's equation is quite clear. Lenders insist on a nominal rate of interest that is equal to the real rate plus whatever inflation is expected to be over the course of the lending period. If the expected rate of inflation is 5 percent per year and the real rate of interest is 4 percent, lenders would generally be unwilling to lend funds at less than 9 percent. If, ex post, the rate of inflation turns out to be 10 percent, the borrower has obtained funds at a *negative* real rate of interest; and lenders will adjust their expectations about inflation in succeeding periods. Thus, inflationary expectations affect nominal interest rates. The implications of the "Fisher effect" will be considered in more detail below, but it is important to note that Fisher discovered a mechanism that could make inflation self-perpetuating. Higher rates of monetary expansion may thus lead, initially, to lower nominal interest rates (through an increase in the supply of loanable funds), but eventually higher *prices* lead, through inflationary expectations, to increases in the nominal rate, and to higher inflation. This principle has become a stock-in-trade of modern monetarists.

Knut Wicksell and Modern Monetary Theory

While some neoclassical macroeconomists remained true to the Marshallian tradition, others attempted to put monetary theory into a Walrasian framework. The most successful at this last task was a Swedish economist, Knut Wicksell (1851–1926). Wicksell opposed the kind of quasi-mechanistic formulations that Fisher advanced. He added two elements to the quantity theory that brought it into the realm of modern monetary economics. First, he took a hint from Thomas Tooke (1779–1858), an early critic of the quantity theory, and asserted money works through *income* to determine the aggregate price level. Second, borrowing from Henry Thornton (chapter 6), Wicksell used Thornton's two-rate analysis to underscore the role of the interest rate in monetary theory.[1] Wicksell's restatement of the quantity theory was an important step toward integrating monetary theory with value theory. He constructed an aggregate demand/aggregate supply framework for investigating changes in prices, describing matters as follows:

> Every rise or fall in the price of a particular commodity presupposes a disturbance of the equilibrium between the supply of and demand for that commodity, whether the disturbance has actually taken place or is merely prospective. What is true in this respect of each commodity separately must doubtless be true of all commodities collectively. A general rise in prices is therefore only conceivable on the supposition that the general demand has for some reason become, or is expected to become, greater than the supply. . . . Any theory of money worthy of the name must be able to show how and why the monetary or pecuniary demand for goods exceeds or falls short of the supply of goods in given conditions. (*Lectures*, vol 2, pp. 159–160)

What is especially noteworthy in this passage is the way in which Wicksell made the transition from the partial-equilibrium approach of Marshall (i.e., supply equals demand for a single product) to the aggregate supply/aggregate demand

[1] Carl Uhr, a leading student of Wicksell, has concluded that Wicksell was probably never exposed to Thornton's writings directly but that he had studied the currency debate between Tooke and Ricardo at length and was most likely exposed to Thornton's ideas through Ricardo (*Economic Doctrines*, p. 200).

framework later employed by Keynes. Moreover, Wicksell responded to the challenge that he set down in the last sentence of the above passage: He showed how monetary demand exceeds or falls short of aggregate supply through the effects of changes in money on cash balances.

Real Balances. In the following passage Wicksell describes vividly the monetary adjustment mechanism known as the real-balance effect. While reading this passage keep in mind that he was talking about the consequences of a decrease in the stock of money:

> Let us suppose that for some reason or other . . . the stock of money is diminished while prices remain temporarily unchanged. The cash balances will gradually appear to be *too small in relation to the new level of prices*. . . . (It is true that in this case I can rely on a higher level of receipts in the future. But meanwhile I run the risk of being unable to meet my obligations punctually, and at best I may easily be forced by shortage of ready money to forego some purchases that would otherwise have been profitable.) I therefore seek to enlarge my balance. This can only be done—neglecting for the present the possibility of borrowing, etc.—through a *reduction* in my *demand* for goods and services, or through an *increase* in the *supply* of my own commodity . . . or through both together. The same is true for all other owners and consumers of commodities. But in fact nobody will succeed in realizing the object at which each is aiming—to increase his cash balance; for the sum of individual cash balances is limited by the amount of the available stock of money, or rather is identical with it. On the other hand, the universal reduction in demand and increase in supply of commodities will necessarily bring about a continuous fall in all prices. This can only cease when prices have fallen to the level at which the cash balances are regarded as adequate. (*Interest and Prices*, pp. 39–40)

By establishing the real-balance effect as the equilibrating mechanism that ensures stability in the wake of monetary disturbances, Wicksell filled in what Don Patinkin called the "missing chapter" in neoclassical monetary theory (see Patinkin, *Money, Interest and Prices*). By emphasizing the relation between savings and investment in his aggregate demand /aggregate supply analysis, Wicksell also rescued the interest rate (as a monetary variable) from the near-oblivion into which it had sunk after Thornton. Wicksell did not accept the interest rate as a purely monetary phenomenon, but he used the two-rate thesis to synthesize nonmonetary theories of the rate of interest, making the divergence between the natural rate and the actual rate the main element of his dynamic analysis.

Wicksell's Cumulative Process. Neoclassical monetary theorists have been criticized for complacently accepting the comparative-static, mechanical conclusion of the Hume-Mill-Fisher quantity theory (i.e., $2M = 2P$). Although a number of neoclassical monetary theorists grasped the significance of the real-balance effect, "they frequently failed," in Patinkin's words, "to provide a systematic dynamic analysis of the way in which the monetary increase generated real-balance effects in the commodity markets, which propelled the economy from its original equilibrium position to its new one" (*Money*, p. 167). Wicksell was the exception. His dynamic analysis, which focused on the interest rate as the point of departure, constitutes what he called the "cumulative process."

Wicksell's dynamic process involves shifts between the normal and actual rates of interest based on short-run discrepancies between aggregate supply and demand. This makes the interrelation between money and product markets explicit.

> If the banks lend their money at materially lower rates than the normal rate as above defined [e.g., in Thornton—see figure 6-1], then in the first place saving will be discouraged and for that reason there will be an increased demand for goods and services for present consumption. In the second place, the profit opportunities of entrepreneurs will thus be increased and the demand for goods and services, as well as for raw materials already in the market for future production, will evidently increase to the same extent as it had previously been held in check by the higher rate of interest. Owing to the increased income thus accruing to the workers, landowners, and the owners of raw materials, etc., the prices of consumption goods will begin to rise. . . . What is still more important is that the rise in prices, whether small or great at first, can never cease so long as the cause which gave rise to it continues to operate; in other words, so long as the loan rate remains below the normal rate. (*Lectures*, vol. 2, pp. 195–196)

By pointing out that the effects of the cumulative process may be irreversible, Wicksell hinted at the role played by expectations in macroeconomic analysis. He maintained that entrepreneurs who had been able to pay higher wages and raw material prices when the loan rate was below the natural rate will, "*even if* [the] *bank rate reverts to the normal natural rate*, on an average be able to offer the same high price, because they have reason to expect the same increased prices for their own products in the future" (*Lectures*, vol. 2, p. 196). Thus, if banks maintain artificially low interest rates, they merely tempt entrepreneurs to bid up the prices of labor and raw materials, and thus the prices of final goods.

Despite his innovations, Wicksell's monetary analysis ran in the same grooves as those laid down by the classical economists. He set out, in fact, to defend the quantity theory against its critics, and he did so effectively for the long-run variant of that theory. He succeeded far better than his predecessors in elaborating a process of adjustment by means of the real-balance effect and in assigning prominent roles to the interest rate and aggregate demand in explaining macroeconomic adjustments to changes in money—an issue of major concern to Keynes.

The Cambridge Equation

We learned in chapter 16 that Marshall founded a Cambridge tradition in partial-equilibrium analysis near the end of the nineteenth century. This tradition extended to monetary theory, but Marshall's incessant delays in publishing his ideas robbed his monetary theory of its novelty by the time it was published. Nevertheless, Marshall spread his ideas concerning the integration of monetary theory and value theory through an oral tradition at Cambridge University. Pigou wrote in his biography of Marshall: "He always taught that the value of money is a function of its supply on the one hand and the demand for it, on the other, as measured by 'the average stock of command over commodities which each person cares to keep in ready form'" (*Memorials*, p. 29). Ironically, Marshall's heirs apparent at Cambridge never succeeded as fully as Wicksell in integrating monetary and value theories. But Marshall's supply-and-demand framework is embodied in the famous Cambridge Equation, which enabled a shift in focus to the demand for money as well as its supply. In this respect Marshall's monetary economics is the spiritual father of the Keynesian theory of liquidity preference (see chapter 21) as well as the modern formulation of the demand for money as a part of a general theory of asset choice.

Marshall taught that the demand for money (i.e., the desired quantity of cash balances) could be expressed at any time as a fraction of income, which led to the familiar equation, $M = KPT$. In this formulation M is the stock of money, which Marshall assumed to be an exogenous variable. The right-hand side of the equation is an expression of the quantity of money supplied: K is the fraction of income that the community seeks to hold in the form of cash balances and demand deposits; P is the general price level; and T is total output. Analytically, K in the cash-balance equation is the reciprocal of V in Fisher's equation of exchange. Thus, both Fisher and Marshall accepted the quantity theory as a fundamental truth, and both concentrated on the medium-of-exchange function of money while neglecting the interest rate.

Neglect of the interest rate led to some serious shortcomings in neoclassical monetary analysis, chief of which was the failure to recognize interdependence between the product and money markets. Wicksell avoided this pitfall, as we have seen, but the too exclusive emphasis by Marshall and his Cambridge circle[2] on the demand for money may have impeded their systematic analysis of the way in which changes in real balances are transmitted into the commodity market. This is curious because the cash-balance effect is inherent in the Cambridge Equation. The equation can be rearranged, in other words, to express an excess supply of money ($E_s = M - KPT$) or an excess demand for money ($E_d = KPT - M$), either one of which is capable of generating a real-balance effect.

Patinkin found it curious that the Cambridge group did not apply the test of stability conditions to the monetary sector of the economy, since they never failed to do so in examining the product markets. This discrepancy is especially obtrusive in the case of Walras, as Patinkin noted in his critique of neoclassical monetary theory:

> Walras was a man who never tired of establishing the stability of his system by elaborating on the corrective forces of excess supply that would be called into play should the price lie above its equilibrium value, and the forces of excess demand that would be called into play should it lie below. He did it when he explained how the market determines the equilibrium prices of commodities; he did it again when he explained how the market determines the equilibrium prices of productive services; and he did it a third time when he explained how the market determines the equilibrium prices of capital goods. But he did not do it when he attempted to explain how the market determines the equilibrium "price" of paper money. And Walras is the rule, not the exception. (*Money*, p. 168)

Inexplicable oversights of this nature tended to preserve the chasm between monetary theory and value theory well into the twentieth century. However, some predecessors of Keynes made headway by explaining the dynamic relation between money, income, and the business cycle.

■ Modern Monetarism: Theory and Policy

With the preceding as background, we now return to the main theme of this chapter and attempt to demonstrate how some of the basic elements of the modern monetarist position are straightforward extensions of earlier works on the quantity theory. As pointed out previously, the popularity of monetarism as a policy prescription was preceded by continuous and persistent contributions (even during the heyday of Keynesianism) to the development of the quantity theory. No writer, perhaps, has defended the monetarist position in more forceful and elegant terms than Nobel laureate Milton Friedman, whose ideas have shaped a generation of "monetarists."

[2] Along with Marshall, this group included A. C. Pigou and D. H. Robertson.

Friedman's Theory of the Demand for Money

In 1956 (during the growing dominance of Keynes's ideas within the academic community) Chicago economist Milton Friedman published a set of innovative essays elaborating and modifying the quantity theory of money (*Studies in the Quantity Theory of Money*). In his essay entitled "The Quantity Theory of Money: A Restatement" (contained in *Studies*) Friedman set out a new version of the demand for money and gave it the following expression:

$$m_d = \alpha\,(Y_p, w, i, P^*, P, u)$$

where the demand for money is presented as a function (α) of permanent income (Y_p), the proportion of human to nonhuman wealth (w), the *nominal* interest rate (i), *expected* changes in the rate of change in the price level (P^*), the actual price level (P), and the preference function for money vis-à-vis other goods (u). Friedman offered this specification as a *theory* of money demand, and set it up in testable form.

An elaboration of all of the independent variables in Friedman's equation would take us too far afield here. (The interested reader is invited to read the original essay.) But several points about the equation are of principal importance. Unlike the older version of the quantity theory, Friedman's restatement is essentially a theory of demand for money, not a theory of prices. In this respect, his approach to monetary theory is similar to Keynes's. There is an important difference, however. Friedman's restatement of the quantity theory rests on a basic premise from capital theory: that "income" is the yield on capital. This means that the concept of income Friedman uses in his construction of the quantity theory is different from that used by Keynes in his income-expenditure model. Friedman called his income measure "permanent income," which is to say that he treats income as a discounted, present-value stream of payments derived from an existing stock of wealth, including human capital. Human capital consists of "qualitative" improvements such as education and training. Keynes neglected wealth almost entirely, which was more appropriate to the type of short-run analysis he was interested in than to the long-run analysis Friedman favored.[3] In the long run, permanent income is a more appropriate variable.

Friedman does not argue that the demand for cash balances (or its reciprocal, velocity) is constant, as earlier naive formulations of the quantity theory implied. But he does argue that money demand is a stable and predictable function of the independent variables, citing empirical support. Hence, he argues that money is still the crucial variable in predicting prices (as well as short-term fluctuations in output and employment, as we shall see). In other words, according to Friedman, if velocity is predictable, changes in the rate of monetary expansion will explain changes in the rate of inflation (or deflation) as well as short-term alterations in output and employment.[4]

On closer examination, it is obvious that Friedman's money-demand equation is an elaboration of the money-demand function we examined earlier in this chapter. It can be simplified to include only income (current, not permanent) and nominal

[3] Keynes's matter-of-fact justification for short-run analysis was that "in the long run, we are all dead." A favorite retort by modern monetarists is that the reason we are dead in the long run is because Keynesian policies of inflation and excessive government have killed us.

[4] Although Friedman's statistical evidence has sparked much controversy, his role as a leading monetary theorist is undisputable. On this point, at least, other leading monetary theorists agree. Harry Johnson has written that "Friedman's application to monetary theory of the basic principle . . . that income is the yield on capital, and capital the present value of income—is probably the most important development in monetary theory since Keynes' *General Theory*" ("Monetary Theory and Policy," p. 350).

interest rates (y and i). While this simplification does not do justice to Friedman's elegant conception, it will make our elementary explanation of "monetarism" easier. For example, a very lucid explanation of inflation emerges from the combination of the Fisher effect and Friedman's conception of money demand.

A Simplified Monetarist Explanation of Inflation

Recall that Fisher said the nominal interest rate is equal to the sum of the real interest rate and the *expected* inflation rate. This immediately raises questions about how expectations are formed. One popular theory about expectations is the so-called *adaptive expectations* theory, which states that price expectations are formed on the basis of past experience with inflation, with more recent past price experience weighing more heavily than that of the distant past. Expectations are dominated by uncertainty about future prices. Laborers, for example, contract for future wages and businesses set future prices on the basis of some (uncertain) expectations about future prices. The adaptive expectations theory says that these expectations will be formed principally by the most recent past experience.

We know that the *nominal* interest rate is partly a function of price expectations and that the demand for cash balances is in turn a function of the nominal interest rate. Higher nominal rates mean higher opportunity costs for holding money, which means a *reduced* demand for cash balances (and vice versa). A simplified explanation for inflation may thus be given utilizing the concepts of adaptive expectations, the Fisher effect, and Friedman's (modified) money-demand function. Assume (1) that there is a constant rate of money expansion by the central bank; (2) that expected inflation rates and actual inflation rates are equal (and equivalent to the rate of monetary expansion); (3) that the nominal interest rate is equal to the real rate plus the rate of inflation (or monetary expansion), which is constant; (4) that actual and desired holdings of cash balances are equal; and (5) that real income is growing at a constant rate. Given these conditions, assume a once-and-for-all increase in the rate of monetary expansion.

The initial results of the increase in monetary expansion are to increase actual cash balances of individuals and firms above their desired levels. This *initially* depresses the nominal rate of interest via the "Wicksell effect" (i.e., an increase in loanable funds temporarily lowers the real rate of interest). The excess of cash balances leads to increased spending on commodities, securities, and all other assets. Actual prices (and nominal wages) begin to rise due to the increased nominal spending. After a time, expectations "adapt" to the price increases, causing the nominal interest rate, which fell initially, to rise. The process does not end until: (1) the new rate of inflation is equal to the new and higher rate of monetary expansion; (2) the nominal interest rate has increased by an amount equal to the difference between the old and the new inflation rate; (3) actual cash balances are again equal to desired cash balances; and (4) the *real* rate of interest is restored to its former level. Notice that the level of cash balances held will be *lower* than before because a higher nominal interest rate means a higher (opportunity) cost of holding money.

There are some obvious implications of this process for economic policy. How often have we heard that "tight money and high interest rates are the causes of inflation"? Some businesspeople and politicians adhere to this naive view. The monetarist version of events tells us that exactly the opposite is the case. While monetary expansion *initially* lowers the nominal interest rate, inflation and the Fisher effect take over and eventually cause nominal interest rates to rise. The only way that interest rates could be depressed over long periods is to enact higher and higher rates of monetary expansion, a very dangerous policy in the view of monetarists.

Friedman is famously quoted as saying, "Inflation is always and everywhere a *monetary phenomenon*," and he has convincingly demonstrated this proposition for the United States in a massive empirical study he and Anna Schwartz published, *A Monetary History of the United States, 1867–1960*. As in the earlier and more naive versions of the quantity theory, inflation can be explained by increased velocity (reduced money-demand growth), reduced income growth, or an increased rate of monetary expansion. In the contemporary monetarist's view, there are limits to the growth of velocity—people can economize just so much on cash balances. Further, the growth in income and employment is, in the longer run, determined by real forces and other factors (see the following section). The remaining culprit is *monetary expansion*. Ultimately the monetarist interpretation of inflation, as we shall see momentarily, is that it is produced by erratic discretionary changes in money growth rates.

Inflation and Unemployment: The Monetarist Reaction

Modern monetarism embraces the problems of employment and income growth and their relation to inflation. A few years after Friedman unveiled his restatement of the quantity theory a British economist, A. W. Phillips, published a paper on the relation between employment and inflation levels, "The Relation between Unemployment and the Rate of Change of Money Wage Rates in the United Kingdom, 1861–1957," which posited an inverse relationship between the unemployment rate and the inflation rate.[5] Phillips concluded that higher and higher inflation rates were required to reduce the unemployment rate by a given percentage. If verified, this circumstance would present the ultimate policy maker's dilemma. Immediately, problems of definition arose, especially concerning unemployment. Economists in the U.S. faced different definitions, one by the U. S. Department of Labor, another by the President's Council of Economic Advisers, and so forth. Which concept should rule?

Eventually strong doubts developed about the predictive nature of the Phillips curve in the face of actual macroeconomic events, such as stagflation—a term used to describe inflation accompanied by low growth, unemployment, or economic recession. In the 1960s Keynesian economics, and the Phillips curve associated with it, made stagflations impossible because high unemployment would reduce demand for goods and services, which would lower prices. Thus, no inflation. Presented with actual stagflation in the 1970s and 1980s, however, economists began to investigate the validity of the Phillips curve more closely.

Friedman once again rose to the occasion and offered an elegant alternative conception of both unemployment and the short-run Phillips curve. In his 1968 presidential address to the American Economic Association ("The Role of Monetary Policy") Friedman argued that the *long-run* Phillips relation was vertical at some *natural* rate of unemployment. That is, in the long run, any particular rate of monetary expansion and inflation has little or nothing to do with the *natural* unemployment rate. The question of what constitutes the natural rate of unemployment was defined by Friedman in the following terms. "It refers," he said,

[5] Actually, as the title of Phillips's paper suggests, he used money wage rates rather than the inflation rate in his relation. Furthermore, it has since been established that Irving Fisher invented the notion that Phillips claimed as his. See Fisher, "Statistical Relation," in the references.

> to that rate of employment which is consistent with the *existing real conditions* in the labor market. It can be lowered by removing obstacles in the labor market, by reducing friction. It can be raised by introducing additional obstacles. The purpose of the concept is to separate the monetary from the nonmonetary aspects of the employment situation—precisely the same purpose that Wicksell had in using the word *natural* in connection with the rate of interest. (*Price Theory*, p. 228)

In Friedman's conception, then, the natural rate of unemployment is determined by all *real* conditions affecting the supply and demand for labor. These factors would include all institutional arrangements, such as degree of unionization, minimum-wage laws, proportion of women in the workforce, status of worker education, and so on.

In the short run, however, Friedman noted that the actual unemployment rate may be higher or lower than the natural rate. To see intuitively how this is possible we need merely return to our analysis of money and inflation in the previous section, changing only the assumption stated there that output and employment remain constant over the adjustment to a new rate of monetary expansion. The key to understanding the short-run-inflation–unemployment relation is to note that after an increase in the rate of money expansion, the price expectations of businesspeople and workers diverge from their actual price experience. Specifically, as individuals begin to rid themselves of excess cash balances, the prices of goods and services rise. Individual entrepreneurs perceive an increase in demand (and price) for their own products (not an increase in the general price level) and produce more, simultaneously hiring more labor at a lower actual real wage. Why will laborers be willing to supply more labor? (Nominal wages may *rise* somewhat, but inflation tends to drive down real wages, indicating a *reduced* quantity of labor input!) The answer is that laborers' perceptions of prices lag behind—workers are, in Keynesian terms, under *money illusion*. In other words, increased *nominal* wages fool laborers into thinking that real wages have increased, and therefore they supply more labor. Hence unemployment falls below the natural rate until laborers (and businesses) catch on and readjust. There is, therefore, a short-run inverse relationship between unemployment and inflation, but in the long run the Phillips curve is vertical at the natural rate of unemployment. Monetarists argue that in the long-run employment and output growth are determined by *real factors* affecting input markets, thus returning to the classical perspective. Altering money supply growth rates affects output and employment only temporarily. However, money supply changes have long-term effects on the rate at which prices change.

Monetarist Economic Policy

Monetarism also carries a strong policy message. The existence of an "expectations component" in the argument means that lags of various kinds exist within the implementation of monetary policy. There are both *inside* and *outside* lags in the monetary policy exercised by central banks. Inside lags exist because it takes time to recognize adverse macroeconomic developments affecting output, employment, and prices, and to administer appropriate corrective measures. Monetary policy may have an advantage over fiscal policy in this regard because, unlike fiscal policy, it does not have to go through a political/legislative process. But the outside lag may present a greater problem. Milton Friedman first called attention to the outside lag—the length of time it takes before actual changes in monetary expansion or contraction are felt on the "target" variables of inflation, output, and employment.

Adjustment of expectations is a time-consuming process. Different studies present conflicting evidence on the matter, but it is generally believed that there is a six- to nine-month lag between alterations in monetary policy and resulting changes in total spending. Output changes are ordinarily thought to be the first target affected, with the full effects of monetary expansion on the rate of inflation following later, taking as long as a year and a half. Comparatively little is known, however, about the formation of expectations and other factors affecting the length of these lags. Thus, it is clear that a good deal of uncertainty surrounds the conduct and effectiveness of monetary policy.

Because monetary policy does not take place in a vacuum, the actions of the Federal Reserve Board must be considered. The Fed's attempt to target interest rates such as the federal funds rate (i.e., to keep it within a certain range) has led to very costly mistakes. When interest rates are pushed upward by excessive government borrowing the Federal Reserve often reacts with a monetary expansion that temporarily lowers the interest rate but lays the groundwork for more upward pressures on interest rates in the future (preceded, of course, by higher inflation rates). This problem has led many monetarists, including, and most especially Friedman, to espouse the targeting of bank reserves and monetary aggregates rather than interest rates. At this point in the new millennium, however, Friedman's criticisms of Federal Reserve policy have failed to change its institutional behavior. At base, monetarists view monetary policy from a "rules-versus-discretion" perspective. Given the state of existing and (likely) future knowledge of macroeconomic processes they strongly question whether discretionary monetary policy can ever create stability. Not surprisingly, the Federal Reserve policy makers resist this allegation.

Rules versus Authority. The United States operates under an independent monetary authority. The members of the Federal Reserve Board are appointed by the president of the United States—with the advice and consent of the Senate—but once chosen, they operate independently of the body politic.[6] Friedman sees in this arrangement a threat to individual liberty because it puts a select few in charge of the most important thing that affects the price level and employment—the nation's money. We might expect Friedman to be led to such a view on the basis of philosophical persuasion alone, but his argument against an independent monetary authority receives added force from investigation of historical monetary data. For example, in his lengthy study with Anna Schwartz, *A Monetary History of the United States, 1867–1960*, Friedman revealed that during the Great Depression the Federal Reserve Board allowed the money stock of the United States to fall by one-third, to which he attributed the severity and duration of the crisis.

A deeper acquaintance with monetary facts in the U.S. and other countries led Friedman to assert that severe depressions have always been accompanied by sharp reductions in the money stock and that sharp reductions in the money stock have always been accompanied by depressions. On the other end of the spectrum, Friedman feels that severe inflations have always been accompanied by sharp increases in the money stock and vice versa. With respect to the Great Depression, Friedman opined:

> The Great Depression in the United States, far from being a sign of the inherent instability of the private enterprise system, is a testament to how much harm can be done by mistakes on the part of a few men when they wield vast power over the monetary system of a country. (*Capitalism and Freedom*, p. 50)

[6] The degree of independence of the Fed (i.e., its freedom from political influence) is frequently called into question by its critics.

Friedman therefore advocates an alternative that has long been in the University of Chicago tradition. He favors automatic rules in place of independent monetary authority. In a favorite parable Friedman compared the past performance of the Federal Reserve Board to the actions of a nervous teenager learning to drive: when pressing on the accelerator (i.e., increasing the money stock), our nervous tyro frequently gives the car too much gas; when stepping on the brakes (reducing the money stock), he or she pushes too hard. In a phrase, monetary overacceleration and overbraking are predictable. Rather than proceeding smoothly on a path of economic growth, discretionary monetary policy subjects the economy to fits and starts, cultivating inflation and/or depression, and harming individuals in the process.

As an effective countermeasure Friedman proposed that the Federal Reserve Board be directed by law to increase the money stock month by month at an annual rate of between 3 and 5 percent. A rate of increase in this range is consistent, he judged, with attainable economic growth and relative price stability. Moreover, it would eliminate the destabilizing effects of, say, a 12 percent increase in the money supply one month and a 3 percent increase the next.

Not surprisingly, many academicians and policy makers regard the rules-versus-authority question with suspicion. Friedman's result, stable economic growth under the monetary rule, depends crucially on the stability of velocity. Friedman has marshaled statistical evidence in support of this assumption, but his critics either dispute the evidence or challenge Friedman's statistical procedures. Some critics contend that while velocity may be stable in the long run, it is not stable in the short run. They therefore argue that discretionary monetary policy is required to head off short-run, destabilizing changes in velocity. Friedman is no stranger to controversy, but when all is said and done, monetarism could hardly have a more effective spokesman.[7] (For yet another view of why government intervention is likely to produce bad results—based in part on monetarism—see the box, The Force of Ideas: Rational Expectations, or "You Can't Fool All of the People All of the Time.")

Supply-Siders and Monetarists—The Bottom Line. This chapter and its preceding one illustrate that much of modern macroeconomics is unsettled territory. Keynesians and post-Keynesians support discretionary manipulation of fiscal or budget policy as the principal tool for macroeconomic stabilization, with discretionary monetary policy in an auxiliary role. Keynesian macroeconomic policy is sometimes referred to as "demand management." Those who take this position see the economy in constant need of manipulation and tinkering, with the success of policy measures taken dependent on a strong governmental apparatus. Monetarists view the problem from the other way around. They see the economy as basically stable and self-regulating, requiring little if any government intervention. They view the proper macroeconomic role of government (especially that of the Federal Reserve) as providing a predictable and stable environment within which unfettered economic processes can work efficiently to maximize economic well-being. Minimal government, balanced budgets, deregulation of business and industry, and a monetary growth rule are all part of the monetarist policy "package." Nevertheless, Keynes influenced both camps by directing attention to, and emphasizing, the "demand side" of the economy.

[7] During his lifetime Friedman's razor-sharp intellect and tenacious debating skills led some admirers to compare him to the philosopher Nietzsche, of whom H. L. Mencken said, "when he took to the floor to argue it was a time to send for ambulances" (in Breit and Ransom, *Academic Scribblers*, p. 259).

The Force of Ideas: Rational Expectations, or "You Can't Fool All of the People All of the Time"

Inasmuch as economics deals with human behavior, expectations are fundamental to economic theory. A family planning to purchase a home will anticipate its long-run earnings prospects and the likely trend of future rents and mortgage rates. In its negotiations with employers, a labor union will base its wage demands in part on what it thinks future inflation will be. In each case, the final individual or group transaction will have an effect on the actual inflation rate, once it feeds through to prices. Intuitively, you might think that expectations are forward-looking. Clearly they involve the (largely unknown) future. But until the 1970s economists modeled expectations as if they were based on the past. For example, it was common practice to posit that next year's inflation rate would be a weighted average of current and past rates. This assumption was dictated by the twin realization that it is impossible to observe expectations directly, but reasonable to suppose that they will be based largely on experience.

The flaw in this reasoning is that it assumes that people would go on believing what they know to be false. Several economists were troubled by this "irrational" argument. In the 1960s John Muth argued that it would be better to assume that people have "rational expectations," meaning that true forward-looking expectations will be based on the best information at hand, and that those shown to be persistently wrong will be discarded.

In the 1970s Robert Lucas (Nobel laureate, 1995) demonstrated the importance of this simple idea. Lucas challenged the validity of government economic models of the economy based on the past behavior of households and firms. He argued that when governments change their policies expectations also change, so that the economy's response to the new policy may be different from what governments expect.

This idea has widespread applicability, but it exerted a particularly strong impact on monetary policy. Until the 1970s governments thought they could buy lower unemployment with a bit more inflation, an idea vigorously attacked by Friedman, as pointed out in this chapter. But Friedman based his argument on backward-looking expectations. By applying rational expectations, Lucas killed the argument for good.

According to rational expectations theory, a short-run inflationary monetary policy will boost jobs only because firms are fooled into thinking that a rise in the price they can charge for their goods signals stronger demand for their products. In fact, it merely signals a rise in the overall price level. In the long-run, under rational expectations, there can be no trade-off between inflation and unemployment because people cannot be fooled forever. They learn from their mistakes. Once people see that inflation has risen, unemployment will return to its former level.

Clearly, the insights provided by Muth and Lucas, as well as the other "rational expectationists," are useful as a warning against naive government policy. But as with all simple yet forceful ideas, rational expectations theory raises many fundamental questions. How are expectations formed? When are governments to be believed? What constitutes efficient information? How do people use information? How can economic models capture the limited ability of people to understand how the economy works?

Partly as a consequence of the rational expectations view, economists are now preoccupied with the issues of credibility and sustainability. Can governments keep their promises, and for how long? We now recognize more explicitly that governments are perpetually twisted on the horns of a dilemma: Although tough policies eventually bring the benefits of low inflation, politicians gain popularity by encouraging a short burst of inflation that temporarily boosts incomes and employment. But if they succumb to this temptation repeatedly, their credibility may be lost. It is likely that the great future battles over massive social programs (e.g., Social Security, Medicare, and Medicaid, etc.) in the United States and elsewhere will pivot on this basic idea.

Theory and policy are almost always affected by actual events. Stagflation occurred in the United Kingdom in the 1960s and 1970s and in the United States in the early 1970s. The difficulty of fitting stagflation within a Keynesian framework led to a greater acceptance of monetarist theories in the 1970s and 1980s. To some extent the pendulum has swung back in the opposite direction as monetarism had increasing difficulty predicting the demand for money and the long period of low inflation and high employment of the 1990s—a kind of reverse of stagflation. Nevertheless, the specter of stagflation continues to haunt Western economies in the twenty-first century.

But in between these pendulum swings within the "demand-side" paradigm, an alternate view of the macroeconomy emerged over the 1970s and the 1980s from another quarter that emphasized supply-side solutions to macroeconomic problems. Writers in this third camp have acquired the name *supply-siders*. Rejecting Keynesian economics and the demand-side orientation of the monetarists, the supply-siders concentrated on the effect that macroeconomic policies have on incentives to save, invest, and acquire capital. Blaming the inflation of the 1970s in part on reduced growth in labor productivity, the supply-siders emphasized factors affecting technology and the labor market.

Supply-siders promote tax and spending cuts and a balanced budget as a major fiscal tonic. The net result, it is hoped, will be the creation of greater incentives to save and invest, thus propelling the economy forward. The deregulation of industry, including reduced business "standards" regulation, an emphasis on private labor-training programs, and reduced social welfare subsidies that create disincentives to work and save are also part of most of the supply-siders' policy prescriptions. The supply-siders seemed to reach the height of their influence during the administration of President Reagan in the United States. Since then, the shift in Washington's mood has been back in the direction of Keynesianism.

■ Conclusion

The French have a saying that "the more things change, the more they remain the same." This maxim appears especially appropriate to an evaluation of modern macroeconomic and monetary theory. Supply-side economics and the fundamentals of modern rational expectations theory (the idea without its technical accoutrements) were the stock-in-trade of Adam Smith and many of the other important classical economists! Labor productivity and capital formation were undeniable foundational elements of classical macroeconomics, which was absorbed by the issue of economic growth and development. Through their analysis of market economies classical economists were led to advocate as little government "policy making" as possible, consistent with the overarching goal of economic development. These "classical" principles are very close to the philosophical and theoretical conceptions of modern supply-siders, monetarists, and rational expectationists. As such, contemporary macroeconomics and monetary theory appear to be returning to the timeless concerns of any economy. However, they have returned far richer. We now know, thanks in large measure to the Keynesian interlude and to the refurbishment of neoclassical ideas by Milton Friedman and the rational expectationists, a great deal more about the workings of the aggregate economy. As such, modern macroeconomics—conceived of as including monetary economics—is a major and ongoing study of the contemporary economist.

References

Breit, William, and Roger Ransom, *The Academic Scribblers*, rev. ed. New York: Holt, 1982.

Fisher, Irving. "A Statistical Relation between Unemployment and Price Changes," *International Labour Review*, vol. 13 (June 1926), pp. 785–792. Reprinted as "I Discovered the Phillip's Curve," *Journal of Political Economy*, vol. 81 (March/April 1973), pp. 496–502.

———. *The Purchasing Power of Money*. New York: A. M. Kelley, 1963 [1911].

———. *The Theory of Interest*. New York: Macmillan, 1930.

Friedman, Milton. *Studies in the Quantity Theory of Money*. Chicago: The University of Chicago Press, 1956.

———. *Capitalism and Freedom*. Chicago: The University of Chicago Press, 1962.

———. "The Role of Monetary Policy," *American Economic Review*, vol. 58 (March 1968), pp. 1–17.

———. *Price Theory*. Chicago: Aldine, 1976.

———, and Anna Schwartz. *A Monetary History of the United States, 1867–1960*. Princeton, NJ: Princeton University Press, 1963.

Johnson, H. G. "Monetary Theory and Policy," *American Economic Review*, vol. 52 (June 1962), pp. 335–384.

Mill, J. S. *Principles of Political Economy*, W. J. Ashley (ed.). New York: A. M. Kelley, 1965 [1848].

Patinkin, Don. *Money, Interest and Prices*, 2d ed. New York: Harper & Row, 1965.

Phillips, A. W. "The Relation between Unemployment and the Rate of Change of Money Wage Rates in the United Kingdom, 1861–1957," *Economica*, vol. 25 (November 1958), pp. 283–299.

Pigou, A. C. (ed.). *Memorials of Alfred Marshall*. London: Macmillan, 1925.

Uhr, Carl G. *Economic Doctrines of Knut Wicksell*. Berkeley: University of California Press, 1962.

Wicksell, Knut. *Lectures on Political Economy*, 2 vols., L. Robbins (ed.). London: Routledge & Kegan Paul, 1935.

———. *Interest and Prices*, R. F. Kahn (trans.). London: Macmillan, 1936.

Notes for Further Reading

An excellent survey of monetary theory that in some respects parallels the one presented in this chapter is contained in Joseph Ascheim and C. Y. Hsieh, *Macroeconomics: Income and Monetary Theory* (Columbus, OH: Merrill, 1969). For a broader sweep, see Charles Rist, *History of Money and Credit Theory from John Law to the Present Day*, J. Degras (trans.) (New York: Macmillan, 1940).

Space does not permit our doing justice to the many talents of Irving Fisher, certainly a prime candidate for "greatest American economist." A glimpse at the personal side of Irving Fisher is provided in J. P. Miller, "Irving Fisher of Yale," in William Fellner, et al. (eds.), *Ten Economic Studies in the Tradition of Irving Fisher* (New York: Wiley, 1967). The same volume also contains an instructive and perceptive assessment of Fisher's theoretical work by Paul Samuelson. Robert W. Dimand, "Irving Fisher and Financial Economics: The Equity Premium Puzzle, the Predictability of Stock Prices, and Intertemporal Allocation Under Risk," *Journal of the History of Economic Thought*, vol. 29 (June 2007), pp 153–166, discusses Fisher's views on financial economics, his personal fortunes in the stock market, the loss of his fortune in the Great Depression, and the resulting decline in his reputation.

Fisher's role as policy maker and presidential adviser is detailed in W. R. Allen, "Irving Fisher, F.D.R., and the Great Depression," *History of Political Economy*, vol. 9 (Winter 1977), pp. 560–587. Fisher's very important foundation for the theory of risk and uncertainty is developed in J. H. Crockett, Jr., "Irving Fisher on the Financial Economics of Uncertainty," *History of Political Economy*, vol. 12 (Spring 1980), pp. 65–82. Frank G. Steindl, "Was Fisher a Practicing Quantity Theorist?" *Journal of the History of Economic Thought*, vol. 19 (Fall 1997), pp. 241–260, says yes (before the Great Depression) and no (after the Great Depression). As a counterpoint to Fisher's views on the quantity theory of money, see N. T. Skaggs, "The Methodological Roots of J. Laurence Laughlin's Anti-Quantity Theory of Money and Prices," *Journal of the History of Economic Thought*, vol. 17 (Spring 1995), pp. 1–21. Laughlin was head of the economics department at the University of Chicago and the leader of anti-quantity theory sentiment in the early twentieth century.

Possibly the best single source of information on Wicksell and his ideas is Carl Uhr's *Economic Doctrines of Knut Wicksell* (see references). See also Ragnar Frisch, *Knut Wicksell: A Cornerstone in Modern Economic Theory* (Oslo, 1951). Torsten Gardlund, *The Life of Knut Wicksell* (Aldershot, UK: Edward Elgar, 1996), provides additional biographical details. John C. Wood (ed.), *Knut Wicksell: Critical Assessments* (London: Routledge, 1994), collected the major secondary literature on Wicksell, showing the richness of his work and the significance of his legacy. See also, S. Stern and B. Thalberg (eds.), *The Theoretical Contributions of Knut Wicksell* (London: Macmillan, 1979). A two-volume collection of Wicksell's economic writings, some previously unpublished, and available in English for the first time, translated from German or Swedish, appeared in 2002–2003 under the title *Knut Wicksell: Essays in Economics*, Bo Sandelin (ed.) (London: Routledge, 2002/2003).

On Wicksell's cumulative process and its significance in monetary theory, see Don Patinkin, "Wicksell's 'Cumulative Process,'" *Economic Journal*, vol. 62 (December 1952), pp. 835–847; same author, "Wicksell's Cumulative Process in Theory and Practice," *Banca Nazionale del Lavaro Review*, vol. 21 (June 1968), pp. 120–131; Claes-Henric Siven, "Capital Theory and Equilibrium in Wicksell's Cumulative Process," *History of Political Economy*, vol. 29 (Summer 1997), pp. 201–217. Also see Mauro Boianovsky, "Wicksell's Business Cycle," *The European Journal of the History of Economic Thought*," vol. 2 (Autumn 1995), pp. 375–411; E. J. Nell, "Wicksell's Theory of Circulation," *Journal of Political Economy*, vol. 75 (August 1967), pp. 386–394; and Jacob Marschak, "Wicksell's Two Interest Rates," *Social Research*, vol. 8 (November 1941), pp. 469–478.

Some other aspects of Wicksell's macroeconomics are discussed by Lars Jonung, "Knut Wicksell's Norm of Price Stabilization and Swedish Monetary Policy in the 1930's," *Journal of Monetary Economics*, vol. 5 (October 1979), pp. 459–496; same author, "Knut Wicksell on Unemployment," *History of Political Economy*, vol. 21 (Spring 1989), pp. 27–42; and William Coleman, "Wicksell on Technical Change and Real Wages," *History of Political Economy*, vol. 17 (Fall 1985), pp. 355–366. Mauro Boianovsky, "Wicksell on Deflation in the Early 1920s," *History of Political Economy*, vol. 30 (Summer 1998), pp. 219–275, concluded that worldwide deflation of the 1920s caused Wicksell to revise some aspects of his cumulative process model.

Alfred Marshall's monetary theories are best described in his *Money, Credit, and Commerce* (New York: A. M. Kelley, 1960 [1923]). Perhaps the best spokesman for the Cambridge group was Marshall's student Pigou. See A. C. Pigou: "The Value of Money," *Quarterly Journal of Economics*, vol. 32 (November 1917), pp. 38–65; "The Monetary Theory of the Trade Cycle," *Economic Journal*, vol. 39 (June 1929), pp. 183–194; and "Marginal Utility and Elasticities of Demand," *Quarterly Journal of Economics*, vol. 50 (May 1936), p. 532. D. A. Walker, "Keynes's Anticipation of Monetarism," *Australian Economic Papers*, vol. 28 (June 1989), pp. 1–15, attempts to place Keynes at the forefront of later developments. Don Patinkin's *Money, Interest and Prices* (see references) is valuable on two counts: (1) it is a monumental effort to fully integrate monetary theory and value theory, and (2) the supplementary notes at the end of the book provide useful information on the historical antecedents of neoclassical monetary theory. While the text is heavy going for undergraduates and possibly even graduates, the notes might be read with much profit.

The literature on modern monetarism and its satellite ideas is vast and growing. J. Huston McCulloch, *Money and Inflation: A Monetarist Approach* (New York: Academic, 1975), provides a useful introduction. A more extensive treatment of the monetarist approach to money and inflation may be found in Leonardo Auernheimer and R. B. Ekelund, Jr., *The Essentials of Money and Banking* (New York: Wiley, 1982). The relation between modern monetarism and classical economics generally, and David Hume in particular, is the subject of Thomas Mayer, "David Hume and Monetarism," *Quarterly Journal of Economics*, vol. 95 (August 1980), pp. 89–101. J. Daniel Hammond, "Labels and Substance: Friedman's Restatement of the Quantity Theory," *History of Political Economy*, vol. 31 (Fall 1999), pp. 449–471, emphasizes Friedman's allegiance to Marshall's methodology and value theory, and his use of the Cambridge cash balances approach. Hsiang-Ke Chao, "Milton Friedman and the Emergence of the Permanent Income Hypothesis," *History of Political Economy*, vol. 35 (Spring 2003), pp. 77–104, explains the development of one of the linchpins of Friedman's restatement of the quantity theory. Gilles Dostaler, "Friedman and Keynes: Divergences and Convergences," *The European Journal of the History of Economic Thought*, vol. 5 (Summer 1998), pp. 317–347, compares the two giants of twentieth century macroeconomics.

Economic history from a monetarist perspective is beautifully exposed in the Friedman–Schwartz volume (see references). The Great Depression, analyzed from this vantage, has stirred up a good deal of controversy. See Milton Friedman and Anna J. Schwartz, *The Great Contraction* (Princeton, NJ: Princeton University Press, 1966); then read Peter Temin's *Did Monetary Factors Cause the Great Depression?* (New York: Norton, 1976).

Rational expectations theory is explained in a clear, nontechnical fashion by Rodney Maddock and Michael Carter, "A Child's Guide to Rational Expectations," *Journal of Economic Literature*, vol. 20 (March 1982), pp. 39–51. Although complex in its advance formulations, the theory of rational expectations developed rapidly over the 1970s: see Thomas Sargent, "Rational Expectations, the Real Rate of Interest, and the Natural Rate of Unemployment," *Brookings Papers in Economic Activity* 2 (1973), pp. 429–472; Thomas Sargent and Neil Wallace, "Rational Expectations and the Theory of Economic Policy," *Journal of Monetary Economics*, vol. 2 (April 1976), pp. 169–184; and Robert E. Lucas, "An Equilibrium Model of the Business Cycle," *Journal of Political Economy*, vol. 83 (December 1975), pp. 1113–1144. Michael C. Lovell, "Tests of the Rational Expectations Hypothesis," *American Economic Review*, vol. 76 (March 1986), pp. 110–124, has attempted to test the conclusions of the theory and found them lacking in empirical support.

James Forder, "The Historical Place of the 'Friedman-Phelps' Expectations Critique," *The European Journal of the History of Economic Thought*, vol. 17 (2010), pp. 493–511, argues that the expectations critique made famous by Friedman and Phelps in the 1960s was actually older, and that it was an established principle by the time Friedman and Phelps wrote. The argument is that the Keynesians caused the confusion by responding to Friedman's arguments about expectations rather than his claims about the natural rate of unemployment, which were two different problems.

Readers interested in learning more about lags and "targets" in monetary (and fiscal) policy would do well to consult L. C. Anderson and J. L. Jordan, "Monetary and Fiscal Actions: A Test of Their Relative Importance in Economic Stabilization," *Federal Reserve Bank of St. Louis Review*, vol. 50 (November 1968), pp. 11–24; see also B. M. Friedman, "Even the St. Louis Model Now Believes in Fiscal Policy," *Journal of Money, Credit and Banking*, vol. 9 (May 1977), pp. 365–367; and J. E. Tanner, "Are the Lags in the Effects of Monetary Policy Variable?" *Journal of Monetary Economics*, vol. 5 (January 1979), pp. 105–121.

For a general introduction to the aspects of supply-side economics see L. R. Klein, "The Supply Side," *American Economic Review*, vol. 68 (March 1978), pp. 1–7. The "Laffer curve"—showing the relation between tax rates and government revenues—has been an integral part of modern supply-side economics. Economist Arthur Laffer argues that lowering tax rates would create additional incentives to work and invest, increased incomes, and increased revenues for government; see A. B. Laffer and R. D. Ranson, "A Formal Model of the Economy," *Journal of Business*, vol. 44 (July 1971), pp. 247–270; and the simplified treatment in Jude Wanniski's "Taxes, Revenues, and the 'Laffer Curve,'" *The Public Interest*, vol. 50 (Winter 1978), pp. 3–16. For a "fiscalist" criticism of Laffer's logic see Walter Heller, "The Kemp-Roth-Laffer Free Lunch," *The Wall Street Journal* (July 12, 1978), p. 20. Whether the Laffer relation exists or not is debatable, but no one denies the onset of a productivity problem in the U.S. economy of the 1970s. An excellent overview of the problem is provided in J. A. Tatom, "The Productivity Problem," *Federal Reserve Bank of St. Louis Review*, vol. 61 (September 1979), pp. 3–16. Also, for contrasting approaches to the productivity problem, see Paul Samuelson and Milton Friedman, "Productivity: Two Experts Cross Swords," *Newsweek* (September 8, 1980), pp. 68–69.

The reemergence of the quantity theory in the 1950s and 1960s, along with the monetarist school that it spawned, is the subject of a spate of papers, all contained in *History of Political Economy*. Three separate papers concerning the effect of statistical and theoretical developments on the early quantity theory may be profitably read as a unit. T. M. Humphrey treats the statistical tests of the theory in the first three decades of this century, stressing that the major contribution of such tests was empirical rather than theoretical in nature. See Humphrey, "Empirical Tests of the Quantity Theory of Money in the United States, 1900–1930," *History of Political Economy*, vol. 5 (Fall 1973), pp. 285–316. Anticipatory and actual contributions to theoretical monetarism are the subjects of two papers about C. F. Bickerdike and Clark Warburton. On Bickerdike's anticipatory developments related to the role of money in business fluctuations see V. J. Tarascio, "Bickerdike's Monetary Growth Theory," *History of Political Economy*, vol. 12 (Summer 1980), pp. 161–173. Clark Warburton was the staunchest defender of monetarism before the seminal writings of Friedman appeared. Although very much out of the mainstream of Keynesian times, Warburton deserves credit for kindling the fires of monetarism when it was most unpopular to do so; see T. F. Cargill's "Clark Warburton and the Development of Monetarism since the Great Depression," *History of Political Economy*, vol. 11 (Fall 1979), pp. 425–449. Finally, Reuven Brenner, "The Concept of Indexation and Monetary Theory," *History of Political Economy*, vol. 11 (Fall 1979), pp. 395–405, identifies important parallels between indexation as a hedge against inflation and the development of monetarism.

23

Austrian Economics

Chapter 14 reviewed the contributions of the "older" Austrian school within the context of a "marginal revolution" in value theory that occurred in the closing decades of the nineteenth century. Historians of economic thought have tended to lump Menger, Jevons, and Walras together as independent discoverers of the same approach to value. This tendency serves to obscure the essential differences in the original intent and design of their respective theoretical constructions and in the influence exerted by each writer, in his own way, on the subsequent development of economic thought. One important difference is that Walras, alone of the three, was the architect of a general-equilibrium system. Joseph Schumpeter singled out this accomplishment as the really important one of the period and concluded that "in itself, the principle of marginal utility is not so important after all as Jevons, the Austrians, and Walras himself believed" (*History*, p. 918). There is some doubt, however, whether the Austrians ever considered the marginal-utility principle alone to be as important as Schumpeter seems to think they did. Research has shown the marginal-utility principle to be *incidental* to Menger's economic analysis, not an integral part of it.[1] Menger nowhere concerned himself with the relative maxima or minima of functions, which many take to be the essence of marginalism. The focus of his economic analysis, instead, was on the study of institutions and the conditions of disequilibrium.

This last concern constitutes a sharp cleavage between the Austrian brand of "neoclassical" economics and the French (Cournot–Dupuit–Walras) or English (Jevons–Marshall) variants of neoclassical theory. Overlooking for the moment the fact that Walras rode the high road of general-equilibrium theory while Marshall took the low road of partial-equilibrium analysis, both showed a theoretical concern for the determination of prices under a hypothetical regime of perfectly free competition. By contrast, Menger did not try to explain prices nor did he assume that competition could be "perfect." He forged no analytical link between "the importance of satisfactions" (i.e., marginal utility) and market prices. In fact, he regarded market prices as superficial and incidental manifestations of much deeper forces at work in the exchange of goods and services. He believed that economics should investigate these deeper forces and essential causes rather than concern itself with mathematical formalism.

Menger's view of human beings and their nature inevitably colored his approach to economic analysis. William Jaffé, an authority on Walras, concluded:

[1] For example, see J. T. Salerno, "The Place of Mises's *Human Action*" in the references.

> Man, as Menger saw him, far from being a "lightning calculator" [Veblen's derogatory phrase], is a bumbling, erring, ill-informed creature, plagued with uncertainty, forever hovering between alluring hopes and haunting fears, and congenitally incapable of making finely calibrated decisions in pursuit of satisfactions. With his attention [thus] unswervingly fixed on reality, Menger could not, and did not, abstract from the difficulties traders face in any attempt to obtain all the information required for anything like a pinpoint equilibrium determination of market prices to emerge, nor did his approach permit him to abstract from the uncertainties that veil the future, even the near future in the conscious anticipation of which most present transactions take place. Neither did he exclude the existence of non-competing groups, or the omnipresence of monopolistic or monopoloid traders in the market. ("Menger," pp. 520–521)

The institutional component is also of paramount importance in the Austrian paradigm, albeit in a different way from that conceived by Veblen. The fundamental goal of Menger's economics was to make social phenomena intelligible in terms of individual goals and plans. Economic and social institutions affect human action by influencing the interaction of individual plans. In Menger's framework an institution is any coordinated pattern of individual interaction. A market or a legal system is an institution, but so is money and so are prices. How does it come about that so many people of diverse backgrounds come to agree on a certain pattern of interaction? How is it possible that so many individual exchanges take place under mutually advantageous conditions without central direction? The Austrian tradition is not a ready-made set of answers to these and other major theoretical questions, but it is instead a way of conceiving "the economic problem." It is a research program with a peculiar gestalt. The key concepts in this particular approach concern the role and influence of subjectivity, time, uncertainty, disequilibrium, process, knowledge, and coordination.

■ The Gestalt of Austrian Economics

Although it was Menger who first gave meaning to the phrase "Austrian economics," his influence went far beyond the national boundaries of his native land. The "Vienna circle" that began with Menger nurtured second-generation Austrians, most notably two émigrés to America, Ludwig von Mises (1881–1973) and Joseph Schumpeter (1883–1950). Mises in turn taught a third generation of economists that includes Friedrich Hayek (1889–1992), Oskar Morgenstern (1902–1977), Fritz Machlup (1902–1983), Paul Rosenstein-Rodan (1902–1985), and Gottfried Haberler (1900–1995). In London, Hayek's influence touched G. L. S. Shackle (1903–1992) and Ludwig Lachmann (1906–1990), the latter also a holder of a Vienna doctorate. In the United States, Mises influenced Israel Kirzner and Murray Rothbard (1926–1995), who attended his seminars at New York University. In this way, successive generations of "Austrians" were propagated and continue to produce long after the geographic connotation of the word ceased to have any substantive meaning.

Modern expositors of the Austrian approach underscore five major points of emphasis that distinguish, in their view, Austrian economics from mainstream neoclassical analysis. The five distinguishing features are: (1) radical subjectivism, (2) methodological individualism, (3) purposive human action, (4) casual-geneticism, and (5) methodological essentialism. Each of these requires some elaboration.

Radical subjectivism is a wide net that ensnares several Austrian themes. Basic to the Austrian approach is the conviction that all underlying permanent relations of economic theory are consequences of human choice. Austrians therefore emphasize the roles of knowledge and error in individual decision making. What is important is that people *differ* with respect to their knowledge, interpretations, expectations, and alertness, so that subjectivism has a much broader meaning than implied merely by personal tastes. All decisions are by their very nature subjective. Certain information cannot be reasonably expected to be held by anyone other than the individual making a decision, e.g., the intensity and form of his or her preferences and expectations. Since decision making is the province of the entrepreneur, entrepreneurship is consequently a major force in Austrian economics.

The most unique and radical aspect of the Austrian approach, however, lies in its emphasis on the primacy of utility and the denial of costs as a coterminous element (with utility) in the determination of value. This last point constitutes the sharpest break with the English variant (Marshall and Jevons) of neoclassical value theory. Essentially, Austrians argue that economic costs are themselves subjective, because they are based on calculations of utility *forgone* whenever a choice is made. In other words, Austrians associate costs with a decision, a neutral act, not with an event or a thing. This means that costs are subordinate to, but inextricably joined with, utility. Costs are subjective because they are perceived by the decision maker. The price paid for an item therefore represents the utility of it to the purchaser alone, not necessarily its utility to anyone else. This line of thought runs against the strict Marshallian tradition that associates costs with events and therefore regards costs as in some sense objective.

Methodological individualism asserts that the most appropriate way to study economic phenomena is at the level of the individual. If economics is a science of choice, then one must look to the chooser to understand economic relations. But aren't some choices collective in the sense that they are made by a body of people (e.g., a committee) rather than by a single individual? There are two responses to this question. One is that any collective decision-making body is composed of persons whose individual decisions make up the collective judgment. The second concerns the nature of aggregates and what kind of information they convey. Austrians argue that aggregates only matter where individual considerations don't matter; yet for Austrians, individual decisions *always* matter. In the final analysis the choice between the study of individual or aggregate choices is at least partly a normative issue, and Austrians are quite explicit about their methodological preference in this regard.

There is an element of teleology in the Austrian approach expressed in their emphasis on *purposive* human action. However, it is a kind of teleology that does not take goals as absolute. Goals may change over time, and they obviously vary from one individual to the next. In this connection, the basic proposition defended by Austrians is that individual choice is not the consequence of some mere gravitational pull toward utility. Rather, individuals act with a purpose, even if that purpose is frequently frustrated by error or imperfect knowledge. In this regard, Austrians reject Benthamite principles, for Bentham saw people as being passively pushed about by pleasure and pain. Austrians regard all choices as forward looking; consequently expectations are very important economic variables. These expectations, along with the purpose behind each person's actions, shape individual plans and the decisions made in order to carry out each plan.

To say that Austrian economics is *causal-genetic* is to say that it emphasizes essences rather than functional relationships. Functionalism stresses the working out of conditions that must be met in order for some end to be fulfilled (e.g., the enumeration of characteristics that constitute the competitive model). Austrians claim to be more interested in the nature and essence of things and less interested in their form. There is an Aristotelian strain that runs through the Austrian approach; for example, attempts to mathematize economic relations are considered fruitless because mathematics is functional and form-oriented and therefore incapable of contributing any real understanding of basic economic relations.

Finally, *methodological essentialism* asserts that the proper method of studying economics is the study of *essences*, not appearances or superficialities. Because economics is a social science, its method must be that which is appropriate to the study of human behavior. Therefore, Austrians reject the application of natural sciences to economics. Hayek coined a word, "scientism" to describe the (illegitimate, in his view) application of principles of natural science to the study of humans. He and other Austrians find this attempt to transfer the methodology of natural science to a social science like economics decidedly *unscientific* because it involves the mechanical and uncritical application of habits of thought to fields different from those in which they have been formed. According to Hayek, "The scientistic as distinguished from the scientific view is not an unprejudiced but a very prejudiced approach which, before it has considered its subject, claims to know what is the most appropriate way of investigating it" (*Counter-Revolution*, p. 24). He maintains that the chief culprits in promoting the slavish imitation of the method and language of science by the social sciences were Saint-Simon and Comte.

Austrian economics, therefore, claims to be *nonscientistic*, and its goals are fairly modest. Unconcerned with predictions, Austrians merely seek to understand human society and to make it more intelligible. Thus, their methodology separates them from mainstream neoclassical economics. (See the box, Method Squabbles 6: Austrians vs. Marshallians: Is There Really a Difference?)

Method Squabbles 6: Austrians vs. Marshallians: Is There Really a Difference?

Some in the contemporary economics profession believe that Austrian economics is an attempt at a "distinction without a difference," that is, only a variation on standard neoclassical (Marshallian) economics. To be sure, Marshallian economics was subsequently modified by the introduction of asymmetric information, uncertainty, and other factors. Nevertheless, conceptual and philosophical differences clearly exist. Examples include the Austrian emphasis on utility as the basis for subjective costs and their emphasis on "human action" in contrast to Marshallian demand and supply analysis. But to be fair, both approaches emphasize rational maximizing and economizing by individuals. The real question comes down to this: Aside from some philosophical concerns, do Austrian economists "do" economics differently than orthodox Marshallians?

There are important differences in the *practice* of Austrian economics, differences that can be traced back to ideas of first-generation Austrians. Consider only two examples from their formulations of microeconomic behavior: the matter of "discontinuities" in consumption and production, and the pervasive uncertainty that attends economic decisions. Recall that Menger, Wieser, and Böhm-Bawerk emphasized fixed proportions in consumption and production. This "lumpiness" attended all consumables and all inputs due to the observed physical impossibility of purchasing final goods or resources "continuously." According to Austrian tenets, mathematics in the form of the differential calculus is inappropriate—actually impossible—in abstracting from real-world processes. There is no smooth Marshallian continuity involved when people make physical additions of goods or resources in consumption and production; therefore it is senseless to pretend that such continuity exists. By this reasoning, the use of calculus will get you into trouble by distorting characteristics of real economic phenomena in the economy. The Austrian rejection of "rational mechanics" and mathematical theorizing stems as much from this observation about the real world as it does from some philosophical preconceptions.

Next, consider the Austrians' (limited) use of modern econometrics. They believe that one cannot apply the methods of the "hard" sciences to economics primarily because of the uncertainty and limited information (emphasized early on by Menger) that attends all market exchange. In an attempt at economic *prediction*, modern Marshallians use probability theory, which is the foundation of statistics and econometrics, to "test" economic theory. But when market activity is viewed as an unfolding process and as a result of human action rather than human design, there is little room for predictability. Thus, the Austrian's primary objective is to describe rather than predict. There is, within this paradigm, not much room or tolerance for modern econometrics. Past events and the data trail they leave (data gathering is yet another problem) cannot be used to make exact predictions of future events within limits of probability acceptable to Austrians. Too much uncertainty exists concerning the future course of events propelled by human action to be able to reduce economic phenomena to mechanistic processes. Rather, Austrians rely on logical and scholastic methods of presenting and analyzing problems, very much in the tradition of how the early Austrians viewed the world. There are, in short, real differences between Austrian and orthodox Marshallian modes of "doing" economics.

A full discussion of every aspect of Austrian economics would take us beyond the aim and scope of this book. We confine ourselves in this chapter to a brief review of several major Austrian themes: money, credit, the trade cycle, and the nature of competition.

■ Ludwig von Mises: The Theory of Money and Credit

Classical economics treated money as neutral in its economic effects (see chapter 6), and Walrasian neoclassical economics does not recognize the uniqueness of money. In Walrasian general-equilibrium models money is merely a *numéraire*—it has no properties distinguishing it from the many nonmoney goods in the model. By contrast, Austrian monetary theory considers money unique because of its intertemporal exchangeability. Hence, the Austrians concentrate on the relative price effects of changes in the money supply. In its contemporary formulation Austrian economics begins with a theory of the evolution of money and concludes with an analysis of the effects of changes in money on the fundamental economic decisions of individuals.

Although Carl Menger (see chapter 14) fashioned a theory of the evolution of money that emphasized the unintended consequences of individual (self-interested) behavior, he did not succeed in solving the question of what determines the value of money. Despite promising efforts by Knut Wicksell (see chapter 22), monetary theory remained separated from value theory until the two were integrated by Ludwig von Mises, one of Böhm-Bawerk's students at the University of Vienna. Mises achieved the integration of monetary and value theory by founding both on the same principle, the marginal utility of subjective individual wants.

Subjective Use Value versus Objective Exchange Value

Mises recognized that the marginal utility of money comes from two separate sources. On the one hand, money has value derived from the value of the goods it can buy. On the other hand, money has a subjective use value of its own because it can be held for future exchange. What we call the value of money in common parlance springs from the ability of money to be exchanged for other things. Mises called this characteristic of money its "objective exchange value" in order to distinguish it from money's subjective use value. Today we call it the purchasing power of money.

How then do we measure the purchasing power of money? Conventional theory advanced the concept of a unitary (aggregate) price level, whereby the purchasing power of money (the reciprocal of the price level) is the outcome of the total volume of transactions in society divided by the velocity of circulation. In terms of the familiar equation of exchange (see chapter 22) where $MV = PT$, the price level P would be derived as follows: $P = MV/T$ and its reciprocal (the purchasing power of money), $1/P = T/MV$. Mises recognized the grain of truth in the quantity theory, namely "the idea that a connection exists between variations in the value of money on the one hand and the supply of it on the other hand," but he said, "beyond this proposition the Quantity Theory can provide us with nothing. Above all, it fails to explain the mechanism of variations in the value of money" (*Theory of Money and Credit*, p. 130).

True to the Austrian tradition, Mises rejected the macroeconomic approach to monetary theory in favor of an individualistic approach. All valuation is done by individuals; therefore the key to understanding the value of money must be in the mind of the individual. The purchasing power of a dollar is the vast *array of goods* that can be purchased with that dollar. This array is heterogeneous and specific. At any point of time a dollar might buy four boxes of salt, three packs of chewing gum, two candy bars, one-half box of laundry detergent, one-tenth of a music compact disc, and so forth and so on. The purchasing power of money therefore cannot be summarized in some unitary price-level figure. At all times a homogeneous good must be defined in terms of its usefulness to the consumer rather than its technological properties. Likewise, price must be related to the specific usefulness of a good, not to its technological properties. An apartment with the same technological properties in Manhattan and in Boise will not have the same price because they are not equally useful to the purchaser. The apartment in New York is more ideally situated to more extensive consumption possibilities and therefore will be more highly priced on the market. Mises emphasized locational (and temporal) aspects in explaining differences in the value of technologically similar goods, and this emphasis complements the Austrian notion that the purchasing power of money is equal to an array of goods.

In applying the theory of marginal utility to the price of money, Mises confronted a thorny analytical problem. When an individual ranks coffee or shoes or vacations on a value scale, he or she values those goods for their direct use in consumption, and each valuation is independent of and prior to its price on the market. However, people hold money not because it can be used directly in consumption but because it can eventually be exchanged for goods that will be used directly. In other words, money is not useful in itself; it is useful because it has a prior exchange value—a preexisting purchasing power. The demand for money therefore not only is *not* independent of its existing market price but derives precisely from its preexisting price in terms of other goods and services. Therein lies the problem. If the demand for money, and hence its utility, depends on its preexisting price or purchasing power, how can that price be explained by the demand? Mises's critics accused him of falling into a circular trap.

Mises avoided the trap by invoking a regression theorem. The demand for money on any given day, say day D, is equal to its purchasing power on the previous day, $D - 1$. The demand for money on the previous day, $D - 1$, in turn is equal to the purchasing power of money on $D - 2$, and so on. In other words, the demand for money always has a historical (i.e., temporal) component. But is this not an infinite regression backward in time? No, Mises answered, we must push the analysis backward only to that point when the commodity used as money was not used as a medium of indirect exchange but was demanded instead solely for its own direct consumption use. Suppose we go back in time to the point when gold was introduced as money. Let us assume that before this day, all trade took place by barter. On the last day of barter, gold had value only for its direct consumption use, but on the first day of its use as money, it took on an additional use as a medium of exchange. In other words, on the first day of its use as a medium of exchange, gold had two dimensions of utility: first, a direct consumption use; and second, a monetary use that had a historical component in its utility.

Evaluating this regression theorem, Murray Rothbard, a student of Mises, pointed out the continuity between Mises and Menger, who emphasized the evolutionary and institutional elements of money:

> Not only does the Mises regression theorem fully explain the current demand for money and integrate the theory of money with the theory of marginal utility, but it also shows that money must have originated in this fashion—on the market—with individuals on the market gradually beginning to use some previously valuable commodity as a medium of exchange. No money could have originated either by a social compact to consider some previously valueless thing as a "money" or by sudden governmental fiat. For in those cases, the money commodity could not have a previous purchasing power, which could be taken into account in the individual's demand for money. In this way, Mises demonstrated that Carl Menger's historical insight into the way in which money arose on the market was not simply a historical summary but a theoretical necessity. ("Austrian Theory of Money," p. 169)

The Effect of Changes in Money on Relative Prices

Utilizing an insight first attributed to Richard Cantillon (see chapter 4), Mises focused his monetary analysis on the effects of changes in the stock of money on economic activity. Once again, he rejected the macroeconomic approach in favor of methodological individualism. In response to the quantity theory advanced by John Locke, Cantillon had argued that the result of an increase in the stock of money will not be uniform across the economy but rather will cause prices to rise at uneven rates in different sectors, thereby changing *relative* prices in the process. Mises combined the marginal-utility theory of money with this "Cantillon effect" to elucidate the impact of changes in the supply of money.

In modern societies, when governments or central banks increase the supply of money, they don't do so in a way that affects everyone equally. Instead, new money is created by the government or by banks to be spent on specific goods and services. The demand for these specific goods rises, thereby raising their prices first. (The elements of this in a Misesian economy should now be clear: As money holdings increase, the marginal utility of money declines so that certain goods are revalued ahead of money on subjective preference scales, pushing the prices of these goods upward.) Gradually the new money ripples through the economy, raising demand and prices as it goes. Income and wealth are thereby redistributed to those who receive the new money early in the process, at the expense of those who receive the new money later, or those who live on fixed incomes and receive none of the new money.

Recognizing these relative price effects and the ensuing wealth redistribution they entail, Mises took a vigorous stand against inflationary expansion of the money supply. Indeed, he argued that because the exchange services of money are not increased by a higher stock of money, inflation will always be a zero-sum game, benefiting some at the expense of others:

> The services money renders are conditioned by the height of its purchasing power. Nobody wants to have in his cash holding a definite number of pieces of money or a definite weight of money; he wants to keep a cash holding of a definite amount of purchasing power. As the operation of the market tends to determine the final state of money's purchasing power at a height at which the supply of and the demand for money coincide, there can never be an excess or a deficiency of money. Each individual and all individuals together always enjoy fully the advantages which they can derive from indirect exchange and the use of money, no matter whether the total quantity of money is great or small. Changes in money's purchasing power generate changes in the disposition of wealth among the various members of society. From the point of view of people eager to be enriched by such changes, the supply of money may be called insufficient or excessive, and the appetite for such gains may result in policies designed to bring about cash-induced alterations in purchasing power. However, the services which money renders can be neither improved nor impaired by changing the supply of money. . . . The quantity of money available in the whole economy is always sufficient to secure for everybody all that money does and can do. (*Human Action*, p. 418)

It is clear from the above passage that Mises's economic analysis made him wary of the potential abuse present in every concentration of economic power. Monetary expansion is a method by which the government, its controlled banking system, and favored political groups are able to partially expropriate the wealth of other groups in society. Having witnessed firsthand the German hyperinflation after World War I, Mises remained skeptical of any government's willingness to show monetary restraint over long periods of time. It is for this reason, and not because he attributed any mystical qualities to gold, that Mises championed a gold standard as the best form of money.

■ F. A. Hayek and the Theory of Business Cycles

Mises's theory of money and credit led to an Austrian theory of business cycles based on changes in the supply of money, a theory elaborated most completely by one of Mises's students, Nobel laureate Friedrich A. Hayek. Like Mises, Hayek broke with the quantity theory tradition because it ignored the effect of money on relative prices. He continued the integration of monetary theory and value theory that Mises had begun by exploring the effect of changes in the supply of money on the *composition* of output, rather than the quantity of output or the aggregate price level.

Hayek's business-cycle theory is a blend of the Austrian theories of money, capital, and prices. In a nutshell, his explanation of the cycle runs like this: A monetary disturbance (e.g., an increase in the money stock) causes interest rates to fall below an equilibrium level, which stimulates investment in capital, thereby reallocating resources away from the production of consumption goods toward production of intermediate (capital) goods. As a consequence, prices of capital goods rise and prices of consumption goods fall. This change in relative prices changes the *structure of production*. (Hayek viewed the entire process of production as a multistage activity through which raw materials pass until they finally emerge as end products;

therefore, a change in the number of stages or a reallocation of resources among the different stages constitutes a change in the structure of production.) Because of the longer time component of capital, such a change in the structure of production leads to overinvestment in "longer" or more "roundabout" methods of production and thereby upsets the coordination of plans between consumers and producers and between savers and investors.

Although Hayek's chief technical contribution to economic theory was his monetary theory, his important conception of equilibrium as the coordination of economic activities became the unifying theme in all of his writings. Coordination is achieved when the plans of all economic decision makers mesh. How does this come about? Decision makers look for signals. The appropriate signals are relative prices. Hayek argued that if relative prices change due to the "natural" forces of technology, tastes, time preference, and so forth, the ensuing adjustments will reestablish a coordinated plan. But purely *monetary* disturbances evoke perverse signals by artificially raising rates of return on certain types of economic activity. These rates of return can only be sustained as long as additional monetary stimulus is forthcoming, so eventually every boom will be followed by a bust.

Hayek centered his business cycle theory on the market signals utilized by savers and investors to make their decisions. He emphasized that although these decisions are arrived at independently, they are interdependent in terms of their implications for equilibrium. Cycles occur when a general inconsistency of plans comes about. In the case of a monetary stimulus, firms tend to switch to more capital-intensive methods at the expense of consumption-goods production, despite the fact that no additional planned savings has taken place. According to Hayek:

> This sacrifice is not voluntary, and is not made by those who will reap the benefit from the new investments. It is made by the consumers in general who, because of the increased competition from the entrepreneurs who have received the additional money, are forced to forego part of what they used to consume. It comes about not because they want to consume less, but because they get less goods for their money income. There can be no doubt that, if their money receipts should rise again, they would immediately attempt to expand consumption to the usual proportion. (*Prices and Production*, p. 57)

Hayek completed his research on monetary theory and business-cycle theory in the 1930s, at a time when Keynesian macroeconomics was ascending. Eventually his monetary theory was eclipsed by the so-called Keynesian revolution. In more recent times, Hayek focused attention on other important analytical issues, especially the role of information in economic activity. This last contribution has shown a greater survival value than Hayek's earlier one, and Hayek has been timely in anticipating a revival and reformulation of contemporary theories of competition. Several aspects of the new theory of competition are discussed in chapter 26, particularly the ideas of knowledge, information, and transaction costs. While present space and organizational structure prevent a complete discussion of Hayek's contribution to this literature, his pioneer efforts have had a major influence on the development of contemporary economic thought.

■ Joseph Schumpeter on Competition, Dynamics, and Growth

Joseph Schumpeter (1883–1950) was a third-generation Austrian economist who rose to prominence as finance minister of the Austrian government. A student of Böhm-Bawerk at the University of Vienna, he later emigrated to the United States in order to avoid Hitler's onslaught. Although steeped in the Austrian microeconomic tradition, Schumpeter reopened a classic macroeconomic line of inquiry—the subject of economic development. In 1911, he published his *Theory of Economic Development*, a book that won critical acclaim in Europe but made little impact on English-speaking economists until it was translated into English in 1934. His second major work, *Business Cycles*, followed in 1939.

Schumpeter blended ideas from Marx, Walras, and the German historian and sociologist, Max Weber, with insights from his Austrian forebearers, Menger, Wieser, and his teacher, Böhm-Bawerk. Like Marx, for whom he professed great admiration, Schumpeter was no mere imitator—although he borrowed ideas from his intellectual heroes he melded them into something uniquely his own. He shared Marx's view that economic processes are organic and that change comes from *within* the economic system, not merely from without. He admired the blend of sociology and economics involved in the writings of Marx and Weber. He also extolled the contribution of Walras, from whom he borrowed the notion of the entrepreneur, but transformed it into an active agent of economic progress, more in keeping with the Austrian/German tradition. Schumpeter therefore made the entrepreneur a dynamic force for economic change, the chief agent who causes *disequilibrium* (i.e., change) in a competitive economy.

Schumpeter regarded economic development as a dynamic process, a disturbing of the economic status quo. Rather than consider economic progress as a mere adjunct to the central body of orthodox economic theory, he saw it as the basis for reinterpreting a vital process that had been crowded out of mainstream economic analysis by the static, general-equilibrium approach. The entrepreneur is a key figure for Schumpeter because, quite simply, he or she is the *persona causa* of economic development. Although the nature of competition may change over time, the essential and pivotal role of the entrepreneur does not.

Entrepreneurs and Innovation

Like Menger and the second-generation Austrians, Schumpeter described competition as a process involving mainly the dynamic (and disequilibrating) innovations of the entrepreneur. Schumpeter used the concept of equilibrium as Weber had used the stationary state—as a theoretical construct, a point of departure. He coined a phrase to describe this equilibrium state: "the circular flow of economic life." Its chief characteristic is that economic life proceeds routinely on the basis of past experience; there are no forces evident for any change of the status quo. Schumpeter described the nature of production and distribution in the circular flow in the following terms:

> In every period only products which were produced in the previous period are consumed, and . . . only products which will be consumed in the following period are produced. Therefore workers and landlords always exchange their productive services for present consumption goods only, whether the former are employed directly or only indirectly in the production of consumption goods. There is no necessity for them to exchange their services of labor and land for future goods or for promises of future consumption goods or to apply for any "advances" of present consumption goods. It is simply a matter of exchange, and not of credit transactions. The element of time plays no part. All products are only products and nothing more. For the individual firm it is a matter of complete indifference

> whether it produces means of production or consumption goods. In both cases the product is paid for immediately and at its full value. (*Economic Development*, pp. 42–43)

In this hypothetical system, the production function is invariant, although factor substitution is possible within the limits of known technological horizons. The only real activity that must be performed in this state is "that of combining the two original factors of production, and this function is performed in every period mechanically as it were, of its own accord, without requiring a personal element distinguishable from [mere] superintendence" (*Economic Development*, p. 45). In this artificial situation, the entrepreneur is a nonentity. There is nothing for him or her to do because equilibrium is automatic and permanent. But such a state of being does not apply to the dynamic world in which we live. Schumpeter wrote in *Capitalism, Socialism, and Democracy* (p. 84) that the really relevant problem is not how capitalism administers existing structures, but how it creates and destroys them. He called this process "creative destruction," and maintained that it is the essence of economic development. In other words, development is a *disturbance* of the circular flow. It occurs in industrial and commercial life, not in consumption. It is a process defined by the carrying out of new combinations in production. It is accomplished by the entrepreneur.

Schumpeter reduced his theory to three elemental and corresponding pairs of opposites: (1) the circular flow (i.e., tendency toward equilibrium) versus a change in economic routine or data, (2) statics versus dynamics, and (3) entrepreneurship versus management. The first pair consists of two real processes; the second, two theoretical apparatuses; the third, two distinct types of conduct. Schumpeter maintained that the essential function of the entrepreneur is distinct from that of capitalist, landowner, laborer, or inventor. The entrepreneur may be any and all of these things, but if so it is by coincidence rather than by nature of function. In principle the entrepreneurial function is not connected to the possession of wealth, even though "the accidental fact of the possession of wealth constitutes a practical advantage" (*Economic Development*, p. 101). Moreover, entrepreneurs do not form a social class, in the technical sense, although in a capitalist society they come to be esteemed for their ability.

Schumpeter admitted that the entrepreneur's basic function is almost always mingled with other functions. "Pure" entrepreneurship is difficult to isolate from other economic activity. But "management" does not describe the truly distinctive role of the entrepreneur. Schumpeter wrote: "The function of superintendence in itself, constitutes no essential economic distinction" (*Economic Development*, p. 20). The function of making decisions is another matter, however. In Schumpeter's theory, the dynamic entrepreneur is the person who innovates, who makes "new combinations" in production. He described innovation in several ways. He first spelled out the kinds of new combinations that underlie economic development. They encompass the following: (1) creation of a new good or new quality of good, (2) creation of a new method of production, (3) the opening of a new market, (4) the capture of a new source of supply, and (5) a new organization of industry (e.g., creation or destruction of a monopoly). Over time, of course, the force of these new combinations dissipates, as the "new" becomes part of the "old" in the circular flow of economic activity. But this does not change the essence of the entrepreneurial function. Schumpeter claimed that people act as entrepreneurs only when they actually carry out new combinations; they lose the character of entrepreneurs as soon as they have built up their business, after which they settle down to running it as other people run their businesses.

Later, Schumpeter defined innovation in a more technical sense by means of the production function. The production function, he said, "describes the way in which quantity of product varies if quantities of factors vary. If, instead of quantities of factors, we vary the form of the function, we have an innovation" (*Business Cycles*, p. 62). Mere cost-reducing adaptations of knowledge lead only to new supply schedules of existing goods, however, so this kind of innovation must involve a new commodity, or one of higher quality. He recognized that the knowledge behind the innovation need not be new. It may be existing knowledge that has not been utilized before. According to Schumpeter:

> There never has been anytime when the store of scientific knowledge has yielded all it could in the way of industrial improvement, and, on the other hand, it is not the knowledge that matters, but the successful solution of the task *sui generis* of putting an untried method into practice—there may be, and often is, no scientific novelty involved at all, and even if it be involved, this does not make any difference to the nature of the process. ("Instability of Capitalism," p. 378)

In Schumpeter's theory, successful innovation requires an act of will, not of intellect. It depends, therefore, on leadership, not intelligence, and it should not be confused with invention. Schumpeter was explicit on this last point:

> To carry any improvement into effect is a task entirely different from the inventing of it, and a task, moreover, requiring entirely different kinds of aptitudes. Although entrepreneurs of course may be inventors just as they may be capitalists, they are inventors not by nature of their function but by coincidence and vice versa. Besides, the innovations which it is the function of entrepreneurs to carry out need not necessarily be any inventions at all. (*Economic Development*, pp. 88–89)

Business Cycles

Schumpeter's emphasis on the entrepreneur as the active agent for change in a competitive economy provides a bridge between the microeconomics of the firm and the macroeconomics of government policy. Within a Schumpeterian framework, the ultimate impact on individual incentives that tax and spending policies exert is felt through the transmission mechanism. Once again, the entrepreneur is the focal point. Citing the experience of the U.S. economy in the 1920s, Schumpeter raised the issue of whether taxes significantly affect the profit motive and economic progress. The United States inaugurated a federal income tax in 1913, so the issue was a timely one in the 1920s. Schumpeter evaluated the effects of a progressive income tax on the entrepreneurial function:

> Any tax on net earnings will tend to shift the balance of choice between "to do or not to do" a given thing. If a prospective net gain of a million is just sufficient to over-balance risks and other disutilities, then that prospective million minus a tax will not be so, and this is as true of a single transaction as it is of series of transactions and of the expansion of an old or the foundation of a new firm. Business management and enterprise . . . will for its maintenance depend, at least in the long run, on the actual delivery, in case of success, of the prizes which that scheme of life holds out, and, therefore, taxes beyond a percentage that greatly varies as to time and place must blunt the profit motive. (*Business Cycles*, pp. 291–292)

True to his intellectual training, Schumpeter always kept an eye on the competitive process, that maelstrom of economic activity that is composed of individual decisions based on reigning economic incentives. He retained the Austrian perspective on macroeconomics, namely that all aggregates represent collective outcomes of individual decisions. The causation runs from the individual to the collective, however, as Menger taught, never the other way around. There may be numerous institutional forces promoting or discouraging economic growth, but a key one, in Schumpeter's judgment, lies in a "do no harm" fiscal policy that includes low and/or declining rates of taxation. In the vernacular of politics, Schumpeter was an early "supply-sider."

Schumpeter's influence on the theory of economic development has been enormous, even among those economists who reject the theory outright. And among economists, especially those lacking historical perspective, the term "entrepreneur" has become virtually synonymous with the name of Schumpeter. As theories of economic change go, Schumpeter's analysis occupies the middle ground between Alfred Marshall and Max Weber. Marshall's theory adapted incrementally to shifts in preference and production functions, the result being a continuous improvement in moral qualities, tastes, and economic techniques. Its shortcoming was that it did not explain business cycles, a deficiency that Marshall's student Keynes set out to remedy. Marshall's approach also implied a theory of unilinear progress, which Schumpeter's theory denies. Weber's theory developed its own set of moral imperatives and used them to explain rapid social and economic transitions that punctuate long periods of historical continuity. Borrowing from Weber Schumpeter postulated the *continuous* occurrence of innovations and waves of adaptation simply because entrepreneurs are always present and are a constant force for change.

Ultimately, the appeal of Schumpeter's theory of economic development derives from its simplicity and its power, characteristics evident in the Schumpeterian phrase: "The carrying out of new combinations we call 'enterprise'; the individual whose function it is to carry them out we call 'entrepreneurs'" (*Economic Development*, p. 74). Yet, despite the importance of Schumpeter's contribution to economic development, his dynamic approach and his holistic vision of economic activity have failed to dominate economic analysis. Conventional economics still works mainly by intellectual specialization and division of labor.

■ Competition and the Market Process

As a result of the combined influence of many economic theorists, but especially Cournot and Walras, "competition" took on a meaning in the nineteenth century quite apart from the practical but ambiguous sense it was given in classical economics. Early use of the term meant simply rivalrous behavior (e.g., in Adam Smith); in other words, two or more parties seeking the same prize, which was usually economic profits. The subtle but lasting influence of Cournot and Walras was to change this notion from what may basically be described as a *process* to what may be described as a *situation*. Emphasis turned away from the institutional setting and the personalities involved and toward the *conditions* that must be fulfilled in order to yield an equilibrium result.[2] Thus, the notion of "perfect competition" emerged, a notion that encapsulated the following conditions: (1) perfect knowledge of every

[2] This development may have been accelerated, as we hinted in chap. 20, by the advent of "imperfect" competition in the works of Chamberlin and Robinson.

relevant utility function of both buyers and sellers and of all relevant prices, (2) an infinitely large number of buyers and sellers, (3) complete and open entry and exit of all firms, (4) constant expectations, and (5) homogeneous products. When these conditions operate, the "competitive equilibrium" results—that is, a uniform price for each good, a "normal" level of profits for each producer, utility maximization for each consumer, and no further tendency for things to change. The assumptions of competition are, therefore, nothing else but the conditions necessary to make equilibrium "determinate."

The "competitive model" so briefly sketched here has performed yeoman service in the evolution of economic theory because it has made it possible to give an exact account of the course of economic events solely with the aid of scientific generalizations. In any analytical study, forces whose operations are known must be separated from those that exhibit no uniform principles. The only satisfactory way of recognizing and accounting for the influence of the latter in the real world is to assume them away and observe what happens in their absence. This method of omission and comparison also offers the best hope that we can gradually extend the range of phenomena over which we can make generalizations. But it should be obvious that this technique requires constant awareness of its limitations as well as its strengths.

It has never been easy to convince people that the way to discover reality is through unreality—yet that is what the neoclassical model of perfect competition requires. Modern Austrians offer an alternative that claims to be more realistic because it attempts to incorporate aspects of the human personality excluded from the neoclassical, mechanistic model. In particular the Austrian approach seeks to deal explicitly with individuals': (1) knowledge about their own tastes and the opportunities available, (2) interpretations of current events and others' actions, (3) expectations about future events and behavior, and (4) alertness to new opportunities previously unrecognized. In the Austrian view the key insight into competition is that different people know different things. The market is a *process* whereby scattered and often contradictory bits of information are assimilated and transmitted to individual market participants; in Hayek's phrase, the competitive market process is a *discovery procedure*. Competition—not in the technical sense of "perfect competition," but in the older sense of rivalry—is the engine that drives the market process down the road to *coordination of individual plans* (the Austrian conception of equilibrium).

Hayek has never tired of pointing out that if all that needed to be known was *already* known, then every market decision would correctly anticipate every other decision and the market would automatically attain full equilibrium. Instead, the market is necessary precisely because it is an institutional device for mobilizing existing knowledge and making it available to market participants who are not omniscient. Taking the argument one step further, Austrians argue that the competitive market process is needed not only to mobilize existing knowledge but also to generate awareness of new opportunities. The discoverers of these new opportunities are the entrepreneurs, who take on a far more crucial role in the Austrian paradigm than was previously assigned to them by classical or neoclassical economics. Indeed, in the Austrian framework, the competitive process is by its very nature an entrepreneurial process.

The standard neoclassical theory employs the concept of "economizing," or maximizing utility subject to given tastes and prices, which is inadequate to explain the search for *new* opportunities, whether they consist of new products or variations on existing ones. Likewise, the terms "prices" and "profits" have a more restricted definition in standard use. Conventional theory assumes that the firm confronts known and given cost and revenue possibilities; that is, profit maximization does not entail discovery of a profit opportunity. Instead, it merely requires calculative action to explain already existing and recognized opportunities.

In the Austrian view, this takes too much for granted. The Austrian approach views prices as (disequilibrium) exchange ratios representing the incomplete discoveries and current errors made up to the moment by profit-seeking entrepreneurs. Thus, market prices offer opportunities for pure profit, and it is up to the alert entrepreneurs to sniff out these opportunities and act on them. This view of profit, significantly, has nothing to do with monopoly power. It is merely the reward for noticing some lack of coordination in the market, and acting on it. As such, it is a necessary incentive for the discovery of new knowledge, not (as in the standard theory) a minimal payment to a disembodied economic agent to stand pat.

■ Advertising and Demand Discovery

In light of the attempts by Chamberlin and Robinson to replace or supplement the notion of perfect competition (see chapter 20), the Austrian approach takes on additional interest. Among contemporary Austrian economists, Israel Kirzner, for one, views the Chamberlin–Robinson reformulation as misguided:

> The new theories failed to perceive that the characteristic features of the real world are simply the manifestations of entrepreneurial competition, a process in which would-be buyers and sellers gropingly seek to discover each other's supply and demand curves. The new theories merely fashioned new equilibrium configurations—based, as was the theory of perfect competition—on given and known demand and supply curves—differing from the earlier theory only in the shapes assigned to these curves. In the course of attempting to account for such market phenomena as quality differentiation, advertising, markets in which few producers were to be found, the new theories were led to conclusions which grossly misinterpret the significance of these phenomena. (*Competition and Entrepreneurship*, p. 29)

The basis for Kirzner's claim is that the theory of monopolistic competition rules out the discovery process. There is no awareness of the need for manufacturers and consumers to experiment in order to find those products and variations that are most wanted. Like the theory it was supposed to supplement, it assumed the market demand to be given beforehand. A second weakness noted by other writers besides Austrians is that the theory offers no explanation of how product differentiation can persist in equilibrium, that is, why rival firms cannot duplicate those product variations that prove successful.

In particular, Austrian economics has provided fresh insights into advertising, which proved to be something of an embarrassment to traditional economic theory. If consumers always have perfect information about the products available, there is no rational explanation for the persistence of advertising. Indeed, it would seem wasteful. To Chamberlin and others, advertising was one way of conveying information to consumers about a product they knew existed. As such, it would be innocuous, even helpful. But persuasion is another matter. Most economists objected to persuasive advertising as unabashed hucksterism. Austrian thinking departs substantially from the conventional view. The Austrians admit that consumers do not always know what products are available, and even if they do, they are not usually informed about their properties. Consequently, the seller has a role in capturing the consumer's attention. But in the Austrian view it doesn't matter whether advertising is purely informational, purely persuasive, or some combination of the two. What matters is that the products are noticed, for then and only then can consumers act entrepreneurially—that is, exercise their decision-making ability.

In a similar fashion, the Austrian notion of monopoly stands outside the orthodox view. Standard theory traditionally assumes that a monopolist's demand curve is known and that his or her ability to raise prices and increase profits depends on the shape of that curve. It is not always explained how monopolists came to know the demand curve, why they are sole producers, and why the threat of competition from other firms does not prevent them from acting as they do. Austrian economists confront these questions from the perspective of demand discovery. They maintain that the presence of monopoly in no way obviates the need for market discovery. Whether or not a firm is a monopolist, it must discover what its customers want and what they are willing to pay for it. Therefore, monopolists are subject to the same competitive market process as other firms. Moreover, monopolists must compete with producers of new and better products even if they do not face competition from producers of the *same* product. Hence it is misleading to characterize monopoly as "the absence of competition." Rather, monopoly implies barriers to entry. Kirzner has said:

> The existence of rivalrous competition requires not large numbers of buyers and sellers but simply *freedom of entry.* Competition places pressure on market participants to discover where and how better opportunities, as yet unnoticed, might be offered to the market. The competitive market process occurs because equilibrium has not yet been attained. This process is thwarted whenever non-market barriers are imposed blocking entry to potential competitors. ("Perils of Regulation," p. 9)

One way to gain an appreciation for the operation of the market process is by reviewing the socialist calculation debate that took place over an extended period of time between Mises and Hayek on the one hand and Oskar Lange and H. D. Dickinson on the other. Mises and Hayek illuminated the enormous difficulties confronting socialist planners trying to emulate the market's result without an actual market in operation. Lange and Dickinson, joined later by Abba Lerner and others, maintained that efficient allocation is achievable under socialism so long as socialist managers follow well-prescribed rules in decision making.

■ The Socialist Calculation Debate

Mises fired the opening salvo in the socialist calculation debate in 1922 by questioning whether socialism was possible at all—whether modern industrialized society could continue to exist if organized along socialist lines. He attacked the basic premise of socialist theorists that the economy could be planned and directed efficiently after a socialist state had abolished money, markets, and the price system. He argued that money prices determined in a market economy were necessary for rational economic calculation. The price system allows resources to freely flow to their most highly valued uses; indeed, it directs resources to their highest valued use. For example, it is technically feasible to construct subway rails out of platinum rather than steel, but to use platinum would be inefficient in the face of less expensive substitutes. Only the price system, representing the competing bids of all potential users of platinum, guarantees that such judgments are made. Without the price system, Mises argued, resources could not be allocated efficiently and the economy would function at a primitive level.

Socialist economists confronted Mises's challenge head-on, with some of the most prominent socialist writers, particularly Oskar Lange and Abba Lerner, acknowledging that Mises had uncovered an important weakness in the socialist theory. Lange even half-seriously proposed that in the future socialist commonwealth a statue be erected to Mises so that no one would forget that prices and markets are essential under socialism, too. But of course, the socialists launched a counterattack. Lange started with a tactical retreat. He claimed that socialism would work if socialist planning were *substituted* for the market mechanism. In other words, the state would set prices for goods and factors of production instead of the market. Managers of state-owned firms would then produce until the marginal cost of their output equaled the "shadow" price of the good. Resources required to produce finished goods would be requisitioned in accordance with this rule, and the state would stand ready to adjust prices in response to any shortages or surpluses that might result.

As clever as this response appeared on the surface, Mises and Hayek now responded with an even more devastating critique. The problem with the state "imitating" the market, they argued, is that the ex ante prices established by government functionaries could never convey accurate information regarding the true opportunity costs associated with resource use. The enormous amount of detailed, specific information required for state-determined prices to match market prices, if it *could* be made available to government bureaucrats, would only be forthcoming at huge transaction costs. In addition, for socialism to approximate market performance, individual incentives would have to be structured to ensure that people within the system would use information and resources efficiently. This could happen only if property were privately owned, a circumstance rejected by socialism.

At its most fundamental level, the socialist calculation debate was a contest over theoretical models. Socialist economic theory is based on Walrasian general-equilibrium models within which the central planning board takes the place of the Walrasian auctioneer. Lange proposed that a central planning board administer resource prices and allow consumer goods to be priced in free markets in order to provide accurate information for factor evaluation. Factor prices would then respond to market eventualities, and the whole process would, by trial and error, simulate the Walrasian *tâtonnement* process. For their part, Mises and Hayek rejected the Walrasian model as unrealistic and inappropriate. In either its pure form or its socialist guise it could not capture enough important features of the real world to make it applicable. In particular, Hayek argued that the information required by the socialist calculation theory can only be ascertained by a continuous process of market discovery. The Austrian criticism was essentially the same as that leveled at the neoclassical model, namely that the proponents of socialism did not understand the *nonparametric* function of prices. Somewhere along the way in the evolution of economic theory, neoclassical economists had forgotten or ignored Cantillon's original vision of the market as an arena in which market participants (i.e., entrepreneurs) nudge prices in the direction of equilibrium by exploiting profit opportunities offered by disequilibrium prices. This vision has been more consistently grasped and maintained by Austrian economists than by any other group. Consequently, they attributed the socialists' myopia to an inappropriate perception of how "perfect" markets operate.

As usual, Hayek gave the most forceful counterargument to the socialist position. In a nutshell, he argued as follows: The information that individuals use to guide their economic activity is vast, detailed, fragmented, and often idiosyncratic.

It is not neatly captured in objective demand and supply functions that are at the ready command of the central planners, because such information is the subject of *continuous discovery* through entrepreneurial action and counteraction. Neoclassical economics stresses only one kind of knowledge—the "engineering knowledge" of technical input-output relations. Austrian economics recognizes and emphasizes the specific knowledge of "time and place," which leads to the perception of profit opportunities in advance of the crowd, as well as the kind of knowledge that enables an individual to conceptualize new methods and new products that may bring large rewards. Market prices in this framework are not parameters. They are the unique and timely results of numerous transactions by individuals possessed of these various bits and forms of knowledge. In turn these prices serve as signals by which decentralized knowledge is collected and coordinated into a systematic whole.

The problem that Mises and Hayek were attacking at base was the effects of different specifications of property rights on individual economic decision making. This is a wide-ranging issue that does not confine itself to the dichotomy between socialism and capitalism. It also pervades the issue of economic regulation, which is a major theme of chapter 24.

Eight decades after the socialist calculation debate began, we may well ask in retrospect how relevant was the controversy. At the end of the twentieth century socialism seemed to be in retreat, but in the new millennium, it seems to be resurgent. As Mark Twain said of himself—"the rumors of my death have been greatly exaggerated"—the same might be said of socialism. Despite claims that they have enlarged the sphere of private market activity and embraced other capitalist reforms, two of the world's largest countries, China and Russia, continue to direct large segments of their economies from the center. And in many underdeveloped countries, authoritarian leaders continue to cling to the socialist model. No one knows what the future holds, but history informs us of two sobering facts about centrally planned economies. First, their economic performance is poor by comparison with capitalist market economies—in some cases, disastrously so. Second, the private sector in socialist economies, usually existing in the form of illegal underground economies, is typically large and important. These facts offer at least a partial vindication of the Austrian critique of socialism.

■ Conclusion

The tradition of economic inquiry begun by Menger continues in the writings of many contemporary economists who adopt the "Austrian" orientation. In this chapter, we have seen that the Austrian tradition is wide-ranging. It starts with the theory of subjective wants, then builds on that primal insight in a methodologically consistent fashion to elucidate broader topics such as money, credit, banking, business cycles, economic development, and the very nature of competition. The distinguishing feature of Austrian macroeconomics is its overriding concern for the microeconomic foundations of macroeconomic principles. While this same concern has been expressed with renewed fervor by many conventional economists in the wake of the perceived failures of Keynesian macroeconomics, many "Austrian" ideas have been ignored by mainstream economic theory. For example, if contemporary monetary economics seems far removed from the concerns of Mises and Hayek, the reason is that it treats all increases in the quantity of money as being essentially alike and assumes that relative prices remain unaltered in the wake of the monetary change. In this way it disregards the question of the transmission mechanism by which the new money makes its impact felt on the macroeconomy.

In the final analysis, the monetarists and the Austrians are closer together than the monetarists and the Keynesians. What the monetarists and the Austrians share is the belief that changes in the quantity of money are the primary cause of aggregate instability. The Austrians, however, have been more sensitive to the ubiquitous effects of changes in relative prices caused by monetary changes. Understanding these differences helps to sort out the various policy proposals that are likely to emanate from each camp. In the face of the Keynesian challenge that "money does not matter," the monetarists have counterattacked that "money does matter." Though unspoken, Mises's monetary theory takes the phrase one step further: In the Austrian view, "money matters all the time!"

References

Hayek, F. A. *Prices and Production*, 2d ed. London: Routledge & Kegan Paul, 1935.

———. *The Counter-Revolution of Science: Studies on the Abuse of Reason*. Indianapolis: Liberty Press, 1979.

Jaffé, William. "Menger, Jevons and Walras De-Homogenized," *Economic Inquiry*, vol. 14 (December 1976), pp. 511–524.

Kirzner, I. M. *Competition and Entrepreneurship*. Chicago: The University of Chicago Press, 1973.

———. "The Perils of Regulation: A Market Process Approach." *Miami: Law and Economics Center Occasional Paper*, 1978.

Mises, Ludwig von. *The Theory of Money and Credit*, H. E. Batson (trans.). New York: The Foundation for Economic Education, 1971 [1912].

———. *Human Action: A Treatise on Economics*. New Haven: Yale University Press, 1949.

Rothbard, M. N. "The Austrian Theory of Money," in E. G. Dolan (ed.), *The Foundations of Modern Austrian Economics*. Kansas City: Sheed & Ward, 1976.

Salerno, J. T. "The Place of Mises's *Human Action* in the Development of Modern Economic Thought," *Quarterly Journal of Austrian Economics*, vol. 2 (Spring 1999), pp. 35–65.

Schumpeter, J. A. "The Instability of Capitalism," *Economic Journal*, vol. 38 (1928), pp. 361–386.

———. *The Theory of Economic Development*, 2d ed., R. Opie (trans.). Cambridge, MA: Harvard University Press, 1934.

———. *Business Cycles*. New York: McGraw-Hill, 1939.

———. *Capitalism, Socialism, and Democracy*, 3d ed. New York: Harper & Row, 1950.

———. *History of Economic Analysis*, E. B. Schumpeter (ed.). New York: Oxford University Press, 1954.

Notes for Further Reading

For an exposition of the Austrian gestalt, see L. H. White, *The Methodology of the Austrian School* (New York: The Center for Libertarian Studies, 1977), and A. H. Shand, *Subjectivist Economics: The New Austrian School* (Exeter: Short Run Press, 1980). See also, E. G. Dolan (ed.), *The Foundations of Modern Austrian Economics* (Kansas City: Sheed & Ward, 1976); S. C. Littlechild, *The Fallacy of the Mixed Economy* (London: Institute for Economic Affairs, 1978); L. S. Moss (ed.), *The Economics of Ludwig von Mises* (Kansas City: Sheed & Ward, 1976); G. P. O'Driscoll, *Economics as a Coordination Problem: The Contributions of Friedrich A. Hayek* (Kansas City: Sheed & Ward, 1977); W. D. Reekie, *Industry, Prices and Markets* (New York: Wiley, 1979); M. J. Rizzo (ed.), *Time,*

Uncertainty and Disequilibrium: Exploration of Austrian Themes (Lexington, MA: Heath, 1979); and L. M. Spadaro, *New Directions in Austrian Economics* (Kansas City: Sheed & Ward, 1978).

Edward Elgar has published several volumes attempting to establish the economic legacy of famous third-generation Austrians; see, *The Legacy of Ludwig Von Mises*, Peter J. Boettke and Peter T. Leeson (eds.) (Cheltenham, UK: Edward Elgar, 2006); *The Legacy of Friedrich A. Hayek*, Peter J. Boettke, Andrew Farant, Greg Ransom, and Gilberto Salgado (eds.) (Cheltenham, UK: Edward Elgar, 2000); and *The Legacy of Joseph A. Schumpeter*, Horst Hanusch (ed.) (Cheltenham, UK: Edward Elgar, 1999). For particularly cogent views from notable "insiders," see Ludwig von Mises, *The Historical Setting of the Austrian School* (New Rochelle, NY: Arlington House, 1969); L. M. Lachmann, "The Importance in the History of Ideas of the Austrian School of Economics," J. H. McCulloch (trans.), *Zeitschrift für Nationalökonomie*, vol. 26 (1966), pp. 152–167; and F. A. Hayek, "Economic Thought: The Austrian School," *International Encyclopedia of the Social Sciences*, vol. 4 (1968), pp. 458–462. Earlene Craver, "The Emigration of the Austrian Economists," *History of Political Economy*, vol. 18 (Spring 1986), pp. 1–32, recounts the early academic careers of third-generation Austrians, especially Mises, Hayek, and Schumpeter.

Mises's magnum opus, *Human Action: A Treatise on Economics* (New Haven, CT: Yale University Press, 1949), is a much-neglected book that still repays careful reading. Eamon Butler, *Ludwig von Mises: Fountainhead of the Modern Microeconomics Revolution* (Brookfield, VT: Gower Publishing, 1988), presents a clear and well-reasoned exposition of the main lines of Mises's work. Mises's opening salvo in the socialist calculation debate has been translated and reprinted in *Collectivist Economic Planning*, F. A. Hayek (ed.) (London: Routledge, 1935). See also Ludwig Mises, *Socialism: An Economic and Sociological Analysis*, J. Kahane (trans.) (New Haven, CT: Yale University Press, 1951). Additional appreciations of the problems involved in socialist planning can be found in G. W. Nutter, "Markets without Property: A Grand Illusion," in *Money, the Market and the State: Essays in Honor of James Muir Waller*, N. A. Beadles and L. A. Drewry, Jr. (eds.) (Athens: University of Georgia Press, 1968); and in D. T. Armentano, "Resource Allocation Problems under Socialism," W. P. Snavely (ed.), *Theory of Economic Systems: Capitalism, Socialism, Corporatism* (Columbus, OH: Merrill, 1969).

The socialist side of the debate was put forth most vigorously by Oskar Lange and F. M. Taylor, *On the Economic Theory of Socialism*, B. E. Lippincott (ed.) (New York: McGraw-Hill, 1964); H. D. Dickinson, *Economics of Socialism* (London: Oxford University Press, 1939); and A. P. Lerner, *The Economics of Control* (New York: Macmillan, 1944). Peter Murrell, "Did the Theory of Market Socialism Answer the Challenge of Ludwig Von Mises? A Reinterpretation of the Socialist Controversy," *History of Political Economy*, vol. 15 (Spring 1983), pp. 92–105, contends that the socialist reply to Mises was not definitive and that modern economics now has the tools to confront the issues Mises raised long ago. For more on this debate, see G. K. Chaloupek, "The Austrian Debate on Economic Calculation in a Socialist Economy," *History of Political Economy*, vol. 22 (Winter 1990), pp. 659–675; Don Lavoie, *Rivalry and Central Planning: The Socialist Calculation Debate Reconsidered* (New York: Cambridge University Press, 1985); and J. T. Salerno, "Ludwig von Mises as Social Rationalist," *Review of Austrian Economics*, vol. 4 (1990), pp. 26–54. Steven Horwitz, "Monetary Calculation and Mises's Critique of Planning," *History of Political Economy*, vol. 30 (Fall 1998), pp. 427–450, concluded that the Austrian position has often been misunderstood—the central issue for Mises was always how prices emerge in a money-using economy. Mateusz Machaj, "Market Socialism and the Property Problem: Different Perspective of the Socialist Calculation Debate," *Quarterly Journal of Austrian Economics*, vol. 10 (Winter 2007), pp. 257–280, presents an updated summary and appreciation of the socialist calculation debate and a careful consideration of the different arguments advanced by the major contributors.

Regarded as one of the preeminent thinkers of the twentieth century, as much for his work outside economics as for his work within, Hayek made contributions to the fields of economics, psychology, political philosophy, and the methodology of the social sciences. Hayek's *The Constitution of Liberty* (Chicago: University of Chicago Press, 1960) has become a classic of its kind; and his three-volume work, *Law, Legislation and Liberty* (Chicago: University of Chicago Press, 1973–79) is destined for the same. The role of psychology in shaping Hayek's thought is the subject of Nicolò De Vecchi, "The Place of Gestalt Psychology in the Making of Hayek's Thought," *History of Political Economy*, vol. 35 (Spring 2003), pp. 135–162. On economics as a coordination problem and the emergence of spontaneous order, see Müfit Sabooglu, "Hayek and Spontaneous Orders," *Journal of the History of Economic Thought*, vol. 18 (Fall 1996), pp. 347–364.

In the first-ever biography of Hayek, Lanny Ebenstein, *Friedrich Hayek: A Biography* (London: Palgrave Macmillan, 2001), attempted to take the full measure of Hayek's accomplishment. A somewhat higher flight has been taken by Bruce Caldwell, *Hayek's Challenge: An Intellectual Biography of F. A. Hayek* (Chicago: University of Chicago Press, 2004). Caldwell is also general editor of *The Collected Works of F. A. Hayek*, a series published by the University of Chicago Press. *Hayek on Hayek: An Autobiographical Dialogue*, Stephen Kresge and Leif Weinar (eds.) (Chicago: University of Chicago Press, 1994), is a complete collection of previously unpublished autobiographical sketches and a wide selection of interviews.

We will not attempt to give an exhaustive bibliography of Hayek's writings here, but see O'Driscoll (*op. cit.*) for more detail. A significant number of Hayek's early and later writings on Austrian themes have been collected and published in three short books: *Prices and Production* (London: Routledge, 1935); *Individualism and Economic Order* (Chicago: University of Chicago Press, 1948); and *New Studies in Philosophy, Politics, and the History of Ideas* (Chicago: University of Chicago Press, 1978). Of general interest, see Bruce Caldwell, "Hayek's Transformation," *History of Political Economy*, vol. 20 (Winter 1988), pp. 513–541; same author, "Why Didn't Hayek Review Keynes's *General Theory*?" *History of Political Economy*, vol. 30 (Winter 1998), pp. 545–569. For a reply to Caldwell's query, see Susan Howson, "Why Didn't Hayek Review Keynes's *General Theory*? A Partial Answer," *History of Political Economy*, vol. 33 (Summer 2001), pp. 369–374. Papers probing the nature of Hayek's business cycle theory include: G. R. Steele, "Hayek's Contribution to Business Cycle Theory: A Modern Assessment," *History of Political Economy*, vol. 24 (Summer 1992), pp. 477–492; Hans-Michael Trautwein, "Money, Equilibrium, and the Business Cycle: Hayek's Wicksellian Dichotomy," *History of Political Economy*, vol. 28 (Spring 1996), pp. 27–55; Harald Hagemann and Hans-Michael Trautwein, "Cantillon and Ricardo Effects: Hayek's Contributions to Business Cycle Theory," *The European Journal of the History of Economic Thought*, vol. 5 (Summer 1998), pp. 292–316; J. P. Cochran and F. R. Glahe, "The Keynes–Hayek Debate: Lessons for Contemporary Business Cycle Theorists," *History of Political Economy*, vol. 26 (Spring 1994), pp. 69–96. Roger W. Garrison, "Overconsumption and Forced Saving in the Mises–Hayek Theory of the Business Cycle," *History of Political Economy*, vol. 36 (Summer 2004), pp. 323–349, attempts to sort out the differences between Mises and Hayek and reconcile the Austrian theory with contemporary macroeconomics.

Although a significant amount of attention has been devoted to Hayek's business cycle theory, much less attention has been lavished on the banking theory underpinning his business cycle model. For a notable exception, see Lawrence H. White, "Why Didn't Hayek Favor Laissez Faire in Banking?" *History of Political Economy*, vol. 31 (Winter 1999), pp. 753–769; and same author, "Hayek's Monetary Theory and Policy: A Critical Reconstruction," *Journal of Money, Credit and Banking*, vol. 31 (February 1999), pp. 109–120. J. S. Ferris and J. A. Galbraith, "On Hayek's Denationalization of Money, Free Banking and Inflation Targeting." *The European Journal of the History of Economic Thought*, vol. 13 (2006), pp. 213-231, examine Hayek's proposals for banking reform.

Various aspects of Hayek's thought covering subjectivism, methodology, and institutions are treated by: William Butos and Roger Koppl, "The Varieties of Subjectivism: Keynes and Hayek on Expectations," *History of Political Economy*, vol. 29 (Summer 1997), pp. 327–359; K.-H. Paqué, "Pattern Predictions in Economics: Hayek's Methodology of the Social Sciences Revisited," *History of Political Economy*, vol. 22 (Summer 1990), pp. 281–294; and P. Garrouste, "Menger and Hayek on Institutions: Continuity and Discontinuity," *Journal of the History of Economic Thought*, vol. 16 (Fall 1994), pp. 270–291. An even broader array of papers was collected from the first conference of the *Association des Historiens de la Tradition Économique Autrichienne* and published under the title, *F. A. Hayek as a Political Economist. Economic Analysis and Values*, Jack Birner, Pierre Garrouste, and Thierry Aimar (eds.) (London: Routledge, 2002).

In many respects, Hayek's *The Road to Serfdom* (Chicago: The University of Chicago Press, 1944), has never lost its relevance. Ben Jackson, "Freedom, the Common Good, and the Rule of Law: Lippmann and Hayek on Economic Planning," *Journal of the History of Ideas*, vol. 73 (January 2012), pp. 47–68, weighs Walter Lippmann's influence in the 1930s and '40s on Hayek's political thought and notes that Lippmann anticipated Hayek's later arguments that: Planning would destroy civil and political freedom, certain legal orders are necessary for the preservation of liberty, and critics of planning should be able to produce a suitable replacement consistent with the previous principle.

Generalized dissatisfaction with Keynesian fiscal policies in the postwar period has generated resurgent interest in Schumpeter and his ideas. Two biographies on Schumpeter and his work are R. L. Allen, *Opening Doors: The Life and Work of Joseph Schumpeter*, 2 vols. (New Brunswick, NJ: Transaction Publishers, 1991), and Richard Swedberg, *Schumpeter: A Biography* (Princeton, NJ: Princeton University Press, 1991), which has received more favorable reviews. Also by Swedberg, "Joseph A. Schumpeter and the Tradition of Economic Sociology," *Journal of Institutional and Theoretical Economics*, vol. 145 (September 1989), pp. 508–524, traces the influence of Weber and Sombart on Schumpeter's thought. Yuichi Shionoya, "Schumpeter on Schmoller and Weber: A Methodology of Economic Sociology," *History of Political Economy*, vol. 23 (Summer 1990), pp. 193–220, is a complement to Swedberg's article. Also see Yuichi Shionoya, *Schumpeter and the Idea of Social Science* (Cambridge University Press, 1997).

Peter Kesting, "The Interdependence between Economic Analysis and Methodology in the Work of Joseph A. Schumpeter," *The European Journal of the History of Economic Thought*, vol. 13 (2006), pp. 387–410, examines Schumpeter's work from a methodological perspective, concluding that Schumpeter's total economic work can be properly understood only from the point of view of methodology. Agnès Festré and Eric Nasica, "Schumpeter on Money, Banking and Finance: an Institutionalist Perspective," *The European Journal of the History of Economic Thought*, vol. 16 (2009), pp. 325–356, claim that an institutional analysis of Schumpeter's theory of money, banking, and finance is natural given his emphasis on economic sociology in his methodological views.

Schumpeter's big themes of entrepreneurship and innovation are explored by Nicolò De Vecchi, *Entrepreneurs, Institutions and Economic Change: The Economic Thought of J. A. Schumpeter* (Cheltenham, UK: Edward Elgar, 1995); Enrico Santarelli and Enzo Pesciarelli, "The Emergence of a Vision: The Development of Schumpeter's Theory of Entrepreneurship," *History of Political Economy*, vol. 22 (Winter 1990), pp. 677–696; and Govidan Parayil, "Schumpeter on Invention, Innovation and Technological Change," *Journal of the History of Economic Thought*, vol. 13 (Spring 1991), pp. 78–89. Mark W. Frank, "Schumpeter on Entrepreneurs and Innovation," *Journal of the History of Economic Thought*, vol. 20 (December 1998), pp. 505–516, denies the dichotomous nature of Schumpeter's entrepreneur. *Joseph Alois Schumpeter: Entrepreneurship, Style and Vision*, Juergen Backhouse (ed.) (Dordrecht, Netherlands: Kluwer Publishers, 2003), offers a somewhat broader sweep; of particular interest in this volume is the chapter by Alexander Ebner, "The Institutional Analysis of Entrepreneurship: Historicist Aspects of Schumpeter's Development Theory," pp. 117–140, which offers a reconstruction of Schumpeter's concept of entrepreneurship in light of the influence of Gustave Schmoller (see chapter 11). Gilles Campagnolo and Christel Vivel, "Before Schumpeter: Forerunners of the Theory of the Entrepreneur in 1900s German Political Economy—Werner Sombart, Friedrich von Wieser," *The European Journal of the History of Economic Thought*, vol. 19, (November 2012), pp. 908–943, question the conceptual connection between Schumpeter, Sombart, and Wieser on entrepreneurship by showing which views these authors shared on the character of the entrepreneur, the role of the entrepreneurial function in the economic process, and the evolution of entrepreneurship until the stage of developed capitalism. They conclude that the entrepreneur is a keystone for *building* capitalism. Joseph T. Salerno, "The Entrepreneur: Real and Imagined." *Quarterly Journal of Austrian Economics*, vol. 11 (2008), pp.188–207, provides an overview of the Austrian approach to the entrepreneur through a textual analysis of the writings of its key proponents and discusses the differences between the approaches taken by Mises and Kirzner. Nicolai J. Foss and Peter G. Klein, *Organizing Entrepreneurial Judgment: A New Approach to the Firm* (Cambridge: Cambridge University Press, 2012), survey Austrian work on the entrepreneur and the theory of the firm, with particular emphasis on Knight's (and Mises's) work on uncertainty and judgment.

The Misesian tradition has been carried on in America by Murray Rothbard and Israel Kirzner. See particularly M. N. Rothbard, *Man, Economy and State: A Treatise on Economic Principles* (New York: Van Nostrand, 1962). Rothbard is also the author of an Austrian-centered history of economic thought, *An Austrian Perspective on the History of Economic Thought*, 2 vols. (Brookfield, VT: Edward Elgar, 1995). Joseph T. Salerno, "The Rebirth of Austrian Economics—In Light of Austrian Economics," *Quarterly Journal of Austrian Economics*, vol. 5 (Winter 2002), pp. 111–128, credits Rothbard with the modern revival of the Austrian School. Kirzner's work is on conspicuous display in I. M. Kirzner, *Competition and Entrepreneurship* (Chicago: The University of Chicago Press, 1973); same author, *Perception, Opportunity and Profit* (Chicago: The University of Chicago Press, 1979); and again, *Discovery and the Capitalist Process* (Chicago: The University of Chicago Press, 1985). For a treatment of advertising (a favorite Austrian theme) that poses a "process" view of competition in contrast to the conventional view, see R. B. Ekelund, Jr., and D. S. Saurman, *Advertising and the Market Process* (San Francisco: Pacific Research Institute for Public Policy, 1988). See also, R. F. Hébert, "Advertising," in Peter Boettke (ed.), *The Elgar Companion to Austrian Economics*, (Aldershot, UK: Edward Elgar, 1994), pp. 389–393.

Ludwig Lachmann reflects an Austrian influence absorbed from Hayek at the London School of Economics; see Lachmann, *Capital, Expectations and the Market Process* (Kansas City: Sheed & Ward, 1977); and same author, "From Mises to Shackle: An Essay on Austrian Economics and the Kaleidic Society," *Journal of Economic Literature*, vol. 14 (March 1976), pp. 54–61.

The Ludwig von Mises Institute located in Auburn, Alabama, is a research and educational center for the Austrian School of economics, following the intellectual tradition of Ludwig von Mises (1881–1973) and Murray N. Rothbard (1926–1995). It conducts a variety of teaching and fellowship programs and offers a vast array of publications, including the *Quarterly Journal of Austrian Economics* and the *Journal of Libertarian Studies*. For representative academic works sponsored by the Mises Institute, see *15 Great Austrian Economists*, R. G. Holcombe (ed.) (Auburn, AL: Ludwig von Mises Institute, 1999); L. H. Rockwell, Jr., *Gold Standard: An Austrian Perspective* (Lexington, MA: D. C. Heath, 1985); John V. Denson (ed.), *Costs of War: America's Pyrrhic Victories* (New Brunswick, NJ: Transaction, 1997); same author, *Reassessing the Presidency: The Rise of the Executive State and the Decline of Freedom* (Auburn, AL: Ludwig von Mises Institute, 2001). The Mises Institute web site, http://mises.org, provides open access to the most comprehensive source of materials and publications on the Austrian school, is linked to classrooms and libraries around the world, and at this writing, attracts more Internet traffic than any other market-oriented, nonprofit organization.

Some works to consult that are not strictly Austrian but bear closely on the nature of subjectivism, especially in regard to costs, include A. A. Alchian, *Economic Forces at Work* (Indianapolis: Liberty Press, 1977), particularly pp. 273–334; J. M. Buchanan, *Cost and Choice* (Chicago: Markham, 1969); and *L. S. E. Essays on Costs*, J. M. Buchanan and G. F. Thirlby (eds.) (New York: New York University Press, 1981). For an Austrian perspective on some of the topics not treated in this chapter, see F. A. Hayek, *Monetary Theory and the Trade Cycle* (New York: A. M. Kelley, 1975); L. M. Lachmann, *Capital and Its Structure* (Kansas City: Sheed & Ward, 1977); R. W. Garrison, *Austrian Macroeconomics: A Diagrammatic Exposition* (Menlo Park, CA: Institute for Humane Studies, 1978); J. R. Hicks, *Capital and Time: A Neo-Austrian Theory* (Oxford: Clarendon Press, 1973); and M. N. Rothbard, *America's Great Depression* (Kansas City: Sheed & Ward, 1975).

G. L. S. Shackle has written at length on the problem of time and uncertainty, notably in *Uncertainty in Economics* (London: Cambridge University Press, 1955), and in *Epistemics and Economics* (London: Cambridge University Press, 1972). T. W. Hutchison and Brian Loasby (a student of Shackle) have sounded related themes, the former in *Knowledge and Ignorance in Economics* (Chicago: The University of Chicago Press, 1977) and the latter in *Choice, Complexity and Ignorance* (London: Cambridge University Press, 1976).

Historical development of the mainstream notion of competition of which the Austrians have been critical is the subject of several papers. See G. J. Stigler, "Perfect Competition, Historically Contemplated," in Stigler (ed.), *Essays in the History of Economics* (Chicago: The University of Chicago Press, 1965); P. J. McNulty, "Economic Theory and the Meaning of Competition," *Quarterly Journal of Economics*, vol. 82 (November 1968), pp. 639–656; and K. G. Dennis, *"Competition" in the History of Economic Thought* (New York: Arno Press, 1977). On the importance and significance of property rights in economic theory, see A. A. Alchian, "Some Economics of Property Rights," in Alchian (ed.), *Economic Forces at Work* (Indianapolis: Liberty Press, 1977); and E. G. Furubotn and S. Pejovich (eds.), *The Economics of Property Rights* (Cambridge, MA: Ballinger, 1974).

The entrepreneur, who assumes such a central role in the neo-Austrian paradigm, emerges chameleon-like from a study of past economic thought. Different writers have conceived the concept and role of this prime economic actor in many different ways, so much so that in contemporary economics the term is often used indiscriminately, or at best, ambiguously. An attempt to review the historical record and to distill meaning and direction for the notion of entrepreneurship is contained in R. F. Hébert and A. N. Link, *The Entrepreneur: Mainstream Views and Radical Critiques*, 2d ed. (New York: Praeger, 1988); and, same authors, *A History of Entrepreneurship* (New York: Routledge, 2009).

24

The New Political Economy
Public Choice and Regulation

The great classical writers, such as Adam Smith, Jeremy Bentham, and John Stuart Mill, considered economics to be a social science in the broadest possible sense. Political economy, as they called the "new" discipline, emphasized the adjective almost as much as the noun. In the eighteenth and early nineteenth centuries economics was an inquiry into human behavior, institutions, policy, and policy formation. As economics progressed through the nineteenth and twentieth centuries, however, the scope of its inquiry gradually narrowed. Indeed, we have now come to the point that in some graduate institutions in the United States and abroad, economics is seen more as a branch of applied mathematics than a social science. In the quest to formalize the subject, political and institutional concerns have often been relegated to second-class status within economics curricula (despite Veblen's influence).

But there have always been economists who maintained an interest in the interface between "politics" (political behavior and institutions) and the motives of self-interested economic actors. For them, "economic" behavior is not limited to pecuniary matters. Why should politicians be regarded as selfless lawgivers, whose actions are exogenous to the economic happenings in society? Are they not like the rest of us, self-interested competitors maximizing returns (power, position, votes, etc.) under certain constraints (reelection, for instance)? The important point is that in seeking to optimize their own interests, politicians have an impact on the entire economic system, for example, through fiscal policy or through the supply of industrial regulation. The germ of these notions—especially the idea of political action as an endogenous force—has always been present in economic literature, but in the past fifty years renewed and intensified interest has been directed toward these issues, and in the process, economics has been reborn as a political and social science.

The purpose of this chapter is to show how the self-interested economic motives postulated by classical and neoclassical economists are applied and extended in contemporary economics. Our focus is on two major contemporary themes—public choice and the economic approach to regulation. Even a cursory investigation of these two important and developing areas reveals a fundamental continuity in economic analysis stretching from Adam Smith to the present. In addition, such active concerns on the part of prominent modern writers are evidence that, despite the recent surge of mathematical formalism in the discipline, economics is not down at the heels as a *social* science.

Public Choice

The "new" term for political economy goes by the name of *public choice*. Modern public choice is a study of the political mechanisms or institutions through which taxes and expenditures are determined; that is, it is a study of the demand for and the supply of *public* goods. Public choice employs the simple analytics of competition to make fact-based statements concerning institutions and events in the public sector. Although the economics of the *private* sector has been well developed over the last two centuries, until recently an analysis of how social goods are supplied and demanded took a back seat to the central concerns of most economists.

Some classical and neoclassical writers, such as Adam Smith, Alfred Marshall, and A. C. Pigou, always paid attention to public finance. However, the Marshallian–Pigovian approach to public finance, antedated as we have seen by a cadre of French engineers, focused on "problem solving" in the provision of *specific* public goods. Moreover, its focus was almost exclusively on the tax side of the fiscal equation. The welfare and efficiency effects of various types of taxes were stock-in-trade for neoclassical (Marshall–Pigou) analysis, but it never occurred to writers in this somewhat insular Anglo-Saxon tradition that fiscal decisions were the result of choice on the part of both demanders and suppliers acting through a process of political filtration.

Modern research has demonstrated conclusively that intellectual efforts to place fiscal theory on more broad-based interdependencies were emerging in Italian and Scandinavian writings in the late nineteenth century. James M. Buchanan, Nobel laureate and founder-pioneer of modern public-choice theory, investigated the classical, Italian tradition in public finance (1880–1940) and contrasted it to the Anglo-Saxon (Marshallian–Pigouvian) model.[1] He wrote:

> As early as the 1880s, Mazzola, Pantaleoni, Sax, and De Viti De Marco made rudimentary efforts to analyze the public economy within an exchange framework. Sax and Mazzola discussed the demand side of public goods by identifying collective as distinct from private wants. Pantaleoni extended the marginal calculus to apply to the legislator who makes choices for both sides of the budget. De Viti De Marco explicitly constructed a model in which the consumers and the suppliers-producers of public goods make up the same community of persons. ("Public Finance," p. 384)[2]

In addition, Swedish economists Knut Wicksell (1851–1926) and Erik Lindahl (1891–1960) were hard at work developing a holistic approach to the public sector, with the goal of explaining the determination of a public budget within a political process rather than treat budgets as the endogenous dictates of a Platonic philosopher-king. Contemporary movements among public-choice theorists to establish the entire fiscal sector of the economy within a general-equilibrium theory owe much to the efforts of these Continental economists.

The emergence of Continental contributions to public-sector equilibrium came as no surprise to Buchanan, because he regarded these developments as a straightforward extension of the emergent neoclassical (marginalist) theory of *private* mar-

[1] Buchanan chronicles this tradition in his essay "La scienza delle finanze: The Italian Tradition in Public Finance" (see references).

[2] Buchanan's essay "Public Finance and Public Choice" (see references) provides a fine introduction to contemporary public choice and its history, as does Randall G. Holcombe's "Concepts of Public Sector Equilibrium" (see references). The spirit of our discussion, as well as some details, follow these two papers closely.

kets in the 1870s (see chapters 14–17). However, the vexatious problem for the historian of economics is to explain what Buchanan termed "the long-continued failure of English-language economists to make comparative extensions of their basic framework or to acknowledge an interest in the continental efforts" ("Public Finance," p. 384). The bridge between these early Continental contributions and the emergence of modern public-choice theory is a long one that has, in the main, spanned the Atlantic and reached bedrock in the United States. Contemporary public-choice theory is essentially an ongoing American achievement, originating in the late 1930s and 1940s.[3] The content of this achievement is both extensive and detailed. Voting theory, for example, is an integral and complex part of public choice. Space constraints in a book such as this prohibit a detailed account of the entire field. We therefore confine our discussion to some simple concepts and areas of concern in public-choice theory so readers might grasp an overview of this developing paradigm in contemporary economics.

Public-Goods Demand and the Median-Voter Model

The theory of public-goods demand is an integral aspect of contemporary public-choice theory. It provides a good example of how economic analysis developed to handle one problem can often be applied to new problems. In this case the theory of public-goods demand is analogous in most respects to the Mill–Marshall joint-supply theory applied to the simultaneous production of such items as beef and hides, mutton and wool, and so on (see chapter 8 for the introduction of the joint-supply model). Originally articulated by Howard Bowen in 1943, the necessary conditions for allocative efficiency in the provision of a public good were developed by Paul Samuelson in 1954 in a classic paper entitled "The Pure Theory of Public Expenditures." A public good in this context may be distinguished from a private good insofar as an individual's consumption of the public good does not reduce all other individuals' *simultaneous* consumption. In the private-good case, if X_T is the total consumption of shoes, then $X_T = x_1 + x_2 + \ldots + x_n$, where $x_1 + x_2$, etc., is the sum of all individuals' consumption of shoes. In the public-goods case, X_p may be total consumption of, say, national defense, and $X_p = x_1 = x_2 = \ldots = x_n$, where all individuals consume the *same* amount of defense. In the latter case, one individual's consumption of defense does not detract from another's, and all consume the *same quantity* of defense.

Units of measurement are obviously important. A "unit" of a good is defined as the minimum quantity of that good required to provide more than one consumer simultaneously with that particular bundle of services that distinguishes the good in question from all other goods. Accordingly, a dozen pencils would not be considered a unit of a public good even though twelve individuals could consume this good simultaneously. The reason is that one pencil is capable of providing the unique bundle of services (writing, erasing, etc.) usually associated with the term "pencil." A unit of pencils would be a private good because its services are provided to only a single individual. A Polaris submarine, on the other hand, can be viewed as a unit of a public good because it provides "safety from nuclear attack" simultane-

[3] The early, seminal American contributions were those of Richard A. Musgrave, "The Voluntary Exchange Theory of Public Economy," Howard R. Bowen, "The Interpretation of Voting in the Allocation of Resources," and Buchanan, "The Pure Theory of Government Finance: A Suggested Approach," (all cited in the references). This ongoing tradition in contemporary American economics persists at the Center for the Study of Public Choice, founded by Buchanan, and in *Public Choice*, a journal devoted to the subject, of which Gordon Tullock is the founding editor.

ously to more than one individual. While the provision of "safety from nuclear attack" as a private good might be possible (individual concrete underground silos, for example), the cost per individual presumably is less when the service is provided as a public good.

Some other characteristics of public goods are important though they are not unique to public goods. For instance, in the public-good case described by Samuelson, the *marginal* cost of supplying additional users would be negligible—sometimes zero—and the exclusion of nonpaying consumers would be impossible. Some goods in the private sector approximate the above cost conditions (a bus trip for a particular journey, perhaps). Moreover, it may always be possible to exclude consumers. Even in the case of national defense it would theoretically be possible to remove nonpayers to (nonprotected) islands in remote areas of the Pacific Ocean, although such exclusion would be costly. The conceptual difficulties of defining a *pure* public good are many, therefore, but these matters need not detain us here. Let us assume that joint-consumption, zero marginal cost, and nonexcludability conditions apply and turn to the Bowen–Samuelson equilibrium of figure 24-1. (Note that the details of this case are analogous to Mill's model of joint supply for jointly produced private goods [such as steers] depicted graphically in figure 8-1.)

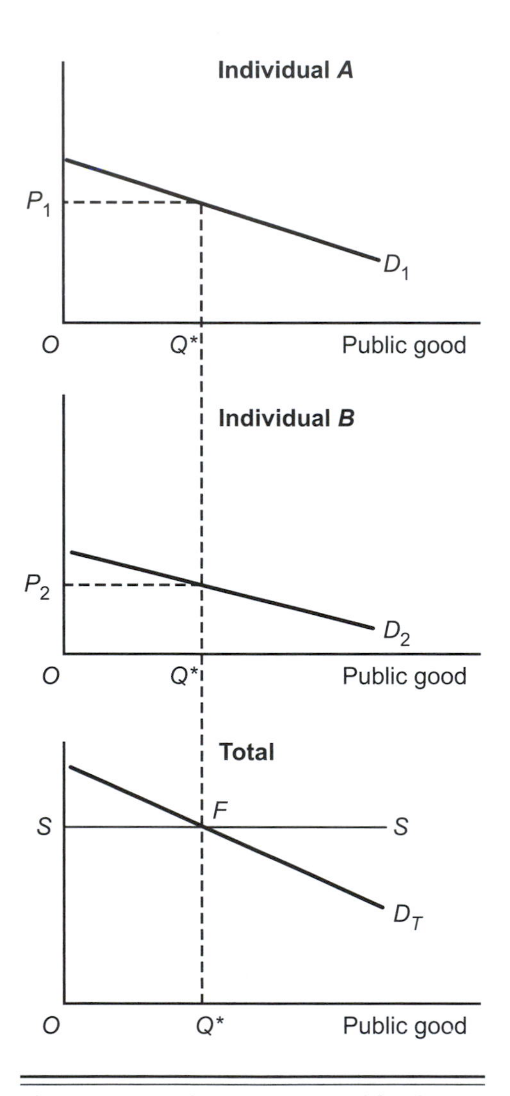

Figure 24-1 The total demand for the public good is the vertical sum of individual demands D_1 and D_2, with each demander consuming Q^* quantity of the good.

The two upper quadrants of figure 24-1 depict the demands for a public good (education, Polaris submarines, etc.) on the part of a closed community of two individuals. These demands are summed vertically in order to get the total demand for the public good shown (with a constant-cost supply curve) in the lowest quadrant of figure 24-1. Insofar as consumption by these two people is noncompeting, the community demand curve for a public good can be obtained by vertical summation of individual demand curves. Individual *A*'s consumption of nuclear submarines does not compete with individual *B*'s. Consumption is simultaneous and "complementary." Most importantly, note that the equilibrium described in the public-goods case with simultaneity of consumption requires (in exact contrast to the private-goods example) that the *same* quantity of the good (Q^*) be consumed by *each* consumer. Different prices are required in equilibrium to get different individuals with different demands to hold Q^* of the commodity. The equilibrium prices would not be equal except in the unlikely event that the two individuals' demands are identical.

Samuelson's description of the demand for public goods is perfectly abstract and general, but in fitting the principle to real-world applications several difficulties emerge. When the good in question is not *purely* public in Samuelson's sense, the optimal size of the consuming group will not be known, and the question that begs answering is: What quantity should be produced (i.e., what Q^*)? In his 1943 paper, Bowen answered:

> It is, of course, no more difficult to obtain information on the cost of producing social goods than to get data on individual goods; but to estimate marginal rates of substitution [public-goods demands] presents serious problems, since it requires the measurement of the preferences for goods which, by their very nature, cannot be subjected to individual consumer choice. ("Interpretation of Voting," pp. 32–33)

In other words, some sort of proxy for public-goods demands is required, and Bowen suggested that under certain conditions, voting (in a democratic setting) is the closest substitute for consumer choice.[4] This insight led to the development of the *median-voter model* (actually a whole set of models), which became a major tool of public-choice theorists in the 1960s and 1970s, owing in large part to the persistent efforts of Kenneth Arrow and Duncan Black. Although the median-voter model is a central element of public-choice theory, it is a fairly technical subject and a full discussion of it would take us too far afield from our present purpose.[5] Nevertheless, the Bowen model and its variants (along with possible complications and problems) may be presented in simple terms.

Any individual's demand for public goods will be determined by two things: (1) the satisfaction he or she expects to receive from various amounts of the good, and (2) the cost to the *individual* of alternative amounts of the public good. In order to look at even a basic model of voting behavior, it is necessary to invoke simplifying assumptions. First, assume that all members of a community actually vote and thereby correctly reveal their individual preferences for the social good. Second, suppose that the total and average cost of the good to the community is known and that it is divided equally among all citizens. Finally, assume with Bowen "that the several curves of individual marginal substitution [i.e., the individual demand curves] are distributed according to the normal law of error" ("Interpretation of Voting," p. 34). This simply means that there are a large number of demand curves and that, for any quantity of the public good provided, there will be demands clustered symmetrically about a mode. Such a community may be illustrated easily in terms of figure 24-2 (on the following page), which shows individual demands clustered about the demand of the median voter. The pro rata tax share (AC/N) is the same for each voter-consumer.

Now consider provision of some quantity of the public good Q_1 in figure 24-2. Clearly for the *same* quantity of the good, different demanders would be willing to

[4] Bowen was not the first economist, and certainly not the last, to deal with this general problem. Harold Hotelling broached the issue of the median voter in 1929 (see references).

[5] The interested reader should consult two works central to the argument, Kenneth Arrow's *Social Choice and Individual Values* and Duncan Black's *The Theory of Committees and Elections* (see "References" and notes for further reading). These works raised the question of the efficiency and workability of majority rule through the median voter in registering individual preferences for social goods. The fascinating intellectual history of the efficiency of voting rules is presented in Black's book. The contributions of the Rev. C. L. Dodgson, better known by his pen name, Lewis Carroll, are particularly interesting (see Black's *Theory*, pp. 189–213).

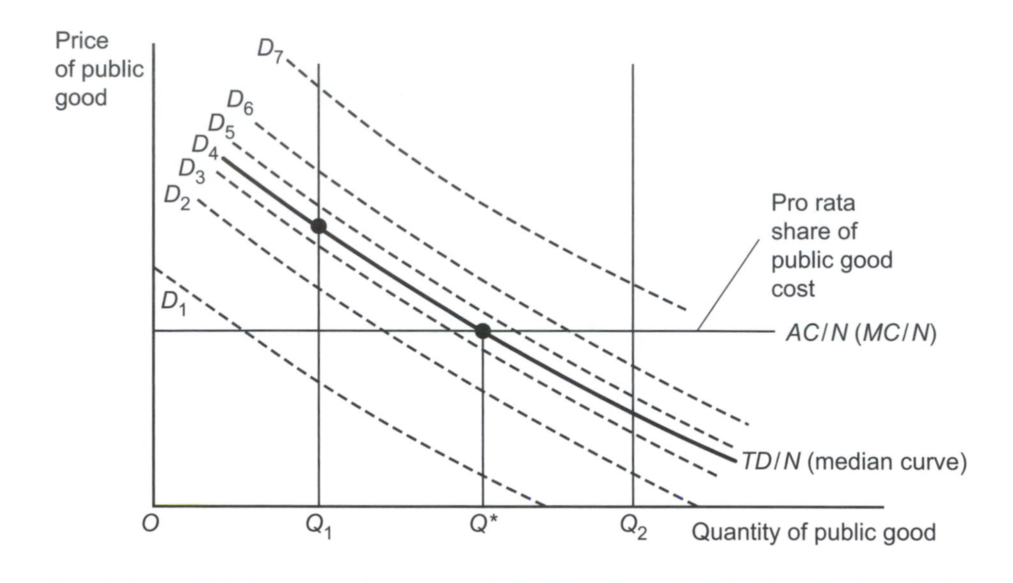

Figure 24-2 At quantity Q_1 of a public good, the median voter values Q at some rate D_4, which is higher than the pro rata tax share. Thus, with majority rule, any Q proposed above Q_1 will win approval and any Q proposed above Q^* will fail to carry.

pay different tax shares. Thus, for Q_1, those who value the good highly would be willing to pay D_7, those placing little value on the public good would only be willing to pay D_1, and so on. The median voter, however, values Q_1 at some rate D_4, which is higher than the pro rata tax share to all taxpayers who receive the public good $AC/N(MC/N)$. Thus, in, say, a town-meeting process employing majority rule, any Q proposed above Q_1 will win approval; any Q proposed above Q^*, such as Q_2, will fail to carry. In this process, the quantity preferred by the median voter, Q^*, will always defeat any other motion.

Under certain circumstances the median-voter process can yield similar results in other variants of the model, such as voting for marginal increases of a public good in a voter referendum, or through elected representatives. In the latter case, if the people are consulted on *particular* policies and if representatives identify with specific issues, the results of the process can approximate those of figure 24-2. Many factors affect voting. Public officials working through certain institutions may upset the results of Bowen equilibrium by manipulating the agenda or simply by representing and voting on a large variety of issues. Thus, majority-rule election processes do not ensure that voter preferences for public goods will be optimized. However, it does seem to be a practical system for approximating voter preferences.

Lindahl Tax Prices and Wicksellian Public Finance

Distribution of the tax share is a crucial feature in the provision of public goods because each individual will demand a good both on the basis of its (marginal) value and on the basis of its cost. The "marginal cost" is simply the share of taxes that the citizen-consumer pays for his or her portion of the output. A major problem in public choice, then, is to devise a means for providing an optimal quantity of any public good such that, for the *single* quantity produced, some distribution of the tax burden may be found that equates the marginal valuation of the good to the marginal tax share for each citizen-consumer. Two early writers on public choice, Erik Lindahl and Knut Wicksell, were interested in different aspects of this question and set out on different analytical paths.

Lindahl Equilibrium. In his 1919 contribution entitled "Just Taxation—A Positive Solution" (part of his book *Die Gerechtigkeit der Besteuerung*), Lindahl treated the problem of tax-share determination as one of bilateral exchange in an "isolated" community with two categories of taxpayers: one "well-to-do" and the other "relatively poor." He saw the distribution of the tax shares as a problem to be settled by "a kind of economic exchange," based on free argument.[6] Lindahl wrote: "[In a] solution in which both parties have equally safeguarded the economic rights to which they are entitled under the existing property order," the price of the collective good "tends to correspond to marginal utility for each interested party" ("Just Taxation," pp. 172–173). This means that tax price will equal the affected voter's (or group of voters') marginal valuation of the public good.

The modern adaptation of Lindahl equilibrium is demonstrated in figure 24-3 (which is constructed in the same manner as figure 24-1, except that the two demand curves and their summation are contained in one graph in figure 24-3).[7] In figure 24-3, D_T is the *vertically* summed demand curve for the public goods, with D_1 and D_2 being the separate demand curves of the two groups. Lindahl equilibrium

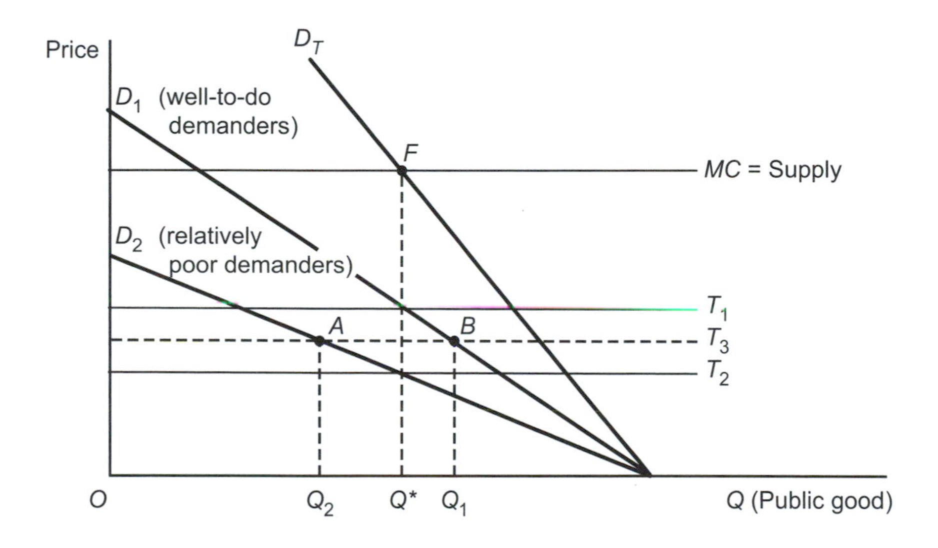

Figure 24-3 Lindahl equilibrium is achieved when well-to-do demanders are charged a marginal tax rate T_1 for Q^* and relatively poor consumers are charged a lower tax rate T_2. At a tax rate of T_3 the poor will prefer Q_2, a less-than-optimal quantity, and the rich will prefer Q_1, a more-than-optimal quantity.

[6] He recognized that because this process was filtered through protagonists in a political process the resultant tax-share distributions would be influenced by the relative power of competing groups, but he assumed initially that such political "blocs" did not influence the model under free exchange.

[7] Figure 24-3 is adapted with modifications from R. G. Holcombe's "Concepts of Public Sector Equilibrium," p. 82.

would occur (through voluntary exchange) when for quantity Q^*, well-to-do demanders are charged a marginal tax rate T_1 and the relatively poor consumers are charged a lower tax rate T_2. Under this tax system, each group is paying a marginal cost (T_1 and T_2, respectively) equal to its marginal valuation of the public good. Efficiency is achieved in the Bowen–Samuelson sense because a single quantity of the good is produced, Q^*, which corresponds to the equation of total demand D_T and marginal cost of production (at point *F* in figure 24-3).

The establishment of Lindahl prices is not necessary in order to obtain efficiency in the production of public goods in the Bowen–Samuelson sense. All that is required for efficiency is that total output of the good be established at point *F* (producing Q^*) in figure 24-3. In order to understand this fact, consider the imposition of some "average" tax rate *T*—one that would be imposed on both groups of demanders and that would cover the costs of producing Q^*. It is easy to see that the well-to-do demanders would prefer this system and would, if possible, foist it on the poor through a political process (Lindahl considered this case). Note, however, that at tax rate T_3 the poor would prefer Q_2, a less-than-optimal quantity of the public good. If the poor were politically powerful, they might force society to take a less-than-optimal quantity of the good.[8] In general, however, a system of Lindahl-tax prices would produce Bowen–Samuelson efficiency—everyone would agree on how much of the public good should be produced. While a Lindahl system is not the only one capable of producing this result, it is the case that a Lindahl model features *unanimous* agreement of the taxed parties in voluntary exchange, given differential tax rates. In developing this feature of his model Lindahl was influenced by his mentor, Knut Wicksell.

Wicksell and Wicksellian Extensions. Swedish economist and reformer Knut Wicksell was probably the most important early progenitor of contemporary public choice. In a lengthy essay titled "A New Principle of Just Taxation" (1896), Wicksell attacked the orthodox approaches to public finance and simultaneously laid the groundwork for both normative and positive public choice. Wicksell emphasized the dual nature of the fiscal side of the economy. In his view, normative comments concerning the welfare effects of alternative tax systems were of no value unless the expenditure side of the fisc (benefits to taxpayers) was simultaneously considered. "Most importantly," as Buchanan pointed out, "Wicksell admonished economists for their failure to recognize the elementary fact that collective or public-sector decisions emerge from a political process rather than from the mind of some benevolent despot" ("Public Finance," p. 385).

Wicksell was chiefly concerned that a fiscal system conform to justice and efficiency. In his view justice and efficiency demanded *unanimity* among all parties that participate in public-sector decisions. Wicksell was unequivocal on this matter:

> When it comes to benefits which are so hard to express numerically, each person can ultimately speak only for himself. It is a matter of comparatively little importance if perchance some individual secures a somewhat greater gain than another so long as everyone gains and no-one can feel exploited from this very elementary

[8] In an ingenious extension of the above problem, Charles M. Tiebout noted in 1956 that people may "vote with their feet" in choosing where to reside ("A Pure Theory of Local Expenditures"—see references). In other words, local communities may be thought of as offering a continuum of public-service quantities. In terms of figure 24-3, given that both groups of demanders face tax rate T_3, the poor would move to a local community offering quantity Q_2 and the well-to-do would seek out one offering Q_1 of public goods. Tiebout's idea certainly offers a testable hypothesis, but there are of course other reasons why citizen-consumers are attracted to specific local communities.

> point of view. But if justice requires no more, it certainly requires no less. In the final analysis, unanimity and fully voluntary consent in the making of decisions provide the only certain and palpable guarantee against injustice in tax distribution. The whole discussion on tax justice remains suspended in mid-air so long as these conditions are not satisfied at least approximately. ("New Principle," p. 90)

According to Wicksell state activity must therefore be of general usefulness; furthermore, the sacrifice must be weighed against the expected utility of the project. Whether individuals favor a project or not depends on a number of variables, such as their position in the income distribution, relative tastes for private versus public consumption, and subjective evaluation of the public project. The tax-price distribution of the costs will determine whether the project would be approved or not. Some distributions of costs would win majority approval and others would not. In a slap against "authoritarian" tax allocations, Wicksell argued that alternative financing and spending proposals should be subject to a public vote of approval. He argued that it would be possible, theoretically, to find a distribution of the costs that would produce *unanimity*. Any other results would provide, in his words, "the sole possible proof that the state activity under consideration would not provide the community with utility corresponding to the necessary sacrifice and should hence be rejected on rational grounds" ("New Principle," p. 90).

Although no other principle would be "just" in Wicksell's system, he did recognize that the ideal of unanimity was not to be expected in practical situations. Society must therefore confront a set of voting-rule options, none of which are efficient in Wicksell's ideal sense. This apparent impasse set the stage for the next advance in the modern literature on public choice. In *The Calculus of Consent* (1962), James Buchanan and Gordon Tullock analyzed less-than-optimal-Wicksellian rules within a framework of methodological individualism. Within this positive (value-free) framework, Buchanan and Tullock modeled the calculus of a utility-maximizing, rational individual as he or she faces the choice of constitutional design. In their model, a "constitution" is simply a set of rules decided on in advance that determines the manner in which future action will be conducted.[9]

The institutions of collective choice in the Buchanan–Tullock conception are themselves variables. They argue:

> The constitutional choice of a rule is taken independently of any single specific decision or set of decisions and is quite rationally based on a long-term view embodying many separate time sequences and many separate collective acts disposing of economic resources. "Optimality" in the sense of choosing the single "best" rule is something wholly distinct from "optimality" in the allocation of resources within a given time span. (*Calculus of Consent*, p. 95)

Optimality, or the determination of the "best" decision rule (e.g., majority rule), takes place in the presence of people's uncertainty concerning their future preferences about a series of individual collective acts or proposals to be voted on. Given such uncertainty about the nature of future preferences, individuals may vote on criteria *unrelated to their respective positions in income distributions*. In other words optimality in the more "dynamic" Buchanan–Tullock framework does not mean the same thing as in Wicksell's time-constrained decision model. Inasmuch as

[9] Moreover, "Collective action is viewed as the action of individuals when they choose to accomplish purposes collectively rather than individually, and the government is seen as nothing more than the set of processes, the machine, which allows such collective action to take place" (Buchanan and Tullock, *Calculus of Consent*, p. 13).

the choices facing the Wicksellian community are later in time than the constitutional choices analyzed by Buchanan and Tullock, his model requires strict unanimity as a condition for optimality (i.e., "justice"). However, at an earlier point a voting rule that is nonoptimal from a Wicksellian perspective can be optimal in the face of future preference uncertainty. Buchanan and Tullock thus provide a theory of constitutions and a design of political institutions that augment the unanimity rule as the sole criterion for efficiency in the narrow Wicksellian sense. Their analysis, especially when combined with the norm of "individualism," has had a large impact on contemporary research on political behavior and institutions.

Bureaucracy, the Supply Side, and Empirical Public Choice

Demand analysis—the interconnections between voting and the demand for public goods—has taken center stage in much of the contemporary public-choice literature. The implicit assumption in this approach is that goods and services demanded in the public sector are *automatically* supplied. However, public goods are supplied by government bureaucracies, which generate incentive mechanisms that have not often been closely scrutinized. Two major exceptions have been the work of the Austrian economist Ludwig von Mises (*Bureaucracy*, 1944) and the more recent study by Gordon Tullock, *The Politics of Bureaucracy* (1965). These books, especially the latter, represent serious attempts to model the process of bureaucratic output and most particularly the motivations and processes by which "public-sector supply" takes place.

How do bureaucrats behave? What are their motivations? Is there a discernible quantity that they optimize in their efforts to supply public goods? These issues and more were taken up by William A. Niskanen, Jr., in his *Bureaucracy and Representative Government* (1971). Reflecting the influence of Tullock, Niskanen views the bureaucrat as an "endogenous" maximizer in the politico/economic arena, not unlike the entrepreneurial suppliers of private goods in the economic marketplace. But one crucial difference stands out. While private entrepreneurs can maximize profits, government bureaucrats cannot legally do so. Though illegal side payments are not unknown in the political arena, it is far more reasonable to posit that the maximand for most bureaucrats is one (or more) of the following: income, prestige, bureau size and/or power, the bureau's budget, promises of a lucrative job after leaving the bureaucracy, and so on. Niskanen assumed that bureaucrats are budget maximizers, and he modeled government bureaus as individual budget-maximizing units. Budget maximization enables the individual bureaucrat to increase his or her salary, change the working environment to his or her liking, or both.

In Niskanen's analysis, bureaus are "nonprofit organizations which are financed . . . by a periodic appropriation or grant" (*Bureaucracy*, p. 15). In essence, a *total* budget is transformed into some level of total output, since marginal adjustments are not feasible within the bureaucratic context. One of the (many) implications of the model is that in their attempt to maximize budget size (and thus the size of the bureau), suppliers will "eat up" the consumer surplus that results from public-goods supply. The sheer growth of bureaucracy is also an obvious implication of this theory. Integrating the theories of public-goods demand and Niskanen's notion of public-goods supply into a "general-equilibrium model" is beset by numerous difficulties, but Niskanen's model has stimulated a good deal of research into the "supply problem," and it has become an ongoing research concern in the economics of public choice.

Public-choice theory has yielded a large number of testable implications and extensions, especially since 1970. Economists have been hard at work expanding and empirically estimating some of these propositions. A very large literature, some of which might be called "empirical public choice" has developed.[10] The list of contributions to this field is long and pertains to such issues as: (1) What are the economics of campaign contributions and how do they affect political competition? (2) How does self-interest lead to length of political terms in office and to the rules of succession? (3) How does an independent judiciary affect cartel behavior? (4) How do economic variables determine entry barriers into politics? (5) How and why are coalitions formed within legislatures? and (6) Why do state and federal legislatures contain more lawyers as representatives than any other occupation? A whole branch of literature has developed on the "political business cycle," attempting to explain how self-interested politicians acting under reelection constraints *cause* swings in inflation, income, and employment. Some of these interesting contributions are discussed below, while others are referenced in the notes for further reading at the end of this chapter.

Empirical Support for the Median-Voter Model. Consider the median-voter model described earlier in this chapter. Assuming there is competition among political parties, it has been shown that whichever party appeals most to the interest of the median voter will be elected. It is not likely that the strongest supporters of a political party will be rewarded in proportion to their contributions. In order to get elected, party members must devise tax-and-spend programs that reallocate benefits from their strongest supporters to the median voter. Randall Holcombe has shown that when tax shares can be offered as part of a political platform, "democracy has a natural bias in favor of electing the political party that has the highest demand for public sector output" ("Public Choice," p. 382). He has also studied the empirical relevance of the Bowen median-voter model (see figure 24-1). Utilizing data from Michigan tax referenda on educational expenditures in 275 elections in 1973, Holcombe provided empirical support for the assertion that the median-voter model is consistent with local governmental referenda on educational expenditures ("Empirical Test," pp. 272–273).

The Economics of Political Representation. Empirical models in public choice have concentrated on testing practical questions. For instance, do methods of paying legislators (as set by a state constitution or by state legislators themselves) determine "outside earnings"? A study by Robert McCormick and Robert Tollison suggests that in higher-paying states, with legislators setting their own salaries, individuals find it less in their own interest to seek outside payments or bribes ("Legislatures as Unions," p. 77). In another interesting empirical study, entitled "Legislators as Taxicabs: On the Value of a Seat in the U.S. House of Representatives," Mark Crain, Thomas Deaton, and Robert Tollison investigated the question of why the size of the U.S. House of Representatives has remained constant at 435 (with the minor exception of a temporary expansion after Alaska and Hawaii were admitted to the Union). The only two constitutional requirements respecting size are that there be (1) no more than one representative per 30,000 population and (2) at least one representative from each state. Given these restrictions the House of Representatives could have held 5,977 members in 1977. Why, then, were there only

[10] See "Public Choice: A Survey," by Dennis C. Mueller, for an annotated discussion of contributions up to 1975 or so (see references).

435? The answer, according to Crain, Deaton, and Tollison, is that legislators are able to restrict their own numbers, much like the situation where taxicabs are controlled in major cities. The result is that economic rents are earned by the existing units of supply—at least partially by the legislators themselves. Thus, some "economic" answers to "political" questions are provided by the axioms of self-interest, the ability of legislators to control their own numbers, and the theory of rent seeking (which is discussed in more detail below).

Agency Problems in Politics. Principles of public choice have also been used to analyze congressional voting and the possibilities that representatives do not always represent the will of the people who elect them. Indeed, one of the major issues in public choice deals with problems relating to agents and principals. The basic problem is how to get the agent to behave in ways that correspond to the interests of the principal. Anyone who has worked in a firm or owned corporate stock, for example, should be familiar with this dilemma. Employees may work in their own interests under certain circumstances and not in the interests of their employer. Left unsupervised, employees may shirk their tasks and engage in activities that enhance their own utility rather than that of the employers. Some examples are: overextending lunch breaks, playing computer games, unauthorized e-mailing, or creating "overtime" situations to boost one's pay. Managers may also work against stockholders' interests, as in the infamous cases of Enron and Tyco, two prominent examples of colossal business failures.

Political representation is beset by the same type of problems and opportunistic behavior that affects businesses. The issue for public-choice scholars is how to get the agents (legislators and the bureaucracies they oversee) to behave in a manner intended by the principals (voters) in a representative democracy. Alternatively, how do representatives respond to election results? In these matters, there are two theoretical camps. Either the legislator is a perfect agent of the people or he or she is a "statesman" independent of the constraints of the electorate. Political scientists have argued that congressional committees use legislative and appointment powers to control bureaucracies (Weingast, "Congressional-Bureaucratic System"). The role of ideology in voting by representatives has been studied also by both political scientists and economists.[11]

This brief discussion of public choice suggests the richness of the emerging literature on the subject. But beyond that, the public-choice paradigm has been a fertile source of advances in the theory of economic regulation. Indeed, an endogenous political process is central to most contemporary theories of economic regulation.

■ The New Political Economy of Regulation

In a distinct and dramatic shift of emphasis from the philosophy of "New Deal liberalism," deregulation of some industries became stylish in the United States among both Democratic and Republican politicians in the 1970s. Historically, regulation of some industries, especially those regarded as natural monopolies (e.g., railroads, electric utilities), has been considered in the "public interest." After the

[11] See James Kau and Paul Rubin, "Self-Interest, Ideology and Logrolling in Congressional Voting"; same authors, *Congressmen, Constituents, and Contributors*; Joseph Kalt and Mark Zupan, "Capture and Ideology in the Economic Theory of Politics"; Sam Peltzman, "Economic Interpretation of Congressional Voting in the Twentieth Century" (all are in the references).

establishment in 1887 of the first large federal regulatory agency (the Interstate Commerce Commission), economists spent great time and effort trying to devise better pricing tools to be implemented in the regulatory process.[12] A vast literature developed on such subjects as marginal-cost pricing, price discrimination, and peak-load pricing, all ostensibly to be of some use in implementing public policy in the regulated areas of the economy. The whole regulatory process was seen as stemming directly from market failure and from the consequent necessity of government actions in the interests of the public. While imperfections in the regulatory process were acknowledged, most economists lined up behind the view that regulation was required due to the presence of "natural monopoly" and, further, that the process could be perfected by successive approximations in control.

Unfolding intellectual events of the 1960s changed all of this within the economics profession and, ultimately, among politicians and the public as well. We have already discussed one of these developments—the emergence of the public-choice paradigm with its emphasis on politicians as endogenous actors in economic processes. It was a logical extension to apply these principles to the regulatory process by means of a theory of rent or profit creation by politicians and regulators ("the government"). The stage was set by two important papers appearing in 1962. George Stigler and Claire Friedland broke the ice with an essay questioning the effects of regulation on such variables as rate levels, the degree of price discrimination, and the rate of return. Their surprising conclusion, based on statistics before and after electrical-utility regulation, was that regulation was almost totally ineffective at controlling the quantities it was designed to control. They noted:

> The theory of price regulation must, in fact, be based upon the tacit assumption that in its absence a monopoly has exorbitant power. If it were true that pure monopoly profits in the absence of regulation would be 10 or 20 percent above the competitive rate of return, so prices would be on the order of 40 to 80 percent above long run marginal cost, there might indeed be some possibility of effective regulation. The electrical utilities do not provide such a possibility. ("What Can Regulators Regulate?" p. 12)

A second contribution was no less influential in questioning long-held beliefs about regulation. Harvey Averch and Leland L. Johnson posited a theory about the firm's actions when facing a regulated rate of return constraint ("Behavior of the Firm under Regulatory Constraint"). They concluded that, from society's point of view, regulated firms would overinvest in fixed capital under certain conditions. Although optimal (i.e., profit maximizing) from the regulated firm's position, too much capital (relative to labor inputs) could force up the costs of utility services to society. The empirical relevance of this Averch–Johnson effect is still being debated by economists and econometricians, but their allegations, along with those of Stigler and Friedland and other writers, helped agitate a general rethinking of the whole regulatory process. This reassessment was, moreover, strongly influenced by the economics of politics and rent seeking.

[12] An early "Chicago school" economist, Henry Simons, went so far as to suggest that failures in the regulatory process demanded government ownership of some industries ("A Positive Program for Laissez Faire"—see references). However, this position is distinct from the modern Chicago view (deregulation plus competitive franchise bidding for rights to supply in some cases), and it is even more distant from the views of a majority of contemporary economists.

Rents, Politics, and Regulation

Before turning to forms of the contemporary theory of regulation, let us review what "rent seeking" means. A basic model is presented in figure 24-4.[13] For simplicity, assume linear demand and marginal-revenue curves plus a constant average- and marginal-cost function. Under competitive conditions, Q_c represents the quantity produced and P_c represents its price. A monopoly, or a legalized cartel sustained by a regulatory system, could have the effect of causing a reduction of output to Q_m, and an increase of price to P_m. It is important to be clear about the nature of the losses. Triangle *AFG* corresponds to a deadweight loss due to monopoly—one that was first noticed by the French engineer Jules Dupuit (see chapter 13). Such a loss is always present whenever price exceeds marginal cost (excise taxes and monopoly prices are analogous in this regard).

But what of area P_cP_mAF? Many economists have claimed these "rents" represent only a redistribution from consumers to the monopolist. In the context of regulatory processes, however, they may be viewed by any given competitor as the value of gaining the franchise.[14] In other words if a single award is given, *each* individual competitor will have an incentive to spend an amount, P_cP_mAF, less an infinitesimal amount, for the exclusive monopoly-granting franchise. Likewise, assuming that

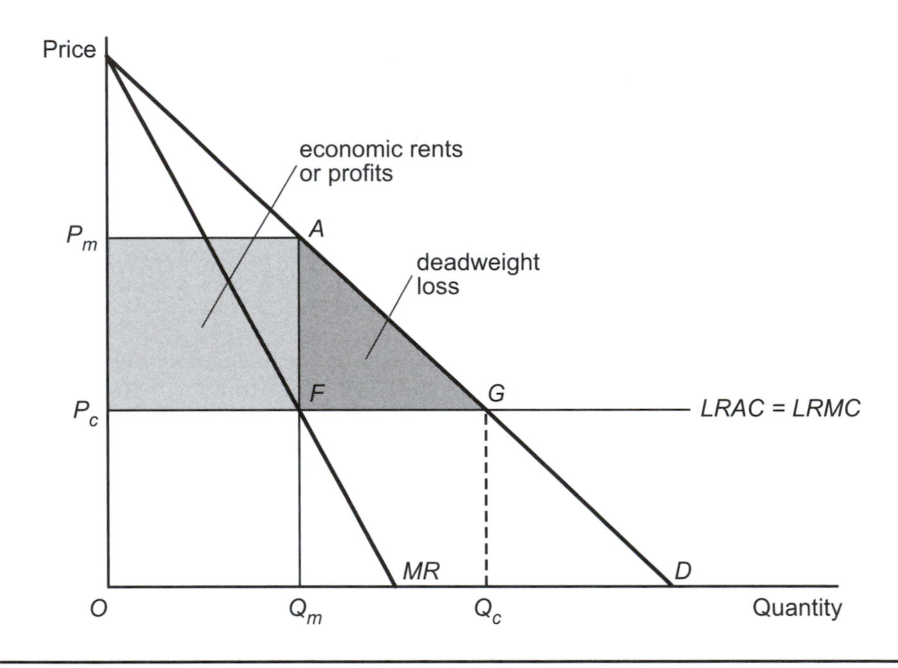

Figure 24-4 In the regulatory process, individual competitors will be willing to spend P_cP_mAF less an infinitesimal amount for the exclusive monopoly rights.

[13] A "rent-seeking" interpretation of the mercantile age was presented in chap. 3, although a specific model, such as figure 24-4, was not developed then.

[14] These "rent-seeking" arguments originated in the writings of Gordon Tullock ("Welfare Costs of Tariffs, Monopolies, and Theft"; "Transitional Gains Gap") and Richard Posner ("Social Costs of Monopoly and Regulation"); see references.

market shares among firms can be cheaply and efficiently devised, a cartel would be willing to bid a similar amount for protection from competition. The disposition and dissipation of these rents could be in lobbying or legal fees. With these principles in mind, let us return to the political and economic interconnections in the regulatory process.

The above argument contains a flaw. Legally, of course, politicians and regulators cannot take bribes, although, as stated earlier, *sub rosa* and illegal side payments have on occasion been unseemly features of government at all levels. Payments from business interests may take other forms, of course, and these motives are the key to the modern theory of regulation. Regulation, like any other good, such as shoes or beer, is demanded and supplied with underlying motives of self-interest. In a provocative paper published in 1971 ("The Theory of Economic Regulation") George Stigler fleshed out a "capture" theory of regulation based on self-interested motives of demanders and suppliers. This view, it must be emphasized, is only superficially similar to the Marxian notion that "capital" uses the state and the political apparatus to capture benefits. In the modern theory, capital or "business" does not always win. Groups of any kind, such as labor, farmers, or consumers, may initiate a regulatory regime or take over an existing one from time to time. In Stigler's view regulation benefits politically effective groups. Let us consider this proposition in more detail.

The Capture Theory. In order to understand the capture theory, we must resolve the issue of who benefits from regulation and who is burdened by it. Regulated firms may benefit from state or federal control to the extent that they receive direct subsidies of money from governing bodies, protection against rival entry into their markets, fixed (minimum) prices that guarantee full cost recovery, or other measures that limit competition. Regulation, however, is almost always a mixed blessing. Regulated industries (railways, electrical utilities, etc.) or occupations (barbers, funeral directors, building contractors, etc.) must pay certain fees and submit to certain rules, regulations, standards of conduct, or other interferences. These are costly and reduce the net return to the regulated firm, but as long as the net benefit is positive and lobbying costs are not prohibitive, those who stand to gain from the regulatory process will logically demand it.

The less obvious question is why would politician-regulators supply regulation? Stated another way, how do businesses go about demanding regulation in a system where outright bribes are illegal? Politically effective coalitions (e.g., labor unions, trade associations, etc.) make their voices heard with votes or campaign contributions. But why are politicians willing to cater to limited interests at the expense of the majority of voters/consumers? The logical answer is that certain characteristics of a democratic political process make it possible for benefits to be concentrated on small numbers while the costs are "diluted" because they are spread over large numbers. Stigler noted that in a democratic process decisions must be taken (through elected representatives) that simultaneously involve all parties—those very interested in a decision, those somewhat interested, and those uninterested ("Theory of Economic Regulation," pp. 10–11). In these circumstances, the larger damage to majorities (i.e., the "deadweight loss" analyzed above) may meet little resistance because the total costs are spread over so many people that the cost to any one person is miniscule.

Information is a good with costs and benefits. Good information makes for better decisions, but it takes time and effort to acquire. Because time is a limited resource an individual has no incentive to acquire costly information on issues of no concern to him or her, yet the individual votes on these issues, ordinarily through a full-time representative affiliated with a political party. As Stigler argues:

> The representative and his party are rewarded for their discovery and fulfillment of the political desires of their constituency by success in election and the perquisites of office. If the representative could confidently await reelection whenever he voted against an economic policy that injured the society, he would assuredly do so. Unfortunately virtue does not always command so high a price. If the representative denies ten large industries their special subsidies of money or governmental power, they will dedicate themselves to the election of a more complaisant successor: the stakes are that important. This does not mean that the representative and his party must find a coalition of voter interests more durable than the anti-industry side of every industry policy proposal. A representative cannot win or keep office with the support of the sum of those who are opposed to: oil import quotas, farm subsidies, airport subsidies, hospital subsidies, unnecessary navy shipyards, an inequitable public housing program, and rural electrification subsidies. ("Theory of Economic Regulation," p. 11)

Politics and the voting process act as gross filters of individual preferences. Regulations of all kinds are simply the result of interactions of self-interested demanders—effective coalitions of individuals who stand to gain from regulation—and political suppliers who must endure periodic reelection constraints.

Does this mean that the "public interest" comes in last in this process? In the modern approach to regulation, the term "public interest" itself takes on a different meaning. The public interest is not some abstract legalism; it is rather a *summation of individuals'* interests on any issue. If transactions costs among consumers were zero, they would most certainly buy out monopolies. In figure 24-4, for example, with a payment of P_cP_mAF consumers could buy off the monopolist and gain triangle AFG, the dead-weight loss. In the imperfect world we inhabit, however, coalition costs are positive and the state is permitted, within the bounds of democracy, to coerce monopolies. As a consequence, economic regulation can reduce the welfare of consumers.

It is important to recognize that regulation does not always support the special interests of industrial market groups. Consumer or environmental groups may also form effective coalitions to affect the political process. Preferences of nonmarket groups may be registered, and different groups may capture the process at different points in time. Identification of the specific configurations of costs and benefits facing demanders and politician-suppliers of regulations is an ongoing task engaging contemporary economists in this field. One of the central problems is to develop a sound single theory of political decision making within bureaucracies. Research on such matters is ongoing.

Politics and the Peltzman Model of Regulation. Sam Peltzman ("Toward a More General Theory of Regulation") engineered the most powerful extension of Stigler's economic theory dealing with the interface between the distribution of economic welfare and the political process. In Peltzman's formulation, consumer welfare is brokered against producer welfare by the political process to produce a regulatory equilibrium level of price and profit. As with Stigler's view, politicians are rewarded with votes, money, and other perquisites—incentives to provide gains for producers. But there is a trade-off: Gains for producers mean losses for consumer-voters, which in turn mean loss of votes for politicians. Therefore, politicians play a "balancing" game between the two groups.

Peltzman's model may be summarized in figure 24-5. Here the politician-regulator's "indifference" curves (i.e., what Peltzman calls "iso-majority" curves) represent the political process at work. Each curve traces out combinations of price and profit that yield the same level of political support. Curves that are higher (ever more northwesterly), such as I_1 versus I_0, denote higher levels of political support. Higher prices (bad for consumers) must be linked with higher profits (good for producers), so that the iso-majority curves are positively sloped. In other words, in order to maintain a given level of political support, votes lost through price increases must be compensated by increases in profits. The conventional profit hill (shown in figure 24-5) shows the amount of wealth that is available for redistribution (from consumers to producers or from producers to consumers). The regulator seeks to mediate between producers and consumers and establishes political equilibrium price and profit levels at point *E*. Note that the regulator does not choose either the competitive optimum (*A*) nor the monopoly optimum (*F*), but rather some intermediate price-profit pair. This result stems from the fact that there will always be a trade-off between consumers' interests and producers' interests that will have political implications for the politician-regulator. Because politicians want to maximize their majorities at election time, there will always be moderation in the kind of business regulation that they establish and support.

This insightful model—which is actually a theory of government as well as a theory of regulation—contains multiple insights. The iso-majority functions depicted in figure 24-5 present a monolithic summary of political preferences and are determined by a variety of factors. Nevertheless, it is the existence of democratically determined legislative rules and the self-interest of politicians that explains

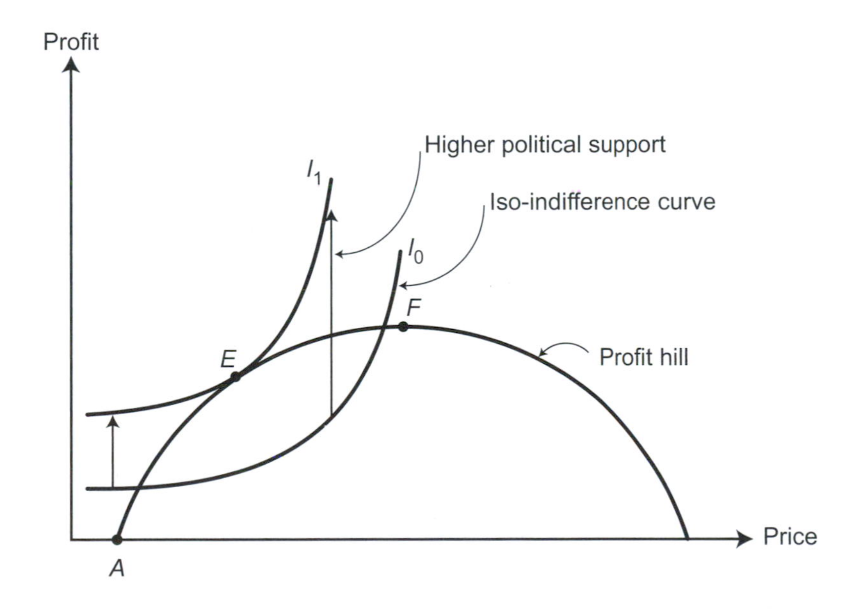

Figure 24-5 Peltzman's model shows that regulation results from the interaction between the profits of the firm (represented by the "profit hill" of businesses) and the political support of politicians (represented by the iso-indifference curves). This interaction generally results in a regulated price *between* monopoly price and competitive price.

the supply of regulation. Likewise, the profit hills in Peltzman's model come from somewhere. Anything that causes these hills to emerge or to change measurably invites regulation and regulatory change as a consequence. Thus, the advent of inventions and new technologies, a sudden shift in relative prices due to cartel formation, the aftermath of a hurricane, economic growth or decline, and the like, can all lead to the establishment of new regulatory regimes. Many empirical implications, moreover, may be developed from Peltzman's model. For example, as Mark Crain and Robert E. McCormick indicate, regulated prices are likely to be lower in jurisdictions in which regulators are elected rather than appointed ("Regulators as an Interest Group"). Peltzman's seminal idea has produced an ongoing and informative inquiry into the nature of the regulatory process.

Other Modern Approaches to Regulation. Historically the case for economic regulation has rested squarely on the presence or absence of "natural monopoly" conditions, that is, a situation in which a firm faces high fixed costs so that its long-run costs per unit fall over large blocks of output. But the modern view rests on a different premise: It suggests that any effective coalition might secure regulation through the political process, regardless of the nature of its cost structure. But what if natural monopoly conditions (i.e., high fixed costs plus declining marginal costs) are present? Does that mean that regulation by some government agency is inevitable?

In a view derived from Sir Edwin Chadwick's nineteenth-century assessment of similar problems (see chapter 10), Harold Demsetz ("Why Regulate Utilities?") questioned the necessity of regulating (in traditional fashion) industries having scale economies in production.[15] Demsetz proposed that formal regulation of utilities would be rendered unnecessary where governments could allow "rivalrous competitors" to bid for the exclusive right to supply the good or service over some indefinite "contract" period. In such a system, as Demsetz demonstrated, the existence of natural monopoly does not imply monopoly price and output, as long as there are an elastic supply of potential bidders and prohibitive collusion costs on the part of potential suppliers.

Under certain restrictive conditions a "competitive" price and output could be achieved by employing Demsetz's idea (see the discussion of Chadwick and figure 10-1 in chapter 10). Critics of this idea have questioned vigorously the concept of franchise bidding as a *substitute* for traditional forms of regulation, judging the franchise-bidding scheme practicably unworkable because of market uncertainty, information and policing costs, ambiguous investment criteria, and so on. Government ownership of certain basic property rights would also be required to make the scheme work. Since it is probable that Demsetz never intended his scheme to serve as a full-fledged theory of regulation, it is not easy to weigh the burden of criticism. There is not much empirical support for the existence of natural monopoly in utilities and other regulated industries, and the "free-market position" on the matter—if there is a unified position—is that *deregulation* and the return of competition to most regulated activities would improve consumer welfare. For a view that contrasts Demsetz's theory to an "Austrian" view of regulation that focuses on risk and uncertainty, see the box, The Force of Ideas: Schumpeter on Risk, Regulation, and Market Processes.

[15] Actually, the modern rediscovery of the "Chadwick principle" was made three years earlier by Gordon Tullock, who applied it to political party competition. See Tullock's "Entry Barriers in Politics" in the references.

The Force of Ideas: Schumpeter on Risk, Regulation, and Market Processes

The concern for regulation and the nature and extent of government involvement in markets is a very old issue, although as we note in this chapter modern writers have taken up the debate with renewed vigor. As is often the case, it is useful to look back at past writers who have informed the debate.

Joseph Schumpeter characterized the market function as an intertemporal competitive process—which implies certain things about the role of government regulation.* According to Schumpeter, *risk* is an unavoidable and natural element of market activity. In discussing problems risk and uncertainty pose to entrepreneurs in a capitalist society Schumpeter said:

> Practically any investment entails . . . certain safeguarding activities such as insuring or hedging. Long-range investing under rapidly changing conditions, especially under . . . the impact of new commodities and technologies, is like shooting at a target that is not only indistinct but moving—and moving jerkily at that. Hence it becomes necessary to resort to such protecting devices as patents or temporary secrecy of processes or, in some cases, long-period contracts secured in advance.†

But when there are "no facilities for insuring against it,"—such as patents; or enforcement of patents is inadequate; or market participants do not have the ability to devise long-term contracts with each other—then risk costs may be recouped (temporarily) by higher prices or aggressively competitive behavior. In other words, Schumpeter stressed that elements of competition that may appear to be anticompetitive from a purely static perspective (patents, etc.) may encourage progress in a more dynamic competitive setting. Expressing a few reservations about the adverse effects of cartels, Schumpeter even characterized a number of static "monopolistic" practices as "natural" tools of dynamic (long-run) competition.

Schumpeter was also alert to the possibilities of utilizing regulatory procedures to subvert the welfare effects of the marketplace. Since government is the only permanent source of monopoly privilege, its regulatory actions should be scrutinized intensively:

> The power to exploit at pleasure a given pattern of demand . . . can under the conditions of intact capitalism hardly persist for a period long enough to matter for the analysis of total output, unless buttressed by public authority. . . . Even railroads and power and light concerns had first to create the demand for their services and, when they had done so, to defend their market against competition.‡

This perspective on market processes provides a forceful case for a clear demarcation between "static" competition and "dynamic" competition. Viewed in a static sense, nongovernmental restrictions on competition are usually considered suboptimal, when in fact they may help regulate the introduction of new technology that improves economic welfare. Government regulation, on the other hand, is the major source of long-term economic rents associated with output reductions and welfare losses. Schumpeter's insights, combined with the modern theory of regulation as discussed in this chapter, remind us that the mere existence of regulation and of intertemporal problems of production and consumption does not constitute proof that the market has failed to work properly.

*For additional discussion of Schumpeter's ideas see Method Squabbles 5 (chapter 21) and chapter 23.
†J. S. Schumpeter, *Capitalism, Socialism, and Democracy*, p. 88.
‡*Capitalism, Socialism, and Democracy*, p. 99.

■ Conclusion

The purpose of this chapter has not been to settle contemporary theoretical disputes in the theory of public choice or regulation. Rather, it has been to demonstrate that new and ongoing inquiries in political economy have utilized and are utilizing the simple models of competition and self-interest sponsored so long ago by Adam Smith. The twist here—and the essential lesson to take from this chapter—is that self-interest as a basic economic motive does not differ in form whether one is buying an ice cream cone or running a campaign for city treasurer. The same motives, in form if not in kind, pervade the activities of all humans. Public-choice theory and application, linking both taxation and expenditures and including the theory of regulation, is a valuable means of transforming economic analysis into other realms of human action. In doing so it is stretching the reaches of the discipline within the original conception of Adam Smith, a conception of economics as part of a broader social and political inquiry.

References

Arrow, Kenneth. *Social Choice and Individual Values*. New York: Wiley, 1951.

Averch, Harvey, and Leland L. Johnson. "Behavior of the Firm under Regulatory Constraint," *American Economic Review*, vol. 52 (December 1962), pp. 1052–1069.

Black, Duncan. *The Theory of Committees and Elections*. London: Cambridge University Press, 1958.

Bowen, Howard R. "The Interpretation of Voting in the Allocation of Resources," *Quarterly Journal of Economics*, vol. 58 (November 1943), pp. 27–48.

Buchanan, J. M. "The Pure Theory of Government Finance: A Suggested Approach," *Journal of Political Economy*, vol. 57 (December 1949), pp. 496–505.

———. "La scienza delle finance: The Italian Tradition in Public Finance," in *Fiscal Theory and Political Economy*. Chapel Hill: University of North Carolina Press, 1960.

———. "Public Finance and Public Choice," *National Tax Journal*, vol. 28 (December 1975), pp. 383–394.

———, and Gordon Tullock. *The Calculus of Consent*. Ann Arbor: The University of Michigan Press, 1962.

Crain, W. Mark, Thomas H. Deaton, and Robert D. Tollison. "Legislators as Taxicabs: On the Value of a Seat in the U.S. House of Representatives," *Economic Inquiry*, vol. 15 (April 1977), pp. 298–302.

———, and Robert E. McCormick. "Regulators as an Interest Group," in James M. Buchanan and Robert D. Tollison (eds.), *The Theory of Public Choice II*. Ann Arbor: University of Michigan Press, 1984, pp. 287–304.

Demsetz, Harold. "Why Regulate Utilities?" *Journal of Law & Economics*, vol. 11 (April 1968), pp. 55–65.

Holcombe, Randall G. "Public Choice and Public Spending," *National Tax Journal*, vol. 31 (December 1978), pp. 373–383.

———. "Concepts of Public Sector Equilibrium," *National Tax Journal*, vol. 33 (March 1980), pp. 77–88.

———. "An Empirical Test of the Median Voter Model," *Economic Inquiry*, vol. 18 (April 1980), pp. 260–275.

Hotelling, Harold. "Stability in Competition," *Economic Journal*, vol. 39 (March 1929), pp. 41–57.

Kalt, Joseph P., and Mark A. Zupan. "Capture and Ideology in the Economic Theory of Politics," *American Economic Review*, vol. 74 (1984), pp. 279–300.

Kau, James B., and Paul H. Rubin. "Self-Interest, Ideology and Logrolling in Congressional Voting," *Journal of Law and Economics*, vol. 22 (1979), pp. 365–384.

———. *Congressmen, Constituents, and Contributors*. Boston: Martinus Nijhoff, 1982.

Lindahl, Erik. "Just Taxation—A Positive Solution," in Richard Musgrave and A. T. Peacock (eds.), *Classics in the Theory of Public Finance*. New York: St. Martin's, 1958 [1919].

McCormick, Robert E., and Robert D. Tollison. "Legislatures as Unions," *Journal of Political Economy*, vol. 86 (February 1978), pp. 63–78.

Mises, Ludwig von. *Bureaucracy*. New Haven, CT: Yale University Press, 1944.

Mueller, Dennis C. "Public Choice: A Survey," *Journal of Economic Literature*, vol. 14 (June 1976), pp. 395–433.

Musgrave, Richard A. "The Voluntary Exchange Theory of Public Economy," *Quarterly Journal of Economics*, vol. 53 (February 1938), pp. 213–237.

Niskanen, William A. *Bureaucracy and Representative Government*. Chicago: Aldine-Atherton Press, 1971.

Peltzman, Sam. "Toward a More General Theory of Regulation," *The Journal of Law & Economics*, vol. 9 (August 1976), pp. 211–240.

———. "An Economic Interpretation of Congressional Voting in the Twentieth Century," *American Economic Review*, vol. 75 (1985), pp. 656–675.

Posner, Richard A. "The Social Costs of Monopoly and Regulation," *Journal of Political Economy*, vol. 83 (August 1975), pp. 807–827.

Samuelson, Paul A. "The Pure Theory of Public Expenditures," *Review of Economics and Statistics*, vol. 36 (November 1954), pp. 387–389.

Schumpeter, J. A. *Capitalism, Socialism, and Democracy*. New York: Harper & Row, 1942.

Simons, Henry. "A Positive Program for Laissez-Faire," in Harry D. Gideonse (ed.), *Public Policy Pamphlet no. 15*. Chicago: The University of Chicago Press, 1934.

Stigler, George J. "The Theory of Economic Regulation," *The Bell Journal of Economics and Management Science*, vol. 2 (Spring 1971), pp. 3–21.

———, and Claire Friedland. "What Can Regulators Regulate? The Case of Electricity," *Journal of Law & Economics*, vol. 5 (October 1962), pp. 1–16.

Tiebout, C. M. "A Pure Theory of Local Expenditures," *Journal of Political Economy*, vol. 64 (October 1956), pp. 416–424.

Tullock, Gordon. "Entry Barriers in Politics," *American Economic Review*, vol. 55 (May 1965), pp. 458–466.

———. *The Politics of Bureaucracy*. Washington: Public Affairs Press, 1965.

———. "The Welfare Costs of Tariffs, Monopolies, and Theft," *Western Economic Journal*, vol. 5 (June 1967), pp. 224–232; also published in James M. Buchanan, Robert D. Tollison, and Gordon Tullock, *Toward a Theory of the Rent-Seeking Society*. College Station: Texas A & M University Press, 1981.

———. "The Transitional Gains Gap," *The Bell Journal of Economics*, vol. 6 (Autumn 1975), pp. 671–678.

Weingast, Barry R. "The Congressional-Bureaucratic System: A Principal Agent Perspective (with Applications to the SEC)," *Public Choice*, vol. 44 (1984), pp. 147–191.

Wicksell, Knut. "A New Principle of Just Taxation," James M. Buchanan (trans.), in Richard Musgrave and A. T. Peacock (eds.), *Classics in the Theory of Public Finance*. New York: St. Martin's, 1958.

Notes for Further Reading

The single best introduction to the literature of public choice is William F. Shughart II and Laura Razzolini, *The Elgar Companion to Public Choice* (Cheltenham, UK: Edward Elgar, 2001). This book contains important papers on such topics as public-choice methodology, constitutional choice, the economics of government branches, and public choice applied to historical episodes. If one chooses to read into the earlier literature, translations of the classics are available. In addition to the writings of Lindahl and Wicksell mentioned in the references to this chapter, Musgrave and Peacock's important volume contains a number of international classics in public finance translated into English. For much insight into the development of public finance see the essays of Maffeo Pantaleoni, Ugo Mazzola, F. Y. Edgeworth, Enrico Barone, and Friedrich von Wieser. A part of the French (Marshall-style) tradition is developed by R. B. Ekelund, Jr., and Robert F. Hébert, "French Engineers, Welfare Economics, and Public Finance in the Nineteenth Century," *History of Political Economy*, vol. 10 (Winter 1978), pp. 636–668.

Contemporary literature on public goods is plentiful. A central question concerns the "competitive provision" of public goods, that is, whether such goods can be supplied competitively and whether such equilibriums are "stable." See J. M. Buchanan, *The Demand and Supply of Public Goods* (Chicago: Rand McNally, 1968); J. G. Head, "Public Goods and Public Policy," *Public Finance*, vol. 17, no. 2 (1962), pp. 197–219; and Harold Demsetz, "The Private Production of Public Goods," *Journal of Law & Economics*, vol. 8 (October 1970), pp. 293–306. In addition to the literature on voting cited in the text, two early papers may be consulted: Duncan Black, "On the Rationale of Group Decision Making," *Journal of Political Economy*, vol. 56 (February 1978), pp. 23–24; and Kenneth Arrow, "A Difficulty in the Concept of Social Welfare," *Journal of Political Economy*, vol. 58 (August 1950), pp. 328–346. Also see T. Nicholas Tideman and Gordon Tullock, "A New and Superior Process for Making Social Choices," *Journal of Political Economy*, vol. 84 (December 1976), pp. 1145–1160.

The "constitutional rules" taken up by Buchanan and Tullock in their extension of Wicksell's optimal tax rules are considered in a somewhat different context in John Rawls, *A Theory of Justice* (Cambridge, MA: Harvard University Press, 1971). Buchanan's reaction to Rawls, in addition to a very sizable contribution to the question, is contained in his *Freedom in Constitutional Contract: Perspectives of a Political Economist* (College Station: Texas A & M University Press, 1977). In addition to Niskanen's major work on bureaucracy, see his "The Peculiar Economics of Bureaucracy," *American Economic Review*, vol. 58 (May 1968), pp. 293–305. Emendations and extensions of Niskanen's work may be found regularly in the journal *Public Choice*; see also Bruce L. Benson, "Why Are Congressional Committees Dominated by 'High-Demand' Legislators?—A Comment on Niskanen's View of Bureaucrats and Politicians," *Southern Economic Journal*, vol. 48 (July 1981), pp. 68–77.

The literature on "empirical public choice" is wonderfully diverse and varied. On the economics of internal organization of legislatures, see W. Mark Crain and Robert D. Tollison, "Campaign Expenditures and Political Competition," *Journal of Law & Economics*, vol. 19 (April 1976), pp. 177–188; Arleen Leibowitz and Robert D. Tollison, "A Theory of Legislative Organization: Making the Most of Your Majority," *Quarterly Journal of Economics*, vol. 95 (March 1980), pp. 261–267; and W. Mark Crain, "On the Structure and Stability of Political Markets," *Journal of Political Economy*, vol. 85 (August 1977), pp. 829–842. An article by Randall G. Holcombe and Asghar Zardkoohi uses a regression model to show that grants are determined by political rather than economic variables; see "The Determinants of Federal Grants," *Southern Economic Journal*, vol. 47 (October 1981), pp. 393–399. An excellent contribution to interest-group theory is provided by Robert E. McCormick and Robert D. Tollison, *Politicians, Legislation, and the Economy: An Inquiry into the Interest-Group Theory of Government* (Leiden: Martinus Nijhoff, 1981).

An important aspect of the empirical public-choice literature has been the modeling of a political business cycle wherein inflation, employment, and disposable income are manipulated by politicians in attempts to win elections. Edward R. Tufte, *Political Control of the Economy* (Princeton, NJ: Princeton University Press, 1978), presents one of the most interesting and comprehensive studies of the electoral cycle. Also see Bruno S.

Frey and Friedrich Schneider, "On the Modeling of Politico-Economic Interdependence," *European Journal of Political Research*, vol. 3 (December 1975), pp. 339–360; same authors, "A Politico-Economic Model of the United Kingdom," *Economic Journal*, vol. 88 (June 1978), pp. 243–253, which employs ex ante measures of actual popularity rather than ex post electoral success as the "independent variable". Richard E. Wagner, "Economic Manipulation for Political Profit: Macroeconomic Consequences and Constitutional Limitations," *Kyklos*, vol. 30 (1977), pp. 395–410, developed a model meshing political manipulations and the monetarist conception of the so-called inflation-unemployment trade-off (i.e., the "Phillips curve"). See W. Mark Crain and Robert B. Ekelund, Jr., "Deficits and Democracy," *Southern Economic Journal*, vol. 44 (April 1978), pp. 813–828, for an empirical study of why deficits are demanded as well as supplied.

Alfred E. Kahn's two-volume study, Volume I: *The Economics of Regulation: Economic Principles*, and Volume II: *Institutional Issues* (New York: Wiley, 1971), provide an excellent summary of the "early" regulation literature and of the institutional structure of broad areas of regulation in the United States through the 1960s. A good survey of post-1962 regulatory theories—those discussed in the present chapter—is contained in the introductory chapters of Bruce M. Owen and Ronald Braeutigam, *The Regulatory Game: Strategic Use of the Administrative Process* (Cambridge: Ballinger, 1978). For an important overview of regulation, in succinct graphical terms, see T. Randolph Beard, David L. Kaserman, and John W. Mayo, "A Graphical Exposition of the Economic Theory of Regulation," *Economic Inquiry*, Oxford University Press, vol. 41 (October 2003), pp. 592–606.

The general topic of rent seeking and its role in regulation and income distribution is covered in *Toward a Theory of the Rent-Seeking Society*, James Buchanan, Robert Tollison, and Gordon Tullock (see references). Empirical papers presenting statistical evidence on rent seeking and regulation have appeared regularly in most academic journals throughout the 1980s and 1990s, especially in journals such as *Journal of Law & Economics*, *Journal of Legal Studies*, *Journal of Regulatory Economics*, and *Public Choice*. A minuscule sample of these papers includes: Deborah Hass-Wilson, "The Effect of Commercial Practice Restrictions: The Case of Optometry," *Journal of Law and Economics*, vol. 32 (April 1986), pp. 165–186; Ann P. Bartel and Lacy Glenn Thomas, "Predation Through Regulation: The Wage and Profit Effects of the Occupational Safety and Health Administration and the Environmental Protection Agency," *Journal of Law and Economics*, vol. 33 (October 1987), pp. 239–264; and Audrey B. Davidson, Elynor D. Davis, and Robert B. Ekelund, Jr., "Political Choice and the Child Labor Statute of 1938: Public Interest or Interest Group Legislation?" *Public Choice*, vol. 82 (1995), pp. 85–106.

The whole question of deregulation has been under constant examination since it became policy in the late 1970s. Again, the literature is voluminous. For an important reason why deregulation has not been a total success, see Robert E. McCormick, William F. Shughart II, and Robert D. Tollison, "The Disinterest in Deregulation," *American Economic Review*, vol. 74 (December 1984), pp. 1075–1079. For an example involving deregulation of the trucking industry, see James M. MacDonald, "Railroad Deregulation, Innovation, and Competition: Effects of the Staggers Act on Grain Transportation," *Journal of Law and Economics*, vol. 35 (April 1989), pp. 63–96. The matter of rent seeking and deregulation is developed in a number of theoretical and practical papers: See R. D. Tollison, "Is the Theory of Rent Seeking Here to Stay?" in C. K. Rowley (ed.), *Democracy and Public Choice* (London: Blackwell, 1987), pp. 143–157. Some reasons why effective cable deregulation has been so difficult to establish may be found in Thomas W. Hazlett, "The Demand to Regulate Franchise Monopoly: Evidence from CATV Rate Deregulation in California," *Economic Inquiry*, vol. 29 (April 1991), pp. 275–296.

Over the 1970s and 1980s, a veritable revolution in the study of industry structure emerged, called "contestable markets theory." The basic argument is simple: When potential competitive rivalry is costless or inexpensive—when entry and exit possibilities exist in a market—and price and output configurations are "sustainable," the market may be characterized as perfectly contestable. The theory of contestable markets may be used to show that the principal conclusion of the traditional competitive model—that price equates to marginal and average cost—may occur when numbers of competitors are as small as two (or even one). In this theory the degree of concentration cannot reveal anything about competitiveness. Under certain conditions even a "natural" monopoly can behave as a competitive firm and industry. This theory holds that the degree of contestability (and not the number of firms) is the benchmark for understanding the competitiveness of markets. See William J. Baumol, John C. Panzar, and Robert D. Willig, *Contestable Markets and the Theory of Industry Structure* (New York: Harcourt Brace Jovanovich, 1982). A number of the papers mentioned in these notes (and others as well) can be found in Robert B. Ekelund, Jr. (ed.), *The Foundations of Regulatory Economics*, 3 vols. (Cheltenham, UK: Edward Elgar, 1998).

Part VI

Back to the Future

The Twenty-First Century

Because the future is unpredictable we can only speculate about the path that economic theory and method will take during the twenty-first century. But we may find some hints in the past. Since the very beginning—including the long prelude to classical economics that we have labeled "preclassical"—the dominant goal of economic theory has been to construct a meaningful, scientific explanation of how society functions. The intellectual children of Adam Smith continue to develop new theories and methods to better explain economic events, including the master's original goal of fathoming the nature and causes of economic growth. It is surprising how often new concerns keep returning to old ideas. Today, for example, theories of economic development often hark back to a central concern of Smith and the English founders—how the impact of institutions such as religion and government affect the well-being of entire nations.

The movement to mathematics and econometrics—a combination of statistics and mathematics used to test and verify theories—is now firmly fixed in economics and will continue throughout the twenty-first century. In chapter 25 you will learn, in very basic terms, the nature of this trend and its major tools. As the twenty-first century spreads out before us, we seek to offer some preliminary assessment of the actual and potential outcomes that mathematics and econometrics might have for the discipline. We have seen clearly in earlier portions of this book that this movement is not new. But the underpinnings of mathematics and econometrics have become so pervasive in professional economic discourse as to cause one to openly wonder whether economics will become another branch of mathematics.

Another distinct trend that will likely continue is the application of microeconomic theory to a broad array of social problems. In chapter 26 you will learn something of the past accomplishments of economists working this venue, and perhaps see opportunities for future research. The chapter focuses on modern developments in demand/consumption theory, and broaches the critical question of the "rationality" assumption in economics brought to the fore by contemporary experiments in psychology. In addition the importance of the economics of information, quality differentiation, and advertising and their relation to consumption technology are treated.

Chapter 27 takes you on an excursion into a few of the major applications of economic theory to matters traditionally relegated to the other social sciences. Here you will see, at least in preliminary fashion how simple economic theory can inform matters in sociology (marriage, dating, etc.), religion (demands for religion, the historical evolution of religion, etc.) art, archeology, anthropology and, not least, politics. These interesting application are the foundation for on-going and interesting extensions of economics as part of the "everyday business of life."

Finally, in chapter 28 you will learn some of the high points of twentieth century economics through a brief survey of Nobel Prize winners in Economic Science. These economists and their winning ideas provide a backdrop for an assessment of the directions of the more distant future. Will core economic theory survive? How has the "technology" for the introduction of economic ideas changed? Will new heterodoxies arise? If so, will there be a schism between political economists (in the tradition of Adam Smith and general social science) and those who regard economics as a pure mathematical science? Only time will tell.

25

Mathematical and Empirical Economics
A Method Revolution

Possibly the most visible aspect of modern economics is the suffusion of ever-expanding new mathematical and statistical techniques into every branch of inquiry. A visit to any university library to investigate the latest in economic research might turn up titles such as the following: "The Economist as Engineer: Game Theory, Experimentation and Computational Tools for Design Economics"; "Recursive Utility and Optimal Growth with Bounded or Unbounded Returns"; "Arrovian Aggregation in Economic Environments: How Much Should We Know About Indifference Surfaces?"; or "On the Nonexistence of Universal Information Structures." These examples are not fabricated but are actual papers in the leading journals. Nobel laureate Gerard Debreu (see references) cited the following journals as playing a major role in the spread of the mathematical technique in economics: *Econometrica* (founded in 1933), *Review of Economic Studies* (1933), *International Economic Review* (1960), *Journal of Economic Theory* (1969), and *Journal of Mathematical Economics* (1974). Others such as the *Journal of Econometrics* (1973) might be added to the list. But these journals, which emphasize the development of technique, grossly underestimate the number of journals and regularly published papers that use and apply mathematical and empirical techniques in economics—papers that number in the tens of thousands of pages each year. Basic economics teaches us that there are costs and benefits to everything. The present chapter seeks briefly to examine some of the applications of mathematic tools to economic study and, as the twenty-first century unfolds before us, to provide a preliminary assessment of the actual and potential outcome of this development for economic science.

Certainly the quest to formalize economic theory and to gauge the power of its predictions is not new. It was a mission and ongoing concern within the discipline throughout the twentieth century and even before. Most, if not all graduate or undergraduate programs in economics require some evidence of proficiency in mathematics and statistics, or econometrics (a combination of economic theory and statistical methods). Advanced students of economics would not be able to read papers in academic journals (such as those listed above and many more) without such proficiency. New mathematical and statistical techniques are rapidly introduced in order to elaborate new economic theories or new tests of earlier economic theories.

The enthusiasm for these developments is somewhat mixed. Some critics argue that the costs of further developments along mathematical/empirical lines heavily outweigh the potential benefits. Others defend these developments and argue that economics cannot and will not ever achieve "scientific" status without continuous cultivation and refinement of technique. Obviously, no definitive prediction of the outcome of these developments in the twenty-first century is possible. But if part of the role of the historian of economic thought is to chronicle and assess major developments in the discipline, the encroaching dominance of technique requires analysis. Specifically, what are the origins of these important developments in method? How and to what end are mathematics and statistics applied in economics and in economic theory? What are the gains and losses from such applications? What is the current state and what is the probable future of mathematical and testing techniques in the profession and in economic inquiry? Since methods of testing economic theory paralleled or followed the acceptance and development of mathematical and statistical techniques, we first devote attention to mathematical methods and their long history in economics.

■ History and Development of Mathematical Economics

From the very beginnings of what we now call economic analysis, economists have attempted to "display" their ideas in order to improve them and to facilitate communication. Much early work was framed in a purely literary style, but numerical and mathematical presentations entered the literature as early as the eighteenth century. Of a fairly substantial mass of international contributions, we provide only three examples worthy of mention. In Italy Cesare Beccaria (1712–1769), a scholar and administrator, established utility as underlying economic behavior in *Dei delitti e delle pene* (1764) and in *Elementi de economia publica* (1771), works he crowned by applying mathematical methods to economic reasoning. In France, a civil engineer, A. N. Isnard (1749–1803), applied a "general equilibrium"/mathematical approach to questions of exchange, production, capital, interest, and foreign trade in *Traité des richesses* (1781). While Ricardo and Malthus were developing a literary approach to classical economics, a British scholar William Whewell (1799–1866) wrote between 1829 and 1831 a *Mathematical Exposition of Some Doctrines of Political Economy*, a book that applied mathematical analysis to Ricardian economics and to capital and input substitution.[1] These and many other amazing contributions were natural developments, since economics not only deals with "tendencies" but also with the numerical calculation of social phenomena.[2] The kind of deduction from which economic theory proceeds clearly invites and encourages researchers to employ mathematics.

Many early advances in the mathematical approach to economic theory did not, fortunately or unfortunately for the history of economics, establish a pattern of acceptability. Augustin Cournot (1801–1877), as we learned in chapter 13, was the real founder of mathematical economics. One could hardly improve, even today, on

[1] These writers are but a small sample. A fuller idea of the achievements of economic innovators with a "technical" bent may be found in chap. 13. Also see the excellent treatment by Theocharis, *Early Developments in Mathematical Economics* (see references).

[2] For example, in the seventeenth century, Sir William Petty developed what he called "Political Arithmetick" to describe a primitive national income account system (see chap. 4). A few decades later, Charles Davenant, building on earlier work by Gregory King, estimated a demand curve (see John Creedy, "On the King–Davenant 'Law' of Demand," in the references).

Cournot's understanding of the role and advantages of using mathematics in economics. The employment of mathematics, in Cournot's embryonic understanding, was not different from the use of words or graphical representations of economic theory. Cournot claimed that Ricardo had only disguised his algebra under "numerical calculations of tedious length" (*Researches*, p. 4). But Cournot knew full well that numerical calculations were not the only or even the major benefits of the use of mathematics. He valued mathematics as a methodological tool, declaring:

> I have said that most authors who have devoted themselves to political economy seem also to have had a wrong idea of the nature of the applications of mathematical analysis to the theory of wealth. They imagined that the use of symbols and formulas could only lead to numerical calculations, and as it was clearly perceived that the subject was not suited to such a numerical determination of values by means of a theory alone, the conclusion was drawn that the mathematical apparatus, if not liable to lead to erroneous results, was at least idle and pedantic. But those skilled in mathematical analysis know that its object is not simply to calculate numbers, but that it is also employed to find the relations between magnitudes which cannot be expressed in numbers and between functions whose law is not capable of algebraic expression. (*Researches*, pp. 2–3)

Good data have always been hard to come by, and very often are costly to generate. This is no less true in our own day as it was in Cournot's. Nevertheless, Cournot appreciated the value of mathematics to facilitate economic intuition about how certain economic values (e.g., price and quantity) were related to each other and to other magnitudes. In his own words, mathematical symbols are able to "facilitate the exposition of problems, to rend it [sic] more concise, to open the way to more extended developments, and to avoid the digressions of vague argumentation" (*Researches*, p. 4). Since the functions developed by Cournot were in finite commodity and price spaces, he effectively used Euclidian geometry (i.e., graphs) to illustrate economic theory alongside algebraic formulations.

■ Common Mathematical Tools Used in Economics

In principle, then, literary, graphical, and mathematical expressions of economic theory do not differ in any fundamental respect. But there are costs and benefits to the use of each means of expression. By way of analogy, consider the use of computer software. Software provides a means to process information; it gets us from "input" to "output." Each software package, whether for word processing or data processing, permits us to transfer inputs to output, and each software package does it differently. Of course, it takes time to learn any given software package, but once learned, the tool may be used again and again for any task that may be adapted to it.

One of the tasks of the economic theorist is to reason deductively from postulates (assumptions about economic behavior) to conclusions about the way the world works—or how some particular facet of it (markets for nurses, for example) functions. Just as there are different types of computer software that provide a means to record and disseminate words and thoughts, there are different ways to get from postulates to conclusions in expressing economic theory. Each kind of software has advantages and disadvantages, just as each mode of economic expression has pluses and minuses.

A purely verbal argument is readily intelligible to the largest audience, but as Cournot recognized, literary exposition has some definite limitations. Literary exposition can lead to digressions and ambiguities. Where elaborate reasoning is required, graphical and mathematical expositions offer more precision. Graphs of economic relations and theories provide a very useful picture and help the economist grasp and extend complex relations. Geometry has taken and still takes economists far as a mode of expressing economic ideas. But graphs also have limits. When problems extend beyond two dimensions (e.g., a demand relation involving changes in prices, quantities, and *income*), graphs become cumbersome, and their usefulness declines. Moreover, graphs are limited to three dimensions, so they are inappropriate to problems involving more than three dimensions. Mathematics and geometry were used by neoclassical writers such as Jevons (chapter 15) and their forerunners (chapter 13) to explicate simple theories of consumer behavior, but as economists began to tackle larger problems (e.g., Walrasian general equilibrium; see chapter 17), new modes of expression ("software") became necessary, and mathematics became a vital tool of the economic theorist. The benefits that mathematics brings to economics are at least threefold: (1) mathematics makes assumptions and premises explicit, thereby eliminating "hidden" biases of theory; (2) it makes the presentation of economic theory more concise and more precise; and (3) it allows the economist to deal more readily with economic problems of more than two dimensions. It was inevitable, therefore, that mathematical theorems of many kinds, some of them exceedingly complex, would become part and parcel of the economist's "software." We cannot treat this subject exhaustively, but we will identify some major, elementary tools here, and we will introduce others (at least intuitively) later in the chapter.

Calculus

Arithmetic and algebra have always been of great value to the economist, but as economics progressed the most useful tools have proven to be differential and integral calculus. We saw previously (chapters 13–17) that early econo-engineers such as Dupuit, Ellet, and Lardner, and later economists such as Jevons, Marshall, and Walras, employed calculus in their contributions. It is of the very nature of economic study to examine magnitudes—quantities supplied and demanded, population, wages, profits, etc.—and whether such magnitudes rise or fall. Purely qualitative economic models deal with direction—up or down. Thus, a hypothesis that states that an increase in demand (supply remaining constant) increases both equilibrium price and quantity makes a *qualitative* statement about the direction of price and quantity. But the issue of *how much* price and quantity will change in response to a change in demand is a *quantitative* question (the answer to which includes the qualitative). Differential calculus, which essentially deals with *rates of change*, is thus the natural tool for the economist to employ in constructing and discussing economic theories, and integral calculus sums these rates of change in order to arrive at total calculations—total population, total quantity demanded or supplied, or total profits.

Consider an example from personal finance. Suppose you are a greenhouse enthusiast and plan to cultivate orchids, eventually for profit. As you add rarer and rarer orchids to your collection, your total expenses rise. The rate of change in your expenditures between, say the 121st and 122nd orchid, is found by taking the "derivative" or "differential" of the total cost curve between these two points. This derivative constitutes your *marginal cost* of adding that extra orchid and it is also, in geometric terms, the tangent to your total cost function. But you may be interested in another question. What is the total cost of your collection between the 200th and 300th orchid? To find this sum you simply add up, or "integrate," the rates of change in expenditures between the 200th and 300th orchids. This simple example suggests how both the differential and integral calculus might be used with either hypothetical or actual data. We might, for example, be interested in federal expenditures on infrastructure throughout the twentieth century. If we have the data, a total expenditures curve could be constructed and the slope at any point in time found by taking the derivative of the total expenditures curve. By contrast, we could find the total expenditure on infrastructure between 2008 and 2012 by *integrating* or finding the area under the total expenditures curve between these two points in time.

Because economic decisions are usually made at the margin, economists are often not as interested in total quantities as they are in marginal quantities. In the theory of the firm, for example, the businessperson is interested in the marginal cost and marginal revenue of this or that action. Differential calculus is uniquely suited to provide such answers. An excellent example is the theory of consumer behavior. The consumer, with a given set of preferences for all goods and services, faces a certain set of prices and is constrained by his or her income. The mathematical procedure that describes the consumer's solution to the problem of utility maximization in these circumstances is called *constrained optimization,* which is a straightforward application of differential calculus. Another example is given by Cournot's theory of profit maximization (see figure 13-1 and related discussion in chapter 13). Cournot specified the solution as requiring the rates of change of the firm's revenue (i.e., marginal revenue) and costs (i.e., marginal costs) to be equal. Marginal revenue and marginal cost are determined by taking the first derivative of the total revenue and total cost functions, respectively, thus providing another illustration of the straightforward application of differential calculus.

Integral calculus finds ready application to basic economic problems, especially in the fields of industrial organization and public finance. The decision whether to provide a new bridge or public park should be informed by, among other things, a calculation and comparison of the economic costs and benefits. A common means of calculating benefits is the computation of consumer surplus (see chapters 13 and 16), by determining the maximum price consumers would be willing to pay for the good or service rather than go without it. The mathematical measure of this aggregate "benefit" is the integral or "summing up" of the benefits of all individuals under the demand curve for the good in question. Once the demand curve is estimated and the costs of the project are calculated, integral calculus provides the economist with a ready-made tool for making an actual calculation and comparison.

Linear Systems and Algebra

Algebra, whether basic or advanced, provides the economist with a wealth of tools or "software" by which to express economic theory. This is especially so when the economist is faced with the task of estimating general-equilibrium (Walrasian) relations and interrelations. A branch of algebra called *matrix algebra* has proved especially useful in dealing with large numbers of equations and variables that summarize or approximate those in a real-world economy.

The combination of linear and matrix algebra provides an estimation procedure that depicts production or consumption (or other) relations as being linear, or as being reducible to, or approximated by, linear relations. The advantage of this procedure is that huge systems of equations can be calculated rapidly by computer to uncover complicated relations in an economic system. A possible disadvantage to using linear relations is that, even as approximations, they may not capture accurately the features of actual production or consumption relations. However, this valuable technique forms the basis for economy-wide models that predict overall economic growth as well as growth in particular economic sectors. A single such model may contain inaccuracies, but fortunately most advanced economies are modeled in a number of ways, giving a better overall prediction of growth and other factors over time. The usefulness of such predictive tools is well established.

■ Cournot's Heirs: Applications of Mathematics to Economic Ideas

Calculus and algebra are two general mathematical tools that have proved useful to the economist. Depending on the nature of the problem, economists have adapted as well many other varieties of mathematical "software" of varying complexity. Calculus, however, has been the tool of choice from the beginning for the simple reason that "small changes" lie at the heart of so many economic problems. The early intellectual descendants of Cournot applied calculus to economic problems in quite ingenious ways. Francis Ysidro Edgeworth (1845–1926), a neoclassical contemporary of Jevons, Marshall, and Walras, was perhaps the premier Anglo-Saxon economist of his era in adapting mathematics to the social sciences (*Mathematical Psychics*). (He dealt with complex, sophisticated, and somewhat obscure problems, which may account for his relative neglect by contemporaries: He applied calculus and other mathematical tools to issues such as monopoly, price discrimination, index numbers, and taxation (see notes for further reading). His long co-editorship of the *Economic Journal*, a duty he shared with John Maynard Keynes, may have had a major impact on the direction of economic method. His admirers all agree, however, that he was without peer in his understanding of (active and reactive) duopoly behavior among competitors and for his invention of the "core" theory of a contracting exchange economy.[3]

Alfred Marshall, although an enthusiastic and capable mathematician, largely eschewed the application of formal mathematics in his academic writings. Marshall's aim was to portray economics as a tool of social change in a way easily understandable by the businessperson and to the intelligent layperson (see chapter 16). He wished his ideas to be accessible to the widest possible audience and saw mathematics as a device that would retard this goal. Yet, while Marshall was reluctant to employ mathematics, his students and successors have taken his (and Léon Walras's) ideas to new heights of mathematical sophistication. In 1934, John R. Hicks (1904–1989) and R. G. D. Allen (1906–1983), in a joint mathematical tour de force, recast Marshallian value theory in terms of calculus. Hicks (subsequently awarded a Nobel Prize in Economics in 1972) later expanded this "new" neoclassical microeconomics in 1939 (*Value and Capital*) to include dynamic and monetary considerations. His rigorous mathematical presentation of key components of economic theory eventually became a standard for modern practice.

Paul A. Samuelson (1915–2009), an American economist who won the Nobel Prize in 1970, has also been an important force for mathematical rigor in economic theory. In his *Foundations of Economic Analysis* (1947), a work stemming from his Harvard doctoral dissertation of six years earlier, Samuelson transformed the style

[3] See Peter Newman's biography of Edgeworth in *The New Palgrave: A Dictionary of Economics* (listed in the references) for a fuller discussion of Edgeworth as a mathematical economist.

of economic analysis from predominantly verbal-graphical exposition to systematic and thorough mathematical treatment. In the *Foundations* and in many other works, Samuelson applied mathematics to general economic theory and to specific elements of that theory, including the theory of consumer behavior, growth and capital theory, welfare economics, and international trade theory. As leaders in the economics profession, Hicks and Samuelson gave legitimacy to mathematical and empirical economics. Moreover, they set the trend that has carried forward into the twenty-first century and shows no signs of abatement.

Linear Mathematical Relations

As suggested above, linear algebra and its elaborations provide an important mathematical tool that finds ready application in economic theory. Numerous early attempts to apply algebra, often in conjunction with calculus, highlight the development of economic theory in the nineteenth century. It might be recalled that Friedrich von Wieser in his book *Natural Value* (1884) introduced a simple system of input-to-value equations in order to determine the productive contribution of each input (chapter 13). His simple, linear equations (for various industry inputs and values) yield a simultaneous algebraic solution. Elaborations on this theme abound in twentieth- and twenty-first century economics.

Linear Programming. One of the most important applications of linear techniques has come through the development of linear programming by mathematicians John von Neumann and George Dantzig in the late 1940s and by economists Robert Dorfman, Paul Samuelson, and Robert Solow in 1958 (see notes for further reading). While linear (and certain forms of nonlinear) programming have been brought to increasingly useful and elaborate states of development, the fundamental idea is basically uncomplicated. Linear programming models represent optimizing behavior as the choice of processes or activities under some set of linear constraints. Dantzig first applied this tool to logistical planning and to the optimal deployment of military forces, but the tool has many other applications in economics and business, especially in choosing least-cost production techniques.

For illustrative purposes, consider a standard problem in microeconomic theory—profit maximization by the firm.[4] Suppose a sporting goods firm produces tennis rackets and barbell sets and that each production requires three machines: types A, B, and C. Arbitrarily we might identify these three types as cutting machines, lathes, and finishing machines. Given the number of machines the firm owns, there is obviously some maximum utilization of that machine to produce (either or both) tennis rackets and barbell sets. Units of these goods require definite numbers of hours of machine use—these are the physical requirements—and, naturally, the firm owns a limited number of each machine. Once these facts are all known, the profit-maximizing firm must choose to produce tennis rackets and barbell sets (called the firm's *choice variables*) within some constraint set by the number of machines the firm owns. The firm is also constrained by the number of machine hours required to produce each of its goods. In other words, the firm is going to be limited by what economists call a *feasible region* of production—combinations of machine hours that will actually produce tennis rackets and barbell sets.

What solution will the firm choose—i.e., how many barbell sets and tennis rackets (or possibly all or one or the other) will the firm actually produce? That choice

[4] The example provided here is adapted from Charles Maurice and Charles Smithson, *Managerial Economics*, chap. 7 (see references).

will depend on the relative profitability of those two items. In general the firm is said to maximize profits subject to physical constraints and availability of machines. Linear iso-profit curves—curves showing profit levels for alternative combinations of the two goods—may be calculated and an exact output of the two goods may be ascertained therefrom. (Naturally there cannot be negative quantities of either good produced.)

This simple example illustrates some fundamental principles of linear programming, but it is only one of many problems that can be treated and solved by linear programming methods. The technique is useful in *any* case involving constrained choice. It has been used repeatedly in problems of cost minimization for given output levels, in the selection of production techniques in industry and agriculture, and in the minimization of transport costs, but it is applicable also to problems involving consumer behavior. It can provide solutions, for example, to the problem of allocating one's work or leisure in order to maximize one's income or satisfaction.

Macroeconomic Applications: Input-Output Analysis. Linear programming is actually an offshoot of a broader mathematical technique called input-output analysis, which was invented by 1973 Nobel laureate Wassily Leontief (1906–1999), an American economist who emigrated from Russia. Input-output analysis is a mathematical technique that emphasizes the general interdependence of inputs and outputs of whole economies, regions, or, indeed, even the entire world. Leontief, who joined the Harvard faculty in 1932, published the first input-output tables for the United States during World War II. His early tables described the American experience between 1919 and 1929 ("Input-Output Analysis"; *The Structure of the American Economy*).

Input-output analysis contains both inductive and deductive components. It draws inductively on actual data and actual interdependencies of all of the various sectors of the economy. These interdependencies, however, are analyzed within mathematical models that facilitate computations and analyses of the effects of exogenous changes such as changes in the composition of final demand or input supplies—the deductive component of input-output investigations. Input-output analysis may also be contrasted with the highly aggregative Keynesian theory (chapter 21), insofar as actual tables are usually based on disaggregated economic data.

As an introduction to this important branch of mathematical analysis, consider an elementary input-output table with only three sectors in a simple economy. Actual input-output tables may contain hundreds of sectors and subsectors describing real-world economies. Ours is represented in table 25-1 and kept simple for illustration. This simple economy contains three interrelated sectors: a food-and-raw-materials sector, a manufacturing sector, and a household sector. Like all input-output tables, table 25-1 is composed of rows and columns arranged in the form of what is called an input-output matrix. (A 3×3 matrix contains three rows and three columns; a 75×75 matrix contains seventy-five rows and an equal number of columns.) Each row and its corresponding column represent one particular sector of the economy, e.g., automobiles, toasters, avocados, and so on. In the simple case described in table 25-1, the agricultural (food-and-raw-materials) sector has produced 1,000 bushels of corn, which are delivered in the various amounts to the sectors listed in the column headings. Two hundred bushels have been retained in the agricultural sector (for replenishment of seed), 100 bushels have been delivered to the manufacturing sector, and 400 bushels have been delivered to the household (final demand) sector. Other sectors, not shown in the table, receive the balance, so

Table 25-1 A Three-Sector Input-Output Matrix*

Sector	Agriculture	Manufacturing	Household	Total
Food and Raw Materials	200	100	400	1,000 bu. corn
Manufacturing	100	150	25	300 tons plastics
Household	250	200	—	450 work-years

*The production requirements of the various sectors of an economy are summarized in rows and columns.

the row does not add up to the total produced. Entries may also be zero for some column sectors since some sectors may deliver nothing to other sectors of the economy. Like the agricultural sector, the manufacturing sector delivers output to other sectors. The manufacturing sector is represented in table 24-1 by a producer of plastics. Thus, we see that manufacturing delivers 100 tons of plastic to the agricultural sector, supplies 25 tons to the household sector, and retains 150 tons for its own use. Each column may be interpreted as displaying the requirements for production in the sector represented. The agriculture column in table 25-1 tells us that the production of 1 bushel of corn requires 1/5 (200/1,000), or 0.20, of a bushel of corn; 1/10 (100/1,000), or 0.10, ton of plastics; and 1/4 (250/1,000), or 0.25, person-year of labor. The production of 1 ton of plastics (reading down column 2) requires 1/3 (100/300), or 0.33, person-year of labor.

While this example may seem artificial, its purpose is to show how the *technical coefficients of production* are built up and arranged in mathematical form. Once the technical coefficients (a fancy term for the production requirements for any good or service) are known, and once final (actual) output is known, equations relating inputs to outputs may be developed. These equations, which can be manipulated through the use of matrix algebra, then provide critical information on *intersectoral* changes in input and production requirements that would emerge, say, if final demand for corn or plastics were to change. The general interdependence of any economic system means that a change in demand in one sector will and must affect many other sectors in the economy. In any real-world economy these interdependent intersectoral changes will have an enormous impact on resource utilization in certain sectors, including employment in specific sectors.[5]

Successes and Failures of Linear Models. Input-output analysis is a useful tool for estimating changes in intersectoral production requirements that emerge from changes in final demands. One early use of Leontief's model, for example, was to predict the extent of steel shortages during World War II. The impact on total production due to technological change in one sector may be estimated by means of the device. Input-output analysis is thus both a descriptive tool that permits the modeling of an economy from actual data and an analytical tool that permits the estimation of intersectoral shortages or surpluses under the assumption of a specific change in final demand or technology. While the technique itself is politically neutral, it obviously lends itself readily to problems of socialist planning and economic development. Be that as it may, Marxist economists did not uncritically accept the technique. Indeed, the Soviet Union's use of computer-driven techniques to determine target outputs and so-called shadow prices for goods did not protect it against

[5] The reader may wish to reexamine Quesnay's *Tableau économique* (see chapter 4) in order to appreciate it as a primitive input-output model.

failure due, in large part, to issues raised by Austrian economists in the socialist calculation debate (see chapter 23). Miscalculations and bureaucratic opportunism (i.e., cheating and fraud) riddled the system, resulting in chronic waiting lines for all manner of goods, including food. Scarcity of food and waiting in long lines to purchase it were not the least important reasons for the final breakup of the Soviet Union in 1991.

The use of linear models in microeconomics and macroeconomics, as exemplified by linear programming and input-out analysis, has been enhanced in a positive manner by the invention and development of the computer. Greater and greater computing capacity—roughly doubling every two years—and the increased speed of calculations have allowed the development of highly sophisticated econometric forecasting models of the economy (famously at the St. Louis Federal Reserve Bank and at MIT). Input-output matrices may now be manipulated and analyzed with hundreds of sectors, thanks to advanced computer technology. In addition, the concepts of linear programming and input-output theory have helped bridge the chasm between the highly aggregative kind of Keynesian macroeconomic theory so popular in the precomputer age and the microeconomic principles of general-equilibrium theory.

Despite rapid advances in technology, however, predictive accuracy has been illusive because the fundamental elements of the economy or most "systems" become more complex through time. Hence theories devised to capture more complex reality become more complex as well—even as computer capabilities are ever increasing. We should be continually mindful that no matter how sophisticated computers become, the quality of "output" (predictions of GDP, employment, inflation, sectoral input requirements, and so on) depends on the quality of the "input" (data derived from varied and sometimes dubious sources). Moreover, no matter how quantitative economics becomes, it remains a social science that involves human, and therefore not strictly predictable, behavior. Actual production and consumption relations may not be strictly reducible to linear functions. In other words, economies or diseconomies may exist in production and consumption patterns in the real world. But these problems do not negate the usefulness of contemporary mathematical techniques. In most cases, some estimation technique is far better than none at all, and estimates can usually be improved over time by better economic theory and intuition, aided by ever-improving methods of calculation. Properly used, linear algebra is a powerful tool that can enlighten and enliven contemporary economic research.

Game Theory

One of the most interesting and important tools of modern economic analysis is the technique called "game theory." Unless huge numbers of competitors act or react in exchange markets of all kinds, some form of mutual interdependence develops. Because we all find ourselves in situations of mutual interdependence every day, the basic problems of competitive games should be familiar to everyone. Anyone who has ever played games of any sort—tennis, soccer, bridge—will immediately recognize the problem. Our actions are interdependent when playing games because the actions of one player affect other players' behavior. Moreover, our *own* behavior is conditioned by what we *expect* other players' reactions to our own behavior to be. Do we go the extra mile in performing our job in expectation that the boss will give us a raise? That depends on how we expect our boss to react to increased productivity. And think of your weekly tennis match with your friend Sam. Respectful of your powerful serve, Sam has learned to stand well behind the baseline when receiving it. This position allows him to return an increasingly high percentage of your serves. Noticing this, you decide to surprise him with a shallow slicing serve. If you serve this way consistently, Sam will likely change his behavior. Sam's actions and yours are clearly interdependent—and recognized to be so. Game theory is a branch of economics that merely formalizes the effects on alternative strategies of mutual interdependence.

The Origins of Game Theory. Cournot (see chapter 13) originated an early form of game theory in the nineteenth century by analyzing the nature of competition between two mineral water sellers. Each competitor's behavior was conditioned on conjectures about how the other seller of mineral water would behave in reaction to the first competitor's actions. Facing demand for a homogeneous product (mineral water), sellers *A* and *B* adjust the quantities they sell assuming that the other will keep quantity constant no matter how much experience he has to the contrary. Each knows the total demand curve for mineral water and each maximizes his own profits under the quantity-constant assumption. As a result (see chapter 13 for a graphical representation) the competitors arrive at an equally shared, combined output equal to $[n/(n + 1)$ (i.e., the monopoly quantity)]. Cournot's model employs a (naive) conjectural variable about a rival's quantity of sales. But in other contexts a conjectural variable could be almost anything—how your boss reacts to your productivity by the amount she pays you, or how Sam reacts to your tennis serve.

The game-theoretic aspects of Cournot's model were fully appreciated early on. The French mathematician, Joseph Bertrand (see notes for further reading) argued in 1883 that Cournot's model would yield different results if it was adapted to include a conjecture about price rather than quantity. In effect Bertrand changed the behavior of each rival to reflect a different conjecture. The new conjecture is: I assume that my competitor will hold price rather than quantity constant (no matter what I do in reaction). It can be demonstrated that such a conjecture would lead to competitive output (where price equals average cost).

A decade after Bertrand offered up his modification, Francis Ysidro Edgeworth added a different perspective to Cournot's original model. He assumed that the duopolist in fact conjectured about price, but that each competitor had an output limitation, so that neither seller could sell all the output that would be demanded under competitive conditions. In this case, equilibrium is unattainable. Because Edgeworth's model anticipates some of the problems that pertain to game theory, it is instructive to consider it in more detail. Let us suppose, as Edgeworth did, that duopolists share a market for mineral water such that each faces a demand curve for *half* the daily market for water. Figure 25-1 on the following page replicates Edgeworth's figure ("Pure Theory of Monopoly," pp. 118–121). RC' is the demand curve for duopolist A and RC is the demand curve for duopolist B. There is a catch, however. A's output limitation is quantity OB' and B's output limitation is OB. Assuming they both start at profit-maximizing price levels, they will share the market equally selling OA' and OA respectively.

Edgeworth asked the question, "What would you do if you were either seller of mineral water?" In order to maximize profits you would lower your price down to Q in figure 25-1 and sell quantity OB' or OB. In this instance Edgeworth's conjecture relates to price: Each competitor thinks the other will hold price constant. By lowering price you take some business away from your competitor. If the output limita-

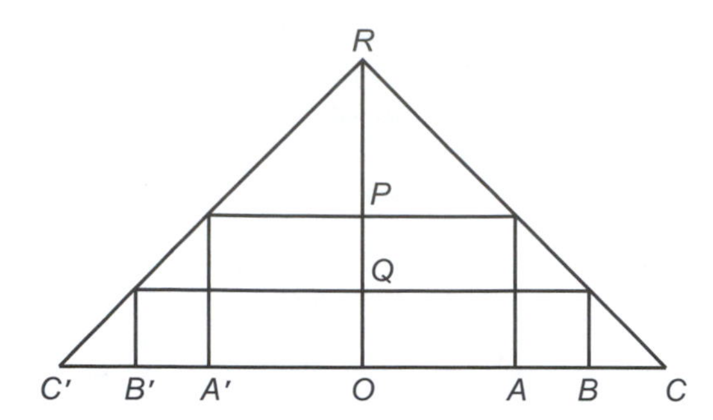

Figure 25-1 Edgeworth's duopolists, each under an output constraint (*OB*′ and *OB* of mineral water), reduce price from *OP*, stealing sales from each other. After price reductions, however, it is in each seller's interest at some point to raise price in order to maximize profit. No equilibrium is stable, however, and price oscillates between *OP* and *OQ*.

tion is such that the whole market cannot be supplied, your rival is free to set a price to "fill out" the market. He would do so in this instance by *raising* price back to the profit-maximizing level (*OP*). As Edgeworth put it, the price-raising competitor "need not fear the competition of his rival, since that rival has already done his worst by putting his whole supply on the market. The best that the rival can now do in his own interest is to follow the example set him and raise his price to [*OP*]" ("Pure Theory," p. 120) and the whole process begins again! Thus, when the conditions of a duopoly game match those specified by Edgeworth, continuous oscillations in price result and equilibrium is not possible.

Edgeworth's model, like Cournot's, was a prelude to future developments. Early models like these, however suggestive, were fairly simplistic concerning the kinds of conjectures that competitors routinely make. In many competitive situations, for example, we expect individuals to eventually realize that collusion is better than competition. Moreover, the early theorists did not establish sets of alternative "payoffs" of one kind or another from particular combinations of actions by competitors. This next step forward is attributed to a mathematician, A. W. Tucker, whose exposition of the "prisoner's dilemma" reached to the core of the modern approach to game theory.

A Prisoner's Dilemma. Consider the following "dilemma." Suppose Bonnie and Clyde—infamous bank robbers of the 1930s who were gunned down for their crimes—return to life to rob banks again. Further suppose that they are caught in the act of robbing a bank but that the FBI only has hard evidence to convict them of some lesser crime. In an attempt to improve their evidence, the FBI sequesters the two prisoners separately and tries to get confessions from them in the following manner. In isolation each prisoner is informed that (1) if he/she confesses, the confessor goes free and the other person gets a big penalty (25 years); (2) if neither confesses, both will receive the light penalty that accompanies the lesser crime (5 years); (3) if both confess, both will receive a severe penalty but of less severity than if only one confesses (15 years). Given the payoffs and the uncertainty, the expected solution is that Bonnie and Clyde both confess to bank robbing.

Economists use a "payoff" matrix like that shown in figure 25-2 to tease out the solution to this problem. The potential prison term for Bonnie is shown on the left side of each individual block, or quadrant, and the potential time served for Clyde is shown on the right side. The police will try to get Bonnie and Clyde to testify against each other. If Clyde confesses, but Bonnie does not confess, Bonnie gets 25 years in the big house and Clyde goes free. Similarly, if Bonnie confesses to the greater crime and Clyde holds out, Bonnie goes free and Clyde gets 25 years. If both refuse to confess, they each get 5 years but if both confess, they each serve 15 years. What is the most likely outcome of this strategy "game" between Bonnie and Clyde? The result depends on the assumptions (conjectural variations) that each makes about the other's behavior. We may reasonably presume (1) that both Bonnie and Clyde want to minimize their time in jail and (2) that neither is concerned about the cost of their decision on the other. Given these two presumptions, the outcome of the game is that both "players" confess.

Look at figure 25-2 and consider the potential years served. What is Bonnie's best strategy? If Clyde confesses, Bonnie gets 15 years if she also confesses; but she gets 25 years if she doesn't. Therefore, Bonnie's best choice is to confess if Clyde confesses. If Clyde does not confess, Bonnie goes free if she confesses and gets 5 years if she doesn't confess. In this instance Bonnie's best choice is to confess if Clyde does not confess. In other words, Bonnie's best strategy is to confess, no matter what Clyde does. The sequester means that Bonnie cannot know Clyde's decision, and can in no way influence his decision, so a confession is the only way for Bonnie to ensure a lesser jail term for herself. You should verify that figure 25-2 shows the same is true for Clyde; his best choice is to confess regardless what Bonnie does. Note, however, that *if the two could communicate*, and *if each could hold the other to his/her word*, the best choice for both Bonnie and Clyde would be to *not confess*. In the terminology of game theory, there is a dominant strategy: Each player has the same best choice, no matter what strategy the other player chooses. In the game represented by figure 25-2, the *dominant strategy* is to confess.

Economic Games. It does not take a leap of imagination to visualize how this kind of "game" can be generalized to other issues, encompassing, for example, actions of love, war, and business. The formal idea of applying Cournot's duopoly

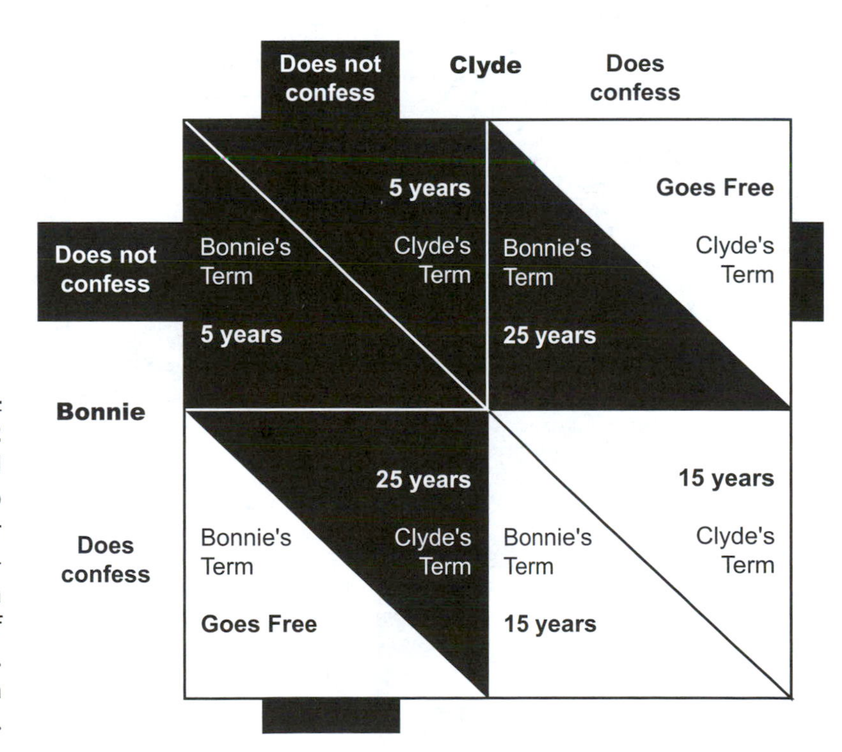

Figure 25-2 If Bonnie and Clyde want to minimize their jail time, the prisoner's dilemma leads both of them to confess. Each receives a 15-year term.

theory to such stratagems was developed in tandem by John von Neumann, a mathematician, and Oskar Morgenstern, an economist, who set forth the principles involved in *The Theory of Games and Economic Behavior* (1944). Economic stratagems that fit this model riddle the conduct of firms, for example, particularly when the products involved are close substitutes. Should Burger King introduce a new low-cal burger, increase advertising, or establish a promotional contest? It depends on how McDonald's or Wendy's will react. Different strategies yield different net profit results in this regard.

Consider yet another example spawned by the prisoner's dilemma. From time to time auto manufacturers increase the warranty period applied to new cars. Warranties are a method of making new cars more attractive to buyers, but they are costly to institute because they increase production costs, which lowers profits. What compels automakers to resort to this measure to increase sales? Game theory helps explain the self-interests involved. Figure 25-3 is a payoff matrix that presents a hypothetical situation in which two auto manufacturers, Toyota and General Motors, are trying to maximize profits. The numbers in the grids represent profits in millions of dollars. Toyota and General Motors could maximize joint profits in grid A where neither manufacturer provides extended warranties. In this instance industry profits total $120 million dollars (GM earns $55 million; Toyota earns $65 million). Similarly, total profits are $100 million in grids B and C and $90 million in grid D. Acting independently, however, both General Motors and Toyota could make higher profits.

General Motors would maximize profits in grid B ($70 million) by providing new warranty protection when its competitor does not. Consider the company's options. Regardless of Toyota's behavior, GM's profits are higher when it offers

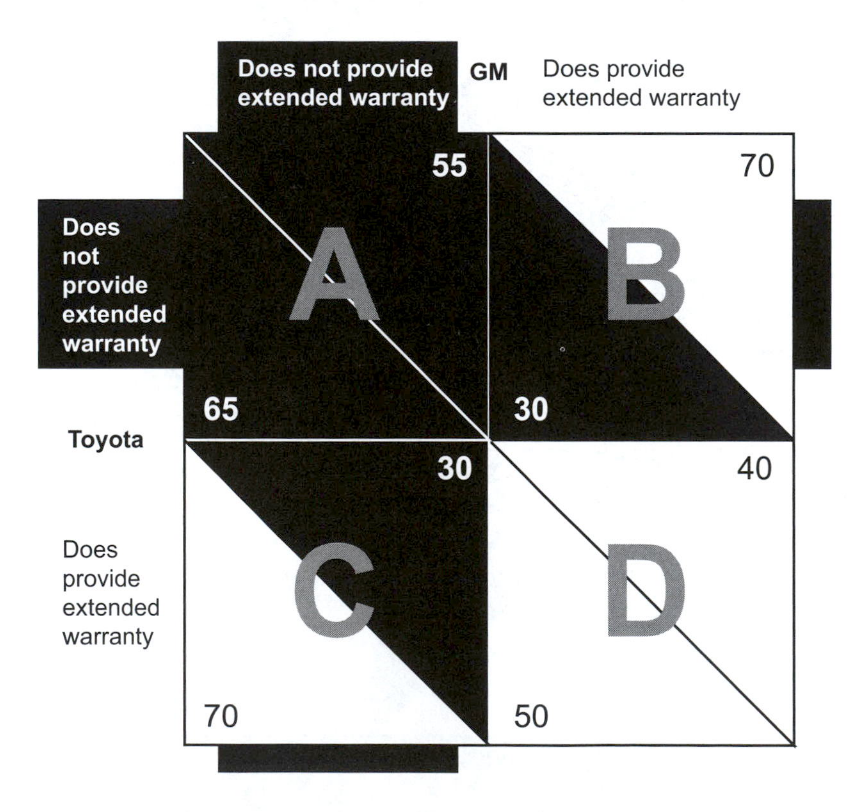

Figure 25-3 Automakers are depicted in a "game" to maximize profits. While they will earn lower total profit ($90 million) from doing so, game theory predicts that individual decisions on the part of both firms to maximize their profit will lead to the introduction of warranties.

extended warranties. If GM offers a warranty and Toyota does not, its profit is $70 million. If it offers a warranty and Toyota does too, GM's profit drops to $40 million. However, if GM elects *not* to offer the warranty and Toyota does, GM's profit falls to $30 million. Toyota's management, assessing the possibilities, will reach the same conclusion, namely that it will always be better off by offering the warranty. Independent decisions to maximize profits by each firm will lead to the introduction of warranties. This means that the sum of profits between the two firms will be lower ($90 million) than it would have been if each firm did not offer warranties ($120 million). In other words, they are "prisoners" of a game.

While such behavior may benefit auto consumers at the expense of General Motors' and Toyota's stockholders, the problem for stockholders could be avoided if the manufacturers were allowed to communicate and to reach grid A in figure 25-3. Communication in this case, as in the case of the prisoner's dilemma, would produce a different solution, but such collusion is usually prohibited by antitrust laws.

Complexities of Economic Games. In the simple illustration of figure 25-3, the game between General Motors and Toyota has a stable outcome, an equilibrium solution. In this simple case, the participants minimize their opponents' maximum—what von Neumann and Morgenstern called a minimax solution. More complex games—those with more players and multiple strategies—may not result in stable equilibria. Indeed, modern mathematical developments in game theory must deal with numerous complexities, some of which are illustrated in the following three paragraphs.

Strategy outcomes depend on prospects for collusion and the time frame involved. Clearly, Bonnie and Clyde or GM and Toyota would be better off with a collusive agreement. As shown in figure 25-3, a move to grid A would make both GM and Toyota better off than they would be under the case where both provide the extended warranty (grid D). Collusion is problematic, however. Information costs may be high, or legal prohibitions may exist. Time is also an important consideration. The two games represented above are one-shot games; in each case, each party has just one chance to make the best decision. If these games were played repeatedly, perhaps both parties in each game would eventually decide to do what's best for both. In other words, the element of time is bound to the prospects for collusion. Tacit collusive solutions—or outcomes without specific, formal agreement—exist when, over an indefinite period of time, firms recognize that their own interests will best be served by maximizing joint or combined profits (or other payoffs). In the latter case, however, antitrust laws may be able to punish or prevent collusion.

Collusive agreements, whether formal or informal, will always tend to collapse when the number of players increases, for two reasons. The first reason is that cheating is more likely as the number of players increases. The second is that the costs of any group decision-making process rise as the number of decision makers increases. When products are homogeneous (e.g., eggs), collusion is easier to organize because there is less need for advertising and other means of product differentiation. However, in cases where firms offer a range of products and services, sometimes only slightly differentiated (e.g., burger franchises, auto manufacturers, banking), competitive strategies to increase market shares and profits are not only possible but extremely probable. In such cases game-theoretic solutions are more difficult to achieve.

Even in a two-player game, the type of conjectures that one makes about the other is of critical importance to the solution. When the time horizon facing two rivals is finite—that is, when the game has a known end point—the outcome is shaped by the principle of *backward induction*. Backward induction results from an incentive to cheat in the final period of the game. Suppose the Toyota and GM game concerning warranties (figure 25-3) is expected to last three periods. If the two firms have somehow arrived at the collusive solution (grid A) for two periods, it would be in either GM's or Toyota's best interest to cheat in the third and final period. Why? To do so would mean bigger profits for the cheater—but only if the other does not cheat. If you think your rival will cheat in the third period, then you have an incentive to get there first—to cheat in the second period. If you think your rival will cheat in the second period, then you will cheat in the first period. The collusive, or joint profit-maximizing, solution tends to break down when the end period of the game is known. Each player has an incentive to cheat before the joint profit-maximizing solution has a chance to get off the ground, rendering the outcome in such a case identical to the outcome of a one-shot game.

Experimental Economics, Mathematics, and Game Theory

The foregoing paragraphs describe some of the problems we might expect in the "real world" when game theory is applied to markets. In essence, there are an infinite number of games that might be played depending on the circumstances in particular markets. The analyst of game-theoretic behavior must be able to know or control an enormous amount of information in order to model competition effectively in particular markets. With the advent of global competition (i.e., "players" from around the world), the collection of such information—much of it by nature kept secret—is virtually impossible.

Despite the complexity presented by many actual situations, simple game-theoretic models provide many insights into the problems of small-numbers competition. Moreover, the game-theoretic approach has inspired new directions in economic analysis. Experimental economics is nothing less than the working out of game-theoretic principles in a "laboratory" setting. Models testing the kind of competitive situations discussed with respect to figures 25-2 and 25-3 have been replicated experimentally. Vernon Smith, Nobel laureate in 2002, and Charles Plott have been pioneers in the development of such models, using both human and animal subjects. Economists John Kagel and Raymond Battalio have used laboratory rats to verify fundamental principles of microeconomic theory (see notes for further reading and the final chapter in this book). Other economists have met laboratory success with monkeys and birds as "economic" actors who respond to work/reward payoffs. Many simple experiments of this kind lead to competitive equilibria, but more complicated experiments are likely to yield multiple equilibria or "indeterminate" outcomes.[6] Even though game theory is still in a developmental stage, some economists believe it forms, or will eventually form, the foundation for modern microeconomics, replacing neoclassical economics in part or *in toto.* (This claim is evaluated in the box, Method Squabbles 7: Modern Neoclassical Economics: Is It Simply a Math "Problem"?)

It must be freely admitted that the issues raised by mathematical models and experimental testing are exceedingly complex, and this complexity often inhibits determinate solutions. When complications such as imperfect information between traders or the presence of third-party bargainers are introduced, solutions become

[6] F. Y. Edgeworth recognized that the mathematical conditions of exchange in any exchange-based economy form a "core" principle on which economic theory rests. Edgeworth advanced the notion of an individual preference function, or "indifference curve." Underlying the preference function are the individual's calculations regarding the number and kind of trades that will maximize his or her utility. At least implicitly, Edgeworth anticipated the kind of multiple equilibria that sometimes emerges from game theory.

Method Squabbles 7: Modern Neoclassical Economics: Is It Simply a Math "Problem"?

Even if they vehemently deny it, some economists increasingly behave as if economics is just another "math problem." An undergraduate degree in mathematics is not only suggested but in essence is required for admission to many university graduate economics programs. Students are routinely taught the elements of game and set theory as a foundation for microeconomic theory. Dissertations are increasingly written on new techniques, eschewing real world "problem analysis" altogether. These techniques, moreover, are most often not adaptable to any form of testing beyond mere "suggestions" of applicability.

At the opposite extreme are those who seek refuge in a total retreat from formalism. These economists might thereby embrace various forms of "evolutionary economics"; join attacks on the assumptions of "classic" neoclassicism; substitute a variety of imperfect-knowledge assumptions; dismiss the "rationality" postulate; and denounce utilitarianism. Some on this side hold that economics must, in effect, become a science of "change" and not a science of "constrained maximization" motivated by utility and profit calculations.

A middle ground probably offers a more defensible position. To the extent that the activities of any methodological camp yield testable propositions or otherwise improve insights into the economic process, these developments are of great, and sometimes enormous, value for understanding economic behavior and processes. But as new means of "discovery" (i.e., gaining knowledge of the economic world) there is yet no single technique or set of techniques equal to the neoclassical method—a method that emphasizes how unfettered markets increase or improve social welfare.

Sympathy for the view that neoclassical economics is too simplistic in its representation of constrained maximization as the modus operandi of individual choice does not obviate the fact that neoclassical economics is actually a method for discovery.* Problems are no less thorny today than they were in Alfred Marshall's day. At present, a "piecemeal" approach to problems in which variables are examined one at a time is the only fruitful method for obtaining answers. Indeed, most contemporary mathematical techniques use this method in one form or another. Among other things, this method of reasoning became a foundation for the development of modern probabilistic econometrics. One would not think of answering a question such as, "Do new gun laws reduce crime?" or "Would a new state excise tax on hotels reduce tourism?" without invoking the neoclassical method of analysis and verification. All sciences, however inexact the methods of testing, need an organizing principle and, for better or worse, the neoclassical paradigm provides that foundation for economics.

Neoclassical economics has survived even as it has been amended by reductions in the level of abstraction, by econometric advances, and by other important discoveries generated by Nobel laureates such as George Akerlof, Gary Becker, James Buchanan, Jr., Ronald Coase, Milton Friedman, Friedrich von Hayek, Michael Spence, George Stigler, and William Vickrey, as well as by lesser mortals. Mathematical formalism and advanced general-equilibrium theorizing, on the one hand, and "deconstructions" of economic theory, on the other, have not changed the central nature of what economists do when they seek answers to practical problems. Contrary to those who would proclaim that neoclassical economics is dead, it is quite alive and not even "smelling funny."

*Present dissatisfaction with the state of contemporary economics has led in some quarters to the view that the science has become a mere "grab bag" of ideas. See, for example, David Colander, "The Death of Neoclassical Economics" (references). However, we maintain that the organizing principles implied in the term "neoclassical" remain cogent and meaningful, if for no other reason than that this is the form in which economics is taught to undergraduates and that the practice retains force in the conduct of economic research.

indeterminant. Some of the most complex and elaborate tools of mathematics have been applied to these issues. Tools such as game theory, set theory, and measure theory, which call into play fixed-point theorems and other forms of advanced mathematics, have all been used to analyze technical questions raised by Edgeworth's theory of contracting. Indeed, several Nobel prizes have been awarded for contributions related to this issue, such as those received by Kenneth J. Arrow in 1972 and Gerard Debreu in 1983.

As old and new mathematical tools have influenced the current direction of technical economic theory, so have mathematics and statistics established a new area in contemporary economic inquiry. The high-minded aim of the inquiry is nothing less than to make economics "scientific," in the same way that the physical sciences are so regarded. This has induced more and more economists to emulate the successful techniques of the physical sciences. In other words, more and more emphasis has been placed on "testing" the validity of economic hypotheses.

■ Empiricism in Economics: Testing Economic Theory

Much empirical economics today involves econometrics, the examination of data with the use of mathematical and statistical techniques to see how well it "fits" economic theory. Done properly, econometrics has the power to "verify" economic theory within certain degrees of confidence. Its object is both to explain and to predict economic behavior within the context of an accepted theory. Within the limits of statistical inference and probability, econometrics attempts to test economic theory using historical data and to forecast economic events utilizing a combination of economic theory and economic data.

Descriptive Statistics and Economic Theory

Attempts to enliven economic theory with real-world facts—often called "descriptive statistics"—is centuries old. An interesting early example involves the efforts of the political arithmeticians of the late seventeenth and early eighteenth centuries to come to grips with quantitative data concerning national output, the balance of trade, consumer demand, and a variety of other subjects. One of the earliest and best-known illustrations of empirical economics comes from research on consumer demand conducted by Gregory King (1648–1712) and Charles Davenant (1656–1714). King, called by Nobel laureate Richard Stone "the first great economic statistician," established the empirical foundations of the inverse relationship between price and quantity purchased. This "law," which was refined considerably by Charles Davenant, appeared in Davenant's mercantilist treatise of 1699, *An Essay upon the Probable Methods of Making a People Gainers in the Balance of Trade*. Davenant's version of the demand law, which we now refer to as the "King–Davenant law of demand," is as follows:

> We take it, that a defect in the harvest may raise the price of corn in the following proportions:

Defect		Above the common rate
1 tenth	Raises	3 tenths
2 tenths	the	8 tenths
3 tenths	Price	1.6 tenths
4 tenths		2.8 tenths
5 tenths		4.5 tenths

> So that when corn rises to treble the common rate, it may be presumed that we want above 1/3 of the common produce; and if we should want 5/10, or half the common produce, the price would rise to near five times the common rate. (*Political and Commercial Works*, pp. 224–225)

King's actual statement of the demand relation was considerably less sophisticated than Davenant's, but it is clear that both writers drew on observations of actual price and quantity behavior. Although this early attempt at estimating a statistical demand curve was naive and quite obviously simplistic, it nevertheless demonstrates the desire to establish economic theory on firm empirical foundations.

During the nineteenth century the field of descriptive statistics made great strides. Besides applications of statistical theory to such problems as population and public health, the technological revolution in transportation provided a backdrop for statistical investigations of a purely economic type. Early railway engineers from Europe and America attempted to identify cost data in order to assess the costs and benefits of existing railroads and proposed rail systems. The American engineer Charles Ellet (see chapters 13 and 18) was a pioneer in this regard. In contributions published between 1840 and 1844 (see notes for further reading), Ellet attempted to determine a "predictive" total cost function for a "typical" American railroad. He did this by collecting data and building up the constants in an equation for rail costs involving various components of railway expenses.

William Stanley Jevons (see chapter 15) also advanced the subject of descriptive statistics in his famous essays of the 1860s on commercial fluctuations and on price series. Jevons improved the notion of index numbers and the nature of sampling techniques. But as Stephen M. Stigler has remarked in his assessment of Edgeworth, "Jevons's lack of use and development of probability-based statistical methods in his empirical work was typical of even the best efforts before the 1880s" ("Francis Ysidro Edgeworth, Statistician," p. 288).

Getting (Tentative) Answers: The Method of Neoclassical Theory and Empiricism

An array of methods for analyzing economic problems exists today. It cannot be said, therefore, that there is one model or method for analyzing economic issues and problems. But it can be said that there is a *dominant* method for analyzing problems and testing for results. For want of a better description, the dominant method of economic investigation today is one that integrates neoclassical economic theory with modern statistical analysis.[7] Neoclassical economics, which we traced to French economists Cournot and Dupuit (chapter 13) and others (chapter 18), was raised to new prominence by Alfred Marshall (chapter 16). Often the individual tools that Marshall developed are allowed to overshadow the analytical method he propounded. That method is one in which economic "tendencies" are discovered by examining one element of a problem at a time while holding all others constant. Marshall's methodology is one in which not all factors are specified (nor can they be) within a theory, and where some of the unspecified factors may measurably alter predicted results.

Marshall regarded economic science as a *procedure* for scientific discovery. He maintained that it is the business of science to collect, arrange, and analyze facts.

[7] Economists are divided on what to call this dominant method and on the method itself. Sutton calls it the "standard paradigm" (*Marshall's Tendencies*), while others would like to proclaim the death of neoclassical economics in the wake of other methods of discovery (game theory, simulation, experimental economics, and so on). See references and notes for further reading.

We draw inferences from facts and improve theories in the process. But Marshall did not think that economics could be a science such as physics or chemistry where controlled experiments are possible. Rather, while certain methods of these "hard" sciences could be useful in economics, he believed economic science was more like meteorology, which involved a much "looser" form of testing and prediction. Marshall cited the study of ocean tides as akin to the study of economics. John Stuart Mill and others also favored this analogy, and Dupuit used it to explain the nature of economic science as early as 1860 (see chapter 18). The reason for the vicissitudes of tides, Dupuit explained, is because there are regular actions that scientists know how to calculate and others that still elude them, despite the best efforts of science. There may always be variables outside the research paradigm that could upset the behavior of regular (scientific) forces.

Seeing economic science this way encouraged the development of modern methods of econometrics to determine, probabilistically, which factors do and which do not alter results. The dominant empirical method of discovery today remains that which combines economic and statistical investigation of variables using the method established by Dupuit, Marshall, and many other neoclassicists. The statistical technique favored for this kind of study is regression analysis.

Regression Analysis

Suppose we observe two quantities moving in particular ways. Let's say that you own a hamburger stand and that you observe that as you raise the price (X) of your hamburgers, the quantity you sell (Y) *rises*. Are you justified in concluding that the demand for your hamburgers is *upward sloping*? The simple answer is no. On the basis of incentives and self-interest, this result would violate common sense and is not what economists expect. But there are other reasons to deny this illogical conclusion. There are many factors besides price that affect the quantity taken of your hamburgers. We know that X and Y are related in some way. But does a change in X cause a change in Y or does a change in Y cause a change in X? Or does some other factor cause or affect both X and Y? (Z might equal income of potential customers around your hamburger joint). There are a huge number of possible changes that might explain your observation. Suppose a new business paying high wages has recently moved into your area. That could shift the demand curve for your product to the right, so that what you are observing might be rightward equilibrium movements along your supply curve. This possibility illustrates the so-called *identification problem* in empirical studies—the identification of cause and effect. The supply and demand for any good may be altered by numerous factors. But simply because we observe two variables moving together (*correlation* is the statistical term), the observation does not imply that one *causes* the other. Correlation, in other words, does not imply causation.

Most behavioral issues are explained by multiple causes, and the "real-world" data collected by the economist or analyst do not easily give up truths concerning cause and effect. This is precisely why economists favor regression analysis. Regression analysis is an econometric tool commonly used to gauge a relationship between a dependent variable and one or more independent variables. If you wished, for example, to study the effect of advertising expenditures on the levels of concentration in some industry or set of industries you might set up the following symbolic relationship:

$$C_i = B_0 + B_1A_i + e_i \ (i = 1,\ldots,n)$$

where C_i is a measure of industrial concentration in some (ith) industry, B_0 is a constant, A_i is a measure of advertising intensity in the ith industry, and e_i is a catchall (error) term designed to capture discrepancies in the posited relationship. In this equation, C is the dependent variable (it is posited to *depend* on the independent variables), and advertising intensity is the independent variable—the one (or ones) theorized to determine the values of or the dependent variable, C_i. The B values, such as B_1, which measures the strength of the marginal effect of advertising intensity on industrial concentration in this simple example, are estimated from available data. While B values may be estimated in a number of ways, the most common estimation procedure is called "the method of least squares."

Simple regression means that the regression equation contains only one independent variable, as shown in the above expression. In effect, our equation seeks to determine the impact of a one-unit change in advertising intensity on industry concentration, which, of course, could be positive or negative. The impact is measured by a regression coefficient (B), which is a number that contains two pieces of information. In addition to indicating whether the proposed relationship is positive or negative, it indicates how the dependent variable would change when the independent variable (advertising intensity in our example) changes by one unit. This number, it must always be remembered, is only an estimate of the theorized cause-and-effect relation. The researcher employing this technique can never be entirely certain that the coefficient reflects the true relationship. He or she can be confident only that the estimate is correct within certain (probabilistic) intervals (i.e., a 5 percent confidence interval means that the technique will yield the correct answer 95 percent of the time).

Other important issues often raise more complex statistical questions. Reconsider the simple relationship between concentration and advertising. If our theory is that advertising intensity causes concentration, can we be sure that a positive and significant B_1 coefficient is conclusive evidence of that result? Might it not be the case that industries that are more profitable can afford to advertise more, or that more profitable industries are more concentrated? Insofar as other variables may affect industrial concentration besides the one posited in a simple regression, econometricians most often test such theories with multiple regression techniques. *Multiple regression* includes more than one explanatory (independent) variable and is usually of the following general form:

$$Y_i = B_0 + B_1X_{1_i} + B_2X_{2_i} + \ldots B_kX_{k_i} + e_i \text{ (where } i = 1, \ldots, n)$$

This equation describes n observations and the relation between some dependent variable, Y, and k independent variables. Returning to our advertising-industrial concentration example, for example, we might express concentration in some industry as a function of (or relating to) advertising intensity, the profitability of the industry, and the amount of product differentiation associated with the industry, together with other factors. A multiple regression technique would allow the experienced investigator to give a reliable judgment of the impact of the various factors affecting industry concentration—within specified limits of confidence. Contemporary theoretical econometrics is concerned chiefly with the development of more powerful tools so that complex equations such as these can be better fitted to the data. As indicated above, however, regression techniques are incapable of providing conclusive proof of selected hypotheses. We can never be 100 percent sure that an estimator captures true relationships. Nevertheless, econometrics can develop statistical techniques that add confidence to estimates. All manner of problems, social and economic, are routinely investigated in this manner. Does the death penalty deter murder? More generally, do increased expenditures on law enforcement deter crime? Do more liberal divorce laws increase the incidence of divorce? Does a liberalized tax deduction for charitable giving increase such giving? Econometric testing, within limits, provides some answers to these and many more interesting questions in economics and social science (see notes for further reading).

The Quest for Knowledge: Modern Econometrics

The search for improved techniques has been a vital part of the development of econometrics. Late in the nineteenth century and early in the twentieth century, certain key economists distinguished themselves in this respect. In Britain, G. U. Yule (1813–1886) pioneered economic and social science applications of statistics, whereas in the United States, Henry L. Moore (1869–1958) championed empirical methods in his studies of business cycles and agricultural production (see notes for further reading). Moore was particularly influential in fostering a zeal for econometric studies among a number of important students, particularly Henry Schulz (1893–1938), whose *Theory and Measurement of Demand* (1938) became an early twentieth-century classic.

A natural inquiry for those interested in measurement involved the aggregative aspects of the economy, especially as the ascendance of Keynesian economics in the post–World War II period spurred interest in developing measurements for the national income accounts, inflation, and employment. Many pioneers of measured sector performance in the economy went on to win the Nobel Prize in Economics after it was inaugurated in 1969. Names such as Simon Kuznets (winner in 1971), Wassily Leontief (1973), James Meade (1977), and Sir Richard Stone (1984) have all been heralded for work in measuring performance in key sectors of the economy. Thus, it was the quest for knowledge about the overall economy that was a primary impetus for econometric research. While the empirical nature of economic theory and the quest to measure the macroeconomy was the subject of accelerated attention in the late nineteenth and early twentieth centuries, the formal recognition of econometric research as a distinctive field of economics may be traced to the year 1933.

In 1933 a distinguished international coterie of scholars founded the Econometric Society and its journal, *Econometrica*, which is dedicated to the pursuit of empirical economics. Harold Hotelling (1895–1973), a prominent American economist and statistician, and Ragnar Frisch (1895–1973), a Norwegian economist and subsequent Nobel Prize winner (1969), were among the founders.[8] The society and its journal have supported research for more than three-quarters of a century on the theory and method of testing economic ideas. On occasion, inadequate methods have been attacked (e.g., Frisch presented devastating early critiques of measurement errors). At the same time, new and superior testing tools have been generated (e.g., the development of probabilistic rationalizations of regression analysis and the use of probabilities to develop maximum-likelihood estimation methods). These developments continue to the present day, not only in the first wave of the econometric journals, but also in a number of later journals devoted to the subject that have appeared in the wake of *Econometrica*'s success.

[8] Hotelling and Frisch were critically important to early efforts, but there were many other pioneers. A survey of Nobel Prize winners in Economic Science includes many of these names as well as an indication of the international flavor of econometric and measurement inquiry. The latter would include Jan Tinbergen (cowinner in 1969), Leonid Kantorovich and Tjalling Koopmans (cowinners in 1975), Robert Solow (1987), Trygve Haavelmo (1989), and Harry Markowitz (1990).

■ Conclusion

No abbreviated survey of mathematical and empirical techniques could possibly do justice to the full range of their use in modern economics. The reader is invited to pick up almost any current economics journal to savor the flavor of quantitative economics today. Virtually no area of modern microeconomic or macroeconomic theory has remained untouched by mathematical and empirical methods. Mathematical and econometric tools have permeated the microeconomic subfields of labor, public finance, and antitrust and government regulation, to name a few. Macroeconomic model building and forecasting of national income, inflation, and employment would be inconceivable without such tools.

Historians of economic thought are in a unique position to address critical questions related to these ongoing developments. A meaningful evaluation must rest on the advantages (benefits) and deficiencies (costs) of this development as it relates to some conception of *progress* in economics. Is the purpose of formulating analytical tools to make economics "scientific" or is it merely to create a means to help us answer important economic and social questions? The chief argument for continued mathematic formalization of economics is that the discipline cannot become truly scientific until it attains the rigor and completeness of science—in other words, until its fundamental propositions have been tested and proven. Theory without verification or potential verification is of limited usefulness. Facts without theory are meaningless.

Some economists have strong reservations concerning this view. Critics argue that the nature of social science, of which economics is a part, makes exact formulation and verification impossible. Many of the central problems of contemporary econometrics relate to inexact or incomplete formalizations of economic theory and to various insufficiencies in sample data and in the random errors inherent to the measurement of variables. Modern econometric techniques are, generally speaking, most appropriate when data samples are large; yet in many instances, large-sample data do not exist. Thus, the quantities and qualities of economic data are often insufficient to the task. In contrast to conditions in the physical and natural sciences, the collection of most economic data is not predetermined or predesigned to fit tests of economic theory. Indeed, most economic data are collected by government agencies for far less specific purposes, often for purely political reasons. While inadequate theory and poor data are not sufficient reasons in themselves to reject quantitative method, some critics argue that the design costs and the collection costs necessary to secure high-quality data are prohibitive.

Numerous critics, especially neo-Austrian and institutional economists, argue that the attempt to make economics a science through mathematical formalization and empirical verification is illusory. In the opinion of these critics, the fruits of decades-long intellectual investment in mathematical and statistical techniques have been small, if not negative. According to this argument, these futile attempts at rendering economics scientific have engendered widespread distrust of the economic pronouncements of policy makers and an almost total breakdown in communication between "mainstream" economists and other social scientists. Even worse, mathematics and calculation in the hands of those equipped with tools but with few or no creative ideas about problems or policies can lead economists away from the basic truths about markets and market functioning. The march to socialism, so the argument goes, is likely to be led by "calculators" who have no practical understanding of how real-world markets function. In this view, mathematics inevitably diverts attention away from the basic truths of the economic process, as developed by its founders.

There is some growing awareness of the dangers of technical pursuits as substitutes for the study of economics, a subject we will return to in the final chapter of this book. Some skepticism is undoubtedly healthy, and yet the complete or substantial abandonment of formalization and aggressive testing would be as much a mistake as its uncritical acceptance. Of all people, economists must avoid this pitfall because they, more than other scientists, deal with quantities at the margin. An appreciation of the limits to mathematics and econometric technique fosters an understanding of their correct and useful place in economic science. So long as these limits are understood, the value of mathematics and econometrics in formulating and testing economic ideas is very great.

References

Colander, David. "The Death of Neoclassical Economics," *Journal of the History of Economic Thought*, vol. 22 (June 2000), pp. 127–143.

Cournot, Augustin. *Researches into the Mathematical Principles of the Theory of Wealth*, N. T. Bacon (trans.). New York: A. M. Kelley, 1960 [1838].

Creedy, John. "On the King–Davenant 'Law' of Demand," *Scottish Journal of Political Economy*, vol. 33 (July 1986), pp. 193–212.

Davenant, Charles. *The Political and Commercial Works of That Celebrated Writer Charles D'Avenant, Relating to the Trade and Revenue of England*, collected and revised by Sir Charles Whitworth in five volumes, vol. 2. London: Farnborough Gregg, 1967.

Debreu, Gerard. "Mathematical Economics," in John Eatwell, Murray Milgate, and Peter Newman (eds.), *The New Palgrave: A Dictionary of Economics*, vol. 3. London: Macmillan, 1987, pp. 399–404.

Edgeworth, F. Y. *Mathematical Psychics: An Essay on the Application of Mathematics to the Moral Sciences*. London: Kegan Paul, 1881.

———. "The Pure Theory of Monopoly," *Papers Relating to Political Economy*, 3 vols. London: Macmillan, 1925.

Hicks, J. R. *Value and Capital*. Oxford: Oxford University Press, 1939.

———, and R. G. D. Allen. "A Reconsideration of the Theory of Value," *Economica*, vol. 1 (February, May 1934), pp. 52–76, 196–219.

Leontief, Wassily. *The Structure of the American Economy: 1919–1929*. Oxford: Oxford University Press, 1941.

———. "Input-Output Analysis," in John Eatwell, Murray Milgate, and Peter Newman (eds.), *The New Palgrave: A Dictionary of Economics*, vol. 2. London: Macmillan, 1987, pp. 860–864.

Maurice, Charles, and Charles Smithson. *Managerial Economics*, 3d ed. New York: McGraw-Hill, 1988.

Newman, Peter. "Francis Ysidro Edgeworth," in John Eatwell, Murray Milgate, and Peter Newman (eds.), *The New Palgrave: A Dictionary of Economics*, vol. 2. London: Macmillan, 1987, pp. 84–98.

Samuelson, P. A. *Foundations of Economic Analysis*. Cambridge, MA: Harvard University Press, 1947.

Stigler, Stephen M. "Francis Ysidro Edgeworth, Statistician," *Journal of the Royal Statistical Society*, ser. A, vol. 141 (1978), pp. 287–322.

Sutton, John. *Marshall's Tendencies: What Can Economists Know?* Cambridge, MA: MIT Press, 2000.

Theocharis, Reghinos D. *Early Developments in Mathematical Economics*, 2d. ed. Philadelphia: Porcupine Press, 1983.
Von Neumann, John, and Oskar Morgenstern. *Theory of Games and Economic Behavior.* Princeton, NJ: Princeton University Press, 1944.

Notes for Further Reading

Any introduction to the vast literature of economics containing formalized mathematics and econometrics must begin with a grasp of certain essentials. Although several basic texts contain excellent treatments of mathematical economics, the following two are especially noteworthy and useful to upper-division or first-year graduate students: Alpha Chiang, *Fundamental Methods of Mathematical Economics* (New York: McGraw-Hill, 1967); and Akira Takayama, *Mathematical Economics* (Cambridge: Cambridge University Press, 1985). Those interested in basic calculus applied to consumer demand should master the mathematical appendix to Hicks's *Value and Capital* (see references). Similarly, those seeking an introduction to econometrics along with knowledge of basic statistics, should consult G. S. Maddala, *Introduction to Econometrics* (New York: Macmillan, 1988); and Domodar Gujarati, *Basic Econometrics*, 2d ed. (New York: McGraw-Hill, 1988). Another very useful reference is William H. Greene's *Econometric Analysis*, 7th ed. (Upper Saddle River, NJ: Prentice-Hall, 2012).

Early works in mathematical economics and descriptive statistics (the handmaiden of modern econometric techniques) tended to be isolated contributions until the late nineteenth and early twentieth centuries. The most cited example of an early empirical statement of demand is the King–Davenant law of demand, but both the priorities of the two writers and the quality of their statements have been debated. Two papers deal with these issues: John Creedy, "On the King–Davenant 'Law' of Demand" (see references); and A. M. Endres, "The King–Davenant 'Law' in Classical Economics," *History of Political Economy*, vol. 19 (Winter 1987), pp. 621–638. See also A. M. Endres, "The Functions of Numerical Data in the Writings of Graunt, Petty, and Davenant," *History of Political Economy*, vol. 17 (Summer 1985), pp. 245–264.

The splendid work of Cournot is graced not only by his contributions to mathematical economics, but also by a treatise on probabilities. Reghinos D. Theocharis provides excellent coverage of mathematical economics in its infancy (see references and Theocharis, *The Development of Mathematical Economics: From Cournot to Jevons* [London: Macmillan, 1993]). Those interested in early attempts by engineers to measure cost functions should examine Charles Ellet, "Cost of Transportation on Railways," *Journal of the Franklin Institute of the State of Pennsylvania* (September, December 1842; November 1843); and R. B. Ekelund, Jr., "Economic Empiricism in the Writing of Early Railway Engineers," *Explorations in Economic History*, vol. 9 (Winter 1971), pp. 179–196.

W. S. Jevons, *Investigations in Currency and Finance*, H. S. Foxwell (ed.) (London: Macmillan, 1884), provides a starting point for the "middle" period of mathematico-statistical writings in economics. But pride of place should go to F. Y. Edgeworth. In addition to his *Mathematical Psychics* (see references), Edgeworth produced an enormous literature, largely published in the *Economic Journal*, devoted to the application of mathematical tools to index numbers, theories of taxation, the theory of monopoly and price discrimination, and theories of economic welfare. Many, but not all, of these papers are contained in Edgeworth, *Papers Relating to Political Economy* (see references). The birth of modern statistics in the writings of Galton, Pearson, and Edgeworth is detailed by S. M. Stigler, *The History of Statistics: The Measurement of Uncertainty before 1900* (Cambridge, MA: Harvard University Press, 1986), who takes his readers on a journey strewn with multiple attempts to obtain improved measurement in fields as diverse as astronomy, psychology, heredity, and the social sciences. Stigler's book reads like a well-crafted mystery story, in which the author demonstrates how the development of modern tools of correlation and regression analysis, which required sound analyses of probability and measurements of uncertainty, were remarkably slow in flowering. The key figures in the drama, as Stigler shows, were Francis Galton, Karl Pearson and, most importantly, Edgeworth.

Edgeworth's theory of the "core" exchange conditions in an economy and its importance in modern economic theory are set forth in lucid fashion by Peter Newman in *The New Palgrave* (see references), and on a more technical plane in *The Theory of Exchange* (Englewood Cliffs, NJ: Prentice-Hall, 1965). Also see John Creedy, *Edgeworth and the Development of Neoclassical Economics* (Oxford: Basil Blackwell, 1986). Alberto Baccini, "Edgeworth on the Foundations of Ethics and Probability," *The European Journal of the History of Economic Thought*, vol. 14 (2007), pp. 79–96, argues that Edgeworth's utilitarianism and his probability theory share a common theme: the search for an encompassing epistemological basis for the social sciences.

Henry L. Moore, the American pioneer in statistics and econometrics, made several important contributions, e.g., "The Statistical Complement of Pure Economics," *Quarterly Journal of Economics*, vol. 23 (November 1908), pp. 1–33; *Generating Economic Cycles* (New York: Macmillan, 1923); and same author, *Synthetic Economics* (New York: Macmillan, 1929). See George J. Stigler, "Henry L. Moore and Statistical Economics," in *Essays in the History of Economics* (Chicago: University of Chicago Press, 1965), for more details on Moore's place in the history of mathematical economics. Jeff Biddle, "Statistical Economics, 1900–1950," *History of Political Economy*, vol. 31 (Winter 1999), pp. 607–651, conveys a sense of the "standard practice" in statistical economics and how it changed in the first half of the twentieth century.

The foundations for the mathematics of linear programming were established by the great mathematician John von Neumann in the 1920s and 1930s and brought to fruition by George B. Danzig in his work entitled *Programming in a Linear Structure* (Washington, DC: U.S.A.F. 1948). Salim Rashid, "John von Neumann and Scientific Method," *Journal of the History of Ideas*, vol. 68 (July 2007), pp. 501–527, argues that in regard to the relation between mathematics and economics von Neumann eventually settled on a pragmatic (engineering) approach, where math is justified by its applications. Robert Dorfman, Paul Samuelson, and Robert Solow, *Linear Programming and Economic Analysis* (New York: McGraw-Hill, 1958), show how linear programming can be applied to economic analysis. An excellent basic introduction to the subject of linear programming may be found in Christopher Thomas and Charles Maurice, *Managerial Economics* (New York: McGraw-Hill, 2004).

Olav Bjerkholt and Ariane Dupont, "Ragnar Frisch's Conception of Econometrics," *History of Political Economy*, vol. 42 (Spring 2010), pp. 21–73, draw on largely unknown documents to elaborate Frisch's scientific views, how he aimed at modeling economics on physics by transferring methodological principles, and on the methods he proposed for economics, such as his axiomatization approach, his structural modeling approach (which became a cornerstone for macroeconomics), his refined explication of concepts such as static/dynamic, micro/macro, and equilibrium, and his concern with the probabilistic nature of the real economic world. See also, same authors, "Ragnar Frisch and the Probability Approach," in Marcel Boumans, Ariane Dupont-Kieffer, and Duo Qin (eds.), *Histories on Econometrics*, Annual Supplement to volume 43, *History of Political Economy* (Durham, NC: Duke University Press, 2011), which contains thirteen essays dealing with the history of econometrics.

Prior to his book-length contribution to input-output analysis mentioned in this chapter, Wassily Leontief published the elements of his famous idea in an article entitled "Quantitative Input-Output Relations in the Economic System of the United States," *Review of Economics and Statistics*, vol. 18 (August 1936), pp. 105–125. This complicated topic was made more comprehensible by William H. Miernyk, *The Elements of Input-*

Output Analysis (New York: Random House, 1965). Miernyk not only clearly develops the analytical principle involved but also shows how to apply it in regional, interregional, and international contexts, concluding his discussion with a lucid review of the mathematics required by the technique (e.g., matrices and determinants). Chious-shuang Yan, *Introduction to Input-Output Economics* (New York: Holt, Rinehart and Winston, 1969), is another useful source on the subject.

Cournot's duopoly model was the genesis of game theory, but others helped to refine his idea. For those who read French, see Joseph L. F. Bertrand, "*Théorie mathématique de la richesse sociale* par Léon Walras; *Recherches sur les principes mathématiques de la théorie des richesses* par Augustin Cournot," *Journal des savants* (Septembre 1883), pp. 499–508. Besides the modern classic work by von Neumann and Morgenstern, Martin Shubik, in *Game Theory in the Social Sciences, Concepts and Solutions* (Cambridge, MA: MIT Press, 1982), and same author, *A Game Theoretic Approach to Political Economy* (Cambridge, MA: MIT Press, 1984), outlines the many applications of game theory, actual and potential. The important field of experimental economics got a boost when Vernon L. Smith won the 2002 Nobel Prize in Economics "for having established laboratory experiments as a tool in empirical economic analysis, especially in the study of alternative market mechanisms." (He shared the prize with Daniel Kahneman of Princeton University). The interested reader may wish to dig into the literature produced by Smith on experiments relating to auctions, electricity pricing, public goods provisions, and a plethora of issues. For a sample, see Vernon L. Smith. "An Experimental Study of Competitive Market Behavior," *Journal of Political Economy*, vol. 70 (April 1962), pp. 111–137; same author, "Experiments with a Decentralized Mechanism for Public Good Decisions," *American Economic Review*, vol. 70 (September 1980), pp. 584–599; *Bargaining and Market Behavior*, Vernon L. Smith (ed.) (Cambridge, UK: Cambridge University Press, 2000).

Some of the more arresting laboratory economic "experiments" have been conducted by the late Professor Raymond C. Battalio, Professor John Kagel, and others. In addition to more "conventional" experiments, they employed rats and pigeons to test economic theories. Parts of their fascinating results may be found in the following papers: R. C. Battalio and John Kagel, "Demand Curves for Animal Consumers," *Quarterly Journal of Economics*, vol. 66 (February 1981); "Commodity Choice Behavior with Pigeons as Subjects," *Journal of Political Economy*, vol. 89 (February 1981); "Consumption-Leisure Trade-offs of Animal Workers," *American Economic Review*, vol. 71 (February 1981); same authors, with D. MacDonald, "Animal Choices Over Uncertain Outcomes: Some Initial Experimental Results," *American Economic Review*, vol. 75 (September 1985). Also see John B. Van Huyck, Raymond C. Battalio, and Richard O. Beil, "Tacit Coordination Games, Strategic Uncertainty, and Coordination Failure," *American Economic Review*, vol. 80 (March 1990), pp. 234–248; and, same authors, "Strategic Uncertainty, Equilibrium Selection, and Coordination Failure in Average Opinion Games," *Quarterly Journal of Economics*, vol. 106 (August 1991), pp. 885–911.

Readers who wish to learn more about a particular mathematical technique or about the application of mathematics to a particular area of economic theory might profitably consult *The New Palgrave: A Dictionary of Economics* (see references). In general, the entries provide readable, nontechnical introductions to particular subject areas written by specialists (and sometimes by the pioneers themselves). Another excellent basic source on such matters is William Baumol, *Economic Theory and Operations Analysis*, 4th ed. (Englewood Cliffs, NJ: Prentice-Hall, 1977). Baumol's chapter-length treatments of such subjects as game theory and linear programming, not to mention his succinct statements of the mathematical concepts used in developing them, are masterpieces of clarity and brevity. Those in search of shorthand definitions of terms and concepts used in mathematical economics should consult W. A. Skrapek, B. M. Korkie, and T. E. Daniel, *Mathematical Dictionary for Economics and Business Administration* (Boston: Allyn & Bacon, 1976).

26

Changing the Boundaries of Microeconomics
Demand, Consumption, and "Rationality"

Microeconomics in the static-equilibrium traditions established by Marshall and Walras has enjoyed and still enjoys great prestige in modern economic theory. But as we saw in chapter 24, economists have ventured beyond the standard neoclassical theory of competition into such "new" realms as the nature of market disequilibrium, the development of modern public-choice theory, and the reevaluation of the theories of regulation and industrial organization. Many of the new analytical twists can be ascribed to what might be termed a "Chicago" school of thought, led over the past three decades mainly by economists George Stigler (1911–1991) and Gary Becker (b. 1930), who have systematically rehabilitated most of the standard Marshallian premises.

Marshall, it might be recalled, made many important simplifying assumptions regarding markets. Specifically, he abstracted from quality differences in products, costly consumer information, the costs of time forgone in consuming and producing goods, and the locations of sellers and buyers. The novelty of much contemporary microeconomic theory consists of (1) providing a formal analysis of how market outcomes change when we relax these and other simplifying assumptions about consumers and firms and (2) applying these new tools to interesting and novel questions that were previously thought to be beyond the purview of economists (e.g., crime, drug use, family relations, and so on).

Additionally, whole new fields of inquiry have evolved to challenge the very fundamentals of economics. Finding the traditional assumptions wanting, contemporary economic theorists engage in "prospect theory," "happiness theory," neuroeconomics, and experimental economics—fields that attempt to integrate psychology with economic choice. Whether these new areas, which have been graced by Nobel prizes, will revolutionize the science is an open question, however.

This chapter reviews a small sample of these new developments in economic theory. These intellectual "novelties" serve as examples of how past ideas continually shape present and future ideas. On closer examination, many novel tools are found to be refinements of earlier principles discovered in the classical and neoclassical periods. For example, the new theory of household production pioneered by Gary Becker rests on the principles of utility maximization established by Jevons,

Menger, and Walras. Further extensions of earlier theories of costs and benefits have resulted in economic theories of marriage, child rearing, and crime. Like other scientists, economists build the present and the future on the contributions of the past.

■ Modern Consumption Technology

Traditional neoclassical microeconomics imposes a distinct cleavage between producers and consumers, whereas contemporary microeconomics treats the cleavage as an oversimplification of the process by which goods are purchased and consumed.

The Household as a Factory

Gary Becker established a trend in microeconomics by treating the household as analogous to a small factory—one that "combines capital goods, raw materials and labour to clean, feed, procreate and otherwise produce useful commodities" ("Theory of the Allocation of Time," p. 496). In this surprisingly broad approach, an individual consumer becomes part of both household production and consumption. One of the most important insights of this approach recognizes that the production and consumption of goods (children are sometimes regarded as consumer goods in Becker's model) *take time*. Time is an opportunity cost that must be calculated along with the market price of any good or activity in making economic decisions. Earlier economists (e.g., Senior, Böhm-Bawerk, Marshall) also understood the nature of time as both a resource and a constraint, but their concepts were sometimes vague, and they never fully integrated them into mainstream economic theory the way that Becker does.

Figure 26-1 gives a schematic view of the combination of market goods and time necessary to produce ultimate goods or services ("commodities"). Just as it takes inputs of human resources, capital, and time to bring children to adulthood, the production and consumption of any *ultimate* good or service may be viewed as combining inputs to consume an output. If we identify an ultimate good consumed by an individual, such as "healthful behavior," we see that the production of such a good requires the combination of numerous "market goods" (those purchased directly by consumers in the marketplace) and time inputs. Athletic equipment, health foods of all sorts, medical services, and time spent in doing exercises and in consuming health-related goods are all *inputs* in a process that yields the ultimate good. The individual or the household transforms these inputs into outputs through a production function.

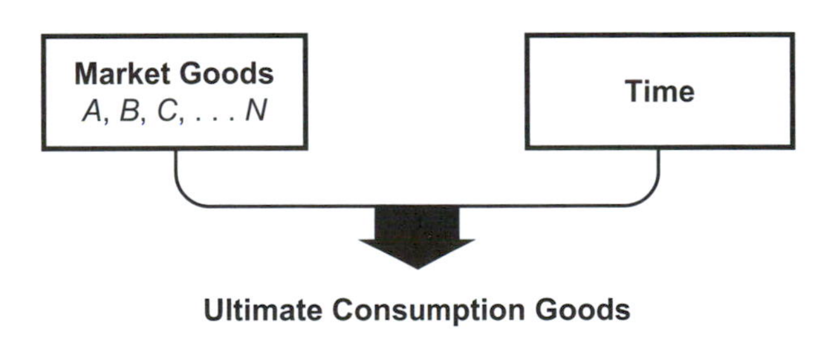

Figure 26-1 The household as a miniature factory combines market goods and time to produce ultimate consumption goods.

Ultimate consumption is therefore a function of both market goods and time inputs. Since it takes time to see a play, read a book, or consume a meal, the full price of these activities must include the opportunity cost of using time to engage in these consumption activities. The measurement of this opportunity cost can be approximated by the market wage of the individual under consideration. Assume, for example, that an individual who can make $10 an hour in market work is choosing between a restaurant meal that takes an hour and a fast-food meal that takes fifteen minutes. Assume further that the money cost of both meals is $6. While both meals require the same money outlay, the full price of consumption differs between the two alternatives. The full price of the fast-food meal is $8.50 ($6 plus $2.50 in forgone income) versus $16 for the restaurant meal ($6 plus $10 in forgone income). The determining factor in the individual's final decision will be the amount of utility each meal produces per (full-cost) dollar of expenditure.

This approach has the benefit of highlighting the full costs of household production, which are usually obscured from view. The value of household production—producing and raising children, performing household chores and maintenance activities, etc.—may also be expressed in terms of opportunity costs. Also, when the cost of time is placed on an equal footing with the cost of market goods, new insights into the traditional choice between work and leisure (now a choice between market work, leisure, and household production) and new views of the consumption patterns of households in terms of both quantity and quality are made possible.

The implications of the new consumer theory are expressed in several ways. As earnings from market work rise (with equal reductions in other income), the opportunity cost of in-home production increases, and we expect to see more goods and less time used in household production. In general, the development and widespread use of time-reducing appliances may be explained partly by this phenomenon. Greater use of child-care services, outside contracting for household services, and the emergence of condominiums and other low-maintenance housing (and lawn care) arrangements are all related to wage and earnings increases over time.

Another implication of this new theory of consumer behavior involves *patterns* of consumption. As family incomes rise, family members tend to substitute goods-intensive commodities and activities for time-intensive ones. In effect, economic growth generates a bias against time-intensive production and consumption within the household. The development of time-saving devices and products is, in some measure, a reflection of the increased opportunity cost of time-intensive consumptions. The decline of time-intensive gourmet cooking and the substitution of high-quality frozen foods and take-out meals, all suitable for time-saving microwave cooking, are manifestations of the effect that Becker emphasizes.

Many modern inventions are successful because they permit substitutions that allow people to economize by reallocating time-intensive consumptions. The growth of airline travel, portable computers, smart phones, digital video recorders, and audio books provide everyday examples. In other words, not only do households combine market goods and time inputs as raw materials (e.g., a piano, printed music, and piano lessons) to produce ultimate goods (e.g., music appreciation), but the *proportions* in which they are combined change over time as market wage rates and incomes change.[1]

[1] The assumption of taste stability is examined within the framework of a household production function by George Stigler and Gary Becker in their paper "*De Gustibus Non Est Disputandum*" (see references). In addition, Stigler and Becker give form to their concept by investigating the implications of taste stability for "addictions," custom and tradition, advertising, fashions, and fads.

The Economics of Information

The modern theory of consumption technology has let another genie out the bottle. In a Marshallian world, consumers are assumed to be immediately aware, at zero cost, of any price differences in a given market for a given product. By buying low and selling high, they will drive market price to a single, uniform value. One price for a product will prevail when a perfectly competitive market is in equilibrium.

In 1961 George J. Stigler enlarged and developed the argument that information is an economic good that is costly to produce and obtain ("Economics of Information"). For example, when gas stations provide information by posting prices they must pay for the construction of the signs, including raw materials and labor. Furthermore, consumers must spend valuable time (and other resources) looking for, and comparing, the prices that are posted. Since information concerning prices is costly to produce and obtain in most markets, transaction prices will be "dispersed" (more than one price) for the same commodity *even when the market is in equilibrium*.

A Simple Information Model. Figure 26-2 provides a framework for understanding the economics of information. The marginal cost to the consumer of searching for a lower price for some particular good or service is represented by MC in figure 26-2. Since additional search time is typically more costly at the margin, MC rises over time. If you are in the market for a used car, for example, the marginal cost of your search can be thought of as the costs associated with visiting and negotiating with one or more used-car dealers. The level of the MC curve will naturally vary across goods. It will be low, for example, when shopping for appliances on the Internet, but it will be high when searching for a new home.

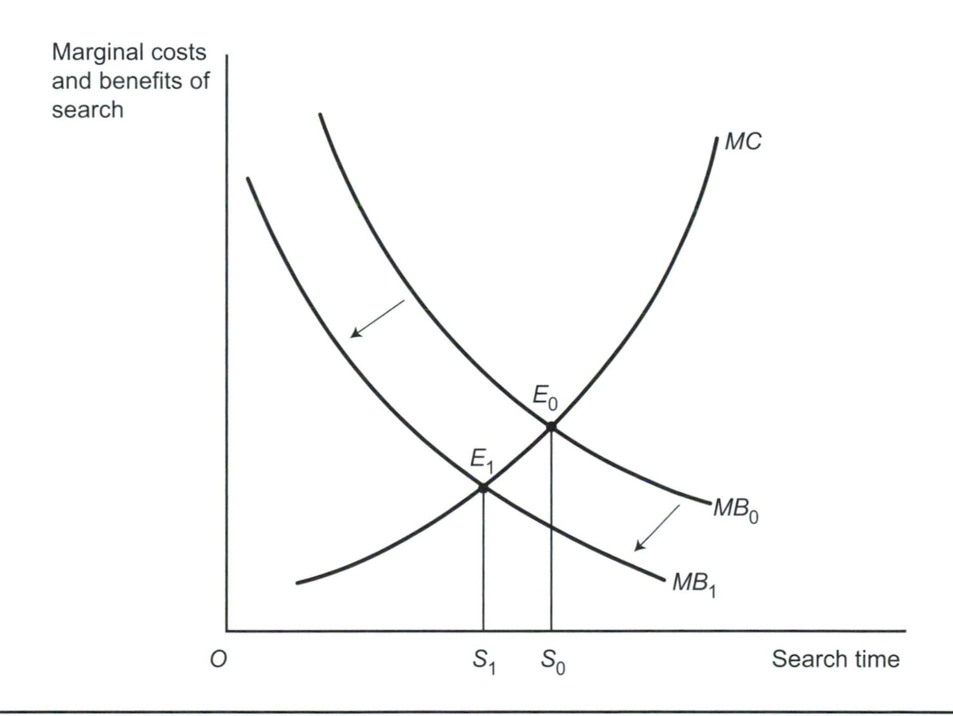

Figure 26-2 The provision of information reduces optimal search time spent acquiring goods and services. Advertising is an example of such information provision.

The marginal benefit curve (MB_0) depicts the marginal benefit to the consumer of searching for a lower price. As a consumer checks the prices of more and more sellers, the prospect of finding a lower price from the next seller declines, therefore MB_0 declines as search time increases. The marginal benefit of additional search time also varies across markets. For example, additional search time will be rewarded at a higher level if the purchase involves a high-ticket item (e.g., houses, central air-conditioning/heating systems, boats, or automobiles) than it will for low-ticket items (e.g., toothpicks, lipstick, or chewing gum). Generally, the smaller the share of a consumer's budget represented by any single expenditure, the less the benefit of additional search time; that is, the location of the MB_0 curve in figure 26-2 will be further to the southwest.

The consumer will search until the marginal cost (MC) of search time equals the marginal benefit (MB_0) of search time. This coincides with the point of optimal or efficient search time, shown by point E_0 in figure 26-2. At levels of marginal cost and benefit to the left of point E_0 (ignore point E_1 and curve MB_1 for the moment), the extra benefits of more search time exceed the extra costs. To the right of point E_0, the marginal costs of search time exceed the marginal benefits. Point E_0 represents the correct or equilibrium amount of search time for a given consumer for some particular good or service. Consumers employ such optimal search procedures in their shopping behavior, not so much in the rigid fashion of the diagram, but in an intuitive, instinctive manner. Since point E will not be the same for all consumers for all products or services, the fact that information about prices is costly to produce and to obtain means that in most markets there will be a dispersion of final transaction prices and not a single price for a product at all locations.[2] Again, as stressed in earlier examples, this line of reasoning recognizes time as part of the *full cost* of consuming goods and services.

A New Role for Advertising. Strong attachment to the competitive model that assumes homogeneous products and perfect information leads to overt criticism of advertising as wasteful and/or unnecessary. In contrast, the new economics of search time provides a rational explanation for the existence of advertising. In this new approach advertising is a low-cost means of producing information. We have seen that gathering information is costly in terms of time forgone and that time has an implicit value. In the simplest of terms, advertising saves the consumer time in his or her effort to acquire information about prices or qualities of products.

Consider an example in which a consumer starts without any knowledge whatsoever about prices for a desired product. Each additional hour of search time requires that the individual sacrifice utility in the form of time forgone. Hence, the marginal cost of the search rises, as shown along curve MC in figure 26-2. The curve MB_0 represents the marginal benefit to search time (i.e., information gained), assuming that the consumer knows nothing about existing prices. Optimal search time is therefore S_0 for this consumer.

By comparison, consider a situation in which a consumer starts with some (but not complete) knowledge of prices, obtained, for example, through newspaper advertising. In this case additional search time will probably not yield price differen-

[2] Common sense and personal experience support the idea of search costs. The following experiment may be conducted in any community. Collect the prices for a single product of a particular quality such as a specific brand and size of aspirin or toothpaste at six or seven different stores. An array of prices will likely be observed across locations, which is a result consistent with Stigler's thesis. Real-cost differences to consumers may therefore provide a plausible explanation for different *money* prices of a particular good or service.

tials as large as that obtained in the previous case in which the consumer started with a zero knowledge base. Therefore, the additional benefit to any given amount of search time (in terms of finding price reductions) is less in the case where the consumer starts with some price information. Marginal benefits to search time in this second case may be depicted as MB_1, reflecting the fact that for any given amount of search time, additional benefits to search time are less if consumers have some information ahead of time. We can conclude therefore that the existence of advertising reduces the amount of time consumers spend in searching for lower prices. If consumers spend less time searching for lower prices, they necessarily have more time left to devote to other, more desirable activities such as earning income from market work, producing goods at home, or partaking in leisure activities.

There are, in effect, two sacrifices involved in consuming most goods: (1) the money price of the good and (2) the value of time forgone in search and other transaction costs. Together these elements constitute the full price of any good or service. In the informed modern view, advertising economizes on search time and therefore lowers the full price of goods and services.

Issues Concerning the Quality of Goods and Services

Modern microeconomics examines information, how it affects consumer demand, and its links to advertising and search time in highly creative ways. One innovation classifies goods according to how they affect the generation and retrieval of information. Phillip Nelson (see references) distinguishes between search goods and experience goods. *Search goods* are those whose characteristics are readily determined before purchase, while *experience goods* are those whose characteristics are primarily determined after purchase. In general, consumers demand less information for search goods, such as gasoline at gas stations, fast food, or toothpaste. Such goods are typically purchased frequently, and the consumer usually has good information about their qualities. Experience goods, on the other hand, are often purchased infrequently and tend to be of higher value. We expect more information to be demanded and supplied for experience goods than for search goods.

Think of it this way. Would you demand more information about a box of breakfast cereal or about a new refrigerator? In the case of the cereal we pretty much know what to expect regarding product quality before we buy. But in the case of the refrigerator we will typically learn its quality dimensions only after we buy and use it—which sometimes can be a long time after purchase. Consequently, sellers of refrigerators have incentives to provide something extra in order to enhance sales. They must provide information about the quality of the product as well. Advertising is one way of providing the requisite information that consumers demand in an effort to reduce search costs for experience goods. Highly personal sales efforts and various forms of quality assurance may also characterize the sale of experience goods.

There are yet other types of goods whose quality cannot be discerned even after purchase. These are called *credence goods*. Some examples are: services of psychologists, psychiatrists, fortune-tellers, palm-readers, or organized churches. In particular, credence goods are those for which consumers face high costs in deciding the right amount to buy, determining the quality of what has been purchased, or some combination of the two. As explained by the developers of this idea, Michael Darby and Edi Karni ("Free Competition"), we expect a higher degree of fraud in the sale of credence goods because it is difficult to substantiate claims of quality. Fraud is achieved in large part by selling a lower-quality product or service than the consumer believes he or she is buying, with the actual quality impossible or very costly to discover or verify. Many different religions promise widely varying qualities of an afterlife, but how are we to determine these qualities of the ultimate product and how much of it to "purchase"?

While most goods are predominately of one type or another (search, experience, or credence), it is the case that some goods may contain elements of each characteristic. Moreover, the dissection of goods and services by type leads us to particular inferences about the provision of information. The placement and type of advertising, for example, is typically determined by the dominant characteristic. Under normal circumstances we do not expect Steinway & Sons to advertise their pianos for sale in *Sports Illustrated*; but we do expect Nike to advertise their shoes there. Our expectations about the kind and quality of information in ads—whether in magazines, in newspapers, on TV, on the Internet, or even on billboards—will depend on the type of good for which we typically search. We will expect a higher proportion of quality information (i.e., years in business, seller reputation, licenses and certifications) for credence goods (e.g., pest control services) than for search goods (e.g., outdoor barbecue cookers). Other things equal, moreover, typical buyer characteristics, such as age and gender, are often considered by sellers and will determine the amount and kind of advertising in which sellers engage.[3]

Naturally, when the likelihood of fraud increases, we can expect institutions and exchange arrangements to emerge that promise to reduce the threat. Consumers can often quickly discover intrinsic and subjective qualities of credence goods by repeat purchases, or by reliance on third-party quality assessments (e.g., J. D. Power & Associates, *Consumer Reports*, customer reviews). Sellers may resort to "money-back guarantees," warranties, and service contracts to assuage doubts about product quality. For a fee, automobile assessment shops will give independent quality assessments of used cars. Licensing of doctors, dentists, opticians, hospitals, and many other service providers are yet another means of quality assurance. These market and institutional arrangements help provide information to consumers that may prevent or reduce fraud. In sum, the quality of goods and services has become a major focus of contemporary economic analysis.

Innovations in Demand Theory

Standard Marshallian demand theory assumes that consumers purchase goods and services that are desired for the direct utility that they convey, an approach that has been modified by more recent developments. Thus, the household is now portrayed as purchasing combinations of market goods *and* time to produce more ultimate and desirable commodities. A separate, but related, new development in modern demand theory emphasizes the attributes of goods and services rather than the good or service itself. This new perspective holds that consumers do not demand market goods for their direct utility but for the utility derived from certain combinations of utility-producing *characteristics*. This feature of demand is represented in figure 26-3, where a single market good (A) produces multiple characteristics or joint dimensions (a, b, c, . . . , n characteristics).

The demand for characteristics is a fact of everyday experience. Many goods are capable of satisfying utility on the basis of several different dimensions. For exam-

[3] Some empirical evidence exists on advertising intensities and qualities associated with the distinction of search, experience, and credence goods (see notes for further reading).

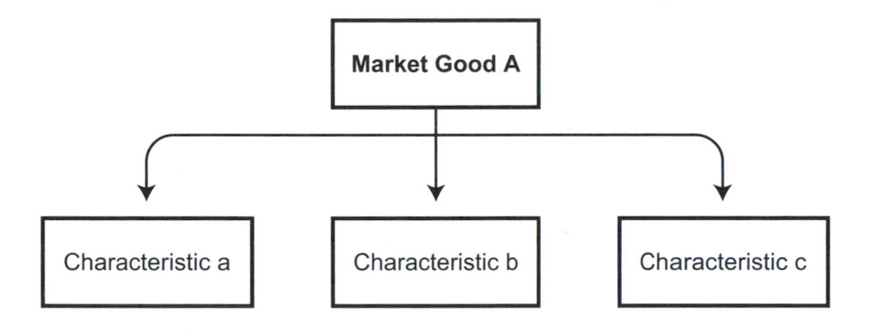

Figure 26-3 Modern demand theory emphasizes that individuals do not demand market goods per se, but the characteristics and attributes provided by market goods.

ple, individuals purchase automobiles for prestige and status, not merely for transportation. A Porsche produces these characteristics in different proportions than a small economy car, which, in turn, produces characteristics in different proportions than a Cadillac or Lincoln. The point, commonly attributed to Kelvin Lancaster (1924–1999), is that consumers actually demand jointly produced characteristics rather than products or services themselves ("New Approach to Consumer Theory"). This new approach has some clear advantages over the traditional Marshallian analysis of demand. For example, it provides a basis for examining goods that are obviously related but that cannot be compared easily (or at all) in standard theory. Motorcycles, bicycles, subways, buses, taxis, railroads, airlines, and walking shoes all provide one or more of the characteristics of automobiles, and yet standard theory provides no meaningful way to compare them.

Lancaster's approach to consumer behavior, along with Becker's innovations discussed earlier, serve to remind economists that the purchase of market goods is merely an intermediate step to the satisfaction of some more ultimate want. The demand for market goods is therefore a derived demand—the demand for an automobile or a subway token is *derived* from a demand for certain utility-creating attributes (e.g., transportation and other things) provided by the good or service. It must be remembered that quality itself is one of those attributes. This enlarged focus on goods as bundles of characteristics, where the characteristics are numerous and variable, sheds light on the sometimes sudden emergence (and rapid disappearance) of market goods in the consumption bundles of individuals or households.

In sum, new developments relating to consumer behavior, including nuances of the kind discussed here, dot the landscape of modern literature in microeconomics. As with most new economic ideas, these, too, have been robed in the formal dress of mathematical models, and the result has been to expose the limitations of the new developments as well as their relevance to real-world situations. On balance, however, the modern theory of consumer behavior has widened the boundaries of microeconomic theory.

■ Newer Theories of the Firm

Broadly speaking, the economic function of a firm is to combine economic resources in order to produce goods and services demanded by consumers. Standard theory tells us firms that succeed in meeting these demands efficiently survive and prosper while those that do not incur losses and fail. In traditional economic theory, cost curves based on resource productivity are combined with demand and other revenue curves to make models of firms categorized by market structure (i.e., competitive, monopolistic, or variations thereof), as seen in chapter 20, for example. This sort of analysis *describes* firms and their behavior, but it does not answer a more fundamental question: Why do firms exist at all?

All advanced economies are based on the division of labor. In a market economy the division of labor is vented in an incredible array of activities based on the different skills and talents of individuals. But what mechanism or mechanisms ensure that such consumables as food, clothing, and airline travel are produced when and where they are wanted? The answer is found in the concept of economic coordination. In order to explain why firms exist, *market coordination* must be distinguished from *firm coordination*. Market coordination exists when the price system *directly* provides signals (through supply and demand) that guide production and consumption. Firm coordination exists when the division of labor is carried on and directed by managers. Market coordination is by nature decentralized, whereas firm coordination is by nature centralized. Firm coordination is therefore not unlike central planning in a socialist economy. Within the firm, resources are not bought and sold but are transferred through managerial directives.

In the language of economics, a firm is a voluntary institution characterized by free contract. Employees agree voluntarily to follow the dictates of managers, but these "commands" are but a figure of speech. Successful managers must mimic the price system by transferring and allocating resources in an efficient manner, given the prices of equivalent resources "outside" the firm. But if market and firm coordination are so similar, why are firms necessary at all? Why do some automobile manufacturers purchase tires for their cars rather than make their own? Why do some firms purchase advertising and travel services from outside agencies (i.e., other firms) rather than produce them within the firm? Why is market coordination used for some resource inputs and firm coordination used for others? Contemporary microeconomics seeks to provide satisfactory answers to such questions.

Why Firms? The Coasian Perspective

In a classic paper published in 1937 entitled "The Nature of the Firm," Nobel laureate Ronald Coase (b. 1910) proposed a simple and elegant answer to the question: Why are firms necessary? He argued that firms emerge and exist as a least-cost means of economic coordination. Economic coordination is a two-sided coin. There are costs to using market coordination. The hiring of inputs (e.g., temporary labor) typically involves transaction costs, search costs, and negotiation costs. If contracts are used, they must be negotiated as well as policed. The other side of the coin is that market coordination provides certain benefits. For example, it may enable a firm to act more nimbly and flexibly by hiring labor for one day at a time. When firms hire "temps" they are using market coordination rather than firm coordination.

At some point, however, market coordination may give way to firm coordination. Entrepreneurs begin to use firm coordination when a comparison of the costs and benefits between alternative forms of coordination indicates positive benefits to coordination *within* rather than without. It may pay to organize clerical tasks *within* the firm by hiring a worker on a regular, longer-term basis rather than on a part-time basis. A firm therefore emerges as a conglomeration of resources that are gathered together under the centralized (quasi-socialistic) direction of a manager because it is cheaper than organizing and directing resources through overt (outside) market mechanisms.

The next compelling question is: When do firms stop growing in size? Coase argued that firms face a limit to growth in the form of rising marginal costs of organization and direction. When the net benefits derived from internal organization and direction fall below the net benefits of organizing tasks through market contracts, the firm stops growing and again resorts to market coordination. Economic reality rarely presents us with an either/or situation, however. Many firms use *both* forms of resource coordination simultaneously. Market coordination may be more efficient for some specialized tasks, e.g., a "temp" to type rarely needed legal documents, whereas frequent and repetitive tasks may be accomplished at lower cost by a full-time worker with a wide array of office skills. As a practical matter, therefore, each task within the firm may be examined from the standpoint of whether the net benefits derived from inside coordination exceed those derived from outside coordination.

Team Production and Shirking in the Firm

Coase's innovative theory of the firm has spawned a number of theoretical extensions. One of the more promising off-shoots of the theory has been the "team production" view of how activities are organized within firms. Most of the activities of firms, including the production of goods and services, involve team effort—and a team, like a chain, is only as strong as its weakest link. How, then, can the firm prevent its team members from shirking or engaging in unproductive behavior? One answer has been given by Armen Alchian and Harold Demsetz, who maintain that the manager acts as a team monitor to ensure efficiency in those instances where several individuals or groups must work together to accomplish a task ("Production, Information Costs and Economic Organization").

Specialization, as Adam Smith recognized long ago, leads to increased productivity. But people have an incentive to shirk if no one polices their behavior. At the same time workers stand to benefit from being monitored because their returns are, to a large degree, adversely affected by the shirking behavior of other members of the team. These circumstances explain the emergence of a manager as someone given the responsibility to reward superior performance and to discipline those who shirk.

In the absence of team production, individual producers are disciplined by the actions of rivals, that is, by market competition. A worker can shirk, but he or she bears the full costs of such behavior by receiving lower earnings. In such circumstances, an internal monitor is not necessary. Firms that employ monitors obviously face increased costs over those that do not, so it is only when the benefits of increased productivity to team production outweigh the costs of monitoring the team that team production replaces individual production. In the evolutionary scheme of things, when teams can produce goods and services at a lower cost than individuals can, firms emerge and prosper. The Alchian–Demsetz view therefore regards a firm as the logical consequence of positive net benefits that derive from team production even in the face of the higher costs of monitoring team performance.

This concept of manager-as-monitor-of-team-production raises some rather obvious questions. For instance, who will monitor the manager? Doesn't the manager also have an incentive to shirk? The institutional composition of the firm provides answers to these questions, particularly in what it reveals about the pattern of incentives, both positive and negative, given to managers. On the one hand, managers are disciplined by the market. If they perform poorly, monitor-managers will be fired and competing managers will be installed by owners or stockholders. On the other hand, managers can be rewarded as residual claimants who share in the profits or rewards of team production. Managers thus have both negative and positive incentives to be efficient monitors of team production.

Interest in the economics of information as a central part of the newer microeconomics has raised a number of provocative issues related to the quality of products as well. The central question concerns the determination of product quality and the kind of information buyers and sellers have before the purchase of products. If sellers possess information that buyers do not have regarding product quality, they may have incentives to sell substandard products or services. This rather obvious observation has generated various approaches to the issue of product quality.

Entrepreneurship Redux

Resurgent issues involving the nature of the firm and product quality raised anew questions about the essence and vitality of entrepreneurship. On the one hand Lancaster's characteristics-based demand theory is strongly evocative of Dupuit's treatment of demand in an earlier era (see chapter 13). Both writers opened up broad opportunities for the entrepreneur to be creative in the "formation/manipulation" of products in attempts to form effective profit strategies. On the other hand, Coase's view of the firm offers an explanation for vertical integration. Entrepreneurs in a Coasian firm are tasked with maintaining administrative arrangements that supplant the market mechanism. They are merely required to calculate administrative versus market costs and adjust their organizations accordingly in line with the profit motive. They do not face uncertainty, nor is their function to be proactive; it is to be reactive. The chief merit of Coase's theory is the illumination of transaction costs and how they affect the nature of the firm. Its implications for entrepreneurship are limited.

On this point a contrast between Coase and Knight (see chapter 20) on the theory of the firm is instructive. Coase's theory focused on the execution of economic activity rather than its conception and planning. Knight emphasized conception and planning, stressing how the presence of uncertainty induces major changes in the organon of economic theory. "With uncertainty present," Knight wrote, "doing things, the actual execution of activity, becomes in a real sense a *secondary* part of life: the primary problem or function is deciding what to do and how to do it" (*Risk*, p. 268; emphasis added). Knight recognized that producers take the responsibility of forecasting consumers' wants, but he insisted that "the work of forecasting and at the same time a large part of the technological direction and control of production are still further concentrated upon a very narrow class of the producers, and we meet with a new economic functionary, the entrepreneur" (p. 268).

Knight traced major changes in the basic form of business organization to the rise of the entrepreneur class. Internal organization of a business cannot be entrusted to chance or to purely mechanical formulas in the face of uncertainty. Entrepreneurs are required to make discretionary decisions. Firms are compelled to recognize the disparity among individuals regarding intellect, judgment, and venturesomeness. The successful business must establish an organizational structure to promote successful decision making. It does so, according to Knight, by encouraging the confident and venturesome to assume the risk that the doubtful and timid wish to avoid. In a phrase, entrepreneurs "insure" the latter group by guaranteeing them a specified income in return for a share of the enterprise's outcome.

In sum, the Knightian firm exists because the real world cannot meet all the conditions for competitive equilibrium dictated by economic theory. Knight held that the price system is effective in allocating resources among alternative uses but that it does not establish the *pattern* of alternative uses, which is established by entrepreneurs. Thus, the essence of entrepreneurship is judgment, born of uncertainty. "Any degree of effective exercise of judgment, or making decisions," Knight wrote, "is in a free society coupled with a corresponding degree of uncertainty-bearing, of taking the responsibility for those decisions" (*Risk*, p. 271). This responsibility is expressed in the collateral guarantees of fixed remuneration given to resource suppliers by the entrepreneur.

Knight's theory of entrepreneurship is the logical extension of Cantillon's early and rich insight into how markets work, but it is also a logical antecedent to Coase's theory. The opportunity for transactions to take place must exist before the cost of such transactions can be used to explain the nature of the firm. Coase's analysis takes for granted the primary question of what to produce. Insofar as it emphasizes calculation rather than judgment, it provides no meaningful way to distinguish the entrepreneur from other hired inputs. In other words, Coase worked within the confines of standard, neoclassical price theory. He adopted the static, general-equilibrium method of analysis, which abstracts from time and uncertainty. As a theory of the firm, his analysis is imaginative and insightful. As a theory of the entrepreneur, however, it is limited in scope and substance.

To explain the anomaly of why firms exist in a regime of perfect competition Knight pushed economic analysis outside the standard neoclassical paradigm. In place of the perfect foresight hypothesized in static, general-equilibrium models, he substituted entrepreneurial judgment. He made uncertainty the cornerstone of his theory, and he adopted Cantillon's concept of uncertainty (refined to distinguish between insurable and uninsurable risks). This practice places uncertainty at the point of final consumer goods and services. One can almost hear the echo of Cantillon in the following passage:

> [T]he main uncertainty which affects the entrepreneur is that connected with the sale price of his product. His position in the price system is typically that of a purchaser of productive services at present prices to convert into finished goods for sale at the prices prevailing when the operation is finished. There is no uncertainty as to the prices of the things he buys. He bears the technological uncertainty as to the amount of physical product he will secure, but the probable error in calculations of this sort is generally not large; the gamble is in the price factor in relation to the product. (*Risk*, pp. 317–318)

Thus, for Knight (as compared to Coase), output price uncertainty accounts for the unique nature of the firm. Transaction costs do not enter the picture at this stage of inquiry, because they are secondary to the originative acts of (1) deciding what goods are to be produced and (2) establishing the appropriate administrative organization to do so. Whereas Coase took markets for granted, Knight wished to understand the dynamic problem of how markets are created. He believed the creation of markets is an entrepreneurial function. Prices allocate resources, but they don't create markets—entrepreneurs do. From Knight's perspective, therefore, the price system could never be viewed as a complete substitute for the entrepreneur.

What mattered most to Coase was finding the reason why the price mechanism should be superseded, and he could not discover this reason in Knight's treatment of the firm. Coase's perceptive analysis of transaction costs eventually spawned a new literature that embellished the idea of the entrepreneur as contractor.[4] Thanks to him, the transactions-cost literature has flowered in contemporary microeconomic theory. Nevertheless, his criticisms of Knight were mostly misplaced because he did not understand the genuine nature of Knight's inquiry.

Like Schumpeter, Knight was interested in explaining the nature of economic progress in a market system, the chief components of which are firms and entrepreneurs. By firm he meant a basic form of business organization in which the entrepreneur takes direction, control, and responsibility. Contracting alone does not capture the full role of the entrepreneur for Knight because "in the world as it is the interests affected by contracts are never all represented in the agreements" (*Risk*, p. 353). In Knight's view, entrepreneurs are more than contractors. They are specialists at bearing uncertainty, and while the contract is one way to reduce uncertainty, some uncertainty can never be eliminated. For Knight, therefore, the size of firms depends, among other things, on the available supply of entrepreneurial qualities.

Markets, Information, and "Lemons"

Ever since the pathbreaking work of Friedrich Hayek (see chapter 23), economists have become acutely aware that markets are mechanisms for generating and disseminating information. It follows that economic markets work best when there is an unimpeded flow of accurate, reliable information between potential buyers and sellers. Within the informational framework of the market, price is a "signal" that conveys important information about quality, and about the relationship between wants on the one hand and available supplies on the other. But how reliable is this signal? Information can be asymmetric: Sellers may have more or better information than buyers, or vice versa. One of the more interesting extensions of modern microeconomics attempts to grapple with this important problem.

A good example of what we mean is provided by the automobile market.[5] It is difficult for an automobile buyer to obtain complete information before making a purchase. A new car may be dependable and trouble-free, or it may turn out to need repairs continually. Cars in the latter category are known as "lemons." Unfortunately, the customer usually does not know beforehand whether or not a car is a lemon. Under such circumstances, the reputation of the seller becomes a basis for customers to make decisions about which automobiles to purchase.

Consider the used-car market, where the potential for "lemons" is particularly great. Among other things, used-car buyers demand previously owned automobiles on the basis of their price and on the probability that they will provide reliable transportation (i.e., not be a "lemon"). If the initial price of used cars does not clear the market, the resulting "signal" is that an imbalance exists between quantity supplied and quantity demanded. In the absence of informational barriers, the price would readily adjust to accommodate the demand to the supply, or vice versa. This normal process may be short-circuited, however, if buyers have inadequate information. Suppose that price is "too high" (i.e., quantity supplied exceeds quantity demanded). Sellers' attempts to eliminate the surplus by lowering price may not

[4] The classic reference to the "nexus of contracts" theory of the firm is Armen A. Alchian and Harold Demsetz; see also, Michael Jensen and William Meckling, Paul Rubin, Benjamin Klein and Keith Leffler, all cited in the references. More recently, Yoram Barzel (see references) has used this approach to explore the moral hazard aspects of entrepreneurship. In a more fundamental historical sense, the idea of the entrepreneur as contractor harks back to Bentham.

[5] See George Akerlof, "Market for 'Lemons'" (references).

succeed because customers may perceive that the cars offered for sale at a lower price are more likely to be "lemons." This may lead to aggressive "discounting" at the wholesale level, so that the average used car sells below its normally depreciated value. But discounting has a potentially adverse side effect in that below-normal prices of used cars may discourage owners of higher-quality used cars from selling, thereby reducing the number of potential welfare-enhancing trades that take place between willing buyers and sellers.

The problem of asymmetric information is particularly resistant in certain markets. In such cases, circumstances emerge over time, which serve to mitigate the "lemons" problem. Thus, the reputation of the seller becomes an important criterion for the prospective purchaser. Auto dealers with good reputations for honoring promises through warranties or guarantees gain an advantage over unreliable, fly-by-night firms. Airlines with better safety records gain customers over those with weak safety records, and so forth. Markets may be imperfect, therefore, but they remain vibrant and, left to themselves, are usually capable of generating compensating features that promote overall welfare between market participants.

■ Nontraditional Approaches: Prospect Theory, Happiness Theory, and Neuroscience

New approaches to human behavior that challenge fundamental principles of economics—specifically the utility-maximization approach to consumer demand and valuation—have been growing over the last three decades through the efforts of psychologists. While traditional economic theory clings to its standard assumptions of rational behavior, self-interest, and stable preference (utility) functions, Daniel Kahneman and Amos Tversky have attempted a revision of utility theory ("prospect theory") that some economists feel may someday form the basis of a "new economics." Spawned from this revision of utility theory is another new approach, "happiness theory"—that is, discovering what makes people happy. Foundational to these theories is neuroscience, which has tentacles in social and behavioral sciences. We briefly touch neuroscientific techniques that assert human behavior is not always rational.

Prospect Theory

The new approach to utility, demand, and value is outlined in Kahneman and Tversky's famous paper, "Prospect Theory: An Analysis of Decision under Risk" (2000 [1979]). The fruit of their efforts culminated in Kahneman winning the Nobel Prize in Economics in 2002. Tversky died in 1996, but Kahneman continues to develop their joint line of reasoning. He argues that people are limited in their choices by the information available at a given moment; they sometimes depart from the economist's view of rationality, and their behavior is never as consistent and logical as economists assume it to be. People can be generous. They can place the happiness or welfare of others (wife, husband, partner, poor and/or downtrodden people) into their "utility function." They may engage in "conspicuous consumption," as Veblen claimed, deriving utility from keeping up with, or outspending, their peers. The psychologists also argue that over time tastes are unstable. Preferences change, maybe even frequently, upsetting one of the standard assumptions of traditional economic theory.

Kahneman and Tversky set out to examine how individuals make choices in *their* world, as opposed to the world of the economists.[6] According to Kahneman:

> If you prefer an apple to a banana, then you also prefer a 10% chance to win an apple to a 10% chance to win a banana. The apple and the banana stand for any objects of choice (including gambles) and the 10% chance stands for any probability. Economists adopted expected utility theory in a dual role: as a logic that prescribes how decisions should be made, and as a description of how Econs make choices. Amos [Tverskky] and I were psychologists, however, and we set out to understand how Humans actually make risky choices without assuming anything about their rationality. (*Thinking Fast and Slow*, pp. 270–271)

The Kahneman–Tversky approach seeks to develop a utility theory more firmly rooted in psychology than allowed by the earlier Bernoulli-based theory that undergirds economics.[7] Whereas the economist assumes that individuals start with a reference point when evaluating decisions or probabilities, prospect theory assumes that individuals must first identify *outcomes* that they believe are equivalent, such as the probability of getting two more apples to the probability of losing two less bananas. But it should be obvious that whatever one's reference point will depend on how one values apples and bananas and how many apples and bananas the individual possesses when asked. In other words, behavior and decisions cannot be assumed, they must be analyzed given some reference point—which, in general, will be different for different individuals. If two individuals who each earn $100,000 a year are each given a $25,000 raise, the psychological valuation of the raise is likely to be different for each of them. The psychological value of the raise may well depend on how comparable workers are compensated or on the consumption patterns of one's peer group (Veblen again).

Prospect theory may be explicated within the simple framework of a coin toss. Suppose the gamble is that you win $150 if the coin comes up heads, but you lose $100 if it comes up tails. Would you take the bet? Kahneman and Tversky recognize that you have a different reference point if your wealth is $30,000 than if it is $5 million, yet the expected value of the gamble is the same. They observed that many individuals would not take the bet, because "for most people the fear of losing $100 is more intense than the hope of gaining $150." They concluded that "losses loom larger than gains and that people are *loss averse*" (Kahneman, *Thinking*, p. 284).

Loss aversion is a central tenet of prospect theory. The other key principles are: Acts of evaluation are relative to a neutral reference point, and changes in wealth are subject to diminishing sensitivity (e.g., the subjective difference between $900 and $1,000 is much smaller than the difference between $100 and $200).[8] These three principles come into play in figure 26-4, which shows the psychological values of gains and losses in Kahneman's theoretical framework. In this figure, psychological satisfaction (value) is represented on the vertical axis and outcomes or dollar

[6] In order to draw distinctions between two types of decision makers Kahneman and Tversky use terminology invented by Richard Thaler, who dubbed the two types "Econs" and "Humans." Econs are those who behave as economists assume, Humans decide on the basis of "prospects." (see references).

[7] Daniel Bernoulli (1700–1782), was a Swiss mathematician and physicist, whose invention of the St. Petersburg Paradox provided the basis for the economic theories of risk aversion, risk premium and utility. The St. Petersburg paradox is a classical situation where a naive decision criterion (which takes only the expected value into account) would recommend a course of action that no (real) rational person would be willing to take.

[8] This principle is somewhat different from the principle of the diminishing marginal utility of money.

amounts on the horizontal axis. The neutral reference point is at the intersection of the vertical and horizontal axes. The S-shape of the curve represents diminishing sensitivity to gains and losses. Kahneman points out that the two curves that form the S around the reference point are not symmetrical due to loss aversion—the slope of the function changes abruptly at the reference point showing that the response to losses is stronger than the response to corresponding gains (*Thinking*, pp. 282–283).

Figure 26-4 shows that from a neutral reference point the positive psychological value of a $100 gain (NE quadrant) is less than the negative psychological value of a $100 loss (SW quadrant), or that a person fears the resulting loss to a greater extent than he or she welcomes the resulting gain. By inference, this person would not take a bet with the fifty-fifty prospect of winning $150 or losing $100. Not all individuals are necessarily loss averse with this gamble. Each individual is required to establish some benchmark in evaluating the alternatives. That benchmark will be different for different individuals and for different benchmark levels of income as well. Life sometimes forces us to take chances. Will the object of your affection say "yes" or "no" to a date? Will you get that part in the school play? Should a lawyer accept you as a client? Decisions must be made. Sometimes all the alternatives one faces are bad. It is believed that individuals become less "loss averse" in such instances (desperation?). However, other things equal, in prospect theory a certain outcome is preferred to an uncertain one. This is not the general case in traditional theory.

It should be obvious that prospect theory undermines generally accepted principles of economic reasoning. Loss aversion might explain the fact that our valuation of possessions may change over time in either direction, suggesting that the utility derived from them also varies over time. We may purchase a piece of art for $1,000 today but not wish to sell it for $2,000 a month later. However, it remains to be seen whether prospect theory can be more robust in promoting economic understanding. So far, it has not come close to overturning the existing paradigm of economics, which remains steadfastly committed to the rationality principle.

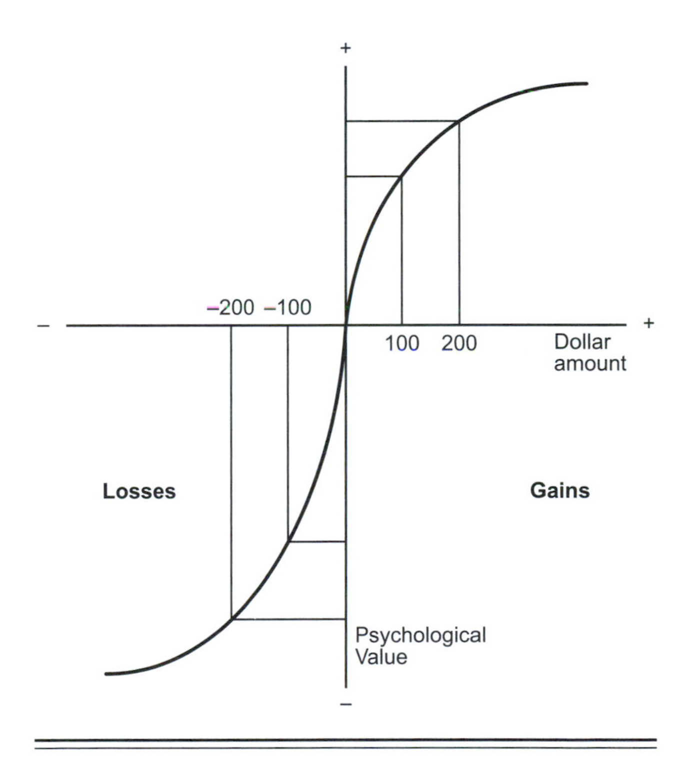

Figure 26-4 The psychological value of gains and losses based on evaluation from a neutral reference point, diminishing sensitivity to changes in wealth, and loss aversion.

Nevertheless, the human dimensions of social behavior are indeed complex, offering perhaps large opportunities to integrate economics and psychology in meaningful ways. At this writing, prospect theory represents a supplemental rather than an integral tool of economic analysis. It is confined mostly to the world inside of the laboratory, where experiments are conducted to test whether animal "consumers" are "rational" or "irrational." The weight of these experiments has been to show that the behavioral assumptions involving rational behavior are minimal insofar as they apply to animals as well as humans. Prospect theory has far to go if it is to revolutionize economic theory. At least one critic argues that it is "not ready-made for economic applications," (Barberis, "Thirty Years," p. 174). We shall have to wait and see its lasting impact, if any. (For now, we invite you to take a look at the box, The Force of Ideas: Veblen Redux and the Behaviorists, to see parallels in the divergence from traditional economic methodology.)

The Force of Ideas: Veblen Redux and the Behaviorists

The traditional nexus of economic theory (repeatedly exercised in this book) has been jolted, but not replaced, by the "behavioral economics" of psychologists and experimentalists. Other assaults on traditional notions of utility maximization have included the argument that higher pecuniary income (or GDP) may not be a good indicator of "happiness." But readers might recall from chapter 19 that dissent from methodological orthodoxy was alive and well a century ago in the core of Veblenian "institutional" economics, which proffered a basic and (necessarily) less sophisticated "take" on human nature quite similar to modern methodological critics. Consider only two of Veblen's conceptions for comparison: rationality and emulation.

Veblen attacked the "rationality postulate" enshrined in neoclassical and Austrian economics. As he put it, human beings were more than simply "lightening fast calculators" (see chapter 19). The self-interested nature of individuals was operative to an extent but it was assumed, not proven, to be the central driver of economic behavior. Standard economic theory assumed that human nature was unalterable and divorced from

> the cultural elements involved in the theoretical scheme, elements that are of the nature of institutions, human relations governed by use and wont in whatever kind and connexion, are not subject to inquiry but are taken for granted as pre-existing in a finished, typical form and as making up a normal and definitive economic situation, under which and in terms of which human intercourse is necessarily carried on. ("Limitations," p. 157)

In short, just as Kahneman and Tversky argued, Veblen suggested that human behavior was complex and that habits and instincts played a heuristic role in choice. Heuristic "short-cuts" to thinking—explainable perhaps in the wired system of the brain—constitute what Veblen called instincts and habits. A major criticism of neoclassical economics, Veblen argued, is that rather than admit that knowledge is "bounded" by instincts and habits, neoclassical economics simply assume them away. The modern behaviorists are reprising similar arguments.

The importance of relativity in gauging satisfaction (utility) was also stressed by Veblen, although he gave the subject of utility an "anthropological" twist. In early stages of civilization honor and esteem were achieved by the possession of wealth or property, whether obtained from one's own efforts or through inheritance. In the emerging pecuniary economy—where making money becomes a contrast to making goods—a new "propensity" arises in human nature. Says Veblen:

> Under the regime of individual ownership the most available means of visibly achieving a purpose is that afforded by the acquisition and accumulation of goods; and as the self-regarding antithesis between man and man reaches fuller consciousness, the

propensity for achievement—the instinct of workmanship—tends more and more to shape itself into a straining to surpass others in pecuniary achievement. Relative success, tested by an invidious pecuniary comparison with other men, becomes the conventional end of action. (*Theory*, pp. 39–40)

What Veblen terms "conspicuous leisure" coupled with "conspicuous consumption" becomes an elusive "end" to human behavior. When one has finally caught up with "the Joneses," the Joneses, or at least some of them, advance further in consumption or pecuniary wealth, and one's satisfaction (or utility) is lowered because of his or her new *relative* position.

These attributes of human nature mean that the kind of rationality and utility maximization proffered in traditional theory, as well as substitute theories advanced by today's behaviorists and psychologists, miss the mark in analyzing economic activity and results. If utility cannot dependably be linked to higher GDP or income or wealth, the connection between happiness and overall well-being is questionable. While these matters cannot be fully discussed here, we note that "new" investigative tools, however intriguing, have not replaced traditional economic notions of rationality and utility maximization any more than Veblen succeeded in displacing Marshallian and Austrian neoclassicism. Identifying parallels in economic criticism, however, reminds us that traditional methods of economics have been under close scrutiny in much the same manner over time.

Happiness Theory

Something called "happiness theory" is an offshoot of the Kahneman–Tversky emphasis on "experienced" utility rather than hypothesized utility. In this field one does not *assume* that an individual is "happy" to some degree, or attempt to measure happiness in money; one simply *asks* the individual. The basic idea here, not unlike "prospect theory," is that happiness and well-being have nonpecuniary as well as pecuniary dimensions. (Once more, traditional theory assumes that individuals rationally maximize income or wealth.) Like prospect theory happiness theory is an attempt to integrate psychology with economics, while calling on empirical results from specialized and global studies. Happiness "theorists" look at actual data to see how people behave. From observations they derive the (sometimes not too surprising) conclusions that married or partnered people are happier or more satisfied than single people; that the employed are happier than the unemployed; that (for example) Danes are happier than U.S. citizens; and many other conclusions that might seem obvious to the casual observer (for details see Frey, *Happiness, A Revolution in Economics*, and Layard, *Happiness: Lessons from a New Science*).

One critical aspect of both "happiness" theory and "prospect" theory must be carefully examined—the stability of preferences at any moment and over time. One speculation on this matter is the "Easterlin Paradox," formulated by Richard Easterlin ("Does Economic Growth Improve the Human Lot?") in 1974. The Easterlin Paradox holds that more per-capita income is not related positively to happiness, at least at higher income levels. While empirical evidence since Easterlin's paper does not support his hypothesis (rather some studies indicate a positive correlation between per capita income and happiness even at higher levels of income), Easterlin's reasoning is nevertheless important, because it relates to a so-called relative income hypothesis.[9] One part of this idea is based on acculturation—the idea that

[9] See notes for further reading at the end of this chapter.

individuals become accustomed to higher levels of income through time. By the acculturation principle people may be made happier by higher income in the short run, but over time they find that other people's incomes have increased along with theirs, leaving their *relative* position (and happiness level) about the same. Clearly, it can be shown that very wealthy countries contain happier people than very poor countries, but that is not what the relative income hypothesis is about. The utility of increases in income adjusts to former levels through time.

The relative income hypothesis is associated with the issue of "interdependent utility functions," which is the notion that one person's utility is linked to the utility experienced by others, especially one's friends or associates. An increase in the status or income or wealth of A, may cause a decrease in the utility of individuals B through N, leaving the group A though N no better off. Based on this premise, if your salary rises and your coworkers' does not, the group's utility does not change. If you purchase a new Porsche and your friends do not, the group's utility remains the same.[10] Acceptance of this notion has led to proposals to tax luxury goods and higher incomes (Frank, *Luxury Fever*), actions that meet with criticism and resistance on grounds that taxes violate economic freedom and lead to distortions in the allocation of resources (Salerno, "Clamping Down on the Joneses"). It goes without saying that taxation reduces welfare—a consequence that would have to be set against any increases that would come from taxes on luxury goods or higher incomes. According to Frey, "keeping up with the Joneses" in income or wealth or luxury goods has counterparts in the attainment of political power, awards (such as the Pulitzer or Nobel prizes), educational "status," distinction in the arts and in scholarship, and in many other areas (*Happiness*, p. 172). The important point is that such behavior does not comport with the traditional "economic" assumption of rationality.

Neuroscience

Another avenue to explaining human behavior has been the scientific approach called "neuroscience." Neuroscience measures brain activity in various ways to identify both pleasure and pain and the degrees of pleasure and pain from some stimuli. In other words, neuro research is aimed at finding the source and measurement of "utility" and "happiness." Neuroscience uses various methods to "explain" happiness by way of brain "imaging." The electroencephalogram measures stimuli from outside the brain. Other techniques, such as the MRI (magnetic resonance imaging) or PET (positron emission tomography) scans measure blood or blood characteristics to arrive at conclusions concerning action or intelligence. Rather than just assume that humans are rational calculators, neuroscience studies *Homo sapiens* as an intuitive, emotional, and "nonrational," being capable of making nonrational (in an economic sense) decisions.

Neuroscience, happiness theory, and prospect theory have raised interesting and important issues in economic theory, but the broad brush of "nonrational" human behavior has yet to alter the fundamentals of economic teaching. Instead the science of choice as elaborated within traditional economics is subjected to reality tests by ever-expanding and improving econometric techniques (see chapter 25). Calculations using the "nonrational" assumptions discussed above have been tested by experimentation on groups of people (students), animals (rats and pigeons), field surveys, government surveys, and international data sets. Still in its infancy, the

[10] This idea should sound familiar if you have digested the narrative, "The Force of Ideas: Veblen Redux and the Behaviorists" in this chapter.

new behavioral economics and the results to date have yet to be given the "real-world" scrutiny that traditional economic theory has been put through over an extended period of time. Nontraditional assumptions concerning behavior may yet hold promise for "revolutionizing" economics, but a radical reorientation of economic thinking does not appear to be in the cards anytime soon.

Conclusion

Contemporary microeconomics teems with many provocative issues and interesting applications. To borrow Hemingway's aphorism about Paris, today's microeconomics is a movable and ever-changing feast. In this chapter we have tried to convey the flavor of several new developments relating to consumption and demand. Even a small taste of the feast conveys the clear and correct impression that economic theory has made and is making giant leaps in the direction of "realism." Economists are learning to recognize and to account for all kinds of actual market circumstances that were held in abeyance by earlier writers. This is not, of course, to criticize the genuine pioneers of microeconomic theory such as Marshall, Jevons, or Walras. Rather, it is evidence that the operation of markets is a more complex process than could be handled by the earlier conceptual apparatus. In reality, the modern directions of microeconomic theory are testimony to the ongoing nature of earlier contributions and the vibrancy of economics.

References

Akerlof, George A. "The Market for 'Lemons': Quality Uncertainty and the Market Mechanism," *Quarterly Journal of Economics*, vol. 84 (August 1970), pp. 488–500.

Alchian, Armen A., and Harold Demsetz. "Production, Information Costs, and Economic Organization," *American Economic Review*, vol. 62 (December 1972), pp. 777–795.

Barberis, Nicholas C. "Thirty Years of Prospect Theory in Economics: A Review and Assessment," *Journal of Economic Perspectives*, vol. 27 (Winter 2013), pp. 173–196.

Barzel, Yoram. "The Entrepreneur's Reward for Self-Policing," *Economic Inquiry*, vol. 25 (January 1987), pp. 103–116.

Becker, Gary S. "A Theory of the Allocation of Time," *The Economic Journal*, vol. 75 (September 1965), pp. 493–517.

Coase, Ronald H. "The Nature of the Firm," *Economica*, vol. 4 (November 1937), pp. 386–405.

Darby, Michael, and Karni, Edi. "Free Competition and the Optimal Amount of Fraud," *Journal of Law and Economics*, vol. 16 (April 1973), pp. 67–88.

Easterlin, Richard. "Does Economic Growth Improve the Human Lot? Some Empirical Evidence," in Paul David and Melvin Reder (eds), *Nations and Household in Economic Growth: Essays in Honour of Moses Abramowitz*. Amsterdam: Academic Press, 1974.

Frank, Robert. *Luxury Fever: Why Money Fails to Satisfy in an Era of Excess*. New York: Free Press, 1999.

Frey, Bruno S. *Happiness: A Revolution in Economics*. Cambridge, MA: The MIT Press, 2008.

Jensen, Michael C., and William H. Meckling. "A Theory of the Firm: Governance, Residual Claims, and Organizational Forms," *Journal of Financial Economics*, vol. 3 (October 1976), pp. 305–360.

Kahneman, Daniel. *Thinking Fast and Slow*. New York: Farrar, Straus and Giroux 2011.

———, and Amos Tversky. "Prospect Theory: An Analysis of Decision Under Risk," in Daniel Kahneman and Amos Tversky, *Choices, Values, and Frames*. Cambridge, UK: Cambridge University Press, 2000 [1979], pp. 17–43.

Klein, Benjamin, and Keith Leffler. "The Role of Market Forces in Assuring Contractual Performance," *Journal of Political Economy*, vol. 89 (1981), pp. 615–641.

Knight, Frank H., *Risk, Uncertainty and Profit*. New York: Houghton-Mifflin, 1921.

Lancaster, Kelvin J. "A New Approach to Consumer Theory," *Journal of Political Economy*, vol. 74 (April 1966), pp. 132–157.

Layard, Richard. *Happiness: Lessons from a New Science*. London: Penguin Books, 2005.

Nelson, Phillip. "Information and Consumer Behavior," *Journal of Political Economy*, vol. 78 (1970), pp. 311–329.

———. "Advertising as Information," *Journal of Political Economy*, vol. 82 (1974), pp. 729–754.

Rubin, Paul. "The Theory of the Firm and the Structure of the Franchise Contract," *Journal of Law and Economics*, vol. 21 (1978), pp. 223–233.

Salerno, Joseph. "Clamping Down on the Joneses," *Mises Daily*, August 21, 2012. Ludwig von Mises Institute. http://mises.org/daily/6155/Clamping-Down-on-the-Joneses.

Stigler, George J. "The Economics of Information," *Journal of Political Economy*, vol. 69 (June 1961), pp. 213–225.

———, and Gary S. Becker. "De Gustibus Non Est Disputandum," *American Economic Review*, vol. 67 (March 1977), pp. 76–90.

Thaler, Richard H., and Cass R. Sunstein. *Nudge: Improving Decisions about Health, Wealth, and Happiness*. New Haven, CT: Yale University Press.

Veblen, Thorstein. *The Theory of the Leisure Class*, with an introduction by John Kenneth Galbraith. Boston: Houghton Mifflin Company, 1973 [1899].

———. "The Limitations of Marginal Utility," *Journal of Political Economy* (1909), in Wesley C. Mitchell, *What Veblen Taught*, New York: A. M. Kelley, 1964.

Notes for Further Reading

No short narrative of contemporary trends in the microeconomic analysis of demand, consumption, and "rationality" (or any other subject) could possibly do justice to the ideas themselves. As always, there is no substitute for the original sources. One source stands out in bringing the largest number of original papers on the "new" microeconomics together under one cover: see William Breit, Harold M. Hochman, and Edward Saueracker (eds.), *Readings in Microeconomics* (St. Louis: Times Mirror/Mosby College Publishing, 1986). For another excellent compendium of original essays on the "new microeconomics" and its broad applicability, see Richard B. McKenzie and Gordon Tullock, *The New World of Economics: Explorations into the Human Experience*, 3d ed. (Homewood, IL: Irwin, 1981). The authors take up such matters as marriage, child production, law, crime, presidential elections, and college and university education, examining each issue as a straightforward application of basic microeconomic principles. The principles underlying "nonrational" theorizing in economics are well covered in the Kahneman and Frey texts listed in the references to this chapter.

The relation between goods quality, advertising, and information is an ongoing subject of contemporary microeconomics. In addition to the papers by Stigler, Nelson, and Darby and Karni cited above in the references, empirical papers on the nature of goods and information transmission exist. On the issue of search and experience goods, see three papers by David Laband: "Advertising as Information: An Empirical Note," *Review of Economics and Statistics*, vol. 68 (August 1986), pp. 517–521; "The Durability of Informational Signals and the Content of Advertising," *Journal of Advertising*, vol. 18 (March 1989), pp. 13–18; and "An Objective Measure of Search versus Experience Goods," *Economic Inquiry*, vol. 29 (July 1991), pp. 497–509. Robert B. Ekelund, Jr., Franklin G. Mixon, Jr., and Rand W. Ressler, "Advertising and Information: An Empirical Study of Search, Experience and Credence Goods," *The Journal of Economic Studies*, vol. 22

(1995), pp. 33–43; extend this discussion to include credence goods as well. The concept of a "meta-credence" good—one that goes beyond the existence of a simple credence good—is applied to religion by Robert B. Ekelund, Jr., Robert F. Hébert, and Robert D. Tollison, *The Marketplace of Christianity* (Cambridge: The MIT Press, 2006).

Many other important innovations in resource allocation and the theory of the firm and firm operations bear careful study. In our view, one of the most interesting extensions of time costs and resource allocation involves the problem of welfare dissipation under differing schemes of distribution and retrade. A central contribution that clearly reveals the implicit costs of queuing is that of Yoram Barzel, "A Theory of Rationing by Waiting," *Journal of Law & Economics*, vol. 17 (April 1974), pp. 73–95. Harvey Leibenstein, "Allocative Efficiency vs. 'X-Efficiency,'" *American Economic Review*, vol. 56 (June 1966), pp. 392–415, raises and evaluates the question of whether firms minimize costs as assumed in orthodox theory. Problems relating property rights and contracting to firm size and organization have been developed in a number of contributions by Oliver E. Williamson: see, for example, "Hierarchical Control and Optimum Firm Size," *Journal of Political Economy*, vol. 56 (April 1967), pp. 123–138; and *Markets and Hierarchies* (New York: The Free Press, 1975). The modern approach to the theory of the firm is evaluated and expanded in an unpublished doctoral dissertation by Donald J. Boudreaux, *Contracting, Organization, and Monetary Instability: Studies in the Theory of the Firm* (Auburn University, 1986). A contemporary brief for the generally positive contribution of advertising to efficient market functioning and information provision is given in Robert B. Ekelund, Jr., and David S. Saurman, *Advertising and the Market Process: A Modern Economic View* (San Francisco: Pacific Research Institute for Public Policy, 1988).

The intrusion of modern microeconomic theory into other realms of social behavior is evident by the success of Stephen D. Levitt and Steven J. Dubner's *Freakonomics: A Rogue Economist Explores the Hidden Side of Everything* (New York: HarperCollins, 2005). One of the "politically incorrect" arguments set forth therein by Levitt, an economist at the University of Chicago, is that the dramatic lowering of the crime rate in the 1990s—usually attributed to more police resources, passage of mandatory sentencing laws, and so forth—may have been a result instead, or as well, of the institutionalization of legalized abortions following the 1973 Supreme Court decision, *Roe v. Wade*. Pushing the envelope ever further, Levitt utilizes conventional economic tools to analyze Internet dating, sumo wrestling, student cheating on standardized examinations, and why drug dealers live with their mothers.

The revolution in microeconomic theory—especially that related to property rights, the modern theory of the firm, and rent-seeking and interest group behavior—has spawned an enormous amount of interest in neoinstitutional economics. The work of Nobel laureate Douglass North has already been mentioned in connection with the extension of microeconomic theory to the development of institutions (see chapter 19, notes for further reading). In addition to the works cited there, see North, *Institutions, Institutional Change and Economic Performance* (Cambridge: Cambridge University Press, 1990); and same author, "Institutions and Economic Growth: An Historical Introduction," *World Development*, vol. 17 (1991), pp. 1319–1332. Also see Steve Pejovich, *Economic Analysis of Institutions and Systems* (Dordrecht: Kluwer Academic Publishers, 1995); and for a view that argues that neoclassical economics (even as expanded in modern settings) is not up to the task of providing a workable theory of institutions, see Eirik G. Furubotn, *Future Development of the New Institutional Economics: Extension of the Neoclassical Model or New Construct?* (Jena: Max Planck Institute for Research into Economic Systems, 1994).

Finally, the father of research on cognitive behavior, including what is now labeled behavioral economics was Herbert Simon (1916–2001) who won the Nobel Prize in Economics in 1978. Simon introduced the concept of "bounded rationality," which simply indicates that individuals have limited abilities to compute all possible information when making decisions. Individuals (and organizations) must make decisions based on necessarily limited information. See Simon, "A Behavioral Model of Rational Choice," *Quarterly Journal of Economics*, vol. 69 (1955), pp. 99–188.

The central questions are: Do individuals act "rationally" when they choose on the basis of limited information and what is the nature of choice? A traditional interpretation would be that we do not act on the basis of cost and benefit. Information is costly with uncertain benefits. We do not invest in information concerning a decision when the costs of attaining that information exceed the benefits. This does not suggest that investigations into cognition are worthless; only that there are competing approaches to "rationality." And from a scientific perspective, brain mapping is a promising area of research on decision making and "happiness," although it has hardly borne much fruit. Without question many decisions are made heuristically—through "shortcuts" in mental processing. (We do not have to go through all the mental steps to explain our tooth cleaning behavior every morning—it is done "automatically.") But how these shortcuts affect decision making is not always clear. The question and results of "happiness research" are also problematic. The challenge to stable preference functions may be substantive, but many of the conclusions to the hypothesis that luxury goods should be taxed or that happiness surveys justify higher taxes on higher incomes are debatable. In the limit, according to economist Thomas DiLorenzo, "happiness research" is really a crusade to persuade the public that poverty and servitude to the state are superior to prosperity and freedom" ("The Trojan Horse of 'Happiness Research,'" *Mises Daily*, June 9, 2011. Ludwig von Mises Institute, http://mises.org/daily/5356). The idea that one person's increase in utility from buying a Porsche is counterbalanced by her friend's disutility from that purchase—providing grounds for taxing Porsches or income—is also soundly attacked by economist Joseph T. Salerno who calls the research of Robert Frank (see references) "pseudoscientific social welfare." According to Salerno, "The plain truth is that these policies constitute an attempt to forcibly impose the arbitrary values of an arrogant and self-appointed intellectual elite on the most intensely private affairs of the productive majority who are choosing to spend their money according to their own preferences and personal-welfare evaluations" (see references). Thus, the new developments surrounding the fundamental basis of economics—traditional rationality, self-interest, and utility maximization—are something of an ongoing process. Some of the conclusions are appealing but many are highly questionable. For example, Barberis (see References) concludes that, while prospect theory may have some applications in risk and insurance, it is unlikely to find general application within general economics or economic policy. With respect to the latter view, also see the comments of Gary Becker, "Interview with Gary Becker," Federal Reserve Bank of Minneapolis (June 14, 2002), at http://www.minneapolisfed.org/pubs/region/02-06/becker.cfm. These approaches will undoubtedly continue to elicit comments both positive and negative as the twenty-first century progresses.

27

The Resurgence of Economics as a Social Science

New developments in consumption theory introduced in chapter 26, including a potentially fundamental alteration in how economists approach utility, demand, and preferences (e.g., Becker's theory of full price, Bruno Frey's and Richard Layard's happiness theories, and Daniel Kahneman's and Amos Tversky's "prospect theory") are only part of the ambitious reach of economic analysis in contemporary economics. Much to the chagrin of other social scientists—some of whom regard the economist's reach into sociology, anthropology, and political science as "poaching"—contemporary economic analysis is in fact shedding new light on issues from the fields of art, sociology, religion, and politics. Concepts such as "full price" (i.e., money price plus value of time foregone) and implicit (nonpecuniary) markets have been integrated into traditional economics, and newer concepts of search, signaling, and information theory have been introduced. Indeed, economics is moving toward an integration of the social sciences envisioned centuries ago by Adam Smith and John Stuart Mill.

Arguably, economics is the queen of the social sciences. A brief look at the index of Adam Smith's *Wealth of Nations* conveys its enormous scope. Smith dealt with religion, politics, literature, history, and many other matters. Yet, possibly as a consequence of specialization and division of labor, contemporary economics has increasingly enriched the technical aspects of the field. Perhaps as a backlash to the ever-growing technical nature of economic inquiry, a contrary movement is afoot with the aim to reintegrate economics—specifically modern and received economic theory—with issues that have, through the past two centuries, been cleaved from economic inquiry. These matters concern, among other things, history, sociology, anthropology (especially archeology and culture) and politics.

The present chapter surveys, albeit briefly, some of the new developments linking economics to social and cultural phenomena. We first discuss a few of the applications of economic analysis to sociology, specifically to the sociology of mating and the family. Next we consider some of the inroads that economics has taken to increase our understanding of aspects of culture—art, religion, and primitive societies. Finally, we consider some of the links between economics and practical politics, revisiting some of the issues previously raised in chapter 24.

■ Economics and Sociology

As economics spread its wings in the twentieth century it began to engulf issues that were formerly considered strictly within the purview of sociology. Nobel laureate Gary Becker (*Economic Approach to Human Behavior*) has been at the forefront of developments involving economic theories of social interactions and family organization. While sociologists and psychologists typically view the family as a complex set of interpersonal activities and relations, Becker treats it as a form of economic organization. In the language of the economist, marriage is a two-party, incompletely defined contract carrying explicit and implicit obligations. In this view prenuptial dating is an investment in information about prospective mates. Being "in love" implies interdependent utility functions, inasmuch as most successful marriages are made by people who have a sense of mutual caring and whose preferences and values are closely related.

The economic theory of the family maintains that a "head of household," who cares for the welfare of family members, directs and allocates household resources in Pareto-optimal fashion (see chapter 17). All family members have incentives to act in a way that maximizes the household head's utility function. This arrangement allows every family member to be better off than he or she would be in isolation. Becker constructs the household head's single utility function in a way that captures the utility of the entire household, so that the resulting function represents the collective utility of the family. Within this context decisions are made regarding the transformation of leisure into household work or market work, as suggested in chapter 26. The sociological-psychological category of "role-playing" within the family unit finds a place in this analysis as a consequence of specialization based on rational economic principles of cost and choice. This approach is not without ardent critics, but Becker's insights give meaning to a number of social phenomena that sociologists have been at pains to understand and explain. Marriage rates and birthrates can be understood within this framework, but before marriage, or partnership, and child rearing come dating and mating.

The Economics of Dating and Mating

Sociologists often treat dating as "ritualistic" behavior—one of the oldest rituals known to humanity. Certainly, dating and mating practices have a long and successful history as adaptive survival techniques to protect children. However, economists bring a different perspective. The process of dating and mating is an organized activity that takes place within a highly competitive environment of searching and acquiring information (see chapter 26). We refer here to contemporary practices and activity.

Information, like any product or service is never free, a principle that applies as much to finding a suitable mate or partner as it does to automobiles. Costs of searching for a mate include the opportunity costs of time, clothing, grooming, and entertainment expenses, to name a few. Internet "niche" dating services (e.g., "It's Just Lunch," "Christian Mingle," "Our Time") provide an alternative means of search but require subscription fees or other payments. On the one hand, at the margin search costs rise with the time spent searching. On the other, given your stock of information the marginal benefits of finding a mate or "permanent" companion declines with time spent searching. From an economic perspective finding the "right" mate and the optimal search time will occur where marginal cost equals marginal benefits.

"Personality assessments" are routinely a part of Internet dating and are cost lowering, but indirect measures of personality, habits, outlook, and philosophy are more difficult to determine. On entering the dating-market game most people put on their "best face," and many are inclined to exaggerate their "genuine" physical and psychological traits, a fact that might help account for early divorce in some instances. (Two of the biggest Internet deceptions are reputedly the self-described female as "blonde" and exaggeration of earned income by the self-described male.) Given high information costs, the process of self-selection takes place through *signals* as well as information provided by character-identifying facts and institutions. The whole system is devised to *reduce information costs among the market participants in their search for a date or a mate*.

Mating signals take different forms. Where you go to college and what your major is tell a lot about you as a potential mate by signaling probable IQ, parents' income or wealth, and parents' socioeconomic status. Religious preferences (or lack thereof) also provide vital signals. Each organization to which a prospective mate belongs (e.g., garden club, sky-diving club, Rotary, book-of-the-month club) reveals something of his or her personality and character. Signals therefore provide information that tends to lower search costs and improve selection of dates, mates, or companions.

In a market economy institutions/agencies/arrangements continuously arise in order to lower the costs of search, and independent, disinterested evaluators emerge. "Matchmakers" are a staple of some Jewish communities to this day. Internet matchmaking has become a thriving industry, providing detailed profiles of physical, emotional, and social preferences. Dating agencies will record your height, weight, taste for sushi, music and entertainment preferences, and so on, matching people of like characteristics. "Personals" are carried by many newspapers for couplings of various kinds. Singles bars that cater to different age groups, young and old, education levels, and income brackets dot the urban landscape. Bars and clubs for gays, lesbians, transvestites, and transgendered individuals exist in large part to reduce information costs. The bottom line is that contemporary dating occurs within a highly organized economic market in which institutions emerge to reduce the costs and increase the benefits of searching for a mate.

Marriage as an Economic Contract

Given biological and other kinds of specialization, there has always been an economic aspect to marriage. In medieval times love was one of the least compelling reasons people got married; among the upper classes marriage was a means of promoting "mergers" for the maintenance of family dynasties. Even today, in some non-Western societies, marriages are "arranged" by parents without consideration of intimate feelings between the betrothed.

Becker sees marriage as a frequent (though not universal) outcome of the dating game. It can therefore be studied as a long-term, written, oral, or implicit contract between (mainly) two parties to produce and nurture children and to satisfy other wants of a household unit. This "economic" definition of marriage as contract lends itself to civil unions, gay marriage, and cohabitation, as well as traditional family formation. A key point is that an individual's success at fulfilling the contract is determined in large part by how successful he or she is in searching for a mate (see Becker's *A Treatise on the Family*; or Richard Posner's *Sex and Reason* for in-depth discussion of this process).

Viewing marriage as an incompletely defined contract that is entered into according to the perceived costs and benefits of the participants makes it possible to bring those costs and benefits explicitly into the decision nexus. On the cost side, marriage means that each partner sacrifices some independence and makes many compromises regarding personal habits, friendships, and the nature and direction of expenditures. On the benefit side, marriage facilitates the production and rearing of children by providing love, companionship, nurture, and reciprocal caring. In addition to these benefits, however, marriage often provides an opportunity to enjoy the economic gains from specialization and division of labor. Until recently in the United States, most familial division of labor made the male marriage partner the primary breadwinner through outside-the-home employment, while the female partner specialized in household production and child rearing. As long as skills vary widely between spouses, the gains to husband and wife from specialization and trade are positive and potentially large.

Changing cultural values and in particular the feminist movement have changed the traditional familial configuration for a significant number of individuals. Laws and practices have greatly lessened discrimination against women in the workplace. Women have, in increasing numbers, become engineers, lawyers, and physicians. In many areas of the marketplace, opportunities for educational attainment and other investments in human capital have been expanded for women. The result is that skill levels of men and women are drawing closer together. With men and women having more and more similar skills, the economic gains from specialization and trade between men and women within the organizational framework of marriage are clearly reduced. Holding constant all other noneconomic factors, economic theory predicts that a reduction of the gains to marriage will lead to a decline in marriage rates and an increase in divorce rates—precisely the experience of many developed nations in recent times.

As more women have entered the workforce and as family incomes have risen, we have observed another phenomenon with economic implications: a decline in the birthrate. Population growth requires a sustained demand for children on the part of parents. Long ago the classical economists argued that income increases would encourage an increase in the production of children, which, if you remember Ricardo's scenario, would eventually lead to the stationary state. Becker's analysis goes beyond the simple Malthusian framework of population growth by adding an important additional consideration: It is not only the level of income that explains population growth but also the relative "price" of children.

The full cost of raising children depends on both the direct expenditures incurred and the *opportunity* costs borne by parents. These opportunity costs increase as family income increases, particularly as the mother's market wage increases. Consequently, economic growth often contains a bias against child production. In most underdeveloped countries, especially those surviving on subsistence agriculture, children represent direct labor inputs and are considered valuable to their parents as a source of labor. Low wages in such countries keep the opportunity costs of having children at a low level. By contrast, in advanced economies the "price" of additional children is high because children are less valuable to their parents as direct labor inputs, and because parents' opportunity costs are high. Instead of raising an additional child, parents may decide to improve their own living standards and/or that of their existing children by spending more on education, housing, or a wide array of other goods. In part, then, rational economic decision making and a novel application of the law of demand explain low birthrates in developed nations and high birthrates in underdeveloped countries.

Despite these recent forays into areas traditionally considered outside the province of economics, no economist, including Becker, argues that economics is the sole or even the central factor in explaining sociological phenomena. Rather, contemporary microeconomics offers additional insights into certain aspects of human behavior that complement and/or supplement explanations proposed by other social scientists. This same economic approach has reached into other allied areas, not usually considered "economic," such as art, religion, archeology, and politics.

■ Economics and Art

Practical economic questions are evident in the art market, especially issues involving the production of art, and buying and selling all types of art through galleries and auction houses. Because private data on gallery transactions or "out-of-market" sales arranged privately between collectors are not generally available, most studies of art purchases and sales have been principally limited to use of auction data, supplemented by anecdotal materials.[1] One area of interest (as one might expect from economists) is the question of how remunerative art investments could be in a portfolio of investments. A study by Jianping Mei and Michael Moses ("Art as an Investment") suggests that some kinds and genres of art (for example, Impressionist, Modern, American) outperform others and therefore may be suitable for inclusion in a diversified investment portfolio. Other writers have suggested that certain segments of the art market are countercyclical (i.e., prices and sales go up when the market turns downward and vice versa), thereby suggesting that art can be used to "balance" a portfolio of investments (as is often said of precious metals). Yet, other investigations, including a massive study of over one million art transactions at auction by Luc Renneboog and Christophe Spaenjers ("Buying Beauty"), find only a modest rate of return (about 3.97 percent) per year on art investments. When storage, insurance, and other costs are taken into account, not to mention risk or variance in value, art "investment" does not appear so appealing. A missing element in the investment approach is *how* value is determined. Surely there is an implicit "consumption" value to owning and looking at fine art and other art objects. The full "return" to holding art, therefore, cannot be only an investment return—it must also include an implicit return in terms of utility gained. Ongoing studies are attempting to gain traction in this regard.

In addition to more traditional studies concerning art and its investment rate of return, contemporary economics is able to provide insights into other issues that might seem outside the purview of economics. Museum attendance, for example, yields to this approach. Conventional wisdom says that museums tend to prosper in upswings in the cycles of income and economic growth. But a study by Skinner, Ekelund, and Jackson ("Museums, Funding, and Business") shows that insofar as attendance is concerned the opposite is correct. Museum attendance actually increases during downturns in the business cycle and decreases during upswings in incomes and growth. This of course causes problems for museums since donations and grants typically follow the business cycle, causing increased expenditures for art venues at the very time of lowered revenues. One proposed remedy would make

[1] The inability to utilize price data from art galleries is not the only problem in the empirical study of art markets. Auction houses only record prices of art objects that are in private hands or are being "deaccessioned" by museums. In the case of American art, many (most) of the highest quality pieces are and have been in museum collections for the past one hundred years, which must be taken into account in identifying correlations between price and suggestions of quality of art at auction.

grants from private and public organizations (such as the National Endowment for the Arts) countercyclical rather than procyclical. Economic analysis can inform the phenomenon of countercyclical attendance; obviously people have more "time on their hands" when unemployed (during a recession). But to an economist, it is the *value* of time that matters. Some museums impose an entry fee, others do not. All things considered, the full entry price is lower when one is unemployed whether or not an entry fee is charged. When the value of time falls, the full price of every activity, including recreation, also falls, leading to greater consumption. This is one reason for the enormous growth in motion picture attendance during the Great Depression. (Child actor Shirley Temple and comedian Buster Keaton kept America smiling in the 1930s in part due to a lower *full price* of movie admittance.)

Economics has been able to shed new light on other poorly understood aspects of the art market as well. Conventional wisdom has it that the value of an artist's work rises at or around his or her death—the so-called "death effect." Economic theory, aided and abetted by Nobel laureate Ronald Coase, offers at least one plausible reason for this phenomenon. Coase's analysis of the "durable goods monopolist" has direct and important relevance to the art market ("Durability and Monopoly"). He asked a simple question: Are monopolies always successful and if not, why not? To learn the answer, consider the actions of two diverse groups: real estate developers and artists (of any kind). Assume that real estate developers have exclusive ownership and control over portions of land that are particularly desirable for housing development. To make it even simpler, assume that some individual (or collection of individuals) exerts monopoly control of all the land in America, which the monopolist can sell at rates identified by the demand curve in Figure 27-1.

If we assume that the total amount of land available is Q_c, the monopolist would want to sell Q_m land and charge customers the monopoly price P_m. But in actuality who would pay P_m for a plot of land? On reflection, a "durable goods monopolist" would not be able to charge more than the competitive price for land (P_c). Market imperatives would force the monopolist to devise some means of guaranteeing buyers that Q_mQ_c of land will not be sold so as to protect the value of their investment. Coase indicated a number of ways that this might be accomplished. Guaranteed "buy- backs," leasing arrangements, and giving away Q_mQ_c for nonmarket purposes (public parks, for example) might allow the monopolist to charge monopoly price P_m. The set-aside land would be taken off the market to warrant the "quality" of the land sold. Otherwise, the durable goods monopolist *cannot behave as a monopolist at all*—he or she must charge the *competitive* price.

This principle applies to artists as well because most artists find themselves in the position of the durable goods monopolist who can only imperfectly make contractual arrangements with demanders of their art. Although some living artists (e.g., Janet Fish or Chuck Close) charge top dollar for their work, the *average* artist makes only between $17,000 and $25,000 per year from his or her art sales. Each artist is, in effect, a durable goods monopolist having at least some degree of monopoly over his or her style. Some artists enter contractual arrangements to guarantee that they will not "overproduce" their art, which would have the effect of driving down its price. Artists who work in duplicative media (woodcuts, lithographs, linocuts, prints, and so on) typically limit the edition of particular works, destroying plates at the end of a run as a warranty to consumers of the value of their purchase. Artists may also limit their output by frequently changing their styles. (Picasso (1881–1973) famously went through numerous styles: for example, blue period, rose period, cubism, and neoclassical). Additionally, some artists "advertise" that a por-

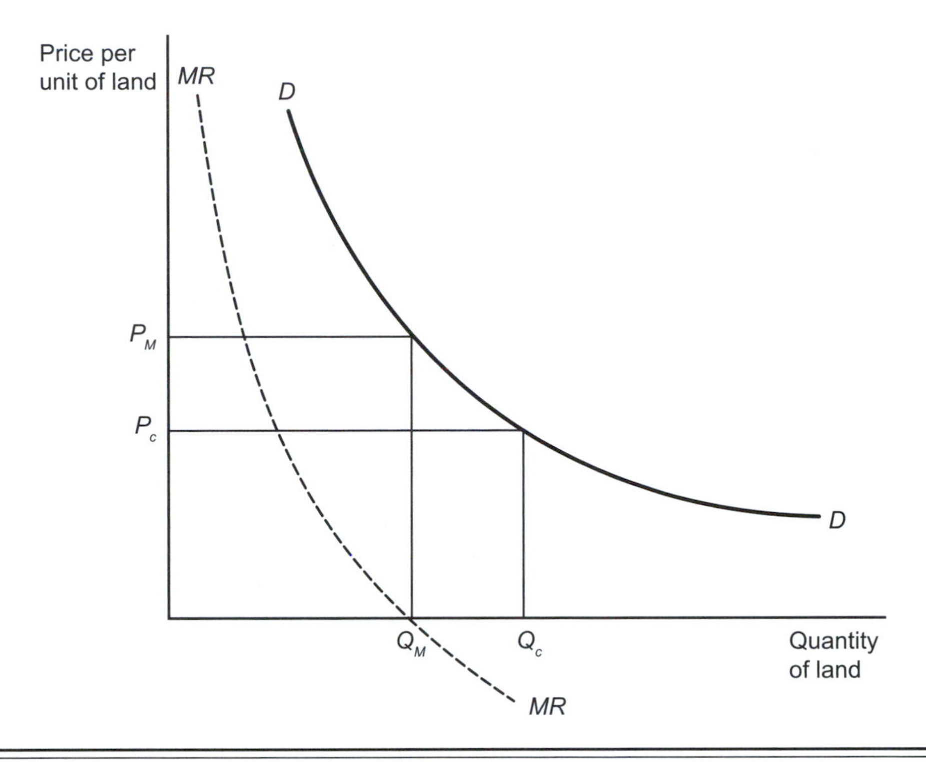

Figure 27-1 Demand and marginal revenue functions facing a land monopolist.

tion of their output will not enter traditional markets (through their dealers). During his lifetime, Mexican artist Rufino Tamayo (1899–1991) behaved like the land developer who created “set-asides” in the example above. He established separate museums to display his artistic output in Mexico (in Oaxaca and Mexico City). Pablo Picasso’s legacies and endowments of hundreds of pictures in France and Spain both before and after his death also established that “nonmarket” part of his output.

This economic principle has intuitive content as well. One of the reasons for a spike in the price of an artist’s work at his or her death is the obvious fact that no further output (short of fakes) will be forthcoming from the deceased artist. Sometimes this “death effect” on an artist’s prices is offset (or postponed) by the posthumous release of the artist’s atelier—those unsold pieces stored by the artist prior to his or her death. In general, however, no ironclad arrangements can be made between suppliers and demanders during the artist’s lifetime to assure that the artist will not spoil the market by overproduction. Hence, the prospect of devaluation will, *ceteris paribus*, keep prices and returns at competitive levels, and this may be one reason for the “starving artist” syndrome. In other words, some would-be monopolists who have exclusive control over particular resources and/or talents cannot always be successful at capturing the consumer surplus that monopoly pricing permits. This does not mean that other factors do not enter the art market that would have the contrary effects described above. “Hot” artists with aggressive dealers and vigorous advertising can stimulate demand while artists are alive—a common feature of the New York art market for example. But prices are determined by both supply and demand and the supply effect described above is always a factor in this market.

■ Economics and Religion

Religion in some form or fashion has been a staple of virtually all known societies. It is likely that the prehistorical beliefs and rituals of *Homo sapiens* (and possibly *Homo neanderthalensis*) were infused with "supernatural" speculation, magic, myth, and sacrifice almost as long as people walked upright. Religion entered the realm of economics in formal fashion when Adam Smith (see chapter 5) made it part of his inquiry into the nature of economic development. Smith, a staunch Presbyterian, believed participatory "bottom–up" religions that allowed competition among sects would lead to efficiency in provision of desirable services to congregants. In contemporary times, the focus (thanks in large part to Becker's extension of the "rationality postulate") has shifted toward economic rationality in the study of religion.

During the long hiatus between Adam Smith and Gary Becker sociologists steadily and persistently enriched the field. Max Weber's provocative study appeared in German in 1904–1905 (*The Protestant Ethic and the Spirit of Capitalism*) and was followed shortly by Émile Durkheim's *The Elementary Forms of Religious Life* in 1915. What economics adds to the discussion is the persistent analysis of religious behavior as an exercise in rational choice—that is, decisions involving resources of money and time. Religion, in other words, like many other products available in a market context, provides utility. Some prominent sociologists, such as Rodney Stark, Andrew M. Greeley, and William Sims Bain (see notes for further reading), have acknowledged the usefulness of an economic model of rational choice and embraced its insights in advancing their sociological studies of religion and religious behavior. Inasmuch as we cannot deal extensively with the ever-increasing multiplicity of contemporary economic studies of religion—both as a microeconomic phenomenon and as related to economic growth—we reserve our discussion in this chapter to two topics: the matter of religion as a cult and the application of industrial organization to the history of religion.

Cult Behavior

The Beckerian approach to religion (an activity or *implicit* market that requires both demanders and suppliers to expend time and money) was embraced initially by Corry Azzi and Ronald G. Ehrenberg ("Household Allocation"), and later in a somewhat different context by Laurence R. Iannaccone ("Sacrifice and Stigma"). Azzi and Ehrenberg developed a model of religious participation based on Becker's theory of household consumption, using empirical data on statewide church membership and a survey sample of church attendance. They tested a number of propositions that were traditionally in the purview of sociologists, such as male versus female participation in church-related activities (women participate more) and the age distribution of church attendance (attendance is positively related to age). Their approach allows that individuals allocate their resources (time and goods) to both temporal and "afterlife" consumption. (Afterlife consumption, consisting of heaven, eternal peace, communion with God, and so on, is a function of time engaged in religious activities during one's lifetime.) By connecting membership in time-intensive religions to households with lower alternative time costs (lower wages imply a lower cost of engaging in nonwage activity), Azzi and Ehrenberg were able to explain why religions that are less time intensive grow faster in the United States than more time-intensive religions. While some of their conclusions have been challenged (statistically), their study had an important catalytic effect on further research.

Lawrence Iannaccone extended the Azzi-Ehrenberg approach by including human capital (i.e., knowledge, familiarity with ritual and dogma, etc.) and inferring that the service ("product") sold was something more than simply an afterlife. Defining a specific stock of religious experience that an individual has built up at any given time as a function of previous activities and experiences, Iannaccone raised the possibility that religion can be a kind of addiction that can grow over time, making it likely that individuals adhere to the faith they were born into. (However, recent evidence from Pew Research indicates a growing degree of switching from one sect to another religion, or to no religion.) Importantly, Iannaccone's theoretical apparatus was aimed at a problem of mounting concern in religion markets: the issue of cults. Early on, Adam Smith believed that religious cults had the potential to create civil disorder and unrest, and he clearly understood that membership in religious organizations had "club" effects—that is, that the utility a person receives from his or her consumption of a club good depends on the number of other persons with whom he or she must share its benefits. Iannaccone recognized that this meant sects, clubs, or churches inevitably face a free-rider problem—the prospect that some members will receive the benefits of membership without bearing the proportionate costs.

Iannaccone argued that strictness is the mechanism used by religious sects to control the free-rider problem. He explained, for example, why some people prefer religions that demand greater sacrifice—that is, why individuals might choose strictness over leniency. He argued that religious sects turn to strictness as a means of controlling the free-rider problem because the cost of monitoring group utility-reducing behavior is high. Imposing strictures such as shaven heads, colored robes, or meeting in isolated locations might mitigate the problem. These strictures make it easier for cult members to police noncult behavior. A member must go all in or not at all because violations of these strictures will result in dismissal from the cult. Note, however, that while such membership rules (which may also apply to terrorists of one sort or another) may help control free riding in small groups, the problem cannot be monitored easily in large churches.

Industrial Organization and Religion

In order to introduce religion into a market framework Azzi and Ehrenberg defined the religious product as "an afterlife." This idea does not transfer easily to cult analysis, however, which has labored to identify a "product." There are both private and public aspects to the religious product, but (at least from the standpoint of Christianity) "promises of eternal salvation" comprise a large part of what religion is selling. This "promise" is what might be termed a "meta-credence good." Recall from chapter 26, credence goods require that certain types of assurances be given in order to satisfy purchasers about the quality of the product, because its genuineness cannot be determined either before or after the sale. By its very nature, the promise of an "other worldly" experience cannot be verified by earthly expenditure of resources. This puts the "product" beyond the terms of normal credence goods (such as psychiatric counseling), hence the designation, meta-credence good. Attempts may be made to establish assurances for the faithful (e.g., grand medieval cathedrals), but no church offers a money-back guarantee to a soul dissatisfied with his or her afterlife experience.

The admission that the product(s) of religion are "bought and sold" implies that religious behavior can be analyzed within the context of an implicit market. That means that churches can be viewed as economic organizations that establish governance, modes of production, selling techniques, competitive strategies, and market shares. This "industrial organization" approach can be traced back at least to Adam Smith. Although it can be applied to any religion, it has been applied most extensively to Christianity (see Ekelund, Hebert and Tollison, *Marketplace*). History recounts how Christianity rose, against long odds, as a fledgling competitor in a faith market dominated by varieties of late Greek and Roman Gnosticism. Robert Ekelund and Robert Tollison assert that the success of Christianity can be traced to the fact that it offered a superior "product" (*Economic Origins of Roman Christianity*). Christian theology established an "other-worldly" reward for those who lead a good life on earth. At a historical epoch when the vast majority of people were downtrodden and without much hope of accumulating material wealth the appeal of such a product should be obvious. The church that offered this product grew as it took advantage of its product appeal and then enlisted the efforts of missionary entrepreneurs (such as St. Paul) who reached out to "customers" everywhere, gentile and Jew, rich and poor, advantaged and disadvantaged.

The diverse forms of early Christian belief that took hold over the first three hundred years after Christ were eventually melded into a single belief system by the Council of Nicea in 325, convened by Emperor Constantine. The economic argument is that Constantine recognized the opportunity to reduce the agency and policing costs of the Roman state by adopting a uniform religion with a coherent, but simple, set of rules. Accordingly, he went about confiscating all "non-Nicean" Christian assets and those of "pagan" temples as well. Later in the fourth century he made Christianity the official religion of the Roman Empire, giving it new impetus as additional lands were conquered and conquered tribes were converted to the new religion. Missionaries were extremely effective in creating "outposts" or "missions" far from Constantinople and Rome. This effectively created a "top-down," vertically integrated church. The hierarchy that was put in place established Rome and the pope at the top of the organizational structure; monasteries and parish churches were downstream firms that marketed the "product."

In part because of this organizational structure the power of the Roman Church grew steadily, cemented through what might be called reciprocity—civil governments protected the Roman papacy in return for the Church's legitimization of particular civil governments. The descendents of Charles Martel, whose military victory at Tours in 732 prevented the Muslim takeover of the European continent, established the Carolingian dynasty that further consolidated the interests of the Roman Church (often called the Western Church). By 800, when Charlemagne was crowned Holy Roman Emperor, the Church had managed to acquire vast quantities of the lands of Europe and England. Over the next few centuries, conflicts with the Eastern Church (established in Eastern Europe and non-European areas) were settled in favor of Rome, the Roman bishop assumed titular leadership of the Church, the Viking invasions were quelled, and the Church became the monopoly religion of vast reaches of the European continent.

The Roman Church behaved as a monopoly roughly over the period 1100–1500. It used its interpretive powers to manipulate doctrine and interpret Scriptures in order to repatriate revenues from both civil governments and its downstream church divisions. The rules regarding marriage were expanded beyond existing civil requirements in order to thwart dynastic families from usurping the power of the Church. At one point marriage could not be within the fifth degree of kinship, although exemptions were often granted when it favored Rome's interests. The usury doctrine was invoked when the Church borrowed money but waived when the Church lent money (Ekelund et al., *Sacred Trust*). The doctrine of purgatory provided an opportunity for the Church to gain revenues through the sale of indulgences, and auricular confession was a means to warrant passage to heaven for the penitent. The Church ultimately acquired large parts of what became Italy (the Papal States) and commanded about one-third of the arable land of Western Europe. In sum, the medieval Roman Church became, in economic structure, a vertically integrated, global corporation.

But monopolies, even large ones, are difficult to sustain over time. The doctrine of purgatory, which provided a convenient avenue for growing Church revenue through the sale of indulgences, also led to many abuses. At first indulgences were granted to living sinners. Later such indulgences were extended to the dead and to the long dead. One could lessen purgatory time of one's deceased grandfather (for example) by donating money to the Church—an indulgence purchase. At one point indulgences were used as a kind of "nonwage payment" to Crusaders to induce them to fight so the Church could gain access to lands it did not control. To many, such as Martin Luther, the Church became a venal institution.

Roman Church abuses, combined with Gutenberg's invention of the printing press in the mid-1400s, encouraged Martin Luther in 1517 to enter the religion market as a competing "firm." He was the first, but not the last, to successfully challenge the monopoly position of the Roman Church. The history of religion from the sixteenth century to the present is a history of ever-changing faiths, each seeking out a peculiar niche in a vast religious market. New religious organizations were sometimes sponsored by monarchs, but more the product differentiation was accomplished by religious entrepreneurs—Luther, Huldrych Zwingli, John Calvin, John Knox, and others. The pattern was repeated over time. By some counts, more than two thousand religious firms currently compete in the market for Christianity, which is only one of the world's religions. Thus, Christianity is constantly being modified, adapted, and reinterpreted according to religious demands that are themselves determined by factors such as income, education, and the state of science. Even as secularism (the rejection of religious faith and worship) extends its reach in the developed world, the number of religious entrepreneurs continues to grow, along with the number of new sects, often through schism. A theory of economic and industrial organization and the new economic history, while never the entire story, continues to shed light on these developments.

■ Economics and Archeology

The fundamental importance of property rights has been known from the days of the ancient Greeks. Whereas Plato denied private property to the ruling class (only), Aristotle (see chapter 2) was a staunch defender of private property as a means of preserving social harmony and encouraging economic efficiency. In addition, private property rights establish built-in incentives to conserve and protect limited resources. As is sometimes the case, the benefits of private property are not appreciated until the privilege of ownership is gone. In the middle ages sections of land were set aside for "common grazing" of farm animals. The predictable result was that no one had an incentive to preserve and protect lands for the future. In modern times, increasing environmental concerns have raised awareness of problems with common property. In essence, when everybody owns something each individual behaves as if no one owns it. The resulting behavior leads to what economists call the "tragedy of the commons." The tragedy arises because, as Armen Alchian explained, individual costs and benefits in such instances differ from society's costs and benefits ("Property Rights").

While the problem has long been known to economists, its implications stretch beyond economics. Archeologists and biologists, have discovered environmental problems in primitive cultures that can be traced back to the tragedy of the commons. Whereas a market system based on private property rights assignment might have resolved some of these issues, failure to establish private property rights led to perverse incentives and, ultimately, to what was identified as market failure.[2] The tragedy of the commons explains how and why some animals have become extinct due to overhunting or destruction of habitat. Some examples of the famously extinct are the Mauritian dodo, the North American passenger pigeon, the New Zealand moa, the Falkland Islands wolf, Darwin's Galapagos mouse, the Caribbean monk seal, the Tasmanian emu, and many more. Jared Diamond recounts how in prehistoric times the wooly mammoth and many other species were overhunted and eventually disappeared ("The American Blitzkrieg").

Scientists have analyzed other cases involving common property that should serve as notice and warning to human populations concerning *slow*, nondramatic changes in resource use. The rather sudden disappearance of the Anasazi Indians from Chaco Canyon in New Mexico may have resulted from the systematic deforestation over many years of the areas surrounding their settlements. Common property provides no incentives to conserve scarce natural resources necessary to support civilizations. Jared Diamond analyzed the fascinating and dramatic case of Easter Island in the Pacific Ocean, once peopled by a great, isolated civilization. Only about 65 square miles, and known for its massive but partially destroyed stone heads, this island is possibly the most inaccessible and isolated piece of land in the world. Diamond investigated its fate from the perspective of modern science, poring through the accumulated studies of biologists, paleontologists, geneticists, pollen analysts, archeologists, and other researchers.[3]

Myth has always surrounded Easter Island and the mysterious monolithic statues found there. Speculations abound. It has been claimed that the statues were built by aliens from another planet or that the island was settled by highly developed societies of American Indians. Science has debunked these speculations. Linguists and radiocarbon dating of materials confirm the islanders were Polynesian. Other scientific evidence is that human activity began around A.D. 400 to 700, with the period of statue construction occurring between 1200 and 1500. At the height of its culture, the island supported an agrarian population of approximately seven thousand people. Scientists have found evidence of abundant plant species, including fiber from which rope could be made and large trees that could be used to transport the stones to the sites where they were carved (facing outward). Chickens were plentiful and boat-building materials were available to harvest porpoises and other fish from the sea.

[2] Other areas of anthropology have not escaped the long arm of economics either. See two provocative papers, one on insurance (or lack thereof) in primitive societies by Richard Posner ("Theory of Primitive Society") and the other on how economic incentives affected primitive hunter cultures by Vernon Smith ("Economics of the Primitive Hunter Culture"); both are in the references and are discussed in notes for further reading.

[3] This section draws heavily from Diamond's essay, "Easter Island's End" (see references). His analytical method is repeated with additional examples in *Collapse: How Societies Choose to Fail or Succeed* (see references). Some of Diamond's conclusions concerning Easter Island have been challenged by Carl Lipo and Terry Hunt, *The Statues that Walked* (see references).

So, what happened to this once-creative and thriving civilization? According to Diamond, destruction of the forests began as early as 800, when palms and other trees and scrubs began to disappear because their wood was used as fuel. The *pau-pau* tree, used for making rope, declined in number, and the forests were cleared to increase the cultivation of crops. Native birds were overharvested and their numbers declined, which led to reduced pollination of trees, plants, and scrubs. As this long but steady process continued, the population grew faster than it could be sustained with declining available resources. According to Diamond:

> People [of Easter Island] also found it harder to fill their stomachs, as land birds, large sea snails, and many seabirds disappeared. Because timber for building seagoing canoes vanished, fish catches declined and porpoises disappeared from the table. Crop yields also declined, since deforestation allowed the soil to be eroded by rain and wind, dried by the sun, and its nutrients to be leeched from it. Intensified chicken production and cannibalism replaced only part of all those lost foods. Preserved statuettes with sunken cheeks and visible ribs suggest that people were starving. ("Easter Island's End," p. 6)

The decline of Easter Island was clearly tragic. Chaos ensued, and by about 1700 the native population had fallen to about one-tenth its peak level. Warring tribes desecrated the monuments and denuded the island; today it supports a population of only about 1,000–1,500 people. The Easter islanders were victims of the tragedy of the commons.

The tragedy of the commons has modern faces as well. The country of Haiti has been denuded of trees as more and more wood was taken for fuel and other uses without efficient resource management that would have allowed replacement of this renewable resource. The owners of moas (large flightless birds related to the ostrich), once a source of nutrition to New Zealanders, would have had an incentive to preserve stocks for reproduction, but the moa population disappeared in the face of common property assignment. Without ownership no one conserves for the future when it is personally costly and not very beneficial to do so. Gorillas, redwood trees, deer, elephants, and oysters sometimes met similar fates in different locales. For obvious reasons, no one worries much about the extinction of dairy cattle because legal rights to them are clearly defined. Ownership is a useful principle of economic efficiency and conservation. Loose definitions of property rights are less productive, and the absence of property rights can be destructive, as the above examples indicate.

■ Economics and Politics

Contemporary economics also has reached into political science. The field of public choice, as we learned in chapter 24, is a study of how political mechanisms or institutions affect decisions concerning taxing and spending by government. It explains the demand for public goods and formally expresses the impact of the median voter. Our earlier discussion also contained lessons about the supply of "political goods" in bureaucracies and political institutions, but it did not detail the clear analogies between rational behavior in economic markets and political markets. A public-choice approach to politics is based on the idea that political actors are no different from anyone else: They behave in predictable ways and seek to obtain their goals efficiently.

The two arenas of human activity, economics and politics, differ in one important respect: The private market is a proprietary setting—one in which individuals bear the economic consequences of their decisions; whereas the political arena is a non-proprietary setting—one in which individuals do not always bear the full economic consequences of their decisions. For example, the political entrepreneur who devises a new program or policy does not bear the full costs of the program if it is a failure; nor does he or she reap all the benefits if it is a success. That is not the case with an individual who buys a car that might be a "lemon" (see chapter 26) or a firm that makes an ill-advised decision to expand. In the market economy individuals and firms must internalize all the costs and benefits of their economic decisions. Politicians operate under a different set of rules. "Pork barrel" expenditures by Congress may benefit a politician at election time but may harm all members of society when the projects must be paid for through future taxes and/or deficits. Politicians may be said to behave under a "reelection constraint," which often means spending now (to get those votes) while "kicking the can down the road" insofar as paying for the projects. Defenders of democracy are wont to say that offending politicians will be "voted out," but economically, that may not be practical or even possible in some cases.

Voting

Consider how economic rationality affects the voting process. Consumers make marginal choices in economic markets, but voters must evaluate package deals in political markets. A consumer of market goods can buy one more, or one less, pencil, hot dog, or computer—i.e., purchases are made at the margin and in (relatively) small increments. But an electoral process works differently. Voters typically face all-or-nothing alternatives involving one political platform or bundle of policies over another. In these package deals a voter usually ends up choosing a number of items he or she does not want in order to get a few things he or she does want. This may seem efficient in that it reduces the number of individual decisions to be made, but with many candidates and issues on the ballot at the same time, voting in a political market also leads to greater complexity and cost in exercising choice.

Another important difference is that under private market rules and actions, consumption tends to be frequent and repetitive, so that learning takes place and feedback is timely. One shops for groceries frequently so that the ability to discard bad products and try new ones is apparent. In (democratic) politics, voting is infrequent and irregular, with voters typically casting their votes every year or every two, four, or six years, as the case may be. This "discontinuity" makes it more difficult for the voter to identify reliable policies and candidates.

These two factors add up to the principle that voters have little incentive to be informed. Voting is a political choice that is far more complicated than economic choice. Voters have difficulty evaluating candidates and issues, and public costs and benefits cannot be easily internalized. Therefore, voters have little incentive to gather information about their public choices. How can the average voter hope to obtain the information needed to make rational decisions about international conflicts, energy sources, foreign aid, welfare, the money supply, jobs, and so on? Voters are quite rationally uninformed about such matters; they estimate that the costs exceed the benefits of being fully informed. Indeed, they may become free riders by not gathering information, not voting, and letting those who do vote make the choices for them. If the choices of other voters happen to be beneficial to nonvoters, the nonvoters benefit without bearing any of the costs.

An economic analysis of the voting process has important implications. On the one hand politicians do not typically receive very useful information from constituents because voters are not well informed and therefore do not transmit their wants effectively. On the other hand, politicians do not have an incentive to be precise or firm regarding their position on various public issues. Politicians who are vague about their "commitments" are therefore more likely to be rewarded with reelection. Pork barrel spending that can be targeted to particular states or congressional districts also improves one's chances of reelection. Nevertheless, the transmission of information in political markets is less direct. In economic markets, if consumers want more carrots, they can effectively signal producers by buying more (using dollar "votes," if you will). In political markets, if voters want more domestic spending and less defense spending, it is difficult and costly to make this preference known to politicians.

Interest Groups

Political science and economic theory also have much to say about the impact of interest groups, as alluded to in chapter 24. The behavior of interest groups helps explain a significant amount of government activity. George Stigler ("Theory of Economic Regulation") and Sam Peltzman ("Toward a More General Theory of Regulation") maintain that interest groups will form in order to obtain benefits from politicians in the form of regulation. The democratic state has the power to coerce monopolies and to enact regulations that favor one group over another (e.g., Wall Street instead of Main Street). But interest groups that lobby legislators for special rules or regulations face organizational costs as well.

There are multiple regulations capable of producing benefits to special interest groups: licensing, quotas, subsidies, as well as taxes and entry barriers. The history of physicians' attempts in the United States to organize is particularly instructive. Toward the end of the nineteenth century many physicians complained that rogue competitors were tainting the market for medical services by preying on the ignorant and threatening the safety of consumers. They called for an organization to put an end to these threats. But organizations are difficult and costly to form and maintain. One difficulty is posed by the free-rider problem. Individual doctors have an incentive to remain outside the interest group because if the group succeeds at some objective—say restricting the number of doctors and thereby raising the price of medical services—the nonmembers benefit without paying membership dues or fees. The benefits "spill over" to the doctors who did not join the group. Interest groups seek ways to restrict benefits to members for such reasons.

Free riding makes the formation of interest groups difficult, but by no means impossible. The physicians' groups successfully organized and their representatives went to state legislatures seeking licensing statues for physicians. In some states, physicians were able to eliminate competition from chiropractors in this manner. Restrictive licensing elevated "legal" physicians' prices and profits to an artificial level because there were fewer competitors in the market. Without government's help in reducing competition, these higher profits would be competed away in the long run. Learning from the experience, doctors have managed to extend a network of regulations to increase their profits. They have established quotas (through entrance exams) on admissions to medical school; restricted the number of hospitals, or interns at hospitals; and limited the duties and responsibilities of nurses to below their technical competency.

Actions by interest groups to restrict supply operate on one side of the market while leaving the market vulnerable to changes in demand. Population increases and federal Medicare and Medicaid programs have increased the demand for physicians, yet the increased demand cannot be met due to state and federal regulations that favor incumbent physicians. Much of the so-called crisis in medical care in the United States finds its origin in these circumstances. Similar situations occur in other markets as well: lawyers, dentists, drug companies, florists (in Louisiana), morticians, and so on. While the benefits of regulations are usually proclaimed loudly, the costs are most often muted or ignored. Most, if not all, regulations result in higher product/service prices achieved through a *coercive* political process paid for by voter-consumers.

Plato recognized eons ago that such welfare transfers are endemic in a democracy. Why do such arrangements that transfer wealth from consumers to professions, businesses, and industries, persist? Politicians serve as brokers by pairing up demanders and suppliers of wealth transfers in political markets. A political miscalculation that transfers too much power to one group or another may raise the probability that the errant politician will be replaced in the next election, but incumbents are hard to dislodge. Interest-group politicians are supported by votes and money to repel election challenges in the next election. Legislators find it easy to be persuaded by powerful interest groups because the benefits they bestow are narrowly focused on members of the favored group but the costs are widely dispersed among (mostly uninformed) voters. Protests are therefore likely to be weak and muted. In sum, the political market allows power and influence (i.e., political goods) to be bought and sold to the detriment of broader, social interests. In the process, politicians subvert the general welfare, consumers pay higher than competitive prices, and societal economic growth is restricted.

■ Conclusion

Despite sometimes shrill complaints of economic imperialism from other social scientists, incursions of economics into sociology, history, and allied social sciences have not attempted to replace but to supplement the work and research of kindred social scientists. The payoff to introducing the rationality postulate into the other social sciences will ultimately have to be determined, but the hope is that it adds a new dimension to its human understanding in the complex arena of social phenomena and behavior. (See the box: Method Squabbles: Traditional Economics under Fire (Again): The New Pushback, for an example of one scholar who believes that an emphasis on economic reasoning to interpret history is a backward approach.)

Method Squabbles: Traditional Economics under Fire (Again): The New Pushback

Traditional economics has never been without critics from within and without the profession. In chapter 26 we saw that the rationality and standard utility maximization postulates have been challenged by contemporary behaviorists. But while proceeding apace, these "internal" challenges to conventional economic theory have not displaced standard neoclassical analysis. In general, "received theory," based on classical and neoclassical contributions, remains the basis for the applications of economics to the other social sciences such as those considered in this chapter and in the last chapter (e.g., Becker's theory of household production). There has been some "pushback" from the other social sciences and the humanities, including attacks on applications of economic theory to historical questions (cliometrics).

One of the most vehement and questionable critics is Francesco Boldizzoni (see notes for further reading) who decries the application of economic theory and statistical methods to history as usurpation of the traditional European-Marxist-historical traditions of investigation.

Boldizzoni regards the incursions of economics into allied fields (perpetrated by an "all-star" list of prominent economists, such as Robert Fogel, Douglass North, Gary Becker, and Richard Posner) as an essentially *American* push of the liberal political tradition of investigations in social sciences. He asserts the primacy of institutions, environments, time and place, and other sociological elements, and rejects the self-interest axiom. Boldizzoni wishes to replace economic man/woman with sociological man/woman, which implies that some meta-theory must be carved out of actual events for each era or episode if we are to truly understand economic history and the development of human societies.

Intellectual history tells us, however, that Boldizzoni's method of inquiry reduces economic history and behavior to mere prose—a narrative that is always anecdotal and never falsifiable. The suggestion that neoclassical economics be replaced by a vague theory derived from "facts" (induction) is an old one that, despite being repeated through the past two centuries, offers no example of success. Criticisms of this ilk have existed from the time of the Industrial Revolution. Romantics and Marxists challenged economic theory in the classical period as a justification of the status quo in income distribution, and assaulted the wages-fund doctrine as "trickle-down economics" gone bad (see chapters 11 and 12). The German and British "historical schools" raised similar objections, and their critiques were to some extent revisited later by American institutionalists (see chapter 19). None of this dissent has halted the trajectory of contemporary economics and its new applications to history, sociology, anthropology, or culture. "Theory" without facts is sterile, and facts without (falsifiable) theory is nonsense. No able economist would reject the value of multiple approaches to history and the other social sciences. However, it is unlikely that "external criticisms" will divert economics from its current path of intellectual integration and incorporation. Boldizzoni has merely added one more weak voice of dissent to a lonely chorus.

Whatever the outcome, the assumption that individuals respond to full prices in both explicit and implicit markets has carried economics further (and further) into the areas of social science. This has been demonstrated particularly with regard to dating, mating, marriage, and household production. Judging by derivative literature, it would also appear that economics can advance our understanding of religious behavior, particularly in regard to how religious institutions supply products to their consumers. Moreover, conventional economic theory has shown early promise in understanding culture and the arts, as well as biological and evolutionary effects of common versus private property arrangements. The "tragedy of the commons" makes societal collapse understandable in a number of cases.

Perhaps nothing is more emblematic of the success of economics in penetrating new fields than the fact that some journals are now focused exclusively on narrow fields of economic inquiry. The *Journal of Cultural Economics* regularly publishes works on the economics of the arts. The *Journal for the Scientific Study of Religion* is a forum for research and publication on the economics of religion. The directions of twenty-first century economics cannot be fully anticipated (see the following chapter), but clearly there is a move toward economics embracing matters that have been traditionally, but myopically, claimed as nonmarket behavior. Economists have slowly but surely discovered that much nonmarket activity submits to the same organizing principles and logical outcomes as market activity.

References

Alchian, Armen. "Property Rights," *The Concise Encyclopedia of Economics*. Library of Economics and Liberty http://www.econlib.org/library/Enc/PropertyRights.html.

Azzi, Corey, and Ronald Ehrenberg. "Household Allocation of Time and Religiosity: Replication and Extension," *Journal of Political Economy*, vol. 85 (1975), pp. 415–423.

———. *The Economic Approach to Human Behavior*. Chicago: University of Chicago Press, 1976.

———. *A Treatise on the Family*. Cambridge: Harvard University Press, 1981.

Coase, Ronald. "Durability and Monopoly," *Journal of Law and Economics*, vol. 15 (1972), pp. 143–149.

Diamond, Jared. "The American Blitzkrieg: A Mammoth Undertaking," *Discover* (June 1987), pp. 82–88.

———. "Easter Island's End," *Discover* (August 1995), pp. 63–69.

———. *Collapse: How Societies Choose to Fail or Succeed*, (rev. ed.). New York: Penguin Books, 2011.

Durkheim, Émile. *The Elementary Forms of Religious Life: A Study in Religious Sociology*, Joseph Ward Swain (trans.). New York: Macmillan, 1915.

Ekelund, R. B. Jr., Robert F. Hébert, Robert D. Tollison, Gary M. Anderson, and Audrey B. Davidson. *Sacred Trust*. New York: Oxford University Press, 1996.

Ekelund, R. B. Jr., Robert F. Hébert, and Robert D. Tollison. *The Marketplace of Christianity*. Cambridge: MIT Press, 2006.

Ekelund, R. B. Jr., and Robert D. Tollison. *Economic Origins of Roman Christianity*. Chicago: University of Chicago Press, 2011.

Iannaccone, Lawrence. "Sacrifice and Stigma: Reducing Free-Riding in Cults, Communes and Other Collectives," *Journal of Political Economy*, vol. 100 (1992), pp. 271–292.

Lipo, Carl, and Terry Hunt. *The Statues that Walked*. New York: Simon and Schuster Digital Sales, 2011.

Mei, Jianping, and Michael Moses. "Art as an Investment and the Underperformance of Masterpieces," *American Economic Review*, vol. 92 (2002), pp. 1656–1668.

Peltzman, Sam. "Toward a More General Theory of Regulation," *Journal of Law and Economics*, vol. 19 (August 1976), pp. 211–240.

Posner, Richard A. *Sex and Reason*. Cambridge: Harvard University Press, 1994.

———. "A Theory of Primitive Society with Special Reference to Law," *Journal of Law and Economics*, vol. 23 (1980), pp. 1–53.

Renneboog, Luc, and Christophe Spaenjers. "Buying Beauty: On Prices and Returns in the Art Market," *Management* Science, vol. 59 (2013), pp. 36–53.

Skinner, Sarah J., Robert B. Ekelund, Jr., and John D. Jackson. "Museums, Funding, and Business," *American Journal of Economics and Sociology*, vol. 68 (2009), pp. 491–516.

Smith, Vernon. "Economics of the Primitive Hunter Culture with Applications to Pleistocene Extinction and the Rise of Agriculture," *Journal of Political Economy*, vol. 83 (August 1975), pp. 727–755.

Stigler, George. "The Theory of Economic Regulation," *The Bell Journal of Economics and Management Science*, vol. 2 (Spring 1971), pp. 3–21.

Weber, Max. The *Protestant Ethic and the Spirit of Capitalism*, Talcott Parsons (trans.), foreword by R. H. Tawney. London: George Allen & Unwin, 1930.

Notes for Further Reading

Economists such as Gary Becker, Nobel laureate in economics (1991), and Richard Posner have by themselves and by demonstration helped extend the reach of modern economics. In a long series of papers and books Becker has redefined the scope of economics to include much of what has been considered the province of sociology. In particular Becker has set the economic principles of time costs and household maximization at the center of labor theory and consumer behavior. His work on marriage, courtship, family, and divorce is far reaching and profound. See Becker, *Economic Approach to Human Behavior* (see references); and same author, *A Treatise on the Family* (see references), plus individual papers referenced therein. Posner has also penetrated "anthropological" and "sociological" topics with the vigor (and rigor) of modern economic analysis. See Posner, *Sex and Reason* (see references); and with specific reference to the AIDS crisis, Posner and Thomas J. Philipson, *Private Choices and Public Health: The AIDS Epidemic in an Economic Perspective* (Cambridge, MA: Harvard University Press, 1993).

Economics and the arts is a major component of the broader designation, "cultural economics." The *Journal of Cultural Economics* is devoted to economic aspects of culture, including music, museums, movies, opera and theater, visual arts, government subsidies of the arts, and myriad other issues. James Heilbrun and Charles M. Gray, *The Economics of Art and Culture* (New York: Cambridge University Press, 2d ed., 2001), provide an overview of the literature cascade that has been forthcoming in this field. Art markets have received a great deal of attention. Mark Blaug, "Where Are We Now on Cultural Economics," *Journal of Economic Surveys*, vol. 15 (April 2001), pp. 123–143, offers a survey of recent developments. Another useful compendium of papers is, *Economic Engagements with Art*, Neil De Marchi and Craufurd D. W. Goodwin (eds.), Annual Supplement to Volume 31, *History of Political Economy* (Durham and London: Duke University Press, 1999). Other useful references are William D. Grampp, *Pricing the Priceless: Art, Artists, and Economics* (New York: Basic Books, 1989); *The Economics of Art Museums*, Martin Feldstein (ed.) (Chicago: University of Chicago Press, 1991); *Economics of the Arts: Selected Essays*, Victor A. Ginsburgh and Pierre-Michel Menger (eds.) (Amsterdam: Elsevier, 1996); Bruno S. Frey and Werner W. Pommerehne, *Muses and Markets: Explorations in the Economics of the Arts* (Oxford: Basil Blackwell, 1989).

Cultural economics, especially as it relates to the arts, has brought a number of issues to the fore. One issue is whether price estimates published online and in auction catalogues are "efficient," i.e., do they accurately express the values of art and other objects? For a treatment of this issue, see R. B. Ekelund, Jr., R. W. Ressler, and J. K. Watson, "Estimates, Bias and 'No Sales' in Latin-American Art Auctions 1977–1996," *Journal of Cultural Economics*, vol. 22 (1998), pp. 33–42; and R. B. Ekelund, Jr., John D. Jackson, and Robert D. Tollison, "Are Art Auction Estimates Biased?" *Southern Economic Journal* (forthcoming 2013). For an alternative approach to price estimation, see Clare McAndrew, Rex Thompson, and James L. Smith, "The Impact of Reservation Prices on the Perceived Bias of Expert Appraisals of Fine Art," *Journal of Applied Econometrics*, vol. 27 (2012), pp. 235–252. Whether art is a good "investment" is the subject of lively debate inasmuch as art has consumption value as well as appreciation potential. Two excellent papers on this subject are those of Jianping Mei and Michael Moses (see references); and same authors, "Vested Interest and Biased Price Estimates: Evidence from an Auction Market," *The Journal of Finance*, vol. 60 (2005), pp. 2409–2435.

The economics of religion has clearly "arrived" judging by the growing output of papers on the subject (and on the new designation granted to the field by the *Journal of Economic Literature*. In addition to the works cited in the references to this chapter, a good place to begin an in-depth study is Lawrence Iannaccone, "Introduction to the Economics of Religion," *Journal of Economic Literature*, vol. 36 (1998), pp. 1465–1495. Insofar as religion is concerned the rationality postulate is embraced by (some) sociologists as well. In particular, see Rodney Stark, *The Rise of Christianity: How the Obscure, Marginal Jesus Movement Became the Dominant Religious Force in the Western World in a Few Centuries* (San Francisco: HarperOne, 1997); and same author, *Cities of God: The Real Story of How Christianity Became an Urban Movement and Conquered Rome* (San

Francisco: HarperOne, 2006). Rachael M. McCleary, *The Oxford Handbook on the Economics of Religion* (New York: Oxford University Press, 2011), is a vital collection of papers on the subject. Also see, same author, "Religion and Political Economy in an International Panel," *Journal for the Scientific Study of Religion*, vol. 45 (2006), pp. 149–175; and, Rachael McCleary and Robert J. Barro, "Religion and Economy," *Journal of Economic Perspectives*, vol. 20 (Spring 2006), pp. 49–72. The subject of religion itself has generated a massive literature comprised of works in history, sociology, anthropology, psychology, and (maybe) surprisingly, biology. On the latter see Pascal Boyer, *Religion Explained: The Evolutionary Origins of Religious Thought* (New York: Basic Books, 2001); and Andrew Newberg, Eugene D'Aquili, and Vince Rause, *Why God Won't Go Away: Brain Science and the Biology of Belief* (New York: Ballantine, 2001). Ryu Susato, "Taming 'The Tyranny of Priests': Hume's Advocacy of Religious Establishments," *Journal of the History of Ideas*, vol. 73 (April 2012), pp. 273–293, provides an interesting contrast between Hume and Smith on religion.

Jared Diamond is a geographer whose proficiency graces other fields. His studies that are particularly amenable to economic analysis deal with the collapse of Easter Island, the decline of the Anasazi, the dissolution of the Mayan culture, and the withering of a Greenland colony (see *Collapse* in the references). His earlier Pulitzer-prize winning book, *Guns, Germs and Steel* (New York: W. W. Norton, rev. ed., 2005), examines how geography and environment created the first great spread of civilization in Eurasia. Diamond emphasizes the nature of plants and animals (in terms of their availability and adaptability to domestication) as inducing "east to west" movement of population and civilization and discouraging "north to south" settlement. Diamond's thesis easily fits into the economist's full-costs-and-benefits model that yields an adjunct explanation. Just as economists sometimes are charged with economic determinism, Diamond has been criticized for "environmental determinism."

Some questions in archeology and anthropology yield easily to economic analysis. Richard A. Posner ("Theory of Primitive Society" in the references), one of the founders of the law and economics paradigm, contributed a brilliant paper on the role that insurance (or its lack) plays on the structure of primitive (that is, nonliterate) societies. Posner shows how the structure of society and family is altered when no market insurance exists. Vernon Smith (references) attributes the decimation of large animals (e.g., bison, mastodon, and mammoth) by Paleolithic hunters to the "tragedy of the commons." Using archeological and anthropological evidence Smith compares free access (open property rights where "first come, first served" reigns) to controlled access to resources using strict ownership. One of the most interesting recent excursions by economists into anthropology and genetics is a paper on human prehistory by Quamrul Ashraf and Oded Galor, "The 'Out of Africa' Hypothesis, Human Genetic Diversity and Comparative Economic Development," *American Economic Review*, vol. 103 (2013), pp. 1–46, which presents empirical evidence that the prehistoric exodus of *Homo sapiens* out of Africa and the varieties of genetic diversity that followed had long-term effects on rates of economic development around the world.

The economics of politics finds its most ready application in today's society, but that should not be surprising in a discipline that began as "political economy." It is interesting to speculate on how a rapidly changing digital technology might affect *changes* in democratic processes. Direct or participatory democracy, in which each citizen has an opportunity to cast his or her vote on all public issues, is often held up as an ideal method of reaching political consensus. Attempts to approach this ideal include Athenian democracy (the agora), the New England Town Meeting, and the Swiss cantons. Such attempts at the ideal have fallen short, however, due to the costs of organizing large groups. But the advent of relatively inexpensive computers, "smart" phones and other methods of digital communication have lowered the cost of direct voting. These developments are foretold in a paper by James C. Miller, III, "A Program for Direct and Proxy Voting in the Legislative Process," *Public Choice* 6 (Fall 1969), pp. 107–113. While information costs on the part of voters remain high, they might be mitigated by engaging "specialist proxies" to represent voters on issues such as regulation, taxes, defense, and so forth. The proxies could be engaged by contracts of varying length, with the highest proxy specialists engaging the narrowest interests but subject to quick recall in the event of poor performance.

There are other interesting ideas that might lower costs of more efficient decision making. One idea that has commonsense appeal but has failed to gain traction would be to *increase* the number of voter's representatives. The minimum number of people that a member of the House of Representatives can represent is 30,000, but there currently is no maximum. In 2013 the actual number of citizens represented by each elected solon is 700,000 on average. Individuals' preferences would be better represented if there were *more* representatives per electoral district, which would allow representatives to better know their constituents' preferences. The downside, however, is that with larger numbers of representatives, consensus may be more difficult to achieve. These and other problems are discussed by George S. Ford, Mark Thornton, and Marc Ulrich, "Constituency Size and the Growth of Public Expenditures: The Case of the United Kingdom, *Journal of Public Finance and Public Choice (PFPC)/ Economia delle svelte pubbliche*, vol. 24 (2006), pp. 127–141. Also see Mark Thornton, "The Case for Bigger Government," *The Lew Rockwell Show*, November 17, 2008. Lew Rockwell interviews Dr. Mark Thornton (podcast) http://www.lewrockwell.com/lewrockwell-show/2008/11/17/69-the-case-for-bigger-government/.

The extension of economic analyses into allied fields shows no signs of abating, despite "pushback" from some avidly "territorial" social scientists. Cliometrics, the use of economic theory and quantitative tools to study history and social phenomena, has established a foothold in the United States and, increasingly, in Europe and elsewhere. Some European scholars persist in questioning the value of the kind of economic analysis found in contemporary economic history by such scholars as Gary Becker, Robert Fogel, and Douglass C. North, who have seen their life's work crowned by Nobel prizes.

It would appear that European methods in social sciences are fundamentally sociological in nature—focused primarily on collectivist institutions as driving forces in society—whereas economists (primarily, but not exclusively American) predominately take an individualist approach that concentrates on the consequences and implications of rational behavior, full prices, and implicit markets. One critique stands out for its defense of the study of history and institutions as a mass of "facts" without falsifiable theory. Francesco Boldizzoni, *The Poverty of Clio* (Princeton: Princeton University Press, 2011), argues against the implied "takeover" of history and other social sciences by economists. It is an odd and idiosyncratic book, displaying massive confusion and misrepresentation of economists' forays into other social sciences, as it assumes that economists accept the economic approach to historical questions as the only explanation of the unfolding of events. Boldizzoni's call for a "renewal of methods" (p. 170) is a thinly veiled plea for a return to the kind of methods advanced by German and English historical "schools" and Karl Marx (see chapters 11 and 12 in this text).

Some criticisms of applying economics to the social sciences have been even more vigorous than Boldizzoni's. Church historian Ramsay MacMullen ("The Translation of History into Economics," *Journal of Interdisciplinary History*, 43 [2012], 289–294) looks with extreme disdain on economists and sociologists (in particular) who use rational-choice theory to study religion and its history. His criticism stems from the extension of traditional areas of inquiry into the realm of implicit markets, full-price, and "goods" under the rubric of utility production. But such applications have helped economists to understand facets of markets for art, marriage, politics, anthropology, and religion. MacMullen also makes the erroneous observation that analysis based on nonrational behavior—exemplified by the interesting insights of Kahneman and Tversky (see chapter 26)—has displaced the modern approach that has been used with respect to religion and in other applications of economics to the social sciences. Yet, in a recent assessment of Kahneman's nonrational "prospect theory," based on its influence during the last thirty years, Barberis (see references chapter 26) concluded, "Even prospect theory's most ardent fan would concede that economic analysis based on this theory is unlikely to replace the analysis that we currently present in our introductory textbooks" (p. 195). Studies using Kahneman's ideas have been limited principally to risk and insurance and especially to laboratory experiments, not to "real-world" experience or historical testing. Psychology, in this instance, appears to have given far less to economics than economics has given to the other social sciences. It bears repeating that in modern science facts without theory are meaningless, and theory without facts is unconvincing. The resurgence of economics as a social science does not mean that facts are irrelevant, only that they must be assembled in a coherent method to be considered alongside the efforts of historians, sociologists, and anthropologists.

28

Quo Vadis?
Economics in the Twenty-First Century

"I think, therefore I am," wrote the philosopher René Descartes, thereby underscoring the centrality of ideas in the panorama of human existence and activity. This book is about ideas—some that have stood the test of time and some that have not. But a history of ideas, in any field, raises certain critical questions. What, exactly, *are* ideas? How do they originate? Once shaped, what directions do ideas take? Do ideas matter in the history of humankind, and does a grasp of ideas help us understand events and historico-institutional change? Are ideas and "ideologies" the same thing? Finally, what are the ideas that are shaping twenty-first century economics and what are their likely "fates"? Up to this point, our lengthy review of important ideas in the history of economic thought has avoided raising such questions much less posing even tentative answers. Indeed, answers to such questions are not easily derived. But at the end of our historical survey, we pause to consider the nature and consequences of economic ideas and the method of analysis that economists choose in plying their trade. For insight into these issues, we look first to the assembly of economists who have captured their science's highest honor—the Nobel Prize in Economics.

Nobel Laureates and Economics

Economics has been cultivated as a separate science since Adam Smith penned *The Wealth of Nations* in 1776. Since that time, economists have expanded the horizons of economic theory and policy in virtually all areas of inquiry. In 1969, Sweden's Nobel Prize Committee, long vested with the authority to award Nobel Peace Prizes, instituted the Sveriges Riksbank Prize in Economic Science in Memory of Alfred Nobel. Winners have received recognition for many different kinds of contributions and applications: macroeconomics, econometrics, general equilibrium theory, economic history, economic development, input-output analysis, institutional economics, allocation theory, money, national-income accounting, administration, industrial organization, public finance, market design, and financial economics. Prizes for these contributions provide outward signposts that economics is an ongoing activity of varied scope and widespread interest. They also hark to the past and point to the future—simultaneously supplying indirect evidence that contemporary advances continue to build on earlier contributions and provide new directions in the twenty-first century. Table 28-1 lists the Nobel Prize winners in economics from 1969 through 2012, along

Table 28-1 Nobel Prize Winners in Economic Science

1969 RAGNAR FRISCH (Econometrics)
Oslo University
JAN TINBERGEN (Econometrics)
The Netherlands School of Economics

1970 PAUL A. SAMUELSON (Partial and General Equilibrium Theory)
Massachusetts Institute of Technology

1971 SIMON KUZNETS (Economic Growth and Economic History)
Harvard University

1972 JOHN R. HICKS (General Equilibrium Theory)
Oxford University
KENNETH J. ARROW (General Equilibrium Theory)
Harvard University

1973 WASSILY LEONTIEFF (Input-Output Analysis)
Harvard University

1974 GUNNAR MYRDAL (Macroeconomics and Institutional Theory)
University of Stockholm
FRIEDRICH A. HAYEK (Macroeconomics and Institutional Theory)
University of Freiburg

1975 LEONID KANTOROVICH (Theory of Optimum Allocation of Resources)
Moscow Academy of Sciences
TJALLING J. KOOPMANS (Theory of Optimum Allocation of Resources)
Yale University

1976 MILTON FRIEDMAN (Macroeconomics)
University of Chicago

1977 BERTIL OHLIN (International Economics)
Stockholm School of Economics
JAMES E. MEADE (International Economics)
Cambridge University

1978 HERBERT A. SIMON (Administrative/Management Science)
Carnegie-Mellon University

1979 THEODORE W. SCHULTZ (Economic Development)
University of Chicago
W. ARTHUR LEWIS (Economic Development)
Princeton University

1980 LAWRENCE R. KLEIN (Macroeconometrics)
University of Pennsylvania

1981 JAMES TOBIN (Macroeconomics)
Yale University

1982 GEORGE J. STIGLER (Industrial Organization)
University of Chicago

1983 GERARD DEBREU (General Equilibrium Theory)
University of California, Berkeley

1984 J. RICHARD STONE (National Income Accounting)
Cambridge University

1985 FRANCO MODIGLIANI (Macroeconomics)
Massachusetts Institute of Technology

1986 JAMES M. BUCHANAN, Jr. (Public Finance)
George Mason University

1987 ROBERT M. SOLOW (Economic Growth Theory)
Massachusetts Institute of Technology

1988 MAURICE ALLAIS (Partial and General Equilibrium Theory)
École Nationale Supérieure des Mines de Paris

1989 TRYGVE HAAVELMO (Econometrics)
Oslo University

1990 HARRY M. MARKOWITZ (Financial Economics)
City University, New York
MERTON M. MILLER (Financial Economics)
University of Chicago
WILLIAM F. SHADE (Financial Economics)
Stanford University

1991 RONALD H. COASE (Theory of Institutions)
University of Chicago

1992 GARY S. BECKER (Microeconomics and Economic Sociology)
University of Chicago

1993 ROBERT W. FOGEL (Economic History)
University of Chicago

1993 DOUGLASS C. NORTH (Economic History)
Washington University, St. Louis

1994 JOHN C. HARSANYI (Game Theory)
University of California, Berkeley
JOHN F. NASH (Game Theory)
Princeton University
REINHARD SELTEN (Game Theory)
University of Bonn

1995 ROBERT LUCAS (Macroeconomics)
University of Chicago

1996 JAMES A MIRRLEES (Economics of Information)
Cambridge University

1996 WILLIAM VICKREY (Economics of Information)
Columbia University

1997 ROBERT C. MERTON (Financial Economics)
Harvard University
MYRON S. SCHOLES (Financial Economics)
Stanford University

1998 AMARTYA SEN (Welfare Economics)
Cambridge University

1999 ROBERT A. MUNDELL (International Economics)
Columbia University

2000 JAMES J. HECKMAN (Econometrics)
University of Chicago
DANIEL L. McFADDEN (Econometrics)
University of California, Berkeley

2001 GEORGE A. AKERLOF (Economics of Information)
University of California, Berkeley
A. MICHAEL SPENCE (Economics of Information)
Stanford University
JOSEPH E. STIGLITZ (Economics of Information)
Columbia University

2002 DANIEL KAHNEMAN (Economic Psychology and Experimental Economics)
Princeton University

2002 VERNON L SMITH (Economic Psychology and Experimental Economics)
George Mason University

2003 ROBERT F. ENGLE (Econometrics)
New York University
CLIVE W. J. GRANGER (Econometrics)
University of California, San Diego

2004 FINN E. KYDLAND (Macroeconomics)
Carnegie Mellon University

2004 EDWARD C. PRESCOTT (Macroeconomics)
Arizona State University

2005 ROBERT F. AUMANN (Game Theory)
Hebrew University
THOMAS C. SCHELLING (Game Theory)
University of Maryland

2006 EDMUND S. PHELPS (Macroeconomics)
Columbia University

2007 LEONID HURWICZ (Market Design
University of Minnesota
ERIC S. MASKIN (Market Design)
Princeton University
ROGER B. MYERSON (Market Design)
University of Chicago

2008 PAUL KRUGMAN (International Economics)
Princeton University

2009 ELINOR OSTROM (Institutional Economics)
Indiana University /Arizona State University
OLIVER E. WILLIAMSON (Institutional Economics)
University of California, Berkeley

2010 PETER A. DIAMOND (Economics of Search)
Massachusetts Institute of Technology
DALE T. MORTENSEN (Economics of Search)
Northwestern University
CHRISTOPHER A. PISSARIDES (Economics of Search)
London School of Economics & Political Science

2011 THOMAS J. SARGENT (Macroeconomics)
New York University
CHRISTOPHER A. SIMS (Macroeconomics)
Princeton University

2012 ALVIN E. ROTH (Market Design)
Harvard University
LLOYD S. SHAPLEY (Market Design)
University of California, Los Angeles

with a parenthetical description of their contributions cited by the prize selection committee. Why is this instructive? No book on the history of economics can hope to accurately predict the future direction of economic inquiry. Nevertheless, the achievements of the past may contain useful hints.[1]

The preponderance of econometrics, economic dynamics and growth theory, macroeconomic theory, general equilibrium analysis, and, more recently, game theory certainly provides a clue to the directions of modern economics. Individuals within these categories are difficult to classify because there is wide variation in interests and results. Nevertheless, they are united in a common *technical* approach to economic problem solving. This shared technique emphasizes mathematical reasoning and empirical research. Empirical studies of macroeconomic (economy-wide) behavior have become more and more complex through time, as have investigations in public finance and game theory. The quest to understand the underlying interrelationships of aggregate economies and the causes of and factors relating to economic growth will continue—if not through easily testable hypotheses, then through mathematical designs and simulations. Game theory and experimental economics, so clearly recognized by the Nobel Institute, are other fields of important research being carried out at major universities around the world. Much of this work requires solid grounding in advanced mathematics. As economics stretches its mathematical muscle, we may expect more and more of such activity.

There is, however, another side to the past as prologue to the future. We might call it the "movement to reinvigorate economics as a social science." Some of the prize winners have shown the ability to incorporate technical economics and empiricism into their explorations of the interstices of economics, history, politics, sociology, and anthropology. A few examples will suffice to emphasize this point. James M. Buchanan, Jr., developed a contractual and constitutional framework for studying decision making by economic and political agents. George J. Stigler proposed that market outcomes could not be studied apart from an integration of economic and political interests and the incentives faced by each. Douglass C. North has persistently attempted to treat changes in institutions as endogenous factors in bringing about historical change. Robert W. Fogel has introduced quantitative methods into the study of economic history to enrich our understanding and appreciation of the subject. Ronald Coase has underscored the importance of property rights in ongoing studies of historical and contemporary institutions. William Vickrey, James Mirrlees, George Akerlof, Michael Spence, and Joseph Stiglitz have enriched our understanding of the operation of economic markets by recognizing and exploring transactions and information costs. Elinor Ostrom approached science as a form of artisanship and enriched our understanding of common-pool problems and the tragedy of the commons. Rather than dance around the periphery of economic theory, these contributions penetrate to the core of received economic analysis. Among other things, they make the subject of history, sociology, political science, psychology, and anthropology more robust. For this reason, we expect that contemporary economics will continue to find increasing application in allied fields of interest.

[1] The interested reader is directed to the Nobel prize site at http://nobelprize.org/economics/ for a wealth of information concerning each winner, including the "acceptance" speech and articles related to the particular economist. More importantly perhaps, eighteen of the winners themselves provided an analysis of his "evolution as an economist" in a lecture series given at Trinity University (San Antonio, Texas). These delightful and important presentations are reproduced in William Breit and Barry T. Hirsch (eds.), *Lives of the Laureates* (see references). A common theme of this diverse group of winners, if there is one, is that they embarked on economics as a career and as a means of confronting social and economic problems of the real world.

The ideas and theoretical extensions of Gary Becker have been particularly provocative as we saw in chapters 26 and 27. The application of economics to nontraditional, nonmarket behavior, including marriage, family, dating, and so forth has, judging from recent contributions to economics literature, stimulated many similar avenues of research. Drawing heavily on biological and other social sciences, contemporary writers have applied the premises of self-interest and economic rationality to an ever-widening array of issues, including sexual drives, polygamy, abortion, and motherhood.[2] Nobel Prize winning economists have helped spawn whole new areas of interface, including two thriving areas, "law and economics" and the "economics of religion."[3] It would therefore appear that the interface of economics with sociology and other social sciences will receive continued attention for some time to come.

Finally, economics both informs and is informed by psychology. Game theory with its myriad possible conjectures about behavior in market and nonmarket contexts most certainly employs assumptions about psychological behavior. Do individuals always react in the rational manner posited by economists? Is rationality, like information, limited? How do individuals behave under uncertainty? Experimental economics—as exemplified in the work of Nobel laureates Daniel Kahneman (see chapter 26) and Vernon L. Smith—whether it involves game theory or other types of controlled experiments, relies heavily on psychological premises and laboratory designs. The nature and form of these kinds of studies show no signs of letting up as economics winds its way through this millennium.

George Stigler reminded us that "Contemporary fame does not ensure lasting fame—the leaders of what prove to be scientific fads receded from even the histories of the science" (in Breit and Hirsch, *Lives*, p. 79). There is no guarantee that all (or any) of the central ideas and achievements of the latter part of the twentieth century or the beginning years of the twenty-first century will have a lasting impact. The worlds of science and social sciences are filled with "also-rans" and "never-rans." Our purpose in examining a few of the ideas of the elite coterie of Nobel Prize winners has been to at least acknowledge those economists who are currently recognized by the profession as having made important contributions. While these past achievements might serve to indicate which way the intellectual winds are blowing, we know from the contemporary state of meteorology that winds change often and unpredictably. The evolution of the economics profession and the technology surrounding it also has changed dramatically since its origins in the eighteenth century.

■ The Transmission of Ideas and the New "Technology" of Economics

Any "count" of economists working today must be approximate. Some estimates put the number of professional economists worldwide at between 40,000 and 65,000. The American Economic Association (AEA) constitutes the largest organized group of economists, although there are many organizations devoted to the study and practice of economics in both the United States and around the world. The amount of economic literature produced annually also grows apace. There were, for example, about 100 journals indexed by the AEA in 1924, 140 in 1968, 300 in 2005, and about 350 in 2012 (a number that includes an estimate for e-journals).

[2] See in particular works and writings of Richard A. Posner, including *Sex and Reason* (references).

[3] The area of law and economics owes much to Ronald Coase and to other writers as well: see Richard A. Posner, *The Economics of Justice* (references).

Membership in the AEA mushroomed in the past 40 years from 4,000 to about 20,000. Founded in Saratoga, New York, in 1886, the AEA once drew members primarily from academics, but it now contains an increasing number of business economists and "government" economists affiliated with federal, state, and local agencies. Professional associations of all kinds have flourished during the twentieth and into the twenty-first centuries. Many hold annual meetings for communicating ideas. Abstracts of papers, indices of economic journals, translation services, books, monographs, specialized associations (e.g., the Econometrics Society, the Public Choice Society, the Association for Cultural Economics, the History of Economics Society, etc.), regional associations (e.g., Southern, Western and Eastern Economic Association, etc.) have all established networks within which knowledge is generated and shared.

This aim of this book has been to chronicle major economic ideas of the past. We have said little about how ideas are created and manipulated, accepted and rejected, through time. Yet, the *transmission* of ideas is a key ingredient in progress, and it is instructive to analyze changes in the generation of economic thought over the past two-and-a-half centuries. Technology and its global reach have clearly and dramatically altered the methods for transmitting ideas of all kinds, including economic ideas (see Stigler, Stigler, and Friedland, "Journals of Economics").

The Internet is growing in its use as a device to spread information, but before it came of age the popular press served as a vehicle for "advertising" ideas with economic content. The British popular and periodical press, in particular, produced (at least for the "educated layperson") a continuous flow of economic commentary and information during the nineteenth and twentieth centuries, and continues to do so today. Established in 1843 to campaign on one of the great political issues of the day, *The Economist* remains a major organ for the dissemination of economic news and ideas. During the heyday of classical economics substantial debates were conducted in the press. Critical issues such as the Corn Laws, the Poor Laws, and the Factory Acts were seriously debated by McCulloch, Malthus, Ricardo, and the Mills (father and son). Jeremy Bentham and Edwin Chadwick (chapters 9 and 10) were deeply engaged in police and criminal justice reform as well as in other issues. John Stuart Mill (chapter 8) debated and ostensibly "recanted" the wages-fund doctrine in an English periodical, the *Fortnightly Review*. Interchanges on many economic issues were enacted in the periodical and popular press across Europe. Reading rooms (often clubs with a small fee) emerged to accommodate an increasingly educated populace.

Naturally, the spread of literacy quickened the pace of economic knowledge, but during its earliest formative years economics was commonly traduced in books and pamphlets. Near the end of the nineteenth century professional economics journals began to make inroads as a dominant vehicle for the dissemination of knowledge among an expanding number of academic specialists. In the United States the *Quarterly Journal of Economics* was established in 1886; followed by the *Journal of Political Economy* in 1892; and the *American Economic Review* in 1896. In England the *Economic Journal* was established in 1891, under the auspices of the Royal Economic Society. Other countries, France, Germany, and Italy in particular, also have long, rich traditions of economic publications, but the twentieth century witnessed the rising hegemony of English-language periodicals in economics.

Although economics journals never displaced books in the transmission of new ideas and theories, a noticeable shift toward periodical literature occurred in the first half of the twentieth century. Journal literature was typically more concise, conveniently brief, imposed shorter lead times in the presentation of novel ideas, and instituted a quality-control measure in the form of the referee process. While a few specialist journals emerged in this time period, the premier research found its way into the major outlets mentioned above.

Traditionally, and almost without exception, papers and books having the greatest impact on economic thought were singly authored. That all began to change as the number of economists (however defined) increased and as mathematics, statistics, and econometrics invaded the economics profession, circumstances that accelerated in the 1970s and 1980s, continuing apace today (Laband and Piette, "Relative Impacts of Economics Journals: 1970–1990"). Simultaneously the "fields" that constitute economics expanded greatly, with new fields emerging and old fields subdividing. As a consequence the number of journals proliferated to accommodate the ever-expanding fields of specialization within economics proper. In 2013, the *Journal of Economic Literature* listed hundreds of "fields" and "subfields." As a consequence of expansion in the number of "niche" journals in economics the legacy journals have experienced increased competition and have, in some instances, relinquished specialized contributions to specialized journals.

These developments have generated an area of inquiry within the economics profession that might be called "economic technology," a field designed to study the efficiency and operation of the intellectual transmission of economic theory and policy. Contributions to this field examine important issues relative to how economic ideas are promulgated. Whereas it might be expected that specific applications of economic analysis in various subfields would provide fertile ground for innovations in general economic theory (a bottom-up process), the hierarchy of journals and the multiplication of subfields may have encouraged the reverse (a top-down process).

The multiplication of economics journals has engendered questions regarding the quality of different journals and the value of economic articles in the production and spread of knowledge. Typically, the articles that economists submit to academic and business journals are subjected to scrutiny from journal editors and unpaid referees who are assigned to evaluate the papers submitted. Does this practice add value to the papers (judged by citations)? Based on evidence he collected in correspondence with journal editors, David Laband argues that referees do in fact add value to economic research ("Is There Value-Added from the Review Process"). Economics journal editors "match" the research topics submitted with recognized experts in the relevant domain. (The "experts" themselves had to "earn their spurs" by succeeding within the same kind of editorial gauntlet.) This process bestows a great deal of power on editors as well as referees. Questions of favoritism arise. Laband and Piette ("Favoritism versus Search") did not find evidence of favoritism, but anecdotal evidence is not always persuasive, and doubts most likely remain.

Transmission of new, creative, and influential ideas does not always proceed smoothly and efficiently. Joshua Gans and George Shepherd ("How the Mighty Have Fallen") studied the academic biographies of Nobel laureates and winners of the John Bates Clark Medal (an AEA award given to an outstanding economist under the age of 40). They found that famous economists such as Nobel laureates James Tobin, Bertil Ohlin, and Milton Friedman had their research *rejected* by journal editors at one time or another. Nobel laureate George Akerlof, who received the Nobel Prize for his fundamental contribution to the economics of information and exchange, had his highly influential article, "The Market for 'Lemons': Quality, Uncertainty and the Market Mechanism," rejected four times before it was finally accepted in the *Quarterly Journal of Economics*!

Not surprisingly specialization in authorship has accompanied specialization in economics. In this respect, economics has trended toward common practice in the "hard" sciences such as chemistry and biology. David Laband and Robert Tollison looked at the dramatic rise in coauthorship in economics and the hard sciences. They discovered that prior to 1950 practically no papers in the major economic journals were coauthored, but by the first decade of the twenty-first century almost 80 percent of the papers in economic journals had two or more authors. The practice is more compelling in technical areas, such as macroeconomic theory and policy, than in economic history or history of economic thought, but the significant issue is that writers often find that specialization necessarily limits their range of knowledge and technique. A theorist will work with an econometrician to produce a paper that would (hopefully) be better than if either attempted to write alone—a straightforward application of the law of comparative advantage. Laband and Tollison concluded that while formal collaboration in terms of number of coauthored papers may be greater in biology than economics, informal collaboration—passing draft papers around to colleagues and friends for evaluation—is far greater in economics ("Intellectual Collaboration," pp. 655–656).

Looking backward, it seems evident that the invention of the printing press spurred certain "revolutions" (the Protestant Revolution, for instance). Looking forward we might expect the digital age to have similar consequences—perhaps especially in economics because the full cost of computation has been dramatically reduced. In the 1960s simple regression, a vital tool of the econometrician, was very time consuming. Now, thanks to modern technology, thousands of complex econometric computations may be done in less than a minute. This advance has in itself sponsored greater econometric testing of complex econo/mathematical relations. Digital technology has greatly increased accessibility to economic knowledge. (The writing of this book was made considerably easier than earlier editions because of so much useful information readily available on the Internet and because of the efficiency of today's word processing features.) Other things equal, lower research costs should lead to more research, thus feeding the expansion of knowledge.

Within the university community the future path of economics is uncertain. Undergraduate emphasis on mathematics and econometrics in university curricula has met with some resistance. Laband and Piette speculate on "whether the strong market showing (popularity) of the *Journal of Economic Perspectives*, with its emphasis on [nonmathematical] presentation of arguments and findings in essay form reflects a widespread reaction within the profession to the mathematical emphasis" ("Relative Impacts," pp. 244–286) so prevalent today. It remains to be seen whether the increased knowledge output wrought by new technologies will translate into progress in economic policy and understanding. The growing hegemony of mathematics and econometrics within the discipline of economics will be a critical issue.

■ Ideas, Ideology, and History

How do we asses an idea in terms of how it will affect the future? How much attention should we devote to ideology—the study of ideas? What is an idea, anyway? We cannot afford to ignore semantics. Dictionary definitions run the gamut from hazy perception, opinion, or belief, to detailed plan. We can probably agree that an idea is the product of mental activity. Ideas are therefore notions that actually or potentially exist in the mind. What about ideology? One definition is that it is the study of ideas, but a more popular meaning is that it comprises a *set* of ideas, doctrines, or beliefs that form the basis of some cultural, political, or economic system. Ideas and ideology can be understood as generalities, without reference to particular subject matter, or as specifics within a narrow field. Economic ideas, as you may have silently observed throughout this book, might include a new technology or knowledge base that finds application in a market framework. In a practical sense, someone with a new idea potentially or actually increases the welfare of someone else, or what amounts to the same thing, reduces transaction costs for somebody. A new way to *produce* or *package* cat food constitutes a new idea. Better ways to *distribute* cat food to customers also reduces costs to consumers—and likewise constitutes a new idea. This book has surveyed and evaluated many ideas—not about cat food, to be sure, but about the varied theoretical elements of an economy and the numerous institutions that affect market behavior. For example, Adam Smith presented an analytical framework for economic development; John Stuart Mill championed a politico-economic formula for judging the desirability of public policy; Karl Marx advanced a historico-economic paradigm for structural change; Alfred Marshall developed a set of analytical tools useful to businesspeople and those seeking solutions to economic problems. This list is not exhaustive. The history of economics is a history of ideas because ideas form the raw material of any academic discipline.

We have said little about ideology throughout this book. Yet, ideology cannot be ignored. Without it, Marx's analysis of a capitalist economy is incomplete, for example. Social classes tend to coalesce around particular interests, with each group of interests more often than not confronting an opposing interest group. This observation applies to "capitalist" and "socialist" ideologies alike. "Ideology" is the teacher's friend—it is a convenient device for ordering and categorizing ideas—but as a moving force of history, its role is far from clear-cut.

Perhaps the question is not whether we can precisely define ideas or ideology, but whether ideas have consequences in shaping individual activity of an economic and social nature. The conventional wisdom states that ideas shape the modern world. But as usual, timing is everything. For example, history reveals that certain musical or artistic ideas "floated about" for long periods of time in relative obscurity or outright neglect before they were "rediscovered." One of the world's most revered composers, J. S. Bach, lapsed into obscurity in his time, relegating status to his (far) less talented offspring, only to be rediscovered in the Romantic age by great musicians of another generation, such as Felix Mendelssohn. Closer to the present, twelve-tone music, a strikingly inventive conception developed by Arnold Schoenberg early in the twentieth century, has yet to really "catch on."[4] These examples also raise the issue of the "dating" of revolutions. Do they occur when the idea is first expressed or, alternatively, when it is generally accepted—sometimes generations after the idea is first expressed?

Economic ideas—while of enormous potential importance to society—may catch on only when circumstances warrant. For all of the anticipations of "under-

[4] George Stigler argued that influencing contemporaries is the only chance to become successful in influencing science, citing the neglected genius of Gossen and Cournot who were only recognized later (Breit and Hirsch, *Lives*, p. 79). Likewise, contemporary fame does not ensure lasting fame. We demure on Stigler's first point, inasmuch as later "revolutions" are often sparked from gleanings of past discoveries. Moreover, sciences and arts are often built from accretions to knowledge, rather than by revolutions.

consumption" arguments in the nineteenth century, and even after Keynes's development of it in the *General Theory* (1936) during a deep depression, persistent and habitual deficit spending by Western central governments did not occur until the 1970s and 1980s. Likewise, the issue of peak-load pricing in the supply of public utilities (electricity and telecommunications), firmly established in French economic literature decades earlier, did not find practical application in the United States until the 1960s. Moreover, analytical concepts such as "external economies and diseconomies" (see chapter 16) preceded by almost a hundred years the recent mobilization of public opinion regarding environmental concerns.

There are several impediments to a complete understanding of how ideas influence history. One of the most basic is the fact that the chain of causation is ambiguous. Do ideas lead to events or do events precipitate ideas? More pointedly, do *ideas* or *events* explain history? Do ideas *lead* change, with events following, or vice versa? Or is it that *sometimes* ideas are leading variables and other times lagging variables? These questions are significant, at least from a pedagogic standpoint. Current pedagogy distinguishes between economic history (i.e., study of events and their economic consequences) and intellectual history (e.g., the history of economic thought). It appears that history can be read from either perspective. For example, it could plausibly be argued that Adam Smith (chapter 5), armed with the concepts of free markets and laissez-faire, was merely establishing an economic theory based on observed events in the world of English commerce that had been underway for a century or more. The same may also have been true of the Physiocrats (chapter 4) in eighteenth-century France. At the same time, economic ideas that appear to be novel at one historical moment may have been hotly debated within academic circles for years before coming to the fore or before actually stirring action. Again drawing on Smith, his liberating idea that a basically free market could and would supply an organizing principle that would improve economic welfare in a commercial society, was the consequence of a philosophic inquiry stretching over two centuries during which leading intellectuals searched for an answer to the Hobbesian dilemma: that the only alternative to social chaos was an all-powerful central government. The world of science—from the production of the atomic bomb to the realization of space travel—offers many examples of a similar nature.

In scientific pursuits, of course, technological prerequisites are always required. No matter how fertile the mind of famed futurist author H. G. Wells, space travel and rocketry did not become viable until other ideas and circumstances (inventions, mathematical developments, war, etc.) precipitated action. Actualization of scientific pursuits demands appropriate economic circumstances, which underscores a critical point: Market incentives empower ideas to be actualized through self-interested individuals or groups of individuals who seek to profit from supplying products or services to a large body of consumers. Technological feasibility insists on economic feasibility (i.e., the benefits to some individual or group must exceed the costs) before actualization takes place.

Nobel laureate George Stigler (1911–1991) stirred the troubled waters of these issues more than any other modern historian of economic thought. In a collection of essays entitled *The Economist as Preacher* (1982), Stigler emphasized the role of self-interest in explaining the influence of economists. Stigler believed that economists, as preachers, are received well "in the measure that [they] preach what the society wishes to hear" (p. 13). Economists, for example, are virtually unanimous in their advocacy of free trade between nations, but their stance has little impact unless free trade improves the welfare of those people who are in a position to enact laws to maintain it. Economists and other enlightened citizens may therefore decry protectionist legislation as mistaken, but Stigler warns that economists in particular should be wary of taking such a position. In his words, "the discipline [economics] that assumes man to be a reasonably efficient utility maximizer is singularly ill-suited to assuming that the political activity of men bears little relationship to their desires" (*Economist as Preacher*, p. 9). In other words, the world may be full of "errant" policies from the economist's perspective, but such policies are not mistaken in the eyes of their supporters.

The thorny question of when do ideas become action occupied Hamlet no less than countless other individuals who have contemplated the meaning of life. Shakespeare put these words into Hamlet's troubled mind:

> And thus the native hue of resolution
> Is sicklied o'er with the pale cast of thought,
> And enterprises of great pith and moment
> With this regard their currents turn awry,
> And lose the name of action.

Although we may never be able to satisfactorily answer the question of when ideas become action, we are able to extract a valuable lesson from our survey of the history of economics: *Ideas become action* (i.e., receive a trial in the marketplace) *within context—within a framework of policies, constraints, or ground rules that are established through a political process conducted by self-interested politicians and interest groups*. Metaphorically, there is an institutional skin that envelopes every ideational corpse.

A holistic understanding of historical change, therefore, must be informed not only by ideas and ideologies but by institutional parameters that establish the incentives that ultimately motivate ideas and actions. Ideas and ideology alone are not enough. Indeed, despite recognition that ideas and ideology may be of great importance in explaining particular movements or policies, the debate over the dominance of ideology versus incentives has not run its course. The outcome, if indeed one results, is critical to the ongoing activities of many contemporary economists seeking to fathom the mysteries of economic development. Although it is generally admitted that a political sector is integral to an explanation of institutional change and in particular regulatory policies, evidence of ideology effecting legislation is inconclusive (see Kalt and Zupan, "Capture"; Kau and Rubin, "Self-Interest"; Lott and Bronars, "Time"). Depending on how it is defined, ideology itself may well be the result of past and present "economizing"—the assessment of costs and benefits.

■ Does Method Matter?

Throughout this book you have been confronted with various "Method Squabbles," or conflicting views, approaches, and procedures championed by different economists. The purpose of highlighting differences has been to inform, not confuse (although that is a calculated risk). When ideas become generally accepted they have a tendency over time to become fixed in the public mind. New practitioners invest time and talent in learning the prevailing technique (ideology?), and as a consequence, they acquire a vested interest in certain operational procedures. Although this is a natural progression, the danger is that accepted ideas may become rigid *doctrines*, and their adherents in turn become doctrinaire. The intellectual rigidity engendered by such doctrinism thwarts further ideational progress by stifling tolerance for opposing points of view. Such is the "noxious influence of authority" that Jevons (chapter 15) complained of in his day. At the heart of this issue is the question of what is the appropriate method of economic inquiry.

Economists, like other scientists, have worked in concert for well over two centuries to build society's "knowledge base." The slow but steady accretions to this body of economic knowledge have been the subject of this book. Knowledge has a way of growing exponentially, in part because of the specialization and division of labor applied to its construction and in part because of technological advance. The modern age has witnessed a proliferation of outlets for research in economics and a huge increase in the number of individuals identifying themselves as economists. While economists at American universities have led the way since the twentieth century (winning, for example, all but a few of the Nobel Prizes granted in economics between 1969 and 2012), contributions to economic analysis have come from many different quarters of the globe. In the context of our survey of the history of economic thought, two important, interrelated questions beg to be answered: (1) How "new" is it? and (2) Does its form encourage or constrain creativity in economic ideas?

"Keeping the record straight" has always been a major activity of the intellectual historian, and every practitioner can cite examples of an idea's fiery tail. For example, Richard Cantillon and other preclassical writers have emerged as clear anticipators of Adam Smith. An eighteenth-century engineer, A. N. Isnard, is now known to have anticipated Walras on general equilibrium theory (see Jaffé, *A. N. Isnard*). In the post–World War II period, John von Neumann, a mathematician, and Oskar Morgenstern, an economist, teamed up to develop game theory as an edifice constructed on Cournot's foundation (see chapter 13). James Buchanan (chapter 24) pioneered the field of public choice after he discovered and translated an earlier essays by Knut Wicksell and Antonio De Viti De Marco. Modern economists have expanded the horizons of economic theory and policy in virtually all areas of inquiry. These areas include the application of mathematics to economic theory; the application of economic analysis to political behavior; and the economic analysis of crime, the environment, taxes, health, safety, insurance, finance, labor, and product quality. And, as we have seen, even areas previously reserved for sociology, such as dating, mating, and marriage, have yielded to the economist's deft touch (chapter 27). Albeit it reluctantly in some instances, most of the other social sciences are yielding in some measure to economic analysis. The historian of economic thought, by nature a generalist rather than a specialist, is in a unique position to evaluate the importance, creativity, and originality of these contributions.

Increasingly the history of economic thought is lumped with methodology, and the two are treated as companion fields of inquiry. It is therefore difficult to avoid judgments about economic method. The hallmark of modern economic inquiry in the first decades of this millennium is its mathematical character, which has invaded virtually all areas of modern microeconomic or macroeconomic theory, including the subfields of labor, public finance, and antitrust and government regulation, to name a few. Contemporary macroeconomic model building and forecasting of national income and employment would be inconceivable without such tools. Courses in mathematics and econometrics form the basis of most (not all) graduate curricula at major and minor universities around the world. It is legitimate to ask whether creativity and originality take a backseat in the wake of widespread use of this tool to express and develop modern economic ideas.

A meaningful evaluation must rest on the costs and benefits, the advantages and shortcomings, of this development as it relates to a concept of progress in economics. The chief argument for continued formalization and mathematization of economics is that the discipline cannot become truly scientific unless and until it attains the rigor and complexity of science—in other words, until its fundamental propositions have been tested and proven. The contemporary consensus (however loose) is that theory without verification (at least potential verification) is of limited usefulness and that facts without theory forged in the logic of mathematics are meaningless. Many "mainstream" economists argue, therefore, that increased respect for economics as a separate, scientific discipline will only come about by the steady application of rigorous mathematical and statistical tools.

Some economists (including a few who have been the most ardent practitioners of the mathematical method) have voiced strong reservations about this view. They argue that the nature of *social* science makes exact formulation and verification impossible. The *power* of econometrics to predict, and mathematics to illuminate, is the overarching issue. Some of the central problems of contemporary econometrics relate to inexact or incomplete formalizations of economic theory and to various inadequacies in data samples and in the random errors inherent in the measurement of social variables. Modern econometric techniques are, generally speaking, most appropriate when data samples are large; yet, in many instances, large-sample data sets simply do not exist. Thus, the quantities and qualities of economic data are often ill-suited to the task at hand. In contrast to conditions in the physical and natural sciences, the collection of most economic data is not predetermined or predesigned to fit various tests of economic theory. Indeed, much economic data is collected by government agencies for less-specific purposes, often for purely political reasons. While inadequate theory and poor data are not sufficient reasons in themselves to reject quantitative methods, some critics argue that the design costs and the collection costs required to secure high-quality data are prohibitive. Moreover, many economists are neither trained nor disposed to *generate* data that would be more suitable to the solution of compelling problems. Many econometricians are *consumers* (of data) rather than *producers*.

Some critics of contemporary economic method, especially those of institutionalist or neo-Austrian persuasion (chapter 23), argue that the attempt to make economics a science through mathematical formalization and empirical verification is illusory. In their opinion, the actual return to decades-long intellectual investment in mathematical and statistical techniques has been small, if not negative. According to this argument, these futile attempts to make economics scientific have spawned widespread distrust of the economic pronouncements of policy makers and an almost total breakdown in communication between economists and other social scientists. Even worse, mathematics and calculation techniques in the hands of those equipped with tools but not ideas may lead economists away from basic truths about markets and market functioning. In this view, mathematics inevitably diverts attention away from the fundamental truths of the economic process originally formulated by Adam Smith and refined by a host of other writers considered in this book. At age 102, Nobel laureate Ronald Coase may be in a unique experiential position to assess the present state of economics. Coase spins a cautionary tale:

> Economics as currently presented in textbooks and taught in the classroom does not have much to do with business management, and still less with entrepreneurship. The degree to which economics is isolated from the ordinary business of life is extraordinary and unfortunate. That was not the case in the past.
>
> [But] in the 20th century, economics consolidated as a profession; economists could afford to write exclusively for one another. At the same time, the field experi-

> enced a paradigm shift, gradually identifying itself as a theoretical approach of economization and giving up the real-world economy as its subject matter. . . . The tools used by economists to analyze business firms are too abstract and speculative to offer any guidance to entrepreneurs and managers in their constant struggle to bring novel products to consumers at low cost.
>
> This separation of economics from the working economy has severely damaged both the business community and the academic discipline. Since economics offers little in the way of practical insight, managers and entrepreneurs depend on their own business acumen, personal judgment, and rules of thumb in making decisions. In times of crisis, when business leaders lose their self-confidence, they often look to political power to fill the void. Government is increasingly seen as the ultimate solution to tough economic problems, from innovation to employment.
>
> Economics thus becomes a convenient instrument the state uses to manage the economy, rather than a tool the public turns to for enlightenment about how the economy operates. ("Saving Economics from the Economists")

Another critical issue with respect to economic method may be identified in the oversimplified questions: What *is* contemporary economics and by what adjective should it be identified? Developments in late twentieth- and early twenty-first-century economics, such as those discussed in the latter chapters of this book, have had profound effects on both the study and the directions of the discipline. Neoclassical economics is, at least approximately, what the entering university student learns in his or her first courses and even later in the undergraduate curriculum. These ideas are embodied in the rationality assumptions within consumption and production theory, the assumption of perfect information among participants, and the mechanics of equilibrium theory. But given the programs of study at most universities around the world, and the current requirements of the discipline, the student aspiring to professional status would be well served by the equivalent of a university undergraduate degree in mathematics. Advanced classes introduce a variety of technical models—many of which discard the abstract assumptions of mid-twentieth-century neoclassical economics, such as perfect information, rationality, open competition, and so on. Game theory, by its very nature, deals with a small number of rivals, for example, not the large numbers of buyers and sellers assumed in purely competitive markets. Is this "modern" or "contemporary" neoclassical economics, or is it merely *ad hoc* learning—i.e., a "cafeteria" approach to questions dealing with economic reasoning?

■ Is Schism in the Cards for Economics?

Economics may well be at a crossroads of sorts. Will encroaching technical refinement become the essence of economics? Alternatively, will economics become merely another mathematics problem? Or will the ever-present demands for policy analysis—economics in the service of society, if you will—prevent a complete descent into barrenness? The answer to *both* questions may well be yes!

There is a persistent danger that highly technical but sterile analysis tends to be self-perpetuating. Despite the perceived failure of esoteric lines of inquiry to achieve much progress, those who have made heavy human capital investments in mathematical and econometric techniques have a strong incentive to perpetuate the "mystique of the cognoscenti." Moreover, the formalization of economics too often raises entry barriers in academics, whereby graduate curriculum requirements, university hiring standards, journal editorial policies, and professional recognition hinge on the mastery and application of mathematical and empirical techniques. Some observers believe that the cultivation of technique for technique's sake has fostered an environment wherein intellectual fads readily come and go. The shelf life of such fads is often notoriously short. As soon as today's new technique fails to live up to the unrealistic expectations placed on it, it falls out of favor, only to grease the skids for a new fad to replace it. Economists who indulge in the latest fad run the risk of becoming obsolete, and quickly so. Worse yet, the ongoing process tends to drive a wedge between those who regard economics as a powerful, though somewhat imprecise, behavioral science, and those who regard the discipline as a branch of applied mathematics. Some skeptics believe the very survival of economics will ultimately require a formal split between the "economists" and the "mathematicians."

Recognition of these problems as they relate to the development of creative ideas in the discipline of economics appears to be increasing. Some years back, there was evidence of a slowdown in the production of formal mathematical articles that abound in contemporary economics literature.[5] Genuine understanding of the correct and useful place in economic science of mathematic and econometric techniques is based on an awareness and appreciation of the limits of mere technique. So long as these limits are understood (and respected), the value of mathematics and econometrics in formulating and testing certain economic ideas is potentially great. The choice should not be between "poetry" and "advanced mathematics." The trick is to forge ideas with meaningful economic content on the one hand and to avoid shunning economic problems merely because they are not easily amenable to mathematical manipulation on the other. If economic science as applied mathematics becomes unable to address and provide at least tentative answers to perpetual economic policy questions, it will most likely lead to cleavage between political economy and economics as a mathematical science. Whether this will happen cannot be predicted at this time, but a schism within the profession is a real possibility.

There is no cleavage, however, between the progress of economics as a science of scarcity and welfare maximization and the progress of the "hard sciences." Notably there have been three great revolutions in the progress of humankind: the Agricultural Revolution of about 10,000 years ago, the Industrial Revolution that burgeoned in the seventeenth and eighteenth centuries and has been ongoing ever since, and the digital/biological/atomic revolution that began in the last century and continues into the present. Individuals and societies adapt to such cataclysmic changes. We are on the threshold of the latest revolution, which recognizes time as a vital resource. Consider what resource savings have been produced by digital and satellite communications that make available massive quantities of (global) information at our fingertips. Where will it ultimately lead? In the future, cars may "drive themselves," in the process generating more time savings and possibly reducing transportation costs. Breakthroughs in medicine and medical technology will invariably mean longer productive life spans. Robotics, artificial intelligence, and the unlocking of the human genome will have critical impacts on products, markets, and economic behavior (see Kaku, *Physics of the Future*). But economic markets have evolved throughout history to deal with such dislocations and institutional changes, and there is no reason to think they will not do so again, if not completely stifled by unwise and improvident policy.

No science is perfect, and perfect truth, as Protagoras told us eons ago, is always elusive, whether it is sought in physics, sociology, microbiology, meteorol-

[5] See the interesting comments of mathematical economist and 1983 Nobel laureate Gerard Debreu ("Mathematical Economics," pp. 401–403).

ogy, or economics. Progress in economic ideas critically depends on the use and application of many methods of science and on the progressive adaptation to both large- and small-scale revolutions. It depends, in short, on the kind of methodological pluralism that has been demonstrated in the broad expanse of economic inquiry over time—the kind of pluralism that is perhaps best exemplified through study and knowledge of the history of economic theory and method.

References

Breit, William, and Barry Hirsch (eds.). *Lives of the Laureates: Eighteen Nobel Economists*, 4th ed. Cambridge, MA: The MIT Press, 2004.

Coase, Ronald. "Saving Economics from the Economists," *Harvard Business Review* (December 2012). http://hbr.org/2012/12/saving-economics-from-the-economists/ar/1.

Debreu, Gerard. "Mathematical Economics," in J. Eatwell, M. Milgate, and P. Newman (eds.), *The New Palgrave: A Dictionary of Economics*, vol. 3, pp. 399–404. London: Macmillan, 1987.

Ekelund, Robert B., Jr., Robert F. Hébert, and Robert D. Tollison. *The Marketplace of Christianity*. Cambridge, MA: The MIT Press, 2006.

Gans, Joshua S. and George B. Shepherd "How the Mighty Have Fallen: Rejected Classic Articles by Leading Economists," *Journal of Economic Perspectives*, vol. 8 (Winter 1994), pp. 165–180.

Jaffé, William. "A. N. Isnard: Progenitor of the Walrasian General Equilibrium Model," *History of Political Economy*, vol. 1 (Spring 1969), pp. 19–43.

Kaku, Michio. *Physics of the Future: How Science will Shape Human Destiny and our Daily Lives by the Year 2100*. New York: Doubleday, 2012.

Kalt, J. P., and M. A. Zupan. "Capture and Ideology in the Economic Theory of Politics," *American Economic Review*, vol. 74 (June 1984), pp. 279–300.

Kau, J. B., and P. H. Rubin. "Self-Interest, Ideology and Log Rolling in Congressional Voting," *Journal of Law and Economics*, vol. 22 (October 1979), pp. 365–384.

Laband, David N. "Is There Value-Added from the Review Process in Economics? Preliminary Evidence from Authors," *Quarterly Journal of Economics*, vol. 103 (May 1990), pp. 341–352.

———., and Michael J. Piette. "Favoritism versus Search for God Papers: Empirical Evidence Regard the Behavior of Journal Editors," *Journal of Political Economy*, vol. 102 (1994), pp. 194–203.

———. "The Relative Impacts of Economics Journals: 1970–1990," in Joshua S. Gans (ed.), *Publishing Economics: Analyses of the Academic Journal Market in Economics*. Cheltenham, UK: Edward Elgar, 2000.

———., and Robert D. Tollison. "Intellectual Collaboration," *Journal of Political Economy*, vol. 108 (2000), pp. 632–662.

———. "Alphabetized Coauthorship," *Applied Economics*, vol. 38 (2006), pp. 1649–1653.

Lott, John, and S. G. Bronars. "Time Series Evidence on Shirking in the U.S. House of Representatives," *Public Choice*, vol. 76 (1993), pp. 125–150.

Posner, Richard A. "A Theory of Primitive Society with Special Reference to Law," *Journal of Law and Economics*, vol. 23 (1980), pp. 1–53.

———. *Sex and Reason*. Cambridge, MA: Harvard University Press, 1992.

———. *The Economics of Justice*. Cambridge, MA: Harvard University Press, 1981.

Smith, Vernon L. "The Primitive Hunter Culture, Pleistocene Extinction, and the Rise of Agriculture," *Journal of Political Economy*, vol. 83 (1975), pp. 727–756.

Stigler, George J. *The Economist as Preacher and Other Essays*. Chicago: University of Chicago Press, 1982.

———., Stephen M. Stigler, and Claire Friedland. "The Journals of Economics," *Journal of Political Economy*, vol. 103 (1995), pp. 331–359.

Name Index

Subject Index